your Thill/Bovée?

Balanced Presentation of Fundamentals

Excellence in Business

Communication

Eighth Edition

John Thill
Courtland Bovée

ISBN: 0-13-615750-5

Excellence in Business Communication Custom One-Color Option

The Core

Optional Chapters

Contact your local PH Rep for more information on the custom/core option.

Excellence in Business Communication

EIGHTH EDITION

Excellence in Business Communication

EIGHTH EDITION

JOHN V. THILL
Chairman and Chief Executive Officer
Global Communication Strategies

COURTLAND L. BOVÉE
Professor of Business Communication
C. Allen Paul Distinguished Chair
Grossmont College

PEARSON

Prentice
Hall

Pearson Education International

Editor-in-Chief: David Parker
Product Development Manager: Ashley Santora
Assistant Editor: Keri Molinari
Marketing Manager: Jodi Bassett
Marketing Assistant: Ian Gold
Senior Managing Editor: Judy Leale
Associate Managing Editor: Renata Butera
Production Project Manager: Carol Samet
Permissions Project Manager: Charles Morris
Senior Operations Supervisor: Arnold Vila
Art Director: Steve Frim
Interior Design: Heather Peres
Director, Image Resource Center: Melinda Patelli
Manager, Rights and Permissions: Zina Arabia
Manager, Visual Research: Beth Brenzel
Image Permissions Coordinator: Joanne Dippel
Photo Researcher: Teri Stratford
Composition: GGS Book Services
Full-Service Project Management: Jeanine Furino, GGS Book Services
Printer/Binder: Quebecor/Versailles

Credits and acknowledgments borrowed from other sources and reproduced, with permission, in this textbook appear on page AC-1.

If you purchased this book within the United States or Canada you should be aware that it has been wrongfully imported without the approval of the Publisher or the Author.

Pearson Prentice Hall™ is a trademark of Pearson Education, Inc.
Pearson® is a registered trademark of Pearson plc
Prentice Hall® is a registered trademark of Pearson Education, Inc.

Pearson Education LTD., London
Pearson Education Singapore, Pte. Ltd
Pearson Education, Canada, Ltd
Pearson Education—Japan
Pearson Education Australia PTY, Limited

Pearson Education North Asia Ltd
Pearson Educación de Mexico, S.A. de C.V.
Pearson Education Malaysia, Pte. Ltd.
Pearson Education, Upper Saddle River, New Jersey

10 9 8 7 6 5 4 3 2 1
ISBN-13: 978-0-13-714383-2
ISBN-10: 0-13-714383-4

Contents in Brief

Contents

PART V   WRITING EMPLOYMENT MESSAGES AND INTERVIEWING FOR JOBS   543

15   BUILDING CAREERS AND WRITING RÉSUMÉS   544

16   INTERVIEWING FOR EMPLOYMENT AND FOLLOWING UP   580

GIVING STUDENTS VITAL HANDS-ON EXPERIENCE WITH THE FULL RANGE OF PRINT AND ELECTRONIC MEDIA

The eighth edition of *Excellence in Business Communication* offers an unsurpassed collection of contemporary model documents that reflect the entire spectrum of print and electronic communication media. Students entering today's workforce are expected to use a wide range of tools, from instant messaging to blogging to podcasting, and *Excellence in Business Communication* provides the hands-on experience they need to meet employer expectations.

The annotations that accompany every model document help students understand how to apply the principles discussed in the chapter. Both the documents and the annotations have been extensively revised and improved in response to reviewer input.

Annotations show students the specific elements that make messages successful.

Uses an informative headline to summarize the news

Restates the news in the opening, providing more details

Provides a point of reference for regular readers of the blog

Continues to provide additional layers of detail

WHAT'S NEW IN THIS EDITION

With business communication evolving so rapidly, textbooks and learning packages need to evolve just as quickly. Here are the highlights of the extensive revisions in this edition:

- In this edition, students learn from dozens of practical examples in a variety of media, including blogs, wikis, and podcasts, that show both effective and ineffective communication efforts.

- A unique new chapter (Chapter 7) on crafting messages for electronic media covers e-mail, instant messaging, blogging, and podcasting. Coverage of wikis was added to the teamwork chapter, and writing website content was added to the report writing section.

Complex topics are clearly explained in both text and visuals.

- New coverage of audience psychology (in Chapter 1) gives students important insights into how audiences receive, process, and respond to messages.

- Expanded coverage of visual communication (in Chapter 12) helps students understand the growing importance of visual media in business today. Key topics include visual symbolism, visual design principles, and the ethics of visual design.

- The text now has more emphasis on strategic and managerial communication, with slightly less focus on tactical, transactional communication.

- Cases have long been a popular pedagogical feature, and the eighth edition now offers more than 140 cases, including more than 100 short-message cases, short- and long-report cases, PowerPoint cases, and employment-message cases. More than one-third of the cases are new in this edition. Cases feature virtually every significant medium now used in business, including e-mail, instant messaging, text messaging, social networking, blogging, webpages, voice mail, and podcasting.

- A new career planning Prologue features advice on creating employment portfolios and using this course as a way to create work samples to show potential employers. To help students select appropriate projects for their portfolios, numerous "Portfolio Builder" exercises and cases are highlighted throughout the book.

- The entire text was thoroughly revised for clarity and conciseness. Even with an additional chapter and all these major additions and updates, the total word count in this edition is more than 12,000 words lower than in the previous edition.

The following pages itemize the extensive improvements in every chapter.

Numerous quick reference tables and checklists offer practical advice for successful communication.

Table 7.2	TIPS FOR EFFECTIVE BUSINESS BLOGGING
Tip	**Why It's Important**
Have a clear plan before you start blogging.	Without a clear plan, your blog is likely to wander from topic to topic without providing compelling information or building a sense of community with your audience.
Post frequently.	The whole point of a blog is fresh material; if you don't have a constant supply of new information or new links, create a traditional website instead.
Make it about your customers and the issues that are important to them.	Readers want to know how your blog will help them, entertain them, or give them a chance to communicate with others who have similar interests.
Write in an authentic voice; never create an artificial character who supposedly writes a blog.	*Flogs*, or fake blogs, violate the spirit of blogging, show disrespect for your audience, and will turn audiences against you as soon as they uncover the truth.
Link generously—but carefully.	Providing interesting links to other blogs and websites is a fundamental aspect of blogging, but think twice before putting these links in your blog. Make sure the links will be of value to your readers, and make sure they don't point to material that could damage your reputation.
Keep it brief.	Most online readers don't have the patience to read lengthy reports.

Chapter-by-Chapter Changes and Improvements

Feature	Chapter 1	Chapter 2	Chapter 3	Chapter 4
Learning objectives	More emphasis on understanding the communication process and how audiences receive and process messages	More emphasis on collaborative writing and wikis for team communication	More emphasis on improving intercultural communication skills	Comparable to 7th edition
Chapter-opening vignette and chapter-closing simulation	**Updated:** Six Apart, one of the leaders in blogging technology	**Updated:** The Container Store, a growing retail chain with a reputation for excellent teamwork	**Updated:** IBM, highly regarded for its successful diversity initiatives	**Updated:** *The Complete Idiot's Guides*, a publishing phenomenon built around audience needs
Chapter content (subject areas that were added, clarified, expanded, streamlined, or updated for this edition)	• *Inside the Mind of Your Audience*, new section that explains how audiences receive, process, and respond to messages • New section on legal aspects of communication, including intellectual property concerns • Virtual communities • Technology highlight box on Web 2.0	• Collaborative writing technologies, including content management systems and wikis • Updated coverage of meeting technologies • IM now covered in new Chapter 7	• Expanded coverage of appreciating diversity in religion and in ability differences • Use of assistive technologies for communicating with people with disabilities	• Streamlined coverage of media types • New coverage of visual media • Revised coverage of electronic media
Model documents and other exhibits	• **Revised:** Communication process (Fig. 1.5) • **New:** Audience-centered communication (Fig. 1.7) • **New:** Becoming an effective business communicator (Fig. 1.8)	• **New:** Using a wiki for collaborative communication (Fig. 2.1) • **Updated:** Shared workspaces (Fig. 2.2) • **Updated:** Typical meeting agenda (Fig. 2.4) • **Updated:** Typical minutes of a meeting (Fig. 2.5) • **New:** Virtual meetings in a virtual world (Fig. 2.7)	• **New:** Languages of the world (language map) (Fig. 3.1)	• **New:** Visual media (Fig. 4.5) • **New:** Electronic oral media (Fig. 4.6) • **Updated:** E-mail message with improved organization (Fig. 4.8) • **Updated:** Message demonstrating a diplomatic organization plan (Fig. 4.9) • **New:** Media advantages and disadvantages (Table 4.1)
End-of-chapter exercises	• New exercise on audience psychology	• New exercise on voice mail	Comparable to 7th edition	• New exercises on ethical choices and blogging for profit
End-of-chapter cases	N/A	N/A	N/A	N/A

Chapter-by-Chapter Changes and Improvements

Feature	Chapter 5	Chapter 6	Chapter 7	Chapter 8 (formerly Chapter 7)
Learning objectives	More emphasis on building credibility	Comparable to 7th edition	New chapter	Comparable to 7th edition
Chapter-opening vignette and chapter-closing simulation	**Updated:** Creative Commons, a new approach to copyrights for digital publishing	**New:** Mercedes-AMG's multimedia website	**New:** The Southwest Airlines team-written blog	**Updated:** Cone, Inc., which specializes in crafting positive messages for corporate and nonprofit clients
Chapter content (subject areas that were added, clarified, expanded, streamlined, or updated for this edition)	• Clarified coverage of denotation and connotation • E-mail messages now covered in Chapter 7	• Coverage of RSS newsfeeds now in Chapter 7	New content: • Choosing electronic media for brief messages • Creating effective e-mail messages • Creating effective instant messages and text messages • Creating effective business blogs • Creating effective podcasts • Distributing blog and podcast content	Comparable to 7th edition
Model documents and other exhibits	• **New:** Fostering a positive relationship with an audience (Fig. 5.2) • **New:** Choosing effective words (Fig. 5.3) • **New:** Unified paragraphs (Fig. 5.4) • **Revised:** Weeding out obsolete phrases (Table 5.3)	• **New:** Improving a customer letter through careful revision (Fig. 6.2) • **New:** Revised customer letter (Fig. 6.3) • **New:** Revision marks in Microsoft Word (Fig. 6.4) • **New:** Comments attached to a PDF file (Fig. 6.5) • **New:** Ineffective and effective document design (Fig. 6.6) • **New:** A typical business memo (Fig. 6.7)	New figures and tables: • E-mail for business communication • IM for business communication • Video blogging • Elements of an effective business blog • The podcasting process • The syndication process for blogs • Viewing blog headlines in newsreader software • Tagging on a social bookmarking site • Tips for effective e-mail messages • Tips for effective business blogging	• **New:** Routine messages (Fig. 8.1) • **New:** Effective message requesting action (Fig. 8.2) • **New:** Effective IM response to information request (Fig. 8.5) • **New:** News release announcing positive news (Fig. 8.9) • **New:** Congratulating business partners (Fig. 8.10)
End-of-chapter exercises	• New exercises on the "you" attitude, topic sentences, and transitions	• New exercises on revision, readability, document design, ethics, and global audiences	• 40 new questions and exercises	• New exercise on writing requests
End-of-chapter cases	N/A	N/A	25 new cases	13 new cases

Chapter-by-Chapter Changes and Improvements

Feature	Chapter 9 (formerly Chapter 8)	Chapter 10 (formerly Chapter 9)	Chapter 11 (formerly Chapter 10)	Chapter 12 (formerly Chapter 11)
Learning objectives	More emphasis on the importance of ethics and etiquette in negative messages	More emphasis on identifying objections before writing persuasive messages	Comparable to 7th edition	More emphasis on effective writing for the web
Chapter-opening vignette and chapter-closing simulation	**Updated:** KMPG, which had to make a strategic decision about apologizing for illegal accounting practices	**New:** ClubMom, the first online social network for mothers	**New:** Tesco, the leading grocery retailer in the UK, and its extensive audience research program	**New:** Tellabs, a major producer of Internet equipment, and its highly regarded annual reports
Chapter content (subject areas that were added, clarified, expanded, streamlined, or updated for this edition)	• Expanded coverage of ethics and etiquette in the preparation and delivery of negative messages	• Revised coverage of audience motivation • Revised coverage of anticipating objections	• More on research ethics, including *pretexting* • Organizing website content • The challenge of finding information in the hidden Internet • Taking advantage of innovative research technologies, including desktop and enterprise search, research and content managers, social bookmarking, and research newsfeeds	• Drafting online content • Revised and expanded coverage of visual communication, including visual design principles, visual symbolism, and the ethics of visual design
Model documents and other exhibits	Comparable to 7th edition	• **New:** Explaining the benefits of product features (Fig. 10.4) • **New:** The spectrum of emotional and logical appeals (Fig. 10.5) • **New:** Flexible communication on the web (Fig. 10.6) • **New:** Human needs that influence motivation (Table 10.1)	• **Revised:** Direct approach versus indirect approach in an introduction (Fig. 11.3) • **New:** Information architecture (Fig. 11.9) • **Updated:** Important resources for business research (Table 11.3) • **Updated:** Best of Internet searching (Table 11.4)	• **Updated:** Choosing the right tone for business reports (Fig. 12.2) • **New:** Effective report expressing action plan in the close (Fig. 12.4) • **New:** Visual symbolism (Fig. 12.7) • **New:** Ineffective and effective visual designs (Fig. 12.8) • **New:** Mapping using geographic information system (Fig. 12.16b) • **New:** Diagram (Fig. 12.17)
End-of-chapter exercises	• New exercises on buffers, ethics, etiquette, and company culture	• New exercises on avoiding hard sells, anticipating objections, podcasting, writing persuasive subject lines, and building credibility	Comparable to 7th edition	• New exercises on online composition and visual design
End-of-chapter cases	10 new cases	9 new cases	N/A	Comparable to 7th edition

Chapter-by-Chapter Changes and Improvements

Feature	Chapter 13 (formerly Chapter 12)	Chapter 14 (formerly Chapter 13)	Chapter 15 (formerly Chapter 14)	Chapter 16 (formerly Chapter 15)
Learning objectives	Comparable to 7th edition	Comparable to 7th edition	More emphasis on the importance of networking, résumé fraud, and résumé formats	Comparable to 7th edition
Chapter-opening vignette and chapter-closing simulation	**Updated:** Bill & Melinda Gates Foundation and the role reports and proposals play in the operation of one of the world's premiere charitable organizations	**Updated:** Hewlett-Packard using oral presentations to win a $3 billion order	**New:** Hersha Hospitability Management's use of an applicant tracking system	**Updated:** Google's continuing search for the best technical and business talent in the online industry
Chapter content (subject areas that were added, clarified, expanded, streamlined, or updated for this edition)	• Revising web content	• New coverage of adapting presentations based on the audience's emotional state • Revised coverage of creating navigation and support slides, including title, agenda, program detail, and blueprint slides	• Updated advice on staying abreast of business and financial news, including subscribing to blogs and podcasts • Preparing reference sheets • Expanded coverage of networking, including using online social networks • Creating PDF and PowerPoint versions of résumés • Material on career planning is now in the new Prologue	• Updated coverage of situation, behavioral, and working interview formats • New section on interview media, describing telephone, e-mail, IM, virtual, and video interviews
Model documents and other exhibits	• **New:** Report synopsis (Fig. 13.3)	• **New:** Distractions from decorative artwork (Fig. 14.5) • **Updated:** Presentation slide master (Fig. 14.7) • **Updated:** Slide sorter view (Fig. 14.8) • **New:** Navigation and support slides (Fig. 14.9) • **New:** Moving blueprint slides (Fig. 14.10)	• **New:** Combination résumé (Fig. 15.5)	• **New:** Finding out about an organization and a job opportunity (Table 16.2)
End-of-chapter exercises	• New exercises on structuring solicited proposals and revising for clarity and conciseness	• New exercises on using PowerPoint animation (students can download a presentation file to analyze), making presentations at trade shows, and techniques for improving vocal delivery	• New exercises on HTML résumés and creating a vidcast to accompany a résumé	• New exercises on handling qualification weaknesses in an interview and matching personality to company culture
End-of-chapter cases	6 new cases	4 new cases	Comparable to 7th edition	Comparable to 7th edition

A COMPLETE TEACHING AND LEARNING SOLUTION

Excellence in Business Communication has helped millions of students master essential skills for succeeding in the workplace. The eighth edition extends that tradition by offering an unmatched set of tools that simplify teaching, promote active learning, and stimulate critical thinking. These components work together at four levels to provide seamless coverage of vital knowledge and skills:

- **Previewing.** Each chapter prepares students with clear learning objectives and a brief compelling vignette featuring a successful professional role model.

- **Developing.** Chapter content develops, explains, and elaborates on concepts with a concise, carefully organized presentation of textual and visual material. The three-step process of planning, writing, and completing is clearly explained and reinforced throughout the text in examples ranging from e-mail messages to blogs to formal reports.

- **Enhancing.** Contemporary examples, many accompanied by the three-step diagram adapted to each message, show students the specific elements that contribute to—or detract from—successful messages.

- **Reinforcing.** Hundreds of realistic business English exercises and activities let students practice vital skills and put newfound knowledge to immediate use. Interactive document makeovers let students experience firsthand the elements that make a document successful, giving them the insights they need to analyze and improve their own business messages. Communication cases, most featuring real companies, encourage students to think about contemporary business issues as they put their skills to use in a variety of media, including blogging and podcasting.

At every stage of the learning experience, *Excellence in Business Communication* provides the tools that instructors and students need to succeed.

Features That Help Students Build Essential Knowledge and Skills	Previewing	Developing	Enhancing	Reinforcing
Learning objectives (beginning of chapter)	•			
On the Job vignettes (beginning of chapter)	•			
Concise presentations of fundamentals (within chapter)		•		
Managerial perspectives on key topics (within chapter)		•		
Three-step writing process diagrams (within chapter)		•		
Real-life examples (within chapter)			•	
Annotated model documents (within chapter)			•	
Highlight boxes (within chapter)			•	
Handbook of Grammar, Mechanics, and Usage (end of book)			•	
Margin notes (within chapter)				•
Checklists (within chapter)				•
On the Job simulations (end of chapter)				•
Learning Objectives Checkup (end of chapter				•

Features That Help Students Build Essential Knowledge and Skills	Previewing	Developing	Enhancing	Reinforcing
Apply Your Knowledge questions (end of chapter)				•
Practice Your Knowledge activities and exercises (end of chapter)				•
Expand Your Knowledge web resources (end of chapter)				•
Cases (following Chapters 7, 8, 9, 10, 13, 14, 15, and 16)				•
Document Makeovers (online)				•
Interactive study guide (online)				•
Peak Performance Grammar and Mechanics (online)				•

UP-TO-DATE COVERAGE OF IMPORTANT TOPICS

Covering teamwork, listening, ethics, and etiquette to the latest communication technologies, *Excellence in Business Communication* has always helped instructors and students stay on the leading edge of contemporary practice. That emphasis continues in the eighth edition, with innovative coverage of audience psychology, electronic media, and visual communication.

Audience Psychology (Chapter 1)

Too many business professionals, particularly early in their careers, make avoidable mistakes caused by poor understanding of how audiences receive, process, and respond to incoming messages. The eighth edition addresses this challenge with unique new coverage of audience psychology. These concepts are tightly integrated with a discussion of the communication process that includes a graphic (Figure 1.8) that clearly identifies the skills communicators need to succeed at every stage of the process.

Electronic Media (Chapter 7)

Businesses continue to adopt virtually any technology that promises faster and more effective communication, and the past couple years have seen astounding changes in business media habits. Practically overnight, blogs, wikis, and podcasts have moved from the high-tech fringe into the business mainstream. *Excellence in Business Communication* further extends its lead in technology coverage with a unique new chapter, "Crafting Messages for Electronic Media," that helps students adapt the skills they're learning to these new media.

Visual Media and Visual Communication Design (Chapters 4 and 12)

Technology isn't the only fundamental change occurring in the world of business communication. In recent years, more communicators have discovered the power of visual media, both to convey complex ideas quickly and to connect with audiences whose verbal skills might be insufficient for traditional, text-heavy messages.

Chapter 4 introduces students to visual media, and Chapter 12 expands on this with coverage of visual literacy, principles of effective visual design, and the ethics of visual communication.

Why should I care about CRM?

XPLANAT|ONS® by XPLANE®

As seen in Business 2.0 | ©2001 xplane.com

Compelling real-life examples show students how principles such as visual design are put to use.

Communication Technology

Vital topics in communication technology are interwoven throughout the text, reflecting the expectations and opportunities in today's workplace:

- Aggregators
- Assistive technologies
- Autocompletion and autocorrection
- Automated reputation analysis
- Blogging
- Commenting tools
- Computer animation
- Content management systems
- Crowdsourcing
- Desktop publishing
- Desktop search engines
- Digital photography
- Electronic forms
- Electronic presentations
- E-mail
- E-mail hygiene
- Enterprise IM
- Enterprise search engines
- Enterprise wikis
- E-portfolios
- Extranets
- Geographic information systems
- Global Positioning Systems (GPSs)
- Graphic design software
- Groupware
- Hidden Internet
- HTML résumé production
- Hyperlinks
- Instant messaging
- Intellectual property rights
- Interactive media

- Internet telephony (VoIP)
- Interview simulators
- Intranets
- Knowledge management systems
- Linked and embedded documents
- Machine translation
- Mobile blogs
- Multimedia documents
- Multimedia presentations
- Natural language search
- Newsfeeds
- Online brainstorming systems
- Online chat systems
- Online research techniques
- Online survey tools
- Opt-in e-mail
- PDF documents
- Peer-to-peer networking
- Podcasting
- Podcatchers
- Proposal writing software
- Research and content managers
- Résumé scanning systems
- RSS
- Screencasting
- Search and metasearch engines
- Security and privacy concerns in electronic media
- Shared online workspaces
- Short messaging service (SMS)
- Social bookmarking

- Social media
- Social networking
- Streaming media
- Syndication
- Tagging
- Templates and style sheets
- Text messaging
- Translation software
- Video blogging
- Video podcasts
- Videoconferencing and telepresence

- Virtual agents and bots
- Voice synthesis and recognition
- Web 2.0
- Web content management systems
- Web directories
- Web-based virtual meetings
- Webcasting
- Website accessibility
- Wikis
- Wireless networks (Wi-Fi and WiMAX)
- Wizards

VERSATILE RESOURCES FOR INSTRUCTORS AND STUDENTS

The multimedia *Excellence in Business Communication* package helps instructors and students take full advantage of the latest advances in instructional technology.

Business Communication Headline News

Stay on top of hot topics, important trends, and new technologies with **Business Communication Headline News**, which uses the newest Internet technologies to deliver late-breaking news in headlines with concise summaries. You can scan incoming items in a matter of seconds and simply click through to read the full articles that interest you.

This free service offers numerous ways to enhance lectures and student activities:

- Keep current with the latest information and trends in the field
- Easily update your lecture notes with fresh material
- Create visuals for your classroom presentations
- Supplement your lectures with cutting-edge handouts
- Gather podcasts, online video, and other new media examples to use in the classroom
- Enhance your research projects with the newest data
- Compare best practices from other instructors
- Improve the quality and effectiveness of your teaching by reading about new teaching tips and techniques

While visiting the website, you also get free access to these powerful instructional resources:

- The **Business Communication Web Directory**, available only on this site, where you'll find more than 240 topics and more than 5,000 links, with a search engine for the site to help you find exactly what you want.
- Thirty-six **Business Communication Newsletters** updated every 15 minutes, each devoted to a specific topic, such as business correspondence, blogging, e-mail, podcasting, and instant messaging.

- **Business Communication News Links**, with links to dozens of business communication topics from sources including Google News, Live Search, Ask.com, Clipmarks, and Yahoo! News.

- **The Business Communication Library**, available only on this site, where you'll find dozens of articles on a wide variety of topics, with a newsfeed available to alert you to new articles.

- **Business Communication Search**, featuring a revolutionary approach to searching developed by Bovée and Thill that lets you quickly access more than 325 search engines. The tool uses a simple, attractive, intuitive, interface, engineered to help business communication instructors find precisely what they want, whether it's PowerPoint files, Adobe Acrobat PDFs, Microsoft Word documents, or Excel files.

- **Business Communication Multimedia Resources**, with thousands of PowerPoint presentations, online videos, podcasts, and photographs from Google Video, Dailymotion, Yahoo! Images, Podscope, Podzinger, and many more. Download these resources today and use them in your classes tomorrow.

- **Textbook Resources**, where students can find textbook resources such as podcasts and PowerPoints.

You can subscribe to Business Communication Headline News and get delivery by e-mail, MyYahoo or Google homepage, RSS newsreader, mobile phone, instant messenger, MP3, and a host or other options. Learn more today by visiting www.businesscommunicationblog.com.

Authors' E-Mail Hotline for Faculty

Integrity, excellence, and responsiveness are the authors' hallmarks. That means providing you with textbooks that are academically sound, creative, timely, and sensitive to instructor and student needs. As an adopter of *Excellence in Business Communication*, you are invited to use the authors' E-mail Hotline (hotline@businesscommunicationblog.com) if you ever have a question or concern related to the text or its supplements.

Instructor's Resource Center

At www.prenhall.com/irc, instructors can access a variety of print, digital, and presentation resources available with this text in downloadable format. Registration is simple and gives you immediate access to new titles and new editions. As a registered faculty member, you can download resource files and receive immediate access and instructions for installing course management content on your campus server.

If you ever need assistance, our dedicated technical support team is ready to help with the media supplements that accompany this text. Visit www.247.prenhall.com for answers to frequently asked questions and toll-free user support phone numbers.

The following supplements are available to adopting instructors (for detailed descriptions, please visit www.prenhall.com/irc):

- **Instructor's Resource Center (IRC) on CD-ROM**—ISBN: 0136019390

- **Printed Instructor's Manual with Video Guide**—ISBN: 0136019366

- **Printed Test Item File**—ISBN: 0136018912

- **TestGen Test Generating Software**—Available at the IRC (online).

- **PowerPoint Slides**—Both basic and enhanced versions are available at the IRC (online or on CD-ROM).

- **Classroom Response Systems (CRS)**—Available at the IRC (both online and on CD-ROM); learn more at www.prenhall.com/crs.
- **Image Bank**—Visit the IRC on CD-ROM for this resource
- **Custom Videos on DVD**—ISBN: 0136006957
- **Transparency Package**—ISBN: 0136018904

OneKey Online Courses: Convenience, Simplicity, and Success

OneKey offers complete teaching and learning online resources in one place. OneKey is all that instructors need to plan and administer courses, and OneKey is all that students need for anytime, anywhere access to online course material. Conveniently organized by textbook chapter, these resources save time and help students reinforce and apply what they have learned. OneKey is available in three course management platforms: Blackboard, CourseCompass, and WebCT.

OneKey resources include

- **Learning modules** (Each section within each chapter offers a 5-question pretest, a summary for review, an online learning activity, and a 10-question posttest.)
- **Peak Performance Grammar and Mechanics***
- **Two versions of Document Makeovers*** (One version feeds your grade book, and one provides student practice.)
- **Access to Mydropbox.com**
- **Peer review software**

OneKey requires an access code, which can be shrink-wrapped free of charge with new copies of this text. Please contact your local sales representative for the correct ISBN. Codes may also be purchased separately at www.prenhall.com/management.

Companion Website

This text's Companion Website, at www.prenhall.com/thill, contains valuable resources for both students and professors, including access to a student version of the PowerPoint package, an online study guide, the "English–Spanish Audio Glossary of Business Terms," the "Handbook of Grammar, Mechanics, and Usage," and the "Business Communication Study Hall," which allow students to brush up on several aspects of business communication—grammar, writing skills, critical thinking, report writing, résumés, and PowerPoint development.

Student Study Guide

This study guide includes a variety of review questions and study quizzes. Page references to the review questions and quizzes are included.

---

*Instructors who wish to use "Peak Performance Grammar and Mechanics" and "Document Makeovers" but not the rest of the OneKey content can access these features in a special section of the Companion Website. This section requires an access code, which you can ask to have shrink-wrapped free of charge with new copies of this text. Please contact your local sales representative for the correct ISBN. Codes may also be purchased separately at www.prenhall.com/management.

VangoNotes

Study on the go with VangoNotes (www.VangoNotes.com), detailed chapter reviews in downloadable MP3 format. Now wherever you are and whatever you're doing, you can study on the go by listening to the following for each chapter of your textbook:

- **Big Ideas**—Your "need to know" for each chapter
- **Key Terms**—Audio "flashcards"—help you review key concepts and terms
- **Rapid Review**—Quick-drill session—use it right before your test

VangoNotes are *flexible:* Download all the material (or only the chapters you need) directly to your MP3 player. And VangoNotes are *efficient:* Use them in your car, at the gym, walking to class, wherever you go. So get yours today, and get studying.

CourseSmart eTextbooks Online

CourseSmart is an exciting new *choice* for students looking to save money. As an alternative to purchasing the print textbook, students can purchase an electronic version of the same content and save up to 50% off the suggested list price of the print text. With a CourseSmart eTextbook, students can search the text, make notes online, print out reading assignments that incorporate lecture notes and bookmark important passages for later review. For more information, or to purchase access to the CourseSmart eTextbook, visit wwwcoursesmart.com.

FEEDBACK

The authors and the product team would appreciate hearing from you! Let us know what you think about this textbook by writing to college_marketing@prenhall.com. Please include "Feedback about Thill/Bovée 8e" in the subject line.

For any questions related to this product, please contact our customer service department online, at www.247.prenhall.com.

ACKNOWLEDGMENTS

The eighth edition of *Excellence in Business Communication* reflects the professional experience of a large team of contributors and advisors.

Reviewers

Our thanks to the many individuals whose valuable suggestions and constructive comments contributed to the success of this book. The authors are deeply grateful to Janet Adams, Minnesota State University–Mankato; Gus Amaya, Florida International University; Anita S. Bednar, Central State University; Donna Cox, Monroe Community College; Sauny Dills, California Polytechnic State University–San Luis Obispo; Ruthann Dirks, Emporia State University; Cynthia Drexel, Western State College; Mary DuBoise, DeVry University–Dallas; J. Thomas Dukes, University of Akron; Karen Eickhoff, University of Tennessee; Lindsay S. English, Ursuline College; Mike Flores, Wichita State University; Charlene A. Gierkey, Northwestern Michigan College; Sue Granger, Jacksonville State University; Bradley S. Hayden,

Western Michigan University; Joyce Hicks, Valparaiso University; Michael Hignite, Southwest Missouri State; Mark Hilton, Lyndon State College; Cynthia Hofacker, University of Wisconsin–Eau Claire; Louise C. Holcomb, Gainesville College; Larry Honl, University of Wisconsin–Eau Claire; Kenneth Hunsaker, Utah State University; Sandie Idziak, University of Texas; Robert O. Joy, Central Michigan University; Paula R. Kaiser, University of North Carolina–Greensboro; Paul Killorin, Portland Community College; Linda M. LaDuc, University of Massachusetts–Amherst; Jennifer Loney, Portland State University; Al Lucero, East Tennessee State University; Rachel Mather, Adelphi University; Linda McAdams, Westark Community College; Melinda McCannon, Gordon College; Bronna McNeely, Midwestern State University; William McPherson, Indiana University of Pennsylvania; Russ Meade, Tidewater Community College; Betty Mealor, Abraham Baldwin College; Mary Miller, Ashland University; Joe Newman, Faulkner University; Barbara Oates, Texas A&M University; Richard Profozich, Prince George's Community College; Brian Railsback, Western Carolina University; John Rehfuss, California State University–Sacramento; Joan C. Roderick, Southwest Texas State University; Salvatore Safina, University of Wisconsin; Jean Anna Sellers, Fort Hays State University; Andrea Smith–Hunter, Siena College; Carol Smith White, Georgia State University; Karen Sneary, Northwestern Oklahoma State University; Jeanne Stannard, Johnson County Community College; Terisa Tennison, Florida International University; Michael Thompson, Brigham Young University; Betsy Vardaman, Baylor University; Robert von der Osten, Ferris State University; Karl V. Winton, Marshall University; Billy Walters, Troy State University; George Walters, Emporia State University; John L. Waltman, Eastern Michigan University; F. Stanford Wayne, Southwest Missouri State; Robert Wheatley, Troy State University; Rosemary B. Wilson, Washtenaw Community College; Beverly C. Wise, SUNY–Morrisville; Aline Wolff, New York University; and Bonnie Yarbrough, University of North Carolina–Greensboro. We also appreciate the notable talents and distinguished contributions of Deborah Valentine, Emory University; Anne Bliss, University of Colorado–Boulder; Carolyn A. Embree, University of Akron; Carla L. Sloan, Liberty University; Doris A. Van Horn Christopher, California State University–Los Angeles; and Susan S. Rehwaldt, Southern Illinois University.

Reviewers of Document Makeovers

We sincerely thank the following reviewers for their assistance with the Document Makeover feature: Lisa Barley, Eastern Michigan University; Marcia Bordman, Gallaudet University; Jean Bush-Bacelis, Eastern Michigan University; Bobbye Davis, Southern Louisiana University; Cynthia Drexel, Western State College; Kenneth Gibbs, Worcester State College; Ellen Leathers, Bradley University; Diana McKowen, Indiana University; Bobbie Nicholson, Mars Hill College; Andrew Smith, Holyoke Community College; Jay Stubblefield, North Carolina Wesleyan College; and Dawn Wallace, South Eastern Louisiana University.

Reviewers of Model Documents

The many model documents in the text and their accompanying annotations received invaluable review from Dacia Charlesworth, Robert Morris University; Diane Todd Bucci, Robert Morris University; Estelle Kochis, Suffolk County Community College; Sherry Robertson, Arizona State University; Nancy Goehring, Monterey Peninsula College; James Hatfield, Florida Community College at Jacksonville; and Avon Crismore, Indiana University.

Personal Acknowledgments

We wish to extend a heartfelt thanks to our many friends, acquaintances, and business associates who provided materials or agreed to be interviewed so that we could bring the real world into the classroom.

A very special acknowledgment goes to George Dovel, whose superb editorial skills, distinguished background, and wealth of business experience assured this project of clarity and completeness. Also, recognition and thanks to Jackie Estrada for her outstanding skills and excellent attention to detail. Her creation of the "Peak Performance Grammar and Mechanics" material is especially noteworthy. Paul Straley's keen eye enhanced the quality of the text throughout.

We also feel it is important to acknowledge and thank the Association for Business Communication, an organization whose meetings and publications provide a valuable forum for the exchange of ideas and for professional growth.

In addition, we would like to thank the supplement authors who prepared material for this new edition. They include Myles Hassell, University of New Orleans, who created the PowerPoint package and developed material for the study guide; William Peirce, Prince George's Community College, who developed material for the Internet study guide and OneKey Learning Modules; and Jay Stubblefield, North Carolina Wesleyan College, who wrote the test bank.

We want to extend our warmest appreciation to the devoted professionals at Prentice Hall. They include Jerome Grant, president; David Parker, editor-in-chief; Anne Howard, executive marketing manager; Ashley Santora, product development manager; Keri Molinari, assistant editor; all of Prentice Hall Business Publishing; and the outstanding Prentice Hall sales representatives. Finally, we thank Judy Leale, senior managing editor of production, and Renata Butera, associate managing editor, for their dedication; and we are grateful to Jeanine Furino, senior production editor at GGS Book Services, and Janet Slowik, art director, for their superb work.

John V. Thill

Courtland L. Bovée

Prologue

BUILDING A CAREER WITH YOUR COMMUNICATION SKILLS

USING THIS COURSE TO HELP LAUNCH YOUR CAREER

Few courses offer the two-for-the-price-of-one value you get from a business communication class. Not only will the skills you develop in this course be vital to your business career, they'll also play a key role in launching your career. As you'll see in Chapters 15 and 16, every activity in the job search process relies on communication, and the better you can communicate, the more successful you'll be in landing interesting and rewarding work.

This brief prologue sets the stage by helping you understand today's dynamic workplace, the steps you can take to adapt to the job market, and the importance of creating an employment portfolio. Take a few minutes to read these sections while you think about the career you hope to create for yourself.

UNDERSTANDING TODAY'S DYNAMIC WORKPLACE

Social, political, and financial events continue to change workplace conditions from year to year, so the job market you read about this year might not be the same market you try to enter a year or two from now. However, you can count on a few forces that are likely to affect your entry into the job market and your career success in years to come:[1]

- **Stability.** Your career probably won't be as stable as careers were in your parents' generation. In today's business world, your career will be affected by globalization, mergers and acquisitions, short-term mentality driven by the demands of stockholders, ethical upheavals, and the relentless quest for lower costs. On the plus side, new opportunities, new companies, and even entire industries can appear almost overnight, so while your career might not be as predictable as careers used to be, it could well be more of an adventure.

- **Lifetime employment.** The idea of *lifetime employment*, in which employees spend their entire working lives with a single firm that takes care of them throughout their careers, is all but gone in many industries. Boeing, the Chicago-based aerospace giant, speaks of lifetime *employability* rather than lifetime employment, putting the responsibility on employees to track market needs and keep their skills up to date—and even change careers if necessary. In fact, most U.S. employees will not only change employers multiple times but will even change careers anywhere from three to five times over their working lives.

- **Growth of small business.** Small business continues to be the primary engine of job creation in the United States, so chances are good that you'll work for a small firm at some point. One expert predicts that before long, 80 percent of the U.S. labor force will be working for firms employing fewer than 200 people.

- **Increase in independent contractors.** The nature of employment itself is changing for many people. As companies try to become more flexible, more employees

xxxiii

Would you like to pursue a career in business but have the flexibility to work from home? Many professionals now do so, as either independent contractors or corporate employees who telecommute.

are going solo and setting up shop as independent contractors, sometimes selling their services back to the very companies they just left.

- **Changing view of job-hopping.** Given all the changes, job-hopping doesn't have quite the negative connotation it once had. Even so, you still need to be careful about jumping at every new opportunity that promises more money or prestige. Recruiting and integrating new employees takes time and costs money, and most employers are reluctant to invest in someone who has a history of switching jobs numerous times without good reason.

What do all these forces mean to you? First, take charge of your career—and stay in charge of it. Understand your options, have a plan, and don't count on others to watch out for your future. Second, as you will learn throughout this course, understanding your audience is key to successful communication, starting with understanding how employers view today's job market.

How Employers View Today's Job Market

From the employer's perspective, the employment process is always a question of balance. Maintaining a stable workforce can improve practically every aspect of business performance, yet many employers feel they need the flexibility to shrink and expand payrolls as business conditions change. Employers obviously want to attract the best talent, but the best talent is often expensive and vulnerable to offers from competitors, so there are always financial trade-offs to consider.

Employers also struggle with the ups and downs of the economy, just as employees do. When unemployment is low, the balance of power shifts to employees, and employers have to compete in order to attract and keep top talent. When unemployment is high, the power shifts back to employers, who can afford to be more selective and less accommodating. In other words, pay attention to the economy whenever you're job hunting; at times you can be more aggressive, but at other times you should be more accommodating.

Rather than look for lifelong employees for every position, many employers now fill some needs by hiring temporary workers or engaging contractors on a project-by-project basis. Many U.S. employers are now also more willing to move jobs to less expensive labor markets outside the country and to recruit globally to fill positions in the United States. Both trends have stirred controversy, especially in the technology sector, as U.S. firms recruit top engineers and scientists from other countries while shifting mid- and low-range jobs to India, China, Russia, and other countries with lower wage structures.[2]

What Employers Look for in Job Applicants

Given the forces in the contemporary workplace, employers are looking for people who can adapt to the new dynamics of the business world, survive and thrive in fluid and uncertain situations, and continue to learn throughout their careers. Companies want team players with strong work records, leaders who are versatile, and employees with diversified skills and varied job experience.[3] In addition, most employers expect college graduates to be sensitive to cultural differences and to have a sound understanding of international affairs.[4] In fact, in some cases, your chances of being hired are better if you have studied abroad, have learned another language, or can otherwise demonstrate an appreciation of other cultures.

ADAPTING TO TODAY'S JOB MARKET

Adapting to the workplace is a lifelong process of seeking the best fit between what you want to do and what employers are willing to pay you to do. For instance, if money is more important to you than anything else, you can certainly pursue jobs that promise high pay; just be aware that most of these jobs require years of experience, and many produce a lot of stress, require frequent travel, or have other drawbacks you'll want to consider. In contrast, if location, lifestyle, intriguing work, or other factors are most important to you, you may well have to sacrifice some level of pay to achieve them. You need to know what you want to do, what you have to offer, and how to make yourself more attractive to employers.

What Do You Want to Do?

Economic necessities and the vagaries of the marketplace will influence much of what happens in your career, of course; nevertheless, it's wise to start your employment search by examining your own values and interests. Identify what you want to do first and then see whether you can find a position that satisfies you at a personal level while also meeting your financial needs.

- **What would you like to do every day?** Research occupations that interest you. Find out what people really do every day. Ask friends, relatives, or alumni from your school. Read interviews with people in various professions to get a sense for what their careers are like.

- **How would you like to work?** Consider how much independence you want on the job, how much variety you like, and whether you prefer to work with products, machines, people, ideas, figures, or some combination thereof. Do you prefer constant change or a predictable role?

- **What specific compensation do you expect?** What do you hope to earn in your first year? What's your ultimate earnings goal? Are you willing to settle for less money in order to do something you really love?

- **Can you establish some general career goals?** Consider where you'd like to start, where you'd like to go from there, and the ultimate position you'd like to attain.

- **What size company would you prefer?** Do you like the idea of working for a small, entrepreneurial operation or a large corporation?

- **What sort of corporate culture are you most comfortable with?** Would you be happy in a formal hierarchy with clear reporting relationships? Or do you prefer less structure? Do you prefer teamwork or individualism? Do you like a competitive environment?

- **What location would you like?** Would you like to work in a city, a suburb, a small town, an industrial area, or an uptown setting? Do you favor a particular part of the country? Another country?

Filling out the assessment in Table 1 might help you get a clearer picture of the nature of work you would like to pursue in your career.

Table 1 — CAREER SELF-ASSESSMENT

What work-related activities and situations do you prefer? Evaluate your preferences in each of the following areas and use the results to help guide your job search.

Activity or Situation	Strongly Agree	Agree	Disagree	No Preference
1. I want to work independently.	_____	_____	_____	_____
2. I want variety in my work.	_____	_____	_____	_____
3. I want to work with people.	_____	_____	_____	_____
4. I want to work with technology.	_____	_____	_____	_____
5. I want physical work.	_____	_____	_____	_____
6. I want mental work.	_____	_____	_____	_____
7. I want to work for a large organization.	_____	_____	_____	_____
8. I want to work for a nonprofit organization.	_____	_____	_____	_____
9. I want to work for a small family business.	_____	_____	_____	_____
10. I want to work for a service business.	_____	_____	_____	_____
11. I want to start or buy a business someday.	_____	_____	_____	_____
12. I want regular, predictable work hours.	_____	_____	_____	_____
13. I want to work in a city location.	_____	_____	_____	_____
14. I want to work in a small town or suburb.	_____	_____	_____	_____
15. I want to work in another country.	_____	_____	_____	_____
16. I want to work outdoors.	_____	_____	_____	_____
17. I want to work in a structured environment.	_____	_____	_____	_____
18. I want to avoid risk as much as possible.	_____	_____	_____	_____
19. I want to enjoy my work, even if that means making less money.	_____	_____	_____	_____
20. I want to become a high-level corporate manager.	_____	_____	_____	_____

What Do You Have to Offer?

Knowing what you *want* to do is one thing. Knowing what you *can* do is another. You may already have a good idea of what you can offer employers. If not, some brainstorming can help you identify your skills, interests, and characteristics. Start by jotting down 10 achievements you're proud of, such as learning to ski, taking a prize-winning photo, tutoring a child, or editing your school paper. Think carefully about what specific skills these achievements demanded of you. For example, leadership skills, speaking ability, and artistic talent may have helped you coordinate a winning presentation to your school's administration. As you analyze your achievements, you'll begin to recognize a pattern of skills. Which of them might be valuable to potential employers?

Next, look at your educational preparation, work experience, and extracurricular activities. What do your knowledge and experience qualify you to do? What have you learned from volunteer work or class projects that could benefit you on the job? Have you held any offices, won any awards or scholarships, mastered a second language?

Take stock of your personal characteristics. Are you aggressive, a born leader? Or would you rather follow? Are you outgoing, articulate, great with people? Or do you prefer working alone? Make a list of what you believe are your four or five most important qualities. Ask a relative or friend to rate your traits as well.

If you're having difficulty figuring out your interests, characteristics, or capabilities, consult your college placement office. Many campuses administer a variety of tests to help students identify interests, aptitudes, and personality traits. These tests won't reveal your "perfect" job, but they'll help you focus on the types of work best suited to your personality.

How Can You Make Yourself More Valuable?

While you're figuring out what you want from a job and what you can offer an employer, you can take positive steps now toward building your career. First, look for volunteer projects, temporary jobs, freelance work, or internships that will help expand your experience base and skill set. These temporary assignments not only help you gain valuable experience and relevant contacts but also provide you with important references and with items for your employment portfolio (see the following section).[5]

Second, consider applying your talents to *crowdsourcing* projects, in which companies and nonprofit organizations invite the public to contribute solutions to various challenges. For example, Fellowforce (www.fellowforce.com) posts projects involving advertising, business writing, photography, graphic design, programming, strategy development, and other skills.[6] Even if your contributions aren't chosen, you still have solutions to real business problems that you can show to potential employers as examples of your work.

Third, learn more about the industry or industries in which you want to work and stay on top of new developments. Join networks of professional colleagues and friends who can help you keep up with trends and events. Many professional societies have student chapters or offer students discounted memberships. Take courses and pursue other educational or life experiences that would be difficult to get while working full time.

Even after an employer hires you, it's a good idea to continue improving your skills, in order to distinguish yourself from your peers and to make yourself more valuable to current and potential employers. Acquire as much technical knowledge as you can, build broad-based life experience, and develop your social skills. Learn to respond to change in positive, constructive ways; doing so will help you adapt if your "perfect" career path eludes your grasp. Learn to see each job, even so-called entry-level jobs, as an opportunity to learn more and to expand your knowledge, experience, and social skills. Share what you know with others instead of hoarding knowledge in the hope of becoming indispensable; helping others excel is a skill, too.[7]

BUILDING AN EMPLOYMENT PORTFOLIO

Employers want proof that you have the skills to succeed on the job, but even if you don't have much relevant work experience, you can use your college classes to assemble that proof. Simply create and maintain an *employment portfolio*, which is a collection of projects that demonstrate your skills and knowledge. You can create both a *print portfolio* and an *e-portfolio*; both can help with your career effort. A print portfolio gives you something tangible to bring to interviews, and it lets you collect project results that might not be easy to show online, such as a handsomely bound report.

An e-portfolio is a multimedia presentation of your skills and experiences.[8] Think of it as a website that contains your résumé, work samples, letters of recommendation, articles you may have written, and other information about you and your skills. Be creative. For example, a student who was pursuing a degree in meteorology added a video clip of himself delivering a weather forecast.[9] The portfolio can be burned on a CD-ROM for physical distribution or, more commonly, posted online—whether it's a personal website, your college's site (if student pages are available), or a networking site such as www.collegegrad.com or www.portfolios.com. To see a selection of student e-portfolios from colleges around the United States, go to www.businesscommunicationblog.com and click on "Textbook Resources." Locate *Excellence in Business Communication*, 8th ed., click on "Prologue," and then click on "Student E-Portfolios."

Starting in Chapter 7, pay close attention to the activities and cases marked "Portfolio Builder." These items will make particularly good samples of not only your communication skills but your ability to understand and solve business-related challenges. By combining these projects with samples from your other courses, you can create a compelling portfolio by the time you're ready to start interviewing. Your portfolio is also a great resource for writing your résumé because it reminds you of all the great work you've done over the years. Moreover, you can continue to refine and expand your portfolio throughout your career; many professionals use e-portfolios to advertise their services, for instance (see Figure 1).

As you assemble your portfolio, collect anything that shows your ability to perform, whether it's in school, on the job, or in other venues. However, you *must* check with an employer before including any items you created while you were an employee. Many business documents contain confidential information that companies don't want distributed to outside audiences.

For each item you add to your portfolio, write a brief description that helps other people understand the meaning and significance of the project. Include items such as these:

- **Background.** Why did you undertake this project? Was it a school project, an article you wrote on your own initiative, or something else?

- **Project objectives.** Explain the project's goals, if relevant.

- **Collaborators.** If you worked with others, be sure to mention that and discuss team dynamics, if appropriate. For instance, if you led the team or worked with others long distance as a *virtual team*, point that out.

- **Constraints.** Sometimes the most impressive thing about a project is the time or budget constraints under which it was created. If these apply to a project, consider mentioning them in a way that doesn't sound like an excuse for poor quality. If you had only one week to create a website, for example, you might say, "One of the intriguing challenges of this project was the deadline; I had only one week to design, compose, test, and publish this material."

- **Outcomes.** If the project's goals were measurable, what was the result? For example, if you wrote a letter soliciting donations for a charitable cause, how much money did you raise?

- **Learning experience.** If appropriate, describe what you learned during the course of the project.

FIGURE 1
Professional Portfolio

FIGURE 1
Professional Portfolio
Claudia Volpi, a creative director
and writer based in Santa Monica,
California, uses Portfolios.com to
host her professional portfolio.
From the thumbnail images on
the front page, viewers can click
to see samples of her work, such
as this television commercial.
They can also click to learn more
about her background and
qualifications.

Keep in mind that the portfolio itself is a communication project, too, so be sure
to apply everything you learn in this course about effective communication and good
design. Also, assume that every potential employer will find your e-portfolio site
(even if you don't tell them about it), so don't include anything that could come back
to haunt you.

To get started, first check with the career center at your college; many schools
now offer e-portfolio systems for their students. (Some schools now require e-portfolios, so you may already be building one.) You can also find plenty of advice online;
search for "e-portfolio" or "student portfolio." Finally, consider reading *Portfolios for
Technical and Professional Communicators* by Herb J. Smith and Kim Haimes-Korn.
This book is intended for communication specialists, but it offers great advice for
anyone who wants to create a compelling employment portfolio.

Best wishes for success in this course and in your career!

Part I
Understanding the Foundations of Business Communication

Achieving Success Through Effective Business Communication

Learning Objectives

AFTER STUDYING THIS CHAPTER, YOU WILL BE ABLE TO

1 Explain why effective communication is important to your success in today's business environment

2 Describe the five characteristics of effective business communication

3 Identify eight communication skills that successful employers expect from their employees

4 List five ways in which business communication differs from social communication

5 Describe six strategies for communicating more effectively on the job

6 Explain what must occur for an audience to successfully receive, decode, and respond to messages

7 Explain four strategies for using communication technology successfully

8 Discuss the importance of ethics in business communication, and differentiate between ethical dilemmas and ethical lapses

On the Job

COMMUNICATING AT SIX APART

MENA TROTT HELPS REDEFINE THE NATURE OF COMMUNICATION

Many people transform personal interests into successful business enterprises. Mena Trott used her hobby to help start a revolution. She was among the first wave of web users to keep a *web log*, or *blog*, an online journal that can cover any topic from politics to pets. As the popularity of her blog grew, the rudimentary blogging tools available at the time couldn't keep up. Trott and her husband, Ben, decided to create their own software that would handle high-volume blogging—and make it easy for anyone to blog.

Through both the company she co-founded with her husband, Ben, and her own widely read blog, Six Apart's Mena Trott is an influential figure in the world of blogging.

The Trotts' first product, Movable Type, caught on quickly as web users around the world welcomed the opportunity to become instant online publishers. Before long, Ben and Mena had become first-name celebrities in the "blogosphere," and an effort that had started as an extension of a hobby soon grew into a multinational company. (The Trotts named their new company Six Apart in honor of the fact that the two of them were born just six days apart.)

With help from companies such as Six Apart, bloggers began to influence virtually every aspect of contemporary life, from politics to journalism to business. The best of the business blogs tear down the barriers that can make companies seem impersonal or unresponsive to customers. Companies ranging from Boeing to General Motors to Microsoft now use blogs to put a human face on commercial organizations, and millions of people read these blogs to keep up on the latest news about the products and companies that interest them.

Blogging is changing so rapidly that it's hard to predict what the future holds for Six Apart, but Trott summed up the impact of blogging when she said, "I can't imagine where we'll be in a year, let alone five years, but I'm certain web logging is here to stay."[1]

www.sixapart.com

ACHIEVING SUCCESS IN TODAY'S COMPETITIVE ENVIRONMENT

Your career success depends on effective communication.

Successful professionals such as Mena Trott (profiled in the chapter opener) will tell you that to succeed in business today, you need the ability to communicate with people both inside and outside your organization. Whether you are competing to get the job you want or to win the customers your company needs, your success or failure depends to a large degree on your ability to communicate. In fact, if you're looking for a surefire way to stand out from your competition in the job market, improving your communication skills may be the single most important step you can take. Employers often express frustration at the poor communication skills of many employees—particularly recent college graduates who haven't yet learned how to adapt their casual communication style to the professional business environment. If you learn to write well, speak well, listen well, and recognize the appropriate way to communicate in various business situations, you'll gain a major advantage that will serve you throughout your career.[2]

Communication is vital to every company's success.

Whether you are posting entries on a blog, giving a formal presentation, or chatting with co-workers at lunch, you are engaging in **communication**, the process of transferring information from a sender to a receiver. The essence of communication is sharing—providing data, information, and insights in an exchange that benefits both you and the people with whom you are communicating.[3] Effective communication helps businesses in many ways. These benefits include[4]

- Stronger decision making and faster problem solving

- Earlier warning of potential problems

- Increased productivity and steadier workflow

- Stronger business relationships

- Clearer and more persuasive marketing messages

- Enhanced professional images for both employers and companies

- Lower employee turnover and higher employee satisfaction

- Better financial results and higher return for investors

No matter what your level in the organization, you have an important communication role.

Effective communication strengthens the connection between a company and all of its **stakeholders**, those groups affected in some way by the company's actions: customers, employees, shareholders, suppliers, neighbors, the community, and the nation.[5] Conversely, when communication breaks down, the results can be anything from time wasting to tragic. At every stage of your career, communication will help you succeed, and the higher you rise in your organization, the more important it becomes. In fact, top managers spend as much as 85 percent of their time communicating with others.[6]

Communicating in Organizational Settings

Messages flow into, through, and out of business organizations in a variety of ways. **Internal communication** takes place between people inside a company, whereas **external communication** takes place between a company and outside parties. In addition, messages travel over both *formal* and *informal* channels (see Figure 1.1).

Formal communication follows the structure of the organization.

Every organization has a **formal communication network**, in which ideas and information flow along the lines of command (the hierarchical levels) in the company's organization structure (see Figure 1.2). Throughout the internal formal network, information travels in three directions. *Downward communication* flows from executives to employees, conveying executive decisions and providing information

	Internal	**External**
Formal	Planned communication among insiders (such as memos, reports, e-mail, instant messages, executive blogs, conference calls, and presentations) that follows the company's chain of command	Planned communication with outsiders (such as letters, reports, speeches, websites, instant messages, news releases, advertising, and executive blogs)
Informal	Casual communication among employees (such as e-mail, instant messages, face-to-face conversations, phone calls, team blogs, and wikis) that do not follow the company's chain of command	Casual communication with suppliers, customers, investors, and other outsiders (such as face-to-face conversations, e-mail, instant messages, phone calls, and customer-support blogs)

FIGURE 1.1
Forms of Communication
Business communication can be both formal or informal and internal or external. As you can see from this chart, many of the same tools can be used in any of these four situations.

that helps employees do their jobs. *Upward communication* flows from employees to executives, providing insight into problems, trends, opportunities, grievances, and performance—thus allowing executives to solve problems and make intelligent decisions. *Horizontal communication* flows between departments to help employees share information, coordinate tasks, and solve complex problems.[7]

Every organization also has an **informal communication network**—a *grapevine*—that operates anywhere two or more employees are in contact, from the lunchroom to the golf course to the company's e-mail and instant messaging (IM) systems. Some executives are wary of the informal network, but savvy managers tap into it to spread and receive informal messages.[8] Smart managers also know that a particularly active grapevine is a sign that the formal communication network is not providing the information employees believe they need.

Grapevines flourish when employees don't receive information they want or need.

FIGURE 1.2
Formal Communication Network
A formal communication network is defined by the official relationships between the various job positions in the organization. Messages can flow upward (from a lower-level employee to a higher-level employee), downward (from a higher-level employee to a lower-level employee), and horizontally (across the organization, between employees at the same or similar levels).

→ Examples of downward communication
→ Examples of upward communication
→ Examples of horizontal communication

External communication flows into and out of the organization by both formal means (carefully prepared letters, announcements, and so on) and informal means (meeting potential sales contacts at industry gatherings or networking at social events). In fact, informal exchanges are now considered so important that a new class of technology has sprung up to enable them. Just as Facebook, MySpace, and similar **social networking technologies** help students and other individuals connect, software and websites such as Spoke Connect, LinkedIn.com, and Ryze.com help businesspeople connect. These business-oriented solutions typically work by indexing e-mail and IM address books, calendars, and message archives, then looking for connections between names.[9]

The concept of social networking is also evolving in some companies into the form of *virtual communities* or *communities of practice* that link employees with similar professional interests throughout the company and, occasionally, with customers and suppliers as well. For example, the heavy-equipment manufacturer Caterpillar has more than 2,700 such communities that discuss problems and share insights into improving quality and productivity.[10]

Recognizing Effective Communication

Effective business documents share five key attributes.

You can have the greatest ideas in the world, but they're no good to your company or your career if you can't express them clearly and persuasively. To make your messages effective, make them practical, factual, concise, clear, and persuasive:[11]

- **Provide practical information.** Give recipients useful information, whether it's to help them perform a desired action or understand a new company policy. For instance, if you review the various product blogs on Six Apart's website (www.sixapart.com/about/ourblogs), you'll see that every posting helps advance the cause of blogging in some way—and as blogging continues to grow, so do the business opportunities for Six Apart.

- **Give facts rather than vague impressions.** Use concrete language, specific detail, and information that is clear, convincing, accurate, and ethical. Even when an opinion is called for, present compelling evidence to support your conclusion.

- **Present information in a concise, efficient manner.** Rather than dump everything on the reader, highlight the most important information. Audiences respond better to messages that clarify and summarize effectively.

- **Clarify expectations and responsibilities.** Write messages to generate a specific response from a specific audience. Clearly state what you expect from audience members or what you can do for them.

- **Offer compelling, persuasive arguments and recommendations.** Show your readers precisely how they will benefit from responding to your message the way you want them to.

Keep these five important characteristics in mind as you review Figures 1.3 and 1.4 (see pages 8–9). At first glance, both e-mails appear to be well constructed, but Figure 1.3 is far less effective, as the comments (in blue) explain. In contrast, Figure 1.4 shows how an effective message can help everyone work more efficiently.

Understanding What Employers Expect from You

Employers are constantly evaluating your communication skills.

No matter how good you are at accounting, engineering, law, or whatever professional specialty you pursue, employers expect you to be competent at a wide range of communication tasks. In fact, employers start judging your ability to communicate before you even show up for your first interview, and the process of evaluation never really stops. Fortunately, the skills that employers expect from you are the same skills that will help you advance in your career:

- Organizing ideas and information logically and completely
- Expressing ideas and information coherently and persuasively
- Listening to others effectively
- Communicating effectively with people from diverse backgrounds and experiences
- Using communication technologies effectively and efficiently
- Following accepted standards of grammar, spelling, and other aspects of high-quality writing and speaking
- Communicating in a civilized manner that reflects contemporary expectations of business etiquette
- Communicating ethically, even when choices aren't crystal clear

You'll have the opportunity to practice all these skills throughout this course—but don't stop there. Successful professionals continue to hone communication skills throughout their careers.

> The same skills that employers expect from you will also help you advance in your career.

Understanding Why Business Communication Is Unique

If you have some experience in the business world, you already know that business communication is often more complicated and demanding than your typical social communication with family, friends, and school associates. Expectations are higher on the job, and the business environment is so complex that your messages can fail for reasons that never even occurred to you before. Business communication is affected by such factors as the increasing value of information, the globalization of business and increase in workforce diversity, the pervasiveness of technology, the evolution of organizational structures, and the growing reliance on teamwork.

> The complexity of business communication makes it vulnerable to factors such as
> - growing value of information
> - globalization and diversity
> - technology
> - teamwork
> - organizational structures
> - communication barriers

The Increasing Value of Business Information   As competition for jobs, customers, and resources continues to grow, the importance of information continues to escalate as well. Even companies not usually associated with the so-called Information Age often rely on **knowledge workers**: employees at all levels of an organization who specialize in acquiring, processing, and communicating information. Three examples will give you an idea of the value of information in today's economy:

> Information has become one of the most important resources in business today.

- **Competitive insights.** The more a company knows about its competitors and their plans, the better its ability to adjust its own business plans.
- **Customer needs.** Most companies invest significant time and money in the effort to understand the needs of their customers, and this information needs to be analyzed and summarized in order to develop goods and services that better satisfy customer needs.
- **Regulations and guidelines.** Today's businesses must understand and follow a wide range of government regulations and guidelines covering such areas as employment, environment, taxes, and accounting. In the field of accounting and finance, for instance, executives say that communication skills are more important than ever before, not only for the increasing requirements of government reporting but also for the increase in interdepartmental collaboration.[12]

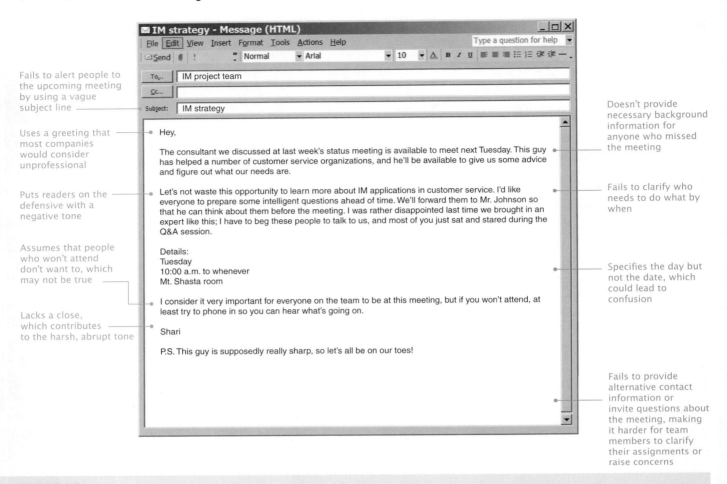

Fails to alert people to the upcoming meeting by using a vague subject line

Uses a greeting that most companies would consider unprofessional

Puts readers on the defensive with a negative tone

Assumes that people who won't attend don't want to, which may not be true

Lacks a close, which contributes to the harsh, abrupt tone

Doesn't provide necessary background information for anyone who missed the meeting

Fails to clarify who needs to do what by when

Specifies the day but not the date, which could lead to confusion

Fails to provide alternative contact information or invite questions about the meeting, making it harder for team members to clarify their assignments or raise concerns

IM strategy - Message (HTML)

To...: IM project team
Subject: IM strategy

Hey,

The consultant we discussed at last week's status meeting is available to meet next Tuesday. This guy has helped a number of customer service organizations, and he'll be available to give us some advice and figure out what our needs are.

Let's not waste this opportunity to learn more about IM applications in customer service. I'd like everyone to prepare some intelligent questions ahead of time. We'll forward them to Mr. Johnson so that he can think about them before the meeting. I was rather disappointed last time we brought in an expert like this; I have to beg these people to talk to us, and most of you just sat and stared during the Q&A session.

Details:
Tuesday
10:00 a.m. to whenever
Mt. Shasta room

I consider it very important for everyone on the team to be at this meeting, but if you won't attend, at least try to phone in so you can hear what's going on.

Shari

P.S. This guy is supposedly really sharp, so let's all be on our toes!

FIGURE 1.3
Ineffective Business Communication
At first glance, this e-mail message looks like a reasonable attempt at communicating with the members of a project team. However, review the blue annotations to see just how many problems the message really has.

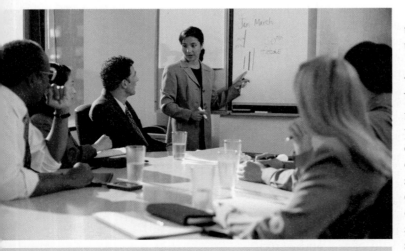

Successful companies know that diverse workforces can create powerful competitive advantages, but such workforces require closer attention to communication in order to eliminate barriers between groups with different communication styles.

No matter what the specific type of information, the better you understand it, use it, and communicate it to others, the more competitive you and your company will be.

The Globalization of Business and the Increase in Workforce Diversity   Today's businesses increasingly reach across international borders to market their products, partner with other businesses, and employ workers and executives—an effort known as **globalization**. Many U.S. companies rely on exports for a significant portion of their sales, sometimes up to 50 percent or more, so managers and employees in these firms need to communicate with many other cultures. Moreover, thousands of companies from all around the world vie for a share of the massive U.S. market, so chances are you'll do business with or even work for a company based in another country at some point in your career.

As people and products cross borders, businesses of all shapes and sizes are paying more attention to **workforce**

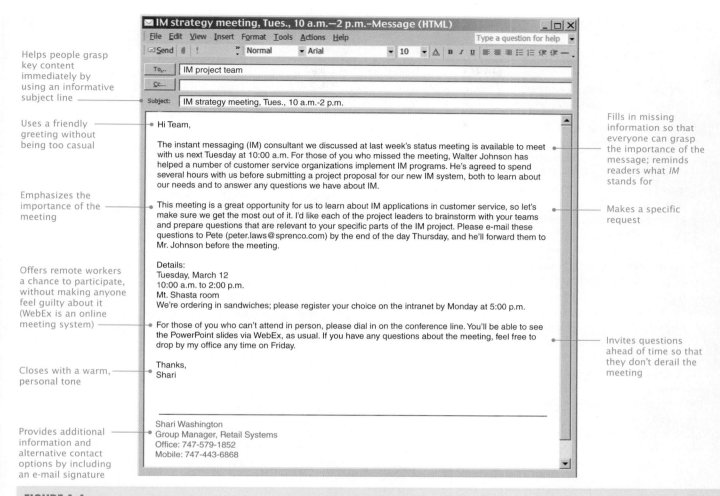

Helps people grasp key content immediately by using an informative subject line

Uses a friendly greeting without being too casual

Emphasizes the importance of the meeting

Offers remote workers a chance to participate, without making anyone feel guilty about it (WebEx is an online meeting system)

Closes with a warm, personal tone

Provides additional information and alternative contact options by including an e-mail signature

Fills in missing information so that everyone can grasp the importance of the message; reminds readers what *IM* stands for

Makes a specific request

Invites questions ahead of time so that they don't derail the meeting

FIGURE 1.4
Effective Business Communication
This improved version of the e-mail message from Figure 1.3 does a much better job of communicating the information people need in order to effectively prepare for the meeting.

diversity—all the differences among the people who work together, including differences in age, gender, sexual orientation, education, cultural background, religion, life experience, and so on. As Chapter 3 discusses, successful companies realize two important facts: (1) The more diverse their workforce, the more attention they need to pay to communication; and (2) a diverse workforce can yield a significant competitive advantage by fostering new ideas and new communication skills.

People with different cultural backgrounds and life experiences may have different communication styles.

The Pervasiveness of Technology   The blogging innovations provided by Mena Trott and her colleagues at Six Apart represent another important theme in contemporary business communication: the influence of technology in virtually every aspect of the field (see "Using the Power of Technology: Is Web 2.0 the Future or the Past Revisited?"). However, taking advantage of technology requires time, energy, and frequent improvement of skills. If your level of technical expertise doesn't keep up with that of your colleagues and co-workers, the imbalance can put you at a disadvantage and complicate the communication process. Throughout this course, you'll learn how to use numerous technological tools and systems more effectively.

Technology can help or hinder communication, depending on how it's designed and used.

The Evolution of Organizational Structures   Every business has a particular structure that defines the relationships between the various people and departments within the organization. These relationships in turn affect the nature and quality of

USING THE POWER OF TECHNOLOGY

Is Web 2.0 the Future or the Past Revisited?

Take your pick: (a) It unleashes the power of the individual while harnessing the collective wisdom of crowds; it shifts the web from consumption to contribution; and far into the future it "will be recognized as the largest, most complex, and most surprising event on the planet." (b) It is a load of baloney that at best is meaningless marketing nonsense and at worst is an attempt to repackage failed business models from the dot-com boom of the late 1990s.

"It" is Web 2.0. Defining Web 2.0 is difficult, and estimating its eventual impact on business is even harder. Web 2.0 could be described as a shift in the philosophy and technology of the World Wide Web, from static, isolated, and tightly controlled websites to connected, interactive, user-driven services. However, the term is used so widely and so loosely that no accepted definition has yet emerged.

Communication technologies often included under the Web 2.0 umbrella include blogging, podcasting, wikis, and newsfeeds; you'll learn more about them in Chapter 7. Among the companies frequently cited as examples of the Web 2.0 approach are the news website Digg.com (www.digg.com), which allows users to select the most important news stories from around the world; the social bookmarking site del.icio.us (http://del.icio.us), which helps web surfers find interesting and

useful websites; and YouTube (www.youtube.com), the wildly popular video sharing service. YouTube in particular is a good example of *user-generated content*, in which individual consumers create a website's content. *Conversational media* (in which individuals communicate back and forth rather then passively accepting content from a corporation) and *citizen journalism* (in which everyday people can contribute video clips, blog postings, and other news items) are other Web 2.0 concepts.

Web 2.0 detractors generally don't dispute the value of these sites and tools; rather, they question whether Web 2.0 is really the profound philosophical shift in human behavior that some of its proponents seem to claim—and whether a whole class of profitable businesses can be built around the concept. While that debate rages on, here's some pragmatic advice: Take advantage of these powerful new communication tools without getting too caught up in what exactly Web 2.0 means or where it might be going.

CAREER APPLICATIONS

1. Read several online opinions that promote or downplay the importance of Web 2.0 (you can find a number of links in the "Web 2.0" article on Wikipedia, www.wikipedia.org).

2. After reading those opinions, write your own one- or two-sentence description of Web 2.0. (Good luck! This could prove to be a challenging assignment.)

Organizations with tall structures may unintentionally restrict the flow of information.

communication throughout the organization. *Tall structures* have many layers of management between the lowest and highest positions, so they can suffer communication breakdowns and delays as messages are passed up and down through multiple layers.[13]

Flatter organizational structures usually make it easier to communicate effectively.

To overcome such problems, many businesses are adopting *flat structures* that reduce the number of layers. With fewer layers, communication generally flows faster and with fewer disruptions and distortions. On the other hand, with fewer formal lines of control and communication in these organizations, individual employees are expected to assume more responsibility for communication—particularly in the horizontal direction, from department to department across the company.

In the pursuit of speed and agility, some businesses have adopted flexible organizations that pool the talents of employees and external partners. For instance, when launching a new product, a company may supplement the efforts of internal departments with help from a public relations firm, an advertising agency, a marketing consultant, a web developer, and a product distributor. With so many individuals and organizations involved in the project, everyone must share the responsibility for giving and getting necessary information, or communication will break down.

Corporate cultures with an open climate benefit from free-flowing information and employee input.

Regardless of the particular structure a company uses, communication efforts will also be influenced by the organization's **corporate culture**, the mixture of values, traditions, and habits that give a company its atmosphere and personality. Successful companies encourage employee contributions by ensuring that communication flows freely down, up, and across the organization chart. Open climates encourage candor and honesty, helping employees feel free enough to admit their mistakes, disagree with the boss, and share negative or unwelcome information. For example, at Great Circle, a travel company based in Boston, employees are expected to practice "open and courageous communication" with each other and company management—even when that means asking executives to explain mistakes and bad decisions.[14]

The Growing Reliance on Teamwork   You'll probably find yourself on a number of teams throughout your career, as a full-time assignment or as part of a temporary project. Teams are commonly used in business today, but they're not always successful—and a key reason that teams fail to meet their objectives is poor communication. Chapter 2 offers insights into the complex dynamics of team communication and identifies skills you need to be an effective communicator in group settings.

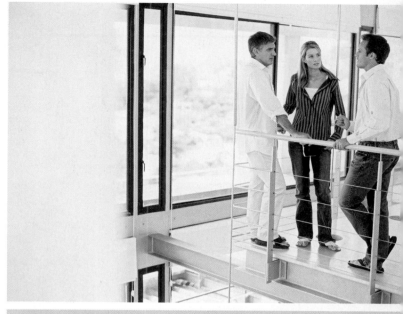

Open cultures promote the flow of information. In fact, some modern office buildings are even designed to encourage casual interaction and impromptu meetings.

COMMUNICATING MORE EFFECTIVELY ON THE JOB

Communication in today's business environment is clearly a challenge, but a careful combination of strategies can improve your ability to communicate effectively. The most important of these strategies are connecting with your audience, minimizing distractions, adopting an audience-centered approach, improving your basic communication skills, using constructive feedback, and being sensitive to business etiquette.

Working in a team makes you even more responsible for communicating effectively.

Connecting with Your Audience

No matter what the circumstances, successful communication is all about making connections with your audience. You have no doubt had experiences in which a single word or even just a glance successfully communicated what you wanted to say— as well as experiences in which you talked for hours or sent what seemed like a million text messages but just couldn't get your audience to understand your message. Why do some efforts succeed while others fail?

Human communication is a complex process with many opportunities for messages to get lost, ignored, or misinterpreted. Fortunately, by understanding this process, you can improve the odds that your messages will reach their intended audiences and produce their intended effects.

Overview of the Communication Process   By viewing communication as a process (see Figure 1.5), you can identify and improve the skills you need in order to be more successful—and you can recognize the many places and ways in which communication can fail. (Note that the original version of this process model was created to describe electronic communication,[15] but it provides helpful insights into any form of communication.) Many variations on this process model exist, but these eight steps provide a practical overview:

Viewing communication as a process helps you identify steps you can take to improve your success as a communicator.

1. **The sender has an idea.** You conceive an idea and want to share it. Whether a communication effort will ultimately be effective starts right here, depending on the nature of the idea, the composition of the audience and your relationship to

FIGURE 1.5
The Communication Process
These eight steps illustrate how ideas travel from sender to receiver. The process is presented in more detail in the following pages, and Figure 1.8 on page 21 offers advice on improving your skills at each step.

these people, and your motivation for wanting to share the idea. For example, if an idea will benefit your department or company and your motivation is to make a contribution, the communication process is off to a strong start. In comparison, if the idea is poorly conceived (perhaps you haven't considered the financial impact of a proposal) or your motivation is suspect (perhaps you're more interesting in "scoring points" with the boss than really contributing), the communication will be more difficult and possibly unsuccessful.

2. **The sender encodes the idea as a message.** When you put your idea into a message (words, images, or a combination of both) that your receiver will understand, you are **encoding** it. Much of the focus of this course is on developing the skills needed to successfully encode your ideas into effective messages. Encoding can fail for a number of reasons, including poor word choices that confuse or anger the audience, imagery that evokes unintended emotional responses, and cultural differences that result in the same words and images meaning different things to different people.

3. **The sender produces the message in a transmittable medium.** With the appropriate message to express your idea, you now need some way to present that message to your intended audience. As you'll read in Chapter 4, media for transmitting messages can be divided into *oral, written, visual,* and various *electronic* forms of the other three. As an experienced user of communication media, you already know that this step requires careful decision making and at least some level of technical skills. Misguided media choices or insufficient technical skills can undermine the best intentions. For instance, a desire to keep everyone informed of every important detail in a project can lead to e-mail overload—and a breakdown in communication as people struggle to keep track of all the messages and the inevitable response threads. In contrast, many companies now find that a blog is a much better way to keep teams informed because this medium can dramatically reduce the number of messages required.

4. **The sender transmits the message through a channel.** Just as technology continues to multiply the number of media options at your disposal, it also continues to provide new **communication channels** you can use to transmit your messages. The distinction between medium and channel can get a bit murky, but think of medium as the *form* a message takes and channel as the system used to

deliver the message. The channel can be a face-to-face conversation, the Internet, another company—any system capable of delivering messages.

5. **The audience receives the message.** If all goes well, your message survives the trip through the channel and arrives at your intended audience. However, mere arrival at the destination is not a guarantee that the message will be noticed or understood correctly. As "How Audiences Receive Messages" explains, many messages are either ignored or misinterpreted as noise.

6. **The audience decodes the message.** If the message is actually received, the audience then needs to extract your idea from the message, a step known as **decoding**. "How Audiences Decode Messages" takes a closer look at this complex and subtle step in the process.

7. **The audience responds to the message.** By crafting your messages in ways that show the benefits of responding, you can increase the chances that your audiences will respond as you'd like them to. However, as "How Audiences Respond to Messages" points out, audiences need to remember your message long enough to act on it, they need to be able to act on it as you want them to, and they need to be motivated to respond.

8. **The audience provides feedback.** Aside from responding (or not responding) to the message, audience members may also give **feedback** that helps you evaluate the effectiveness of your communication effort. Sometimes feedback can be subtle and hard to interpret; a listener looking away while you're talking might be confused and embarrassed to let it show, might be angry and trying to control his or her emotions, might be deeply interested in what you're saying and considering the implications, or might simply be bored. Other times, feedback is direct and easy to interpret, as when someone says he or she doesn't understand you, thinks your idea is brilliant, or can't hear you.

The following sections take a closer look at two important aspects of the process: environmental barriers that can block or distort messages and the steps audiences take to receive, decode, and respond to messages.

Barriers in the Communication Environment Within any communication environment, messages can be disrupted by a variety of **communication barriers**:

- **Noise and distractions.** External distractions range from poor acoustics to uncomfortable meeting rooms to crowded computer screens with instant messages and reminders popping up all over the place. The common habit of *multitasking*, attempting more than one task at a time, is a recipe for distractions. Internal distractions are thoughts and emotions that prevent audiences from focusing on incoming messages. For instance, a person worried about losing his job might ignore any message that doesn't apply to his immediate concerns.

- **Competing messages.** Having your audience's undivided attention is a rare luxury. In many cases, you must compete with other messages that are trying to reach your audience at the same time. Too many messages can result in **information overload**, which not only makes it difficult to discriminate between useful and useless information but also amplifies workplace stress.[16]

- **Filters.** Messages can be blocked or distorted by *filters*, which are any human or technology intervention between the sender and the receiver. Filtering can be both intentional (such as automatically filing e-mail messages based on sender or content) or unintentional (such as an overly aggressive spam filter that deletes legitimate e-mail). As you read earlier, the structure and culture of an organization can also inhibit the flow of vital messages. And, in some cases, the people or

Communication barriers include
- Noise and distractions
- Competing messages
- Filters
- Channel breakdowns

companies you rely on to deliver a message can distort it, either accidentally or to meet their own needs.

- **Channel breakdowns.** Sometimes the channel simply breaks down and fails to deliver your message at all. A colleague you were counting on to deliver a message to your boss might have forgotten to do so, a brochure you sent to a customer might have gotten lost in the mail, or a computer server might have crashed and prevented your blog from displaying.

As a communicator, try to be aware of any barriers that could prevent your messages from reaching their intended audiences. And make sure you haven't unintentionally built barriers around yourself. If people don't feel that you are approachable for any reason, they'll avoid communicating with you—even regarding messages that you need to hear.[17]

Inside the Mind of Your Audience After a message survives the journey through the communication channel and reaches its intended audience, it encounters a whole new set of challenges. Understanding how audiences receive, decode, and respond to messages will help you create more effective messages.

To actually receive a message, audience members need to sense it, select it, and perceive it as a message.

How Audiences Receive Messages Messages often reach the intended audience but have no effect whatsoever. For an audience member to actually receive a message, three events need to occur: the receiver has to *sense* the presence of a message, *select* it from all the other messages clamoring for attention, and *perceive* it as an actual message (as opposed to random, pointless noise).[18] You can appreciate the magnitude of this challenge by driving down any busy street in a commercial section of town. You'll encounter literally hundreds of messages—billboards, posters, store window displays, thumping car stereos, pedestrians waving or talking on mobile phones, horns honking, street signs, traffic lights, and so on. However, you sense, select, and perceive only a small fraction of these messages. In fact, if you *didn't* ignore most of them, you would be one very dangerous driver!

Today's business audiences are much like drivers on busy streets. They are inundated with so many messages and so much noise that they miss or ignore many of the messages intended for them. The good news is that through this course, you will learn a variety of techniques to craft messages that get noticed. In general, follow these five principles to increase your chances of success:

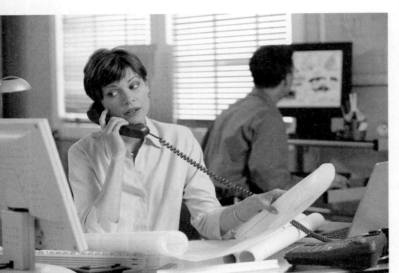

Trying to send and receive multiple messages simultaneously is so distracting that it can actually reduce a worker's functioning intelligence level.

To improve the odds that your messages will be successfully perceived by your audience, pay close attention to expectations, ease of use, familiarity, empathy, and technical compatibility.

- **Consider audience expectations.** Deliver messages using the media and channels that the audience expects. Of course, sometimes going *against* expectations can stimulate audience attention, which is why advertisers sometimes do wacky and creative things to get your attention. However, for most business communication efforts, following the expectations of your audience is the most efficient way to get your message across.

- **Ensure ease of use.** Even if audiences are actively looking for your messages, they probably won't see your messages if you make them hard to find. Poorly designed websites with confusing navigation are common culprits in this respect.

- **Emphasize familiarity.** Use words, images, and designs that are familiar to your audience. For example, most visitors to business websites now expect to see information about the company on a page called "About Us."

- **Practice empathy.** Make sure your messages "speak to the audience" by clearly addressing *their* wants and needs—not yours. People are much more inclined to notice messages that relate to their individual concerns.[19]

- **Design for compatibility.** With so many messages delivered electronically these days, be sure to verify technical compatibility with your audience. For instance, if your website requires visitors to have the Adobe Flash capability on their computers, you won't reach audience members who don't have that software.

How Audiences Decode Messages Even though a message may have been received by the audience, it still doesn't "mean" anything until the recipient decodes it and assigns meaning to it. Unfortunately, there is no guarantee that your audience will assign the same meaning that you intended. Even well-crafted, well-intentioned communication efforts can fail at this stage because assigning meaning is a highly personal process affected by culture, individual experience, learning and thinking styles, hopes, fears, and even temporary moods. Moreover, audiences tend to extract the meaning they *expect* to get from a message, even if it's the opposite of what the sender intended.[20] In fact, rather than extracting *your* meaning, it's more accurate to state that audience members re-create *their* own meaning—or meanings—from the message.

> Decoding a message to assign meaning to it is a complicated and often highly personal process.

As you'll discover in Chapter 3, culture shapes people's views of the world in profound ways, from determinations of right and wrong to details such as the symbolic meanings attached to specific colors. For instance, because U.S. culture celebrates youth and individual accomplishment, it is "natural" for people raised in the United States to admire young, independent-minded leaders who rebel against older, established ways of doing business. Compare this approach to that in places such as Japan, where people generally place a higher value on respect for older colleagues, consensus decision making, and group accomplishment. Given these differences, a younger colleague's bold proposal to radically reshape business strategy could be interpreted more positively in one culture than in the other—quite independent of the proposal's merits alone.

At an individual level, beliefs and biases also influence the meaning that audiences extract from messages. For instance, our minds organize incoming sensations into a mental map that represents our individual **perception** of reality. If a detail does not quite fit for any reason, people are inclined to distort the information rather than rearrange their pattern—a process known as **selective perception**.[21] For example, a manager who believes wholeheartedly in a particular business strategy might distort or ignore evidence that suggests the strategy is failing.

> Selective perception occurs when people ignore or distort incoming information to fit their preconceived notions of reality.

Language differences also influence received meaning. If you ask an employee to send you a report on sales figures "as soon as possible," does that mean within 10 seconds, 10 minutes, or 10 days? By clarifying expectations and resolving any potential ambiguities in your messages, you can reduce the odds of such interpretation uncertainties. The more experiences you share with another person, the more likely you are to share perception and thus share meaning (see Figure 1.6).

Individual thinking styles are another important factor in decoding messages. For example, even though business decisions are supposedly made on the basis of objective analysis and clear logic, emotion and intuition (reaching conclusions without using rational processes) can influence the interpretation of messages. Let's say you return from a sales trip with a hunch that several major customers may start buying more products from your firm, and you share that optimistic assessment with your colleagues. Someone who tends to respond to the emotional element in messages and to put a lot of faith in "gut feel" may conclude that sales are about to increase. Someone else with a more cautious, analytical approach may view your input as an interesting bit of data but hardly proof of an imminent increase.

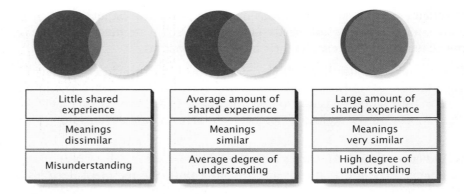

Little shared experience	Average amount of shared experience	Large amount of shared experience
Meanings dissimilar	Meanings similar	Meanings very similar
Misunderstanding	Average degree of understanding	High degree of understanding

FIGURE 1.6
How Shared Experience Affects Understanding
The more your audience members share your experiences—personal, professional, and cultural— the more likely they will be to extract the same meanings that you encode in your messages.

Audiences will likely respond to a message if they remember it, if they're able to respond, and if they're properly motivated to respond.

How Audiences Respond to Messages You are almost there. Your message has been delivered, received, and correctly decoded. Now what? Will audience members respond in the way you'd like them to? Probably—if three events occur.

First, the recipient has to *remember* the message long enough to act on it. Simplifying greatly, memory works in several stages: *Sensory memory* momentarily captures incoming data from the senses; then, whatever the recipient pays attention to is transferred to *short-term memory*. Information in short-term memory will quickly disappear if it isn't transferred to *long-term memory*, which can be done either actively (such as by memorizing a list of items) or passively (such as when a new piece of information connects with something else the recipient already has stored in long-term memory). Finally, the information needs to be *retrieved* when the recipient needs to act on it.[22] In general, people find it easier to remember and retrieve information that is important to them personally or professionally. Consequently, by communicating in ways that are sensitive to your audience's wants and needs, you greatly increase the chance that your messages will be remembered and retrieved.

Second, the recipient has to be *able* to respond as you wish. Obviously, if recipients simply cannot do what you want them to do, such as paying for a product you are promoting, they will not respond according to your plan. By understanding your audience (see Chapter 4), you can work to minimize these scenarios.

By explaining why audiences will benefit by responding to your messages, you'll increase their motivation to respond.

Third, the recipient has to be *motivated* to respond. You'll encounter many situations in which your audience has the option of responding but isn't required to—the record company may or may not offer your band a contract, the boss may or may not respond to your request for a raise, and so on. The good news is that you often have a fair amount of influence over whether the recipient will respond as you'd like. Throughout this course, you'll learn the techniques for crafting messages that motivate readers to respond.

Minimizing Distractions

Overcome distraction by
- Using common sense and courtesy
- Not sending unnecessary messages
- Not isolating yourself
- Informing receivers of message priority

Although distractions are a major problem in business communication, everyone in the organization can help overcome them. A small dose of common sense and courtesy goes a long way. Turn off that mobile phone before you step into a meeting. Don't talk across the tops of cubicles when people inside them are trying to work. Be sensitive to personal differences, too; for instance, some people enjoy working with music on, but music is an enormous distraction for others.[23]

Take steps to insulate yourself from distractions, too. Don't let e-mail, IM, or telephones interrupt you every minute of the day. Set aside time to attend to a number of messages at once so that you can think and focus the rest of the time.

Make sure the messages you send are necessary. E-mail in particular has made it too easy to send too many messages or send messages to the people who don't need them. In fact, one of the reasons that blogging is taking off so quickly in business is that it can significantly reduce internal e-mail traffic.[24]

In addition, if you must send a message that isn't urgent or crucial, let people know so that they can prioritize. If a long report requires no action from recipients, tell them up-front so that they don't have to search through it, looking for action items. Also, most systems let you mark messages as urgent; however, use this feature only when it's truly needed. Too many so-called urgent messages that aren't particularly urgent will lead to annoyance and anxiety, not action.

Finally, try to overcome emotional distractions by recognizing your own feelings and by anticipating emotional reactions from others.[25] When a situation may cause tempers to flare, choose your words carefully. As a receiver, avoid placing blame and reacting subjectively.

Emotionally charged situations require extra care when communicating.

Adopting an Audience-Centered Approach

Using an **audience-centered approach** means focusing on and caring about the members of your audience, making every effort to get your message across in a way that is meaningful to them (see Figure 1.7). This approach is also known as adopting the **"you" attitude**, in contrast to messages that are about "me." Learn as much as possible about the biases, education, age, status, style, and personal and professional concerns of your receivers. If you're addressing strangers and unable to find out more about them, try to project yourself into their position by using your common sense and imagination. This ability to relate to the needs of others is a key part of *emotional intelligence*, widely considered to be a vital characteristic of successful managers and leaders.[26] The more you know about the people you're communicating with, the easier it will be to concentrate on their needs—which, in turn, will make it easier for them to hear your message, understand it, and respond positively.

Keeping your audience's needs in mind helps you ensure successful messages.

If you haven't had the opportunity to communicate with a diverse range of people in your academic career so far, you might be surprised by the different communication styles you will encounter on the job. Recognizing and adapting to your audience's style will improve not only the effectiveness of your communication but also the quality of your working relationship.[27] The audience-centered approach is emphasized throughout this book, so you'll have plenty of opportunity to practice this approach to communicating more effectively.

Fine-Tuning Your Business Communication Skills

Your skills as a communicator will be as much a factor in your business success as anything else you'll do. No matter what your skill level, opportunities to improve are easy to find. Many employers provide communication training in both general skills and specific scenarios, but don't wait. Use this course to begin mastering your skills now.

Work on your communication skills before you start or restart your business career.

Lack of experience may be the only obstacle between you and effective communication. Perhaps you're worried about having a limited vocabulary or uncertain about questions of grammar, punctuation, and style. If you're intimidated by the idea of writing an important document or appearing before a group, you're not alone. Everyone gets nervous about communicating from time to time, even people you may think of as "naturals." People aren't born writing and speaking well; they master these skills through study and practice. Even simple techniques, such as keeping a reading log and writing practice essays, will improve not only your writing skills but also your overall performance in school.[28]

This course lets you practice in an environment that provides honest and constructive feedback. You'll have ample opportunity to plan and produce documents, collaborate in teams, listen effectively, improve nonverbal communication, and communicate across cultures—all skills that will serve your career well.

TYPEPAD | MOVABLE TYPE | LIVEJOURNAL | **ABOUT US** | SUPPORT

ABOUT SIX APART
News & Events
Management
History
Offices
Jobs
Press Center
Our Blogs

TypePad Update & Lessons Learned

MENA'S CORNER

Mena Trott is president and a co-founder of Six Apart.

Mena's Corner is my chance to show the inner workings of a start-up and give the outside world a glimpse into our challenges, our achievements, and our professional passions.

ARCHIVES BY MONTH:
December 2005
November 2005
October 2005
September 2005
August 2005
July 2005
June 2005
May 2005
April 2005
February 2005
January 2005
December 2004
October 2004
August 2004
July 2004
May 2004
April 2004
March 2004

XML Feed

BLOG NOW!
Fully-featured.

Mena | November 17, 2005

During the last month, we've been very open about TypePad's performance problems and the solutions we're implementing to bring the service up to a high standard. We're happy to say that, since things have stabilized, we've been able to offer compensation to our customers for the inconvenience caused by slow service and downtime.

As Barak said in his email and post, we offer our sincere apologies for any inconvenience and hope that customers of TypePad view the compensation as fair.

Not only did the people here at Six Apart feel the pain of poor performance (as employees and users), but we also spent a great deal of time reading customer emails, comments and posts which helped us understand that every customer is different. Some customers didn't want any compensation, they just wanted us to spend resources fixing the problems; others felt that the performance of TypePad hindered their businesses and personal communications; and some didn't notice any service degradation at all.

So, what are the lessons?

- **Read what your customers have to say**
  This is the most obvious piece of advice, but the most important. Customers who are invested in a service usually want the company that's supporting them to succeed. The best advice comes from your customers, and they aren't afraid to tell it like it is. That said...

- **Ignore the tone of nasty complaints, but pay attention to the underlying messages**
  When people are disappointed, their frustrations are often expressed in the form of anger. But at the same time, the fact that they took the time to write what they feel rather than shrugging it off indicates a deep desire for a solution, not just blame. We're all human and the nasty stuff hurts, but we love passionate users, so that involves taking the good and the bad comments in stride.

- **Understand that the people giving feedback represent many who remain silent**
  For every person who complains, realize that there are probably ten people conscious of the problem but not interested in speaking out

Offers links to related discussions so that anyone landing on this page can get the full story

Assures customers that their concerns and feedback were taken seriously

Helps everyone benefit from the experience (the list continues down the screen)

FIGURE 1.7
Audience-Centered Communication
After an upgrade to its TypePad blog-hosting system resulted in a period of poor performance for customers, Six Apart's Mena Trott and her staff communicated openly and honestly with customers. They explained what happened, acknowledged customer frustrations, apologized for the inconvenience, offered compensation, and kept their audience up to date. Trott and her colleagues even shared what the experience had taught them as managers and communicators—insights that can help customers handle their own business communication challenges.

Giving—and Responding to—Constructive Feedback

Constructive feedback focuses on improvement, not on personal criticism.

You will encounter many situations in which you are expected to give and receive feedback regarding communication efforts. Whether giving or receiving criticism, be sure you do so in a constructive way. **Constructive feedback**, sometimes called *constructive criticism*, focuses on the process and outcomes of communication, not on the people involved (see Table 1.1). In contrast, **destructive feedback** delivers criti-

GIVING CONSTRUCTIVE FEEDBACK		Table 1.1
How to Be Constructive	*Explanation*	
Think through your suggested changes carefully.	Because many business documents must illustrate complex relationships between ideas and other information, isolated and superficial edits can do more harm than good.	
Discuss improvements rather than flaws.	Instead of saying "this is confusing," explain how the writing can be improved to make it clearer.	
Focus on controllable behavior.	Because the writer may not have control over every variable that affected the quality of the message, focus on those aspects the writer can control.	
Be specific.	Comments such as "I don't get this" or "Make this clearer" don't identify what the writer needs to fix.	
Keep feedback impersonal.	Focus comments on the message, not the person who created it.	
Verify understanding.	Ask for confirmation from the recipient to make sure that the person understood your feedback.	
Time your feedback carefully.	Make sure the writer will have sufficient time to implement the changes you suggest.	
Highlight any limitations your feedback may have.	If you didn't have time to give the document a thorough edit, or if you're not an expert in some aspect of the content, let the writer know so that he or she can handle your comments appropriately.	

cism with no effort to stimulate improvement.[29] For example, "This proposal is a confusing mess, and you failed to convince me of anything" is destructive feedback. Your goal is to be more constructive: "Your proposal could be more effective with a clearer description of the construction process and a well-organized explanation of why the positives outweigh the negatives." When giving feedback, avoid personal attacks and give the person clear guidelines for improvement.

When you receive constructive feedback, resist the immediate urge to defend your work or deny the validity of the feedback. Remaining open to criticism isn't easy when you've poured your heart and soul into a project, but feedback is a valuable opportunity to learn and improve. Try to disconnect your emotions from the work and view it simply as something you can make better. Many writers also find it helpful to step back, think about the feedback for a while, and let their emotions settle down before diving in to make corrections. Of course, don't automatically assume that even well-intentioned feedback is necessarily correct. You have the responsibility for the final quality of the message, so make sure that any suggested changes are valid ones.

> Try to react unemotionally when you receive constructive feedback.

Being Sensitive to Business Etiquette

In today's hectic, competitive world, the notion of **etiquette** (the expected norms of behavior in a particular situation) can seem outdated and unimportant. However, the way you conduct yourself can have a profound influence on your company's success and your career. When executives hire and promote you, they

> Understanding communication etiquette can help you avoid needless blunders.

expect your behavior to protect the company's reputation. The more you understand such expectations, the better chance you have of avoiding career-damaging mistakes.

Throughout this book, you'll encounter advice for a variety of business situations, but even if you don't know the specific expectations in a given situation, some general guidelines will get you through any rough spots. Start by being sensitive to the fact that people can have different expectations about the same situation. Something you find appalling or embarrassing might be business as usual for a colleague, and vice versa. Moreover, etiquette expectations don't always make sense, nor are they always fair in the eyes of everyone concerned. For example, some high-ranking women executives say some male colleagues who aren't bothered when men use coarse language (particularly words and phrases with sexual undertones) often view such language as unacceptable from women. These women acknowledge that the situation isn't fair, but they've learned to work within the prevailing behavior norms in order to avoid hindering their careers.[30]

Respect, courtesy, and common sense will get you through most etiquette challenges on the job.

Long lists of etiquette "rules" can be overwhelming, and you'll never be able to memorize all of them. Fortunately, you can count on three principles to get you through just about any situation: respect, courtesy, and common sense. Moreover, these principles will encourage forgiveness if you do happen to make a mistake. As you encounter new situations, take a few minutes to learn the expectations of the other people involved. Travel guidebooks are a great source of information about norms and customs in other countries. Check to see if your library has online access to the CultureGram database, or review the country profiles at **www.kwintessential.co.uk**. Don't be afraid to ask questions, either. People will respect your concern and curiosity. You'll gradually accumulate considerable knowledge, which will help you feel comfortable and be effective in a wide range of business situations.

Applying What You've Learned to the Communication Process

With these additional insights into what makes communication succeed, take another look at the communication process model. Figure 1.8 identifies the key challenges in the process and summarizes the steps you can take along the way to become a more effective communicator.

USING TECHNOLOGY TO IMPROVE BUSINESS COMMUNICATION

Communicating in today's business environment requires at least a basic level of technical competence.

Today's businesses rely heavily on technology to improve the communication process. Companies and employees who use technology wisely can communicate more effectively and therefore compete more successfully.

You will find technology discussed extensively throughout this book, with specific advice on using both common and emerging tools to meet communication challenges. The four-page photo essay "Powerful Tools for Communicating Effectively" (on pages 22–25) offers an overview of the technologies that connect people in offices, factories, and other business settings.

Anyone who has used a computer knows that the benefits of technology are not automatic. Poorly designed or inappropriately used technology can hinder communication more than it helps. To communicate effectively, learn to keep technology in perspective, use technological tools productively, spend time and money on technology wisely, and disengage from the computer frequently to communicate in person.

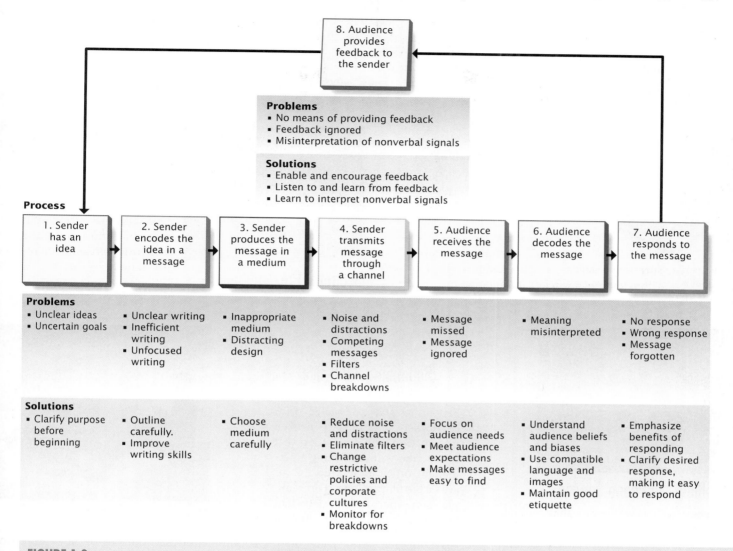

FIGURE 1.8

Becoming an Effective Business Communicator

The communication process presents many opportunities for messages to get lost, distorted, or misinterpreted as they travel from sender to receiver. Fortunately, you can take action at every step in the process to increase your chances of success.

Keeping Technology in Perspective

Technology is an aid to interpersonal communication, not a replacement for it. Technology can't think for you or communicate for you, and if you lack some essential skills, technology probably can't fill in the gaps. Your spell checker is happy to run all your words through the dictionary, but it doesn't know whether you're using the correct words or crafting powerful sentences.

Don't rely too much on technology or let it overwhelm the communication process.

The sheer number of possibilities in many technological tools can get in the way of successful communication. For instance, the content of a message may be obscured if an electronic presentation is overloaded with visual effects. Moreover, if technological systems aren't adapted to user or organizational needs, people won't adapt to the technology—they won't use it effectively or, worse, they won't use it at all. Perhaps even more ominously, some workers are beginning to show signs of information technology addiction—possibly to the point of craving the stimulation of being connected practically around the clock, even while on vacation.[31]

Powerful Tools for Communicating Effectively

The tools of business communication evolve with every new generation of digital technology. Selecting the right tool for each situation can enhance your business communication in many ways. In today's flexible office settings, communication technology helps people keep in touch and stay productive. When co-workers in different cities need to collaborate, they can meet and share ideas without costly travel. Manufacturers use communication technology to keep track of parts, orders, and shipments—and to keep customers well-informed. Those same customers can also communicate with companies in many ways at any time of day or night.

Wireless Networks

Laptop PCs with wireless access let workers stay connected to the network from practically anywhere within the office—any desk, any conference room. This technology offers high-speed Internet access within range of a wireless access point.

Electronic Presentations

Combining a color projector with laptop or personal digital assistant (PDA) running the right software lets people give informative busine presentations that are enhanced w sound, animation, and even web s hyperlinks. Having everything in electronic form also makes it easy customize a presentation or to ma last-minute changes.

Follow-Me Phone Service

To be reachable without juggling multiple forwarding numbers, some people have follow-me phone service. Callers use one number to reach the person anywhere— at the office, a remote site, a home office. The system automatically forwards calls to a list of preprogrammed numbers and transfers unanswered calls to voice mail.

Redefining the Office

Technology makes it easier for people to stay connected with co-workers and retrieve needed information. Some maintain that connection without having a permanent office, a desktop PC, or even a big filing cabinet. For example, Sun Microsystems lets staff members choose to work either at the main office or at remote offices called "drop-in centers." Many Sun facilities have specially equipped "iWork" areas that can quickly reconfigure phone and computer connections to meet individual requirements.

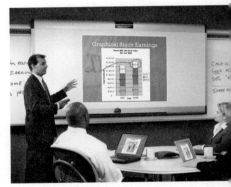

Electronic Whiteboards

Electronic whiteboards can capture, store and e-mail the results of brainstorming sessions and other meetings. The newest versions work with electronic presentatio too, letting users write and draw directly displayed slides.

Intranets

Businesses use Internet technologies to create an intranet, a private computer network that simplifies information sharing within the company. Intranets can handle company e-mail, instant messaging (IM), websites, and even Internet phone connections. To ensure the security of company communication and information, intranets are shielded from the public Internet.

Communicating in the Office

Wikis

Wikis promote collaboration by simplifying the process of creating and editing online content. Anyone with access (some wikis are private, while some are public) can add and modify pages as new information becomes available.

Web-Based Meetings

Workers can actively participate in web-based meetings by logging on from a desktop PC, laptop, or mobile phone. Websites such as WebEx help users integrate voice, text, and video, and let them share applications such as Microsoft PowerPoint and Microsoft Word in a single browser window.

Collaborating

Working in teams is essential in almost every business. Teamwork can become complicated, however, when team members work in different parts of the company, in different time zones, or even for different companies. Technology helps bridge the distance by making it possible to brainstorm, attend virtual meetings, and share files from widely separated locations. Communication technology also helps companies save money on costly business travel without losing most of the benefits of face-to-face collaboration.

Internet Videophone

Person-to-person video calling has long been possible through popular instant messaging programs. Internet videophone services do even more, letting multiple users participate in a videoconference without the expense and complexity of a full-fledged videoconferencing system. Some services are flexible enough to include telecommuters who have broadband Internet connections.

Shared Workspace

Online workspaces such as eRoom and Groove make it easy for far-flung team members to access shared files anywhere, any time. Accessible through a browser, the workspace contains a collection of folders and has built-in intelligence to control which team members can read, edit, and save specific files.

Communicating Remotely

Videoconferencing and Telepresence

Less costly than travel, videoconferencing provides many of the same benefits as an in-person meeting. Advanced systems include telepresence and robot surrogates, which use computers to "place" participants in the room virtually, letting them see and hear everyone while being seen and heard themselves. Such realistic interaction makes meetings more productive.

RFID

Throughout the distribution chain, from factories to ships to warehouses to retail shelves, companies can replace manual tracking and reporting with automated systems that monitor small radio-frequency identification (RFID) tags attached to goods and containers.

Extranets

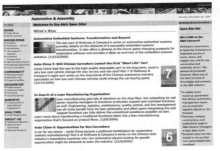

Extranets are secure, private computer networks that use Internet technology to share business information with suppliers, vendors, partners, and customers. Think of an extranet as an extension of the company intranet that is available to people outside the organization by invitation only.

Sharing the Latest Information

Companies use a variety of communication technologies to create products and services and deliver them to customers. The ability to easily access and share the latest information improves the flow and timing of supplies, lowers operating costs, and boosts financial performance. Easy information access also helps companies respond to customer needs by providing them timely, accurate information and service and by delivering the right products to them at the right time.

Wireless Warehouses

Communication technology is a key source of competitive advantage for shipping companies such as FedEx and UPS. Hand-worn scanners use wireless links to help warehouse personnel access instant information that lets them process more packages in less time at transit hubs.

Package Tracking

Senders and receivers often want frequent updates when packages are in transit. Handheld devices such as the FedEx PowerPad enhance customer service by letting delivery personnel instantly upload package data to the FedEx network. The wireless PowerPad also aids drivers by automatically receiving weather advisories.

Communicating About Products and Services

Supply Chain Management

Advanced software applications let suppliers, manufacturers, and retailers share information—even when they have incompatible computer systems. Improved information flow increases report accuracy and helps each company in the supply chain manage stock levels.

Over-the-Shoulder Support

For online shoppers who need instant help, many retail websites make it easy to connect with a live sales rep via phone or instant messaging. The rep can provide quick answers to questions and, with permission, can even control a shopper's browser to help locate particular items.

Help Lines

Some people prefer the personal touch of contact by phone. Moreover, some companies assign preferred customers special ID numbers that let them jump to the front of the calling queue. Many companies are addressing the needs of foreign-language speakers by connecting them with external service providers who offer multilingual support.

Interacting

Maintaining an open dialog with customers is a great way to gain a better understanding of their likes and dislikes. Today's communication technologies make it easier for customers to interact with a company whenever, wherever, and however they wish. A well-coordinated approach to phone, web, and in-store communication helps a company build stronger relationships with its existing customers, which increases the chances of doing more business with each one.

Corporate Blogs

Web-based journals let companies offer advice, answer questions, and promote the benefits of their products and services. Elements of a successful blog include frequent updates and the participation of knowledgeable contributors. Adding a subtle mix of useful commentary and marketing messages helps get customers to read or listen to them.

Podcasting

With the portability and convenience of downloadable audio and video recordings, podcasts have quickly become a popular means of delivering everything from college lectures to marketing messages. Podcasts are also used for internal communication, replacing conference calls, newsletters, and other traditional communication vehicles.

Communicating with Customers

In-Store Kiosks

Staples is among the retailers that let shoppers buy from the web while they're still in the store. Web-connected kiosks were originally used to let shoppers custom-configure their PCs, but the kiosks also give customers access to roughly 8,000 in-store items as well as to the 50,000 products available online.

Using Technological Tools Productively

Employees who are comfortable using communication technologies have a competitive advantage in today's marketplace.

Communication technologies can save time and money, but they can also waste time and money if not used efficiently. You don't have to become an expert to use most communication technologies efficiently, but you will need to be familiar with the basic features and functions of the tools you are expected to use on the job.

Another major productivity consideration is personal use of IM, blogging, music players, and other technological tools (and toys) on the job. Few companies go to the extreme of banning all personal use of such technologies while at work or of trying to restrict employees' personal blogs, but every company needs to address this issue. For instance, inappropriate web surfing not only distracts employees from work responsibilities but also can leave employers open to lawsuits for sexual harassment if inappropriate images are displayed in or transmitted around the company.[32] In addition, e-mail and instant messages are considered legal documents and can be used as evidence in lawsuits or criminal trials.[33] Blogging has created another set of managerial challenges, given the risk that employee blogs can expose confidential information or damage a firm's reputation in the marketplace. With all of these technologies, the best solution lies in clear policies that are enforced evenly for all employees.[34] Finally, remember that every communication tool, from e-mail to IM to micro-blogging tools such as Twitter, can be used productively or wastefully. Make sure that technology enhances the communication effort rather than overwhelms or disrupts it.

Reconnecting with People Frequently

No matter how much technology is involved, communication is still about people connecting with people.

In spite of their efficiency and speed, technological tools may not be the best choice for every communication situation. Even in the best circumstances, technology can't match the rich experience of person-to-person contact. Let's say you IM a colleague, asking how she did with her sales presentation to an important client, and her answer comes back simply as "Fine." What does *fine* mean? Is an order expected soon? Did she lose the sale and doesn't want to talk about it? Was the client rude, and she does not want to talk about it? If you reconnect with her, perhaps visit her in person, she might provide additional information, or you might be able to offer advice or support during a difficult time.

Moreover, most human beings need to connect with other people. You can create amazing documents and presentations without ever leaving your desk or meeting anyone in person. But if you stay hidden behind technology, people won't get to know you nearly as well. You may be funny, bright, and helpful, but you're just a voice on the phone or a name on a document until people can interact with you in person. As technological options increase, people seem to need the human touch even more.

MAKING ETHICAL COMMUNICATION CHOICES

Ethics are the accepted principles of conduct that govern behavior within a society. Put another way, ethical principles define the boundary between right and wrong. Former Supreme Court Justice Potter Stewart defined ethics as "knowing the difference between what you have a right to do and what is the right thing to do."[35] To make the right choices as a business communicator, you have a responsibility to think through not only what you say but also the consequences of saying it.

Of course, people in a society don't always agree on what constitutes ethical behavior. For instance, the emergence of **stealth marketing**, in which customers don't know they're being marketed to, has raised a new set of concerns about ethics. One common stealth-marketing technique is sending people into public places to use particular products in a conspicuous manner and then discuss them with strangers—as

though they were just regular people on the street, when in fact they are employed by a marketing firm. Another is paying consumers or rewarding them with insider information and other benefits to promote products to their friends without telling the friends it's a form of advertising. Critics complain that such techniques are deceptive because they don't give their targets the opportunity to raise their instinctive defenses against the persuasive powers of marketing messages.[36]

Ethical behavior is a companywide concern, of course; but because communication efforts are the public face of a company, they are subjected to particularly rigorous scrutiny from regulators, legislators, investors, consumer groups, environmental groups, labor organizations, and anyone else affected by business activities. **Ethical communication** includes all relevant information, is true in every sense, and is not deceptive in any way. In contrast, unethical communication can include falsehoods and misleading information (or can withhold important information). Here are some examples of unethical communication:[37]

Any time you try to mislead your audience, the result is unethical communication.

- **Plagiarism. Plagiarism** is presenting someone else's words or other creative product as your own. Note that plagiarism can also be illegal if it violates a **copyright**, which is a form of legal protection for the expression of creative ideas.[38]

- **Selective misquoting.** Deliberately omitting damaging or unflattering comments to paint a better picture of you or your company is unethical if the picture you create is untruthful.

- **Misrepresenting numbers.** Statistics and other data can be unethically manipulated by increasing or decreasing numbers, exaggerating, altering statistics, or omitting numeric data.

- **Distorting visuals.** Images can also be manipulated in unethical ways, such as making a product seem bigger than it really is or changing the scale of graphs and charts to exaggerate or conceal differences.

In contrast, an ethical message is accurate and sincere. It avoids language and images that manipulate, discriminate, or exaggerate. On the surface, such ethical practices appear fairly easy to recognize, but deciding what is ethical can be a considerable challenge in complex business situations.

Distinguishing Ethical Dilemmas from Ethical Lapses

Every company has responsibilities to its stakeholders, and those various groups often have competing interests. An **ethical dilemma** involves choosing between alternatives that aren't clear-cut. Perhaps two conflicting alternatives are both ethical and valid, or perhaps the alternatives lie somewhere in the gray area between clearly right and clearly wrong. Suppose you are the chief executive of a company whose sales are declining, and you might be forced to reduce costs by laying off 100 employees. You've decided to wait two months before making this tough decision. Here's your dilemma: Do you tell the workforce now that 100 jobs could disappear in the near future? Telling them now would give people more time to look for new jobs and adjust their finances—clearly a good thing. However, if you tell them now, vital employees nervous about their future could jump ship, which could drive sales down even more—clearly not a good thing. And what if you tell them now and many people leave but then sales improve enough in the next two months that you can avoid the layoffs? You will have unnecessarily disrupted many careers and families. Situations such as these often have no clear answer.

An ethical dilemma is a choice between alternatives that may all be ethical and valid.

In contrast, an **ethical lapse** is a clearly unethical (and frequently illegal) choice. In 2004, several insurance companies were accused of misleading military personnel at Fort Benning in Georgia, Camp Pendleton in California, and other bases around the country. Many of these young men and women thought they were signing up for

An ethical lapse is knowing that something is wrong and doing it anyway.

savings programs when in fact they were buying extremely expensive and frequently unnecessary life insurance policies. The policies were often sold during mandatory financial training sessions for the soldiers, who were given no time to read the documents they signed. After the situation was brought to national attention by the *New York Times* and other news media, at least two of the companies involved, Madison National Life Insurance Company and American Amicable Life Insurance, began issuing full refunds.[39]

With both internal and external communication efforts, the pressure to produce results or justify decisions can make unethical communication a tempting choice. Compare the messages in Figures 1.9 and 1.10, in which the results of a marketing research project are presented to company executives.

Ensuring Ethical Communication

Ensuring ethical business communication requires three elements: ethical individuals, ethical company leadership, and the appropriate policies and structures to support employees' efforts to make ethical choices.[40] Moreover, these three elements need to work in harmony. If employees see company executives making unethical decisions and flouting company guidelines, they might conclude that the guidelines are meaningless and emulate their bosses' unethical behavior.

Responsible employers establish clear ethical guidelines for their employees to follow.

Employers have a responsibility to establish clear guidelines for ethical behavior, including business communication. In a recent global survey by the International

FIGURE 1.9
Unethical Communication
The writers of this memo clearly wanted the company to continue funding their pet project, even though the marketing research didn't support such a decision. By comparing this memo with the version shown in Figure 1.10, you can see how the writers twisted the truth and omitted evidence in order to put a positive spin on the research.

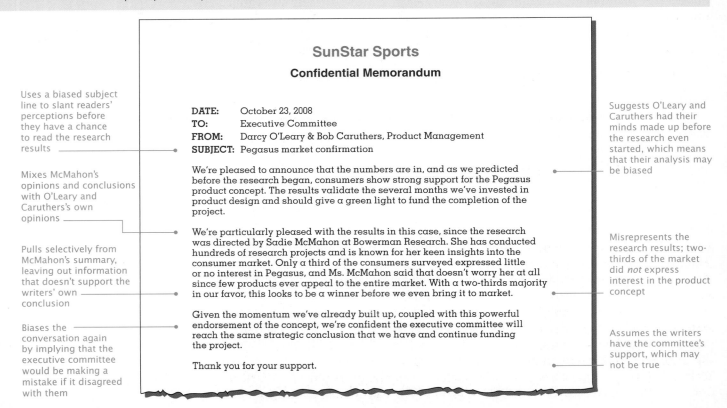

Uses a biased subject line to slant readers' perceptions before they have a chance to read the research results

Mixes McMahon's opinions and conclusions with O'Leary and Caruthers's own opinions

Pulls selectively from McMahon's summary, leaving out information that doesn't support the writers' own conclusion

Biases the conversation again by implying that the executive committee would be making a mistake if it disagreed with them

Suggests O'Leary and Caruthers had their minds made up before the research even started, which means that their analysis may be biased

Misrepresents the research results; two-thirds of the market did *not* express interest in the product concept

Assumes the writers have the committee's support, which may not be true

SunStar Sports

Confidential Memorandum

DATE: October 23, 2008
TO: Executive Committee
FROM: Darcy O'Leary & Bob Caruthers, Product Management
SUBJECT: Pegasus market confirmation

We're pleased to announce that the numbers are in, and as we predicted before the research began, consumers show strong support for the Pegasus product concept. The results validate the several months we've invested in product design and should give a green light to fund the completion of the project.

We're particularly pleased with the results in this case, since the research was directed by Sadie McMahon at Bowerman Research. She has conducted hundreds of research projects and is known for her keen insights into the consumer market. Only a third of the consumers surveyed expressed little or no interest in Pegasus, and Ms. McMahon said that doesn't worry her at all since few products ever appeal to the entire market. With a two-thirds majority in our favor, this looks to be a winner before we even bring it to market.

Given the momentum we've already built up, coupled with this powerful endorsement of the concept, we're confident the executive committee will reach the same strategic conclusion that we have and continue funding the project.

Thank you for your support.

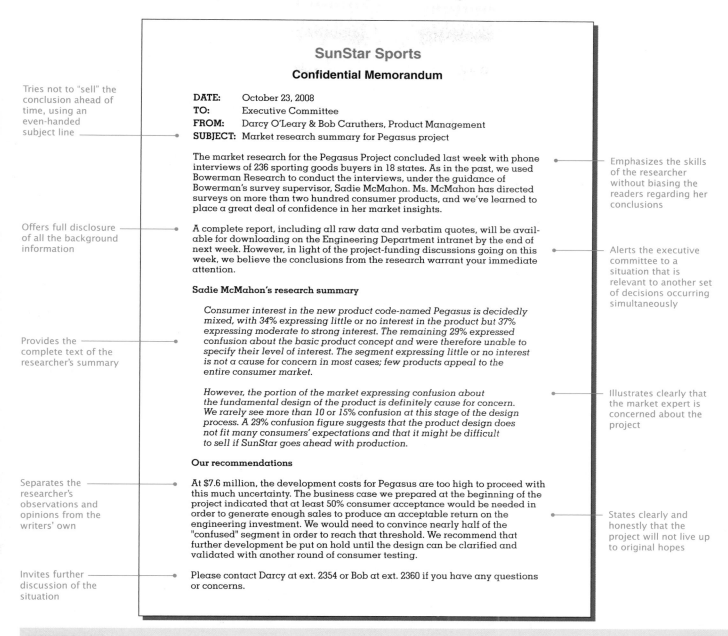

Tries not to "sell" the conclusion ahead of time, using an even-handed subject line

Offers full disclosure of all the background information

Provides the complete text of the researcher's summary

Separates the researcher's observations and opinions from the writers' own

Invites further discussion of the situation

Emphasizes the skills of the researcher without biasing the readers regarding her conclusions

Alerts the executive committee to a situation that is relevant to another set of decisions occurring simultaneously

Illustrates clearly that the market expert is concerned about the project

States clearly and honestly that the project will not live up to original hopes

SunStar Sports
Confidential Memorandum

DATE: October 23, 2008
TO: Executive Committee
FROM: Darcy O'Leary & Bob Caruthers, Product Management
SUBJECT: Market research summary for Pegasus project

The market research for the Pegasus Project concluded last week with phone interviews of 236 sporting goods buyers in 18 states. As in the past, we used Bowerman Research to conduct the interviews, under the guidance of Bowerman's survey supervisor, Sadie McMahon. Ms. McMahon has directed surveys on more than two hundred consumer products, and we've learned to place a great deal of confidence in her market insights.

A complete report, including all raw data and verbatim quotes, will be available for downloading on the Engineering Department intranet by the end of next week. However, in light of the project-funding discussions going on this week, we believe the conclusions from the research warrant your immediate attention.

Sadie McMahon's research summary

Consumer interest in the new product code-named Pegasus is decidedly mixed, with 34% expressing little or no interest in the product but 37% expressing moderate to strong interest. The remaining 29% expressed confusion about the basic product concept and were therefore unable to specify their level of interest. The segment expressing little or no interest is not a cause for concern in most cases; few products appeal to the entire consumer market.

However, the portion of the market expressing confusion about the fundamental design of the product is definitely cause for concern. We rarely see more than 10 or 15% confusion at this stage of the design process. A 29% confusion figure suggests that the product design does not fit many consumers' expectations and that it might be difficult to sell if SunStar goes ahead with production.

Our recommendations

At $7.6 million, the development costs for Pegasus are too high to proceed with this much uncertainty. The business case we prepared at the beginning of the project indicated that at least 50% consumer acceptance would be needed in order to generate enough sales to produce an acceptable return on the engineering investment. We would need to convince nearly half of the "confused" segment in order to reach that threshold. We recommend that further development be put on hold until the design can be clarified and validated with another round of consumer testing.

Please contact Darcy at ext. 2354 or Bob at ext. 2360 if you have any questions or concerns.

FIGURE 1.10
Ethical Communication
This version of the memo shown in Figure 1.9 presents the evidence in a more honest and ethical manner.

Association of Business Communicators, 70 percent of communication professionals said their companies clearly define what is considered ethical and unethical behavior. On a somewhat less positive note, slightly fewer than half said their companies encourage open discussion of ethical issues and dilemmas.[41]

Many companies establish an explicit ethics policy by using a written **code of ethics** to help employees determine what is acceptable. A code is often part of a larger program of employee training and communication channels that allow employees to ask questions and report instances of questionable ethics. For example, United Technologies, a large aerospace and defense company based in Hartford, Connecticut, offers employees, customers, and suppliers a confidential way to report suspected fraud and other ethical concerns. The people who share their concerns through the program then receive a written response that explains how the situation was resolved.[42] To ensure ongoing compliance with their codes of ethics, many companies also conduct **ethics audits** to monitor ethical progress and to point out any weaknesses that need to be addressed.

However, whether or not formal guidelines are in place, every employee has the responsibility to communicate in an ethical manner. In the absence of clear guidelines, ask yourself the following questions about your business communications:[43]

- Have you defined the situation fairly and accurately?

- What is your intention in communicating this message?

- What impact will this message have on the people who receive it, or who may be affected by it?

- Will the message achieve the greatest possible good while doing the least possible harm?

- Will the assumptions you've made change over time? That is, will a decision that seems ethical now seem unethical in the future?

- Are you comfortable with your decision? Would you be embarrassed if it were printed in tomorrow's newspaper or spread across the Internet?

If you can't decide whether a choice is ethical, picture yourself explaining it to someone whose opinion you value.

If all else fails, think about a person whom you admire and ask yourself what he or she would think of your decision. If you wouldn't be proud to describe your choice to someone you admire and respect, you may be making a poor ethical choice.

Ensuring Legal Communication

Business communication is governed by a wide variety of laws designed to ensure accurate, complete messages.

In addition to ethical guidelines, business communication is also bound by a wide variety of laws and regulations, including the following areas:

- **Promotional communication.** Marketing specialists need to be aware of the many laws that govern truth and accuracy in advertising. These laws address such issues as false and deceptive advertising, misleading or inaccurate labels on product packages, and "bait and switch" tactics in which a store advertises a lower-priced product to lure consumers into a store but then tries to sell them a more expensive item.[44] Chapter 10 explores this area in more detail.

- **Contracts.** A **contract** is a legally binding promise between two parties, in which one party makes a specified offer and the other party accepts. Contracts are fundamental to virtually every aspect of business, from product sales to property rental to credit cards and loans to professional service agreements.[45]

- **Employment communication.** A variety of local, state, and federal laws govern communication between employers and both potential and current employees. For example, job descriptions must be written in a way that doesn't intentionally or unintentionally discriminate against women, minorities, or people with disabilities.[46]

- **Intellectual property.** In an age when instant global connectivity makes it effortless to copy and retransmit electronic files, the protection of intellectual property has become a widespread concern. **Intellectual property (IP)**

Document Makeover

IMPROVE THIS MEMO

To practice correcting drafts of actual documents, visit your online course or the access-code-protected portion of the Companion Website. Click on "Document Makeovers," then click on Chapter 1. You will find a memo that contains problems and errors related to what you've learned in this chapter about improving business communication. Use the Final Draft decision tool to create an improved version of this memo. Check the message for ethical communication and an audience-centered approach.

includes patents, copyrighted materials, trade secrets, and even Internet domain names.[47] Bloggers need to be particularly careful about IP protection, given the carefree way that some post the work of others without offering proper credit. For guidelines on this hot topic, get the free *Legal Guide for Bloggers* at www.eff.org/bloggers/lg.

- **Financial reporting.** Finance and accounting professionals, particularly those who work for publicly traded companies (those that sell stock to the public), must adhere to stringent reporting laws. For instance, a number of corporations have recently been targets of government investigations and shareholder lawsuits for offering misleading descriptions of financial results and revenue forecasts.

- **Defamation.** Negative comments about another party raise the possibility of **defamation**, the intentional communication of false statements that damage character or reputation.[48] (Written defamation is called *libel*; spoken defamation is called *slander*.) Someone suing for defamation must prove (1) that the statement is false, (2) that the language is injurious to the person's reputation, and (3) that the statement has been published.

   If you have any doubts about the legality of any message you intend to distribute, ask for advice from your company's legal department. A small dose of caution can prevent huge legal headaches and protect your company's reputation in the marketplace.

APPLYING WHAT YOU'VE LEARNED

At the beginning of this chapter, you met Six Apart's Mena Trott in "On the Job: Communicating at Six Apart." Trott is just one of the many real business professionals you'll meet throughout this book—people who successfully handle the same communication challenges you'll face on the job. Each chapter opens with one of these slice-of-life vignettes, and as you read through each chapter, think about the person and the company highlighted in the vignette. Become familiar with the various concepts presented in the chapter, and imagine how they might apply to the featured scenario.

   At the end of each chapter, you'll take part in an innovative simulation called "On the Job: Solving Communication Dilemmas." You'll play the role of a person working in the highlighted organization, and you'll face situations you'd encounter on the job. You will be presented with several communication scenarios, each with several possible courses of action. It's up to you to recommend one course of action from each scenario as homework, as teamwork, as material for in-class discussion, or in a host of other ways. These scenarios let you explore various communication ideas and apply the concepts and techniques from the chapter.

   Now you're ready for the first simulation. As you tackle each problem, think about the material you covered in this chapter and consider your own experience as a communicator. You'll probably be surprised to discover how much you already know about business communication.

On the Job

SOLVING COMMUNICATION DILEMMAS AT SIX APART

As president of Six Apart, Mena Trott plays a vital role in keeping communication flowing and making sure everyone receives necessary information by helping employees overcome potential barriers to effective communication.

To assist her with a growing workload of internal and external communication tasks, she has recently hired you as assistant with special responsibilities for communication. Use your knowledge of communication to choose the best response for each of the following situations. Be prepared to explain why your choice is best.

1. One of the reasons for Six Apart's success is its friendly, open style of communication with its customers, even those occasional customers who make unrealistic demands or expect special treatment. Unfortunately, you've learned that some of the customer service representatives have been letting their emotions get in the way when dealing with these difficult customers. Several customers have complained about rude treatment. You're sensitive to the situation because you know that customer service can be a difficult job. However, having a reputation for hostile customer service could spell doom for the company, so you need to communicate your concerns immediately. Which of the following sentences would be the best way to begin an e-mail message to the customer service staff?
   a. "We must all work harder at serving customers in an efficient, timely manner."
   b. "The growing problem of abusive customer communications must stop immediately—after all, without customers, we have no revenue; without revenue, you have no jobs."
   c. "Positive customer support is one of our most important competitive advantages, but it has come to management's attention that some of you are ruining the company's reputation by mistreating customers."
   d. "Thank you for your continued efforts at supporting our customers; I know this can be a challenging task at times."

2. Six Apart has developed a corporate culture that reflects both the engaging personalities of Ben and Mena Trott and the generally informal "vibe" of the blogosphere. However, as the company continues to grow, new employees bring a variety of communication styles and expectations. In particular, the new accounting manager tends to communicate in a formal, distant style that some company old-timers find off-putting and impersonal. Several of these people have expressed concerns that the new manager "doesn't fit in," even though she's doing a great job otherwise. How should you respond?
   a. Tell these people to stop complaining; the accounting manager is doing her job well, and that's what counts.
   b. In a private conversation with the accounting manager, explain the importance of fitting into the corporate culture and give her a four-week deadline to change her style.
   c. In a private conversation with the accounting manager, explain the reasoning behind the company's informal culture and its contribution to the company's success; suggest that she might find her work here more enjoyable if she modifies her approach somewhat.
   d. Allow the accounting manager to continue communicating in the same style; after all, that's her personal style, and it's not up to the company to change it.

3. A false rumor has begun circulating online that Six Apart plans to sell one of its product lines to a competitor and lay off most of the employees who currently work on those products. Trott asks your advice in handling the situation. Which of the following would you recommend?
   a. Try to plant a counter-rumor on the online grapevine so that the employees who are worried about their jobs will get the right message the same way they got the wrong one.
   b. Immediately schedule a companywide, in-person meeting to set the record straight, emphasizing to everyone in the firm that Six Apart has no plans to shed that product line.
   c. Post a message on Mena's Corner (her blog on the Six Apart website), setting the record straight and assuring the workforce that all jobs are safe; employees and customers alike are accustomed to getting information from her blog, so it's the right way to communicate this message.
   d. Ignore the rumor. Like all other false rumors, it will eventually die out.

4. As Microsoft, Google, and other major companies join the market for blogging software and services, Six Apart is forced to lower its prices to remain competitive. Unfortunately, lower prices mean the company will have to lower its operating costs if it is to remain profitable, and employee salaries are the single biggest cost. The management team has decided to enact a 10 percent salary reduction for the next six months and then re-evaluate the company's financial health at that point. However, some of the executives are convinced that the salary reductions will have to continue for a year at least—and perhaps even be permanent. In light of this knowledge, which of the following communication strategies would best balance the needs of the company and the needs of the employees?
   a. Tell employees that the 10 percent pay cut will last six months, without implying that it could last longer or even be permanent. If employees worry that their income could be reduced permanently, they'll start looking for other jobs now, which will be a big drain on worker productivity and make the financial situation even worse.
   b. Tell employees that the 10 percent pay cut *is scheduled* to last six months, leaving open the possibility that it could last longer without stating so.
   c. Explain that the pay reduction is likely to be permanent, even if you're not sure that will be the case; it's better to give employees the worst possible news and then offer a pleasant surprise if the situation works out more favorably than expected.
   d. Tell employees that the pay cut will last for six months, at which point the management team will evaluate the situation and decide if the cut needs to be extended beyond that. Explain that you'd like to be able to provide more solid information, but the uncertainties in the market make that unrealistic. The best that you can do is tell employees everything you know—and don't know.

Learning Objectives Checkup

Assess your understanding of the principles in this chapter by reading each learning objective and studying the accompanying exercises. For fill-in-the-blank items, write the missing text in the blank provided; for multiple-choice items, circle the letter of the correct answer. You can check your responses against the answer key on page AK-1.

Objective 1.1: Explain why effective communication is important to your success in today's business environment.

1. Your ability to communicate can help your company
   a. Become more efficient
   b. Increase quality
   c. Improve responsiveness
   d. Become more innovative
   e. Do all of the above
2. As your career advances and you achieve positions of greater responsibility with an organization, your communication skills will
   a. Become less important because you will delegate these tasks
   b. Become more important because you will communicate about increasingly important matters to larger and larger audiences
   c. Remain as important as they were during the early stages of your career

Objective 1.2: Describe the five characteristics of effective business communication.

3. Effective business messages are
   a. Entertaining, blunt, and persuasive
   b. Practical, objective, concise, clear, and persuasive
   c. Personal, clear, and challenging
4. Why is it important for a business message to clearly state expectations regarding who is responsible for doing what in response to the message?
   a. To make sure other employees don't avoid their responsibilities
   b. To make sure that the person who sent the message isn't criticized if important tasks don't get completed
   c. To eliminate confusion by letting each affected person know what his or her specific responsibilities are

Objective 1.3: Identify eight communication skills that successful employers expect from their employees.

5. Which of the following skills does the chapter identify as those that employers are likely to expect?
   a. Organizing ideas and information
   b. Programming HTML webpages
   c. Designing graphics for reports and websites
   d. Expressing and presenting ideas coherently and persuasively
   e. Training other employees
   f. Using communication technologies
   g. Communicating in at least three languages
   h. Communicating in an ethical manner

Objective 1.4: List five ways in which business communication differs from social communication.

6. How has teamwork affected business communication in recent years?
   a. Businesses have decided that team-based communication is inefficient, and most companies have stopped using teams.
   b. Businesses increasingly rely on teams, but most companies have communication specialists who are responsible for communication within each team.
   c. Businesses increasingly rely on teams, and they expect every member of a team to be able to communicate effectively in a team setting.
   d. Innovative businesses use blogs as the primary means of communicating in teams.
7. The evolution toward flatter organizational structures is affecting communication by
   a. Reducing the workload of upper managers by reducing the number of messages they receive
   b. Reducing the number of layers of management
   c. Giving employees more responsibility for communication
   d. Slowing down business decisions and processes
8. Which of the following is a common barrier to successful communication?
   a. Distractions
   b. Information overload
   c. Perceptual differences
   d. All of the above
9. Successful companies tend to view workforce diversity as
   a. A legally mandated requirement
   b. An opportunity to learn more about markets and communicate more effectively with various market segments
   c. An unavoidable cost of doing business
   d. A reason to outsource more business functions in order to reduce the confusion created by diversity
10. Which of the following is the most accurate characterization of current business use of communication technology?
    a. Companies can't afford to waste money on new technology, so few have adopted e-mail, instant messaging, blogs, and other tools that many consumers use.
    b. Only large companies use technologies such as e-mail and websites.
    c. Technology affects virtually every aspect of business communication today.
    d. The use of technology always improves the effectiveness of communication.

Objective 1.5: Describe six strategies for communicating more effectively on the job.

11. An audience-centered approach to communication
    a. Starts with the assumption that the audience is always right
    b. Improves the effectiveness of communication by focusing on the information needs of the audience

c. Is generally a waste of time because it doesn't accommodate the needs of the sender

d. Always simplifies the tasks involved in planning and creating messages

12. Constructive feedback focuses on _____ rather than criticism.

13. Sensitivity to business etiquette
    a. Reduces the chance of interpersonal blunders that might negatively affect communication
    b. Is considered by most companies to be a waste of time in today's fast-paced markets
    c. Is now legally required in all 50 states
    d. Always increases the cost of business communication

Objective 1.6: Explain what must occur for an audience to successfully receive, decode, and respond to messages.

14. In order for audience members to successfully receive messages, they must first _____ the presence of the message, then _____ it from other sensory input, and then _____ it as a message.

15. In order for the receiver of a message to respond in the manner desired by the sender, the receiver needs to
    a. Remember the message
    b. Be able to respond to the message
    c. Have the motivation to respond to the message
    d. Do all of the above

Objective 1.7: Explain four strategies for using communication technology successfully.

16. Successful users of business communication technology make sure that it _____ the communication effort rather than overwhelms or disrupts it.

17. Learning how to use communication technologies effectively
    a. Helps you focus on communicating rather than on the tool being used
    b. Forces you to focus on the tool rather than on the communication process
    c. Is a waste of time for anyone with top management aspirations
    d. Is no longer necessary

18. Reconnecting frequently with colleagues and customers in person
    a. Is widely considered an inappropriate use of time, given all the electronic options now available
    b. Is frowned on by successful managers
    c. Is critical because it helps ensure that technology doesn't hinder human interaction

Objective 1.8: Discuss the importance of ethics in business communication, and differentiate between ethical dilemmas and ethical lapses.

19. Ethical communication
    a. Is the same thing as legal communication
    b. Costs more because there are so many rules to consider
    c. Is important only for companies that sell to consumers rather than to other businesses
    d. Is important because communication is the public face of a company

20. An ethical _____ exists when a person is faced with two conflicting but ethical choices; an ethical _____ occurs when a person makes an unethical choice.

Apply Your Knowledge

1. Why do you think good communication in an organization improves employee attitudes and performance? Explain briefly.

2. Is it possible for companies to be too dependent on communication technology? Explain briefly.

3. How can a lack of shared experience between sender and receiver result in communication failures?

4. As a manager, how can you impress on your employees the importance of strong business ethics when dealing with colleagues, customers, and the general public?

5. **Ethical Choices** Because of your excellent communication skills, your boss always asks you to write his reports for him. When you overhear the CEO complimenting him on his logical organization and clear writing style, he responds as if he'd written all those reports himself. What kind of ethical choice does your boss's response represent? What can you do in this situation? Briefly explain your solution and your reasoning.

Practice Your Knowledge

MESSAGE FOR ANALYSIS

Read the following blog posting and then (1) analyze whether the message is effective or ineffective (be sure to explain why) and (2) revise the message so that it follows this chapter's guidelines.

It has come to my attention that many of you are lying on your time cards. If you come in late, you should not put 8:00 on your

card. If you take a long lunch, you should not put 1:00 on your time card. I will not stand for this type of cheating. I simply have no choice but to institute an employee monitoring system. Beginning next Monday, video cameras will be installed at all entrances to the building, and your entry and exit times will be logged each time you use electronic key cards to enter or leave.

Anyone who is late for work or late coming back from lunch more than three times will have to answer to me. I don't care if you had to take a nap or if you girls had to shop. This is a place of business, and we do not want to be taken advantage of by slackers who are cheaters to boot.

It is too bad that a few bad apples always have to spoil things for everyone.

EXERCISES

For active links to all websites discussed in this chapter, visit this text's website at **www.prenhall.com/thill**. Locate your book and click on its "Companion Website" link. Then select Chapter 1 and click on "Featured Websites." Locate the name of the page or the URL related to the material in the text. Please note that links to sites that become inactive after publication of the book will be removed from the "Featured Websites" section.

1.1 Effective Business Communication: Understanding the Difference Bring to class a sales message that you received in the mail or via e-mail. Comment on how well the communication
   a. Provides practical information
   b. Gives facts rather than impressions
   c. Clarifies and condenses information
   d. States precise responsibilities
   e. Persuades others and offers recommendations

1.2 Internal Communication: Planning the Flow For the following tasks, identify the necessary direction of communication (downward, upward, horizontal), suggest an appropriate type or types of communication (casual conversation, formal interview, meeting, workshop, web conference, instant messaging, memo, blog, bulletin board notice, and so on), and briefly explain your suggestions.
   a. As human resources manager, you want to announce details about this year's company picnic.
   b. As director of internal communication, you want to convince top management of the need for an internal executive blog.
   c. As production manager, you want to make sure that both the sales manager and the finance manager receive your scheduling estimates.
   d. As marketing manager, you want to help employees throughout the company understand the marketplace and customer needs.

1.3 Communication Networks: Formal or Informal? An old college friend phoned you out of the blue to say, "Truth is, I had to call you. You'd better keep this under your hat, but when I heard my company was buying you guys out, I was dumbfounded. I had no idea that a company as large as yours could sink so fast. Your group must be in pretty bad shape over there!" Your stomach suddenly turned queasy, and you felt a chill go up your spine. You'd heard nothing about any buyout, and before you could even get your college friend off the phone, you were wondering what you should do. Of the following, choose one course of action and briefly explain your choice.
   a. Contact your CEO directly and relate what you've heard.
   b. Ask co-workers whether they've heard anything about a buyout.
   c. Discuss the phone call confidentially with your immediate supervisor.
   d. Keep quiet about the whole thing. (There's nothing you can do about the situation anyway.)

1.4 Ethical Choices In less than a page, explain why you think each of the following is or is not ethical.
   a. Keeping quiet about a possible environmental hazard you've just discovered in your company's processing plant
   b. Overselling the benefits of instant messaging to your company's management; they never seem to understand the benefits of technology, so you believe it's the only way to convince them to make the right choice
   c. Telling an associate and close friend that she'd better pay more attention to her work responsibilities, or management will fire her
   d. Recommending the purchase of excess equipment to use up your allocated funds before the end of the fiscal year so that your budget won't be cut next year

1.5 The Changing Workplace: Personal Expression at Work Blogging has become a popular way for employees to communicate with customers and other parties outside the company. In some cases, employee blogs have been quite beneficial for both companies and their customers by providing helpful information and "putting a human face" on otherwise formal and imposing corporations. However, in some other cases, employees have been fired for posting information that their employers said was inappropriate. One particular area of concern is criticism of the company or individual managers. Should employees be allowed to criticize their employers in a public forum such as a blog? In a brief e-mail message, argue for or against company policies that prohibit any critical information in employee blogs.

1.6 Internet Cisco is a leading manufacturer of equipment for the Internet and corporate networks and has developed a code of ethics that it expects employees to abide by. Visit the company's website, at **www.cisco.com**, and find the *Code of Conduct*. In a brief paragraph, describe three specific examples of things you could do that would violate these provisions; then list at least three opportunities that Cisco provides its employees to report ethics violations or ask questions regarding ethical dilemmas.

1.7 Communication Etiquette Potential customers frequently visit your production facility before making purchase decisions. You and the people who report to you in the sales department have received extensive training in etiquette issues because you deal with high-profile clients so frequently. However, the rest of the workforce has not received such training, and you worry that someone might inadvertently say or do something that would offend one of these potential customers. In a two-paragraph e-mail, explain to the general manager why you think anyone who might come in contact with customers should receive basic etiquette training.

1.8 Ethical Choices Knowing that you have many friends throughout the company, your boss relies on you for feedback concerning employee morale and other issues affecting the staff. She recently approached you and asked you to start reporting any behavior that might violate company polices, from taking office supplies home to making personal long-distance calls. List the issues you'd like to discuss with her before you respond to her request.

1.9 Formal Communication: Self-Introduction Write an e-mail message or prepare an oral presentation, introducing yourself to your instructor and your class. Include such things as your background, interests, achievements, and goals. If you write an e-mail message, keep it under one normal screen in length, and use Figure 1.4 as a model for the format. If you prepare an oral presentation, plan to speak for no more than two minutes.

1.10 Teamwork Your boss has asked your work group to research and report on corporate child-care facilities. Of course, you'll want to know who (besides your boss) will be reading your report. Working with two team members, list four or five other things you'll want to know about the situation and about your audience before starting your research. Briefly explain why each of the items on your list is important.

1.11 Communication Process: Analyzing Miscommunication Use the eight phases of the communication process to analyze a miscommunication you've recently had with a co-worker, supervisor, classmate, teacher, friend, or family member. What idea were you trying to share? How did you encode and transmit it? Did the receiver get the message? Did the receiver correctly decode the message? How do you know? Based on your analysis, identify and explain the barriers that prevented your successful communication in this instance.

1.12 Ethical Choices You've been given the critical assignment of selecting the site for your company's new plant. After months of negotiations with landowners, numerous cost calculations, and investments in ecological, social, and community impact studies, you are about to recommend building the new plant on the Lansing River site. Now, just 15 minutes before your big presentation to top management, you discover a possible mistake in your calculations: Site-purchase costs appear to be $500,000 more than you calculated, nearly 10 percent over budget. You don't have time to recheck all your figures, so you're tempted to just go ahead with your recommendation and ignore any discrepancies. You're worried that management won't approve this purchase if you can't present a clean, unqualified solution. You also know that many projects run over their original estimates, so you can probably work the extra cost into the budget later. On your way to the meeting room, you make your final decision. In a few paragraphs, explain the decision you made.

1.13 Communication Etiquette In group meetings, some of your colleagues have a habit of interrupting and arguing with the speaker, taking credit for ideas that aren't theirs, and shooting down ideas they don't agree with. You're the newest person in the group and not sure if this is accepted behavior in this company, but it concerns you both personally and professionally. Should you go with the flow and adopt their behavior or stick with your own communication style, even though you might get lost in the noise? In two paragraphs, explain the pros and cons of both approaches.

Expand Your Knowledge

LEARNING MORE ON THE WEB

CHECK OUT THESE RESOURCES AT THE BUSINESS WRITER'S FREE LIBRARY

www.mapnp.org/library/commskls/cmm_writ.htm
The Business Writer's Free Library is a terrific resource for business communication material. Categories of information include basic composition skills, basic writing skills, correspondence, reference material, and general resources and advice. Log on and read about the most common errors in English, become a word detective, ask Miss Grammar, review samples of common forms of correspondence, fine-tune your interpersonal skills, join a newsgroup, and more. Follow the links and improve your effectiveness as a business communicator.

1. What are some strategies for communicating with an uncooperative audience?

2. What is the value of diversity in the workplace?
3. Why is bad etiquette bad for business?

SURFING YOUR WAY TO CAREER SUCCESS

Bovée and Thill's Business Communication Headline News offers links to hundreds of online resources that can help you with this course, your other college courses, and your career. Visit www.businesscommunicationblog.com and click on "Web Directory." The "Communication" section connects you to a variety of websites and articles on basic communication skills, communication challenges on the job, and intriguing topics such as communication ethics and disinformation. Identify three websites from this section that could be useful in your business career. For each site, write a two-sentence summary of what the site offers and how it could help you launch and build your career.

Learn Interactively

INTERACTIVE STUDY GUIDE

Visit www.prenhall.com/thill, then locate your book and click on its "Companion Website" link. Select Chapter 1 to take advantage of the interactive "Chapter Quiz" to test your knowledge of chapter concepts. Receive instant feedback on whether you need additional studying. Also, visit the "Study Hall," where you'll find an abundance of valuable resources that will help you succeed in this course.

PEAK PERFORMANCE GRAMMAR AND MECHANICS

"Peak Performance Grammar and Mechanics" is a special feature accompanying your text that helps you evaluate and improve your knowledge of the various parts of speech and of *mechanics*, basic style issues such as capitalization, abbreviation, spelling, numbers, and the use of italics. If your instructor has required the use of this feature, either in your online course or on CD, you can improve your skill with nouns by using the "Peak Performance Grammar and Mechanics" module. Click "Grammar Basics," then "Nouns and Pronouns." Take the Pretest to determine whether you have any weak areas. Then review those areas in the Refresher Course. Take the Follow-Up Test to check your grasp of nouns. For an extra challenge or advanced practice, take the Advanced Test. Finally, for additional reinforcement, go to the "Improve Your Grammar, Mechanics, and Usage" section that follows and complete those exercises.

Improve Your Grammar, Mechanics, and Usage

The following exercises help you improve your knowledge of and power over English grammar, mechanics, and usage. Turn to the Handbook of Grammar, Mechanics, and Usage at the end of this book and review all of Section 1.1 (Nouns). Then look at the following 10 items. Underline the preferred choice within each set of parentheses. (Answers to these exercises appear on page AK-3.)

1. She remembered placing that report on her (*bosses, boss's*) desk.
2. We mustn't follow their investment advice like a lot of (*sheep, sheeps*).
3. Jones founded the company back in the early (*1990's, 1990s*).
4. Please send the (*Joneses, Jones'*) a dozen of the following: (*stopwatchs, stopwatches*), canteens, and headbands.
5. Our (*attorneys, attornies*) will talk to the group about incorporation.
6. Make sure that all (*copys, copies*) include the new addresses.
7. Ask Jennings to collect all (*employee's, employees'*) donations for the Red Cross drive.
8. Charlie now has two (*sons-in-law, son-in-laws*) to help him with his two online (*business's, businesses*).
9. Avoid using too many (*parentheses, parenthesis*) when writing your reports.
10. Follow President (*Nesses, Ness's*) rules about what constitutes a (*weeks, week's*) work.

For additional exercises focusing on nouns, go to www.prenhall.com/thill, then locate your text and click on its "Companion Website" link. Click on Chapter 1, click on "Additional Exercises to Improve Your Grammar, Mechanics, and Usage," then click on "1. Possessive nouns" or "2. Antecedents."

Chapter 2

Communicating in Teams and Mastering Listening and Nonverbal Communication Skills

Learning Objectives

AFTER STUDYING THIS CHAPTER, YOU WILL BE ABLE TO

1 Highlight the advantages and disadvantages of working in teams

2 Identify eight guidelines for successful collaborative writing

3 Explain how wiki technology can help teams collaborate

4 Explain how group dynamics can affect team effectiveness

5 Describe how meeting technologies can help participants communicate more successfully

6 Describe the listening process, and explain how good listeners overcome barriers at each stage of the process

7 Clarify the importance of nonverbal communication, and briefly describe six categories of nonverbal expression

8 Discuss the role of business etiquette, both in the workplace and in social settings

On the Job

COMMUNICATING AT THE CONTAINER STORE

SOLID TEAMWORK + EFFECTIVE COMMUNICATION = A GREAT SHOPPING EXPERIENCE

Let's face it: Frontline jobs in retail don't have the greatest reputation. For employees, these positions often combine low pay with high stress, leading to rapid burnout and frequent turnover. From a customer's perspective, retail employees seem to fall into two categories: unmotivated rookies or aggressive sellers who seem more intent on getting their commissions than helping customers.

When they founded The Container Store, Garrett Boone and Kip Tindell set out to shatter these expectations by creating a pleasant, welcome working and shopping experience. As millions of frustrated consumers know all too well, though, delivering great customer service isn't easy. The Container Store manages to do so through respect for employees, open communication, and a structure that promotes teamwork over individual competition.

Daily "huddles" at The Container Store, informal meetings among team members, reinforce company values and let people exchange important information.

When selecting new employees, for instance, the company engages in a comprehensive interviewing and selection process to find the perfect person for each position, driven by the belief that one great employee equals three good ones. At The Container Store, a great employee is self-motivated, team oriented, and passionate about customer service. Most new hires are former customers, in fact, so they're already fans of the company before they join.

That emphasis on teamwork is reinforced twice a day, before opening and after closing, through a meeting called "the huddle." Similar to a huddle in football, it helps to give everyone a common purpose: set goals, share information, boost morale, and bond as a team. Team-building efforts are further encouraged by participation in community outreach activities, such as school supply drives, and through purely recreational activities dreamed up by the employees on the Fun Committee.

Through a commitment to teamwork and effective communication, The Container Store paves the way for its employees to deliver great customer service. Tindell believes that full, open communication with employees takes courage but says, "The only way that people feel really, really a part of something is if they know everything."[1]

www. containerstore. com

IMPROVING YOUR PERFORMANCE IN TEAMS

Team members have a shared mission and are collectively responsible for their work.

You may never work in a retail operation such as The Container Store (profiled in the chapter opener), but chances are quite good that your career will involve working in teams and other group situations that will test your communication skills. A **team** is a unit of two or more people who share a mission and the responsibility for working to achieve a common goal.[2] Companies can create *formal teams* that become part of the organization's structure, or they can establish *informal teams* that aren't part of the formal organization but are created to solve particular problems, work on specific activities, or encourage employee participation.

Two popular types of informal teams are problem-solving teams and task forces.

Problem-solving teams and **task forces** are informal teams that assemble to resolve specific issues and then disband when their goal has been accomplished. Such teams are often *cross-functional*, pulling together people from a variety of departments with different areas of expertise and responsibility. The resulting diversity of opinions and interests can lead to tensions that highlight the need for effective communication. For instance, consider a cross-functional team charged with making a product more competitive in the marketplace. A representative from the sales department might complain that the product's price is too high because manufacturing has not done enough to lower production costs. Someone from manufacturing might counter that costs are already as low as possible but perhaps the sales department doesn't know how to sell the product effectively. Balancing these competing interests and opinions without letting them boil over into personal animosity requires skill at listening, speaking, and writing.

Committees are formal teams that usually have a long life span and can become a permanent part of the organizational structure. Committees typically deal with regularly recurring tasks, such as an executive committee that meets monthly to plan strategy and review results.

Effective communication is essential to every aspect of team performance.

Whatever the purpose and function of your team, you and your fellow team members must be able to communicate effectively with each other and with people outside your team. As Chapter 1 points out, this ability often requires taking on additional responsibility for communication: sharing information with team members, listening carefully to their inputs, and crafting messages that reflect the team's collective ideas and opinions. Increasingly, this communication takes place long distance, with **virtual teams** connecting from remote locations using a variety of meeting technologies (see "Using Meeting Technologies" on page 51).

Advantages and Disadvantages of Teams

When teams are successful, they improve productivity, creativity, employee involvement, and even job security.[3] Teams are frequently at the core of **participative management**, the effort to involve employees in the company's decision making. Getting employees involved in the daily operation of their own stores is one of the central principles of participative management at The Container Store, as managers and employees share vital business information every day. A successful team can provide a number of advantages:[4]

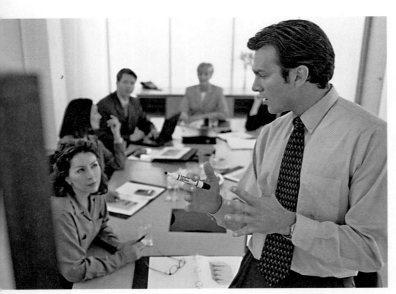

Companies in fast-moving industries rely on teams to work closely and quickly to solve problems and capitalize on market opportunities.

- **Increased information and knowledge.** By pooling the resources of several individuals, teams have access to more information in the decision-making process.

- **Increased diversity of views.** Team members can bring a variety of perspectives to the decision-making process.

Keep in mind, however, that unless these diverse viewpoints are guided by a shared goal, the multiple perspectives can actually hamper a team's efforts.[5]

- **Increased acceptance of a solution.** Those who participate in making a decision are more likely to support the decision enthusiastically and encourage others to accept it.

- **Higher performance levels.** Working in teams can unleash new levels of creativity and energy in workers who share a sense of purpose and mutual accountability. Effective teams can be better than top-performing individuals at solving complex problems.[6] Furthermore, teams fill an individual worker's need to belong to a group, reduce employee boredom, increase feelings of dignity and self-worth, and reduce stress and tension between workers.

> Effective teams can pool knowledge, take advantage of diverse viewpoints, and increase acceptance of solutions the team proposes.

Although teamwork has many advantages, it also has a number of potential disadvantages. At their worst, teams are unproductive and frustrating, and they waste everyone's time. Teams need to be aware of and work to counter the following disadvantages:

- **Groupthink.** Groupthink occurs when pressures to conform with accepted norms of behavior cause individual team members to withhold contrary or unpopular opinions. The result can be decisions that are worse than ones the team members might have made individually.

- **Hidden agendas.** Some team members may have a **hidden agenda**—private, counterproductive motives, such as a desire to take control of the group or to undermine someone else on the team.

- **Free riders.** Some team members may be **free riders**—individuals who don't contribute their fair share to the group's activities.

- **Cost.** Another important drawback to teamwork is the high cost of coordinating group activities. Aligning schedules, arranging meetings, and coordinating individual parts of a project can eat up a lot of time and money.

> Teams need to avoid the negative impact of groupthink, hidden agendas, free riders, and excessive costs.

Characteristics of Effective Teams

To be effective collaborators in a team setting, you and your colleagues should recognize that each individual brings valuable assets, knowledge, and skills to the team. Strong collaborators are willing to exchange information, examine issues, and work through conflicts that arise. They trust each other, working toward the greater good of the team and organization rather than focusing on personal agendas.[7]

The most effective teams have a clear objective and a shared sense of purpose, communicate openly and honestly, reach decisions by consensus, think creatively, and know how to resolve conflict.[8] Learning these team skills takes time and practice, so U.S. companies now teach teamwork more frequently than any other aspect of business.[9]

In contrast, unsuccessful teamwork can waste time and money, generate lower-quality work, and frustrate both managers and employees. A lack of trust is cited as the most common reason for the failure of teams. This lack of trust can result from team members who are suspicious of one another's motives or ability to contribute.[10] Another common reason for failure is poor communication, particularly when teams operate across cultures, countries, and time zones.[11] Poor communication can also result from basic differences in conversational styles. Some people expect conversation to follow an orderly pattern in which team members wait their turns to speak. Others view conversation as more spontaneous and are comfortable with an overlapping, interactive style.[12]

Team Communication

Collaborating on reports, websites, presentations, and other communication projects gives teams the opportunity to capitalize on each person's unique presentation and communication skills. In other words, the collective energy and expertise of the team can be used to create something that transcends what each individual could do otherwise.[13] However, collaborating on team messages requires special effort; the following section offers a number of guidelines to help you write well as a team.

Collaborative Writing Guidelines

In any collaborative effort, it's important to recognize that team members coming from different backgrounds may have different work habits or concerns: A technical expert may focus on accuracy and scientific standards, whereas an editor may be more concerned about organization and coherence. In addition, team members differ in writing styles and personality traits—two factors that can complicate the creative nature of communication.

To collaborate effectively, everyone involved must be flexible and open to other opinions, focusing on team objectives rather than on individual priorities.[14] Successful writers know that most ideas can be expressed in many ways, so they avoid the "my way is best" attitude. The following guidelines will help you collaborate more successfully:[15]

> Successful collaboration requires a number of steps, from selecting the right partners and agreeing on project goals to establishing clear processes and avoiding writing as a group.

- **Select collaborators carefully.** Choose a combination of people who have the experience, information, and talent needed for each project.

- **Agree on project goals before you start.** Starting without a clear idea of what you hope to accomplish inevitably leads to frustration and wasted time.

- **Give your team time to bond before diving in.** If people haven't had the opportunity to work together before, make sure they can get to know each other before being asked to collaborate.

- **Clarify individual responsibilities.** Because team members will be depending on each other, make sure individual responsibilities are clear, including who is supposed to do what and by when.

- **Establish clear processes.** Make sure everyone knows how the work will be done, including checkpoints and decisions to be made along the way.

- **Avoid writing as a group.** The actual composition is the only part of developing team messages that does not usually benefit from group participation. Group writing is often a slow, painful process that delivers bland results. Plan, research, and outline together but try to assign the actual writing to one person or divide larger projects among multiple writers. And if you divide the writing, try to have one person do a final revision pass to ensure a consistent style.

- **Make sure tools and techniques are ready and compatible across the team.** If you plan to use technology for sharing or presenting materials, test the system before work begins. (See the following section for more on collaboration technologies.)

- **Check to see how things are going along the way.** Don't assume that everything is working just because you don't hear anything negative.

> Collaboration tools include multiauthor blogs, content management systems, and wikis.

Collaborative Writing Technologies

A variety of collaboration tools exist to help teams write, including group review and commenting features in word processors, multiauthor blogs, and **content management systems** that organize and control the content for websites. Each of these tools addresses specific needs, but none offers quite the level of direct collaboration as the wiki. A **wiki**, from the Hawaiian word for

FIGURE 2.1
Using a Wiki for Collaborative Communication
The "[EDIT]" links on this webpage are telltale signs of a wiki—in this case, the online user's manual for the WordPress blogging system. Anyone who wants to contribute can expand and improve the instructions and advice that benefit the entire community of WordPress users.

quick, is a website that allows anyone with access to add new material and edit existing material (see Figure 2.1). Public wikis allow anyone to edit pages; private wikis are accessible only by permission. For instance, Yahoo! uses private wikis to facilitate communication among hundreds of team members around the world involved in creating and documenting new services.[16]

Key benefits of wikis include simple operation—writers don't need to know any of the techniques normally required to create web content—and the freedom to post new or revised material without prior approval. This approach is quite different from a content management system, in which both the organization of the website and the *workflow* (the rules for creating, editing, reviewing, and approving content) are tightly controlled.[17] But with a wiki, if you see a way to improve a particular page or want to add a new page, you simply edit or write using your web browser, and it's done. A content management system is a great way to maintain consistent presentation on a company's primary public website, whereas wikis allow teams to collaborate with speed and flexibility.

Enterprise wiki systems extend the wiki concept with additional features for business use that ensure information quality and confidentiality without losing the speed

Benefits of wikis include simple operation and the ability to post new or revised material instantly, without a formal review process.

and flexibility of a wiki. For instance, *access control* lets a team leader identify who is allowed to read and modify the wiki. *Change monitoring* alerts team members when significant changes or additions are made. And *rollback* allows a team to "travel back in time" to see all previous versions of pages.[18]

To use a wiki productively, keep these points in mind:[19]

- Contributors need to let go of traditional expectations of authorship, including individual recognition.

- Team members sometimes need to be encouraged to edit and improve each other's work.

- The focus of wikis is on text content; formatting and design options are usually quite limited.

- Many wikis provide both editing and commenting capabilities, and participants should use the appropriate tool for each.

- New users should take advantage of the *sandbox*, if available; this is a "safe," non-published section of the wiki where team members can practice editing and writing.

Shared workspaces give team members instant access to shared resources and information.

Of course, most teams work on a wide variety of documents and other files, from traditional word processing files to spreadsheets and so on. To facilitate collaboration on a broad scale, many teams now take advantage of **groupware**, computer-based systems that let people communicate, share files, present materials, and work on documents simultaneously. **Shared workspaces** are online "virtual offices" that give everyone on a team access to the same set of resources and information: databases, calendars, project plans, pertinent instant messaging and e-mail exchanges, shared reference materials, and team-created documents (see Figure 2.2). Workspaces such as Documentum eRoom, Microsoft SharePoint, and IBM Lotus Team Workspace create a seamless environment for collaboration.

FIGURE 2.2
Shared Workspaces
Shared workspaces, such as this example from Microsoft's SharePoint system, give virtual teams instant access to the documents, calendars, and other files and information needed for successful collaboration.

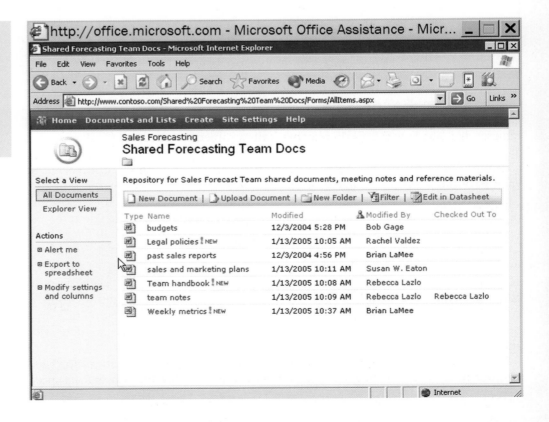

Most groupware systems also have built-in intelligence to control which team members can read, edit, and save specific files. *Revision control* goes one step further: It allows only one person at a time to check out a given file or document and records all the changes that person makes. This feature prevents two people from independently editing the same report at the same time and creating two versions of the same document.[20]

Group Dynamics

The interactions and processes that take place among the members of a team are called **group dynamics**. Productive teams tend to develop rules of interaction that are conducive to business. Often unstated, these rules become group **norms**—informal standards of conduct that members share and that guide member behavior. For example, some teams develop a casual approach to schedules, with members routinely showing up 10 or 15 minutes late for meetings, while other teams expect strict adherence to time commitments.

Teams with a strong sense of identity and cohesiveness can develop overly strong expectations for group behavior, with little tolerance for deviations from those norms. Such strong identity can lead to higher levels of commitment and performance. Unfortunately, it can also lead to groupthink or make it difficult for new members to fit in. Group dynamics are affected by several factors: the roles that team members assume, the current phase of team development, the team's success in resolving conflict, and its success in overcoming resistance.

Group dynamics are the interactions and processes that take place in a team.

Assuming Team Roles   Members of a team can play various roles, which fall into three categories (see Table 2.1). Members who assume **self-oriented roles** are motivated mainly to fulfill personal needs, so they tend to be less productive than other members. Surprisingly, "dream teams" composed of multiple superstars often don't perform as well as one might expect because high-performing individuals can have trouble putting the team's needs ahead of their own.[21] In addition, highly skilled and experienced people with difficult personalities might not contribute as they could for the simple reason that other team members may avoid interacting with them.[22] Far more likely to contribute to team goals are members who assume **team-maintenance roles** to help everyone work well together and those who assume **task-oriented roles** to help the team reach its goals.[23]

Each member of a group plays a role that affects the outcome of the group's activities.

Roles can also change over time. For instance, in a self-directed team with no formal leader, someone may assume a task-oriented leadership role early in the team's evolution. If this person doesn't prove to be a capable leader, someone else may emerge as a leader as the group searches for more effective direction.[24]

Allowing for Team Evolution   Teams typically evolve through a number of phases on their way to becoming productive (see Figure 2.3). One common model identifies five phases:[25]

Teams typically evolve through phases; a common model of this growth includes orientation, conflict, brainstorming, emergence, and reinforcement.

1. **Orientation.** Team members socialize, establish their roles, and begin to define their task or purpose. Many companies use a variety of team-building exercises and activities to help teams break down barriers and develop a sense of shared purpose.[26] Note that team building can be a particular challenge with geographically dispersed virtual teams because the members may never meet in person. Establishing a "team operating agreement" that sets expectations for online meetings, communication processes, and decision making can help teams overcome the disadvantages of distance.[27]

2. **Conflict.** Team members begin to discuss their positions and become more assertive in establishing their roles. Disagreements and uncertainties are natural in this phase.

Table 2.1	TEAM ROLES PEOPLE PLAY		
	Dysfunctional	**Functional**	
	Self-Oriented Roles	*Team-Maintenance Roles*	*Task-Facilitating Roles*
	Controlling: Dominating others by exhibiting superiority or authority	**Encouraging:** Drawing out other members by showing verbal and nonverbal support, praise, or agreement	**Initiating:** Getting the team started on a line of inquiry
	Withdrawing: Retiring from the team either by becoming silent or by refusing to deal with a particular aspect of the team's work	**Harmonizing:** Reconciling differences among team members through mediation or by using humor to relieve tension	**Information giving or seeking:** Offering (or seeking) information relevant to questions facing the team
	Attention seeking: Calling attention to oneself and demanding recognition from others	**Compromising:** Offering to yield on a point in the interest of reaching a mutually acceptable decision	**Coordinating:** Showing relationships among ideas, clarifying issues, summarizing what the team has done
	Diverting: Focusing the team's discussion on topics of interest to the individual rather than on those relevant to the task		**Procedure setting:** Suggesting decision-making procedures that will move the team toward a goal

3. **Brainstorming.** Team members air all the options and discuss the pros and cons fully. At the end of this phase, members begin to settle on a single solution to the problem. Note that while group brainstorming remains a highly popular activity in today's companies, it may not always be the most productive way to generate new ideas. Some research indicates that having people brainstorm individually and then bring their ideas to a group meeting is more successful.[28]

4. **Emergence.** Consensus is reached when the team finds a solution that is acceptable enough for all members to support (even if they have reservations).

5. **Reinforcement.** The team clarifies and summarizes the agreed-upon solution. Members receive their assignments for carrying out the group's decision, and they make arrangements for following up on those assignments.

FIGURE 2.3
Phases of Group Development
Groups generally progress through several stages on their way to becoming productive and reaching their objectives.

1. Orientation	2. Conflict	3. Brainstorming	4. Emergence	5. Reinforcement
Team members get to know each other and establish roles.	Different opinions and perspectives begin to emerge.	Team members explore their options and evaluate alternatives.	The team reaches a consensus on the chosen decision.	Team harmony is re-established and plans are made to put the decision into action.

You may also hear the process defined as *forming, storming, norming, performing,* and *adjourning,* the phases identified by researcher Bruce Tuckman when he proposed one of the earliest models of group development.[29] Note that stages are a general framework for team development. Some teams may move forward and backward through several stages before they become productive, and other teams may be productive right away, even while some or all members are in a state of conflict.[30]

Resolving Conflict   Conflict can arise for a number of reasons. Team members may believe that they need to compete for money, information, or other resources. Or members may disagree about who is responsible for specific tasks. Various members can also bring ideas that are equally good but incompatible. Poor communication can lead to misunderstanding, and intentionally withholding information can undermine trust. Basic differences in values, attitudes, and personalities may lead to arguments. Power struggles may result when one member questions the authority of another or when people with limited authority attempt to increase their power or exert more influence. Conflict can also arise because individuals or teams are pursuing different goals.[31]

Conflict can be either constructive or destructive. Conflict is constructive if it forces important issues into the open, increases the involvement of team members, and generates creative ideas for the solution to a problem. Constructive conflict can prod teams to higher performance, in fact. Teamwork isn't necessarily about happiness and harmony; even teams that have some interpersonal friction can excel with effective leadership and team players committed to strong results. As teamwork experts Andy Boynton and Bill Fischer put it, "Virtuoso teams are not about getting polite results."[32]

In contrast, conflict is destructive if it diverts energy from more important issues, destroys morale, or divides the team.[33] Destructive conflict can lead to *win-lose* or *lose-lose* outcomes, in which one or both sides lose, to the detriment of the entire team. If you approach conflict with the idea that both sides can satisfy their goals to at least some extent (a *win-win strategy*), you can often minimize losses for everyone. For the win-win strategy to work, though, everybody must believe that (1) it's possible to find a solution that both parties can accept, (2) cooperation is better for the organization than competition, (3) the other party can be trusted, and (4) greater power or status doesn't entitle one party to impose a solution.

To craft a win-win solution, start by considering the other party's needs. Find out what the other party considers acceptable. Search for mutually satisfactory solutions or compromises, the results of which are better for the team overall.[34] In many cases, the resolution process is chiefly an exchange of opinions and information that gradually leads to a mutually acceptable solution.[35]

Here are seven measures that can help team members successfully resolve conflict:

> Conflict in teams can be either constructive or destructive.

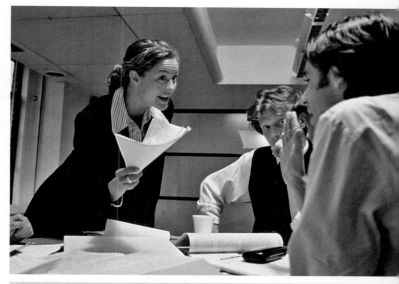

Conflict is an inevitable part of working in teams, but an effective team knows how to keep destructive conflict from distracting the team from its objectives.

- **Proaction.** Deal with minor conflict before it becomes major conflict.

- **Communication.** Get those directly involved in the conflict to participate in resolving it.

- **Openness.** Get feelings out in the open before dealing with the main issues.

- **Research.** Seek factual reasons for the problem before seeking solutions.

- **Flexibility.** Don't let anyone lock into a position before considering other solutions.

- **Fair play.** Don't let anyone avoid a fair solution by hiding behind the rules.
- **Alliance.** Get opponents to fight together against an "outside force" instead of against each other.

When you encounter resistance or hostility, try to maintain your composure and address the other person's emotional needs.

Overcoming Resistance   Resistance to change is a particular type of conflict that can affect work in teams. Some resistance is clearly irrational, such as when people resist any kind of change, whether it makes sense or not. Sometimes, however, the resistance is perfectly logical. A change may require someone to relinquish authority or give up comfortable ways of doing things. In any event, you can help overcome resistance with calm, reasonable communication:

- **Express understanding.** You might say, "I can understand that this change might be difficult, and if I were in your position, I might be reluctant myself." Help the other person relax and talk about his or her anxiety so that you have a chance to offer reassurance.[36]
- **Bring resistance out into the open.** When people are noncommittal and silent, they may be tuning you out without even knowing why. Continuing with your argument is futile. Deal directly with the resistance, without accusing. You might say, "You seem cool to this idea. Have I made some faulty assumptions?" Such questions force people to face and define their resistance.[37]
- **Evaluate others' objections fairly.** Don't simply repeat yourself. Focus on what the other person is expressing, both the words and the feelings. Get the person to open up so that you can understand the basis for the resistance. Others' objections may raise legitimate points that you'll need to discuss, or they may reveal problems that you'll need to minimize.[38]
- **Hold your arguments until the other person is ready for them.** Getting your point across depends as much on the other person's frame of mind as it does on your arguments. You can't assume that a strong argument will speak for itself. By becoming more audience centered, you will learn to address the other person's emotional needs first.

MAKING YOUR MEETINGS MORE PRODUCTIVE

Much of the communication you'll participate in will take place in meetings.

Many business meetings waste time and money as a result of poor planning.

Meetings are a primary communication venue for today's businesses, whether held in formal conference rooms, in informal settings such as The Container Store's daily huddles, or on the Internet as *virtual meetings*. Well-run meetings can help solve problems, develop ideas, and identify opportunities. Much of your workplace communication will occur in small-group meetings; therefore, your ability to contribute to the company and to be recognized for those contributions will depend on your meeting skills.

Unfortunately, many meetings are unproductive. In one study, senior and middle managers reported that only 56 percent of their meetings were actually productive and that 25 percent of them could have been replaced by a phone call or a memo.[39] The three most frequently reported problems with meetings are getting off the subject, not having an agenda, and running too long.[40] You can help ensure productive meetings by preparing carefully, conducting meetings efficiently, and using meeting technologies wisely.

Document Makeover

IMPROVE THIS E-MAIL MESSAGE

To practice correcting drafts of actual documents, visit your online course or the access-code-protected portion of the Companion Website. Click on "Document Makeovers," then click on Chapter 2. You will find an e-mail message that contains problems and errors related to what you've learned in this chapter about communicating in teams. Use the Final Draft decision tool to create an improved version of the e-mail. Check the message for clarity, relevance of topics to meeting participants, proper approach to group collaboration, and communication of meeting etiquette.

Preparing for Meetings

Careful preparation helps you avoid the two biggest meeting mistakes: (1) holding a meeting when a blog posting or another message would do the job and (2) holding a meeting without a specific goal in mind. Before you even begin preparing for a meeting, make sure it's truly necessary. Once you're sure, proceed with four preparation tasks:

- **Identify your purpose.** Although many meetings have multiple purposes, most are one of two types: *Informational meetings* involve sharing information and perhaps coordinating action. *Decision-making meetings* involve persuasion, analysis, and problem solving. Whatever your purpose, make sure it is clear and clearly communicated to all participants.

- **Select participants for the meeting.** If the session is purely informational and one person will do most of the talking, you can invite a large group. For problem-solving and decision-making meetings, invite only those people who are in a direct position to help the meeting reach its objective. The more participants, the more comments and confusion you're likely to get and the longer the meeting will take. However, make sure you invite all the key decision makers, or your meeting will fail to satisfy its purpose.

- **Choose the time and the facility.** For working sessions, morning meetings are usually more productive than afternoon sessions. Also, consider the seating arrangements: Are rows of chairs suitable, or do you need a conference table or some other setting? Plus, give some attention to details such as room temperature, lighting, ventilation, acoustics, and refreshments; any of these seemingly minor details can make or break a meeting.

- **Set the agenda.** The success of any meeting depends on the preparation of the participants. Distribute a carefully written agenda to participants, giving them enough time to prepare as needed (see Figure 2.4). A productive agenda answers three key questions: (1) What do we need to do in this meeting to accomplish our goals? (2) What issues will be of greatest importance to all participants? (3) What information must be available in order to discuss these issues?[41]

> To ensure a successful meeting, decide on your purpose ahead of time, select the right participants, choose the time and facility carefully, and set a clear agenda.

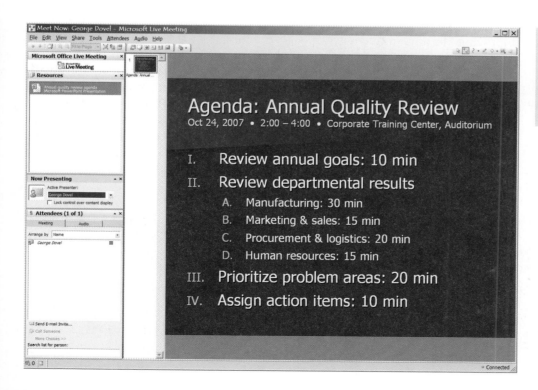

FIGURE 2.4
Typical Meeting Agenda
Agenda formats vary widely, depending on the complexity of the meeting and the presentation technologies used.

Leading and Participating in Meetings

Everyone shares the responsibility for successful meetings.

Everyone in a meeting shares the responsibility for keeping the meeting productive and making it successful. If you're the designated leader of a meeting, however, you have an extra degree of responsibility and accountability. To ensure productive meetings, be sure to do the following:

- **Keep the discussion on track.** A good meeting draws out the best ideas and information the group has to offer. Good leaders guide, mediate, probe, stimulate, and summarize as the situation demands.

- **Follow agreed-upon rules.** Business meetings run the gamut from informal to extremely formal, complete with detailed rules for speaking, proposing new items to discuss, voting on proposals, and so on. The larger the meeting, the more formal you'll need to be to maintain order. Formal meetings use **parliamentary procedure**, a time-tested method for planning and running effective meetings. The best-known guide to this procedure is *Robert's Rules of Order*.

- **Encourage participation.** On occasion, some participants will be too quiet and others too talkative. The quiet participants may be shy, they may be expressing disagreement or resistance, or they may be working on unrelated tasks. Draw them out by asking for their input on issues that pertain to them. For the overly talkative, simply say that time is limited and others need to be heard from.

- **Participate actively.** If you're a meeting participant, try to contribute to both the subject of the meeting and the smooth interaction of the participants. Use your listening skills and powers of observation to size up the interpersonal dynamics of the people, then adapt your behavior to help the group achieve its goals. Speak up if you have something useful to say, but don't monopolize the discussion or talk simply to bring attention to yourself.

- **Close effectively.** At the conclusion of the meeting, verify that the objectives have been met; if they have not, arrange for follow-up work as needed. Make sure all participants agree on the outcome and give people a chance to clear up any misunderstandings.

To review the tasks that contribute to productive meetings, refer to "Checklist: Improving Meeting Productivity."

For formal meetings, it's good practice to appoint one person to record the *minutes*, a summary of the important information presented and the decisions made during a meeting. If your company doesn't have a specific format for minutes, follow the generic format shown in Figure 2.5. Key elements include a list of those present and a list of those who were invited but didn't attend, followed by the times the meeting started and ended, all major decisions reached at the meeting, all assignments of tasks to meeting participants, and all subjects that were deferred to a later meeting. In

✓ CHECKLIST: Improving Meeting Productivity

A. Prepare carefully.

- ✓ Make sure the meeting is necessary.
- ✓ Decide on your purpose.
- ✓ Select participants carefully.
- ✓ Choose the time and facility.
- ✓ Set the agenda.

B. Lead effectively and participate fully.

- ✓ Keep the meeting on track.
- ✓ Follow agreed-upon rules.
- ✓ Encourage participation.
- ✓ Participate actively.
- ✓ Close effectively.

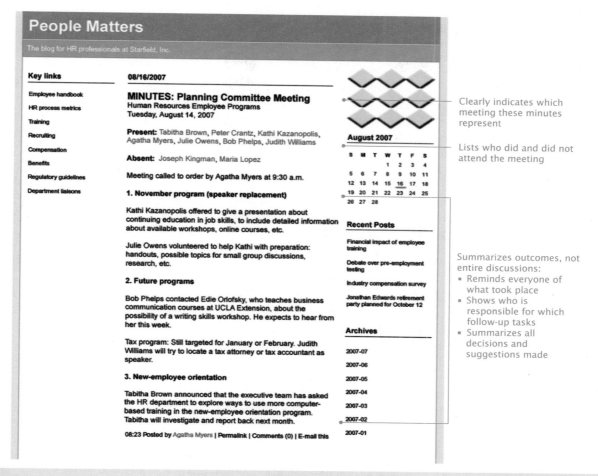

People Matters

The blog for HR professionals at Starfield, Inc.

Key links

Employee handbook

HR process metrics

Training

Recruiting

Compensation

Benefits

Regulatory guidelines

Department liaisons

08/16/2007

MINUTES: Planning Committee Meeting
Human Resources Employee Programs
Tuesday, August 14, 2007

Present: Tabitha Brown, Peter Crantz, Kathi Kazanopolis, Agatha Myers, Julie Owens, Bob Phelps, Judith Williams

Absent: Joseph Kingman, Maria Lopez

Meeting called to order by Agatha Myers at 9:30 a.m.

1. November program (speaker replacement)

Kathi Kazanopolis offered to give a presentation about continuing education in job skills, to include detailed information about available workshops, online courses, etc.

Julie Owens volunteered to help Kathi with preparation: handouts, possible topics for small group discussions, research, etc.

2. Future programs

Bob Phelps contacted Edie Orlofsky, who teaches business communication courses at UCLA Extension, about the possibility of a writing skills workshop. He expects to hear from her this week.

Tax program: Still targeted for January or February. Judith Williams will try to locate a tax attorney or tax accountant as speaker.

3. New-employee orientation

Tabitha Brown announced that the executive team has asked the HR department to explore ways to use more computer-based training in the new-employee orientation program. Tabitha will investigate and report back next month.

08:23 Posted by Agatha Myers | Permalink | Comments (0) | E-mail this

August 2007

S	M	T	W	T	F	S
			1	2	3	4
5	6	7	8	9	10	11
12	13	14	15	16	17	18
19	20	21	22	23	24	25
26	27	28				

Recent Posts

Financial impact of employee training

Debate over pre-employment testing

Industry compensation survey

Jonathan Edwards retirement party planned for October 12

Archives

2007-07
2007-06
2007-05
2007-04
2007-03
2007-02
2007-01

Clearly indicates which meeting these minutes represent

Lists who did and did not attend the meeting

Summarizes outcomes, not entire discussions:
- Reminds everyone of what took place
- Shows who is responsible for which follow-up tasks
- Summarizes all decisions and suggestions made

FIGURE 2.5
Typical Minutes of a Meeting
The use of intranet and blog postings is a common way to distribute meeting minutes. The specific format of the minutes is less important than making sure you record all the key information, particularly regarding responsibilities that were assigned during the meeting.

addition, the minutes objectively summarize important discussions, noting the names of those who contributed major points. Outlines, subheadings, and lists help organize the minutes; additional documentation (such as tables or charts submitted by meeting participants) is noted in the minutes and attached. Many companies now post meeting minutes on intranet sites or blogs for easy reference.

Using Meeting Technologies

You can expect to use a variety of meeting-related technologies throughout your career. Learn how to use these tools effectively, and you'll become a more effective contributor and leader in all your meetings.

Some meeting technologies assist with local, or on-site, meetings, in which everyone is in the same room at the same time. For example, **electronic whiteboards** capture meeting notes and create files that can be printed, e-mailed, and archived. Electronic presentations are used extensively in business; you'll learn more about them in Chapter 14.

Most of the recent innovations in meeting technology are in support of **virtual meetings**, in which participants interact remotely. Virtual meeting technologies

Virtual meeting technologies range from instant messaging to videoconferencing to web-based systems.

encompass a wide range of tools that let team members in different locations interact without the disruption, risk, and cost of travel.[42] Instant messaging and **teleconferencing**, in which three or more people are connected by phone simultaneously, are the simplest forms of virtual meetings. When you are invited to participate in a teleconference, you are typically given a special phone number and a meeting access code, which ensures the privacy of the session.

Videoconferencing combines audio communication with live video, letting team members see each other, demonstrate products, and transmit other visual information. Videoconferencing can take place either over the Internet or through dedicated networks with specially built rooms in the involved locations.

The most sophisticated **web-based meeting systems** combine the best of instant messaging, shared workspaces, and videoconferencing with other tools such as *virtual whiteboards* that let teams collaborate in real time (see Figure 2.6). Using such systems, attendees can log on from a desktop or laptop PC, a PDA, or even a web-enabled mobile phone from almost anywhere in the world.

Technology continues to create intriguing opportunities for online interaction. For instance, one of the newest virtual tools is *online brainstorming*, in which companies conduct "idea campaigns" to generate new ideas from people across the organization. These range from small team meetings to huge events such as IBM's giant InnovationJam, in which 100,000 IBM employees, family members, and customers from 160 countries were invited to brainstorm online for three days.[43]

Companies are also beginning to experiment with virtual meetings and other communication activities in *virtual worlds* such as Second Life (www.secondlife.com). In much the same way that gamers can create and control characters (often known as *avatars*) in a multiplayer video game, professionals can create online versions of themselves to participate in meetings, training sessions, sales presentations, and other activities (see Figure 2.7). For example, the computer company Sun Microsystems created the Sun Pavilion in Second Life. This virtual arena provides a place for Sun executives and invited guests to present information and share ideas.[44]

Companies continue to look for innovative ways to promote communication and collaboration while reducing the cost and hassle of meetings.

FIGURE 2.6
Web-Based Meetings
Online meetings offer powerful tools for communication, but you need to be proficient at using these tools if you are to be effective during online meetings.

FIGURE 2.7
Virtual Meetings in a Virtual World
Virtual reality environments such as Second Life let presenters transcend the limits of physical reality. Here at Sun Microsystem's pavilion in Second Life, a presenter floats in front of a giant version of a computer chip. In real life, such a chip would be smaller than a postage stamp, making it impossible for the audience to see important details.

IMPROVING YOUR LISTENING SKILLS

The importance of listening, whether in meetings and other business contexts or in your personal life, is self-evident: If a receiver won't or can't listen, the speaker's message simply won't get through. Some 80 percent of top executives say that listening is the most important skill needed to get things done in the workplace.[45]

Effective listening strengthens organizational relationships, enhances product delivery, alerts the organization to opportunities for innovation, and allows the organization to manage growing diversity in the workforce and in the customers it serves.[46] Companies whose employees and managers listen effectively stay informed, up to date, and out of trouble. Conversely, poor listening skills can cost companies millions of dollars a year as a result of lost opportunities, legal mistakes, and other errors. Effective listening is vital to the process of building trust not only between organizations but also between individuals.[47] Throughout your career, effective listening will give you a competitive edge, enhancing your performance and thus the influence you have within your company.

Listening is one of the most important skills in the workplace.

Recognizing Various Types of Listening

Understanding the nature of listening is the first step toward improving your listening skills. People listen in a variety of ways, which influences what they hear and the meaning they extract. In fact, relying on a single approach to listening limits your effectiveness. A people-oriented listener might miss important information about an upcoming deadline, whereas an action-oriented listener might miss an important clue that there's a personal problem brewing between two team members.[48] As you read about the major types of listening, reflect on your own inclination as a listener and consider how learning to use several methods could make your listening more effective.

The primary goal of **content listening** is to understand and retain the speaker's message. For example, Henry Nordhoff, CEO of the San Diego–based pharmaceutical company Gen-Probe, has a business background and relies on content listening to gather technical information from the scientists whose work he oversees.[49] When you're listening for content, the emphasis is on information and understanding. Ask questions to clarify the material and probe for details. Because you're not evaluating

To be a good listener, adapt the way you listen to suit the situation.

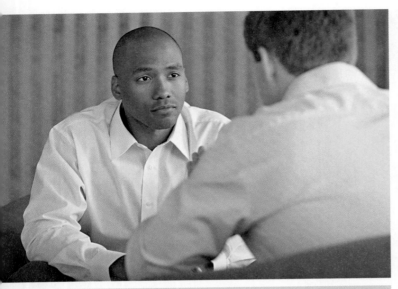

When you engage in empathic listening, you pay attention to feelings, needs, and wants—not just the spoken words.

at this point, it doesn't matter whether you agree or disagree, approve or disapprove—only that you understand. Try to overlook the speaker's style and any limitations in the presentation; just focus on the information.[50]

The goal of **critical listening** is to understand and evaluate the meaning of the speaker's message on several levels: the logic of the argument, the strength of the evidence, the validity of the conclusions, the implications of the message for you and your organization, the speaker's intentions and motives, and the omission of any important or relevant points. If you're skeptical, ask questions to explore the speaker's point of view and credibility. Be on the lookout for bias that could color the way the information is presented and be careful to separate opinions from facts.[51]

The goal of **empathic listening** is to understand the speaker's feelings, needs, and wants so that you can appreciate his or her point of view, regardless of whether you share that perspective. By listening in an empathic way, you help the individual vent the emotions that prevent a calm, clear-headed approach to the subject. Sometimes the only thing an upset colleague is looking for is somebody to listen, so avoid the temptation to jump in with advice unless the person specifically asks for it. Also, don't judge the speaker's feelings and don't try to tell the person he or she shouldn't feel this or that emotion. Instead, let the speaker know that you appreciate his or her feelings and understand the situation. After you establish that connection, you can then help the speaker move on to search for a solution.[52]

No matter what mode they are using at any given time, effective listeners try to engage in **active listening**, making a conscious effort to turn off their own filters and biases to truly hear and understand what the other party is saying. They ask questions or summarize the speaker's message to verify key points and encourage the speaker through positive body language and supportive feedback.[53]

Understanding the Listening Process

Listening is a far more complex process than most people think. As a consequence, most of us aren't very good at it. Given such complexity, it's no wonder most of us listen at or below a 25 percent efficiency rate, remember only about half of what's said during a 10-minute conversation, and forget half of that within 48 hours.[54] Furthermore, when questioned about material we've just heard, we are likely to get the facts mixed up.[55]

Listening involves five steps: receiving, decoding, remembering, evaluating, and responding.

Why is such a seemingly simple activity so difficult? The answer lies in the complexity of the process. Listening follows the same sequence as the general communication process model you explored in Chapter 1 (page 12), with the added burden that it happens in real time. To listen effectively, you need to successfully complete five separate steps:[56]

1. **Receiving.** You start by physically hearing the message and acknowledging it. Physical reception can be blocked by noise, impaired hearing, or inattention. Some experts also include nonverbal messages as part of this stage because these factors influence the listening process as well.

2. **Decoding.** Your next step is to assign meaning to sounds, which you do according to your own values, beliefs, ideas, expectations, roles, needs, and personal history.

3. **Remembering.** Before you can act on the information, you need to store it for future processing. As you learned in Chapter 1, incoming messages must first be

captured in short-term memory, and then they are transferred to long-term memory for more permanent storage.

4. **Evaluating.** With the speaker's message captured, your next step is to evaluate it by applying critical thinking skills. You separate fact from opinion and evaluate the quality of the evidence.

5. **Responding.** After you've evaluated the speaker's message, you react. If you're communicating one-on-one or in a small group, the initial response generally takes the form of verbal feedback. If you're one of many in an audience, your initial response may take the form of applause, laughter, or silence. Later on, you may act on what you have heard.

If any one of these steps breaks down, the listening process becomes less effective or even fails entirely. As both a sender and a receiver, you can reduce the failure rate by recognizing and overcoming a variety of physical and mental barriers to effective listening.

Overcoming Barriers to Effective Listening

Good listeners look for ways to overcome potential barriers throughout the listening process (see Table 2.2). For instance, simply working to avoid interrupting the speaker removes many potential barriers. If you have questions, wait until the speaker has finished speaking. And rustling papers, tapping on your PDA, or checking your watch—these are just a few of the many nonverbal behaviors that can interrupt a speaker and hamper listening for everyone.

Selective listening is one of the most common barriers to effective listening. If your mind wanders, you may stay tuned out until you hear a word or phrase that gets your attention once more. But by that time, you're unable to recall what the speaker *actually* said; instead, you remember what you *think* the speaker probably said.[57]

Good listeners actively try to overcome the barriers to successful listening.

DISTINGUISHING EFFECTIVE LISTENERS FROM INEFFECTIVE LISTENERS	Table 2.2

Effective Listeners	*Ineffective Listeners*
• Listen	• Listen passively
• Take careful and complete notes	• Take no notes or take ineffective notes
• Make frequent eye contact with the speaker (depends on culture to some extent)	• Make little or no eye contact
• Stay focused on the speaker and the content	• Allow their minds to wander; are easily distracted
• Mentally paraphrase key points to maintain attention level and ensure comprehension	• Fail to paraphrase
• Adjust listening style to the situation	• Listen with the same style, regardless of the situation
• Give the speaker nonverbal cues (such as nodding to show agreement or raising eyebrows to show surprise or skepticism)	• Fail to give the speaker nonverbal feedback
• Save questions or points of disagreement until an appropriate time	• Interrupt whenever they disagree or don't understand
• Overlook stylistic differences and focus on the speaker's message	• Are distracted by or unduly influenced by stylistic differences; are judgmental
• Make distinctions between main points and supporting details	• Are unable to distinguish main points from details
• Look for opportunities to learn.	• Assume they already know everything that's important to know.

Your mind can process information much faster than most speakers talk.

One reason listeners' minds tend to wander is that people think faster than they speak. Most people speak at about 120 to 150 words per minute, but listeners can process audio information at up to 500 words per minute.[58] In other words, your brain has a lot of free time whenever you're listening and, if left unsupervised, it will find a thousand other things to think about. Make a conscious effort to focus on the speaker and use the extra time to analyze what you hear or prepare questions you want to ask.

Overcoming such interpretation barriers can be difficult because you may not even be aware of them. As Chapter 1 notes, selective perception leads listeners to mold messages to fit their own conceptual frameworks. Listeners sometimes make up their minds before fully hearing the speaker's message, or they engage in defensive listening—protecting their self-esteem by tuning out anything that doesn't confirm their view of themselves.

Even when your intentions are the best, you can still misinterpret incoming messages if you and the speaker don't share enough language or experience. Lack of common ground is why misinterpretation is so frequent between speakers of different native languages, even when they're trying to speak the same language. When listening to a speaker whose native language or life experience is different from yours, try to paraphrase that person's ideas. Give the speaker a chance to confirm what you think you heard or to correct any misinterpretation.

When information is crucial and you can't record it in some way, use memory techniques to make sure you don't forget it.

Overcoming memory barriers is a slightly easier problem to solve, but it takes some work. If the information is crucial, try to record it in some fashion. If you do need to memorize something, you can hold information in short-term memory by repeating it silently or organizing a long list of items into several shorter lists. To store information in long-term memory, four techniques can help: (1) associate new information with something closely related (such as the restaurant in which you met a new client), (2) categorize the new information (for example, alphabetize the names of products you're trying to remember), (3) visualize words and ideas as pictures, and (4) create mnemonics such as acronyms or rhymes. Note that all four techniques have an important factor in common: You have to *do* something to make the information stick.

For a reminder of the steps you can take to overcome listening barriers, see "Checklist: Overcoming Barriers to Effective Listening."

IMPROVING YOUR NONVERBAL COMMUNICATION SKILLS

Nonverbal communication supplements spoken language.

Nonverbal communication is the interpersonal process of sending and receiving information, both intentionally and unintentionally, without using written or spoken language. Nonverbal signals play three important roles in communication. The first is complementing verbal language: Nonverbal signals can strengthen a verbal message

✓ CHECKLIST: Overcoming Barriers to Effective Listening

- ✓ Control whatever barriers to physical reception you can (such as avoiding interrupting speakers by asking questions or by exhibiting disruptive nonverbal behaviors).
- ✓ Avoid selective listening by trying to focus on the speaker and analyzing what you hear.
- ✓ Keep an open mind by avoiding any prejudgment and by not listening defensively.
- ✓ Try to paraphrase the speaker's ideas, giving that person a chance to confirm or correct your interpretation.
- ✓ Don't count on your memory; write down or record important information.
- ✓ Improve your short-term memory by repeating information or breaking it into shorter lists.
- ✓ Improve your long-term memory through association, categorization, visualization, and mnemonics.

(when nonverbal signals match words), weaken a verbal message (when nonverbal signals don't match words), or replace words entirely.

The second role for nonverbal signals is revealing truth. In fact, nonverbal communication often conveys more to listeners than the words you speak—particularly when they're trying to decide how you really feel about a situation or when they're trying to judge your credibility and aptitude for leadership.[59] However, even the power of nonverbal cues is not infallible when it comes to detecting truth. In one recent study, most people failed to detect dishonest speech roughly half the time; only a tiny fraction of the population are able to consistently detect when people are lying to them.[60]

Nonverbal cues help you ascertain the truth of spoken information.

The third role for nonverbal signals is conveying information efficiently. Nonverbal signals can convey both nuance and rich amounts of information in a single instant. For instance, in a tough situation, a colleague who rolls her eyes and cracks a wry smile could be saying, "Yes, we're in a bind again, but we've worked our way through problems before. Let's skip the cheerleading and motivational speaking and just get down to work."

Recognizing Nonverbal Communication

Paying special attention to nonverbal signals in the workplace will enhance your ability to communicate successfully. Moreover, as you interact with business associates from other backgrounds, you'll discover that some nonverbal signals don't necessarily translate across cultures. You'll learn more about cultural influences on nonverbal communication in Chapter 3. The range and variety of nonverbal signals are almost endless, but you can grasp the basics by studying six general categories:

Nonverbal signals include facial expression, gesture and posture, vocal characteristics, personal appearance, touch, and time and space.

- **Facial expression.** Your face is the primary site for expressing your emotions; it reveals the type and the intensity of your feelings.[61] Your eyes are especially effective for indicating attention and interest, influencing others, regulating interaction, and establishing dominance.[62]

- **Gesture and posture.** By moving or not moving your body, you express both specific and general messages, some voluntary and some involuntary. Many gestures—a wave of the hand, for example—have a specific and intentional meaning. Other types of body movement are unintentional and express a more general message. Slouching, leaning forward, fidgeting, and walking briskly are all unconscious signals that reveal whether you feel confident or nervous, friendly or hostile, assertive or passive, powerful or powerless.

- **Vocal characteristics.** Your voice carries both intentional and unintentional messages. Consider the sentence "What have you been up to?" If you repeat that question, changing your tone of voice and stressing various words, you can consciously convey quite different messages. However, your voice can also reveal things of which you are unaware. Your tone and volume, your accent and speaking pace, and all the little *ums* and *ahs* that creep into your speech say a lot about who you are, your relationship with the audience, and the emotions underlying your words.

- **Personal appearance.** People respond to others on the basis of their physical appearance—sometimes fairly and other times unfairly. Although an individual's body type and facial features impose limitations, most people are able to control their appearance to some degree. Grooming, clothing, accessories, style—you can control all of these. Adopt the style of the people you want to impress.

- **Touch.** Touch is an important way to convey warmth, comfort, reassurance—or control. Touch is so powerful, in fact, that it is governed by cultural customs that establish who can touch whom and how in various circumstances. In the United States and Great Britain, for instance, people usually touch less frequently than people in France or Costa Rica. Even within each culture's norms, however, individual

Dressing too casually or too formally for a given business setting can send a signal that you don't understand or don't respect the situation.

attitudes toward touch can vary widely. A manager might be comfortable using hugs to express support or congratulations, but his or her subordinates could interpret those hugs as either a show of dominance or sexual interest.[63] Touch is a complex subject. The best advice: When in doubt, don't touch.

- **Time and space.** Like touch, time and space can be used to assert authority, imply intimacy, and send other nonverbal messages. For instance, some people try to demonstrate their own importance or disregard for others by making other people wait; others show respect by being on time. The manipulation of space works in a similar way. When top executives gather for lunch in a private dining room, they send a strong signal to all the employees crowding into the cafeteria downstairs. The decision to respect or violate someone's "private space" is another powerful nonverbal signal. Again, attitudes toward time and space vary from person to person and culture to culture (see Chapter 3).

Using Nonverbal Communication Effectively

Work to make sure your nonverbal signals match the tone and content of your spoken communication.

Paying attention to nonverbal cues will make you a better speaker and a better listener. When you're talking, be more conscious of the nonverbal cues you could be sending (see "Sharpening Your Career Skills: Sending the Right Signals"). Are they effective without being manipulative? Consider a situation in which an employee has come to you to talk about a raise. This situation is a stressful one for the employee, so don't say you're interested in what she has to tell you and then spend your time glancing at your computer or checking your watch. Conversely, if you already know you won't be able to give her the raise, be honest in expressing your emotions. Don't overcompensate for your own stress by smiling too broadly or shaking her hand too vigorously. Both nonverbal signals would raise her hopes without justification. In either case, match your nonverbal cues to the tone of the situation.

SHARPENING YOUR CAREER SKILLS

Sending the Right Signals

The nonverbal signals you send can enhance—or undermine—your verbal message, so make sure to use nonverbal cues to your advantage. In U.S. business culture, the following signals are key to building and maintaining professional credibility:

- *Eye behavior.* Maintain direct, but not continuous, eye contact. Don't look down before responding to a question, and be careful not to shift your eyes around. Don't look away from the other person for extended periods, and try not to blink excessively.

- *Gestures.* When using gestures to emphasize points or convey the intensity of your feelings, keep them spontaneous, unrehearsed, and relaxed. Keep your hands and elbows away from your body, and avoid hand-to-face gestures, throat clearing, fidgeting, and tugging at clothing. Don't lick your lips, wring your hands, tap your fingers, or smile out of context.

- *Posture.* Assume an open and relaxed posture. Walk confidently, with grace and ease. Stand straight, with both feet on the floor, and sit straight in your chair without slouching. Hold your head level, and keep your chin up. Shift your posture while communicating, leaning forward and smiling as you begin to answer a question. Avoid keeping your body rigid or otherwise conveying a sense of tension.

- *Voice.* Strive for a conversational style, while speaking at a moderately fast rate. Use appropriate variation in pitch, rate, and volume. Avoid speaking in a monotone. Avoid sounding flat, tense, or nasal. Do your best to avoid *ahs* or *ums*, repeating words, interrupting or pausing mid-sentence, omitting parts of words, and stuttering.

CAREER APPLICATIONS

1. What message might you get if your boss smiles but looks away when you ask if you'll be getting a raise this year? Explain your interpretation of these nonverbal signals.

2. Would you be reluctant to hire a job candidate who stares intently at you through an entire job interview? Why or why not?

✓ CHECKLIST: Improving Nonverbal Communication Skills

A. Understand the roles that nonverbal signals play in communication.

✓ Nonverbal signals complement verbal language by strengthening, weakening, or replacing words.

✓ Nonverbal signals often reveal the truth, sometimes conveying more to listeners than spoken words.

B. Recognize nonverbal communication signals.

✓ Note that facial expressions (especially eye contact) reveal the type and intensity of a speaker's feelings.

✓ Watch for cues from gesture and posture.

✓ Listen for vocal characteristics that signal who the speaker is, the speaker's relationship with the audience, and the emotions underlying the speaker's words.

✓ Recognize that listeners are influenced by physical appearance.

✓ Be careful with physical contact; touch can convey positive attributes but can also be interpreted as dominance or sexual interest.

✓ Pay attention to the use of time and space.

Also consider the nonverbal signals you send when you're not talking—the clothes you wear, the way you sit, the way you walk. Are you talking like a serious business professional but dressing like you belong in a dance club or a frat house? Avoiding eye contact, keeping your hands in your pockets, and failing to sit or stand up straight can tell people that you lack confidence in yourself or interest in others.[64]

When you listen, be sure to pay attention to the speaker's nonverbal cues. Do they amplify the spoken words or contradict them? Is the speaker intentionally using nonverbal signals to send you a message that he or she can't put into words? Be observant but don't assume that you can "read someone like a book." Nonverbal signals are powerful, but they aren't infallible. Contrary to popular belief, just because someone doesn't look you squarely in the eye doesn't mean he or she is lying.[65] If something doesn't feel right, ask the speaker an honest and respectful question; doing so may clear everything up, or it may uncover issues you need to explore further. See "Checklist: Improving Nonverbal Communication Skills" for a summary of key ideas regarding nonverbal skills.

What signals does your personal appearance send?

DEVELOPING YOUR BUSINESS ETIQUETTE

By now you may have noticed a common thread running through the topics of successful team efforts, productive meetings, effective listening, and nonverbal communication: All these activities depend on mutual respect and consideration among all participants. As Chapter 1 notes, etiquette is now considered an essential business skill. Nobody wants to work with someone who is rude to colleagues or an embarrassment to the company. Moreover, shabby treatment of others in the workplace can be a huge drain on morale and productivity.[66] Poor etiquette can drive away customers, investors, and other critical audiences—and it can limit your career potential. Here are some key etiquette points to remember when you're in the workplace and out in public.

Business Etiquette in the Workplace

Knowing how to behave and how to interact with people in business will help you appear polished, professional, and confident.[67] Understanding business etiquette also helps you put others at ease so that they are comfortable enough to do business with you.[68] Both of these factors will be major contributors to your career success.

Attention to basic business etiquette will help your career at every stage.

Personal appearance can have considerable impact on your success in business.

For instance, rightly or wrongly, your personal appearance often has considerable impact on your career success. Pay attention to the style of dress where you work and adjust your style to match. Expectations for specific jobs, companies, and industries can vary widely. The financial industries tend to be more formal than high technology, for instance, and sales and executive positions usually come with more formal expectations than positions in engineering or manufacturing. Observe others carefully and don't be afraid to ask for advice. If you're not sure, dress moderately and simply—earn a reputation for what you can *do*, not for what you can wear. Table 2.3 offers some general guidelines on assembling a business wardrobe that's cost-effective and flexible.

In addition to your clothing, grooming affects the impression you give others in the workplace. Pay close attention to cleanliness and avoid using products with powerful scents, such as perfumed soaps, colognes, shampoos, and after-shave lotions (many people are bothered by these products, and some are allergic to them). Shampoo frequently, keep hands and nails neatly manicured, use mouthwash and deodorant, and make regular trips to a hair stylist.[69] Some companies have specific policies regarding hairstyles, which you may be expected to follow.[70]

Something as simple as your smile also affects the way people do business with you. When you smile, do so genuinely. A fake smile is obvious because the timing is frequently off, and the expression fails to involve all the facial muscles that a genuine smile would.[71] However, certain occasions require smiling, such as when you're introduced to someone, when you give or receive a compliment, and when you applaud someone's efforts.[72]

Plan phone calls as carefully as you plan meetings.

Phone skills have a definite impact on your success. Phone calls lack the visual richness of face-to-face conversations, so you have to rely on your attitude and tone of voice to convey confidence and professionalism. Table 2.4 summarizes helpful tips for placing and receiving phone calls in a confident, professional manner.

If you're accustomed to using your mobile phone anywhere and everywhere, get ready to change your habits. Mobile phones are causing so much disruption in the workplace that some senior executives now ban their use in meetings.[73] Even if

Table 2.3   ASSEMBLING A BUSINESS WARDROBE

1 Smooth and Finished (Start with this)	2 Elegant and Refined (To column 1, add this)	3 Crisp and Starchy (To column 2, add this)	4 Up-to-the-Minute Trendy (To column 3, add this)
1. Wear well-tailored clothing that fits well. 2. Keep buttons, zippers, and hemlines in good repair. 3. Keep shoes shined and in good condition. 4. Make sure the fabrics you wear are clean, are carefully pressed, and do not wrinkle easily. 5. Choose colors that flatter your height, weight, skin tone, and style.	1. Choose form-fitting (but not skin-tight) clothing—not swinging or flowing fabrics, frills, or fussy trimmings. 2. Choose muted tones and soft colors or classics, such as the dark blue suit or the basic black dress. 3. If possible, select a few classic pieces of jewelry (such as a string of pearls or diamond cuff links) for formal occasions.	1. Wear blouses or shirts that are or appear starched. 2. Choose closed top-button shirts or button-down shirt collars, higher-neckline blouses, long sleeves with French cuffs and cuff links. 3. Wear creased trousers or longer skirt hemline. 4. Wear jackets that complement an outfit and lend an air of formality to your appearance. Avoid jackets with more than two tones—one color should dominate.	1. Add trendy clothing items to your wardrobe often. 2. Choose bold colors (but sparingly so that you won't appear garish). 3. Embellish your look with trendy jewelry and hairstyles.

Table 2.4	QUICK TIPS FOR IMPROVING YOUR PHONE SKILLS		
General Tips	*Placing Calls*	*Receiving Calls*	*Using Voice Mail*
Use frequent verbal responses that show you're listening ("Oh yes," "I see," "That's right").	Be ready before you call so that you don't waste the other person's time.	Answer promptly and with a smile so that you sound friendly and positive.	When recording your own outgoing message, make it brief and professional.
Increase your volume just slightly to convey your confidence.	Minimize distractions and avoid making noise that could annoy the other party.	Identify yourself and your company (some companies have specific instructions for what to say when you answer).	If you can, record temporary greetings on days when you are unavailable all day so that callers will know you're gone for the day.
Don't speak in a monotone; vary your pitch and inflections so people know you're interested.	Identify yourself and your organization, briefly describe why you're calling, and verify that you've called at a good time.	Establish the needs of your caller by asking, "How may I help you?" If you know the caller's name, use it.	Check your voice-mail messages regularly and return all necessary calls within 24 hours.
Slow down when conversing with people whose native language isn't the same as yours.	Don't take up too much time. Speak quickly and clearly, and get right to the point of the call.	If you can, answer questions promptly and efficiently; if you can't help, tell them what you can do for them.	Leave simple, clear messages with your name, number, purpose for calling, and times when you can be reached.
Stay focused on the call throughout; others can easily tell when you're not paying attention.	Close in a friendly, positive manner and double-check all vital information such as meeting times and dates.	If you must forward a call or put someone on hold, explain what you are doing first.	State your name and telephone number slowly so that the other person can easily write them down; repeat both if the other person doesn't know you.
		If you forward a call to someone else, try to speak with that person first to verify that he or she is available and to introduce the caller.	Be careful what you say; most voice-mail systems allow users to forward messages to anyone else in the system.
		If you take a message for someone else, be complete and accurate, including the caller's name, number, and organization.	Replay your message before leaving the system to make sure it is clear and complete.

mobile phones aren't banned in your office, don't let yours become a source of annoyance to your colleagues.

Business Etiquette in Social Settings

From business lunches to industry conferences, you represent your company when you're out in public, so make sure your appearance and actions are appropriate to the situation. Get to know the customs of the culture when you meet new people. In North America, a firm handshake is expected when two people meet, whereas a respectful bow of the head is more appropriate in Japan. If you are expected to shake hands, be aware that the passive "dead fish" handshake creates an extremely negative impression. Also, women and men should shake hands on equal terms; the days of a woman offering just her fingertips are long gone in the business world. If you are physically able, always stand when shaking someone's hand.

When introducing yourself, include a brief description of your role in the company. When introducing two other people, speak their first and last names clearly, then try to offer some information (perhaps a shared professional interest) to help

You represent your company when you're out in public, so etiquette continues to be important.

these two people ease into a conversation.[74] Generally speaking, the lower-ranking person is introduced to the senior-ranking person, without regard to gender.[75] When you're introduced to someone, repeat the person's name as soon as possible. Doing so is both a compliment and a good way to remember it.[76]

Business is often conducted over meals, and knowing the basics of dining etiquette will make you more effective in these situations.[77] Choose foods that are easy to eat; you don't want to wrestle with a lobster while trying to carry on a conversation. If a drink is appropriate, save it for the end of the meal. Leave business papers under your chair until entrée plates have been removed; the business aspect of the meal doesn't usually begin until then.

Just as in the office, when you use your mobile phone in public, you send the message that people around you aren't as important as your call and that you don't respect your caller's privacy.[78] If it's not a matter of life and death—literally—wait until you're back in the office.

Finally, always remember that business meals are a forum for business, period. Don't get on your soapbox about politics, religion, or any other topic likely to stir up emotions. Don't complain about work, don't ask deeply personal questions, avoid profanity, and be careful with humor—a joke that entertains some people could easily offend others.

On the Job

SOLVING COMMUNICATION DILEMMAS AT THE CONTAINER STORE

After joining The Container Store, you quickly demonstrated your skills on the sales floor and soon earned an invitation to enter the company's management training program. With that training completed, you couldn't be more excited to take over your first store and begin the managerial phase of your career. That's the good news. The bad news is that the store you've been assigned to developed some morale problems under the previous manager, and you have some challenges ahead to restore a sense of teamwork and positive communication. Apply the concepts you learned in this chapter to the following challenges.

1. The eight employees who now report to you once had a reputation for being a tight-knit, supportive team, but you quickly figure out this that team is in danger of becoming dysfunctional. For example, minor issues that functional teams routinely handle, from cleaning up the lunch area to helping each other on the sales floor, frequently generate conflict within this group. What steps should you take to help your crew return to positive behavior?

   a. Give the team the task of healing itself, without getting directly involved. Explain the steps necessary in forming an effective team and then let them figure out how to make it happen.
   b. Lead the "team restoration" project yourself so that you can mediate whatever conflicts arise, at least until the team is able to function on its own in a more positive manner.
   c. Don't try to interfere; the negative behaviors were probably caused by an ineffective manager in the

past, but now that you're in charge, the team will return to positive behavior under your enlightened guidance.
   d. Your professional reputation and the store's sales are on the line, so you don't have time for the niceties of team building. Sit down with the group and demand that the negative, unprofessional behavior stop immediately.

2. While you're trying to figure out how to handle the overall team situation, you notice that the morning and evening huddles often degenerate into little more than complaint sessions. Workers seem to gripe about everything from difficult customers to the temperature in the store. Some of these sound like valid business issues that might require additional training or other employee support efforts; others are superficial issues that you suspect are simply by-products of the negative atmosphere. How should you handle complaints during the huddles?

   a. Try to defuse each complaint with humor; after a while, employees will begin to lighten up and stop complaining so much.
   b. Ask employees to refrain from complaining during the huddles; after all, these are important business meetings, not random social gatherings.
   c. Set up a whiteboard and write down each issue that is raised. After you've compiled a list over the course of a week or so, add a problem-solving segment to each huddle, in which you and the team tackle one issue per meeting to determine

the scope of each problem and identify possible solutions.

d. Whenever a complaint is raised, stop the huddle and confront the person who raised the issue. Challenge him or her to prove that the problem is a real business issue and not just a personal complaint. By doing this, you will not only identify the real problems that need to be fixed but also discourage people from raising petty complaints that shouldn't be aired in the workplace.

3. After observing the staff in action for a couple weeks and interviewing several dozen shoppers, you conclude that some employees are more effective than others when it comes to listening to customers and helping them find the right solutions to their individual needs. For instance, a few customers complained that the store employees who waited on them "did not seem to hear what I was saying," and several others said that "they expected me to know the names of every product in the store before they could help me." You recognize these as classic listening challenges, and you want to work with the corporation's training specialists to design a short course in effective listening. Which of the following strategies will you emphasize in the course?

a. Content listening is the best strategy because it is the only way to find out exactly what customers need. Train employees to filter out small talk and listen carefully for the precise terms customers use to describe the products they need and then work to match those needs with the store's vast inventory of products.

b. Because research shows that customers who enjoy the shopping experience in a store tend to stay longer and buy more, you should encourage employees to focus on empathic listening. By creating emotional bonds with shoppers, rather than jumping right in to talk about products, the sales staff will make shoppers more comfortable, which will eventually lead to increased sales.

c. One of the issues your interviews uncovered is that customers often don't know exactly what they're looking for, either because they don't know what some products are called or because they simply don't know what's available in the marketplace. Consequently, critical listening—looking beyond the words and phrases customers use to identify the true needs they are trying to express—should be the primary focus.

d. No single listening strategy is appropriate for all customers in all situations, so the best approach is to train employees to quickly assess each customer encounter in order to determine the best listening style to use. Design the training to help employees identify the clues they can use to decide how to proceed with each customer. For instance, if a couple walks in arguing about whether they should even be spending money on organizational products, the best approach

might be empathic listening: Defuse the negative emotions and encourage the shoppers to focus on their storage needs. In contrast, straightforward content listening is best for a customer who walks in with a printout from The Container Store website and asks to see a specific product.

4. First impressions can make or break the sale in retailing, and those impressions are created by everything from the cleanliness of the parking lot to the personal appearance of the store employees. Four job candidates are waiting outside your office, and you have a few moments to observe them before inviting them in for an initial interview (you can see them through the glass wall but can't hear them). Based on the following descriptions, which of these people seems like the best fit for The Container Store? Why?

a. Candidate A: A woman who is dressed perfectly for an interview at The Container Store. Her appearance is contemporary "business casual" but a notch or two more formal than the store employees, which suggests that she appreciates and shows respect for the business situation she finds herself in. However, you are slightly troubled by the fact that she's listening to her iPod and has kicked off her shoes and tucked her feet under her while she waits in the chair.

b. Candidate B: A man who has also dressed the part, although this candidate's behavior is nothing like the relaxed, carefree attitude that Candidate A is showing. He seems to be juggling multiple tasks at once: checking notes on a PDA, organizing a collection of papers he pulled from his briefcase, reattaching several sticky notes that keep falling loose, and fiddling with a mobile phone that he has answered at least twice in the few minutes you've been watching.

c. Candidate C: A woman who closed the notebook she was scanning in order to help Candidate B with some problem he was having with his mobile phone. (If you had to guess, he was having trouble figuring out how to silence the ringer.) After their interaction, they shake hands and appear to be introducing themselves with cordial smiles. Unfortunately, although the city is suffering through record high temperatures, her sundress and sandals strike you as a bit too casual for a job interview.

d. Candidate D: A man wearing what appears to be a finely tailored, conservative suit. His appearance is more dignified and businesslike than the other three, and he knows how to dress for success—carefully knotted tie, starched shirt, perfect posture, the works. He keeps to himself and avoids bothering the other candidates, although his facial expressions make it clear that he disapproves of the noise Candidate B is making with his mobile phone.

Learning Objectives Checkup

Assess your understanding of the principles in this chapter by reading each learning objective and studying the accompanying exercises. For fill-in-the-blank items, write the missing text in the blank provided; for multiple-choice items, circle the letter of the correct answer. You can check your responses against the answer key on page AK-1.

Objective 2.1: Highlight the advantages and disadvantages of working in teams.

1. Teams can achieve a higher level of performance than individuals alone because
   a. They combine the intelligence and energy of multiple individuals
   b. Motivation and creativity flourish in team settings
   c. They involve more input and a greater diversity of views, which tends to result in better decisions
   d. They do all of the above
2. Which of the following is a potential disadvantage of working in teams?
   a. Teams always stamp out creativity by forcing people to conform to existing ideas and practices.
   b. Teams increase a company's clerical workload because of the additional government paperwork required for administering workplace insurance.
   c. Team members are never held accountable for their individual performance.
   d. Social pressure within the group can lead to groupthink, in which people go along with a bad idea or poor decision even though they may not really believe in it.

Objective 2.2: Identify eight guidelines for successful collaborative writing.

3. Which of the following is the best way for a team of people to write a report?
   a. Each member should plan, research, and write his or her individual version and then the group can select the strongest report.
   b. The team should divide and conquer—one person doing the planning, one doing the research, one doing the writing, and so on.
   c. To ensure a true group effort, every task from planning through final production should be done as a team, preferably with everyone in the same room at the same time.
   d. Research and plan as a group but assign the actual writing to one person, or at least assign separate sections to individual writers and have one person edit them all to achieve a consistent style.
4. Which of the following steps should be completed before anyone from the team does any planning, researching, or writing?
   a. The team should agree on the project's goals.
   b. The team should agree on the report's title.
   c. To avoid compatibility problems, the team should agree on which word processor or other software will be used.

d. The team should always step away from the work environment and enjoy some social time in order to bond effectively before starting work.

Objective 2.3: Explain how wiki technology can help teams collaborate.

5. Which of the following are key benefits of using wikis for collaborative communication?
   a. The ability to post web content without needing to learn the conventional tools and techniques for creating webpages
   b. The ability for managers to ensure that messages posted on webpages consistently follow the strategic messaging plan
   c. The freedom for anyone with access to post new or revised material quickly, without waiting for approval
   d. The ability to impose strict workflow rules on team communication
   e. Both a and c
   f. Both b and d

Objective 2.4: Explain how group dynamics can affect team effectiveness.

6. Self-oriented roles are a type of _____ behavior in group settings.
7. Which of the following is the most accurate description of groupthink?
   a. The ability of teams to generate more new ideas than a single employee can
   b. A situation in which team members value harmony more than effective decision making
   c. The ability of teams to uncover hidden agendas and ensure open, constructive communication
   d. The existence of peer pressure in group settings
8. Conflict in team settings can be beneficial when it is _____ but harmful when it is _____.

Objective 2.5: Describe how meeting technologies can help participants communicate more successfully.

9. Online meeting technologies allow geographically dispersed teams to conduct _____ meetings over the Internet.

Objective 2.6: Describe the listening process, and explain how good listeners overcome barriers at each stage of the process.

10. After receiving messages, listeners _____ what they've heard by assigning meaning to the sounds.
11. If you're giving an important presentation and notice that many of the audience members look away when you try to make momentary eye contact, which of the following is most likely going on?
    a. These audience members don't want to challenge your authority by making direct eye contact.
    b. You work with a lot of shy people.
    c. The information you're presenting is making your audience uncomfortable in some way.

d. The audience is taking time to carefully think about the information you're presenting.

12. If you don't agree with something the speaker says in a large, formal meeting, the best response is to
   a. Signal your disagreement by folding your arms across your chest and staring defiantly back at the speaker
   b. Use your mobile phone or PDA to begin sending text messages to other people in the room, explaining why the speaker is wrong
   c. Immediately challenge the speaker so that the misinformation is caught and corrected
   d. Quietly make a note of your objections and wait until a question-and-answer period to raise your hand

Objective 2.7: Clarify the importance of nonverbal communication, and briefly describe six categories of nonverbal expression.

13. Nonverbal signals can be more influential than spoken language because
   a. Body language is difficult to control and therefore difficult to fake, so listeners often put more trust in such cues than in the words a speaker uses
   b. Nonverbal signals communicate faster than spoken language, and most people are impatient
   c. Body language saves listeners from the trouble of paying attention to what a speaker is saying

14. Which of the following is true about nonverbal signals?
   a. They can strengthen a spoken message.
   b. They can weaken a spoken message.
   c. They can replace spoken messages.
   d. All of the above.

Objective 2.8: Discuss the role of business etiquette, both in the workplace and in social settings.

15. Which of the following is the best characterization of etiquette in today's business environment?
   a. Business etiquette is impossible to generalize because every company has its own culture; you have to make it up as you go along.
   b. With ferocious international competition and constant financial pressure, etiquette is an old-fashioned luxury that businesses simply can't afford today.
   c. Ethical businesspeople don't need to worry directly about etiquette because ethical behavior automatically leads to good etiquette.
   d. Etiquette plays an important part in the process of forming and maintaining successful business relationships.

16. If you forgot to shut off your mobile phone before stepping into a business meeting and you receive a call during the meeting, the most appropriate thing to do is to
   a. Lower your voice to protect the privacy of your phone conversation
   b. Answer the phone then quickly hang it up to minimize the disruption to the meeting
   c. Excuse yourself from the meeting and find a quiet place to talk
   d. Continue to participate in the meeting while taking the call; this shows everyone that you're an effective multitasker

17. Your company has established a designated "quiet time" from 1:00 to 3:00 every afternoon, during which office phones, instant messaging, and e-mail are disabled so that people can concentrate on planning, researching, writing, and other intensive tasks without being interrupted. However, a number of people continue to flout the guidelines by leaving their mobile phones on, saying their families and friends need to be able to reach them. With all the various ring tones going off at random, the office is just as noisy as it was before. What is the best response?
   a. Agree to reactivate the office phone system if everyone will shut off their mobile phones but have all incoming calls routed through a receptionist who will take messages for all routine calls and deliver a note if an employee truly is needed in an emergency.
   b. Give up on quiet time; with so many electronic gadgets in the workplace today, you'll never achieve peace and quiet.
   c. Get tough on the offenders by confiscating mobile phones whenever they ring during quiet time.
   d. Without telling anyone, simply install one of the available mobile phone jamming products that block incoming and outgoing mobile phone calls.

18. Constantly testing the limits of your company's dress and grooming standards sends a strong signal that you
   a. Don't understand or don't respect your company's culture
   b. Are a strong advocate for worker's rights
   c. Are a creative and independent thinker who is likely to generate lots of successful business ideas
   d. Represent the leading edge of a new generation of enlightened workers who will redefine the workplace according to contemporary standards

Apply Your Knowledge

1. How can nonverbal communication help you run a meeting? How can it help you call a meeting to order, emphasize important topics, show approval, express reservations, regulate the flow of conversation, and invite a colleague to continue with a comment?

2. Whenever your boss asks for feedback during department meetings, she blasts anyone offering criticism,

which causes people to agree with everything she says. You want to talk to her about it, but what should you say? List some of the points you want to make when you discuss this issue with your boss.

3. Is conflict in a team good or bad? Explain your answer.

4. At your last department meeting, three people monopolized the entire discussion. What can you do at the next

meeting to encourage other department members to voluntarily participate?

5. **Ethical Choices** Strange instant messages occasionally pop up on your computer screen during your team's virtual meetings, followed quickly by embarrassed apologies from one of your colleagues in another city. You eventually figure out that this person is working from home, even though he says he's in the office; moreover, the messages suggest that he's running a sideline business from his home. You're concerned about the frequent disruptions, not to mention your colleague's potential ethical violations. What should you do? Explain your choice.

Practice Your Knowledge

MESSAGE FOR ANALYSIS

A project leader has made notes about covering the following items at the quarterly budget meeting. Prepare a formal agenda by putting these items into a logical order and rewriting, where necessary, to give phrases a more consistent sound.

- Budget Committee Meeting to be held on December 12, 2008, at 9:30 A.M.
- I will call the meeting to order.
- Real estate director's report: A closer look at cost overruns on Greentree site.
- The group will review and approve the minutes from last quarter's meeting.
- I will ask the finance director to report on actual versus projected quarterly revenues and expenses.
- I will distribute copies of the overall divisional budget and announce the date of the next budget meeting.
- Discussion: How can we do a better job of anticipating and preventing cost overruns?
- Meeting will take place in Conference Room 3, with WebEx active for remote employees.
- What additional budget issues must be considered during this quarter?

EXERCISES

For active links to all websites discussed in this chapter, visit this text's website at www.prenhall.com/thill. Locate your book and click on its "Companion Website" link. Then select Chapter 2 and click on "Featured Websites." Locate the name of the page or the URL related to the material in the text. Please note that links to sites that become inactive after publication of the book will be removed from the "Featured Websites" section.

2.1 **Teamwork** With a classmate, attend a local community or campus meeting where you can observe a group discussion, vote, or other group action. During the meeting, take notes individually and, afterward, work together to answer the following questions.

a. What is your evaluation of this meeting? In your answer, consider (1) the leader's ability to articulate the meeting's goals clearly, (2) the leader's ability to engage members in a meaningful discussion, (3) the group's dynamics, and (4) the group's listening skills.

b. How did group members make decisions? Did they vote? Did they reach decisions by consensus? Did those with dissenting opinions get an opportunity to voice their objections?

c. How well did the individual participants listen? How could you tell?

d. Did any participants change their expressed views or their votes during the meeting? Why might that have happened?

e. Did you observe any of the communication barriers discussed in Chapter 1? If so, identify them.

f. Compare the notes you took during the meeting with those of your classmate. What differences do you notice? How do you account for these differences?

2.2 **Team Communication: Overcoming Barriers** Every month, each employee in your department is expected to give a brief oral presentation on the status of his or her project. However, your department has recently hired an employee with a severe speech impediment that prevents people from understanding most of what he has to say. As department manager, how will you resolve this dilemma? Please explain.

2.3 **Team Development: Resolving Conflict** Describe a recent conflict you had with a team member at work or at school and explain how you resolved it. Did you find a solution that was acceptable to both of you and to the team?

2.4 **Ethical Choices** During team meetings, one member constantly calls for votes before all the other members have voiced their views. As the leader, you asked this member privately about his behavior. He replied that he was trying to move the team toward its goals, but you are concerned that he is really trying to take control. How can you deal with this situation without removing the member from the group?

2.5 **Online Communication: Staying on Track with Blog Replies** As the leader of a product development team, you write a daily blog to inform team members of questions, concerns, and other developments related to your project. Team members are always encouraged to reply to your online posts, but lately a number of people have been wandering off track with their replies, raising new issues in the middle of a discussion thread or posting on matters unrelated to the item to which they're replying. As a result, the blog is becoming less useful for everyone because individual message threads no longer stick to a single topic. Write a brief blog posting, three or four sentences at most, courteously reminding everyone why it's important to stick to the subject at hand when replying to blog items.

2.6 Internet Visit the PolyVision website, at www. websterboards.com, and read about electronic whiteboards. What advantages do you see in using this kind of whiteboard during a meeting? Draft a short e-mail to your boss outlining the product's advantages.

2.7 Telephones and Voice Mail Late on a Friday afternoon, you learn that the facilities department is going to move you—and your computer, your desk, and all your files—to another office first thing Monday morning. However, you have an important client meeting scheduled in your office for Monday afternoon, and you need to finalize some contract details on Monday morning. You simply can't lose access to your office at this point, and you're more than a little annoyed that your boss didn't ask you before approving the move. He has already left for the day, but you know he usually checks his voice mail over the weekend so you decide to leave a message asking him to cancel the move or at least call you at home as soon as possible. Using the voice mail guidelines listed in Table 2.4, plan your

message. (Use an imaginary phone number as your contact number and make up any other details you need for the call.) As directed by your instructor, submit either a written script of the message or a podcast recording of the actual message.

2.8 Nonverbal Communication: Analyzing Written Messages Select a business letter and envelope that you have received at work or home. Analyze their appearance. What nonverbal messages do they send? Are these messages consistent with the content of the letter? If not, what could the sender have done to make the nonverbal communication consistent with the verbal communication?

2.9 Nonverbal Communication: Analyzing Body Language Describe what the following body movements suggest when someone exhibits them during a conversation. How do such movements influence your interpretation of spoken words?
a. Shifting one's body continuously while seated
b. Twirling and playing with one's hair
c. Sitting in a sprawled position
d. Rolling one's eyes
e. Extending a weak handshake

2.10 Listening Skills: Self-Assessment How good are your listening skills? Use the following chart to rate yourself on each element of listening. Then examine your ratings to identify where you are strongest and where you can improve, using the tips in this chapter.

Element of Listening	Always	Frequently	Occasionally	Never
1. I look for areas of interest when people speak.				
2. I focus on content rather than delivery.				
3. I wait to respond until I understand the content.				
4. I listen for ideas and themes, not isolated facts.				
5. I take notes only when needed.				
6. I really concentrate on what speakers are saying.				
7. I stay focused even when the ideas are complex.				
8. I keep an open mind despite emotionally charged language.				

2.11 Etiquette: Coaching New Hires As the local manager of an international accounting firm, you place a high priority on professional etiquette. Not only does it communicate respect to your clients, but it also instills confidence in your firm by showing that you and your staff are aware of and able to meet the expectations of almost any audience. Earlier today, you took four recently hired college graduates to lunch with an important client. You've done this for years, and it's

usually an upbeat experience for everyone, but today's lunch was a disaster. One of the new employees made not one, not two, but *three* calls on his mobile phone during lunch. Another interrupted the client several times and even got into a mild argument. The third employee kept making sarcastic jokes about politics, making everyone at the table uncomfortable. And the fourth showed up dressed like she was expecting to bale hay or work in coal mine, not have a business lunch in a posh restaurant. You've already called the client to apologize, but now you need to coach these employees on proper business etiquette. Draft a brief

memo to these employees, explaining why etiquette is so important to the company's success—and their individual careers.

Expand Your Knowledge

LEARNING MORE ON THE WEB
MAKING MEETINGS WORK WITH THE 3M MEETING NETWORK

www.3m.com/meetingnetwork

The 3M Meeting Network contains a wide selection of articles on planning meetings, designing activities to build teamwork, and making better presentations. Click on "Articles & Advice," find the appropriate articles, and then answer the following questions.

1. How can you know if a meeting should be held or not?
2. How can good leaders show they trust the group's ability to perform successfully?
3. What are the advantages and disadvantages of "open space" meetings, which take place without formal agendas or facilitation?

SURFING YOUR WAY TO CAREER SUCCESS

Bovée and Thill's Business Communication Headline News offers links to hundreds of online resources that can help you with this course, your other college courses, and your career. Visit www.businesscommunicationblog.com and click on "Web Directory." The "Business Communication" section connects you to a variety of websites and articles on business English and business writing, as well as such important topics as information overload, company culture, company image, and business etiquette. Identify three websites from this section that could be useful in your business career. For each site, write a two-sentence summary of what the site offers and how it could help you launch and build your career.

Learn Interactively

INTERACTIVE STUDY GUIDE

Go to the Companion Website at www. prenhall.com/thill and locate your book, then click on "Companion Website." Select Chapter 2 to take advantage of the interactive "Chapter Quiz" to test your knowledge of chapter concepts. Receive instant feedback on whether you need additional studying. Also, visit the "Study Hall," where you'll find an abundance of valuable resources that will help you succeed in this course.

PEAK PERFORMANCE GRAMMAR AND MECHANICS

If your instructor has required the use of "Peak Performance Grammar and Mechanics," either in your online course or on

CD, you can improve your skill with pronouns by using the "Peak Performance Grammar and Mechanics" module. Click on "Grammar Basics" and then "Nouns and Pronouns." Take the Pretest to determine whether you have any weak areas. Then review those areas in the Refresher Course. Take the Follow-Up Test to check your grasp of pronouns. For an extra challenge or advanced practice, take the Advanced Test. Finally, for additional reinforcement, go to the "Improve Your Grammar, Mechanics, and Usage" section that follows and complete those exercises.

Improve Your Grammar, Mechanics, and Usage

The following exercises help you improve your knowledge of and power over English grammar, mechanics, and usage. Turn to the Handbook of Grammar, Mechanics, and Usage at the end of this book and review all of Section 1.2 (Pronouns). Then look at the following 10 items. Underline the preferred choice within each set of parentheses. (Answers to these exercises appear on page AK-3.)

1. The sales staff is preparing guidelines for (*their, its*) clients.

2. Few of the sales representatives turn in (*their, its*) reports on time.
3. The board of directors has chosen (*their, its*) officers.
4. Gomez and Archer have told (*his, their*) clients about the new program.
5. Each manager plans to expand (*his, their, his or her*) sphere of control next year.
6. Has everyone supplied (*his, their, his or her*) Social Security number?

7. After giving every employee (*his, their, a*) raise, George told (*them, they, all*) about the increased workload.

8. Bob and Tim have opposite ideas about how to achieve company goals. (*Who, Whom*) do you think will win the debate?

9. City Securities has just announced (*who, whom*) it will hire as CEO.

10. Either of the new products would readily find (*their, its*) niche in the marketplace.

For additional exercises focusing on pronouns, go to www.prenhall.com/thill then locate your text and click on its "Companion Website" link. click on Chapter 2, click on "Additional Exercises to Improve your Grammar, Mechanics, and Usage," then click on "3. Case of pronouns" or "4. Possessive pronouns."

Chapter 3

Communicating in a World of Diversity

Learning Objectives

AFTER STUDYING THIS CHAPTER, YOU WILL BE ABLE TO

1 Discuss the opportunities and challenges of intercultural communication

2 Define culture and explain how culture is learned

3 Define ethnocentrism and stereotyping and give three suggestions for overcoming these limiting mindsets

4 Explain the importance of recognizing cultural variations and list eight categories of cultural differences

5 Discuss steps you can take to improve your intercultural communication skills

6 Outline strategies for studying other cultures

7 List seven recommendations for writing clearly in multilanguage business environments

On the Job

COMMUNICATING AT IBM

ENSURING SUCCESS BY EMBRACING DIVERSITY

The "I" in IBM stands for "International," but it could just as easily stand for "Intercultural," as a testament to the computer giant's long-standing commitment to embracing diversity. Ron Glover, IBM's vice president of global workforce diversity, knows from years of experience that communicating successfully across cultures is no simple task, however—particularly in a company that employs more than 325,000 people and sells to customers in roughly 175 countries around the world.

Language alone presents a formidable barrier to communication when you consider that IBM's employees speak more than 165 languages. But language is just one of many elements that play a role in communication between cultures. Differences in age, ethnic background, gender, sexual orientation, physical ability, and economic status can all affect the communication process. Glover emphasizes that "to operate successfully, we must be especially mindful of how we respect and value differences among people in countries and regions." He recognizes that these differences represent both a challenge and an opportunity, and a key part of his job is helping IBM executives and employees work together in a way that transforms their cultural differences into a critical business strength. Diversity, he explains, is "an essential aspect of IBM's broader business strategy."

Throughout its long history of employing and working with people from a variety of cultures, IBM

Ron Glover oversees IBM's efforts to build competitive advantage by capitalizing on the benefits of a diverse workforce.

has learned some powerful lessons. Perhaps the most significant is its conclusion that successfully managing a diverse workforce and competing in a diverse marketplace start with embracing those differences, not trying to ignore them or pretending they don't affect interpersonal communication. Take Ron Glover's advice when he says that even if your company never does business outside the United States, "you will need to effectively engage differences to remain viable in the economy of the future."[1]

www.ibm.com

UNDERSTANDING THE OPPORTUNITIES AND CHALLENGES OF COMMUNICATION IN A DIVERSE WORLD

Effective intercultural communication
- Opens up business opportunities around the world
- Improves the contributions of employees in a diverse workforce

IBM's experience (profiled in the chapter opener) illustrates the challenges and opportunities for business professionals who know how to communicate with diverse audiences. Although the concept is often framed in terms of ethnic background, a broader and more useful definition of **diversity** includes "all the characteristics and experiences that define each of us as individuals."[2] As you'll learn in this chapter, these characteristics and experiences can have a profound effect on the way businesspeople communicate.

To a large degree, these effects on communication are the result of fundamental differences between cultures. **Intercultural communication** is the process of sending and receiving messages between people whose cultural background could lead them to interpret verbal and nonverbal signs differently. Every attempt to send and receive messages is influenced by culture, so to communicate successfully, you need a basic grasp of the cultural differences you may encounter and how you should handle them. Your efforts to recognize and surmount cultural differences will open up business opportunities throughout the world and maximize the contribution of all the employees in a diverse workforce.

The Opportunities in a Global Marketplace

You will communicate with people from other cultures throughout your career.

Thousands of U.S. businesses depend on exports for significant portions of their revenues. Every year, these companies export roughly $700 billion in materials and merchandise, along with billions more in personal and professional services. If you work in one of these companies, you may well be called on to visit or at least communicate with a wide variety of people who speak languages other than English and who live in cultures quite different from what you're used to (see Figure 3.1). Of the top ten export markets for U.S. products, only three (Canada, Great Britain, and Singapore) have English as an official language, and two of those three (Canada and Singapore) have more than one official language.[3]

In the global marketplace, most natural boundaries and national borders are no longer the impassable barriers they once were. Domestic markets are opening to worldwide competition as businesses of all sizes look for new growth opportunities outside their own countries. For example, automotive giant Ford markets to customers in some 130 countries, providing websites that offer local information, usually in the local language.[4]

The Advantages of a Diverse Workforce

The diversity of today's workforce brings distinct advantages to businesses:
- A broader range of views and ideas
- A better understanding of diverse, fragmented markets
- A broader pool of talent from which to recruit

Over the past few decades, many innovative companies have changed the way they approach diversity, from seeing it as a legal requirement to seeing it as a strategic opportunity to connect with customers and take advantage of the broadest possible pool of talent.[5] Smart business leaders such as IBM's Ron Glover recognize the competitive advantages of a diverse workforce that offers a broader spectrum of viewpoints and ideas, helps companies understand and identify with diverse markets, and enables companies to benefit from a wider range of employee talents. As Renee Wingo of Virgin Mobile USA, a mobile phone operator based in Warren, New Jersey, puts it, "You're not going to create any magic as a manager unless you bring together people with diverse perspectives who aren't miniversions of you."[6]

Diversity is simply a fact of life for all companies. The United States has been a nation of immigrants from the beginning, and that trend continues today. The Western and Northern Europeans who made up the bulk of immigrants during the nation's early years now share space with people from across Asia, Africa, Eastern

FIGURE 3.1
Languages of the World
This map illustrates the incredible array of languages used around the world. Each dot represents the geographic center of the more than 6,900 languages tracked by the linguistic research firm SIL International. Even if all of your business communication takes place in English, you will interact with audiences who speak a variety of other native languages.

Europe, and other parts of the world. By 2010 recent immigrants will account for half of all new U.S. workers.[7] Even the term *minority*, as it applies to nonwhite residents, makes less and less sense every year: In two states (California and New Mexico) and several dozen large cities, Caucasian Americans no longer constitute a clear majority.[8] Nor is this pattern of immigration unique to the United States: Workers from Africa, Asia, and the Middle East are moving to Europe in search of new opportunities, while workers from India, the Philippines, and Southeast Asia contribute to the employment base of the Middle East.[9]

Differences in everything from age and gender to religion and ethnic heritage to geography and military experience enrich the workplace. Both immigration and workforce diversity create advantages—and challenges—for business communicators throughout the world.

The Challenges of Intercultural Communication

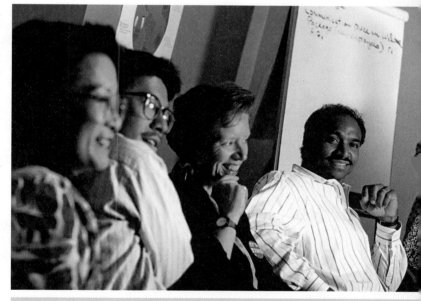

Communication among people of diverse cultural backgrounds and life experiences is not always easy, but doing it successfully can create tremendous strategic advantages.

Diversity affects how business messages are conceived, planned, sent, received, and interpreted in the workplace. Today's increasingly diverse workforce encompasses a wide range of skills, traditions, backgrounds, experiences, outlooks, and attitudes toward work—all of which can affect employee behavior on the job. Supervisors face the challenge of communicating with these diverse employees, motivating them, and fostering cooperation and harmony among them. Teams face the challenge of working together closely, and companies are challenged to coexist peacefully with business partners and with the community as a whole.

Culture influences everything about communication, including

- Language
- Nonverbal signals
- Word meaning
- Time and space issues
- Rules of human relationships

The interaction of culture and communication is so pervasive that separating the two is virtually impossible. The way you communicate—from the language you speak and the nonverbal signals you send to the way you perceive other people—is influenced by the culture in which you were raised. The meaning of words, the significance of gestures, the importance of time and space, the rules of human relationships—these and many other aspects of communication are defined by culture. To a large degree, your culture influences the way you think, which naturally affects the way you communicate as both a sender and a receiver.[10] So you can see that intercultural communication is much more complicated than simply matching language between sender and receiver. It goes beyond mere words to beliefs, values, and emotions.

Throughout this chapter, you will encounter examples of how communication styles and habits vary from one culture to another. These examples are intended to illustrate the major themes of intercultural communication, not to give an exhaustive list of styles and habits of any particular culture. With an understanding of these major themes, you'll be prepared to explore the specifics of any culture.

ENHANCING YOUR SENSITIVITY TO CULTURE AND DIVERSITY

The good news is that you're already an expert in culture, at least in the culture you grew up with. You understand how your society works, how people are expected to communicate, what common gestures and facial expressions mean, and so on. The bad news is that because you're such an expert in your own culture, your communication is largely automatic; that is, you rarely stop to think about the communication rules you're following. An important step toward successful intercultural communication is becoming more aware of these rules and of the way they influence your communication. A good place to start is to understand what culture is.

Understanding the Concept of Culture

Culture is a shared system of symbols, beliefs, attitudes, values, expectations, and behavior norms.

Culture is a shared system of symbols, beliefs, attitudes, values, expectations, and norms for behavior. People's cultural background influences the way they prioritize what is important in life, helps define their attitudes toward what is appropriate in any given situation, and establishes rules for their behavior.[11] One study suggests that people from different cultures even view the world—literally—in different ways. Shown a variety of pictures, Chinese subjects focused more on the whole picture and the harmony of elements within it, whereas North Americans of European descent focused more on the dominant, individual objects in the scene.[12]

You belong to several cultures, each of which affects the way you communicate.

Actually, everyone belongs to several cultures. In addition to the culture you share with all the people who live in your own country, you belong to other cultural groups, including an ethnic group, possibly a religious group, and perhaps a profession that has its own special language and customs. With its large population and long history of immigration, the United States is home to a vast array of cultures. As one indication of this diversity, the inhabitants of this country now speak more than 160 languages.[13] In contrast, Japan is much more homogeneous, having only a few separate cultural groups.[14]

Cultures can differ widely and vary in their rate of change, their degree of complexity, and their tolerance toward outsiders. These differences affect the level of trust and openness that you can achieve when communicating with people of other cultures.

As you grow up in a culture, you are taught who you are and how best to function in that culture by the group's members. Sometimes you are explicitly told which behaviors are acceptable; at other times you learn by observing which values work best in a particular group. In these ways, culture is passed on from person to person and from generation to generation.[15]

In addition to being automatic, cultures tend to be *coherent*; that is, they appear to be fairly logical and consistent when viewed from the inside. For instance, the notion of progress is deeply embedded in the culture of the United States. Those who achieve are admired and rewarded, and those who don't are sometimes viewed negatively, even if they live happy and contented lives. Such coherence generally helps a culture function more smoothly internally, although it can create disharmony between cultures that don't view the world in the same way.

Finally, cultures also tend to be complete, providing their members with most of the answers to life's big questions. This idea of completeness dulls or even suppresses curiosity about life in other cultures. Therefore, such completeness can complicate communication with other cultures.[16]

Overcoming Ethnocentrism and Stereotyping

Ethnocentrism is the tendency to judge all other groups according to the standards, behaviors, and customs of one's own group. Given the automatic influence of one's own culture, when people compare their culture to others, they often conclude that their own group is superior.[17] An even more extreme reaction is **xenophobia**, a fear of strangers and foreigners. Clearly, businesspeople who take these views are not likely to communicate successfully across cultures.

Distorted views of other cultures or groups also result from **stereotyping**, assigning a wide range of generalized attributes to an individual on the basis of membership in a particular culture or social group. Whereas ethnocentrism and xenophobia represent negative views of everyone in a particular group, stereotyping is more a matter of oversimplifying and of failing to acknowledge individuality. For instance, assuming that an older colleague will be out of touch with the youth market and that a younger colleague can't be an inspiring leader is an example of stereotyping age groups.

Those who want to show respect for other people in their business communications need to adopt a more positive viewpoint, in the form of **cultural pluralism**—the practice of accepting multiple cultures on their own terms. When crossing cultural boundaries, you'll be even more effective if you move beyond simple acceptance and adapt your own communication style to that of the new cultures you encounter—even integrating aspects of those cultures into your own.[18] A few simple habits can help you avoid the negativity of ethnocentrism and the oversimplification of stereotyping:

- **Avoid assumptions.** Don't assume that others will act the same way you do, use language and symbols the same way you do, or even operate from the same values and beliefs. For instance, in a comparison of the 10 most important values in three cultures, people from the United States had no values in common with people from Japanese or Arab cultures.[19]

- **Avoid judgments.** When people act differently, don't conclude that they are in error or that their way is invalid or inferior.

- **Acknowledge distinctions.** Don't ignore the differences between another person's culture and your own.

Unfortunately, overcoming ethnocentrism and stereotyping is no simple task, even for people who are highly motivated to do so. You may need to change lifelong beliefs about yourself and your culture. Moreover, recent research suggests that people often have beliefs and biases that they're not even consciously aware of—and that may even conflict with the beliefs they *think* they have. (To see if you have some of these *implicit beliefs*, visit the Project Implicit website, at **https://implicit.harvard.edu/implicit**, and take some of the simple online tests.)[20]

Cultures tend to offer views of life that are coherent (internally logical) and complete (answer all of life's big questions).

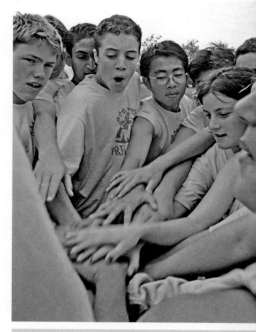

Participation in group activities is an important method of learning about a culture's rules and expectations.

Ethnocentrism is the tendency to judge all other groups according to the standards, behaviors, and customs of one's own group.

Xenophobia is a fear of strangers.

Stereotyping is assigning generalized attributes to an individual on the basis of membership in a particular group.

Cultural pluralism is the acceptance of multiple cultures on their own terms.

Recognizing Variations in a Diverse World

Cultural differences can lead to miscommunication in the workplace.

Whenever you communicate, your instinct is to encode your message using the assumptions of *your* culture. However, members of your audience decode your message according to the assumptions of *their* culture (see "Communicating Across Cultures: Test Your Intercultural Knowledge"). Consequently, the greater the difference between cultures, the greater the chance for misunderstanding.[21] From using brand names that are obscene slang in another language to misunderstanding attitudes about worker-manager relationships, companies around the world have made mistakes that have damaged relationships and lost sales. You can learn to avoid such blunders by recognizing and accommodating eight main types of cultural differences: contextual, legal and ethical, social, nonverbal signals, gender, age, religion, and ability.

Cultural context is the pattern of physical cues, environmental stimuli, and implicit understanding that conveys meaning between members of the same culture.

High-context cultures rely heavily on nonverbal actions and environmental setting to convey meaning; low-context cultures rely more on explicit verbal communication.

Contextual Differences Every attempt at communication occurs within a **cultural context**, the pattern of physical cues, environmental stimuli, and implicit understanding that conveys meaning between two members of the same culture. However, cultures around the world vary widely in the role that context plays in communication (see Figure 3.2).

In a **high-context culture** such as that of South Korea or Taiwan, people rely less on verbal communication and more on the context of nonverbal actions and environmental setting to convey meaning. For instance, a Chinese speaker expects the receiver to discover the essence of a message and uses indirectness and metaphor to provide a web of meaning.[22] In high-context cultures, the rules of everyday life are

COMMUNICATING ACROSS CULTURES

Test Your Intercultural Knowledge

Even well-intentioned businesspeople can make mistakes if they aren't aware of simple but important cultural differences. Can you spot the erroneous assumptions in these scenarios?

1. You're tired of the discussion and you want to move on to a new topic. You ask your Australian business associate, "Can we table this for a while?" To your dismay, your colleague ignores the request and keeps right on discussing the topic.
2. You finally made the long trip overseas to meet the new German director of your division. Despite slow traffic, you arrive only four minutes late. His door is shut, so you knock on it and walk in. The chair is too far away from the desk, so you pick it up and move it closer. Then you lean over the desk, stick out your hand and say, "Good morning, Hans, it's nice to meet you." Why is his reaction so chilly?
3. Your meeting went better than you'd ever expected. In fact, you found the Japanese representative for your new advertising agency to be very agreeable; she said yes to just about everything. When you share your enthusiasm with your boss, he doesn't appear very excited. Why?

Here's what went wrong in each situation:

1. To "table" something in Australia means to bring it forward for discussion, the opposite of the usual U.S. meaning. The

English that's spoken in Australia is closer to British than to U.S. English.
2. You've just broken four rules of German polite behavior: punctuality, privacy, personal space, and proper greetings. In time-conscious Germany, you should never arrive even a few minutes late. Also, Germans like their privacy and space, and many adhere to formal greetings of "Frau" and "Herr," even if the business association has lasted for years.
3. The word *yes* may not always mean "yes" in the Western sense. Japanese people may say *yes* to confirm they have heard or understood something but not necessarily to indicate that they agree with it. You'll seldom get a direct no. Some of the ways that Japanese people say no indirectly include "It will be difficult," "I will ask my supervisor," "I'm not sure," "We will think about it," and "I see."

CAREER APPLICATIONS

1. Have you ever been on the receiving end of an intercultural communication error, such as when someone inadvertently used an inappropriate gesture or figure of speech? How did you respond?
2. If you had arrived late at the office of the German colleague, what would have been a better way to handle the situation?

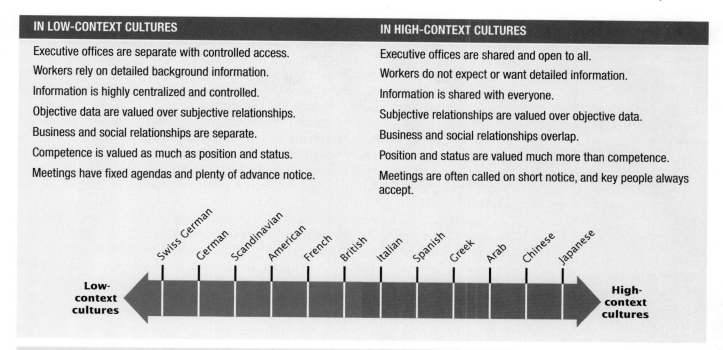

IN LOW-CONTEXT CULTURES	IN HIGH-CONTEXT CULTURES
Executive offices are separate with controlled access.	Executive offices are shared and open to all.
Workers rely on detailed background information.	Workers do not expect or want detailed information.
Information is highly centralized and controlled.	Information is shared with everyone.
Objective data are valued over subjective relationships.	Subjective relationships are valued over objective data.
Business and social relationships are separate.	Business and social relationships overlap.
Competence is valued as much as position and status.	Position and status are valued much more than competence.
Meetings have fixed agendas and plenty of advance notice.	Meetings are often called on short notice, and key people always accept.

Low-context cultures ← Swiss German · German · Scandinavian · American · French · British · Italian · Spanish · Greek · Arab · Chinese · Japanese → High-context cultures

FIGURE 3.2
How Cultural Context Affects Business
Cultural context influences the nature of business communication in many ways. Note that these are generalized assessments of each culture; contextual variations can be found within each culture and from one individual to another.

rarely explicit; instead, as individuals grow up, they learn how to recognize situational cues (such as gestures and tone of voice) and how to respond as expected.[23] The primary role of communication is building relationships, not exchanging information.[24]

In a **low-context culture** such as the United States or Germany, people rely more on verbal communication and less on circumstances and cues to convey meaning. A British speaker feels responsible for transmitting the meaning of the message and often places sentences in chronological sequence to establish a cause-and-effect pattern.[25] In a low-context culture, rules and expectations are usually spelled out through explicit statements such as "Please wait until I'm finished" or "You're welcome to browse."[26] The primary task of communication in low-context cultures is exchanging information.[27]

Contextual differences are apparent in the way cultures approach situations such as decision making, problem solving, and negotiating. For instance, in lower-context cultures, businesspeople tend to focus on the results of the decisions they face, a reflection of the cultural emphasis on logic and progress. Will this be good for our company? For my career? In comparison, higher-context cultures emphasize the means or the method by which the decision will be made. Building or protecting relationships can be as important as the facts and information used in making the decisions.[28] Consequently, negotiators working on business deals in such cultures may spend most of their time together building relationships rather than hammering out contractual details.

Whether you're making a decision, solving a problem, or negotiating a business deal, the communication tactics that work well in a high-context culture may backfire in a low-context culture and vice versa. The key to success is understanding why the other party is saying and doing particular things and then adapting your approach accordingly.

Low-context cultures tend to value written agreements and interpret laws strictly, whereas high-context cultures view adherence to laws as being more flexible.

Cultural differences can complicate ethical choices.

Legal and Ethical Differences   Cultural context also influences legal and ethical behavior. For example, because low-context cultures value the written word, they consider written agreements binding. But high-context cultures put less emphasis on the written word and consider personal pledges more important than contracts. They also tend to take a more flexible approach regarding adherence to the law, whereas low-context cultures would adhere to the law strictly.[29]

As you conduct business around the world, you'll find that legal systems and ethical standards differ from culture to culture. In the United Kingdom and the United States, for instance, someone is presumed innocent until proved guilty, a principle rooted in English common law. However, in Mexico and Turkey, someone is presumed guilty until proved innocent, a principle rooted in the *Napoleonic Code*.[30]

Similarly, bribing government officials appears to be a fairly common practice in countries such as Kenya, where businesspeople and consumers alike find themselves forced to pay *kitu kidogo* ("something small") to government officials in order to gain admittance to a hospital, receive a driver's license, or accomplish myriad other objectives of daily life.[31] Similar traditions exist in other countries, such as *huilu* in China, *vzyatka* in Russia, *baksheesh* in the Middle East, and *una mordida* ("a small bite") in Mexico.[32] In contrast, U.S. law prohibits U.S. companies from paying bribes, even in countries where the practice is accepted (or expected).[33]

Making ethical choices across cultures can seem complicated, but you can keep your messages ethical by applying four basic principles:[34]

- **Actively seek mutual ground.** Both parties must be flexible and must avoid insisting that an interaction take place strictly in terms of one culture or another.

- **Send and receive messages without judgment.** To allow information to flow freely, both parties must recognize that values vary from culture to culture, and they must trust each other.

Honesty and respect are cornerstones of ethical communication, regardless of culture.

- **Send messages that are honest.** To ensure that the information is true, both parties must see things as they are—not as they would like them to be. Both parties must work to recognize their own personal and cultural biases.

- **Show respect for cultural differences.** To protect the basic human rights of both parties, each must understand and acknowledge the other's needs and preserve each other's dignity.

Whereas formal rules of etiquette are explicit and well defined, informal rules are learned through observation and imitation.

Social Differences   The nature of social behavior varies among cultures, sometimes dramatically. Wal-Mart learned this lesson the hard way when the giant retailer tried to expand into Germany. Store clerks resisted the company requirement of always smiling at customers—a cornerstone of customer relationship strategies in the United States—because doing so was sometimes misinterpreted by customers as flirting. Wal-Mart dropped the requirement but, after a number of other cultural and strategic missteps, eventually left the German market.[35]

In addition to the factors already discussed, social rules can vary from culture to culture in the following areas:

- **Attitudes toward work and success.** For example, many U.S. residents hold the view that material comfort earned by individual effort is a sign of superiority and that people who work hard are better than those who don't (see Figure 3.3).

Respect and rank are reflected differently from culture to culture in the way people are addressed and in their working environment.

- **Roles and status.** Culture dictates, or at least tries to dictate, the roles that people play, including who communicates with whom, what they communicate, and in what way. For example, in some countries, women still don't play a prominent role in business, and women executives who visit those countries may find that they're not taken seriously as businesspeople.[36]

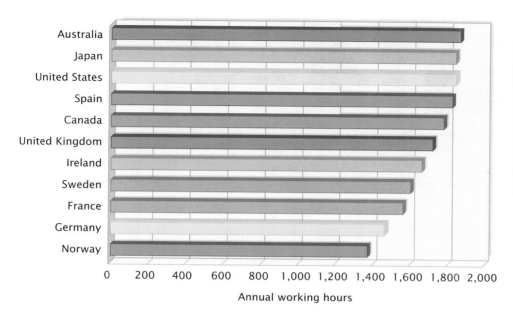

- **Use of manners.** What is polite in one culture may be considered rude in another. For instance, asking a colleague "How was your weekend?" is a common way of making small talk in the United States, but the question sounds intrusive to people in cultures in which business and private lives are seen as totally separate. As another example, if you're invited to visit someone's home in India "any time," you should make an unexpected visit without waiting for a definite invitation. Failure to take the "any time" invitation literally would be an insult, a sign that you don't care to develop the friendship.

  The rules of polite behavior vary from country to country.

- **Concepts of time.** Business runs on schedules, deadlines, and appointments, but these matters are regarded differently from culture to culture. People in low-context cultures view time as a limited resource and tend to treat schedules as rigid requirements. However, executives from high-context cultures often see time as more flexible and often take care not to damage relationships in pursuit of deadlines. Consequently, the workday isn't expected to follow a rigid, preset schedule.[37] Similarly, the hard-charging, round-the-clock style of some U.S. businesspeople doesn't mesh well in cultures that put a higher value on relaxed personal and social time.[38]

  Attitudes toward time, such as adherence to meeting schedules, can vary throughout the world.

Nonverbal Differences   As discussed in Chapter 2, nonverbal communication can be a reliable guide to determining the meaning of a message. However, this notion of reliability is valid only when the communicators belong to the same culture. For instance, the simplest hand gestures change meaning from culture to culture. A gesture that communicates good luck in Brazil is the equivalent of giving someone "the finger" in Colombia.[39] In fact, the area of gestures is so complicated that entire books have been written about it. Don't assume that the gestures you grew up with will translate to another culture; doing so could lead to embarrassing mistakes (see Figure 3.4).

From colors to facial expression, nonverbal elements add yet another layer of richness and complexity to intercultural communication. When you have the opportunity to interact with people in another culture, the best advice is to study the culture in advance, then observe the way people behave in the following areas:

- **Greetings.** Do people shake hands, bow, or kiss lightly (on one side of the face or both)?

  Nonverbal differences can vary widely from culture to culture.

- **Personal space.** When people are conversing, do they stand closer together or farther away than you are accustomed to?

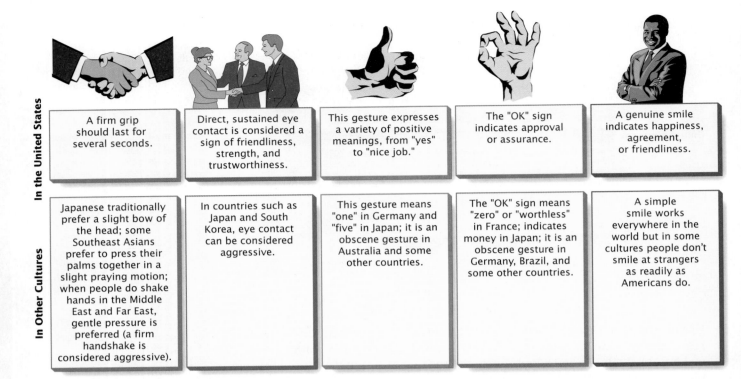

In the United States

A firm grip should last for several seconds.	Direct, sustained eye contact is considered a sign of friendliness, strength, and trustworthiness.	This gesture expresses a variety of positive meanings, from "yes" to "nice job."	The "OK" sign indicates approval or assurance.	A genuine smile indicates happiness, agreement, or friendliness.

In Other Cultures

Japanese traditionally prefer a slight bow of the head; some Southeast Asians prefer to press their palms together in a slight praying motion; when people do shake hands in the Middle East and Far East, gentle pressure is preferred (a firm handshake is considered aggressive).	In countries such as Japan and South Korea, eye contact can be considered aggressive.	This gesture means "one" in Germany and "five" in Japan; it is an obscene gesture in Australia and some other countries.	The "OK" sign means "zero" or "worthless" in France; indicates money in Japan; it is an obscene gesture in Germany, Brazil, and some other countries.	A simple smile works everywhere in the world but in some cultures people don't smile at strangers as readily as Americans do.

FIGURE 3.4
Avoiding Nonverbal Mishaps
These examples illustrate some of the many nuances of nonverbal communication across cultures. Even smiling isn't quite as simple as it might seem. Americans tend to smile at strangers more often than people in many other cultures, so they are sometimes put off by what they consider unfriendly responses from strangers. Conversely, people from other cultures can be put off by the American habit of frequent smiling, which some view as insincere.

- **Touching.** Do people touch each other on the arm to emphasize a point or slap each other on the back to show congratulation? Or do they refrain from touching altogether?

- **Facial expressions.** Do people shake their heads to indicate "no" and nod them to indicate "yes"? This is what people are accustomed to in the United States, but it is not universal.

- **Eye contact.** Do people make frequent eye contact or avoid it? Frequent eye contact is often taken as a sign of honesty and openness in the United States, but in other cultures, it can be a sign of aggressiveness or lack of respect.

- **Posture.** Do people slouch and relax in the office and in public, or do they sit up straight?

- **Formality.** In general, does the culture seem more or less formal than yours?

Following the lead of people who grew up in the culture is not only a great way to learn but a good way to show respect as well.

A culture's views on youth and aging affect how people communicate with one another.

Age Differences   In U.S. culture, youth is associated with strength, energy, possibilities, and freedom. In contrast, age is too often associated with declining powers and a loss of respect and authority—even though older workers can offer broader experience, the benefits of important business relationships nurtured over many years, and high degrees of "practical intelligence"—the ability to solve complex, poorly defined problems.[40]

In contrast, in cultures that value age and seniority, longevity earns respect and increasing power and freedom. For instance, in many Asian societies, the oldest employees hold the most powerful jobs, the most impressive titles, and the greatest degree of freedom and decision-making authority. If a younger employee disagrees with one of these senior executives, the discussion is never conducted in public. The notion of "saving face," of avoiding public embarrassment, is too strong. Instead, if a senior person seems to be in error about something, other employees will find a quiet, private way to communicate whatever information they feel is necessary.[41]

As with all other diversity issues, the solution to age-related conflicts can be found in respecting one another and working toward common goals. As Virginia Byrd, a veteran career counselor from Encinitas, California, put it, "It's a real blessing to have different generations in our workplaces. There is so much we can share, if we make the effort."[42]

Gender Differences   The perception of men and women in business varies from culture to culture. In the United States today, women find a much wider range of business opportunities than existed just a few decades ago. For instance, women are now chief executive officers (CEOs) of a number of leading corporations, including PepsiCo, Archer Daniels Midland, eBay, Kraft Foods, Avon, MTV, and Xerox.[43] However, such opportunity is not the case in more tradition-oriented societies, where men tend to hold most or all of the positions of authority and women are expected to play a more subservient role. Female executives who visit other cultures may not be taken seriously until they successfully handle challenges to their knowledge, capabilities, and patience.[44]

As more women enter the workforce and take on positions of increasing responsibility, it's important for company leaders to revisit assumptions and practices.[45] For instance, company cultures that have been dominated by men for years may have adopted communication habits that some women have difficulty relating to—such as the frequent use of sports metaphors or the acceptance of coarse language.

Whatever the culture, evidence suggests that men and women tend to have slightly different communication styles. Broadly speaking, men tend to emphasize content in their communication efforts whereas women place a higher premium on relationship maintenance.[46] This difference can create friction when two parties in a conversation have different needs and expectations from the interchange. Again, these are broad generalizations that do not apply to every person in every situation, but keeping them in mind can help men and women overcome communication hurdles in the workplace.

Religious Differences   Religion is a dominant force in many cultures and the source of many differences between cultures.[47] The effort to accommodate employees' life interests on a broader scale has led a number of companies to address the issue of religion in the workplace. As one of the most personal and influential aspects of life, religion does bring potential for controversy in a work setting. On the one hand, some employees feel they should be able to express their beliefs in the workplace and not be forced to "check their faith at the door" when they come to work. On the other hand, companies want to avoid situations in which openly expressed religious differences may cause friction between employees or distract employees from their responsibilities. To help address such concerns, firms such as Ford, Intel, Texas

Communication styles and expectations can vary widely between age groups, putting extra demands on teams that include workers of varying ages.

Men tend to emphasize content in their messages, and woman tend to emphasize relationship maintenance.

Document Makeover

IMPROVE THIS LETTER

To practice correcting drafts of actual documents, visit your online course or the access-code-protected portion of the Companion Website. Click on "Document Makeovers," then click on Chapter 3. You will find a letter that contains problems and errors related to what you've learned in this chapter about developing effective intercultural communication skills. Use the Final Draft decision tool to create an improved version of this letter. Check the message for a communication style that keeps the message brief; does not become too familiar or informal; uses transitional elements appropriately; and avoids slang, idioms, jargon, and technical language.

Instruments, and American Airlines allow employees to form faith-based employee-support groups as part of their diversity strategies. In contrast, Procter & Gamble is among the companies that don't allow organized religious activities at their facilities.[48] As more companies work to establish inclusive workplaces, and as more employees seek to integrate religious convictions into their daily work, you can expect to see this issue being discussed at many companies in the coming years.

Ability Differences   Colleagues and customers with disabilities that affect communication represent an important aspect of the diversity picture. People whose hearing, vision, or physical ability to operate computers is impaired can be at a significant disadvantage in today's workplace.

As with other elements of diversity, success starts with respect for individuals and sensitivity to differences. Employers can also invest in a variety of **assistive technologies** that help people with disabilities perform activities that might otherwise be difficult or impossible. These technologies include devices and systems that help people communicate orally and visually, interact with computers and other equipment, and enjoy greater mobility in the workplace. For example, web designers can emphasize *web accessibility*, taking steps to make websites more accessible to people with limited vision. Assistive technologies create a vital link for thousands of employees with disabilities, giving them the opportunity to pursue a greater range of career paths and giving employers access to a broader base of talent. With the United States heading for a potentially serious shortage of workers, the economy will benefit from everyone who can make a contribution; assistive technologies will be an important part of the solution.[49]

Adapting to U.S. Business Culture

If you are a recent immigrant to the United States or grew up in a culture outside the U.S. mainstream, you can apply all of the concepts and skills in this chapter to help you adapt to U.S. business culture. Here are some key points to remember as you become accustomed to business communication in this country:[50]

- **Individualism.** In contrast to cultures that value group harmony and group success, U.S. culture generally expects individuals to succeed by their own efforts, and it rewards individual success. Even though teamwork is emphasized in many companies, competition between individuals is expected and even encouraged in many cases.

- **Equality.** Although the country's historical record on equality has not always been positive and inequalities still exist, treating all people equally is considered a core U.S. value. This applies to race, gender, social background, and even age. To a greater degree than people in many other cultures, Americans believe that every person should be given the opportunity to pursue whatever dreams and goals he or she may have in life.

- **Privacy and personal space.** People in the United States are accustomed to a fair amount of privacy, and this includes their "personal space" at work. For example, they expect you to knock before entering a closed office and to avoid asking questions about personal beliefs or activities until they get to know you well.

- **Time and schedules.** U.S. businesses value punctuality and the efficient use of time. For instance, meetings are expected to start and end at designated times.

- **Religion.** The United States does not have an official state religion. Many religions are practiced throughout the country, and people are expected to respect each other's beliefs.

- **Communication style.** Communication tends to be direct and to focus on content and transactions, not relationships or group harmony.

These are generalizations, of course. Any nation of 300 million people will exhibit a wide variety of behaviors. However, following these guidelines will help you succeed in most business communication situations.

IMPROVING YOUR INTERCULTURAL COMMUNICATION SKILLS

Communicating successfully from one culture to another requires a variety of skills (see Figure 3.5). You can improve your intercultural skills throughout your entire career by studying other cultures and languages, respecting preferences for communication styles, learning to write and speak clearly, listening carefully, knowing when to use interpreters and translators, and helping others adapt to your culture.

Improving intercultural skills is a career-long effort.

Studying Other Cultures

Effectively adapting your communication efforts to another culture requires not only knowledge about the culture but also the ability and the motivation to change your personal habits as needed.[51] In other words, it's not a simple task. Unfortunately, a thorough knowledge of another culture and its communication patterns (both verbal and nonverbal) can take years to acquire. Fortunately, you don't need to learn about

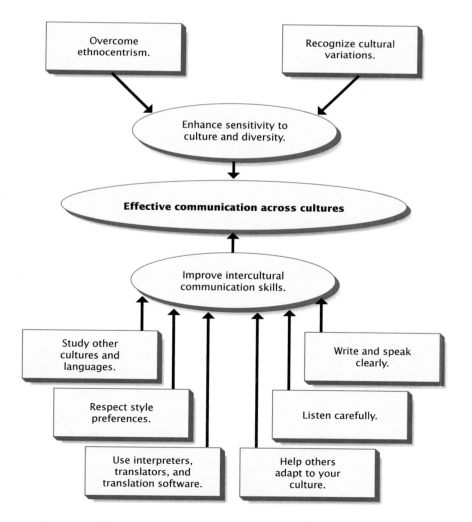

FIGURE 3.5
Components of Successful Intercultural Communication
Communicating in a diverse business environment is not always an easy task, but you can continue to improve your sensitivity and build your skills as you progress in your career.

the whole world all at once. Many companies appoint specialists for specific countries or regions, giving you a chance to focus on fewer cultures at a time. Some firms also provide resources to help employees prepare for interaction with other cultures. On IBM's global workforce diversity intranet site, for instance, employees can click on the "GoingGlobal" link to learn about customs in specific cultures.[52]

Even a small amount of research and practice will help you get through many business situations. In addition, most people respond positively to honest effort and good intentions, and many business associates will help you along if you show an interest in learning more about their cultures.

Mistakes in intercultural communication happen. When they do, apologize (if appropriate), ask about the accepted way, and move on.

Try to approach situations with an open mind and a healthy sense of humor. When you make a mistake, simply apologize, if appropriate, ask the other person to explain the accepted way, and then move on. As business becomes ever more global, even the most tradition-bound cultures are learning to deal with outsiders more patiently and overlook the occasional cultural blunder.[53]

Numerous websites and books offer advice on traveling to and working in specific cultures. Also try to sample newspapers, magazines, and even the music and movies of another country. For instance, a movie can demonstrate nonverbal customs even if you don't grasp the language. (However, be careful not to rely solely on entertainment products. If people in other countries based their opinions of American culture only on Hollywood's silly teen flicks and violent action movies, what sort of impression do you imagine they'd get?) For some of the key issues to research before doing business in another country, refer to Table 3.1.

Studying Other Languages

Consider what it must be like to work at IBM, where the global workforce speaks more than 165 languages. Without the ability to communicate in more than one language, how could this diverse group of people ever conduct business? As commerce continues to become more globalized, the demand for multilingual communicators continues to grow as well. Some countries have emphasized language diversity more than others over the years. For instance, in the Netherlands, with its long history of international trade, fluency in multiple languages is considered an essential business skill.[54] Shifts in business patterns can dramatically affect language learning, too. As U.S. companies continue to outsource a variety of business functions to facilities in India, many Indians now view English skills as an important career asset. Conversely, the growing international status of China as a manufacturing powerhouse is prompting many professionals in the United Sates and other countries to learn Mandarin, the official language in China.[55]

Many U.S. companies find that they must be able to conduct business in languages other than English.

In addition, a number of U.S. companies are teaching their English-speaking employees a second language to facilitate communication with their co-workers. The Target retail chain is among those sponsoring basic Spanish classes for English-speaking supervisors of immigrant employees. Elsewhere around the country, enrollment is growing in specialized classes such as health-care Spanish and Spanish for professionals.[56]

If you have a long-term business relationship with people of another culture, it is helpful to learn at least some basic words and phrases of their language.

Even if your colleagues or customers in another country speak your language, it's worth the time and energy to learn common phrases in theirs. Learning the basics not only helps you get through everyday business and social situations but also demonstrates your commitment to the business relationship. After all, the other person probably spent years learning your language.

Finally, don't assume that two countries speaking the same language speak it the same way. The French spoken in Quebec and other parts of Canada is often noticeably different from the French spoken in France. Similarly, it's often said that the United States and the United Kingdom are two countries divided by a common language. For instance, *period* (punctuation), *elevator*, and *gasoline* in the United States are *full stop*, *lift*, and *petrol* in the United Kingdom.

Table 3.1	DOING BUSINESS IN OTHER COUNTRIES

Action	Details to Consider
Understand social customs	• How do people react to strangers? Are they friendly? Hostile? Reserved? • How do people greet each other? Should you bow? Nod? Shake hands? • How do you express appreciation for an invitation to lunch, dinner, or someone's home? Should you bring a gift? Send flowers? Write a thank-you note? • Are any phrases, facial expressions, or hand gestures considered rude? • How do you attract the attention of a waiter? Do you tip the waiter? • When is it rude to refuse an invitation? How do you refuse politely? • What topics may or may not be discussed in a social setting? In a business setting? • How do social customs dictate interaction between men and women? Between younger people and older people?
Learn about clothing and food preferences	• What occasions require special clothing? • What colors are associated with mourning? Love? Joy? • Are some types of clothing considered taboo for one gender or the other? • How many times a day do people eat? • How are hands or utensils used when eating? • Where is the seat of honor at a table?
Assess political patterns	• How stable is the political situation? • Does the political situation affect businesses in and out of the country? • Is it appropriate to talk politics in social or business situations?
Understand religious and folk beliefs	• To which religious groups do people belong? • Which places, objects, actions, and events are sacred? • Do religious beliefs affect communication between men and women or between any other groups? • Is there a tolerance for minority religions? • How do religious holidays affect business and government activities? • Does religion require or prohibit eating specific foods? At specific times?
Learn about economic and business institutions	• Is the society homogeneous or heterogeneous? • What languages are spoken? • What are the primary resources and principal products? • Are businesses generally large? Family controlled? Government controlled? • What are the generally accepted working hours? • How do people view scheduled appointments? • Are people expected to socialize before conducting business?
Appraise the nature of ethics, values, and laws	• Is money or a gift expected in exchange for arranging business transactions? • Do people value competitiveness or cooperation? • What are the attitudes toward work? Toward money? • Is politeness more important than factual honesty?

Respecting Preferences for Communication Style

Communication style—including the level of directness, the degree of formality, preferences for written versus spoken communication, and other factors—varies widely from culture to culture. Knowing what your communication partners expect can help you adapt to their particular style. Once again, watching and learning are the best ways to improve your skills. However, you can infer some generalities from what you already know about a culture. For instance, U.S. workers typically prefer an open and direct communication style; they find other styles frustrating or suspect. Directness is also valued in Sweden as a sign of efficiency; but, unlike discussions in the United States, heated debates and confrontations are unusual. Italian, German, and French executives don't soften up colleagues with praise before they criticize—doing so seems manipulative to them. However, professionals from high-context cultures, such as Japan or China, tend to be less direct.[57]

Business correspondence in other countries is often more formal than the style used by U.S. businesspeople (see Figure 3.6). Of course, if you carry formality to extremes, you'll sound unnatural.

Business correspondence is often more formal in other countries than it is in the United States.

FIGURE 3.6
Effective German Business Letter (Translated)
In Germany, business letters usually open with a reference to the business relationship and close with a compliment to the recipient. In this letter written by a supplier to a nearby retailer, you can see that the tone is more formal than would typically be used in the United States.

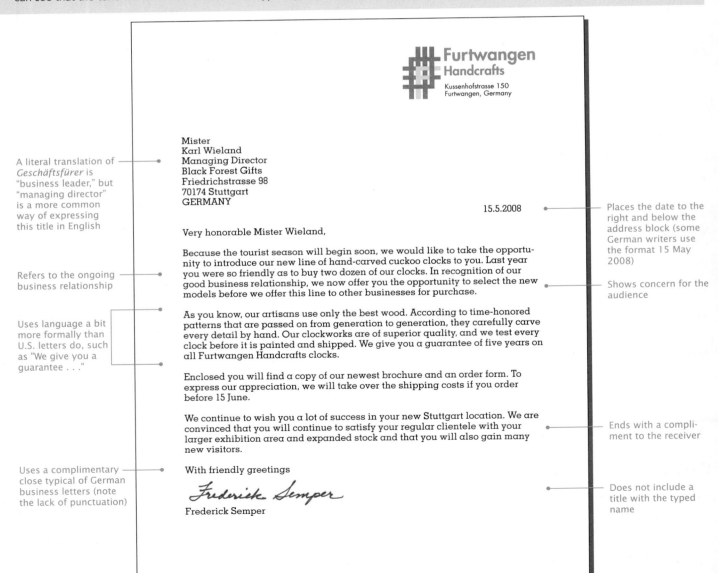

A literal translation of *Geschäftsfürer* is "business leader," but "managing director" is a more common way of expressing this title in English

Refers to the ongoing business relationship

Uses language a bit more formally than U.S. letters do, such as "We give you a guarantee . . ."

Uses a complimentary close typical of German business letters (note the lack of punctuation)

Places the date to the right and below the address block (some German writers use the format 15 May 2008)

Shows concern for the audience

Ends with a compliment to the receiver

Does not include a title with the typed name

Furtwangen Handcrafts
Kussenhofstrasse 150
Furtwangen, Germany

Mister
Karl Wieland
Managing Director
Black Forest Gifts
Friedrichstrasse 98
70174 Stuttgart
GERMANY

15.5.2008

Very honorable Mister Wieland,

Because the tourist season will begin soon, we would like to take the opportunity to introduce our new line of hand-carved cuckoo clocks to you. Last year you were so friendly as to buy two dozen of our clocks. In recognition of our good business relationship, we now offer you the opportunity to select the new models before we offer this line to other businesses for purchase.

As you know, our artisans use only the best wood. According to time-honored patterns that are passed on from generation to generation, they carefully carve every detail by hand. Our clockworks are of superior quality, and we test every clock before it is painted and shipped. We give you a guarantee of five years on all Furtwangen Handcrafts clocks.

Enclosed you will find a copy of our newest brochure and an order form. To express our appreciation, we will take over the shipping costs if you order before 15 June.

We continue to wish you a lot of success in your new Stuttgart location. We are convinced that you will continue to satisfy your regular clientele with your larger exhibition area and expanded stock and that you will also gain many new visitors.

With friendly greetings

Frederick Semper

Frederick Semper

Writing and Speaking Clearly

When writing to businesspeople from another culture, familiarize yourself with their communication preferences and adapt your approach, style, and tone to meet their expectations. Follow these recommendations:[58]

- **Use simple, precise language.** For instance, the word *rich* has at least half a dozen different meanings, whereas *wealthy* has exactly one, leaving no room for ambiguity.

- **Be brief.** Use simple sentences and short paragraphs, breaking information into smaller chunks that are easier for your reader to capture and translate.[59]

- **Use transitional elements.** Help readers follow your train of thought by using plenty of transitional words and phrases.

- **Address international correspondence properly.** Refer to Tables A.3 through A.5 in Appendix A for an explanation of different address elements and salutations commonly used in certain foreign countries.

- **Cite numbers and dates carefully.** In the United States, 12-05-08 means December 5, 2008, but in many other countries (and in some professions in the United States), it means May 12, 2008. Dates in Japan and China are usually expressed with the year first, followed by the month and then the day. Similarly, 1.000 means one with three decimal places in the United States and Great Britain, but it means one thousand in many European countries.

- **Avoid slang, idiomatic phrases, and business jargon.** Everyday speech and writing are full of slang and **idiomatic phrases**, phrases that mean more than the sum of their literal parts. Examples from U.S. English include "off the top of my head" and "more bang for the buck." Your audience may have no idea what you're talking about when you use such phrases.

- **Avoid humor and other references to popular culture.** Jokes and references to popular entertainment usually rely on subtle cultural issues that might be completely unknown to your audience.

Speaking clearly and getting plenty of feedback are two of the keys to successful intercultural conversations.

Although some of these differences may seem trivial, meeting the expectations of an international audience illustrates knowledge of and respect for the other cultures (see Figures 3.7 and 3.8).

To be more effective in intercultural conversations, remember these tips: (1) Speak slowly and clearly separate each word; (2) don't rephrase until it's obviously necessary (immediately rephrasing something you've just said doubles the translation workload for the listener); (3) look for and ask for feedback to make sure your message is getting through; (4) don't talk down to the other person by overenunciating words or oversimplifying sentences; and (5) at the end of the conversation, double-check to make sure you and the listener agree on what has been said and decided.

Listening Carefully

Languages vary considerably in the significance of tone, pitch, speed, and volume. The English word *progress* can be a noun or a verb, depending on which syllable you accent. In Chinese, the meaning of the word *mà* changes

Experienced international speakers such as Google CEO Eric Schmidt are careful to incorporate culture and language variations into their communication efforts.

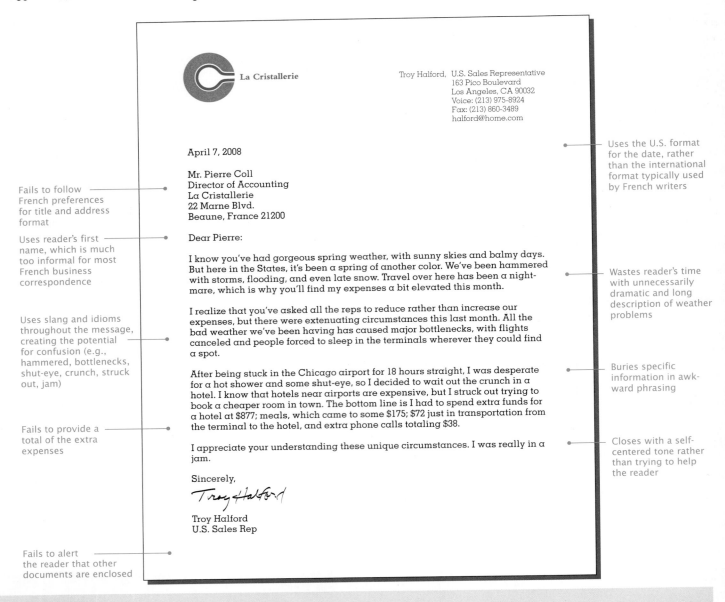

Uses the U.S. format for the date, rather than the international format typically used by French writers

Fails to follow French preferences for title and address format

Uses reader's first name, which is much too informal for most French business correspondence

Uses slang and idioms throughout the message, creating the potential for confusion (e.g., hammered, bottlenecks, shut-eye, crunch, struck out, jam)

Wastes reader's time with unnecessarily dramatic and long description of weather problems

Buries specific information in awkward phrasing

Fails to provide a total of the extra expenses

Closes with a self-centered tone rather than trying to help the reader

Fails to alert the reader that other documents are enclosed

FIGURE 3.7
Ineffective Intercultural Letter
This letter from a U.S. sales representative to a manager in France exhibits several intercultural mistakes, including the informal tone and use of American slang. Compare this with the improved version in Figure 3.8.

depending on the speaker's tone; it can mean *mother*, *pileup*, *horse*, or *scold*. Regular Arabic speech can sound excited or angry to an English-speaking U.S. listener.[60] Conversely, businesspeople from Japan tend to speak more softly than Westerners.

To listen more effectively in intercultural situations, accept what you hear without judgment and let people finish what they have to say.

With some practice, you can start to get a sense of vocal patterns. The key is simply to accept what you hear first, without jumping to conclusions about meaning or motivation. Let other people finish what they have to say. If you interrupt, you may miss something important. You'll also show a lack of respect. If you do not understand a comment, ask the person to repeat it. Any momentary awkwardness you might feel in asking for extra help is less important than the risk of unsuccessful communication.

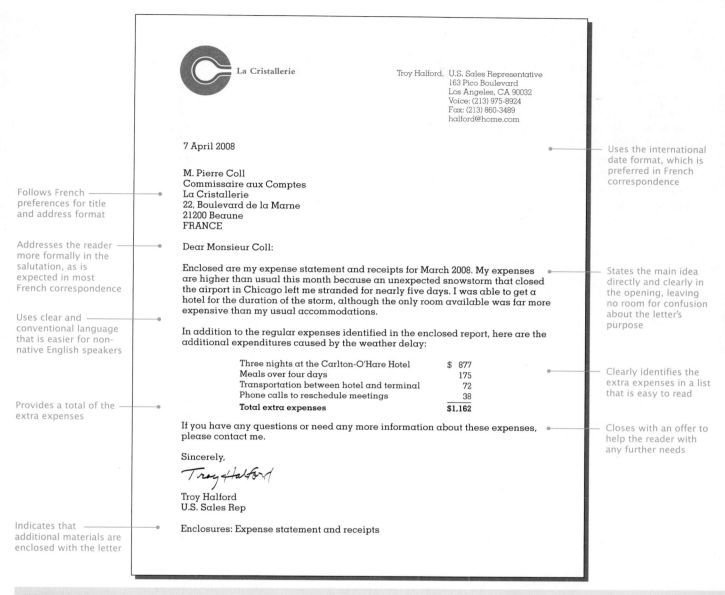

La Cristallerie

Troy Halford, U.S. Sales Representative
163 Pico Boulevard
Los Angeles, CA 90032
Voice: (213) 975-8924
Fax: (213) 860-3489
halford@home.com

7 April 2008

M. Pierre Coll
Commissaire aux Comptes
La Cristallerie
22, Boulevard de la Marne
21200 Beaune
FRANCE

Dear Monsieur Coll:

Enclosed are my expense statement and receipts for March 2008. My expenses are higher than usual this month because an unexpected snowstorm that closed the airport in Chicago left me stranded for nearly five days. I was able to get a hotel for the duration of the storm, although the only room available was far more expensive than my usual accommodations.

In addition to the regular expenses identified in the enclosed report, here are the additional expenditures caused by the weather delay:

Three nights at the Carlton-O'Hare Hotel	$ 877
Meals over four days	175
Transportation between hotel and terminal	72
Phone calls to reschedule meetings	38
Total extra expenses	**$1,162**

If you have any questions or need any more information about these expenses, please contact me.

Sincerely,

Troy Halford
Troy Halford
U.S. Sales Rep

Enclosures: Expense statement and receipts

*Annotations (left):*
Follows French preferences for title and address format

Addresses the reader more formally in the salutation, as is expected in most French correspondence

Uses clear and conventional language that is easier for non-native English speakers

Provides a total of the extra expenses

Indicates that additional materials are enclosed with the letter

*Annotations (right):*
Uses the international date format, which is preferred in French correspondence

States the main idea directly and clearly in the opening, leaving no room for confusion about the letter's purpose

Clearly identifies the extra expenses in a list that is easy to read

Closes with an offer to help the reader with any further needs

FIGURE 3.8
Effective Intercultural Letter
This version of the letter to a manager in France follows French standards for correspondence and is also easier to read and to scan.

Using Interpreters, Translators, and Translation Software

You may encounter business situations that require using an *interpreter* (for spoken communication) or a *translator* (for written communications). In addition, most customers expect to be addressed in their native language, particularly concerning advertising, warranties, repair and maintenance manuals, and product labels—and local government regulations may require it.

Keeping up with current language usage in a given country or culture is also critical. Landor Associates, a leading marketing agency, usually engages three native-language speakers to review translated materials to make sure the sense of the message is compatible with current usage and slang.[61] Some companies also use *back-translation* to ensure accuracy. Once a translator encodes a message into another language, a different translator retranslates the message into the original language.

✓ CHECKLIST: Improving Intercultural Communication Skills

✓ Study other cultures so that you can appreciate cultural variations.

✓ Study the languages of people with whom you communicate, even if you can learn only a few basic words and phrases.

✓ Help nonnative speakers learn your language.

✓ Respect cultural preferences for communication style.

✓ Write clearly, using brief messages, simple language, generous transitions, and appropriate international conventions.

✓ Avoid slang, humor, and references to popular culture.

✓ Speak clearly and slowly, giving listeners time to translate your words.

✓ Ask for feedback to ensure successful communication.

✓ Listen carefully and ask speakers to repeat anything you don't understand.

✓ Use interpreters and translators for important messages.

Machine translation uses computerized intelligence (such as software or specialized websites) to translate material from one language to another.

This back-translation is then compared with the original message to uncover any errors or discrepancies.

The time and cost required for professional translation has encouraged the development of **machine translation**, any form of computerized intelligence used to translate one language to another. Dedicated software tools and online services such as WorldLingo (www.worldlingo.com) offer some form of automated translation. Major search engines such as AltaVista and Google let you request a translated version of the websites you find. Although none of these tools promises translation quality on a par with human translators, they can be quite useful with individual words and short phrases, and they can give you the overall gist of a message.[62]

Helping Others Adapt to Your Culture

Whether a younger person is unaccustomed to the formalities of a large corporation or a colleague from another country is working on a team with you, look for opportunities to help people fit in and adapt their communication style. For example, if a nonnative English speaker is making mistakes that could hurt his or her credibility, you can offer advice on the appropriate words and phrases to use. Most language learners truly appreciate this sort of assistance, as long as it is offered in a respectful manner. Moreover, chances are that while you're helping, you'll learn something about the other person's culture and language, too.

You can also take steps to simplify the communication process. For example, oral communication in a second language is usually more difficult than written forms, so instead of asking a foreign colleague to provide information in a conference call, you could set up an intranet site where the person can file a written report. Similarly, using instant messaging, e-mail, or blogging is often easier for colleagues with different native languages than participating in live conversations.

For a brief summary of ideas to improve intercultural communication in the workplace, see "Checklist: Improving Intercultural Communication Skills."

On the Job

SOLVING COMMUNICATION DILEMMAS AT IBM

Ron Glover is responsible for overall diversity planning and strategy at IBM, but every manager throughout the company is expected to foster a climate of inclusion and support for employees of every cultural background. As a team leader in one of IBM's software development labs, you're learning to exercise sound business judgment and use good listening skills to help resolve situations that arise within your diverse group of employees. How would you address each of these challenges?

1. Joo Mi Kang, a recent immigrant from South Korea, is a brilliant programmer who continues to impress everyone with her technical innovations. Unfortunately, she usually doesn't do a good job of documenting her code, an admittedly tedious process in which programmers are supposed to write descriptions of what they've created and explain how it works so that other people can come in later and fix it if needed. You suspect from seeing some of her e-mails that she has trouble writing in English. What should your first step be?

   a. Send her an e-mail reminding her of the need to document her code; attach a copy of her job description.
   b. Suggest that she find a tutor to help her develop her English skills.
   c. Visit her in her office and discuss the situation; ask if she understands the importance of documenting her code and whether she has encountered any difficulty in doing so.
   d. Assign several other programmers the task of pitching in to take care of her documentation chores.

2. Your employees are breaking into ethnically based cliques. Members of ethnic groups eat together, socialize together, and often chat in their native languages while they work. You appreciate how these groups give their members a sense of community, but you worry that these informal communication channels are alienating nonmembers and fragmenting the flow of information. How do you encourage a stronger sense of community and teamwork across your department?

   a. Ban the use of languages other than English at work.
   b. Do nothing. This is normal behavior, and any attempt to disrupt it will only generate resentment.
   c. Structure work assignments and other activities (such as volunteer projects) in ways that bring people from the various cultural groups into regular contact with one another and make them more dependent on one another as well.
   d. Send all your employees to diversity training classes.

3. Vasily Pevsner, a Russian immigrant, has worked in the department for five years. He works well alone, but he resists working with other employees, even in team settings where collaboration is expected. How do you handle the situation?

   a. Stay out of the way and let the situation resolve itself. Pevsner has to learn how to get along with the other team members.
   b. Tell the rest of the team to work harder at getting along with Pevsner.
   c. Tell Pevsner he must work with others or he will not progress in the company.
   d. Talk privately with Pevsner and help him understand the importance of working together as a team. During the conversation, try to uncover why he doesn't participate more in team efforts.

4. IBM boasts one of the most highly educated workforces in the world, and your department is no exception. However, you've been surprised at the confusion that some of your memos and other written messages have generated lately. You suspect your casual and often humorous writing style might be the culprit and decide to "test drive" a different writing style. You've drafted four versions of a blog posting that explains a new policy aimed at keeping software projects on schedule as they near completion. Which of these do you choose and why?

   a. "As each new project nears completion, I recognize how hard you all try to keep projects on schedule, even with the last-minute problems that are always part of software projects. To lighten your workload during the hectic final phase, you'll no longer be expected to attend routine department meetings or tend to other nonessential tasks during the final four weeks of each project."
   b. "As each new project races toward the finish line, I appreciate that all of you work like dogs to keep projects on schedule, even with the inevitable glitches and gremlins that always seem to attack software projects at the last minute. Good news: During the last four weeks of every project, you'll be excused from nonessential tasks such as routine department meetings so that you can focus on your programming work (admit it—I know you hate coming to these meetings anyway!)."
   c. "As usual, the solution to all of life's problems can be found on television! While watching the Raiders–Chiefs game yesterday, I realized that we need to have our own version of the two-minute drill. To help avoid schedule slippage during the crazy final few weeks of each project, team members will be excused from routine meetings and other nonessential tasks not directly related to their project responsibilities."
   d. "As you should all be aware, numerous entities both internal and external to the corporation rely on us for timely project completion. While the inherent nature of software development presents unexpected difficulties during the final stages of a project, it is incumbent upon us to employ every tactic possible to avoid significant completion delays. Henceforth, team members will be excused from nonessential tasks during the final four weeks of every development project."

Learning Objectives Checkup

Assess your understanding of the principles in this chapter by reading each learning objective and studying the accompanying exercises. For fill-in-the-blank items, write the missing text in the blank provided; for multiple-choice items, circle the letter of the correct answer. You can check your responses against the answer key on page AK-1.

Objective 3.1: Discuss the opportunities and challenges of intercultural communication.

1. Which of the following factors is a significant reason U.S. business professionals often need to understand the cultures of other countries?
   a. Recent changes to government regulations require cultural education before companies are granted export licenses.
   b. The U.S. economy has been shrinking for the past 20 years, forcing companies to look overseas.
   c. Many countries require business executives to be fluent in at least two languages.
   d. Thousands of U.S. companies, including many of the largest corporations in the country, rely on markets in other countries for a significant portion of their sales.

2. Which of the following is a benefit of a multicultural workforce?
   a. Providing a broader range of viewpoints and ideas
   b. Giving companies a better understanding of diverse markets
   c. Enabling companies to recruit workers from the broadest possible pool of talent
   d. All of the above

3. A culturally rich workforce, composed of employees representing a wide range of ethnicities, religions, ages, physical abilities, languages, and other factors
   a. Always slows down the decision-making process
   b. Can be more challenging to manage but can pay off in a variety of important ways
   c. Is easier to manage because so many new ideas are present
   d. Is a concern only for companies that do business outside the United States

Objective 3.2: Define culture, and explain how culture is learned.

4. Culture is defined as
   a. A distinct group that exists within a country
   b. A shared system of symbols, beliefs, attitudes, values, expectations, and norms for behavior
   c. The pattern of cues and stimuli that convey meaning between two or more people
   d. Serious art forms such as classical music, painting, sculpture, drama, and poetry

5. Which of the following is *not* an example of a cultural group?
   a. Hindus

   b. Wrestling fans
   c. Television viewers
   d. Members of a fraternity

6. Culture is learned from
   a. Family members
   b. Explicit teaching by others in the culture
   c. Observations of the behavior of others in the culture
   d. All of the above

Objective 3.3: Define ethnocentrism and stereotyping, and give three suggestions for overcoming these limiting mindsets.

7. _____ is the tendency to judge all other groups according to the standards, behaviors, and customs of one's own group.

8. _____ is the mistake of assigning a wide range of generalized attributes to individuals on the basis of their membership in a particular culture or social group, without considering an individual's unique characteristics.

9. Which of the following is one of several techniques you can use to make sure you don't fall into the traps of ethnocentrism and stereotyping?
   a. Minimize interactions with people whose cultures you don't understand.
   b. Make sure that the people you work with clearly understand your culture.
   c. Insist that every employee who works for you strictly follows the company's guidelines for intercultural communication.
   d. Avoiding making assumptions about people in other cultures.

Objective 3.4: Explain the importance of recognizing cultural variations, and list eight categories of cultural differences.

10. In business, recognizing cultural differences is important because
    a. Doing so helps reduce the chances for misunderstanding
    b. Someone from another culture may try to take advantage of your ignorance
    c. If you don't, you'll be accused of being politically incorrect
    d. Doing so helps you become more ethnocentric

11. An example of low-context cultural communication would be
    a. Someone from China using metaphors to convey meaning
    b. Someone from Greece insisting on reaching agreement on every detail of a deal
    c. Someone from Canada vigorously arguing his point of view in a problem-solving situation
    d. Someone from Japan encouraging socializing before entering into official negotiations

12. Which of the following is generally true about high-context cultures?
    a. Employees work shorter hours in such cultures because context allows them to communicate less often.
    b. People rely less on verbal communication and more on the context of nonverbal actions and environmental setting to convey meaning.
    c. People rely more on verbal communication and less on the context of nonverbal actions and environmental setting to convey meaning.
    d. The rules of everyday life are explicitly taught to all people within the culture.
13. Contextual differences between cultures refer to
    a. The degree to which various cultures rely on verbal or nonverbal actions to convey meaning
    b. Whether cultures emphasize written or spoken communication
    c. The role of the Internet (including e-mail and instant messaging) in international communication
    d. Attitudes toward work and success
14. Differing attitudes toward greetings, personal space, touching, facial expression, eye contact, posture, and formality are common examples of _____ differences between cultures.

Objective 3.5: Discuss steps you can take to improve your intercultural communication skills.

15. When communicating orally to those who speak English as a second language, you should make it a habit to always
    a. Immediately rephrase every important point you make in order to the give your listeners two options to choose from
    b. Speak louder if listeners don't seem to understand you
    c. Ignore the other person's body language
    d. Rephrase your key points if you observe body language that suggests a lack of understanding

Objective 3.6: Outline strategies for studying other cultures.

16. Understanding the nuances of a culture can take years to learn, so the best approach when preparing to communicate with people in a culture that you don't know well is to
    a. Learn as much as you can from websites, travel guides, and other resources and not be afraid to ask for help while you are communicating in that new culture
    b. Learn as much as you can from websites, travel guides, and other resources but never ask for help because doing so will only show everyone how ignorant you are
    c. Learn as much as you can from TV shows and movies that feature the other culture; the combination of spoken words, visuals, and music is the best way to learn a culture
    d. Not worry about cultural variations; you'll never have time to understand them all, so your energy is better spent on other business issues

Objective 3.7: List seven recommendations for writing clearly in multilanguage business environments.

17. When writing for audiences who don't speak the same native language as you speak, you can improve communication by
    a. Spelling out numbers rather than writing them as figures
    b. Using simple sentences and careful word choices
    c. Using long paragraphs to reduce the number of visual breaks on the page
    d. Doing all of the above
18. When you are writing for multilanguage audiences, humor
    a. Should be used often because it makes your audience feel welcome on a personal level
    b. Should rarely, if ever, be used because humor is one of the most difficult elements of communication to encode or decode in a second language
    c. Should never be used because movies and other entertainment products rarely cross over national boundaries
    d. Should be used at least once per letter to show that you appreciate your audience as human beings

Apply Your Knowledge

1. What are some of the intercultural differences that managers of a U.S.-based firm might encounter during a series of business meetings with a China-based company whose managers speak English fairly well?
2. What are some of the intercultural communication issues to consider when deciding whether to accept a job in an overseas branch of a U.S. company? How about a job in the United States with a local branch of a foreign-owned firm? Explain.
3. How do you think company managers from a country that has a relatively homogeneous culture might react when they do business with the culturally diverse staff of a company based in a less homogeneous country? Explain your answer.
4. Your company has relocated to a U.S. city where Vietnamese culture is strongly established. Many of your employees will be from this culture. What can you do to improve communication between your management and the Vietnamese Americans you are currently hiring?
5. **Ethical Choices** Your office in Turkey desperately needs the supplies that have been sitting in Turkish customs for a month. Should you bribe a customs official to speed up delivery? Explain your decision.

Practice Your Knowledge

MESSAGE FOR ANALYSIS

Your boss wants to send a brief e-mail message welcoming employees recently transferred to your department from the company's Hong Kong branch. They all speak English, but your boss asks you to review his message for clarity. What would you suggest your boss change in the following e-mail message—and why? Would you consider this message to be audience centered? Why or why not?

I wanted to welcome you ASAP to our little family here in the States. It's high time we shook hands in person and not just across the sea. I'm pleased as punch about getting to know you all, and I for one will do my level best to sell you on America.

EXERCISES

For active links to all websites discussed in this chapter, visit this text's website at **www.prenhall.com/thill**. Locate your book and click on its "Companion Website" link. Then select Chapter 3 and click on "Featured Websites." Locate the name of the page or the URL related to the material in the text. Please note that links to sites that become inactive after publication of the book will be removed from the "Featured Websites" section.

3.1 Intercultural Sensitivity: Recognizing Variations You represent a Canadian toy company that's negotiating to buy miniature truck wheels from a manufacturer in Osaka, Japan. In your first meeting, you explain that your company expects to control the design of the wheels as well as the materials that are used to make them. The manufacturer's representative looks down and says softly, "Perhaps that will be difficult." You press for agreement, and to emphasize your willingness to buy, you show the prepared contract you've brought with you. However, the manufacturer seems increasingly vague and uninterested. What cultural differences may be interfering with effective communication in this situation? Explain.

3.2 Ethical Choices A U.S. manager wants to ship machine parts to a West African country, but a government official there expects a special payment before allowing the shipment into the country. How can the two sides resolve their different approaches without violating U.S. rules against bribing foreign officials? On the basis of the information presented in Chapter 1, would you consider this situation an ethical dilemma or an ethical lapse? Please explain.

3.3 Teamwork Working with two other students, prepare a list of 10 examples of slang (in your own language) that might be misinterpreted or misunderstood during a business conversation with someone from another culture. Next to each example, suggest other words you might use to convey the same message. Do the

alternatives mean *exactly* the same as the original slang or idiom?

3.4 Intercultural Communication: Studying Cultures Choose a specific country, such as India, Portugal, Bolivia, Thailand, or Nigeria, with which you are not familiar. Research the culture and write a brief summary of what a U.S. manager would need to know about concepts of personal space and rules of social behavior in order to conduct business successfully in that country.

3.5 Multicultural Workforce: Bridging Differences Differences in gender, age, and physical abilities contribute to the diversity of today's workforce. Working with a classmate, role-play a conversation in which
  a. A woman is being interviewed for a job by a male personnel manager
  b. An older person is being interviewed for a job by a younger personnel manager
  c. An employee who is a native speaker of English is being interviewed for a job by a hiring manager who is a recent immigrant with relatively poor English skills
How did differences between the applicant and the interviewer shape the communication? What can you do to improve communication in such situations?

3.6 Intercultural Sensitivity: Understanding Attitudes As the director of marketing for a telecommunications firm based in Germany, you're negotiating with an official in Guangzhou, China, who's in charge of selecting a new telephone system for the city. You insist that the specifications be spelled out in the contract. However, your Chinese counterpart seems to have little interest in technical and financial details. What can you do or say to break this intercultural deadlock and obtain the contract so that both parties are comfortable?

3.7 Cultural Variations: Ability Differences You are a new manager at K & J Brick, a masonry products company that is now run by the two sons of the man who founded it 50 years ago. For years, the co-owners have invited the management team to a wilderness lodge for a combination of outdoor sports and annual business planning meetings. You don't want to miss the event, but you know that the outdoor activities weren't designed for someone with your physical impairments. Draft a short memo to the rest of the management team, suggesting changes to the annual event that will allow all managers to participate.

3.8 Culture and Time: Dealing with Variations When a company knows that a scheduled delivery time given by an overseas firm is likely to be flexible, managers may buy in larger quantities or may order more often to avoid running out of product before the next delivery. Identify three other management decisions that may be influenced by differing cultural concepts of time and describe them in a brief e-mail message to your instructor.

3.9 Intercultural Communication: Using Interpreters Imagine that you're the lead negotiator for a company that's trying to buy a factory in Prague, the capital of the Czech Republic. Although you haven't spent much time in the country in the past decade, your parents grew up near Prague, so you understand and speak the language fairly well. However, you wonder about the advantages and disadvantages of using an interpreter anyway. For example, you may have more time to think if you wait for an intermediary to translate the other side's position. Decide whether to hire an interpreter and then write a brief e-mail message (two or three paragraphs) explaining your decision.

3.10 Internet: Translation Software Explore the powers and limitations of computer translation at Babel Fish, http://babelfish.altavista.com. In the box labeled "Translate a block of text," enter a sentence such as "We are enclosing a purchase order for four dozen computer monitors." In the drop-down menu choose "English to Spanish" and click on "Translate." Once you've read the Spanish version, cut and paste it into the "text for translation" box, select "Spanish to English," and click on "Translate." Try translating the same English sentence into German, French, or Italian and then back into English. How do the results of each translation differ? What are the implications for the use of automated translation services and back-translation? How could you use this website to sharpen your intercultural communication skills? Summarize your findings in a brief report.

3.11 Intercultural Communication: Improving Skills You've been assigned to host a group of Swedish col-lege students who are visiting your college for the next two weeks. They've all studied English, but this is their first trip to your area. Make a list of at least eight slang terms and idioms they are likely to hear on campus. How will you explain each phrase? When speaking with the Swedish students, what word or words might you substitute for each slang term or idiom?

3.12 Intercultural Communication: Podcasting Your company was one of the first to use the Apple iPod and other digital music players as business communication tools. Executives often record messages (such as monthly sales reports) as digital audio files and post them on the company's intranet site, a technique known as *podcasting*. Employees from the 14 offices in Europe, Asia, and North America then download the files to their music players and listen to the messages while riding the train to work, eating lunch at their desks, and so on. Your boss asks you to draft the opening statement for a podcast that will announce a revenue drop caused by intensive competitive pressure. She reviews your script and hands it back with a gentle explanation that it needs to be revised for international listeners. Improve the following statement in as many ways as you can:

> *Howdy, comrades. Shouldn't surprise anyone that we took a beating this year, given the insane pricing moves our knucklehead competitors have been making. I mean, how those clowns can keep turning a profit is beyond me, what with steel costs still going through the roof and labor costs heating up—even in countries where every-body goes to find cheap labor—and hazardous waste disposal regs adding to operating costs, too.*

Expand Your Knowledge

LEARNING MORE ON THE WEB
CULTURAL SAVVY FOR COMPETITIVE ADVANTAGE

www.executiveplanet.com

Want to be more competitive when doing business across bor-ders? Executive Planet offers quick introductions to expected business practices in a number of countries, from setting up appointments to giving gifts to negotiating deals. Visit www.executiveplanet.com and browse the country reports to answer the following questions.

1. What sort of clothes should you pack for a business trip to Mexico that will include both meetings and social events?
2. You've been trying to sell your products to a Saudi Arabian company whose executives treat you to an extravagant evening of dining and entertainment. Can you take this as a positive sign that they're likely to buy from you?

3. You collect antique clocks as a hobby, and you plan to give one of your favorites to the president of a Chinese company you plan to visit. Would such a gift likely help or hurt your relationship with this person?

SURFING YOUR WAY TO CAREER SUCCESS

Bovée and Thill's Business Communication Headline News offers links to hundreds of online resources that can help you with this course, your other college courses, and your career. Visit www.businesscommunicationblog.com and click on "Web Directory." The "Intercultural Communication" section connects you to a variety of websites and articles on intercultural communication, international business etiquette, English as a second language, and language barriers. Identify three websites from this section that could be useful in your business career. For each site, write a two-sentence summary of what the site offers and how it could help you launch and build your career.

Learn Interactively

INTERACTIVE STUDY GUIDE

Visit www.prenhall.com/thill, then locate your book and click on its "Companion Website" link. Select Chapter 3 to take advantage of the interactive "Chapter Quiz" to test your knowledge of chapter concepts. Receive instant feedback on whether you need additional studying. Also, visit the "Study Hall," where you'll find an abundance of valuable resources that will help you succeed in this course.

PEAK PERFORMANCE GRAMMAR AND MECHANICS

If your instructor has required the use of "Peak Performance Grammar and Mechanics," either in your online course or on CD, you can improve your skill with verbs by using the "Peak Performance Grammar and Mechanics" module. Click on "Grammar Basics" and then "Verbs." Take the Pretest to determine whether you have any weak areas. Then review those areas in the Refresher Course. Take the Follow-Up Test to check your grasp of verbs. For an extra challenge or advanced practice, take the Advanced Test. Finally, for additional reinforcement, go to the "Improve Your Grammar, Mechanics, and Usage" section that follows and complete those exercises.

Improve Your Grammar, Mechanics, and Usage

The following exercises help you improve your knowledge of and power over English grammar, mechanics, and usage. Turn to the Handbook of Grammar, Mechanics, and Usage at the end of this book and review all of Section 1.3 (Verbs). Then look at the following 10 items. Circle the letter of the preferred choice in the following groups of sentences. (Answers to these exercises appear on page AK-3.)

1. Which sentence contains a verb in the present perfect form?
   a. I became the resident expert on repairing the copy machine.
   b. I have become the resident expert on repairing the copy machine.
2. Which sentence contains a verb in the simple past form?
   a. She knows how to conduct an audit when she came to work for us.
   b. She knew how to conduct an audit when she came to work for us.
3. Which sentence contains a verb in the simple future form?
   a. Next week, call John to tell him what you will do to help him set up the seminar.
   b. Next week, call John to tell him what you will be doing to help him set up the seminar.
4. Which sentence is in the active voice?
   a. The report will be written by Leslie Cartwright.
   b. Leslie Cartwright will write the report.
5. Which sentence is in the passive voice?
   a. The failure to record the transaction was mine.
   b. I failed to record the transaction.
6. Which sentence contains the correct verb form?
   a. Everyone upstairs receives mail before we do.
   b. Everyone upstairs receive mail before we do.
7. Which sentence contains the correct verb form?
   a. Neither the main office nor the branches is blameless.
   b. Neither the main office nor the branches are blameless.
8. Which sentence contains the correct verb form?
   a. C&B Sales are listed in the directory.
   b. C&B Sales is listed in the directory.
9. Which sentence contains the correct verb form?
   a. When measuring shelves, 7 inches is significant.
   b. When measuring shelves, 7 inches are significant.
10. Which sentence contains the correct verb form?
    a. About 90 percent of the employees plans to come to the company picnic.
    b. About 90 percent of the employees plan to come to the company picnic.

For additional exercises focusing on verbs, go to www.prenhall.com/thill, then locate your text and click on its "Companion Website" link. Click on Chapter 3, click on "Additional Exercises to Improve Grammar, Mechanics and Usage," and then click on "5. Verb tenses," "6. Transitive and intransitive verbs," or "7. Voice of verbs."

Part II

Applying the Three-Step Writing Process

Planning Business Messages

Learning Objectives

AFTER STUDYING THIS CHAPTER, YOU WILL BE ABLE TO

1 Describe the three-step writing process

2 Explain why it's important to define your purpose carefully and list four questions that can help you test that purpose

3 Describe the importance of analyzing your audience and identify the six factors you should consider when developing an audience profile

4 Discuss gathering information for simple messages and identify three attributes of quality information

5 List factors to consider when choosing the most appropriate medium for your message

6 Explain why good organization is important to both you and your audience

7 Summarize the process for organizing business messages effectively

On the Job

COMMUNICATING AT THE COMPLETE IDIOT'S GUIDES

BUILDING A PUBLISHING EMPIRE BY PUTTING THE READER FIRST

How many times have you become frustrated with some new electronic device, turned to the user manual for help—and gotten even more frustrated?

Joe Kraynak, the successful writer of such helpful books as *The Complete Idiot's Guide to PCs* and *The Complete Idiot's Guide to Microsoft Office 2000*, is on your side. He thinks people are right to criticize the manuals that come with personal computers, mobile phones, and other complex products. Many high-tech products make intelligent people feel, well, like idiots. That frustration with ineffective attempts at explaining complex topics has fueled the rapid growth of the cheekily titled *Idiot's Guide* series, which now covers hundreds of subjects.

In Kraynak's mind, the problem is that too many product manuals are written without enough attention to the reader's real needs. The engineers or technicians who often do the writing are intimately familiar

Its tongue-in-cheek name aside, the Idiot's Guide *series has grown to hundreds of volumes on the strength of its clear, audience-focused writing.*

with their products and technologies, and they sometimes mistakenly assume that readers are, too. This disregard for what readers need can lead not only to inadequate explanations of new topics but also to overuse of befuddling jargon and acronyms. Moreover, too many manuals focus on descriptions of products when what readers really want are explanations of how to use them.

"I try to put myself in the shoes of a new user, to think like somebody I know," says Kraynak. He advises other writers to do the same. What essential information do your readers need first? Which less-important details can wait until later? What style of writing will be most effective? You may not write books on the latest high-tech gadgets, but all business messages can suffer from the same flaws that plague so many user manuals. Follow Kraynak's example, and your readers will grow to count on you for clear messages, too.[1]

www.idiotsguides.com

UNDERSTANDING THE THREE-STEP WRITING PROCESS

The problems that Joe Kraynak (profiled in the chapter opener) describes aren't limited to high-tech product manuals. All too often, people writing about finances, government regulations, business processes, and other important topics fail to understand and accommodate their readers' needs. The result is confusing, frustrating messages that don't help the reader—or the writer, for that matter. Fortunately, by following a proven process, you can learn to create effective messages that will not only satisfy audience needs but also highlight your skills as a perceptive, quality-conscious business leader.

Following the three-step writing process (see Figure 4.1) will help ensure that your messages are *effective* (meeting your audience's needs and getting your points across) and *efficient* (making the best use of your time and your audience's time).

The three-step writing process consists of planning, writing, and completing a message.

- **Step 1: Planning business messages.** To plan any message, first *analyze the situation* by defining your purpose and developing a profile of your audience. Once you're sure what you need to accomplish with your message, *gather information* that will meet your audience's needs. Next, *select the right medium* (oral, written, visual, or electronic) to deliver your message. With those three factors in place, you're ready to *organize the information* by defining your main idea, limiting your scope, selecting a direct or an indirect approach, and outlining your content. Planning messages is the focus of this chapter.

- **Step 2: Writing business messages.** Once you've planned your message, *adapt to your audience*. Be sensitive to your audience's needs by adopting the "you"

FIGURE 4.1
The Three-Step Writing Process
This three-step process will help you create more effective messages in any medium. As you get more practice with the process, it will become easier and more automatic.

Planning

Analyze the Situation
Define your purpose and develop an audience profile.

Gather Information
Determine audience needs and obtain the information necessary to satisfy those needs.

Select the Right Medium
Select the best medium for delivering your message.

Organize the Information
Define your main idea, limit your scope, select a direct or an indirect approach, and outline your content.

1

Writing

Adapt to Your Audience
Be sensitive to audience needs, by using a "you" attitude, politeness, positive emphasis, and bias-free language. Build a strong relationship with your audience by establishing your credibility and projecting your image. Control your style with a conversational tone, plain English, and appropriate voice.

Compose the Message
Choose strong words that will help you create effective sentences and coherent paragraphs.

2

Completing

Revise the Message
Evaluate content and review readability and then edit and rewrite for conciseness and clarity.

Produce the Message
Use effective design elements and suitable layout for a clean, professional appearance.

Proofread the Message
Review for errors in layout, spelling, and mechanics.

Distribute the Message
Deliver your message using the chosen medium; make sure all documents and all relevant files are distributed successfully.

3

attitude, being polite, emphasizing the positive, and using bias-free language. Build strong relationships with your audience by establishing your credibility and projecting your company's image. Be sure to control your style by using a conversational tone, plain English, and the correct voice. Then you're ready to *compose your message* by choosing strong words, creating effective sentences, and developing coherent paragraphs. Writing business messages is discussed in Chapter 5.

- **Step 3: Completing business messages.** After writing your first draft, *revise your message* by evaluating the content, reviewing readability, and then editing and rewriting until your message comes across concisely and clearly, with correct grammar, proper punctuation, and effective format. Next, *produce your message*. Put it into the form that your audience will receive, and review all design and layout decisions for an attractive, professional appearance. *Proofread* the final draft for typos, spelling errors, and other mechanical problems. Finally, *distribute your message*, using the best combination of personal and technological tools. Completing business messages is discussed in Chapter 6.

Throughout this book, you'll learn how to apply these steps to a wide variety of business messages: short messages such as e-mails and blog postings (Chapters 7 through 10), longer messages such as reports (Chapters 11 through 13), oral presentations (Chapter 14), and the employment messages you can use to build a great career (Chapters 15 and 16).

Optimizing Your Writing Time

The more you use the three-step writing process, the more intuitive and automatic it will become. You'll also get better at allotting your time for each task during a writing project. As a general rule, try using roughly half your time for planning and about a quarter of your time for writing. Reserve the remaining quarter of your time for completing the project, so that you don't shortchange important completion steps such as revising, producing, proofreading, and distributing.[2]

Of course, these time allotments will be significantly different for different projects. For example, if you already know your material intimately, the planning step may take less than half your time. Or, if you're delivering your message via multimedia such as a CD-ROM or an interactive website, the completion step could take far longer than a quarter of your time.

Seasoned professionals understand that there is no right or best way to write all business messages. As you work through the writing process presented in this chapter and in Chapters 5 and 6, try not to view it as a list of how-to directives but as a way to understand the various tasks involved in effective business writing.[3]

Planning Effectively

As soon as the need to create a message appears, inexperienced communicators are often tempted to dive directly into writing. However, even a few minutes of planning can sometimes save hours of rework and frustration later on. Even if you have only 20 or 30 minutes to prepare and send a message, work through all three steps quickly to ensure that your time is well used. Analyzing your audience helps you to find and assemble the facts they're looking for and to deliver that information in a concise and compelling way. Planning your message also reduces indecision as you write and helps eliminate work as you review and revise.

As a starting point, try to use half your time for planning, one-quarter for writing, and one-quarter for completing your messages.

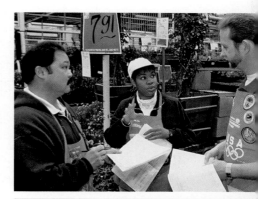

Home Depot, the world's largest home improvement retailer, keeps its operations running smoothly by carefully planning communication efforts and designing messages that meet the needs of its customers, suppliers, and employees.

Trying to save time by skimping on planning usually costs you more time in the long run.

ANALYZING YOUR SITUATION

A successful message starts with a clear purpose that connects the sender's needs with the audience's needs. Identifying your purpose and your audience is usually a straightforward task for simple, routine messages; however, this task can be more demanding in more intricate situations. For instance, if you need to communicate about a shipping problem between your Beijing and Los Angeles factories, your purpose might be simply to alert upper management to the situation, or it might involve asking the two factory managers to explore and solve the problem. These two scenarios have different purposes and different audiences, so they naturally yield dramatically different messages. If you launch directly into writing without clarifying your purpose and your audience, you'll waste time and energy, and you'll probably generate a less effective message.

Defining Your Purpose

Your general purpose may be to inform, to persuade, or to collaborate.

All business messages have a **general purpose**: to inform, to persuade, or to collaborate with the audience. This purpose helps define the overall approach you need to take, including the information you need to gather, your choice of medium (or media), and even the way you organize your message. For instance, having a clear purpose is key to the success of Joe Kraynak's work on *The Complete Idiot's Guide to Computer Basics*; he knows he isn't trying to turn readers into computer experts but, rather, is helping them understand how to use their computers more successfully.

The general purpose also determines the appropriate degree of audience participation and the amount of control you have over your message. Informing your audience requires little interaction (see Figure 4.2). Audience members absorb the information and accept or reject it, but they don't contribute to message content; you control the message. To persuade your audience, you require a moderate amount of participation, such as giving people the chance to ask questions so that you can address any doubts; nevertheless, you need to retain a moderate amount of message control. Finally, to collaborate with audience members, you need maximum participation. Your control of the message is reduced because you must adjust to new, unexpected input and reactions.

To determine the specific purpose, think of how the audience's ideas or behavior should be affected by the message.

Within the scope of its general purpose, each message also has a **specific purpose**, which identifies what you hope to accomplish with your message and what your audience should do or think after receiving your message. For instance, is your goal simply to update your audience on an event, or do you want audience members to take immediate action? State your specific purpose as precisely as possible, even identifying which audience members should respond, how they should respond, and when.

FIGURE 4.2
The Relationship Between General Purpose and Communicator Control
Your control over a message is inversely related to the degree of audience participation. The more participation from the audience, the less control you have and vice versa.

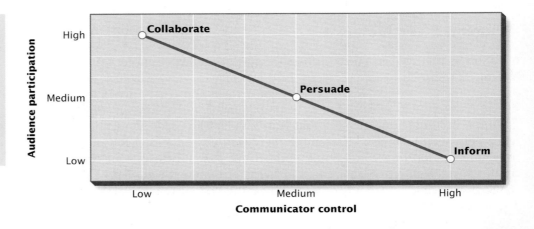

After you have defined your specific purpose, you can decide whether that purpose merits the time and effort required for you to prepare and send the message. Test your purpose by asking four questions:

- **Will anything change as a result of your message?** Make sure you don't contribute to information overload by sending messages that won't change anything. For instance, if you don't like your company's latest advertising campaign but you're not in a position to influence it, sending a critical message to your colleagues won't change anything and won't benefit anyone.

- **Is your purpose realistic?** If your purpose involves a radical shift in action or attitude, go slowly. Consider proposing a first step so that your message acts as the beginning of a learning process.

- **Is the time right?** Think through the potential impact of your message—both intentional and unintentional—to see whether this is a good time to send it. Many professions and departments have recurring cycles in their workloads, and messages sent during peak times may be ignored. Similarly, employees in departments that are in the midst of reorganization, layoffs, or other changes won't be able to give your message their full attention.

- **Is your purpose acceptable to your organization?** Your company's business objectives may dictate whether a purpose is acceptable. For instance, you may be tempted to fire off a stern reply to a particularly unpleasant customer, suggesting that the person take his or her business elsewhere, but doing so may go against your company's priorities of retaining all current customers.

When you are satisfied that you have a clear and meaningful purpose and that this is a smart time to proceed, your next step is to understand the members of your audience and their needs.

> Defer a message or do not send it at all if
> - Nothing will change as a result of sending it
> - The purpose is not realistic
> - The timing is not right
> - The purpose is not acceptable to your organization

Developing an Audience Profile

Before your audiences will take the time to read or hear your messages, they need to be interested in what you're saying. They need to see what's in it for them: How will listening to your advice or doing what you ask help them, personally or professionally? The more you know about your audience, their needs, and their expectations, the more effectively you'll be able to communicate with them.

If you're communicating with someone you know well, audience analysis is relatively easy. You can identify the person's needs and predict his or her reaction to any given message without a lot of research. On the other hand, your audience could be made up of strangers—potential customers or suppliers you've never met, a new boss, or new employees. In these situations, you need to learn more in order to adjust your message appropriately. For an example of the kind of information you need to compile in an audience analysis, see Figure 4.3. To conduct an audience analysis, take the following steps:

- **Identify your primary audience.** For some messages, certain audience members may be more important than others. Don't ignore the needs of less influential members but make sure you address the concerns of the key decision makers.

- **Determine audience size and geographic distribution.** A message aimed at 10,000 people spread around the globe will probably require a different approach than one aimed at a dozen people down the hall.

- **Determine audience composition.** Look for similarities and differences in culture, language, age, education, organizational rank and status, attitudes, experience, motivations, and any other factors that could affect the successful reception and decoding of your message.

> Ask yourself some key questions about your audience members:
> - Who are they?
> - How many people do you need to reach?
> - How much do they already know about the subject?
> - What are their expectations and preferences?
> - What is their probable reaction to your message?

FIGURE 4.3
Audience Analysis Helps You Plan Your Message
For simple, routine messages, you usually don't need to analyze your audience in depth. However, for complex messages or messages for indifferent or hostile audiences, take the time to study their information needs and potential reactions to your message.

Audience analysis notes

Project: A report recommending that we close down the on-site exercise facility and subsidize private memberships at local health clubs.

- **Primary audience:** Nicole Perazzo, vice president of operations, and her supervisory team.

- **Size and geographic distribution:** Nine managers total; Nicole and five of her staff are here on site; three other supervisors are based in Hong Kong.

- **Composition:** All have experience in operations management, but several are new to the company.

- **Level of understanding:** All will no doubt understand the financial considerations, but the newer managers may not understand the importance of the on-site exercise facility to many of our employees.

- **Expectations and preferences.** They're expecting a firm recommendation, backed up with well-thought-out financial rationale and suggestions for communicating the bad news to employees. For a decision of this magnitude, a formal report is appropriate; e-mail distribution is expected.

- **Probable reaction.** From one-on-one discussions, I know that several of the managers receiving this report are active users of the on-site facility and won't welcome the suggestion that we should shut it down. However, some nonexercisers generally think it's a luxury the company can't afford. Audience reactions will range from highly positive to highly negative; the report should focus on overcoming the highly negative reactions since they're the ones I need to convince.

If audience members have different levels of understanding of the topic, aim your message at the most influential decision makers.

- **Gauge audience members' level of understanding.** If audience members share your general background, they'll probably understand your material without difficulty. If not, your message will need an element of education, and deciding how much information to include can be a challenge. Include only enough information to accomplish the specific purpose of your message; and if the members of your audience have various levels of understanding, gear your coverage to your primary audience.

- **Understand audience expectations and preferences.** Will members of your audience expect complete details or just a summary of the main points? Do they want an e-mail message, or will they expect a formal report? In general, the higher up the organization your message goes, the fewer details people want to see, simply because they have less time to read them.

You need to take a gradual approach and have plenty of evidence to win over a skeptical audience.

- **Forecast probable audience reaction.** As you'll read later in the chapter, audience reaction affects message organization. If you expect a favorable response, you can state conclusions and recommendations up front and offer minimal supporting evidence. If you expect skepticism, you can introduce conclusions gradually and with more proof.

GATHERING INFORMATION

With a clear picture of who your audience is, your next step is to assemble the information that you will include in your message. For simple messages, you may already have all the information at hand, but more complex messages can require considerable research and analysis before you're ready to begin writing. Chapter 11 explores formal techniques for finding, evaluating, and processing information. You can often use a variety of informal techniques to gather insights and focus your research efforts:

- **Consider other viewpoints.** Putting yourself in someone else's position helps you consider what that person may be thinking, feeling, or planning.

- **Read reports and other company documents.** Consider annual reports, financial statements, news releases, blogs, marketing reports, and customer surveys for helpful information. Find out whether your company has a *knowledge-management system*, a centralized database that collects the experiences and insights of employees throughout the organization.

- **Talk with supervisors, colleagues, or customers.** Fellow workers and customers may have information you need, or they may know what your audience will be interested in.

- **Ask your audience for input.** If you're unsure of what audience members need from your message, ask them. Admitting you don't know but want to meet their needs will impress an audience more than guessing and getting it wrong.

Uncovering Audience Needs

Joe Kraynak organizes his writing to overcome a common flaw in manuals for technical products: providing too little of the right information (how to use the equipment) and too much of the wrong information (how the equipment works). In many situations, your audience's information needs are readily apparent, such as when a consumer sends an e-mail asking a specific question. In other cases, your audience may be unable to articulate exactly what is needed. If someone makes a vague or broad request, ask questions to narrow the focus. If your boss says, "Find out everything you can about Interscope Records," ask which aspect of the company and its business is most important. Asking a question or two often forces the person to think through the request and define more precisely what is required.

Also, try to think of information needs that your audience may not have expressed. Suppose you've been asked to compare two health insurance plans for your firm's employees, but your research uncovered a third alternative that might be even better than the first two. You could then expand your report to include a brief explanation of why the third plan should be considered and then compare it to the two original plans.

> If someone gives you a vague request, ask questions to clarify it before you plan a response.

> Include any additional information that may be helpful, even though the requester didn't specifically ask for it.

Providing Required Information

After you've defined your audience's information needs, be sure you satisfy those needs completely. One good way to test the thoroughness of your message is to use the **journalistic approach**: Check to see whether your message answers *who, what, when, where, why,* and *how*. Using this test, you can quickly tell whether a message fails to deliver—such as this message requesting information from employees:

> Test the completeness of your planned message by making sure it will answer the key questions *who, what, when, where, why,* and *how*.

> We are exploring ways to reduce our office space leasing costs and would like your input on a proposed plan in which employees who telecommute on alternate days could share offices. Please let me know what you think of this proposal.

The message fails to tell employees everything they need to know in order to provide meaningful responses. The *what* could be improved by identifying the specific information points the writer needs from employees (such as whether individual telecommuting patterns are predictable enough to allow scheduling of shared offices). The writer also doesn't specify *when* the responses are needed or *how* the employees should respond. By failing to address such points, the request is likely to generate a variety of responses, some possibly helpful but some probably not.

To gauge the quality of the information you provide in your messages, check to ensure that the information is accurate, ethical, and pertinent.

Be Sure the Information Is Accurate   Inaccurate information in business messages can cause a host of problems, from embarrassment and lost productivity to serious safety and legal issues. Inaccurate information may persist for months or years after you distribute it, or you may commit the organization to promises it isn't able to keep—and the error could harm your reputation as a reliable businessperson.

You can minimize mistakes by double-checking every piece of information you collect. If you are consulting sources outside the organization, ask yourself whether they are current and reliable. Be particularly careful when using sources you find on the Internet. As you'll see in Chapter 11, the simplicity of online publishing and common lack of editorial oversight call for extra care in using online information. Be sure to review any mathematical or financial calculations. Check all dates and schedules and examine your own assumptions and conclusions to be certain they are valid.

> Be certain that the information you provide is accurate and that the commitments you make can be kept.

Be Sure the Information Is Ethical   By working hard to ensure the accuracy of the information you gather, you'll also avoid many ethical problems in your messages. If you do make an honest mistake, such as delivering information you initially thought to be true but later found to be false, contact the recipients of the message immediately and correct the error. No one can reasonably fault you in such circumstances, and most people will respect your honesty.

> Ethics should guide your decisions when determining how much detail to include in your message.

Messages can also be unethical if important information is omitted. Of course, as a business professional, you may have legal or other sound business reasons for not including every detail about every matter. So just how much detail should you include? Make sure you include enough detail to avoid misleading your audience. If you're unsure how much information your audience needs, offer as much as you believe best fits your definition of complete and then offer to provide more upon request.

Be Sure the Information Is Pertinent   When gathering information for your message, remember that some points will be more important to your audience than others. They will appreciate your efforts to prioritize the information they need and filter out the information they don't. Moreover, by focusing on the information that concerns your audience the most, you increase your chances of accomplishing your own communication goals.

> Try to figure out what points will especially interest your audience and then give those points the most attention.

If you don't know your audience or if you're communicating with a large group of people with diverse interests, use common sense to identify points of interest. Audience factors such as age, job, location, income, and education can give you a clue. If you're trying to sell memberships in a health club, you might adjust your message for athletes, busy professionals, families, and people in different locations or in different income brackets. The comprehensive facilities and professional trainers would appeal to athletes, whereas the low monthly rates would appeal to college students on tight budgets.

> Rely on common sense if you don't know enough about your audience members to know exactly what will interest them.

Some messages necessarily reach audiences with a diverse mix of educational levels, subject awareness, and other variables. In these cases, your only choice is to try to accommodate the likely range of audience members (see Figure 4.4).

FIGURE 4.4

An Audience-Focused Report (Selected Pages)

These two pages from a local water district's annual water quality report do a good job of presenting a technical subject to the general public (all of the households in this particular city). Notice how the report presents scientific information accurately but supplements that with clear explanations of what the information means and how it pertains to water users.

SELECTING THE RIGHT MEDIUM

Selecting the best medium for your message can make the difference between effective and ineffective communication.[4] A **medium** is the form through which you choose to communicate your message. You may choose to talk with someone face to face, post to a blog, send e-mail, or create a webcast—and there are many other media from which to choose.

In fact, media categories have become increasingly blurred in recent years, with the advent of so many options that include multimedia formats. For the sake of discussion, you can divide media into oral, written, visual, and electronic (which often combines several media types).

Oral Media

Oral communication is best when you need to encourage interaction, express emotions, or monitor emotional responses.

Primary oral media include face-to-face conversations, interviews, speeches, and in-person presentations and meetings. By giving communicators the ability to see, hear, and react to each other, traditional oral media are useful for encouraging people to ask questions, make comments, and work together to reach a consensus or decision. In particular, experts recommend that managers engage in frequent "walk-arounds," chatting with employees to get input, answer their questions, and interpret important business events and trends.[5]

Of course, if you don't want a lot of questions or interaction, oral media can be an unwise choice. However, consider your audience carefully before deciding to limit interaction by choosing a different medium. As a manager, you will encounter unpleasant situations (declining an employee's request for a raise, for example) in which sending an e-mail message or otherwise avoiding personal contact will seem appealing. However, in many such cases, you owe the other party the opportunity to ask questions or express concerns. Moreover, facing the tough situations in person will earn you a reputation as an honest, caring manager.

The higher you rise in an organization, the more time you spending talking and listening. Your ability to communicate with people from virtually any background will be key to your success.

Written Media

Memos are short, printed messages for internal audiences; letters are short, printed messages for external audiences.

Written messages take many forms, from traditional memos to glossy reports that rival magazines in production quality. Most letters and memos are relatively brief documents, generally one or two pages, although some run much longer. **Memos** are used for the routine, day-to-day exchange of information within an organization. Because of their open construction and informal method of delivery (such as being placed in baskets), memos are less private than letters. In many organizations, e-mail messages, blogs, and other electronic media have largely replaced paper memos.

Letters are brief written messages sent to recipients outside the organization. In addition to conveying a particular message, they perform an important public relations function in fostering good working relationships with customers, suppliers, and others. Many organizations rely on form letters to save time and money on routine communication. Form letters are particularly handy for such one-time mass mailings as sales messages about products, information about organizational activities, and goodwill messages such as seasonal greetings.

Reports and proposals are usually longer than memos and letters, although both can be created in memo or letter format. These documents come in a variety of lengths, ranging from a few pages to several hundred, and are usually fairly formal in tone. Chapters 13 through 15 discuss reports and proposals in detail.

Visual Media

Although you probably won't work with many messages that are purely visual (with no text), the importance of visual elements in business communication continues to grow. Traditional business messages rely primarily on text, with occasional support from graphical elements such as charts, graphs, or diagrams to help illustrate points discussed in the text. However, many business communicators are discovering the power of messages in which the visual element is dominant and supported by small amounts of text. For the purposes of this discussion, you can think of *visual media* as any formats in which one or more visual elements play a central role in conveying the message content (see Figure 4.5).

Messages that combine powerful visuals with supporting text can be effective for a number of reasons. Today's audiences are pressed for time and bombarded with messages, so anything that communicates quickly is welcome. Visuals are also effective at describing complex ideas and processes because they can reduce the work required for an audience to identify the parts and relationships that make up the whole. Also, in a multilingual business world, diagrams, symbols, and other images can lower communication barriers by requiring less language processing. Finally, visual images can be easier to remember than purely textual descriptions or explanations.

In some situations, a message that is predominantly visual with text used to support the illustration can be more effective than a message that relies primarily on text.

FIGURE 4.5
Visual Media
In traditional business messages, visual elements usually support the text. However, in some instances, the message can be presented more effectively by reversing that relationship—basing the message on a dominant visual and using text to support that image. (*CRM* stands for *customer relationship management*, a category of software that helps companies manage their interactions with customers.)

Why should I care about CRM?

XPLANATIONS® by XPLANE®

1. A customer orders 10 new servers through sales. When the salesperson enters the order into the CRM software, the CRM database is updated with this new sale information.

Customer — 10 servers / Order — Sales

2. If there's a problem, the customer can call a support line and enter a customer identification number. This prompts the CRM software to call up the customer's history and route the call to the most appropriate agent, who can upsell the customer based on its purchasing history.

Where's the %#&@!! "on" switch? / Customer ID

Call center support

3. If a customer decides to buy additional products online, the CRM database will recognize the customer and make unique purchase suggestions or offers based on its purchasing history.

Send me 20 new servers. / Customer ID

Latest version of server? Upgrade memory for old servers?

Company website

CRM Software / CRM Database

Customer data / Update / Sales ideas / Customer history / Sales ideas / Customer history

4. Using CRM analytics software, the company can track customer trends from call center data and act to fix problems or anticipate new ones.

23% of customers can't find the "on" switch.

Data

Redesign

As seen in Business 2.0 | ©2001 xplane.com

Electronic Media

The range of electronic media is broad and continues to grow even broader, from telephones and podcasts to blogs and wikis to e-mail and text messaging. When you want to make a powerful impression, using electronic media can increase the excitement and visual appeal with computer animation, video, and music.

The growth of electronic communication options is both a blessing and a curse for business communicators. On the one hand, you have more tools than ever before to choose from, with more ways to deliver rational and emotional content. On the other hand, the sheer range of choices can complicate your job because you often need to choose among multiple media, and you need to know how to use each medium successfully. You'll learn more about using electronic media throughout this book (and in Chapter 7, in particular); for now, here is a quick overview of the major electronic media now used in business:

- **Electronic versions of oral media.** These include telephone calls, teleconferencing (when three or more people join the same call), voice mail messages, audio recordings such as compact discs and podcasts, and even online speaking characters (see Figure 4.6). The simple telephone call is still a vital communication link for many organizations, but even it has joined the Internet age, thanks to *Internet telephony*, also known by the technical term VoIP (which stands for *Voice over IP*, the Internet Protocol). More than 100 million people worldwide now use Skype, which offers free basic phone service over the Internet.[6] Although telephone calls can't convey all the nonverbal signals of an in-person conversation, they can convey quite a few, including tone of voice, laughter, pauses, and so on. Voice mail is a handy way to send brief messages when an immediate response isn't crucial, but it's a poor choice for lengthy messages because the information is difficult to retrieve. You'll learn about podcasts, perhaps the most significant business audio advancement of recent years, in Chapter 7.

- **Electronic versions of written media.** These range from e-mail and instant messages to blogs, websites, and wikis. Instant messaging (IM) is rapidly overtaking e-mail in some companies. At IBM, for instance, employees send more than 5 million instant messages a month.[7] *Text messaging*, a phone-based instant messaging medium that has long been popular with consumers in Asia and Europe, is finally catching on in the United States.[8] Even documents that were once distributed on paper are now easily transferred electronically, thanks to Adobe's portable document format (PDF). Faxes have been replaced by other electronic options in many cases, although they still have a role in business communication. Internet-based fax services, such as eFax, lower the cost of faxing by eliminating the need for a dedicated fax line and fax machine.

To use many electronic media options successfully, a person must have at least some degree of technical skill.

Electronic media offer an ever-expanding array of ways to deliver oral, written, and visual messages.

Electronic written media have largely replaced traditional written media in many companies.

FIGURE 4.6
Electronic Oral Media
Many websites now feature talking animated figures, sometimes called *avatars*, offering website visitors a more engaging experience.

- **Electronic versions of visual media.** These can include electronic presentations (using Microsoft PowerPoint and other software), computer animation (using software such as Adobe Flash to create animated sequences for websites), and video. Businesses have made extensive use of video (particularly for training, new product promotions, and executive announcements) for years—first on tape, then on DVD, and now online. Video is also incorporated in podcasting, creating *vidcasts*, and in blogging, including *video blogs* (*vlogs*) and *mobile blogs* (*moblogs*).[9] **Multimedia** refers to use of two or more media to craft a single message, typically some combination of audio, video, text, and visual graphics.

Factors to Consider When Choosing Media

Choosing the right medium for each message is a question of balancing your needs with your audience's needs (see Table 4.1). Be sure to consider how your message is affected by the following factors:

- **Media richness.** Richness is a medium's ability to (1) convey a message through more than one *informational cue* (visual, verbal, vocal), (2) facilitate feedback, and (3) establish personal focus. The richest medium is face-to-face communication; it's personal, it provides immediate feedback (verbal and nonverbal), and it conveys the emotion behind a message.[10] Multimedia presentations and multimedia webpages are also quite rich, with the ability to present images, animation, text, music, sound effects, and other elements. Many electronic media are also *interactive*, in that they enable audiences to participate in the communication process. For example, a website can allow visitors to select the types of information they want to see, to provide feedback, or use a variety of online calculators or other tools. At the other end of the richness continuum are the leanest media— those that communicate in the simplest ways, provide no opportunity for audience feedback, and aren't personalized (see Figure 4.7). Use the richest media to send nonroutine or complex messages, to humanize your presence throughout the organization, to communicate caring to employees, and to gain employee commitment to company goals. Use leaner media to send simple, routine messages.

  > The richest media use more than one informational cue, facilitate feedback, and establish a personal focus on each audience member.

- **Message formality.** Your media choice affects the style and tone of your message. For instance, to share simple information with employees, you would probably send an e-mail message or post an announcement on a blog rather than write a formal printed memo or make a face-to-face presentation.

- **Media limitations.** Every medium has limitations. For example, although face-to-face communication is one of the richest media, it's also one of the most restrictive because you and your audience must be in the same place at the same time.[11] Similarly, IM is perfect for communicating simple, straightforward messages, but it is ineffective for sending complex ones.

- **Sender intentions.** Your choice of medium influences your audience's perception of your intentions. If you want to emphasize the formality of your message, use a more formal medium such as a memo or a letter. To convey emotion, consider a visual medium such as a personal speech or a videoconference. For immediate feedback, meet face to face, make a phone call, or use IM.[12]

  > Your media choices themselves can send a message to your audience.

- **Urgency and cost.** Electronic media have lowered the cost of transmitting messages, but in some instances (usually involving printed messages), you need to weigh cost versus delivery time. For instance, local couriers and delivery services such as FedEx, UPS, and DHL can deliver printed materials quickly, but they tend to cost much more than regular mail.

- **Audience preferences.** Make sure to consider which medium or media your audience expects or prefers.[13] What would you think if your college tried to deliver

  > When choosing the appropriate medium, don't forget to consider your audience's expectations.

Table 4.1   MEDIA ADVANTAGES AND DISADVANTAGES

Media	Advantages	Disadvantages
Oral	• Provide opportunity for immediate feedback • Allow a certain ease of interaction • Involve rich nonverbal cues (both physical gesture and vocal inflection) • Allow you to express the emotion behind your message	• Restrict participation to those physically present • Unless recorded, provide no permanent, verifiable record of the communication • Reduce communicator's control over the message • Other than for messages that are prewritten and rehearsed, offer no opportunity to revise or edit your spoken words
Written	• Allow you to plan and control your message • Reach geographically dispersed audiences • Offer a permanent, verifiable record • Minimize the distortion that can accompany oral messages • Can be used to avoid immediate interactions • De-emphasize any inappropriate emotional components	• Usually not conducive to speedy feedback • Lack the rich nonverbal cues provided by oral media • Often take more time and more resources to create and distribute • Elaborate printed documents can require special skills in preparation and production
Visual	• Can convey complex ideas and relationships quickly • Often less intimidating than long blocks of text • Can reduce the burden on the audience to figure out how the pieces fit	• Can require artistic skills to design • Require some technical skills to create • Can require more time to create than equivalent amount of text • More difficult to transmit and store than simple textual messages
Electronic	• Deliver messages quickly • Reach geographically dispersed audiences • Offer the persuasive power of multimedia formats • Can increase accessibility and openness in an organization	• Are easy to overuse (sending too many messages to too many recipients) • Privacy risks and concerns (exposing confidential data; employer monitoring of e-mail and IM; accidental forwarding) • Security risks (viruses; spyware) • Productivity concerns (frequent interruptions; non-business web surfing)

FIGURE 4.7
Media Richness
Business media vary widely in terms of *richness*, which encompasses the number of informational cues available, their ability to incorporate feedback, and the degree to which they can be personalized.

Leaner: fewer cues, no interactivity, no personal focus

Standard reports, Static webpages, Mass media, Posters & signs — Custom reports, Letters & memos, E-mail & IM, Wikis, Blogs, Podcasts — Telephone calls, Teleconferencing, Video (including vodcasts, vlogs, video IM) — Face-to-face conversations, Multimedia presentations, Multimedia webpages, Virtual reality

Richer: multiple cues, interactive, personalized

your diploma by fax? You'd expect the college to hand the diploma to you at graduation or mail it to you. In addition, some cultures tend to favor one channel over another. For example, the United States, Canada, and Germany emphasize written messages, whereas Japan emphasizes oral messages—perhaps because its high-context culture carries so much of the message in nonverbal cues and "between-the-lines" interpretation.[14]

After you select the best medium for your purpose, situation, and audience, you are ready to start thinking about the organization of your message.

ORGANIZING YOUR INFORMATION

For anything beyond the simplest messages, organization can make the difference between success and failure. Compare the two versions of the message in Figure 4.8. The ineffective version exhibits several common organization mistakes: taking too long to get to the point, including irrelevant material, getting ideas mixed up, and leaving out necessary information.

As you'll see in the following chapters, various types of messages may require different organizational schemes. Nevertheless, in every case, you can organize your message in a logical and compelling way by recognizing the importance of good organization, defining your main idea, limiting your scope, choosing either a direct or an indirect approach, and outlining your content.

To organize a message
- Define your main idea
- Limit the scope
- Choose the direct or indirect approach
- Group your points

Recognizing the Importance of Good Organization

At best, poor organization creates unnecessary work for your readers, forcing them to piece together your message in a sensible way. At worst, poor organization leads readers to form inaccurate conclusions or tempts them to stop reading or listening. If you gain a reputation as a disorganized communicator, people will begin to ignore your messages and question your thinking skills. In other words, poorly organized messages are bad for business and bad for your career.

Poor organization can waste time, reduce efficiency, and damage relationships.

Effective organization also saves you time and consumes less of your creative energy. Your draft goes more quickly because you don't waste time putting ideas in the wrong places or composing material that you don't need. You may also use your organizational plan to get advance input from your audience. That way, you can be sure you're on the right track *before* you spend hours working on your draft. Furthermore, if you're working on a large, complex project, you can use your organization plan to divide the writing job among co-workers.

In addition to helping you, good organization helps the members of your audience in three key ways. First, it helps your audience understand your message. By making your main point clear at the outset and by presenting information logically, a well-organized message satisfies your audience's need for information.

Good organization helps audience members understand your message, accept your message, and save time.

Second, good organization helps your audience accept your message. Effective messages often require a bit more than simple, clear logic. A diplomatic approach helps receivers accept your message, even if it's not exactly what they want to hear (see Figure 4.9).

Third, good organization saves your audience time. Well-organized messages are efficient. They contain only relevant ideas, and they are brief. Moreover, all the information in a well-organized message is in a logical place. Audience members receive only the information they need, and because that information is presented as accessibly and succinctly as possible, audience members can follow the thought pattern without a struggle. Before you can even begin arranging the information in your message, take a moment to define your main idea.

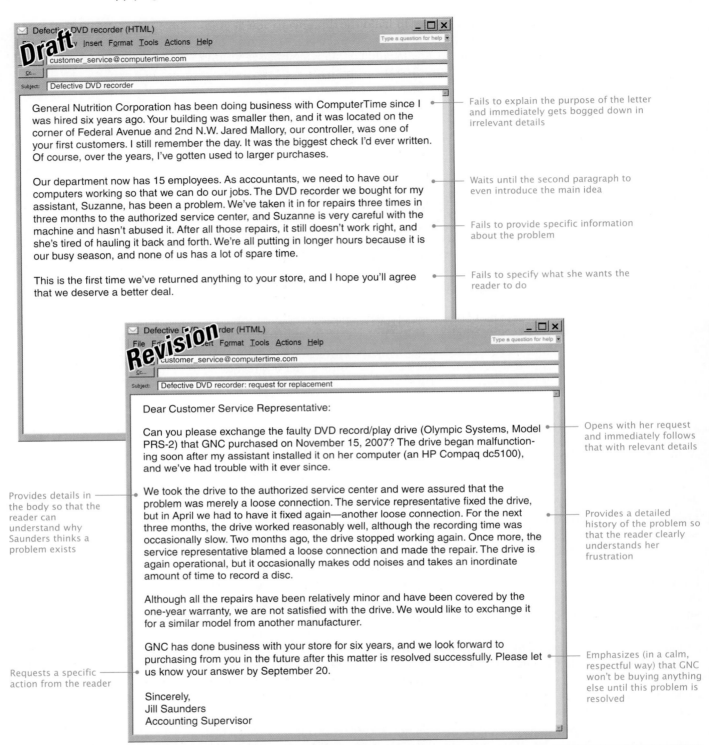

The revised version of this e-mail is clear and efficient, presenting only the necessary information in a logical sequence.

Draft

☑ Defective DVD recorder (HTML) _ ☐ ✕

File ... Insert Format Tools Actions Help   Type a question for help ▾

To: customer_service@computertime.com
Cc...
Subject: Defective DVD recorder

General Nutrition Corporation has been doing business with ComputerTime since I was hired six years ago. Your building was smaller then, and it was located on the corner of Federal Avenue and 2nd N.W. Jared Mallory, our controller, was one of your first customers. I still remember the day. It was the biggest check I'd ever written. Of course, over the years, I've gotten used to larger purchases.

Our department now has 15 employees. As accountants, we need to have our computers working so that we can do our jobs. The DVD recorder we bought for my assistant, Suzanne, has been a problem. We've taken it in for repairs three times in three months to the authorized service center, and Suzanne is very careful with the machine and hasn't abused it. After all those repairs, it still doesn't work right, and she's tired of hauling it back and forth. We're all putting in longer hours because it is our busy season, and none of us has a lot of spare time.

This is the first time we've returned anything to your store, and I hope you'll agree that we deserve a better deal.

- Fails to explain the purpose of the letter and immediately gets bogged down in irrelevant details

- Waits until the second paragraph to even introduce the main idea

- Fails to provide specific information about the problem

- Fails to specify what she wants the reader to do

Revision

☑ Defective DVD recorder (HTML) _ ☐ ✕

File Edit ... ert Format Tools Actions Help   Type a question for help ▾

To: customer_service@computertime.com
Cc...
Subject: Defective DVD recorder: request for replacement

Dear Customer Service Representative:

Can you please exchange the faulty DVD record/play drive (Olympic Systems, Model PRS-2) that GNC purchased on November 15, 2007? The drive began malfunctioning soon after my assistant installed it on her computer (an HP Compaq dc5100), and we've had trouble with it ever since.

We took the drive to the authorized service center and were assured that the problem was merely a loose connection. The service representative fixed the drive, but in April we had to have it fixed again—another loose connection. For the next three months, the drive worked reasonably well, although the recording time was occasionally slow. Two months ago, the drive stopped working again. Once more, the service representative blamed a loose connection and made the repair. The drive is again operational, but it occasionally makes odd noises and takes an inordinate amount of time to record a disc.

Although all the repairs have been relatively minor and have been covered by the one-year warranty, we are not satisfied with the drive. We would like to exchange it for a similar model from another manufacturer.

GNC has done business with your store for six years, and we look forward to purchasing from you in the future after this matter is resolved successfully. Please let us know your answer by September 20.

Sincerely,
Jill Saunders
Accounting Supervisor

- Opens with her request and immediately follows that with relevant details

- Provides details in the body so that the reader can understand why Saunders thinks a problem exists

- Provides a detailed history of the problem so that the reader clearly understands her frustration

- Emphasizes (in a calm, respectful way) that GNC won't be buying anything else until this problem is resolved

- Requests a specific action from the reader

FIGURE 4.8
E-Mail Message with Improved Organization
The revised version of this e-mail is clear and efficient, presenting only the necessary information in a logical sequence.

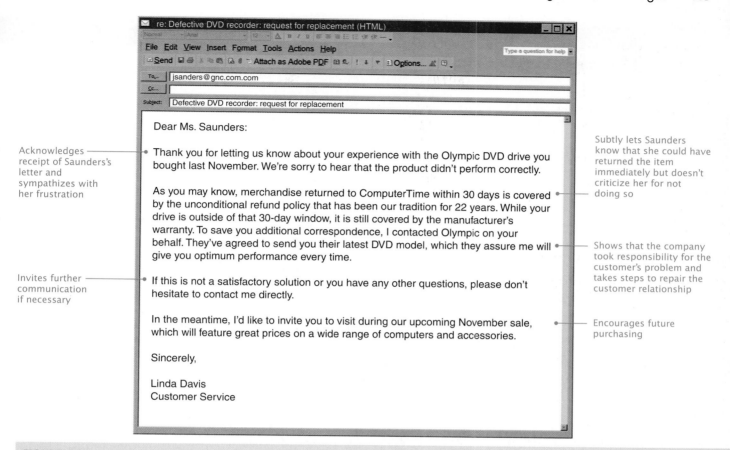

Acknowledges receipt of Saunders's letter and sympathizes with her frustration

Invites further communication if necessary

Subtly lets Saunders know that she could have returned the item immediately but doesn't criticize her for not doing so

Shows that the company took responsibility for the customer's problem and takes steps to repair the customer relationship

Encourages future purchasing

FIGURE 4.9
Message Demonstrating a Diplomatic Organization Plan
In the case of ComputerTime's response to Jill Saunders's request for a replacement product from a different manufacturer, ComputerTime isn't able to do exactly what Saunders requested (it has arranged a replacement from the same manufacturer instead). Consequently, the response letter from Linda Davis has a negative aspect to it, but the style of the letter is tactful and positive.

Defining Your Main Idea

The broad subject, or **topic**, of every well-organized business message can be condensed to one idea, whether it's soliciting the executive committee for a larger budget or apologizing to a client for an incident of poor customer service. Your entire message supports, explains, or demonstrates your **main idea**—a specific statement about the topic of your message (see Table 4.2).

Your main idea may be obvious when you're preparing a brief message with simple facts that have little emotional impact on your audience. If you're responding to a request for information, your main idea may be simply "Here is what you wanted." However, defining your main idea is more complicated when you're not sure what to tell your audience—either because you don't fully understand the topic yourself or you're not sure what the audience needs to know. In addition, in longer documents and presentations, you often need to unify a mass of material, so you need to define a main idea that encompasses all the individual points you want to make. Finding a common thread through all these points can be a challenge. Sometimes you won't even be sure what your main idea is until you sort through the information. For

The topic is the broad subject; the main idea makes a statement about the topic.

Defining your main idea is more difficult when you're trying to persuade someone or convey disappointing information.

Table 4.2	DEFINING TOPIC AND MAIN IDEA		
General Purpose	*Specific Purpose*	*Topic*	*Main Idea*
To inform	Teach customer service representatives how to file insurance claims	Insurance claims	Proper filing saves the company time and money.
To persuade	Convince top managers to increase spending on research and development	Funding for research and development	Competitors spend more than we do on research and development.
To collaborate	Solicit ideas for a companywide incentive system that ties wages to profits	Incentive pay	Tying wages to profits motivates employees and reduces compensation costs in tough years.

tough assignments like these, consider a variety of techniques to generate creative ideas:

- **Brainstorming.** Working alone or with others, generate as many ideas and questions as you can without stopping to criticize or organize. After you capture all these pieces, look for patterns and connections to help identify the main idea and clusters of supporting ideas. If your assignment is to find a way to increase sales, for example, you might find a cluster of ideas relating to new products, another relating to advertising strategies, and another related to pricing. Identifying such clusters helps you see the major issues and zero in on the most important idea.

- **Journalistic approach.** Introduced earlier in the chapter, the journalistic approach asks *who, what, when, where, why,* and *how* questions to distill major ideas from piles of unorganized information.

- **Question-and-answer chain.** Start with a key question, from the audience's perspective, and work back toward your message. In most cases, you'll find that each answer generates new questions until you identify the information that needs to be in your message.

- **Storyteller's tour.** Some writers find it easier to talk through a communication challenge before they try to write. Pretend you're giving a colleague a guided tour of your message and record what you say. Then listen to your talk, identify ways to tighten and clarify the message, and repeat the process. Working through this recording several times will help you distill the main idea down to a single concise message.

- **Mind mapping.** You can generate and organize ideas using a graphic method called mind mapping. Start with a main idea and then branch out to connect every other related idea that comes to mind (see Figure 4.10).

Limiting Your Scope

The **scope** of your message is the range of information you present, the overall length, and the level of detail—all of which need to correspond to your main idea. In Joe Kraynak's case, because computers are complicated devices that could fill an entire encyclopedia with descriptive detail, he limits his scope carefully—providing only enough information to fulfill his specific purpose of helping people use computers more successfully.

Limit the number of support points; having fewer stronger points is a better approach than using many weaker points.

If your audience expects you to deliver a message of a certain length (such as a 10-page report or a 10-minute presentation), be sure to test your main idea statement against this length limitation. You may find that you have a compelling main idea but

FIGURE 4.10
Using the Mind-Mapping Technique to Plan a Writing Project
Mind mapping is a helpful technique for identifying and organizing the many ideas and pieces of information that a complex writing task usually entails. Software (MindJet's MindManager in this case) makes it easy to create graphical output—such as this diagram, which shows the writer's own concerns about a report, her insights into the audience's concerns, and several issues related to writing and distributing the report.

that there's no way you can cover it adequately in the space or time allowed. You'll need to narrow your main idea or, if appropriate, use this first message to provide a high-level overview of your material and then deliver additional supporting information by some other means.

Whatever the length of your message, limit the number of major support points to half a dozen or so—and if you can get your idea across with fewer points, all the better. Listing 20 or 30 support points may feel as if you're being thorough, but your audience will view such detail as disorganized and rambling. Instead, look for ways to group supporting points under major headings, such as finance, customers, competitors, employees, or whatever is appropriate for your subject. You may need to refine your major support points so that you have a smaller number with greater impact.

If your message needs to be brief, your main idea will have to be easy to understand and easy to accept. However, if your message is long, you can develop the major points in more detail. How much space you need to communicate and support your main idea depends on your subject, your audience members' familiarity with the material, their receptivity to your conclusions, and your credibility. You'll need fewer words to present routine information to a knowledgeable audience that already knows and respects you. You'll need more words to build a consensus about a complex and controversial subject, especially if the members of your audience are skeptical or hostile strangers.

Choosing Between Direct and Indirect Approaches

After you've defined your ideas, you're ready to decide on the sequence you will use to present your points. You have two basic options for identifying the sequence in which you present those points:

- **Direct approach (deductive).** When you know your audience will be receptive to your message, use a **direct approach**: Start with the main idea (such as a recommendation, a conclusion, or a request) and follow that with your supporting evidence.

Use a direct approach if the audience's reaction is likely to be positive; use an indirect approach if it is likely to be negative.

- **Indirect approach (inductive).** When your audience will be skeptical about or even resistant to your message, use an **indirect approach**: Start with the evidence first and build your case before presenting the main idea.

Audience reaction can range from eager to unwilling.

To choose between these two alternatives, analyze your audience's likely reaction to your purpose and message (see Figure 4.11). Bear in mind, however, that Figure 4.11 presents only general guidelines; always consider the unique circumstances of each message and audience situation. For example, although an indirect approach may be best when you're sending bad news to outsiders, if you're writing a message to a close associate, you may want to get directly to the point, even if your message is unpleasant. The following sections offer more insight on choosing the best approach for routine and positive messages, negative messages, and persuasive messages.

Routine and Positive Messages   The most straightforward business messages are *routine* and *positive* messages. Routine messages involve the daily matters of operating a business, from placing orders to updating employees about process changes. Positive messages convey some sort of good news, whether you're announcing a price cut, accepting an invitation, or congratulating a colleague. In most instances, your audience will be pleased to hear from you. When you're providing routine information as part of your regular business, your audience will probably be neutral—neither pleased nor displeased.

Aside from being easy to understand, routine messages are easy to prepare. In most cases, you use a direct approach. In the opening, state your main idea directly. If you have good news to share, conveying that right away puts your audience members in a positive frame of mind and encourages them to be receptive to whatever else you have to say. The body of your message can then provide all necessary details. The close is cordial and emphasizes your good news or makes a statement about the specific action desired. Routine and positive messages are discussed in greater detail in Chapter 8.

FIGURE 4.11
Choosing Between the Direct and Indirect Approaches
Think about the way your audience is likely to respond before choosing your approach.

	Direct approach	**Indirect approach**	
Audience Reaction	Eager/interested/ pleased/neutral	Displeased	Uninterested/unwilling
Message Opening	Start with the main idea, the request, or the good news.	Start with a neutral statement that acts as a transition to the reasons for the bad news.	Start with a statement or question that captures attention.
Message Body	Provide necessary details.	Give reasons to justify a negative answer. State or imply the bad news, and make a positive suggestion.	Arouse the audience's interest in the subject. Build the audience's desire to comply.
Message Close	Close with a cordial comment, a reference to the good news, or a statement about the specific action desired.	Close cordially.	Request action.

Negative Messages   Unfortunately, being a business communicator also means you'll face situations in which you need to deliver bad news. Because your audience will be disappointed, these messages usually benefit from the indirect approach—putting the evidence first and building up to the main idea. This approach strengthens your case as you go along, not only making the receiver more receptive to the eventual conclusion but also treating the receiver in a more sensitive manner, which helps you retain as much goodwill as possible. Astute businesspeople know that every person they encounter could be a potential customer, supplier, or contributor or could influence someone who is a customer, supplier, or contributor.

Successful communicators take extra care with their negative messages. They often open with a neutral statement that acts as a transition to the reasons for the bad news. In the body, they give the reasons that justify the negative answer, announcement, or information before they state or imply the bad news. And they are always careful to close cordially.

The challenge of negative messages lies in being honest but kind. You don't want to sacrifice ethics and mislead your audience, nor do you want to be overly blunt. To achieve a good mix of candor and kindness, focus on some aspect of the situation that makes the negative news a little easier to take.

Keep in mind that the indirect approach is neither manipulative nor unethical. As long as you can be honest and reasonably brief, you're often better off opening a bad-news message with a neutral point and putting the negative information after the explanation. Then, if you can close with something fairly positive, you're likely to leave the audience feeling at least neutral—not great but not hostile either (which is often about all you can hope for when you must deliver bad news). Negative messages are discussed further in Chapter 9.

In many situations, you can cushion the blow of negative news by introducing it with other, more positive information.

Using the indirect approach gives you an opportunity to get your message across to an uninterested or skeptical audience.

Persuasive Messages   Persuasive messages present a special communication challenge because you're asking your audience to give, do, or change something, whether it's buying a product or agreeing to fund a new project. Before you try to persuade people to do something, you try to capture their attention and get them to consider your message with an open mind. Make an interesting point and provide supporting facts that encourage your audience to continue paying attention. In most persuasive messages, the opening mentions a reader benefit, refers to a problem that the recipient may have, poses a question, or mentions an interesting statistic. Then the body builds interest in the subject and arouses audience members' desire to comply. Once you have them thinking, you can introduce your main idea. The close is cordial and requests the desired action. Persuasive messages are discussed at greater length in Chapter 10.

Persuasive messages can be challenging because you're generally asking your audience to give up something, such as time, money, power, and so on.

Outlining Your Content

After you have chosen the right approach, it's time to figure out the most logical and effective way to present your major points and supporting details. Even if you've resisted creating outlines in your school assignments over the years, try to get into the habit of creating outlines when you're preparing business messages. You'll save time, get better results, and do a better job of navigating through complicated business situations. Even if you're just jotting down three or four points on a notepad, making a plan and sticking to it will help you cover the important details. For a look at some of the

Document Makeover

IMPROVE THIS LETTER

To practice correcting drafts of actual documents, visit your online course or the access-code-protected portion of the Companion Website. Click on "Document Makeovers" and then click on Chapter 4. You will find a letter that contains problems and errors related to what you've learned in this chapter about planning and organizing business messages. Use the Final Draft decision tool to create an improved version of this letter. Check the document for audience focus, the right choice of medium, and the proper choice of direct or indirect approach.

USING THE POWER OF TECHNOLOGY

Create and Collaborate with Powerful Outlining Tools

Experienced business communicators recognize the power of a well-planned outline. However, outlining doesn't have to be the dull exercise you may remember from book reports and other school projects. Today's outlining tools, such as Microsoft Word's outline mode, make it easy to organize and reorganize ideas quickly. Some can even help ignite your creativity and generate new ideas.

For example, by following a consistent scheme of headings and subheadings, you can quickly add, delete, and rearrange sections to make sure your overall structure is logical and coherent. Also, if you ever feel like you've gotten lost in a long document after you've started writing, you can find your way again by shifting to outline mode. Collapse the outline down to just the first-level headings, then expand one level at a time—it's a great way to rediscover the shape of the forest when you're lost in the trees. Using outlining software is also a powerful way to study the layout of a website because you can see the entire structure underneath the homepage and make sure that your visitors won't get lost in or frustrated by confusing navigation.

For complex reports, you'll often need to collaborate on the outline with one or more colleagues who may be in differ-

ent locations around the world. Groupware collaboration tools let multiple people work on an outline at the same time, often with integrated IM so that you can brainstorm and evaluate ideas on the fly. Rather than sending the outline around via e-mail and letting each person modify it individually—which can create endless rounds of revision and compromise—using a groupware outliner lets everyone contribute, argue, and collaborate all at once.

CAREER APPLICATIONS

1. Assume that your boss has asked you to deliver a presentation summarizing a report you've just completed. She says you don't need to start from scratch, though. Figure out the steps needed to transfer your report structure from Microsoft Word to Microsoft PowerPoint.

2. Product designers use a process called *reverse engineering* to find out how a finished product is put together. You can do the same thing with finished articles and reports to see how they're organized. Cut and paste the text of a substantial online news article into your word processor and then distill it down to an outline. Do you see any ways to improve the organization of the article?

A good way to visualize how all the points will fit together is to construct an outline.

most powerful outlining tools available today, see "Using the Power of Technology: Create and Collaborate with Powerful Outlining Tools."

When you're preparing a longer, more complex message, an outline is indispensable because it helps you visualize the relationships among the various parts. Without an outline, you may be inclined to ramble. As you're describing one point, another point may occur to you, so you describe it as well. One detour leads to another, and before you know it, you've forgotten the original point and wasted precious time and energy. With an outline to guide you, however, you can communicate in a more systematic way. Following an outline also helps you insert transitions so that your message is coherent and your audience can understand the relationships among your ideas.

You're no doubt familiar with the basic outline formats that identify each point with a number or letter and that indent certain points to show which ones are of equal status. A good outline divides a topic into at least two parts, restricts each subdivision to one category, and ensures that each subdivision is separate and distinct (see Figure 4.12).

You may want to experiment with other organizational schemes in addition to traditional outlines.

Another way to visualize the outline of your message is to create an organization chart similar to the charts used to show a company's management structure (see Figure 4.13). You show the main idea in the highest-level box and, like a top executive, to establish the big picture. The lower-level ideas, like lower-level employees, provide the details. All the ideas are logically organized into divisions of thought, just as a company is organized into divisions and departments.[15] Using a visual chart instead of a traditional outline has many benefits. Charts help you (1) see the various levels of ideas and how the parts fit together, (2) develop new ideas, and (3) restructure your information flow. The mind-mapping technique used to generate ideas works in a similar way.

Alphanumeric Outline

I. First major point
  A. First subpoint
  B. Second subpoint
    1. Evidence
    2. Evidence
      a. Detail
      b. Detail
    3. Evidence
  C. Third subpoint
II. Second major point
  A. First subpoint
    1. Evidence
    2. Evidence
  B. Second subpoint

Decimal Outline

1.0 First major point
  1.1 First subpoint
  1.2 Second subpoint
    1.2.1 Evidence
    1.2.2 Evidence
      1.2.2.1 Detail
      1.2.2.2 Detail
    1.2.3 Evidence
  1.3 Third subpoint
2.0 Second major point
  2.1 First subpoint
    2.1.1 Evidence
    2.1.2 Evidence
  2.2 Second subpoint

FIGURE 4.12
Two Common Outline Forms
Your company may have a tradition of using a particular outline form for formal reports and other documents. If not, either of these two approaches will work for almost any writing project.

Whichever outlining or organizing scheme you use, start your message with the main idea, follow that with major supporting points, and then illustrate these points with evidence.

Start with the Main Idea   The main idea helps you establish the goals and general strategy of the message, and it summarizes two vital things: (1) what you want your audience members to do or think and (2) why they should do so. Everything in your message either supports the main idea or explains its implications. As discussed earlier in this chapter, some messages state the main idea quickly and directly, whereas other messages delay the main idea until after the evidence is presented.

State the Major Points   Now it's time to support your main idea with the major points that clarify and explain your ideas in more concrete terms. If your purpose is to inform and the material is factual, your major points may be based on something physical or financial—something you can visualize or measure, such as activities to be performed, functional units, spatial or chronological relationships, or parts of a whole. When you're describing a process, the major points are almost inevitably steps in the process. When you're describing an object, the major points often correspond to the parts of the object. When you're giving a historical account, major points represent events in the chronological chain. If your purpose is to persuade or to collaborate, select major points that develop a line of reasoning or a logical argument that proves your central message and motivates your audience to act.

Major supporting points clarify your main idea.

You can divide major points according to physical relationships, the description of a process, the components of an object, or a historical chronology.

Illustrate with Evidence   After you've defined the main idea and identified supporting points, you're ready to illustrate each point with specific evidence that helps audience members understand and remember the more abstract concepts

FIGURE 4.13
Organization Chart Method for Outlining
Consider the organization chart approach when you're faced with a large variety of facts, figures, and other bits of information and aren't quite sure how they all may relate to one another. Gathering pieces of evidence together under major points allows a clearer picture of the main idea to emerge.

you're presenting. For example, if you're advocating that your company increase its advertising budget, you can support your major point by providing evidence that your most successful competitors spend more on advertising than you do. You can also describe a case in which a particular competitor increased its advertising budget and achieved an impressive sales gain. Then you can show that over the past five years, your firm's sales have gone up and down in response to the amount spent on advertising.

If you're developing a long, complex message, you may need to carry the outline down several levels. Remember that every level is a step along the chain from the abstract to the concrete, from the general to the specific. The lowest level contains the evidence, the individual facts and figures that tie the generalizations to the observable, measurable world. The higher levels are the concepts that reveal why those facts are significant.

Up to a point, the more evidence you provide, the more conclusive your case will be. If your subject is complex and unfamiliar or if your audience is skeptical, you may need a lot of facts and figures to demonstrate your points. On the other hand, if your subject is routine and your audience is positively inclined, you can be more sparing with the evidence. You want to provide enough support to be convincing but not so much that your message becomes boring or inefficient.

> Each major support point must itself be supported with enough specific evidence to be convincing but not so much that your message becomes long and boring.

Table 4.3 — SIX TYPES OF DETAIL

Type of Detail	Example	Comment
Facts and figures	Sales are strong this month. We have two new contracts worth $5 million and a good chance of winning another worth $2.5 million.	Adds more credibility than any other type. Can become boring if used excessively. Most common type used in business.
Example or illustration	We've spent four months trying to hire recent accounting graduates, but so far, only one person has joined our firm. One candidate told me that she would love to work for us, but she can get $5,000 more a year elsewhere.	Adds life to a message, but one example does not prove a point. Idea must be supported by other evidence as well.
Description	Upscale hamburger restaurants target burger lovers who want more than the convenience and low prices of a McDonald's. These places feature wine and beer, half-pound burgers, and generous side dishes (nachos, potato skins). "Atmosphere" is key.	Helps audience visualize the subject by creating a sensory impression. Does not prove a point, but clarifies it and makes it memorable. Begins with overview of function; defines its purpose, lists major parts, and explains how it operates.
Narration	Under former management, executives worked in blue jeans, meetings rarely started on time, and lunches ran long. When Jim Wilson became CEO, he completely overhauled the operation. A Harvard MBA who favors Brooks Brothers suits, Wilson has cut the product line in half and chopped $12 million off expenses.	Works well for attracting attention and explaining ideas, but lacks statistical validity.
Reference to authority	I discussed this idea with Jackie Loman in the Chicago plant, and she was very supportive. As you know, Jackie has been in charge of that plant for the past six years. She is confident that we can speed up the number 2 line by 150 units an hour if we add another worker.	Bolsters a case while adding variety and credibility. Works only if "authority" is recognized and respected by audience.
Visual aids	Graphs, charts, tables	Helps audience grasp specific data. Used more in memos and reports than in letters.

✓ CHECKLIST: Planning Business Messages

A. Analyze the situation.

✓ Determine whether the purpose of your message is to inform, persuade, or collaborate.
✓ Identify what you want your audience to think or do.
✓ Make sure your purpose is worthwhile and realistic.
✓ Make sure the time is right for your message.
✓ Make sure your purpose is acceptable to your organization.
✓ Identify the primary audience.
✓ Determine audience size and composition.
✓ Estimate your audience's level of understanding and probable reaction to your message.

B. Gather information.

✓ Decide whether to use formal or informal techniques for gathering information.
✓ Find out what your audience wants to know.

✓ Provide all required information and make sure it's accurate, ethical, and pertinent.

C. Select the best medium for your message.

✓ Understand the advantages and disadvantages of oral, written, visual, and electronic media.
✓ Consider media richness, formality, media limitations, sender intentions, urgency, cost, and audience preference.

D. Organize your information.

✓ Define your main idea.
✓ Limit your scope.
✓ Choose a direct or an indirect approach.
✓ Outline content by starting with the main idea, adding major points, and illustrating with evidence.

Another way to keep your audience interested is to vary the type of detail you include. As you draft your message, try to incorporate the methods described in Table 4.3. Switch from facts and figures to narration, add a dash of description, throw in some examples or a reference to authority. If it makes sense, you can reinforce all these details with visual aids. Think of your message as a stew: a mixture of ingredients seasoned with a blend of spices. Each separate flavor adds to the richness of the whole.

If your schedule permits, try to put aside your outline for a day or two before you begin composing your first draft. Then review it with a fresh eye, looking for opportunities to improve the flow of ideas. For a reminder of the planning tasks involved in preparing your messages, see "Checklist: Planning Business Messages."

On the Job

SOLVING COMMUNICATION DILEMMAS AT THE COMPLETE IDIOT'S GUIDES

Joe Kraynak's audience-centered approach to writing books has been so successful that he's hired you as a research assistant to help with a variety of new projects. He has also offered to mentor you as you begin your own career as a business writer, and you'll have the opportunity to write sections for several of his books as well. Use what you've learned in this chapter to solve these planning dilemmas.

1. Kraynak's next project is writing a how-to book for the enormously popular Motorola Razr phone, a stylish model that includes everything from video playback to Bluetooth wireless capability for adding wireless headsets and other accessories. The writer's challenge is balancing the needs of several types of

users, including people who've never used a mobile phone before, people who have used mobile phones but don't care about advanced features, and "power users" who want to use every feature possible in every way imaginable. You've sketched out several outlines and need to select the one you'll recommend to Kraynak.

a. Organize the book in five sections: (1) an introduction to mobile phones (which readers can skip if they choose), (2) a quick graphical overview of the phone that identifies all the buttons and other features, (3) a guide to basic operation of the phone, (4) a guide to advanced capabilities, and (5) a short glossary/index that defines the various features and functions and refers readers to more information in sections 1 to 4.

b. Organize the entire book like an encyclopedia, describing the phone's individual features and functions in detail and in alphabetical order. This way, people can quickly find information about the phone, no matter how much experience they have.

c. Write three books in one: (1) an introductory guide that explains the basic concepts of using a mobile phone, along with instructions on basic operation; (2) an experienced user's guide that covers just the instructions on basic operation; and (3) a power user's guide that covers the basic operation as well as all the advanced features. This book will be considerably longer, but it'll give each audience exactly what it needs.

d. Advise Kraynak to turn down the project; there's no way anybody can write a single book that addresses the needs of so many different audiences.

2. One of the keys to Kraynak's success is identifying areas in which inexperienced product users are likely to need extra information and explanation. For the Razr book, he has asked for your help in pinpointing those issues. Unfortunately, the publisher has him on a tight schedule, and you have only one day to conduct this research. Which of the following should you do?

a. Study the manual that Motorola provides with the Razr; that document is likely to have all the information you need.

b. Visit as many online blogs, customer support websites, and discussion groups (such as Google Groups) as you can, scanning for questions that people seem to have about using the Razr phone.

c. Interview every mobile phone owner you know, asking them to recall the questions they had when they first started using their current phones. Although many of them won't be Razr owners, the questions might be similar enough to help.

d. Use the Razr yourself for a day, trying to approach it the same way a new user would: What questions do you have when you first open the box? Can you figure out how to charge the battery and get the phone ready for use? Is it easy to add new names to the phone book? and so on. By putting yourself in the readers' shoes, you can identify all the questions they're likely to have.

3. Books aren't the only documents that authors such as Joe Kraynak have to write, of course. The business of being a writer involves a wide range of business communication efforts, including memos, letters, e-mails, progress reports, and proposals, to name a few. While you're working on the Razr book, Kraynak comes up with the idea of a website that would provide helpful information for all popular mobile phones. The site would take advantage of the strong consumer awareness of the *Idiot's Guide* brand name but have the advantage of being much easier to update than a printed book. However, he has heard from another author that the editors of the *Idiot's*

Guide series aren't interested in online publishing at this point, since they're busy and successful with printed books. However, you think the new website idea could be a winner for everyone (the publisher, Kraynak, and you), so you offer to draft a proposal on the issue. Which of these organizing approaches should you take? Why?

a. Launching a big, commercial website is a serious business decision. Come right out and say what you propose and then back that up with details in the body of the message. The audience will study the supporting details and then evaluate your idea on its merits alone.

b. They don't want to publish online? Everybody wants to publish online—and virtually everybody is doing so. Your proposal needs to be not only direct but also blunt: If the *Idiot's Guide* series doesn't create such as website, somebody else surely will. Without exactly saying so, you need to convey the message that only an idiot would ignore an opportunity like this for the *Idiot's Guide* series.

c. Your proposal should take an indirect approach because the readers will initially be resistant to the idea. Moreover, it would be bad form to dictate precisely what the solution should be, so write only in general terms (such as "the opportunity for online publishing is significant") and let the readers reach a conclusion on their own (as in, deciding specifically to create an *Idiot's Guide* website for popular phones).

d. If the proposal doesn't quickly address the audience's reservations regarding web publishing, audience members won't bother to read the details or consider the proposal. Consequently, an indirect approach is best. Start by announcing that you've identified a business opportunity that is ideal for *Idiot's Guide* but needs to be acted upon soon, or a competitor will get there first. After you've captured the audience's attention with that intriguing opening, continue with your persuasive argument in favor of the website (including, for instance, the possibility that the website will increase the demand for books).

4. Kraynak emphasizes that the website proposal needs to provide enough evidence to be convincing but not so much that it becomes long and tiresome to read. Which of the following support points does *not* belong in the proposal? Why not?

a. A list of companies that would possibly be interested in advertising on the website, along with an estimate of the advertising revenue the site might be able to generate

b. A brief history of online publishing, from the days before the World Wide Web to the latest in blogging

c. A plan for updating the website content as new phone models are released

d. An estimate of the number of mobile phone owners who are likely to use such a website

Learning Objectives Checkup

Assess your understanding of the principles in this chapter by reading each learning objective and studying the accompanying exercises. For fill-in-the-blank items, write the missing text in the blank provided; for multiple-choice items, circle the letter of the correct answer. You can check your responses against the answer key on page AK-1.

Objective 4.1: Describe the three-step writing process.

1. The three major steps in the three-step writing process are
   a. Writing, editing, and producing
   b. Planning, writing, and completing
   c. Writing, editing, and distributing
   d. Organizing, defining your purpose, and writing

2. The first step of the three-step writing process is
   a. Writing the first draft
   b. Organizing your information
   c. Planning your message
   d. Preparing an outline

3. The purpose of limiting your scope when planning a writing project is to
   a. Make your job easier
   b. Reduce the number of things you need to think about
   c. Make sure your memos are never longer than one page
   d. Make sure that your message stays focused on the main idea and any necessary supporting details

4. Which of the following tasks should you do when you're planning a writing project?
   a. Define your purpose
   b. Revise carefully to make sure you haven't made any embarrassing mistakes
   c. Choose words and sentences carefully to make sure the audience understands your main idea
   d. Do all of the above

5. The _____ of a message indicates whether you intend to use the message to inform, to persuade, or to collaborate.

Objective 4.2: Explain why it's important to define your purpose carefully, and list four questions that can help you test that purpose.

6. After you've defined the purpose of your message, which of the following questions should you ask yourself before continuing the writing process?
   a. Will anything change as a result of my delivering this message?
   b. Is this message realistic?
   c. Is this the right time to deliver this message?
   d. Is this message acceptable to my organization?
   e. All of the above

7. If you were to write a letter to a manufacturer complaining about a defective product and asking for a refund, your general purpose would be
   a. To inform
   b. To persuade
   c. To collaborate
   d. To entertain

Objective 4.3: Describe the importance of analyzing your audience, and identify the six factors you should consider when developing an audience profile.

8. No matter what the message is or the audience you want to reach, you should always
   a. Determine the information your audience needs in order to grasp your main idea
   b. Learn the names of everyone in the target audience
   c. Estimate the percentage of audience members who are likely to agree with your message
   d. Determine a complete demographic profile of your audience

9. If audience members will vary in terms of the amount of information they already know about your topic, your best approach is to
   a. Provide as much extra information as possible to make sure everyone gets every detail
   b. Provide just the basic information; if your audience needs to know more, they can find out for themselves
   c. Gear your coverage to your primary audience and provide the information most relevant to them
   d. Include lots of graphics

Objective 4.4: Discuss gathering information for simple messages, and identify three attributes of quality information.

10. To make sure you have provided all the necessary information, use the journalistic approach, which is to
    a. Interview your audience about its needs
    b. Check the accuracy of your information
    c. Verify whether your message answers the questions *who*, *what*, *when*, *where*, *why*, and *how*
    d. Make sure your information is ethical

11. To determine whether the information you've gathered is good enough, verify that it is
    a. Accurate
    b. Ethical
    c. Pertinent to the audience's needs
    d. All of the above

12. If you realize you have given your audience incorrect information, the most ethical action would be to
    a. Say nothing and hope no one notices
    b. Wait until someone points out the error and then acknowledge the mistake
    c. Post a correction on your website
    d. Contact the audience immediately and correct the error

Objective 4.5: List factors to consider when choosing the most appropriate medium for your message.

13. A medium's ability to convey a message using more than one informational cue, to facilitate feedback, and to establish personal focus is a measure of its _____.

14. Which of the following choices would be best for communicating a complex policy change to employees in a company with offices all over the world?
    a. A teleconference followed by an e-mail message
    b. Instant messaging (IM)
    c. A traditional typed memo sent via regular postal mail
    d. A website posting with an e-mail message alerting employees to the change and directing them to the website for more information

Objective 4.6: Explain why good organization is important to both you and your audience.

15. Which of the following is an important benefit of taking time to organize your business messages?
    a. You can delay the actual writing.
    b. You save time and conserve creative energy because the writing process is quicker.
    c. Organizing your thoughts and information saves you the trouble of asking colleagues for input.
    d. In many cases, you can simply send a detailed outline and save the trouble of writing the document.

Objective 4.7: Summarize the process for organizing business messages effectively.

16. Starting with the main idea and then offering supporting evidence is known as the _____ approach.
17. Starting with evidence first and building toward your main idea is know as the _____ approach.
18. When your audience is likely to have a skeptical or even hostile reaction to your main idea, you should generally use
    a. An indirect approach
    b. A direct approach
    c. An open-ended approach
    d. A closed approach

Apply Your Knowledge

1. Some writers argue that planning messages wastes time because they inevitably change their plans as they go along. How would you respond to this argument? Briefly explain.
2. As a member of the public relations department, what medium would you recommend using to inform the local community that your toxic-waste cleanup program has been successful? Why?
3. Would you use a direct or an indirect approach to ask employees to work overtime to meet an important deadline? Please explain.
4. Which approach—direct or indirect—would you use to let your boss know that you'll be out half a day this week to attend your father's funeral? Why?

5. **Ethical Choices** A day after sending an e-mail to all 1,800 employees in your company regarding income tax implications of the company's retirement plan, you discover that one of the sources you relied on for your information plagiarized from other sources. You quickly double-check all the information in your message and confirm that it is accurate. However, you are concerned about using plagiarized information, even though you did nothing wrong. Write a brief e-mail message to your instructor, explaining how you would handle the situation.

Practice Your Knowledge

MESSAGE FOR ANALYSIS

A writer is working on an insurance information brochure and is having trouble grouping the ideas logically into an outline. Prepare the outline, paying attention to appropriate subordination of ideas. If necessary, rewrite phrases to make them all consistent.

Accident Protection Insurance Plan
- Coverage is only pennies a day
- Benefit is $100,000 for accidental death on common carrier
- Benefit is $100 a day for hospitalization as result of motor vehicle or common carrier accident
- Benefit is $20,000 for accidental death in motor vehicle accident

- Individual coverage is only $17.85 per quarter; family coverage is just $26.85 per quarter
- No physical exam or health questions
- Convenient payment—billed quarterly
- Guaranteed acceptance for all applicants
- No individual rate increases
- Free, no-obligation examination period
- Cash paid in addition to any other insurance carried
- Covers accidental death when riding as fare-paying passenger on public transportation, including buses, trains, jets, ships, trolleys, subways, or any other common carrier
- Covers accidental death in motor vehicle accidents occurring while driving or riding in or on automobile, truck, camper, motor home, or nonmotorized bicycle

EXERCISES

For active links to all websites discussed in this chapter, visit this text's website at **www.prenhall.com/thill**. Locate your book and click on its "Companion Website" link. Then select Chapter 4 and click on "Featured Websites." Locate the name of the page or the URL related to the material in the text. Please note that links to sites that become inactive after publication of the book will be removed from the "Featured Websites" section.

4.1 Planning Messages: General and Specific Purpose Make a list of communication tasks you need to accomplish in the next week or so (for example, a job application, a letter of complaint, a speech to a class, an order for some merchandise). For each, determine a general and a specific purpose.

4.2 Planning Messages: Specific Purpose For each of the following communication tasks, state a specific purpose. (If you have trouble, try beginning with "I want to . . .")

   a. A report to your boss, the store manager, about the outdated items in the warehouse
   b. A memo to clients about your booth at the upcoming trade show
   c. A letter to a customer who hasn't made a payment for three months
   d. A memo to employees about the department's high mobile phone bills
   e. A phone call to a supplier to check on an overdue parts shipment
   f. A report to future users of the computer program you have chosen to handle the company's mailing list

4.3 Message Planning Skills: Self-Assessment How good are you at planning business messages? Use the chart below to rate yourself on each element of planning an audience-centered business message. Then examine your ratings to identify where you are strongest and where you can improve, using the tips in this chapter.

4.4 Planning Messages: Audience Profile For each communication task that follows, write brief answers to three questions: Who is my audience? What is my audience's general attitude toward my subject? What does my audience need to know?

   a. A final-notice collection letter from an appliance manufacturer to an appliance dealer that is 3 months behind on payments, sent 10 days before initiating legal collection procedures
   b. An unsolicited e-mail message asking readers to purchase computer disks at near-wholesale prices
   c. An advertisement for peanut butter
   d. Fliers to be attached to doorknobs in the neighborhood, announcing reduced rates for chimney cleaning or repairs
   e. A cover letter sent along with your résumé to a potential employer
   f. A website that describes the services offered by a consulting firm that helps accounting managers comply with government regulations

4.5 Meeting Audience Needs: Necessary Information Choose a fairly simple electronic device (such as a digital music player or digital camera) that you know how to operate well. Write two sets of instructions for operating the device: one set for a reader who has never used that type of device and one set for someone who is generally familiar with that type of machine but has never operated the specific model. Briefly explain how your two audiences affect your instructions.

4.6 Selecting Media: Defining the Purpose List five messages you have received lately, such as direct-mail promotions, letters, e-mail messages, phone solicitations, and class lectures. For each, determine the general and the specific purpose; then answer the following questions: (a) Was the message well timed? (b) Did the sender choose an appropriate medium for the message? (c) Was the sender's purpose realistic?

4.7 Selecting Media: Identifying an Audience Barbara Marquardt is in charge of public relations for a cruise line that operates out of Miami. She is shocked to read a letter in a local newspaper from a disgruntled passenger, complaining about the service and entertainment

Element of Planning	Always	Frequently	Occasionally	Never
1. I start by defining my purpose.	_____	_____	_____	_____
2. I analyze my audience before writing a message.	_____	_____	_____	_____
3. I investigate what my audience wants to know.	_____	_____	_____	_____
4. I check that my information is accurate, ethical, and pertinent.	_____	_____	_____	_____
5. I consider my audience and purpose when selecting media.	_____	_____	_____	_____

on a recent cruise. Marquardt will have to respond to these publicized criticisms in some way. What audiences will she need to consider in her response? What medium should she choose? If the letter had been published in a travel publication widely read by travel agents and cruise travelers, how might her course of action differ? Summarize your recommendations in an e-mail message.

4.8 Teamwork: Audience Analysis Your team has been studying a new method for testing the durability of your company's power tools. Now the team needs to prepare three separate reports on the findings: first, a report for the administrator who will decide whether to purchase the equipment needed for this new testing method; second, a report for the company's engineers who design and develop the hand tools; and third, a report for the trainers who will be showing workers how to use the new equipment. To determine the audience's needs for each of these reports, the team has listed the following questions: (1) Who are the readers? (2) Why will they read my report? (3) Do they need introductory or background material? (4) Do they need definitions of terms? (5) What level or type of language is needed? (6) What level of detail is needed? (7) What result does my report aim for? Working with two other students, answer the questions for each of these audiences and summarize your analysis in a brief report:
a. The administrator
b. The engineers
c. The trainers

4.9 Internet: Planning Your Message Go to the PepsiCo website, at www.pepsico.com, and follow the link to the latest annual report. Then locate and read the chairman's letter. Who is the audience for this message? What is the general purpose of the message? What do you think this audience wants to know from the chairman of PepsiCo? Summarize your answers in a brief (one-page) memo or oral presentation.

4.10 Message Organization: Outlining Your Content Using the improved version of the GNC e-mail message in Figure 4.8, draw an organizational chart similar to the one shown in Figure 4.13. Fill in the main idea, the major points, and the evidence provided in this message. (Note: Your diagram may be smaller than the one provided in Figure 4.13.)

4.11 Message Organization: Limiting Scope Suppose you are preparing to recommend that top management install a new heating system that uses the cogeneration process. The following information is in your files. Eliminate topics that aren't essential; then arrange the other topics so that your report will give top managers a clear understanding of the heating system and a balanced, concise justification for installing it.
a. History of the development of the cogeneration heating process
b. Scientific credentials of the developers of the process

c. Risks assumed in using this process
d. Your plan for installing the equipment in your building
e. Stories about its successful use in comparable facilities
f. Specifications of the equipment that would be installed
g. Plans for disposing of the old heating equipment
h. Costs of installing and running the new equipment
i. Advantages and disadvantages of using the new process
j. Detailed 10-year cost projections
k. Estimates of the time needed to phase in the new system
l. Alternative systems that management may wish to consider

4.12 Message Organization: Choosing an Approach Indicate whether a direct or an indirect approach would be best in each of the following situations and then briefly explain why. Would e-mail be an inappropriate medium for any of these messages? Explain.
a. A letter asking when next year's automobiles will be put on sale locally
b. A letter from a recent college graduate requesting a letter of recommendation from a former instructor
c. A letter turning down a job applicant
d. An announcement that because of high air-conditioning costs, the plant temperature will be held at 78°F during the summer
e. A final request to settle a delinquent debt

4.13 Message Organization: Audience Focus If you were trying to persuade people to take the following actions, how would you organize your argument?
a. You want your boss to approve your plan for hiring two new people.
b. You want to be hired for a job.
c. You want to be granted a business loan.
d. You want to collect a small amount from a regular customer whose account is slightly past due.
e. You want to collect a large amount from a customer whose account is seriously past due.

4.14 Ethical Choices: Providing Information Your supervisor, whom you respect, has asked you to withhold important information that you think should be included in a report you are preparing. Disobeying him could be disastrous for your relationship and your career. Obeying him could violate your personal code of ethics. What should you do? On the basis of the discussion in Chapter 1, would you consider this situation to be an ethical dilemma or an ethical lapse? Please explain.

4.15 Three-Step Process: Other Applications In an e-mail message to your instructor, explain how the material discussed in this chapter can also apply to meetings, as discussed in Chapter 2. (Hint: Review the section headings in Chapter 4 and think about making your meetings more productive.)

Expand Your Knowledge

LEARNING MORE ON THE WEB
READY TO MAKE A BUCK ON BLOGGING?
www.problogger.net

Millions of people now blog for fun, but a few are figuring out how to earn part or all of their income from their blogging efforts. ProBlogger (www.problogger.net) can help you get started with advice on setting up a blog, using Google's popular AdSense program, and identifying multiple ways to generate income with a blog. Explore ProBlogger's advice to answer these questions:

1. What are the various ways bloggers can make money from their work?
2. How can you go about choosing a topic for your blog?
3. How can the Google AdSense program help bloggers cover their costs and perhaps even turn a profit?

SURFING YOUR WAY TO CAREER SUCCESS

Bovée and Thill's Business Communication Headline News offers links to hundreds of online resources that can help you with this course, your other college courses, and your career. Visit www.businesscommunicationblog.com and click on "Web Directory." The "Writing Process" section connects you to a variety of websites and articles on planning, writing, revision, audience analysis, and brainstorming. Identify three websites from this section that could be useful in your business career. For each site, write a two-sentence summary of what the site offers and how it could help you launch and build your career.

Learn Interactively

INTERACTIVE STUDY GUIDE

Visit www.prenhall.com/thill, then locate your book and click on its "Companion Website" link. Select Chapter 4 to take advantage of the interactive "Chapter Quiz" to test your knowledge of chapter concepts. Receive instant feedback on whether you need additional studying. Also, visit the "Study Hall," where you'll find an abundance of valuable resources that will help you succeed in this course.

PEAK PERFORMANCE GRAMMAR AND MECHANICS

If your instructor has required the use of "Peak Performance Grammar and Mechanics," either in your online course or on CD, you can improve your skill with adjectives by using the

"Peak Performance Grammar and Mechanics" module. Click on "Grammar Basics" and then "Adjectives and Adverbs." Take the Pretest to determine whether you have any weak areas. Then review those areas in the Refresher Course. Take the Follow-Up Test to check your grasp of adjectives. For an extra challenge or advanced practice, take the Advanced Test. Finally, for additional reinforcement, go to the "Improve Your Grammar, Mechanics, and Usage" section that follows and complete those exercises.

Improve Your Grammar, Mechanics, and Usage

The following exercises help you improve your knowledge of and power over English grammar, mechanics, and usage. Turn to the Handbook of Grammar, Mechanics, and Usage at the end of this book and review all of Section 1.4 (Adjectives). Then look at the following 10 items. Underline the preferred choice within each set of parentheses. (Answers to these exercises appear on page AK-3.)

1. Of the two products, this one has the (*greater, greatest*) potential.
2. The (*most perfect, perfect*) solution is *d*.
3. Here is the (*interesting, most interesting*) of all the ideas I have heard so far.
4. The (*hardest, harder*) part of my job is firing people.
5. A (*highly placed, highly-placed*) source revealed Dotson's (*last ditch, last-ditch*) efforts to cover up the mistake.
6. A (*top secret, top-secret*) document was taken from the president's office last night.
7. A (*30 year old, 30-year-old*) person should know better.
8. The two companies are engaged in an (*all-out no-holds-barred; all-out, no-holds-barred*) struggle for dominance.
9. A (*tiny metal; tiny, metal*) shaving is responsible for the problem.
10. You'll receive our (*usual cheerful prompt; usual, cheerful, prompt; usual cheerful, prompt*) service.

For additional exercises focusing on adjectives, go to www.prenhall.com/thill, then locate your text and click on its "Companion Website" link. Click on Chapter 4, click on "Additional Exercises to Improve Your Grammar, Mechanics and Usage," and then click on "8. Adjectives."

Chapter 5

Writing Business Messages

Learning Objectives

AFTER STUDYING THIS CHAPTER, YOU WILL BE ABLE TO

1 Explain the importance of adapting your messages to the needs and expectations of your audience

2 Explain why establishing credibility is vital to the success of your communication efforts

3 Discuss four ways of achieving a businesslike tone with a style that is clear and concise

4 Briefly describe how to select words that are not only correct but also effective

5 Explain how sentence style affects emphasis within your message

6 List five ways to develop coherent paragraphs

On the Job

COMMUNICATING AT CREATIVE COMMONS

REDEFINING TWO CENTURIES OF COPYRIGHT LAW FOR THE DIGITAL AGE

Have you ever noticed that tiny © symbol on books, DVDs, music CDs, and other media products? This symbol means that the person or organization who created the item has *copyright* protection—the exclusive legal right to produce, distribute, and sell that creation. Anyone who wants to resell, redistribute, or adapt such works usually needs to secure permission from the current copyright holder.

However, what if you *want* people to remix the song you just recorded? Or suppose you need a few photos for a website or a short piece of music for a training video? Other than for limited personal and educational use, a conventional copyright requires every person to negotiate a contract for every application or adaptation of every piece of work he or she wants to use.

The search for some middle ground between "all rights reserved" and simply giving your work away led Stanford University law professor Lawrence Lessig to co-found Creative Commons. This nonprofit organization's goal is to provide a simple, free, and legal way

Lawrence Lessig, co-founder of Creative Commons, uses a variety of communication vehicles to convince copyright owners to explore new ways of sharing and protecting their creative works.

for musicians, artists, writers, teachers, scientists, and others to collaborate and benefit through the sharing of art and ideas. Instead of the everything-or-nothing approach of traditional copyright, Creative Commons offers a more flexible range of "some rights reserved" options.

Through books, articles, and speeches, Lessig has been a tireless promoter of the Creative Commons concept, working to convince people that society benefits from the free exchange of art and ideas and that overuse of the copyright law is endangering not only creative expression but also important scientific research. The message is clearly getting through: Within the first year, more than a million of these innovative license agreements were initiated for musical works, short films, educational materials, novels, and more. This approach can't solve the entire dilemma of copyrights in the digital age, but it has already created a better way for creative people to communicate and collaborate.[1]

www.creativecommons.org

BRINGING YOUR IDEAS TO LIFE

As they work to persuade their audiences to consider new forms of copyright protection, Lawrence Lessig and his colleagues at Creative Commons (profiled in the chapter opener) realize it takes more than just a great idea to change the way people think. Expressing ideas clearly and persuasively will be key to your success as well.

Having completed the planning phase (see Chapter 4), you're ready to choose the words and craft the sentences and paragraphs that will carry your ideas to their intended audiences. Figure 5.1 lists the tasks involved in adapting to your audience and composing your message.

ADAPTING TO YOUR AUDIENCE

Audiences want to know how your messages will benefit them.

Whether consciously or not, audiences greet most incoming messages with a question: "What's in this for me?" If your intended audience members think a message does not apply to them or doesn't meet their needs, they won't be inclined to pay attention to it. Follow the example set by the Creative Commons website, which addresses a diverse audience of artists, lawyers, and business professionals but fine-tunes specific messages for each group of people. By adapting your communication to the needs and expectations of your audiences, you'll provide a more compelling answer to the "What's in this for me?" question and improve the chances of your message being successful.

A good relationship with your audience is essential to effective communication.

Note that adapting your message is not always a simple task. Some situations require you to balance competing or conflicting needs—for example, when you're trying to convince people to change their minds or when you're delivering bad news. To successfully adapt your message to your audience, try to be sensitive to your audience's needs, build a strong relationship with your audience, and control your style to maintain a professional tone.

FIGURE 5.1
Step Two in the Three-Step Writing Process: Write Your Messages
The second step in the three-step writing process includes two vital tasks: adapting to your audience and composing your message.

Planning → Writing → Completing

Adapt to Your Audience
Be sensitive to audience needs, by using a "you" attitude, politeness, positive emphasis, and bias-free language. Build a strong relationship with your audience by establishing your credibility and projecting your image. Control your style with a conversational tone, plain English, and appropriate voice.

Compose the Message
Choose strong words that will help you create effective sentences and coherent paragraphs.

1   2   3

Being Sensitive to Your Audience's Needs

Even in simple messages intended merely to share information, it's possible to use all the right words and still not be sensitive to your audience members and their needs. You can improve your audience sensitivity by adopting the "you" attitude, maintaining good standards of etiquette, emphasizing the positive, and using bias-free language.

Using the "You" Attitude   Chapter 1 introduces the notion of audience-centered communication and the "you" attitude—that is, by speaking and writing in terms of your audience's wishes, interests, hopes, and preferences. On the simplest level, you can adopt the "you" attitude by replacing terms that refer to yourself and your company with terms that refer to your audience. In other words, use *you* and *yours* instead of *I, me, mine, we, us,* and *ours*:

> The "you" attitude is best implemented by expressing your message in terms of the audience's interests and needs.

Instead of This	Write This
To help us process this order, we must ask for another copy of the requisition.	So that your order can be filled promptly, please send another copy of the requisition.
We are pleased to announce our new flight schedule from Atlanta to New York, which is any hour on the hour.	Now you can take a Delta flight from Atlanta to New York any hour on the hour.
We offer MP3 players with 50, 75, or 100 gigabytes of storage capacity.	Select your MP3 player from three models with 50, 75, or 100 gigabytes of storage capacity.

When business messages use an "I" or "we" attitude, they risk sounding selfish and uninterested in the audience. The message is all about the sender, and the audience is just expected to go along with it. Even so, using *you* and *yours* requires finesse. If you overdo it, you're likely to create some rather awkward sentences, and you run the risk of sounding overly enthusiastic and artificial.[2]

The "you" attitude is not intended to be manipulative or insincere. It's an extension of the audience-centered approach. In fact, the best way to implement the "you" attitude is to sincerely think about your audience when composing your message.

Nor is the "you" attitude simply a matter of using one pronoun rather than another; it's a matter of genuine empathy. You can use *you* 25 times in a single page and still ignore your audience's true concerns. In other words, it's the thought and sincerity that count, not the pronoun *you*. If you're talking to a retailer, try to think like a retailer; if you're dealing with a production supervisor, put yourself in that position; if you're writing to a dissatisfied customer, imagine how you would feel at the other end of the transaction.

Be aware that on some occasions, it's better to avoid using the word *you*, particularly if doing so will sound overly authoritative or accusing:

> Avoid using *you* and *yours* when doing so
> - Makes you sound dictatorial
> - Makes someone else feel guilty
> - Goes against your organization's style

Instead of This	Write This
You failed to deliver the customer's order on time.	The customer didn't receive the order on time.
	or
	Let's figure out a system that will ensure on-time deliveries.
You must correct all five copies by noon.	All five copies must be corrected by noon.

As you practice using the "you" attitude, be sure to consider the attitudes of other cultures and the policies of your organization. In some cultures, it is improper to single out one person's achievements because the whole team is responsible for the outcome; in that case, using the pronoun *we* or *our* (when you and your audience are part of the same team) would be more appropriate. Similarly, some companies have a tradition of avoiding references to *you* and *I* in formal messages and reports.

Maintaining Standards of Etiquette You know how it feels to be treated inconsiderately; when that happens, you probably react emotionally and then pay less attention to the offending message. By being courteous to members of your audience, you show consideration for them and foster a more successful environment for communication.

On occasions when you experience frustration with co-workers, customers, or others you deal with, you may be tempted to respond in blunt terms. However, venting your emotions rarely improves the situation and can damage your reputation. Demonstrate your diplomatic skills by controlling your emotions and communicating calmly and politely:

Although you may be tempted now and then to be brutally frank, try to express the facts in a kind and thoughtful manner.

Instead of This	Write This
Once again, you've managed to bring down the entire website through your incompetent programming.	Let's review the last website update so that we can find out how to improve the process.
You've been sitting on our order for two weeks, and we need it now!	Our production schedules depend on timely delivery of parts and supplies, but we have not yet received the order you promised to deliver two weeks ago. Please respond today with a firm delivery commitment.

Use extra tact when communicating with people higher up in the organization or outside the company.

Of course, some situations require more diplomacy than others. If you know your audience well, a less formal approach may be more appropriate. In contrast, when you are communicating with people who outrank you or with people outside your organization, an added measure of courtesy is usually needed.

Written communication and most forms of electronic media generally require more tact than oral communication (see Figure 5.2). When you're speaking, your words are softened by your tone of voice and facial expression. Plus, you can adjust your approach according to the feedback you get. If you inadvertently offend someone in writing or in a podcast, for example, you usually don't get the immediate feedback you would need to resolve the situation. In fact, you may never know that you offended your audience.

You can communicate negative news without being negative.

Emphasizing the Positive During your career, you will have many occasions to communicate bad news—maybe dozens or hundreds of times. As you rise through the ranks of management, you will encounter situations in which unpleasant news can significantly affect the personal and financial well-being of employees, customers, and investors. However, there is a big difference between delivering negative news and being negative. When the tone of your message is negative, you put unnecessary strain on business relationships, which can cause people to distance themselves from you and your ideas.

If you're facing a potentially negative situation, look for ways to soften the blow or emphasize positive aspects of a situation. For example, when Alaska Airlines instituted surcharges for heavy luggage in an attempt to reduce injuries to baggage handlers, the company presented the change to passengers with posters that said, "Pack Light & Save."[3] By presenting the situation as an opportunity to save money rather than as an added cost of travel, Alaska worked to maintain a positive relationship

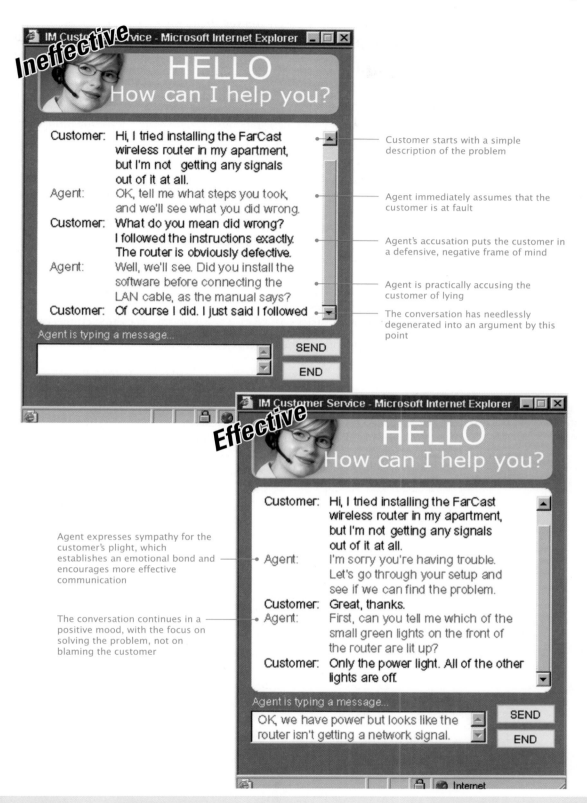

FIGURE 5.2

Fostering a Positive Relationship with an Audience

In the "ineffective" example, notice how the customer service agent's unfortunate word choices immediately derail this instant messaging exchange. In the "effective" example, a more sensitive approach allows both people to focus on solving the problem.

with its customers. Never try to hide the negative news but always be on the lookout for positive points that will foster a good relationship with your audience:[4]

Instead of This	Write This
It is impossible to repair your laptop today.	Your computer can be ready by Tuesday. Would you like a loaner until then?
We apologize for inconveniencing you during our remodeling.	The renovations now under way will help us serve you better.
We wasted $300,000 advertising in that magazine.	Our $300,000 advertising investment did not pay off; let's analyze the experience and apply the insights to future campaigns.

When you are offering criticism or advice, focus on what the person can do to improve.

When you find it necessary to criticize or correct, don't dwell on the other person's mistakes. Avoid referring to failures, problems, or shortcomings. Focus instead on what the person can do to improve:

Instead of This	Write This
The problem with this department is a failure to control costs.	The performance of this department can be improved by tightening cost controls.
You failed to provide all the necessary information on the previous screen.	Please review the items marked in red on the previous screen so that we can process your order as quickly as possible.

Show your audience members how they will benefit from listening to and complying with your message.

If you're trying to persuade audience members to buy a product, pay a bill, or perform a service for you, emphasize what's in it for them. Don't focus on why *you* want them to do something. An individual who sees the possibility for personal benefit is more likely to respond positively to your appeal:

Instead of This	Write This
We will notify all three credit reporting agencies if you do not pay your overdue bill within 10 days.	Paying your overdue bill within 10 days will prevent a negative entry on your credit record.
I am tired of seeing so many errors in the customer-service blog.	Proofreading your blog postings will help you avoid embarrassing mistakes that generate more customer-service complaints.

Try to avoid words with negative connotations; use meaningful euphemisms instead.

In general, try to state your message without using words that may hurt or offend your audience. Substitute *euphemisms* (mild terms) for those that have unpleasant associations. You can be honest without being harsh. Gentle language won't change the facts, but it will make them more acceptable:

Instead of This	Write This
Cheap merchandise	Economy merchandise
Failing	Underperforming
Fake	Imitation or faux

On the other hand, don't carry euphemisms to extremes, or your audience will view your efforts as insincere. And if you're too subtle, people won't know what you're talking about. If employees need to become 10 percent more productive to save the company from bankruptcy, don't tell them they need to "make positive performance adjustments"—tell them they need to become 10 percent more productive. Also, when using euphemisms, you walk a fine line between softening the blow and hiding the facts. It would be unethical to speak to your local community about "manufacturing by-products" when you're really talking about your plans for disposing of toxic waste. Such an attempt to hide the facts would likely backfire, damaging your business image and reputation. Even if it is unpleasant, people respond better to an honest message delivered with integrity than they do to a sugarcoated message that obscures the truth.

Using Bias-Free Language   Chapter 3 points out that you are often unaware of the influence of your own culture on your behavior. Any bias present in your culture is likely to show up in your language, often in subtle ways that you may not even recognize. However, chances are that your audience will take note.

Avoid biased language that may offend your audience.

Bias-free language avoids words and phrases that unfairly and even unethically categorize or stigmatize people in ways related to gender, race, ethnicity, age, or disability. Contrary to what some may think, biased language is not simply about "labels." To a significant degree, language reflects the way we think and what we believe, and biased language may well perpetuate the underlying stereotypes and prejudices that it represents.[5] Moreover, because communication is all about perception, being fair and objective isn't enough; to establish a good relationship with your audience, you must also *appear* to be fair.[6] Good communicators make every effort to avoid biased language (see Table 5.1):

- **Gender bias.** Avoid sexist language by using the same labels for everyone, regardless of gender. (Don't call a woman *chairperson* and then call a man *chairman*.) Reword sentences to use *they* or to use no pronoun at all rather than refer to all individuals as *he*. Note that the preferred title for women in business is *Ms.*, unless the individual asks to be addressed as *Miss* or *Mrs.* or has some other title, such as *Dr.*

- **Racial and ethnic bias.** Avoid language suggesting that members of a racial or an ethnic group have stereotypical characteristics. The best solution is to avoid identifying people by race or ethnic origin unless such a label is relevant to the matter at hand—and it rarely is.

- **Age bias.** Mention the age of a person only when it is relevant. Moreover, be careful of the context in which you use words that refer to age. Such words carry a variety of positive and negative connotations—and not only when referring to people beyond a certain age. For example, *young* can imply youthfulness, inexperience, or even immaturity, depending on how it's used.

- **Disability bias.** As with other labels, physical, mental, sensory, or emotional impairments should never be mentioned in business messages unless those conditions are directly relevant to the subject. If you must refer to someone's disability, put the person first and the disability second.[7] For example, by saying "employees with physical handicaps," not "handicapped employees," you focus on the whole person, not the disability. Finally, never use outdated terminology such as *crippled* or *retarded*.

Building Strong Relationships with Your Audience

Focusing on your audience's needs is vital to effective communication, but you also have your own priorities as a communicator. Sometimes these needs are obvious and direct, such as when you're appealing for a budget increase for your department. At other times, the need may be more subtle. For instance, you might want to demonstrate your understanding of the marketplace or your company's concern for the natural environment. Two key efforts help you address your own needs while building positive relationships with your audience: establishing your credibility and projecting your company's image.

Table 5.1 — OVERCOMING BIAS IN LANGUAGE

Examples	Unacceptable	Preferable
Gender Bias		
Using words containing "man"	Man-made	Artificial, synthetic, manufactured, constructed
	Mankind	Humanity, human beings, human race, people
	Manpower	Workers, workforce
	Businessman	Executive, manager, businessperson
	Salesman	Sales representative, salesperson, clerk
	Foreman	Supervisor
Using female-gender words	Actress, stewardess	Actor, flight attendant
Using special designations	Woman doctor, male nurse	Doctor, nurse
Using "he" to refer to "everyone"	The average worker . . . he	The average worker . . . he or she
Identifying roles with gender	The typical executive spends four hours of his day in meetings.	Most executive spend four hours a day in meetings.
	the consumer . . . she	consumers . . . they
	The nurse/teacher . . . she	nurses/teachers . . . they
Identifying women by marital status	Norm Lindstrom and Maria	Norm Lindstrom and Maria Drake
	Norm Lindstrom and Ms. Lindstrom	Mr. Lindstrom and Ms. Drake
Racial/Ethnic Bias		
Assigning stereotypes	My African-American assistant speaks more articulately than I do.	My assistant speaks more articulately than I do.
	Jim Wong is an unusually tall Asian	Jim Wong is tall.
Identifying people by race or ethnicity	Mario M. Cuomo, Italian American politician and ex-governor of New York	Mario M. Cuomo, politician and ex-governor of New York
Age Bias		
Including age when irrelevant	Mary Kirazy, 58, has just joined our trust department.	Mary Kirazy has just joined our trust department.
Disability Bias		
Putting the disability before the person	Crippled workers face many barriers on the job.	Workers with physical disabilities face many barriers on the job.
	An epileptic, Tracy has no trouble doing her job.	Tracy's epilepsy has no effect on her job performance.

People are more likely to react positively to your message when they have confidence in you.

Establishing Your Credibility   Audience responses to your messages depend heavily on your **credibility**, a measure of your believability based on how reliable you are and how much trust you evoke in others. With audiences who already know you, you've already established some degree of credibility, based on past communication efforts. As long as you haven't let people down in the past, they are inclined to accept each new message from you. However, with audiences who don't know you, you need to establish credibility before they'll accept—or perhaps even pay attention to—

your messages. To build, maintain, or repair your credibility, emphasize the following characteristics:

- **Honesty.** Demonstrating honesty and integrity will earn you the respect of your audiences, even if they don't always agree with or welcome your messages.

- **Objectivity.** Show that you can distance yourself from emotional situations and look at all sides of an issue.

- **Awareness of audience needs.** Let your audiences know that you understand what's important to them.

- **Credentials, knowledge, and expertise.** Audiences need to know that you have whatever it takes to back up your message, whether it's education, professional certification, special training, past successes, or simply the fact that you've done your research.

- **Endorsements.** An *endorsement* is a statement on your behalf by someone who is accepted by your audience as an expert. If your audiences don't know anything about you, try to get assistance from someone they do know and trust.

- **Performance.** Demonstrating impressive communication skills is not enough; people need to know they can count on you to get the job done.

- **Sincerity.** When you offer praise, don't use hyperbole, such as "you are the most fantastic employee I could ever imagine." Instead, point out specific qualities that warrant praise.

To enhance your credibility, emphasize such factors as honesty, objectivity, and awareness of audience needs.

In addition, audiences need to know that you believe in yourself and your message. If you lack faith in yourself, you're likely to communicate an uncertain attitude that undermines your credibility. In contrast, if you are convinced that your message is sound, you can state your case with authority so that your audience has no doubts. Try to avoid phrases such as *if*, *hope*, and *trust*, which can drain the audience's confidence in your message:

Document Makeover

IMPROVE THIS LETTER

To practice correcting drafts of actual documents, visit your online course or the access-code-protected portion of the Companion Website. Click on "Document Makeovers" and then click on Chapter 5. You will find a letter that contains problems and errors related to what you've learned in this chapter about establishing a good relationship with your audience. Use the Final Draft decision tool to create an improved version of this letter. Check the document for the "you" attitude, positive language, communication etiquette, bias-free language, and phrases that establish credibility.

Instead of This	Write This
We hope this recommendation will be helpful.	We're glad to make this recommendation.
If you'd like to order, please visit our website	To order, please visit our website.
We trust that you'll want to extend your service contract.	By extending your service contract, you can continue to enjoy top-notch performance from your equipment.

Finally, keep in mind that credibility can take days, months, or even years to establish—and it can be wiped out in an instant. An occasional mistake or letdown is usually forgiven, but major lapses in honesty or integrity can destroy your reputation. On the other hand, when you do establish credibility, communication becomes much easier because you no longer have to spend time and energy convincing people that you are a trustworthy source of information and ideas.

Projecting Your Company's Image When you communicate with outsiders, on even the most routine matter, you serve as the spokesperson for your organization. The impression you make can enhance or damage the reputation of the entire company.

Whether you're blogging, updating a website, or even just exchanging IM with a customer, you are responsible for projecting your company's preferred image to the outside world.

Your *style* involves all the choices you make to express yourself; your *tone* is the overall impression your messages create.

Most business messages aim for a conversational style that is warm but still businesslike.

Consequently, the interests and preferred communication style of your company must take precedence over your own views and personal communication style.

Many organizations have specific communication guidelines that show everything from the correct use of the company name to preferred abbreviations and other grammatical details. Specifying a desired style of communication is more difficult, however. Observe more experienced colleagues to see how they communicate and never hesitate to ask for editorial help to make sure you're conveying the appropriate tone. For instance, with clients entrusting thousands or millions of dollars to it, an investment firm communicates in a style quite different from that of a clothing retailer. And a clothing retailer specializing in high-quality business attire communicates in a different style than a store catering to the latest trends in casual wear.

Controlling Your Style and Tone

Your communication **style** involves the choices you make to express yourself: the words you select, the manner in which you use those words in sentences, and the way you build paragraphs from individual sentences. Your style creates a certain **tone**, or overall impression, in your messages. You can vary your style to sound forceful or objective, personal or formal, colorful or dry. The right choice depends on the nature of your message and your relationship with the reader. Although style can be refined during the revision phase (see Chapter 6), you'll save time and a lot of rewriting if you use a style that allows you to achieve the desired tone from the start.

Using a Conversational Tone   The tone of your business messages can range from informal to conversational to formal. If you're in a large organization and you're communicating with your superiors or with customers, your tone may tend to be more formal and respectful.[8] However, that formal tone might sound distant and cold if used with close colleagues or in organizations that value informality.

Compare the three versions of the message in Table 5.2. The first is too formal and stuffy for today's audiences, whereas the third is too casual for any audience other than close associates or friends. The second message demonstrates the conversational tone used in most business communication—using plain language that sounds businesslike without being stuffy or full of jargon. You can achieve a conversational tone by following these guidelines:

- **Avoid obsolete and pompous language.** Business language used to be much more formal than it is today, but some out-of-date phrases still find their way into communication efforts. You can avoid using such language if you ask yourself, "Would I say this if I were talking with someone face to face?" Similarly, avoid using big words, trite expressions, and overly complicated sentences to impress others. Such pompous language sounds self-important (see Table 5.3).

- **Avoid preaching and bragging.** Few things are more irritating than know-it-alls who like to preach or brag. However, if you do need to remind your audience of something that should be obvious, try to work in the information casually, perhaps in the middle of a paragraph, where it will sound like a secondary comment rather than a major revelation. Also, avoid bragging about your accomplishments or those of your organization (unless your audience is a part of your organization).

- **Be careful with intimacy.** Most business messages should avoid intimacy, such as sharing personal details or adopting an extremely casual, unprofessional tone. However, when you do have a close relationship with your audience, such as among the members of a close-knit team, a more intimate tone is sometimes appropriate and even expected.

- **Be careful with humor.** Humor can be an effective tool to inject interest into dry subjects or take the sting out of negative news, but it can easily backfire and divert

Table 5.2 — FORMAL, CONVERSATIONAL, AND INFORMAL TONES

Formal Tone	Conversational Tone	Informal Tone
Reserved for the most formal occasions	*Preferred for most business communication*	*Reserved for communication with friends and close associates*
Dear Ms. Navarro:	Dear Ms. Navarro:	Hi Gabriella:
Enclosed please find the information that was requested during our telephone communication of May 14. As was mentioned at that time, Midville Hospital has significantly more doctors of exceptional quality than any other health facility in the state.	Here's the information you requested during our phone conversation on Friday. As I mentioned, Midville Hospital has the best doctors and more of them than any other hospital in the state.	Hope all is well. Just sending along the information you asked for. As I said on Friday, Midville Hospital has more and better doctors than any other hospital in the state.
As you were also informed, our organization has quite an impressive network of doctors and other health-care professionals with offices located throughout the state. In the event that you should need a specialist, our professionals will be able to make an appropriate recommendation.	In addition, we have a vast network of doctors and other health professionals with offices throughout the state. If you need a specialist, we can refer you to the right one.	We also have a large group of doctors and other health professionals with offices close to you at work or at home. Need a specialist? We'll refer you to the right one.
In the event that you have questions or would like additional information, you may certainly contact me during regular business hours.	If you would like more information, please call me between 9:00 and 5:00, Monday through Friday.	Just give me a ring if you want to know more; I'm in the office from 9:00 to 5:00, Monday through Friday.
Most sincerely yours,	Sincerely,	Take care,
Samuel G. Berenz	Samuel G. Berenz	Sam

attention from your message. The humor must be connected to the point you're trying to make; business messages are not a forum for sharing jokes. Never use humor in formal messages or when you're communicating across cultural boundaries. If you don't know your audience well or you're not skilled at using humor in a business setting, don't use it at all. When in doubt, leave it out.

WEEDING OUT OBSOLETE PHRASES — Table 5.3

Obsolete Phrase	Up-to-Date Replacement
We are in receipt of	*We received*
Kindly advise	*Please let me/us know*
Attached please find	*Enclosed is or I/We have enclosed*
It has come to my attention	*I have just learned or [Someone] has just informed me*
The undersigned	*I/We*
In due course	*(Specify a specific time or date.)*
Permit me to say that	*(Omit; just say whatever you need to say.)*
Pursuant to	*(Omit; just say whatever you need to say.)*
In closing, I'd like to say	*(Omit; just say whatever you need to say.)*
We wish to inform you that	*(Omit; just say whatever you need to say.)*
Please be advised that	*(Omit; just say whatever you need to say.)*

Using Plain English   What do you think this sentence is trying to say?

> We continually exist to synergistically supply value-added deliverables such that we may continue to proactively maintain enterprise-wide data to stay competitive in tomorrow's world.[9]

If you don't have any idea what it means, you're not alone. However, this is a real sentence from a real company, written in an attempt to explain what the company does and why. This sort of incomprehensible, buzzword-filled writing is driving a widespread call to use *plain English*.

Audiences can understand and act on plain English without reading it over and over.

Plain English is a way of presenting information in a simple, unadorned style so that your audience can easily grasp your meaning, without struggling through specialized, technical, or convoluted language. Because it's close to the way people normally speak, plain English is easily understood by anyone with a basic education. The Plain English Campaign (a nonprofit group in England campaigning for clear language) defines *plain English* as language "that the intended audience can read, understand and act upon the first time they read it."[10] You can see how this definition supports using the "you" attitude and shows respect for your audience.

On the Creative Commons website, for instance, licensing terms are available in two versions: a complete document that spells out contractual details in specific legal terms that meet the needs of legal professionals, and a second version, labeled "human-readable," which explains the licensing terms in nontechnical language that anyone can understand.[11]

Even though readers overwhelmingly appreciate plain English and its merits have been demonstrated in a variety of audience tests,[12] murky, pompous, and unnecessarily complex writing is still more common than it should be. One reason is that writers are sometimes unsure about their own writing skills and about the impact their messages will have. They mistakenly believe that packaging simple ideas in complex writing makes their messages seem more impressive. Another reason is inadequate planning, which results in messages that meander in search of a conclusion. A third reason is that some writers intentionally try to create distance between themselves and their audiences. Whatever the cause, the result of unnecessarily complex writing is always the same: ineffective communication that wastes time, wastes money, and annoys everyone who comes in contact with it.

Even though plain English is intended for audiences who speak English as their primary language, plain English can also help you simplify the messages you prepare for audiences who speak English only as a second or even third language. For example, by choosing a word that has only one interpretation, you will communicate more clearly with an intercultural audience (see "Communicating Across Cultures: Communicating with a Global Audience on the Web").[13]

Bear in mind that plain English doesn't have to be simplistic, dull, or imprecise. The point is to be clear, not lifeless. Also, be sure to consider the needs and expectations of your audience. For instance, scientific, technical, legal, and other specialized messages often require specialized terminology. Use these specific terms whenever you need to; just be sure to use them in clearly constructed sentences and well-organized paragraphs.

Selecting Active or Passive Voice   Your choice of active or passive voice also affects the tone of your message. You are using **active voice** when the subject performs the action and the object receives the action: "John rented the office." You're using **passive voice** when the subject receives the action: "The office was rented by John." As you can see, the passive voice combines the helping verb *to be* with a form of the verb that is usually similar to the past tense. When you use active sentences, your messages generally sound less formal and make it easier for readers to figure out who performed the action (see Table 5.4). In contrast, passive voice de-emphasizes the subject and implies that the action was done by something or someone.

COMMUNICATING ACROSS CULTURES

Communicating with a Global Audience on the Web

Reaching an international audience on the web involves more than simply offering translations of the English language. Successful global sites address the needs of international customers in five ways:

1. *Consider the reader's perspective.* Many communication elements that you take for granted may be interpreted differently by audiences in other countries. Should you use the metric system, different notations for times or dates, or even different names for countries? For example, German citizens don't refer to their country as *Germany*; it's *Deutschland* to them. Review the entire online experience and look for ways to improve communication, including such helpful tools as interactive currency converters and translation dictionaries.

2. *Take cultural differences into account.* For instance, because humor is rooted in cultural norms, U.S. humor may not be so funny to Asian or European readers. Avoid idioms and references that aren't universally recognized, such as "putting all your eggs in one basket" or "out of the frying pan and into the fire."

3. *Keep the message clear.* Use simple words and sentences and write in the active voice. Define abbreviations, acro-

nyms, and words an international audience may not be familiar with.

4. *Complement language with visuals.* Use drawings, photos, and other visuals to help communicate when words alone may not get the message across.

5. *Consult local experts.* Seek the advice of local experts about phrases and references that may be expected. Even terms as simple as *homepage* differ from country to country. Spanish readers refer to the "first page," or *página inicial*, whereas the French term is "welcome page," or *page d'accueíl*.

CAREER APPLICATIONS

1. Visit Sony's Global Headquarters website, at www.sony.net, and examine Sony's music-oriented websites for Argentina, France, and Germany. How does Sony "localize" each country's site?

2. Compare Sony Music's international sites to IBM's global webpages, at www.ibm.com. How does Sony's approach differ from IBM's? Do both corporations successfully address the needs of a global audience? Write a two-paragraph summary that compares the international sites of both companies.

Table 5.4	**CHOOSING ACTIVE OR PASSIVE VOICE**

In general, avoid passive voice in order to make your writing lively and direct

Dull and Indirect in Passive Voice	Lively and Direct in Active Voice
The new procedure was developed by the operations team.	The operations team developed the new procedure.
Legal problems are created by this contract.	This contract creates legal problems.
Reception preparations have been undertaken by our PR people for the new CEO's arrival.	Our PR people have begun planning a reception for the new CEO.

However, passive voice is helpful when you need to be diplomatic or want to focus attention on problems or solutions rather than on people

Accusatory or Self-congratulatory in Active Voice	More Diplomatic in Passive Voice
You lost the shipment.	The shipment was lost.
I recruited seven engineers last month.	Seven engineers were recruited last month.
We are investigating the high rate of failure on the final assembly line.	The high rate of failures on the final assembly line is being investigated.

Active sentences are usually stronger than passive ones.

Use passive sentences to soften bad news, to put yourself in the background, or to create an impersonal tone.

Using the active voice helps make your writing more direct, livelier, and easier to read. In contrast, the passive voice is not wrong grammatically, but it is often cumbersome, can be unnecessarily vague, and can make sentences longer. In most cases, the active voice is your best choice.[14] Nevertheless, using the passive voice can help you demonstrate the "you" attitude in some situations:

- **When you want to be diplomatic about pointing out a problem or an error of some kind.** The passive version seems less like an accusation.

- **When you want to point out what's being done without taking or attributing either credit or blame.** The passive version shifts the spotlight away from the person or persons involved.

- **When you want to avoid personal pronouns in order to create an objective tone.** The passive version may be used in a formal report, for example.

For example, to explain its 90-day limit on product returns, Gap says the following on its website: "Merchandise returned more than 90 days after the purchase date will not be eligible for a return,"[15] instead of saying something like "You cannot return products more than 90 days after the purchase date." The second half of Table 5.4 illustrates several other situations in which the passive voice helps you focus your message on your audience.

COMPOSING YOUR MESSAGE

With these insights into how you can adapt to your audience, you're ready to begin composing your message. Composition is much easier if you've already figured out what to say and in what order (refer to the outlining advice in Chapter 4). However, you may also discover as you move along that you can improve on your outline. Feel free to rearrange, delete, and add ideas, as long as you don't lose sight of your purpose.

As you compose your first draft, try to let your creativity flow. Don't try to write and edit at the same time and don't worry about getting everything perfect. Make up words if you can't think of the right word, draw pictures, talk out loud—do whatever it takes to get the ideas out of your head and onto your computer screen or a piece of paper. You'll have time to revise and refine the material later before showing it to anyone. In fact, many writers find it helpful to establish a personal rule of *never* showing a first draft to anyone. By working in this "safe zone," away from the critical eyes of others, your mind will stay free to think clearly and creatively.

If you get stuck and feel unable to write, try to overcome writer's block by jogging your brain in creative ways. The introduction is often the hardest part to write, so put it aside and work on whichever parts of the document you're most comfortable with at any given moment. In most cases, you don't need to write the sections in any particular order.[16] Work on nontext elements such as graphics or your cover page. Give yourself a mental break by switching to a different project. When you're feeling refreshed, the words will probably start flowing again, your mind will engage, and the writing will come easier.

As you create and refine your messages, learn to view your writing at three levels: strong words, effective sentences, and coherent paragraphs.

Choosing Strong Words

Correctness is the first consideration when choosing words.

Effective messages depend on carefully chosen words, whether you select them during your first draft or edit them in later.[17] First, pay close attention to correctness. The "rules" of grammar and usage can be a source of worry for all writers because many of these rules are complex and can evolve over time. Even professional editors and grammarians occasionally have questions about correct usage, and they sometimes disagree about the answers. For example, the word *data* is the plural form of *datum*, yet some experts now prefer to treat *data* as a singular noun when it's used in nonscientific material to refer to a body of information.

Although debating the finer points of usage may seem like nitpicking, using words correctly is important. If you make grammatical or usage errors, you lose credibility with your audience—even if your message is otherwise correct. Poor grammar implies that you're uninformed, and audiences put less faith in an uninformed source. Worse still, poor grammar can imply that you don't respect your audience enough to get things right. Even if an audience is broad-minded enough to withhold such a judgment, grammatical errors are distracting.

Using correct grammar enhances your image.

If you have doubts about what is correct, look up the answer and use the proper form of expression. Check the Handbook of Grammar, Mechanics, and Usage at the end of this book, or consult any of the many special reference books and resources available in libraries, in bookstores, and on the Internet. Most authorities agree on the basic conventions.

Just as important as selecting the correct word is selecting the most suitable word for the job at hand. Naturally, using the right words is important in life-and-death situations. But even when you're dealing with less perilous circumstances, the right words can make all the difference in the success of your communication efforts. Word effectiveness is generally more difficult to achieve than correctness, particularly in written communication. Even professional writers with decades of experience continue to work at their craft to use functional and content words correctly and to find words that communicate well (see Figure 5.3).

Effectiveness is the second consideration when choosing words.

Using Functional and Content Words Correctly   Words can be divided into two main categories. **Functional words** express relationships, and each has only one unchanging meaning in any given context. Functional words include conjunctions,

Functional words (conjunctions, prepositions, articles, and pronouns) express the relationships among content words (nouns, verbs, adjectives, and adverbs).

FIGURE 5.3
Choosing Effective Words
Through the use of such words and phrases as *paradise, at their own pace, smooth,* and *trouble-free,* The Moorings conveys a sense of relaxed adventure on its website.

prepositions, articles, and pronouns. Your main concern with functional words is to use them correctly. **Content words** are multidimensional and, therefore, frequently subject to various interpretations. They include nouns, verbs, adjectives, and adverbs. These words carry the meaning of a sentence. In your sentences, content words are the building blocks, and functional words are the mortar that holds them together. In the following sentence, all the content words are underlined:

> <u>Carlo Firenze noted</u> that <u>custom ringtones have generated several billion dollars</u> in <u>sales so far</u>, but <u>he isn't sure</u> if this <u>momentum will transfer</u> to <u>other mobile data services</u>.

Both functional words and content words are necessary, but your effectiveness as a communicator depends largely on your ability to choose the right content words for your message.

Content words have both a denotative (explicit, specific) meaning and a connotative (implicit, associative) meaning.

Denotation and Connotation Content words have both a denotative and a connotative meaning. The **denotative meaning** is the literal, or dictionary, meaning. The **connotative meaning** includes all the associations and feelings evoked by the word.

The denotative meaning of *desk* is "a piece of furniture with a flat work surface and various drawers for storage." The connotative meaning of *desk* may include thoughts associated with work or study, but the word *desk* has fairly neutral connotations—neither strong nor emotional. However, some words have much stronger connotations than others. For example, the connotations of the word *fail* are negative and can carry strong emotional meaning. If you say that the sales department *failed* to meet its annual goal, the connotative meaning suggests that the group is inferior, incompetent, or below some standard of performance. However, the reason for not achieving 100 percent might be an inferior product, incorrect pricing, or some other factor outside the control of the sales department. In contrast, by saying that the sales department achieved 85 percent of its goal, you clearly communicate that the results were less than expected—without triggering all the negative emotions associated with *failure*.

The more abstract a word is, the more it is removed from the tangible, objective world of things that can be perceived with the senses.

Abstraction and Concreteness Words vary dramatically in the degree of abstraction or concreteness they convey. An **abstract word** expresses a concept, quality, or characteristic. Abstractions are usually broad, encompassing a category of ideas, and they are often intellectual, academic, or philosophical. *Love, honor, progress, tradition,* and *beauty* are abstractions, as are such important business concepts as *productivity, profits, quality,* and *motivation*. In contrast, a **concrete word** stands for something you can touch, see, or visualize. Most concrete terms are anchored in the tangible, material world. *Chair, table, horse, rose, kick, kiss, red, green,* and *two* are concrete words; they are direct, clear, and exact. Incidentally, technology continues to generate new words and new meanings that describe things that don't have a physical presence but are nonetheless concrete: *software, database, signal,* and *code* are all concrete terms as well.

Use concrete, specific terms whenever possible; use abstractions only when necessary.

You might assume that concrete words are better than abstract words because they are more precise, but that isn't always the case. For example, try to rewrite this sentence without using the underlined abstract words:

> We hold these <u>truths</u> to be <u>self-evident</u>, that all men are <u>created equal</u>, that they are <u>endowed</u> by their <u>Creator</u> with certain <u>unalienable Rights</u>, that among these are <u>Life</u>, <u>Liberty</u>, and the <u>Pursuit of Happiness</u>.

As you can see, the Declaration of Independence needs abstractions, and so do most business messages. (You'll also note that *men* would be replaced with *people* or another gender-neutral term, had this sentence been written in the 21st century rather than the 18th century.) Abstractions let you rise above the common and tangible.

Even though they're indispensable, abstractions can be troublesome. They tend to be fuzzy and subject to multiple interpretations. Moreover, it isn't always easy to get readers excited about ideas, especially ideas that are unrelated to concrete experience. The best way to minimize such problems is to blend abstract terms with concrete ones, the general with the specific. State the concept and then pin it down with details expressed in more concrete terms. Save the abstractions for ideas that cannot be expressed any other way.

Because words such as *small*, *numerous*, *sizable*, *near*, *soon*, *good*, and *fine* are imprecise, try to replace them with terms that are more specific. Instead of referring to a *sizable loss*, talk about a *loss of $32 million*.

Finding Words That Communicate Well   By practicing your writing, learning from experienced writers and editors, and reading extensively, you'll find it easier to choose words that communicate exactly what you want to say. When you compose your business messages, think carefully to find the most effective words for each situation (see Table 5.5):

> Try to use words that are powerful and familiar.

- **Choose powerful words.** Choose words that express your thoughts clearly, specifically, and dynamically. Nouns and verbs are the most concrete words and should do most of the communication work in your messages. Verbs are especially powerful because they tell what's happening in the sentence, so make them dynamic and specific. For instance, you could replace *fall* with *slide*, *slip*, *plummet*, *drop*, or *decline* to suggest the magnitude of the decrease. Here's another helpful clue: If you find yourself using a lot of adjectives and adverbs, you're probably trying to compensate for weak nouns and verbs. Saying that *sales plummeted* is stronger and more efficient than saying *sales dropped dramatically* or *sales experienced a dramatic drop*.

- **Choose familiar words.** You'll communicate best with words that are familiar to both you and your readers. Efforts to improve a situation can be *ameliorative*, to be sure, but saying they are *helpful* is a lot more effective. Moreover, trying to use an unfamiliar word for the first time in an important document can lead to embarrassing mistakes.

- **Avoid clichés and buzzwords.** Although familiar words are generally the best choice, beware of terms and phrases so common or so trendy that they have lost some of their power to communicate. Don't follow the example of writers who use these tired phrases because they don't want to invest the energy required for original writing, or they worry too much about keeping up with the latest trendy language.[18]

> Avoid clichés and trendy buzzwords in your writing and use jargon only when your audience is completely familiar with it.

- **Use jargon carefully.** Handle technical or professional terms with care. Although jargon has a bad reputation in general, it's usually an efficient way to communicate within specific groups that understand their own special terms. After all, that's how jargon develops in the first place, as people with similar interests develop ways to communicate complex ideas quickly. For instance, when a recording engineer wants to communicate that a particular piece of music is devoid of reverberation and other sound effects, it's a lot easier to simply describe the track as "dry." Of course, to people who aren't familiar with such insider terms, jargon is meaningless and intimidating—one more reason it's important to understand your audience before you start writing.

Remember, you improve your business writing skills through imitation and practice. As you read for business or pleasure, make a note of the words you think are effective and keep them in a file. Look through your file before drafting your next

Table 5.5 — FINDING WORDS THAT COMMUNICATE WITH POWER

Avoid Weak Phrases	Use Strong Terms
Wealthy businessperson	Tycoon
Business prosperity	Economic boom
Hard times	Slump

Avoid Unfamiliar Words	Use Familiar Words
Ascertain	Find out, learn
Consummate	Close, bring about
Peruse	Read, study
Circumvent	Avoid
Increment	Growth, increase
Unequivocal	Certain

Avoid Clichés and Buzzwords	Use Plain Language
An uphill battle	A challenge
Writing on the wall	Prediction
Call the shots	Be in charge
Take by storm	Attack
Cost an arm and a leg	Expensive
A new ballgame	Fresh start
Fall through the cracks	Be overlooked
Think outside the box	Be creative
Run it up the flagpole	Offer for consideration
Eat our own dog food	Use our own products
Mission critical	Vital
Disintermediate	Get rid of

message, and try using some of these words in your document. You may be surprised how they can strengthen your writing.

Creating Effective Sentences

Arranging your words in effective sentences is the next step in creating powerful messages. Start by selecting the optimum type of sentence and then arrange words to emphasize the most important point in each sentence.

Choosing from the Four Types of Sentences   Sentences come in four basic varieties: simple, compound, complex, and compound–complex. A **simple sentence** has one main *clause* (a single subject and a single predicate), although it may be expanded by nouns and pronouns serving as objects of the action and by modifying

A simple sentence has one main clause.

phrases. Here's a typical example (with the subject underlined once and the predicate verb underlined twice):

> Profits <u>increased</u> in the past year.

A **compound sentence** has two main clauses that express two or more independent but related thoughts of equal importance, usually joined by *and*, *but*, or *or*. In effect, a compound sentence is a merger of two or more simple sentences (independent clauses) that are related. For example:

> Wage <u>rates</u> <u>have declined</u> by 5 percent, and employee <u>turnover</u> <u>has been</u> high.

A compound sentence has two main clauses.

The independent clauses in a compound sentence are always separated by a comma or by a semicolon (in which case the conjunction—*and*, *but*, or *or*—is dropped).

A **complex sentence** expresses one main thought (the independent clause) and one or more subordinate thoughts (dependent clauses) related to it, often separated by a comma. The subordinate thought, which comes first in the following sentence, could not stand alone as a valid sentence:

> Although you may question Gerald's conclusions, <u>you</u> <u>must admit</u> that his research is thorough.

A complex sentence has one main clause and one subordinate clause.

A **compound–complex sentence** has two main clauses, at least one of which contains a subordinate clause:

> Profits <u>have increased</u> in the past year, and although you may question Gerald's conclusions, <u>you</u> <u>must admit</u> that his research is thorough.

A compound–complex sentence has two main clauses and at least one dependent clause.

When constructing a sentence, choose the form that matches the relationship of the ideas you want to express. If you have two ideas of equal importance, express them as two simple sentences or as one compound sentence. However, if one of the ideas is less important than the other, place it in a dependent clause to form a complex sentence. For example, although the following compound sentence uses a conjunction to join two ideas, they aren't truly equal:

> The chemical products division is the strongest in the company, and its management techniques should be adopted by the other divisions.

By making the first thought subordinate to the second, you establish a cause-and-effect relationship. The following complex sentence is therefore much more effective because it clearly explains why the other divisions should adopt the chemical division's management techniques:

> Because the chemical products division is the strongest in the company, its management techniques should be adopted by the other divisions.

To make your writing as effective as possible, strive for variety and balance using all four sentence types. If you use too many simple sentences, you won't be able to properly express the relationships among your ideas, and your writing will sound

Writing is most effective if it balances all four sentence types.

choppy and abrupt. If you use too many long, compound sentences, your writing will sound monotonous. On the other hand, an uninterrupted series of complex or compound–complex sentences is hard to follow.

Using Sentence Style to Emphasize Key Thoughts   In every message, some ideas are more important than others. You can emphasize key ideas through your sentence style. One obvious technique is to give important points the most space. When you want to call attention to a thought, use extra words to describe it. Consider this sentence:

> The chairperson called for a vote of the shareholders.

To emphasize the importance of the chairperson, you might describe her more fully:

> Having considerable experience in corporate takeover battles, the chairperson called for a vote of the shareholders.

You can increase the emphasis even more by adding a separate short sentence to augment the first:

> The chairperson called for a vote of the shareholders. She has considerable experience in corporate takeover battles.

You can also call attention to a thought by making it the subject of the sentence. In the following example, the emphasis is on the person:

> *I* can write letters much more quickly using a computer.

However, when you change the subject, the computer takes center stage:

> The *computer* enables me to write letters much more quickly.

Another way to emphasize an idea is to place it either at the beginning or at the end of a sentence:

Less emphatic: We are cutting the *price* to stimulate demand.

More emphatic: To stimulate demand, we are cutting the *price*.

In complex sentences, the placement of the dependent clause hinges on the relationship between the ideas expressed. If you want to emphasize the idea, put the dependent clause at the end of the sentence (the most emphatic position) or at the beginning (the second most emphatic position). If you want to downplay the idea, bury the dependent clause within the sentence.

Most emphatic: The electronic parts are manufactured in Mexico, *which has lower wage rates than the United States.*

Emphatic: *Because wage rates are lower in Mexico,* the electronic parts are manufactured there.

Margin notes:

Emphasize parts of a sentence by
- Devoting more words to them
- Putting them at the beginning or at the end of the sentence
- Making them the subject of the sentence

Dependent clauses can determine emphasis.

Least emphatic: Mexico, *which has lower wage rates*, was selected as the production site for the electronic parts.

Techniques such as these give you a great deal of control over the way your audience interprets what you have to say.

Crafting Unified, Coherent Paragraphs

After arranging powerful words in effective sentences, your next step is to arrange those sentences into coherent paragraphs. Paragraphs organize sentences related to the same general topic. Readers expect each paragraph to focus on a single unit of thought and to be a logical link in an organized sequence of the thoughts that make up a complete message. By carefully arranging the elements of each paragraph, you help your readers grasp the main idea of your document and understand how the specific pieces of support material back up that idea (see Figure 5.4).

Elements of the Paragraph   Paragraphs vary widely in length and form, but the typical paragraph contains three basic elements: a topic sentence, support sentences that develop the topic, and transitional words and phrases.

FIGURE 5.4
Unified Paragraphs
In two brief paragraphs, Whirlpool assured its trade partners (retailers and commercial laundries) that business would continue as usual after its acquisition of rival Maytag.

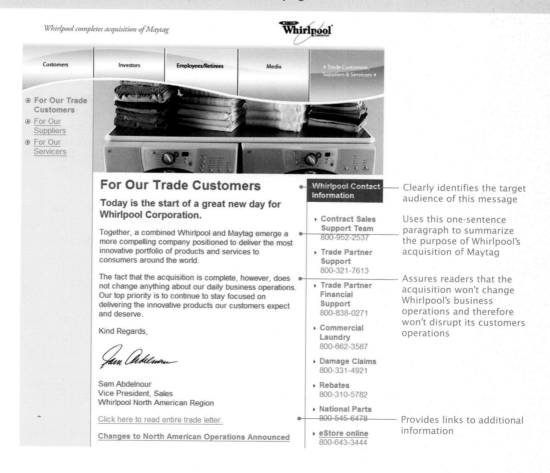

Most paragraphs consist of
- A topic sentence that reveals the subject of the paragraph
- Related sentences that support and expand the topic
- Transitional elements that help readers move between sentences and paragraphs

Topic Sentence An effective paragraph is *unified*; it deals with a single topic. The sentence that introduces that topic is called the **topic sentence**. In informal and creative writing, the topic sentence may be implied rather than stated. In business writing, the topic sentence is generally explicit and is often the first sentence in the paragraph. The topic sentence gives readers a summary of the general idea that will be covered in the rest of the paragraph. The following examples show how a topic sentence can introduce the subject and suggest the way that subject will be developed:

> The medical products division has been troubled for many years by public relations problems. [In the rest of the paragraph, readers will learn the details of the problems.]
>
> Relocating the plant in New York has two main disadvantages. [The disadvantages will be explained in subsequent sentences.]
>
> To get a refund, please supply us with the following information. [The details of the necessary information will be described in the rest of the paragraph.]

In addition to helping your readers, topic sentences help you as a writer because they remind you of the purpose of each paragraph and thereby help you stay focused. In fact, a good way to test the effectiveness of your writing is to prepare a summary version that consists of only the first sentence of each paragraph. If this summary communicates the essence of your message in a sensible, compelling way, you've probably done a good job of presenting your information.[19]

Support Sentences In most paragraphs, the topic sentence needs to be explained, justified, or extended with one or more support sentences. These related sentences must all have a bearing on the general subject and must provide enough specific details to make the topic clear:

> The medical products division has been troubled for many years by public relations problems. Since 2004 the local newspaper has published 15 articles that portray the division in a negative light. We have been accused of everything from mistreating laboratory animals to polluting the local groundwater. Our facility has been described as a health hazard. Our scientists are referred to as "Frankensteins," and our profits are considered "obscene."

The support sentences are all more specific than the topic sentence. Each one provides another piece of evidence to demonstrate the general truth of the main thought. Also, each sentence is clearly related to the general idea being developed, which gives the paragraph its unity. A paragraph is well developed when (1) it contains enough information to make the topic sentence convincing and interesting and (2) it contains no extraneous, unrelated sentences.

Transitional Elements In addition to being unified and well supported, effective paragraphs are *coherent*; that is, they are arranged in a logical order so that the audience can easily follow the train of thought. You achieve coherence by using transitions that show the relationship between paragraphs and among sentences within paragraphs. For example, did you notice how this paragraph began? The transitional phrase "In addition to…" helped move you from the previous discussion to this new topic.

Transitions are words or phrases that tie together ideas by showing how one thought is related to another and by alerting the reader to what lies ahead. They not only help readers understand the connections you're trying to make but also smooth your writing. In fact, effective transitions are one of the hallmarks of polished, effective writing.

Ideally, you begin planning transitions while you're outlining, as you decide how the various ideas and blocks of information will be arranged and connected.[20] You can establish transitions in a variety of ways:

- **Use connecting words.** Use words such as *and, but, or, nevertheless, however, in addition,* and so on.

- **Echo a word or phrase from a previous paragraph or sentence.** "A system should be established for monitoring inventory levels. *This system* will provide . . . ."

- **Use a pronoun that refers to a noun used previously.** "Ms. Arthur is the leading candidate for the president's position. *She* has excellent qualifications."

- **Use words that are frequently paired.** "The machine has a *minimum* output of . . . .Its *maximum* output is . . . ."

Transitional elements include
- Connecting words (conjunctions)
- Repeated words or phrases
- Pronouns
- Words that are frequently paired

Some transitional elements serve as mood changers, such as alerting the reader that the tone of the message is about to change from negative to positive or vice versa. Some announce a total contrast with what's gone on before, some announce a cause–effect relationship, and some signal a change in time. Here is a list of common transitions:

Additional detail: moreover, furthermore, in addition, besides, first, second, third, finally

Cause–effect: therefore, because, accordingly, thus, consequently, hence, as a result, so

Comparison: similarly, here again, likewise, in comparison, still

Contrast: yet, conversely, whereas, nevertheless, on the other hand, however, but, nonetheless

Condition: although, if

Illustration: for example, in particular, in this case, for instance

Time sequence: formerly, after, when, meanwhile, sometimes

Intensification: indeed, in fact, in any event

Summary: in brief, in short, to sum up

Repetition: that is, in other words, as I mentioned earlier

Consider using a transition whenever it could help the reader understand your ideas and follow you from point to point. You can use transitions inside paragraphs to tie related points together and between paragraphs to ease the shift from one distinct thought to another. In longer reports, a transition that links major sections or chapters is often a complete paragraph that serves as a mini-introduction to the next section or as a summary of the ideas presented in the section just ending. Here's an example:

Given the nature of this product, our alternatives are limited. As the previous section indicates, we can stop making it altogether, improve it, or continue with the current model. Each of these alternatives has advantages and disadvantages, which are discussed in the following section.

This paragraph makes it clear to the reader that the analysis of the problem (offered in the previous section) is now over and that the document is making a transition to an analysis of alternatives (to be offered in the next section).

Keep in mind that transitions are not a substitute for effective organization. Put your ideas into a strong framework first and then use transitions to link them together even more strongly.

Five Ways to Develop a Paragraph   Unification and coherence strongly depend on how you develop your paragraphs. Use a structure that is familiar to your readers, appropriate to the idea you're trying to portray, and suited to your purpose. Five of the most common development techniques are illustration, comparison or contrast, cause and effect, classification, and problem and solution (see Table 5.6).

In practice, you'll occasionally combine two or more methods of development in a single paragraph. For instance, you could begin by using illustration, shift to comparison or contrast, and then shift to problem and solution. However, when combining approaches, do so carefully so that you don't lose readers partway through the

Table 5.6 — FIVE TECHNIQUES FOR DEVELOPING PARAGRAPHS

Technique	Description	Example
Illustration	Giving examples that demonstrate the general idea	Some of our most popular products are available through local distributors. For example, Everett & Lemmings carries our frozen soups and entrees. The J. B. Green Company carries our complete line of seasonings, as well as the frozen soups. Wilmont Foods, also a major distributor, now carries our new line of frozen deserts.
Comparison or contrast	Using similarities or differences to develop the topic	When the company was small, the recruiting function could be handled informally. The need for new employees was limited, and each manager could comfortably screen and hire her or his own staff. However, our successful bid on the Owens contract means that we will be doubling our labor force over the next six months. To hire that many people without disrupting our ongoing activities, we will create a separate recruiting group within the human resources department.
Cause and effect	Focusing on the reasons for something	The heavy-duty fabric of your Wanderer tent probably broke down for one of two reasons: (1) a sharp object punctured the fabric, and without reinforcement, the hole was enlarged by the stress of pitching the tent daily for a week or (2) the fibers gradually rotted because the tent was folded and stored while still wet.
Classification	Showing how a general idea is broken into specific categories	Successful candidates for our supervisor trainee program generally come from one of several groups. The largest group, by far, consists of recent graduates of accredited business management programs. The next largest group comes from within our own company, as we try to promote promising staff workers to positions of greater responsibility. Finally, we do occasionally accept candidates with outstanding supervisory experience in related industries.
Problem and solution	Presenting a problem and then discussing the solution	Selling handmade toys online is a challenge because consumers are accustomed to buying heavily advertised toys from major chain stores or well-known websites such as Amazon.com. However, if we develop an appealing website, we can compete on the basis of product novelty and quality. In addition, we can provide unusual crafts at a competitive price: a rocking horse of birch, with a hand-knit tail and mane; a music box with the child's name painted on the top; a real teepee, made by Native American artisans.

paragraph. In addition, instead of settling for the first approach that comes to mind, consider the alternatives. Think through various methods before committing yourself, or even write several test paragraphs to see which method works best. By avoiding the easy habit of repeating the same old paragraph pattern time after time, you can keep your writing fresh and interesting.

USING TECHNOLOGY TO COMPOSE AND SHAPE YOUR MESSAGES

Careful and informed use of technology can help you compose and shape better messages in less time. As you probably know, today's software (including word processors and online publishing systems for websites and blogs) provides a wide range of tools to help writers compose documents:

> Take full advantage of your software's capabilities to help you produce effective, professional messages in less time.

- **Style sheets and templates.** *Style sheets* are master lists of predefined styles (typeface, type size, and so on) for headlines, paragraph text, and so on. (Here, the word *style* should not be confused with *writing style*, discussed earlier in the chapter.) Many organizations provide employees with approved style sheets to ensure a consistent look for all company documents. Moreover, style sheets can eliminate hours of design time by making many of your choices for you. *Templates* can go beyond style sheets by defining such factors as page design, available fonts, and other features. A template can include *boilerplate*, a section of text that is reused from document to document. (Depending on the version of Microsoft Word you're using, style sheets may have been replaced by templates.)

- **Autocompletion.** A software feature called *autocompletion* (or something similar) inserts a ready-made block of text when you type the first few characters. For example, instead of typing your company's name, address, phone number, fax number, e-mail address, and website URL, you can set the software to enter all this information as soon as you type the first three letters of the company name.

- **Autocorrection.** Another automatic feature in some programs instantly corrects spelling and typing errors and converts text to symbols, such as converting (c) to the © copyright symbol. However, autocorrection may make changes that you *don't* want made, such as when you type a lettered list with (a), (b), and (c)—and you really want (c), not a copyright symbol.

- **File merge and mail merge.** Today's software makes it easy to combine files—an especially handy feature when several members of a team write different sections of a report. For particularly complex reports, you can set up a master document that merges a number of subdocuments automatically when it's time to print. *Mail merge* lets you personalize form letters by inserting names and addresses from a database.

- **Endnotes, footnotes, indexes, and tables of contents.** Your computer can help you track footnotes and endnotes, renumbering them every time you add or delete references. For a report's indexes and table of contents, you can simply flag the items you want to include, and the software assembles the lists for you.

- **Wizards.** Many programs offer *wizards* that guide you through the process of creating letters, résumés, webpages, and other common documents.

As with other forms of communication technology, using these tools efficiently and effectively requires some balance. You need to learn enough about the features to be handy with them, without spending so much time that the tools distract the writing process. For a reminder of the tasks involved in writing your messages, see "Checklist: Writing Business Messages."

✓ CHECKLIST: Writing Business Messages

A. Adapt to your audience.

✓ Use the "you" attitude.
✓ Maintain good etiquette through polite communication.
✓ Emphasize the positive whenever possible.
✓ Use bias-free language.
✓ Establish your credibility in the eyes of your audience.
✓ Project your company's preferred image.
✓ Use a conversational but still professional and respectful tone.
✓ Use plain English for clarity.

B. Compose your message.

✓ Choose strong words that communicate efficiently.
✓ Make sure you use functional and content words correctly.

✓ Pay attention to the connotative meaning of your words.
✓ Balance abstract and concrete terms to convey your meaning accurately.
✓ Avoid clichés and trendy buzzwords.
✓ Use jargon only when your audience understands it and prefers it.
✓ Vary your sentence structure for impact and interest.
✓ Develop coherent, unified paragraphs.
✓ Use transitional elements generously to help your audience follow your message.

On the Job

SOLVING COMMUNICATION CHALLENGES AT CREATIVE COMMONS

To achieve their mission of popularizing a new approach to copyrighting songs, artwork, literature, and other creative works, Lawrence Lessig and his staff at Creative Commons need to convince people that the traditional approach to copyright doesn't meet the needs of today's digital society. This is no small challenge: Not only do they need to convince people to reconsider more than 200 years of legal precedent and habit, they also need to communicate with an extremely diverse audience—everyone from lawyers and business managers to artists, writers, musicians, and scientists. After graduating with a business degree, you've joined Creative Commons as a communication intern for a year before entering law school. Apply your knowledge of effective writing to the following four scenarios.[21]

1. Creative Commons offers several varieties of its "Sampling" license, which makes it easier for artists to give other people the opportunity to use snippets of their work in new creative works. Digitally sampling pieces of existing songs for use in new songs is common today, but sampling also applies to photographs, graphic designs, and any other work that people might want to borrow from. Which of the following does the best job of describing the Sampling and Sampling Plus licenses and the key difference between the two?

   a. Both the Sampling and Sampling Plus licenses allow people to take pieces of your work and reuse them in new creative works for any purpose other than advertising. Sampling Plus also allows people to copy and distribute your entire work for noncommercial purposes only.

   b. Sampling is more restrictive than Sampling Plus because it forbids the copying and distribution of your entire work. Both licenses allow people to use pieces of your work for any purpose other than advertising.

   c. Unlike the Sampling license, Sampling Plus allows people to copy and distribute your entire work, although for noncommercial purposes only (e.g., they can't resell it or use it in advertising).

   d. The Sampling Plus license also gives people the right to copy and distribute your entire work, although for noncommercial purposes only (e.g., they can't resell it or use it in advertising).

2. A key part of the communication challenge for Creative Commons is translating legal documents into language that musicians, artists, and others with no legal training can easily understand. Which of the following does the best job of adapting the following legal phrase (which is part of the licensing contracts) into language for a general audience?

   The above rights may be exercised in all media and formats whether now known or hereafter devised. The above rights include the right to make such modifications as are technically necessary to exercise the rights in other media and formats.

a. The rights granted by this licensing contract extend to any current or future media, and you also have the right to modify the material as needed to meet the technical needs of any media.

b. You may use this material in any present or future media and modify it as needed to work with any media.

c. Be advised that your rights within the scope of this contract include the right to use this material in any media that either exists now or might be devised in the future. Moreover, you are also granted the right to modify the material as any current or future media might technically demand.

d. You are hereby granted the right to use this material in any media, including modifications required by that media.

3. The single most important concept in the Creative Commons approach is the idea of a spectrum of possibilities between *all rights reserved* (a conventional copyright) and *no rights reserved* (being in the *public domain*, where anybody is free to use material in any way they please). Review the structure of the following four sentences and choose the one that does the best job of emphasizing the importance of the "spectrum of possibilities."

a. Conventional copyrights, in which the creator reserves all rights to a work, and the public domain, in which the creator gives up all rights, represent two black-and-white extremes.

b. Between the all-or-nothing extremes of a conventional copyright and being in the public domain, Creative Commons sees a need for other possibilities.

c. The primary contribution of Creative Commons is developing a range of possibilities between the extremes of *all rights reserved* (conventional copyright) and *no rights reserved* (public domain).

d. The black-and-white choice of *all rights reserved* (conventional copyright) and *no rights reserved* (public domain) does not meet everyone's needs, so Creative Commons is developing a range of possibilities between these two extremes.

4. Like many other organizations these days, Creative Commons must occasionally deal with online rumors spread by bloggers who aren't always sure of their facts. You've been asked to reply to an e-mail query from a *Wall Street Journal* reporter who read a blog rumor that Creative Commons's real objective is to destroy ownership of all copyrights. Which of the following has the right style and tone for your response?

a. That blog posting is an absolute crock. The person who wrote it is either a liar or a fool.

b. As our website and other materials strive to make clear, the objective of Creative Commons is to work within the framework of existing copyright law but to establish a range of possibilities for people whose needs aren't met by conventional copyright choices.

c. You wouldn't believe how much time and energy we have to spend defending ourselves against idiotic rumors like this.

d. Creative Commons has never expressed, in print or in online materials, nor in any speeches or presentations given by any of our current or former staff or board members, any plans or strategies that would allow anyone to reach a valid conclusion that our intent is to weaken existing copyright protections.

Learning Objectives Checkup

Assess your understanding of the principles in this chapter by reading each learning objective and studying the accompanying exercises. For fill-in-the-blank items, write the missing text in the blank provided; for multiple-choice items, circle the letter of the correct answer. You can check your responses against the answer key on page AK-1.

Objective 5.1: Explain the importance of adapting your messages to the needs and expectations of your audience.

1. Why should you take the time to adapt your messages to your audience?

a. People are more inclined to read and respond to messages that they believe apply to them and their concerns.

b. Adapting messages to audiences is corporate policy in nearly all large companies.

c. Adapting your message saves time during planning and writing.

d. You can manipulate audience responses more easily by adapting your messages.

2. How is your audience likely to respond to a message that doesn't seem to be about their concerns or that is written in language they don't understand?

a. They will ignore the message.

b. If they read the message, they will be less inclined to respond in a positive way.

c. They will assume that the writer doesn't respect them enough to adapt the message.

d. All of the above could occur.

Objective 5.2: Explain why establishing credibility is vital to the success of your communication efforts

3. Credibility is a measure of

a. Your power within the organization

b. The length of time the audience has known you

c. Your confidence

d. The audience's perception of your believability

4. If you have developed a reputation for missing deadlines on projects you manage, which of the following statements would do the best job of helping to rebuild your credibility? [You have previously committed to a project completion date of April 1.]

    a. No April foolin' this time; we'll be finished by April 1.

    b. After analyzing past projects, I now realize that a failure to clarify project objectives up front created significant delays down the line. In order to meet the April 1 deadline, I will make sure to clarify the objective as soon as the team assembles.

    c. I plan to work extra hard this time to make sure we will be finished by April 1.

    d. I hope that we will be finished by April 1.

Objective 5.3: Discuss four ways of achieving a businesslike tone with a style that is clear and concise.

5. A good way to achieve a businesslike tone in your messages is to

    a. Use formal business terminology, such as "In re your letter of the 18th"

    b. Brag about your company

    c. Use a conversational style that is not intimate or chatty

    d. Use plenty of humor

6. Plain English is

    a. Never recommended when speaking with people for whom English is a second language

    b. A movement toward using "English only" in American businesses

    c. A way of writing and arranging technical materials to make them more understandable

    d. An attempt to keep writing at a fourth- or fifth-grade level

7. If you want to avoid attributing blame or otherwise calling attention to a specific person, the _____ voice is a more diplomatic approach.

8. The _____ voice usually makes sentences shorter, more direct, and livelier.

Objective 5.4: Briefly describe how to select words that are not only correct but also effective.

9. Which of the following defines the connotative meaning of the word *flag*?

    a. A flag is a piece of material with a symbol of some kind sewn on it.

    b. A flag is a symbol of everything that a nation stands for.

    c. A flag is fabric on a pole used to mark a geographic spot.

    d. A flag is an object used to draw attention.

10. Which of the following is a concrete word?

    a. Little

    b. Mouse

    c. Species

    d. Kingdom

11. If you're not sure about the meaning of a word you'd like to use, which of the following in the most appropriate way to handle the situation?

    a. Your readers probably have instant access to online dictionaries these days, so go ahead and use the word.

    b. Use the word but include a humorous comment in parentheses saying that you're not really sure what this big, important word means.

    c. Either verify the meaning of the word or rewrite the sentence so that you don't need to use it.

    d. Find a synonym in a thesaurus and use that word instead.

12. Using jargon is

    a. Often a good idea when discussing complex subjects with people who are intimately familiar with the subject and common jargon relating to it

    b. Never a good idea

    c. A good way to build credibility, no matter what the purpose of the message

    d. A sign of being an "insider"

Objective 5.5: Explain how sentence style affects emphasis within your message.

13. What is the most emphatic place to put a dependent clause?

    a. At the end of the sentence

    b. At the beginning of the sentence

    c. In the middle of the sentence

    d. Anywhere in the sentence

14. Devoting a lot of words to a particular idea shows your audience that

    a. The idea is complicated

    b. The idea is the topic sentence

    c. The idea is important

    d. The idea is new and therefore requires more explanation

Objective 5.6: List five ways to develop coherent paragraphs.

15. When developing a paragraph, keep in mind

    a. That you should stick to one method of development within a single paragraph

    b. That once you use one method of development, you should use that same method for all the paragraphs in a section

    c. That your choice of technique should take into account your subject, your intended audience, and your purpose

    d. All of the above

16. To develop a paragraph by illustration, give your audience enough _____ to help them grasp the main idea.

17. Paragraphs organized by comparison and contrast point out the _____ or _____ between two or more items.

18. To explain the reasons something happened, which of these paragraph designs should you use?

    a. Cause–effect

    b. Opposition and argument

    c. Classification

    d. Prioritization

Apply Your Knowledge

1. How can you apply the "you" attitude when you don't know your audience personally?
2. When composing business messages, how can you be yourself and project your company's image at the same time?
3. What steps can you take to make abstract concepts such as *opportunity* feel more concrete in your messages?
4. Should you bother using transitional elements if the logical sequence of your message is already obvious? Why or why not?
5. **Ethical Choices** Eleven million people in the United States are allergic to one or more food ingredients. Every year, 30,000 of these people end up in the emergency room after suffering allergic reactions, and hundreds of them die. Many of these tragic events are tied to poorly written food labels that either fail to identify dangerous allergens or use scientific terms that most consumers don't recognize.[22] Do food manufacturers have a responsibility to ensure that consumers read, understand, and follow warnings on food products? Explain your answer.

Practice Your Knowledge

MESSAGE FOR ANALYSIS

Read the following e-mail draft and then (1) analyze the strengths and weaknesses of each sentence and (2) revise the document so that it follows this chapter's guidelines. The message was written by the marketing manager of an online retailer of baby-related products in the hope of becoming a retail outlet for Inglesina strollers and high chairs. As a manufacturer of stylish, top-quality products, Inglesina (based in Italy) is extremely selective about the retail outlets through which it allows its products to be sold.

Our e-tailing site, www.BestBabyGear.com, specializes in only the very best products for parents of newborns, infants, and toddlers. We constantly scour the world looking for products that are good enough and well-built enough and classy enough—good enough that is to take their place alongside the hundreds of other carefully selected products that adorn the pages of our award-winning website, www.bestbabygear.com. We aim for the fences every time we select a product to join this portfolio; we don't want to waste our time with onesey-twosey products that might sell a half dozen units per annum—no, we want every product to be a top-drawer success, selling at least one hundred units per specific model per year in order to justify our expense and hassle factor in adding it to the abovementioned portfolio. After careful consideration, we thusly concluded that your Inglesina lines meet our needs and would therefore like to add it.

EXERCISES

For active links to all websites discussed in this chapter, visit this text's website at **www.prenhall.com/thill**. Locate your book and click on its "Companion Website" link. Then select Chapter 5 and click on "Featured Websites." Locate the name of the page or the URL related to the material in the text. Please note that links to sites that become inactive after publication of the book will be removed from the "Featured Websites" section.

5.1 Audience Relationship: Courteous Communication Substitute a better phrase for each of the following:
   a. You claim that
   b. It is not our policy to
   c. You neglected to
   d. In which you assert
   e. We are sorry you are dissatisfied
   f. You failed to enclose
   g. We request that you send us
   h. Apparently you overlooked our terms
   i. We have been very patient
   j. We are at a loss to understand

5.2 Audience Relationship: The "You" Attitude Rewrite these sentences to reflect your audience's viewpoint:
   a. Your e-mail order cannot be processed; we request that you use the order form on our website instead.
   b. We insist that you always bring your credit card to the store.
   c. We want to get rid of all our 15-inch LCD screens to make room in our warehouse for the new 19-, 23-, and 35-inch monitors. Thus, we are offering a 25 percent discount on all sales of 15-inch models this week.
   d. I am applying for the position of fact-checker in your editorial office. I feel my grades prove that I am bright and capable, and I think I can do a good job for you.
   e. As requested, we are sending the refund for $25.
   f. If you cared about doing a good job, you would've made the extra effort required to learn how to use the machinery properly.
   g. Your strategy presentation this morning absolutely blew me away; there's no way we can fail with all the brilliant ideas you've pulled together—I'm so glad you're running the company now!
   h. Regarding your e-mail message from September 28 regarding the slow payment of your invoice, it's important for you to realize that we've just undergone

a massive upgrade of our accounts payable system and payments have been delayed for everybody, not just you.

i. I know I'm late with the asset valuation report, but I haven't been feeling well and I just haven't had the energy needed to work through the numbers yet.

j. With all the online news sources available today, I can't believe you didn't know that MyTravel and Thomas Cook were in merger talks—I mean, you don't even have to get up from your computer to learn this!

5.3 Audience Relationship: Emphasize the Positive Revise these sentences to be positive rather than negative:

a. To avoid the loss of your credit rating, please remit payment within 10 days.

b. We don't make refunds on returned merchandise that is soiled.

c. Because we are temporarily out of Baby Cry dolls, we won't be able to ship your order for 10 days.

d. You failed to specify the color of the blouse that you ordered.

e. You should have realized that waterbeds will freeze in unheated houses during winter. Therefore, our guarantee does not cover the valve damage, and you must pay the $9.50 valve-replacement fee (plus postage).

5.4 Audience Relationship: Emphasize the Positive Provide euphemisms for the following words and phrases:

a. Stubborn

b. Wrong

c. Stupid

d. Incompetent

e. Loudmouth

5.5 Audience Relationship: Bias-Free Language Rewrite each of the following to eliminate bias:

a. For an Indian, Maggie certainly is outgoing.

b. He needs a wheelchair, but he doesn't let his handicap affect his job performance.

c. A pilot must have the ability to stay calm under pressure, and then he must be trained to cope with any problem that arises.

d. Candidate Renata Parsons, married and the mother of a teenager, will attend the debate.

e. Senior citizen Sam Nugent is still an active salesman.

5.6 Ethical Choices Your company has been a major employer in the local community for years, but shifts in the global marketplace have forced some changes in the company's long-term direction. In fact, the company plans to reduce local staffing by as much as 50 percent over the next 5 to 10 years, starting with a small layoff next month. The size and timing of future layoffs have not been decided, although there is little doubt that more layoffs will happen at some point. In the first draft of a letter aimed at community leaders, you write that "this first layoff is part of a continuing series of staff reductions anticipated over the next several years." However, your boss is concerned about

the vagueness and negative tone of the language and asks you to rewrite that sentence to read "this layoff is part of the company's ongoing efforts to continually align its resources with global market conditions." Do you think this suggested wording is ethical, given the company's economic influence in the community? Explain your answer in an e-mail message to your instructor.

5.7 Message Composition: Controlling Style Rewrite the following e-mail to customer Betty Crandall so that it conveys a helpful, personal, and interested tone:

> We received your order complaint via our website response system. Owing to the fact that you neglected to include the size of the dress you ordered, please be advised that no shipment of your order was made, but the aforementioned shipment will occur at such time as we are in receipt of the aforementioned information.

5.8 Message Composition: Selecting Words Write a concrete phrase for each of these vague phrases:

a. Sometime this spring

b. A substantial saving

c. A large number attended

d. Increased efficiency

e. Expanded the work area

f. Flatten the website structure

5.9 Message Composition: Selecting Words List terms that are stronger than the following:

a. Ran after

b. Seasonal ups and downs

c. Bright

d. Suddenly rises

e. Moves forward

5.10 Message Composition: Selecting Words As you rewrite these sentences, replace the clichés with fresh, personal expressions:

a. Being a jack-of-all-trades, Dave worked well in his new general manager job.

b. Moving Leslie into the accounting department, where she was literally a fish out of water, was like putting a square peg into a round hole, if you get my drift.

c. I knew she was at death's door, but I thought the doctor would pull her through.

d. Movies aren't really my cup of tea; as far as I am concerned, they can't hold a candle to a good book.

e. It's a dog-eat-dog world out there in the rat race of the asphalt jungle.

5.11 Message Composition: Selecting Words Suggest short, simple words to replace each of the following:

a. Inaugurate

b. Terminate

c. Utilize

d. Anticipate

e. Assistance

f. Endeavor

g. Ascertain

h. Procure

i. Consummate

j. Advise

k. Alteration

l. Forwarded

m. Fabricate

n. Nevertheless

o. Substantial

5.12 Message Composition: Selecting Words Write up-to-date, less-stuffy versions of these phrases; write *none* if you think there is no appropriate substitute or "delete" if the phrase should simply be deleted:

a. As per your instructions

b. Attached herewith

c. In lieu of

d. In reply I wish to state

e. Please be advised that

5.13 Message Composition: Creating Sentences Suppose that end-of-term frustrations have produced this e-mail message to Professor Anne Brewer from a student who believes he should have received a B in his accounting class. If this message were recast into three or four clear sentences, the teacher might be more receptive to the student's argument. Rewrite the message to show how you would improve it:

> *I think that I was unfairly awarded a C in your accounting class this term, and I am asking you to change the grade to a B. It was a difficult term. I don't get any money from home, and I have to work mornings at the Pancake House (as a cook), so I had to rush to make your class, and those two times that I missed class were because they wouldn't let me off work because of special events at the Pancake House (unlike some other students who just take off when they choose). On the midterm examination, I originally got a 75 percent, but you said in class that there were two different ways to answer the third question and that you would change the grades of students who used the "optimal cost" method and had been counted off 6 points for doing this. I don't think that you took this into account, because I got 80 percent on the final, which is clearly a B. Anyway, whatever you decide, I just want to tell you that I really enjoyed this class, and I thank you for making accounting so interesting.*

5.14 Message Composition: Creating Sentences Rewrite each sentence so that it is active rather than passive:

a. The raw data are entered into the customer relationship management system by the sales representative each Friday.

b. High profits are publicized by management.

c. The policies announced in the directive were implemented by the staff.

d. Our computers are serviced by the Santee Company.

e. The employees were represented by Janet Hogan.

5.15 Message Composition: Writing Paragraphs In the following paragraph, identify the topic sentence and the related sentences (those that support the idea of the topic sentence):

> *Sync in a snap with Auto-Sync. By default, iTunes automatically copies your entire music library to iPod and deletes songs on iPod that are not listed in iTunes. Or you can use Playlist Sync and select the playlists you want to sync with your iPod. If you have more songs in your iTunes library than you can fit on your iPod, let iTunes create a playlist to fill your iPod, or just update your iPod by dragging over individual songs.[23]*

Now add a topic sentence to this paragraph:

> *Our analysis of the customer experience should start before golfers even drive through the front gate here at Glencoe Meadows; it should start when they phone in or log onto our website to reserve tee times. When they do arrive, the first few stages in the process are also vital: the condition of the grounds leading up to the clubhouse, the reception they receive when they drop off their clubs, and the ease of parking. From that point, how well are we doing with check-in at the pro shop, openings at the driving range, and timely scheduling at the first tee? Then there's everything associated with playing the course itself and returning to the clubhouse at the end of the round.*

5.16 Teamwork Working with four other students, divide the following five topics among yourselves and each write one paragraph on your selected topic. Be sure each student uses a different technique when writing his or her paragraph: One student should use the illustration technique, one the comparison or contrast technique, one a discussion of cause and effect, one the classification technique, and one a discussion of problem and solution. Then exchange paragraphs within the team and pick out the main idea and general purpose of the paragraph one of your teammates wrote. Was everyone able to correctly identify the main idea and purpose? If not, suggest how the paragraph could be rewritten for clarity.

a. Types of digital cameras (or dogs or automobiles) available for sale

b. Advantages and disadvantages of eating at fast-food restaurants

c. Finding my first full-time job

d. Good qualities of my car (or house, or apartment, or neighborhood)

e. How to make a dessert recipe (or barbecue a steak or make coffee)

5.17 Internet Download the Securities and Exchange Commission (SEC) publication, *A Plain English Handbook*, at **www.sec.gov/pdf/plaine.pdf**. In one or two sentences, summarize what the SEC means by the phrase "plain English." Now read the SEC's online advice about how to invest in mutual funds. Does this document follow the SEC's plain-English guidelines? Can you suggest any improvements for the organization, words, sentences, or paragraphs?

5.18 **Message Organization: Transitional Elements** Add transitional elements to the following sentences to improve the flow of ideas. (Note: You may need to eliminate or add some words to smooth out your sentences.)

a. Steve Case saw infinite possibilities in online business. Steve Case was determined to turn his vision into reality. The techies scoffed at his strategy of building a simple Internet service for ordinary people. Case doggedly pursued his dream. He analyzed other online services. He assessed the needs of his customers. He responded to their desires for an easier way to access information over the Internet. In 1992, Steve Case named his company America Online (AOL). Critics predicted the company's demise. By the end of the century, AOL was a profitable powerhouse. An ill-fated merger with Time Warner was a financial disaster and led to Case's ouster from the company.

b. Facing some of the toughest competitors in the world, Harley-Davidson had to make some changes. The company introduced new products. Harley's management team set out to rebuild the company's production process. New products were coming to market, and the company was turning a profit. Harley's quality standards were not on par with those of its foreign competitors. Harley's costs were still among the highest in the industry. Harley made a U-turn and restructured the company's organizational structure. Harley's efforts have paid off.

c. Whether you're indulging in a doughnut in New York or California, Krispy Kreme wants you to enjoy the same delicious taste with every bite. The company maintains consistent product quality by carefully controlling every step of the production process. Krispy Kreme tests all raw ingredients against established quality standards. Every delivery of wheat flour is sampled and measured for its moisture content and protein levels. Krispy Kreme blends the ingredients. Krispy Kreme tests the doughnut mix for quality. Krispy Kreme delivers the mix to its stores. Financial critics are not as kind to the company as food critics have been. Allegations of improper financial reporting have left the company's future in doubt.

5.19 **Ethical Choices** Under what circumstances would you consider the use of terms that are high in connotative meaning to be ethical? When would you consider it to be unethical? Explain your reasoning.

Expand Your Knowledge

LEARNING MORE ON THE WEB
COMPOSE A BETTER BUSINESS MESSAGE

http://owl.english.purdue.edu

At Purdue University's Online Writing Lab (OWL), you'll find tools to help you improve your business messages. For advice on composing written messages, for help with grammar, and for referrals to other information sources, you'd be wise to visit this site. Purdue's OWL offers online services and an introduction to Internet search tools. You can also download a variety of handouts on writing skills. Check out the resources at the OWL homepage and then answer the following questions:

1. Explain why positive wording in a message is more effective than negative wording. Why should you be concerned about the position of good news or bad news in your written message?
2. What six factors of tone should you consider when conveying your message to your audience?
3. What points should you include in the close of your business message? Why?

SURFING YOUR WAY TO CAREER SUCCESS

Bovée and Thill's Business Communication Headline News offers links to hundreds of online resources that can help you with this course, your other college courses, and your career. Visit www.businesscommunicationblog.com and click on "Web Directory." The "Working with Words" section connects you to a variety of websites and articles on abstract versus concrete words, abusive words, bias-free writing, euphemisms, obsolete language, plain English, and profane words. Identify three websites from this section that could be useful in your business career. For each site, write a two-sentence summary of what the site offers and how it could help you launch and build your career.

Learn Interactively

INTERACTIVE STUDY GUIDE

Visit www.prenhall.com/thill, then locate your book and click on its "Companion Website" link. Select Chapter 5 to take advantage of the interactive "Chapter Quiz" to test your knowledge of chapter concepts. Receive instant feedback on whether you need additional studying. Also, visit the "Study Hall," where you'll find an abundance of valuable resources that will help you succeed in this course.

**PEAK PERFORMANCE GRAMMAR
AND MECHANICS**

If your instructor has required the use of "Peak Performance Grammar and Mechanics," either in your online course or on CD, you can improve your skill with adverbs by using the "Peak Performance Grammar and Mechanics" module. Click on "Adverbs." Take the Pretest to determine whether you have any weak areas. Then review those areas in the Refresher Course. Take the Follow-Up Test to check your grasp of adverbs. For an extra challenge or advanced practice, take the Advanced Test. Finally, for additional reinforcement, go to the "Improve Your Grammar, Mechanics, and Usage" section that follows and complete those exercises.

Improve Your Grammar, Mechanics, and Usage

The following exercises help you improve your knowledge of and power over English grammar, mechanics, and usage. Turn to the Handbook of Grammar, Mechanics, and Usage at the end of this book and review all of Section 1.5 (Adverbs). Then look at the following 10 items. Underline the preferred choice within each set of parentheses. (Answers to these exercises appear on page AK-3.)

1. Their performance has been (*good/well*).
2. I (*sure/surely*) do not know how to help you.
3. He feels (*sick/sickly*) again today.
4. Customs dogs are chosen because they smell (*good/well*).
5. The redecorated offices look (*good/well*).
6. Which of the two programs computes (*more fast, faster*)?
7. Of the two we have in stock, this model is the (*best, better*) designed.
8. He doesn't seem to have (*any, none*).
9. That machine is scarcely (*never, ever*) used.
10. They (*can, can't*) hardly get replacement parts for this equipment (*any, no*) more.

For additional exercises focusing on adverbs, go to www. prenhall.com/thill, then locate your text and click on its "Companion Website" link. Click on Chapter 5, click on "Additional Exercises to Improve Your Grammar, Mechanics and Usage," and then click on "9. Adverbs."

Chapter 6

Completing Business Messages

Learning Objectives

AFTER STUDYING THIS CHAPTER, YOU WILL BE ABLE TO

1 Discuss the value of careful revision and list the main tasks involved in completing a business message

2 List four writing techniques you can use to improve the readability of your messages

3 Describe the steps you can take to improve the clarity of your writing

4 Discuss why it's important to make your messages concise and give four tips on how to do so

5 Explain how design elements help determine the effectiveness of your documents

6 Highlight the types of errors to look for when proofreading

7 Discuss the most important issues to consider when distributing your messages

On the Job

COMMUNICATING AT MERCEDES-AMG

PROMOTING "POWERFUL LUXURY" THROUGH CAREFUL COMMUNICATION DESIGN

Every business message tries to create a particular impression in the minds of the audience, but what if the impression you want to create is how it feels to drive one of the world's most luxurious cars that has been customized with one of the world's most powerful engines? Merely saying the words "power" and "luxury" isn't likely to be very convincing in today's advertising saturated world.

The German firm Mercedes-AMG is revered among automotive connoisseurs for its high-performance engines, which are available in AMG-Mercedes models. To promote the newest models, the marketing communication specialists at Mercedes-AMG knew they needed to go beyond mere words and photos to use every media option and design technique possible to reach their target audience. The company goal was to create immersive experiences that build an emotional connection between the AMG brand and automotive enthusiasts. The result was an innovative multimedia website that won the Webby award from the International Academy of Digital Arts and Sciences, considered by many to be the online media equivalent of an Oscar or Emmy.

When visitors "start" the virtual engine to begin a virtual tour of the Mercedes-AMG factory in Affalterbach, Germany, their web browsers even shake slightly, to suggest the physical sensation of firing up the mighty AMG engine they can hear growling through

Elegant design and attention to every detail of text, graphics, audio, and video convey a message of sophisticated quality on the Mercedes-AMG website.

their computer speakers. Visitors "drive" to the factory via online video, then enter various buildings to learn more about Mercedes-AMG products.

The message of powerful luxury is delivered in ways that business communicators could only dream about even a few years ago, but with ageless attention to quality. In every respect—word choices, color palette, photography, audio, video, and interactive features—the website reflects the renowned "fit and finish" of the cars it represents.[1]

www.mercedes-amg.com

MOVING BEYOND YOUR FIRST DRAFT

First drafts are rarely as effective as they could be.

Your business messages may not require the sophisticated design or technology of the Mercedes-AMG website (profiled in the chapter opener), but they can benefit from the same rigorous attention to detail in the third step of the three-step writing process: completing your messages.

Once you've completed the first draft of your message, you may be tempted to breathe a sigh of relief, send the message on its way, and move on to the next project. Resist that temptation. Successful communicators recognize that the first draft is rarely as tight, clear, and compelling as it needs to be. Careful revision can mean the difference between a rambling, unfocused message and a lively, direct message that gets results. Figure 6.1 lists the tasks in the third step of the three-step writing process: revising your message to achieve optimum quality and then producing, proofreading, and distributing it.

REVISING YOUR MESSAGE

Even simple, short messages can usually benefit from a quick revision pass.

The nature of the revision task varies somewhat, depending on the medium you're using and the nature of your message. For informal messages to internal audiences, particularly when using instant messaging, text messaging, e-mail, or blogging, the revision process is often as simple as quickly looking over your message to correct any mistakes before sending or posting it. However, don't fall into the common trap of thinking that these electronic media are so new and different and informal that you don't need to worry about grammar, spelling, clarity, and other fundamentals of good writing. These qualities can be even *more* important in electronic media, not less, particularly if these messages are the only contact your audience has with you. Audiences are likely to equate the quality of your writing with the quality of your

FIGURE 6.1
Step Three in the Three-Step Writing Process: Complete Your Messages
Resist the temptation to cut corners when performing the tasks in the third step of the three-step writing process. You've spent a lot of time and energy planning and writing a strong message, so make sure it is produced and delivered with professional quality.

Planning | Writing | Completing

1   **2**   **3**

Revise the Message
Evaluate content and review readability and then edit and rewrite for conciseness and clarity.

Produce the Message
Use effective design elements and suitable layout for a clean, professional appearance.

Proofread the Message
Review for errors in layout, spelling, and mechanics.

Distribute the Message
Deliver your message using the chosen medium; make sure all documents and all relevant files are distributed successfully.

thinking, decision making, and other business skills. Moreover, even minor errors can cause confusion, frustration, and costly delays.

Fortunately, revising simple messages doesn't take much time or effort. With instant messaging, for example, you need only a second or two to scan each message to make sure you haven't said something clumsy or incorrect.

With more complex messages, try to put your draft aside for a day or two before you begin the revision process so that you can approach the material with a fresh eye. Then start with the "big picture," making sure that the document accomplishes your overall goals. Next, move to finer points, such as readability, clarity, and conciseness. Compare the letters in Figures 6.2 and 6.3 for an example of how careful revision can improve a customer letter.

> If you have time, put your draft aside for a day or two before you begin the revision process.

Evaluating Your Content, Organization, Style, and Tone

When you begin the revision process, focus your attention on content, organization, style, and tone. To evaluate the content of your message, ask yourself these questions:

- Is the information accurate?

- Is the information relevant to your audience?

- Is there enough information to satisfy your readers' needs?

- Is there a good balance between general information (giving readers enough background information to appreciate the message) and specific information (giving readers the details they need to understand the message)?

When you are satisfied with the content of your message, review its organization by asking yourself another set of questions:

- Are all your points covered in the most logical order?

- Do the most important ideas receive the most space, and are they placed in the most prominent positions?

- Would the message be more convincing if it were arranged in another sequence?

- Are any points repeated unnecessarily?

- Are details grouped together logically, or are some still scattered through the document?

With the content in place and effectively organized, next consider whether you have achieved the right style and tone for your audience. Is your writing formal enough to meet the audience's expectations, without being too formal or academic? Is it too casual for a serious subject? Does your message emphasize the audience's needs over your own?

Spend a few extra moments on the beginning and end of your message; these sections have the greatest impact on the audience. Be sure that the opening is relevant, interesting, and geared to the reader's probable reaction. In longer messages, check to see that the first few paragraphs establish the subject, purpose, and organization of the material. Review the conclusion to be sure that it summarizes the main idea and leaves the audience with a positive impression.

> The beginning and end of a message have the greatest impact on your readers, so spend a few extra minutes on them.

Reviewing for Readability

When you're satisfied with the content, organization, style, and tone of your message, make a second pass to look at its readability. Most professionals are inundated with more reading material than they can ever hope to consume, and they'll appreciate your efforts to make your documents easier to read. You'll benefit from this effort,

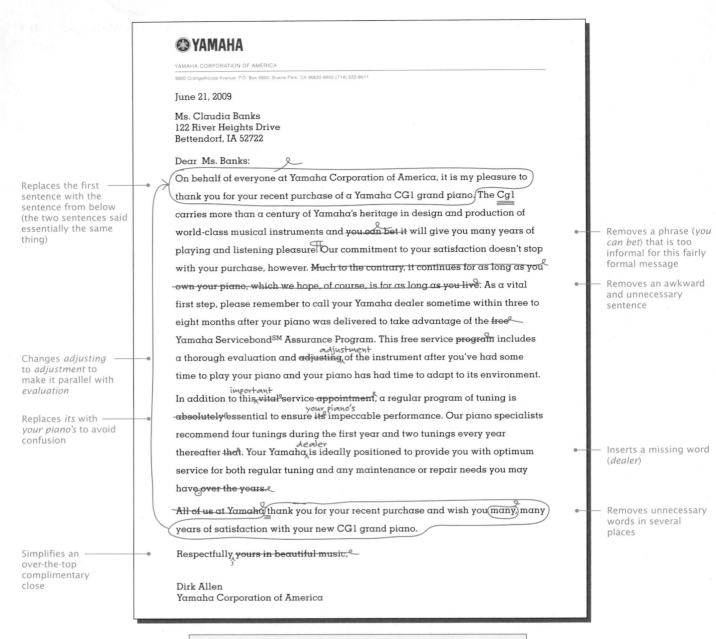

FIGURE 6.2

Improving a Customer Letter Through Careful Revision

Careful revision makes this draft shorter, clearer, and more focused. These *proofreading symbols* (see Appendix C) are still widely used when printed documents are edited and revised. However, in many instances, you'll use the electronic markup features in your word processor or other software, as shown in Figure 6.4 on page 178.

YAMAHA CORPORATION OF AMERICA

6600 Orangethorpe Avenue, P.O. Box 6600, Buena Park, CA 90622-6600 (714) 522-9011

June 21, 2009

Ms. Claudia Banks
122 River Heights Drive
Bettendorf, IA 52722

Dear Ms. Banks:

Thank you for your recent purchase. We wish you many years of satisfaction with your new CG1 grand piano. The CG1 carries more than a century of Yamaha's heritage in design and production of world-class musical instruments and will give you many years of playing and listening pleasure.

Our commitment to your satisfaction doesn't stop with your purchase, however. As a vital first step, please remember to call your Yamaha dealer sometime within three to eight months after your piano was delivered to take advantage of the Yamaha Servicebond℠ Assurance Program. This free service includes a thorough evaluation and adjustment of the instrument after you've had some time to play your piano and your piano has had time to adapt to its environment.

In addition to this important service, a regular program of tuning is essential to ensure your piano's impeccable performance. Our piano specialists recommend four tunings during the first year and two tunings every year thereafter. Your Yamaha dealer is ideally positioned to provide you with optimum service for both regular tuning and any maintenance or repair needs you may have.

Respectfully,

Dirk Allen
Yamaha Corporation of America

FIGURE 6.3
Revised Customer Letter
This revised letter provides the requested information more clearly, in a more organized fashion, with a friendlier style, and with precise mechanics.

too: If you earn a reputation for well-crafted documents that respect the audience's time, people will pay more attention to your work.

You may be familiar with one of the many indexes that have been developed over the years in an attempt to measure readability. For example, the Flesch-Kincaid Grade Level score computes reading difficulty relative to grade-level achievement. A score of 10 suggests that a document can be read and understood by the average 10th grader. Most business documents score in the 8–11 range. Technical documents often score in the 12–14 range. A similar scoring system, the Flesch Reading Ease score, ranks documents on a 100-point scale; the higher the score, the easier the document is to read. Both of these measurements are built into Microsoft Word, making them easy for most business communicators to use.

Readability formulas can give you a helpful indication, but they can't measure everything that affects readability.

Readability indexes offer a useful reference point, but they are all limited by what they are able to measure: word length, number of syllables, sentence length, and paragraph length. They can't measure any of the other factors that affect readability, such as audience analysis, writing clarity, and document design. Compare these two paragraphs:

> Readability indexes offer a useful reference point, but they are all limited by what they are able to measure: word length, number of syllables, sentence length, and paragraph length. They can't measure any of the other factors that affect readability, from "you" orientation to writing clarity to document design.
>
> Readability indexes can help. But they don't measure everything. They don't measure whether your writing clarity is good. They don't measure whether your document design is good or not. Reading indexes are based on word length, syllables, sentences, and paragraphs.

The first paragraph scores 12.0 on grade level and 27.4 on reading ease, meaning it is supposedly rather difficult to read. The second paragraph scores much better on both grade level (8.9) and reading ease (45.8). However, the second example is choppy, unsophisticated, poorly organized, and much less satisfying to read. As a general rule, then, don't assume that a piece of text is readable if it scores well on a readability index—or that it is difficult to read if it doesn't score well.

The effort to make your documents more readable will pay for itself in greater career success.

Beyond shortening words and sentences, you can improve the readability of a message by making the document easy to skim. Most business audiences—particularly influential senior managers—skim longer documents, looking for key ideas, conclusions, and recommendations. If they determine that a document contains valuable information or requires a response, they will read it more carefully when time permits. You can adopt a number of techniques to make your message easier to skim: varying sentence length, using shorter paragraphs, using lists and bullets instead of narrative, and adding effective headings and subheadings.

To keep readers' interest, use a variety of long, medium, and short sentences.

Varying Your Sentence Length Variety is a creative way to make your messages interesting and readable. By choosing words and sentence structure with care, you can create a rhythm that emphasizes important points, enlivens your writing style, and makes your information appealing to your reader. For example, a short sentence that highlights a conclusion at the end of a substantial paragraph of evidence makes your key message stand out. Effective messages, therefore, usually use a mixture of sentences that are short (up to 15 words or so), medium (15–25 words), and long (more than 25 words).

Each sentence length has its advantages. Short sentences can be processed quickly and are easier for nonnative speakers and translators to interpret. Medium-length sentences are useful for showing the relationships among ideas. Long sentences are often the best way to convey complex ideas, list multiple related points, or summarize or preview information.

Of course, each sentence length also has disadvantages. Too many short sentences in a row can make your writing choppy. Medium sentences lack the punch of short sentences and the informative power of longer sentences. Long sentences are usually harder to understand than short sentences because they are

Document Makeover

IMPROVE THIS LETTER

To practice correcting drafts of actual documents, visit your online course or the access-code-protected portion of the Companion Website. Click on "Document Makeovers" and then click on Chapter 6. You will find a letter that contains problems and errors related to what you've learned in this chapter about revising messages. Use the Final Draft decision tool to create an improved version of this letter. Check the message for organization, readability, clarity, and conciseness.

packed with information and ideas. Because readers can absorb only a few words per glance, longer sentences are also more difficult to skim. Thus, the longer your sentence, the greater the possibility that the reader who skims it will not read enough words to process its full meaning. By choosing the best sentence length for each communication need and remembering to mix sentence lengths for variety, you'll get your points across while keeping your messages lively and interesting.

Keeping Your Paragraphs Short   Large blocks of text can be visually daunting, so the optimum paragraph length is short to medium in most cases. Unless you break up your thoughts somehow, you'll end up with lengthy paragraphs that are guaranteed to intimidate even the most dedicated reader. Short paragraphs, generally 100 words or fewer (this paragraph has 88 words), are easier to read than long ones, and they make your writing look inviting. They help audiences read more carefully, too. You can also emphasize ideas by isolating them in short, forceful paragraphs.

> Short paragraphs are easier to read than long ones.

However, don't go overboard with short paragraphs. Be careful to use one-sentence paragraphs only occasionally and only for emphasis. Also, if you need to divide a subject into several pieces in order to keep paragraphs short, be sure to help your readers keep the ideas connected by guiding them with plenty of transitional elements.

Using Lists and Bullets to Clarify and Emphasize   An effective alternative to using conventional sentences is to set off important ideas in a **list**—a series of words, names, or other items. Lists can show the sequence of ideas, heighten their impact visually, and increase the likelihood that a reader will find the key points. In addition, lists help simplify complex subjects, highlight main points, break up a page or screen visually, ease the skimming process for busy readers, and give readers a breather. Consider the difference between the following two approaches to the same information:

> Lists are effective tools for highlighting and simplifying material.

Narrative	**List**
Owning your own business has many potential advantages. One is the opportunity to pursue your own personal passion. Another advantage is the satisfaction of working for yourself. As a sole proprietor, you also have the advantage of privacy because you do not have to reveal your financial information or plans to anyone.	Owning your own business has three advantages: • Opportunity to pursue personal passion • Satisfaction of working for yourself • Financial privacy

When creating a list, you can separate items with numbers, letters, or bullets (a general term for any kind of graphical element that precedes each item). Bullets are generally preferred over numbers, unless the list is in some logical sequence or ranking or you need to refer to specific items in the list elsewhere. The following three steps need to be performed in the order indicated, and the numbers make that clear:

1. Find out how many employees would like on-site day-care facilities.
2. Determine how much space the day-care center would require.
3. Estimate the cost of converting a conference room for the on-site facility.

Lists are easiest to locate and read if the entire numbered or bulleted section is set off by a blank line before and after, as the preceding examples demonstrate.

Furthermore, when using lists, make sure to introduce them clearly so that people know what they're about to read. Of course, you can also add further discussion after the list. One way to introduce lists is to make them a part of the introductory sentence:

> The board of directors met to discuss the revised annual budget. To keep expenses in line with declining sales, the directors voted to
> - Cut everyone's salary by 10 percent
> - Close the employee cafeteria
> - Reduce travel expenses

Another way to introduce a list is to precede it with a complete introductory sentence, followed by a colon:

> The decline in company profit is attributable to four factors:
> - Slower holiday sales
> - Increased transportation and fuel costs
> - Higher employee wages
> - Slower inventory turnover

Regardless of the format you choose, the items in a list should be parallel; that is, they should all use the same grammatical pattern. For example, if one list item begins with a verb, every list item should begin with a verb. If one item is a noun phrase, every one should be a noun phrase:

Nonparallel List Items	**Parallel List Items**
• Improve our bottom line	• Improving our bottom line
• Identification of new foreign markets for our products	• Identifying new foreign markets for our products
• Global market strategies	• Developing our global market strategies
• Issues regarding pricing and packaging size	• Resolving pricing and packaging issues

Parallel forms are easier to read and skim. You can create parallelism by repeating the pattern in words, phrases, clauses, or entire sentences (see Table 6.1).

Table 6.1   ACHIEVING PARALLELISM

Method	Example
Parallel words	The letter was approved by Clausen, Whittaker, Merlin, and Carlucci.
Parallel phrases	We are gaining market share in supermarkets, in department stores, and in specialty stores.
Parallel clauses	I'd like to discuss the issue after Vicki gives her presentation but before Marvin shows his slides.
Parallel sentences	In 2006, we exported 30 percent of our production. In 2007, we exported 50 percent.

Adding Headings and Subheadings   A **heading** is a brief title that tells readers about the content of the section that follows. **Subheadings** are subordinate to headings, indicating subsections within a major section. Headings and subheadings serve these important functions:

- **Organization.** Headings show your reader at a glance how the document is organized. They act as labels to group related paragraphs together and effectively organize your material into short sections.

- **Attention.** Informative, inviting, and in some cases intriguing headings grab the reader's attention, make the text easier to read, and help the reader find the parts he or she needs to read—or skip.

- **Connection.** Using headings and subheadings together helps readers see the relationship between main ideas and subordinate ones so that they can understand your message more easily. Moreover, headings and subheadings visually indicate shifts from one idea to the next.

Headings fall into two categories. **Descriptive headings**, such as "Cost Considerations," identify a topic but do little more. **Informative headings**, such as "A New Way to Cut Costs," put your reader right into the context of your message.

Informative headings guide readers to think in a certain way about the topic. They are also helpful in guiding your work as a writer, especially if written in terms of questions you plan to address in your document. Well-written informative headings are self-contained, which means readers can read just the headings and subheadings and understand them without reading the rest of the document. For example, "Introduction" conveys little information, whereas the heading "Staffing Shortages Cost the Company $150,000 Last Year" provides a key piece of information and captures the reader's attention. Whatever types of headings you choose, keep them brief and use parallel construction as you would for an outline, lists, or a series of words.

Editing for Clarity and Conciseness

After you've reviewed and revised your message for readability, your next step is to make sure your message is as clear and as concise as possible. To ensure clarity, look closely at your paragraph organization, sentence structure, and word choices. Do your paragraphs have clear topic sentences? Are the transitions between ideas obvious? Then ask yourself whether your sentences are easy to decipher. Are your statements simple and direct? Perhaps a sentence is so complicated that readers can't unravel it. Next, review your word choices. You might have chosen a word that is so vague that readers can interpret it in several ways. Perhaps pronouns or tenses switch midsentence so that readers lose track of who is talking or when an event took place.[2]

See Table 6.2 for examples of the following tips:

- **Break up overly long sentences.** Don't connect too many clauses with *and* or *or*. If you find yourself stuck in a long sentence, you're probably trying to make the sentence do more than it can reasonably do, such as expressing two dissimilar thoughts or peppering the reader with too many pieces of supporting evidence at once. (Did you notice how difficult this long sentence was to read?) You can often clarify your writing by separating a string of items into individual sentences.

- **Rewrite hedging sentences.** Sometimes you have to write *may* or *seems* to avoid stating a judgment as a fact. However, when you have too many such hedges, you come across as being unsure of what you're saying.

- **Impose parallelism.** When you have two or more similar ideas to express, make them parallel. Repeating the same grammatical construction shows that the ideas

---

Margin notes:

Use headings to grab the reader's attention and organize material into short sections.

Informative headings are generally more helpful than descriptive ones.

Use the same grammatical form for each heading.

Clarity is essential to getting your message across accurately and efficiently.

Don't be afraid to present your opinions without qualification.

When you use the same grammatical pattern to express two or more ideas, you show that they are comparable thoughts.

Table 6.2 — REVISING FOR CLARITY

Issues to Review	Ineffective	Effective
Overly Long Sentences Taking compound sentences too far	The magazine will be published January 1, and I'd better meet the deadline if I want my article included because we want the article to appear before the trade show.	The magazine will be published January 1. I'd better meet the deadline because we want the article to appear before the trade show.
Hedging Sentences Overqualifying sentences	I believe that Mr. Johnson's employment record seems to show that he may be capable of handling the position.	Mr. Sims had been drenched with rain, bombarded with telephone calls, and shouted at by his boss.
Unparallel Sentences Using dissimilar construction for similar ideas	Mr. Simms had been drenched with rain, bombarded with telephone calls, and his boss shouted at him.	Mr. Sims had been drenched with rain, bombarded with telephone calls, and shouted at by his boss.
	To waste time and missing deadlines are bad habits.	Wasting time and missing deadlines are bad habits.
Dangling Modifiers Placing modifiers close to the wrong nouns and verbs	Walking to the office, a red sports car passed her.	A red sports car passed her while she was walking to the office.
	Reduced by 25 percent, Europe had its lowest semiconductor output in a decade.	Europe reduced semiconductor output by 25 percent, its lowest output in a decade.
Long Noun Sequences Stringing too many nouns together	The window sash installation company will give us an estimate on Friday.	The company that installs window sashes will give us an estimate on Friday.
Camouflaged Verbs Changing verbs and nouns into adjectives	The manager undertook implementation of the rules.	The manager implemented the rules.
	Verification of the shipments occurs weekly.	We verify shipments weekly.
Changing verbs into nouns	reach a conclusion about	conclude
	give consideration to	consider
Sentence Structure Separating subject and predicate	A 10% decline in market share, which resulted from quality problems and an aggressive sales campaign by Armitage, the market leader in the Northeast, was the major problem in 2007.	The major problem in 2007 was a 10% loss of market share, which resulted from both quality problems and an aggressive sales campaign by Armitage, the market leader in the Northeast.
Separating adjectives, adverbs, or prepositional phrases from the words they modify	Our antique desk lends an air of strength and substance with thick legs and large drawers.	With its thick legs and large drawers, our antique desk lends an air of strength and substance.
Awkward References	The Law Office and the Accounting Office distribute computer supplies for legal secretaries and beginning accountants, respectively.	The Law Office distributes computer supplies for legal secretaries; the Accounting Office distributes those for beginning accountants.
Too Much Enthusiasm	We are extremely pleased to offer you a position on our staff of exceptionally skilled and highly educated employees. The work offers extraordinary challenges and a very large salary.	We are pleased to offer you a position on our staff of skilled and well-educated employees. The work offers challenges and an attractive salary.

are related, of similar importance, and on the same level of generality. Parallelism is discussed earlier in this chapter in the section on lists.

- **Correct dangling modifiers.** Sometimes a modifier is not just an adjective or an adverb but an entire phrase modifying a noun or a verb. Be careful not to leave this type of modifier *dangling*, with no connection to the subject of the sentence. The first ineffective example under "Dangling Modifiers" in Table 6.2 implies that the red sports car has an office and the legs to walk there. The second example shows one frequent cause of dangling modifiers: passive construction.

- **Reword long noun sequences.** When multiple nouns are strung together as modifiers, the resulting sentence can be hard to read. You may be trying too hard to create the desired effect. See if a single well-chosen word will do the job. If the nouns are all necessary, consider moving one or more to a modifying phrase, as shown in Table 6.2. Although you add a few more words, your audience won't have to work as hard to understand the sentence.

- **Replace camouflaged verbs.** Watch for words that end in *-ion*, *-tion*, *-ing*, *-ment*, *-ant*, *-ent*, *-ence*, *-ance*, and *-ency*. These endings often change verbs into nouns and adjectives, requiring you to add a verb in order to get your point across. To prune and enliven your messages, use verbs instead of noun phrases.

- **Clarify sentence structure.** Keep the subject and predicate of a sentence as close together as possible. When the subject and predicate are far apart, readers may need to read the sentence twice to figure out who did what. Similarly, adjectives, adverbs, and prepositional phrases usually make the most sense when they're placed as close as possible to the words they modify.

  Subject and predicate should be placed as close together as possible, as should modifiers and the words they modify.

- **Clarify awkward references.** In an effort to save words, business writers sometimes use expressions such as *the above-mentioned*, *as mentioned above*, *the aforementioned*, *the former*, *the latter*, and *respectively*. These words cause readers to jump from point to point, which hinders effective communication. You'll often be more successful using specific references (such as "as described in the second paragraph on page 22"), even if that means adding a few more words.

- **Moderate your enthusiasm.** An occasional adjective or adverb to intensify and emphasize your meaning is fine, but too many can degrade your writing and damage your credibility.

  Showing enthusiasm for ideas is fine, but be careful not to go so far that you sound unprofessional or unbelievable.

Readers appreciate conciseness, in addition to clarity, in business messages. The good news is that most first drafts can be cut by as much as 50 percent.[3] By reorganizing your content, improving the readability of your document, and correcting your sentence structure for clarity, you will have already eliminated most of the excess. Now it is time to examine every word you've written. As you begin your editing task, simplify, prune, and strive for order. See Table 6.3 for examples of the following tips:

- **Delete unnecessary words and phrases.** To test whether a word or phrase is essential, try the sentence without it. If the meaning doesn't change, leave it out. For instance, *very* is often simply clutter. There's no need to call someone "very methodical." The person is either methodical or not. In addition, avoid the clutter of too many or poorly placed relative pronouns (*who*, *that*, *which*). Even articles can be excessive (such as repeating *the* in a list of items). However, well-placed relative pronouns and articles prevent confusion, so make sure you don't obscure the meaning of the sentence by removing them.

  Make your documents tighter by removing unnecessary words.

- **Shorten long words and phrases.** Short words are generally more vivid and easier to read than long ones. Shorter phrases are easier to process and understand quickly. Remember, though, the idea is to use short, simple words and phrases, *not* simple concepts.[4]

Table 6.3 — REVISING FOR CONCISENESS

Issues to Review	Ineffective	Effective
Unnecessary Words and Phrases		
Using wordy phrases	for the sum of	for
	in the event that	if
	prior to the start of	before
	in the near future	soon
	at this point in time	now
	due to the fact that, in view of the fact that	because
	until such time as	when
	with reference to	about
Using too many relative pronouns	Cars that are sold after January will not have a six-month warranty.	Cars sold after January will not have a six-month warranty.
	Employees who are driving to work should park in the underground garage.	Employees driving to work should park in the underground garage.
Using too few relative pronouns	The project manager told the engineers last week the specifications were changed.	The project manager told the engineers last week that the specifications were changed.
		The project manager told the engineers that last week the specifications were changed.
Long Words and Phrases		
Using overly long words	During the preceding year, the company accelerated productive operations.	Last year the company sped up operations.
	The action was predicated on the assumption that the company was operating at a financial deficit.	The action was based on the belief that the company was losing money.
Using wordy phrases rather than infinitives	If you want success as a writer, you must work hard.	To succeed as a writer, you must work hard.
	The employer increased salaries so that she could improve morale.	The employer increased salaries to improve morale.
Redundancies		
Repeating meanings	absolutely complete	complete
	basic fundamentals	fundamentals
	follows after	follows
	free and clear	free
	refer back	refer
	repeat again	repeat
	collect together	collect
	future plans	plans
	return back	return
	important essentials	essentials
	end result	result
	actual truth	truth
	final outcome	outcome
Using double modifiers	modern, up-to-date equipment	modern equipment
It Is/There are Starters	It would be appreciated if you would sign the lease today.	Please sign the lease today.
Starting sentences with *it* or *there*	There are five employees in this division who were late to work today.	Five employees in this division were late to work today.

- **Eliminate redundancies.** In some word combinations, the words tend to say the same thing. For instance, "visible to the eye" is redundant because *visible* is enough without further clarification; "to the eye" adds nothing.

- **Recast "It is/There are" starters.** If you start a sentence with an indefinite pronoun such as *it* or *there*, odds are the sentence could be shorter and more active. For instance, "We believe…" is a stronger opening than "It is believed that…"

Sometimes you'll find that the most difficult problem in a sentence can be solved by simply removing the problem itself. When you come upon a troublesome element, ask yourself, "Do I need it at all?" Possibly not. In fact, you may find that it was giving you so much grief precisely because it was trying to do an unnecessary job.[5] When you remove the troublesome element, the afflicted sentence will spring to life and breathe normally. Take advantage of the "undo" and "redo" functions in your software to experiment with adding and removing various elements.

For a reminder of the tasks involved in revision, see "Checklist: Revising Business Messages."

Using Technology to Revise Your Message

When it's time to revise and polish your message, your word processor can help you add, delete, and move text, using functions such as *cut and paste* (taking a block of text out of one section of a document and pasting it in somewhere else) and *search and replace* (finding words or phrases and changing them if you need to). Be careful using this feature, though; choosing the "replace all" option can result in some unintended errors. For example, finding *power* and replacing all occurrences with *strength* will also change the word *powerful* to *strengthful*.

Software tools such as *revision marks* and *commenting* keep track of proposed editing changes electronically and provide a history of a document's revisions. In Microsoft Word, the revisions appear in a different text color than the original text (see Figure 6.4), giving you a chance to review changes before accepting or rejecting

✓ CHECKLIST: Revising Business Messages

A. Evaluate content, organization, style, and tone.

- ✓ Make sure the information is accurate, relevant, and sufficient.
- ✓ Check that all necessary points appear in logical order.
- ✓ Verify that you present enough support to make the main idea convincing and interesting.
- ✓ Be sure the beginning and end are effective.
- ✓ Make sure you've achieved the right tone.

B. Review for readability.

- ✓ Consider using a readability index but be sure to interpret the answer carefully.
- ✓ Use a mix of short and long sentences.
- ✓ Keep paragraphs short.
- ✓ Use bulleted and numbered lists to emphasize key points.
- ✓ Make the document easy to scan with headings and subheadings.

C. Edit for clarity.

- ✓ Break up overly long sentences and rewrite hedging sentences.
- ✓ Impose parallelism to simplify reading.
- ✓ Correct dangling modifiers.
- ✓ Reword long noun sequences and replace camouflaged verbs.
- ✓ Clarify sentence structure and awkward references.
- ✓ Moderate your enthusiasm to maintain a professional tone.

D. Edit for conciseness.

- ✓ Delete unnecessary words and phrases.
- ✓ Shorten long words and phrases.
- ✓ Eliminate redundancies.
- ✓ Rewrite sentences that start with "It is" or "There are."

FIGURE 6.4
Revision Marks in Microsoft Word
Microsoft Word, the most commonly used word processing software in business offices, offers handy tools for reviewing draft documents. In this example, text to be added is underlined, and text to be deleted is struck through. The writer can then choose to accept or reject each suggested change.

Spell checkers, grammar checkers, and computerized thesauruses can all help with the revision process, but they can't take the place of good writing and editing skills.

them. Adobe Acrobat lets you attach comments to PDF files (see Figure 6.5). (Note that Adobe Acrobat is not the same product as the free Adobe Reader.) Using revision marks and commenting features is also a great way to keep track of editing changes made by team members. Both Word and Acrobat let you use different colors for each reviewer, as well, so you can keep everyone's comments separate.

In addition to the many revision tools, four software functions can help bring out the best in your documents. First, a *spell checker* compares your document with an electronic dictionary, highlights unrecognized words, and suggests correct spellings. Spell checkers are wonderful for finding typos, but they are no substitute for good spelling skills. For example, if you use *their* when you mean to use *there*, your spell checker won't notice because *their* is spelled correctly. Plus, some of the "errors" that the spell checker indicates may actually be proper names, technical words, words that you misspelled on purpose, web addresses, or simply words the spell checker doesn't know. It's up to you to decide whether each flagged word should be corrected or left alone, to find the errors that your spell checker has overlooked, and to catch problems that the spell checker itself might introduce (such as inserting unwanted hyphens or suggesting incorrect word replacements).

Second, a computer *thesaurus* gives you alternative words, just as a printed thesaurus does. A computer thesaurus is much faster and lets you try multiple alternatives in just a few seconds to see which works best. The best uses of any thesaurus, printed or computerized, are to find fresh, interesting words when you've been using the same word too many times and to find words that most accurately convey your intended meaning. Don't fall into the temptation of using your thesaurus to find impressive words to spice up your writing; if you're not comfortable using a word, it won't sound natural in your documents.

Third, a *grammar checker* tries to do for your grammar what a spell checker does for your spelling. Because the program doesn't have a clue about what you're trying

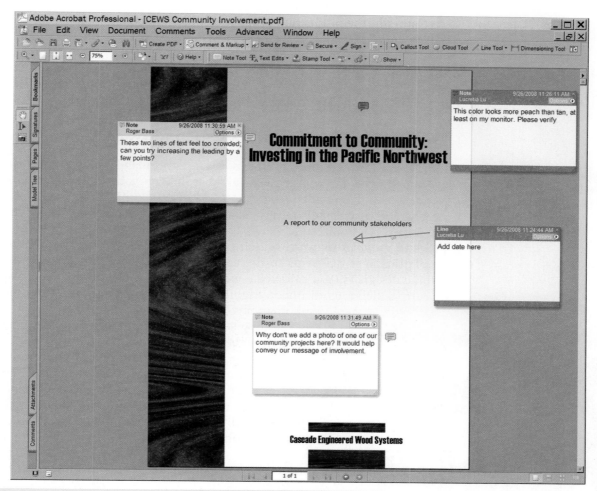

FIGURE 6.5
Comments Attached to a PDF File
Adobe Acrobat lets reviewers attach comments to a document in PDF format.

to say, it can't tell whether you've said it clearly or completely. However, grammar checkers can highlight items you should consider changing, such as passive voice, long sentences, and words that tend to be misused.

Fourth, a *style checker* can also monitor your word and sentence choices and suggest alternatives that might produce more effective writing. For instance, the style-checking options in Microsoft Word range from basic issues, such as spelling out numbers and using contractions, to more subjective matters, such as sentence structure and the use of technical terminology.

By all means, use any software tools that you find helpful when revising your documents. Just remember that it's unwise to rely on them to do all your revision work, and you're responsible for the final product.

PRODUCING YOUR MESSAGE

Now it's time to put your hard work on display. The *production quality* of your message—the total effect of page or screen design, graphical elements, typography, and so on—plays an important role in the effectiveness of your message. A polished, inviting design not only makes your material easier to read but also conveys a sense of professionalism and importance.[6]

> The quality of your document or screen design affects both readability and audience perceptions of you and your message.

Naturally, the production task varies widely, depending on the medium you've chosen and the degree of formality you need to achieve. In the simplest media, such as text messaging, you have virtually nothing to do. With instant messaging and e-mail, you can control a variety of aspects, such as type size and color. With documents prepared with a word processor, your options multiply considerably—particularly if you plan to deliver the documents electronically.

Adding Graphics, Sound, Video, and Hypertext

Take advantage of your word processor's ability to incorporate visual elements in your documents.

Today's word processors and other software tools make it easy to produce impressive documents and online materials that enliven your messages with full-color pictures, sound and video recordings, and hypertext links. The software for creating business visuals falls into two basic groups: *presentation software*, which helps you create electronic slide shows for in-person or online meetings (see Chapter 14), and *graphics software*, which ranges from basic tools that help you create simple business diagrams to the comprehensive tools preferred by artists and graphic designers. You can create graphics yourself, use digital photographs, add *clip art* (collections of uncopyrighted images), or scan in printed drawings or photographs.

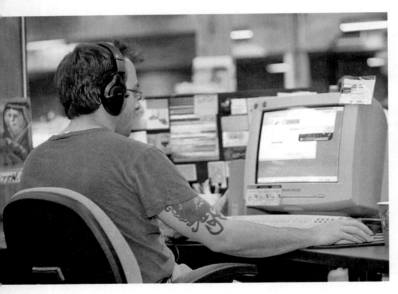

By embedding multimedia elements in reports and other documents, you can enhance your messages with audio and video.

Adding sound bites or video clips to electronic documents can be an effective way to help get your message across. Several systems let you record brief messages and attach them to particular places in a document. The reader then clicks on a speaker icon to play each comment.

You can use Hypertext Markup Language (HTML) to insert hyperlinks into your documents. Readers can easily jump from one document to another by clicking on such a link. They can go directly to a website, jump to another section of your document, or go to a different document or program altogether. Suppose you're preparing a report on this year's budget. Rather than include pages and pages of budget details from prior years, you can connect to them using hyperlinks. If readers need to access specific details, they can simply click on the appropriate links. Using hyperlinks, you can customize your documents to meet the individual information needs of your readers—just as you can on a webpage. Of course, you have to make sure that the file (or the software program used to open that file) is included with your electronic document, installed on the recipient's computer, or accessible via a network connection.

Designing for Readability

Design affects the impression your message makes.

Design affects readability in two important ways. First, if used carefully, design elements can improve the effectiveness of your message. If used poorly, design elements can act as barriers, blocking your communication. For example, people age 65 and over are the fastest-growing segment of online consumers in the United States, but many websites don't take into account the natural changes that occur in eyesight as people age. Older people often find it difficult to read the small type that is common on websites—and many websites make the even greater mistake of preventing viewers from enlarging type size in their browsers.[7]

Second, visual design itself sends a nonverbal message to the audience, influencing their perceptions of the communication before they read a single word (see Figure 6.6). For example, the elegant style of the Mercedes-AMG website conveys a

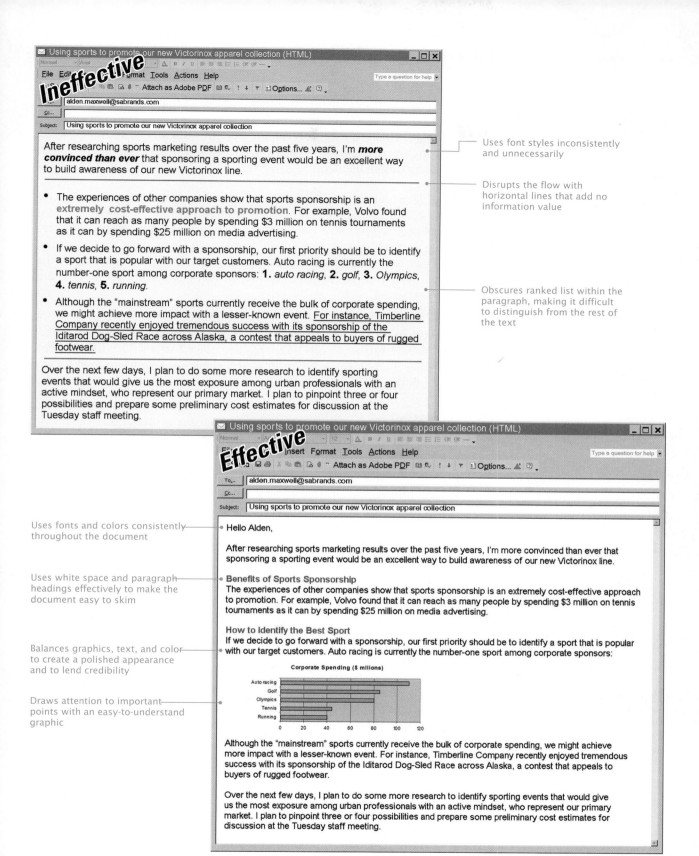

Ineffective

☑ Using sports to promote our new Victorinox apparel collection (HTML)

Normal   Arial

File   Edit   Format   Tools   Actions   Help   Type a question for help

          Attach as Adobe PDF   Options...

alden.maxwell@sabrands.com

Cc...

Subject: Using sports to promote our new Victorinox apparel collection

After researching sports marketing results over the past five years, I'm **more convinced than ever** that sponsoring a sporting event would be an excellent way to build awareness of our new Victorinox line.

• The experiences of other companies show that sports sponsorship is an extremely cost-effective approach to promotion. For example, Volvo found that it can reach as many people by spending $3 million on tennis tournaments as it can by spending $25 million on media advertising.

• If we decide to go forward with a sponsorship, our first priority should be to identify a sport that is popular with our target customers. Auto racing is currently the number-one sport among corporate sponsors: **1.** *auto racing*, **2.** *golf*, **3.** *Olympics*, **4.** *tennis*, **5.** *running*.

• Although the "mainstream" sports currently receive the bulk of corporate spending, we might achieve more impact with a lesser-known event. For instance, Timberline Company recently enjoyed tremendous success with its sponsorship of the Iditarod Dog-Sled Race across Alaska, a contest that appeals to buyers of rugged footwear.

Over the next few days, I plan to do some more research to identify sporting events that would give us the most exposure among urban professionals with an active mindset, who represent our primary market. I plan to pinpoint three or four possibilities and prepare some preliminary cost estimates for discussion at the Tuesday staff meeting.

Uses font styles inconsistently and unnecessarily

Disrupts the flow with horizontal lines that add no information value

Obscures ranked list within the paragraph, making it difficult to distinguish from the rest of the text

Effective

☑ Using sports to promote our new Victorinox apparel collection (HTML)

Normal   12

File   Insert   Format   Tools   Actions   Help   Type a question for help

          Attach as Adobe PDF   Options...

To...   alden.maxwell@sabrands.com

Cc...

Subject: Using sports to promote our new Victorinox apparel collection

Hello Alden,

After researching sports marketing results over the past five years, I'm more convinced than ever that sponsoring a sporting event would be an excellent way to build awareness of our new Victorinox line.

Benefits of Sports Sponsorship
The experiences of other companies show that sports sponsorship is an extremely cost-effective approach to promotion. For example, Volvo found that it can reach as many people by spending $3 million on tennis tournaments as it can by spending $25 million on media advertising.

How to Identify the Best Sport
If we decide to go forward with a sponsorship, our first priority should be to identify a sport that is popular with our target customers. Auto racing is currently the number-one sport among corporate sponsors:

Corporate Spending ($ millions)

Auto racing
Golf
Olympics
Tennis
Running
          0   20   40   60   80   100   120

Although the "mainstream" sports currently receive the bulk of corporate spending, we might achieve more impact with a lesser-known event. For instance, Timberline Company recently enjoyed tremendous success with its sponsorship of the Iditarod Dog-Sled Race across Alaska, a contest that appeals to buyers of rugged footwear.

Over the next few days, I plan to do some more research to identify sporting events that would give us the most exposure among urban professionals with an active mindset, who represent our primary market. I plan to pinpoint three or four possibilities and prepare some preliminary cost estimates for discussion at the Tuesday staff meeting.

Uses fonts and colors consistently throughout the document

Uses white space and paragraph headings effectively to make the document easy to skim

Balances graphics, text, and color to create a polished appearance and to lend credibility

Draws attention to important points with an easy-to-understand graphic

FIGURE 6.6

Ineffective and Effective Document Design

Compare these two e-mail screens. They contain virtually the same information but send dramatically different messages to the reader. The unprofessional appearance of the "ineffective" version makes it uninviting and difficult to read. The amateurish use of color is distracting. In contrast, the "effective" version is clear, inviting, and easy to either read entirely or scan quickly.

message that matches the nature of the products themselves. The black, silver, gray, and white color palette sends a distinctly different message than a website with wild, clashing colors would send.

Effective design helps you establish the tone of your document and helps guide your readers through your message. To achieve an effective design, pay careful attention to the following design elements:

For effective design, pay attention to
- *Consistency*
- *Balance*
- *Restraint*
- *Detail*

- **Consistency.** Throughout each message, be consistent in your use of margins, typeface, type size, and spacing (such as in paragraph indents, between columns, and around photographs). Also be consistent when using recurring design elements, such as vertical lines, columns, and borders. In many cases, you'll want to be consistent not only within a message but also across multiple messages; that way, audiences who receive messages from you recognize your documents and know what to expect.

- **Balance.** To create a pleasing design, balance the space devoted to text, artwork, and white space. Balance is a subjective issue. One document may have a formal, rigid design in which the various elements are placed in a grid pattern, while another may have a less formal design in which elements flow more freely across the page—and both could be in balance.

- **Restraint.** Strive for simplicity in design. Elegant simplicity, using only enough text, graphics, audio, and video to get each point across, is one of the reasons the Mercedes-AMG website is so effective. Don't clutter your message with too many design elements, too much highlighting, too many colors, or too many decorative touches. Let "simpler" and "fewer" be your guiding concepts.

- **Detail.** Pay attention to details that affect your design and thus your message. For instance, headings and subheadings that appear at the bottom of a column or page can annoy readers when the promised information doesn't appear until the next column or page. Also, narrow columns with too much space between words can be distracting.

If you will be designing a lot of documents that go beyond simple memos and reports, consider taking a course in page layout or graphic design to make the most of your creative efforts. However, even without special training, you can make your printed and electronic messages more effective by understanding the use of white space, margins and line justification, typefaces, and type styles.

White space separates elements in a document and helps guide the reader's eye.

White Space   Any space free of text or artwork, whether in print or online, is considered **white space** (note that "white space" isn't necessarily white). These unused areas provide visual contrast and important resting points for your readers. White space includes the open area surrounding headings, margins, vertical space between columns, paragraph indents or extra space between unindented paragraphs, and horizontal space between lines of text. To increase the chance that readers will read your messages, be generous with white space; it makes pages and screens feel less intimidating and easier to read.[8]

Most business documents use a flush-left margin and a ragged-right margin.

Margins and Justification   Margins define the space around text and between text columns. They're influenced by the way you place lines of type, which can be set (1) justified (flush on the left and flush on the right), (2) flush left with a ragged-right margin, (3) flush right with a ragged-left margin, or (4) centered. Justified type "darkens" your message's appearance because the uniform line lengths lack the white space created by ragged margins. It also tends to make your message look more formal and less like a personalized message. Justified type is often considered more difficult to read because large gaps can appear between words and because more words are hyphenated. (Excessive hyphenation is distracting and hard to follow.) Even so, many magazines, newspapers, and books use justified type because it can accommodate more text in a given space. These professionally published documents also have an advantage most business communicators don't have: the time and skill needed to carefully adjust character and word spacing in order to eliminate problems caused by justification.

Flush-left, ragged-right type "lightens" your message's appearance. It gives a document an informal, contemporary feeling of openness. Spacing between words is the same, and only long words that fall at the ends of lines are hyphenated.

Centered type is rarely used for text paragraphs but is commonly used for headings and subheadings. Flush-right, ragged-left type is rarely used in business documents.

Typefaces   **Typeface** or **font** refers to the physical design of letters, numbers, and other text characters. Typeface style influences the tone of your message, making it look authoritative or friendly, businesslike or casual, classic or modern, and so on (see Table 6.4). Be sure to choose fonts that are appropriate for your message. Most computers offer dozens of font choices, but most of these are inappropriate for general business usage.

Serif typefaces have small crosslines (called serifs) at the ends of each letter stroke. Serif typefaces such as Times Roman are commonly used for text; they can look busy and cluttered when set in large sizes for headings or other display treatments. Typefaces with rounded serifs can look friendly; those with squared serifs can look official.

Sans serif typefaces have no serifs (*sans* is French for "without"). Typefaces such as Helvetica and Arial are ideal for display treatments that use larger type. Sans serif typefaces can be difficult to read in long blocks of text. They look best when surrounded by plenty of white space—as in headings or in widely spaced lines of text.

For most documents, you shouldn't need to use more than two typefaces, although if you want to make captions or other text elements stand out, you can use another font.[9] You can't go too far wrong with a sans serif typeface (such as Arial) for heads and subheads and a serif typeface (such as Times New Roman) for text and captions. Using too many typefaces clutters a document and can produce an amateurish look (see Figure 6.6).

> Serif typefaces are commonly used for text; sans serif typefaces are commonly used for headings.

TYPEFACE PERSONALITIES: SERIOUS TO CASUAL TO PLAYFUL		Table 6.4
Serif Typefaces (best for text)	**Sans Serif Typefaces (best for headlines; some work well for text)**	**Specialty Typefaces (for decorative purposes only)**
Bookman Old Style	Arial	ANNA
Century Schoolbook	**Eras Bold**	Bauhaus
Courier	Franklin Gothic Book	*Edwardian*
Garamond	Frutiger	*Lucida Handwriting*
Rockwell	Gill Sans	Euclid Fraktur
Times Roman	Verdana	**STENCIL**

Type Styles   *Type style* refers to any modification that lends contrast or emphasis to type, including boldface, italic, underlining, and other highlighting and decorative styles. Using boldface type for subheads breaks up long expanses of text. You can also boldface isolated words in the middle of a text block to draw more attention to them. However, if you set too many words in boldface, you may create a "checkerboard" appearance within a paragraph and darken the overall appearance of your message, making it look heavy and uninviting.

Use italic type for emphasis. Although italics are sometimes used when irony or humor is intended, quotation marks are usually best for that purpose. Italics can also be used to set off a quote and are often used in captions. Boldfaced type and italics are most effective when reserved for key words—those that help readers understand the main point of the text. A good example of using boldface type effectively is found in the revision tips listed under the heading "Editing for Clarity and Conciseness" on pages 173–177 of this chapter. Here the boldfaced type draws attention to the key tips, followed by a short, regular-typeface explanation of each tip.

> Avoid using any type style that inhibits your audience's ability to read your messages.

As a general rule, avoid using any style in a way that slows your audience's progress through the message. For instance, underlining or using all-uppercase letters can interfere with your reader's ability to recognize the shapes of words, improperly placed boldface or italicized type can slow down your reader, and shadowed or outlined type can seriously hinder legibility.

Make sure the size of your type is proportionate to the importance of your message and the space allotted. For most business messages, use a type size of 10 to 12 points for regular text and 12 to 18 points for headings and subheadings (a point is approximately 1/72 inch). Resist the temptation to reduce your type size to squeeze in text or to enlarge it to fill up space. Type that is too small is hard to read, whereas extra-large type looks unprofessional. Be particularly careful with small type online; high-resolution computer screens can reduce this type even further, making it extremely difficult to read.

Using Technology to Produce Your Message

The production tools you have at your disposal vary widely, depending on the software and systems you're using. Some IM and e-mail systems offer limited formatting and production capabilities, whereas most word processors now offer some capabilities that rival professional publishing software for many day-to-day business needs. *Desktop publishing* software such as QuarkXPress and Adobe InDesign goes beyond word processing, offering more advanced layout capabilities designed to accommodate photos, technical drawings, and other elements. (These programs are used mainly by design professionals.) For online content, web publishing and blogging systems make it easy to produce great-looking pages quickly. Multimedia production tools such as Microsoft Producer let you combine slides, audio commentary, video clips, and other features into computer-based presentations that once cost thousands of dollars to create.

> Learning to use the basic features of your communication tools will help you produce better messages in less time.

No matter what system you're using, become familiar with the basic formatting capabilities. A few hours of exploration on your own or an introductory training course can dramatically improve the production quality of your documents. Depending on the types of messages you're creating, you'll benefit from being proficient with the following features:

- **Templates and style sheets.** As Chapter 5 notes, you can save a tremendous amount of time during production by using templates and style sheets. Many companies provide these to their employees to ensure a consistent look and feel for all print and online documents.

- **Page setup.** Use page setup to control margins, orientation (*portrait* is vertical; *landscape* is horizontal), and the location of *headers* and *footers* (text and graphics that repeat at the top and bottom of every page).

- **Column formatting.** Most business documents use a single column of text per page, but multiple columns can be an attractive format for documents such as newsletters. Columns are also handy for formatting long lists.

- **Paragraph formatting.** Take advantage of the various paragraph formatting controls to enhance the look of your documents. For instance, you can offset quotations by increasing margin width around a single paragraph, subtly compress line spacing to fit a document on a single page, or use hanging indents to offset the first line of a paragraph.

- **Numbered and bulleted lists.** Let your word processor or online publishing system do the busywork of formatting numbered and bulleted lists. It can also automatically renumber lists when you add or remove items, saving you the embarrassment of misnumbered lists.

- **Tables.** Tables are great for displaying any information that lends itself to rows and columns: calendars, numeric data, comparisons, and so on. Use paragraph and font formatting thoughtfully within tables for the best look.

- **Pictures, text boxes, and objects.** Word processors let you insert a wide variety of pictures (using industry-standard formats, such as JPEG and GIF). *Text boxes* are small blocks of text that stand apart from the main text; they are great for captions, callouts, margin notes, and so on. *Objects* can be anything from a spreadsheet to a sound clip to an engineering drawing. Similarly, blogging systems, wikis, and other web development tools let you insert a variety of pictures, audio and video clips, and other multimedia elements.

> Paragraph formatting gives you greater control over the look of your documents.

By improving the appearance of your documents with these tools, you'll improve your readers' impressions of you and your messages, too.

Formatting Formal Letters and Memos

Formal business letters usually follow certain design conventions, as the letter in Figure 6.3 (see page 169) illustrates. Most business letters are printed on *letterhead stationery*, which includes the company's name, address, and other contact information. The first thing to appear after the letterhead is the date, followed by the inside address, which identifies the person receiving the letter. Next is the salutation, usually in the form of *Dear Mr.* or *Ms. Last Name*. The message comes next, followed by the complimentary close, usually *Sincerely* or *Cordially*. And last comes the signature block: space for the signature, followed by the sender's printed name and title. Your company will probably have a standard format to follow for letters, possibly along with a template in Microsoft Word or whatever word processor is standard in the organization. For in-depth information on letter formats, see Appendix A: "Format and Layout of Business Documents."

> Business letters typically have the following elements:
> - Preprinted letterhead stationery
> - Date
> - Inside address
> - Salutation
> - Complimentary close
> - Signature block

Like letters, business memos usually follow a preset design (see Figure 6.7), and your employer will probably have a standard format or template for you to use. Most memos begin with a title such as *Memo*, *Memorandum*, or *Interoffice Correspondence*. Following that are usually four headings: *Date*, *To*, *From*, and *Subject*. (*Re:*, short for *Regarding*, is sometimes used instead of *Subject*.) Memos usually don't use a salutation, complimentary close, or signature, although signing your initials next to your name on the *From* line is standard practice in most companies. Bear in mind that memos are often distributed without sealed envelopes, so they are less private than most other message formats.

> Many companies use a printed form or word processor template for memos.

Uses standard company memo stationery with title indicating that this is a memo

Uses four standard headings for memos

Does not begin with a salutation

Carnival

INTERNAL MEMORANDUM

DATE: June 11, 2008
TO: Lauren Eastman
FROM: Brad Lymans
SUBJECT: Capacity for Carnival Corporation Cruise Ships

Here is the capacity data you requested along with a brief explanation of the figures:

Cruise Brand	Number of Ships	Passenger Capacity	Primary Market
Carnival	15	30,020	North America
Holland America	10	13,348	North America
Costa	7	9,200	Europe
Cunard	2	2,458	Worldwide
Seabourn	6	1,614	North America
Windstar	4	756	North America
Airtours-Sun	4	4,352	Europe
Total	48	61,748	

All passenger capacities are calculated based on two passengers per cabin, even though some cabins can accommodate three or four passengers.

Cruising capacity has grown in recent years, and management expects it to continue because all the major cruise companies are planning to introduce new ships into service. Carnival Corporation will build 16 additional cruise ships over the next five years, increasing the company's passenger capacity by 36,830, which will bring the total to 98,578.

To utilize this new capacity, we must increase our share of the overall vacation market. Keep in mind that demand for cruises may be affected by (1) the strength of the countries where the ships operate; (2) political instability in areas where the ships travel; and (3) adverse incidents involving cruise ships in general.

Please let me know if you have any further questions or need any additional data.

Does not include a complimentary close or a signature block

FIGURE 6.7
A Typical Business Memo
This document shows the elements usually included in a formal business memo. Note that in many instances today, this information would be transmitted via e-mail instead of a printed memo.

PROOFREADING YOUR MESSAGE

Your credibility is affected by your attention to the details of mechanics and form, so proofread carefully.

Imagine that you're a quality inspector for a car company. As each car rolls off the assembly line, you make sure the engine runs properly, the doors close tightly, the paint shines to glossy perfection, and so on. All the work is supposedly final, but you look closely just in case. Your company's reputation is at stake, and you don't want to let a faulty product out the door. Think of proofreading as the quality inspection stage for your documents, as your last chance to make sure your document is ready to carry your message—and your reputation—to the intended audience.

Look for two types of problems: (1) undetected mistakes from the writing, design, and layout stages; and (2) mistakes that crept in during production. For the first category, you can review format and layout guidelines in Appendix A on page A-1 and brush up on writing basics with the Handbook of Grammar, Mechanics, and

Usage on page H-1. The second category can include anything from computer glitches such as missing fonts or misaligned page elements to problems with the ink used in printing. Be particularly vigilant with complex documents and complex production processes that involve teams of people and multiple computers. Strange things can happen as files move from computer to computer, especially when lots of graphics and different fonts are involved.

Far from being a casual scan up and down the page (or screen, for online material), proofreading should be a methodical procedure in which you look for specific problems that might occur. Start by reviewing the advice in "Sharpening Your Career Skills: Proofread Like a Pro to Create Perfect Documents." You might also find it helpful to create a checklist of items to review; this can be handy when you need to review one of your own documents or you're asked to review someone else's work.

The amount of time you need to spend on proofing depends on the length and complexity of the document and the situation. A typo in an e-mail message to your team may not be a big deal; but a typo in a financial report, a contract, or a medical file certainly could be serious. As with every other task in the writing process, practice

> A methodical approach to proofreading will help you find the problems that need to be fixed.

> Plan to spend plenty of time proofing documents that are long, complex, and important.

SHARPENING YOUR CAREER SKILLS

Proofread Like a Pro to Create Perfect Documents

Before you click on "Send" or tote that stack of reports off to the shipping department, make sure your document represents the best possible work you can do. Your colleagues will usually overlook errors in everyday e-mails, but higher-profile mistakes in messages to outside audiences can damage your company and hinder your career.

Use these techniques from professional proofreaders to help ensure high-quality output:

- *Make multiple passes.* Go through the document several times, focusing on a different aspect each time. The first pass may be to look for omissions and errors in content; the second pass may be to check for typographical, grammatical, and spelling errors; and a final pass could be for layout, spacing, alignment, colors, page numbers, margins, and other design features.

- *Use perceptual tricks.* You've probably experienced the frustration of reading over something a dozen times and still missing an obvious error that was staring you right in the face. This happens because your brain has developed a wonderful skill of subconsciously supplying missing pieces and correcting mistakes when it "knows" what is supposed to be on the page. To keep your brain from tricking you, you need to trick it by changing the way you process the visual information. Try (1) reading each page backward, from the bottom to the top; (2) placing your finger under each word and reading it silently; (3) making a slit in a sheet of paper that reveals only one line of type at a time; (4) reading the document aloud and pronouncing each word carefully; and (5) temporarily reformatting the document so that it looks fresh to your eyes.

- *Double-check high-priority items.* Double-check the spelling of names and the accuracy of dates, addresses, and any number that could cause grief if incorrect (such as telling a potential employer that you'd be happy to work for $5,000 a year when you meant to say $50,000).

- *Give yourself some distance.* If possible, don't proofread immediately after finishing a document; let your brain wander off to new topics and then come back fresh later on.

- *Be vigilant.* Avoid reading large amounts of material in one sitting and try not to proofread when you're tired.

- *Stay focused.* Concentrate on what you're doing. Try to block out distractions and focus as completely as possible on your proofreading task.

- *Review complex electronic documents on paper.* Some people have trouble proofreading webpages, online reports, and other electronic documents on-screen. If you have trouble, try to print the materials so you can review them on paper.

- *Take your time.* Quick proofreading is not careful proofreading.

CAREER APPLICATIONS

1. Why is it so valuable to have other people proofread your documents?

2. Proofread the following sentence: aplication of thse methods in stores in San Deigo nd Cinncinati have resultted in a 30 drop in roberies an a 50 precent decling in violnce there, acording ot thedevelpers if the securty sytem, Hanover brothrs, Inc.

✓ CHECKLIST: Proofing Business Messages

A. Look for writing errors.

✓ Typographical mistakes
✓ Misspelled words
✓ Grammatical errors
✓ Punctuation mistakes

B. Look for missing elements.

✓ Missing text sections
✓ Missing exhibits (drawings, tables, photographs, charts, graphs, online images, and so on)
✓ Missing source notes, copyright notices, or other reference items

C. Look for design, formatting, and programming mistakes.

✓ Incorrect or inconsistent font selections
✓ Column sizing, spacing, and alignment
✓ Margins
✓ Special characters
✓ Clumsy line and page breaks
✓ Page numbers
✓ Page headers and footers
✓ Adherence to company standards
✓ Links (make sure they're active and link to the correct pages)
✓ Downloadable files (make sure they're stored in the appropriate folder so audiences can access them)

helps: You become not only more familiar with what errors to look for but also more skilled in identifying those errors. See "Checklist: Proofing Business Messages" for a handy list of items to review during proofing.

DISTRIBUTING YOUR MESSAGE

With the production finished, you're ready to distribute your message. As with every other aspect of business communication, your options for distribution multiply with every advance in technology. In some cases, the choice is obvious: Just hit the Send button in your e-mail program, and your message is on its way. In other cases, such as when you have a 100-page report with full-color graphics or a complex multimedia presentation, you need to plan the distribution carefully so that your message is received by everyone who needs it—and only those who need it. When planning your distribution, consider the following factors:

Consider cost, convenience, time, security, and privacy when choosing a distribution method.

- **Cost.** Cost won't be a concern for most messages, but for lengthy reports or multimedia productions, it may well be. Printing, binding, and delivering reports can be an expensive proposition, so weigh the cost versus the benefits before you decide. If you're trying to land a million-dollar client, spending $1,000 on presentation materials could be a wise investment.

- **Convenience.** How much work is involved for you and your audience? Although it's easy to attach a document to an e-mail message, things might not be so simple for the people on the other end. They may not have access to a printer, might be accessing your message from slow wireless connections or on handheld devices with tiny screens, or might not have the software needed to open your file. If you're sending large files as IM or e-mail attachments, consider using a file-compression utility such as WinZip or StuffIt to shrink the file first. For extremely large files, see whether your audience would prefer a CD-ROM instead.

- **Time.** How soon does the message need to reach the audience? Don't waste money on overnight delivery if the recipient won't read the report for a week.

- **Security and privacy.** The convenience offered by IM, e-mail, blogs, and other technologies needs to be weighed against security and privacy concerns. For the most sensitive documents, your company will probably restrict the people who can receive the documents and the means you can use to distribute them. In addition, most computer users are wary of opening attachments these days. Instead of sending Word files (which are vulnerable to macro viruses and other risks), consider converting your Word documents to PDF files that can be viewed using Adobe Reader.

Chapter 7 offers more advice on distributing podcasts, blogs, and other messages in electronic formats.

On the Job

SOLVING COMMUNICATION DILEMMAS AT MERCEDES-AMG

You've just joined the Mercedes-AMG marketing team as a communication specialist. Your duties include creating new material for the Mercedes-AMG website and, occasionally, reviewing materials created by your colleagues. Using what you've learned in this chapter about completing messages, address the following challenges.[10]

1. You've been asked to review the following statement that concerns the protection of personal data collected from website visitors (Daimler is the parent company of Mercedes-Benz, so its name appears in all legal documentation):

   As a worldwide leader in the automotive industry, Daimler uses a wide variety of technical and organizational security measures in order to protect the data we have under our control. We employ these measures in order to protect against accidental or intentional manipulation, loss, or destruction. We also use these measures in order to protect said collected data against access by persons unauthorized to access such information. Of course, we constantly strive to maintain the latest and most sophisticated data protection possible, so our security procedures are continually enhanced as new technology becomes available.

   Which of the following revisions is the best way to shorten this statement to 50 words or fewer (it is currently 94 words) without losing any essential information?

   a. Daimler promises to protect your privacy whenever you enter personal data on our website.
   b. Daimler uses a wide variety of technical and organizational security measures in order to protect the data we have under our control against accidental or intentional manipulation, loss, destruction, or unauthorized access. Our security procedures are continually enhanced as new technology becomes available.
   c. As a worldwide leader in the automotive industry, Daimler protects the data we have under our control against accidental or intentional manipulation,

   loss, or destruction. We also use these measures in order to protect said collected data against access by persons unauthorized to access such information.
   d. Daimler uses a wide variety of technical and organizational security measures in order to protect the data we have under our control against accidental or intentional manipulation, loss, or destruction. We also use these measures in order to protect said collected data against access by persons unauthorized to access such information. Of course, we constantly strive to maintain the latest and most sophisticated data protection possible, so our security procedures are continually enhanced as new technology becomes available.

2. In a section that discusses the history of AMG from its founding as a manufacturer of race car engines, the Mercedes-AMG website includes the following sentence: "The technology transfer from the race circuit to the road is still an integral part of the company's philosophy, which is to the benefit of every Mercedes-AMG customer." Which of these revised statements does the best job of communicating this message without using the term *technology transfer*?

   a. Every Mercedes-AMG customer benefits from the technologies we develop for race cars.
   b. It has always been the philosophy of Mercedes-AMG to transfer technologies we develop for the race track to the road, which benefits every Mercedes-AMG customer.
   c. Making sure customers benefit from our racing experience has always been an important part of Mercedes-AMG's philosophy.
   d. Transferring technologies developed for racing to our regular passenger cars remains an integral part of the company's philosophy.

3. Although your manager speaks English as a second language, he is an accomplished communicator and adamant about clear writing. He circled the following sentence in your draft of a report but left you to figure out what is wrong: "We have implemented improvements in quality control at every stage of the manufacturing process." How should you revise the sentence?

a. We have implemented improvements in quality control at every phase of the manufacturing process.
b. At every stage of the manufacturing process, we have implemented improvements in quality control.
c. We have improved quality control at every stage of the manufacturing process.
d. At every stage, we have implemented improvements in quality control of the manufacturing process.

4. While reviewing a draft of a new promotional brochure, you find a paragraph that you believe would be more effective as a bulleted list:

The exclusive character of the new Mercedes-Benz CL 63 AMG two-door coupé is immediately reflected in the high-tech equipment package: AMG body styling, AMG 19-inch light-alloy wheels, AMG sports suspension with Active Body Control, AMG high-performance braking system, the distinctive AMG interior as well as the Mercedes-Benz PRE SAFE® anticipatory occupant protection system, which uses radar to recognize potentially dangerous situations and automatically adjust the vehicle's speed to avoid collisions.

Which of the following does the most effective job of communicating this information in list form? (Remember that Mercedes-AMG models are special adaptations of standard Mercedes-Benz models.)

a. The exclusive character of the new Mercedes-Benz CL 63 AMG two-door coupé is immediately reflected in the high-tech equipment package:
   • AMG body styling
   • AMG 19-inch light-alloy wheels
   • AMG sports suspension with Active Body Control
   • AMG high-performance braking system
   • Distinctive AMG interior
   • Mercedes-Benz PRE SAFE® anticipatory occupant protection system, which uses radar to recognize potentially dangerous situations and automatically adjust the vehicle's speed to avoid collisions

b. The exclusive character of the new Mercedes-Benz CL 63 AMG two-door coupé is immediately reflected in the high-tech equipment package, which features a number of unique AMG features:
   • Body styling
   • 19-inch light-alloy wheels
   • Sports suspension with Active Body Control
   • High-performance braking system
   • Distinctive interior
In addition, every Mercedes-AMG model features such Mercedes-Benz innovations as the PRE SAFE® anticipatory occupant protection system, which uses radar to recognize potentially dangerous situations and automatically adjust the vehicle's speed to avoid collisions.

c. The exclusive character of the new Mercedes-Benz CL 63 AMG two-door coupé is immediately reflected in the high-tech equipment package:
   • AMG features:
      • Body styling
      • 19-inch light-alloy wheels
      • Sports suspension with Active Body Control
      • High-performance braking system
      • Distinctive interior
   • Mercedes-Benz features:
      • Innovations such as the PRE SAFE® anticipatory occupant protection system, which uses radar to recognize potentially dangerous situations and automatically adjust the vehicle's speed to avoid collisions

Learning Objectives Checkup

Assess your understanding of the principles in this chapter by reading each learning objective and studying the accompanying exercises. For fill-in-the-blank items, write the missing text in the blank provided; for multiple-choice items, circle the letter of the correct answer. You can check your responses against the answer key on page AK-1.

Objective 6.1: Discuss the value of careful revision, and list the main tasks involved in completing a business message.

1. Which of these is the most important reason you should take care to revise messages before sending them?
   a. Revising shows your audience how hard you work.
   b. Revising lowers the word count.
   c. Revising makes it cheaper to e-mail messages.
   d. Revising can usually make your messages more successful.

2. Which of the following is not one of the main tasks involved in completing a business message?
   a. Drafting the message
   b. Revising the message
   c. Producing the message
   d. Proofreading the message

Objective 6.2: List four writing techniques you can use to improve the readability of your messages.

3. Regarding sentence length, the best approach for business messages is to
   a. Keep all sentences as short as possible

b. Make most of your sentences long since you will usually have complex information to impart
c. Vary the length of your sentences
d. Aim for an average sentence length of 35 words

4. Regarding paragraph length, the best approach for business messages is to
a. Keep paragraphs short
b. Make most of your paragraphs long since that is standard practice in business writing
c. Make most of your paragraphs one sentence in length
d. Aim for an average paragraph length of 200 words

5. Regarding the use of lists, the best approach for business messages is to
a. Avoid using lists except where absolutely necessary
b. Make sure listed items are in parallel form
c. Use numbered lists rather than bulleted ones
d. Do all of the above

6. Which of the following is not an informative heading?
a. Why We Need a New Distributor
b. Five Challenges Facing Today's Distributors
c. Distributors Are a Better Choice for Us Than Wholesalers
d. Distributor Choices

Objective 6.3: Describe the steps you can take to improve the clarity of your writing.

7. Which of the following sentences contains hedging words?
a. It appears that we may have a problem completing the project by May 20.
b. There is a possibility that the project might be done by May 20.
c. It seems that the project could possibly miss its completion date of May 20.
d. All of the above contain hedging words.

8. Which of the following sentences lacks parallelism?
a. Consumers can download stock research, electronically file their tax returns, create a portfolio, or choose from an array of recommended mutual funds.
b. Consumers can download stock research, can electronically file their tax returns, create a portfolio, or they can choose from an array of recommended mutual funds.
c. Consumers can download stock research, can electronically file their tax returns, can create a portfolio, or can choose from an array of recommended mutual funds.
d. Consumers can download stock research, they can electronically file their tax returns, they can create a portfolio, or they can choose from an array of recommended mutual funds.

9. Which of the following sentences does not have a dangling modifier?
a. Lacking brand recognition, some consumers are wary of using Internet-only banks.
b. Because Internet-only banks lack brand recognition, some consumers are wary of using them.
c. Because of a lack of brand recognition, some consumers are wary of using Internet-only banks.
d. All have dangling modifiers.

Objective 6.4: Discuss why it's important to make your messages concise, and give four tips on how to do so.

10. When editing for conciseness, you should look for
a. Unnecessary words and phrases
b. Dangling modifiers
c. Lack of parallelism
d. Awkward references

11. Which of the following is not an example of a redundancy?
a. Visible to the eye
b. Free gift
c. Very useful
d. Repeat again

Objective 6.5: Explain how design elements help determine the effectiveness of your documents.

12. A well-designed document
a. Includes a wide variety of typefaces
b. Balances the space devoted to text, artwork, and white space
c. Fills as much of the available space as possible with text and art
d. Does all of the above

13. Any blank areas in a document are referred to as _____.

14. Type that is "justified" is
a. Flush on the left and ragged on the right
b. Flush on the right and ragged on the left
c. Flush on both the left and the right
d. Centered

15. A sans serif typeface would be best for
a. The headings in a report
b. The text of a report
c. Both the headings and the text of a report
d. Elements such as footnotes and endnotes

Objective 6.6: Highlight the types of errors to look for when proofreading.

16. When proofreading, you should look for errors in
a. Spelling and punctuation
b. Grammar and usage
c. Typography and format
d. All of the above

Objective 6.7: Discuss the most important issues to consider when distributing your messages.

17. As a general rule, the cost of distributing a business message should be balanced against
a. The importance and urgency of the message
b. The length of the message
c. Your career goals as they relate to the message
d. The number of recipients

18. Which of the following concerns is the most important to consider when distributing messages through electronic media such as e-mail?
a. The difficulty of reading on-screen
b. Privacy and security
c. Differences between flat-panel and CRT monitors
d. The difficulty of keeping e-mail addresses current

Apply Your Knowledge

1. Why is it helpful to put your first draft aside for a while before you begin the editing process?
2. Given the choice of only one, would you prefer to use a grammar checker or a spell checker? Why?
3. Why is it important to spend extra time reviewing and polishing the beginning and end of a message?
4. Which distribution method would you choose for a highly confidential strategic planning report that needs to be sent to top executives at six locations in North America, Asia, and Europe? You can make it available as an electronic file or a printed document, depending on the distribution method. Explain your choice.
5. **Ethical Choices** What are the ethical implications of murky, complex writing in a document that explains how customers can appeal the result of a decision made in the company's favor during a dispute?

Practice Your Knowledge

MESSAGES FOR ANALYSIS

Read the following messages, then (1) analyze the strengths and weaknesses of each sentence and (2) revise each document so that it follows the guidelines in this chapter and in Chapters 4 and 5.

MESSAGE 6.A

As an organization, the North American Personal Motorsports Marketing Association has committed ourselves to helping our members—a diverse group comprising of dealers of motorcycles, all-terrain vehicles, Snowmobiles, and personal watercraft—achieve their business objectives. Consequently, our organization, which usually goes under the initials NAPMMA, has the following aims, goals, and objectives. Firstly, we endeavor to aid or assist our members in reaching their business objectives. Second, NPAMMA communicates ("lobbying" in slang terms) with local, state, and national governmental agencies and leaders on issues of importance to our members. And lastly, we educate the motorsports public, that being current motorsports vehicle owners, and prospective owners of said vehicles, on the safe and enjoyable operation of they're vehicles.

MESSAGE 6.B

To access this message, visit **www.businesscommunication blog.com** and click on "Textbook Resources." Locate *Excellence in Business Communication*, 8th ed., click on Chapter 6, and then select Page 192, Message 6.B. Download and open the Microsoft Word document. Using the various page, paragraph, and font formatting options available in your word processor, modify the formatting of the document so that its visual tone matches the tone of the message.

EXERCISES

For active links to all websites discussed in this chapter, visit this text's website, at **www.prenhall.com/thill**. Locate your book and click on its "Companion Website" link. Then select Chapter 6 and click on "Featured Websites." Locate the name of the page or the URL related to the material in the text. Please note that links to sites that become inactive after publi-cation of the book will be removed from the "Featured Websites" section.

6.1 Message Readability: Writing Paragraphs Rewrite the following paragraph to vary the lengths of the sentences and to shorten the paragraph so it looks more inviting to readers:

> *Although major league baseball remains popular, more people are attending minor league baseball games because they can spend less on admission, snacks, and parking and still enjoy the excitement of America's pastime. Connecticut, for example, has three AA minor league teams, including the New Haven Ravens, who are affiliated with the St. Louis Cardinals; the Norwich Navigators, who are affiliated with the New York Yankees; and the New Britain Rock Cats, who are affiliated with the Minnesota Twins. These teams play in relatively small stadiums, so fans are close enough to see and hear everything, from the swing of the bat connecting with the ball to the thud of the ball landing in the outfielder's glove. Best of all, the cost of a family outing to see rising stars play in a local minor league game is just a fraction of what the family would spend to attend a major league game in a much larger, more crowded stadium.*

6.2 Message Readability: Using Bullets Rewrite the following paragraph using a parallel bulleted list and one introductory sentence:

> *Our forensic accounting services provide the insights needed to resolve disputes, recover losses, and manage risk intelligently. One of our areas of practice is insurance claims accounting and preparation services, designed to help you maximize recovery of insured value. Another practice area is dispute advisory, in which we can assist with discovery, expert witness testimony, and economic analysis. A third practice: construction consulting. This service helps our clients understand why large-scale construction projects fail to meet schedule or budget requirements. Fourth, we offer general investigative and forensic account-*

ing services, including fraud detection and proof of loss analysis.[11]

6.3 Revising Messages: Clarity Break these sentences into shorter ones:

a. The next time you write something, check your average sentence length in a 100-word passage, and if your sentences average more than 16 to 20 words, see whether you can break up some of the sentences.

b. Don't do what the village blacksmith did when he instructed his apprentice as follows: "When I take the shoe out of the fire, I'll lay it on the anvil, and when I nod my head, you hit it with the hammer." The apprentice did just as he was told, and now he's the village blacksmith.

c. Unfortunately, no gadget will produce excellent writing, but using a yardstick like the Fog Index gives us some guideposts to follow for making writing easier to read because its two factors remind us to use short sentences and simple words.

d. Know the flexibility of the written word and its power to convey an idea, and know how to make your words behave so that your readers will understand.

e. Words mean different things to different people, and a word such as *block* may mean city block, butcher block, engine block, auction block, or several other things.

6.4 Revising Messages: Conciseness Cross out unnecessary words in the following phrases:

a. Consensus of opinion
b. New innovations
c. Long period of time
d. At a price of $50
e. Still remains

6.5 Revising Messages: Conciseness Revise the following sentences, using shorter, simpler words:

a. The antiquated calculator is ineffectual for solving sophisticated problems.

b. It is imperative that the pay increments be terminated before an inordinate deficit is accumulated.

c. There was unanimity among the executives that Ms. Jackson's idiosyncrasies were cause for a mandatory meeting with the company's personnel director.

d. The impending liquidation of the company's assets was cause for jubilation among the company's competitors.

e. The expectations of the president for a stock dividend were accentuated by the preponderance of evidence that the company was in good financial condition.

6.6 Revising Messages: Conciseness Use infinitives as substitutes for the overly long phrases in these sentences:

a. For living, I require money.

b. They did not find sufficient evidence for believing in the future.

c. Bringing about the destruction of a dream is tragic.

6.7 Revising Messages: Conciseness Rephrase the following in fewer words:

a. In the near future
b. In the event that
c. In order that
d. For the purpose of
e. With regard to
f. It may be that
g. In very few cases
h. With reference to
i. At the present time
j. There is no doubt that

6.8 Revising Messages: Conciseness Condense these sentences to as few words as possible:

a. We are of the conviction that writing is important.

b. In all probability, we're likely to have a price increase.

c. Our goals include making a determination about that in the near future.

d. When all is said and done at the conclusion of this experiment, I'd like to summarize the final windup.

e. After a trial period of three weeks, during which time she worked for a total of 15 full working days, we found her work was sufficiently satisfactory so that we offered her full-time work.

6.9 Revising Messages: Modifiers Remove all the unnecessary modifiers from these sentences:

a. Tremendously high pay increases were given to the extraordinarily skilled and extremely conscientious employees.

b. The union's proposals were highly inflationary, extremely demanding, and exceptionally bold.

6.10 Revising Messages: Hedging Rewrite these sentences so that they no longer contain any hedging:

a. It would appear that someone apparently entered illegally.

b. It may be possible that sometime in the near future, the situation is likely to improve.

c. Your report seems to suggest that we might be losing money.

d. I believe Nancy apparently has somewhat greater influence over employees in the e-marketing department.

e. It seems as if this letter of resignation means you might be leaving us.

6.11 Revising Messages: Indefinite Starters Rewrite these sentences to eliminate the indefinite starters:

a. There are several examples here to show that Elaine can't hold a position very long.

b. It would be greatly appreciated if every employee would make a generous contribution to Mildred Cook's retirement party.

c. It has been learned in Washington today from generally reliable sources that an important announcement will be made shortly by the White House.

d. There is a rule that states that we cannot work overtime without permission.

e. It would be great if you could work late for the next three Saturdays.

6.12   Revising Messages: Parallelism Present the ideas in these sentences in parallel form:

a. Mr. Hill is expected to lecture three days a week, to counsel two days a week, and must write for publication in his spare time.

b. She knows not only accounting, but she also reads Latin.

c. Both applicants had families, college degrees, and were in their thirties, with considerable accounting experience but few social connections.

d. This book was exciting, well written, and held my interest.

e. Don is both a hard worker and he knows bookkeeping.

6.13   Revising Messages: Awkward References Revise the following sentences to delete the awkward references:

a. The vice president in charge of sales and the production manager are responsible for the keys to 34A and 35A, respectively.

b. The keys to 34A and 35A are in executive hands, with the former belonging to the vice president in charge of sales and the latter belonging to the production manager.

c. The keys to 34A and 35A have been given to the production manager, with the aforementioned keys being gold embossed.

d. A laser printer and an inkjet printer were delivered to John and Megan, respectively.

e. The walnut desk is more expensive than the oak desk, the former costing $300 more than the latter.

6.14   Revising Messages: Dangling Modifiers Rewrite these sentences to clarify the dangling modifiers:

a. Running down the railroad tracks in a cloud of smoke, we watched the countryside glide by.

b. Lying on the shelf, Ruby saw the seashell.

c. Based on the information, I think we should buy the property.

d. Being cluttered and filthy, Sandy took the whole afternoon to clean up her desk.

e. After proofreading every word, the memo was ready to be signed.

6.15   Revising Messages: Noun Sequences Rewrite the following sentences to eliminate the long strings of nouns:

a. The focus of the meeting was a discussion of the bank interest rate deregulation issue.

b. Following the government task force report recommendations, we are revising our job applicant evaluation procedures.

c. The production department quality assurance program components include employee training, supplier cooperation, and computerized detection equipment.

d. The supermarket warehouse inventory reduction plan will be implemented next month.

e. The State University business school graduate placement program is one of the best in the country.

6.16   Revising Messages: Sentence Structure Rearrange the following sentences to bring the subjects closer to their verbs:

a. Trudy, when she first saw the bull pawing the ground, ran.

b. It was Terri who, according to Ted, who is probably the worst gossip in the office (except for Tom, of course), mailed the wrong order.

c. William Oberstreet, in his book *Investment Capital Reconsidered*, writes of the mistakes that bankers through the decades have made.

d. Judy Schimmel, after passing up several sensible investment opportunities, despite the warnings of her friends and family, invested her inheritance in a jojoba plantation.

e. The president of U-Stor-It, which was on the brink of bankruptcy after the warehouse fire, the worst tragedy in the history of the company, prepared a press announcement.

6.17   Revising Messages: Camouflaged Verbs Rewrite each sentence so that the verbs are no longer camouflaged:

a. Adaptation to the new rules was performed easily by the employees.

b. The assessor will make a determination of the tax due.

c. Verification of the identity of the employees must be made daily.

d. The board of directors made a recommendation that Mr. Ronson be assigned to a new division.

e. The auditing procedure on the books was performed by the vice president.

6.18   Producing Messages: Design Elements Review a copy of the syllabus your instructor provided for this course. Which design elements were used to improve readability? Can you identify ways to make the document easier to read or more user friendly in general? Create your own version, experimenting with different design elements and design choices. How do your changes affect readability? Exchange documents with another student and critique each other's work.

6.19   Web Design Visit the stock market page of Bloomberg's website, at www.bloomberg.com, and evaluate the use of design in presenting the latest news. What design improvements can you suggest to enhance readability of the information posted on this page? Summarize your recommendations in an e-mail message to your instructor.

6.20   Teamwork Team up with another student and exchange your revised versions of Message 6.A (see the exercises under "Messages for Analysis"). Review the assignment to be sure the instructions are clear. Then read and critique your teammate's revision to see whether it can be improved. After you have critiqued each other's work, take a moment to examine the way you expressed your comments and the way you felt listening to the other student's comments. Can you identify ways to improve the critiquing process in situations such as this?

6.21 Proofreading Messages: E-Mail Proofread the following e-mail message and revise it to correct any problems you find:

> *Our final company orrientation of the year will be held on Dec. 20. In preparation for this sesssion, please order |20 copies of the Policy handbook, the confindentiality agreement, the employee benefits Manual, please let me know if you anticipate any delays in obtaining these materials.*

6.22 Ethical Choices The time and energy required for careful revision can often benefit you or your company directly, such as by increasing the probability that website visitors will buy your products. But what about situations in which the quality of your writing and revision work really doesn't stand to benefit you directly? For instance, assume that you are putting a notice on your website, informing the local community about some upcoming construction to your man-ufacturing plant. The work will disrupt traffic for nearly a year and generate a significant amount of noise and air pollution, but knowing the specific dates and times of various construction activities will allow people to adjust their commutes and other activities to minimize the negative impact on their daily lives. However, your company does not sell products in the local area, so the people affected by all this are not potential customers. Moreover, providing accurate information to the surrounding community and updating it as the project progresses will take time away from your other job responsibilities. Do you have an ethical obligation to keep the local community informed with accurate, up-to-date information? Why or why not? Explain your position in a memo to your instructor.

6.23 Revising for International Audiences Revise the following message to improve its readability for non-native speakers of English:

> *After being trialled in a number of primary and secondary schools across the country, Podium is bringing podcasting within the reach of everyone, giving teachers and pupils the chance to create podcasts quickly and easily.*[12]

Expand Your Knowledge

LEARNING MORE ON THE WEB

WRITE IT RIGHT: TIPS TO HELP YOU RETHINK AND REVISE

www.powa.org

Are you sure that readers perceive your written message as you intended? If you want help revising a message that you're completing, use the Paradigm Online Writing Assistant (POWA). With this interactive writer's guide, you can select topics to get tips on how to edit your work, reshape your thoughts, and rewrite for clarity. Read discussions about perfecting your writing skills, complete one of the many online activities provided to reinforce what you've learned, or join the Forum to talk about writing. At POWA's website, you'll learn how to improve the final draft of your message. Explore POWA's advice and then answer the following questions:

1. Why is it better to write out ideas in a rough format and later reread your message to revise its content? When revising your message, what questions can you ask about your writing?

2. Name the four elements of the "writing context." Imagine that you're the reader of your message. What questions might you ask?

3. When you revise a written message, what is the purpose of "tightening"? What is one way to tighten your writing as you complete a message?

SURFING YOUR WAY TO CAREER SUCCESS

Bovée and Thill's Business Communication Headline News offers links to hundreds of online resources that can help you with this course, your other college courses, and your career. Visit www.businesscommunicationblog.com and click on "Web Directory." The "Interpersonal" section connects you to a variety of websites and articles on effective questions, interpersonal dialogs, listening, and feedback. Identify three websites from this section that could be useful in your business career. For each site, write a two-sentence summary of what the site offers and how it could help you launch and build your career.

Learn Interactively

INTERACTIVE STUDY GUIDE

Visit www.prenhall.com/thill, then locate your book and click on its "Companion Website" link. Select Chapter 6 to take advantage of the interactive "Chapter Quiz" to test your knowledge of chapter concepts. Receive instant feedback on whether you need additional studying. Also, visit the "Study Hall," where you'll find an abundance of valuable resources that will help you succeed in this course.

PEAK PERFORMANCE GRAMMAR AND MECHANICS

If your instructor has required the use of "Peak Performance Grammar and Mechanics," either in your online course or on

CD, you can improve your skill with prepositions, conjunctions, and articles by using the "Peak Performance Grammar and Mechanics" module. Click on "Grammar Basics" and then click on "Prepositions, Conjunctions, and Articles." Take the Pretest to determine whether you have any weak areas. Then review those areas in the Refresher Course. Take the Follow-Up Test to check your grasp of prepositions, conjunctions, and articles. For an extra challenge or advanced practice, take the Advanced Test. Finally, for additional reinforcement, go to the "Improve Your Grammar, Mechanics, and Usage" section that follows and complete those exercises.

Improve Your Grammar, Mechanics, and Usage

The following exercises help you improve your knowledge of and power over English grammar, mechanics, and usage. Turn to the Handbook of Grammar, Mechanics, and Usage at the end of this textbook and review Section 1.6.1 (Prepositions). Then look at the following 10 items. Underline the preferred choice within each set of parentheses. (Answers to these exercises appear on page AK-3.)

1. Where was your argument (*leading to, leading*)?
2. I wish he would get (*off, off of*) the phone.
3. U.S. Mercantile must become (*aware, aware of*) and sensitive to its customers' concerns.
4. Dr. Namaguchi will be talking (*with, to*) the marketing class, but she has no time for questions.
5. Matters like this are decided after thorough discussion (*among, between*) all seven department managers.

6. We can't wait (*on, for*) their decision much longer.
7. Their computer is similar (*to, with*) ours.
8. This model is different (*than, from*) the one we ordered.
9. She is active (*in not only, not only in*) a civic group but also in an athletic organization.
10. Carolyn told Jorge not to put the used inkjet cartridges (*in, into*) the trash can.

For additional exercises focusing on prepositions, go to www.prenhall.com/thill, then locate your text and click on its "Companion Website" link. Click on Chapter 6, click on "Additional Exercises to Improve Your Grammar, Mechanics, and Usage," and click on "10. Prepositions."

Part III

Crafting Brief Messages

Chapter 7

Crafting Messages for Electronic Media

Learning Objectives

AFTER STUDYING THIS CHAPTER, YOU WILL BE ABLE TO

1 Compare the strengths and weaknesses of the print and electronic media available for short messages

2 Identify the qualities of an effective e-mail subject line

3 Explain how overuse of e-mail can reduce productivity

4 Identify guidelines for successful instant messaging (IM) in the workplace

5 Describe the role of blogging in business communication today

6 Explain why identifying your audience, purpose, and scope is vital to successful blogging

7 Explain how to adapt the three-step writing process for podcasts

8 Describe the syndication process and explain how it helps you distribute blog and podcast content

On the Job

COMMUNICATING AT SOUTHWEST AIRLINES

ONLINE UPROAR TRIGGERS CHANGE IN COMPANY POLICY

Southwest Airlines's blog is usually a love fest—or a "luv" fest, to use one of the company's favorite words. In fact, the blog's official title is "Nuts About Southwest." A typical post might highlight the community service efforts of a group of employees or congratulate a team of Southwest mechanics for winning gold at the Aviation Maintenance Olympics. Devoted customers post enthusiastic comments on nearly every article, and many seem to have bonded in virtual friendship with the nearly 30 Southwest employees who take turns writing the blog.

Bill Owens probably didn't expect a bubbly reception to a rather workaday post titled "Why can't I make reservations further in advance?" in which he calmly explained why the company usually didn't let customers make reservations as far into the future as other airlines do.

But he probably wasn't expecting the response he did get, either. In his words, "Talk about sticking your head in a hornet's nest!" Instead of the usual dozen or so happy responses to a typical post, he received several hundred responses—and many expressed disappointment, unhappiness, and downright anger. Customers described one scenario after another in which they had a real need to book travel farther in advance than Southwest allowed, and many complained that the policy was forcing them to fly other airlines. Some Southwest employees chimed in, too, expressing their frustration with not being able to meet customer needs at times.

After bravely and patiently addressing specific customer responses over a period of several months, Owens responded with a new post titled "I blogged.

TAKE OFF/LANZATE EDUCATION TRAVEL AWARD

By: Christine Ortega - Manager Corporate Community Affairs

Have you heard of the Take Off!/ ¡Lanzate! Education travel award? For the third year in a row, Southwest Airlines is offering travel to disadvantaged students who travel away from home to attend college. The cool thing about this award is that Latino students can use the ticket(s) to bring a parent or loved one to visit them at school, or they can jet home to see the family.

Maria Elena Cruz pictured in the photo was a past recipient. Her interest in Mexican Anthropology ties to strong family roots where her family hailed from a line of Mexican huichol chiefs. She was totally thrilled to receive the tickets as the best school for her field of study in Mexican Anthropology, was in Austin, TX. A Californian from a home of modest means, Maria Elena felt a tremendous relief to know that she would be able to stay connected to her family, and could not believe she was selected! She thought that there was little chance anyone would care about her dream to obtain her Masters so far from home.

The other good news is that the deadline to apply for the travel award has been extended to June 29. If you know a Latino student

SOUTHWEST AIRLINES BLOG
Nuts about Southwest is all about our Employees, Customers, airplanes, and airports. We really are **Nuts about Southwest** and we hope that our Readers will share that passion by posting their own comments.

For more information about the blog and participating, please visit our User Guide.

SYNDICATE THIS BLOG

RSS   + newsgator
ATOM + MY YAHOO!

≽DING≼

Exclusive Southwest Offers Right on Your Desktop

Vote for Us in the Blogger's Choice Awards

Southwest Airlines's multiauthor blog, Nuts About Southwest, features a variety of entertaining writers from around the company.

You flamed. We changed." In this message, he explained that the company had listened and was changing its scheduling policies to better accommodate customer needs.

In fact, feedback from blog readers is so important that Southwest CEO Colleen Barrett considers the blog a "customer service laboratory" that helps the company learn how to better serve its customers.[1]

www. blogsouthwest. com

CHOOSING ELECTRONIC MEDIA FOR BRIEF MESSAGES

Southwest's experience with customer feedback (profiled in the chapter opener) is just one of many cases in which electronic media are changing business communication. In recent years, the options for sending short business messages have expanded considerably, from traditional printed memos and letters to a variety of electronic formats. When a new communication technology appears, creative businesspeople usually find a way to apply it to business challenges.

You are likely to encounter the following short-message media on the job in the next few years:

Today you have multiple options for sending short messages:
- Printed memos
- Printed letters
- E-mail messages
- Instant messages
- Text messages
- Blog postings
- Podcasts

- **Memos and letters.** Printed memos (for internal communication) and letters (for external communication) have been primary communication vehicles for hundreds of years. In many companies, e-mail and other electronic media have largely replaced traditional printed memos. Letters are still used often for external communication, but electronic media are replacing many letters as well. For more on formatting printed letters and memos, see Chapter 6 and Appendix A.

- **E-mail.** Thanks to its high speed and low cost, e-mail is now a primary medium for most companies. However, as technologies continue to evolve and users tire of fighting the flood of spam, viruses, and other problems related to e-mail, this medium is in turn being replaced in many instances by instant messaging, blogging, wikis (see Chapter 2), and other tools that provide better support for instant communication and real-time collaboration.

- **Instant messaging (IM).** After consumers around the world began to adopt IM as a faster and simpler alternative to e-mail, businesses weren't far behind; computer-based IM usage now rivals e-mail in many companies. IM offers even greater speed than e-mail as well as simple operation and—so far at least—fewer problems with unwanted messages or security and privacy problems.

- **Text messaging.** Phone-based text messaging offers the near-instantaneous communication of IM, with the added advantage of almost universal portability. Of course, small screen sizes and the lack of a regular keyboard on most phone devices make text messaging somewhat less convenient than computer-based IM. Text messaging is just beginning to make inroads into business communication, with marketing messages being one of the first applications.[2]

- **Blogs.** From internal communication among small teams to executive blogs with thousands of readers, blogs are now common in business communication. The ability to update content quickly and easily makes blogs a natural medium when communicators need to get messages out in a hurry; bloggers can also publish information to vast audiences with relatively little effort.

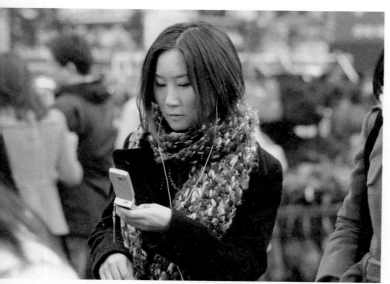

Text messaging is beginning to take off as an advertising and customer communication medium, although it is still not as widespread in business as computer-based instant messaging.

- **Podcasts.** You may be familiar with podcasts as the online equivalent of recorded radio or video broadcasts (video podcasts are often called vidcasts or vodcasts). Businesses are now using podcasts to replace or supplement conference calls, training courses, and other communication activities. (Note that although the term podcast was derived from *iPod*, podcasts are in no way restricted to Apple's digital music players. Any device capable of playing the audio or video file, including computers, PDAs, many phones, and who-knows-what new devices in the future, can play podcasts.) Podcasts offer a simple way for anyone to publish audio or video messages. They do require somewhat more work to create than blogs, and high-quality podcasts require a modest set of specialized equipment and plenty of network bandwidth.

Carleton University in Ottawa, Ontario, Canada, reaches students all over the world with its lecture vodcasts.

When considering the various electronic media now available, it's important to recognize that they are more than just new tools in your communication toolkit. Because they (a) make it easy for almost anyone to communicate with a global audience, (b) usually provide a quick and effortless way for audiences to respond to messages, and (c) are easy to forward and link all over the Internet, electronic media are changing the very nature of business communication. Customers are no longer content to be passive listeners in a one-way process controlled by business. They now expect to be active participants in a real conversation—and not only with companies but with other customers. Blogs, podcasts, bookmarking and tagging sites (such as del.icio.us and Digg), photo- and video-sharing sites (such as Flickr and YouTube), wikis, and other electronic tools should be viewed as **social media**, in which all participants can contribute to the conversation.[3] Today's smart companies are learning how to adapt their communication efforts to this new media landscape and to welcome customers' participation.

However, while most of your business communication is likely to be via electronic means, don't automatically dismiss the benefits of printed messages. Here are several situations in which you should use a printed message over electronic alternatives:

- **When you want to make a formal impression.** For special messages, such as sending congratulations or condolences, the formality of printed documents usually makes them a much better choice than electronic messages.

- **When you are legally required to provide information in printed form.** Business contracts and government regulations sometimes require that information be provided on paper. The laws that cover such disclosures continue to evolve, so make sure you consult with your firm's legal staff if you're not sure.

- **When you want to stand out from the flood of electronic messages.** Ironically, the rapid growth of electronic messages creates an opportunity for printed memos and letters. If your audience's computers are overflowing with e-mail, IM, and newsfeeds, a printed message could stand out enough to get noticed.

Obviously, if your audience doesn't have access to electronic media or you don't have the necessary e-mail or IM addresses, you'll also need to use a printed message.

The following sections offer advice on using e-mail, IM, blogging, and podcasting for business communication. And for a brief look at some of the other interesting communication technologies that you may encounter on the job, see "Using the Power of Technology: More Ways to Spread the Message."

Consider using printed messages when you want to create a more formal impression, to accompany other physical material, to stand out from electronic messages, or when you are legally or contractually required to do so.

USING THE POWER OF TECHNOLOGY

More Ways to Spread the Message

Businesses invest significant amounts of money in technologies designed to improve both internal and external communication. In some instances, technologies such as *electronic data interchange* and its newer web-based equivalents replace the human element in the communication process. In others, technology attempts to enhance human communication by increasing mobility, lowering cost, improving responsiveness, or creating new capabilities. Here are some of the most intriguing communication-enhancement technologies:

- *Voice synthesis and recognition.* The human voice will always be central to business communication, but that doesn't mean two human beings are required for every conversation. *Voice synthesis* regenerates a human speaking voice from computer files that represent words or parts of words. *Voice recognition* converts human speech to computer-compatible data. Both technologies continue to improve every year, with richer vocabularies and more human-sounding voices.

- *Virtual agents. Virtual agents*, also known as *bots* (derived from the word *robot*), are a class of automated tools that perform a variety of communication tasks, such as answering customer service questions and responding to requests for electronic documents. They can function in either voice-based (over the telephone) or text-based (via IM or text messaging) environments.

- *Mobile communication.* If you're accustomed to studying on the go, you'll fit right into today's untethered work environment. In some cases, mobile workers don't even have traditional offices, using temporary cubicles at work, home offices, cars, airports, and even new Internet-equipped airplanes for office space. Geographic data from a **global positioning system (GPS)** are also creating new forms of mobile communication, such as location-based advertising (getting an advertisement on your mobile phone from a store you're walking past, for instance) and remote monitoring of medical patients and trucking fleets.

- *Networking advances.* You might already be using some of the new networking technologies that help businesspeople communicate and collaborate. **Peer-to-peer (P2P) computing** lets multiple PCs communicate directly so that they can share files or work on large problems simultaneously. **Wireless networking** extends the reach of the Internet with wireless access points that connect to PCs and handheld devices via radio signals. Wireless networking extends the reach of the Internet through the commonly used *Wi-Fi* technology for local area networks and the emerging *WiMAX* standard, which can cover entire metropolitan areas.

CAREER APPLICATIONS

1. Have you ever encountered a bot or a voice-recognition system when you expected to reach a human being (such as reaching a voice-response system when you telephoned a business)? Describe the situation and purpose of your "conversation." Were you satisfied with the outcome of the conversation? Why or why not?

2. What are the ethical implications of using GPS to track the movement of employees such as truck drivers?

CREATING EFFECTIVE E-MAIL MESSAGES

Chances are you already have quite a bit of experience using e-mail, but e-mail in the workplace is a more formal medium than you are probably accustomed to for personal communication (see Figure 7.1). Consequently, it's important to approach e-mail as a professional communication medium and an important company resource, as explained in the following section.

Treating E-Mail as a Professional Communication Medium

Business e-mail messages are more formal than the e-mail messages you send to family and friends.

The most important single point to recognize about e-mail in the workplace is that the nature of business e-mail is dramatically different from that of personal e-mail. The expectations of writing quality are higher, and the consequences of bad writing or poor judgment in the use of e-mail can be much more serious. For example, e-mail and other electronic documents have the same legal weight as printed documents. In numerous instances in recent years, e-mail and other electronic message forms have

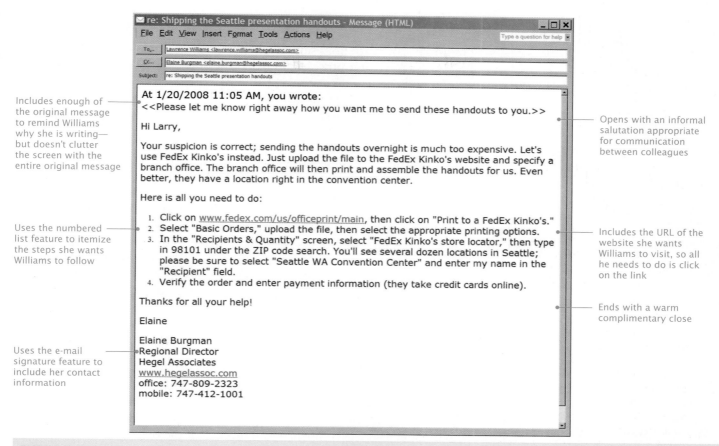

Includes enough of the original message to remind Williams why she is writing—but doesn't clutter the screen with the entire original message

Uses the numbered list feature to itemize the steps she wants Williams to follow

Uses the e-mail signature feature to include her contact information

Opens with an informal salutation appropriate for communication between colleagues

Includes the URL of the website she wants Williams to visit, so all he needs to do is click on the link

Ends with a warm complimentary close

FIGURE 7.1
E-Mail for Business Communication
In this response to an e-mail query from a colleague, Elaine Burgman takes advantage of her e-mail system's features to create an efficient and effective message.

been used as evidence in lawsuits and criminal investigations involving everything from sexual harassment to financial fraud.[4]

Legal hazards are only one of the serious risks that e-mail presents. Other concerns include the possibility of disclosing confidential information and exposing company networks to security problems. To minimize the potential for trouble, many companies now have formal e-mail policies that specify how employees can use e-mail, including restrictions against using company e-mail service for personal messages and sending material that might be deemed objectionable. More than one-quarter of U.S. employers have terminated employees for misuse of company e-mail systems, according to one recent survey.[5] In addition, roughly the same percentage of employers now monitor internal e-mail, and half of them monitor external e-mail. This monitoring can involve both automated scans using software programmed to look for sensitive content and manual scans in which security staff actually read selected e-mail messages.[6]

Regardless of formal policies, every e-mail user has a responsibility to avoid actions that could cause trouble, from downloading virus-infected software to sending objectionable photographs. *E-mail hygiene* refers to all the efforts that companies are making to keep e-mail clean and safe—from spam blocking and virus protection to content filtering.[7] Make sure you understand what your employer expects from you and follow those guidelines.

E-mail presents considerable legal hazards, and many companies have formal e-mail policies.

Adapting the Three-Step Process for Successful E-Mail

E-mail messages can range from simple one-paragraph memos to multipage reports, and the three-step writing process can help you in every instance. With practice, you'll be able to complete the various planning, writing, and completing tasks in a matter of minutes for most messages—which will be a significant benefit to your career. In addition to the skills you've practiced in Chapters 4 through 6, apply the guidelines in the following sections.

Attention to etiquette is vital with e-mail communication.

Planning E-Mail Messages   The ease of e-mail communication is its greatest strength—and its greatest weakness. Because sending e-mail is so easy, it is often overused and misused. Consequently, attention to e-mail etiquette is essential, and that starts in the planning stage. Most importantly, make sure every e-mail you send is necessary so that you don't contribute to the deluge of messages of dubious importance. Many busy professionals now struggle to keep up with the flow of e-mail messages—some report receiving as many as 50 messages an hour from colleagues and clients.[8] The flood of messages from an expanding array of electronic sources can significantly affect employees' ability to focus on their work. In one recent study, in fact, workers exposed to a constant barrage of e-mail, IM, and phone calls experienced an average 10-point drop in their functioning IQ.[9] You can help keep electronic messages from causing problems in your organization by following the tips in Table 7.1.

Do your part to stem the flood of e-mail by making sure you don't send unnecessary messages or cc people who don't really need to see particular messages.

When analyzing your audience, think twice before sending copies to multiple recipients with the *cc* (courtesy copy) function. Let's say you send a message to your boss and cc five colleagues simply because you want them to see that you're giving the boss some good information. Those five people now not only have to read your message but might also feel compelled to reply so that the boss doesn't think they're being negligent. Then everyone will start replying to *those* replies, and on and on. What should have been a single message exchange between you and your boss quickly turns into a flurry of messages that wastes everybody's time.

Finally, be sure to respect the chain of command. In many companies, any employee can e-mail anyone else, including the president and CEO. However, take care that you don't abuse this freedom. For instance, when corresponding with superiors, don't send an e-mail complaint straight to the top just because it's easy to do so. Your e-mail will usually be more effective if you follow the organizational hierarchy and give each person a chance to address the situation in turn.

Writing E-Mail Messages   Too many people, particularly young professionals accustomed to using electronic media for personal communication, assume that the standards and expectations of business communication don't apply to e-mail. Even some seasoned businesspeople advocate a general disregard for punctuation, grammar, spelling, and other conventions in e-mail writing because paying attention to such details takes too much time.

Granted, you don't need to compose perfect works of literature to inform people that lunch will be served in the conference room, but as a general rule, the time you might save with careless e-mail writing won't make up for the damage it can do to your career.[10] First, haphazard planning and sloppy writing may require less time for writers, but they usually demand *more* time from readers forced to dig the meaning out of misspelled words, confusing sentences, and disjointed paragraphs. Making readers do work you should have done is the very antithesis of the "you" attitude. Second, people who care about effective communication—a group that includes most senior executives, the people who often decide whether you'll get promoted and how much you'll get paid—often judge the quality of your *work* by the quality of your *writing*. Third, at the click of somebody else's mouse, e-mail messages can

TIPS FOR EFFECTIVE E-MAIL MESSAGES

Table 7.1

Tip	Why It's Important
When you request information or action, make it clear what you're asking for, why it's important, and how soon you need it; don't make your reader write back for details.	People will be tempted to ignore your messages if they're not clear about what you want or how soon you want it.
When responding to a request, either paraphrase the request or include enough of the original message to remind the reader what you're replying to.	Some businesspeople get hundreds of e-mail messages a day and may need to be reminded what your specific response is about.
If possible, avoid sending long, complex messages via e-mail.	Long messages are easier to read as printed reports or web content.
Adjust the level of formality to the message and the audience.	Overly formal messages to colleagues are perceived as stuffy and distant; overly informal messages to customers or top executives are perceived as disrespectful.
Activate a signature file, which automatically pastes your contact information into every message you create.	You save the trouble of retyping vital information and ensure that recipients know how to reach you through other means.
Don't let unread messages pile up in your in-basket.	You'll miss important information and create the impression that you're ignoring other people.
Never type in all caps.	ALL CAPS ARE INTERPRETED AS SCREAMING.
Don't overformat your messages with background colors, colored type, unusual fonts, and so on.	Such messages can be difficult and annoying to read on-screen.
Remember that messages can be forwarded anywhere and saved forever.	Don't let a moment of anger or poor judgment haunt you the rest of your career.
Use the "return receipt requested" feature only for the most critical messages.	This feature triggers a message back to you whenever someone receives or opens your message; many consider this an invasion of privacy.
Make sure your computer has up-to-date virus protection.	One of the worst breaches of "netiquette" is unknowingly infecting other computers because you haven't bothered to protect your own system.
Pay attention to grammar, spelling, and capitalization.	Some people don't think e-mail needs formal rules, but careless messages make you look unprofessional and can annoy readers.
Use acronyms sparingly.	Shorthand such as IMHO (in my humble opinion) and LOL (laughing out loud) can be useful in informal correspondence with colleagues, but don't use them in other messages.

travel to places you never imagined, including the CEO's computer screen, a newspaper, a lawyer's office, or any number of websites and blogs. Always assume that whatever you write in an e-mail message could become public knowledge inside or outside the firm.

Writing Effective Subject Lines The subject line in an e-mail might seem like a minor detail, but it's actually one of the most important parts of every e-mail message because it helps recipients decide which messages to read and when to read them. Missing or poorly written subject lines often result in messages being deleted without even being opened. To capture your audience's attention, make sure your subject line is informative and compelling. Go beyond simply describing or classifying your message; use the opportunity to build interest with keywords, quotations, directions, or questions:[11]

Ineffective Subject Line	Effective Subject Line
July sales results	July sales results: good news and bad news
Tomorrow's meeting	Be ready for some tough questions at Friday's meeting
Marketing reports	Marketing reports are due Monday morning
Employee parking	Revised resurfacing schedule for parking lot
Status report	Website redesign is falling behind schedule

Consider the first of these examples. "July sales results" accurately describes the content of the message, but "July sales results: good news and bad news" is more intriguing. Readers will want to know why some news is good and some is bad. "Status report" doesn't even specify which project the report is about, whereas "Website redesign is falling behind schedule" identifies the project and alerts people to a problem.

Also, if you and someone else are replying back and forth based on the same original message, periodically modify the subject line of your message to reflect the revised message content. When numerous messages have identical subject lines, trying to find a particular one can be confusing and frustrating. For instance, if you come up with a solution to the scheduling problem on the website redesign project, modify the subject line to read something like "Website redesign: staffing solution" so that people can find that specific message when they need to.

Keeping Your Emotions Under Control Given the spontaneous nature of e-mail (and other electronic media), you will sometimes need to work hard to keep your emotions from getting the best of you when you're writing. A message that contains insensitive, insulting, or critical comments is called a *flame*. If you're angry, calm down before composing an e-mail message. If you do write an emotionally charged message, let it sit for at least a day and then revise it or even delete it. Ask yourself two questions: First, "Would I say this to my audience face to face?" And second, "Am I comfortable with this message becoming a permanent part of the company's communication history?" Remember that a living, breathing human being is on the receiving end of your communication—and that your message can be forwarded easily and stored forever.

Completing E-Mail Messages   The revision, production, and proofing you've studied earlier all apply to e-mail messages. Again, don't let the speed and simplicity of e-mail lull you into thinking that careless writing is acceptable. Particularly for important messages, a few moments of revising and proofing might save you hours of headaches and damage control. Also, lean in favor of simplicity when it comes to producing your e-mail messages. A clean, easily readable font, in black on a white background, is sufficient for nearly all e-mail messages.

Take advantage of your e-mail system's ability to include a *signature* (most corporate systems support this). This is a small text file that is automatically appended to your outgoing messages. Use it to include your full name, job title, company, and contact information. A signature gives your messages a more professional appearance and makes it easy for others to communicate with you through other channels.

When you're ready to distribute your message, pause to verify what you're doing before you click Send. Double-check your addressees to make sure you've included everyone necessary—and no one else. Did you click Reply All when you meant to click Reply? The difference could be embarrassing or even career threatening. Don't include people in the cc (courtesy copy) or bcc (blind courtesy copy) fields unless you know how these features work. (Everyone who receives the message can see who is on the cc line but not who is on the bcc line.) Also, don't set the message priority to "high" or "urgent" unless your message is truly urgent.

To review the tips and techniques for successful e-mail, see "Checklist: Creating Effective E-Mail Messages."

CREATING EFFECTIVE INSTANT MESSAGES AND TEXT MESSAGES

While e-mail is here to stay as a business medium, its disadvantages—including viruses, spam, and rampant overuse—are driving many people to explore alternatives.[12] One of the most important of those alternatives is instant messaging (IM). For both routine communication and exchanges during online meetings, IM is now widely used throughout the business world and is beginning to overtake and even replace e-mail for internal communication in many companies.[13] Business-grade IM systems offer a range of capabilities, including basic chat, *presence awareness* (the ability to quickly see which people are at their desks and available to IM), remote display of documents, video capabilities, remote control of other computers, automated newsfeeds from blogs and websites, and automated bot capabilities (see page 202).[14]

IM is taking the place of e-mail for routine communication in many companies.

✓ CHECKLIST: Creating Effective E-Mail Messages

A. Treat e-mail as a professional communication medium.

- ✓ Remember that business e-mail is more formal than personal e-mail.
- ✓ Recognize that e-mail messages carry the same legal weight as other business documents.
- ✓ Follow company e-mail policy; understand the restrictions your company places on e-mail usage.
- ✓ Practice good e-mail hygiene by not opening suspicious messages, keeping virus protection up to date, and following other guidelines.

B. Adapt the three-step process for effective e-mail.

- ✓ Make sure every e-mail you send is necessary.
- ✓ Don't cc or bcc anyone who doesn't really need to see the message.

- ✓ Follow the chain of command.
- ✓ Pay attention to the quality of your writing and use correct grammar, spelling, and punctuation.
- ✓ Make your subject lines informative by clearly identifying the purpose of your message.
- ✓ Make your subject lines compelling by wording them in a way that intrigues your audiences.
- ✓ Update the subject line if you reply to the same message back and forth multiple times.
- ✓ Keep your emotions under control.
- ✓ Don't mark messages as "urgent" unless they truly are urgent.

Phone-based text messaging is fast and portable but not as versatile as computer-based IM.

Text messaging is beginning to find applications in business as well. Although both IM and text messaging perform the similar function of nearly instantaneous communication between devices, IM is primarily a computer-based technology, whereas text messaging is primarily a phone-based technology. (Of course, as often happens, continuing innovation blurs the lines between technologies, and now you can send a text message to a phone from your computer and so on.) Text messaging has long been popular in other parts of the world, where it is often referred to as *short messaging service* (*SMS*) and phones have had texting capability for years. With text messaging now well entrenched among young consumers in North America, expanded business applications are likely to follow. In addition to person-to-person communication between colleagues, text messaging is taking off in such areas as marketing (alerting customers about new sale prices, for example) and entertainment (such as letting viewers predict the outcome of sporting events or place votes on reality television programs).[15]

Because IM is currently more versatile and more widely used in business than text messaging, the following sections focus on IM. However, as text messaging evolves along with wireless devices and networking, you can expect that many of the benefits, risks, and guidelines that pertain to IM will eventually pertain to text messaging as well.

Understanding the Benefits and Risks of IM

IM offers many benefits:
- Rapid response
- Lower cost
- Ability to mimic conversation
- Wide availability

The benefits of IM include its rapid response to urgent messages, lower cost than phone calls and e-mail, ability to mimic conversation more closely than e-mail, and availability on a wide range of devices, from PCs to mobile phones to PDAs.[16] In addition, because it more closely resembles real conversation, IM doesn't get misused as a broadcast method as often as e-mail does.[17]

Of course, wherever technology goes, trouble seems to follow. The potential drawbacks of IM include security problems (the risks of computer viruses and the worry that sensitive messages might be intercepted by outsiders), the need for *user authentication* (making sure that online correspondents are really who they appear to be), the challenge of logging messages for later review and archiving, and incompatibility between competing IM systems. Fortunately, with the growth of *enterprise instant messaging* (*EIM*), IM systems designed for large-scale corporate use, many of these problems are being overcome. Security remains an ongoing concern, however, with attacks on IM systems, both public and corporate, continuing to rise.[18] A new breed of virus spread by bots is a particular concern. IM users who fall prey to these bots believe they are chatting with a trusted correspondent when in fact they are exchanging information with an automated bot that imitates human IM chat. The bot encourages the user to download a file or otherwise expose his or her computer to malicious software and then spreads the virus through the user's IM address book.[19]

Adapting the Three-Step Process for Successful IM

Although instant messages are often conceived, written, and sent within a matter of seconds, the principles of the three-step process still apply:

- **Planning instant messages.** View every IM exchange as a conversation; while you may not deliberately plan every individual statement you make or question you pose, take a moment to plan the overall exchange. If you're requesting something, think through exactly what you need and the most effective way to ask for it. If someone is asking you for something, consider his or her needs and your ability to meet them before you respond. And although you rarely organize instant messages

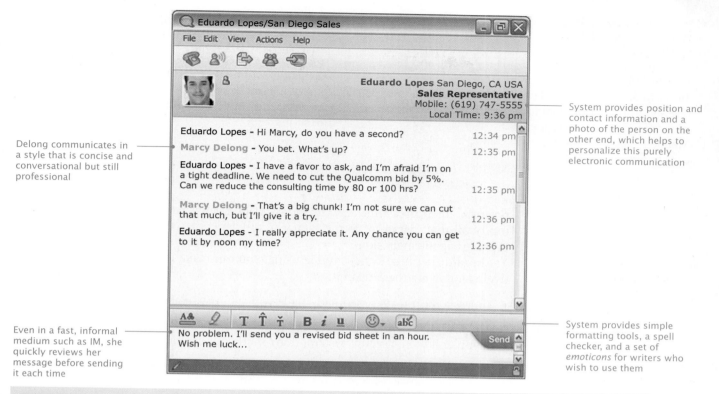

Delong communicates in a style that is concise and conversational but still professional

System provides position and contact information and a photo of the person on the other end, which helps to personalize this purely electronic communication

Even in a fast, informal medium such as IM, she quickly reviews her message before sending it each time

System provides simple formatting tools, a spell checker, and a set of *emoticons* for writers who wish to use them

FIGURE 7.2

Instant Messaging for Business Communication
Instant messaging is widely used in business, but you should not use the same informal style of communication you probably use for IM with your friends and family.

in the sense of creating an outline, try to deliver information in a coherent, complete way that minimizes the number of individual messages required.

- **Writing instant messages.** As with e-mail, the appropriate writing style for business IM is more formal than the style you may be accustomed to with personal IM or text messaging. You should generally avoid IM acronyms (such as "FWIW" for "for what it's worth" or "HTH" for "hope that helps") except when communicating with close colleagues. In the IM exchange in Figure 7.2, notice how the participants communicate quickly and rather informally but still maintain good etiquette and a professional tone. This style is even more important if you or your staff use IM to communicate with customers and other outside audiences. In the coming years, business IM writing may become less formal, but for now, the best approach is to maintain a businesslike style and tone.

- **Completing instant messages.** One of the biggest attractions of IM is that the completing step is so easy. You don't have to produce the message in the usual sense, and distribution is as simple as clicking the Send button. However, don't skip over the revising and proofreading tasks. Quickly scan each message before you send to make sure you don't have any missing or misspelled words and that your message is clear and complete.

To use IM effectively, keep in mind some important behavioral issues: the potential for constant interruptions, the ease of accidentally mixing personal and business messages, the risk of being out of the loop (if a hot discussion or an impromptu meeting flares up when you're away from your PC or other IM device), and the "vast

When using IM, be aware of the potential for constant interruptions and wasted time.

✓ CHECKLIST: Using IM Productively

✓ Pay attention to security and privacy issues and be sure to follow all company guidelines.

✓ Treat IM as a professional communication medium, not an informal, personal tool; avoid using IM slang with all but close colleagues.

✓ Maintain good etiquette, even during simple exchanges.

✓ Protect your own productivity by making yourself unavailable when you need to focus.

✓ In most instances, don't use IM for confidential messages, complex messages, or personal messages.

potential for wasted time" (in the words of MIT labor economist David Autor). On top of all that, users are at the mercy of other people's typing abilities, which can make IM agonizingly slow.[20]

Regardless of the system you're using, you can make IM more efficient and effective by following these tips:[21]

Understand the guidelines for successful business IM before you begin to use it.

- Unless a meeting is scheduled, make yourself unavailable when you need to focus on other work.

- If you're not on a secure system, don't send confidential information.

- Be extremely careful about sending personal messages—they have a tendency to pop up on other people's computers at embarrassing moments.

- Don't use IM for important but impromptu meetings if you can't verify that everyone concerned will be available.

- Unless your system is set up for it, don't use IM for lengthy, complex messages; e-mail is better for those.

- Try to avoid carrying on multiple IM conversations at once to minimize the chance of sending messages to the wrong people.

- If your IM system has filters for *spim*, the IM version of e-mail spam, make sure they're active and up to date.[22]

To review the advice for effective IM in the workplace, see "Checklist: Using IM Productively."

CREATING EFFECTIVE BUSINESS BLOGS

Blogs have a unique ability to encourage interaction with a large, geographically dispersed audience.

To an extent perhaps unmatched by any other medium, blogs can engage large, widely distributed audiences. In a sense, a blog combines the global reach and reference value of a conventional website with the conversational exchanges of e-mail or IM. Good business blogs pay close attention to several important elements:

- **Communicating with personal style and an authentic voice.** Most business messages designed for large audiences are carefully scripted and written in a "corporate voice" that is impersonal and objective. In contrast, successful business blogs are written by individuals and exhibit their personal style. Audiences relate to this fresh approach and often build closer emotional bonds with the blogger's organization as a result. For instance, Microsoft's Channel 9 video blog, or *vlog* (http://channel9.msdn.com), features online informal video clips in which several of the company's technical experts answer questions and criticisms from software developers. Channel 9 and other employee blogs are credited with helping to repair Microsoft's reputation among software customers.[23]

FIGURE 7.3
Video Blogging
With the addition of video, blogging becomes a true multimedia experience that gives bloggers an easy way to share sights and sounds with their audiences. Here, Ford Motor Company integrates video blogging with elements of a conventional website.

- **Delivering new information quickly.** Today's blogging tools let you post new material within minutes of writing it or filming it (see Figure 7.3). Not only does this feature allow you to respond quickly when needed—such as during a corporate crisis—it also lets your audiences know that an active conversation is taking place. Blogs that don't offer a continuous stream of new and interesting content are quickly ignored in today's online environment.

- **Choosing topics of peak interest to audiences.** Successful blogs cover topics that readers care about. For instance, General Motors's popular FastLane blog (http://fastlane.gmblogs.com) features top executives writing about GM cars and responding to questions and criticisms from car enthusiasts. The people who read the blog and write comments obviously care about cars and want the latest information from GM.[24]

- **Encouraging audiences to join the conversation.** Not all blogs invite comments, although most do. These comments can be a valuable source of news, information, and insights. In addition, the relatively informal nature of blogging seems to make it easier for companies to let their guard down and converse with their audiences. Of course, not all comments are helpful or appropriate, which is why many bloggers review all comments and select the most helpful or interesting ones to post.

Given the unique ability of blogs to convey topical information quickly and in a conversational format, their rapid adoption by businesses in virtually every industry

Most business blogs invite readers to leave comments.

The business applications of blogs include a wide range of internal and external communication tasks.

Moblogs are blogs adapted for display on mobile devices such as phones.

should come as no surprise. The following sections offer an overview of the business applications of blogging, and Table 7.2 offers a number of suggestions for successful blogging.

Understanding the Business Applications of Blogging

Blogs are a potential solution whenever you have a continuing stream of information to share with an online audience—and particularly when you want the audience to have the opportunity to respond. Here are some of the many ways businesses are using blogs:[25]

- **Project management and team communication.** Using blogs is a good way to keep project teams up to date, particularly when team members are geographically dispersed. For instance, the trip reports that employees file after visiting customers or other external parties can be enhanced vividly with *mobile blogs*, or *moblogs*. Thanks to the convenience of camera phones and other multimedia wireless devices, employees on the go can send text, audio, images, and video to their colleagues. Conversely, mobile employees can also stay in touch with their team blogs using handheld devices.

- **Company news.** On a broader scale, companies can use blogs to keep employees informed about general business matters, from facility news to benefit updates. Blogs also serve as online community forums, giving everyone in the company a chance to raise questions and voice concerns.

- **Customer support.** Building on the tradition of online customer support forums that have been around since the earliest days of the Internet, customer support blogs answer questions, offer tips and advice, and inform customers about new products.

- **Public relations and media relations.** Many company employees and even high-ranking executives now share company news with both the general public and journalists via their blogs. The "Nuts About Southwest" blog featured at the beginning of the chapter is a great example.

- **Recruiting.** Using a blog is a great way to let potential employees know more about your company, the people who work there, and the nature of the company culture.

- **Policy and issue discussions.** Executive blogs in particular provide a public forum for discussing legislation, regulations, and other broad issues of interest to an organization.

- **Crisis communication.** Using blogs is a convenient way to provide up-to-the-minute information during emergencies, correct misinformation, or respond to rumors.

- **Market research.** Blogs can be a clever way to solicit feedback from customers and experts in the marketplace. In addition to using their own blogs for research, today's companies need to monitor blogs that are likely to discuss them, their executives, and their products. Negative product reviews, rumors, and other information can spread across the globe in a matter of hours, and managers need to know what the online community is saying—whether it's positive or negative. *Reputation analysts* such as Evolve24 (**www.evolve24.com**) have developed ways to automatically monitor blogs and other online sources to see what people are saying about their corporate clients.[26]

Table 7.2 — TIPS FOR EFFECTIVE BUSINESS BLOGGING

Tip	Why It's Important
Have a clear plan before you start blogging.	Without a clear plan, your blog is likely to wander from topic to topic without providing compelling information or building a sense of community with your audience.
Post frequently.	The whole point of a blog is fresh material; if you don't have a constant supply of new information or new links, create a traditional website instead.
Make it about your customers and the issues that are important to them.	Readers want to know how your blog will help them, entertain them, or give them a chance to communicate with others who have similar interests.
Write in an authentic voice; never create an artificial character who supposedly writes a blog.	*Flogs*, or fake blogs, violate the spirit of blogging, show disrespect for your audience, and will turn audiences against you as soon as they uncover the truth.
Link generously—but carefully.	Providing interesting links to others blogs and websites is a fundamental aspect of blogging, but think twice before putting these links in your blog. Make sure the links will be of value to your readers, and make sure they don't point to material that could damage your reputation.
Keep it brief.	Most online readers don't have the patience to read lengthy reports.
Don't post anything you wouldn't want the entire world to see.	Future employers, government regulators, competitors, journalists, and community critics are just a few of the people who might see what you've written. Assume that anything you write will be spread through the online world.
Don't engage in blatant product promotion.	Readers who think they're being advertised to will stop reading.
Take time to write compelling, specific headlines for your postings.	Readers usually decide within a couple of seconds whether to read your postings; boring or vague headlines will turn them away instantly.
Pay attention to spelling, grammar, and mechanics.	No matter how smart or experienced you are, poor-quality writing undermines your credibility with discriminating audiences.
Respond to criticism openly and honestly.	Hiding sends the message that you don't have a valid response to the criticism. If your critics are wrong, patiently explain why you think they're wrong. If they are right, explain how you'll fix the situation.
Listen and learn.	If you don't take the time to analyze the comments people leave on your blog or the comments other bloggers make about you, you're missing out on one of the most valuable aspects of blogging.
Respect intellectual property.	Presenting the work of others as your own is not only unethical but can violate copyright laws.
Be scrupulously honest and careful with facts.	Honesty is an absolute requirement for every ethical business communicator, of course, but you need to be extra careful online because inaccuracies (both intentional and unintentional) are likely to be discovered quickly and shared widely.

- **Brainstorming.** Online brainstorming via blogs offers a way for people to toss ideas around and build on each other's contributions.
- **Viral marketing.** The interconnected nature of the blogosphere makes it a natural vehicle for spreading the word about your company and your products. Bloggers often make it a point to provide links to other blogs and websites that interest them, giving marketers a great opportunity to spread their messages. *Viral market-*

Blogs are an ideal medium for viral marketing, the organic spread of messages from one audience member to another.

ing refers to the transmission of messages in much the same way that biological viruses are transmitted from person to person.

- **E-mail replacement.** As spam filters and message overload make it more difficult to reach people via e-mail, many companies have turned to blogs as a way to distribute information to customers and other audiences. Using *newsfeeds* from a company's blog (see page 219), audiences can subscribe to categories of information that interest them. These messages are then delivered via an *aggregator*, bypassing the increasingly clogged e-mail channel.

- **News syndication.** Blogging also allows both individuals and companies to become publishers of news and other information. For example, by subscribing to the update service at www.businesscommunicationblog.com, the student resource site for this textbook, you can get the latest news about business communication skills and tools. Syndication is explained on page 219.

The uses of blogs are limited only by your creativity, so be on the lookout for new ways you can use them to foster positive relationships with colleagues, customers, and other important audiences (see Figure 7.4).

Adapting the Three-Step Process for Successful Blogging

The three-step writing process is easy to adapt to blogging tasks. The planning step is particularly important if you're considering starting a blog because you're planning an entire communication channel, not just a single message. Pay close attention to your audience, your purpose, and your scope:

- **Audience.** Except for team blogs and other efforts with an obvious and well-defined audience, defining your target audience can be a challenge. You want an audience large enough to justify the time you'll be investing but narrow enough that you can provide a clear focus for the blog. For instance, if you work for a firm that develops computer games, would you focus your blog on "hardcore" players, the type who spend thousands of dollars on super-fast PCs optimized for video games, or would you broaden the reach to include all video gamers? The decision often comes down to business strategy.

- **Purpose.** Unlike a personal blog, in which you typically write about whatever interests you, a business blog needs to have a business-related purpose that is important to your company and to your chosen audience. Moreover, the purpose has to "have legs"—that is, it needs to be something that can drive the blog's content for months or years—rather than focus on a single event or issue of only temporary interest. For instance, if you're a technical expert, you might create a blog to give the audience tips and techniques for using your company's products more effectively—a never-ending subject that's important to both you and your audience. This would be the *general purpose* of your blog; each posting would have a *specific purpose* within the context of that general purpose. Finally, if you are not writing an official company blog but rather blogging as an individual employee, make sure you understand your employer's blogging guidelines. As with e-mail and IM, more and more companies are putting policies in place to prevent employee mistakes with blogging.[27]

- **Scope.** As with your audience, defining the scope of your blog can be a bit tricky. You want to cover a subject area that is broad enough to offer discussion possibilities for months or years but narrow enough to have an identifiable focus. For instance, GM's FastLane blog is about GM cars only—not GM's stock price, labor negotiations, and so on. Moreover, the scope of your blog needs to remain fairly

Before you launch a blog, make sure you have a clear understanding of your target audience, the purpose of your blog, and the scope of subjects you plan to cover.

The headline and tagline combine to clearly indicate the source and the nature of this blog

Postings can be either complete articles or introductions that have links to the complete pieces

Postings are accompanied by a line that indicates who posted the material and when; most blogs also allow visitors to comment on posts

A calendar with hotlinks is one way to provide quick access to postings from previous days

Related and interesting links, to both regular websites and other blogs, are a feature of nearly every blog

Many blogs offer a search box to let visitors find past articles

Most blogs provide one or more ways for readers to subscribe via a newsfeed

FIGURE 7.4
Elements of an Effective Business Blog
Blogs exist in many forms and formats, but visitors expect a few basic elements, such as access to archives, links to related information, and a convenient way to subscribe to an automatic newsfeed. Note the style and tone of the writing in this blog; it is far more engaging and conversational than the traditional "corporate voice." Moreover, it is about the *customers*, not the *company*.

stable so that you can build an audience over time. If you start out discussing product support but then shift to talking about your company's advertising programs, you'll probably lose readers along the way.

After you begin writing your blog (or posting messages to a multiauthor blog that someone else has created), the careful planning needs to continue with each message. Unless you're posting to a restricted-access blog, such as an internal blog on a company intranet, you can never be sure who might see your posts. Other bloggers might link to them months or years later.

Write in a comfortable, personal style. Blog audiences don't want to hear from your company; they want to hear from *you*. Bear in mind, though, that *comfortable* does not mean *careless*. Sloppy writing damages your credibility. In addition, while audiences expect you to be knowledgeable in the subject area your blog covers, you

Write blog postings in a comfortable—but not careless—style.

✓ CHECKLIST: Blogging for Business

✓ Consider using a blog whenever you have a continuing stream of information to share with an online audience.

✓ Identify an audience that is broad enough to justify the effort but narrow enough to have common interests.

✓ Identify a purpose that is comprehensive enough to provide fuel for a continuing stream of posts.

✓ Consider the scope of your blog carefully; make it broad enough to attract an audience but narrow enough to keep you focused.

✓ Communicate with a personal style and an authentic voice but don't write carelessly.

✓ Deliver new information quickly.

✓ Choose topics of peak interest to your audience.

✓ Encourage audiences to join the conversation.

✓ Offer a newsfeed option so that subscribers can get automatic updates.

don't need to know everything about a topic. If you don't have all the information yourself, provide links to other blogs and websites that supply relevant information. In fact, many blog audiences consider carefully screened links to be an essential part of blogging.

Completing messages for your blog is usually quite easy. Evaluate the content and readability of your message, proofread to correct any errors, and post using your blogging system's tools for doing so. If your blog doesn't already have one, be sure to include one or more *newsfeed* options so that your audience can automatically receive headlines (and summaries, if you choose) of new blog posts (see "Distributing Blog and Podcast Content" on page 218).

"Checklist: Blogging for Business" summarizes some of the key points to remember when creating and writing a business blog, and you can always get updated advice from some of the many blogs and websites dedicated to blogging.

CREATING EFFECTIVE PODCASTS

Podcasting can be used to deliver a wide range of audio and video messages.

Podcasting offers a number of interesting possibilities for business communication. Its most obvious use is to replace existing audio and video messages, such as one-way teleconferences in which a speaker provides information without expecting to engage in conversation with the listeners. Training is another good use of podcasting. One of the first podcasts recorded by technical experts at IBM gave other employees advice on setting up blogs, for example.[28] Sales representatives who travel to meet with potential customers can listen to audio podcasts or view video podcasts to get the latest information on their companies' products. Podcasts are also an increasingly common feature on blogs, letting audiences listen to or watch recordings of their favorite bloggers. New services can even transcribe blogs into podcasts and vice versa.[29]

As more businesspeople become comfortable with podcasting, it should find applications in a variety of new areas, wherever audio or video content can convey business messages effectively. For instance, real estate agents can record audio podcasts that potential homebuyers can listen to while walking through houses. Marketing departments can replace expensive printed brochures with video podcasts that demonstrate new products in action. Human resources departments can offer video tours of their companies to entice new recruits.

Adapting the Three-Step Process for Successful Podcasting

Although it might not seem obvious at first, the three-step writing process adapts quite nicely to podcasting. You've already chosen the medium, so focus the planning step on analyzing the situation, gathering the information you'll need, and organizing your material. One vital planning step depends on whether you intend to create podcasts for limited use and distribution (such as a weekly audio update to your virtual team) or you plan to create a *podcasting channel* with regular recordings on a consistent theme, designed for a wider public audience. As with planning a blog, if you intend to create a podcasting channel, be sure to think through the range of topics you want to address over time to verify that you have a sustainable purpose. If you plan to comment on the stock market or breaking news in your industry, for instance, you'll have a recurring source of topics to discuss. In contrast, if you plan to share marketing ideas for small business owners, make sure you have or can find plenty of ideas over time so that your podcasting efforts don't run out of steam. If you bounce from one theme to another over time, you risk losing your audience.[30]

> Steering devices such as transitions, previews, and reviews are vital in podcasts.

As you organize and begin to think about the words or images you'll use as content, pay close attention to previews, transitions, and reviews. These steering devices are especially vital in audio and video recordings because these formats lack the "street signs" (such as headings) that audiences rely on in print media. Moreover, scanning back and forth to find specific parts of an audio or video message is much more difficult than with textual messages, so you need to do everything possible to make sure your audience successfully receives and interprets your message on the first try.

> Generous use of previews, transitions, and reviews helps podcast audiences follow the thread of your recording.

One of the attractions of podcasting is the conversational, person-to-person feel of the recordings, so unless you need to capture exact wording, speaking from an outline and notes rather than a prepared script is often the best choice. However, no one wants to listen to rambling podcasts that struggle to make a point, so don't try to make up your content on the fly. Effective podcasts, like effective stories, have a clear beginning, middle, and end.

In the completing step, keep in mind that making edits is much more difficult with audio or video than with textual media. Take extra care to revise your script or think through your speaking notes before you begin to record. You don't want to get halfway through the recording process and realize that you should have said something else in the introduction.

> Plan your podcast content carefully; edits are much more difficult to make in podcasts than in textual messages.

Finally, consider integrating your podcasting efforts with a related blog. Not only can you provide additional information, you can use the commenting feature of the blog to encourage feedback from your audience.[31]

Assembling a Podcasting System

The equipment needed to record podcasts depends on the degree of production quality you want to achieve. For the most basic podcasts, such as those you might record for internal audiences, most contemporary personal computers probably have the equipment you need: a low-cost microphone (most laptop computers now have built-in microphones), a sound card to convert the microphone signal to digital format (most computers have them now), and some recording software (free versions are available online). Many handheld digital recorders can also record audio files that you can upload to a PC for editing and distribution.

However, a basic system might not deliver the audio quality or production flexibility you need for a public podcast. For instance, the microphone built into your laptop can't reproduce sound nearly as well as a professional-quality microphone can, and because it's physically located on the computer, the built-in microphone will pick up the noise

With a few upgrades beyond a basic computer, you can assemble a studio capable of producing professional-quality podcasts.

FIGURE 7.5
The Podcasting Process
Creating a podcast requires a few easy steps, and basic podcasts can be created using free or low-cost hardware and software.

For basic podcasts, your computer probably has most of the hardware you already need, and you can download recording software.

For higher-quality podcasts, you'll probably need additional hardware and software.

from the computer's fan. Similarly, the low-cost sound cards built into many computers can add a significant amount of noise to your signal.[32]

If you need higher production quality or greater flexibility, you'll need additional pieces of hardware and software, such as an audio processor (to filter out extraneous noise and otherwise improve the audio signal), a mixer (to combine multiple audio or video signals), a better microphone, and more sophisticated recording and editing software (see Figure 7.5). You may also need to improve the acoustics of the room in which you are recording, to minimize echoes, noise, and other problems. To learn more about the technical requirements of podcasting, pick up one of the many new books on the subject. Some of them even come with free recording software.[33]

For a quick review of the key points of business podcasting, see "Checklist: Planning and Producing Business Podcasts."

DISTRIBUTING BLOG AND PODCAST CONTENT

With today's blog and podcast technologies, you can easily reach a vast audience— an audience that can continue to grow if your "fans" spread the word for you. To distribute effectively, get into the mindset of *publishing*, rather than sending, your content.

✓ CHECKLIST: Planning and Producing Business Podcasts

✓ Consider podcasting whenever you have the opportunity to replace existing audio or video messages.

✓ If you plan a podcast channel with a regular stream of new content, make sure you've identified a theme or purpose that is rich enough to sustain your effort.

✓ Pay close attention to previews, transitions, and reviews to help prevent your audience from getting lost.

✓ Decide whether you want to improvise your podcast or speak or film from a written script.

✓ If you improvise, do enough planning and organization to avoid floundering and rambling in search of a point.

✓ Remember that editing is much more difficult to do with audio or video than with textual media and plan your content and recording carefully.

✓ Consider linking your podcast to a blog in order to provide additional information and a forum for audience feedback.

✓ Syndicate your podcast, if appropriate, via RSS enclosures.

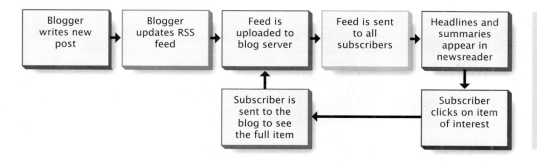

FIGURE 7.6
The Syndication Process for Blogs
The publish/subscribe model lets bloggers reach a potentially vast audience and lets audiences automatically acquire fresh content from an unlimited number of sources.

Publishing Your Content

As with newspapers and magazines, blog and podcast publishing requires some action from both the publisher and the subscriber. The publisher creates the content and submits it to a distribution channel, which delivers it to anyone who has chosen to subscribe. This process of publication for blogs and podcasts is often referred to as **syndication** (see Figure 7.6).[34] As a publisher, you initiate syndication by creating a **feed**, or *newsfeed*, a file that contains information about the items you have written or recorded. In the case of podcasts, the audio or video file is enclosed within the feed file as well. Several formats now exist for these feeds; the most common is known as **RSS**, which is short for *really simple syndication*. (Although this process sounds fairly technical, popular blogging and podcasting systems take care of most of the details for you.) The benefit of syndication via an RSS feed is that you have the potential to build up a vast audience over time, provided that you offer compelling content and make that content easy to find.

> Syndication is the process of distributing blog and podcast content via feeds.

On the receiving end, audiences subscribe to your content through a piece of software called an **aggregator** or a *newsreader*. (*Aggregating* is simply another word for *collecting*.) Basic aggregators can collect messages with both text and static images, and some aggregators specialize in certain types of media. Aggregators specifically for podcasts are usually called **podcatchers**. Whenever you create a feed for a new blog post or podcast, your subscribers are automatically alerted via the feed. In the case of blogs, aggregators usually display a headline and brief summary of your post. Anyone who wants to read the full item can click on the headline to be directed back to your blog to see the entire post (see Figure 7.7). In the case of podcasts, subscribers can choose to have new podcasts downloaded to their computer or other device automatically, or they can download them manually. For audiences, the key benefit of syndication is automatically collecting interesting content from many sources in a variety of formats. In a sense, it's like creating personal versions of the Internet.

> Aggregators automatically collect information about new blog postings and podcasts.

Connecting with Audiences

This publish/subscribe process generally works nicely when publishers and subscribers take the necessary steps to send and receive content. Of course, both parties need to find each other in the first place. This connection can happen in a variety of ways. The most fundamental step for blog publishers is to add the feed capability to their blogs so that interested audiences can easily subscribe through their aggregators. Bloggers and podcasters can also take advantage of services such as FeedBurner, www.feedburner.com, which make sure files are properly formatted and help publicize content.[35]

> Adding feed capability is the most important step in staying connected with your blog or podcast audiences.

Beyond that, publishers can get themselves listed in a variety of directories, some of which specialize in blogs (such as Technorati, www.technorati.com),

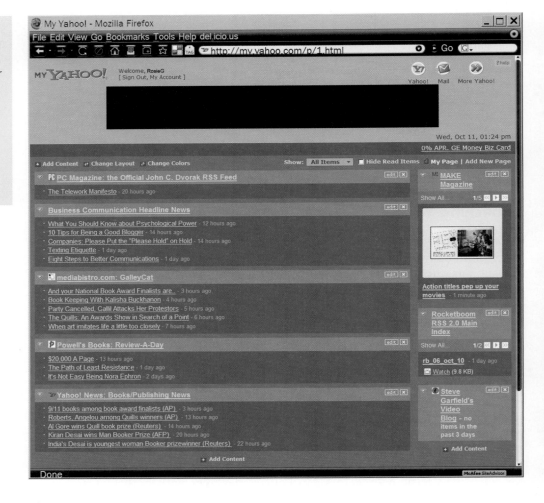

others in podcasts (such as Juice, http://juicereceiver.sourceforge.net), some in only video feeds (such as FireAnt, www.fireant.tv), and others in two or more media types (such as Mefeedia, http://mefeedia.com, which covers podcasts and vodcasts).

Tagging involves assigning descriptive words to each post of a podcast.

Content creators can also make their material easier to find through **tagging**, which involves assigning descriptive words to each post or podcast. For instance, for a blog posting on clever techniques for attracting new employees, you might tag the post with the word *recruiting*. Visitors to your blog who want to read everything you've written about recruiting just click on that word to see all your posts on that subject. Tagging can also help audiences locate your posts on blog trackers such as Technorati or on *social bookmarking* or *social news* sites such as del.icio.us, http://del.icio.us (see Figure 7.8), and Digg, www.digg.com. You can read more about social bookmarking as a research tool in Chapter 11.

Bloggers can help each other find audiences by listing favorite blogs in their blogrolls.

Bloggers can also help each other by identifying blogs they themselves read. This list, called a *blogroll*, can be found on many blogs. In addition, when bloggers comment on individual posts on other blogs, they can also use a feature called *trackback* to let readers of the original post know that other bloggers have commented on it. Both blogrolls and trackbacks help "spread the word" for bloggers by showing audiences other blogs they might like as well.

New capabilities and services emerge constantly in the world of online media, and this chapter has provided just a broad overview. To learn the latest on blogging, podcasting, and other new media choices, visit www.businesscommunicationblog.com, click on "Web Directory," then click on "Business Communication," and then click on the subject of interest.

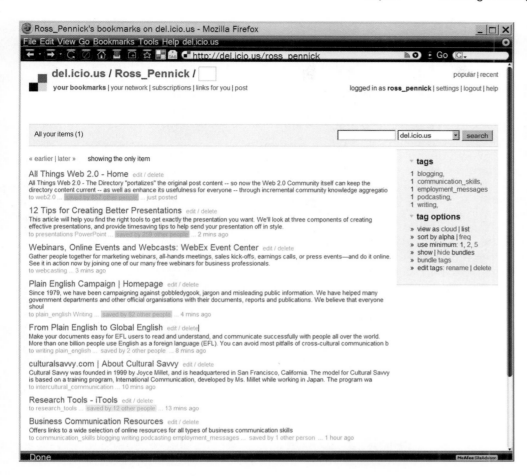

FIGURE 7.8

Tagging on a Social Bookmarking Site
Tagging lets bloggers and podcasters identify the content of their messages to make it easier for audiences to find items of interest. Sites such as del.icio.us also let audiences apply their own tags to items they've selected (indicated by the "to" line in each entry), making it easier for them to categorize content and share their choices with other del.icio.us users.

On the Job

SOLVING COMMUNICATION DILEMMAS AT SOUTHWEST AIRLINES

You recently joined the corporate communications group at Southwest Airlines, and one of your responsibilities is overseeing the Nuts About Southwest blog. Study the scenarios that follow and apply what you learned about blogging in this chapter to choose the best course of action.

1. Pressure is building to stop the practice of moderating the blog by reviewing reader comments and selecting which ones will appear on the blog. You've received a number of adamant messages saying that Nuts About Southwest won't be a "real" blog until anyone is allowed to write any sort of comment without being "censored" by the company. However, you know that every blog is vulnerable to rude, inappropriate, and irrelevant comments, and you don't want Nuts About Southwest to turn into a free-for-all shouting match. Which of the following messages should you post on the blog to explain that the current policy of reviewing and filtering comments will continue?

a. There are plenty of free-for-all blogs and websites on the Internet; if you want to rant and rave, I suggest you try one of those.

b. Please bear in mind that this blog is a Southwest company commercial communication endeavor and, as such, it must adhere to company standards for communication style. I therefore regret to inform you that we cannot allow a free-form, unmonitored exchange as part of this blog.

c. Our blog; our rules. Seriously, though, this is a professional communication channel designed primarily to give Southwest employees the opportunity to share their thoughts with customers and vice versa. As such, we need to make sure that primary messaging effort doesn't get lost in the noise that can flare up in unregulated online forums.

d. Every web surfer knows that online discussions can get a little out of hand at times, degenerating into shouting matches, name calling, and off-topic rants. In order to continue providing the congenial, information-driven blog that readers have come to expect, we believe it is necessary to exercise a minimal amount of control over the content.

2. Southwest's change in scheduling policy (allowing customers to reserve seats slightly farther into the future) placated many customers but not everyone. Some still want to book travel up to a year or more in advance. You don't want to ignore these complaints, but the company has decided that scheduling that far out just isn't feasible. You therefore decide to post a few representative complaints and respond to them as best you can. In addition to letting customers know that the schedule window won't be extended that far, you'd like to curtail any further discussion on this topic. Which of the following would be the best way to respond to these complaints?

   a. Folks, you don't really understand how complicated running an airline truly is. You can't just slap a time schedule together and have it magically happen. Every single flight involves a flight crew, a ground crew, catering, gates at both ends, fees, clearances, you name it. Zillions of details have to be coordinated for every flight we put on the schedule, and it's a major job. We manage to handle 3,000 flights a day, so trust us; we know what we're doing.

   b. Thanks for your input. We realize air travel isn't as smooth or as simple as we'd all like, so it's helpful to hear from all of our valued customers. I'll make sure the rest of the scheduling team reads your comments, and if anything changes in the scheduling policy, I'll post the new information here immediately.

   c. Thanks for taking the time to post your comments. You're certainly welcome to book your travel on other airlines if you need to nail down a reservation 6 to 12 months into the future. However, I should warn you that the farther into the future you make a reservation, the greater the chances that the airline will change the schedule on you. Let's say it's January 10, and you want to book a flight from Denver to San Jose on December 20. Fine, you're all set. Then along comes October or November, and the airline realizes it needs that plane for the Denver to Chicago leg on December 20 instead. What happens then? You get a phone call or e-mail saying "Sorry, we've had to book you on a different flight at a different time." What's the point of nailing down your plans 11 or 12 months in advance if they're just going to change on you?

   d. Thanks for taking the time to post your comments. When we're considering the scheduling question, let's remember why all of us—employees included—are nuts about flying Southwest: low fares, predictable schedules, and on-time performance. In order to maintain those benefits, we've learned over the years that we need to make certain choices about how we run the airline. One of those choices is to operate a shorter

reservation window than many other airlines. I realize this doesn't meet the needs of every passenger in every situation, but experience shows that it's the best way to make most passengers happy most of the time. In that light, I hope the decision not to extend scheduling beyond six months makes sense to everyone.

3. The multiauthor concept generally works well for Nuts About Southwest. It divides the writing workload, and it gives readers the opportunity to hear from a variety of voices across the company. One member of the team is retiring, so you need to recruit a new blogger to replace her. Your plan is to send an e-mail message to everyone in the company, providing a brief reminder of the blog's purpose, describing the writing style you're looking for, and inviting interested writers to submit sample blog entries for evaluation. Which of the following paragraphs is the best way to describe the preferred writing style for the blog? (This message is for employees only; it won't be seen by the public.)

   a. Nuts About Southwest has connected with thousands of readers because the writing is *engaging* (people want to read and respond), *personal* (readers want to get to know real, live human beings, not a faceless corporation), *honest* (we don't sugarcoat anything or hide from criticism), and *friendly* (our readers want to enjoy the experience).

   b. What kind of writing are we looking for? Well, let me tell you exactly what we need. We need writing that is above all (a) engaging—it makes people *want* to read and become involved in the conversation. Plus, (b), the writing must be *personal*; we don't need anybody to repeat "the company line" here; we want *your unique* thoughts and opinions. However, (c), we, of course (!), need writing that is consistent with Southwest's culture that combines honesty with friendliness.

   c. You should be able to produce copy that meets the following criteria: Your writing must be engaging, personal, honest, and friendly. Writing that does not meet these criteria, no matter how well written in other respects, will not be accepted for online publication.

   d. I'll be short and to the point: the writing we want for this blog must be engaging, personal, honest, and friendly.

4. For the sample blog entries you solicited in your e-mail message, you asked candidates to start their entries with a brief paragraph introducing themselves. Which of the following seems like the most compatible style for Nuts About Southwest?

   a. Hi everyone! I'm Janice McNathan, and I couldn't be more excited to be joining the Nuts About Southwest blog cuz—hey, I'm nuts! I've worked at some goofball companies before, but nobody has as much fun as the loonies here at Southwest, so I know I'm going to have a great time writing for this blog!

b. Howdy folks, Charlie Parker here. No, not the famous jazz musician! I'm just a lowly fuel inventory auditor here in Dallas. Pretty much, I keep tabs on the fuel that goes into our planes and I make sure we get the best deals possible and all the paperwork stays in order. I can't promise any exciting stories of adventure like the pilots and other people write here, but I'll keep my eyes peeled around the airport here, and maybe something interesting will come up.

c. I'm Rick Munoz, and I've always wanted to be a professional writer. My career sort of took a detour, though, and I wound up as a programmer who works behind the scenes at the Southwest website. I really appreciate this opportunity to hone my craft, and who knows—maybe this will be the break I need to make it as a "real" writer. You'll be able to say "I knew that guy before he became famous!"

d. Excuse me while I wipe the grease off my hands; I don't want to mess up this shiny new keyboard! Hi, I'm Kristal Yan, an airframe and powerplant mechanic at Southwest's facility in Oakland, California. I've been an avid reader of Nuts About Southwest since it started, and I really look forward to participating in this wonderful worldwide conversation. I hope to provide some interesting observations from a mechanic's perspective, and I hope you'll feel free to ask any questions you may have about how we keep Southwest's planes running smoothly and safely.

Learning Objectives Checkup

Assess your understanding of the principles in this chapter by reading each learning objective and studying the accompanying exercises. For fill-in-the-blank items, write the missing text in the blank provided; for multiple-choice items, circle the letter of the correct answer. You can check your responses against the answer key on page AK-2.

Objective 7.1: Compare the strengths and weaknesses of the print and electronic media available for short messages.

1. To express sympathy to the family of one of your employees who recently died in a traffic accident, which of these media would you choose and why?
   a. Printed memo
   b. Printed letter
   c. E-mail
   d. Instant message

2. Which of the following best describes an advantage of computer-based instant messaging over phone-based text messaging?
   a. A computer keyboard and full-size display make IM more convenient to use than text messaging.
   b. IM is cheaper because everybody has computers these days.
   c. IM is faster than text messaging.
   d. Computer-based IM is currently available in more languages than phone-based text messaging.

Objective 7.2: Identify the qualities of an effective e-mail subject line.

3. Which of the following is true of e-mail subject lines?
   a. Only "newbies" bother to use them anymore.
   b. Subject lines should never give away the content of the message because no one will bother to read it if they already know what the message is about.
   c. They can make the difference between a message being read right away, skipped over for later attention, or ignored entirely.
   d. They should always be in all caps to get the audience's attention.

4. To capture attention in your e-mail messages, be sure to
   a. Make your subject line longer than you would in a printed memo
   b. Avoid key words, quotations, directions, or questions
   c. Make your subject line informative and compelling
   d. Retain the same subject line in multiple e-mails on the same topic, no matter how the content changes

5. Which of the following is the most effective e-mail subject line?
   a. Production line: wiring issues
   b. Wiring errors in production: let's analyze the problem and explore solutions
   c. Wiring errors on the production line MUST STOP NOW!
   d. Careless workers → unhappy customers → fewer customers → fewer employees

Objective 7.3: Explain how overuse of e-mail can reduce productivity.

6. If you wanted to compliment the head of your department on the presentation she made to a major customer last week, which of the following would be the wisest course of action?
   a. Use bcc to send the message to everyone else in the department without the boss knowing that you did so.
   b. Use e-mail but don't cc anyone else in the department.
   c. Make sure you cc everyone in the department so they can share in congratulating the boss as well.
   d. Send the boss a memo instead so that the communication will stay private and avoid disrupting other people in the department.

7. You work in a customer service department, answering e-mails from customers. This morning you received an angry message from a customer who has a legitimate complaint about your company's warranty policies. After responding to the message as best you can, which of the following steps should you take?
   a. Forward the message to your immediate supervisor and suggest that the company might want to reconsider its warranty policies.
   b. Forward the message to the CEO and suggest that the company might want to reconsider its warranty policies.
   c. Forward the message to everyone in the department so they are aware of the problem with the warranty policy.
   d. Delete the customer's message; you can't fix the warranty policy.

8. The _____ address line on an e-mail message sends the message to additional recipients and lets everyone see who is receiving the message; the _____ address line also sends the message to additional recipients, but no one can see that these recipients are receiving the message.

Objective 7.4: Identify guidelines for successful instant messaging (IM) in the workplace.

9. Which of the following reasons help explain why IM usage is overtaking e-mail in some companies?
   a. People don't have to be so formal when they use IM; it saves time to use acronyms and emoticons and to avoid using capitalization, punctuation, and other time wasters.
   b. IM works better as a broadcast mechanism than e-mail.
   c. IM is faster than e-mail and mimics human conversation better than e-mail, so many people find it a more natural way to communicate.
   d. IM systems let you communicate using different colors of text, which is vital for highlighting key points and conveying nonverbal aspects that are impossible to communicate in e-mail.

10. Which of these statements best describes how the three-step writing process applies to IM?
    a. Because there is no planning step and no completing step in IM, the three-step process does not apply.
    b. The real beauty of IM in the business world is that people don't have to spend so much time composing; they just zap out whatever is on their minds and get back to work.
    c. The three-step process for IM works exactly the same way as it does with letters, memos, and reports. Every message requires audience analysis, information gathering, and outlining.
    d. IM exchanges should be planned the same way conversations are planned to minimize confusion and the number of messages required. And instant messages don't have to be great works of literature, but they do need to be efficient and effective, so some degree of care in writing and revising is important.

11. Which of the following message types are most appropriate for IM?
    a. Long, complex messages
    b. Brief conversational messages
    c. Confidential or highly personal messages
    d. All of the above

Objective 7.5: Describe the role of blogging in business communication today.

12. Which of the following is a good strategy for using blogs to promote products and services?
    a. Write in a style that is personal and conversational; minimize direct promotion of your products and services. Focus instead on topics that your customers and potential customers find helpful and interesting.
    b. In order to cut through the noise in the blogosphere, promote your products and services constantly. If you don't, your competitors will drown you out.
    c. Make sure the blog matches all other corporate communications in both style and content; customers get confused when a company communicates in more than one style.
    d. Blogs should never be used for marketing and selling.

13. Which of the following best describes the idea of an "authentic voice" in blogging?
    a. A writing style that is scrupulously precise and free from technical and grammatical errors
    b. The voice of a real, living, breathing human being, communicating to other human beings on a personal level
    c. Writing that is always highly emotional so as to counteract the dehumanizing logic and linear thinking that dominates business today
    d. A detached, professional voice that is careful not to take sides, voice opinions, or otherwise inject elements into the conversation that could disturb or disappoint audiences

14. Blogs are a natural tool for _____, the transmission of messages in a voluntary, organic way from one interested party to another.

Objective 7.6: Explain why identifying your audience, purpose, and scope is vital to successful blogging.

15. Which of the following best describes the optimum audience of a blog?
    a. Always the largest audience possible
    b. Only people who are experts in the subject matter so that comments and discussions aren't pulled off track by "newbies" who don't know what they are talking about
    c. An audience large enough to justify the time required to maintain the blog but narrow enough to ensure a clear focus
    d. Whatever audience happens to find the blog on the web

16. Which of these is *not* a good general purpose for a blog?
    a. Sharing news from the racing circuit, describing how the racers we sponsor are faring and how they use our products
    b. Commenting on economic and social policy decisions that affect the national and international business environment

c. Explaining to the local community why we've decided not to expand employment at the Nampa facility

d. Describing the work going on in our research and development labs

Objective 7.7: Explain how to adapt the three-step writing process for podcasts.

17. If one of the attractions of podcasting is its spontaneous, conversational feel, why should podcasters take the time to plan their recordings?

    a. Individual podcasts that aren't well thought out can end up being rambling, confusing, and repetitive.

    b. Podcasts are more difficult to edit than textual messages, so it's important to do enough planning to help avoid major mistakes.

    c. If you don't plan ahead, you could run out of ideas and therefore have no reason to continue podcasting.

d. All of the above are reasons to plan podcasts.

18. A/an _____ is an ongoing series of podcasts on the same general topic.

Objective 7.8: Describe the syndication process, and explain how it helps you distribute blog and podcast content.

19. _____ is the process of publishing blog and podcast content to the web so that audiences can find your content and be automatically updated when new content is available.

20. Which of these tools is used to collect new blog postings, podcasts, and other fresh content automatically?

    a. A newsreader or aggregator

    b. A feeder

    c. A news scooper

    d. An RSS publisher

Apply Your Knowledge

1. Are instant messaging and blogging replacing many instances of e-mail for the same reasons that e-mail replaced many instances of printed memos and letters? Explain your answer.

2. If one of the benefits of blogging is the personal, intimate style of writing, is it a good idea to limit your creativity by adhering to conventional rules of grammar, spelling, and mechanics? Why or why not?

3. In your work as a video game designer, you know that eager players search the web for any scrap of information they can find about upcoming releases. In fact, to build interest, your company's public relations department carefully doles out small bits of information in the months before a new title hits the market. However, you and others in the company are also concerned about competitors getting their hands on all this "prerelease" information. If they learn too much too soon, they can use the information to improve their own products more quickly. You and several other designers and programmers maintain blogs that give players insights into game design techniques and that occasionally share tips and tricks. You have thousands of readers, and you know your blog helps build customer loyalty. The company president wants to ban blogging entirely so that bloggers don't accidentally share too much

prerelease information about upcoming games. Would this be a wise move? Why or why not?

4. Should podcasting be considered as a potential replacement for your company's employee newsletter, which is currently sent by e-mail? Why or why not?

5. **Ethical Choices** Your boss wants you to send a message to the production staff, thanking all 60 members for their hard work and overtime to get the new manufacturing line set up and running on schedule. Your boss has been working a lot of overtime herself, and she's been under a lot of pressure. She wants to send the thank-you message by e-mail and asks you to work on the wording. You think each member of the production staff should receive a formal printed letter to keep for future promotions or other jobs. You know your boss won't like being interrupted about an issue that she thinks is off her desk, and you know how valuable her time is.

    a. Should you draft the letter and produce 60 copies so that you don't have to bother your boss?

    b. Should you simply draft the e-mail message as requested to save everyone time?

    c. Should you discuss the issue with your boss, regardless of taking her away from the tasks she so desperately needs to get done?

Practice Your Knowledge

MESSAGES FOR ANALYSIS

Review the following messages and then (1) analyze the strengths and weaknesses of each message and (2) revise as indicated.

MESSAGE 7.A: IMPROVING IM SKILLS

Review this IM exchange and explain how the customer service agent could have handled the situation more effectively:

Agent: Thanks for contacting Home Exercise Equipment. What's up?

Customer: I'm having trouble assembling my home gym.

Agent: I hear that a lot! LOL

Customer: So is it me or the gym?

Agent: Well, let's see <grin>. Where are you stuck?

Customer: The crossbar that connects the vertical pillars doesn't fit.

Agent: What do you mean doesn't fit?

Customer: It doesn't fit. It's not long enough to reach across the pillars.

Agent: Maybe you assembled the pillars in the wrong place. Or maybe we sent the wrong crossbar.

Customer: How do I tell?

Agent: The parts aren't labeled so could be tough. Do you have a measuring tape? Tell me how long your crossbar is.

MESSAGE 7.B: DRAFTING EFFECTIVE BLOG POSTS.

Revise this blog post based on what you've learned in this chapter:

[headline]

We're DOOMED!!!!!
[post]

I was at the Sikorsky plant in Stratford yesterday, just checking to see how things were going with the assembly line retrofit we did for them last year. I think I saw the future, and it ain't pretty. They were demo'ing a prototype robot from Motoman that absolutely blows our stuff out of the water. They wouldn't let me really see it, but based on the 10-second glimpse I got, it's smaller, faster, and more maneuverable than any of our units. And when I asked about the price, the guy just grinned. And it wasn't the sort of grin designed to make me feel good.

I've been saying for years that we need to pay more attention to size, speed, and maneuverability instead of just relying on our historical strengths of accuracy and payload capacity, and you'd have to be blind not to agree that this experience proves me right. If we can't at least show a design for a better unit within two or three months, Motoman is going to lock up the market and leave us utterly in the dust.

Believe me, being able to say "I told you so" right now is not nearly as satisfying as you might think!!

MESSAGE 7.C: PLANNING A BETTER PODCAST.

To access this message, visit **www.businesscommunication blog.com** and click on "Textbook Resources." Locate *Excellence in Business Communication*, 8th ed., click on Chapter 7, and select Page 226, Message 7.C. Download and listen to this podcast. Identify at least three ways in which the podcast could be improved and draft a brief e-mail message that you could send to the podcaster with your suggestions for improvement.

EXERCISES

For active links to all websites discussed in this chapter, visit this text's website, at **www.prenhall.com/thill**. Locate your book and click on its "Companion Website" link. Then select Chapter 7 and click on "Featured Websites." Locate the name of the page or the URL related to the material in the text. Please note that links to sites that become inactive after publication of the book will be removed from the "Featured Websites" section.

7.1   Choose Your Medium: Selecting the Best Technology for a Message For each of these message needs, choose a medium that you think would work effectively and explain your choice. (More than one medium could work in some cases; just be able to support your particular choice.)
a. A technical support service for people trying to use their digital music players
b. A message of condolence to the family of an employee who passed away recently
c. A message from the CEO of a small company, explaining that she is leaving the company to join a competitor
d. A series of observations on the state of the industry
e. A series of messages, questions, and answers surrounding the work of a project team

7.2   E-Mail: Making Subject Lines Informative Using your imagination to make up whatever details you need, revise the following e-mail subject lines to make them more informative.
a. New budget figures
b. Marketing brochure—your opinion
c. Production schedule

7.3   E-Mail: Message Outlining a New Employee Procedure The following e-mail message contains numerous errors related to what you've learned about planning and writing business messages. Using the information it contains, write a more effective version.

TO: Felicia August <fb_august@evertrust.com>
SUBJECT: Those are the breaks, folks

Some of you may not like the rules about break times; however, we determined that keeping track of employees while they took breaks at times they determined rather than regular breaks at prescribed times was not working as well as we would have liked it to work. The new rules are not going to be an option. If you do not follow the new rules, you could be docked from your pay for hours when you turned up missing, since your direct supervisor will not be able to tell whether you were on a "break" or not and will assume that you have walked away from your job. We cannot be responsible for any errors that result from your inattentiveness to the new rules. I have already heard complaints from some of you and I hope this memo will end this issue once and for all. The decision has already been made.

Starting Monday, January 1, you will all be required to take a regular 15-minute break in the morning and again in the afternoon, and a regular thirty-minute lunch at the times specified by your supervisor, NOT when you think you need a break or when you "get around to it."

There will be no exceptions to this new rule!

Felicia August
Manager
Billing and accounting

7.4   Instant Messaging: Let's Get Professional Your firm, which makes professional paint sprayers, uses IM extensively for internal communication and frequently for external communication with customers and suppliers as well. Several customers have recently forwarded copies of messages they've received from your staff, asking if you know how casually some employees were treating this important medium. You decide to revise parts of several messages to show your staff a more appropriate writing style. Rewrite these sentences, making up any information you need, to convey a more businesslike style and tone. (Look up the acronyms online if you need to.)

a. IMHO, our quad turbo sprayer is best model 4U.

b. No prob; happy2help!

c. FWIW, I use the L400 myself & it rocks

d. Most cust see 20–30% reduct in fumes w/this sprayer —— of course, YMMV.

7.5 Blogging: Keeping Emotions Under Control The members of the project team of which you are the leader have enthusiastically embraced blogging as a communication medium. Unfortunately, as emotions heat up during the project, some of the blog postings are getting too casual, too personal, and even sloppy. Because your boss and other managers around the company also read this project blog, you don't want the team to look unprofessional in anyone's eyes. Revise the following blog posting so that it communicates in a more businesslike manner while retaining the informal, conversational tone of a blog. (Be sure to correct any spelling and punctuation mistakes you find as well.)

> Well, to the profound surprise of absolutely nobody, we are not going to be able meet the June 1 commitment to ship 100 operating tables to Southeast Surgical Supply. (For those of you who have been living in a cave the past six month, we have been fighting to get our hands on enough high-grade chromium steel to meet our production schedule.) Sure enough, we got news, this morning that we will only get enough for 30 tables. Yes, we look lik fools for not being able to follow through on promises we made to the customer, but no, this didn't have to happpen. Six month's ago, purchasing warned us about shrinking supplies and suggested we advance-buy as much as we would need for the next 12 months, or so. We naturally tried to followed their advice, but just as naturally were shot down by the bean counters at corporate who trotted out the policy about never buying more than three months worth of materials in advance. Of course, it'll be us- - -not the bean counters who'll take the flak when everybody starts asking why revenues are down next quarter and why Southeast is talking to our friends at Crighton Manuf!!! Maybe, some day this company will get its head out of the sand and realize that we need to have some financial flexibility in order to compete.

7.6 Blogging: Blog Post Informing Employees About an Office Relocation From what you've learned about effective blogging as well as planning and writing business messages in general, you should be able to iden-

tify numerous errors made by the writer of the following blog posting. After identifying the flaws, draft a version that fixes them.

Get Ready!

> We are hoping to be back at work soon, with everything running smoothly, same production schedule and no late projects or missed deadlines. So you need to clean out your desk, put your stuff in boxes, and clean off the walls. You can put the items you had up on your walls in boxes, also.
>
> We have provided boxes. The move will happen this weekend. We'll be in our new offices when you arrive on Monday.
>
> We will not be responsible for personal belongings during the move.
>
> Posted by David Burke at 10:42 AM 09–27–08

7.7 Podcasting: Where Are We Going with This, Boss? You've recently begun recording a weekly podcast to share information with your large and far-flung staff. After a month, you ask for feedback from several of your subordinates, and you're disappointed to learn that some people stopped listening to the podcast after the first couple weeks. Someone eventually admits that many staffers feel the recordings are too long and rambling, and the information they contain isn't valuable enough to justify the time it takes to listen. You aren't pleased, but you want to improve. An assistant transcribes the introduction to last week's podcast so you can review it. You immediately see two problems. Revise the introduction based on what you've learned in this chapter.

> So there I am, having lunch with Selma Gill, who just joined and took over the Northeast sales region from Jackson Stroud. In walks our beloved CEO with Selma's old boss at Uni-Plex; turns out they were finalizing a deal to co-brand our products and theirs and to set up a joint distribution program in all four domestic regions. Pretty funny, huh? Selma left Uni-Plex because she wanted to sell our products instead, and now she's back selling her old stuff, too. Anyway, try to chat with her when you can; she knows the biz inside and out and probably can offer insight into just about any sales challenge you might be running up against. We'll post more info on the co-brand deal next week; should be a boost for all of us. Other than those two news items, the other big news this week is the change in commission reporting. I'll go into the details in minute, but when you log onto the intranet, you'll now see your sales results split out by product line and industry sector. Hope this helps you see where you're doing well and where you might beef things up a bit. Oh yeah, I almost forgot the most important bit. Speaking of our beloved CEO, Thomas is going to be our guest of honor, so to speak, at the quarterly sales meeting next week and wants an update on how petroleum prices are affecting customer behavior. Each district manager should be ready with a brief report. After I go through the commission reporting scheme, I'll outline what you need to prepare.

Expand Your Knowledge

LEARNING MORE ON THE WEB
READY TO START BLOGGING?

Blogging is easy to do if you have the right information. Start with the helpful tutorials at www.website101.com/RSS-Blogs-Blogging. More than 30 brief articles cover everything from creating a blog to attracting more readers to setting up RSS newsfeeds. Learn the techniques for adding audio and photo files to your blog. Review how search engines treat blogs and how you can use search engines to help more people find your blog. Then answer the following questions.

1. What are five ways to attract more readers to your blog?
2. Why are blogs good for marketing?
3. What is a newsfeed and why is it a vital part of blogging?

SURFING YOUR WAY TO CAREER SUCCESS

Bovée and Thill's Business Communication Resources for Students offers links to hundreds of online resources that can help you with this course, your other college courses, and your career. Visit www.buscommresources.com and click on "Web Directory." The "Letters, Memos, E-Mail, Instant Messages, Blogs, and Web Content" section connects you to a variety of websites and articles on routine, positive, and negative messages; persuasive messages; letters and memos; e-mail; IM; blogging; and web writing. Identify three websites from this section that could be useful in your business career. For each site, write a two-sentence summary of what the site offers and how it could help you launch and build your career.

Learn Interactively

INTERACTIVE STUDY GUIDE

Visit www.prenhall.com/thill, then locate your book and click on its "Companion Website" link. Select Chapter 7 to take advantage of the interactive "Chapter Quiz" to test your knowledge of chapter concepts. Receive instant feedback on whether you need additional studying. Also, visit the "Study Hall," where you'll find an abundance of valuable resources that will help you succeed in this course.

PEAK PERFORMANCE GRAMMAR AND MECHANICS

If your instructor has required the use of "Peak Performance Grammar and Mechanics," either in your online course or on CD, you can continue to improve your skill with prepositions, conjunctions, and articles by using the "Peak Performance Grammar and Mechanics" module. Click on "Grammar Basics" and then click on "Prepositions, Conjunctions, and Articles." Take the Pretest to determine whether you have any weak areas. Then review those areas in the Refresher Course. Take the Follow-Up Test to check your grasp of prepositions, conjunctions, and articles. For an extra challenge or advanced practice, take the Advanced Test. Finally, for additional reinforcement, go to the "Improve Your Grammar, Mechanics, and Usage" section that follows and complete those exercises.

Improve Your Grammar, Mechanics, and Usage

The following exercises help you improve your knowledge of and power over English grammar, mechanics, and usage. Turn to the Handbook of Grammar, Mechanics, and Usage at the end of this book and review Section 1.6.1 (Prepositions), Section 1.6.2 (Conjunctions), and Section 1.6.3 (Articles and Interjections). Then look at the following 10 items. Circle the letter of the preferred choice in the following groups of sentences. (Answers to these exercises appear on page AK-3.)

1. a. The response was not only inappropriate but it was also rude.
   b. The response was not only inappropriate but also rude.
2. a. Be sure to look the spelling up in the dictionary.
   b. Be sure to look up the spelling in the dictionary.

3. a. We didn't get the contract because our proposal didn't comply with the RFP.
   b. We didn't get the contract because our proposal didn't comply to the RFP.
4. a. Marissa should of known not to send that e-mail to the CEO.
   b. Marissa should have known not to send that e-mail to the CEO.
5. a. The Phalanx 1000 has been favorably compared to the Mac iBook.
   b. The Phalanx 1000 has been favorably compared with the Mac iBook.
6. a. What are you looking for?
   b. For what are you looking?

7. a. Have you filed an SEC application?
   b. Have you filed a SEC application?
8. a. The project turned out neither to be easy nor simple.
   b. The project turned out to be neither easy nor simple.
9. a. If you hire me, you will not regret your decision!
   b. If you hire me, you will not regret your decision.
10. a. This is truly an historic event.
    b. This is truly a historic event.

For additional exercises focusing on conjunctions, articles, and prepositions, go to www.prenhall.com/thill, then locate your text and click on its "Companion Website" link. Click on Chapter 7, click on "Additional Exercises to Improve Your Grammar, Mechanics, and Usage," and click on "11. Conjunctions, Articles, and Interjections."

Cases

Applying the Three-Step Writing Process to Cases
Apply each step to the following cases, as assigned by your instructor.

Planning

Analyze the Situation
Identify both your general purpose and your specific purpose. Clarify exactly what you want your audience to think, feel, or believe after receiving your message. Profile your primary audience, including their backgrounds, differences, similarities, and likely reactions to your message.

Gather Information
Identify the information your audience will need to receive, as well as other information you may need in order to craft an effective message.

Select the Right Medium
The medium is identified for each case here, but when on the job, make sure your medium is both acceptable to the audience and appropriate for the message.

Organize the Information
Define your main idea, limit your scope, choose a direct or indirect approach, and outline necessary support points and other evidence.

Writing

Adapt to Your Audience
Show sensitivity to audience needs with a "you" attitude, politeness, positive emphasis, and bias-free language. Understand how much credibility you already have—and how much you may need to establish. Project your company's image by maintaining an appropriate style and tone. Consider cultural variations and the differing needs of internal and external audiences.

Compose the Message
For written messages, draft your message using clear but sensitive words, effective sentences, and coherent paragraphs. For podcasts, outline your message and draft speaking notes to ensure smooth recording; use plenty of previews, transitions, and review to help audiences follow along.

Completing

Revise the Message
Evaluate content and review readability, then edit and rewrite for conciseness and clarity.

Produce the Message
For written messages, use effective design elements and suitable layout for a clean, professional appearance. For podcasts, record your messages using whatever equipment you have available (professional podcasts may require upgraded equipment).

Proofread the Message
Review for errors in layout, spelling, and mechanics. Listen to podcasts to check for recording problems.

Distribute the Message
Deliver your message using the chosen medium; make sure all documents and all relevant files are distributed successfully.

1   **2**   **3**

Blogging SKILLS

1. Selling without selling: Blog posting about a GPS rescue Promoting products through customer success stories can be a great marketing tactic, as long as you keep the customer as the "star" of the story and don't promote the product too blatantly. You've recently joined Garmin, a leading manufacturer of electronic navigation equipment, including a popular line of handheld global positioning system (GPS) devices used by hikers, kayakers, and others who venture off the beaten path.

Your task: As a communication specialist, your responsibilities include writing blog postings that highlight dramatic stories in which people used Garmin GPS units to rescue themselves or others from potentially dangerous situations. Visit Garmin's website, at www.garmin.com, click on "Company," "What's New" and then "GPS Adventures" (or access the page directly at www.garmin.com/whatsNew/adventures.html). Select a customer story that involves a wilderness rescue in which a Garmin product played an important role. Using the information provided by the customer, rewrite the story in the third person (changing "I" or "we" references to "he," "she," or "they") for an audience that isn't familiar with the product in question. Subtly work in references to the product and the benefits it provided in this scenario, but keep the focus on the customer. Limit yourself to 400 words.

Blogging SKILLS

2. Come on to Comic-Con: Explaining the benefits of attending Comic-Con International is an annual convention that highlights a wide variety of pop culture and entertainment media, from comic books and collectibles to video games and movies. From its early start as a comic book convention that attracted several hundred fans and publishing industry insiders, Comic-Con has become a major international event with more than 100,000 attendees.

Your task: Several readers of your pop culture blog have been asking for your recommendation about visiting Comic-Con in San Diego next summer. Write a two- or three-paragraph posting for your blog that explains what Comic-Con is and what visitors can expect to experience at the convention. Be sure to address your posting to fans, not industry insiders. You can learn more at www.comic-con.org.[36]

E-Mail SKILLS

3. Keeping the fans happy: Analyzing advertising on ESPN.com ESPN leads the pack both online and off. Its well-known cable television sports channels are staple fare for sports enthusiasts, and ESPN.com (http://espn.go.com) is the leader in sports websites, too. Advertisers flock to ESPN.com because it delivers millions of visitors in the prime 18- to 34-year-old demographic group. With a continually refreshed offering of sporting news, columnists, video replays, and fantasy leagues (online competitions in which participants choose players for their teams, and the outcome is based on how well the real players do in actual live competition), ESPN.com has become one of the major advertising venues on the web.

As an up-and-coming web producer for ESPN.com, you're concerned about the rumblings of discontent you've heard from friends and read in various blogs and other sources. ESPN.com remains popular with millions of sports fans, but some say they are getting tired of all the ads—both ads on the site itself and pop-up ads. A few say they are switching to other websites with fewer advertising intrusions. Your site traffic numbers are holding fairly steady for now, but you're worried that the few visitors leaving ESPN.com might be the start of a significant exodus in the future.

Your task: Write an e-mail message to your manager, expressing your concern about the amount of advertising content on ESPN.com. Acknowledge that advertising is a vital source of revenue, but share what you've learned about site visitors who claim to be migrating to other sites. Offer to lead a comprehensive review effort that will compare the advertising presence on ESPN.com with that of other sports websites and explore ways to maintain strong advertising sales without alienating readers.[37]

4. That's not the way things really are: Correcting economic misinformation As the CEO of a small manufacturing company, your interests and responsibilities range far beyond the four walls of the factory. You have to be in tune with the global economy, politics, taxation policies, and other external forces that affect your company and your employees. Along with your peers in other companies, you've learned to speak out on issues—particularly when you believe that misguided government policies or misinformed public opinions threaten the viability of your company, your industry, and the economy as a whole.

An item in this morning's newspaper certainly got your attention. A prominent national political leader claimed that job-growth figures in recent years prove that the government's economic policies are working. The economy is in reasonably good shape, considering the battering it has taken in recent years, but you believe the situation would improve considerably if the government would address a variety of issues, from health-care costs to economic incentives for investing in manufacturing upgrades. Moreover, you know that the politician's claim about job growth is only partly true. Yes, the U.S. economy added nearly 2 million new jobs in the past five years, but a recent *BusinessWeek* article pointed out that virtually all those jobs were in health care. Not only did all other industries not add jobs as a whole, but the dramatic rise in health-care employment suggests no end to the rise in health-care costs.

Your task: Write a brief letter (no more than 300 words) to the editor of the newspaper. Correct the impression that job growth is occurring throughout the economy and encourage political leaders to address problems that you believe continue to limit growth in other industries, including health-care costs, taxation policies in the manufacturing sector, and unfair competitive practices from companies in certain other countries. Make up whatever information you need to back up your claims.[38]

E-Mail SKILLS

5. Must be an opportunity in here somewhere: The growing market of women living without husbands For the first time in history (aside from special situations such as major wars), more than half—51 percent—of all U.S. adult women now live without a spouse. (In other words, they live alone, with roommates, or as part of an unmarried couple.) Twenty-five percent have never married, and 26 percent are divorced, widowed, or married but living apart from their spouses. In the 1950s and into the 1960s, only 40 percent of women lived without a spouse, but every decade since, the percentage has increased. In your work as a consumer trend specialist for Seymour Powell (www.seymourpowell.com), a product design firm based in London that specializes in the home, personal, leisure, and transportation sectors, it's your business to recognize and respond to demographic shifts such as this.

Your task: With a small team of classmates, brainstorm possible product opportunities that respond to this trend. In an e-mail to be sent to the management team at Seymour Powell, list your ideas for new or modified products that might sell well in a society in which more than half of all adult women live without a spouse. For each idea, provide a one-sentence explanation of why you think the product has potential.[39]

E-Mail SKILLS | Portfolio BUILDER

6. Help is on the way: Encouraging Ford dealers The "Big Three" U.S. automakers—General Motors, Chrysler, and Ford—haven't had much good news to share lately. Ford, in particular, has been going through a rough time, losing billions of dollars and being overtaken in sales volume by Toyota.

Your task: Write an e-mail to be sent to all Ford dealers in North America, describing an exciting new model about to be introduced to the public. For this exercise, you can use either an upcoming Ford model you have researched in the automotive media or a fictitious car of your own imagination (make sure it's something that could conceivably be introduced by Ford).[40]

Blogging SKILLS

7. Legitimate and legal: Defending technology sales to Chinese police agencies Cisco, a leading manufacturer of computer networking equipment, is one of several technology companies that have been criticized recently for selling high-tech equipment to police agencies in China. After the Chinese government killed hundreds of protestors in Tiananmen Square in 1989, U.S. officials began restricting the export of products that could be used by Chinese security forces. The restrictions cover a range of low-tech devices, from helmets and handcuffs to fingerprint powder and teargas, but not certain high-tech products, such as the networking equipment that Cisco sells, which can conceivably be used by security forces in ways that violate human rights. Critics contend that

by not restricting products such as Cisco's, the U.S. government is not enforcing the full intent of the restrictions. Moreover, they suggest that Cisco could be enabling abuse. For example, its Chinese marketing brochure promotes the equipment's ability to "strengthen police control."

Your task: Write a brief post for the Cisco executive blog that explains the following points: The company rigorously follows all U.S. export regulations; the company's marketing efforts in China are consistent with the way it markets products to other police organizations throughout the world; the products are simply tools, and like all other tools, they can be applied in good or bad ways, and responsible application is the customer's responsibility, not Cisco's; if Cisco didn't sell this equipment to the Chinese government, another company from another country would.[41]

IM SKILLS

8. The very definition of confusion: Helping consumers sort out high-definition television High-definition television can be a joy to watch—but, oh, what a pain to buy. The field is littered with competing technologies and arcane terminology that is meaningless to most consumers. Moreover, it's nearly impossible to define one technical term without invoking two or three others, leaving consumers swimming in an alphanumeric soup of confusion. The manufacturers themselves can't even agree on which of the *18* different digital TV formats truly qualify as "high definition." As a sales support manager for Crutchfield (www.crutchfield.com), a leading online retailer of audio and video systems, you understand the frustration buyers feel; your staff is deluged daily by their questions.

Your task: To help your staff respond quickly to consumers who ask questions via Crutchfield's online IM chat service, you are developing a set of "canned" responses to common questions. When a consumer asks one of these questions, a sales advisor can simply click on the ready-made answer. Start by writing concise, consumer-friendly definitions of the following terms: *resolution*, *HDTV*, *1080p*, and *HDMI*. (Visit Crutchfield's educational site, www.crutchfieldadvisor.com, and click on "Learn About Home Theater & A/V" to learn more about these terms. Answers.com and CNET.com are two other handy sources.)[42]

Podcasting SKILLS | Portfolio BUILDER

9. Based on my experience: Recommending your college or university With any purchase decision, from a restaurant meal to a college education, recommendations from satisfied customers are often the strongest promotional messages.

Your task: Write a script for a one- to two-minute podcast (roughly 150 to 250 words) explaining why your college or university is a good place to get an education. Your audience is high school juniors and seniors. You can choose to craft a general message, something that would be useful to all prospective students, or you can focus on a specific academic discipline, the athletic program, or some other important aspect of your college experience. Either way, make sure your introductory comments make it clear whether you are offering a general recommendation or a specific recommendation. If your instructor asks you to do so, record the podcast and submit the file electronically.

Podcasting SKILLS

10. Based on my experience: Suggestions for improving your college or university Every organization, no matter how successfully it operates, can find ways to improve customer service.

Your task: Write a script for a one- to two-minute podcast (roughly 150 to 250 words) identifying at least one way in which your college experience could have been or still could be improved through specific changes in policies, programs, facilities, or other elements. Your audience is the school's administration. Offer constructive criticism and specific arguments why your suggestions would help you—and possibly other students as well. Be sure to focus on meaningful and practical opportunities for improvement. If your instructor asks you to do so, record the podcast and submit the file electronically.

Blogging SKILLS

11. Look sharp: Travel safety tips for new employees As the travel director for a global management consulting firm, your responsibilities range from finding the best travel deals to helping new employees learn the ins and outs of low-risk, low-stress travels. One of the ways in which you dispense helpful advice is through an internal blog.

Your task: Research advice for safe travel and identify at least six tips that every employee in your company should know. Write a brief blog posting that introduces and identifies the six tips.

E-Mail SKILLS

12. Your work does matter: Encouraging an unhappy colleague You certainly appreciate your company's "virtual team" policy of letting employees live wherever they want while using technology to communicate and collaborate. The company is headquartered in a large urban area, but you get to live in the mountains, only a step or two away from some of the best fly fishing in the world. Most of the time, this approach to work couldn't get any better.

However, the lack of face-to-face contact with your colleagues definitely has disadvantages. For example, when a teammate seems to be upset about something, you wish you could go for a walk with the person and talk it out rather than relying on phone calls, e-mail, or IM. In the past couple weeks, Chris Grogan, the graphic designer working with you on a new e-commerce website project, seems to be complaining about everything. His negative attitude is starting to wear down the team's enthusiasm at a critical point in the project. In particular, he has complained several times that no one on the

team seems to care about his design work. It is rarely mentioned in team teleconferences, and no one asks him about it. That part is true, actually, but the reason is that there is nothing wrong with his work—some critical technical issues unrelated to the graphic design are consuming everyone's attention.

Your task: After a couple unsuccessful attempts at encouraging Grogan over the phone, you decide to write a brief e-mail message to assure him of the importance of his work on this project and the quality of his efforts. Let him know that graphic design is a critical part of the project's success and that as soon as those technical issues are resolved and the project is completed, everyone will have a chance to appreciate his contribution to the project. Make up whatever details you need to craft your message.

E-Mail SKILLS

13. She's one of us: Promoting a new lifestyle magazine Consumers looking for beauty, health, and lifestyle magazines have an almost endless array of choices, but even in this crowded field, Logan Olson found her own niche. Olson, who was born with congenital heart disease, suffered a heart attack at age 16 that left her in a coma and caused serious brain damage. The active and outgoing teen had to relearn everything from sitting up to feeding herself. As she recovered, she looked for help and advice in conquering such daily challenges as finding fashionable clothes that were easier to put on and makeup that was easier to apply. Mainstream beauty magazines didn't seem to offer any information for young women with disabilities, so she started her own magazine. Oprah Winfrey has *Oprah*, and now Logan Olson has *Logan*. The magazine not only gives young women tips on buying and using a variety of products but lets women with disabilities know there are others out there like them, facing and meeting the same challenges.

Your task: Write a promotional e-mail message to be sent to young women with disabilities as well as families and friends who might like to give gift subscriptions, promoting the benefits of subscribing to *Logan*. You can learn more about *Logan* at www.loganmagazine.com.[43]

E-Mail SKILLS | Portfolio BUILDER

14. We're the one: Explaining why a company should hire your firm You work for Brainbench (www.brainbench.com), one of many companies that offer employee screening services. Brainbench's offerings include a variety of online products and consulting services, all designed to help employers find and develop the best possible employees. For example, Brainbench's Pre-Hire Testing products help employers test for job skills, communication skills, personality, and employment history red flags (such as chronic absenteeism or performance problems). Employers use these test results to either screen out candidates entirely or ask focused interview questions about areas of concern.

Sonja Williamson, the human resources director of a large retail company, has just e-mailed your sales team. She would like an overview of the Pre-Hire Testing products and some background on your company.

Your task: Write an e-mail response to Williamson's query. Be sure to thank her for her interest, briefly describe the Pre-Hire Testing products, and summarize Brainbench's qualifications. Include at least one hyperlink to the Brainbench website and consider attaching one or more PDF files from the website as well.

E-Mail SKILLS

15. Firing the customer: When a particular customer is always wrong Many companies operate on the principle that the customer is always right, even when the customer *isn't* right. They take any steps necessary to ensure happy customers, lots of repeat sales, and a positive reputation among potential buyers. Overall, this is a smart and successful approach to business. However, most companies eventually encounter that one nightmare customer who drains so much time, energy, and profits that the only sensible option is to refuse the customer's business. For example, the nightmare customer might be someone who constantly berates you and your employees, repeatedly makes outlandish demands for refunds and discounts, or simply requires so much help that you not only lose money on this person but you also no longer have enough time to help your other customers. "Firing" a customer is an unpleasant step that should be taken only in the most extreme cases and only after other remedies have been attempted (such as talking with the customer about the problem), but it is sometimes necessary for the well-being of your employees and your company.

Your task: If you are currently working or have held a job in the recent past, imagine that you've encountered just such a customer. If you don't have job experience to call on, imagine that you work in a retail location somewhere around campus or in your neighborhood. Identify the type of behavior this imaginary customer exhibits and the reasons the behavior can no longer be accepted. Write a brief e-mail message to the customer to explain that you will no longer be able to accommodate him or her as a customer. Calmly explain why you have had to reach this difficult decision. Maintain a professional tone by keeping your emotions in check.

Podcasting SKILLS

16. Podcasting pitch: Training people to sell your favorite product What product do you own (or use regularly) that you can't live without? It could be something as seemingly minor as a favorite pen or something as significant as a medical device that you literally can't live without. Now imagine you're a salesperson for this product; think about how you would sell it to potential buyers. How would you describe it and how would you explain the benefits of owning it? After you've thought about how you would present the product to others, imagine that you've been promoted to sales manager, and it is your job to train other people to sell the product.

Your task: Write the script for a brief podcast (200 to 300 words) that summarizes for your sales staff the most important points to convey about the product. Imagine that they'll listen to your podcast while driving to a customer's location or preparing for the day's activity in a retail store (depending on the nature of the product). Be sure to give your staffers a concise overview message about the product and several key support points.

E-Mail SKILLS

17. Time to think: E-mail requesting a change in your workload The description of your job as a global marketing manager for New Balance is full of responsibilities that require creative thinking, from predicting consumer and retailing trends to establishing seasonal priorities for the global merchandising effort. You love these challenges—in fact, they're the main reason you took the job at this respected maker of athletic shoes and apparel. Unfortunately, between department meetings, status reports, budgets, and an endless array of other required chores, you hardly have time to think at all, much less engage in the sort of unstructured, "blue sky" thinking that is crucial to creative strategizing. You have virtually no time at work for such thinking, and after 50 or 60 hours a week at the office or on the road, you're too exhausted to brainstorm on your own time.

Your task: Write an e-mail to your boss, Paul Heffernan, the executive vice president of global marketing, persuading him that you need to reshuffle your assignments to free up more time to think. This is a tricky request because you know that Heffernan faces the same challenge. However, you're convinced that by spending less time on tasks that could be done by someone else (or perhaps shouldn't be done at all), you'll be able to do a better job of creating marketing strategies—and maybe even set a good example for other New Balance executives. You have a preliminary list of changes you'd like to make, but you know you need to discuss the entire scope of your job with Heffernan before finalizing the list. Your purpose: Invite him to lunch to begin a discussion of reshaping your responsibilities.[44]

E-Mail SKILLS

18. Mercedes merchandise: Message announcing exclusive online gift shop Mercedes-Benz owners take their accessories seriously, which is why you get angry letters and e-mails when they buy Mercedes-branded merchandise that turns out to be fake. Even though your company has nothing to do with these low-quality, unauthorized knock-offs, customers sometimes blame you anyway. To battle the problem, Mercedes has opened an online store where every item comes with a certificate of authenticity that it was manufactured by a Mercedes-approved partner and meets Mercedes quality standards. At **www.mbusi.com**, the website for the Mercedes-Benz manufacturing plant in Tuscaloosa, Alabama, shoppers can follow the "Store" link to the online gift shop. But first they need to know it exists.

Your task: As assistant for Steve Beaty, vice president of accessories marketing, draft an e-mail message to registered Mercedes owners, telling them about the online gift shop. Visit the website to learn more about it and then write the message using a style you think suits the car manufacturer's image.

▌Team
▌SKILLS

19. Measuring suppliers: E-mail requesting reviews at Microsoft Microsoft evaluates employees regularly to determine their performance; why not do the same with the independent contractors the company hires to perform key functions? Nearly every department uses outside providers these days—a practice called *outsourcing*. So if there's a gap between what Microsoft expects from contractors and what the contractors actually deliver, shouldn't Microsoft tell them how they can improve their performance?

You've been discussing these questions all morning in a meeting with other members of the Employee Services Group. Your boss is convinced that regular reviews of independent contractors are essential.

"It's all about improving clarity in terms of goals and expectations," he says, adding that if contractors receive constructive feedback, Microsoft can develop good relationships with them instead of having to look for new service suppliers all the time.

Your boss assigns your team the task of informing all Microsoft departments that they'll be required to evaluate subcontractors every six months, beginning immediately. The goal of the review is to determine the performance of independent contractors so that Microsoft can (1) give them constructive feedback and continue a strong relationship or (2) end the relationship if service is substandard. Departments will need to rate each contractor on a scale of 1 (poor) to 5 (excellent) for each of several factors that your group is going to determine. Departments will be sending their reports to Roxanna Frost, group program manager for Microsoft's Executive Management and Development Group.

Your task: Working as a team with your classmates, develop a list of factors that will help you rate the overall service of independent contractors. You'll need to consider cost, quality of work, innovation, delivery, and other factors similar to those you'd encounter in a job performance review. Then compose an e-mail to all Microsoft department managers: Explain the new review requirements and include your list of factors to be rated on the 1-to-5 scale.[45]

▌IM
▌SKILLS

20. Yes, we do purple: Instant message from Lands' End When clothing retailer Lands' End offered its 2,500 telephone service representatives the chance to train on its new instant messaging system, "Lands' End Live," you jumped at the opportunity. As it turned out, so many volunteered for the new training that the company had to give preference to a few hundred who'd been on the job longest. You were one of the lucky ones.

Now you've had months of practice answering messages like the one you just received from a customer named Alicia. She wants to know if she can have a red Polartec Aircore-200 Scarf custom monogrammed—not in the standard, contrasting, wheat-colored thread, but in radiant purple—as a gift for her husband, whose favorite colors are red and purple.

On its website, Lands' End promises to fulfill nonstandard monogram requests "if technical limitations allow." You've done a quick check and, yes, her husband can have his initials in bright purple on the red background.

Your task: Write the instant message reply to Alicia, telling her the good news.[46]

▌E-Mail
▌SKILLS

21. No exaggeration: Short e-mail describing internship duties You've been laboring all summer at an internship, learning how business is conducted. You've done work nobody else wanted to do, but that's okay. Even the smallest tasks can make a good impression on your future résumé.

This morning, your supervisor asks you to write a description of the job you've been doing. "Include everything, even the filing," she suggests, "and address it to me in an e-mail message." She says a future boss might assign such a task prior to a performance review. "You can practice describing your work without exaggeration—or too much modesty," she says, smiling.

Your task: Using good techniques for short messages and relying on your real-life work experience, write an e-mail that will impress your supervisor. Make up any details you need.

▌Blogging
▌SKILLS

22. Meet the parents: Blog posting announcing the acquisition of Golden West As the human resources director for Golden West Financial, you know how proud your fellow employees are to work for one of the most admired banking companies in the United States. Golden West, which serves retail customers through its World Savings Bank branches across the West, was founded in Oakland, California, in the 1960s by the husband-and-wife team of Herbert and Marion Sandler. For decades, Golden West flourished as an independent company, but in 2006, the Sandlers decided to sell Golden West to Wachovia, a financial giant based in Charlotte, North Carolina.

Over the coming weeks, you'll provide Golden West employees with more information about the impact of the huge deal, but for now, you want them to be aware of four key points:

- The deal allows Golden West to expand beyond its core offering of home mortgages to provide other financial services that its customers have requested for some time.

- The Sandlers carefully selected Wachovia because of its compatible values of integrity, customer-first business practices, and teamwork.

- World Savings Bank operations will continue from existing locations under the existing World Savings Bank brand name. New financial services from Wachovia will be added over time.

- The company's commitment to providing excellent career opportunities for women and minorities will not change.[47]

Your task: Write a short posting for Golden West's internal blog, announcing the deal and communicating the four aforementioned key points listed (in your own words). Close by telling your colleagues how excited you are about the deal and that you'll be providing more information in the day and weeks ahead.

E-Mail SKILLS

23. Environmental planning: E-mail announcing a committee meeting You've probably worked as a volunteer on a committee or with team members for class assignments. You know how hard it is to get a diverse group of individuals together for a productive meeting. Maybe you've tried different locations—one member's home or a table at the library. This time you're going to suggest a local restaurant.

The committee you're leading is a volunteer group planning a trash-clearing project at an area park. Your meeting goal is to brainstorm ways to encourage public participation in this environmental event, to be held next Earth Day.

Your task: Develop a short e-mail message telling committee members about the meeting. Include time, date, duration, and location (choose a place you know). Mention the meeting goal to encourage attendance.

Podcasting SKILLS

24. Why me? Introducing yourself to a potential employer While writing the many letters and e-mail messages that are part of the job search process, you find yourself wishing that you could just talk to some of these companies so your personality could shine through. Well, you've just gotten that opportunity. One of the companies that you've applied to has e-mailed you back, asking you to submit a two-minute podcast introducing yourself and explaining why you would be a good person to hire.

Your task: Identify a company that you'd like to work for after graduation and select a job that would be a good match for your skills and interests. Write a script for a two-minute podcast (two minutes represents roughly 250 words for most speakers). Introduce yourself and the position you're applying for, describe your background, and explain why you think you're a good candidate for the job. Make up any details you need. If your instructor asks you to do so, record the podcast and submit the file.

25. "Hi, my name is . . .": Introducing yourself on a business network Business networking websites such as www.linkedin.com, www.ryze.com, and www.spoke.com have become popular places for professionals to make connections that would be difficult or impossible to make without the Internet. (You might be familiar with MySpace.com or Friendster.com, sites that help individuals meet through networks of people they already know and trust.) These business-oriented sites follow the same principle, but instead of using them to find new friends or dates, you use them to find new customers, new suppliers, or other important business connections. For instance, you might find that the ideal contact person in a company you'd like to do business with is the aunt of your boss's tennis partner.

An important aspect of business networking is being able to provide a clear description of your professional background and interests. For example, a manufacturing consultant can list the industries in which she has experience, the types of projects she has worked on, and the nature of work she'd like to pursue in the future (such as a full-time position for a company or additional independent projects).

Your task: Write a brief statement introducing yourself, including your educational background, your job history, and the types of connections you'd like to make. Feel free to "fast forward" to your graduation and list your degree, the business specialty you plan to pursue, and any relevant experience. If you have business experience already, feel free to use that information instead. Make sure your statement is clear, concise (no more than two sentences), and compelling so that anyone looking for someone like you would want to get in touch with you after reading your introduction.

Chapter 8

Writing Routine and Positive Messages

Learning Objectives

AFTER STUDYING THIS CHAPTER, YOU WILL BE ABLE TO

1 Apply the three-step writing process to routine and positive messages

2 Outline an effective strategy for writing routine requests

3 Explain how to ask for specific action in a courteous manner

4 Describe a strategy for writing routine replies and positive messages

5 Discuss the importance of knowing who is responsible when granting claims and requests for adjustment

6 Explain how creating informative messages differs from responding to information requests

7 Describe the importance of goodwill messages and explain how to make them effective

On the Job

COMMUNICATING AT CONE, INC.

USING POSITIVE MESSAGES TO POSITIVELY AFFECT THE LIVES OF HUNGRY CHILDREN

Considering the number of corporate scandals in recent years, it's easy to forget that thousands of companies continue to conduct business ethically and work to make significant contributions in their communities. Ready to assist them in their efforts to help others is Carol Cone of Cone, Inc., a Boston-based agency that specializes in *cause branding*, linking corporate brands to socially beneficial programs.

One of Cone's biggest success stories has been publicizing the efforts of ConAgra Foods, which took up the cause of child hunger in the United States through its

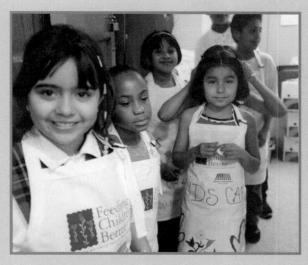

ConAgra's Feeding Children Better program supports thousands of children every year, and the company's public relations agency uses these successes to focus nationwide attention on the problems of childhood hunger.

Feeding Children Better program. A centerpiece of those efforts is Kids Cafés, an after-school program that serves free, hot, nutritious meals to kids in need. Since it became the national sponsor of Kids Cafés, ConAgra has funded 150 new Kids Cafés, each one providing more than 10,000 meals per year. ConAgra also aids in the battle against childhood hunger by helping to improve the distribution of donated food nationwide.

Cone focuses news releases, web content, and other messages on the three main goals of the program: (1) getting food to children who need it, (2) repairing breakdowns in food distribution, and (3) raising national awareness about child hunger. ConAgra and Cone have received numerous awards for their good work and effective communication, such as the Corporate Citizenship Award from the U.S. Chamber of Commerce and the Cause Marketing Halo Award.

What makes Cone's messages so effective? Simply calling attention to ConAgra's good deeds would be a positive business result, but doing so would primarily benefit ConAgra, not the various hunger relief programs. Instead, Cone puts her news releases to work by highlighting ConAgra's progress toward the goal of eradicating childhood hunger, thereby helping her client accomplish even more positive outcomes through the use of positive messages.[1]

www.coneinc.com

USING THE THREE-STEP WRITING PROCESS FOR ROUTINE AND POSITIVE MESSAGES

Regardless of the subject matter of your business messages, you can make them more effective by following the example of Carol Cone (profiled in the chapter opener) to stay focused on your business goals and to emphasize the audience's concerns. Like Cone, you'll be composing numerous routine and positive messages during the typical business day. In fact, most business communication is about routine matters: customer orders, company policies, employees, products, operations, and so on. The three-step writing process gives you a great way to produce these messages effectively and efficiently.

Step 1: Plan Your Message

Even simple, routine messages can benefit from thoughtful planning.

Even though planning routine and positive messages may take only a few minutes, the four tasks of planning still apply. First, analyze the situation, making sure that your purpose is clear and that you know enough about your audience to craft a successful message. Second, gather the information your audience needs to know. Including all necessary information the first time saves you and your audience the trouble of follow-up messages to fill in the gaps. Third, select the right medium for the message and the audience. Fourth, organize your information effectively. This task includes defining your main idea, limiting your scope, selecting a direct or an indirect approach, and outlining your content. Throughout this chapter, you'll learn more about performing all four of these tasks for a variety of routine and positive message types.

Step 2: Write Your Message

With all messages, you need to adapt to your audience by being sensitive to their needs: Maintain the "you" attitude, be polite, emphasize the positive, and use bias-free language. To strengthen your relationship with your audience, establish your credibility and project your company's image. And keep in mind that even if you normally use a conversational tone, some messages may need to be more formal than others. Finally, use plain English and try to use the active voice as much as possible.

With some practice, You'll be able to compose most routine messages quickly. Your main idea is probably well defined already; just be sure you stick to it by limiting the scope of your message (see Figure 8.1).

For routine requests and positive messages
- *Open by stating the request or main idea*
- *Give necessary details in the body*
- *Close with a cordial request for specific action*

In most cases, your readers will be interested or at least neutral, so you can usually adopt the direct approach for routine and positive messages: Open with a clear statement of the main idea, include all necessary details in the body, and then close cordially. Keep in mind that even though these messages are the least complicated to write, communicating across cultural boundaries can be a challenge, especially if you're not familiar with the cultural differences involved.

Step 3: Complete Your Message

No matter how brief or straightforward your message, maximize its impact by giving yourself plenty of time to revise, produce, proofread, and distribute it. First, revise your message by evaluating content and organization to make sure you've said what you want to in the order you want to say it. Review your message's readability. Edit and rewrite to make it concise and clear. Second, design your document to suit your purpose and your audience. Even simple messages can benefit from careful font selection, the wise use of white space, and other design choices. Next, proofread the

FIGURE 8.1
Routine Messages
Routine and positive messages
are best conveyed using a direct
approach. Google uses this blog
to keep users of its AdWords
search engine advertising system
up to date on maintenance
interruptions and other important
news.

final version of your message, looking for typos, errors in spelling and mechanics, alignment problems, poor print quality, and so on. Finally, choose a distribution method that balances cost, convenience, time, security, and privacy. Refer to Chapter 7 for the most common media formats for brief messages.

MAKING ROUTINE REQUESTS

Making requests—for information, action, products, adjustments, or other matters— is a routine part of business. In most cases, your audience will be prepared to comply, as long as you're not being unreasonable or asking people to do something they would expect you to do yourself. By applying a clear strategy and tailoring your approach to each situation, you'll be able to generate effective requests quickly.

Strategy for Routine Requests

Like all other business messages, routine requests have three parts: an opening, a body, and a close. Using the direct approach, open with your main idea, which is a clear statement of your request. Use the body to give details and justify your request. Finally, close by requesting specific action.

Take care that your direct approach doesn't come across as abrupt or tactless.

State Your Request Up Front   Begin routine requests by placing your request first; up front is where it stands out and gets the most attention. Of course, getting right to the point should not be interpreted as a license to be abrupt or tactless:

- **Pay attention to tone.** Even though you expect a favorable response, the tone of your initial request is important. Instead of demanding action ("Send me the latest personnel cost data"), soften your request with words such as *please* and *I would appreciate*.

- **Assume that your audience will comply.** An impatient demand for rapid service isn't necessary. You can generally make the assumption that your audience will comply with your request once the reason for it is clearly understood.

- **Be specific.** State precisely what you want. For example, if you request the latest market data from your research department, be sure to say whether you want a one page summary or 100 pages of raw data.

Explain and Justify Your Request   Use the body of your message to explain your initial request. Make the explanation a smooth and logical outgrowth of your opening remarks. If possible, point out how complying with the request could benefit the reader. For instance, if you would like some assistance interpreting complex quality-control data, you might point out how a better understanding of quality-control issues would improve customer satisfaction and ultimately lead to higher profits for the entire company.

Using a list format helps readers sort through multiple questions or requests.

Whether you're writing a formal letter or a simple instant message, you can use the body of your request to list a series of questions. This list of questions helps organize your message and helps your audience identify the information you need. Just keep in mind a few basics:

- **Ask the most important questions first.** If cost is your main concern, you might begin with a question such as "What is the cost for shipping the merchandise by air versus truck?" Then you might want to ask more specific but related questions about, say, discounts for paying early.

- **Ask only relevant questions.** To help expedite the response to your request, ask only questions that are central to your main request. Doing so will generate an answer sooner and make better use of the other person's time.

- **Deal with only one topic per question.** If you have an unusual or complex request, break it down into specific, individual questions so that the reader can address each one separately. Don't put the burden of untangling a complicated request on your reader. This consideration not only shows respect for your audience's time but also gets you a more accurate answer in less time.

Close request messages with
- A request for some specific action
- Information about how you can be reached
- An expression of appreciation

Request Specific Action in a Courteous Close   Close your message with three important elements: (1) a specific request, (2) information about how you can be reached (if it isn't obvious), and (3) an expression of appreciation or goodwill. When you ask readers to perform a specific action, ask that they respond by a specific time, if appropriate (for example, "Please send the figures by April 5 so that I can return first-quarter results to you before the May 20 conference."). Plus, by including your phone number, e-mail address, office hours, and other contact information, you help your readers respond easily.

Conclude your message by sincerely expressing your goodwill and appreciation. However, don't thank the reader "in advance" for cooperating. If the reader's reply warrants a word of thanks, send it after you've received the reply. To review, see "Checklist: Writing Routine Requests."

✓ CHECKLIST: Writing Routine Requests

A. State your request up front.

✓ Write in a polite, undemanding, personal tone.
✓ Use the direct approach because your audience will probably respond favorably to your request.
✓ Be specific and precise in your request.

B. Explain and justify your request.

✓ Justify the request or explain its importance.
✓ Explain any potential benefits of responding.
✓ Ask the most important questions first.

✓ Break complex requests into individual questions that are limited to only one topic each.

C. Request specific action in a courteous close.

✓ Make it easy to comply by including appropriate contact information.
✓ Express your gratitude.
✓ Clearly state any important deadlines for the request.

Common Examples of Routine Requests

The various types of routine requests are innumerable, from asking favors to requesting credit. However, many of the routine messages that you'll be writing will likely fall into a few main categories: asking for information and action, asking for recommendations, and making claims and requesting adjustments.

Asking for Information and Action   When you need to know about something, elicit an opinion from someone, or request a simple action, you usually need only ask. In essence, simple requests say

• What you want to know or what you want readers to do

• Why you're making the request

• Why it may be in your readers' interest to help you

If your reader is able to do what you want, such a straightforward request gets the job done quickly. Follow the direct approach by opening with a clear statement of your reason for writing. In the body, provide whatever explanation is needed to justify your request. Then close with a specific description of what you expect and include a deadline, if appropriate (see Figure 8.2). In some situations, readers might be unwilling to respond unless they understand how the request benefits them, so be sure to include this information in your explanation. You can assume some shared background when communicating about a routine matter to someone in the same company.

In contrast to requests sent internally, those sent to people outside the organization usually adopt a more formal tone. Such requests are often in letter form, although some are sent via e-mail. These messages are usually short and simple but still formal and professional, like the following request for information:

Dear Bioverse:

Please provide additional information on distribution opportunities for your Healthy Ponds product line, as mentioned on your website. Enviro Domestic is a 20-year-old firm with a well-established design, retail, and service presence in the Oklahoma City area, and we believe your bioremediation products would make a compelling addition to our offerings.

— Makes overall request in polite question form (no question mark)

— Identifies the writer's affiliation and reason for writing

Planning

Writing

Completing

Analyze the Situation
Verify that purpose is to request information from company managers.

Gather Information
Gather accurate, complete information about local competitive threats.

Select the Right Medium
Choose e-mail for this internal message, which also allows the attachment of a Word document to collect the information.

Organize the Information
Clarify that the main idea is collecting information that will lead to a better competitive strategy, which will in turn help the various district managers.

Adapt to Your Audience
Show sensitivity to audience needs with a "you" attitude, politeness, positive emphasis, and bias-free language. Writer already has credibility as manager of the department.

Compose the Message
Maintain a style that is conversational but still businesslike, using plain English and appropriate voice.

Revise the Message
Evaluate content and review readability; avoid unnecessary details.

Produce the Message
Simple e-mail format is all the design this message needs.

Proofread the Message
Review for errors in layout, spelling, and mechanics.

Distribute the Message
Deliver the message via the company's e-mail system.

1   **2**   **3**

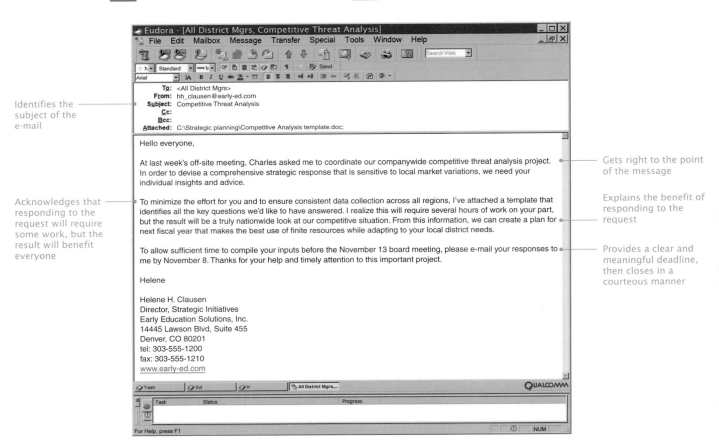

Identifies the subject of the e-mail

Acknowledges that responding to the request will require some work, but the result will benefit everyone

Gets right to the point of the message

Explains the benefit of responding to the request

Provides a clear and meaningful deadline, then closes in a courteous manner

FIGURE 8.2   Effective Message Requesting Action
In this e-mail request to district managers across the country, Helene Clausen asks them to fill out an attached information collection form. Although the request is not unusual and responding to it is part of the managers' responsibility, Clausen asks for their help in a courteous manner and points out the benefits of responding.

In particular, we would appreciate answers to the following questions:

1. Do you offer exclusive regional distribution contracts?
2. Do you offer factory training for sales and service specialists?
3. Do you plan to expand beyond water bioremediation solutions into other landscaping products?

Please let us hear from you by February 15.

Specifies exactly what the writer wishes to know to assist the recipient in responding

Closes with a polite request and a specific answer deadline

A more complex request might require not only greater detail but also information on how responding will benefit the reader.

Sometimes you may need to reestablish a relationship with former customers or suppliers. In many cases, when customers are unhappy about some purchase or about the way they were treated, they don't complain; they simply stay away from the offending business. Thus, a letter of inquiry might encourage customers to use idle credit accounts, offering them an opportunity to register their displeasure and then be able to move on to a good relationship. In addition, a customer's response to such an inquiry may give you insights into ways to improve your products and customer service. Even if they have no complaint, customers still welcome this type of personal attention.

The purpose of some routine requests to customers is simply to reestablish communication.

Asking for Recommendations

The need to inquire about people arises often in business. For example, before awarding credit, contracts, jobs, promotions, scholarships, and so on, companies often ask applicants to supply references. If you're applying for a job, and your potential employer asks for references, you may want to ask a close personal or professional associate to write a letter of recommendation. Or, if you're an employer considering whether to hire an applicant, you may want to write directly to the person the applicant named as a reference.

Companies ask applicants to list references who can vouch for their ability, skills, integrity, character, and fitness for the job. Before you volunteer someone's name as a reference, ask permission to do so. Some people don't want you to use their names, perhaps because they don't know enough about you to feel comfortable writing a letter or because they or their employers have a policy of not providing recommendations.

Always ask for permission before using someone as a reference.

Because requests for recommendations and references are routine, you can organize your inquiry using the direct approach. Open your message by clearly stating why the recommendation is required (if it's not for a job, be sure to explain what it is for) and that you would like your reader to write the letter. If you haven't had contact with the person for some time, use the opening to trigger the reader's memory of the relationship you had, the dates of association, and any special events that might bring a clear and favorable picture of you to mind. Consider including an updated résumé if you've had significant career advancement since your last contact.

Refresh the memory of any potential reference you haven't been in touch with for a while.

Close your message with an expression of appreciation and the full name and address of the person to whom the letter should be sent. When asking for an immediate recommendation, you should also mention the deadline. Always be sure to enclose a stamped, preaddressed envelope as a convenience to the other party. Figure 8.3 provides an example of a request that follows these guidelines.

Making Claims and Requesting Adjustments

If you're dissatisfied with a company's product or service, you can opt to make a **claim** (a formal complaint) or request an **adjustment** (a settlement of a claim). In either case, it's important to maintain a professional tone in all your communication, no matter how angry or frustrated you are. Keeping your cool will help you get the situation resolved sooner.

Planning

Writing

Completing

Analyze the Situation
Verify that the purpose is to request a recommendation letter from a college professor.

Gather Information
Gather information on classes and dates to help the reader recall you and to clarify the position you seek.

Select the Right Medium
The letter format gives this message an appropriate level of formality, although many professors prefer to be contacted by e-mail.

Organize the Information
Messages like this are common and expected, so a direct approach is fine.

Adapt to Your Audience
Show sensitivity to audience needs with a "you" attitude, politeness, positive emphasis, and bias-free language.

Compose the Message
Style is respectful and businesslike, while still using plain English and appropriate voice.

Revise the Message
Evaluate content and review readability; avoid unnecessary details.

Produce the Message
Simple memo format is all the design this message needs.

Proofread the Message
Review for errors in layout, spelling, and mechanics.

Distribute the Message
Deliver the message via postal mail or e-mail if you have the professor's e-mail address.

1   **2**   **3**

1181 Ashport Drive
Tate Springs, TN 38101
March 14, 2008

Professor Lyndon Kenton
School of Business
University of Tennessee, Knoxville
Knoxville, TN 37916

Dear Professor Kenton:

I recently interviewed with Strategic Investments and have been called for a second interview for their Analyst Training Program (ATP). They have requested at least one recommendation from a professor, and I immediately thought of you. May I have a letter of recommendation from you?

As you may recall, I took BUS 485, Financial Analysis, from you in the fall of 2006. I enjoyed the class and finished the term with an "A." Professor Kenton, your comments on assertiveness and cold-calling impressed me beyond the scope of the actual course material. In fact, taking your course helped me decide on a future as a financial analyst.

My enclosed résumé includes all my relevant work experience and volunteer activities. I would also like to add that I've handled the financial planning for our family since my father passed away several years ago. Although I initially learned by trial and error, I have increasingly applied my business training in deciding what stocks or bonds to trade. This, I believe, has given me a practical edge over others who may be applying for the same job.

If possible, Ms. Blackmon in Human Resources needs to receive your letter by March 30. For your convenience, I've enclosed a preaddressed, stamped envelope.

I appreciate your time and effort in writing this letter of recommendation for me. It will be great to put my education to work, and I'll keep you informed of my progress. Thank you for your consideration in this matter.

Sincerely,

Joanne Tucker

Joanne Tucker

Enclosure

Includes information near the opening to refresh the reader's memory about this former student

Gives a deadline for response and includes information about the person expecting the recommendation

Opens by stating the purpose of the letter and making the request, assuming the reader will want to comply with the request

Refers to résumé in the body and mentions experience that could set applicant apart from other candidates

Mentions the preaddressed, stamped envelope to encourage a timely response

FIGURE 8.3 Effective Letter Requesting a Recommendation
This writer uses a direct approach when asking for a recommendation from a former professor. Note how she takes care to refresh the professor's memory because the class was taken a year and a half ago. She also indicates the date by which the letter is needed and points to the enclosure of a stamped, preaddressed envelope.

In addition, be sure to document your initial complaint and every correspondence after that.

In most cases, and especially in your first message, assume that a fair adjustment will be made and use a direct request. Open with a straightforward statement of the problem. In the body, give a complete, specific explanation of the details; provide

In claim letters
- Explain the problem and give details
- Provide backup information
- Request specific action

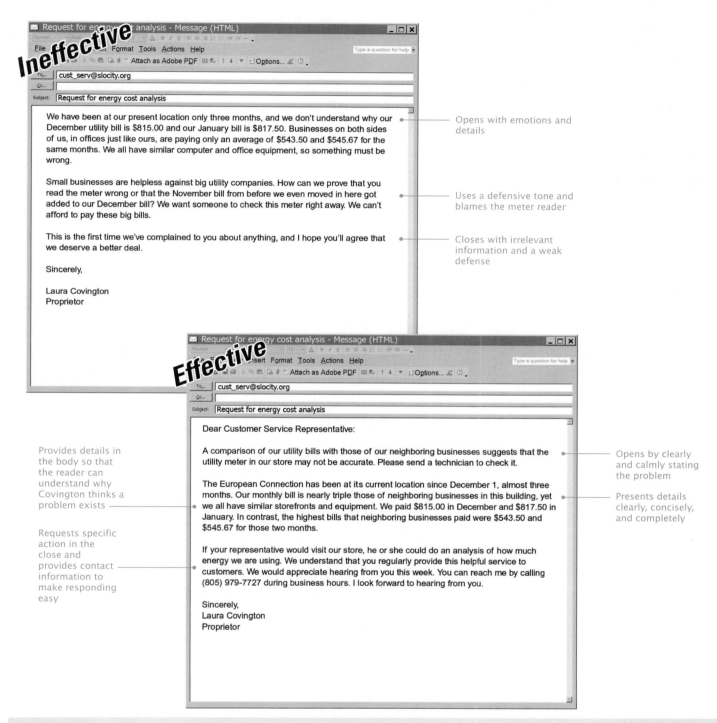

Ineffective

To... cust_serv@slocity.org
Subject: Request for energy cost analysis

We have been at our present location only three months, and we don't understand why our December utility bill is $817.50 and our January bill is $817.50. Businesses on both sides of us, in offices just like ours, are paying only an average of $543.50 and $545.67 for the same months. We all have similar computer and office equipment, so something must be wrong.

Small businesses are helpless against big utility companies. How can we prove that you read the meter wrong or that the November bill from before we even moved in here got added to our December bill? We want someone to check this meter right away. We can't afford to pay these big bills.

This is the first time we've complained to you about anything, and I hope you'll agree that we deserve a better deal.

Sincerely,

Laura Covington
Proprietor

Opens with emotions and details

Uses a defensive tone and blames the meter reader

Closes with irrelevant information and a weak defense

Effective

To... cust_serv@slocity.org
Subject: Request for energy cost analysis

Dear Customer Service Representative:

A comparison of our utility bills with those of our neighboring businesses suggests that the utility meter in our store may not be accurate. Please send a technician to check it.

The European Connection has been at its current location since December 1, almost three months. Our monthly bill is nearly triple those of neighboring businesses in this building, yet we all have similar storefronts and equipment. We paid $815.00 in December and $817.50 in January. In contrast, the highest bills that neighboring businesses paid were $543.50 and $545.67 for those two months.

If your representative would visit our store, he or she could do an analysis of how much energy we are using. We understand that you regularly provide this helpful service to customers. We would appreciate hearing from you this week. You can reach me by calling (805) 979-7727 during business hours. I look forward to hearing from you.

Sincerely,
Laura Covington
Proprietor

Provides details in the body so that the reader can understand why Covington thinks a problem exists

Requests specific action in the close and provides contact information to make responding easy

Opens by clearly and calmly stating the problem

Presents details clearly, concisely, and completely

FIGURE 8.4

Ineffective and Effective Versions of a Claim
Note the difference in tone and information content in these two versions. The ineffective version is emotional and unprofessional, whereas the effective version communicates calmly and clearly.

✓ CHECKLIST: Making Claims and Requesting Adjustments

✓ Maintain a professional tone, even if you're extremely frustrated.
✓ Open with a straightforward statement of the problem.
✓ Provide specific details in the body.
✓ Present facts honestly and clearly.

✓ Politely summarize the desired action in the close.
✓ Clearly state what you expect as a fair settlement or ask the reader to propose a fair adjustment.
✓ Explain the benefits of complying with the request, such as your continued patronage.

---

any information an adjuster would need to verify your complaint. In your close, politely request specific action or convey a sincere desire to find a solution. And, if appropriate, suggest that the business relationship will continue if the problem is solved satisfactorily.

Be prepared to document your claim. Send copies and keep the original documents.

Companies usually accept the customer's explanation of what's wrong, so it is important to be entirely honest when filing claims. Also, be prepared to back up your claim with invoices, sales receipts, canceled checks, dated correspondence, and any other relevant documents. Send copies and keep the originals for your files.

If the remedy is obvious, tell your reader exactly what you expect from the company, such as exchanging incorrectly shipped merchandise for the right item or issuing a refund if the item is out of stock. In some cases, you might ask the reader to resolve a problem. However, if you're uncertain about the precise nature of the trouble, you could ask the company to make an assessment and then advise you on how the situation could be fixed. Supply your contact information so that the company can discuss the situation with you, if necessary. Compare the ineffective and effective versions in Figure 8.4 for an example of making a claim.

A rational, clear, and courteous approach is best for any routine request. To review the tasks involved in making claims and requesting adjustments, see "Checklist: Making Claims and Requesting Adjustments."

SENDING ROUTINE REPLIES AND POSITIVE MESSAGES

Just as you'll make numerous requests for information and action throughout your career, you'll also respond to such requests from other people. When responding positively to a request, sending routine announcements, or sending a positive or goodwill message, you have several goals: to communicate the information or the good news, answer all questions, provide all required details, and leave your reader with a good impression of you and your firm.

Strategy for Routine Replies and Positive Messages

Use a direct approach for positive messages.

Like requests, a routine reply or positive message has an opening, a body, and a close. Because readers receiving these messages will generally be interested in what you have to say, you usually use the direct approach. Place your main idea (the positive reply or the good news) in the opening, use the body to explain all the relevant details, and close cordially—perhaps highlighting a benefit to your reader.

Prepare your audience for the detail that follows by beginning your positive message with the main idea or good news.

Start with the Main Idea   By opening routine and positive messages with the main idea or good news, you're preparing your audience for the detail that follows. Try to make your opening clear and concise. Although the following introductory statements make the same point, one is cluttered with unnecessary information that buries the purpose, whereas the other is brief and to the point:

Instead of This	**Write This**
I am pleased to inform you that after careful consideration of a diverse and talented pool of applicants, each of whom did a thorough job of analyzing Trask Horton Pharmaceuticals's training needs, we have selected your bid.	Trask Horton Pharmaceuticals has accepted your bid to provide public speaking and presentation training to the sales staff.

The best way to write a clear opening is to have a clear idea of what you want to say. Before you put one word on paper, ask yourself, "What is the single most important message I have for the audience?"

Provide Necessary Details and Explanation   Use the body to explain your point completely so that your audience won't be confused or doubtful about your meaning. As you provide the details, maintain the supportive tone established in the opening. This tone is easy to continue when your message is entirely positive, as in this example:

> Your educational background and internship have impressed us, and we believe you would be a valuable addition to Green Valley Properties. As discussed during your interview, your salary will be $4,300 per month, plus benefits. Please plan to meet with our benefits manager, Paula Sanchez, at 8 a.m. on Monday, March 21. She will assist you with all the paperwork necessary to tailor our benefit package to your family situation. She will also arrange various orientation activities to help you acclimate to our company.

However, if your routine message is mixed and must convey mildly disappointing information, put the negative portion of your message into as favorable a context as possible:

Try to embed any negative information in a positive context.

Instead of This	**Write This**
No, we no longer carry the Sportsgirl line of sweaters.	The new Olympic line has replaced the Sportsgirl sweaters that you asked about. Olympic features a wider range of colors and sizes and more contemporary styling.

In this example, the more complete description is less negative and emphasizes how the recipient can benefit from the change. Be careful, though: You can use negative information in this type of message *only* if you're reasonably sure the audience will respond positively. Otherwise, use the indirect approach (discussed in Chapter 9).

If you are communicating to a customer, you might also want to use the body of your message to assure the customer of the wisdom of his or her purchase selection (without being condescending or self-congratulatory). Using such favorable comments, often know as *resale*, is a good way to build customer relationships. These comments are commonly included in acknowledgments of orders and other routine announcements to customers, and they are most effective when they are relatively short and specific:

> The zipper on the laptop carrying case you purchased is double-stitched and guaranteed for the life of the product.
>
> The KitchenAid mixer you ordered is our best-selling model. It should meet your cooking needs for many years.

Document Makeover

IMPROVE THIS E-MAIL MESSAGE

To practice correcting drafts of actual documents, visit your online course or the access-code-protected portion of the Companion Website. Click on "Document Makeovers," then click on Chapter 8. You will find an e-mail message that contains problems and errors related to what you've learned in this chapter about routine, good news, and goodwill messages. Use the Final Draft decision tool to create an improved version of this routine e-mail. Check the message for skilled presentation of the main idea, clarity of detail, appropriate use of resale, and the inclusion of a courteous close.

End with a Courteous Close Your message is most likely to succeed if your readers are left feeling that you have their best interests in mind. You can accomplish this task either by highlighting a benefit to the audience or by expressing appreciation or goodwill. If follow-up action is required, clearly state who will do what next. See "Checklist: Writing Routine Replies and Positive Messages" to review the primary tasks involved in this type of business message.

Common Examples of Routine Replies and Positive Messages

As with routine requests, you'll encounter the need for a wide variety of routine replies and positive messages. You can expect to write letters or e-mail messages for most routine messages directed to people outside the company, although e-mail and instant messaging (with live operators or automated bots) are gaining popularity in customer-service applications. Most routine and positive messages fall into six main categories: answers to requests for information and action, grants of claims and requests for adjustment, recommendations, informative messages, good-news announcements, and goodwill messages.

Answering Requests for Information and Action Every professional answers requests for information and action from time to time. If the response to a request is a simple yes or some other straightforward information, the direct plan is appropriate. A prompt, gracious, and thorough response will positively influence how people think about you and the organization you represent (see Figure 8.5).

To handle repetitive queries quickly and consistently, companies usually develop form responses that can be customized as needed (see Figure 8.6). These ready-made message templates can be printed forms, word processor documents, e-mail templates, or blocks of instant messaging text that can be dropped into a messaging window with the click of a mouse.

✓ CHECKLIST: Writing Routine Replies and Positive Messages

A. Start with the main idea.
- ✓ Be clear and concise.
- ✓ Identify the single most important message before you start writing.

B. Provide necessary details and explanation.
- ✓ Explain your point completely to eliminate any confusion or lingering doubts.
- ✓ Maintain a supportive tone throughout.

- ✓ Embed negative statements in positive contexts or balance them with positive alternatives.
- ✓ Talk favorably about the choices the customer has made.

C. End with a courteous close.
- ✓ Let your readers know that you have their personal well-being in mind.
- ✓ If further action is required, tell readers how to proceed and encourage them to act promptly.

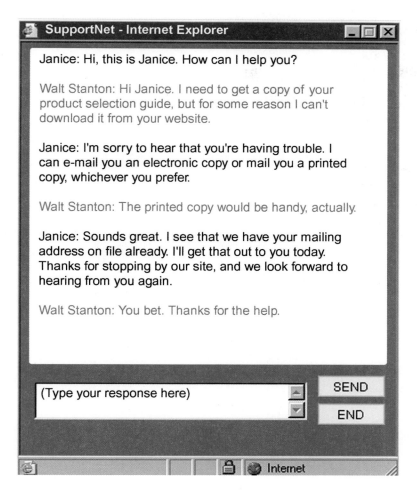

SupportNet - Internet Explorer

Janice: Hi, this is Janice. How can I help you?

Walt Stanton: Hi Janice. I need to get a copy of your product selection guide, but for some reason I can't download it from your website.

Janice: I'm sorry to hear that you're having trouble. I can e-mail you an electronic copy or mail you a printed copy, whichever you prefer.

Walt Stanton: The printed copy would be handy, actually.

Janice: Sounds great. I see that we have your mailing address on file already. I'll get that out to you today. Thanks for stopping by our site, and we look forward to hearing from you again.

Walt Stanton: You bet. Thanks for the help.

(Type your response here)

SEND

END

Internet

FIGURE 8.5
Effective IM Response to an Information Request
This quick and courteous exchange is typical of IM communication in such areas as customer service and technical support. The agent (Janice) solves the problem quickly and leaves the customer with a positive impression of the company.

When you're answering requests and a potential sale is involved, you have three main goals: (1) to respond to the inquiry and answer all questions, (2) to leave your reader with a good impression of you and your firm, and (3) to encourage the future sale. The following message meets all three objectives:

Here is the brochure "Entertainment Unlimited" that you requested. This booklet describes the vast array of entertainment options available to you with an Ocean Satellite Device (OSD).

> Starts with a clear statement of the main point

On page 12 of "Entertainment Unlimited" you'll find a list of the 338 channels that the OSD brings into your home. You'll have access to movie, sports, and music channels; 24-hour news channels; local channels; and all the major television networks. OSD gives you a clearer picture and more precise sound than those old-fashioned dishes that took up most of your yard—and OSD uses only a small dish that mounts easily on your roof.

> Presents key information immediately, along with resale and sales promotion

More music, more cartoons, more experts, more news, and more sports are available to you with OSD than with any other cable or satellite connection in this region. Yes, it's all there, right at your fingertips.

> Encourages readers to take one more step toward a purchase by highlighting product benefits

Just call us at 1-800-786-4331, and an OSD representative will come to your home to answer your questions. You'll love the programming and the low monthly cost. Call us today!

> Points toward the sale confidently

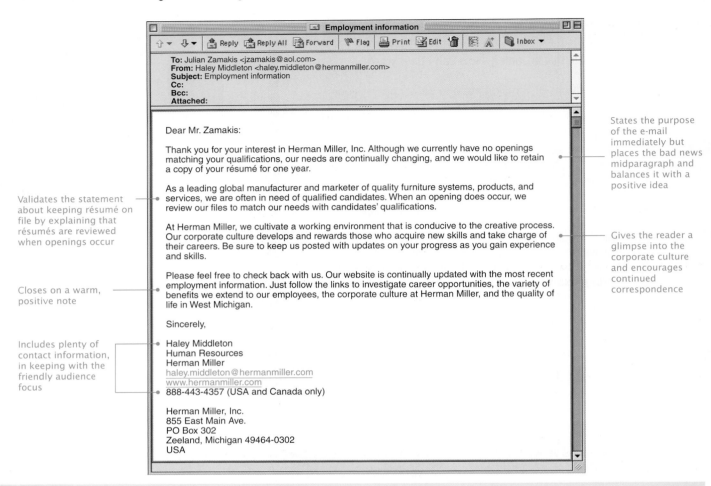

FIGURE 8.6
Personalized Reply to a Request for Information
This e-mail message personalizes a standardized response by including the recipient's name in the greeting.

Granting Claims and Requests for Adjustment   Even the best-run companies make mistakes, from shipping the wrong order to billing a customer's credit card inaccurately. In other cases, a customer or a third party might be responsible for a mistake, such as misusing a product or damaging a product in shipment. Each of these events represents a turning point in your relationship with your customer. If you handle the situation well, your customer is likely to be even more loyal than before because you've proven that you're serious about customer satisfaction. However, if a customer believes that you mishandled a complaint, you'll make the situation even worse. Dissatisfied customers often take their business elsewhere without notice and tell numerous friends and colleagues about the negative experience. A transaction that might be worth only a few dollars by itself could cost you many times that amount in lost business. In other words, every mistake is an opportunity to improve a relationship.

Few people go to the trouble of requesting an adjustment unless they actually have a problem, so most businesses start from the assumption that the customer is correct. From there, your response to the complaint depends on your company's policies for resolving such issues and your assessment of whether the company, the customer, or some third party is at fault.

Responding to a Claim When Your Company Is at Fault Before you respond after your company has made a mistake, make sure you know your company's policies, which might even dictate specific legal and financial steps to be taken. For serious problems that go beyond routine errors, your company should have a *crisis management plan* that outlines communication steps both inside and outside the organization (see Chapter 9).

Most routine responses should take your company's specific policies into account and address the following points:

- **Acknowledge receipt of the customer's claim or complaint.** Even if you can't solve the problem immediately, at least let the other party know that somebody is listening.

- **Take (or assign) personal responsibility for setting matters straight.** Customers want to know that someone is listening and responding.

- **Sympathize with the customer's inconvenience or frustration.** Letting the customer see that you're on his or her side helps defuse the emotional element of the situation.

- **Explain precisely how you have resolved or plan to resolve the situation.** If you can respond exactly as the customer requested, be sure to communicate that. If you can't, explain why.

- **Take steps to repair the relationship.** Keeping your existing customers is almost always less expensive than acquiring new customers, so look for ways to mend the relationship and encourage future business.

- **Follow up to verify that your response was correct.** Follow-up not only helps improve customer service but also gives you another opportunity to show how much you care about your customer.

In addition to these positive steps, maintain professional demeanor by avoiding some key negative steps as well: Don't blame anyone in your organization by name; don't make exaggerated, insincere apologies; don't imply that the customer is at fault; and don't promise more than you can deliver.

As with requests for information or action, companies often create customizable templates for granting claims and requests for adjustment. In the following example, a large mail-order clothing company created an e-mail form to respond to customers who complain that they haven't received exactly what was ordered:

> Your e-mail message concerning your recent Klondike order has been forwarded to our director of order fulfillment. Your complete satisfaction is our goal, and a customer service representative will contact you within 48 hours to assist with the issues raised in your letter.
>
> In the meantime, please accept the enclosed $5 gift certificate as a token of our appreciation for your business. Whether you're skiing or driving a snowmobile, Klondike Gear offers you the best protection from wind, snow, and cold—and Klondike has been taking care of customers' outdoor needs for over 27 years.
>
> Thank you for taking the time to write to us. Your input helps us better serve you and all our customers.

Annotations (right margin):
- Acknowledges receipt of the customer's message
- Explains what will happen next and when, without making promises the writer can't keep
- Takes steps to repair the relationship and ensure continued business
- Closes with a statement of the company's concern for all its customers

Responding to a Claim When the Customer Is at Fault Communication about a claim is a delicate matter when the customer is clearly at fault. You can (1) refuse the claim and attempt to justify your refusal or (2) simply do what the customer asks. If you refuse the claim, you may lose your customer—as well as many of the customer's friends and colleagues, who will hear only one side of the dispute. You must weigh the cost of making the adjustment against the cost of losing future business from one or more customers.

When granting an unjustified claim, maintain a respectful and positive tone while informing the customer that the claim was a result of misuse or mistreatment of the product.

At the Alexandria, Virginia, bank Burke & Hebert, CEO Hunt Burke and his staff communicate in a friendly, audience-focused way that helps the bank enjoy almost fanatical customer loyalty.

If you choose to grant a claim, you can open with the good news: You're replacing the merchandise or refunding the purchase price. However, the body needs more attention. Your job is to make the customer realize that the merchandise was mistreated, but you want to avoid being condescending ("Perhaps you failed to read the instructions carefully") or preachy ("You should know that wool shrinks in hot water"). The dilemma is this: If the customer fails to realize what went wrong, you may commit your firm to an endless procession of returned merchandise; but if you insult the customer, your cash refund will have been wasted because you'll lose your customer anyway. Close in a courteous manner that expresses your appreciation for the customer's business (see Figure 8.7).

Responding to a Claim When a Third Party Is at Fault Sometimes neither your company nor your customer is at fault. For example, ordering a book from Amazon.com involves not only Amazon.com but also a delivery service such as FedEx or the U.S. Postal Service, the publisher and possibly a distributor of the book, a credit card issuer, and a company that processes credit card transactions. Any one of these other partners might be at fault in the event of a problem, but the customer is likely to blame Amazon.com because that is the entity primarily responsible for the transaction.

No general scheme applies to every case involving a third party, so evaluate the situation carefully and know your company's policies before responding. For instance, an online retailer and the companies that manufacture its merchandise might have an agreement which specifies that the manufacturers automatically handle all complaints about product quality. However, regardless of who eventually resolves the problem, if customers contact you, you need to respond with messages that explain how the problem will be solved. Pointing fingers is unproductive and unprofessional; resolving the situation is the only issue customers care about. See "Checklist: Granting Claims and Adjustment Requests" to review the tasks involved in these kinds of business messages.

✓ CHECKLIST: Granting Claims and Adjustment Requests

A. Responding when your company is at fault

✓ Be aware of your company's policies in such cases before you respond.

✓ For serious situations, refer to the company's crisis management plan.

✓ Start by acknowledging receipt of the claim or complaint.

✓ Take or assign personal responsibility for resolving the situation.

✓ Sympathize with the customer's frustration.

✓ Explain how you have resolved the situation (or plan to).

✓ Take steps to repair the customer relationship.

✓ Verify your response with the customer and keep the lines of communication open.

B. Responding when the customer is at fault

✓ Weigh the cost of complying with or refusing the request.

✓ If you choose to comply, open with the good news.

✓ Use the body of the message to respectfully educate the customer about steps needed to avoid a similar outcome in the future.

✓ Close with an appreciation for the customer's business.

C. Responding when a third party is at fault

✓ Evaluate the situation and review your company's policies before responding.

✓ Avoid placing blame; focus on the solution.

✓ Regardless of who is responsible for resolving the situation, let the customer know what will happen to resolve the problem.

Planning

Analyze the Situation
Verify that the purpose is to grant the customer's claim, tactfully educate him, and encourage further business.

Gather Information
Gather information on product care, warranties, and resale information.

Select the Right Medium
An e-mail message is appropriate in this case because the customer contacted the company via e-mail.

Organize the Information
You're responding with a positive answer, so a direct approach is fine.

1

Writing

Adapt to Your Audience
Show sensitivity to audience needs with a "you" attitude, politeness, positive emphasis, and bias-free language.

Compose the Message
Maintain a style that is respectful while still managing to educate the customer on product usage and maintenance.

2

Completing

Revise the Message
Evaluate content and review readability; avoid unnecessary details.

Produce the Message
Emphasize a clean, professional appearance.

Proofread the Message
Review for errors in layout, spelling, and mechanics.

Distribute the Message
E-mail the reply.

3

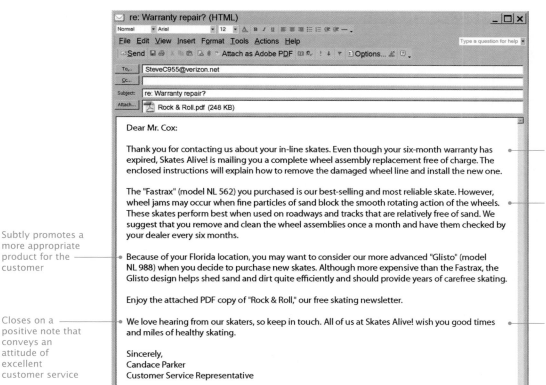

Subtly promotes a more appropriate product for the customer

Closes on a positive note that conveys an attitude of excellent customer service

Acknowledges reader communication, keeps opening positive by avoiding words such as problem, and conveys the good news right away

Explains the problem without blaming the customer by avoiding the pronoun *you* and by suggesting ways to avoid future problems

Gives the reader a glimpse into the corporate culture and encourages continued correspondence

FIGURE 8.7   Responding to a Claim When the Buyer Is at Fault
In the interest of positive customer relationships, this company agreed to provide replacement parts for a customer's in-line skates, even though the product is outside its warranty period. (For the sake of clarity, the content of the customer's original e-mail message is not reproduced here.)

Providing Recommendations When writing a letter of recommendation, your goal is to convince readers that the person being recommended has the characteristics necessary for the job, project assignment, scholarship, or other objective the person is seeking. A successful recommendation letter contains a number of relevant details:

- The candidate's full name

- The position or other objective the candidate is seeking

- The nature of your relationship with the candidate

- An indication of whether you're answering a request from the person or taking the initiative to write

- Facts and evidence relevant to the candidate and the opportunity

- A comparison of this candidate's potential with that of peers, if available (for example, "Ms. Jonasson consistently ranked in the top 10 percent of her class")

- Your overall evaluation of the candidate's suitability for the opportunity

As surprising as this might sound, the most difficult recommendation letters to write are often those for truly outstanding candidates. Your audience will have trouble believing uninterrupted praise for someone's talents and accomplishments. To enhance

PRACTICING ETHICAL COMMUNICATION

What's Right to Write in a Recommendation Letter?

Recommendation letters are classified as routine messages, but with all the legal troubles they can get employers into these days, they've become anything but routine. Over the years, employees have won thousands of lawsuits that charged former employers with defamation related to job recommendations. In addition to charges of defamation—which can be successfully defended if the "defamatory" statements are proven to be true—employers have been sued for retaliation by ex-employees who believed that negative letters were written expressly for purposes of revenge. And as if that weren't enough, employers have even sued each other over recommendation letters when the recipient of a letter believed the writer failed to disclose important negative information.

No wonder many companies now refuse to divulge anything more than job titles and dates of employment. But even that doesn't always solve the problem: Ex-employees have been known to sue for retaliation when their employers refused to write on their behalf. (This refusal to write recommendations also causes problems for hiring companies. If they can't get any real background information on job candidates, they risk hiring employees who lack the necessary skills or who are disruptive or even dangerous in the workplace.)

For companies that let managers write recommendations, what sort of information should or should not be included? Even though the majority of states now have laws protecting companies against recommendation-related lawsuits when the employer acts in good faith, individual cases vary so much that

no specific guidelines can ever apply to all cases. However, asking yourself the following questions before drafting a recommendation letter will help you avoid trouble:

- Does the party receiving this personal information have a legitimate right to it?

- Does all the information I've presented relate directly to the job or benefit being sought?

- Have I put the candidate's case as strongly and as honestly as I can?

- Have I avoided overstating the candidate's abilities or otherwise misleading the reader?

- Have I based all my statements on firsthand knowledge and provable facts?

No matter what the circumstances, experts also advise that you always consult your human resources or legal department for advice.

CAREER APPLICATIONS

1. A former employee was often late for work but was an excellent and fast worker who got along well with everyone. Do you think it's important to mention the tardiness to potential employers? If so, how will you handle it?

2. Step outside yourself for a moment and write a letter of recommendation about you from a former employer's perspective. Make sure your letter embodies honesty, integrity, and prudence.

your credibility—and the candidate's—illustrate your general points with specific examples that point out the candidate's abilities and fitness for the job opening.

Most candidates aren't perfect, however, and you'll need to decide how to handle each situation that comes your way. Omitting a reference to someone's shortcomings may be tempting, especially if the shortcomings are irrelevant to the demands of the job in question. Even so, you have an obligation to refer to any serious shortcoming that could be related to job performance. You owe it to your audience, to your own conscience, and even to better-qualified candidates. You don't have to present the shortcomings as simple criticisms, however. A good option is to list them as areas for improvement or as areas the person might be working on now.

The danger in writing a critical letter is that you might inadvertently engage in *libel*, publishing a false and malicious written statement that injures the candidate's reputation. On the other hand, if that negative information is truthful and relevant, it may be unethical and even illegal to omit it from your recommendation (see "Practicing Ethical Communication: What's Right to Write in a Recommendation Letter?").

If you must refer to a shortcoming, you can best protect yourself by sticking to the facts, avoiding value judgments, and placing your criticism in the context of a generally favorable recommendation, as in Figure 8.8. In this letter, the writer supports all statements and judgments with evidence.

Before you dash off any recommendation letter, even for someone you know closely and respect without reservation, keep in mind that every time you write a recommendation, you're putting your own reputation on the line. If the person's shortcomings are so pronounced that you don't think he or she is a good fit for the job, the only choice is to not write the letter at all. Unless your relationship with the person warrants an explanation, simply suggest that someone else might be in a better position to provide a recommendation.

> A serious shortcoming cannot be ignored in letters of recommendation, but beware of being libelous:
> - Include only relevant, factual information
> - Avoid value judgments
> - Balance criticisms with favorable points

Creating Informative Messages   All companies send routine informative messages such as reminder notices and policy statements. For instance, you may need to inform employees of organizational changes or tell customers about new shipping and return policies. Use the opening of informative messages to state the purpose (to inform) and briefly mention the nature of the information you are providing. Unlike the replies discussed earlier, informative messages are not solicited by your reader, so make it clear up front why the reader is receiving this particular message. Provide the necessary details in the body and end your message with a courteous close.

Most informative communications are neutral. That is, they stimulate neither a positive nor a negative response from readers. For example, when you send departmental meeting announcements and reminder notices, you'll generally receive a neutral response from your readers (unless the purpose of the meeting is unwelcome). Simply present the factual information in the body of the message and don't worry too much about the reader's attitude toward the information.

Some informative messages may require additional care. For instance, policy statements or procedural changes may be good news for a company, perhaps by saving money. However, it may not be obvious to employees that such savings may make available additional employee resources or even pay raises. In instances in which the reader may not initially view the information positively, use the body of the message to highlight the potential benefits from the reader's perspective.

> When writing informative messages
> - State the purpose in the opening and briefly mention the nature of the information you are providing
> - Provide necessary details in the body
> - End with a courteous close

Announcing Good News   To develop and maintain good relationships, smart companies recognize that it's good business to spread the word about positive developments. These can include opening new facilities, hiring a new executive, introducing new products or services, or sponsoring community events—such as the announcements that Carol Cone and her staff write for ConAgra and other clients. Because good news is always welcome, use the direct approach.

November 14, 2008

Ms. Clarice Gailey
Director of Operations
McNally and Associates, Inc.
8688 Southgate Ave.
Augusta, GA 30906

Dear Ms. Gailey:

[Clearly states candidate's full name and the main point of the letter in the opening]

I am pleased to recommend Talvin Biswas for the marketing position at McNally and Associates. Mr. Biswas has worked with Discovery Communications as an intern for the past two summers while working toward his degree in marketing and advertising. His duties included customer correspondence, web content updates, and direct-mail campaign planning.

[Specifies duration and nature of relationship in the body to give weight to the evaluation]

As his supervisor, in addition to knowing his work here, I also know that Mr. Biswas has served as secretary for the International Business Association at the University of Michigan. He tutored other international students in the university's writing center. His fluency in three languages (English, French, and Hindi) and thorough knowledge of other cultures will make him an immediate contributor to your international operation.

Although a quiet, introspective young man, Mr. Biswas will not hesitate to contribute ideas when invited to do so. In addition, because Mr. Biswas learns quickly, he will learn your company's routine with ease.

[Closes by inviting reader to discuss the candidate further]

[Begins the close by summarizing the supportive evaluation]

Mr. Biswas will make an excellent addition to your staff at McNally and Associates. If I can provide any additional information, please call or fax me at the numbers above. If you prefer to communicate by e-mail, my address is ramsey@discovery.com.

Sincerely,

Lim Sok Ramsey
Vice President, Strategy and Development

FIGURE 8.8
Effective Recommendation Letter
This letter clearly states the nature of the writer's relationship to the candidate and provides specific examples to support the writer's endorsements.

Writing to a successful job applicant is one of the most pleasant good-news messages you might have the opportunity to write. The following example uses the direct approach and provides information that the recipient needs:

[Announces news in a friendly, welcoming tone]

Welcome to Lake Valley Rehabilitation Center. A number of excellent candidates were interviewed, but your educational background and recent experience at Memorial Hospital make you the best person for the position of medical records supervisor.

[Confirms important details]

As we discussed, your salary is $39,200 a year. We would like you to begin on Monday, February 1. Please come to my office at 9 a.m. I will give you an in-depth orientation to Lake Valley and discuss the various company benefits available to you. You can also sign all the necessary employment documents.

After lunch, Vanessa Jackson will take you to the medical records department and introduce you to your staff. I look forward to seeing you on February 1.

← Explains the first day's routine to ease the new employee's uncertainty

Job-offer letters should be reviewed by legal experts familiar with employment law because they can be legally binding contracts.

Although messages like these are pleasant to write, they require careful planning and evaluation in order to avoid legal troubles. For instance, messages that imply lifetime employment or otherwise make promises about the length or conditions of employment can be interpreted as legally binding contracts, even if you never intended to make such promises. Similarly, downplaying potentially negative news (such as rumors of a takeover) that turns out to affect the hired person in a negative way can be judged as fraud. Consequently, experts advise that a company's legal staff either scrutinize each offer letter or create standardized content to use in such letters.[2]

Good-news announcements are usually communicated via a letter or a **news release**, also known as a *press release*, a specialized document used to share relevant information with the local or national news media. (News releases are also used to announce negative news, such as plant closings.) In most companies, news releases are usually prepared or at least supervised by specially trained writers in the public relations department. The content follows the customary pattern for a positive message: good news followed by details and a positive close. However, traditional news releases have a critical difference: You're not writing directly to the ultimate audience (such as the readers of a newspaper); you're trying to interest an editor or a reporter in a story, and that person will then write the material that is eventually read by the larger audience. To write a successful news release, keep the following points in mind:[3]

- Above all else, make sure your information is newsworthy and relevant to the specific publications or websites to which you are sending it. Editors are overwhelmed with news releases, so those without real news content are disposed of quickly—and can damage the writer's credibility, too.

- Focus on one subject; don't try to pack a single news release with multiple, unrelated news items.

- Put your most important idea first. Don't force editors to hunt for the news.

- Be brief: Break up long sentences and keep paragraphs short.

- Eliminate clutter, such as redundancy and extraneous facts.

- Be as specific as possible.

- Minimize self-congratulatory adjectives and adverbs; if the content of your message is newsworthy, the media professionals will be interested in the news on its own merits.

- Follow established industry conventions for style, punctuation, and format.

As with many other aspects of business communication, the process of creating and distributing news releases and other media materials is continually improved by technological advances. Online distribution systems such as PR Newswire and BusinessWire make it easy for even the smallest companies to reach editors and reporters at the most prominent publications around the world. Many companies also create special media pages on their websites that contain their latest news releases, company background information, and archives of past news releases.

FIGURE 8.9
Announcing Positive News
Blogs have become a popular mechanism for announcing positive company news. Some companies even forgo the traditional news release in favor of controlling and distributing such messages themselves.

Up until recently, news releases were intended only for members of the news media and crafted in a way to provide information to reporters who would then write their own articles if the subject matter was interesting to their readers. Thanks to the Internet, however, the nature of the news release is changing. Many companies now view it as general-purpose tool for communicating directly with customers and other audiences, writing *direct-to-consumer news releases* (see Figure 8.9). As new-media expert David Meerman Scott puts it, "Millions of people read press releases directly, unfiltered by the media. You need to be speaking directly to them."[4]

Goodwill is the positive feeling that encourages people to maintain a business relationship.

Fostering Goodwill All business messages should be written with an eye toward fostering goodwill among business contacts, but some messages are written primarily and specifically to build goodwill. You can use these messages to enhance your relationships with customers, colleagues, and other businesspeople by sending friendly—even unexpected—notes with no direct business purpose.

Make sure your compliments are sincere and honest.

Effective goodwill messages must be sincere and honest. Otherwise, you'll appear to be interested in personal gain rather than in benefiting customers, fellow workers, or your organization. To come across as sincere, avoid exaggerating, and back up any compliments with specific points. In addition, readers often regard more restrained praise as being more sincere:

Instead of This	**Write This**
Words cannot express my appreciation for the great job you did. Thanks. No one could have done it better. You're terrific! You've made the whole firm sit up and take notice, and we are ecstatic to have you working here.	Thanks again for taking charge of the meeting in my absence and doing such an excellent job. With just an hour's notice, you managed to pull the legal and public relations departments together so that we could present a united front in the negotiations. Your dedication and communication abilities have been noted and are truly appreciated.

Sending Congratulations One prime opportunity for sending goodwill messages is to congratulate individuals or companies for significant business achievements—perhaps for being promoted or for attaining product sales milestones (see Figure 8.10). Other reasons for sending congratulations include the highlights in people's

Taking note of significant events in someone's personal life helps cement a business relationship.

FIGURE 8.10
Congratulating Business Partners
Goodwill messages serve a variety of business functions. In this announcement, Business Objects congratulates several of its customers for achieving a level of excellence in *business intelligence* (the acquisition and application of information to business decisions).

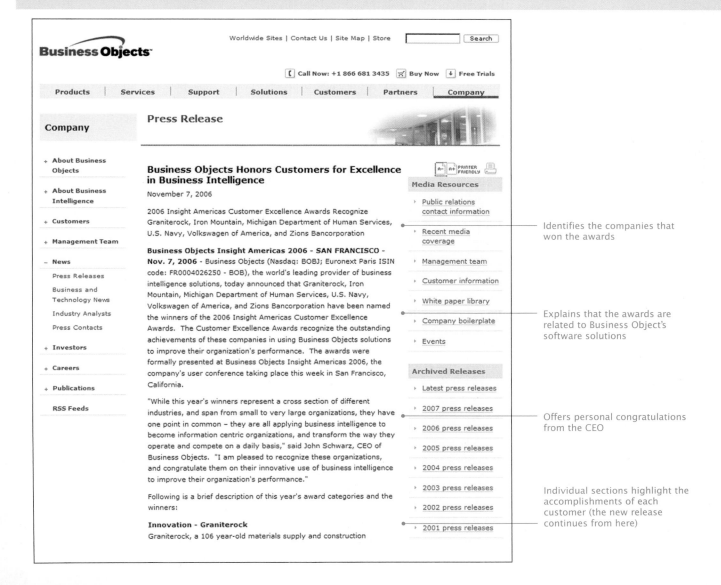

Identifies the companies that won the awards

Explains that the awards are related to Business Object's software solutions

Offers personal congratulations from the CEO

Individual sections highlight the accomplishments of each customer (the new release continues from here)

personal lives, such as weddings, births, graduations, and success in nonbusiness competitions. You may congratulate business acquaintances on their own achievements or on the accomplishments of a spouse or child. You may also take note of personal events, even if you don't know the reader well. If you're already friendly with the reader, a more personal tone is appropriate.

Congratulations can also be incorporated into promotional campaigns, such as when companies send messages to new parents or to recent homebuyers. Some companies even develop a mailing list of potential customers by assigning an employee to clip newspaper announcements of births, engagements, weddings, and graduations or to obtain information on real estate transactions in the local community. Then they introduce themselves by sending out a form letter that might read like this:

> Congratulations on your new home! All of us at Klemper Security Solutions hope it brings you and your family many years of security and happiness.
>
> Please accept the enclosed *Homeowner's Guide to Home Security* with our compliments. It lists a number of simple steps you can take to keep your home, your family, and your possessions safe.

This simple message has a natural, friendly tone, even though the sender has never met the recipient.

An effective message of appreciation documents a person's contributions.

Sending Messages of Appreciation   An important managerial quality is the ability to recognize the contributions of employees, colleagues, suppliers, and other associates. Your praise does more than just make the person feel good; it encourages further excellence. Moreover, a message of appreciation may become an important part of someone's personnel file. So when you write a message of appreciation, try to specifically mention the person or people you want to praise. The brief message that follows expresses gratitude and reveals the happy result:

> Thank you and everyone on your team for the heroic efforts you took to bring our servers back up after last Friday's flood. We were able to restore business right on schedule first thing Monday morning. You went far beyond the level of contractual service in restoring our data center within 16 hours. I would especially like to highlight the contribution of networking specialist Julienne Marks, who worked for 12 straight hours to reconnect our Internet service. If I can serve as a reference in your future sales activities, please do not hesitate to ask.

The primary purpose of condolence messages is to let the audience know that you and the organization you represent care about the person's loss.

Offering Condolences   In times of serious trouble and deep sadness, well-written condolences and expressions of sympathy can mean a great deal to people who've experienced loss. Granted, this type of message is difficult to write, but don't let the difficulty of the task keep you from responding promptly.

Open a condolence message with a brief statement of sympathy, such as "I was deeply sorry to hear of your loss" in the event of a death, for example. In the body, mention the good qualities or the positive contributions made by the deceased. State what the person meant to you or your colleagues. In closing, you can offer your condolences and your best wishes. Here are a few general suggestions for writing condolence messages:

- **Keep reminiscences brief.**   Recount a memory or an anecdote (even a humorous one), but don't dwell on the details of the loss lest you add to the reader's anguish.

- **Write in your own words.**   Write as if you were speaking privately to the person. Don't quote "poetic" passages or use stilted or formal phrases. If the loss is a death, refer to it as such rather than as "passing away" or "departing."

✓ CHECKLIST: Sending Goodwill Messages

✓ Be sincere and honest.
✓ Don't exaggerate or use vague, grandiose language; support positive statements with specific evidence.
✓ Use congratulatory messages to build goodwill with clients and colleagues.
✓ Send messages of appreciation to emphasize how much you value the work of others.

✓ When sending condolence messages, open with a brief statement of sympathy followed by an expression of how much the deceased person meant to you or your firm (as appropriate); close by offering your best wishes for the future.

- **Be tactful.** Mention your shock and dismay but remember that bereaved and distressed loved ones take little comfort in lines such as "Richard was too young to die" or "Starting all over again will be so difficult." Try to strike a balance between superficial expressions of sympathy and painful references to a happier past or the likelihood of a bleak future.

- **Take special care.** Be sure to spell names correctly and be accurate in your review of facts. Try to be prompt.

- **Write about special qualities of the deceased.** You may have to rely on reputation to do this, but let the grieving person know you valued his or her loved one.

- **Write about special qualities of the bereaved person.** A pat on the back helps a bereaved family member feel more confident about handling things during such a traumatic time.[5]

Supervisor George Bigalow sent the following condolence letter to his administrative assistant, Janice Case, after learning of the death of Janice's husband:

> My sympathy to you and your children. All your friends at Carter Electric were so very sorry to learn of John's death. Although I never had the opportunity to meet him, I do know how very special he was to you. Your tales of your family's camping trips and his rafting expeditions were always memorable.

To review the tasks involved in writing goodwill messages, see "Checklist: Sending Goodwill Messages."

On the Job

SOLVING COMMUNICATION DILEMMAS AT CONE, INC.

In addition to serving hot meals, the Kids Café program provides a safe, nurturing environment that keeps kids out of trouble during the risky afternoon hours from 3:00 to 6:00. To make that time more valuable, many Kids Cafés have started offering sports, crafts, mentoring, and tutoring. These activities require qualified volunteers who are willing to spend a few hours each week working with the kids. To staff the tutoring program, ConAgra has asked Cone to create a recruiting campaign that will attract volunteers qualified to help with math, English, and science homework. As part of your job supervising the recruiting campaign, how would you handle these challenges?

1. One of the most important recruiting tools will be a letter addressed to current monetary donors, asking them to give as little as three hours a month. Donors in such situations are often asked to volunteer their time, so you can safely assume that the request will be received as a routine matter. Which of the following sounds like the best way to begin this letter?

   a. Money may make the world go 'round, but time is what our kids really need. Just a few hours a week is all we're asking for.

   b. Everyone involved with the Kids Café program sincerely appreciates your generous financial support, and I thank you personally as well. Since you've already demonstrated your commitment to the children, could we ask you to consider donating a few hours of your time every week as a tutor?

   c. Think of how easily we all waste three or four hours every week—whether it's watching pointless television shows or gabbing on the telephone. Wouldn't you welcome the opportunity to make something wonderful happen with a few of those wasted hours?

   d. As a successful adult, you've no doubt experienced one of those moments when you ask yourself, "Could I make a difference in a child's life by teaching?" Just think of the sense of satisfaction that such a wonderful experience could bring to your life.

2. You've finished writing your opening and the body of the letter, which includes information about the volunteering program and the experience of being a tutor. Which of these closes would be the best way to conclude your letter?

   a. If you can lend a hand to our volunteer efforts by tutoring children in these subjects, please contact me by July 20 (my e-mail address and phone number are shown below). Thank you once again for your kind financial support, and I hope we'll be able to add you to our list of volunteer tutors as well.

   b. Please let me know if you'd be interested in helping out with the tutoring program. After all, anybody can write a check. Real heroes give of themselves—their time, their energy, and their skills.

   c. If you can lend a hand to our volunteer efforts by tutoring children in these subjects for two to four hours a week, or if you might be interested but want to know more about the program, please contact me by July 20 (my e-mail address and phone number are shown below). Thank you once again for your kind financial support, and I hope we'll be able to add you to our list of volunteer tutors as well.

   d. Thank you once again for your kind financial support, and I hope we'll be able to add you to our list of volunteer tutors as well. I look forward to hearing from you.

3. It's nine months later, and the recruiting program has been a success. Most Kids Cafés have filled their volunteer openings, and some are expanding the tutoring program to other subjects because so many people volunteered. Now it's time write a letter to thank everyone who helps the children by volunteering their time every week. Each letter will include two free movie passes as a gesture of appreciation, and each will be personally signed by the CEO of ConAgra. Which of these openings is the best way to start this letter of appreciation?

   a. Executives such as myself are constantly asked to volunteer for a variety of community organizations, so I know how challenging it can be to find those free hours in your schedule every week—even if you're not busy running a multibillion-dollar corporation.

   b. You are a miracle worker! Not many people are equipped with the skills, dedication, and commitment to the children that it takes to be a volunteer tutor, but you are definitely in that select company.

   c. Helping people is what it's all about, isn't it? And now it's time for the good folks at ConAgra to help you in return with these FREE movie passes. Enjoy!

   d. On behalf of everyone at ConAgra and everyone involved in the Kids Café program, please accept my sincere thanks for the time you've taken out of your busy schedule to help tutor the children at Kids Café. It's a small token, to be sure, but please accept these movie passes. I hope you'll find time to relax for a few hours with someone special.

4. One of the volunteer tutors from the Kids Café near your office has e-mailed you with a request to write a letter of recommendation for him. He says you have inspired him so much that not only does he want to work in the public relations field, he wants to apply for a writing position at Cone. You're simultaneously flattered—he's a wonderful young man—and pleased to be an inspiration, but he just hasn't worked out as an English tutor because his own writing skills are too limited. In fact, you've been searching for other volunteer opportunities for him so that you can transfer him out of the tutoring program. How should you handle his request?

   a. Ignore the request. The volunteer will get the message that you don't think his skills are sufficient to work at Cone.

   b. Write the letter but carefully avoid any direct endorsement of the volunteer's writing skills. Instead, focus on his ability to work with others, his commitment to helping the community, and his record of dependability.

   c. Telephone the volunteer and explain that PR agencies have extremely high expectations for writers and that his chances of being hired could be improved through some formal training and additional writing experience.

   d. Reply by e-mail with an explanation that you don't really have time to write the letter now, but you'll try to get to it when things calm down.

Learning Objectives Checkup

Assess your understanding of the principles in this chapter by reading each learning objective and studying the accompanying exercises. For fill-in-the-blank items, write the missing text in the blank provided; for multiple-choice items, circle the letter of the correct answer. You can check your responses against the answer key on page AK-2.

Objective 8.1: Apply the three-step writing process to routine and positive messages.

1. When it comes to routine messages, you can
   a. Skip the planning stage
   b. Keep the planning stage brief
   c. Begin by gathering all the information you'll need
   d. Begin by choosing the channel and medium

2. When writing routine messages, you
   a. Can assume that your readers will be interested or neutral
   b. Should open with an "attention getter"
   c. Should use the indirect approach with most audiences
   d. Need not allow much time for revision, production, or proofreading

Objective 8.2: Outline an effective strategy for writing routine requests.

3. When writing a routine request, you begin
   a. With a personal introduction, such as "My name is Lee Marrs, and I am . . ."
   b. With a vague reference to what you are writing about, such as "I have something to ask you."
   c. With a strong demand for action
   d. By politely stating your request

4. What should you do when asking questions in a routine request?
   a. Begin with the least important question and work your way up to the most important question.
   b. Include all possible questions about the topic, even if the list gets long.
   c. Deal with only one topic per question.
   d. Do all of the above.

5. Which of the following should you do when closing a routine request?
   a. Be sure to thank the reader "in advance" for complying with the request.
   b. Ask the reader to respond by a specific and appropriate time.
   c. Ask any remaining questions you have.
   d. Do all of the above.

Objective 8.3: Explain how to ask for specific action in a courteous manner.

6. A courteous close contains
   a. A specific request
   b. Information about how you can be reached (if it isn't obvious)
   c. An expression of appreciation or goodwill
   d. All of the above

Objective 8.4: Describe a strategy for writing routine replies and positive messages.

7. If you are making a routine reply to a customer, it's a good idea to
   a. Leave out any negative information
   b. Include resale information to assure the customer of the wisdom of his or her purchase
   c. Leave out sales promotion material, which would be tacky to include
   d. Do all of the above

8. A positive message should open with a clear and concise statement of _____.

9. If a message has both positive and negative elements, you should
   a. Always start with the bad news to get it out of the way first
   b. Write two separate messages; never mix good and bad news
   c. Put the bad news in a postscript (p.s.) at the bottom of the letter
   d. Try to put the negative news in a positive context

Objective 8.5: Discuss the importance of knowing who is responsible when granting claims and requests for adjustment.

10. Which of the following is not among the recommended elements to include in your message if you are responding to a claim or complaint when your company is at fault?
    a. An acknowledgement that you received the customer's claim or complaint
    b. An expression of sympathy for the inconvenience or loss the customer has experienced
    c. An explanation of how you will resolve the situation
    d. Complete contact information for your corporate legal staff

11. If a customer who is clearly at fault requests an adjustment, you should
    a. Ignore the request; the customer is clearly wasting your time
    b. Carefully weigh the cost of complying with the request against the cost of denying it and then decide how to respond based on the overall impact on your company
    c. Always agree to such requests because unhappy customers spread bad publicity about a company
    d. Suggest in a firm but professional tone that the customer take his or her business elsewhere in the future

12. If a third party (such as a shipping company) is at fault when one of your customers makes a claim or requests an adjustment, the best response is to
    a. Follow the terms of whatever customer service agreement your company has with the third party
    b. Explain to the customer that your company is not at fault

c. Always grant the request; after all, it's your customer, and the customer holds you responsible

d. Forward the message to the third party as quickly as possible

Objective 8.6: Explain how creating informative messages differs from responding to information requests.

13. Which of the following is generally true about informative messages?
   a. Audiences always request informative messages.
   b. Your audience may or may not be expecting informative messages and may or may not be motivated to read them.
   c. Audiences don't request informative messages, so they always reject them when they arrive.
   d. Informative messages are always positive.

Objective 8.7: Describe the importance of goodwill messages, and explain how to make them effective.

14. The purpose of goodwill messages is to
   a. Generate sales
   b. Impress others
   c. Make yourself feel better
   d. Enhance relationships with customers, colleagues, and other businesspeople

15. The most effective goodwill messages
   a. Always try to find an "angle" that benefits the sender in addition to the receiver
   b. Avoid details and focus on the emotions of the situation
   c. Are sincere and honest
   d. Do all of the above

Apply Your Knowledge

1. Why is it good practice to explain why replying to a request could benefit the reader?

2. Your company's error cost an important business customer a new client; you know it, and your customer knows it. Do you apologize, or do you refer to the incident in a positive light without admitting any responsibility? Briefly explain.

3. You've been asked to write a letter of recommendation for an employee who worked for you some years ago. You recall that the employee did an admirable job, but you can't remember any specific information at this point. Should you write the letter anyway? Explain.

4. Every time you send a direct-request e-mail message to Ted Jackson, who works in another department in your company, he delays or refuses to comply. You're beginning to get impatient. Should you send Jackson a memo to ask what's wrong? Complain to your supervisor about Jackson's uncooperative attitude? Arrange a face-to-face meeting with Jackson? Bring up the problem at the next staff meeting? Explain your answer.

5. **Ethical Choices** You have a complaint against one of your suppliers, but you have no documentation to back it up. Should you request an adjustment anyway? Why or why not?

Practice Your Knowledge

MESSAGES FOR ANALYSIS

Read the following documents and then (1) analyze the strengths and weaknesses of each sentence and (2) revise each document so that it follows this chapter's guidelines.

MESSAGE 8.A: REQUESTING ROUTINE INFORMATION FROM A BUSINESS

Our college is closing its dining hall for financial reasons, so we want to do something to help the students prepare their own food in their dorm rooms if they so choose. Your colorful ad in Collegiate Magazine caught our eye. We need the following information before we make our decision:

- *Would you be able to ship the microwaves by August 15th? I realize this is short notice, but our board of trustees just made the decision to close the dining hall last week, and we're scrambling around trying to figure out what to do.*
- *Do they have any kind of a warranty? College students can be pretty hard on things, as you know, so we will need a good warranty.*

- *How much does it cost? Do you give a discount for a big order?*
- *Do we have to provide a special outlet?*
- *Will students know how to use them, or will we need to provide instructions?*

As I said before, we're on a tight time frame and need good information from you as soon as possible to help us make our decision about ordering. You never know what the board might come up with next. I'm looking at several other companies also, so please let us know ASAP.

MESSAGE 8.B: MAKING CLAIMS AND REQUESTS FOR ADJUSTMENT

At a local business-supply store, I recently purchased your Negotiator Pro for my computer. I bought the CD because I saw your ad for it in Macworld magazine, and it looked as if it might be an effective tool for use in my corporate seminar on negotiation.

Unfortunately, when I inserted it in my office computer, it wouldn't work. I returned it to the store, but since I had already opened it, they refused to exchange it for a CD that would work or give me a refund. They told me to contact you and that you might be able to send me a version that would work with my computer.

You can send the information to me at the letterhead address. If you cannot send me the correct disk, please refund my $79.95. Thanks in advance for any help you can give me in this matter.

MESSAGE 8.C: RESPONDING TO CLAIMS AND ADJUSTMENT REQUESTS WHEN THE CUSTOMER IS AT FAULT

We read your letter requesting your deposit refund. We couldn't figure out why you hadn't received it, so we talked to our maintenance engineer as you suggested. He said you had left one of the doors off the hinges in your apartment in order to get a large sofa through the door. He also confirmed that you had paid him $5.00 to replace the door since you had to turn in the U-Haul trailer and were in a big hurry.

This entire situation really was caused by a lack of communication between our housekeeping inspector and the maintenance engineer. All we knew was that the door was off the hinges when it was inspected by Sally Tarnley. You know that our policy states that if anything is wrong with the apartment, we keep the deposit. We had no way of knowing that George just hadn't gotten around to replacing the door.

But we have good news. We approved the deposit refund, which will be mailed to you from our home office in Teaneck, New Jersey. I'm not sure how long that will take, however. If you don't receive the check by the end of next month, give me a call.

Next time, it's really a good idea to stay with your apartment until it's inspected as stipulated in your lease agreement. That way, you'll be sure to receive your refund when you expect it. Hope you have a good summer.

MESSAGE 8.D: LETTER OF RECOMMENDATION

Your letter to Kunitake Ando, President of Sony, was forwarded to me because I am the human resources director. In my job as head of HR, I have access to performance reviews for all of the Sony employees in the United States. This means, of course, that I would be the person best qualified to answer your request for information on Nick Oshinski.

In your letter of the 15th, you asked about Nick Oshinski's employment record with us because he has applied to work for your company. Mr. Oshinski was employed with us from January 5, 1998, until March 1, 2008. During that time, Mr. Oshinski received ratings ranging from 2.5 up to 9.6, with 10 being the top score. As you can see, he must have done better reporting to some managers than to others. In addition, he took all vacation days, which is a bit unusual. Although I did not know Mr. Oshinski personally, I know that our best workers seldom use all the vacation time they earn. I do not know if that applies in this case.

In summary, Nick Oshinski performed his tasks well depending on who managed him.

EXERCISES

For active links to all websites discussed in this chapter, visit this text's website at www.prenhall.com/thill. Locate your book and click on its "Companion Website" link. Then select

Chapter 8 and click on "Featured Websites." Locate the name of the page or the URL related to the material in the text. Please note that links to sites that become inactive after publication of the book will be removed from the "Featured Websites" section.

8.1 Revising Messages: Directness and Conciseness Revise the following short e-mail messages so that they are more direct and concise; develop a subject line for each revised message.

a. I'm contacting you about your recent e-mail request for technical support on your cable Internet service. Part of the problem we have in tech support is trying to figure out exactly what each customer's specific problem is so that we can troubleshoot quickly and get you back in business as quickly as possible. You may have noticed that in the online support request form, there are a number of fields to enter your type of computer, operating system, memory, and so on. While you did tell us you were experiencing slow download speeds during certain times of the day, you didn't tell us which times specifically, nor did you complete all the fields telling us about your computer. Please return to our support website and resubmit your request, being sure to provide all the necessary information; then we'll be able to help you.

b. Thank you for contacting us about the difficulty you had collecting your luggage at Denver International Airport. We are very sorry for the inconvenience this has caused you. As you know, traveling can create problems of this sort regardless of how careful the airline personnel might be. To receive compensation, please send us a detailed list of the items that you lost and complete the following questionnaire. You can e-mail it back to us.

c. Sorry it took us so long to get back to you. We were flooded with résumés. Anyway, your résumé made the final 10, and after meeting three hours yesterday, we've decided we'd like to meet with you. What is your schedule like for next week? Can you come in for an interview on June 15 at 3:00 p.m.? Please get back to us by the end of this workweek and let us know if you will be able to attend. As you can imagine, this is our busy season.

d. We're letting you know that because we use over a ton of paper a year and because so much of that paper goes into the wastebasket to become so much more environmental waste, starting Monday, we're placing white plastic bins outside the elevators on every floor to recycle that paper and, in the process, minimize pollution.

8.2 Revising Messages: Directness and Conciseness Rewrite the following sentences so that they are direct and concise. If necessary, break your answer into two sentences.

a. We wanted to invite you to our special 40% off by-invitation-only sale; the sale is taking place on November 9.

b. We wanted to let you know that we are giving a tote bag and a voucher for five iTunes downloads with every $50 donation you make to our radio station.

c. The director planned to go to the meeting that will be held on Monday at a little before 11 a.m.

d. In today's meeting, we were happy to have the opportunity to welcome Paul Eccelson, who reviewed the shopping cart function on our website and offered some great advice; if you have any questions about these new forms, feel free to call him at his office.

8.3 Internet Visit the Workplace eCards section of the Blue Mountain site at **www.bluemountain.com** and analyze one of the electronic greeting cards bearing a goodwill message of appreciation for good performance. Under what circumstances would you send this electronic message? How could you personalize it for the recipient and the occasion? What would be an appropriate close for this message?

8.4 Teamwork With another student, identify the purpose and select the most appropriate medium for communicating the following written messages. Next, consider how the audience is likely to respond to each message. Based on this audience analysis, determine whether the direct or indirect approach would be effective for each message and explain your reasoning.

a. A notice to all employees about the placement of recycling bins by the elevator doors

b. The first late-payment notice to a good customer who usually pays his bills on time

8.5 Revising Messages: Conciseness, Courteousness, and Specificity Critique the following closing paragraphs. How would you rewrite each to be concise, courteous, and specific?

a. I need your response sometime soon so I can order the parts in time for your service appointment. Otherwise, your air-conditioning system may not be in tip-top condition for the start of the summer season.

b. Thank you in advance for sending me as much information as you can about your products. I look forward to receiving your package in the very near future.

c. To schedule an appointment with one of our knowledgeable mortgage specialists in your area, you can always call our hotline at 1-800-555-8765. This is also the number to call if you have more questions about mortgage rates, closing procedures, or any other aspect of the mortgage process. Remember, we're here to make the home-buying experience as painless as possible.

8.6 Ethical Choices Your company markets a line of automotive accessories for people who like to "tune" their cars for maximum performance. A customer has just written a furious e-mail, claiming that a supercharger he purchased from your website didn't deliver the extra engine power he expected. Your company has a standard refund process to handle situations such as this, and you have the information you need to inform the customer about that. You also have information that could help the customer find a more compatible supercharger from one of your competitors, but the customer's e-mail message is so abusive that you don't feel obligated to help. Is this an appropriate response? Why or why not?

Expand Your Knowledge

LEARNING MORE ON THE WEB

RECOMMENDED ADVICE FOR RECOMMENDATION LETTERS

http://businessmajors.about.com

Whether you're continuing on to graduate school or entering the workforce with your undergraduate degree, recommendation letters could play an important role in the next few steps of your career. From selecting the people to ask for recommendation letters to knowing what makes an effective letter, About.com extends the advice offered in this chapter with real-life examples and suggestions. Visit About.com's Business Majors website and click on "Recommendation Letters." Read the advice you find and answer the following questions:

1. What is a good process for identifying the best people to ask for recommendation letters?

2. What information should you provide to letter writers to help them produce credible and compelling letters on your behalf?

3. What are the most common mistakes you need to avoid with recommendation letters?

SURFING YOUR WAY TO CAREER SUCCESS

Bovée and Thill's Business Communication Headline News offers links to hundreds of online resources that can help you with this course, your other college courses, and your career. Visit **www.businesscommunicationblog.com** and click on "Web Directory." The "Communication on the Job" section connects you to a variety of websites and articles on committees and teams, group communication, team conflict, negotiation, office politics, and the grapevine. Identify three websites from this section that could be useful in your business career. For each site, write a two-sentence summary of what the site offers and how it could help you launch and build your career.

Learn Interactively

INTERACTIVE STUDY GUIDE

Visit www.prenhall.com/thill, then locate your book and click on its "Companion Website" link. Select Chapter 8 to take advantage of the interactive "Chapter Quiz" to test your knowledge of chapter concepts. Receive instant feedback on whether you need additional studying. Also, visit the "Study Hall," where you'll find an abundance of valuable resources that will help you succeed in this course.

PEAK PERFORMANCE GRAMMAR AND MECHANICS

If your instructor has required the use of the "Peak Performance Grammar and Mechanics," either in your online course or on a CD, you can improve your skill with

sentences by using the "Peak Performance Grammar and Mechanics" module. Click on "Sentences." Take the Pretest to determine whether you have any weak areas. Then review those areas in the Refresher Course. Take the Follow-Up Test to check your grasp of sentences. For an extra challenge or advanced practice, take the Advanced Test. Finally, for additional reinforcement, go to the "Improve Your Grammar, Mechanics, and Usage" section that follows and complete those exercises.

Improve Your Grammar, Mechanics, and Usage

The following exercises help you improve your knowledge of and power over English grammar, mechanics, and usage. Turn to the Handbook of Grammar, Mechanics, and Usage at the end of this book and review all of Section 1.7 (Sentences). Then look at the following 10 items. Circle the letter of the preferred choice within each group of sentences. (Answers to these exercises appear on page AK-3.)

1. a. Joan Ellingsworth attends every stockholder meeting. Because she is one of the few board members eligible to vote.
   b. Joan Ellingsworth attends every stockholder meeting. She is one of the few board members eligible to vote.
2. a. The executive director, along with his team members, is working quickly to determine the cause of the problem.
   b. The executive director, along with his team members, are working quickly to determine the cause of the problem.
3. a. Listening on the extension, details of the embezzlement plot were overheard by the security chief.
   b. Listening on the extension, the chief overheard details of the embezzlement plot.
4. a. First the human resources department interviewed dozens of people. Then it hired a placement service.
   b. First the human resources department interviewed dozens of people then it hired a placement service
5. a. Andrews won the sales contest, however he was able to sign up only two new accounts.
   b. Andrews won the sales contest; however, he was able to sign up only two new accounts.

6. a. To find the missing file, the whole office was turned inside out.
   b. The whole office was turned inside out to find the missing file.
7. a. Having finally gotten his transfer, he is taking his assistant right along with him.
   b. Having finally gotten his transfer, his assistant is going right along with him.
8. a. Irving was recruiting team members for her project, she promised supporters unprecedented bonuses.
   b. Because Irving was recruiting team members for her project, she promised supporters unprecedented bonuses.
9. a. He left the office unlocked overnight. This was an unconscionable act, considering the high crime rate in this area lately.
   b. He left the office unlocked overnight. An unconscionable act, considering the high crime rate in this area lately.
10. a. When it comes to safety issues, the abandoned mine, with its collapsing tunnels, are cause for great concern.
    b. When it comes to safety issues, the abandoned mine, with its collapsing tunnels, is cause for great concern.

For additional exercises focusing on sentences, go to www.prenhall.com/thill, then locate your text and click on its "Companion Website" link. Click on Chapter 8, click on "Additional Exercises to Improve Your Grammar, Mechanics and Usage," and click on "12. Longer sentences," "13. Sentence fragments," "15. Misplaced modifiers," or "24. Transitional words and phrases."

Cases

Applying the Three-Step Writing Process to Cases

Apply each step to the following cases, as assigned by your instructor.

Planning

Analyze the Situation
Identify both your general purpose and your specific purpose. Clarify exactly what you want your audience to think, feel, or believe after receiving your message. Profile your primary audience, including their backgrounds, differences, similarities, and likely reactions to your message.

Gather Information
Identify the information your audience will need to receive, as well as other information you may need in order to craft an effective message.

Select the Right Medium
Make sure the medium is both acceptable to the audience and appropriate for the message.

Organize the Information
Choose a direct or indirect approach based on the audience and the message; most routine requests and routine and positive messages should employ a direct approach. Identify your main idea, limit your scope, then outline necessary support points and other evidence.

Writing

Adapt to Your Audience
Show sensitivity to audience needs, by using a "you" attitude, politeness, positive emphasis, and bias-free language. Understand how much credibility you already have—and how much you may need to establish. Project your image by maintaining an appropriate style and tone.

Compose the Message
Draft your message using powerful words, effective sentences, and coherent paragraphs.

Completing

Revise the Message
Evaluate content and review readability and then edit and rewrite for conciseness and clarity.

Produce the Message
Use effective design elements and suitable layout for a clean, professional appearance.

Proofread the Message
Review for errors in layout, spelling, and mechanics; verify overall document quality.

Distribute the Message
Deliver your message using the chosen medium; make sure all documents and all relevant files are distributed successfully.

1   **2**   **3**

ROUTINE REQUESTS

E-Mail SKILLS

1. **Breathing life back into your biotech career: E-mail requesting a recommendation** After five years of work in the human resources department at *Cell Genesys* (a company that is developing cancer treatment drugs), you were laid off in a round of cost-cutting moves that rippled through the biotech industry in recent years. The good news is that you found stable employment in the grocery distribution industry. The bad news is that in the three years since you left Cell Genesys, you have truly missed working in the exciting biotechnology field and having the opportunity to be a part of something as important as helping people recover from life-threatening diseases. You know that careers in biotech are uncertain, but you have a few dollars in the bank now, and you're willing to ride that rollercoaster again.

Your task: Draft an e-mail to Calvin Morris, your old boss at Cell Genesys, reminding him of the time you worked together and asking him to write a letter of recommendation for you.[6]

IM SKILLS

2. Transglobal exchange: Instant message request for information from Chinese manufacturer Thank goodness your company, Diagonal Imports, chose the Sametime enterprise instant messaging software produced by IBM Lotus. Other products also allow you to carry on real-time exchanges with colleagues on the other side of the planet, but Sametime supports bidirectional machine translation, and you're going to need it.

The problem is that production on a popular line of decorative lighting appliances produced at your Chinese manufacturing plant inexplicably came to a halt last month. As the product manager in the United States, you have many resources you could call on to help, such as new sources for faulty parts. But you can't do anything if you don't know the details. You've tried telephoning top managers in China, but they're evasive, telling you only what they think you want to hear.

Finally, your friend Kuei-chen Tsao has returned from a business trip. You met her during your trip to China last year. She doesn't speak English, but she's the line engineer responsible for this particular product: a fiber-optic lighting display that features a plastic base with a rotating color wheel. As the wheel turns, light emitted from the spray of fiber-optic threads changes color in soothing patterns. Product #3347XM is one of Diagonal's most popular items, and you've got orders from novelty stores around the United States waiting to be filled. Kuei-chen should be able to explain the problem, determine whether you can help, and tell you how long before regular shipping resumes.

Your task: Write the first of what you hope will be a productive instant message exchange with Kuei-chen. Remember that your words will be machine translated.[7]

Text-Messaging SKILLS

3. Tracking the new product buzz: Text message to colleagues at a trade show The vast Consumer Electronics Show (CES) is the premier promotional event in the industry. More than 130,000 industry insiders from all over the world come to see the exciting new products on display from nearly 1,500 companies—everything from video game gadgets to Internet-enabled refrigerators with built-in computer screens. You've just stumbled on a video game controller that has a built-in webcam to allow networked gamers to see and hear each other while they play. Your company also makes game controllers, and you're worried that your customers will flock to this new controller-cam. You need to know how much buzz is circulating around the show: Have people seen it? What are they saying about it? Are they excited about it?

Your task: Compose a text message to your colleagues at the show, alerting them to the new controller-cam and asking them to listen for any buzz it might be generating among the attendees at the Las Vegas Convention Center and the several surrounding hotels where the show takes place. Here's the catch: Your text-messaging service limits messages to 160 characters, including spaces and punctuation, so your message can't be any longer than this.[8]

4. Step on it: Letter to Floorgraphics requesting information about underfoot advertising You work for Alberta Greenwood, owner of Better Bike and Ski Shop. Yesterday, Alberta met with the Schwinn sales representative, Tom Beeker, who urged her to sign a contract with Floorgraphics. That company leases floor space from retail stores and creates and sells floor ads to manufacturers such as Schwinn. Floorgraphics will pay Alberta a fee for leasing the floor space, as well as a percentage for every ad it sells. Alberta was definitely interested and turned to you after Beeker left.

"Tom says that advertising decals on the floor in front of the product reach consumers right where they're standing when making a decision," explained Alberta. "He says the ads increase sales from 25 to 75 percent."

You both look down at the dusty floor, and Alberta laughs. "It seems funny that manufacturers will pay hard cash to put their names where customers are going to track dirt all over them! But if Tom's telling the truth, we could profit three ways: from the leasing fee, the increased sales of products being advertised, and the share in ad revenues. That's not so funny."

Your task: Alberta Greenwood asks you to write a letter for her signature to CEO Richard Rebh at Floorgraphics, Inc. (5 Vaughn Dr., Princeton, NJ 08540) asking for financial details and practical information about the ads. For example, how will you clean your floors? Who installs and removes the ads? Can you terminate the lease if you don't like the ads?[9]

5. Air rage fiasco: Letter requesting refund from British Airways "There we were, cruising over the Atlantic, and the guy just went berserk! I couldn't believe it!" Samantha Alberts, vice president of sales at Richter Office Solutions, is standing over your desk, describing the scene for you. You notice that your boss is still pale and shaky, even though it's Monday and the "incident" happened last Friday.

She was flying back from a conference in London to make a presentation at your New York branch, before heading back home to San Francisco on Saturday. She admits it was a crushing schedule and probably foolish to plan to prepare her notes on the plane, but she never expected this.

"So how did it start?" you ask mildly, hoping your calm will help steady her nerves. She's got another meeting in two hours.

"Well, I didn't notice anything until this guy leaped up and lunged for the flight attendant with both fists flailing. But later I heard that he'd been viewing offensive images on his laptop and that other passengers complained that they could see the screen. When the steward politely asked him to stop, the guy went nuts! He was a stocky, red-faced, bull-necked guy, and it took six crew members to handcuff him and strap him into a back-row seat. Maybe he was drunk or on drugs, I don't know, but he just kept screaming, 'I'm going to kill you!' and hitting people with his head, which was bleeding everywhere.

"Finally a passenger who was a pediatrician came forward and offered to administer a sedative to the guy. Thank goodness. Otherwise we would've been listening to his profanity for the next 10 hours . . . ." she trails off. "You know, I thought he was a hijacker and I was going to die on that plane."

"So did they arrest him?"

"As soon as we got on the ground. Police cars were everywhere. He just kept mumbling, 'I thought they were going to kill me.'" She shudders. "But the flight attendants and airline officials were wonderful. They told us to write to the airline, explain the details, and ask for a refund. Of course, I was late and unprepared for my meeting. Thank goodness it wasn't a client! When they heard about my 'air rage' encounter, the folks in our home office just handed me a cup of strong coffee and sat me down on a couch with a blanket."

Your task: You always handle Samantha's travel arrangements, and she's left you with her ticket stubs and other documents. Write the letter requesting a refund to British Airways Ticket Refunds USA, 75-20 Astoria Blvd., Jackson Heights, NY 11370. (Make up any necessary times, dates, or flight numbers.)[10]

6. Unhappy customer: Claim letter requesting an adjustment As a consumer, you've probably bought something that didn't work right or paid for a service that did not turn out the way you expected. Maybe it was a pair of jeans with a rip in a seam that you didn't find until you got home or a watch that broke a week after you bought it. Or maybe your family hired a lawn service to do some yard work—and no one from the company showed up on the day promised; and when the gardeners finally appeared, they did not do what they'd been hired for but did other things that wound up damaging valuable plants.

Your task: Choose such an incident from your own experience and write a claim letter asking for a refund, repair, replacement, or other adjustment. You'll need to include all the details of the transaction, plus your contact address and phone number. If you can't think of such an experience, make up details for an imaginary situation. If your experi-

ence is real, you might want to mail the letter. The reply you receive will provide a good test of your claim-writing skills.

E-Mail SKILLS

7. A juicy position: E-mail requesting information about careers at Jamba Juice You did not expect to find a job while working out at 24-Hour Fitness, but you're willing to explore an opportunity when it appears. As you were buying a smoothie at the Jamba Juice bar inside the gym, you overheard the manager talking about the company's incentives for employees, especially those interested in becoming managers. You ask her about it, and she suggests you visit the company's website (www.jambajuice.com) for more information.

You're still in business school, and you need a part-time job. Finding one at a company that offers a good future after graduation would be even better than simply earning some money to keep you going now. You check the Jamba Juice website. You discover that the juice-bar chain has created a good reputation in the health, fitness, and nutrition industry. Also, you can submit your résumé online for an entry-level job. That sounds promising. If you could start now while finishing your degree, you'd be in a prime spot for promotion once you graduate. You start to wonder if Jamba Juice could be a long-term career opportunity.

Your task: Write an e-mail message requesting additional information about careers and advancement at Jamba Juice. First, visit www.jambajuice.com to learn all that you can about the company; then compose your message. Specifically, ask for information about career long-term advancement beyond the store level, to corporate management. You might want to mention that you're still in school, studying business (make up any details you need).[11]

E-Mail SKILLS

8. Blockbuster shake-up: Message requesting information from retail managers Everyone knew there was trouble at Blockbuster's new headquarters in Dallas when CEO Bill Fields, a former Wal-Mart whiz, suddenly resigned. Then Sumner Redstone and Tom Dooley (chairman and deputy chairman of Blockbuster's parent company, Viacom) flew in to assess the damage wrought by Fields's departure. They started by giving orders—particularly to you, Fields's former executive assistant.

Before Fields resigned to take a position with Hudson's Bay Company in Canada, his strategy had been to boost Blockbuster's sagging movie and game rentals by establishing a new niche as a "neighborhood entertainment center." Using strategies he'd learned at Wal-Mart, he ordered the reconfiguration of more than 1,000 Blockbuster outlets, surrounding the cash registers with flashy displays of candy, potato chips, magazines, tie-in toys, and new and used DVDs for sale. His stated goal was to add $1 in retail purchases to every rental transaction. Meanwhile, he also relocated Blockbuster's headquarters from Florida to Dallas, losing 75 percent of the company's top staff when they declined to make the move. Then Fields initiated the construction of an 818,000-square-foot warehouse 25 miles outside Dallas to centralize a new, highly sophisticated distribution operation (Fields's special expertise) for Blockbuster's 3,600 North American outlets. But revenues were still falling.

Redstone and Dooley's new plan is to get Blockbuster back into its core business of movie and game rentals. "This is still a healthy, growing business," Dooley insists. He believes that consumers coming in to rent movies and games were confused by the array of retail products that greeted them.

Dooley and Redstone have been hiring new headquarters staff at the rate of about 50 people per week, they've been to the warehouse construction site, they've ordered outlets to rearrange merchandise to emphasize rentals, and now they've turned to you. "We've got a job you'll love," Dooley smiles. "We want to know what our store managers know, and we want you to ask them."

Your task: Briefly state the purpose of your message. Then draft an e-mail request asking retail managers if customers walk out when current hits aren't available, whether the emphasis on retail products affected cash flow, and whether sales and rental figures have changed now that the clutter has been removed. Ask them: Where's the cash coming from—movie and game rentals, movie and game sales, or candy bars? Dooley says, "I want a full report from every manager by the end of next week!" To get that kind of cooperation, be sure to organize your questions effectively.[12]

ROUTINE MESSAGES

Blogging SKILLS

9. Here's how it will work: Explaining the brainstorming process Austin, Texas, advertising agency GSD&M Advertising brainstorms new advertising ideas using a process it calls *dynamic collaboration*. A hand-picked team of insiders and outsiders is briefed on the project and given a key question or two to answer. The team members then sit down at computers and anonymously submit as many responses as they can within five minutes. The project moderators then pore over these responses, looking for any sparks that can ignite new ways of understanding and reaching out to consumers.

Your task: For these brainstorming sessions, GSD&M recruits an eclectic mix of participants from inside and outside the agency—figures as diverse as economists and professional video gamers. To make sure everyone understands the brainstorming guidelines, prepare a message to be posted on the project blog. In your own words, convey the following four points as clearly and succinctly as you can:

- **Be yourself.** We want input from as many perspectives as possible, which is why we recruit such a diverse array of participants. Don't try to get into what you believe is the mindset of an advertising specialist; we want you to approach the given challenge using whatever analytical and creative skills you normally employ in your daily work.

- **Create, don't edit.** Don't edit, refine, or self-censor while you're typing during the initial five-minute session. We don't care if your ideas are formatted beautifully, phrased poetically, or even spelled correctly. Just crank 'em out as quickly as you can.

- **It's about the ideas, not the participants.** Just so you know up front, all ideas are collected anonymously. We can't tell who submitted the brilliant ideas, the boring ideas, or the already-tried-that ideas. So while you won't get personal credit, you can also be crazy and fearless. Go for it!

- **The winning ideas will be subjected to the toughest of tests.** Just in case you're worried about submitting ideas that could be risky, expensive, or difficult to implement—don't fret. As we narrow down the possibilities, the few that remain will be judged, poked, prodded, and assessed from every angle. In other words, let us worry about containing the fire; you come up with the sparks.[13]

Podcasting SKILLS Portfolio BUILDER

10. Listening to business: Using the iPod to train employees As a training specialist in Winnebago Industry's human resources department, you're always on the lookout for new ways to help employees learn vital job skills. While watching a production worker page through a training manual while learning how to assemble a new recreational vehicle, you get what seems to be a great idea: Record the assembly instructions as audio files that workers can listen to while performing the necessary steps. With audio instructions, they wouldn't need to keep shifting their eyes between the product and the manual—and constantly losing their place. They could focus on the product and listen for each instruction. Plus, the new system wouldn't cost much at all; any computer can record the audio files, and you'd simply make them available on an intranet site for download into iPods or other digital music players.

Your task: You immediately run your new idea past your boss, who has heard about podcasting but doesn't think it has any place in business. He asks you to prove the viability of the idea by recording a demonstration. Choose a process that you engage in yourself—anything from replacing the strings on a guitar to sewing a quilt to changing the oil in a car—and write a brief (one page or less) description of the process that could be recorded as an audio file. Think carefully about the limitations of the audio format as a replacement for printed text (for instance, do you need to tell people to pause the audio while they perform a time-consuming task?). If directed by your instructor, record your instructions as a podcast.

Portfolio BUILDER

11. Got it covered? Letter from American Express about SUV rentals You can always tell when fall arrives at American Express—you are deluged with complaints from customers who have just received their summer vacation bills. Often these angry calls are about a shock-inducing damage repair bill from a car rental agency. Vacation car rentals can be a lot more complicated than most people think. Here's what happens.

Your credit card customers are standing at the Hertz or Avis counter, ready to drive away, when the agent suggests an upgrade to, say, a Ford Expedition or another large SUV. Feeling happy-go-lucky on vacation, your customers say, "Why not?" and hand over their American Express card.

As they drive off in large vehicles that many are unaccustomed to handling, 9 out of 10 are unaware that the most common accidents among rental cars take place at low speeds in parking lots. Plus, the upgraded vehicle they're driving is no longer fully covered either by their regular auto insurance or

by the secondary car rental insurance they expect from American Express. If they've agreed to pay the additional $10 to $25 a day for the car rental agency's "collision and liability damage wavier fee," they will be able to walk away from any accident with no liability. Otherwise, they're running a costly risk.

Soon they pull into a shopping mall with the kids to pick up the forgotten sunscreen and sodas, where they discover that luxury road-warrior mobile is not so easy to park in stalls designed in the 1970s and 1980s, when compact cars were all the rage. *Thwack*—there goes the door panel. *Crunch*—a rear bumper into a light post. *Wham!* There goes the family bank account, but they don't realize it yet—not until they receive the bill from the rental agency, the one that comes *after* their auto insurance and credit card companies have already paid as much as they're going to pay for damages.

Auto insurers typically provide the same coverage for rentals as you carry on your own car. When customers use their credit card to pay for car rentals, American Express offers secondary protection that generally covers any remaining, unpaid damages. But there are important exceptions. Neither insurance nor credit card companies will pay the "loss of vehicle use fees" that car rental agencies always tack on. These fees can run into thousands of dollars, based on the agency's revenue losses while the car is in the repair shop. When your customers are billed for this fee, they invariably call you, angrily demanding to know why American Express won't pay it. And if they've rented an SUV, they're even angrier.

American Express Green and Gold cards provide secondary coverage up to $55,000, and the Platinum card extends that to $75,000. But large SUVs such as the Ford Expedition, the GMC Yukon, and the Chevrolet Suburban are not covered at all. Such exclusions are common. For instance, Diners Club specifically excludes "high-value, special interest or exotic cars"—such as the Ferraris, Maseratis, and even Rolls Royces that are urged on customers by rental agencies.

Your task: As assistant vice president of customer service, you'd like to keep the phone lines cooler this summer and fall. It's April, so there's still time. Write a form letter to be sent to all American Express customers, urging them to check their rental car coverages, advising them against renting vehicles that are larger than they really require, and encouraging them to consider paying the rental agency's daily loss waiver fees.[14]

12. Mind your own e-mail: Message outlining electronic privacy policy at the *Los Angeles Times* When you stepped into your office at the *Los Angeles Times* this morning, the place was buzzing with gossip about a reporter in the paper's Moscow bureau. Apparently, he'd been snooping into his fellow reporters' e-mail. To catch him, supervisors there set up a sting operation, planting an exchange of phony e-mail messages with the Jerusalem bureau, which cooperated in catching the snoop. The bogus e-mail referred to "shrinking travel allowances."

The suspect took the bait, apparently using a co-worker's password to view the e-mail. When he later mentioned the new travel rules, he was slapped with a reassignment back to Los Angeles, to an as-yet-undesignated job—probably writing obituaries, or so the rumormongers in your office have decided.

The *Los Angeles Times* has always observed strict discipline with regard to journalistic ethics. But because journalists traditionally hold confidentiality in high regard, management assumed that e-mail privacy needed no special rules or enforcement policies. Clearly, that assumption was wrong. In the past, the company casually conveyed a list of common-sense e-mail guidelines such as not using the system for personal business; being aware that employee e-mail is not invisible to computer system administrators or even managers; not using derogatory language, obscenity, or copyrighted material; and so on. Now, a strict privacy policy will be added to the list, and it will be sent out to bureau managers in an official memo.

As an employee of the newspaper's legal department, you've been handed the task of writing the memo to managers. Outline the company's policy for handling e-mail privacy violations. Management has already decided the penalties: reassignment, suspension without pay, or termination of employment. What you'll be communicating is how the new penalties are to be implemented. You will also suggest that managers immediately introduce these new rules to employees in a special meeting and that they routinely explain all the rules and guidelines to new hires.

For a first offense, the penalty will be a verbal warning in a personal meeting with a direct supervisor, which will also be entered in writing in the employee's human resources file. For a second offense, the penalty will be reassignment or suspen-

sion without pay, for a period to be determined by the employee's supervisor (who will know best the most appropriate length of time). A third offense will result in immediate termination without severance pay.

Your task: Address your memo to news bureau managers (who oversee editorial offices around the globe). Outline the company's policy for handling employees who violate e-mail privacy rules. Explain that a more detailed company-issued policy memo covering all issues will be in their hands in a few weeks and must be posted at each bureau in an area visible to employees. For managerial reference in the meantime, list the penalties for privacy violations and the appropriate sequence for applying them.[15]

■ E-Mail ■ Portfolio
** SKILLS   BUILDER**

13. Temper, temper: E-mail to Metro Power employees about technology failures This is the third time in two months that your company, Metro Power, has had to escort an employee from the building after a violent episode. Frankly, everyone is a little frightened by this development. As a human resources administrator, you have the unhappy task of trying to quell the storm.

Metro Power rarely fires employees, preferring to transfer them to new responsibilities, which may either draw out their finer points (and prove better for everyone in the long run) or help them decide to seek greener pastures. But in three cases, you had no choice. In one incident, a man punched out his computer screen after the system failed. In another, a man threw his keyboard across the room when he couldn't get access to the company's intranet. And in a third incident, a woman kicked a printer while screaming obscenities.

In all three cases, co-workers were terrified by these sudden outbursts. Too many disgruntled workers have committed too many violent acts against others in recent years; and whenever workers lose their temper on the job these days, it causes great fear—not to mention financial losses from the destruction of property and the disruption of workflow.

People are on edge at Metro Power right now. Rising energy costs, public and government scrutiny, and cries of price gouging are causing additional work and stress for all your employees. Plus, too much overtime, unrealistic expectations for overworked departments, and high demands on sensitive equipment are contributing to the problem. Tempers are frayed, and nerves strained. You're concerned that these three incidents are just the tip of the iceberg.

Your department head suggests that you write a reminder to all employees about controlling tempers in the workplace. "Tell them that technology glitches are commonplace and not some unholy disaster. And remind them to report routine computer failures to Bart Stone. He'll get to them in due course."

You say nothing to contradict her idea, but you wonder how to do what she asks without sounding trite or condescending. You don't want to sound like some nagging parent; if you do, no one will pay attention to your message. You sigh deeply as your boss strolls calmly back to her office. You're fairly certain that every employee already knows about reporting computer failures to Bart Stone, assistant director of information services.

Even so, you can think of a few suggestions that might be helpful, such as taking a walk to cool down and recognizing that machines, like humans, are not infallible. You want cooler heads to prevail, but that's just the sort of cliché you'd like to avoid in your message.

Your task: Write the e-mail message to all employees. Instead of uttering platitudes or wagging your finger, include preventive maintenance tips for office equipment, such as turning off systems at night, keeping food and liquids away from keyboards, making use of dusting sprays and special cloths, and so on. Your boss also asked you to make it clear that abusive behavior will be reprimanded, so include that point in a tactful way.[16]

ROUTINE REPLIES

**■ E-Mail ■ Portfolio
 SKILLS   BUILDER**

14. Window shopping at Wal-Mart: Offering advice to the webmaster Wal-Mart has grown to international success because it rarely fails to capitalize on a marketing scheme, and

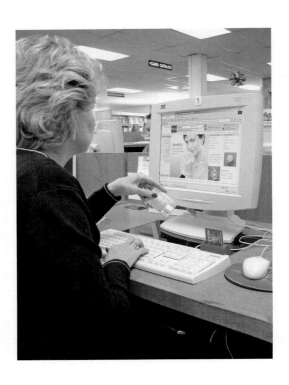

its website is no exception. To make sure the website remains effective and relevant, the webmaster asks various people to check out the site and give their feedback. As administrative assistant to Wal-Mart's director of marketing, you have just received a request from the webmaster to visit Wal-Mart's website and give your feedback.

Your task: Visit www.walmart.com and do some online "window shopping." As you browse through the site, consider the language, layout, graphics, and overall ease of use. In particular, look for aspects of the site that might be confusing or frustrating—annoyances that could prompt shoppers to abandon their quests and head to a competitor such as Target. Summarize your findings and recommendations in an e-mail message to the webmaster.

15. The special courier: Letter of recommendation for an old friend In today's mail, you get a letter from Non-Stop Messenger Service, 899 Sparks St., Ottawa, Ontario K1A 0G9, Canada. It concerns a friend of yours who has applied for a job. Here is the letter:

Kathryn Norquist has applied for the position of special courier with our firm, and she has given us your name as a reference. Our special couriers convey materials of considerable value or confidentiality to their recipients. It is not an easy job. Special couriers must sometimes remain alert for periods of up to 20 hours, and they cannot expect to follow the usual "three square meals and a full night's sleep" routine because they often travel long distances on short notice. On occasion, a special courier must react quickly and decisively to threatening situations.

For this type of work, we hire only people of unquestioned integrity, as demonstrated both by their public records and by references from people, like you, who have known them personally or professionally.

We would appreciate a letter from you, supplying detailed answers to the following questions: (1) How long and in what circumstances have you known the applicant? (2) What qualities does she possess that would qualify her for the position of special courier? (3) What qualities might need to be improved before she is put on permanent assignment in this job?

As vice president of human resources at DHL, you know how much weight a strong personal reference can carry, and you don't really mind that Kathryn never contacted you for permission to list your name—that's Kathryn. You met her during your sophomore year at San Diego State University— that would have been 1994—and you two were roommates for several years after. Her undergraduate degree was in journalism, and her investigative reporting was relentless. You have never known anyone who could match Kathryn's stamina when she was on a story. Of course, when she was between stories, she could sleep longer and do less than anyone else you have ever known.

After a few years of reporting, Kathryn went back to school and earned her MBA from the University of San Diego.

After that, you lost track of her for a while. Somebody said that she had joined the FBI—or was it the CIA?—you never really knew. You received a couple of postcards from Paris and one from Madrid.

Two years ago, you met Kathryn for dinner. Only in town for the evening, she was on her way to Borneo to "do the text" for a photographer friend of hers who worked for *National Geographic*. You read the article last year on the shrinking habitat for orangutans. It was powerful.

Although you're in no position to say much about Kathryn's career accomplishments, you can certainly recommend her energy and enthusiasm, her ability to focus on a task or an assignment, her devotion to ethics, and her style. She always seems unshakable—organized, thorough, and honorable—whether digging into political corruption or trudging the jungles of Borneo. You're not sure that her free spirit would flourish in a courier's position, and you wonder if she is a bit overqualified for the job. But knowing Kathryn, you're confident she wouldn't apply for a position unless she truly wanted it.

Your task: Supplying any details you can think of, write as supportive a letter as possible about your friend Kathryn to Roscoe de la Penda, Human Resources Specialist, Non-Stop Messenger.

E-Mail SKILLS

16. Red dirt to go: Positive e-mail reply from Paradise Sportswear As the owner of Paradise Sportswear in Hawaii, Robert Hedin was nearly done in by Hurricane Iniki in 1992, which wiped out his first silk-screened and airbrushed T-shirt business. He tried again, but then Hawaii's red dirt started seeping into his warehouse and ruining his inventory. Finally, a friend suggested that he stop trying to fight Mother Nature. Hedin took the hint: He mortgaged his condo and began producing Red Dirt Shirts, all made with dye created from the troublesome local dirt.

Bingo. Hedin's Red Dirt Sportswear designs are so popular, they're being snapped up by locals and tourists in Hedin's eight Paradise Sportswear retail outlets and in every Kmart on the islands. Hedin even added a new line, Lava Blues, made with real Hawaiian lava rock.

"You can make 500 shirts with a bucket of dirt," grins Hedin as he shows you around the operation on your first day. He's just a few years away from the usual retirement age, but he looks like a kid who's finally found the right playground.

Recently, Hedin decided to capitulate to all the requests he's received from retail outlets on the mainland. Buyers kept coming to the islands on vacation, discovering Hedin's "natural" sportswear, and begging him to set up a deal. For a long time, his answer was no; he simply couldn't handle the extra work. But now he's hired you.

As special sales representative, you'll help Hedin expand slowly into this new territory, starting with one store. Whole-saling to the local Kmarts is easy enough, but handling all the arrangements for shipping to the mainland would be too much for the current staff. So you'll start with the company Hedin has chosen to become the first mainland retailer to sell Red Dirt and Lava Blues sportswear: Surf's Up in Chicago, Illinois—of all places. The boss figures that with less competition than he'd find on either coast, his island-influenced sportswear will be a big hit in Chicago, especially in the dead of winter.

Your task: Write a positive response to the e-mail received from Surf's Up buyer Ronald Draeger, who says he fell in love with the Paradise clothing concept while on a surfing trip to Maui. Let him know he'll have a temporary exclusive and that you'll be sending a credit application and other materials by snail mail. His e-mail address is surfsup@insnet.com.[17]

E-Mail SKILLS

17. Auto-talk: E-mail messages for Highway Bytes computers to send automatically You are director of customer services at Highway Bytes, which markets a series of small, handlebar-mounted computers for bicyclists. These Cycle Computers do everything, from computing speed and distance traveled to displaying street maps. Serious cyclists love them, but your company is growing so fast that you can't keep up with all the customer service requests you receive every day. Your boss wants not only to speed up response time but also to reduce staffing costs and allow your technical experts the time they need to focus on the most difficult and important questions.

You've just been reading about automated response systems, and you quickly review a few articles before discussing the options with your boss. Artificial intelligence researchers have been working for decades to design systems that can actually converse with customers, ask questions, and respond to requests. Some of today's systems have vocabularies of thousands of words and the ability to understand simple sentences. For example, *chatterbots* are automated bots that can actually mimic human conversation. (You can see what it's like to carry on a conversation with some of these bots by visiting **www.botspot.com**, clicking on Artificial Life Bots, and then selecting Chatterbots.)

Unfortunately, even though chatterbots hold a lot of promise, human communication is so complex that a truly automated customer service agent could take years to perfect (and may even prove to be impossible). However, the simplest automated systems are called *autoresponders*, or *on-demand e-mail*. They are fast and extremely inexpensive. They have no built-in intelligence, so they do nothing more than send back the same reply to every message they receive.

You explain to your boss that although some of the messages you receive require the attention of your product specialists, many are simply requests for straightforward information. In fact, the customer service staff already answers some 70 percent of e-mail queries with three ready-made attachments:

- **Installing Your Cycle Computer.** This attachment gives customers advice on installing the Cycle Computer the first time or reinstalling it on a new bike. In most cases, the computer and wheel sensor bolt directly to the bike without modification, but certain bikes do require extra work.

- **Troubleshooting Your Cycle Computer.** This attachment provides a step-by-step guide to figuring out what might be wrong with a malfunctioning Cycle Computer. Most problems are simple, such as dead batteries or loose wires, but others are beyond the capabilities of your typical customer.

- **Upgrading the Software in Your Cycle Computer.** This attachment tells customers how to attach the Cycle Computer to their home or office PC and download new software from Highway Bytes.

Your boss is enthusiastic when you explain that you can program your current e-mail system to look for specific words in incoming messages and then respond, based on what it finds. For example, if a customer message contains the word *installation*, you can program the system to reply with the *Installing Your Cycle Computer* attachment. This reconfigured system should be able to handle a sizable portion of the hundreds of e-mails your customer service group gets every week.

Your task: First, draft a list of keywords that you want your e-mail system to look for. You need to be creative and spend some time with a thesaurus. Identify all the words and word combinations that could identify a message as pertaining to one of the three subject areas. For instance, the word *attach*

would probably indicate a need for the installation material, whereas *new software* would most likely suggest a need for the upgrade attachment. Second, draft three short e-mail messages, one to accompany each of the ready-made attachments, explaining that the attached document answers the most common questions on a particular subject (installation, troubleshooting, or upgrading). Your messages should invite recipients to write back if the attached document doesn't solve the problem—and don't forget to provide the e-mail address: support2@highwaybytes.com. Third, draft a fourth message to be sent out whenever your new system is unable to figure out what the customer is asking for. Simply thank the customer for writing and explain that the query will be passed on to a customer service specialist who will respond shortly.

E-Mail SKILLS

18. Lighten up: E-mail reply to a website designer at Organizers Unlimited When Kendra Williams, owner of Organizers Unlimited, wanted to create a website to sell her Superclean Organizer, she asked you, her assistant, to find a designer. After some research, you found three promising individuals. Williams chose Pete Womack, whose résumé impressed both of you. Now he's e-mailed his first design proposal, and Williams is not happy.

"I detest cluttered websites!" she explodes. "This homepage has too many graphics and animations, too much 'dancing baloney.' He must have included at least a megabyte of bouncing cotton balls and jogging soap bars! Clever, maybe, but we don't want it! If the homepage takes too long to load, our customers won't wait for it, and we'll lose sales."

Williams's dislike of clutter is what inspired her to invent the Superclean Organizer in the first place, a neat device for organizing bathroom items.

Your task: "You found him," says Williams. "Now you can answer and tell him what's wrong with this design." Before you write the e-mail reply to Womack explaining the need for a simpler homepage, read some of the articles offering tips at www.sitepoint.com. On the homepage, under "Before You Code," select "Site Planning." Under "Design and Layout," select "Design Principles." Use the ideas you find to support your message.[18]

E-Mail SKILLS

19. Shopping for talent: Memo at Clovine's recommending a promotion You enjoy your duties as manager of the women's sportswear department at Clovine's—a growing chain of moderate to upscale department stores in south Florida. You especially enjoy being able to recommend someone for a promotion. Today, you received an e-mail message from Rachel Cohen, head buyer for women's apparel. She is looking for a smart, aggressive employee to become assistant buyer for the women's sportswear division. Clovine's likes to promote from within, and Rachel is asking all managers and supervisors for likely candidates. You have just the person she's looking for.

Jennifer Ramirez is a salesclerk in the designer sportswear boutique of your main store in Miami, and she has caught your attention. She's quick, friendly, and good at sizing up a customer's preferences. Moreover, at recent department meetings, she has shared some insightful observations about fashion trends in south Florida.

Your task: Write an e-mail reply to Rachel Cohen, head buyer, women's sportswear, recommending Jennifer Ramirez and evaluating her qualifications for the promotion. Rachel can check with the human resources department about Jennifer's educational and employment history; you're mainly interested in conveying your positive impression of Jennifer's potential for advancement.

20. Impressive trainee: Letter of recommendation for a top-notch intern As a project manager at Orbitz, one of the largest online travel services in the world, you've seen plenty of college interns in action. However, few have impressed you as much as Maxine "Max" Chenault. For one thing, she learned how to navigate the company's content management system virtually overnight and always used it properly, whereas other interns sometimes left things in a hopeless mess. She asked lots of intelligent questions about the business. You've been teaching her blogging and website design principles, and she's picked them up rapidly. Moreover, she is always on time, professional, and eager to assist. Also, she didn't mind doing mundane tasks.

On the downside, Chenault is a popular student. Early on, you often found her busy on the phone planning her many social activities when you needed her help. However, after you had a brief talk with her, this problem vanished.

You'll be sorry to see Chenault leave when she returns to school in the fall, but you're pleased to respond when she asks you for a letter of recommendation. She's not sure where she'll apply for work after graduation or what career path she'll choose, so she asks you to keep the letter fairly general.

Your task: Working with a team of your classmates, discuss what should and should not be in the letter. Prepare an outline based on your discussion and then draft the letter.

21. Satellite farming: Letter granting credit from Deere & Company This is the best part of your job with Deere & Co. in Moline, Illinois: saying yes to a farmer. In this case, it's Arlen Ruestman in Toluca, Illinois. Ruestman wants to take advantage of new farming technology. Your company's GreenStar system uses GPS satellite technology to let farmers know exactly where they are as they drive equipment across

their fields. For farmers like Ruestman, that means a new ability to micromanage even as many as 10,000 acres of corn or soybeans.

For instance, using the GreenStar system, farmers can map and analyze characteristics such as acidity, soil type, or crop yields from a given area. Using this information, they know exactly how much herbicide or fertilizer to spread over precisely which spot—eliminating waste and achieving better results. With cross-referencing and accumulated data, farmers can analyze why crops are performing well in some areas and not so well in others. Then they can program farm equipment to treat only the problem area—for example, spraying a new insect infestation 2 yards wide, 300 yards down the row.

Some farms have already saved as much as $10 an acre on fertilizers alone. For 10,000 acres, that's $100,000 a year. Once Ruestman retrofits your GreenStar precision package on his old combine and learns all its applications, he should have no problem saving enough to pay off the $7,350 credit account you're about to grant him.

Your task: Write a letter to Ruestman (P.O. Box 4067, Toluca, IL 61369), informing him of the good news.[19]

POSITIVE MESSAGES

Blogging SKILLS   Portfolio BUILDER

22. Leveraging the good news: Blog announcement of a prestigious professional award You and your staff in the public relations (PR) department at Epson of America were delighted when the communication campaign you created for the new PictureMate Personal Photo Lab (www.epson.com/picturemate) was awarded the prestigious Silver Anvil award by the Public Relations Society of America. Now you'd like to give your team a pat on the back by sharing the news with the rest of the company.

Your task: Write a one-paragraph message for the PR department blog (which is read by people throughout the company but is not accessible outside the company) announcing the award. Take care not to "toot your own horn" as the manager of the PR department. Use the opportunity to compliment the rest of the company for designing and producing such an innovative product.[20]

23. Intercultural condolences: Letter conveying sympathy at IBM You've been working for two years as administrative assistant to Ron Glover, vice president of global workforce diversity at IBM in Armonk, New York. Chana Panichpapiboon has been with Glover even longer than you have, and, sadly, her husband was killed (along with 19 others) in a bus accident yesterday. The bus skidded on icy pavement into a deep ravine, tipping over and crushing the occupants before rescue workers could get to them.

You met Surin last year at a company banquet. You can still picture his warm smile and the easy way he joked with you and others over chicken Florentine, even though you were complete strangers to him. He was only 32 years old, and he left Chana two children, a 12-year-old boy, Arsa, and a 10-year-old girl, Veera. His death is a terrible tragedy.

Normally, you'd write a condolence letter immediately. But Chana is a native of Thailand, and so was Surin. You know you'd better do a little research first. Is Chana Buddhist or Catholic? Is there anything about the typical Western practice of expressing sympathy that might be inappropriate? Offensive?

After making some discreet inquiries among Chana's closest friends at work, you've learned that she is Theravada Buddhist, as are most people in Thailand. From a reference work in the company library about doing business around the world, you've gleaned only that, in the beliefs of many people in Thailand, "the person takes precedence over rule or law" and "people gain their social position as a result of karma, not personal achievement," which means Chana may believe in reincarnation. But the book also says that Theravada Buddhists are free to choose which precepts of their religion, if any, they will follow. So Chana's beliefs are still a mystery.

You do know that her husband was very important to her and much loved by all their family. That, at least, is universal. And you're toying with a phrase you once read, "The hand of time lightly lays, softly soothing sorrow's wound." Is it appropriate?

Your task: You've decided to handwrite the condolence note on a blank greeting card you've found that bears a peaceful, "Eastern-flavor" image. You know you're risking a cultural gaffe, but at least you won't commit the greater offense of not writing at all. Choose the most sincere wording you can, which should resonate through any differences in custom or tradition.[21]

the news release "Adobe Wins Platinum Certification Awarded by U.S. Green Building Council," available on the Adobe website, at **www.adobe.com/aboutadobe/pressroom**. Select a few key details from this news release to include in your message.[22]

25. Congrats on that: Complimenting a former business acquaintance for national recognition You pull the new issue of *Fortune* magazine out of the stack of mail and are quite pleased to see Indra Nooyi on the cover. Not only was Nooyi recently appointed CEO of PepsiCo, but *Fortune* has just named her the most powerful woman in American business. You got to know her briefly when PepsiCo acquired your previous employer, Quaker Oats, in 2001. You haven't spoken to her since then, but you have followed her accomplishments in the business media.

Your task: Write a brief letter (no more than one page) congratulating Nooyi on her promotion to CEO and on being recognized by *Fortune*. Make up any details you need to create a credible message. You can learn more about Nooyi's career and accomplishments in the news release "PepsiCo's Board of Directors Appoints Indra K. Nooyi as Chief Executive Officer Effective October 1, 2006," on the PepsiCo website, **www.pepsico.com** (look under News, PepsiCo Releases, 2006). Address the letter to Indra Nooyi, CEO, PepsiCo, Inc., 700 Anderson Hill Road, Purchase, NY 10577.

26. Our sympathy: Condolence letter to an Aetna underwriter As chief administrator for the underwriting department of Aetna Health Plans in Walnut Creek, California, you're facing a difficult task. One of your best underwriters, Hector Almeida, recently lost his wife in an automobile accident (he and his teenage daughter weren't with her at the time). Because you're the boss, everyone in the close-knit department is looking to you to communicate the group's sympathy and concern.

Someone suggested a simple greeting card that everyone could sign, but that seems so impersonal for someone you've worked with every day for nearly five years. So you decided to

Blogging SKILLS | **Portfolio BUILDER**

24. Green is the new green: Blog update on energy savings Adobe Systems is well known as the maker of Acrobat, Photoshop, Flash, and other programs that are fundamental tools in the Internet Age. It is also becoming well known as one of the "greenest" companies in the country, adopting a variety of techniques and technologies that have not only reduced its energy usage considerably but also cut nearly $1 million a year from its utility bills. In 2006, Adobe became the first company ever to receive the Platinum Certification from the U.S. Green Building Council.

Your task: Write a one- or two-paragraph post for an internal blog at Adobe, letting employees know how well the company is doing in its efforts to reduce energy usage and thanking employees for the energy-saving ideas they've submitted and the individual efforts they've made to reduce, reuse, and recycle. Learn more about the company's accomplishments by searching for write a personal note on behalf of the whole department. Although you met Hector's wife, Rosalia, at a few company functions, you knew her mostly through Hector's frequent references to her. You didn't know her well, but you do know important things about her life, which you can celebrate in the letter.

Right now, he's devastated by the loss. But if anyone can overcome this tragedy, Hector can. He's always determined to get a job done, no matter what obstacles present themselves, and he does it with an upbeat attitude. That's why everyone in the office likes him so much.

You also plan to suggest that when he returns to work, he might like to move his schedule up an hour so that he'll have more time to spend with his daughter, Lisa, after school. It's your way of helping make things a little easier for them during this period of adjustment.

Your task: Write the letter to Hector Almeida, who lives at 47 West Ave., #10, Walnut Creek, CA 94596. (Feel free to make up any details you need.)[23]

Chapter 9

Writing Negative Messages

Learning Objectives

AFTER STUDYING THIS CHAPTER, YOU WILL BE ABLE TO

1 Apply the three-step writing process to negative messages

2 Explain the differences between the direct and the indirect approaches to negative messages, including when it's appropriate to use each one

3 Identify the risks of using the indirect approach and explain how to avoid such problems

4 Adapt negative messages for internal and external audiences

5 Explain the importance of maintaining high standards of ethics and etiquette when delivering negative messages

6 Explain the role of communication in crisis management

7 List three guidelines for delivering negative news to job applicants and give a brief explanation of each one

On the Job

COMMUNICATING AT KPMG

DOES AN APOLOGY MAKE GOOD BUSINESS SENSE?

When businesses make mistakes, should they apologize? Traditional thinking says they can't afford to because doing so is an admission of guilt that can be used against them in lawsuits. However, an emerging school of thought says that apologizing isn't as risky as previously believed and that courts tend to show leniency toward companies that express remorse after making mistakes.

The large accounting firm KPMG recently faced this situation when the Internal Revenue Service ruled that certain *tax shelters* (investments created primarily to reduce tax burdens) the company had been recommending for some of its wealthy clients were illegal. Soon after, KPMG faced a criminal investigation and multiple lawsuits from individual clients who accused the company of encouraging them to break the law. Just a few years earlier, KPMG competitor Arthur Andersen had been convicted in criminal matters of a different type and had collapsed as a result, putting 85,000 people out of work.

When the accounting firm KPMG publicly apologized for the illegal actions of some of its partners (one of whom, Jeffrey Eischeid, is shown here leaving the courthouse), the admission of guilt helped save the firm from potentially devastating criminal charges but might well have worked against it in numerous client lawsuits.

KPMG faced a classic dilemma. If it apologized in an effort to avoid criminal prosecution, that might be seen as an admission of guilt that could be used against it in all those civil suits.

Apparently deciding that the risk of a possible criminal charge was greater than the risk of apologizing, the company issued the following statement: "KPMG takes full responsibility for the unlawful conduct by former KPMG partners . . . and we deeply regret that it occurred." The apology seemed to help, as the firm avoided a criminal indictment by agreeing to pay a fine of nearly a half-billion dollars and agreeing to get out of the tax shelter business. However, the admission of guilt was welcomed by lawyers representing KPMG clients. "It's stunning. Obviously, it's very helpful," said one. That optimism seemed warranted, as the firm was later forced to pay most of its tax shelter clients a total of more than $150 million, and lawsuits from the remaining clients are likely to drag on for years.[1]

www.us.kpmg.com

USING THE THREE-STEP WRITING PROCESS FOR NEGATIVE MESSAGES

Chances are slim that you'll ever need to issue a message like KPMG's (profiled in the chapter opener), but communicating other kinds of negative news is a fact of life for all business professionals, from rejecting job applicants to telling customers that shipments will be late to turning down speaking invitations.

When you need to send a negative message, you have five goals: (1) to convey the bad news; (2) to gain acceptance for the bad news; (3) to maintain as much goodwill as possible with your audience; (4) to maintain a good image for your organization; and (5) if appropriate, to reduce or eliminate the need for future correspondence on the matter (however, in a few cases, you want to encourage discussion). Five goals are clearly a lot to accomplish in one message. However, by learning some simple techniques and following the three-step process, you can develop negative messages that reduce the stress for everyone involved and improve the effectiveness of your communication efforts.

Step 1: Plan Your Message

When planning negative messages, you can't avoid the fact that your audience does not want to hear what you have to say. To minimize the damage to business relationships and to encourage the acceptance of your message, analyze the situation carefully to better understand the context in which the recipient will process your message.

Be sure to consider your purpose thoroughly—whether it's straightforward (such as rejecting a job application) or more complicated (such as drafting a negative performance review, in which you not only give the employee feedback on past performance but also help the person develop a plan to improve future performance). Similarly, your audience profile can be simple and obvious in some situations (such as rejecting a credit request) and far more complex in others (such as telling a business partner that you've decided to terminate the partnership).

With a clear purpose and your audience's needs in mind, identify and gather the information your audience will need in order to understand and accept your message. Negative messages can be intensely personal to the recipient, and in many cases, recipients have a right to expect a thorough explanation of your answer (although that isn't always the case). For instance, if one of your hardworking employees has asked for a raise but you don't think her performance warrants it, you can carefully explain the difference between hard work and productive results to help her accept your message.

Selecting the right medium is critical. For instance, experts advise that bad news for employees be delivered in person whenever possible, both to show respect for the employees and to give them an opportunity to ask questions. Of course, delivering bad news is never easy, and an increasing number of managers appear to be using e-mail and other electronic media to convey negative messages to employees.[2] However, employees are more likely to accept messages and maintain respect for the sender if bad news is delivered in person.

Defining your main idea in a negative message is often more complicated than simply saying no. For instance, in the case of the hardworking employee who requested a raise, your message might go beyond saying no to explaining how she can improve her performance by working smarter, not just harder.

Step 2: Write Your Message

When you are adapting a negative message to your audience, pay close attention to effectiveness and diplomacy. After all, your audience does not want to hear what you have to say and might disagree strongly with you, so messages perceived to be

Five goals of negative messages:
- Give the bad news
- Ensure acceptance of the bad news
- Maintain reader's goodwill
- Maintain organization's good image
- Reduce future correspondence on the matter

Analysis, investigation, and adaptation help you avoid alienating your readers.

When preparing negative messages, choose the medium with care.

unclear or unkind will amplify the audience's stress. Maintain a "you" attitude, strive for polite language that emphasizes the positive whenever appropriate, and make sure your word choice is without bias. For more advice, see "Adapting to Your Audience" on page 291.

If your credibility hasn't already been established with the audience, lay out your qualifications for making the decision in question. Recipients of negative messages who don't think you are credible are more likely to challenge your decision or reject your message. And, as always, projecting and protecting your company's image are prime concerns; if you're not careful, a negative answer could spin out of control into negative feelings about your company.

When you use language that conveys respect and avoids an accusing tone, you protect your audience's pride. This kind of communication etiquette is always important, but it demands special care with negative messages. Moreover, you can ease the sense of disappointment by using positive words rather than negative, counterproductive ones (see Table 9.1).

You're likely to spend more time on word, sentence, and paragraph choices for negative messages than for any other type of business writing. People who receive negative messages often look for subtle shades of meaning, seeking flaws in your reasoning or other ways to challenge the decision. By writing clearly and sensitively, you can take some of the sting out of bad news and help your reader accept the decision and move on.

Step 3: Complete Your Message

Your need for careful attention to detail continues as you complete your message. Revise your content to make sure everything is clear, complete, and concise—bearing in mind that even small flaws are magnified as readers react to your negative news. Produce clean, professional documents and proofread carefully to eliminate mistakes. Finally, be especially sure that your negative messages are delivered promptly and successfully; waiting for bad news is difficult enough, without wondering whether a message was lost.

Audiences often expect significant negative messages to be delivered in person. Here, Ford Motor Company Executive Vice President and Chief Financial Officer Donat R. Leclair announces the closing of up to 14 manufacturing plants and layoffs of up to 30,000 employees.

CHOOSING POSITIVE WORDS	Table 9.1

Examples of Negative Phrasings	Positive Alternatives
Your request *doesn't make any sense.*	Please clarify your request.
The *damage* won't be fixed for a week.	The item will be repaired next week.
Although it wasn't our *fault,* there will be an *unavoidable delay* in your order.	We will process your order as soon as we receive an aluminum shipment from our supplier, which we expect to happen within 10 days.
You are clearly *dissatisfied.*	I recognize that the product did not live up to your expectations.
I was *shocked* to learn that you're unhappy.	Thank you for sharing your concerns about your shopping experience.
Unfortunately, we haven't received it.	The item hasn't arrived yet.
The enclosed statement is *wrong.*	Please verify the enclosed statement and provide a correct copy.

DEVELOPING NEGATIVE MESSAGES

As you apply the three-step writing process to negative messages, keep three important aspects in mind. First, before you organize the main points of a message, determine whether it will be better to use the direct or indirect approach. Second, before actually composing your message, be sensitive to variations across cultures or between internal and external audiences. Third, to fulfill the spirit of audience focus, be sure you maintain high ethical standards.

Choosing the Best Approach

You've been choosing between direct and indirect approaches to deliver negative messages your entire life. When you come right out and tell somebody some bad news, you're using the direct approach. When you try to ease your way into the conversation before delivering the bad news, you're using the indirect approach. To choose an approach for negative business messages, ask yourself the following questions:

You need to consider a variety of factors when choosing between direct and indirect approaches.

- **Will the bad news come as a shock?** The direct approach is fine for business situations in which people readily acknowledge the possibility of receiving bad news. However, if the bad news might come as a shock to readers, use the indirect approach to help them prepare for it.

- **Does the audience prefer short messages that get right to the point?** If you know that your boss always wants brief messages that get right to the point, even when they deliver bad news, use the direct approach.

- **How important is this news to the audience?** For minor or routine scenarios, the direct approach is nearly always best. However, if the audience has an emotional investment in the situation or the consequences are considerable, the indirect approach is less jarring.

- **Do you need to maintain a close working relationship with the audience?** The indirect approach makes it easier to soften the blow of bad news and can therefore be the better choice when you need to preserve a good relationship.

- **Do you need to get the audience's attention?** If someone hasn't responded to repeated messages, the direct approach can help you get his or her attention.

- **What is your organization's preferred style?** Some companies have a distinct communication style, ranging from blunt and direct to gentle and indirect. However, going against expectations can be an effective way to get people's attention in a dramatic way. When Coca-Cola CEO E. Neville Isdell wanted to let both insiders and outsiders know that the company's continuing sales slump was due to more than just temporary market factors, he issued uncharacteristically blunt statements such as saying that the company suffers from "a people deficit and a skills deficit."[3]

- **How much follow-up communication do you want?** If you want to discourage a response from your reader, the direct approach signals the finality of your message more effectively. However, if you use the indirect approach to list your reasons before announcing a decision, you leave the door open for a follow-up response from the person—which might actually be the best strategy at times. For example, if you're rejecting a project team's request for funding, you might be wise to invite the team to provide any new information that could encourage you to reconsider your decision.

No matter which approach you choose for a given message, don't lose sight of your purpose and your audience. A sensitive, personal tone can be more important to your readers than your choice of message organization.[4]

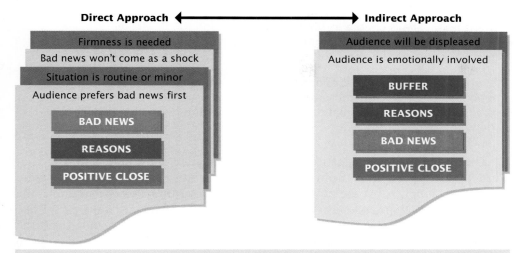

Direct Approach ⟵⟶ **Indirect Approach**

Direct Approach column:
- Firmness is needed
- Bad news won't come as a shock
- Situation is routine or minor
- Audience prefers bad news first
  - BAD NEWS
  - REASONS
  - POSITIVE CLOSE

Indirect Approach column:
- Audience will be displeased
- Audience is emotionally involved
  - BUFFER
  - REASONS
  - BAD NEWS
  - POSITIVE CLOSE

FIGURE 9.1
Choosing the Indirect or Direct Approach for Negative Messages
Analyze the situation carefully before choosing your approach to organizing negative messages.

Using the Direct Approach Effectively   A negative message using the direct approach opens with the bad news, proceeds to the reasons for the situation or the decision, and ends with a positive statement aimed at maintaining a good relationship with the audience (see Figure 9.1). Depending on the circumstances, the message may also offer alternatives or a plan of action to fix the situation under discussion. Stating the bad news at the beginning can have two advantages: (1) It makes a shorter message possible, and (2) it requires less time for the audience to reach the main idea of the message.

> Use the direct approach when your negative answer or information will have minimal personal impact.

Open with a Clear Statement of the Bad News No matter what the news is, come right out and say it. However, even if the news is likely to be devastating, maintain a calm, professional tone that keeps the focus on the news and not on individual failures or other personal factors. Also, if necessary, remind the reader why you're writing, as in these examples:

> Please modify our standing order for the FL-205 shipping cases from 3,000 per month to 2,500 per month.

Reminds the reader that your company has a standing order and announces the change immediately

> Transnation Life is unable to grant your application for SafetyNet term life insurance.

Reminds the reader that he or she applied for life insurance with your firm and announces your decision

> In spite of everyone's best efforts to close more sales this past quarter, revenue fell 14 percent compared to the third quarter last year.

Introduces the topic of sales with a personal acknowledgment to the staff and then delivers the news directly and immediately

Notice how the third example still manages to ease into the bad news, even though it delivers the bad news directly and quickly. In all three instances, the recipient gets the news immediately without reading the reasons that the news is bad.

Provide Reasons and Additional Information In most cases, you follow the direct opening with an explanation of why the news is negative:

> Please modify our standing order for the FL-205 shipping cases from 3,000 per month to 2,500 per month. The FL-205 continues to meet our needs for medical packaging, but our sales of that product line have leveled off.

Reassures the reader that the product in question is still satisfactory but is no longer needed in the same quantity

Offers a general explanation as the reason the application was denied and discourages further communication on the matter →

Transnation Life is unable to grant your application for SafetyNet term life insurance. The SafetyNet program has specific health history requirements that your application does not meet.

Lets readers know why the news is negative and reassures them that job performance is not the reason →

In spite of everyone's best efforts to close more sales this past quarter, revenue fell 14 percent compared to the third quarter last year. Reports from the field offices indicate that the economic downturn in Asia has reduced demand for our products.

The amount of detail you should provide depends on your relationship with the audience.

The extent of your explanation depends on the nature of the news and your relationship with the reader. In the first example, for instance, a company wants to assure its longtime supplier that the product is still satisfactory. In the second example, the insurance company provides a general reason for the denial because listing a specific health issue might encourage additional communication from the reader, and the company's decision is final. In the third example, the explanation points out why the news is bad and also reassures employees that no one in the firm is personally responsible for the failure.

However, you will encounter some situations in which explaining negative news is neither appropriate nor helpful, such as when the reasons are confidential, excessively complicated, or irrelevant to the reader. To maintain a cordial working relationship with the reader, you might want to explain why you can't provide the information.

Should you apologize when delivering bad news? As the KPMG vignette at the beginning of the chapter illustrates, the answer isn't quite as simple as one might think. The notion of *apology* is hard to pin down. To some people, it simply means an expression of sympathy that something negative has happened to another person. At the other extreme, it means admitting fault and taking responsibility for specific compensations or corrections to atone for the mistake.

Some experts have advised that a company should never apologize, even when it knows it has made a mistake, as the apology might be taken as a confession of guilt that could be used against the company in a lawsuit. This is the dilemma KPMG faced when deciding how to respond to illegal actions taken by a few of its employees. However, several states have laws that specifically prevent expressions of sympathy from being used as evidence of legal liability. In fact, judges, juries, and plaintiffs tend to be more forgiving of companies that express sympathy for wronged parties; moreover, an apology can help repair a company's reputation. Recently, some prosecutors have begun pressing executives to publicly admit guilt and apologize as part of the settlement of criminal cases—unlike the common tactic of paying fines but refusing to admit any wrongdoing.[6]

During an investigation into charges that representatives of the company spied on journalists and company directors, HP CEO Mark Hurd, shown here testifying before a congressional committee investigating the affair, apologized to both the victims of the privacy invasions and HP employees.[5]

The best general advice in the event of a serious mistake or accident is to immediately and sincerely express sympathy and offer help if appropriate, without admitting guilt; then seek the advice of your company's lawyers before elaborating. As one recent survey concluded, "The risks of making an apology are low, and the potential reward is high."[7]

Close on a Positive Note After you've explained the negative news, close the message in a positive but still honest and respectful manner:

Reinforces the relationship you have with the reader and provides a positive view toward the future—without unduly promising a return to the old level of business →

Please modify our standing order for the FL-205 shipping cases from 3,000 per month to 2,500 per month. The FL-205 continues to meet our needs for medical packaging, but our sales of that product line have leveled off. We appreciate the great service you provide and look forward to continuing our business relationship with you.

> Transnation Life is unable to grant your application for SafetyNet term life insurance. The SafetyNet program has specific health history requirements that your application does not meet. We wish you success in finding coverage through another provider.
>
> In spite of everyone's best efforts to close more sales this past quarter, revenue fell 14 percent compared to the third quarter last year. Reports from the field offices indicate that the economic downturn in Asia has reduced demand for our products. However, I continue to believe that we have the best product for these customers, and we'll continue to explore ways to boost sales in these key markets.

(margin note) Ends on a respectful note, knowing that life insurance is an important subject for the reader, but also makes it clear that the company's decision is final

(margin note) Helps readers respond to the news by letting them know that the company plans to fix the situation, even if the plan for doing so isn't clear yet

Notice how all three examples deliver bad news quickly and efficiently without being disrespectful or overly apologetic. Consider offering your readers an alternative solution if you can. Depending on the situation, you might also explain how you or your organization plan to respond to the negative news.

Using the Indirect Approach Effectively   The indirect approach helps readers prepare for the bad news by presenting the reasons for it first. However, don't assume that the indirect approach is meant to obscure bad news, delay it, or limit your responsibility. Rather, the purpose of this approach is to ease the blow and help readers accept the situation. When done poorly, the indirect approach can be disrespectful and even unethical. But when done well, it is a good example of audience-oriented communication crafted with attention to ethics and etiquette.

(margin note) Use the indirect approach when some preparation will help your audience accept your bad news.

Open with a Buffer   Messages using an indirect approach open with a **buffer**: a neutral, noncontroversial statement that establishes common ground with your reader (refer to Figure 9.1). Some critics believe that using a buffer is manipulative and unethical—and even dishonest. However, buffers are unethical only if they're insincere or deceptive. Showing consideration for the feelings of others is never dishonest.

(margin note) A well-written buffer establishes common ground with the reader.

A poorly written buffer might trivialize the reader's concerns, divert attention from the problem with insincere flattery or irrelevant material, or mislead the reader into thinking your message actually contains good news. A good buffer, on the other hand, can express your appreciation for being considered (if you're responding to a request), assure your reader of your attention to the request, or indicate your understanding of the reader's needs. A good buffer also needs to be relevant and sincere.

(margin note) Poorly written buffers mislead or insult the reader.

Consider these possible responses to a manager of the order-fulfillment department who requested some temporary staffing help from your department (a request you won't be able to fulfill):

> Our department shares your goal of processing orders quickly and efficiently.

(margin note) Establishes common ground with the reader and validates the concerns that prompted the original request—without promising a positive answer

> As result of the last downsizing, every department in the company is running shorthanded.

(margin note) Establishes common ground, but in a negative way that downplays the recipient's concerns

> You folks are doing a great job over there, and I'd love to be able to help out.

(margin note) Potentially misleads the reader into concluding that you will comply with the request

> Those new state labor regulations are driving me crazy over here; how about in your department?

(margin note) Trivializes the reader's concerns by opening with an irrelevant issue

Only the first of these buffers can be considered effective; the other three are likely to damage your relationship with the other manager—and lower his or her

Table 9.2	TYPES OF BUFFERS	
Buffer Type	**Strategy**	**Example**
Agreement	Find a point on which you and the reader share similar views.	We both know how hard it is to make a profit in this industry.
Appreciation	Express sincere thanks for receiving something.	Your check for $127.17 arrived yesterday. Thank you.
Cooperation	Convey your willingness to help in any way you realistically can.	Employee Services is here to assist all associates with their health insurance, retirement planning, and continuing education needs.
Fairness	Assure the reader that you've closely examined and carefully considered the problem, or mention an appropriate action that has already been taken.	For the past week, we have carefully monitored those using the photocopying machine to see whether we can detect any pattern of use that might explain its frequent breakdowns.
Good news	Start with the part of your message that is favorable.	A replacement knob for your range is on its way, shipped February 10 via UPS.
Praise	Find an attribute or an achievement to compliment.	The Stratford Group clearly has an impressive record of accomplishment in helping clients resolve financial reporting problems.
Resale	Favorably discuss the product or company related to the subject of the letter.	With their heavy-duty, full-suspension hardware and fine veneers, the desks and file cabinets in our Montclair line have become a hit with value-conscious professionals.
Understanding	Demonstrate that you understand the reader's goals and needs.	So that you can more easily find the printer with the features you need, we are enclosing a brochure that describes all the Panasonic printers currently available.

opinion of you. Table 9.2 shows several types of effective buffers you could use to tactfully open a negative message.

Given the damage that a poorly composed buffer can do, consider every buffer carefully before you send it. Is it respectful? Is it relevant? Is it neutral, implying neither yes nor no? Does it provide a smooth transition to the reasons that follow? If you can answer yes to every question, you can proceed confidently to the next section of your message. However, if a little voice inside your head tells you that your buffer sounds insincere or misleading, it probably is, in which case you'll need to rewrite it.

Provide Reasons and Additional Information An effective buffer serves as a stepping-stone to the next part of your message, in which you build up the explanations and information that will culminate in your negative news. The nature of the information you provide is similar to that of the direct approach—it depends on the audience and the situation—but the way you portray this information necessarily differs because your reader doesn't know your conclusion yet.

An ideal explanation section leads readers to your conclusion before you come right out and say it. In other words, before you actually say no, the reader has followed your line of reasoning and is ready for the answer. By giving your reasons effectively, you help maintain focus on the issues at hand and defuse the emotions that always accompany significantly bad news.

As you lay out your reasons, guide your reader's response by starting with the most positive points first and moving forward to increasingly negative ones. Be concise but provide enough detail for the audience to understand your reasons. You need to convince your audience that your decision is justified, fair, and logical. If appropriate, you can use the explanation section to suggest how the negative news might in fact benefit your reader in some way—but only if this is true and only if you can do so without offending your audience.

Avoid hiding behind company policy to cushion your bad news. If you say, "Company policy forbids our hiring anyone who does not have two years' supervisory experience," you imply that you won't consider anyone on his or her individual merits. Skilled and sympathetic communicators explain company policy (without referring to it as "policy") so that the audience can try to meet the requirements at a later time. Consider this response to an employee:

> Because these management positions are quite challenging, the human relations department has researched the qualifications needed to succeed in them. The findings show that the two most important qualifications are a bachelor's degree in business administration and two years' supervisory experience.

Phrase your reasons to signal the negative news ahead.

Don't hide behind "company policy" when you deliver bad news.

Shows the reader that the decision is based on a methodical analysis of the company's needs and not on some arbitrary guideline

Establishes the criteria behind the decision and lets the reader know what to expect

The paragraph does a good job of stating reasons for the refusal:

- It provides enough detail to logically support the refusal.

- It implies that the applicant is better off avoiding a program in which he or she might fail.

- It explains the company's policy as logical rather than arbitrary.

- It doesn't offer an apology for the decision because no one is at fault.

- It avoids negative personal expressions (such as "You do not meet our requirements").

Well-written reasons are
- Detailed
- Tactful
- Individualized
- Unapologetic if no one is at fault
- Positive

Even valid, well-thought-out reasons won't convince every reader in every situation. However, if you've done a good job of laying out your reasoning, you've done everything you can to prepare the reader for the main idea, which is the negative news itself.

Continue with a Clear Statement of the Bad News After you've prepared the audience to receive the bad news, the next task is to present the news as clearly and as kindly as possible. Three techniques are especially useful for saying no. First, de-emphasize the bad news:

- Minimize the space or time devoted to the bad news—without trivializing it or withholding any important information.

- Subordinate bad news in a complex or compound sentence ("My department is already shorthanded, so I'll need all my staff for at least the next two months"). This construction pushes the bad news into the middle of the sentence, the point of least emphasis.

- Embed bad news in the middle of a paragraph or use parenthetical expressions ("Our profits, which are down, are only part of the picture").

To handle bad news carefully
- De-emphasize the bad news visually and grammatically
- Use a conditional statement, if appropriate
- Tell what you did do, not what you didn't do

However, keep in mind that it's possible to abuse de-emphasis. For instance, if the primary point of your message is that profits are down, it would be inappropriate to marginalize that news by burying it in the middle of a sentence. State the negative news clearly and then make a smooth transition to any positive news that might balance the story.

Second, use a conditional (*if* or *when*) statement to imply that the audience could have received, or might someday receive, a favorable answer ("When you have more managerial experience, you are welcome to reapply"). Such a statement could motivate applicants to improve their qualifications.

Third, emphasize what you can do or have done rather than what you cannot do. Say "We sell exclusively through retailers, and the one nearest you that carries our merchandise is . . ." rather than "We are unable to serve you, so please call your nearest dealer." Also, by implying the bad news, you may not need to actually state it ("The five positions currently open have been filled with people whose qualifications match those uncovered in our research"). By focusing on the facts and implying the bad news, you make the impact less personal.

Don't disguise bad news when you emphasize the positive.

When implying bad news, however, be sure your audience will be able to grasp the entire message—including the bad news. Withholding negative information or overemphasizing positive information is unethical and unfair to your reader. If an implied message might lead to uncertainty, state your decision in direct terms. Just be sure to avoid overly blunt statements that are likely to cause pain and anger:

Instead of This	Write This
I *must refuse* your request.	I will be out of town on the day you need me.
We *must deny* your application.	The position has been filled.
I *am unable* to grant your request.	Contact us again when you have established . . .
We *cannot afford to* continue the program.	The program will conclude on May 1.
Much as I would like to attend . . .	Our budget meeting ends too late for me to attend.
We *must turn down* your extension request.	Please send in your payment by June 14.

Close on a Positive Note As in the direct approach, the conclusion of the indirect approach is your opportunity to emphasize your respect for your audience, even though you've just delivered unpleasant news. Express best wishes without ending on a falsely upbeat note. If you can find a positive angle that's meaningful to your audience, by all means consider adding it to your conclusion. However, don't try to pretend that the negative news didn't happen or that it won't affect the reader. Suggest alternative solutions if such information is available. In a message to a customer or potential customer, an ending that includes resale information or sales promotion may also be appropriate. If you've asked readers to decide between alternatives or to take some action, make sure that they know what to do, when to do it, and how to do it. Whatever type of conclusion you use, follow these guidelines:

A positive close
- *Builds goodwill*
- *Offers a suggestion for action*
- *Provides a look toward the future*

- **Avoid a negative or uncertain conclusion.** Don't refer to, repeat, or apologize for the bad news and refrain from expressing any doubt that your reasons will be accepted. (Avoid statements such as "I trust our decision is satisfactory.")

- **Limit future correspondence.** Encourage additional communication *only* if you're willing to discuss your decision further. (If you're not, avoid wording such as "If you have further questions, please write.")

- **Be optimistic about the future.** Don't anticipate problems that haven't occurred yet. (Avoid statements such as "Should you have further problems, please let us know.")

- **Be sincere.** Steer clear of clichés that are insincere in view of the bad news. (If you can't help, don't say, "If we can be of any help, please contact us.")

- **Be confident.** Don't show any doubt about keeping the person as a customer. (Avoid phrases such as "We hope you will continue to do business with us.")

Finally, keep in mind that the close is the last thing audience members have to remember you by. Even though they're disappointed, leave them with the impression that they were treated with respect.

Adapting to Your Audience

Even more than other business messages, negative messages require that you maintain your audience focus and be as sensitive as possible to audience needs. Therefore, you may need to adapt your message to cultural differences or to the differences between internal and external audiences.

Cultural Variations Bad news is unwelcome in any language, but the conventions for conveying it to business associates can vary considerably from country to country. For instance, French business letters are traditionally quite formal and writer oriented, often without reference to audience needs or benefits. Moreover, when the news is bad, French writers take a direct approach. They open with a reference to the problem or previous correspondence and then state the bad news clearly. While they don't refer to the audience's needs, they often do apologize and express regret for the problem.[8]

> Expectations for the handling of bad news vary from culture to culture.

In contrast, Japanese letters traditionally open with remarks about the season, business prosperity, or health. When the news is bad, these opening formalities serve as the buffer. Explanations and apologies follow, and then comes the bad news or refusal. Japanese writers protect their readers' feelings by wording the bad news ambiguously. Western readers may even misinterpret this vague language as a condition of acceptance rather than as the refusal it actually is.[9] In short, if you are communicating across cultures, you'll want to use the tone, organization, and other cultural conventions that your audience expects. Only then can you avoid the inappropriate or even offensive approaches that could jeopardize your business relationship.[10]

Internal Versus External Audiences Internal audiences frequently have expectations for negative messages that differ from those of external audiences. In some cases, the two groups can interpret the news in different or even opposite ways. For example, employees will react negatively to news of an impending layoff, but company shareholders might welcome the news as evidence that management is trying to control costs. In addition, if a negative message such as a layoff is being sent to internal and external audiences, employees will not only expect more detail but will also expect to be informed before the public is told.

> Compared to external audiences, internal audiences often expect more detail in negative messages.

Negative messages to outside audiences require attention to the diverse nature of the audience and the concern for confidentiality of internal information. A single message might have a half-dozen audiences, all with differing opinions and agendas. You may not be able to explain things to the level of detail that some of these people want if doing so would release proprietary information such as future product plans.

> You may need to adjust the content of negative messages for various external audiences.

Maintaining High Standards of Ethics and Etiquette

All business messages demand attention to ethics and etiquette, of course, but these considerations take on special importance when you are delivering bad news—for several reasons. First, a variety of laws and regulations dictate the content and delivery of many business messages with potentially negative content, such as the release of financial information by a public company. Second, negative messages can have a significant negative impact on the lives of those receiving them. Even if the news is conveyed legally and conscientiously, good ethical practice demands that these situations be approached with care and sensitivity. Third, emotions often run high when negative messages are involved, for both the sender and the receiver. Senders need to not only manage their own emotions but also consider the emotional state of their audiences.

Sharing bad news effectively requires commitment from everyone in the organization.

The challenge of sending—and receiving—negative messages fosters a tendency to delay, downplay, or distort the bad news.[11] However, doing so may be unethical, if not illegal. In recent years, numerous companies have been sued by shareholders, consumers, employees, and government regulators for allegedly withholding or delaying negative information in such areas as company finances, environmental hazards, and product safety. In many of these cases, the problem was slow, incomplete, or inaccurate communication between the company and external stakeholders. In others, problems stemmed from a reluctance to send or receive negative news within the organization.

Effectively sharing bad news within an organization requires commitment from everyone involved. Employees must commit to sending negative messages when necessary, and to doing so in a timely fashion, even when that is unpleasant or difficult. Conversely, managers must commit to maintaining open communication channels, truly listening when employees have negative information to share, and not punishing employees who deliver bad news.

The impulse to want to believe that everything is fine can be strong, and managers who are so inclined can fail to perceive or respond to negative messages from their employees. The energy company BP (formerly British Petroleum) recently experienced such breakdowns when managers didn't act on warnings from employees in the company's Alaska oil pipeline and Texas refining operations. After years of intense efforts by the company to reduce maintenance costs, corrosion and other problems led to a large oil spill along its Alaska pipeline and a tragic accident at its Texas refinery. Some employees said the emphasis on saving money was so strong that safety warnings sometimes went unheeded up the chain of command. Said one, "A scream at our level is, if anything, a whisper at their level."[12]

Although BP employees were not discouraged from reporting bad news, in corporate cultures that don't encourage open communication, employees who fear retribution may go to great lengths to avoid sending bad-news messages. In such dysfunctional environments, failure breeds still more failure because decision makers don't get the honest, objective information they need to make wise choices.[13] In contrast, managers in open cultures expect or even demand that their employees bring them bad news whenever it happens so that corrective action can be taken. Whatever the case, if you need to transmit bad news up the chain of command, don't try to pin the blame on anyone in particular. Simply emphasize the nature of the problem—and a solution, if possible. This tactic will help you earn a reputation as an alert problem solver rather than just a complainer.[14]

Document Makeover

IMPROVE THIS MEMO

To practice correcting drafts of actual documents, visit your online course or the access-code-protected portion of the Companion Website. Click on "Document Makeovers," then click on Chapter 9. You will find a memo that contains problems and errors related to what you've learned in this chapter about handling negative messages. Use the Final Draft decision tool to create an improved version of this memo. Check the message for the use of buffers, apologies, explanations, subordination, embedding, positive action, conditional phrases, and upbeat perspectives.

Finally, recognize that some negative news scenarios will test your self-control and tempt you to respond with a personal attack. However, keep in mind that negative messages can have a lasting impact on the people who receive them and the people who send them. As a communicator, you have a responsibility to minimize the negative impact of your negative messages through careful planning and sensitive, objective writing. As much as possible, focus on the actions or conditions that led to the negative news, not on personal shortcomings or character issues. Develop a reputation as a professional who can handle the toughest situations with dignity.

For a reminder of successful strategies for creating negative messages, see "Checklist: Creating Negative Messages."

> Negative news situations can put your sense of self-control and business etiquette to the test.

EXPLORING COMMON EXAMPLES OF NEGATIVE MESSAGES

The following sections offer examples of the most common negative messages, dealing with topics such as routine business matters, organizational news, and employment messages.

✓ CHECKLIST: Creating Negative Messages

A. Choose the best approach.

- ✓ Consider using the direct approach when the audience is aware of the possibility of negative news, when the reader is not emotionally involved in the message, when you know that the reader would prefer the bad news first, when you know that firmness is necessary, and when you want to discourage a response.
- ✓ Consider using the indirect approach when the news is likely to come as a shock or surprise, when your audience has a high emotional investment in the outcome, and when you want to maintain a good relationship with the audience.

B. For the indirect approach, open with an effective buffer.

- ✓ Establish common ground with the audience.
- ✓ Validate the request, if you are responding to a request.
- ✓ Don't trivialize the reader's concerns.
- ✓ Don't mislead the reader into thinking the coming news might be positive.

C. Provide reasons and additional information.

- ✓ Explain why the news is negative.
- ✓ Adjust the amount of detail to fit the situation and the audience.

- ✓ Avoid explanations when the reasons are confidential, excessively complicated, or irrelevant to the reader.
- ✓ If appropriate, state how you plan to correct or respond to the negative news.
- ✓ Seek the advice of company lawyers if you're unsure what to say.

D. Clearly state the bad news.

- ✓ State the bad news as positively as possible, using tactful wording.
- ✓ De-emphasize the bad news by minimizing the space devoted to it, subordinating it, or embedding it.
- ✓ If your response might change in the future if circumstances change, explain the conditions to the reader.
- ✓ Emphasize what you can or have done rather than what you can't or won't do.

E. Close on a positive note.

- ✓ Express best wishes without being falsely positive.
- ✓ Suggest actions readers might take, if appropriate, and provide them with necessary information.
- ✓ Encourage further communication only if you're willing to discuss the situation further.
- ✓ Keep a positive outlook on the future.

Sending Negative Messages on Routine Business Matters

As you progress in your career and become more visible in your industry and community, you will receive a wide variety of invitations to speak at private or public functions or to volunteer your time for a variety of organizations. In addition, routine business matters such as credit applications and requests for adjustment will often require you to make negative responses. Neither you nor your company will be able to say yes to every request, so crafting negative responses quickly and graciously is an important skill for many professionals.

When turning down an invitation or a request for a favor, consider your relationship with the reader.

Refusing Routine Requests   When you are unable to meet a request, your primary communication challenge is to give a clear negative response without generating negative feelings or damaging either your personal reputation or the company's. As simple as these messages may appear to be, they can test your skills as a communicator because you often need to deliver negative information while maintaining a positive relationship with the other party.

Saying no is a routine part of business and shouldn't reflect negatively on you. If you said yes to every request that crossed your desk, you'd never get any work done. The direct approach will work best for most routine negative responses. It not only helps your audience get your answer quickly and move on to other possibilities but also helps you save time because the direct approach is often easier to write than the indirect approach.

The indirect approach works best when the stakes are high for you or for the receiver, when you or your company has an established relationship with the person making the request, or when you're forced to decline a request that you might have said yes to in the past (see Figure 9.2).

Consider the following points as you develop your routine negative messages:

- **Manage your time carefully.** Focus your time on the most important relationships and requests and get in the habit of crafting quick standard responses for less important situations.

- **If the matter is closed, don't imply that it's still open.** If your answer is truly no, don't use phrases such as "Let me think about it and get back to you" as a way to delay saying no.

- **Offer alternative ideas if you can.** If you can help, great. However, remember to use your time wisely in such matters. Unless the relationship is vital to your company, you probably shouldn't spend time researching alternatives for the other person.

If you aren't in a position to offer additional information or assistance, don't imply that you are.

- **Don't imply that other assistance or information might be available if it isn't.** Don't close your negative message with a cheery but insincere "Please contact us if we can offer any additional assistance." An empty attempt to mollify hostile feelings could simply lead to another request you'll have to refuse.

Handling Bad News About Transactions   Bad news about transactions, the sale and delivery of products and services, is always unwelcome and usually unexpected. Such messages have three goals: to modify the customer's expectations, to explain how you plan to resolve the situation, and to repair whatever damage might have been done to the business relationship.

Some negative messages regarding transactions carry significant business ramifications.

The specific content and tone of each message can vary widely, depending on the nature of the transaction and your relationship with the customer. Telling an individual consumer that his new sweater will be arriving a week later than you promised is a much simpler task than telling General Motors that 30,000 transmission parts will be a week late, especially when you know the company will be forced to idle a multimillion-dollar production facility as a result.

Your approach to bad news about business transactions depends on the customer's expectations.

If you haven't done anything specific to set the customer's expectations—such as promising delivery within 24 hours—the message simply needs to inform the cus-

Planning

Analyze the Situation
Verify that the purpose is to decline a request and offer alternatives; audience is likely to be surprised by the refusal.

Gather Information
Determine audience needs and obtain the necessary information.

Select the Right Medium
For formal messages, printed letters on company letterhead are best.

Organize the Information
Main idea is to refuse the request so limit your scope to that; select an indirect approach based on the audience and the situation.

1

Writing

Adapt to Your Audience
Adjust the level of formality based on degree of familiarity with the audience; maintain a positive relationship by using the "you" attitude, politeness, positive emphasis, and bias-free language.

Compose the Message
Use a conversational but professional style and keep the message brief, clear, and as helpful as possible.

2

Completing

Revise the Message
Evaluate content and review readability to make sure the negative information won't be misinterpreted; make sure your tone stays positive without being artificial.

Produce the Message
Emphasize a clean, professional appearance on company letterhead.

Proofread the Message
Review for errors in layout, spelling, and mechanics.

Distribute the Message
Deliver your message using the chosen medium.

3

---

927 Dawson Valley Road, Tulsa, Oklahoma 74151
Voice: (918) 669-4428   Fax: (918) 669-4429
www.infotech.com

March 6, 2008

Dr. Sandra Wofford, President
Whittier Community College
333 Whittier Avenue
Tulsa, OK 74150

Dear Dr. Wofford:

[Buffers negative response by demonstrating respect and recapping the request] → Infotech has been happy to support Whittier Community College in many ways over the years, and we appreciate the opportunities you and your organization provide to so many deserving students. Thank you for considering our grounds for your graduation ceremony on June 3.

We would certainly like to accommodate Whittier as we have in years past, but our companywide sales meetings will be held this year during the weeks of May 29 and June 5. With over 200 sales representatives and their families from around the world joining us, activities will be taking place throughout our facility. ← *[States a meaningful reason for the negative response, without apologizing (because the company is not at fault)]*

[Suggests an alternative, showing that Kwan cares about the college and has given the matter some thought] → My assistant, Robert Seagers, suggests you contact the Municipal Botanical Gardens as a possible graduation site. He recommends calling Jerry Kane, director of public relations.

We remain firm in our commitment to you, President Wofford, and to the fine students you represent. Through our internship program, academic research grants, and other initiatives, we will continue to be a strong corporate partner to Whittier College and will support your efforts as you move forward. ← *[Closes by emphasizing the importance of the relationship and the company's continuing commitment]*

Sincerely,

May Yee Kwan

May Yee Kwan
Public Relations Director

lc

FIGURE 9.2 Effective Letter Declining a Favor

May Yee Kwan's company has a long-standing relationship with the college Sandra Wofford represents and wants to maintain that positive relationship, but she can't meet this particular request. To communicate negative news, she therefore uses an indirect approach. If Kwan and Wofford shared a closer relationship (if they worked together in a volunteer organization, for instance), the direct approach might have been more appropriate.

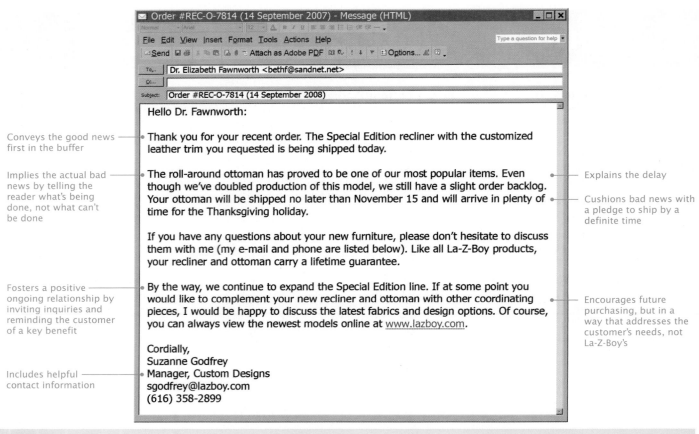

Conveys the good news first in the buffer

Implies the actual bad news by telling the reader what's being done, not what can't be done

Fosters a positive ongoing relationship by inviting inquiries and reminding the customer of a key benefit

Includes helpful contact information

Explains the delay

Cushions bad news with a pledge to ship by a definite time

Encourages future purchasing, but in a way that addresses the customer's needs, not La-Z-Boy's

FIGURE 9.3

Effective E-Mail Advising of a Back Order
This message, which is a combination of good and bad news, uses the indirect approach—with the good news serving as a buffer for the bad news. In this case, the customer wasn't promised delivery by a certain date, so the writer simply informed the customer when to expect the rest of the order. The writer also took steps to repair the relationship and encourage future business with her firm.

tomer, with little or no emphasis on apologies (see Figure 9.3). (Bear in mind, though, in this age of online ordering and overnight delivery, customers have become conditioned to expect instantaneous fulfillment of nearly every transaction, even if you haven't promised anything.)

If you've failed to meet expectations that you set for the customer, you should consider including an element of apology.

If you did set the customer's expectations and now find that you can't meet them, your task is more complicated. In addition to resetting the customer's expectations and explaining how you'll resolve the problem, you may need to include an element of apology. The scope of the apology depends on the magnitude of the mistake. For the customer who ordered the sweater, a simple apology followed by a clear statement of when the sweater will arrive would probably be sufficient. For larger business-to-business transactions, the customer may want an explanation of what went wrong to determine whether you'll be able to perform as you promise in the future.

To help repair the damage to the relationship and encourage repeat business, many companies offer discounts on future purchases, free merchandise, or other considerations. Even modest efforts can go a long way to rebuilding a customer's confidence in your company. However, you don't always have a choice. Business-to-business purchasing contracts often include performance clauses that legally entitle the customer to discounts or other restitution in the event of late delivery. To review the concepts covered in this section, see "Checklist: Handling Bad News About Transactions."

✓ **CHECKLIST: Handling Bad News About Transactions**

✓ Reset the customer's expectations regarding the transaction.

✓ Explain what happened and why, if appropriate.

✓ Explain how you'll resolve the situation.

✓ Repair any damage done to the business relationship, perhaps offering future discounts, free merchandise, or other considerations.

✓ Offer a professional, businesslike expression of apology if your organization made a mistake.

Refusing Claims and Requests for Adjustment   Almost every customer who makes a claim or requests an adjustment is emotionally involved; therefore, the indirect method is usually the best approach for a refusal. Your job as a writer is to avoid accepting responsibility for the unfortunate situation and yet avoid blaming or accusing the customer. To steer clear of these pitfalls, pay special attention to the tone of your letter. A tactful and courteous message can build goodwill even while denying the claim (see Figure 9.4).

Use the indirect approach in most cases of refusing a claim.

When refusing a claim, avoid language that might have a negative impact on the reader. Instead, demonstrate that you understand and have considered the complaint carefully. Then, even if the claim is unreasonable, rationally explain why you are refusing the request. Remember, don't apologize and don't hide behind "company policy." End the message on a respectful and action-oriented note.

When refusing a claim
- Demonstrate your understanding of the complaint
- Explain your refusal
- Suggest alternative action

If you deal with enough customers over a long enough period, chances are you'll get a request that is particularly outrageous. You might even be positive that the person is being dishonest. However, you need to control your emotions and approach the situation as calmly as possible to avoid saying or writing anything that the recipient might interpret as defamation. Someone suing for defamation must prove (1) that the statement is false, (2) that the language is injurious to the person's reputation, and (3) that the statement has been published. To avoid being accused of defamation, follow these guidelines:

- Refrain from using any kind of abusive language or terms that could be considered defamatory.

- Provide accurate information and stick to the facts.

- Never let anger or malice motivate your messages.

- Consult your company's legal advisers whenever you think a message might have legal consequences.

- Communicate honestly and make sure that you believe what you're saying is true.

- Emphasize a desire for a good relationship in the future.

You can help avoid committing defamation by not responding emotionally or abusively.

Most importantly, remember that nothing positive can come out of antagonizing a customer, even one who has verbally abused you or your colleagues. Reject the claim or request for adjustment and move on to the next challenge. For a brief review of the tasks involved when refusing claims, see "Checklist: Refusing Claims."

✓ **CHECKLIST: Refusing Claims**

✓ Use an indirect approach because the reader is expecting or hoping for a positive response.

✓ Indicate your full understanding of the nature of the complaint.

✓ Explain why you are refusing the request, without hiding behind company policy.

✓ Provide an accurate, factual account of the transaction.

✓ Emphasize ways things should have been handled rather than dwell on the reader's negligence.

✓ Avoid any appearance of defamation.

✓ Avoid expressing personal opinions.

✓ End with a positive, friendly, helpful close.

✓ Make any suggested action easy for readers to comply with.

Planning

Writing

Completing

1

Analyze the Situation
Verify that the purpose is to refuse a warranty claim and offer repairs; audience's likely reaction will be disappointment and surprise.

Gather Information
Gather information on warranty policies and procedures, repair services, and resale information.

Select the Right Medium
Choose the best medium for delivering your message; for formal messages, printed letters on company letterhead are best.

Organize the Information
Your main idea is to refuse the claim and promote an alternative solution; select an indirect approach based on the audience and the situation.

2

Adapt to Your Audience
Adjust the level of formality based on degree of familiarity with the audience; maintain a positive relationship by using the "you" attitude, politeness, positive emphasis, and bias-free language.

Compose the Message
Use a conversational but professional style and keep the message brief, clear, and as helpful as possible.

3

Revise the Message
Evaluate content and review readability to make sure the negative information won't be misinterpreted; make sure your tone stays positive without being artificial.

Produce the Message
Emphasize a clean, professional appearance appropriate for a letter on company stationery.

Proofread the Message
Review for errors in layout, spelling, and mechanics.

Distribute the Message
Deliver your message using the chosen medium; make sure the reader receives any necessary support documents as well.

Buffers the bad news by emphasizing a point the reader and writer both agree on

States bad news indirectly, tactfully leaving the repair decision to the customer

Closes by blending sales promotion with an acknowledgment of the customer's interests

Puts company's policy in a favorable light

Helps soothe the reader with a positive alternative

NUMBER ONE IN ENTERTAINMENT

Village Electronics
68 Lake Itasca Boulevard • Hannover, MN 55341
Voice: (612) 878-1312 • Fax: (612) 878-1316

May 2, 2008

Mr. Daniel Lindmeier
849 Cedar St.
Lake Elmo, MN 55042

Dear Mr. Lindmeier:

Thank you for your letter about the battery release switch on your JVC digital camera. Village Electronics believes, as you do, that electronic equipment should be built to last. That's why we stand behind our products with a 90-day warranty.

Even though your JVC camera is a year old and therefore out of warranty, we can still help. Please package your camera carefully and ship it to our store in Hannover. Include your complete name, address, phone number, and a brief description of the malfunction, along with a check for $35 for an initial examination. After assessing the unit, we will give you a written estimate of the needed parts and labor. Then just let us know whether you want us to make the repairs—either by phone or by filling out the prepaid card we'll send you with the estimate.

If you choose to repair the unit, the $35 will be applied toward your bill, the balance of which is payable by check or credit card. JVC also has service centers available in your area. If you would prefer to take the unit to one of them, please see the enclosed list.

Thanks again for inquiring about our service. I've also enclosed a catalog of our latest cameras and accessories, in which you'll find information about JVC's "Trade-Up Special." If you're ready to move up to one of the newest cameras, JVC will offer a generous trade-in allowance on your current model.

Sincerely,

Walter Brodie

Walter Brodie
Customer Service Manager

Enclosures: List of service centers
Catalog

FIGURE 9.4 Effective Letter Refusing a Claim
Daniel Lindmeier, who purchased a digital video camera from Village Electronics a year ago, wrote to say that the unit doesn't work properly and to inquire about the warranty. He incorrectly believed that the warranty covers one year, when it actually covers only three months. In this response, Walter Brodie uses an indirect approach to convey the bad news and to offer additional helpful information.

Sending Negative Organizational News

As a manager, you may need to issue negative announcements regarding some aspect of your products, services, or operations. Most of these scenarios have unique challenges that must be addressed on a case-by-case basis, but the general advice offered here applies to all of them. One key difference among all these messages is whether you have time to plan the announcement. The following section addresses those negative messages that you do have time to plan for, and "Communicating in a Crisis" offers advice on communication during emergencies.

Communicating Under Normal Circumstances   Businesses must convey a range of negative messages regarding their ongoing operations. As you plan such messages, take extra care to consider all your audiences and their unique needs. Consider that a significant negative event such as a plant closing can affect hundreds or thousands of people in many organizations. Employees need to find new jobs, get training in new skills, or perhaps get emergency financial help—issues that need to be addressed. For example, when Michael Gannaway, CEO of Pillowtex, informed employees that efforts to save the bedding company had failed and that it was shutting down, his letter included phone and web contacts employees could use to get assistance.[15] Outside the company, school districts may have to adjust budgets and staffing levels if many of your employees plan to move in search of new jobs. Your customers need to find new suppliers. Your suppliers may need to find other customers of their own. Government agencies may need to react to everything from a decrease in tax revenues to an influx of people seeking unemployment benefits.

> Negative organizational messages to external audiences can require extensive planning.

When making negative announcements, follow these guidelines:

- **Match your approach to the situation.** A modest price increase won't shock most customers, so the direct approach is fine. However, canceling a product that people count on is another matter, so building up to the news via the indirect approach might be better.

- **Consider the unique needs of each group.** As the plant closing example illustrates, various people have different information needs.

- **Give each audience enough time to react as needed.** For instance, employees, particularly high-level professionals and managers, may need three to six months or more to find new jobs.

> Give people as much time as possible to react to negative news.

- **Give yourself enough time to plan and manage a response.** Chances are you're going to be hit with complaints, questions, or product returns after you make your announcement, so make sure you're ready with answers and additional follow-up information.

- **Look for positive angles but don't exude false optimism.** If eliminating a seldom-used employee benefit means employees will save money, by all means promote that positive angle. On the other hand, laying off 10,000 people does not give them "an opportunity to explore new horizons." It's a traumatic event that can affect employees, their families, and their communities for years. The best you may be able to do is to thank people for their past support and to wish them well in the future.

- **Minimize the element of surprise whenever possible.** This step can require considerable judgment on your part, as well as awareness of any applicable laws. In general, if you recognize that current trends are pointing toward negative results sometime in the near future, it's often best to let your audience know ahead of time.

> Ask for legal help and other assistance if you're not sure how to handle a significant negative announcement.

- **Seek expert advice if you're not sure.** Many significant negative announcements have important technical, financial, or legal elements that require the expertise of lawyers, accountants, or other specialists.

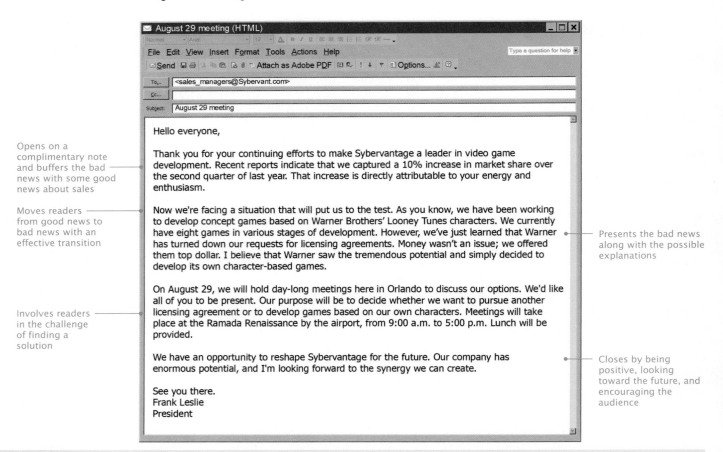

Opens on a complimentary note and buffers the bad news with some good news about sales

Moves readers from good news to bad news with an effective transition

Involves readers in the challenge of finding a solution

Presents the bad news along with the possible explanations

Closes by being positive, looking toward the future, and encouraging the audience

FIGURE 9.5

Effective E-Mail Providing Bad News About Company Operations
In this message to employees at Sybervantage, Frank Leslie shares the unpleasant news that a hoped-for licensing agreement with Warner Brothers has been rejected. Rather than dwell on the bad news, he focuses on options for the future. The upbeat close diminishes the effect of the bad news without hiding or downplaying the news itself.

Negative situations will test your skills as a communicator and leader. People may turn to you and say, "Okay, so things are bad; now what do we do?" Inspirational leaders try to seize such opportunities as a chance to reshape or reinvigorate the organization, and they offer encouragement to those around them (see Figure 9.5).

Communicating in a Crisis   Some of the most critical instances of business communication occur during crises, which can include anything from incidents of product tampering to industrial accidents, crimes or scandals involving company employees, on-site hostage situations, or terrorist attacks. During a crisis, employees, their families, the surrounding community, and others will demand information; in addition, rumors can spread unpredictably and uncontrollably (see "Using the Power of Technology: Controlling Online Rumors"). You can also expect the news media to descend quickly, asking questions of anyone they can find.

Although you can't predict these events, you can prepare for them. Analysis of corporate crises over the past several decades reveals that companies that respond quickly with the information people need tend to fare much better in the long run than those that go into hiding or release inconsistent or incorrect information.[16] In contrast, poor communication can increase victims' trauma and damage company reputations. After an explosion at International Coal Group's Sago coal mine in West Virginia in 2006, one or more rescuers apparently began to spread the word that

USING THE POWER OF TECHNOLOGY

Controlling Online Rumors

Ah, the miracles of the Internet: spam, viruses, spyware, stolen bandwidth, hacked databases full of confidential information—all offering ruin and nuisance at the speed of light. If you work in corporate communications, you can add rapid-fire rumor mongering to that list.

Consumers can now share rumors and complaints through e-mail, instant messaging, blogs, chat rooms, newsgroups, complaint websites such as **www.planetfeedback.com**, and "corporate hate" sites such as **www.paypalsucks.com** and **www.allstateinsurancesucks.com**. On the positive side, consumers who feel they have been treated unfairly can use the public exposure as leverage. Many companies appreciate the feedback from these sites, too, and even buy complaint summaries so they can improve products and services.

Nevertheless, many of these venues don't verify rumors or complaints. E-mail is probably the worst offender in this respect because messages are so easy to forward en masse. Among the classic and recent rumors spread online: McDonald's soft-serve ice cream contains pig fat, products from Coca-Cola and PepsiCo are tainted, perfume samples arriving in the mail are poisonous, bananas from Costa Rica carry flesh-eating bacteria, the small letter *k* on Snapple labels means the company supports the Ku Klux Klan, and Carmex lip balm has (take your pick) addictive ingredients or either an acid or ground glass fibers that damage your lips so you have to use more. Every one of these rumors is false.

Controlling false rumors is difficult, but you can help contain them by (1) responding quickly with clear information distributed in any way you can, (2) tracking down and responding to rumors wherever they appear, (3) enlisting the help of government agencies such as the Centers for Disease Control and Prevention (**www.cdc.gov**) and debunking sites such as **www.snopes.com**, and (4) even digging back through e-mail threads and responding personally to everyone who passed the message along. Moreover, don't wait for bad news to find you; monitor complaint sites and newsgroups so that you can jump on false information faster.

CAREER APPLICATIONS

1. A legitimate complaint about one of your products on planetfeedback.com also contains a statement that your company "doesn't care about its customers." How should you respond?

2. A few bloggers are circulating false information about your company, but the problem is not widespread—yet. Should you jump on the problem now and tell the world the rumor is false, even though most people haven't heard it yet? Explain your answer.

12 trapped miners were still alive. Family and friends gathered in joyous anticipation to meet their loved ones when they returned to the surface. Tragically, the information was wrong; 11 of the 12 were in fact dead. Even though the company quickly realized the report from the mine was wrong, no one updated the family members for several more hours, and they were understandably crushed when they finally learned the truth. Investigators criticized the company and government officials for their disorganized communication effort and lack of control over outgoing messages.[17]

The key to successful communication efforts during a crisis is having a **crisis management plan**. In addition to defining operational procedures to deal with the crisis itself, this plan also outlines communication tasks and responsibilities, which can include everything from media contacts to news release templates (see Table 9.3). The plan should clearly specify which people are authorized to speak for the company, contact information for all key executives, and a list of the media outlets and technologies that will be used to disseminate information. Many companies now go one step further by regularly testing crisis communications in realistic practice drills that last a full day or more.[18]

Anticipation and planning are key to successful communication in a crisis.

Sending Negative Employment Messages

Most managers must convey bad news about individual employees from time to time. Recipients have an emotional stake in your message, so taking an indirect approach is usually advised. In addition, you should use care in choosing the media you use for these messages. For instance, e-mail and other written forms let you control the message and avoid personal confrontation, but one-on-one conversations are more sensitive and facilitate questions and answers.

Table 9.3 — HOW TO COMMUNICATE IN A CRISIS

When a Crisis Hits:

Do	Don't
Prepare for trouble ahead of time by identifying potential problems, appointing and training a response team, and preparing and testing a crisis management plan.	Don't blame anyone for anything.
Get top management involved as soon as the crisis hits.	Don't speculate in public.
Set up a news center for company representatives and the media that is equipped with phones, computers, and other electronic tools for preparing news releases and online updates. At the news center, take the following steps:	Don't refuse to answer questions.
• Issue frequent news updates, and have trained personnel available to respond to questions around the clock.	Don't release information that will violate anyone's right to privacy.
• Provide complete information packets to the media as soon as possible.	Don't use the crisis to pitch products or services.
• Prevent conflicting statements and provide continuity by appointing a single person trained in advance to speak for the company.	Don't play favorites with media representatives.
• Tell receptionists and other employees to direct all media calls to the designated spokesperson in the news center.	
Tell the whole story—openly, completely, and honestly. If you are at fault, apologize.	
Demonstrate the company's concern by your statements and your actions.	

Refusing Requests for Recommendation Letters   As Chapter 8 notes (page 254), many companies now refuse to write recommendation letters—especially for people whose job performance has been unsatisfactory. When sending refusals to prospective employers who have requested information about past employees, your message can be brief and direct:

Implies that company policy prohibits the release of any more information but does provide what information is available

Ends on a positive note

> Our human resources department has authorized me to confirm that Yolanda Johnson worked for Tandy, Inc., for three years, from June 2005 to July 2007. Best of luck as you interview applicants.

This message doesn't need to say, "We cannot comply with your request." It simply gets down to the business of giving readers the information that is allowable.

Refusing an applicant's direct request for a recommendation letter is another matter. Any refusal to cooperate may seem to be a personal slight and a threat to the applicant's future. Diplomacy and preparation help readers accept your refusal:

Uses the indirect approach since the other party is probably expecting a positive response

Announces that the writer cannot comply with the request, without explicitly blaming it on "policy"

Offers to fulfill as much of the request as possible and offers an alternative

Ends on a positive note

> Thank you for letting me know about your job opportunity with Coca-Cola. Your internship there and the MBA you've worked so hard to earn should place you in an excellent position to land the marketing job.
>
> Although we do not send out formal recommendations here at PepsiCo, I can certainly send Coca-Cola a confirmation of your employment dates. And if you haven't considered this already, be sure to ask several of your professors to write evaluations of your marketing skills. Best of luck to you in your career.

This letter tactfully avoids hurting the reader's feelings because it makes positive comments about the reader's recent activities, implies the refusal, suggests an alternative, and uses a polite close.

Rejecting Job Applications Tactfully telling job applicants that you won't be offering them employment is another frequent communication challenge. Poorly written rejection letters can have negative consequences, ranging from the loss of qualified candidates for future openings to the loss of potential customers (not only the rejected applicants but also their friends and family).[19] Badly phrased rejection letters can even invite legal troubles. When delivering bad news to job applicants, follow three guidelines:[20]

Poorly written rejection letters tarnish your company's reputation and can even invite legal troubles.

- **Choose your approach carefully.** Experts disagree on whether a direct or an indirect approach is best for rejection letters. On the one hand, job applicants know they won't get many of the positions they apply for, so negative news during a job search is not generally a shock. On the other hand, people put their hopes and dreams on the line when they apply for work, so job applicants have a deep emotional investment in the process—which is one of the factors to consider in using the indirect approach. If you opt for the direct approach, try not to be brutally blunt in the opening. Tell your reader that the position has been filled rather than saying, "Your application has been rejected." If you opt for the indirect approach, be careful not to mislead the reader or delay the bad news for more than a sentence or two. A simple "Thank you for considering ABC as the place to start your career" is a quick, courteous buffer that shows your company is flattered to be considered. Don't mislead the reader in your buffer by praising his or her qualifications in a way that could suggest good news is soon to follow.

- **Clearly state why the applicant was not selected.** Make your rejection less personal by stating that you hired someone with more experience or whose qualifications match the position requirements more closely.

- **Close by suggesting alternatives.** If time permits, you might suggest other positions for which the applicant is qualified or professional organizations that could help the applicant find employment.

Compare the ineffective and effective versions of the message in Figure 9.6 to see how this writer followed these guidelines.

Resist the temptation to not respond to applicants. Some companies are now so swamped with e-mailed résumés and online applications that they no longer have time to respond to them all. However, a failure to respond to job applicants has traditionally been viewed as a fairly serious breach of business etiquette. Responding is not only good for your company's image but also initiates conversations that might lead to successful hiring when you have the right opportunities for the right people.[21]

Giving Negative Performance Reviews The main purpose of a **performance review** is to improve employee performance by (1) emphasizing and clarifying job requirements; (2) giving employees feedback on their efforts toward fulfilling those requirements; and (3) guiding continued efforts by developing a plan of action, which includes rewards and opportunities. Performance reviews help companies set organizational standards and communicate organizational values.[22]

An important goal of any performance evaluation is to give the employee a plan of action for improving his or her performance.

Criticizing others is difficult for most people, but discussing shortcomings is a necessary first step to improvement for both an employee and an organization. When you need to give a negative performance review, follow these guidelines:[23]

- **Confront the problem right away.** Avoiding mention of performance problems usually only makes them worse—and it robs the employee of the opportunity to improve. Moreover, if you don't document problems when they occur, you may make it more difficult to terminate employment later on if the situation comes to that.[24]

- **Plan your message.** Be clear about your concerns and include examples of the employee's specific actions. Think about any possible biases you may have and get feedback from others. Collect and verify all relevant facts (both strengths and weaknesses).

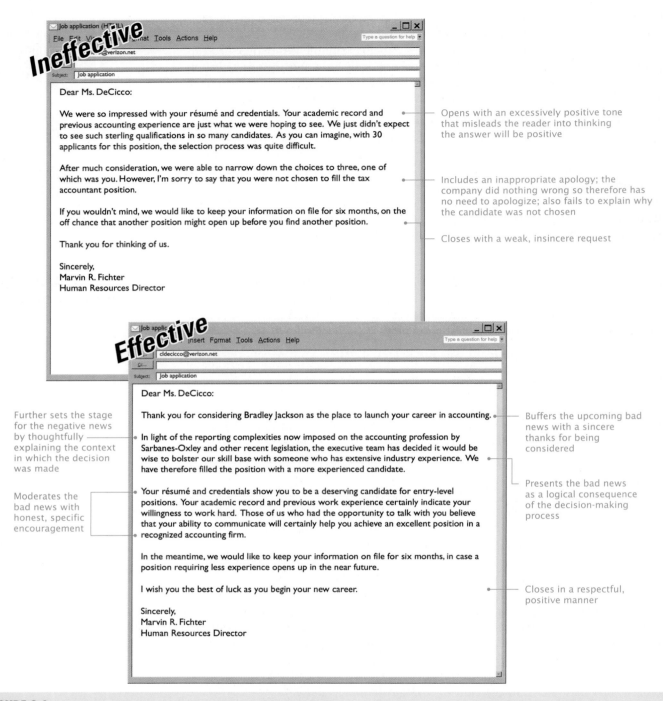

FIGURE 9.6

Ineffective and Effective E-Mails Rejecting a Job Application
This e-mail response was drafted by Marvin Fichter to communicate the bad news to Carol DeCicco following her interview with Bradley & Jackson. After reviewing the first draft, Fichter made several changes to improve the communication. The revised e-mail helps DeCicco understand that (1) she would have been hired if she'd had more tax experience and (2) she shouldn't be discouraged.

Address performance problems in private.

- **Deliver the message in private.** Whether in writing or in person, be sure to address the performance problem privately. Don't send performance reviews by e-mail or fax. If you're reviewing an employee's performance face to face, conduct that review in a meeting arranged expressly for that purpose and consider holding that meeting in a conference room or some other neutral area.

- **Focus on the problem.** Without attacking the employee, discuss the problems caused by his or her performance and explain how it doesn't meet expectations established for the position. Identify the consequences of continuing poor performance and show that you're committed to helping solve the problem.

- **Ask for a commitment from the employee.** Help the employee understand that planning for and making improvements are the employee's responsibility. However, finalize decisions jointly so that you can be sure any action to be taken is achievable. Set a schedule for improvement and for following up with evaluations of that improvement.

Even if an employee's performance has been disappointing, you would do well to begin by mentioning some good points in your performance review. Then clearly and tactfully state how the employee can better meet the responsibilities of the job. If the performance review is to be effective, be sure to suggest ways that the employee can improve.[25] Remember that the ultimate goal is not to criticize but to help the employee succeed.

Terminating Employment   The decision to terminate employees is rarely easy or simple, but doing it effectively is an important managerial responsibility. When writing a termination message, you have three goals: (1) present the reasons for this difficult action, (2) avoid statements that might expose the company to a wrongful termination lawsuit, and (3) leave the relationship between the terminated employee and the firm as favorable as possible. For both legal and personal reasons, present specific justification for asking the employee to leave.[26] Your company's lawyers will be able to tell you whether the employee's performance is legal grounds for termination.

Make sure that all your reasons are accurate and verifiable. Avoid words that are open to interpretation, such as *untidy* and *difficult*. You can help protect personal feelings as you end the relationship by telling the truth about the termination and by helping as much as you can to make the employee's transition as smooth as possible.[27] To review the tasks involved in this type of message, see "Checklist: Writing Negative Employment Messages."

Carefully word a termination letter to avoid creating undue ill will and grounds for legal action.

✓ CHECKLIST: Writing Negative Employment Messages

A. Refusing requests for recommendation letters

- ✓ Don't feel obligated to write a recommendation letter if you don't feel comfortable doing so.
- ✓ Take a diplomatic approach to minimize hurt feelings.
- ✓ Compliment the reader's accomplishments.
- ✓ Suggest alternatives, if available.

B. Rejecting job applications

- ✓ Always respond to applications.
- ✓ If you use a direct approach, take care to avoid being blunt or cold.
- ✓ If you use an indirect approach, don't mislead the reader in your buffer or delay the bad news for more than a sentence or two.
- ✓ Clearly state why the applicant was rejected.
- ✓ Suggest alternatives if possible.

C. Giving negative performance reviews

- ✓ Maintain an objective and unbiased tone.
- ✓ Use nonjudgmental language.
- ✓ Focus on problem resolution.
- ✓ Make sure negative feedback is documented and shared with the employee.
- ✓ Don't avoid confrontations by withholding negative feedback.
- ✓ Ask the employee for a commitment to improve.

D. Terminating employment

- ✓ State your reasons accurately and make sure they are objectively verifiable.
- ✓ Avoid statements that might expose your company to a wrongful termination lawsuit.
- ✓ Consult company lawyers to clarify all terms of the separation.
- ✓ End the relationship on terms as positive as possible.

On the Job

SOLVING COMMUNICATION DILEMMAS AT KPMG

Thanks to your good head for numbers and effective communication skills, you didn't take long to move up to a management position with KPMG. You're now an audit manager in the firm's Louisville, Kentucky, office. (An *audit* is the process of reviewing a firm's accounting records for accuracy and legal compliance.) Your responsibilities range from managing audits for KPMG's clients to helping members of your group develop their skills to coordinating with other managers in cross-functional team efforts. Not surprisingly, communication challenges are frequent and diverse.[28]

1. Another manager in the Louisville office stopped by this morning with a request to borrow two of your best auditors for a three-week emergency. Under normal conditions, you wouldn't hesitate to help, but your team has its own scheduling challenges to deal with. Plus, this isn't the first time this manager has run into trouble, and you are confident that poor project management is the reason. Which of the following is the most diplomatic way to state your refusal while suggesting that your colleague's management skills need improvement?
   a. With the commitments we've made to our own clients, we won't be able to bail you out this time.
   b. I sympathize with the trouble you've gotten yourself into again, I really do, but the commitments we've made to our own clients prevent us from releasing any auditors for temporary assignments.
   c. The commitments we've made to our own clients prevent us from releasing any auditors for temporary assignments. However, I would be happy to meet with you to discuss the techniques I've been using to manage project workloads.
   d. Instead of shifting resources around like usual, why don't we meet to discuss some new strategies for staffing and project management?

2. In business services professions such as public accounting, service providers often work closely with clients for long periods—sometimes even setting up offices at clients' facilities and functioning almost like employees in the client's organization. As in all other professional relationships, personal aspects can enter the relationship over time. In a good situation, the people involved can become friends or social acquaintances, further cementing the business relationship. In a bad situation, even competent professionals can start to rub each other the wrong way at a personal level, which can corrode the business relationship over time. Unfortunately, that has happened with one of your best staff members. Shirley Jackson is widely admired for her technical skills, but a top manager in a client organization has asked you to take her off the project. Although you'd prefer to tell Jackson in per-

son, schedule conflicts dictate that you send her an e-mail. Which of these buffers would be the best way to open the message?
   a. Your work for Comstock Manufacturing continues to be first rate, but you never can tell how these things are going to work out, can you?
   b. If it were up to me, Shirley, I would never deliver a message like this, but Comstock has asked me to re-evaluate the staffing on its auditing projects.
   c. As I've expressed on many occasions, thank you once again for the top-quality work you've done for Comstock Manufacturing over the years.
   d. As you know, Shirley, I continually evaluate the staffing assignments on all our projects to make sure clients are satisfied with the quality of our work and the overall nature of our relationship with them.

3. Although your project management skills are quite good, you do occasionally run into unforeseen circumstances that lead to less-than-ideal results. You underestimated the number of hours required to complete a financial analysis project for an important client. The contract you signed with the client allows a 10 percent overage for such contingencies, but your best guess now is that the total will be 20 to 25 percent over. You have the unpleasant task of explaining to your boss that the project will be coming in over budget and that KPMG will have to absorb the remaining 10 to 15 percent. Which of the following is the best way to communicate that news to your boss?
   a. I messed up, big time. The Southern Petroleum project is going to come in over budget.
   b. The Southern Petroleum project is going to come in at least 20 percent over budget, perhaps 25 percent.
   c. We've recently discovered that Southern Petroleum's accounting system was in far worse shape than I anticipated when I submitted the project proposal, and as a result of the extra work required to reconcile their disorganized records, the project is going to run 20 to 25 percent over budget.
   d. We've recently discovered that Southern Petroleum's accounting system was in far worse shape than I anticipated when I submitted the project proposal. This is clearly not my fault, but as a result of the extra work required to reconcile their disorganized records, the project is going to run 20 to 25 percent over budget.

4. You've found it easy to say "yes" to recommendation letter requests from former employees who were top performers, and you've learned to say "no" to people who didn't perform so well. The requests you

struggle with are from employees in the middle, people who didn't really excel but didn't really cause any trouble, either. You've just received a request from a computer systems specialist who falls smack in the middle of the middle. Unfortunately, he's applying for a job at a firm that you know places high demands on its employees and generally hires the best of the best. He's a great person, and you'd love to help, but in your heart, you know that if by some chance he does get the job, he probably won't last. Plus, you don't want to get a reputation in the industry for recommending weak candidates. How do you set the stage for the negative news?

a. As your former manager, I'd like to think I can still look out for your best interests, and I'm sorry to

say, but based on what I know about the position you're applying for, this might not be the best career move for you at this point.

b. In my view, the responsibility of writing a letter of recommendation goes beyond simply assessing a person's skills; it must consider whether the person is applying for the right job.

c. One of the most important factors I consider when deciding whether to endorse an applicant is whether he or she is pursuing an opportunity that offers a high probability of success.

d. Writing a recommendation letter is a heavy responsibility. After all, I have my own reputation to protect, too.

Learning Objectives Checkup

Assess your understanding of the principles in this chapter by reading each learning objective and studying the accompanying exercises. For fill-in-the-blank items, write the missing text in the blank provided; for multiple-choice items, circle the letter of the correct answer. You can check your responses against the answer key on page AK-2.

Objective 9.1: Apply the three-step writing process to negative messages.

1. Which of the following should be a goal of every negative message?
   a. To convey the bad news clearly
   b. To gain audience acceptance for the news
   c. To maintain as much goodwill as possible with the audience
   d. To maintain a good image for your organization
   e. To reduce or eliminate the need for future correspondence on the matter, if appropriate
   f. None of the above
   g. (a), (c), and (d)
   h. All of the above

2. Which of the following is an effective way to maintain the "you" attitude when crafting negative messages?
   a. Make sure the reader clearly understands that he or she is at fault; after all, recognizing a mistake is the first step toward improvement.
   b. Make it clear that you don't enjoy giving out bad news.
   c. Show respect for the reader by "soft peddling" the negative news, implying it without really coming out and saying it directly.
   d. Show respect for the reader by avoiding negative, accusatory language and emphasizing positives whenever possible.

Objective 9.2: Explain the differences between the direct and the indirect approaches to negative messages, including when it's appropriate to use each one.

3. When using the direct approach with negative messages, you begin with
   a. A buffer
   b. An attention-getter
   c. The bad news
   d. Any of the above

4. An advantage of using the direct approach with negative messages is that it
   a. Saves readers time by helping them reach the main idea more quickly
   b. Eases readers into the message
   c. Is diplomatic
   d. Does all of the above

5. When using the indirect approach with negative messages, you begin with
   a. A buffer
   b. An attention-getter
   c. The bad news
   d. Any of the above

6. Which of the following is an advantage of using the indirect approach with negative messages?
   a. Most readers prefer the direct approach for such messages.
   b. It makes a shorter message possible.
   c. It eases the reader into the message.
   d. It does all of the above.

Objective 9.3: Identify the risks of using the indirect approach, and explain how to avoid such problems.

7. The purpose of using the indirect approach is to
   a. Help the writer avoid the unpleasant task of delivering bad news

b. Help the reader avoid the unpleasant task of receiving bad news
c. Soften the blow of the bad news for the reader
d. Reduce the word count in your messages

8. A/an _____ is a neutral, noncontroversial opening statement that establishes common ground with your reader.

9. Which of the following is a good possibility to consider for use in writing a buffer?
   a. Look for opportunities to express your appreciation for being considered.
   b. Assure your reader of the attention you've paid to his or her request.
   c. Indicate your understanding of the reader's situation.
   d. All of the above are useful approaches.

Objective 9.4: Adapt negative messages for internal and external audiences.

10. When writing negative messages, the key difference to consider between internal and external audiences is
    a. The expectations regarding the message
    b. Their legal standing
    c. The length of time they've been associated with the company
    d. None of the above

11. When a negative message is going to be sent to both internal and external audiences (such as an announcement of a factory closing), which of the following best describes the expectations that internal audiences usually have regarding the timing of the message delivery?
    a. Internal audiences want to receive the news first.
    b. Internal audiences want to receive the news at the same time as the external audience.
    c. Internal audiences want to receive the news after the external audience has received it.
    d. The timing doesn't matter to internal audiences.

Objective 9.5: Explain the importance of maintaining high standards of ethics and etiquette when delivering negative messages

12. Which of the following is an important reason to take particular care to maintain ethics and etiquette when crafting negative messages?
    a. In many cases, the communicator needs to adhere to a variety of laws and regulations when delivering negative messages.
    b. Good ethical practice demands care and sensitivity in the content and delivery of negative messages, as these messages can have a profoundly negative effect on the people who receive them.
    c. Communicators need to manage their own emotions when crafting and distributing negative messages while at the same time considering the emotional needs of their audiences.
    d. All of the above are important reasons to maintain ethics and etiquette in negative messages.

13. Which of the following is most characteristic of organizational cultures that emphasize open communication?

a. Managers are willing to listen to bad news from employees, but they understand if employees don't want to deliver bad news.
b. Managers expect employees to deliver bad news so that corrective action can be taken.
c. Managers reward employees who deliver bad news with extra vacation time, extra pay, or both.
d. None of the above is true.

Objective 9.6: Explain the role of communication in crisis management.

14. Which of the following best characterizes the nature of crisis management planning?
    a. Good managers should be able to anticipate the specific crisis scenarios their companies might encounter and therefore should be able to plan for every crisis in a specific way.
    b. With everything from terrorism to technological disasters, there's no way to anticipate which crisis might hit any given business, so it's a waste of time to plan a response.
    c. Although you can't anticipate the nature and circumstance of every possible crisis, you can prepare by deciding how to handle such issues as communication with employees and the public.
    d. Only negatively focused managers worry about crisis planning; positive managers keep their organizations moving toward company goals.

15. Continuing advances in communication technology make it
    a. Easier to control rumors through Internet filters and other means
    b. More difficult to control rumors
    c. Easier to find the people who start rumors
    d. Illegal to spread false rumors about public corporations

Objective 9.7: List three guidelines for delivering bad news to job applicants, and give a brief explanation of each one.

16. Why do many experts recommend using an indirect approach when rejecting job applicants?
    a. Applicants have a deep emotional investment in the decision.
    b. Laws in most states require an indirect approach.
    c. Indirect approaches are easier to write.
    d. Indirect approaches are shorter.

17. When explaining why an applicant wasn't chosen for a position, you should
    a. Be specific without being too personal, such as explaining that the position requires specific skills that the applicant doesn't yet possess
    b. Point out the person's shortcomings as that's the honest way and the only way the person knows what he or she needs to improve
    c. Be as vague as possible to avoid hurting the person's feelings
    d. Never explain why an applicant wasn't chosen

Apply Your Knowledge

1. Why is it important to end a negative message on a positive note?
2. If company policy changes, should you explain those changes to employees and customers at about the same time? Why or why not?
3. If your purpose is to convey bad news, such as refusing a request, should you take the time to suggest alternatives to your reader? Why or why not?
4. When a company suffers a setback, should you soften the impact by letting out the bad news a little at a time? Why or why not?
5. **Ethical Choices** Is intentionally de-emphasizing bad news the same as distorting graphs and charts to de-emphasize unfavorable data? Why or why not?

Practice Your Knowledge

MESSAGES FOR ANALYSIS

Read the following messages and then (1) analyze the strengths and weaknesses of each sentence and (2) revise each message so that it follows this chapter's guidelines.

MESSAGE 9.A: PROVIDING NEGATIVE NEWS ABOUT TRANSACTIONS

Your spring fraternity party sounds like fun. We're glad you've again chosen us as your caterer. Unfortunately, we have changed a few of our policies, and I wanted you to know about these changes in advance so that we won't have any misunderstandings on the day of the party.

We will arrange the delivery of tables and chairs as usual the evening before the party. However, if you want us to set up, there is now a $100 charge for that service. Of course, you might want to get some of the brothers and pledges to do it, which would save you money. We've also added a small charge for cleanup. This is only $3 per person (you can estimate because I know a lot of people come and go later in the evening).

Other than that, all the arrangements will be the same. We'll provide the skirting for the band stage, tablecloths, bar setup, and, of course, the barbecue. Will you have the tubs of ice with soft drinks again? We can do that for you as well, but there will be a fee.

Please let me know if you have any problems with these changes, and we'll try to work them out. I know it's going to be a great party.

MESSAGE 9.B: REFUSING REQUESTS FOR CLAIMS AND ADJUSTMENTS

I am responding to your letter of about six weeks ago asking for an adjustment on your wireless hub, model WM39Z. We test all our products before they leave the factory; therefore, it could not have been our fault that your hub didn't work.

If you or someone in your office dropped the unit, it might have caused the damage. Or the damage could have been caused by the shipper if he dropped it. If so, you should file a claim with the shipper. At any rate, it wasn't our fault. The parts are already covered by warranty. However, we will provide labor for the repairs for $50, which is less than our cost, since you are a valued customer.

We will have a booth at the upcoming trade show there and hope to see you or someone from your office. We have many new models of hubs, routers, and other computer gear that we're sure

you'll want to see. I've enclosed our latest catalog. Hope to see you there.

MESSAGE 9.C: REJECTING JOB APPLICATIONS

I regret to inform you that you were not selected for our summer intern program at Equifax. We had over a thousand résumés and cover letters to go through and simply could not get to them all. We have been asked to notify everyone that we have already selected students for the 25 positions based on those who applied early and were qualified.

We're sure you will be able to find a suitable position for summer work in your field and wish you the best of luck. We deeply regret any inconvenience associated with our reply.

EXERCISES

For active links to all websites discussed in this chapter, visit this text's website at www.prenhall.com/thill. Locate your book and click on its "Companion Website" link. Then select Chapter 9 and click on "Featured Websites." Locate the name of the page or the URL related to the material in the text. Please note that links to sites that become inactive after publication of the book will be removed from the "Featured Websites" section.

9.1 **Selecting the Approach** Select which approach you would use (direct or indirect) for the following negative messages.
   a. An e-mail message to your boss, informing her that one of your key clients is taking its business to a different accounting firm
   b. An e-mail message to a customer, informing her that one of the books she ordered over the Internet is temporarily out of stock
   c. An instant message to a customer, explaining that the DVD recorder he ordered for his new computer is on back order and that, as a consequence, the shipping of the entire order will be delayed
   d. A blog post to all employees, notifying them that the company parking lot will be repaved during the first week of June and that the company will provide a shuttle service from a remote parking lot during that period
   e. A letter from a travel agent to a customer, stating that the airline will not refund her money for the

flight she missed but that her tickets are valid for one year

f. A form letter from a U.S. airline to a customer, explaining that the company cannot extend the expiration date of the customer's frequent flyer miles even though the customer was living overseas for the past three years and unable to use the miles during that time

g. A letter from an insurance company to a policy-holder, denying a claim for reimbursement for a special medical procedure that is not covered under the terms of the customer's policy

h. A letter from an electronics store, stating that the customer will not be reimbursed for a malfunctioning mobile phone that is still under warranty (because the terms of the warranty do not cover damages to phones that were accidentally dropped from a moving car)

i. An announcement to the repairs department, listing parts that are on back order and will be three weeks late

9.2 **Teamwork** Working alone, revise the following statements to de-emphasize the bad news. (*Hint*: Minimize the space devoted to the bad news, subordinate it, embed it, or use the passive voice.) Then team up with a classmate and read each other's revisions. Did you both use the same approach in every case? Which approach seems to be most effective for each of the revised statements?

a. The airline can't refund your money. The "Conditions" section on the back of your ticket states that there are no refunds for missed flights. Sometimes the airline makes exceptions, but only when life and death are involved. Of course, your ticket is still valid and can be used on a flight to the same destination.

b. I'm sorry to tell you, we can't supply the custom decorations you requested. We called every supplier, and none of them can do what you want on such short notice. You can, however, get a standard decorative package on the same theme in time. I found a supplier that stocks these. Of course, it won't have quite the flair you originally requested.

c. We can't refund your money for the malfunctioning MP3 player. You shouldn't have immersed the unit in water while swimming; the users manual clearly states the unit is not designed to be used in adverse environments.

9.3 **Using Buffers** As a customer service supervisor for a telephone company, you're in charge of responding to customers' requests for refunds. You've just received an e-mail from a customer who unwittingly ran up a $500 bill for long-distance calls after mistakenly configuring his laptop computer to dial an Internet access number that wasn't a local call. The customer says it wasn't his fault because he didn't realize he was dialing a long-distance number. However, you've dealt with this situation before; you know that the customer's Internet service provider warns its customers to choose a local access number because customers are responsible for all long-distance charges. Draft a short buffer (one or two sentences) for your e-mail reply, sympathizing with the customer's plight but preparing him for the bad news (that company policy specifically prohibits refunds in such cases).

9.4 **Internet** Public companies occasionally need to issue news releases announcing or explaining downturns in sales, profits, demand, or other business factors. Search the web to locate a company that has issued a press release that recently reported lower earnings or other bad news and access the news release on that firm's website. Alternatively, find the type of press release you're seeking by reviewing press releases at www.prnewswire.com or www.businesswire.com. How does the headline relate to the main message of the release? Is the release organized according to the direct or the indirect approach? What does the company do to present the bad news in a favorable light—and does this effort seem sincere and ethical to you?

9.5 **Ethical Choices** The insurance company where you work is planning to raise all premiums for health-care coverage. Your boss has asked you to read a draft of her letter to customers announcing the new, higher rates. The first two paragraphs discuss some exciting medical advances and the expanded coverage offered by your company. Only in the final paragraph do customers learn that they will have to pay more for coverage starting next year. What are the ethical implications of this draft? What changes would you suggest?

Expand Your Knowledge

LEARNING MORE ON THE WEB
PROTECT YOURSELF WHEN SENDING NEGATIVE EMPLOYMENT MESSAGES

www.toolkit.cch.com

A visit to CCH's Business Owner's Toolkit can help you reduce your legal liability, whether you are laying off an employee, firing an employee, or contemplating a companywide reduction in your workforce. Find out the safest way to fire someone from a legal standpoint before it's too late. Learn why it's important to docu-

ment disciplinary actions. Discover why some bad news should be given face-to-face and never with a letter or over the phone. Read CCH's advice to find answers to these questions:

1. What should a manager communicate to an employee during a termination meeting?
2. Why is it important to document employee disciplinary actions?
3. What steps should you take before firing an employee for misconduct or poor work?

SURFING YOUR WAY TO CAREER SUCCESS

Bovée and Thill's Business Communication Headline News offers links to hundreds of online resources that can help you with this course, your other college courses, and your career. Visit www.businesscommunicationblog.com and click on "Web Directory." The "Internet and the World Wide Web" sec- tion connects you to a variety of websites and articles on web- site design and development, HTML, web graphics, RSS, wikis, and related topics. Identify three websites from this sec- tion that could be useful in your business career. For each site, write a two-sentence summary of what the site offers and how it could help you launch and build your career.

Learn Interactively

INTERACTIVE STUDY GUIDE

Visit www.prenhall.com/thill, locate your book and click on its "Companion Website" link. Select Chapter 9 to take advan- tage of the interactive "Chapter Quiz" to test your knowledge of chapter concepts. Receive instant feedback on whether you need additional studying. Also, visit the "Study Hall," where you'll find an abundance of valuable resources that will help you succeed in this course.

PEAK PERFORMANCE GRAMMAR AND MECHANICS

If your instructor has required the use of "Peak Perfor- mance Grammar and Mechanics," either in your online course or on CD, you can improve your skill with commas by using the "Peak Performance Grammar and Mechanics" module. Click on "Commas." Take the Pretest to determine whether you have any weak areas. Then review those areas in the Refresher Course. Take the Follow-Up Test to check your grasp of commas. For an extra challenge or advanced practice, take the Advanced Test. Finally, for additional reinforcement, go to the "Improve Your Grammar, Mechanics, and Usage" sec- tion that follows and complete those exercises.

Improve Your Grammar, Mechanics, and Usage

The following exercises help you improve your knowledge of and power over English grammar, mechanics, and usage. Turn to the Handbook of Grammar, Mechanics, and Usage at the end of this book and review all of Section 2.6 (Commas). Then look at the following 10 items. Circle the letter of the preferred choice in the following groups of sentences. (Answers to these exercises appear on page AK-3.)

1. a. Please send us four cases of filters two cases of wing nuts and a bale of rags.
   b. Please send us four cases of filters, two cases of wing nuts and a bale of rags.
   c. Please send us four cases of filters, two cases of wing nuts, and a bale of rags.
2. a. Your analysis, however, does not account for returns.
   b. Your analysis however does not account for returns.
   c. Your analysis, however does not account for returns.
3. a. As a matter of fact she has seen the figures.
   b. As a matter of fact, she has seen the figures.
4. a. Before May 7, 1999, they wouldn't have minded.
   b. Before May 7, 1999 they wouldn't have minded.
5. a. Stoneridge Inc. will go public on September 9 2003.
   b. Stoneridge, Inc., will go public on September 9, 2003.
   c. Stoneridge Inc. will go public on September 9, 2003.
6. a. "Talk to me" Sandra said "before you change a thing."
   b. "Talk to me," Sandra said "before you change a thing."
   c. "Talk to me," Sandra said, "before you change a thing."
7. a. The firm was founded during the long hard recession of the mid-1970s.

b. The firm was founded during the long, hard recession of the mid-1970s.
   c. The firm was founded during the long hard, recession of the mid-1970s.
8. a. You can reach me at this address: 717 Darby St., Scottsdale, AZ 85251.
   b. You can reach me at this address: 717 Darby St., Scottsdale AZ 85251.
   c. You can reach me at this address: 717 Darby St., Scottsdale, AZ, 85251.
9. a. Transfer the documents from Fargo, North Dakota to Boise, Idaho.
   b. Transfer the documents from Fargo North Dakota, to Boise Idaho.
   c. Transfer the documents from Fargo, North Dakota, to Boise, Idaho.
10. a. Sam O'Neill the designated representative is gone today.
    b. Sam O'Neill, the designated representative, is gone today.
    c. Sam O'Neill, the designated representative is gone today.

For additional exercises focusing on commas, go to www. prenhall.com/thill, then locate your text and click on its "Companion Website" link. Click on Chapter 9, click on "Addi- tional Exercises to Improve Your Grammar, Mechanics and Usage," and then click on "14. Fused sentences and comma splices."

Cases

Applying the Three-Step Writing Process to Cases
Apply each step to the following cases, as assigned by your instructor.

Planning

Analyze the Situation
Identify both your general purpose and your specific purpose. Clarify exactly what you want your audience to think, feel, or believe after receiving your message. Profile your primary audience, including their backgrounds, differences, similarities, and likely reactions to your message.

Gather Information
Identify the information your audience will need to receive, as well as other information you may need in order to craft an effective message.

Select the Right Medium
Make sure your medium is both acceptable to the audience and appropriate for the message. Realize that written media are inappropriate for some negative messages.

Organize the Information
Choose a direct or indirect approach based on the audience and the message; many negative messages are best delivered with an indirect approach. If you use the indirect approach, carefully consider which type of buffer is best for the situation. Identify your main idea, limit your scope, and then outline necessary support points and other evidence.

1

Writing

Adapt to Your Audience
Show sensitivity to audience needs with a "you" attitude, politeness, positive emphasis, and bias-free language. Understand how much credibility you already have—and how much you may need to establish. Project your company's image by maintaining an appropriate style and tone. Consider cultural variations and the differing needs of internal and external audiences.

Compose the Message
Draft your message using clear but sensitive words, effective sentences, and coherent paragraphs.

2

Completing

Revise the Message
Evaluate content and review readability, then edit and rewrite for conciseness and clarity.

Produce the Message
Use effective design elements and suitable layout for a clean, professional appearance.

Proofread the Message
Review for errors in layout, spelling, and mechanics.

Distribute the Message
Deliver your message using the chosen medium; make sure all documents and all relevant files are distributed successfully.

3

NEGATIVE MESSAGES ON ROUTINE BUSINESS MATTERS

Telephone SKILLS

1. **When a recall isn't really a recall: Voice recording informing customers that an unsafe product won't be replaced** Vail Products of Toledo, Ohio, manufactured a line of beds for use in hospitals and other institutions where there is a need to protect patients who might otherwise fall out of bed and injure themselves (including patients with cognitive impairments or patterns of spasms or seizures). These "enclosed bed systems" use a netted canopy to keep patients in bed rather than the traditional method of using physical restraints such as straps or tranquilizing drugs. The intent is humane, but the design is flawed: At least 30 patients have become trapped in the various parts of the mattress and canopy structure, and 8 of them have suffocated.

Working with the U.S. Food and Drug Administration (FDA), Vail issued a recall on the beds, as manufacturers often do in the case of unsafe products. However, the recall is not really a recall. Vail will not be replacing or modifying the beds, nor will it accept returns. Instead, the company is urging institutions to move patients to other beds, if possible. Vail has also sent out revised manuals and warning labels to be placed on the beds. The company also announced that it is ceasing production of enclosed beds.

Your task: A flurry of phone calls from concerned patients, family members, and institutional staff is overwhelming the support staff. As a writer in Vail's corporate communications office, you've been asked to draft a short script to be recorded on the company's phone system. When people call the main number, they'll hear "Press 1 for information regarding the recall of Model 500, Model 1000, and Model 2000 enclosed beds." After they press 1, they'll hear the message you're about to write, explaining that although the action is classified as a recall, Vail will not be accepting returned beds, nor will it replace any of the affected beds. The message should also assure customers that Vail has already sent revised operating manuals and warning labels to every registered owner of the beds in question. The phone system has limited memory, and you've been directed to keep the message to 75 words or less.[29]

E-Mail SKILLS   Portfolio BUILDER

2. Message to the boss: Refusing a project on ethical grounds. A not-so-secret secret is getting more attention than you'd really like after an article in *BusinessWeek* gave the world an inside look at how much money you and other electronics retailers make from extended warranties (sometimes called service contracts). The article explained that typically half of the warranty price goes to the salesperson as a commission and that only 20 percent of the total amount customers pay for warranties eventually goes to product repair.

You also know why extended warranties are such a profitable business. Many electronics products follow a predictable pattern of failure: a high failure rate early in their lives, then a "midlife" period during which failures go way down, and concluding with an "old age" period when failure rates ramp back up again (engineers refer to the phenomenon as the *bathtub curve* because it looks like a bathtub from the side—high at both ends and low in the middle). Those early failures are usually covered by manufacturers' warranties, and the extended warranties you sell are designed to cover that middle part of the life span. In other words, many extended warranties cover the period of time during which consumers are *least* likely to need them and offer no coverage when consumers need them *most*. (Consumers can actually benefit from extended warranties in a few product categories, including laptop computers and plasma televisions. Of course, the more sense the warranty makes for the consumer, the less financial sense it makes for your company.)[30]

Your task: Worried that consumers will start buying fewer extended warranties, your boss has directed you to put together a sales training program that will help cashiers sell the extended warranties even more aggressively. The more you ponder this challenge, though, the more you're convinced that your company should change its strategy so it doesn't rely on profits from these warranties so much. In addition to offering questionable value to the consumer, they risk creating a consumer backlash that could lead to lower sales of all your products. You would prefer to voice your concerns to your boss in person, but both of you are traveling on hectic schedules for the next week. You'll have to write an e-mail instead. Draft a brief message explaining why you think the sales training specifically and the warranties in general are both bad ideas.

3. Not this time: Letter denying debit adjustments to Union Bank of California customer You are an operations officer in the ATM Error Resolution Department at Union Bank of California. Your department often adjusts customer accounts for ATM debit errors. Mistakes are usually honest ones—such as a merchant swiping a customer's check debit card two or three times, thinking the first few swipes didn't "take," when they actually did.

Customers having problems on their statements are instructed to write a claim letter to your department that describes the situation and includes copies of receipts. Customers are notified of the outcome within 10 to 20 business days. Usually, you credit their account.

However, you've received a letter from Margaret Caldwell, who maintains several hefty joint accounts with her husband at your bank. Three debits to her checking account were processed on the same day and credited to the same market, Wilson's Gourmet. The debits carry the same transaction reference number, 1440022-22839837109, which is what caught Mrs. Caldwell's attention. But you know that number changes daily, not hourly, so multiple purchases made on the same day often carry the same number. Also, the debits are for different amounts ($23.02, $110.95, and $47.50), so these transactions were not a result of repeated card swipes. No receipts were enclosed.

Mrs. Caldwell writes that the store was trying to steal from her, but you doubt that and decide to contact Wilson's Gourmet. Manager Ronson Tibbits tells you that he's had no problems with his equipment. He also mentions that food shoppers commonly return at different times during the day to make additional purchases, particularly for beverages or merchandise they forgot the first time.

You decide that these charges did not result from a bank or merchant error. It doesn't matter whether Mrs. Caldwell is merely confused or trying to commit an intentional fraud. Bank rules are clear for this situation: You must politely deny her request.

Your task: Write a letter to Margaret Caldwell, 2789 Aviara Parkway, Carlsbad, CA 92008, explaining your refusal of her claim #7899. Keep in mind that you don't want to lose this wealthy customer's business.[31]

IM SKILLS

4. Midair letdown: Instant message about flight cancellations at United Airlines It used to be that airline passengers didn't learn about canceled connecting flights until after they'd landed. Sometimes a captain would announce cancellations just before touching down at a major hub, but how were passengers to notify waiting relatives or business associates on the ground?

As a customer service supervisor for United Airlines, you've just received information that all United flights from Chicago's O'Hare International Airport to Boston's Logan International have been canceled until further notice. A late-winter storm has already blanketed Boston with snow, and freezing rain is expected overnight. The way the weather report looks, United will probably be lodging Boston-bound connecting passengers in Chicago-area hotels tonight. Meanwhile, you'll be using some of United's newest communication tools to notify travelers of the bad news.

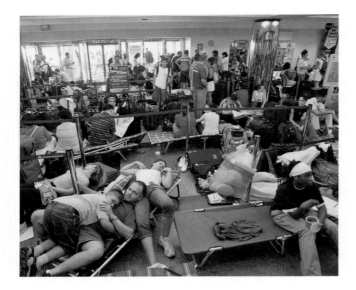

United Airlines now partners with Verizon Airfone to provide JetConnect information services, giving travelers access to instant messaging and other resources while they're airborne. For a small fee, they can plug their laptop computers into the Airfone jack, activating their own instant messaging software to send and receive messages. If they've signed up for United's EasyUpdate flight status notification service, they'll also receive instant message alerts for flight cancellations, delays, seating upgrades, and so on.

Your task: Write the cancellation alert, staying within the 65-word limit of many instant messaging programs. You might want to mention the airline's policy of providing overnight lodging for passengers who planned to use the Boston route as a connecting flight to complete journeys in progress.[32]

IM SKILLS

5. Quick answer: Instant message turning down employee request at Hewlett-Packard If she'd asked you a week ago, Lewinda Johnson might have been granted her request to attend a conference on the use of blogging for business, which is being held in New York City next month. Instead, Johnson waited until you were stuck in this meeting, and she needs your response within the hour. She'll have to take no for an answer: With travel budgets under tight restrictions, you would need at least three days to send her request up the chain of command. Furthermore, Johnson hasn't given you sufficient justification for her attendance since she's already familiar with blogging.

Your task: Write a 60- to 75-word instant message to Lewinda Johnson, declining her request. Decide whether the direct or indirect approach is appropriate.[33]

Blogging SKILLS | Portfolio BUILDER

6. Coffee offer overflow: Undoing a marketing mistake at Starbucks Marketing specialists usually celebrate when target audiences forward their messages to friends and family—essentially acting as unpaid advertising and sales representatives. In fact, the practice of viral marketing (see page 213) is based on this hope. For one Starbucks regional office, however, viral marketing started to make the company just a bit sick. The office sent employees in the Southeast an e-mail coupon for a free iced drink and invited them to share the coupon with family and friends. To the surprise of virtually no one who understands the nature of online life, the e-mail coupon multiplied rapidly, to the point that Starbucks stores all around the country were quickly overwhelmed with requests for free drinks. The company decided to immediately terminate the free offer, a month ahead of the expiration date on the coupon.[34]

Your task: Write a one-paragraph message that can be posted on the Starbucks website and at individual stores, apologizing for the mix-up and explaining that the offer is no longer valid.

7. No deal: Letter from Home Depot to faucet manufacturer As assistant to the vice president of sales for Atlanta-based Home Depot, you attended Home Depot's biannual product-line review held at Tropicana Field in St. Petersburg, Florida. Also attending were hundreds of vendor hopefuls, each eager to become one of the huge retail chain's 25,000 North American suppliers. During individual meetings with a panel of regional and national Home Depot merchandisers, these vendors did their best to win, keep, or expand their spots in the company's product lineup.

Vendors know that Home Depot holds all the cards; so, if they want to play, they have to follow Home Depot rules, offering low wholesale prices and swift delivery. Once chosen, they're constantly re-evaluated—and quickly dropped for infractions such as requesting a price increase or planning to sell directly to consumers via the Internet. They also receive sharp critiques of past performance, which are not to be taken lightly.

A decade ago, General Electric failed to keep Home Depot stores supplied with lightbulbs, causing shortages. Co-founder Bernard Marcus immediately stripped GE of its exclusive, 80-foot shelf space and flew off to negotiate with its Netherlands competitor, Phillips. Two years later, after high-level negotiations, GE lightbulbs were back on Home Depot shelves—but in a position inferior to Phillips's.

Such cautionary tales aren't lost on vendors. However, they know that despite tough negotiating, Home Depot is always looking for variety to please its customers' changing tastes and demands. The sales potential is so enormous that the compromises and concessions are worthwhile. If selected, vendors get immediate distribution in more than 1,700 stores (Home Depot, EXPO, and other subsidiary companies) across the United States, Canada, Mexico, and Puerto Rico.

Still, you've seen the stress on vendor reps' faces as they explain product enhancements and on-time delivery ideas in the review sessions. Their only consolation for this grueling process is that, although merchandisers won't say yes or no on the spot, they let manufacturers know where they stand within a day or two. And the company is always willing to reconsider at the next product-line review—wherever it's held.

Your task: You're drafting some of the rejection letters, and the next one on your stack is to a faucet manufacturer, Roseway Manufacturing, 133 Industrial Ave., Gary, IN 46406. "Too expensive," "substandard plastic handles," and "a design not likely to appeal to Home Depot customers," say the panel's notes. (Knowing what its customers want has put Home Depot in the top 10 of the Fortune 500 list, with $40 billion in annual sales.) Find a way to soften the blow in your rejection letter to Roseway. After all, consumer tastes do change. Direct your letter to Pamela Wilson, operations manager.[35]

8. Suffering artists: Memo declining high-tech shoes at American Ballet Theatre At the American Ballet Theatre (ABT), where you're serving as assistant to Artistic Director Kevin McKenzie, the notion of suffering for the art form has been ingrained since the early 1800s, when the first ballet dancer rose up *en pointe*. Many entrepreneurs are viewing this painful situation with hopeful enthusiasm, especially when they discover that dancers worldwide spend about $150 million annually on their shoes—those "tiny torture chambers" of cardboard and satin (with glued linen or burlap to stiffen the toes). The painful footwear (about $50 a pair) rarely last beyond a single hard performance.

A company the size of ABT spends about $500,000 a year on pointe shoes—plus the cost of a staff physical therapist and all those trips to chiropractors, podiatrists, and surgeons to relieve bad necks, backs, knees, and feet. Entrepreneurs believe there must be room for improvement, given the current advantages of orthopedics, space-age materials, and high-tech solutions for contemporary athletes. There's no denying that ballet dancers are among the hardest-working athletes in the world.

The latest entrepreneur to approach ABT is Eliza Minden of Gaynor Minden, Inc. She wants to provide a solution to the shoe problem. She has approached Michael Kaiser, executive director and a member of ABT's board of governing trustees, with a proposal for providing new, high-performance pointe shoes in exchange for an endorsement.

Minden's alternative pointe shoes offer high-impact support and toe cushions. They're only $90 a pair and can be blow dried back into shape after a performance. When the cost-conscious board member urged the company to give them a try, you were assigned to collect feedback from dancers.

So far, not so good. For example, after a brief trial, one principal ballet dancer said she'd rather numb her feet in icy water, dance through "zingers" of toe pain, and make frequent visits to the physical therapist than wear Minden's shoes. The majority of others agree. Apparently, they *like* breaking in the traditional satin models with hammers and door slams and throwing them away after a single *Coppelia*. Too stiff, they say

of the new shoes. Besides, they're simply not the shoes they grew up with and trained in. Only a few of the company's newest members, such as Gillian Murphy, liked Minden's high-tech shoes. That's not enough for a company endorsement.

You've seen all those feet bleeding backstage. You feel sorry for Minden; it *was* a good idea—just a hard sell among the tradition-oriented dancers.

Your task: McKenzie has asked you to write an internal memo in his name to Michael Kaiser, executive director of the American Ballet Theatre, explaining the dancers' refusal to use the new high-tech Gaynor Minden pointe shoes. In your memo, be sure to include the dancers' reasons as well as your own opinion regarding the matter. You'll need to decide whether to use the direct or the indirect approach; include a separate short note to your instructor justifying your selection of approach.[36]

9. Cyber-surveillance: Memo refusing claim from Silent Watch victim Your business is called Advertising Inflatables, and your specialty is designing and building the huge balloon replicas used for advertising at retail stores, tire outlets, used-car lots, fast-food outlets, fitness clubs, and so on. You've built balloon re-creations of everything from a 50-foot King Kong to a "small" 10-foot pizza.

Not long ago, you installed the "cyber-surveillance" software Silent Watch to track and record employees' computer usage. At the time, you sent out a memo informing all employees that they should limit their computer use and e-mail to work projects only. You also informed them that their work would be monitored. You did not mention that Silent Watch would record every keystroke of their work or that they could be monitored from a screen in your office.

As expected, Silent Watch caught two of the sales staff spending 50 to 70 percent of their time surfing Internet sites unrelated to their jobs. You withheld their pay accordingly, without warning. You sent them a memo, notifying them that they were not fired but were on probation. You considered this wise because when they work, both employees are very good at what they do, and talent is hard to find.

However, now sales representative Jarod Harkington has sent you a letter, demanding reinstatement of his pay and claiming that he was "spied on illegally." On the contrary, company attorneys have assured you that the courts almost always side with employers on this issue, particularly after employees receive a warning such as the one you wrote. The computer equipment belongs to Advertising Inflatables, and employees are paid a fair price for their time.

Your task: Write a letter refusing Mr. Harkington's claim.[37]

E-Mail SKILLS

10. Mobile phone violations: E-mail message to associates at Wilkes Artis Law Firm "Company policy states that personnel are not to conduct business using mobile phones while driving," David Finch reminds you. He's a partner at the law firm Wilkes Artis in Washington, D.C., where you work as his administrative assistant.

You nod, waiting for him to explain. He already issued a memo about this rule last year after a 15-year-old girl was hit and killed by an attorney from another firm. Driving back from a client meeting, the attorney was distracted while talking on her mobile phone. The girl's family sued the firm and won $30 million, but that's not the point. The point is that mobile phones can cause people to be hurt, even killed.

Finch explains, "Yesterday one of our associates called his secretary while driving his car. We can't allow this. According to the National Highway Transportation Safety Administration, 20 to 30 percent of all driving accidents are related to mobile phone usage. From now on, any violation of our mobile phone policy will result in suspension without pay, unless the call is a genuine health or traffic emergency."[38]

Your task: Finch asks you to write an e-mail message to all employees, announcing the new penalty for violating company policy.

NEGATIVE ORGANIZATIONAL NEWS

Blogging SKILLS

11. We're going to catch some flak for this: Alerting employees to the removal of a popular product XtremityPlus is known for its outlandish extreme-sports products, and the Looney Launch is no exception. Fulfilling the dream of every childhood daredevil, the Looney Launch is an aluminum and fiberglass contraption that quickly unfolds to create the ultimate bicycle jump. The product has been selling as fast as you can make it, even though it comes plastered with warning labels proclaiming that its use is inherently dangerous.

As XtremityPlus's CEO, you were nervous about introducing this product, and your fears were just confirmed: You've been notified of the first lawsuit by a parent whose child broke several bones after crash-landing off a Looney Launch.

Your task: Write a post for your internal blog explaining that the Looney Launch is being removed from the market immediately. Tell your employees to expect some negative reactions from enthusiastic customers and retailers, but explain that (a) the company can't afford the risk of additional lawsuits; and (b) even for XtremityPlus, the Looney Launch pushes the envelope a bit too far. The product is simply too dangerous to sell in good conscience.

E-Mail SKILLS

12. Looney Launch coming back to Earth: Informing retailers about the demise of a popular product Now it's time to follow up the internal employee message about the Looney Launch (see Case 11) with a message to the retailers that carry the product.

Your task: Write an e-mail message to retailers explaining that the Looney Launch is being removed from the market and explaining why you've reached this decision. Apologize for the temporary disruption this will cause to their businesses but emphasize that it's the right decision from both legal and social perspectives. Thank them for their continuing efforts to sell XtremityPlus products and assure them that your company will continue to offer exciting and innovative products for extreme-sports enthusiasts.

Blogging SKILLS   Portfolio BUILDER

13. Communicating in a crisis: Informing the local community about a serious accident One of your company's worst nightmares has just come true. EQ Industrial Services (EQIS), based in Wayne, Michigan, operates a number of facilities around the country that dispose, recycle, and transport hazardous chemical wastes. Last night, explosions and fires broke out at the company's Apex, North Carolina, facility, forcing the evacuation of 17,000 local residents.

Your task: It's now Friday, the day after the fire. Write a brief post for the company's blog, covering the following points:

- A fire did break out at the Apex facility at approximately 10 P.M. Thursday.

- No one was in the facility at the time.

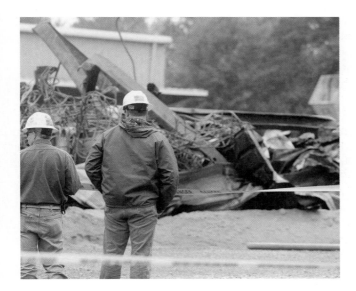

• Because of the diverse nature of the materials stored at the plant, the cause of the fire is not yet known.

• Rumors that the facility stores extremely dangerous chlorine gas and that the fire was spreading to other nearby businesses are not true.

• Special industrial firefighters hired by EQIS have already brought the fire under control.

• Residents in the immediate area were evacuated as a precaution, and they should be able to return to their homes tomorrow, pending permission by local authorities.

• Several dozen residents were admitted to local hospitals with complaints of breathing problems, but most have been released already; about a dozen emergency responders were treated as well.

• At this point (Friday afternoon), tests conducted by the North Carolina State Department of Environment and Natural Resources "had not detected anything out of the ordinary in the air." Conclude by thanking the local police and fire departments for their assistance and directing readers to EQIS's toll-free hot line for more information.[39]

■ E-Mail
▌ SKILLS

14. Low-carb impact: E-mail announcing losses and new products at Monterey Pasta As marketing planning manager for Monterey Pasta Company, you know all about the impact that diet crazes can have on the food industry. When low-carb diets began to catch on, you knew it would be bad news for your firm. In fact, at Wal-Mart and Costco, Monterey Pasta's largest retail customers, sales plummeted nearly 30 percent in just a few months. Your company is not alone; many other tra-

ditional pasta makers are also showing losses because of the new diet preferences. In contrast, your major competitor, American Italian Pasta, introduced a line of low-carb pastas and has continued to enjoy strong sales.

Now management has asked you to issue a revised forecast for fourth-quarter earnings. Previous predictions were for fourth-quarter sales to increase over last year's figures by 7 to 10 percent. Today's forecast from chief financial officer Scott S. Wheeler is for a 3 to 5 percent *decrease* in revenue from last year's fourth-quarter earnings.

However, in the same message, management wants you to announce the release of Monterey Pasta's new Carb-Smart line of fresh pastas, sauces, and prepared entrees. In a company meeting, Monterey Pasta President and CEO Jim Williams announced, "Americans love fresh pasta, but the current wave of low-carb diets has many consumers watching the amount of carbohydrates they consume. Carb-Smart responds to that trend by delivering the flavor and convenience of traditional fresh pasta, but with half the carbs. So carb-counting pasta lovers can now have their ravioli . . . and eat it, too."

Your task: Write an e-mail that announces both the bad news (the declining financial projections) and the good news (the new Carb-Smart line). Your message will go to shareholders, retail customers, distributors, and other interested parties. You can read more about the Carb-Smart line at www.montereygourmetfoods.com/kitchen/carbsmart.[40]

15. Product recall: Letter from Perrigo Company about children's painkiller You work for Perrigo, the leading manufacturer of more than 900 store-brand, over-the-counter (OTC) pharmaceuticals and nutritional products. These items are found beside brand-name products such as Tylenol, Motrin, Benadryl, NyQuil, Centrum, or Ex-Lax, but they're packaged under the name of the store where customers are shopping. They're priced a bit lower but offer comparable quality and effectiveness. For retailers, selling Perrigo products yields a higher profit margin than name brands. For consumers, buying the store brands can mean significant savings.

However, your company has discovered that a batch of its cherry-flavored children's painkiller contains up to 29 percent more acetaminophen than the label indicates—enough to cause an overdose in the young children the product is designed for. Such overdoses can cause liver failure. As of this morning, your marketing department calculates that 6,500 4-ounce bottles of the "children's nonaspirin elixir" (a Tylenol look-alike) are already in the hands of consumers. That leaves some 1,288 bottles still on store shelves.

No one is telling you how this error happened, and it's only been found in lot number 1AD0228. However, finding a guilty party is not so important to your job. You're more concerned about getting the word out fast. Such errors do happen, and the best move is to be immediate and direct, being completely honest with retailers and the public. Full and prompt disclosure is especially crucial when consumers' health is involved, as it always is in your line of business.

The painkiller has been sold under the Kroger label at stores in Alabama, Arkansas, Georgia, Illinois, Indiana, Kentucky, Louisiana, Michigan, Mississippi, Missouri, North Carolina, Ohio, South Carolina, Tennessee, Texas, Virginia, and West Virginia. It was sold under the Hy-Vee label in Illinois, Iowa, Kansas, Minnesota, Missouri, Nebraska, and South Dakota and under the Good Sense label at independent retail chains throughout the United States. Perrigo must notify consumers throughout the United States that they should not give the product to children but, rather, should check the lot number and, if it's from the affected batch, return the bottle to the store they bought it from for a refund.

Your task: As Perrigo's customer service supervisor, you must notify retailers by letter. They've already been told verbally, but legal requirements mandate a written notification. That's good because a form letter to your retail customers can also include follow-up instructions. Explain the circumstances behind the recall and instruct stores to pull bottles from the shelves immediately for return to your company. Perrigo will, of course, reimburse the refunds provided to consumers. Questions should be directed to Perrigo at 1-800-321-0105—and it's okay if retailers give that number to consumers. Be sure to mention all that your company is doing and use resale information.[41]

E-Mail SKILLS / Portfolio BUILDER

16. Sorry, but we don't have a choice: E-mail about monitoring employee blogs You can certainly sympathize with employees when they complain about having their e-mail and instant messages monitored, but you're only implementing a company policy that all employees agree to abide by when they join the company. Your firm, Webcor Builders of San Mateo, California, is one of the estimated 60 percent of U.S. companies with such monitoring systems in place. More and more companies use these systems (which typically operate by scanning messages for keywords that suggest confidential, illegal, or otherwise inappropriate content) in an attempt to avoid instances of sexual harassment and other problems.

As the chief information officer, the manager in charge of computer systems in the company, you're often the target when employees complain about being monitored. Consequently, you know you're really going to hear it when employees learn that the monitoring program will be expanded to personal blogs as well.

Your task: Write an e-mail to be distributed to the entire workforce, explaining that the automated monitoring program is about to be expanded to include employees' personal blogs. Explain that, while you sympathize with employee concerns regarding privacy and freedom of speech, it is the management team's responsibility to protect the company's intellectual property and the value of the company name. Therefore, employees' personal blogs will be added to the monitoring system to ensure that employees don't intentionally or acciden-

tally expose company secrets or criticize management in a way that could harm the company.[42]

Blogging SKILLS / Portfolio BUILDER

17. Removing the obstacles on the on-ramp: Blog posting to Ernst & Young employees Like many other companies these days, the accounting firm Ernst & Young is fighting a brain drain as experienced executives and professionals leave in midcareer to pursue charitable interests, devote more time to family matters, or pursue a variety of other dreams or obligations. The problem is particularly acute among women, because on average they step off the career track more often than men do. As general manager of the largest division in the company, you've been tapped to draft a set of guidelines to make it easier for employees who've taken some time off to move back into the company.

However, as soon as word gets out about what you're planning, several of your top performers, people who've never left the company for personal time off—or "taken the off-ramp," in current buzzword speak—march into your office to complain. They fear that encouraging the "off-rampers" to return isn't fair to the employees who've remained loyal to the firm, as they put it. One goes as far to say that anyone who leaves the company doesn't deserve to be asked back. Two others claim that the additional experience and skills they've gained as they continued to work should guarantee them higher pay and more responsibilities than employees who took time off for themselves.

Your task: As unhappy as these several employees are, the program needs to be implemented if Ernst & Young hopes to bring "off-rampers" back into the company—thereby making sure they don't go to work for competitors instead. However, you also can't afford to antagonize the existing workforce; if the people who've already complained are any indication, you have a sizable morale problem on your hands. You decide that your first step is to clearly explain why the program is necessary, including how it will benefit everyone in the company by making Ernst & Young more competitive. Write a short posting for the company's internal blog explaining that, in spite of the objections some employees have raised, the firm is going ahead with the program as planned. Balance this news (which some employees will obviously view as negative) with positive reassurances that all current employees will be treated fairly in terms of both compensation and promotion opportunities. Close with a call for continued communication on this issue, inviting people to meet with you in person or to post their thoughts on the blog.[43]

Portfolio BUILDER

18. Listen to the music, partner: Delivering an ultimatum to a business associate You're a marketing manager for Stanton, one of the premier suppliers of DJ equipment (turntables, amplifiers, speakers, mixers, and related accessories). Your company's latest creation, the FinalScratch system, has been flying off retailers' shelves. Both professional and amateur DJs love the way that FinalScratch gives them the feel of working with vinyl records by letting them control digital music files from any analog turntable or CD player while giving them access to the endless possibilities of digital music technology. (For more information about the product, go to www.stantondj.com.) Sales are strong everywhere except in Music99 stores, a retail chain in the Mid-Atlantic region. You suspect the cause: The owners of this chain refused to let their salespeople attend the free product training you offered when FinalScratch was introduced, claiming their people were smart enough to train themselves.

To explore the situation, you head out from Stanton headquarters in Hollywood, Florida, on an undercover shopping mission. After visiting a few Music99 locations, you're appalled by what you see. The salespeople in these stores clearly don't understand the FinalScratch concept, so they either give potential customers bad information about it or steer them to products from your competitors. No wonder sales are so bad at this chain.

Your task: You're tempted to pull your products out of this chain immediately, but you know how difficult and expensive it is to recruit new retailers in this market. However, this situation can't go on; you're losing thousands of dollars of potential business every week. Write a letter to Jackson Fletcher, the CEO of Music99 (14014 Preston Pike, Dover, DE 19901) expressing your disappointment in what you observed and explaining that the Music99 sales staff will need to agree to attend product training or else your company's management team will consider terminating the business relationship.

You've met Mr. Fletcher in person once and talked to him on the phone several times, and you know him well enough to know that he will not be pleased by this ultimatum. Music99 does a good job selling other Stanton products—and he'll probably be furious to learn that you were "spying" on his sales staff.[44]

19. Refinancing rules: Letter explaining changes at PeopleFirst.com When you began as a customer service representative at PeopleFirst.com, you worked with only five employees to pioneer a web-based auto loan brokerage. Customers loved it.

From your website, they filled out a single application and faxed in any necessary verification documents. Then PeopleFirst matched them with the best loan for which they qualified, chosen from a variety of lenders. You mailed them a no-obligation "Blank Check" to spend at any auto dealership up to the amount for which they qualified. The loan didn't begin until they spent the check. Later, if rates dropped, they could come back to PeopleFirst.com for refinancing.

All that changed when huge Capital One Financial Corporation bought out PeopleFirst.com. The company changed your name to Capital One Auto Finance and converted all loans to Capital One loans. Under its new policies, Capital One will not refinance its own loans. However, your existing customers aren't charged a prepayment penalty if they want to pay off their loans early by finding (on their own) another lender for refinancing. You might lose some business this way, but Capital One would lose a lot more if it refinanced all its loans every time rates dropped.

Your task: Explain the new policy in a letter to Faviola and Mary Franzone (7200 Poplar Ave., Memphis, TN 38197), who have inquired about refinancing their auto loan at today's lower rates.[45]

Podcasting SKILLS

20. Say good-bye to the concierge: Podcast announcing the end of a popular employee benefit An employee concierge seemed like a great idea when you added it as an employee benefit last year. The concierge handles a wide variety of personal chores for employees, everything from dropping off their dry cleaning to ordering event tickets to sending flowers. Employees love the service, and you know that the time they save can be devoted to work or family activities. Unfortunately, profits are way down, and concierge usage is up—up so far that you'll need to add a second concierge to keep up with the demand. As painful as it will be for everyone, you decide that the company needs to stop offering the service.

Your task: Script a brief podcast announcing the decision and explaining why it was necessary. Make up any details you need. If your instructor asks you to do so, record your podcast and submit the file.

21. Safe selling: Memo about dangerous scooters at Sports Authority You're not surprised that the Consumer Product Safety Commission (CPSC) has issued a consumer advisory on the dangers of motorized scooters. Unlike a motorcycle or bicycle, a scooter can be mastered by first-timers almost immediately. So both children and adults are hopping on, riding off—without helmets or other safety gear—and turning up with broken arms and legs, scraped faces, and bumped heads.

The popular electric or gas-powered scooters feature two wheels similar to in-line skates and travel 9 to 14 miles per hour. Over a six-month period, says the CPSC, emergency rooms around the country reported 2,250 motorized scooter injuries and 3 deaths. The riders who were killed (ages 6, 11, and 46) might all have lived if they'd been wearing helmets. As a result, some states have already enacted laws restricting scooter operations.

You are a merchandising assistant at Sports Authority, which sells a wide selection of the foot-powered ($25 to $150) and motorized ($350 to $1,000) scooters. Your company is as concerned about the rise in injuries as it is about the CPSC advisory's potential negative effect on sales and legality. Thus, you've been assigned to a team that will brainstorm ideas for improving the situation. For example, one team member has suggested developing a safety brochure to give to customers; another wants to train salespeople to discuss safety issues with customers before they buy.

"We'd like to see increased sales of reflective gear ($6 to $15), helmets ($24), and elbow and knee pads ($19)," a store executive tells your team, "not to improve on our $1.5 billion annual revenue, but to save lives."

Your task: Working with classmates, discuss how Sports Authority can use positive actions (including those mentioned in the case) to soften the effect of the CPSC advisory. Choose the best ideas and decide how to use them in a negative-news memo notifying the chain's 198 store managers about the consumer advisory. Then write the memo your team has outlined.[46]

NEGATIVE EMPLOYMENT MESSAGES

▌Telephone
▌SKILLS

22. Reacting to a lost contract: Phone call rescinding a job offer As the human resources manager at Alion Science and Technology, a military research firm in McLean, Virginia, you were thrilled when one of the nation's top computer visualization specialists accepted your job offer. Claus Gunnstein's skills would have made a major contribution to Alion's work in designing flight simulators and other systems. Unfortunately, the day after he accepted the offer, Alion received news that a major Pentagon contract had been canceled. In addition to letting several dozen current employees know that the company will be forced to lay them off, you need to tell Gunnstein that Alion has no choice but to rescind the job offer.

Your task: Outline the points you'll need to make in a telephone call to Gunnstein. Pay special attention to your opening and closing statements. (You'll review your plans for the phone call with Alion's legal staff to make sure everything you say follows employment law guidelines; for now, just focus on the way you'll present the negative news to Gunnstein. Feel free to make up any details you need.)[47]

23. Juggling diversity and performance: Memo giving a negative performance review at AT&T As billing adjustments department manager at AT&T, you've been trained to handle a culturally diverse workforce. One of your best recent hires is 22-year-old Jorge Gutierrez. In record time, he was entering and testing complex price changes, mastering the challenges of your monumental computerized billing software. He was a real find—except for one problem: His close family ties often distract him from work duties.

His parents immigrated from Central America when Jorge and his sisters were young children, and you understand and deeply respect the importance that family plays in the lives of many Hispanic Americans. However, every morning, Gutierrez's mother calls to be sure he got to work safely. Then his father calls. And three times this month, his younger sister has called him away from work with three separate emergencies. Friends and extended family members seem to call at all hours of the day.

Gutierrez says he's asked friends and family not to call his office number. Now they dial his mobile phone instead. He's reluctant to shut off his mobile phone during work hours in case someone in his family needs him.

At this point, you have given Gutierrez several verbal warnings. You really can't afford to lose him, so you're hoping that a written negative review will give him greater incentive to persuade friends and relatives. You'll deliver the letter in a meeting and help him find ways to resolve the issue within a mutually agreed-upon time frame.

Your task: Write the letter, using suggestions in this chapter to help you put the bad news in a constructive light. Avoid culturally biased remarks or innuendo.

▌E-Mail
▌SKILLS

24. Career moves: E-mail refusing to write a recommendation Tom Weiss worked in the office at Opal Pools and Patios for four months under your supervision (you're office manager). On the basis of what he told you he could do, you started him off as a file clerk. However, his organizational skills proved inadequate for the job, so you transferred him to logging in accounts receivable, where he performed almost adequately. Then he assured you that his "real strength" was customer relations, so you moved him to the complaint department. After he spent three weeks making angry customers even angrier, you were convinced that no place in your office was appropriate for his talents. Five weeks ago, you encouraged him to resign before being formally fired.

Today's e-mail brings a request from Weiss asking you to write a letter recommending him for a sales position with a florist shop. You can't assess Weiss's sales abilities, but you do know him to be an incompetent file clerk, a careless book-keeper, and an insensitive customer service representative. Someone else is more likely to deserve the sales job, so you decide that you have done enough favors for Tom Weiss for one lifetime and plan to refuse his request.

Your task: Write an e-mail reply to Weiss (tomweiss@mailnet.com), indicating that you have chosen not to write a letter of recommendation for him.

25. Bad news for 80: Form letter to unsuccessful job candidates The dean's selection committee screened 85 applications for the position of dean of arts and sciences at your campus. After two rounds of eliminations, the top five candidates were invited to "airport interviews," in which the committee managed to meet with each candidate for an hour. Then the top three candidates were invited to the campus to meet with students, faculty, and administrators.

The committee recommended to the university president that the job be given to Constance Pappas, who has a doctorate in American studies and has been chairperson of the history department at Minneapolis Metropolitan College for the past three years. The president agreed, and Dr. Pappas accepted the offer.

One final task remains before the work of the dean's selection committee is finished: Letters must be sent to the 84 unsuccessful candidates. The four who reached the "airport interview" stage will receive personal letters from the chairperson of the committee. Your job, as secretary of the committee, is to draft the form letter that will be sent to the other 80 applicants.

Your task: Draft a letter of 100 to 200 words. All copies will be individually addressed to the recipients but will carry identical messages.

Portfolio BUILDER

26. What we have here is a failure to communicate: Writing a negative performance review Elaine Bridgewater, the former professional golfer you hired to oversee your golf equipment company's relationship with retailers, knows the business inside and out. As a former touring pro, she has unmatched credibility. She also has seemingly boundless energy, solid technical knowledge, and an engaging personal style. Unfortunately, she hasn't been quite as attentive as she needs to be when it comes to communicating with retailers. You've been getting complaints about voice-mail messages gone unanswered for days, confusing e-mails that require two or three rounds of clarification, and reports that are haphazardly thrown together. As valuable as Bridgewater's other skills are, she's going to cost the company sales if this goes on much longer. The retail channel is vital to your company's survival, and she's the employee most involved in the channel.

Your task: Draft a brief (one page maximum) informal performance appraisal and improvement plan for Bridgewater. Be sure to compliment her on the areas in which she excels but don't shy away from highlighting the areas in which she needs to improve, too: punctual response to customer messages; clear writing; and careful revision, production, and proofreading. Use what you've learned in this course so far to supply any additional advice about the importance of these skills.

Chapter 10

Writing Persuasive Messages

Learning Objectives

AFTER STUDYING THIS CHAPTER, YOU WILL BE ABLE TO

1 Apply the three-step writing process to persuasive messages

2 Identify seven ways to establish credibility in persuasive messages

3 Describe the AIDA model for persuasive messages

4 Distinguish between emotional and logical appeals and discuss how to balance them

5 Explain why it is important to identify potential objections before you start writing persuasive messages

6 Discuss an effective approach to identifying selling points and audience benefits

7 Identify steps you can take to avoid ethical lapses in marketing and sales messages

On the Job

COMMUNICATING AT CLUBMOM

CREATING A BUSINESS BY CONNECTING MOTHERS EVERYWHERE

Few roles in life require more information and insight than parenting. From prenatal care to early childhood development to education to socialization issues, parents are in continuous learning mode as their children grow. Parents also need to learn about themselves as they grow in their roles, from balancing work and home life to nurturing their own relationships. At the same time, parenting can be one of the most isolating experiences for adults, often making it difficult for people to acquire the information and support they need to succeed as parents.

Television personality Meredith Vieira, actor and activist Andrew Shue, and entrepreneur Michael Sanchez pondered this age-old challenge and saw the web as a solution. The three co-founded ClubMom, an online community and information resource that helps mothers find answers, insights—and each other. In addition to providing a huge library of articles, several dozen blogs on various topics, question-and-answer forums, and an online shopping mall, ClubMom includes the MomNetwork, the first social networking site created specifically for mothers.

Information resources and social networks abound on the web, so like any other web start-up, ClubMom faced the challenge of standing apart from the crowd and growing its membership audience large enough to create a viable business. One of the keys to its success is clear, audience-focused messages that make a

ClubMom appeals to new members with a variety of attractive images and brief, upbeat statements that emphasize the benefits of joining.

compelling case for joining ClubMom. Using straightforward statements such as "Join ClubMom and find answers, camaraderie, and support from other moms" and an upbeat but realistic writing style, the company communicates the features of its various online services and the benefits of joining.

The persuasive communication effort certainly seems to have been successful: ClubMom already has more than 2 million members and continues to expand as more mothers join in search of helpful insights and friendly support from their peers.[1]

www.clubmom.com

USING THE THREE-STEP WRITING PROCESS FOR PERSUASIVE MESSAGES

Persuasion is the attempt to change someone's attitudes, beliefs, or actions.

Professionals such as Michael Sanchez, CEO of ClubMom (profiled in the chapter opener) realize that successful businesses rely on persuasive messages in both internal and external communication. Whether you're convincing your boss to open a new office in Europe or encouraging potential customers to try your products, you need to call on your abilities of **persuasion**—the attempt to change an audience's attitudes, beliefs, or actions.[2] Persuasive techniques are a cornerstone of marketing and selling, but even if you never work in those fields, you still need good persuasion skills to advance in your career. Successful professionals also understand that persuasion is not about trickery or getting people to make choices that aren't in their best interest; rather, it lets your audience members know they have a choice and helps them choose to agree with you.[3] As with every other type of business message, the three-step writing process improves persuasive messages.

Step 1: Plan Your Message

In today's message-saturated environment, it's not enough to have a great idea or a great product.

In today's information-saturated business environment, having a great idea or a great product is no longer enough. Every day, untold numbers of good ideas go unnoticed and good products go unsold simply because the messages meant to promote them aren't compelling enough to rise above the competitive noise. Even if audiences agree that your idea or product is attractive, they usually have other options to consider as well, so you will need to convince them that your choice is the best of all the attractive alternatives. Creating successful persuasive messages in these challenging situations demands careful attention to all four tasks in the planning step, starting with an insightful analysis of your purpose and your audience.

Failing to clarify your purpose is a common mistake with persuasive messages.

Analyzing Your Situation   A clear purpose is important in every message, of course, but clarity is doubly important in persuasive messages because you are asking the audience to do something—to take action, make decisions, and so on. Let's say you want to persuade members of top management to support a particular research project. But what does "support" mean? Do you want them to pat you on the back and wish you well? Or do you want them to pull five researchers off another project and assign them to your project? With a clear, specific goal in mind, you'll find it much easier to craft effective persuasive messages.

To persuade successfully, you need to consider both the positive and negative aspects of your proposed solution.

In addition to having a clear purpose, the best persuasive messages are closely connected to the audience's desires and interests.[4] Consider the positives and the negatives—the needs and motivations of your audience members (the reasons they might respond favorably to your message), as well as their concerns and objections (the reasons they might *not* respond favorably). With these two insights as guides, you can work to find common ground with your audience while emphasizing positive points and minimizing negative ones.

Demographics include characteristics such as age, gender, occupation, income, and education.

Psychographics include characteristics such as personality, attitudes, and lifestyle.

To understand and categorize audience needs, you can refer to specific information such as **demographics** (the age, gender, occupation, income, education, and other quantifiable characteristics of the people you're trying to persuade) and **psychographics** (personality, attitudes, lifestyle, and other psychological characteristics). When analyzing your audience members, be sure to take into account their cultural expectations so that you don't undermine your persuasive message by using an inappropriate appeal or by organizing your message in a way that seems unfamiliar or uncomfortable to your audience.

If you aim to change someone's attitudes, beliefs, or actions through a persuasive message, it is vital to understand his or her **motivation**—the combination of forces that drive people to satisfy their needs. Table 10.1 identifies some of the needs that psychologists have identified or suggested as being important in influencing human

Table 10.1 — HUMAN NEEDS THAT INFLUENCE MOTIVATION

Need	*Implications for Communication*
Basic physiological requirements: The needs for food, water, sleep, oxygen, etc.	Everyone has these needs, but the degree of attention an individual gives to them often depends on whether the needs are being met; for instance, an advertisement for sleeping pills will have greater appeal to someone suffering from insomnia than to someone who has no problem sleeping.
Safety and security: The need for protection from bodily harm; the need to know that loved ones are safe; needs for financial security, protection of personal identity, career security, etc.	These needs influence both consumer and business decisions in a wide variety of ways; for instance, advertisements for life insurance often encourage parents to think about the financial security of their children and other loved ones.
Affiliation and belonging: The needs for companionship, acceptance, love, popularity, etc.	The need to feel loved, accepted, or popular drives a great deal of human behavior, from the desire to be attractive to potential mates to wearing the clothing style that a particular social group is likely to approve.
Power and control: The need to feel in control of situations or to exert authority over others	You can see many examples appealing to this need in advertisements: *Take control of your life*, *your finances*, *your future*, *your career*, and so on. Many people who lack power want to know how to get it, and people who have power often want others to know they have it.
Achievement: The need to feel a sense of accomplishment—or to be admired by others for accomplishments	This need can involve both *knowing* (when people experience a feeling of accomplishment) and *showing* (when people are able to show others that they've achieved success); advertising for luxury consumer products frequently appeals to this need.
Adventure and distraction: The need for excitement or relief from daily routine	People vary widely in their need for adventure; some crave excitement—even danger—while others value calmness and predictability. Some needs for adventure and distraction are met *virtually*, such as through horror movies, thriller novels, etc.
Knowledge, exploration, and understanding: The need to keep learning	For some people, learning is usually a means to an end, a way to fulfill some other need; for others, acquiring new knowledge is the goal.
Aesthetic appreciation: The desire to experience beauty, order, symmetry, etc.	Although this need may seem "noncommercial" at first glance, advertisers appeal to it frequently, from the pleasing shape of a package to the quality of the gemstones in a piece of jewelry.
Self-actualization: The need to "be all that one can be," to reach one's full potential as a human being	Psychologists Kurt Goldstein and Abraham Maslow popularized self-actualization as the desire to make the most of one's potential, and Maslow identified it as one of the higher-level needs in his classic hierarchy; even if people met most or all of their other needs, they would still feel the need to self-actualize. An often-quoted example of appealing to this need is the U.S. Army's one-time advertising slogan "Be all that you can be."
Helping others: The need to believe that one is making a difference in the lives of other people	This need is the central motivation in fundraising messages and other appeals to charity.

motivation. Obviously, the more closely a persuasive message aligns with a recipient's existing motivation, the more effective the message is likely to be. For example, if you try to persuade consumers to purchase a product on the basis of its fashion appeal, that message will connect with consumers who are motivated by a desire to be in fashion but probably won't connect with consumers driven more by practical function or financial concerns.

Motivation is a complex psychological subject, and researchers have proposed a variety of theories to help explain why humans are driven to behave as they do. For instance, some theories suggest a process in which people take action to fulfill perceived needs and then evaluate the outcomes of those actions to determine whether the effort was worthwhile:

1. **Need.** The individual senses a need of some sort, from the basic need to earn enough money for food to a need for recognition or self-respect. We are all born with certain needs but can acquire other needs as we grow up, such as a need for achievement, a need for power, or a need to affiliate with compatible friends and colleagues.[5]

2. **Action.** To fulfill the need, the individual takes actions or adopts behaviors that he or she believes will result in the need being satisfied. The *quality* of the action is a matter of choosing which action to take, deciding how much effort to put into the action, and deciding how long to sustain that effort.[6]

3. **Outcome.** The individual observes the outcome of the action (sometimes called the *reward*) and determines whether the effort was worthwhile. Actions that result in positive outcomes are likely to be repeated; those that result in negative outcomes are less likely to be repeated.

Although this is a simplified view of motivation and not all theorists endorse this model, it helps emphasize the importance of understanding your audience's needs and why they would be driven to satisfy those needs. If you don't understand what motivates your audience, you won't be able persuade them to take the actions you'd like them to take. In addition, you can see why following through on the claims or promises made in your message is so vital. If a manager agrees to fund a project that ultimately fails or a customer buys a product that doesn't perform as you said it would, those people are going to be less likely to be persuaded by messages from you in the future.

Gathering Information   Once your situation analysis is complete, you need to gather the information necessary to create a compelling persuasive message. Chapter 11 offers advice on using the latest research techniques to find the information you need.

Selecting the Right Medium   Persuasive messages can be found in virtually every communication medium ever devised, from instant messages and podcasts to radio advertisements and skywriting. For persuasive messages intended for internal audiences, your choice of medium will closely follow the guidelines presented in Chapter 4. However, for marketing and sales messages, your options are far more numerous. In fact, advertising agencies employ media specialists whose only jobs are to analyze the media options available and select the most cost-effective combination for each client and each advertising campaign.

To further complicate matters, various members of your audience might prefer different media for the same message. Some consumers like to do all their car shopping in person, whereas others do most of their car-shopping research online (see "Using the Power of Technology: Building an Audience Through Search Engine Optimization"). Some people don't mind promotional e-mails for products they're interested in; others resent every piece of commercial e-mail they receive. If you can't be sure you can reach most or all of your audience through a single medium, you need to use two or more, such as following up an e-mail campaign with printed letters.

Organizing Your Information   Successful persuasion requires close attention to all four aspects of organizing your information: defining your main idea, limiting your scope, choosing a direct or indirect approach, and grouping your points in a meaningful way. The most effective main ideas for persuasive messages have one thing in common: They are about the receiver, not the sender. For instance, if you're trying to convince others to join you in a business venture, explain how it will help them, not how it will help you.

Businesses continue to find creative new ways to reach target audiences with persuasive messages. If you're a video gamer, you've probably noticed the brand-name products that appear in many of today's games.

You may need to use multiple media to reach your entire audience.

USING THE POWER OF TECHNOLOGY

Building an Audience Through Search Engine Optimization

Have you ever wondered why certain websites appear at the top of the list when you use an online search engine? Or why a site you might expect to find doesn't show up at all? Such questions are at the heart of the one of the most important activities in online communication: *search engine optimization* (SEO). (SEO applies to the *natural* or *organic* search results, not the sponsored, paid results you see above, beside, or below the main search results listing.)

SEO involves three major parties: web users, website owners, and search engine developers such as Google, Yahoo!, and Microsoft. Most web users rely heavily on search engines to find relevant websites for shopping, research, and other online tasks. Website owners often rely on search engines to steer potential customers and other valuable visitors their way. To bring these two parties together while building lots of web traffic and advertising opportunities for themselves, search engine developers constantly fine-tune their engines to produce relevant, helpful search results.

And that's where things get interesting. Using sophisticated—and secret—algorithms, search engines rank search results by relevance to the user's input terms, starting with the most relevant results at the top of the list. Web users typically choose sites that show up in the first few pages of search results, so site owners naturally want to be ranked as high as possible.

Given the secrecy and the high stakes, online search has become something of a cat-and-mouse game in which website owners try to figure out what they can do improve their rankings, while search engine developers work to improve the quality of results—partly by blocking website owners' attempts to "game" the system. For instance, in the early days of online search, some website owners would embed dozens of popular search terms in their websites, even if those terms had nothing to do with their site content. Search engine developers responded with ways to detect such tactics and penalize sites that use them by either lowering the sites' rankings in the search results or leaving them out entirely.

SEO has become a complex topic as search engines and the web itself continue to evolve and as motivated website owners keep looking for ways to boost their rankings. For instance, Google now evaluates more than 100 factors to determine search rankings. Without becoming an expert in SEO, however, you can work toward improving rankings for your website by focusing on three important areas: (1) offer fresh, high-quality, audience-oriented content; (2) use relevant keywords judiciously, particularly in important areas such as the page title that displays at the top of the browser screen; and (3) encourage links to your site from other high-quality sites with relevant content. You can learn more from Google's Webmaster Guidelines, www.google.com/support/webmasters.

CAREER APPLICATIONS

1. Locate a website for any company that sells products to consumers and write a new title for the site's homepage (the title that appears at the top of a web browser). Make the title short enough to read quickly while still summarizing what the company offers. Be sure to use one or more keywords that online shoppers would likely use when searching for the types of products the company sells.

2. Identify three high-quality websites that would be good sites to link to the site you chose in Question 1. For instance, if you chose a website that sells automotive parts and supplies, one of the three linking sites could be a popular blogger who writes about automotive repair. Or if the site you chose sells golf equipment, you might find a sports website that covers the professional golf tours or one that provides information about golf courses around the world.

To limit the scope of each message effectively, include only the information needed to help your audience take the next step toward the ultimate decision or ultimate action you want. In simple scenarios such as persuading teammates to attend a special meeting, you might put everything you have to say into a single, short message. But if you want your company to invest several million dollars in your latest product idea, the scope of your first message might be limited to securing 10 minutes at the next executive committee meeting so that you can introduce your idea and get permission to explore it.

As with routine and negative messages, the best organizational approach to persuasive messages is based on your audience's likely reaction to your message. However, because the nature of persuasion is to convince your audience members to change their attitudes, beliefs, or actions, most persuasive messages use the indirect approach. That means you need to explain your reasons and build interest before asking for a decision or action. Several examples of indirect approaches are presented throughout the chapter.

Limit your scope to include only the information needed to help your audience take the next step toward making a favorable decision.

Use the direct approach if your audience is ready to hear your proposal.

Consider using the direct approach whenever you know your audience is ready to hear your proposal. If your boss wants to change shipping companies and asks for your recommendation, you probably want to open with your choice and then back it up with reasons. Similarly, if there's a good chance your audience members will agree with your message, don't force them to wade through pages of reasoning before seeing your main idea. The direct approach is also called for if you've been building your case through several indirect messages and it's now time to make your request (see Figure 10.1).

If you use the direct approach, keep in mind that even though your audience may be easy to convince, you'll still want to include at least a brief justification or explanation. Don't expect readers to accept your ideas on blind faith. For example, consider the following two openers:

Instead of This	**Write This**
I recommend building our new retail outlet on the West Main Street site.	After comparing the four possible sites for our new retail outlet, I recommend West Main Street as the only site that fulfills our criteria for visibility, proximity to mass transportation, and square footage.

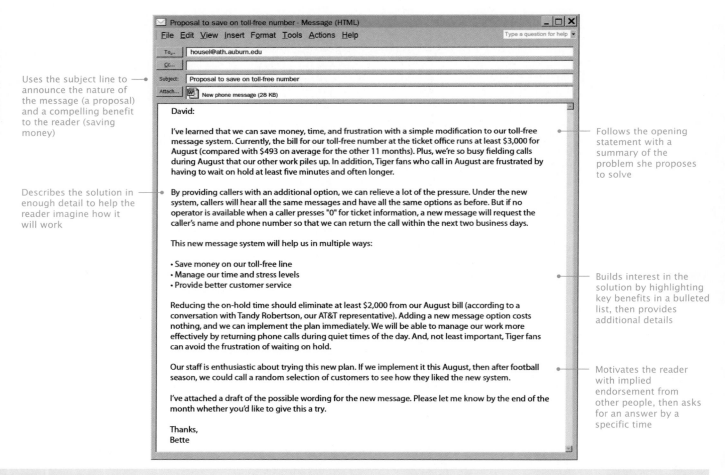

Uses the subject line to announce the nature of the message (a proposal) and a compelling benefit to the reader (saving money)

Describes the solution in enough detail to help the reader imagine how it will work

Follows the opening statement with a summary of the problem she proposes to solve

Builds interest in the solution by highlighting key benefits in a bulleted list, then provides additional details

Motivates the reader with implied endorsement from other people, then asks for an answer by a specific time

FIGURE 10.1
Proposal E-Mail Using a Direct Approach
Bette McGiboney, an administrative assistant to the athletic director of Auburn University, presented a solution to the problem of high phone bills during the month of August. She already has a close relationship with her boss, who is likely to welcome the money-saving idea, so the direct approach is a fast, efficient way to communicate her proposal.

Your choice between the direct and indirect approaches is also influenced by the extent of your authority, expertise, or power in an organization. Generally, the more of these qualities you have in a given situation, the more likely that the direct approach will work for you because audience members are more apt to accept whatever you have to say. Conversely, if you're writing on a subject outside your recognized expertise, or if you're trying to persuade higher-level managers, the indirect approach is usually better because it allows you to build credibility as you present your reasoning.

Your choice of approach is influenced by your authority, expertise, or power within the organization.

Step 2: Write Your Message

Persuasive messages are often uninvited and occasionally even unwelcome, so adopting the "you" attitude is particularly critical when you write them. Most people won't even pay attention to your message, much less respond to it, if it isn't about them. You can encourage a more welcome reception by (1) using positive and polite language, (2) understanding and respecting cultural differences, (3) being sensitive to organizational cultures, and (4) taking steps to establish your credibility.

Persuasive messages are often unexpected or even unwelcome, so the "you" attitude is crucial.

Positive language usually happens naturally with persuasive messages because you're promoting an idea or a product you believe in. However, polite language isn't as automatic as you might think. Don't inadvertently insult the readers by implying that they are incapable of making smart decisions without your wise advice.

Demonstrating an understanding of and respect for cultural differences is crucial to persuasion. For example, an aggressive, hard-sell technique is likely to antagonize a French audience. In Germany, where people tend to focus on technical matters, make sure you provide solid supporting evidence for all messages. In Sweden, audiences tend to focus on theoretical questions and strategic implications, whereas U.S. audiences are usually concerned with more practical matters.[7]

Just as culture within various social groups affects the success of persuasive messages, so too does the culture within various organizations. For instance, some organizations handle disagreement and conflict in an indirect, behind-the-scenes way, whereas others accept and even encourage open discussion and the sharing of viewpoints. When you accept and follow these traditions, you show your audience members that you understand them and respect their values.

Make sure your persuasive messages consider the culture of your audience.

Finally, when trying to persuade a skeptical or hostile audience, you must convince people that you are credible before they will pay much attention to your message. According to recent research, most managers overestimate their own credibility.[8] Chapter 5 lists characteristics essential to building and maintaining your credibility, including honesty, objectivity, awareness of audience needs, knowledge and expertise, endorsements, performance, and communication style. In addition to those elements, you can improve your credibility in persuasive messages with these techniques:

- **Using simple language.** In most persuasive situations, your audience will be cautious, watching for fantastic claims, insupportable descriptions, and emotional manipulation.

Audiences often respond unfavorably to over-the-top language, so keep your writing simple and straightforward.

- **Supporting your message with facts.** Provide objective evidence for the claims and promises you make.

- **Identifying your sources.** Telling your audience where you got your information improves your credibility, especially if your audience already respects those sources.

- **Establishing common ground.** Those beliefs, attitudes, and background experiences that you have in common with members of your audience will help them identify with you.

- **Being objective.** Your ability to understand and acknowledge all sides of an issue helps you present fair and logical arguments in your persuasive message.

- **Displaying your good intentions.** Your willingness to keep your audience's best interests at heart helps you create persuasive messages that are both effective and ethical.

- **Avoiding the "hard sell."** You've no doubt experienced a "hard sell," an aggressive approach that uses strong, emotional language and high-pressure tactics to convince people to make a firm decision in a hurry. Audiences tend to instinctively resist this approach. No one likes being pressured into making a decision, and communicators who take this approach can come across as being more concerned with meeting their own goals than with satisfying the needs of their audiences. In contrast, a "soft sell" is more like a comfortable conversation in which the sender uses calm, rational persuasion to help the recipient make a smart choice.

Step 3: Complete Your Message

The pros know from experience that details can make or break a persuasive message, so they're careful not to skimp on this part of the writing process. For instance, advertisers may have a dozen or more people review a message before it's released to the public.

When you evaluate your content, try to judge your argument objectively and try not to overestimate your credibility. If possible, ask an experienced colleague who knows your audience well to review your draft. Make sure your design elements complement, not detract from, your persuasive argument. In addition, meticulous proofreading will help identify any mechanical or spelling errors that would weaken your persuasive potential. Finally, make sure your distribution methods fit your audience's expectations and preferences.

With the three-step model in mind, you're ready to begin composing persuasive messages, starting with *persuasive business messages* (those that try to convince audiences to approve new projects, enter into business partnerships, and so on), followed by *marketing and sales messages* (those that try to convince audiences to consider and then purchase products and services).

DEVELOPING PERSUASIVE BUSINESS MESSAGES

Persuasive business messages comprise a broad and diverse category, with audiences that range from a single person in your own department to government agencies, investors, business partners, community leaders, and other external groups. Your success as a businessperson is closely tied to your ability to convince others to accept new ideas, change old habits, or act on your recommendations. As you move into positions of greater responsibility in your career, your persuasive messages could start to influence multimillion-dollar investments and the careers of hundreds or thousands of employees. Obviously, you need to match the increase in your persuasive skills with the care and thoroughness of your analysis and planning so that the ideas you convince others to adopt are sound.

Strategies for Persuasive Business Messages

The goals of persuasive business messages are to convince your audiences that your request or idea is reasonable and that it will benefit your readers in some way. Within the context of the three-step process, effective persuasion involves four essential strategies: structuring your message, balancing emotional and logical appeals, rein-

THE AIDA MODEL

Table 10.2

Phase	Objective
Attention	Get the reader's attention with a benefit that is of real interest or value.
Interest	Build the reader's interest by further explaining benefits and appealing to his or her logic or emotions.
Desire	Build desire by providing additional supporting details and answering potential questions.
Action	Motivate the reader to take the next step by closing with a compelling call to action and providing a convenient means for the reader to respond.

forcing your position, and anticipating objections. (Note that all these concepts in this section apply as well to marketing and sales messages, covered later in the chapter.)

Structuring Persuasive Business Messages   As noted earlier, most persuasive messages use the indirect approach. Experts in persuasive communication have developed a number of indirect models for such messages. One of the best known is the **AIDA model**, which organizes messages into these four phases: (1) attention, (2) interest, (3) desire, and (4) action (see Table 10.2). The purpose of the first phase is to get your audience members' attention with a compelling introduction. In the second phase, you raise audience members' interest in your product or idea, and in the third, you increase the audience's desire for the product or willingness to accept your idea. In the fourth phase, you motivate readers to take specific action. Other models exist, but they all follow a pattern similar to this one:

The AIDA model is an effective way to organize most persuasive messages:
- Attention
- Interest
- Desire
- Action

- **Attention.**   Your first objective is to encourage your audience to want to hear about your main idea. Write a brief and engaging opening sentence, with no extravagant claims or irrelevant points. Look for some common ground on which to build your case (see Figure 10.2). And while you want to be positive and confident, make sure you don't start out with a *hard sell*—a pushy, aggressive opening. Doing so often puts audiences on guard and on the defensive.

- **Interest.**   Explain the relevance of your message to your audience. Continuing the theme you started with, paint a more detailed picture of the problem you propose to solve with the solution you're offering (whether it's a new idea, a new process, a new product, or whatever).

- **Desire.**   Help audience members embrace your idea by explaining how the change will benefit them, either personally or professionally. Reduce resistance by identifying and answering in advance any questions the audience might have. If your idea is complex, you might need to explain how you would implement it. Back up your claims in order to increase audience willingness to take the action that you suggest in the next section.

- **Action.**   Suggest the action you want readers to take. Make it more than a statement such as "Please institute this program soon" or "Send me a refund." This is the opportunity to remind readers of the benefits of taking action. The secret of a successful action phase is making the action easy, so if possible, give your readers a couple options for responding, such as a toll-free number to call and a website to visit. Include a deadline, if applicable.

The AIDA model is tailor-made for using the indirect approach, allowing you to save your main idea for the action phase. However, you can also use it for the direct approach, in which case you use your main idea as an attention-getter, build interest

The AIDA model and similar plans are ideal for the indirect approach.

Planning

Analyze the Situation
Verify that the purpose is to solve an ongoing problem, so the audience will be receptive.

Gather Information
Determine audience needs and obtain the necessary information on recycling problem areas.

Select the Right Medium
Verify that an e-mail message is appropriate for this formal communication.

Organize the Information
Limit the scope to the main idea, which is to propose a recycling solution; use an indirect approach to lay out the extent of the problem.

Writing

Adapt to Your Audience
Adjust the level of formality based on the degree of familiarity with the audience; maintain a positive relationship by using the "you" attitude, politeness, positive emphasis, and bias-free language.

Compose the Message
Use a conversational but professional style and keep the message brief, clear, and as helpful as possible.

Completing

Revise the Message
Evaluate content and review readability to make sure the information is clear and complete without being overwhelming.

Produce the Message
Emphasize a clean, professional appearance.

Proofread the Message
Review for errors in layout, spelling, and mechanics.

Distribute the Message
Deliver your message using the chosen medium.

1 **2** **3**

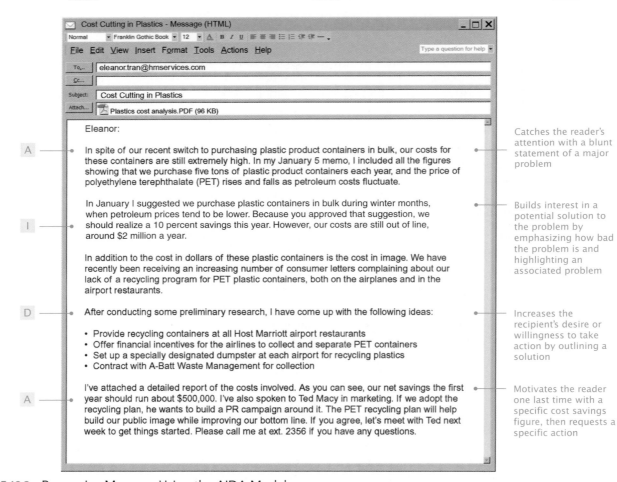

FIGURE 10.2 Persuasive Message Using the AIDA Model

Randy Thumwolt uses the AIDA model in a persuasive message about a program that would try to reduce Host Marriott's annual plastics costs while responding to consumer complaints about the company's recycling record. Note how Thumwolt "sells the problem" before attempting to sell the solution. Few people are interested in hearing about solutions to problems they don't know about or don't believe exist.

with your argument, create desire with your evidence, and reemphasize your main idea in the action phase with the specific action you want your audience to take.

When your AIDA message uses an indirect approach and is delivered by memo or e-mail, keep in mind that your subject line usually catches your reader's eye first. Your challenge is to make it interesting and relevant enough to capture reader attention without revealing your main idea. If you put your request in the subject line, you're likely to get a quick no before you've had a chance to present your arguments.

Instead of This	Write This
Proposal to install new phone message system	Reducing the cost of our toll-free number

You can also see from the AIDA model why it's so important to have a concise, focused purpose for your persuasive messages. If you don't, you'll find it nearly impossible to guide your reader through each phase from attention to action. Focus on your primary goal when presenting your case and concentrate your efforts on accomplishing that one goal. For example, if your main idea is to convince your company to install a new phone-messaging system, leave discussions about switching long-distance carriers until another day—unless it's relevant to your argument.

Balancing Emotional and Logical Appeals   Imagine you're sitting at a control panel with one knob labeled "logic" and another labeled "emotion." As you prepare your persuasive message, you carefully adjust each knob, tuning the message for maximum impact. Too little emotion, and your audience might not care enough to respond. Too much emotion, and your audience might think you are ignoring tough business questions or even being irrational.

Generally speaking, persuasive business messages rely more heavily on logical appeals than on emotional appeals because the main idea is usually to save money, increase quality, or improve some other practical, measurable aspect of business. To find the optimum balance, consider four factors: (1) the actions you hope to motivate, (2) your reader's expectations, (3) the degree of resistance you need to overcome, and (4) how far you feel empowered to go to sell your point of view.[9]

Emotional Appeals As its name implies, an **emotional appeal** calls on audience feelings and sympathies rather than facts, figures, and rational arguments. For instance, you can make use of the emotion surrounding certain words. The word *freedom* evokes strong feelings, as do words such as *success*, *prestige*, *compassion*, *security*, and *comfort*. Such words can help put your audience members in a positive frame of mind and help them accept your message. However, emotional appeals in business messages usually aren't effective by themselves because the audience wants proof that you can solve a business problem. Even if your audience members reach a conclusion based primarily on emotions, they'll look to you to provide logical support as well.

Emotional appeals attempt to connect with the reader's feelings or sympathies.

Logical Appeals A **logical appeal** calls on reasoning and evidence. The basic approach with a logical appeal is to make a claim based on a rational argument supported by solid evidence. When appealing to your audience's logic, you might use three types of reasoning:

Logical appeals are based on the reader's notions of reason; these appeals can use analogy, induction, or deduction.

• **Analogy.** With analogy, you reason from specific evidence to specific evidence. For instance, to convince management to buy a more robust firewall to protect your company's computer network, you might use the analogy of "circling the wagons," as when covered wagons crossing the continent gathered in a circle every night to form a safe space within.

• **Induction.** With inductive reasoning, you work from specific evidence to a general conclusion. To convince your team to change to a new manufacturing process, for example, you could point out that every company that has adopted it has increased profits, so it must be a smart idea.

- **Deduction.** With deductive reasoning, you work from a generalization to a specific conclusion. To persuade your boss to hire additional customer support staff, you might point to industry surveys that show how crucial customer satisfaction is to corporate profits.

Every method of reasoning is vulnerable to misuse, both intentional and unintentional, so verify your rational arguments carefully. For example, in the case of the manufacturing process, are there any other factors that affect the integrity of your reasoning? What if that process works well only for small companies with few products and your firm is a multinational behemoth with 10,000 products? To avoid faulty logic, follow these guidelines:[10]

Logical flaws include hasty generalizations, circular reasoning, attacks on opponents, oversimplifications, false assumptions of cause and effect, faulty analogies, and illogical support.

- **Avoid hasty generalizations.** Make sure you have plenty of evidence before drawing conclusions.

- **Avoid circular reasoning.** *Circular reasoning* is a logical fallacy in which you try to support your claim by restating it in different words. The statement "We know temporary workers cannot handle this task because temps are unqualified for it" doesn't prove anything because the claim and the supporting evidence are essentially identical. It doesn't prove *why* the temps are unqualified.

- **Avoid attacking an opponent.** If your persuasive appeal involves countering a competitive appeal made by someone else, make sure you attack the argument your opponent is making, not his or her character or qualifications.

- **Avoid oversimplifying a complex issue.** Make sure you present all the factors and don't reduce a wide range of choices to a simple "either/or" scenario if that isn't the case.

- **Avoid mistaken assumptions of cause and effect.** If you can't isolate the impact of a specific factor, you can't assume it's the cause of whatever effect you're discussing. The weather improves in spring, and people start playing baseball in spring. Does good weather cause baseball? No. There is a *correlation* between the two—meaning the data associated with them tend to rise and fall at the same time, but there is no *causation*—no proof that one causes the other. The complexity of many business situations makes cause and effect a particular challenge. You lowered prices, and sales went up. Were lower prices the cause? Perhaps, but the increase in sales might have been caused by a better advertising campaign, a competitor's delivery problems, or some other factor.

- **Avoid faulty analogies.** Be sure that the two objects or situations being compared are similar enough for the analogy to hold. For instance, the analogy between circling the wagons and using a network firewall isn't entirely valid because circling the wagons is a temporary move, and computer networks need permanent protection.

- **Avoid illogical support.** Make sure the connection between your claim and your support is truly logical and not based on a leap of faith, a missing premise, or irrelevant evidence.

Choose your words carefully and use abstractions to enhance emotional content.

Reinforcing Your Position   After you've worked out the basic elements of your argument, step back and look for ways to bolster the strength of your position. Can you find more powerful words to convey your message? For example, if your company is in serious financial trouble, talking about *survival* is more powerful emotional appeal than talking about *continued operations*. Using vivid abstractions such as this along with basic facts and figures can bring your argument to life. As with any other powerful tool, though, use vivid language and abstractions carefully and honestly. If the company's survival isn't on the line, don't state or imply that it is.

In addition to individual word choices, consider using *metaphors* and other figures of speech. If you want to describe a quality-control system as being designed to catch every possible product flaw, you might call it a *spider web* to imply that it catches everything that comes its way. Similarly, anecdotes and stories can help your audience grasp the meaning and importance of your arguments. Instead of just listing the number of times the old laptop computers your department uses have failed, you could describe how you lost a sale when your computer broke down during a critical sales presentation.

Beyond specific words and phrases, look for other factors that can reinforce your position. When you're asking for something, your audience members will find it easier to grant your request if they stand to benefit from it as well. For instance, if you're asking for more money to increase your staff, you might offer to lend those new employees to other managers during peak workloads in their departments. The timing of your message can also help. Virtually all organizations operate in cycles of some sort—incoming payments from major customers, outgoing tax payments, seasonal demand for products, and so on. Study these patterns to see whether they might work for or against you. For example, the best time to ask for additional staff might be right after a cyclical period of intense activity that generated complaints about poor customer service, while the experience is still fresh in everyone's mind. If you wait several months for the annual budgeting cycle, the emotional aspect of the experience will have faded, and your request might look like just another cost increase.

> Highlight the direct and indirect benefits of complying with your request.

Anticipating Objections   Even the most powerful persuasive messages can be expected to encounter some initial resistance. The best way to deal with audience resistance is to anticipate as many objections as you can and address them in your initial message before your audience can even bring them up. For instance, if you know that your proposal to switch to lower-cost materials will raise concerns about product quality, address these issues head-on in your message. If you wait until people raise the concern after reading your message, they may gravitate toward a firm no before you have a chance to address their concerns. By addressing such issues right away, you also demonstrate a broad appreciation of the issue and imply confidence in your message.[11] This anticipation is particularly important in written messages, when you don't have the opportunity to detect and respond to objections on the spot.

> Even powerful persuasive messages can encounter resistance from the audience.

To uncover potential audience objections, try some "What if?" scenarios. Poke holes in your own theories and ideas before your audience does. Then find solutions to the problems you've uncovered. Also, recognize that people are more likely to support what they help create, so, if possible, ask your audience members for their thoughts on the subject before you put together your argument. If appropriate, let your audience recommend some solutions. With enough thought and effort, you may even be able to turn problems into opportunities; for example, you may show how your proposal will be more economical in the long run, even though it may cost more now. Just be sure to be thorough, open, and objective about all the facts and alternatives.

Keep in mind that compromise might be your best path to success. Rather than automatically countering audience objections or discounting alternative ideas, listen carefully and then engage your audience in discussion. Chances are, you'll end up with a solution that is even better than your original.

Keep two things in mind when anticipating objections. First, you don't always have to explicitly mention a potential objection. You could simply mention that the lower-cost materials have been tested and approved by the quality-control department rather than acknowledge that some readers might be worried about quality problems. Second, if you expect a hostile audience, one biased against your plan from the beginning, present all sides of the story. As you cover each option, explain the pros and cons. You'll gain additional credibility if you present these options before presenting your recommendation or decision.[12]

> Present both sides of an issue when you expect to encounter strong resistance.

✓ CHECKLIST: Developing Persuasive Messages

A. Get your reader's attention.

✓ Open with an audience benefit, a stimulating question, a problem, or an unexpected statement.
✓ To establish common ground, discuss something your audience can agree with.
✓ Show that you understand the audience's concerns.

B. Build your reader's interest.

✓ Expand and support your opening claim or promise.
✓ Emphasize the relevance of your message to your audience.

C. Increase your reader's desire.

✓ Make audience members want to change by explaining how the change will benefit them.
✓ Back up your claims with relevant evidence.

D. Motivate your reader to take action.

✓ Suggest the action you want readers to take.
✓ Stress the positive results of the action.
✓ Make the desired action clear and easy.

E. Balance emotional and logical appeals.

✓ Use emotional appeals to help the audience accept your message.
✓ Use logical appeals when presenting facts and evidence for complex ideas or recommendations.
✓ Avoid faulty logic.

F. Reinforce your position.

✓ Provide additional evidence of the benefits of your proposal and your own credibility in offering it.
✓ Use abstractions, metaphors, and other figures of speech to bring facts and figures to life.

G. Anticipate objections.

✓ Anticipate and answer potential objections.
✓ Present the pros and cons of all options if you anticipate a hostile reaction.

To review the steps involved in developing persuasive messages, refer to "Checklist: Developing Persuasive Messages."

Common Examples of Persuasive Business Messages

Throughout your career, you'll have numerous opportunities to write persuasive messages within your organization, such as reports suggesting more efficient operating procedures or memos requesting money for new equipment. Similarly, you may produce a variety of persuasive messages for people outside the organization, such as websites shaping public opinions or letters requesting adjustments that go beyond a supplier's contractual obligations. In addition, many of the routine requests you studied in Chapter 8 can become persuasive messages if you want a nonroutine result or believe that you haven't received fair treatment. Most of these messages can be divided into persuasive requests for action, persuasive presentations of ideas, and persuasive claims and requests for adjustment.

Persuasive Requests for Action The bulk of your persuasive business messages will involve requests for action. In some cases, your request will be anticipated or will require minimal effort on the recipient's part, so the direct approach is fine. In others, you'll need to introduce your intention indirectly. Open with an attention-getting device and show readers that you know something about their concerns. Use

Document Makeover

IMPROVE THIS E-MAIL MESSAGE

To practice correcting drafts of actual documents, visit your online course or the access-code-protected portion of the Companion Website. Click on "Document Makeovers" and then click on Chapter 10. You will find an e-mail message that contains problems and errors related to what you've learned in this chapter about writing persuasive messages. Use the "Final Draft" decision tool to create an improved version of this persuasive e-mail request for action. Check the message for its effectiveness at gaining attention, building interest, stimulating desire, motivating action, focusing on the primary goal, and dealing with resistance.

the interest and desire sections of your message to demonstrate that you have good reasons for making such a request and to cover what you know about the situation: the facts and figures, the benefits of helping, and any history or experience that will enhance your appeal. Your goals are (1) to gain credibility and (2) to make your readers believe that helping you will indeed help solve a significant problem. Once you've demonstrated that your message is relevant to your readers, you can close with a request for some specific action or decision (see Figure 10.3).

Persuasive Presentations of Ideas   Most internal persuasive messages focus on getting the audience to make a specific decision or take some specific action. However, you will encounter situations in which you simply want to change attitudes

Sometimes the objective of persuasive messages is simply to encourage people to consider a new idea.

FIGURE 10.3
Persuasive Memo Using the AIDA Model to Request Action
Leslie Jorgensen believes the new Airbus A380 could help Oceana Pacific Airways meet its growth needs while lowering its operating costs. Here she uses the AIDA model to solicit her boss's approval for a study of the plane's market potential. Note that because she also wants to provide some printed materials to support her argument, she opted for a printed memo rather than an e-mail message.

We salute the diversity that makes our supplier partners _____.

unique

insightful

powerful

valuable

successful

From our Associates to our CEO, The Home Depot is dedicated to developing new partnerships with diverse businesses. We want you to join our team. To learn about how you can become a business partner or for more information on our Supplier Diversity Program, call 1-866-SD-AT-THD (732-8843), or visit us at www.homedepot.com/supplierdiversity. We're more than a store... We're an open door.

You can do it.
We can help...

In this magazine ad that promotes the idea of the company's commitment to an ethnically diverse supplier base, The Home Depot used the visual metaphor of diverse species of wood.

or beliefs about a particular topic, without asking the audience to decide or do anything—at least not yet. In complicated, multistep persuasive efforts, the goal of your first message might be nothing more than convincing your audience members to reexamine their opinions or assumptions or to admit the possibility of new ways of thinking.

For instance, the World Wide Web Consortium (a global association that defines many of the guidelines and technologies behind the World Wide Web) has launched a campaign called the Web Accessibility Initiative. Although the consortium's ultimate goal is making websites more accessible to people with disabilities or age-related limitations, a key interim goal is simply making website developers more aware of the need. As part of this effort, the consortium has developed a presentation that highlights the nature of the problems that many web visitors face.[13]

Persuasive Claims and Requests for Adjustment

Although persuasive claims and requests for adjustment are sometimes referred to as *complaint letters*, you don't write them merely to get a complaint off your chest. Your goal is to persuade someone to make an adjustment in your favor. You work toward this goal by demonstrating the difference between what you expected and what you actually received.

Most claim letters are routine messages and use the direct approach discussed in Chapter 8. However, both consumers and business professionals sometimes encounter situations in which they believe they haven't received a fair deal. For instance, you might have purchased a product but didn't use it immediately. When you finally try to use it, you discover it is defective—but the warranty has already expired. You'll need to use persuasive communication to convince the seller that it should replace the product.

Because you've already paid for the product, you obviously can't threaten to withhold payment. Instead, try to convey the essentially negative information in a way that will get positive results. Fortunately, most people in business are open to settling your claim fairly. It's to their advantage to maintain your goodwill and to resolve your problem quickly.

The key ingredients of a good persuasive claim are a complete and specific review of the facts and a confident and positive tone. Assume that the other person is not trying to cheat you and that you have the right to be satisfied with the transaction. Begin persuasive claims by stating the basic problem or reviewing what has been done about the problem so far. Include a statement that you and your audience can agree with or that clarifies what you want to convince your audience about. Be as specific as possible about what you want to happen. Next, give your reader a good reason for granting your claim. Show how your audience is responsible for the problem and appeal to your reader's sense of fair play, goodwill, or moral responsibility. Explain how you feel about the problem but don't get carried away, don't complain too much, and don't make threats. People generally respond more favorably to requests that are calm and reasonable.

DEVELOPING MARKETING AND SALES MESSAGES

Marketing and sales messages use many of the same techniques as persuasive business messages.

Marketing and sales messages use the same basic techniques as other persuasive messages, with the added emphasis of encouraging someone to participate in a commercial transaction. Although the terms *marketing message* and *sales message* are often used interchangeably, they represent separate but related efforts: Marketing messages usher potential buyers through the purchasing process without asking them to make an immediate decision; that's when sales messages take over. Marketing messages focus on such tasks as introducing new brands to the public, providing competitive comparison information, encouraging customers to visit websites for more information, and reminding buyers that a particular product or service is available. In contrast, a sales message makes a specific request for people to purchase a particular product or service.

Most marketing and sales messages, particularly in larger companies, are created and delivered by professionals with specific training in marketing, advertising, sales, or public relations. However, as a manager, you may be called on to review the work of these specialists or even to write such messages in smaller companies, so having a good understanding of how these messages work will help you be a more effective manager. The basic strategies to consider include assessing customer needs; analyzing your competition; determining key selling points and benefits; anticipating purchase objections; applying the AIDA model; and maintaining high standards of ethics, legal compliance, and etiquette.

Assessing Audience Needs

As with every other business message, successful marketing and sales messages start with an understanding of audience needs. Bear in mind that fulfilling customer needs often extends beyond providing the basic product or service. Clothes do far more than simply keep you warm. What you wear makes a statement about who you are, which social groups you want to be associated with (or not), and how you view your relationship with the people around you.

Begin by assessing audience needs, interests, and emotional concerns—just as you would for any other business message. Try to form a mental image of the typical buyer for the product you want to sell. Ask yourself what audience members might want to know about this product. How can your product help them? Are they driven by bottom-line pricing, or is quality more important to them?

Note the advertisements you're exposed to every day. They often focus on just one or two attributes or issues, even if the product or service has many different facets to consider. The purpose of these narrow marketing messages is to grab your attention and then raise your interest level enough to encourage you to conduct further research.

> Purchasing decisions often involve more than just the basic product or service.

Analyzing Your Competition

Marketing and sales messages nearly always compete with messages from other companies trying to reach the same audience. When Chrysler plans a marketing campaign to introduce a new model to current customers, the company knows that its audience has also been exposed to messages from Ford, Honda, Volkswagen, and numerous other car companies. In crowded markets, writers sometimes have to search for words and phrases that other companies aren't already using. They might also want to avoid themes, writing styles, or creative approaches that are too similar to those of competitive messages.

> Most marketing and sales messages have to compete for the audience's attention.

Determining Key Selling Points and Benefits

With some insight into audience needs and existing messages from the competition, you're ready to decide which benefits and features of your product or service to highlight. For all but the simplest products, you want to prioritize the items you plan to discuss. You also want to distinguish between the features of the product and the benefits that those features offer the customers. As Table 10.3 shows, **selling points**

> Selling points focus on the product; benefits focus on the user.

Table 10.3 FEATURES VERSUS BENEFITS

Product Feature	Customer Benefit
Our easy financing plan includes no money down, no interest, and no payments for 24 months.	You can buy what you want right now, even if you have limited cash on hand.
Our marketing communication audit accurately measures the impact of your advertising and public relations efforts.	You can find out whether your message is reaching the target audience and whether you're spending your marketing budget in the best possible manner.
The spools in our fly fishing reels are machined from solid blocks of aircraft-grade aluminum.	Go fishing with confidence: These lightweight reels will stand up to the toughest conditions.

are the most attractive features of an idea or a product, whereas **benefits** are the particular advantages that readers will realize from those features. Selling points focus on the product. Benefits focus on the user.

For example, ClubMom doesn't stress the online networking feature of its services; rather, it stresses the opportunity to connect with other moms who have similar concerns and interests—which is the benefit enabled by the networking feature. A common approach to communicating features and benefits is to show them in a list or a table, identifying each feature and then describing the benefits it offers (see Figure 10.4). Of course, for your message to be successful, your product's distinguishing benefit must correspond to your readers' primary needs or emotional concerns.

Anticipating Purchase Objections

Anticipating objections is crucial to effective marketing and sales messages.

As with persuasive business messages, marketing and sales messages often encounter objections; once again, the best way to handle them is to identify them up-front and try to address as many as you can. Objections can range from high price to low quality to a lack of compatibility with existing products. Perceived risk is another common objection. Consumers might worry that a car won't be safe enough for a family, that a jacket will make them look unattractive, or that a hair salon will botch a haircut. Business buyers might worry about disrupting operations or failing to realize the financial returns on a purchase.

Price can be a particularly tricky issue in any message, whether audience members are consumers or business customers. Whether you highlight or downplay the price of your product, prepare your readers for it. Words such as *luxurious* and *economical* provide unmistakable clues about how your price compares with that of competitors. Such words help your readers accept your price when you finally state it.

If price is a major selling point, give it a position of prominence, such as in the headline or as the last item in a paragraph. If price is not a major selling point, you can handle it in several ways. You could leave the price out altogether or de-emphasize it by putting the figure in the middle of a paragraph that comes well after you've presented the benefits and selling points. Here's an example:

Emphasizes the rarity of the edition to signal value and thus prepares the reader for the big-ticket price that follows

Buries the actual price in the middle of a sentence and ties it in with another reminder of the exclusivity of the offer

> Only 100 prints of this exclusive, limited-edition lithograph will be created. On June 15, they will be made available to the general public, but you can reserve one now for only $350, the special advance reservation price. Simply rush the enclosed reservation card back today so that your order is in before the June 15 publication date.

FIGURE 10.4
Explaining the Benefits of Product Features
On this webpage, Wachovia is careful to explain the customer benefits of its CAP Asset
Management Accounts.

The pros use two other techniques for minimizing price. One is to break a quantity price into units. Instead of saying that a case of motor oil costs $24, you might say that each bottle costs $2. The other technique is to compare your product's price with the cost of some other product or activity: "The cost of owning your own exercise equipment is less than you'd pay for a health-club membership." Your aim is to make the cost seem as small and affordable as possible, thereby minimizing price as a possible objection.

If you've done your homework up front and assessed your audience thoroughly, you should be aware of most of these concerns. You might not be able to address every one of them in your message—if the product or service isn't ideal for the customer, your message can't fix that—but you will be prepared to do the best you can with the product or service you have to promote.

Applying the AIDA Model

Most marketing and sales messages are prepared according to the AIDA model or some variation of it. A typical AIDA-organized message begins with an attention-getting introduction, generates interest by describing some of the product or service's unique features, increases desire by highlighting the benefits that are most appealing to the audience, and closes by suggesting the action the sender would like the audience to take.

You can use a variety of attention-getting devices in marketing and sales messages.

Getting Attention   You can use a wide range of techniques to attract your audience's attention:

- **Your product's strongest benefit.** "Carry a tune (or 2,000)" (for Apple iPod nano)[14]

- **A piece of genuine news.** "Take entertainment to a whole new place" (for Verizon's V CAST service, which lets people download a variety of entertainment services to their mobile phones)[15]

- **A point of common ground with the audience.** "An SUV adventurous enough to accommodate your spontaneity and the gear that comes with it."[16]

- **A personal appeal to the reader's emotions and values.** "The only thing worse than paying taxes is paying taxes when you don't have to."

- **The promise of insider information.** "You may be one of those people who dream of working and living in France and don't know how to go about simply doing it. This guide tells how—from the inside out—others like yourself have managed to work within the French system."[17]

- **The promise of savings.** "Right now, you can get huge savings on a new camera phone."[18]

- **A sample or demonstration of the product.** "Here's your free sample of the new Romalite packing sheet."

- **A solution to a problem.** "This backpack's designed to endure all a kid's dropping and dragging."[19]

Of course, words aren't the only attention-getting device at your disposal. Strong, evocative images are a common attention-getter. With online messages, you have additional options, including audio, animation, and video.

Even more so than in persuasive business messages, it's important to carefully balance emotion and logic in marketing and sales messages. For example, when ClubMom promotes itself to mothers, it strikes a balance between emotional appeals (such as "A few blogs a day keep the insanity away!") and logical appeals (such as "Earn points by shopping with ClubMom partners and through the ClubMom Online Mall and Gift Card Store").[20] Figure 10.5 suggests the range of logical and emotional appeals that marketing messages can achieve, based on the product and the target audience.

To build interest, expand on and support the promises in your attention-getting opening.

Building Interest   Use the interest section of your message to build on the intrigue you created with your opening. This section should also offer support for whatever claims or promises you might have made in the opening. For instance, when Apple introduced a redesigned iPod nano, it started with the headline "Completely remastered" and then continued with these support points:[21]

Itemizes the key improvements in the new iPod nano

Puts music capacity in a position of emphasis, since that—not price—is the major selling point

> A thinner design. Five stylish colors. A brighter display. Up to 24 hours of battery life. Just about the only thing that hasn't changed is the name. In 2GB, 4GB, and 8GB models starting at $149, iPod nano puts up to 2,000 songs in your pocket.

At this point in the message, Apple has substantiated the claim made in the headline and has whetted readers' appetites with some intriguing features and benefits.

To help convince home builders to use its innovative panel system instead of traditional frame construction, Premier Building Systems focuses on logical factors such as cost, efficiency, and quality

FIGURE 10.5
The Spectrum of Emotional and Logical Appeals
All marketing and sales messages strike a balance between logical and emotional appeals. Premier Building Systems, a maker of building materials, relies primarily on logical appeals. At the other extreme, ADiamondIsForever.com relies almost entirely on emotional appeals on its website. Gladiator GarageWorks lies somewhere between these two, emphasizing both the logical and emotional advantages of its garage organizers.

Gladiator GarageWorks uses a combination of logical and emotional appeals by promising to make your garage "a place to work, entertain and show off to your friends and neighbors."

Website photograph used with permission of Whirlpool Corporation

A Diamond Is Forever uses an appeal that is entirely emotional (for instance, it doesn't attempt to promote the investment value of a diamond)

Add details and audience benefits to increase desire for the product or service.

Increasing Desire   To build desire for the product, continue to expand and explain what it offers, how it works, how customers can use it, and so on. On the iPod nano page, Apple continues with more details about the features summarized in the first paragraph of text, such as describing the size and appearance of the new design. Take advantage of whatever medium you are using to continue to offer additional information that will increase audience desire for the product and help you prepare for the action stage. For example, after reading this much about the iPod, some users might want to know more about the iTunes music store, whereas others will want to know about using iPods in their cars. Apple makes it easy to find the information each individual wants. This ability to provide flexible access to information is just one of the reasons the web is such a powerful medium for marketing and sales (see Figure 10.6)

Throughout the body of your message, remember to keep the focus on the audience. When you talk about product features, remember to stress the customer benefits and talk in terms that make sense to users. Listing the capacity of the iPod nano as 2,000 songs is a lot more meaningful for most readers than saying it has 8 gigabytes of memory. Action words give strength to any business message, but they are especially important in sales letters. Compare the following:

Instead of This	**Write This**
The NuForm desk chair is designed to support your lower back and relieve pressure on your legs.	The NuForm desk chair supports your lower back and relieves pressure on your legs.

The second version says the same thing in fewer words and emphasizes what the chair does for the user ("supports") rather than the intentions of the design team ("is designed to support").

To keep readers interested, use strong, colorful language without overdoing it.

To keep readers interested, use colorful verbs and adjectives that convey a dynamic image. Be careful, however, not to overdo it: If you say "Your factory floors will sparkle like diamonds," your audience members will find it hard to believe, which may prevent them from believing the rest of your message.

To increase desire, as well as boost your credibility, provide support for your claims. You can't assume that your audience members will believe what you say just

FIGURE 10.6
Flexible Communication on the Web
Want to try on a thousand pairs of eyeglasses without leaving home? You can, thanks to interactive websites such as FramesDirect.com, which lets you upload a photo of yourself and then see how you look in a variety of eyeglass styles. Flexible media technologies make it easy to adapt promotional messages to the interests of individual audience members.

because you've said it in writing. You'll have to give them proof. Support is especially important if your product is complicated, costs a lot, involves significant risk, or represents some unusual approach.

Creative marketers find many ways to provide support: testimonials from satisfied users, articles written by industry experts, competitive comparisons, product samples and free demonstrations, independent test results, and online movies that show a product in action. You can also highlight guarantees that demonstrate your faith in your product and your willingness to back it up.

Motivating Action   After you have raised enough interest and built up the reader's desire for your offering, you're ready to ask your audience to take action. Whether you want people to pick up the phone to place an order or visit your website to download a free demo version of your software, try to persuade them to do it right away with an effective *call to action*. You might offer a discount for the first 1,000 people to order, put a deadline on the offer, or simply remind them that the sooner they order, the sooner they'll be able to enjoy the product's benefits. Even potential buyers who want the product can get distracted or forget to respond, so encouraging immediate action is important. Make the response action as simple and as risk-free as possible.

After you've generated sufficient interest and desire, you're ready to persuade readers to take the preferred action.

Take care to maintain the respectful, professional tone you've been using up to this point. Don't resort to gimmicks and desperate-sounding pleas for the customer's business. Make sure your final impression is compelling and positive. For instance, in a printed sales letter, the postscript (P.S.) below your signature is often one of the first or last parts people read. Use this valuable space to emphasize the key benefit you have to offer and to emphasize the advantages of ordering soon.

Maintaining High Standards of Ethics, Legal Compliance, and Etiquette

The word *persuasion* has negative connotations for some people, especially in a marketing or sales context. They associate persuasion with dishonest and unethical practices that lead unsuspecting audiences into accepting unworthy ideas or buying unneeded products. However, effective businesspeople view persuasion as a positive force, aligning their own interests with what is best for their audiences. They influence audience members by providing information and aiding understanding, which allows audiences the freedom to choose.[22] Ethical businesspeople inform audiences of the benefits of an idea, a product, or an action so that these audiences can recognize just how well the offering will satisfy a need they truly have. They don't try to trick people into making choices that are not in their best interest.

To maintain the highest standards of business ethics, make every attempt to persuade without manipulating. Choose words that won't be misinterpreted and be sure you don't distort the truth. Adopt the "you" attitude by showing honest concern for your audience's needs and interests. Your consideration of audience needs is more than ethical; it's the proper use of persuasion. That consideration is likely to achieve the response you intend and to satisfy your audience's needs.

As marketing and selling grow increasingly complex, so do the legal ramifications of marketing and sales messages. In the United States, the Federal Trade Commission (FTC) has the authority to impose penalties (ranging from cease-and-desist orders to multimillion-dollar fines) against advertisers who violate federal standards for truthful advertising. Other federal agencies have authority over advertising in specific industries, such as transportation and financial services. Individual states have additional laws that apply. The legal aspects of promotional communication can be quite complex, from state to state and from country to country, and most companies require marketing and sales people to get clearance from company lawyers before

Marketing and sales messages are covered by a wide range of laws and regulations.

sending messages. In any event, pay close attention to the following legal aspects of marketing and sales communication:[23]

- **Marketing and sales messages must be truthful and nondeceptive.** The FTC considers messages to be deceptive if they include statements that are likely to mislead reasonable customers and the statements are an important part of the purchasing decision. Failing to include important information is also considered deceptive. The FTC also looks at *implied claims*—claims you don't explicitly make but that can be inferred from what you do or don't say.

- **You must back up your claims with evidence.** According to the FTC, offering a money-back guarantee or providing letters from satisfied customers is not enough; you must still be able to support your claims with objective evidence such as a survey or scientific study. If you claim that your food product lowers cholesterol, you must have scientific evidence to support that claim.

- **Marketing and sales messages are considered binding contracts in many states.** If you imply or make an offer and then can't fulfill your end of the bargain, you can be sued for breach of contract.

- **In most cases, you can't use a person's name, photograph, or other identity without permission.** Doing so is considered an invasion of privacy. You can use images of people considered to be public figures as long as you don't unfairly imply that they endorse your message.

Before you launch a marketing or sales campaign, make sure you're up to date on the latest regulations affecting spam (or *unsolicited bulk e-mail*, as it's officially known), customer privacy, and data security. New laws are likely to appear in all three areas in the next few years.

Maintaining high ethical standards is a key aspect of good communication etiquette.

Meeting your ethical and legal obligations will go a long way toward maintaining good communication etiquette as well. However, you may still face etiquette decisions within ethical and legal boundaries. For instance, you can produce a marketing campaign that complies with all applicable laws and yet is still offensive or insulting

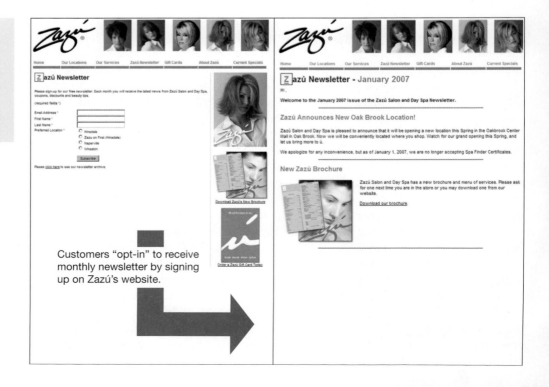

FIGURE 10.7
Opt-In E-Mail Newsletter
Zazú, a salon chain in Illinois, demonstrates the "you" attitude by sending its e-mail newsletter only to clients and other interested parties who have specifically requested it.

Customers "opt-in" to receive monthly newsletter by signing up on Zazú's website.

to your audience. An audience-centered approach, involving respect for your readers and their values, should help you avoid any such etiquette missteps.

Technology also gives communicators new ways to demonstrate sensitivity to user needs. One example is automated updates from blogs and websites, alerting customers to information in which they've expressed an interest. *Opt-in* e-mail newsletters are another technology that shows the "you" attitude at work. Unlike the unwelcome spam messages that litter e-mail inboxes these days, opt-in messages are sent only to those people who have specifically requested information (see Figure 10.7).

> Communication technologies such as opt-in e-mail and blog syndication can help you be sensitive to audience needs.

On the Job

SOLVING COMMUNICATION DILEMMAS AT CLUBMOM

You're the vice president of member services at ClubMom, reporting to CEO Michael Sanchez. In addition to developing new online services, a key part of your job responsibility is crafting messages that describe the new services and persuade members to try them. Use what you've learned in this chapter and in your own experiences as a consumer (and as a parent, if applicable) to address these challenges.

1. You asked one of your staffers to write a benefit statement to communicate the advantages of the Mom-Blogs section of the ClubMom website, which offers more than three dozen blogs on a variety of parenting topics. (You can learn more about the MomBlogs feature at the ClubMom website, www.clubmom.com.) She e-mails the following sentence: "We've worked hard to assemble a team of bloggers who share their knowledge, experience, and opinions on a wide variety of subjects, from pregnancy to schooling to religion." You then write back, explaining why it's important to make marketing messages about the *customer*, not the *company*. Which of these versions best illustrates this vital aspect of the "you" attitude?

   a. The hardworking bloggers at ClubMom share their knowledge, experience, and opinions on a wide variety of subjects, from pregnancy to schooling to religion.
   b. Get insights, information, and thought-provoking opinions from the ClubMom bloggers.
   c. Get insights, information, and thought-provoking opinions from the ClubMom bloggers on a wide variety of subjects, from pregnancy to schooling to religion.
   d. Blogging has rapidly become a popular way for web surfers to get insights, information, and thought-provoking opinions, and the ClubMom blogs will help you, too.

2. A common challenge in marketing communication is distilling a long list of features to a single compelling message that can serve as the product's "headline." Review the following list of features and benefits of the MomNetwork service (extracted from various

communications presented by ClubMom and its business partners):

- The experiences of thousands of moms are now aggregated in a single place online.
- Connect with moms like you; search for moms by personal and family challenges, interests, age of kids, or location.
- Get and give support; find support and swap advice with other moms on a wide range of topics that matter most to you.
- Find the best of what moms have to say; discover thousands of helpful articles, know-how, and tips from ClubMom members and Mom Experts.
- Joining the MomNetwork is absolutely free.
- Setting up your own personal profile is fast and easy.
- Search for moms with similar interests, then send them private messages to establish online conversations.
- Use the My Network feature to collect the names of moms you've connected with online.
- Write as much or as little as you want to share in your personal profile.
- You have complete control over the privacy of your information.

Which of the following statements is the best single-sentence encapsulation of the wide range of benefits that ClubMom offers? Obviously, a single sentence can't communicate every point listed; think more about an initial, high-level message that will entice people to keep reading.

   a. Connecting and collecting; caring and sharing: The online community at ClubMom lets you network with other moms and find information you can use to help make motherhood successful and satisfying.
   b. The online community at ClubMom lets you connect with other moms and find valuable information to help make motherhood successful and satisfying.
   c. ClubMom offers moms everywhere a unique online experience.

d. ClubMom offers the best moms everywhere an absolutely unique online experience, with unparalleled access to valuable knowledge and rewarding camaraderie.

3. Membership in ClubMom is free, so price isn't a potential purchase objection. However, ClubMom does collect a fair amount of information from its members, including information about members themselves, their families, and their product purchase and usage habits. Which of the following statements would you put on the website to encourage anyone who is concerned about privacy and data security to read ClubMom's privacy policy? You can read the policy by clicking on "Privacy Policy" at the bottom of the ClubMom homepage. (Assume that the statement will contain the necessary hyperlink to take visitors to the privacy policy page on the website.)

  a. See why you never have to worry about data security or personal privacy on ClubMom.

b. Learn more about how we protect the information we collect in order to continue making ClubMom a great web destination.

c. We implement SSL for credit card transactions and other sensitive transactions.

d. Like most websites, we collect only the information necessary to provide the valuable services we offer on this website.

4. Which of the following is the most effective call to action to encourage interested moms to sign up for free ClubMom membership?

  a. Sign up for your free Join ClubMom membership today and get knowledge and camaraderie you can't get anywhere else.

  b. Visit ClubMom.com today and learn about the many benefits of free membership.

  c. Every mom belongs in ClubMom; won't you please join today?

  d. ClubMom will change your life in ways you could never have imagined, and it's free!

Learning Objectives Checkup

Assess your understanding of the principles in this chapter by reading each learning objective and studying the accompanying exercises. For fill-in-the-blank items, write the missing text in the blank provided; for multiple-choice items, circle the letter of the correct answer. You can check your responses against the answer key on page AK-2.

Objective 10.1: Apply the three-step writing process to persuasive messages.

1. Which of the following is true about persuasive business messages?
   a. They require government approval before they can be printed or posted on websites.
   b. They are always welcomed by audiences.
   c. They often involve a combination of emotional and logical elements.
   d. They require less planning than any other type of message.

2. Why is the indirect approach often used in persuasive messages?
   a. It is more courteous.
   b. It takes less time.
   c. It is traditional.
   d. It lets the writer build audience interest and desire before asking for action or commitment.

Objective 10.2: Identify seven ways to establish credibility in persuasive messages.

3. Which of the following is not a good way to establish credibility with your audience?
   a. Support your argument with plenty of facts.
   b. Name your sources.

   c. Be enthusiastic and sincere.
   d. Present only your side of the argument to avoid reminding the audience of alternatives.

4. If you lack credibility with an audience, which of the following would be a good technique to use in a persuasive message?
   a. Make your message extremely detailed so the audience will focus on the content.
   b. Include information or endorsements from recognized experts.
   c. Use plenty of humor to help bring the audience over to your side.
   d. Use multimedia to give yourself more ways to get your points across.

Objective 10.3: Describe the AIDA model for persuasive messages.

5. The first phase in the AIDA model is to
   a. Do your research
   b. Gain the audience's attention
   c. Analyze the audience
   d. Call for action

6. The body of a message that follows the AIDA model
   a. Captures the audience's attention
   b. Contains the buffer
   c. Generates interest and heightens desire
   d. Calls for action

7. Which of these is a good way to build desire using the AIDA approach?
   a. Explain how the proposed change will help your audience.

b. Reduce resistance by addressing objections the audience might have.

c. Explain complex ideas or products in more detail.

d. Do all of the above.

8. The final phase of the AIDA method
   a. Provides in-depth information to help generate interest
   b. Reduces resistance by increasing the audience's desire
   c. Calls for action
   d. Captures the audience's attention

Objective 10.4: Distinguish between emotional and logical appeals, and discuss how to balance them.

9. An argument that is based on human feelings is known as a/an _____ appeal.

10. An argument that is based on facts and reason is known as a/an _____ appeal.

11. The best approach to using emotional appeals is usually to
    a. Use them by themselves
    b. Use them in conjunction with logical appeals
    c. Use them only when the audience is particularly hostile
    d. Avoid them in all business messages

12. Which of the following is a type of logical appeal?
    a. Deduction
    b. Induction
    c. Analogy
    d. All of the above

Objective 10.5: Explain why it is important to identify potential objections before you start writing persuasive messages.

13. Why is it important to anticipate objections when planning and writing persuasive messages?
    a. You are legally required to anticipate audience objections in all marketing messages.
    b. By anticipating potential objections, you have the opportunity to address them in a persuasive manner before the audience settles on a firm no answer.
    c. By anticipating potential objections, you have the opportunity to explain to audience members why they are viewing the situation incorrectly.
    d. By anticipating potential objections, you can explain to the audience all the negative consequences of accepting your message.

14. Why is anticipating objections particularly important in written persuasive messages?
    a. Written messages are inherently less believable than oral messages.

b. Responding to questions takes longer in writing than orally.

c. Because they have more time to study them, audiences tend to have more objections to written messages than to messages in other media.

d. You often don't have the opportunity to detect and respond to objections, as you might with an oral message, for instance.

Objective 10.6: Discuss an effective approach to identifying selling points and audience benefits.

15. Prioritizing which features and benefits to write about is
    a. A waste of time because people don't read in sequential order
    b. Important because doing so lets you start with low-priority issues and work your way up to high-priority issues
    c. Important because it helps you focus your message on items and issues that the audience cares about the most
    d. Important because it helps ensure that you remember to talk about every single feature and benefit, no matter how inconsequential

16. What is the relationship between features and benefits?
    a. They are identical.
    b. Features are aspects of an idea or product; benefits are the advantages that readers will realize from those features.
    c. Features tell people how to use a product; benefits tell them how a product differs from the competition.
    d. Features are the primary advantages of a product; benefits are the secondary advantages.

Objective 10.7: Identify steps you can take to avoid ethical lapses in marketing and sales messages.

17. Which of the following steps should you take to make sure your persuasive messages are ethical?
    a. Align your interest with your audience's interests.
    b. Choose words that can't be misinterpreted.
    c. Give the audience the information they need to make an informed decision.
    d. Do all of the above.

18. If it adheres to all applicable federal laws, a marketing or sales message
    a. Is certain to be both legal and ethical
    b. Could still violate some state laws
    c. Could still be unethical
    d. Both b and c

Apply Your Knowledge

1. Why is it important to present both sides of an argument when writing a persuasive message to a potentially hostile audience?

2. How are persuasive messages different from routine messages?

3. When is it appropriate to use the direct organizational approach in persuasive messages?

4. What is likely to happen if your persuasive message starts immediately with a call to action? Why?

5. **Ethical Choices** Are emotional appeals ethical? Why or why not?

Practice Your Knowledge

MESSAGES FOR ANALYSIS

For Message 10.A and Message 10.B, read the following documents and then (1) analyze the strengths and weaknesses of each sentence and (2) revise each document so that it follows this chapter's guidelines.

MESSAGE 10.A: WRITING PERSUASIVE CLAIMS AND REQUESTS FOR ADJUSTMENT

Dear TechStar Computing:

I'm writing to you because of my disappointment with my new multimedia PC display. The display part works all right, but the audio volume is also set too high and the volume knob doesn't turn it down. It's driving us crazy. The volume knob doesn't seem to be connected to anything but simply spins around. I can't believe you would put out a product like this without testing it first.

I depend on my computer to run my small business and want to know what you are going to do about it. This reminds me of every time I buy electronic equipment from what seems like any company. Something is always wrong. I thought quality was supposed to be important, but I guess not.

Anyway, I need this fixed right away. Please tell me what you want me to do.

MESSAGE 10.B: WRITING SALES LETTERS

We know how awful dining hall food can be, and that's why we've developed the "Mealaweek Club." Once a week, we'll deliver food to your dormitory or apartment. Our meals taste great. We have pizza, buffalo wings, hamburgers and curly fries, veggie roll-ups, and more!

When you sign up for just six months, we will ask what day you want your delivery. We'll ask you to fill out your selection of meals. And the rest is up to us. At "Mealaweek," we deliver! And payment is easy. We accept MasterCard and Visa or a personal check. It will save money especially when compared with eating out.

Just fill out the enclosed card and indicate your method of payment. As soon as we approve your credit or check, we'll begin delivery. Tell all your friends about Mealaweek. We're the best idea since sliced bread!

MESSAGE 10.C: CREATING PODCASTS

To access this message, visit www.businesscommunicationblog.com and click on "Textbook Resources." Locate *Excellence in Business Communication*, 8th ed., click on Chapter 10, and select Page 350, Message 10.C. Download and listen to this podcast. Identify at least three ways in which the podcast could be more persuasive and draft a brief e-mail message that you could send to the podcaster with your suggestions for improvement.

EXERCISES

For active links to all websites discussed in this chapter, visit this text's website at www.prenhall.com/thill. Locate your book and click on its "Companion Website" link. Then select Chapter 10 and click on "Featured Websites." Locate the name of the page or the URL related to the material in the text. Please note that links to sites that become inactive after publication of the book will be removed from the "Featured Websites" section.

10.1 Teamwork With another student, analyze the persuasive e-mail message to Eleanor Tran at Host Marriott (Figure 10.2) by answering the following questions:
   a. What techniques are used to capture the reader's attention?
   b. Does the writer use a direct or indirect organizational approach? Why?
   c. Is the subject line effective? Why or why not?
   d. Does the writer use an emotional or a logical appeal? Why?
   e. What reader benefits are included?
   f. How does the writer establish credibility?
   g. What tools does the writer use to reinforce his position?

10.2 Composing Subject Lines Compose effective subject lines for the following persuasive messages:
   a. A recommendation sent by e-mail to your branch manager to install wireless networking throughout the facility. Your primary reason is that management has encouraged more teamwork, but teams often congregate in meeting rooms, the cafeteria, and other places that lack network access—without which they can't do much of the work they are expected to do.
   b. A letter to area residents soliciting customers for your new business, "Meals à la Car," a carryout dining service that delivers from most of the local restaurants. All local restaurant menus are on the Internet. Mom and Dad can dine on egg rolls and chow mein while the kids munch on pepperoni pizza.
   c. An e-mail message to the company president asking that employees be allowed to carry over their unused vacation days to the following year. Apparently, many employees canceled their fourth-quarter vacation plans to work on the installation of a new company computer system. Under their current contract, vacation days not used by December 31 can't be carried over to the following year.

10.3 Ethical Choices Your boss has asked you to post a message on the company's internal blog urging everyone in your department to donate money to the company's favorite charity, an organization that operates a special summer camp for physically challenged children. You wind up writing a lengthy posting packed with facts and heartwarming anecdotes about the camp and the children's experiences. When you must work that hard to persuade your audience to take an action such as donating money to a charity, aren't you being manipulative and unethical? Explain.

10.4 Focusing on Benefits Determine whether the following sentences focus on features or benefits; rewrite as necessary to focus all the sentences on benefits.
   a. All-Cook skillets are coated with a durable, patented nonstick surface.
   b. You can call anyone and talk as long as you like on Saturdays and Sundays with our new FamilyTalk wireless plan.
   c. With 8-millisecond response time, the Samsung LN-S4095D 40-inch LCD TV delivers fast video action that is smooth and crisp.[24]

10.5 Internet Visit the Federal Trade Commission website and read the "Catch the Bandit in Your Mailbox" consumer warning, at www.ftc.gov/bcp/conline/pubs/tmarkg/bandit.shtm. Select one or two marketing or sales letters you've recently received and see whether they contain any of the suspicious content mentioned in the FTC warning. What does the FTC suggest you do with any materials that don't sound legitimate?

10.6 Credibility As the director of human resources in your company, you're desperate for some help. You want to keep the costs of employee benefits under control while making sure you provide employees with a fair benefits package. However, you don't have time to research all the options for health insurance, wellness programs, retirement plans, family counseling, educational benefits, and everything else, so you decide to hire a consultant. You receive the following message from a consultant interested in working with you:

> *I am considered the country's foremost authority on employee health insurance programs. My clients offer universally positive feedback on the programs I've designed for them. They also love how much time I save them—hundreds and hundreds of hours. I am absolutely confident that I can thoroughly analyze your needs and create a portfolio that realizes every degree of savings possible. I invite you to experience the same level of service that has generated such comments as "Best advice ever!" and "Saved us an unbelievable amount of money."*

You'd love to get the results the consultant promises, but these claims don't ring true to you. In fact, the message contains at least a dozen instances in which this writer's credibility might be questioned. Identify as many as you can and explain how you would bolster reader confidence by providing additional or different information.

Expand Your Knowledge

LEARNING MORE ON THE WEB
INFLUENCE AN OFFICIAL AND PROMOTE YOUR CAUSE

http://thomas.loc.gov

At the Thomas site compiled by the Library of Congress, you'll discover voluminous information about federal legislation, congressional members, and committee reports. You can also access committee homepages and numerous links to government agencies, current issues, and historical documents. You'll find all kinds of regulatory information, including laws and relevant issues that might affect you in the business world. Visit the site and stay informed. Maybe you'll want to convince a government official to support a business-related issue that affects you. Explore the data at the Thomas site and find an issue you can use to practice your skills at writing a persuasive message.

1. What key ideas would you include in an e-mail message to persuade your congressional representative to support an issue important to you?
2. In a letter to a senator or member of Congress, what information would you include to convince the reader to vote for an issue related to small business?
3. When sending a message to someone who daily receives hundreds of written appeals, what attention-getting techniques can you use? How can you get support for a cause that concerns you as a businessperson?

SURFING YOUR WAY TO CAREER SUCCESS

Bovée and Thill's Business Communication Headline News offers links to hundreds of online resources that can help you with this course, your other college courses, and your career. Visit www.businesscommunicationblog.com and click on "Web Directory." The "Special Types" section offers links to websites covering crisis management, organizational communication, public and media relations, and advertising and promotion. Identify three websites from this section that could be useful in your business career. For each site, write a two-sentence summary of what the site offers and how it could help you launch and build your career.

Learn Interactively

INTERACTIVE STUDY GUIDE

Visit www.prenhall.com/thill, locate your book and click on its "Companion Website" link. Select Chapter 10 to take advantage of the interactive "Chapter Quiz" to test your knowledge of chapter concepts. Receive instant feedback on whether you need to do additional studying. Also, visit the "Study Hall," where you'll find an abundance of valuable resources that will help you succeed in this course.

PEAK PERFORMANCE GRAMMAR AND MECHANICS

If your instructor has required the use of "Peak Performance Grammar and Mechanics," either in your online course or on CD, you can improve your skill with semicolons and colons by

using the "Peak Performance Grammar and Mechanics" module. Click on "Punctuation I." Take the Pretest to determine whether you have any weak areas. Then review those areas in the Refresher Course. Take the Follow-Up Test to check your grasp of semicolons and colons. For an extra challenge or advanced practice, take the Advanced Test. Finally, for additional reinforcement, go to the "Improve Your Grammar, Mechanics, and Usage" section that follows and complete those exercises.

Improve Your Grammar, Mechanics, and Usage

The following exercises help you improve your knowledge of and power over English grammar, mechanics, and usage. Turn to the Handbook of Grammar, Mechanics, and Usage at the end of this book and review all of Sections 2.4 (Semicolons) and 2.5 (Colons). Then look at the following 10 items. Circle the letter of the preferred choice in the following groups of sentences. (Answers to these exercises appear on page AK-4.)

1. a. This letter looks good; that one doesn't.
   b. This letter looks good: that one doesn't.
2. a. I want to make one thing clear: None of you will be promoted without teamwork.
   b. I want to make one thing clear; none of you will be promoted without teamwork.
   c. I want to make one thing clear: None of you will be promoted; without teamwork.
3. a. The Zurich airport has been snowed in, therefore I can't attend the meeting.
   b. The Zurich airport has been snowed in, therefore, I can't attend the meeting.
   c. The Zurich airport has been snowed in; therefore, I can't attend the meeting.
4. a. His motivation was obvious: to get Meg fired.
   b. His motivation was obvious; to get Meg fired.
5. a. Only two firms have responded to our survey; J. J. Perkins and Tucker & Tucker.
   b. Only two firms have responded to our survey: J. J. Perkins and Tucker & Tucker.
6. a. Send a copy to: Nan Kent, CEO, Bob Bache, president, and Dan Brown, CFO.
   b. Send a copy to Nan Kent, CEO; Bob Bache, president; and Dan Brown, CFO.

   c. Send a copy to Nan Kent CEO; Bob Bache president; and Dan Brown CFO.
7. a. You shipped three items on June 7; however, we received only one of them.
   b. You shipped three items on June 7, however; we received only one of them.
   c. You shipped three items on June 7; however we received only one of them.
8. a. Workers wanted an immediate wage increase: they hadn't had a raise in 10 years.
   b. Workers wanted an immediate wage increase; because they hadn't had a raise in 10 years.
   c. Workers wanted an immediate wage increase; they hadn't had a raise in 10 years.
9. a. His writing skills are excellent however; he needs to polish his management style.
   b. His writing skills are excellent; however, he needs to polish his management style.
   c. His writing skills are excellent: however he needs to polish his management style.
10. a. We want to address three issues; efficiency; profitability; and market penetration.
    b. We want to address three issues; efficiency, profitability, and market penetration.
    c. We want to address three issues: efficiency, profitability, and market penetration.

For additional exercises focusing on semicolons and colons, go to www.prenhall.com/thill, then locate your text and click on its "Companion Website" link. Click on Chapter 10, click on "Additional Exercises to Improve Your Grammar, Mechanics and Usage," and click on "16. Punctuation A."

Cases

Applying the Three-Step Writing Process to Cases
Apply each step to the following cases, as assigned by your instructor.

Planning

Analyze the Situation
Identify both your general purpose and your specific purpose. Clarify exactly what you want your audience to think, feel, or believe after receiving your message. Profile your primary audience, including their backgrounds, differences, similarities, and likely reactions to your message.

Gather Information
Identify the information your audience will need to receive, as well as other information you may need in order to craft an effective message.

Select the Right Medium
Make sure your medium is both acceptable to the audience and appropriate for the message.

Organize the Information
Choose a direct or indirect approach based on the audience and the message; most persuasive messages employ an indirect approach (often following the AIDA model). Identify your main idea, limit your scope, then outline necessary support points and other evidence.

Writing

Adapt to Your Audience
Show sensitivity to audience needs with a "you" attitude, politeness, positive emphasis, and bias-free language. Understand how much credibility you already have—and how much you may need to establish with any particular audience. Project your company's image by maintaining an appropriate style and tone.

Compose the Message
Draft your message using clear but powerful words, effective sentences, and coherent paragraphs. Support your claims with objective evidence; balance emotional and logical arguments.

Completing

Revise the Message
Evaluate content and review readability, then edit and rewrite for conciseness and clarity.

Produce the Message
Use effective design elements and suitable layout for a clean, professional appearance.

Proofread the Message
Review for errors in layout, spelling, and mechanics.

Distribute the Message
Deliver your message using the chosen medium; make sure all documents and all relevant files are distributed successfully.

1   **2**   **3**

PERSUASIVE BUSINESS MESSAGES

 Blogging SKILLS   **Portfolio BUILDER**

1. **That's the point: E-mail encouraging your boss to blog** You've been trying for months to convince your boss, Will Florence, to start blogging. You've told him that top executives in many industries now use blogging as a way to connect with customers and other stakeholders without going through the filters and barriers of formal corporate communications. He was just about convinced—until he read the blog by Bob Lutz, the co-chair and design chief of General Motors.

"Look at this!" he calls from his office. "Bob Lutz is one of the most respected executives in the world, and all these people are criticizing him on his own blog. Sure, a lot of the responses are positive, but quite a few are openly hostile, disagreeing with GM strategy, criticizing the products, criticizing the subjects he chooses for his blog—you name it. If blogging is all about opening yourself up to criticism from every bystander with a keyboard, no way am I going to start a blog."

Your task: Write an e-mail to Florence (w_florence@sprenco.com), persuading him that the freewheeling nature of blog communication is its key advantage, not a disadvantage at all. While they may not always agree with what he has to say, automotive enthusiasts and car buyers respect Lutz for communicating in his own words—and for giving them the opportunity to respond. For background information, read some of the postings from Lutz and other GM executives at http://fastlane.gmblogs.com.[25]

E-Mail SKILLS

2. **Give a little to get a lot: Suggesting free wireless at Starbucks** Like many other students at the University of Wisconsin–Madison, you like to escape from your cramped apartment to work on school projects at local coffee shops. With your wireless-equipped laptop, you hunt for places that offer free wireless so you can access course websites, do research, and occasionally see how Badgers athletic teams are

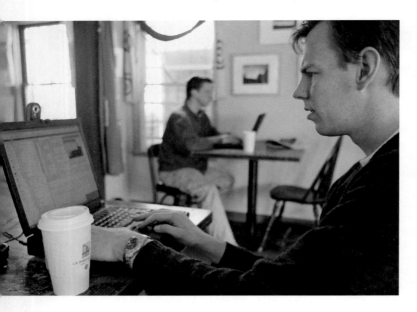

doing. But there's a problem: At the Starbucks right around the corner, you have to pay for wireless access through the service offered by T-Mobile. Several of the locally owned coffeehouses offer free wireless, but the closest one is a mile from your apartment. That's a long walk in a Wisconsin winter.

Your task: Write a persuasive message to Starbucks, suggesting that the company drop its agreement with T-Mobile and offer free wireless instead. Try to convince the firm that free wireless will attract enough additional coffee-buying customers to offset the loss of revenue from wireless—and help Starbucks overcome the "big corporation" image that prompts some coffee drinkers to patronize locally owned establishments instead. While you don't have the data to prove that the cost of offering free wireless would be more than offset by increased coffee sales, at least make a convincing argument that Starbucks should consider making the change. You'll post your message to the Starbucks website, www.starbucks.com, which has a limit of 2,600 characters for such messages.[26]

E-Mail SKILLS

3. Travel turnaround: Memo convincing Travelfest boss to expand client services You are a successful agent with Travelfest, Inc., a full-service travel-management firm. Located in Austin, Texas, Travelfest has four offices and more than 50 employees. Headquarters are downtown, in the lobby of a 35-story office tower. The other three offices are located in major shopping centers in upscale suburbs. The company's business is made up of about 70 percent business travel and 30 percent leisure travel. However, many of the leisure sales also come from corporate customers, so business travelers are clearly your key audience.

Your boss, Gary Hoover, has been working night and day to make up for declining revenues brought about by the loss of airline commissions. He has tried everything, from direct-mail

campaigns to discount coupons to drawings for cruises and weekend getaways. Still, revenues remain flat.

You've been doing some research and analysis of your office's existing customer profiles. You find that many of your customers are middle- to high-income sophisticated travelers, that business travel is bouncing back (with an eye to cheaper fares and less costly accommodations), and that executives often make their own travel arrangements (now that many companies are cutting the cost of maintaining their own travel departments). Your research has triggered some ideas that you believe could substantially increase your revenue from existing customers.

You envision turning your headquarters office into a travel resource for corporate customers. First, you would like to provide as much information as you can on the most popular business destinations—inside and outside the country. You could sell video and audio courses in Spanish, French, German, Japanese, and other languages. And you'd like to introduce a line of travel products, including luggage, maps, travel guides, and electronics—all aimed at the business traveler. You're even thinking about a special area with videos and other educational materials on various cultures and business practices around the world.

You realize your ideas won't generate a lot of direct profit. However, you believe they will get business customers in the door, where you and other agents can sell them travel-management services. If Hoover is willing to try your idea and it works, he may want to do something similar in the suburb offices, perhaps with an emphasis on leisure travel.

Your task: Write an e-mail proposal to Gary Hoover. Outline your ideas and suggest a meeting to discuss them further and determine what market research he'd like you to perform.[27]

E-Mail SKILLS

4. Life's little hassles: E-mail requesting satisfaction It's hard to go through life without becoming annoyed at the way some things work. You have undoubtedly been dissatisfied with a product you've bought, a service you've received, or an action of some elected official or government agency.

Your task: Write a three- to five-paragraph persuasive e-mail request expressing your dissatisfaction in a particular case. Specify the action you want the reader to take.

5. Nap time: Memo requesting space for power nappers at Phidias & Associates It's been one of those days. You were dragging by 10 A.M., ready to slump over into your computer monitor at the Phidias & Associates architectural firm in San Francisco. How are you supposed to be creatively inspired when you can barely get your eyes to focus and your head feels as if it's full of cotton? No, you weren't out partying last night; you've just been working long, late hours on a rush job for one of the firm's biggest clients. If only you could stretch out for a little catnap, you'd be good as new in 15 minutes.

Groggily, you recall an item you tore out of the *Wall Street Journal* a year ago—a paragraph or two in the "Work Week" column, all about companies adding "nap rooms" to help employees recharge during the day. You know that on weekends, a quick nap helps you get a lot more done during the day; and didn't they teach you in school that Thomas Edison kept a cot in his office and got his best ideas when he was napping? And the article quotes an expert, William A. Anthony, author of *The Art of Napping* and professor of rehabilitation counseling at Boston University. He says most people aren't sleep deprived, they're "nap ready."

There are plenty of other precedents and pioneers out there in the business world. At *Macworld* magazine, the human resources director, Shelly Ginenthal, says their two-person nap room was installed all the way back in 1986 and usually has a waiting line. At Yarde Metals in Bristol, Connecticut, President Bruce Yarde says, "A quick little nap can rejuvenate you." He's fighting employee stress with a 25-person nap room. You do some quick research for more evidence and turn up a report from the prestigious National Institutes of Health, indicating that power napping not only helps prevent burnout but also enhances information processing and learning.

Your task: After you've had a good night's sleep, write a memo to Jonas T. Phidias, persuading the senior partner that the distinguished offices of Phidias & Associates could benefit from the addition of a corporate nap room and an organizational embrace of power napping as a way to be more competitive. On a separate page, include a short note to your instructor, justifying your organizational approach (direct or indirect) and your selection of delivery medium (e-mail or interoffice mail).[28]

▌IM ▌SKILLS

6. **Helping children: Instant message holiday fund drive at IBM** At IBM, you're one of the coordinators for the annual Employee Charitable Contributions Campaign. Since 1978, the company has helped employees contribute to more than 2,000 health and human service agencies. These groups may offer child care; treat substance abuse; provide health services; or fight illiteracy, homelessness, and hunger. Some offer disaster relief or care for the elderly. All deserve support. They're carefully screened by IBM, one of the largest corporate contributors of cash, equipment, and people to nonprofit organizations and educational institutions, in the United States and around the world. As your literature states, the program "has engaged our employees more fully in the important mission of corporate citizenship."

During the winter holidays, you target agencies that cater to the needs of displaced families, women, and children. It's not difficult to raise enthusiasm. The prospect of helping children enjoy the holidays—children who otherwise might have nothing—usually awakens the spirit of your most distracted workers. But some of them wait until the last minute and then forget.

They have until December 16 to come forth with cash contributions. To make it in time for holiday deliveries, they can also bring in toys, food, and blankets through Tuesday, December 20. They shouldn't have any trouble finding the collection bins; they're everywhere, marked with bright red banners. But some will want to call you with questions or (hopefully) to make credit card contributions: 800-658-3899, ext. 3342.

Your task: It's December 14. Write a 75- to 100-word instant message encouraging last-minute holiday gifts.[29]

▌E-Mail ▌SKILLS

7. **Tangled web: E-mail to PurelySoftware regarding an online order duplication** Last week you ordered new design software for your boss, Martin Soderburgh, at ArtAlive, the small art consulting business where you work. As he requested, you used his Visa card to order Adobe InDesign and Adobe Photoshop from an Internet vendor, PurelySoftware.com.

When you didn't receive the usual e-mail order confirmation, you called the company's toll-free number. The operator said the company's website was having problems, and he took a second order over the phone: $649 for Adobe InDesign, $564 for Adobe Photoshop, including tax and shipping. Four days later, ArtAlive received two shipments of the software, and your boss's credit card was charged $1,213 twice, for a total of $2,426.

Your task: Technically, you authorized both orders. But you understood during the phone call that the first order was canceled, although you have no written proof. Send a persuasive e-mail to customerservice@purelysoftware.com, requesting (1) an immediate credit to your boss's Visa account and (2) a postage-paid return label for the duplicate order.[30]

▌E-Mail ▌SKILLS

8. **Helping out: Message to Whole Foods Market managers** Whole Foods Market has grown into a nationwide chain by catering to consumer desires for more healthful foods and environmentally sensitive household products. For instance, meats come from animals that were never fed antibiotics, and the cheese is from cows said to be raised on small farms and treated humanely.

Along with selling these products, the company makes a commitment "to the neighborhood and larger community that we serve and in which we live." Whole Foods not only donates 5 percent of after-tax profits to not-for-profit organizations but also financially supports employees who volunteer their time for community service projects. Many Whole Foods stores donate goods and supplies to soup kitchens in their local communities. Company executives want to encourage this type of activity, which reflects the "Whole Foods, Whole People, Whole Planet" corporate motto.

You are the manager of the Whole Foods Market on Ponce de Leon Avenue in Atlanta, Georgia. You've been very successful with a program you developed for donating surplus food to local food banks. Top executives have asked you to help other Whole Foods stores coordinate this effort into a chainwide food donation program, "Whole Foods for Life." Ideally, by streamlining the process chainwide, the company would be able to increase the number of people it helps and get more of its employees involved.

You don't have a great deal of extra money for the program, so the emphasis has to be on using resources already available to the stores. One idea is to use trucks from suburban stores to make the program "mobile." Another idea is to join forces with a retailing chain to give food and clothing to individuals. You've decided that the key will be to solicit input from the other stores so that they'll feel more involved in the final outcome as the larger food-donation program takes shape.

Your task: Write a persuasive e-mail message to all managers at Whole Foods Market, explaining the new program and requesting that they help by pooling ideas they've gleaned from their local experience. Even if they don't have food-donation programs currently in place, you want to hear ideas from them and their employees for this charitable project. With their help, you'll choose the best ideas to develop the new "Whole Foods for Life" program.[31]

▌E-Mail
▌SKILLS

9. No more driving: Telecommuting to Bachman, Trinity, and Smith Sitting in your Dallas office at the accounting firm of Bachman, Trinity, and Smith, clacking away on your computer, it seems as though you could be doing this work from your home. You haven't spoken to any co-workers in more than two hours. As long as you complete your work on time, does your location matter?

As an entry-level accountant, you've participated in on-location audits at major companies for nearly a year now. If your bosses trust you to work while staying at a hotel, why not let you work from home, where you already have an office with computer, phone, and fax machine? You'd love to regain those two hours you lose commuting to and from work every day.

Your task: To support this idea, visit the website of the International Telework Coalition at www.telcoa.org. You'll find statistics and other support for a memo persuading your boss, senior partner Marjorie Bachman, to grant you a six-month trial as a telecommuter.[32]

10. Always urgent: Memo pleading case for hosting a Red Cross blood drive This morning as you drove to your job as food services manager at the Pechanga Casino Entertainment Center in Temecula, California, you were concerned to hear on the radio that the local Red Cross chapter put out a call for blood because national supplies have fallen dangerously low.

During highly publicized disasters, people are emotional and eager to help out by donating blood. But in calmer times, only 5 percent of eligible donors think of giving blood. You're one of those few.

Not many people realize that donated blood lasts for only 72 hours. Consequently, the mainstay of emergency blood supplies must be replenished in an ongoing effort. No one is more skilled, dedicated, or efficient in handling blood than the American Red Cross, which is responsible for half the nation's supply of blood and blood products.

Donated blood helps victims of accidents and disease, as well as surgery patients. Just yesterday you were reading about a girl named Melissa, who was diagnosed with multiple congenital heart defects and underwent her first open-heart surgery at one week of age. Now five years old, she's used well over 50 units of donated blood, and she wouldn't be alive without them. In a thank-you letter, her mother lauded the many strangers who had "given a piece of themselves" to save her precious daughter—and countless others. You also learned that a donor's pint of blood can benefit up to four other people.

Today, you're going to do more than just roll up your own sleeve. You know the local Red Cross chapter takes its Blood Mobile to corporations, restaurants, beauty salons—anyplace willing to host public blood drives. What if you could convince the board of directors to support a blood drive at the casino? The slot machines and gaming tables are usually full, hundreds of employees are on hand, and people who've never visited before might come down to donate blood. The positive publicity certainly couldn't hurt Pechanga's community image. With materials from the Red Cross, you're confident you can organize Pechanga's hosting effort and handle the promotion. (Last year, you headed the casino's successful Toys for Tots drive.)

To give blood, one must be healthy, be at least 17 years old (with no upper age limit), and weigh at least 110 pounds. Donors can give every 56 days. You'll be urging Pechanga donors to eat well, drink water, and be rested before the Blood Mobile arrives.

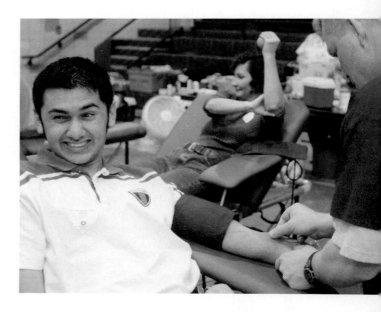

The local Red Cross chapter's mission statement says, in part, that the Red Cross is "a humanitarian organization led by volunteers and guided by the Fundamental Principles of the International Red Cross Movement" that will "prevent and alleviate human suffering wherever it may be found." All assistance is given free of charge, made possible by "contributions of people's time, money, and skills"—and in the case of you and your co-workers, a piece of yourselves.

Your task: Write a memo persuading the Pechanga board of directors to host a public Red Cross blood drive. You can learn more about what's involved in hosting a blood drive at www.givelife.org (click on "Sponsor a Drive"). Ask the board to provide bottled water, orange juice, and snacks for donors. You'll organize food service workers to handle the distribution, but you'll need the board's approval to let your team volunteer during work hours. Use a combination of logical and emotional appeals.[33]

▌E-Mail ▌Portfolio
▌SKILLS ▌BUILDER

11. Message to an angel: Introducing your company to an investor Your new company, WorldConnect Language Services, started well and is going strong. However, to expand beyond your Memphis, Tennessee, home market, you need a one-time infusion of cash to open branch offices in other cities around the Southeast. At the Entrepreneur's Lunch Forum you attended yesterday, you learned about several *angels*, as they are called in the investment community—private individuals who invest money in small companies in exchange for a share of ownership. One such angel, Melinda Sparks, told the audience that she is looking for investment opportunities outside of high technology, where angels often invest their money. She also indicated that she looks for entrepreneurs who know their industries and markets well, who are passionate about the value they bring to the marketplace, who are committed to growing their businesses, and who have a solid plan for how they will spend an investor's money. Fortunately, you meet all of her criteria.

Your task: Draft an e-mail message to Sparks, introducing yourself and your business and asking for a meeting at which you would present your business plan in more detail. Explain that your Memphis office was booked to capacity within two months of opening, thanks to the growing number of international business professionals looking for translators and interpreters. You've researched the entire Southeast region and identified at least 10 other cities that could support a language services office such as yours. Making up whatever other information you need, draft a four-paragraph message following the AIDA method, ending with a request for a meeting within the next four weeks.

▌Blogging ▌Portfolio
▌SKILLS ▌BUILDER

12. Web accessibility advocacy: It's not "World Wide" if it doesn't include everybody Like most other companies today, your firm makes extensive use of the web for internal and external communication. However, after reading about the Web Accessibility Initiative (WAI), you've become concerned that your company's various websites haven't been designed to accommodate people with disabilities or age-related limitations. Fortunately, as one of the company's top managers, you have a perfect forum for letting everyone in the company know how important accessible web design is: Your internal blog is read by the vast majority of employees and managers throughout the company.

Your task: Visit the WAI website, at www.w3.org/WAI, and read the two articles "Introduction to Web Accessibility" (look in the "Introducing Accessibility" section) and "Developing a Web Accessibility Business Case for Your Organization: Overview" in the "Managing Accessibility" section. Using the information you learn in these articles, write a post for your blog that emphasizes how important it is for your company's websites to become more accessible. You don't have direct authority over the company's web developers, so it would be inappropriate for you to request them to take any specific action. Your goal is simply to raise awareness and encourage everyone to consider the needs of the company's online audiences. Don't worry about the technical aspects of web accessibility; focus instead on the benefits of improving accessibility.

▌E-Mail
▌SKILLS

13. Too good to be true: E-mail to Paging South requesting adjustment Paging South offered its pager services for a mere $5 a month. You purchased an inexpensive pager and signed a contract for two years. After you thought your pager phone number was up and running for two weeks, you heard from co-workers and clients that they repeatedly get a busy signal when dialing your pager number. You call Paging South, and they resolve the problem—but doing so takes an additional week. You don't want to be charged for the time the pager was not in service. After discussing the situation with the local manager, she asks you to contact Judy Hinkley at the company's regional business office.

Your task: Send an e-mail message to Hinkley, at Judy@pagingsouth.com, to request an adjustment to your account. Request credit or partial credit for one month of service. Remember to write a summary of events in chronological order, supplying exact dates for maximum effectiveness.

14. Lock legends: Letter requesting refund and damages from Brookstone As a professional photographer, you travel the world for business, leaving from your home base in Williamstown, Massachusetts. Last month it was a trip to Australia, and you thought you'd finally found a way around the "no-locks-on-checked-baggage" rules.

After the World Trade Center attacks of September 11, 2001, the U.S. Travel Security Administration (TSA) forbade airline passengers to check locked luggage. TSA inspectors want easy access so that they can open and check bags for security purposes. But because you carry so much expensive equipment, including numerous camera bags, you've been nervous about the safety of your belongings—not to mention the loss of privacy.

So you were relieved when you read Joe Sharkey's "On the Road" column in the *New York Times* just before your trip. The columnist extolled a newly announced TSA program allowing airline travelers to lock their luggage *if they use special TSA-approved locks*, certified by a company called Travel Sentry. You immediately went to the Brookstone store in Albany after reading its web advertisement for "The luggage locks security won't be cut off. Our Easycheck™ locks are certified by Travel Sentry™ and feature a secure system accepted and recognized by the Transportation Security Administration (TSA). Airport security personnel can now inspect and re-lock your bags quickly and easily." You bought eight locks, at $20 for each set of two.

When you left the Albany airport, TSA inspectors assured you that they had a master key for these locks, just as Sharkey's column had promised they would. But when you got to Melbourne after changing planes in Chicago and Los Angeles, you were stunned to discover the condition of your luggage. One bag was missing the new lock entirely; another was missing the lock and had a rip all along the seam—perhaps from an irritated inspector? Inside a third bag you found its broken Easycheck lock, with a terse TSA inspection notice reminding you that locked baggage is not allowed. On the return trip you tried again, using three of your remaining locks on camera bags. They arrived with no locks and no inspection notices.

You've now called the airports in Chicago and Cleveland, where TSA inspectors told you they'd "never heard of the program." Brookstone will replace the broken lock, but the woman on the phone wasn't sure about the ones that went missing entirely because you have nothing left to bring into the store except your receipt.

Your task: After 10 minutes of listening to music while on hold for the TSA, you've abandoned the idea of a phone complaint to the government agency. You're going to write a letter to Brookstone (120 Washington Ave., Albany, NY 12203)

requesting damages for the ripped luggage (a 24-inch Expandable Ballistic Suitor, $320) and a refund for all eight locks ($80). Six of them were ruined or missing, and your last two are essentially useless.[34]

MARKETING AND SALES MESSAGES

Portfolio BUILDER

15. Your new Kentucky home: Letter promoting the Bluegrass State Like all other states, Kentucky works hard to attract businesses that are considering expanding into the state or relocating entirely from another state. The Kentucky Cabinet for Economic Development is responsible for reaching out to these companies and overseeing the many incentive programs the state offers to new and established businesses.

Your task: As the communication director of the Kentucky Cabinet for Economic Development, you play the lead role in reaching out to companies that want to expand or relocate to Kentucky. Visit www.thinkkentucky.com and download the *Think Kentucky* brochure (look under the "Why Kentucky" link). Identify the eight benefits the state uses to promote Kentucky as a great place to locate a business. Summarize these eight reasons in a form letter that will be sent to business executives throughout the country. Be sure to introduce yourself and your purpose in the letter, and close with a compelling call to action (have them reach you by telephone at 800-626-2930 or by e-mail at econdev@ky.gov). As you plan your letter, try to imagine yourself as the CEO of a company and consider what a complex choice it would be to move to another state.

E-Mail SKILLS

16. Time to lose: Promoting the 6 Week Solution at Curves The Curves franchise has grown quickly over the past several years by catering to women who may not feel at home in traditional gyms. As the owner of a successful Curves health club, you know that information and motivation are often the keys to healthy living in general and weight management in particular. You're excited about a new program the company offers called the Curves 6 Week Solution, a series of classes that help women make better nutrition choices.

Your task: The corporate website offers a nice description of the Curves 6 Week Solution, but it's over 600 words long, and you'd like a shorter version to e-mail to current and prospective clients. Visit that page on the Curves website, www.curves.com/weight_loss, and summarize the description. Aim for no more than 300 words.

17. Give me liberty: Letter persuading customers to remain loyal to Colbar Art For many people in the United States, the Statue of Liberty is something of a tourist cliché, so much a part of New York City's tourist hype that it's taken for granted. But for many immigrants, the first sight of Liberty as they enter the city brings tears along with hopes for a new life. Ovidiu Colea knows the feeling. He immigrated to the United States in the early 1980s after a difficult past that included five long years in a Romanian hard-labor camp for trying to flee a Communist regime.

Colea worked two years as a cab driver to save enough money to start Colbar Art, a company that produces up to 80,000 hand-crafted replicas of the Liberty statue each year. He now helps other immigrants get a start in their new country by hiring them to design and produce Liberty models. Colea pays a royalty to the Liberty–Ellis Island Foundation for using Liberty's image. In fact, during the first year of operation, that royalty amounted to $250,000.

Painstaking labor produces the acrylic and bonded marble statues with a hand-painted patina, and most of that work is done by the very immigrants Lady Liberty welcomes to New York. Colea insists on keeping production in the United States. Although labor costs are cheaper outside the country, he refuses to produce the statues in countries "where there is no liberty or no Statue of Liberty." By keeping jobs in the United States, he's doing his share to keep the American Dream alive.

But the meticulous labor also costs precious production time. With recent high demand for the replicas, the company has fallen behind on orders. To increase production to 120,000 statues per year, the company is leasing more space and training new employees. Meanwhile, the production deficits may continue for several months.

Your task: You work for Colbar Art as assistant manager, and Colea has asked you to write a persuasive form letter to all your customers, explaining the current delays and requesting patience. Be sure to explain the steps the company is taking to solve these delays and describe the quality and creativity that go into the replicas. You can quote Bradford Hill (owner of the Liberty Island gift shop), who says Colbar Art's models represent 65 percent of his sales. Make a convincing argument for your customers to remain loyal to Colbar Art.[35]

IM SKILLS

18. Instant promotion: Text message from Hilton Hotels to frequent guests Hilton Hotels now uses a short messaging service (SMS) to send instant text promotions to customers who've signed up as "HHonors" members. But you work in marketing, and that means you're often struggling to con-

dense elaborate travel packages into 65 enticing words (system maximum).

For example, today's promotion offers "A Golfer's Dream Come True: 'I just played a round of golf by the pyramids!'" For $575 per person per day (double room), valid through January 15, 2008, travelers can stay in the Hilton Pyramids Golf Resort in Cairo, Egypt, for seven nights/eight days, including breakfast, service charge, and tax. They'll be met at the airport, given transportation to the resort, plus two rounds of golf per person at Dreamland Golf course and two rounds of golf per person at Soleimaneia Pyramids Golf & Country Club course. That's 88 words so far.

But you also need to convey that the Dreamland course wraps like a serpent around the Hilton resort. Its lush greens and lakes, designed by Karl Litten, contrast sharply with the golden desert, culminating in a stunning view of the great Pyramids of Giza, one of the seven wonders of the world. The Soleimaneia course features the "biggest floodlit driving course in Egypt." The travel package provides free transportation to this nearby course.

Rates, of course, are subject to availability, and other restrictions may apply. But interested travelers should mention code G7 Pyramids Golf Special when they call Hilton Reservations Worldwide. They can also e-mail RM_PYRAMIDS_GOLF@hilton.com, or call the Cairo hotel directly, at 20 2 8402402. That is, if you can entice them in 65 words.

Your task: Write the persuasive instant message.[37]

Portfolio BUILDER

19. Try it; you just might like it: Convincing consumers to sample beefalo You know enough about human nature to know that people tend to resist new ideas when it comes to food. In your job as public communications director for American Beefalo International, this knowledge presents a professional challenge as you try to convince people to give beefalo a try. The beefalo is a cross between bison (American buffalo) and beef cattle, and even though these animals are primarily cattle (genetically speaking), many consumers are reluctant to give up their familiar beef for something most have never tried.

But here's the good news: Many people are looking for healthful foods, and according to government tests, beefalo is lower in cholesterol, saturated fat, total fat, and calories. Here's a comparison table (based on 100g servings) published on your organization's website:

Meat	Protein (g)	Cholesterol (mg)	Saturated Fats (g)	Total Fat (g)	Calories	Percentage of Calories from Fat
Fish	22.9	47	0.104	0.81	105	6.9
Chicken	31.0	85	1.0	3.5	165	19.5
Pork	29.3	86	3.4	9.7	212	41.0
Beef	25.9	88	8.5	21.5	305	63.6
Beefalo	30.7	58	2.7	6.3	188	30.3

Your task: Write a small flier to be displayed in food stores that sell beefalo cuts. The page size will be 8 1/2 inches tall by 3 3/4 inches wide, so format your word processing page accordingly. Allow room for a photograph, and don't try to cram too much text on the page. Emphasize beefalo as a healthy alternative for people who want to continue enjoying meat in their diets.[36]

20. Selling your idea: Sales letter promoting a product of your own invention You never intended to become an inventor, but you saw a way to make something work more easily, so you set to work. You developed a model, found a way to mass-produce it, and set up a small manufacturing studio in your home. You know that other people are going to benefit from your invention. Now all you need is to reach that market.

Your task: Imagine a useful product that you have invented—perhaps something related to a hobby or sporting activity. List the benefits and features of your imaginary product. Then write a sales letter for it, using what you've learned in this chapter and making up details as you need them.

▌Podcasting SKILLS

21. Listen up: Podcast promoting a podcast station Podcasting, the technique of recording individual sound files that people download from the Internet to listen to on their computers or music players, is quickly redefining the concept of radio. A growing crowd of musicians, essayists, journalists, and others with compelling content use podcasting to reach audiences they can't get to through traditional broadcast radio. The good news is that anyone with a microphone and a computer can record podcasts. That's also the bad news, at least from your perspective as a new podcaster: With so many podcasters now on the Internet, potential listeners have thousands and thousands of audio files to select from.

Your new podcast, School2Biz, offers advice to business students making the transition from college to career. You provide information on everything from preparing résumés to interviewing to finding one's place in the business world and building a successful career. As you expand your audience, you'd eventually like to turn School2Biz into a profitable operation (perhaps by selling advertising time during your podcasts). For now, you're simply offering free advice.

Your task: You've chosen The Podcast Bunker (www.podcastbunker.com) as the first website on which to promote School2Biz. The site also lets podcasters promote their feeds with brief text listings, such as this description of Pet Talk Radio: "A weekly lifestyle show for people with more than a passing interest in pets. Hosted by Brian Pickering & Kaye Browne with Australia's favourite vet Dr Harry Cooper & animal trainer Steve Austin."

Option A: Write a 50-word description of your new podcast, making up any information you need to describe School2Biz. Be sure to mention who you are and why the information you pre-sent is worth listening to. Option B: If your instructor tells you to do so, script and record a brief podcast (no more than three minutes long) that describes and promotes School2Biz.[38]

▌Web Writing SKILLS   ▌Portfolio BUILDER

22. Don't forget print: Using the web to promote Time Inc.'s magazine advertising After a shaky start as the technology matured and advertisers tried to figure out this new medium, online advertising has finally become a significant force in consumer and business marketing. Companies in a wide variety of industries are shifting some of the advertising budgets from traditional media such as television and magazines to the increasing selection of advertising possibilities online—and more than a few companies now advertise almost exclusively online. That's fine for companies that sell advertising time and space for websites and blogs, but your job involves selling advertising in those print magazines that are worried about losing market share to online publishers.

Online advertising has two major advantages that you can't really compete with: interactivity and the ability to precisely target individual audience members. On the other hand, you have several advantages going for you, including the ability to produce high-color photography, the physical presence of print (such as when a magazine sits on a table in a doctor's waiting room), portability, guaranteed circulation numbers, and close reader relationships that go back years or decades in many cases.

Your task: You work as an advertising sales specialist for the Time Inc. division of Time Warner, which publishes more than 150 magazines around the world. Write a brief persuasive message about the benefits of magazine advertising; the statement will be posted on the individual websites of Time Inc.'s numerous magazines, so you can't narrow in on any single publication. Also, Time Inc. coordinates its print publications with an extensive online presence (including thousands of paid online advertisements), so you can't bash online advertising, either.[39]

E-Mail SKILLS   Portfolio BUILDER

23. Insure.com: E-mail promoting a better way to buy insurance The great thing about Insure.com is that no one is obligated to buy a thing, which makes your job in the company's marketing department easier. Free of charge, consumers can log on to your website, ask for dozens of insurance quotes, and then go off and buy elsewhere. They can look at instant price-comparison quotes from more than 200 insurers, covering every kind of insurance from term life and medical to private passenger auto insurance. All rates are guaranteed up-to-the-day accurate against a $500 reward. And so far the online service has received positive press from *Nation's Business, Kiplinger's Personal Finance, Good Housekeeping, The Los Angeles Times, Money, U.S. News & World Report,* and *Forbes.*

Insure.com generates revenues primarily from the receipt of commissions and fees paid by insurers based on the volume of business produced. Customers can purchase insurance from the company of their choice via the Insure.com website, or they can call a toll-free number to speak to one of the company's representatives. The reps are paid salaries versus commissions and do not directly benefit by promoting one insurance company's product over another.

And all this is free. Too bad more people don't know about your services.

Your task: It's your job to lure more insurance customers to Insure.com. You've decided to use direct e-mail marketing (using a list of consumers who have inquired about rates in the past but never committed to purchase anything). Write an e-mail sales message promoting the benefits of Insure.com's services. Be sure your message is suited to e-mail format, with an appropriate subject heading.[40]

Portfolio BUILDER

24. Outsourcing: Letter from Kelly Services offering solutions In 1946, with his dynamic vision and pioneering spirit, William Russell Kelly started a new company to meet the office and clerical needs of Detroit-area businesses. Kelly temporary employees with skills in calculating, inventory, typing, and copying were soon in great demand. During the 1960s, the Kelly Girl became a nationwide icon, synonymous with high-quality temporary employees. The company changed its name to Kelly Services, Inc., in 1966, reflecting the increasing diversity of its services, customers, and employees.

Today, Kelly Services is a global Fortune 500 company that offers staffing solutions including temporary services, staff leasing, outsourcing, and vendor on-site and full-time placement. Kelly provides employees who have a wide range of skills across many disciplines, including office services, accounting, engineering, information technology, law, science, marketing, light industrial, education, health care, and home care.

Workforce needs, in terms of quantity and skills mix, fluctuate greatly. At the same time, employees have adaptable skills and are far more mobile. The result is that more employers and employees alike want flexible staffing arrangements, and temporary staffing is often the best solution.

Companies use Kelly Services to strategically balance workload and workforce during peaks and valleys of demand, to handle special projects, and to evaluate employees prior to making a full-time hiring decision. This dramatic change in business has spurred the rapid growth of the contingent employment industry.

In turn, many individuals are choosing the flexibility of personal career management, increasing options of where, when, and how to work. Many employees now want to fit their work into their lifestyle rather than fit their lifestyle into their work. Therefore, more and more workers are becoming receptive to being contract, temporary, or consulting employees.

The flexibility of a temporary services firm offers advantages to the company and the employee. Both have the opportunity to evaluate one another prior to making a long-term commitment. Kelly Services earns a fee when its employees are hired permanently, but employers find that it's a small price to pay for such valuable preview time, which saves everyone the cost and pain of a bad hiring decision.

Kelly has received many supplier awards for providing outstanding and cost-efficient staffing services, including Chrysler's Gold Award, Ford Motor Company's Q1 Preferred Quality Award, Intel Corporation's Supplier Continuous Quality Improvement (SCQI) Award, and DuPont Legal's Challenge Award.

A job as a marketing manager with Kelly holds challenge and promise. With 2,500 offices in 26 countries, Kelly provides its customers nearly 700,000 employees annually, generating revenue of $4.3 billion in 2003. The company provides staffing solutions to more than 90 percent of the Fortune 500 companies.

As companies increasingly face new competitive pressures to provide better service and quality at lower prices, many are turning to outsourcing suppliers to deliver complete operational management of specific functions or support departments, allowing the company the necessary time to focus on its core competencies. One solution is to choose a single supplier such as the Kelly Management Services (KMS) division to deliver "full service" outsourcing.

KMS combines management experience, people process improvements, technology enhancements, and industry expertise to optimize customer operations and reduce cost. KMS understands the unique challenges companies face in today's increasingly fast-paced business world and can provide customers with services across multiple functional offerings, including call center operations, warehousing, distribution and light assembly, back-office and administrative functions, and mail and reprographic services. The result is a department staffed by employees that can fluctuate as a company's needs change.

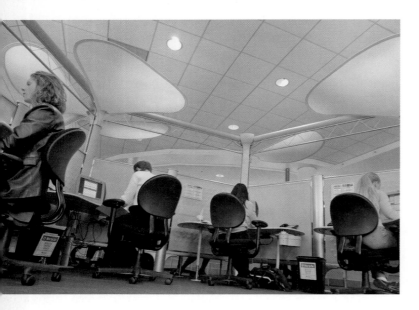

KMS customers who have implemented one service often add others when they see KMS-managed employees performing at high levels and producing substantial cost savings and operational efficiencies. By partnering with an outsourcing supplier such as KMS, companies will experience greater value and cost savings than with in-house operations.

Your task: Write a sales letter to companies similar to Chrysler, Ford, Intel, and DuPont explaining what Kelly has to offer. For current information, visit the Kelly website, at www.kellyservices.com.[41]

Portfolio BUILDER

25. Greener cleaners: Letter promoting environmentally sound Hangers franchise When you told everyone you aspired to work for an environmentally responsible business, you didn't imagine you'd end up in the dry-cleaning business. But now that you are director of franchise development for Hangers Cleaners, you go home every night with a "clean conscience" (your favorite new pun).

Micell Technologies first invented the revolutionary cleaning technology that Hangers Cleaners uses and then in 2001 sold all licensing, all intellectual property, and all interest in Hangers Cleaners to Cool Clean Technologies, which now manufactures the "CO2OL Clean" dry-cleaning machine that your franchise relies on. This breakthrough in dry-cleaning

technology is the first in nearly 50 years—made by Micell co-founders Joseph DeSimone, James McClain, and Timothy Romack. Their new cleaning process uses liquid carbon dioxide (CO_2) and specially developed detergents to clean clothes. The process requires no heat and no further need for the toxic perchloroethylene (perc) or petroleum traditionally used in dry cleaning.

Hangers franchise owners don't have to deal with regulatory paperwork, zoning restrictions, or expensive insurance and taxes for hazardous waste disposal. And unlike petroleum-based solvents, the CO_2 used in the "CO2OL Clean" machine is noncombustible. It's the same substance that carbonates beverages, and it's captured from the waste stream of industries that produce it as a by-product. Moreover, 98 percent of the CO_2 used in a Hangers outlet is recycled and used again, which helps keep prices competitive. The "CO2OL Clean" machine received accolades from the Environmental Protection Agency and was recently rated the best dry-cleaning alternative by a leading consumer products testing group.

You've already sold franchises in 60 locations, from Wilmington, North Carolina, to San Diego, California. Customers love the fact that their clothes don't carry toxic fumes after cleaning, and employees are happy to be working in a safe and cool environment. The process is actually gentler on clothes (no strong solvents or heat), reducing fading and shrinking and helping them last longer. You aren't dry cleaners; you are "garment care specialists."

And beyond the environmental boons, you simply love the design of Hangers stores. When Micell originally established the chain, it hired both dry-cleaning experts and architects to come up with a sleek, modern, high-end retail "look" that features a cool, clean, light-filled interior and distinctive signage out front. It's more akin to a Starbucks than the overheated, toxic-smelling storefront most customers associate with dry cleaning. This high-end look is making it easier to establish Hangers as a national brand, attracting investors and franchisees rapidly as word spreads about the new "greener cleaner."

Your task: Develop a sales letter that can be mailed in response to preliminary inquiries from potential franchise owners. You'll include brochures covering franchise agreements and "CO2OL Clean" specifics, so focus on introducing and promoting the unique benefits of Hangers Cleaners. Your contact information is Hangers Cleaners, 3505 County Road 42 West, Burnsville, MN 55306-3803; phone 952-882-5000; toll-free 866-262-9274.[42]

Part IV

Preparing Reports and Oral Presentations

CHAPTER 11

Planning Reports and Proposals

CHAPTER 12

Writing Reports and Proposals

CHAPTER 13

Completing Reports and Proposals

CHAPTER 14

Designing and Delivering Oral and Online Presentations

Planning Reports and Proposals

Learning Objectives

AFTER STUDYING THIS CHAPTER, YOU WILL BE ABLE TO

1 Adapt the three-step writing process to reports and proposals

2 Distinguish informational reports, analytical reports, and proposals

3 Describe an effective process for conducting business research

4 Define primary and secondary research and explain when you use each method

5 Name nine criteria for evaluating the credibility of an information source

6 Provide five guidelines for conducting an effective online search

7 Outline an effective process for planning and conducting information interviews

8 Explain the differences between drafting a summary, drawing a conclusion, and developing a recommendation

9 Discuss three major ways to organize analytical reports

On the Job

COMMUNICATING AT TESCO

LISTENING TO CUSTOMERS IS PART OF THE RECIPE FOR SUCCESS

Most consumers enjoy the benefits of stiff price competition among their local grocery stores, but the competition is anything but enjoyable for grocery retailers. In the United States, the average grocery store's after-tax profit margin hovers around 1 percent. With so little room for error, grocers need to constantly stay on top of consumer behavior to make sure they offer the right mix of products at the right prices.

Tesco, the leading grocery retailer in the United Kingdom, is not only surviving but thriving in this tough industry. Under the leadership of Richard Brasher, the company's top marketing executive in the United Kingdom, Tesco devotes considerable effort to acquiring and processing information about its customers—information that is used in a variety of reports and other documents to drive both strategic and tactical decisions.

British retail giant Tesco relies on extensive audience research to plan and craft its consumer messages.

For example, when demographic research indicated a growing number of immigrants from Poland, the store reached out to Polish-speaking consumers to learn more about their wants and needs. After a successful experiment on a small scale, Tesco decided to expand its Polish foods selection to as many as 100 other stores. In another instance, the marketing team couldn't figure out why flowers and wine had become such hot sellers during a particular week at the beginning of summer that didn't coincide with any regular holidays. Analysis of sales data revealed that families were buying these items as gifts for their children's teachers at the end of the school year, so the company responded by making sure both items were stocked in plentiful supply during that week.

Tesco is now busy applying its information-driven approach to the competitive U.S. market. After studying the market for two decades, the company decided 2007 was the time to move in. Research reports will continue to play a key role. As the company's website explains, "It's simple—we listen and respond, providing customers with what they tell us they want."[1]

www.tesco.com

365

APPLYING THE THREE-STEP WRITING PROCESS TO REPORTS AND PROPOSALS

Reports can be classified as informational reports, analytical reports, and proposals.

Reports play a significant role in Richard Brasher's success with Tesco (profiled in the chapter opener), as they do in the careers of all other business professionals. Reports fall into three basic categories:

- **Informational reports** offer data, facts, feedback, and other types of information, without analysis or recommendations.

- **Analytical reports** offer both information and analysis, and they can also include recommendations.

- **Proposals** offer structured persuasion for internal or external audiences.

The purpose and content of business reports varies widely; in some cases, you follow a strict guideline, but in others, the organization and format are up to you.

The nature of reports varies widely, from one-page trip reports that follow a standard format to detailed business plans and proposals that can run hundreds of pages. No matter what the circumstances, try to view every business report as an opportunity to demonstrate your understanding of your audience's challenges and your ability to contribute to your organization's success.

The three-step process you studied in Chapters 4 though 6 and applied to short messages in Chapters 7 through 10 is easy to adapt to longer message formats (see Figure 11.1). This chapter addresses the planning step, focusing on two major areas that require special attention in long documents: gathering and organizing informa-

Planning

Analyze the Situation
Clarify the problem or opportunity at hand, define your purpose, develop an audience profile, and develop a work plan.

Gather Information
Determine audience needs and obtain the information necessary to satisfy those needs; conduct a research project if necessary.

Select the Right Medium
Choose the best medium for delivering your message; consider delivery through multiple media.

Organize the Information
Define your main idea, limit your scope, select a direct or an indirect approach, and outline your content using an appropriate structure for an informational report, analytical report, or proposal.

Writing

Adapt to Your Audience
Be sensitive to audience needs with a "you" attitude, politeness, positive emphasis, and bias-free language. Build a strong relationship with your audience by establishing your credibility and projecting your company's image. Control your style with a tone and voice appropriate to the situation.

Compose the Message
Choose strong words that will help you create effective sentences and coherent paragraphs throughout the introduction, body, and close of your report or proposal.

Completing

Revise the Message
Evaluate content and review readability, then edit and rewrite for conciseness and clarity.

Produce the Message
Use effective design elements and suitable layout for a clean, professional appearance; seamlessly combine text and graphical elements.

Proofread the Message
Review for errors in layout, spelling, and mechanics.

Distribute the Message
Deliver your report using the chosen medium; make sure all documents and all relevant files are distributed successfully.

FIGURE 11.1
Three-Step Writing Process for Reports and Proposals
The three-step writing process is especially valuable with reports and proposals. By guiding your work at each step, the process helps you make the most of the time and energy you invest.

tion. Chapter 12 covers the writing step and also includes advice on creating effective visuals for your reports and proposals. Chapter 13 describes the tasks involved in completing reports and proposals.

Analyzing the Situation

The complexity of many reports and the amount of work involved put a premium on carefully analyzing the situation before you begin to write. Pay special attention to your **statement of purpose**, which explains *why* you are preparing the report and *what* you plan to deliver in the report (see Table 11.1).

> Given the length and complexity of many reports, it's crucial to define your purpose clearly so you don't waste time.

The most useful way to phrase a purpose statement is to begin with an infinitive phrase (*to* plus a verb), which helps pin down your general goal (*to inform*, *to identify*, *to analyze*, and so on). For instance, in an informational report, your statement of purpose can be as simple as one of these:

> To identify potential markets for our new phone-based video games
>
> To update the board of directors on the progress of the research project
>
> To submit required information to the Securities and Exchange Commission

Your statement of purpose for an analytical report often needs to be more comprehensive. When Linda Moreno, the cost accounting manager for Electrovision, a high-tech company based in Los Gatos, California, was asked to find ways of reducing employee travel and entertainment costs, she phrased her statement of purpose accordingly:

> Longer reports may have several related purposes.

> . . . to analyze the T&E [travel and entertainment] budget, evaluate the impact of recent changes in airfares and hotel costs, and suggest ways to tighten management's control over T&E expenses.

Because Moreno was assigned an analytical report rather than an informational report, she had to go beyond merely collecting data; she had to draw conclusions and make recommendations. You'll see her complete report in Chapter 13.

PROBLEM OR OPPORTUNITY STATEMENTS VERSUS PURPOSE STATEMENTS		Table 11.1
Problem Statement	**Statement of Purpose**	
Our company's market share is steadily declining.	To explore new ways of promoting and selling our products and to recommend the approaches most likely to stabilize our market share.	
Our current computer network lacks sufficient bandwidth and cannot be upgraded to meet our future needs.	To analyze various networking options and to recommend the system that will best meet our company's current and future needs.	
We need $2 million to launch our new product.	To convince investors that our new business would be a sound investment so that we can obtain desired financing.	
Our current operations are too decentralized and expensive.	To justify the closing of the Newark plant and the transfer of East Coast operations to a single Midwest location in order to save the company money.	

When writing a proposal, you must also be guided by a clear statement of purpose to help focus on crafting a persuasive message. Here are several examples:

> To secure funding in next year's budget for new conveyor systems in the warehouse
>
> To get management approval to reorganize the North American salesforce
>
> To secure $2 million from outside investors to start production of the new titanium mountain bike

Remember, the more specific your purpose statement, the more useful it will be as a guide to planning your report. Furthermore, if you've been assigned the report by someone else, always double-check your statement of purpose with that person to make sure you've interpreted the assignment correctly.

In addition to considering your purpose carefully, you will also want to prepare a *work plan* for most reports and proposals in order to make the best use of your time. For simpler reports, the work plan can be an informal list of tasks and a simple schedule. However, if you're preparing a lengthy report, particularly when you're collaborating with others, you'll want to develop a more detailed work plan. Such a plan might include the following elements:

- Statement of the problem or opportunity (for analytical reports and proposals)
- Statement of the purpose and scope of your investigation
- Discussion of the tasks that need to be accomplished in order to complete the report
- Review of project assignments, schedules, and resource requirements
- Plans for following up after delivering the report

Some work plans also include a tentative outline, if the author has had the opportunity to think through the organization of the report. The work plan in Figure 11.2 includes such an outline.

Gathering Information

The sheer volume of information needed for many reports and proposals requires careful planning—and may even require a separate research project to acquire the data and information you need (see "Supporting Your Messages with Reliable Information" on page 372). To stay on schedule and on budget, be sure to review your statement of purpose and your audience's needs so that you collect all the information you need—and only the information you need.

Selecting the Right Medium

Just as you would for other business messages, select the medium for your report based on the needs of your audience and the practical advantages and disadvantages of the choices available to you. In addition to the general media selection criteria discussed in Chapter 4, consider several points for reports and proposals. First, for many reports and proposals, audiences have specific media requirements, and you might not have a choice. For instance, executives in many corporations now expect to review reports via their in-house intranets, sometimes in conjunction with an *executive dashboard*, a customized online presentation of key operating variables such as revenue, profits, quality, customer satisfaction, and project progress. Second, con-

---

Margin notes:

A detailed work plan saves time and often produces more effective reports.

Some reports require formal research projects to gather all the necessary information.

The best medium for any given report might be anything from a professionally printed and bound document to an online executive dashboard that displays nothing but report highlights.

States the problem clearly enough for anyone to understand without additional research

STATEMENT OF THE PROBLEM
The rapid growth of our company over the past five years has reduced the sense of community among our staff. People no longer feel like part of an intimate organization that values teamwork.

PURPOSE AND SCOPE OF WORK
The purpose of this study is to determine whether a company newsletter would help rebuild a sense of community within the workforce. The study will evaluate the impact of newsletters in other companies and will attempt to identify features that may be desirable in our own newsletter. Such variables as length, frequency of distribution, types of articles, and graphic design will be considered. Costs will be estimated for several approaches, including print and electronic versions. In addition, the study will analyze the personnel and procedures required to produce a newsletter.

Explains exactly what will be covered by the research and included in the final report

Identifies the tasks to be accomplished and does so in clear, simple terms

SOURCES AND METHODS OF DATA COLLECTION
Sample newsletters will be collected from 10 to 20 companies similar to ours in size, growth rate, and types of employees. The editors will be asked to comment on the impact of their publications on employee morale. Our own employees will be surveyed to determine their interest in a newsletter and their preferences for specific features. Production procedures and costs will be analyzed through conversations with newsletter editors, printers, and our website development team.

Offers a preliminary outline to help readers understand the issues that will be addressed in the report

PRELIMINARY OUTLINE
The preliminary outline for this study is as follows:
I. Do newsletters affect morale?
   A. Do people read them?
   B. How do employees benefit?
   C. How does the company benefit?
II. What are the features of good newsletters?
   A. How long are they?
   B. What do they contain?
   C. How often are they published?
   D. How are they designed?
III. How should a newsletter be produced?
   A. Should it be written and edited internally or externally?
   B. Should it be printed or produced electronically?
   C. If electronic, should it be formatted as e-mail, a blog, or regular web content?
IV. What would a newsletter cost?
   A. What would the personnel cost be?
   B. What would the material cost be?
   C. What would outside services cost?
V. Should we publish a company newsletter?
VI. If so, what approach should we take?

Identifies who is responsible for each task and when it will be completed

TASK ASSIGNMENTS AND SCHEDULE
Each phase of this study will be completed by the following dates:

Collect/analyze newsletters	Hank Waters	September 15, 2008
Interview editors by phone	Hank Waters	September 22, 2008
Survey employees	Julienne Cho	September 29, 2008
Develop sample	Hank Waters	October 6, 2008
Develop cost estimates	Julienne Cho	October 13, 2008
Prepare report	Hank Waters	October 20, 2008
Submit final report	Hank Waters	October 24, 2008

FIGURE 11.2
Work Plan for a Report
A formal work plan such as this is a vital tool for planning and managing complex writing projects. The preliminary outline here helps guide the research; the report writers may modify the outline when they begin writing the report.

sider how your audience wants to provide feedback on your report or proposal. Do they prefer to write comments on a printed document or to use the commenting and markup features in a word processing program or Adobe Acrobat? Third, will people need to search through your document frequently or update it in the future? Delivering a report as a word processing file makes both tasks far easier. Fourth, bear in mind that your choice of media also sends a message. For instance, a routine sales report dressed up in expensive multimedia could look like a waste of time and money.

Organizing Your Information

Both the direct and indirect approaches are used in business reports. The direct approach is popular because it is efficient and easy to follow. It can also produce a more forceful report. However, if the audience is unsure about your credibility or is not ready to accept your main idea without first seeing some reasoning or evidence, the indirect approach is a better choice because it gives you a chance to prove your points and gradually overcome audience reservations. The longer the message, though, the less effective the indirect approach is likely to be.

Both approaches have merit, so businesspeople often combine them, revealing their conclusions and recommendations in stages as they go along rather than putting them all first or last (see Figure 11.3).

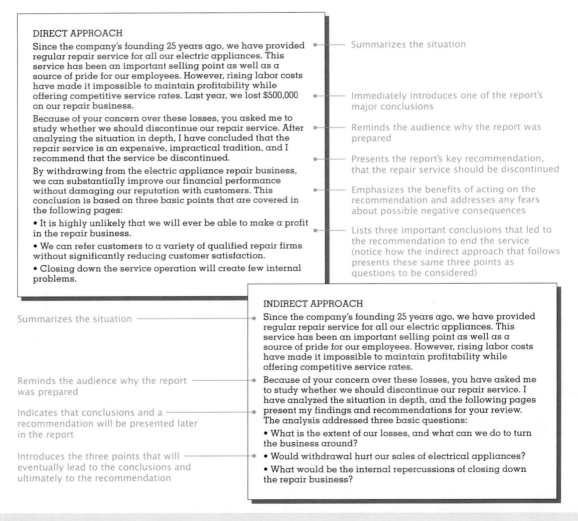

DIRECT APPROACH

Since the company's founding 25 years ago, we have provided regular repair service for all our electric appliances. This service has been an important selling point as well as a source of pride for our employees. However, rising labor costs have made it impossible to maintain profitability while offering competitive service rates. Last year, we lost $500,000 on our repair business.

Because of your concern over these losses, you asked me to study whether we should discontinue our repair service. After analyzing the situation in depth, I have concluded that the repair service is an expensive, impractical tradition, and I recommend that the service be discontinued.

By withdrawing from the electric appliance repair business, we can substantially improve our financial performance without damaging our reputation with customers. This conclusion is based on three basic points that are covered in the following pages:

• It is highly unlikely that we will ever be able to make a profit in the repair business.

• We can refer customers to a variety of qualified repair firms without significantly reducing customer satisfaction.

• Closing down the service operation will create few internal problems.

— Summarizes the situation

— Immediately introduces one of the report's major conclusions

— Reminds the audience why the report was prepared

— Presents the report's key recommendation, that the repair service should be discontinued

— Emphasizes the benefits of acting on the recommendation and addresses any fears about possible negative consequences

— Lists three important conclusions that led to the recommendation to end the service (notice how the indirect approach that follows presents these same three points as questions to be considered)

Summarizes the situation —

Reminds the audience why the report was prepared —

Indicates that conclusions and a recommendation will be presented later in the report —

Introduces the three points that will eventually lead to the conclusions and ultimately to the recommendation —

INDIRECT APPROACH

Since the company's founding 25 years ago, we have provided regular repair service for all our electric appliances. This service has been an important selling point as well as a source of pride for our employees. However, rising labor costs have made it impossible to maintain profitability while offering competitive service rates.

Because of your concern over these losses, you have asked me to study whether we should discontinue our repair service. I have analyzed the situation in depth, and the following pages present my findings and recommendations for your review. The analysis addressed three basic questions:

• What is the extent of our losses, and what can we do to turn the business around?

• Would withdrawal hurt our sales of electrical appliances?

• What would be the internal repercussions of closing down the repair business?

FIGURE 11.3

Direct Approach Versus Indirect Approach in an Introduction
In the direct version of this introduction, the writer quickly presents the report's recommendation, followed by the conclusions that led to that recommendation. In the indirect version, the same topics are introduced in the same order, but no conclusions are drawn about them; the conclusions and the ultimate recommendation appear later, in the body of the report.

Table 11.2 — TYPES OF OUTLINE HEADINGS

Descriptive (Topical) Outline	Informative (Talking) Outline	
	Question Form	Summary Form
I. Industry Characteristics	I. What is the nature of the industry?	I. Flour milling is a mature industry.
A. Annual sales	A. What are the annual sales?	A. Market is large.
B. Profitability	B. Is the industry profitable?	B. Profit margins are narrow.
C. Growth rate	C. What is the pattern of growth?	C. Growth is modest.
1. Sales	1. Sales growth?	1. Sales growth averages less than 3 percent a year.
2. Profit	2. Profit growth?	2. Profits are flat.

When you outline your content, use informative ("talking") headings rather than simple descriptive ("topical") headings (see Table 11.2). When in question or summary form, informative headings force you to really think through the content rather than simply identify the general topic area. Using informative headings will not only help you plan more effectively but also facilitate collaborative writing. A heading such as "Industry characteristics" could mean five different things to the five people on your writing team, so use a heading that conveys a single, unambiguous meaning, such as "Flour milling is a mature industry."

For a quick review of adapting the three-step process to long reports, refer to "Checklist: Adapting the Three-Step Writing Process to Informational and Analytical Reports." The following sections provide specific advice on how to plan informational reports, analytical reports, and proposals.

✓ CHECKLIST: Adapting the Three-Step Writing Process to Informational and Analytical Reports

A. Analyze the situation.

✓ Clearly define your purpose before you start writing.
✓ If you need to accomplish several goals in the report, identify all of them in advance.
✓ Prepare a work plan to guide your efforts.

B. Gather information.

✓ Determine whether you need to launch a separate research project to collect the necessary information.
✓ Reuse or adapt existing material whenever possible.

C. Select the right medium.

✓ Base your decision on audience expectations (or requirements, as the case may be).

✓ Consider the need for commenting, revising, distributing, and storing.
✓ Remember that the medium you choose also sends a message.

D. Organize your information.

✓ Use a direct approach if your audience is receptive.
✓ Use an indirect approach if your audience is skeptical.
✓ Use an indirect approach when you don't want to risk coming across as arrogant.
✓ Combine approaches if doing so will help build support for your primary message.

SUPPORTING YOUR MESSAGES WITH RELIABLE INFORMATION

Many of your business reports will require some level of research.

Audiences expect you to support your message with solid research. As you've probably discovered while doing school projects, research involves a lot more than simply typing a few terms into a search engine. Good research requires a clear process:

1. **Plan your research.** A solid plan yields better results in less time.

2. **Locate the data and information you need.** The research plan tells you *what* to look for; your next step is to figure out *where* the data and information are and *how* to access them.

3. **Process the data and information you've located.** The data and information you find probably won't be in a form you can use immediately and will require some processing, which might involve anything from statistical analysis to resolving the differences between two or more expert opinions.

4. **Apply your findings.** You can apply your research findings in three ways: summarizing information for someone else's benefit, drawing conclusions based on what you've learned, or developing recommendations.

5. **Manage information efficiently.** Many companies today are trying to maximize the return on the time and money they invest in business research by collecting and sharing research results in a variety of computer-based systems, known generally as **knowledge management systems**. At the very least, be sure to share your results with any colleagues who may be able to benefit from them.

You can see the sequence of these steps in Figure 11.4; the following sections offer more details, starting with planning your research.

Planning Your Research

Researching without a plan wastes time and usually produces unsatisfactory results.

Guide your research with a clear problem statement that defines the purpose of your research.

With so much information online these days, it's tempting just to punch some keywords into a search engine and then dig through the results, looking for something, anything, that looks promising. However, this haphazard approach limits your effectiveness (you might not find the right information) and your efficiency (you might spend too much time and money on research).

To avoid expensive and embarrassing research mistakes, start by familiarizing yourself with the subject so that you can frame insightful questions. As you explore

FIGURE 11.4
The Research Process
By following a methodical research process, you can save time and money while uncovering better information.

1 Plan	2 Locate data and information	3 Process data and information	4 Apply your findings	5 Manage information
• Familiarize yourself with the subject; develop problem statement • Identify information gaps • Prioritize research needs • Maintain research ethics and etiquette	• Evaluate sources • Collect secondary information at the library, online, or elsewhere • Collect primary information through surveys and interviews	• Analyze numerical information • Quote, paraphrase, or summarize textual information	• Summarize findings • Draw conclusions • Make recommendations	• Make research results available to others via your company's knowledge management system

the general subject area, try to identify basic terminology, significant trends, important conflicts, influential people, and potential sources of information. Next, develop a **problem statement** that will define the purpose of your research. This statement should explicitly define the decision you need to make or the conclusion you need to reach at the end of the process. For example, Tesco's Richard Brasher might want to know whether consumers are starting to turn away from bottled water because of concerns about cost and the environmental impact of plastic packaging and transportation. His problem statement could be "We need to determine whether we should reduce the number or variety of bottled water brands carried in our stores."

Before you begin your research project, recognize that research carries some significant ethical responsibilities. To avoid ethical lapses, keep the following points in mind:

- **Don't force a specific outcome by skewing your research.** If you go in with strong biases or opinions, you're more likely to favor information that supports your position and gloss over information that doesn't.

- **Respect the privacy of your research participants.** For example, don't observe people without their consent or publicly disclose personal information that you promised to keep private.[2]

- **Document sources and give appropriate credit.** Citing your sources not only is fair to the people who created and provided the information but also helps your audience members confirm your information or explore it in more detail if they so choose.

- **Respect the intellectual property and digital rights of your sources.** *Intellectual property* refers to the ownership of unique ideas that have commercial value in the marketplace.[3] Information you uncover might be protected by copyrights, trademarks, or patents, and depending on the situation, you may not be able to use it without permission.

- **Don't distort information from your sources.** For instance, if an industry expert says that a sales increase is *possible*, don't quote him or her as saying that a sales increase is *probable*.

- **Don't misrepresent who you are or what you intend to do with the research results.** One prominent example of misrepresentation in recent years is known as *pretexting*, which is essentially lying about who you are (such as posing as a journalist) in order to gain access to information that you couldn't get otherwise. Pretexting is not only unethical but also illegal in many instances.[4]

In addition to ethics, research etiquette deserves careful attention, too. For example, respect the time of anyone who agrees to be interviewed or to be a research participant, and maintain courtesy throughout the interview or research process.

Locating Data and Information

The range of sources available to business researchers today is remarkable—almost overwhelming at times. If you have a question about an industry, a company, a market, a new technology, or a financial topic, chances are that somebody else has already researched the subject. Research conducted previously for another purpose is considered **secondary research** when the results are reused in a new project. This secondary information can be anything from magazine articles to survey results. Whenever it is available, review secondary research results that could apply to your research challenge; doing so might save you time and money. Before you use any secondary sources, however, you need to know whether you can trust them, as the following section explains. **Primary research** is new research done specifically for your current project and includes surveys, interviews, observations, and experiments.

Primary research consists of information that you gather specifically for a new research project; secondary research consists of information that others have gathered (and published, in many cases).

Evaluating Sources In every research project, you have the responsibility of verifying the quality of the sources you use. The Internet has made this challenge easier in one respect: It's usually possible to cross-check information by referring to multiple sources. At the same time, online research is more difficult because so much bad information exists on the Internet, from doctored photos to unverified "facts" to biased sources. To avoid tainting your results and damaging your reputation, ask yourself the following questions about each piece of material:

Evaluate your sources carefully to avoid embarrassing and potentially damaging mistakes.

- **Does the source have a reputation for honesty and reliability?** For example, find out how a publication accepts articles and whether it has an editorial board, peer review, or fact-checking procedures. Most traditional, offline publishers have such quality control procedures in place, but many online sources do not.

- **Is the source potentially biased?** To interpret an organization's information, you need to know its point of view.

- **What is the purpose of the material?** For instance, was the material designed to inform others of new research, advance a political position, or promote a product?

- **Is the author credible?** Is the author a professional journalist? An informed amateur? Merely someone with an opinion?

- **Where did the source get *its* information?** Try to find out who collected the data, the methods they used, their qualifications, and their professional reputation.

- **Can you verify the material independently?** Verification can uncover biases or mistakes, which is particularly important when the information goes beyond simple facts to include projections, interpretations, and estimates.

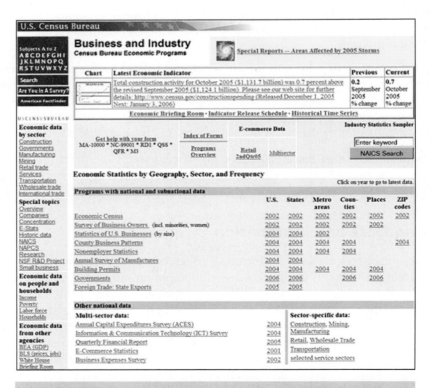

The U.S. Bureau of the Census is a credible source of information.

- **Is the material current?** Make sure you are using the most current information available by checking the publication date of a source.

- **Is the material complete?** Have you accessed the entire document or only a selection from it? If it's a selection, which parts were excluded? Do you need more detail?

You probably won't have time to conduct a thorough background check on all your sources, so focus your efforts on the most important or most suspicious pieces of information.

Conducting Secondary Research Even if you intend to eventually conduct primary research, most projects start with a review of secondary research. Inside your company, you might be able to find a variety of reports, memos, and other documents that could help. Outside the company, business researchers can choose from a wide range of print and online resources. Table 11.3 provides a small sample of the many secondary resources available.[5]

> Before you conduct primary research, see if there is any secondary research you can take advantage of first.

Finding Information at the Library Public, corporate, and university libraries offer an enormous array of business books, electronic databases, newspapers, periodicals, directories, almanacs, and government publications. Some of these printed sources provide information that is not available online, and some of the online sources provide information that is available by subscription. Don't assume you can find everything you need through your own online research. Libraries are also where you'll find one of your most important resources: librarians. Reference librarians are trained in research techniques and can often help you find obscure information you can't find on your own. They can also direct you to many sources of business information:

> Even in the Internet age, libraries offer information and resources you can't find anywhere else—including experienced research librarians.

- **Newspapers and periodicals.** Libraries offer access to a wide variety of popular magazines, general business magazines, *trade journals* (which provide information about specific professions and industries), and *academic journals* (which provide research-oriented articles from researchers and educators). Check with a librarian to see which periodicals are available in print or electronic formats.

- **Business books.** Although less timely than newspapers and periodicals, business books provide in-depth coverage of a variety of business topics. Many libraries now offer online access to their card catalogs so you can see if they have specific titles in their collections.

- **Directories.** Thousands of directories are published in print and electronic formats in the United States, and many include membership information for all kinds of professions, industries, and special-interest groups.

- **Almanacs and statistical resources.** Almanacs are handy guides to factual and statistical information about countries, politics, the labor force, and so on. One of the most extensive, the *Statistical Abstract of the United States*, published annually by the U.S. Department of Commerce, contains statistics about occupations, government, population, health, business, crime, and the environment (also available online at www.census.gov).

- **Government publications.** Information on laws, court decisions, tax questions, regulatory issues, and other governmental concerns is often available in collections of government documents. A librarian can direct you to the information you want.

> Local, state, and federal government agencies publish a huge array of information that is helpful to business researchers.

- **Electronic databases.** Databases offer vast collections of computer-searchable information, often in specific areas, such as business, law, science, technology, and education. Some libraries offer remote online access to some or all databases; for others, you need to visit in person. The following section offers more information on using databases.

Table 11.3 — IMPORTANT RESOURCES FOR BUSINESS RESEARCH

COMPANY, INDUSTRY, AND PRODUCT RESOURCES (URLS ARE PROVIDED FOR ONLINE RESOURCES)

AnnualReports.com. www.reporstgallery.com. Free access to annual reports from thousands of public companies.

Brands and Their Companies/Companies and Their Brands. Contains data on over 400,000 consumer products and 10,000 manufacturers, importers, marketers, and distributors.

CNN/Money. http://money.cnn.com. News, analysis, and financial resources covering companies, industries, and world markets.

Corporate and Industry Research Reports (CIRR). Collection of industry reports produced by industry analysts for investment purposes. Unique coverage includes industry profitability, comparative company sales, market share, profits, and forecasts.

D&B Directories. A variety of directories, including *America's Corporate Families* (ownership connections among companies), *Business Rankings* (25,000 leading companies), *Directory of Service Companies* (over 50,000 companies in the service sector), and *Industrial Guide* (over 120,000 manufacturing companies).

Forbes. Annual Report on American Industry published in first January issue of each year.

Hoover's Handbook of American Business. Profiles of over 500 public and private corporations.

Hoover's Online. www.hoovers.com. Database of 12 million companies worldwide, including in-depth coverage of 35,000 leading companies around the world. Basic information available free; in-depth information requires subscription.

Manufacturing and Distribution USA. Data on thousands of companies in the manufacturing, wholesaling, and retailing sectors.

NAICS Codes. www.census.gov/naics. North American Industry Classification System.

SEC filing. www.sec.gov/edgar.shtml. SEC filings including 10Ks, 10Qs, annual reports, and prospectuses for 35,000 U.S. public firms.

Standard & Poor's Industry Surveys. Concise investment profiles for a broad range of industries. Coverage is extensive, with a focus on current situation and outlook. Includes some summary data on major companies in each industry.

Standard & Poor's Register of Corporations, Directors, and Executives. Index of major U.S. and international corporations. Lists officers, products, sales volume, and number of employees.

Thomas's Register of American Manufacturers. Information on thousands of U.S. manufacturers indexed by company name and product. Also available online at www.thomasnet.com.

U.S. Industrial Outlook. Annual profiles of several hundred key U.S. industries. Each industry report covers several pages and includes tables, graphs, and charts that visually demonstrate how an industry compares with similar industries, including important component growth factors and other economic measures. Currently being transferred online; www.export.gov for latest information.

RESEARCH DIRECTORIES AND INDEXES

Books in Print. Index of books in 62,000 subject categories currently available from U.S. publishers. Indexed by author and title. Professional online version indexes more than 5 million book, audio, and video titles.

Directories in Print. Information on over 15,000 business and industrial directories.

Encyclopedia of Associations. Index of thousands of associations listed by broad subject category, specific subject, association, and location.

Reader's Guide to Periodical Literature. Classic index of general-interest magazines, categorized by subject and author; also available in electronic format.

Ulrich's Periodicals Directory. Listings by title, publisher, editor, phone, and address of over 140,000 publications such as popular magazines, trade journals, government documents, and newspapers. Great for locating hard-to-find trade publications. Also available online by subscription.

PEOPLE
Dun & Bradstreet's Reference Book of Corporate Management. Professional histories of people serving as the principal officers and directors of more than 12,000 U.S. companies.

Who's Who in America. Biographies of living U.S. citizens who have gained prominence in their fields. Related book, *Who's Who in the World*, covers global achievers.

TRADEMARKS
Official Gazette of the United Patent and Trademark Office. Weekly publication (one for trademarks and one for patents) providing official record of newly assigned trademarks and patents, product descriptions, and product names. Also available online at www.uspto.gov.

United States Patent and Trademark Office. www.uspto.gov. Trademark and patent information records.

STATISTICS AND OTHER BUSINESS DATA
Bureau of Economic Analysis. www.bea.gov. Large collection of economic and government data.

Europa—The European Union Online. www.europa.eu.int. A portal that provides up-to-date coverage of current affairs, legislation, policies, and EU statistics.

FedStats. www.fedstats.gov. Access to full range of statistics and information from over 70 U.S. government agencies.

Industry Norms and Key Business Ratios (Dun & Bradstreet). Industry, financial, and performance ratios.

Information Please Almanac. Compilation of broad-range statistical data with strong focus on labor force.

Annual Statement Studies. Industry, financial, and performance ratios published by the Risk Management Association.

Statistical Abstract of the United States. Annual compendium of U.S. economic, social, political, and industrial statistics; also available online at www.census.gov.

STAT-USA. www.stat-usa.gov. Large collection of economic and government data.

The World Almanac and Book of Facts. Facts on economic, social, educational, and political events for major countries.

U.S. Bureau of Labor Statistics. www.bls.gov. Extensive national and regional information on labor and business, including employment, industry growth, productivity, Consumer Price Index (CPI), and overall U.S. economy.

U.S. Census Bureau. www.census.gov. Demographic data on both consumers and businesses based on census data.

COMMERICAL DATABASES (REQUIRE SUBSCRIPTIONS)
Dialog. Hundreds of databases that include areas such as business and finance, news and media, medicine, pharmaceuticals, reference, social sciences, government and regulation, science and technology, and more.

Ebsco. Access to a variety of databases on a wide range of disciplines from leading information providers.

Highbeam. Thousands of full-text newspaper, magazine, and newswire sources, plus maps and photographs.

Gale Business & Company Resource Center. A comprehensive research tool designed for undergraduate and graduate students, job searchers, and investors; offers a wide variety of information on companies and industries.

LexisNexis. Several thousand databases covering legal, corporate, government, and academic subjects.

ProQuest. Thousands of periodicals and newspapers; archives continue to expand through its program to digitize over 5 billion pages of microfilm.

SRDS Media Solutions. A comprehensive database of magazine information and advertising rates, cataloging more than 100,000 U.S. and international media properties.

Conduct online research with extreme care; much of the information online has not been subjected to the same quality controls common in traditional offline publishing.

Finding Information Online The Internet can be a tremendous source of business information, provided that you know where to look and how to use the tools available. **Search engines** identify individual webpages or files that either contain or are tagged with specific words or phrases. Search engines have the advantage of scanning millions or billions of individual webpages and using powerful ranking algorithms to present the pages that are probably the most relevant to your search request.

For all their ease and power, though, search engines have three disadvantages you should be aware of: (1) no human editors are involved to evaluate the quality of the content on these pages; (2) various engines use different search techniques, so one engine might miss a site that another one finds; and (3) search engines can't reach the content on restricted websites (such as the back issues of many professional journals). These out-of-reach pages are sometimes called the *hidden Internet* or the *deep web* because conventional search techniques can't access them. Webpages can be hidden from search engines for a variety of reasons, including password protection, links that some search engines can't follow (such as the links created with Adobe Flash animation software), pages that webmasters block from search engines, and *dynamic pages* that exist only when a visitor submits a query or request on a website. The hidden Internet is estimated to be at least several times larger than the visible Internet, and much of the material you might want to find for some reports could be unreachable through standard search engines.[6]

Web directories rely on human editors to evaluate and select websites.

The good news is that you can get around all three shortcomings of search engines, at least partly, although doing so is sometimes expensive. **Web directories** address the first major shortcoming of search engines by using human editors to categorize and evaluate websites. Directories such as those offered by Yahoo!, About.com, and the Open Directory Project at **www.dmoz.org**, present lists of websites chosen by a team of editors. And as Chapter 7 points out, a number of directories (and search engines) specialize in specific media types, such as Technorati's focus on blogs.

Specialized search capabilities such as Google Book can help you locate texts that might be of value in your research efforts.

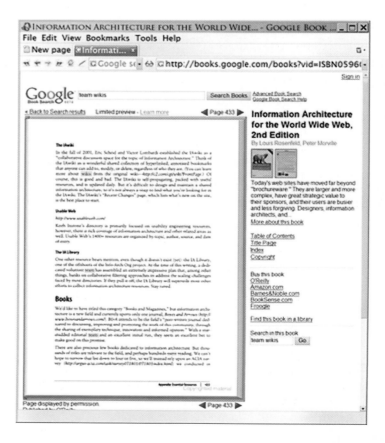

Metasearch engines, or *metacrawlers*, address the second shortcoming of search engines by formatting a search request for the specific requirements of multiple search engines. These versatile tools produce displays that tell you how many hits each engine was able to find for you. Table 11.4 lists some of the most popular search engines, metacrawlers, and directories.

Online databases help address the third shortcoming of search engines by offering access to newspapers, magazines, journals, and other resources. Some databases, such as High Beam (www.highbeam.com), are priced to attract individual users, whereas others, such as LexisNexis (www.lexisnexis.com/corporate) and ProQuest (www.proquest.com), are intended for use by companies, libraries, and other institutions. In addition to periodical databases, specialized databases such as Hoover's (www.hoovers.com) and OneSource's CorpTech (www.corptech.com) offer detailed information on thousands of companies. Also, you can obtain news releases at no charge from PRNewswire (www.prnewswire.com) and Business Wire (www.businesswire.com). Ask your librarian for advice on accessing all these resources.

As search engines, metacrawlers, and databases continue to multiply and offer new ways to find information, using them can become a challenge. Make sure you understand what each search tool expects from you before you enter your query. With a *keyword search*, the engine or database attempts to find items that include all the words you enter. A *Boolean search* lets you define a query with greater precision, using such operators as AND (the search must include the two terms linked by the AND), OR (the search can include either or both words), or NOT (the search ignores items with whatever word comes after NOT). In contrast to keyword and Boolean searches, *natural language searches* let you ask questions in everyday English. For example, "Which video game companies are the most profitable?" is a natural language query. *Forms-based searches* help you create powerful queries by simply filling out an online form that lets you specify such parameters as date ranges, language, Internet domain name, and file and media types.[7]

To make the best use of any search engine or database, keep the following points in mind:

- **Read the instructions.** Unfortunately, there is no universal set of instructions that apply to every search tool, so visit the Help page for advice on how to use a particular tool most effectively.

- **Pay attention to the details.** For instance, some search engines treat *AND* (uppercase) as a Boolean search operator but ignore *and* (lowercase) and conjunctions and articles (called *stopwords*) because they are so common they show up in every webpage or database entry. Again, read the Help page to learn more.

- **Review the search and display options carefully.** Make sure you review all the search options before submitting a search and review the display options when you view the results. For instance, some article databases search only the title unless you specifically ask them to search through the article text as well—a distinction that dramatically affects your results.

- **Try variations of your terms.** If you can't find what you're looking for, try abbreviations (*CEO, CPA*), synonyms (*man, male*), related terms (*child, adolescent, youth*), different spellings (*dialog, dialogue*), singular and plural forms (*woman, women*), nouns and adjectives (*management, managerial*), and open and compound forms (*online, on line, on-line*).

- **Adjust the scope of your search, if needed.** If a search yields little or no information, broaden your search by specifying fewer terms. Conversely, if you're inundated with too many hits, use more terms to narrow your search. For example, "Apple" yields many more hits than "Apple iPod," which yields many more than "Apple iPod nano."

Metacrawlers can save you time by employing multiple search engines at once.

Online databases give you access to the most important resource that search engines usually can't reach: millions of newspaper, magazine, and journal articles.

Make sure you know how each search engine, directory, database, or metacrawler works before you use it.

Table 11.4 — BEST OF INTERNET SEARCHING

Major Search Engines

A9	www.a9.com	Google	www.google.com
AOL Search	http://search.aol.com	Lycos	www.lycos.com
AllTheWeb	www.alltheweb.com	Windows Live	www.live.com
AltaVista	www.altavista.com	Yahoo! search	http://search.yahoo.com
Ask.com	www.ask.com		

Metacrawlers and Hybrid Sites

Clusty	http://clusty.com	Search.com	www.search.com
DogPile	www.dogpile.com	SurfWax	www.surfwax.com
IXQuick	www.ixquick.com	Wakweb	www.wakweb.com
Kartoo	www.kartoo.com	Web Brain	www.webbrain.com
LookSmart	www.looksmart.com	WebCrawler	www.webcrawler.com
Mamma	www.mamma.com	Yahoo!	www.yahoo.com
MetaCrawler	www.metacrawler.com	Zapmeta	www.zapmeta.com
Fazzle	www.fazzle.com	Zworks	www.zworks.com
Infonetware RealTerm Search	www.infonetware.com		

Web Directories and Online Libraries

About.com	www.about.com	Librarians' Index to the Internet	http://lii.org
Answers.com	www.answers.com		
Beaucoup	www.beaucoup.com	Library of Congress	www.loc.gov/rr/business
Digital Librarian	www.digital-librarian.com/business.html	Library Spot	www.libraryspot.com
		Open Directory	www.dmoz.com
Internet Public Library	www.ipl.org	Questia	www.questia.com

News Search Engines

AllTheWeb News	www.alltheweb.com/?cat=news	Newstrawler	www.newstrawler.com
AltaVista News	http://news.altavista.com	Topix	www.topix.net
Digg.com	www.digg.com	World News Network	www.wn.com
Google News	http://news.google.com	Yahoo! News	http://news.yahoo.com

Blog and Podcast Search Engines and Directories

Blinkx	www.blinkx.com	Podcast Bunker	www.podcastbunker.com
Blogdigger	www.blogdigger.com	Podcast Pickle	www.podcastpickle.com
Bloglines	www.bloglines.com	Podcast Network	www.thepodcastnetwork.com
BlogStreet	http://blogstreet.com	PodRazor	www.podrazor.com
Bloogz	www.bloogz.com	Podscope	www.podscope.com
Feedster	www.feedster.com	PodSpider	www.podspider.com
GetAPodcast	www.getapodcast.com	Podzinger	www.podzinger.com
Google video search	http://video.google.com	Technorati	www.technorati.com
Kinja	http://kinja.com	Yahoo! video search	http://video.search.yahoo.com
Podcast Alley	www.podcastalley.com	Waypath	www.waypath.com

Magazine and Periodical Search Engines

FindArticles.com	www.findarticles.com	Google Scholar	http://scholar.google.com
Full Free Text (scholarly articles)	www.freefulltext.com		

As you conduct research throughout your career, keep an eye out for the latest technologies that can help you research more effectively and more efficiently, including these four innovations:

- **Desktop and enterprise search engines.** Unlike conventional search engines, which look for content on the web, **desktop search engines** look for content on a particular computer. These tools are designed to identify and organize the many information and message fragments that most people have stored in various forms on their computers—e-mail messages, IM, PowerPoint presentations, audio and video clips, word processing files, and so on.[8] **Enterprise search engines** perform a similar task but across an entire network of computers.

- **Research and content managers.** A variety of tools known as *research managers*, or *content managers*, can be particularly helpful when your research involves numerous websites. These tools offer such features as letting you save and organize stored website links, providing permanent access to webpages you've visited even if the pages later change or disappear, and automatically generating parts of reports such as tables of contents and bibliographies.[9]

- **Social bookmarking sites.** The social bookmarking sites introduced in Chapter 7 can also assist with research. By highlighting websites, news articles, and other online items that other people find useful, bookmarking sites such as www.digg.com and http://del.icio.us can alert you to helpful resources and offer some indication of what online audiences are interested in at a particular moment in time. When using bookmarking sites for research, don't assume that

Take advantage of the latest research technologies, including desktop and enterprise searches, research and content managers, social bookmarking sites, and newsfeeds.

Desktop search engines are part of the new generation of software tools that can help businesspeople find vital information on company computers. In this example using Copernic Desktop Search (**www.copernic.com**), a user searching for "agreements" found 127 documents in a variety of formats.

all voters use the same terminology to identify things or that the rankings represent any particular segment of the population.[10]

- **Newsfeeds.** Newsfeeds, also discussed in Chapter 7, are an ideal way to stay up to date on fast-moving topics. For example, to stay on top of competitive moves in your industry, you can subscribe to newsfeeds from stock analysts who cover the industry, product user blogs, and blogs published by your competitors.

Proper documentation of the sources you use is both ethical and an important resource for your readers.

Documenting Your Sources   Documenting the secondary sources you use in your writing serves three important functions: It properly and ethically credits the person who created the original material, it shows your audience that you have credible support for your message, and it helps your readers explore your topic in more detail, if desired. Be sure to take advantage of the source documentation tools in your word processing or specialized note-management software, such as Microsoft's OneNote.[11]

You can document your sources through footnotes, endnotes, or some similar system (see Appendix B, "Documentation of Report Sources"). Whatever method you choose, documentation is necessary for such sources as books, articles, tables, charts, diagrams, song lyrics, scripted dialogue, letters, speeches—anything you take from someone else, including ideas and information that you've re-expressed through paraphrasing or summarizing. However, you do not have to cite a source for general knowledge or for specialized knowledge that's generally known among your readers, such as the fact that Nike is a large sporting goods and sportswear company or that computers are pervasive in business today.

Chapter 1 notes that copyright law covers the expression of creative ideas, and copyrights can cover a wide range of materials, including reports and other documents, web content, movies, musical compositions, lectures, computer programs, and even choreographed dance routines. Copyright protection is initiated the moment the expression is put into fixed form. Copyright law does not protect such elements as titles, names, short phrases, slogans, familiar symbols, or lists of ingredients or contents. It also doesn't protect ideas, procedures, methods, systems, processes, concepts, principles, discoveries, or devices, although it does cover their description, explanation, or illustration.[12] However, many of the entities not covered under copyright law are covered under other legal protections, such as patents for devices and processes and trademarks for slogans.

Merely crediting the source is not always enough. According to the *fair use doctrine*, you can use other people's work only as long as you don't unfairly prevent them from benefiting as a result. For example, if you reproduce someone else's copyrighted questionnaire in a report you're writing, even if you identify the source thoroughly, you may be preventing the author from selling a copy of that questionnaire to your readers.

Surveys and interviews are the most common primary research techniques.

Conducting Primary Research   If secondary research can't provide the information and insights you need, you may need to gather the information yourself with primary research. The two most common primary research methods are surveys and interviews. (Other primary techniques are observations and experiments in special situations such as test marketing, but they're not commonly used for day-to-day business research.)

Conducting Surveys   A carefully prepared and conducted survey can provide invaluable insights, but only if it is *reliable* (would produce identical results if repeated) and *valid* (measures what it's supposed to measure). To avoid errors in design and implementation, consider hiring a research specialist for important surveys.

For a survey to produce valid results, it must be based on a representative sample of respondents.

When selecting people to participate in a survey, the most critical task is getting a representative *sample* of the entire population in question. For instance, if you want to know how U.S. consumers feel about something, you can't just survey a few hundred people in a shopping mall. Different types of consumers shop at different times of the day and different days of the week, and many consumers do not shop at malls. The online surveys you see on many websites today potentially suffer from the same *sampling bias*: They capture only the opinions of people who visit the sites and want to participate, which might not be a representative sample of the population. A good handbook on survey research will help you select the right people for your survey, including selecting enough people to have a statistically valid survey.[13]

To develop an effective survey questionnaire, start with the information needs you identified at the beginning of the research process. Then break these points into specific questions, choosing an appropriate type of question for each point (see Figure 11.5). The following guidelines will help you produce results that are valid and reliable:[14]

- **Provide clear instructions.** Entry mistakes will distort your results.

- **Don't ask for information that people can't be expected to remember.** For instance, a question such as "How many times did you go grocery shopping last year?" will generate unreliable answers.

- **Keep the questionnaire short and easy to answer.** Don't expect people to give you more than 10 or 15 minutes of their time.

- **Whenever possible, formulate questions to provide answers that are easy to analyze.** Numbers and facts are easier to summarize than opinions, for instance.

- **Avoid leading questions that could bias your survey.** If you ask, "Do you prefer that we stay open in the evenings for customer convenience?" many people will say yes even if they don't shop in the evenings. Instead, ask, "What time of day do you normally do your shopping?"

- **Avoid ambiguous questions.** If you ask "Do you shop online often?" some people might interpret *often* to mean "every day," whereas others might think it means "once a week" or "once a month."

- **Ask only one thing at a time.** A compound question such as "Do you read books and magazines?" doesn't allow for the respondent who reads one but not the other.

The Internet has become the preferred survey mechanism for many researchers, and dozens of companies now offer online survey services.[15] Compared to traditional mail and in-person techniques, online surveys are usually faster to create, easier to administer, quicker to analyze, and less expensive overall. The interactive capabilities of the web can enhance all kinds of surveys, from simple opinion polls to complex purchase simulations. However, online surveys require the same care as any other type of survey, including being on guard against sampling bias.[16]

Conducting Interviews Getting in-depth information straight from an expert can be a great method for collecting primary information. Interviews can take a variety of formats, from e-mail exchanges to group discussions. For example, Tesco invites thousands of customers to visit its stores every year for meetings known as Customer Question Time, when it asks customers how the company can serve them better.[17]

Be aware that the answers you receive in an interview are influenced by the types of questions you ask, by the way you ask them, and by each subject's cultural and language background. Potentially significant factors include the person's race, gender, age, educational level, and social status.[18]

Ask **open-ended questions** to solicit opinions, insights, and information, such as "Why do you believe that South America represents a better opportunity than Europe for this product line?" Ask **closed questions** to elicit a specific answer, such as yes or

---

Marginal notes:

Provide clear instructions to prevent mistaken answers.

Interviews are easy to conduct but require careful planning to produce useful results.

Choose question types that will generate the specific information you need.

QUESTION TYPE	EXAMPLE
Open-ended	How would you describe the flavor of this ice cream?
Either-or	Do you think this ice cream is too rich? _____ Yes _____ No
Multiple choice	Which description best fits the taste of this ice cream? (Choose only one.) a. Delicious b. Too fruity c. Too sweet d. Too intensely flavored e. Bland f. Stale
Scale	Please mark an *X* on the scale to indicate how you perceive the texture of this ice cream. Too light Light Creamy Too creamy
Checklist	Which of the following ice cream brands do you recognize? (Check all that apply.) _____ Ben & Jerry's _____ Breyers _____ Carvel _____ Dreyer's _____ Häagen-Dazs
Ranking	Rank these flavors in order of your preference, from 1 (most preferred) to 5 (least preferred): _____ Vanilla _____ Cherry _____ Strawberry _____ Chocolate _____ Coconut
Short-answer	In the past 2 weeks, how many times did you buy ice cream in a grocery store? _____ In the past 2 weeks, how many times did you buy ice cream in an ice cream shop? _____

FIGURE 11.5

Types of Survey Questions

For each question you have in your survey, choose the type of question that will elicit the most useful answers.

no. However, don't use too many closed questions in an interview, or the experience will feel more like a simple survey and won't take full advantage of the interactive interview setting.

Think carefully about the sequence of your questions and the subject's potential answers so you can arrange questions in an order that helps uncover layers of information. Also consider providing the other person with a list of questions at least a day or two before the interview, especially if you'd like to quote your subject in writing or if your questions might require your subject to conduct research or think extensively about the answers. If you want to record the interview, ask the person ahead of time and respect his or her wishes.

As soon as possible after the interview, take a few moments to write down your thoughts, go over your notes, and organize your material. Look for important themes, helpful facts or statistics, and direct quotes. If you made a tape recording, *transcribe* it (take down word for word what the person said) or take notes from the tape just as you would while listening to someone in person.

Face-to-face interviews give you the opportunity to gauge the reaction to your questions and observe the nonverbal signals that accompany the answers, but interviews don't necessarily have to take place in person. E-mail interviews are becoming more common, partly because they give subjects a chance to think through their responses thoroughly rather than rushing to fit the time constraints of a face-to-face interview.[19] Also, e-mail interviews might be the only way you will be able to access some experts.

Face-to-face interviews give you the opportunity to gauge nonverbal responses.

In addition to individual interviews, business researchers can also use a form of group interview known as the **focus group**. In this format, a moderator guides a group through a series of discussion questions while the rest of the research team observes through a one-way mirror. The key advantage of focus groups is the opportunity to learn from group dynamics as the various participants bounce ideas and questions off each other. By allowing a group to discuss topics and problems in this manner, the focus group technique can uncover much richer information than a series of individual interviews.[20]

Document Makeover

IMPROVE THIS REPORT

To practice correcting drafts of actual documents, visit your online course or the access-code-protected portion of the Companion Website. Click on "Document Makeovers" and then click on Chapter 11. You will find an informational report that contains problems and errors related to what you've learned in this chapter about planning business reports and proposals. Use the "Final Draft" decision tool to create an improved version of this personal activity report. Check the report for parallel construction, appropriate headings, suitable content, positive and bias-free language, and use of the "you" attitude.

As a reminder of the tasks involved in interviews, see "Checklist: Conducting Effective Information Interviews."

Using Your Research Results

After you've collected all the necessary secondary and primary information, the next step is to transform it into the specific content you need. For simple projects, you may be able to drop your material directly into your report, presentation, or other application. However, when you have gathered a significant amount of information or raw data from surveys, you need to process the material before you can use it. This step can involve analyzing numeric data; quoting, paraphrasing, or summarizing textual material; drawing conclusions; and making recommendations.

After you collect your data, the next step is to convert it into usable information.

✓ CHECKLIST: Conducting Effective Information Interviews

- ✓ Learn about the person you are going to interview.
- ✓ Formulate your main idea to ensure effective focus.
- ✓ Choose the length, style, and organization of the interview.
- ✓ Select question types to elicit the specific information you want.
- ✓ Design each question carefully to collect useful answers.
- ✓ Limit the number of questions you ask.
- ✓ Consider recording the interview if the subject permits.
- ✓ Review your notes as soon as the interview ends.

Mean, median, and mode provide insight into sets of data.

Analyzing Data Business research often produces numeric data, but by themselves, these numbers might not provide the insights managers need in order to make good business decisions. Fortunately, even without advanced statistical techniques, you can use simple arithmetic to help extract meaning from sets of research data. Table 11.5 shows several answers you can gain about a collection of numbers, for instance. The **mean** (which is what most people refer to when they use the term *average*) is the sum of all the items in the group divided by the number of items in that group. The **median** is the "middle of the road," or the midpoint of a series, with an equal number of items above and below. The **mode** is the number that occurs more often than any other in the sample; it's the best answer to a question such as "What is the usual amount?" Each of the three measures can tell you different things about a set of data.

Trends suggest directions or patterns in a series of data points.

It's also helpful to look for **trends**, any repeatable patterns taking place over time, including growth, decline, and cyclical trends that vary between growth and decline. Trend analysis is common in business. By looking at data over a period of time, you can detect patterns and relationships that help you answer important questions. In addition, researchers frequently explore the relationships between subsets of data, using a technique called **cross-tabulation**. For instance, if you're trying to figure out why total sales rose or fell, you might look separately at sales data by age, gender, location, and product type.

Whenever you process numeric data, keep in mind that numbers are easy to manipulate and misinterpret, particularly with spreadsheets and other computer tools. Make sure to double-check all your calculations and document the operation of any spreadsheets you plan to share with colleagues. Also, step back and look at your entire set of data before proceeding with any analysis. Do the numbers make sense based on what you know about the subject? Are there any individual data points that stand out as suspect? Business audiences like the clarity of numbers; it's your responsibility to deliver numbers they can count on.

Quoting a source means reproducing the content exactly and indicating who originally created the information.

Quoting, Paraphrasing, and Summarizing Information You can use textual information from sources in three ways. *Quoting* a source means you reproduce it exactly as you found it, and you either set it off with quotation marks (for shorter passages) or extract it in an indented paragraph (for longer passages). Use direct quotations when the original language will enhance your argument or when rewording the passage would lessen its impact. However, try not to quote sources at great

Table 11.5	THREE TYPES OF DATA MEASURES: MEAN, MEDIAN, AND MODE	
Salesperson	**Sales**	
Wilson	$ 3,000	
Green	5,000	
Carrick	6,000	
Wimper	7,000	Mean
Keeble	7,500	Median
Kemble	8,500	
O'Toole	8,500	Mode
Mannix	8,500	
Caruso	9,000	
Total	$63,000	

length. Too much quoting creates a choppy patchwork of varying styles and gives the impression that all you've done is piece together the work of other people.

You can often maximize the impact of secondary material in your own writing by *paraphrasing* it, restating it in your own words and with your own sentence structures.[21] Paraphrasing helps you maintain a consistent tone while using vocabulary familiar to your audience. Of course, you still need to credit the originator of the information, but not with quotation marks or indented paragraphs.

To paraphrase effectively, follow these tips:[22]

Paraphrasing is expressing someone else's ideas in your own words.

- Reread the original passage until you fully understand its meaning.

- Record your paraphrase on a note card or in an electronic format.

- Use language that your audience is familiar with.

- Check your version with the original source to verify that you have not altered the meaning.

- Use quotation marks to identify any unique terms or phrases you have borrowed exactly from the source.

- Record the source so that you can give proper credit if you use this material in your report.

Summarizing is similar to paraphrasing but presents the gist of the material in fewer words than the original. An effective summary identifies the main ideas and major support points from your source material but leaves out most details, examples, and other information that is less critical to your audience. Like quotations and paraphrases, summaries also require complete documentation of your sources. Summarizing is not always a simple task, and your audience will judge your ability to separate significant issues from less significant details. Identify the main idea and the key support points, and separate these from details, examples, and other supporting evidence (see Table 11.6).

Summarizing is similar to paraphrasing but distills the content into fewer words.

Of course, all three approaches require careful attention to ethics. When quoting directly, take care not to distort the original intent of the material by quoting selectively or out of context. And never resort to plagiarism.

Table 11.6   SUMMARIZING EFFECTIVELY

Original Material (110 Words)	45-Word Summary	22-Word Summary
Our facilities costs spiraled out of control last year. The 23% jump was far ahead of every other cost category in the company and many times higher than the 4% average rise for commercial real estate in the Portland metropolitan area. The rise can be attributed to many factors, but the major factors include repairs (mostly electrical and structural problems at the downtown office), energy (most of our offices are heated by electricity, the price of which has been increasing much faster than for oil or gas), and last but not least, the loss of two sublease tenants whose rent payments made a substantial dent in our cost profile for the past five years.	**Our facilities costs jumped 23% last year,** far ahead of every other cost category in the company and many times higher than the 4% local average. The major factors contributing to the increase are repairs, energy, and the loss of two sublease tenants.	**Our facilities costs jumped 23% last year,** due mainly to rising repair and energy costs and the loss of sublease income.

Main idea
Major support points
Details

Drawing Conclusions A **conclusion** is a logical interpretation of the facts and other information in a report. A sound conclusion is not only logical but flows from the information included in a report, meaning that it should be based on the information included in the report and shouldn't rely on information that isn't in the report. Moreover, if you or the organization you represent have certain biases that influence your conclusion, ethics obligate you to inform the audience accordingly.

Reaching good conclusions based on the evidence at hand is one of the most important skills you can develop in your business career. In fact, the ability to see patterns and possibilities that others can't see is one of the hallmarks of innovative business leaders. Consequently, take your time with this part of the process. Play "devil's advocate" against yourself, attacking your conclusion as an audience might to make sure it stands up to rigorous scrutiny.

Making Recommendations Whereas a conclusion interprets information, a **recommendation** suggests action—what to do in response to the information. The following example illustrates the difference between a conclusion and a recommendation:

Conclusion	Recommendation
On the basis of its track record and current price, I conclude that this company is an attractive buy.	I recommend that we write a letter to the board of directors offering to buy the company at a 10 percent premium over the current market value of its stock.

To be credible, recommendations must be based on logical analysis and sound conclusions. They must also be practical and acceptable to the people who have to make your recommendations work. Finally, when making a recommendation, be certain that you have adequately described the steps needed to implement your recommendation.

PLANNING INFORMATIONAL REPORTS

Informational reports are used to monitor and control operations, to implement policies and procedures, to demonstrate compliance, and to document progress.

Informational reports provide the material that employees, managers, and others need in order to make decisions, take action, and respond to dynamic conditions inside and outside the organization. Although these reports come in dozens of particular formats, they can be grouped into four general categories:

- **Reports to monitor and control operations.** Managers rely on a wide range of reports to see how well their companies are functioning. *Plans* establish expectations and guidelines to direct future action. The most important of these are *business plans* (see "Sharpening Your Career Skills: Creating an Effective Business Plan"). Many business plans are actually a combination of an informational report (describing conditions in the marketplace), an analytical report (analyzing threats and opportunities and recommending specific courses of action), and a proposal (persuading investors to put money into the firm in exchange for a share of ownership). *Operating reports* provide feedback on a wide variety of an organization's functions, including sales, inventories, expenses, shipments, and so on. *Personal activity reports* provide information regarding an individual's experiences during sales calls, industry conferences, market research trips, and so on.

- **Reports to implement policies and procedures.** Reports are the most common vehicle for conveying guidelines, approved procedures, and other organizational decisions. *Policy reports* range from brief descriptions of business procedures to manuals that are dozens or hundreds of pages long. *Position papers* outline an organization's official position on issues that affect the company's success.

- **Reports to demonstrate compliance.** Businesses are required to submit a variety of *compliance reports*, from tax returns to reports that describe the proper handling of hazardous materials.

- **Reports to document progress.** Supervisors, investors, and customers frequently expect to be informed of the status of projects and other activities via *progress reports*.

Figure 11.6 shows the major subcategories within each of the three major report categories, along with examples of the more common types.

SHARPENING YOUR CAREER SKILLS

Creating an Effective Business Plan

The most important report you may ever get the chance to write is a business plan for a new company. A comprehensive business plan forces you to think about personnel, marketing, facilities, suppliers, distribution, and a host of other issues that are vital to your success. If you are starting out on a small scale and using your own money, your business plan may be relatively informal. But at a minimum, you should describe the basic concept of the business and outline its specific goals, objectives, and resource requirements. A formal plan, suitable for use with banks or investors, should cover these points:

- *Summary.* In one or two pages, summarize your business concept. Describe your product or service and its market potential. Highlight some things about your company and its owners that will distinguish your firm from the competition. Summarize your financial projections and the amount of money investors can expect to make on their investment. Be sure to indicate how much money you will need and what it will be spent on.

- *Mission and objectives.* Explain the purpose of your business and what you hope to accomplish—and before you take another step, make sure that this is a mission you can pursue with passion, through thick and thin, with every ounce of commitment and energy you can muster.

- *Company and industry.* Give full background information on the origins and structure of your venture and the characteristics of its industry.

- *Products or services.* Give a complete but concise description of your products or services, focusing on their unique attributes. Explain how customers will benefit from using your products or services instead of those of your competitors.

- *Market and competition.* Provide data that will persuade investors that you understand your target market and can achieve your sales goals. Be sure to identify the strengths and weaknesses of your competitors.

- *Management.* Summarize the background and qualifications of the key management personnel in your company. Include résumés in an appendix.

- *Marketing strategy.* Provide projections of sales and market share and outline a strategy for identifying and contacting customers, setting prices, providing customer services, advertising, and so forth. Whenever possible, include evidence of customer acceptance, such as advance product orders.

- *Design and development plans.* If your product requires design or development, describe the nature and extent of what needs to be done, including costs and possible problems.

- *Operations plan.* Provide information on the facilities, equipment, and labor needed.

- *Overall schedule.* Forecast development of the company in terms of completion dates for major aspects of the business plan.

- *Critical risks and problems.* Identify all negative factors and discuss them honestly.

- *Financial projections and requirements.* Include a detailed budget of start-up and operating costs, as well as projections for income, expenses, and cash flow for the first three years of business. Identify the company's financing needs and potential sources.

- *Exit strategy.* Explain how investors will be able to cash out or sell their investment, such as through a public stock offering, sale of the company, or a buyback of the investors' interest.

A complete business plan obviously requires a considerable amount of work. However, by thinking your way through all these issues, you'll enjoy a smoother launch and a greater chance of success in your new adventure.

CAREER APPLICATIONS

1. Why is it important to identify critical risks and problems in a business plan?

2. Many experts suggest that you write a business plan yourself rather than hire a consultant to write it for you. Why is this a good idea?

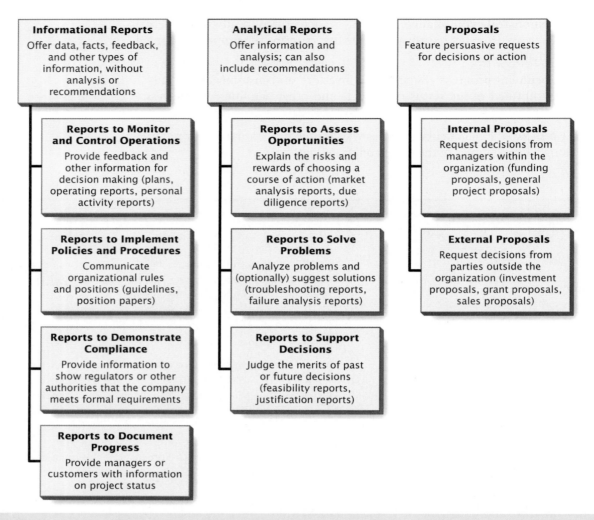

FIGURE 11.6
Common Types of Business Reports and Proposals
You will have the opportunity to read and write many types of reports in your career; here are some of the most common.

Organizing Informational Reports

Informational reports usually use a topical organization.

In most cases, the direct approach is the best choice for informational reports. However, if the information is both surprising and disappointing, such as a project that is behind schedule or over budget, you might consider using the indirect approach to build up to the bad news. Most informational reports use a **topical organization**, arranging material in one of the following ways:

- **Comparison.** If you need to show similarities and differences (or advantages and disadvantages) between two or more entities, organize your report in a way that helps your readers see those similarities and differences clearly.

- **Importance.** Build up from the least important item to most important, or start with the most important item and progress to the least important if you suspect readers are interested in only the most important items.

- **Sequence.** Describe processes or procedures by following the individual steps or stages in order.

- **Chronology.** Describe a development or an event by the order in which things occurred.

- **Spatial orientation.** Describe physical objects or spaces from left to right (or right to left, in some cultures), top to bottom, or outside to inside—in whatever order makes the most sense.

- **Geography.** If location is important, organize your study according to geography, perhaps by region of the world or by area of a city.

- **Category.** If you're asked to review several distinct aspects of a subject, look at one category at a time, such as sales, profit, cost, or investment.

Whichever pattern you choose, use it consistently so that readers can easily follow your discussion from start to finish. Bear in mind, however, that in many instances, you might be expected to follow a particular organization.

Of course, effective informational reports must also be audience centered, logical, focused, and easy to follow, with generous use of previews and summaries. Your audience expects you to sort out the details and separate major points from minor points. In addition, effective reports are honest and objective (compare Figures 11.7 and 11.8).

Organizing Website Content

Many websites, particularly company websites, function as informational reports, offering sections with information about the company, its history, its products and services, its executive team, and so on. While most of what you've already learned about informational reports applies to website writing, the online experience requires some special considerations and practices.

As you begin to plan a website, start by recognizing the unique nature of online communication:

- **Web readers are demanding.** Most site visitors won't bother to dig through poorly organized information. They quickly scan navigation buttons, headings, images, and hyperlinks, looking for possibilities. If nothing looks promising, they're gone.[23]

- **Reading online can be difficult.** Studies show that reading speeds are about 25 percent slower on a monitor than on paper.[24] Reading from computer screens can also be tiring on the eyes, even to the point of causing headaches, double vision, blurred vision, and other physical problems.[25]

- **The web is a nonlinear, multidimensional medium.** Readers of online material move around in any order they please; there often is no beginning, middle, or end. As a web writer, you need to anticipate the various paths your readers will want to follow and to make sure you provide the right hyperlinks in the right places to help readers explore successfully.

Further compounding a web writer's challenge is the fact that many websites have to perform more than one communication function and therefore have more than one purpose. Each of these individual purposes needs to be carefully defined and then integrated into an overall statement of purpose for the entire website. Then, as you develop the site, you need to clearly identify the specific purpose of each section so that readers always know where to find the information they need.[26]

Just as you probably have a number of purposes for a single website, you're likely to have a number of audiences as well. The global reach of the web further complicates the audience analysis issue because you may get visitors from all parts of the world. After you've identified your multiple audiences, you then need to analyze each group's unique information needs and then find a logical way to organize all that

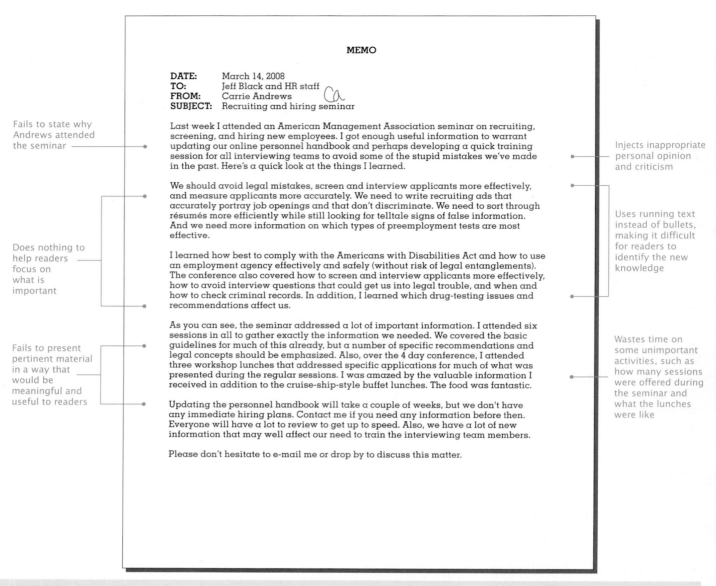

Fails to state why Andrews attended the seminar

Does nothing to help readers focus on what is important

Fails to present pertinent material in a way that would be meaningful and useful to readers

Injects inappropriate personal opinion and criticism

Uses running text instead of bullets, making it difficult for readers to identify the new knowledge

Wastes time on some unimportant activities, such as how many sessions were offered during the seminar and what the lunches were like

MEMO

DATE: March 14, 2008
TO: Jeff Black and HR staff
FROM: Carrie Andrews
SUBJECT: Recruiting and hiring seminar

Last week I attended an American Management Association seminar on recruiting, screening, and hiring new employees. I got enough useful information to warrant updating our online personnel handbook and perhaps developing a quick training session for all interviewing teams to avoid some of the stupid mistakes we've made in the past. Here's a quick look at the things I learned.

We should avoid legal mistakes, screen and interview applicants more effectively, and measure applicants more accurately. We need to write recruiting ads that accurately portray job openings and that don't discriminate. We need to sort through résumés more efficiently while still looking for telltale signs of false information. And we need more information on which types of preemployment tests are most effective.

I learned how best to comply with the Americans with Disabilities Act and how to use an employment agency effectively and safely (without risk of legal entanglements). The conference also covered how to screen and interview applicants more effectively, how to avoid interview questions that could get us into legal trouble, and when and how to check criminal records. In addition, I learned which drug-testing issues and recommendations affect us.

As you can see, the seminar addressed a lot of important information. I attended six sessions in all to gather exactly the information we needed. We covered the basic guidelines for much of this already, but a number of specific recommendations and legal concepts should be emphasized. Also, over the 4 day conference, I attended three workshop lunches that addressed specific applications for much of what was presented during the regular sessions. I was amazed by the valuable information I received in addition to the cruise-ship-style buffet lunches. The food was fantastic.

Updating the personnel handbook will take a couple of weeks, but we don't have any immediate hiring plans. Contact me if you need any information before then. Everyone will have a lot to review to get up to speed. Also, we have a lot of new information that may well affect our need to train the interviewing team members.

Please don't hesitate to e-mail me or drop by to discuss this matter.

FIGURE 11.7
Ineffective Informational Report
While this report looks professional at first glance, it contains weaknesses in tone, content, and formatting. Compare it with the version in Figure 11.8.

material. Professional website designers often use the term **information architecture** to describe the structure and navigational flow of all the parts of a website. In a sense, the information architecture is a three-dimensional outline of the site, showing (1) the vertical hierarchy of pages from the homepage down to the lower level, (2) the horizontal division of pages across the various sections of the site, and (3) the links that tie all these pages together, both internally (between various pages on the site) and externally (between your site and other websites).

As you develop the site architecture, you can begin to simulate how various audiences will use the site and refine the plan to meet everyone's needs (see Figure 11.9). For instance, can potential customers find new product information quickly? In contrast, can existing customers get support or warranty information quickly, without wading through pages of promotion for new products? You can also get a sense of how you need to assist visitors who enter the site at points other than the homepage,

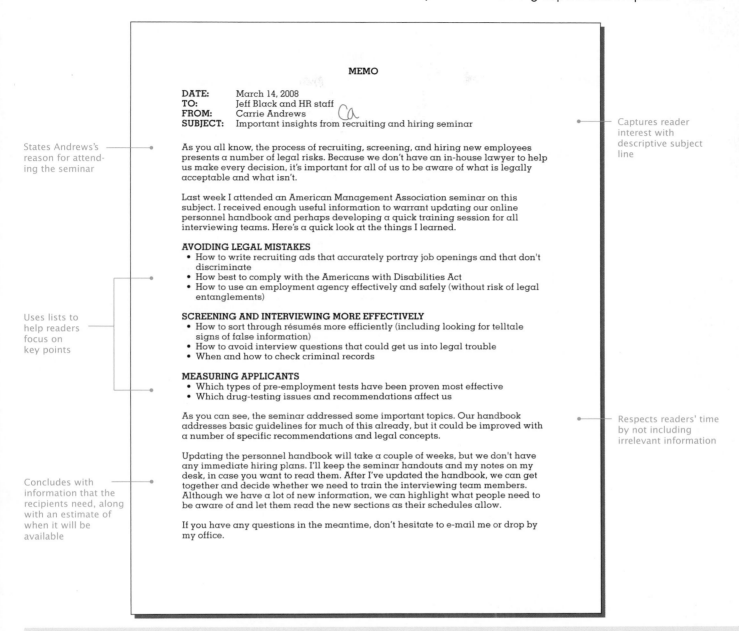

States Andrews's reason for attending the seminar

Uses lists to help readers focus on key points

Concludes with information that the recipients need, along with an estimate of when it will be available

Captures reader interest with descriptive subject line

Respects readers' time by not including irrelevant information

FIGURE 11.8
Effective Informational Report
This version of the report is much easier to read than the version in Figure 11.7 and presents pertinent information in a clear, concise way.

as often happens with search engine links. Accommodating these multiple entry points is one of the most difficult tasks in site design.[27]

To organize your site effectively, keep the following advice in mind:

- **Plan your navigation first.** Don't make the mistake of writing a traditional printed report and then adding links to make it a website. Chances are, you'll need a different structure for the information, so plan your site structure and navigation before you write.[28]

- **Let your readers be in control.** Most readers want to navigate using paths they establish themselves, so create links and pathways that let them explore on their

FIGURE 11.9

Information Architecture
Anyone searching online for the "Green Goodness" brand of nutritional drink would likely land on this specific product page on the Bolthouse Farms website rather than on the company's homepage. However, thanks to careful consideration of information architecture, virtually every site visitor can quickly link to the information in which he or she might be interested.

own. Help your readers by starting with a homepage that clearly points the way to various sections of the site and then offer plenty of descriptive labels, subheads, and previews that let readers figure out where to go next.

- **Break your information into chunks.** Help online readers scan and absorb information by breaking it into self-contained, easily readable chunks that are linked together logically.

PLANNING ANALYTICAL REPORTS

Analytical reports are used to assess opportunities, solve problems, and support decisions.

The purpose of analytical reports is to analyze, to understand, to explain—to think through a problem or an opportunity and figure out how it affects the company and how the company should respond. In many cases, you'll also be expected to make a recommendation based on your analysis. As you saw in Figure 11.6, analytical reports fall into three basic categories:

- **Reports to assess opportunities.** Every business opportunity carries some degree of risk and also requires a variety of decisions and actions in order to capitalize on the opportunity. You can use analytical reports to assess risk and required decisions and actions. For instance, *market analysis reports* are used to judge the likelihood of success for new products or sales. *Due diligence reports* examine the financial aspects of a proposed decision, such as acquiring another company.

- **Reports to solve problems.** Managers often ask for *troubleshooting reports* when they need to understand why something isn't working properly and what needs to be done to fix it. A variation, the *failure analysis report*, studies events that happened in the past, with the hope of learning how to avoid similar failures in the future.

- **Reports to support decisions.** *Feasibility reports* are called for when managers need to explore the ramifications of a decision they're about to make, such as switching materials used in a manufacturing process. *Justification reports* explain a decision that has already been made.

Writing analytical reports presents a greater challenge than writing informational reports because you need to use your reasoning abilities and persuasive skills in addition to your writing skills. With analytical reports, you're doing more than simply delivering information: You're also thinking through a problem or an opportunity and presenting your conclusions. The best writing in the world can't compensate for shaky analysis. When your analysis is complete, you need to present your thinking in a compelling and persuasive manner. Finally, because analytical reports often convince other people to make significant financial and personnel decisions, your reports carry the added responsibility of the consequences of these decisions.

To help define the problem that your analytical report will address, answer these questions:

- What needs to be determined?
- Why is this issue important?
- Who is involved in the situation?
- Where is the trouble located?
- How did the situation originate?
- When did it start?

Clarify the problem in an analytical report by determining what you need to analyze, why the issue is important, who is involved, where the trouble is located, and how and when the problem started.

Not all these questions apply in every situation, but asking them helps you define the problem being addressed and limit the scope of your discussion.

Also try **problem factoring**, dividing the problem into a series of logical, connected questions that try to identify cause and effect. When you speculate on the cause of a problem, you're forming a **hypothesis**, a potential explanation that needs to be tested. By subdividing a problem and forming hypotheses based on available evidence, you can tackle even the most complex situations.

Use problem factoring to divide a complex problem into more manageable pieces.

As with all other business messages, the best organizational structure for each analytical report depends largely on your audience's likely reaction. The three basic structures involve focusing on conclusions, focusing on recommendations, and focusing on logic (see Table 11.7).

Before you choose an approach, determine whether your audience is receptive or skeptical.

	Table 11.7	COMMON WAYS TO STRUCTURE ANALYTICAL REPORTS	

| Element | Focus on Conclusions or Recommendations | Focus on Logical Argument | |
		Use 2 + 2 = 4 Model	Use Yardstick Model
Readers	Are likely to accept	Hostile or skeptical	Hostile or skeptical
Approach	Direct	Indirect	Indirect
Writer credibility	High	Low	Low
Advantages	Readers quickly grasp conclusions or recommendations	Works well when you need to show readers how you built toward an answer by following clear logical steps	Works well when you have a list of criteria (standards) that must be considered in a decision; alternatives are all measured against same criteria
Drawbacks	Structure can make topic seem too simple	Can make report longer	Readers must agree on criteria; can be lengthy because of the need to address all criteria for every alternative

Focusing on Conclusions

Focusing on conclusions is often the best approach when you're addressing a receptive audience.

When writing for audiences that are likely to accept your conclusions—either because they've asked you to perform an analysis or they trust your judgment—consider using a direct approach that focuses immediately on your conclusions. This structure communicates the main idea quickly, but it presents some risks. Even if audiences trust your judgment, they may have questions about your data or the methods you used. Moreover, starting with a conclusion may create the impression that you have oversimplified the situation. You're generally better off taking the direct approach in a report only when your credibility is high—when your readers trust you and are willing to accept your conclusions (see Figure 11.10).

Focusing on Recommendations

When readers want to know what you think they should do, organize your report to focus on recommendations.

A slightly different approach is useful when your readers want to know what they ought to do in a given situation (as opposed to what they ought to conclude). You'll often be asked to solve a problem or assess an opportunity rather than just study it. The actions you want your readers to take become the main subdivisions of your report.

When structuring a report around recommendations, use the direct approach as you would for a report that focuses on conclusions. Then unfold your recommendations using a series of five steps:

1. Establish the need for action in the introduction by briefly describing the problem or opportunity.

2. Introduce the benefit(s) that can be achieved if the recommendation is adopted, along with any potential risks.

3. List the steps (recommendations) required to achieve the benefit, using action verbs for emphasis.

4. Explain each step more fully, giving details on procedures, costs, and benefits; if necessary, also explain how risks can be minimized.

5. Summarize your recommendations.

Opens with the conclusion that the program is a success

Supports the conclusion with evidence from two key areas

Completes the story by highlighting areas that still need improvement

MEASURING QUALITY IMPROVEMENTS

I.   Introduction

II. Conclusion: Outsourcing employee training has reduced costs and improved quality

III. Cost reductions

   A. Exceeded 15 percent cost-reduction goal with 22 percent savings in first year

   B. Achieved actual reduction of 22 percent

   C. Reassigned three staffers who used to work on training full-time

   D. Reduced management time needed to oversee training

   E. Sold the computers that used to be reserved for training

IV. Quality improvements

   A. Employees say they are more confident in 7 out of 10 key skill areas

   B. Measurable mistakes have dropped by 12 percent

V.   Areas needing improvement

   A. Three skill areas still need improvement

   B. Two trainers received approval ratings below 80 percent

   C. Outside trainers aren't always aware of internal company issues

   D. We have lost some flexibility for scheduling courses

VI. Summary

FIGURE 11.10
Preliminary Outline of a Research Report Focusing on Conclusions
Cynthia Zolonka works on the human resources staff of a bank in Houston, Texas. Her company decided to have an outside firm handle its employee training, and a year after the outsourcing arrangement was established, Zolonka was asked to evaluate the results. Her analysis shows that the outsourcing experiment was a success; she opens with that conclusion and supports it with clear evidence. Readers who accept the conclusion can stop reading, and those who desire more information can continue.

Focusing on Logical Arguments

When readers are skeptical or hostile to the conclusion or recommendation you plan to make, use an indirect approach that logically builds toward your conclusion or recommendation. If you guide the audience along a rational path toward the answer, they are more likely to accept it when they encounter it. The two most common logical approaches are known as the *2 + 2 = 4 approach* and the *yardstick approach*.

Logical arguments can follow two basic approaches: 2 + 2 = 4 (adding everything up) and the yardstick method (comparing ideas against a predetermined set of standards).

The 2 + 2 = 4 Approach   The **2 + 2 = 4 approach** is so named because it convinces readers of your point of view by demonstrating that everything adds up. The main points in your outline are the main reasons behind your conclusions and recommendations. You support each reason with the evidence you collected during your analysis. With its natural feel and versatility, the 2 + 2 = 4 approach is generally the most persuasive and efficient way to develop an analytical report for skeptical readers, so try this structure first. You'll find that most of your arguments fall naturally into this pattern.

Try using the 2 + 2 = 4 approach; it's familiar and easy to develop.

As national sales manager of a New Hampshire sporting goods company, Binh Phan was concerned about his company's ability to sell to its largest customers. His boss, the vice president of marketing, shared these concerns and asked Phan to analyze the situation and recommend a solution. As Phan says, "We sell sporting goods to retail chains across the country. Large nationwide chains such as Sports Authority have been revolutionizing the industry, but we haven't had as much success with these big customers as we've had with smaller companies that operate strictly on a local or regional basis. With more and more of the industry in the hands of the large chains, we knew we had to fix the situation."

Phan's troubleshooting report appears in Figure 11.11. The main idea is that the company should establish separate sales teams for these major accounts rather

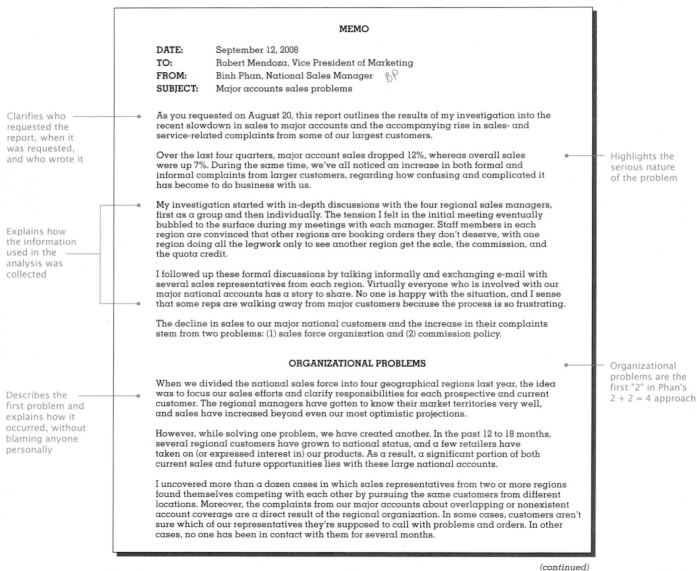

MEMO

DATE:	September 12, 2008
TO:	Robert Mendoza, Vice President of Marketing
FROM:	Binh Phan, National Sales Manager *BP*
SUBJECT:	Major accounts sales problems

Clarifies who requested the report, when it was requested, and who wrote it

As you requested on August 20, this report outlines the results of my investigation into the recent slowdown in sales to major accounts and the accompanying rise in sales- and service-related complaints from some of our largest customers.

Highlights the serious nature of the problem

Over the last four quarters, major account sales dropped 12%, whereas overall sales were up 7%. During the same time, we've all noticed an increase in both formal and informal complaints from larger customers, regarding how confusing and complicated it has become to do business with us.

Explains how the information used in the analysis was collected

My investigation started with in-depth discussions with the four regional sales managers, first as a group and then individually. The tension I felt in the initial meeting eventually bubbled to the surface during my meetings with each manager. Staff members in each region are convinced that other regions are booking orders they don't deserve, with one region doing all the legwork only to see another region get the sale, the commission, and the quota credit.

I followed up these formal discussions by talking informally and exchanging e-mail with several sales representatives from each region. Virtually everyone who is involved with our major national accounts has a story to share. No one is happy with the situation, and I sense that some reps are walking away from major customers because the process is so frustrating.

The decline in sales to our major national customers and the increase in their complaints stem from two problems: (1) sales force organization and (2) commission policy.

ORGANIZATIONAL PROBLEMS

Organizational problems are the first "2" in Phan's 2 + 2 = 4 approach

Describes the first problem and explains how it occurred, without blaming anyone personally

When we divided the national sales force into four geographical regions last year, the idea was to focus our sales efforts and clarify responsibilities for each prospective and current customer. The regional managers have gotten to know their market territories very well, and sales have increased beyond even our most optimistic projections.

However, while solving one problem, we have created another. In the past 12 to 18 months, several regional customers have grown to national status, and a few retailers have taken on (or expressed interest in) our products. As a result, a significant portion of both current sales and future opportunities lies with these large national accounts.

I uncovered more than a dozen cases in which sales representatives from two or more regions found themselves competing with each other by pursuing the same customers from different locations. Moreover, the complaints from our major accounts about overlapping or nonexistent account coverage are a direct result of the regional organization. In some cases, customers aren't sure which of our representatives they're supposed to call with problems and orders. In other cases, no one has been in contact with them for several months.

(continued)

FIGURE 11.11
Analytical Report Using the 2 + 2 = 4 Approach
To make his logical argument clear and compelling, Binh Phan used the 2 +2 = 4 approach.

2

For example, having retail outlets across the lower tier of the country, AmeriSport received pitches from reps out of our West, South, and East regions. Because our regional offices have a lot of negotiating freedom, the three were offering different prices. But all AmeriSport buying decisions were made at the Tampa headquarters, so all we did was confuse the customer. The irony of the current organization is that we're often giving our weakest selling and support efforts to the largest customers in the country.

COMMISSION PROBLEMS

The regional organization problems are compounded by the way we assign commissions and quota credit. Salespeople in one region can invest a lot of time in pursuing a sale, only to have the customer place the order in another region. So some sales rep in the second region ends up with the commission on a sale that was partly or even entirely earned by someone in the first region. Therefore, sales reps sometimes don't pursue leads in their regions, thinking that a rep in another region will get the commission.

For example, Athletic Express, with outlets in 35 states spread across all four regions, finally got so frustrated with us that the company president called our headquarters. Athletic Express has been trying to place a large order for tennis and golf accessories, but none of our local reps seem interested in paying attention. I spoke with the rep responsible for Nashville, where the company is headquartered, and asked her why she wasn't working the account more actively. Her explanation was that last time she got involved with Athletic Express, the order was actually placed from their L.A. regional office, and she didn't get any commission after more than two weeks of selling time.

RECOMMENDATIONS

Our sales organization should reflect the nature of our customer base. To accomplish that goal, we need a group of reps who are free to pursue accounts across regional borders—and who are compensated fairly for their work. The most sensible answer is to establish a national account group. Any customers whose operations place them in more than one region would automatically be assigned to the national group.

In addition to solving the problem of competing sales efforts, the new structure will also largely eliminate the commission-splitting problem because regional reps will no longer invest time in prospects assigned to the national accounts team. However, we will need to find a fair way to compensate regional reps who are losing long-term customers to the national team. Some of these reps have invested years in developing customer relationships that will continue to yield sales well into the future, and everyone I talked to agrees that reps in these cases should receive some sort of compensation. Such a "transition commission" would also motivate the regional reps to help ensure a smooth transition from one sales group to the other. The exact nature of this compensation would need to be worked out with the various sales managers.

3

SUMMARY

The regional sales organization is effective at the regional and local levels but not at the national level. We should establish a national accounts group to handle sales that cross regional boundaries. Then we'll have one set of reps who are focused on the local and regional levels and another set who are pursuing national accounts.

To compensate regional reps who lose accounts to the national team, we will need to devise some sort of payment to reward them for the years of work invested in such accounts. This can be discussed with the sales managers once the new structure is in place.

FIGURE 11.11
(continued)

than continue to service them through the company's four regional divisions. However, Phan knew his plan would be controversial because it required a big change in the company's organization and in the way sales reps are paid. His thinking had to be clear and easy to follow, so he used the 2 + 2 = 4 approach to focus on his reasons.

The yardstick approach compares alternatives to a set of predetermined standards without conducting experiments or evaluating hypotheses.

The Yardstick Approach   The **yardstick approach** is useful when you need to use a number of criteria to decide which option to select from two or more possibilities. With this approach, you begin by discussing the problem or opportunity, and then you list the criteria that will guide the decision. The body of the report then evaluates the alternatives against those criteria. Figure 11.12 is an outline of a feasibility report that uses the yardstick approach, using five criteria to evaluate two alternative courses of action.

The yardstick approach has two potential drawbacks. First, your audience needs to agree with the criteria you're using in your analysis. If they don't, they won't agree with the results of the evaluation. If you have any doubt about their agreement, build consensus before you start your report, if possible, or take extra care to explain why the criteria you're using are the best ones in this particular case. Second, the yardstick approach can get a little boring when you have many options to consider or many criteria to compare them against. One way to minimize the repetition is to compare the options in tables and then highlight the most unusual or important aspects of each alternative in the text so that you get the best of both worlds. This approach allows you to compare all the alternatives against the same yardstick while calling attention to the most significant differences among them.

PLANNING PROPOSALS

The specific formats for proposals are innumerable, but they can be grouped into two general categories. *Internal proposals* request decisions from managers within the organization, such as proposals to buy new equipment or launch new research projects. *External proposals* request decisions from parties outside the organization. Examples of external proposals include *investment proposals*, which request funding from external investors; *grant proposals*, which request funds from government agencies and other sponsoring organizations; and *sales proposals*, which suggest individualized solutions for potential customers and request purchase decisions.

Buyers solicit proposals by publishing a request for proposals (RFP).

The most significant factor in planning a proposal is whether the recipient has asked you to submit a proposal. *Solicited proposals* are generally prepared at the request of external parties that require a product or a service, but they may also be requested by such internal sources as management or the board of directors. Some external parties prepare a formal invitation to bid on their contracts, called a **request for proposals (RFP)**, which includes instructions that specify exactly the type of work to be performed or products to be delivered, along with budgets, deadlines, and other requirements. Suppose that the National Aeronautics and Space Administration (NASA) decides to develop a new satellite. The agency prepares an RFP that specifies exactly what the satellite should accomplish, and it sends the RFP to several aerospace companies, inviting them to bid on the job. The companies respond by preparing proposals that show how they would meet NASA's needs. In most cases, organizations that issue RFPs also provide strict guidelines on what the proposals should include, and you need to follow these guidelines carefully in order to be considered. RFPs can seem surprisingly picky,

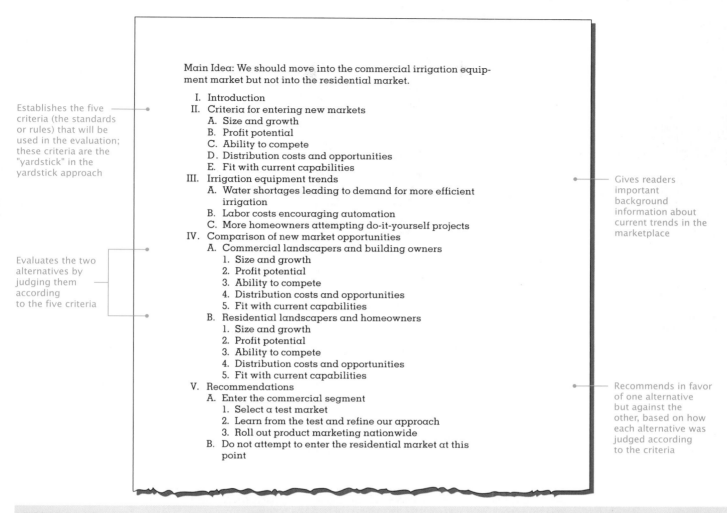

Main Idea: We should move into the commercial irrigation equipment market but not into the residential market.

I. Introduction
II. Criteria for entering new markets
   A. Size and growth
   B. Profit potential
   C. Ability to compete
   D. Distribution costs and opportunities
   E. Fit with current capabilities
III. Irrigation equipment trends
   A. Water shortages leading to demand for more efficient irrigation
   B. Labor costs encouraging automation
   C. More homeowners attempting do-it-yourself projects
IV. Comparison of new market opportunities
   A. Commercial landscapers and building owners
      1. Size and growth
      2. Profit potential
      3. Ability to compete
      4. Distribution costs and opportunities
      5. Fit with current capabilities
   B. Residential landscapers and homeowners
      1. Size and growth
      2. Profit potential
      3. Ability to compete
      4. Distribution costs and opportunities
      5. Fit with current capabilities
V. Recommendations
   A. Enter the commercial segment
      1. Select a test market
      2. Learn from the test and refine our approach
      3. Roll out product marketing nationwide
   B. Do not attempt to enter the residential market at this point

*Annotations (left):*
Establishes the five criteria (the standards or rules) that will be used in the evaluation; these criteria are the "yardstick" in the yardstick approach

Evaluates the two alternatives by judging them according to the five criteria

*Annotations (right):*
Gives readers important background information about current trends in the marketplace

Recommends in favor of one alternative but against the other, based on how each alternative was judged according to the criteria

FIGURE 11.12
Outline of an Analytical Report Using the Yardstick Approach
The report was provided by J. C. Hartley, a market analyst for a large Sacramento company that makes irrigation equipment for farms and ranches. "We've been so successful in the agricultural market that we're starting to run out of customers to sell to," says Hartley. "To keep the company growing, we needed to find another market. Two obvious choices to consider were commercial buildings and residences, but we needed to evaluate them carefully before making a decision."

even to the point of specifying the size of paper to use, but you must follow every detail.

Unsolicited proposals offer more flexibility but a completely different sort of challenge than solicited proposals because recipients aren't expecting to receive them. In fact, your audience may not be aware of the problem or opportunity you are addressing, so before you can propose a solution, you might first need to convince your readers that a problem or an opportunity exists. Consequently, using an indirect approach is often a wise choice for unsolicited proposals.

Regardless of its format and structure, a good proposal explains what a project or course of action will involve, how much it will cost, and how the recipient and his or her organization will benefit. You can see all these elements in Figure 11.13.

MEMO

DATE: July 8, 2008
TO: Jamie Engle
FROM: Shandel Cohen
SUBJECT: Saving $145k/year with an automated e-mail response system

THE PROBLEM:
Expensive and Slow Response to Customer Information Requests

Our new product line has been very well received, and orders have surpassed our projections. This very success, however, has created a shortage of printed brochures, as well as considerable overtime for people in the customer response center. As we introduce upgrades and new options, our printed materials quickly become outdated. If we continue to rely on printed materials for customer information, we have two choices: Distribute existing materials (even though they are incomplete or inaccurate) or discard existing materials and print new ones.

THE SOLUTION:
Automated E-Mail Response System

With minor additions and modifications to our current e-mail system, we can set up an automated system to respond to customer requests for information. This system can save us time and money and can keep our distributed information current.

Automated e-mail response systems have been tested and proven effective. Many companies already use this method to respond to customer information requests, so we won't have to worry about relying on untested technology. Using the system is easy, too: Customers simply send a blank e-mail message to a specific address, and the system responds by sending an electronic copy of the requested brochure.

Benefit #1: Always-Current Information

Rather than discard and print new materials, we would only need to keep the electronic files up to date on the server. We could be able to provide customers and our field sales organization with up-to-date, correct information as soon as the upgrades or options are available.

Benefit #2: Instantaneous Delivery

Almost immediately after requesting information, customers would have that information in hand. Electronic delivery would be especially advantageous for our international customers. Regular mail to remote locations sometimes takes weeks to arrive, by which time the information may already be out of date. Both customers and field salespeople will appreciate the automatic mail-response system.

Benefit #3: Minimized Waste

With our current method of printing every marketing piece in large quantities, we discard thousands of pages of obsolete catalogs, data sheets, and other materials every year. By maintaining and distributing the information electronically, we would eliminate this waste. We would also free up a considerable amount of expensive floor space and shelving that is required for storing printed materials.

(continued)

FIGURE 11.13
Internal Proposal
Shandel Cohen's internal proposal seeks management's approval to install an automatic mail-response system. Because the company manufactures computers, she knows that her boss won't object to a computer-based solution. Also, because profits are always a concern, her report emphasizes the financial benefits of her proposal.

2

Of course, some of our customers may still prefer to receive printed materials, or they may not have access to electronic mail. For these customers, we could simply print copies of the files when we receive such requests. The new Xerox DocuColor printer just installed in the Central Services building would be ideal for printing high-quality materials in small quantities.

Benefit #4: Lower Overtime Costs

In addition to saving both paper and space, we would also realize considerable savings in wages. Because of the increased interest in our new products, we must continue to work overtime or hire new people to meet the demand. An automatic mail-response system would eliminate this need, allowing us to deal with fluctuating interest without a fluctuating workforce.

Cost Analysis

The necessary equipment and software costs approximately $15,000. System maintenance and upgrades are estimated at $5,000 per year. However, those costs are offset many times over by the predicted annual savings:

Printing	$100,000
Storage	25,000
Postage	5,000
Wages	20,000
Total	**$150,000**

Based on these figures, the system would save $130,000 the first year and $145,000 every year after that.

CONCLUSION

An automated e-mail response system would yield considerable benefits in both customer satisfaction and operating costs. If you approve, we can have it installed and running in 6 weeks. Please give me a call if you have any questions.

Margin notes:

Acknowledges one potential shortcoming with the new approach but provides a convincing solution to that as well

Itemizes the cost savings in order to support the $145k/year claim made in the subject line

Summarizes the benefits and invites further discussion

FIGURE 11.13
(continued)

On the Job

SOLVING COMMUNICATION DILEMMAS AT TESCO

As a market development manager working for Richard Brasher, you are responsible for a variety of research, planning, and customer communication projects. Using what you've learned in this chapter about effective research methods and report planning, choose appropriate solutions to these challenges.

1. Tesco has created several online stores (see www.tesco.com) and would like to expand the number of consumers who order goods and services online. Which of the following problem statements best encapsulates the research that would

be needed to devise a plan to attract more online shoppers?

a. Why aren't more consumers buying online?

b. We need to identify whether consumers are buying similar goods and services from competitive websites.

c. We need to understand the behavior of Tesco shoppers—and potential shoppers—in much more detail.

d. We need to identify potential changes to our business strategy and tactics that would prompt more consumers to purchase from Tesco online stores.

2. Which of the following research methods should Tesco use to find out what U.S. consumers think of the Tesco brand name?

   a. Conduct a telephone survey of a carefully selected sample of U.S. residents.
   b. Interview a dozen or so experts in consumer psychology to see what they think about Tesco; they're likely to know much more about how consumers respond to brands than consumers themselves.
   c. Put a brief survey on Tesco's website. Consumers visiting the site are obviously interested in the company, so they are well positioned to comment on it.
   d. Conduct a thorough review of all U.S. magazine and newspaper articles published in the past 12 months, looking specifically for mentions of Tesco.

3. Shoppers often make purchase decisions in the store rather than arriving with a preset list of specific brands to purchase. Brasher would like more information on why consumers choose one brand over another while standing in front of an array of products on the shelf. Is it the brand name? Something about the packaging? The price? Other factors? Which would be the best way to collect this information from at least 500 shoppers?

   a. Install hidden cameras at strategic locations throughout a selected group of Tesco stores; be sure to record audio as well so you can hear what families discuss as they make product selections.
   b. In a selection of stores covering neighborhoods that represent Tesco's overall market, attach brief survey forms to several hundred products throughout each store. Shoppers can fill out the surveys while they wait in the checkout line and hand them to the cashier.
   c. Position data collection personnel throughout a representative selection of stores and interview shoppers just after they've made product selections.
   d. Mail survey forms to 500 U.S. households selected at random.

4. Even though you have been with the company for only three months, you've learned quickly and believe that you have a solid understanding of Tesco's strategic challenges and opportunities. Brasher recently assigned you to write an analytical report on competition in the U.S. grocery market. His directive was to study the major players in the market and assess each one's strengths and weaknesses in preparation for Tesco's major rollout across the country. The report will be distributed to all top executives in the company. In the course of your research, however, you conclude that the entire strategy is a mistake, that the competition in the U.S. market is too strong for Tesco to make any sort of meaningful progress. You believe the company will waste millions, perhaps billions, of dollars on the venture. How should you handle this unexpected conclusion?

   a. The decision to enter the U.S. market has already been made, and it's not your job to question it. Don't mention this conclusion at all in your report.
   b. Discuss your concerns with Brasher before you write your first draft and don't add this conclusion to your report unless he instructs you to do so.
   c. Your conclusion is more important than following Brasher's instructions to the letter. Moreover, your discovery is too important to keep from the executive team. Organize your report with the direct approach, opening immediately with the conclusion and then offering supporting evidence and reasons.
   d. Add your conclusion to the report but organize the report indirectly. Insert your surprising conclusion at the very end of the report, after you've discussed the competitive situation in detail.

Learning Objectives Checkup

Assess your understanding of the principles in this chapter by reading each learning objective and studying the accompanying exercises. For fill-in-the-blank items, write the missing text in the blank provided; for multiple-choice items, circle the letter of the correct answer. You can check your responses against the answer key on page AK-2.

Objective 11.1: Adapt the three-step writing process to reports and proposals.

1. Why is it particularly important in long reports to clearly identify your purpose before you begin writing?
   a. A clear statement of purpose helps you avoid extensive revisions.
   b. A clear statement of purpose gives you the opportunity to clarify the project with the person who assigned you the report.
   c. A clear statement of purpose helps you plan your research by identifying the information you need to gather.
   d. All of the above are important factors.

2. What does it mean to define the *scope* of a project when you're preparing a work plan?
   a. The scope is the range of your investigation and subsequent reporting; you address all the important topics within the defined scope of your project and ignore issues that are outside your scope.

b. The scope refers to the level of detail, in much the same way that microscopes and telescopes provide varying levels of detail.
c. Scope indicates how long you'll spend on the project.
d. None of the above are correct.

Objective 11.2: Distinguish informational reports, analytical reports, and proposals.

3. _____ reports focus on the delivery of facts, figures, and other types of information, without making recommendations or proposing new ideas or solutions.
4. _____ reports assess a situation or problem and recommend a course of action in response.
5. _____ present persuasive messages that encourage readers to take a specific course of action.

Objective 11.3: Describe an effective process for conducting business research.

6. Which of the following is the appropriate first step in any research project?
   a. Evaluate secondary research to see if you can reuse anything from earlier research projects.
   b. Conduct a preliminary phone survey to measure the extent of the issue you're about to research.
   c. Conduct a thorough statistical analysis of any existing data.
   d. Develop a research plan by familiarizing yourself with the subject, identifying information gaps, and prioritizing research needs.
7. Consider the series of values 14, 37, 44, 44, 44, 74, 76, 88, 93, 100, and 112.
   a. The mean is 66.
   b. The median is 74.
   c. The mode is 44.
   d. All of the above are correct.

Objective 11.4: Define primary and secondary research, and explain when you use each method.

8. Research being conducted for the first time is called _____ research.
9. Research that was conducted for other projects but is being considered for a new project is called _____ research.
10. Secondary research is
    a. Generally used before primary research
    b. Generally used after primary research
    c. Generally used at the same time as primary research
    d. Another name for primary research

Objective 11.5: Name nine criteria for evaluating the credibility of an information source.

11. Why does information found on the Internet need to be used with extreme care?
    a. Most sources on the Internet are false.
    b. You can be sued for using anything found online.

c. Online sources often lack the fact-checking and other quality control procedures usually found in traditional offline publishing.
d. Online information often contains computer viruses.

12. Why is it important to understand the purpose for which source material was created?
    a. Knowing the purpose helps alert you to any potential biases.
    b. You are required to indicate this purpose in your bibliography.
    c. The purpose tells you whether the material is copyrighted.
    d. The purpose tells you whether you need to pay usage rights.

13. If you uncover critically important information (the sort that could make or break your company) that is from a credible source and appears to be unbiased, well documented, current, and complete but is the only source of this information you can find, how should you handle this situation in your subsequent reporting?
    a. Use it as you would use any other information.
    b. Use it but clearly indicate the source in your report.
    c. Use it but clearly indicate in your report that this is the only source of the information and you weren't able to verify it through a second, independent source.
    d. Don't use it.

Objective 11.6: Provide five guidelines for conducting an effective online search.

14. Why is it important to fully understand the instructions for using an individual search engine, web directory, database, or other computer-based research tool?
    a. You can be fined if you use these tools improperly.
    b. Most search tools don't return any results if you don't know how to use them.
    c. Using the tool without understanding how it works can produce unpredictable and misleading results.
    d. Today's search tools are so easy to use that you don't need to worry about learning the details.

15. What should you do if your first attempt to find something with a search engine doesn't return anything?
    a. Try again with fewer search terms (which will broaden your search).
    b. Try again with fewer search terms (which will narrow your search).
    c. Try again with more search terms (which will broaden your search).
    d. Try again with more search terms (which will narrow your search).

Objective 11.7: Outline an effective process for planning and conducting information interviews.

16. Recording an interview
    a. Should always be done for legal reasons, regardless of whether the subject consents to be recorded
    b. Should never be done without the subject's permission

c. Is a waste of time if you listen carefully
d. Is always a good idea because it means you don't have to pay close attention during the interview

Objective 11.8: Explain the differences between drafting a summary, drawing a conclusion, and developing a recommendation.

17. A _____ is a shortened version of one or more documents, research results, or other information; it filters out details and presents only the most important ideas.
18. A _____ is your analysis of what the findings mean (an interpretation of the facts).
19. A _____ is your opinion (based on reason and logic) about the course of action that should be taken.

Objective 11.9: Discuss three major ways to organize analytical reports.

20. If you have a long history of success in business and are highly regarded by your audience, which two organizing models will probably be sufficient for most reports to this audience?
    a. Focusing on conclusions or focusing on recommendations
    b. Focusing on conclusions and focusing on troubleshooting
    c. Focusing on logic or focusing on analysis
    d. Focusing on reason and focusing on logic
21. If you need to "walk your audience through" the reasoning that led you to the conclusion or recommendation in your report, you should use an organization that focuses on _____.

Apply Your Knowledge

1. Why must you be careful when using information from a webpage in a business report?
2. Why do you need to evaluate the sources you uncover in your research?
3. If you were writing a recommendation report for an audience that doesn't know you, would you use a direct approach focusing on the recommendation or an indirect approach focusing on logic? Why?
4. Why are unsolicited proposals more challenging to write than solicited proposals?

5. **Ethical Choices** Companies occasionally make mistakes that expose confidential information, such as when employees lose laptop computers containing sensitive data files or webmasters forget to protect confidential webpages from search engine indexes. If you conducted an online search that turned up competitive information on webpages that were clearly intended to be private, what would you do? Explain your answer.

Practice Your Knowledge

MESSAGE FOR ANALYSIS: EVALUATING A REPORT

The Securities and Exchange Commission (SEC) requires every public company to file a comprehensive annual report (form 10-K) electronically. Many companies post links to these reports on their websites, along with links to other company reports. Visit the website of Dell, at www.dell.com, and find the company's most recent annual reports: 10-K and Year in Review (click on "About Dell" on the homepage and then click on the "Investors" link). Compare the style and format of the two reports. For which audience(s) is the Year in Review targeted? Who besides the SEC might be interested in the Annual Report 10-K? Which report do you find easier to read? More interesting? More detailed?

EXERCISES

For active links to all websites discussed in this chapter, visit this text's website at www.prenhall.com/thill. Locate your book and click on its "Companion Website" link. Then select

Chapter 11 and click on "Featured Websites." Locate the name of the page or the URL related to the material in the text. Please note that links to sites that become inactive after publication of the book will be removed from the "Featured Websites" section.

11.1 **Understanding Business Reports and Proposals: How Companies Use Reports** Interview several people working in a career you might like to enter and ask them about the reports they receive and prepare. How do these reports tie in to the decision-making process? Who reads the reports they prepare? Do they write or read electronic, online reports? Summarize your findings in writing, give them to your instructor, and be prepared to discuss them with the class.

11.2 **Understanding Business Reports and Proposals: Report Classification** Using the information presented in this chapter, identify the report type represented by each of the following examples. In addition, write a brief paragraph about each, explaining who the

audience is likely to be, what type of data would be used, and whether conclusions and recommendations would be appropriate.
a. A statistical study of the pattern of violent crime in a large city during the past five years
b. A report prepared by a seed company demonstrating the benefits of its seed corn for farmers
c. A report prepared by an independent testing agency evaluating various types of nonprescription cold remedies
d. A trip report submitted at the end of a week by a traveling salesperson
e. A report indicating how 45 acres of undeveloped land could be converted into an industrial park
f. An annual report to be sent to the shareholders of a large corporation
g. A report from a U.S. National Park wildlife officer to Washington, D.C., headquarters showing the status of the California condor (an endangered species)
h. A written report by a police officer who has just completed an arrest

11.3 Informational Reports: Personal Activity Report Imagine you're the manager of campus recruiting for Nortel, a Canadian telecommunications firm. Each of your four recruiters interviews up to 11 college seniors every day. What kind of personal activity report can you design to track the results of these interviews? List the areas you would want each recruiter to report on and explain how each would help you manage the recruiting process (and the recruiters) more effectively.

11.4 Understanding Your Topic: Subquestions Your boss has asked you to do some research on franchising. Actually, he's thinking about purchasing a few Subway franchises, and he needs some information. Visit www.amazon.com and perform a keyword search on "franchises." Explore some of the books that you find by reading reviews and using the "Search Inside" feature.
a. Use the information to develop a list of subquestions to help you narrow your focus.
b. Write down the names of three books you might purchase for your boss.
c. How can this website assist you with your research efforts?

11.5 Finding Information: Secondary Information Using online, database, or printed sources, find the following information. Be sure to properly cite your source, using the formats discussed in Appendix B (*Hint:* Start with Table 11.3, Important Resources for Business Research.)
a. Contact information for the American Management Association
b. Median weekly earnings of men and women by occupation
c. Current market share for Perrier water
d. Performance ratios for office supply retailers
e. Annual stock performance for Hewlett-Packard
f. Number of franchise outlets in the United States
g. Composition of the U.S. workforce by profession

11.6 Finding Information: Company Information Select any public company and find the following information.
a. Names of the company's current officers
b. List of the company's products or services (if the company has a large number of products, list the product lines instead)
c. Current issues in the company's industry
d. Outlook for the company's industry as a whole

11.7 Finding Information: Secondary Information You'd like to know if it's a good idea to buy banner ads on other websites to drive more traffic to your company's website. You're worried about the expense and difficulty of running an experiment to test banner effectiveness, so you decide to look for some secondary data. Using databases available through your library, identify three secondary sources that might offer helpful data on this issue.

11.8 Finding Information: Search Techniques Analyze any recent school or work assignment that required you to conduct research. How did you approach your investigation? Did you rely mostly on sources of primary information or mostly on sources of secondary information? Now that you have studied this chapter, can you identify two ways to improve the research techniques you used during that assignment? Briefly explain.

11.9 Finding Information: Surveys You work for a movie studio that is producing a young director's first motion picture, the story of a group of unknown musicians finding work and making a reputation in a competitive industry. Unfortunately, some of your friends say that the 182-minute movie is simply too long. Others say they couldn't imagine any sequences to cut out. Your boss wants to test the movie on a regular audience and ask viewers to complete a questionnaire that will help the director decide whether edits are needed and, if so, where. Design a questionnaire that you can use to solicit valid answers for a report to the director about how to handle the audience's reaction to the movie.

11.10 Finding Information: Interviews You're conducting an information interview with a manager in another division of your company. Partway through the interview, the manager shows clear signs of impatience. How should you respond? What might you do differently to prevent this from happening in the future? Explain your answers.

11.11 Teamwork: Evaluating Sources Break into small groups and surf the Internet to find websites that provide business information such as company or industry news, trends, analysis, facts, or performance data. Using the criteria discussed under "Evaluating Your Sources," evaluate the credibility of the information presented at these websites.

11.12 Processing Information: Reading and Taking Notes Select an article from a business magazine such as *BusinessWeek*, *Fortune*, *Forbes*, *Fast Company*, or *Business 2.0*. Read the article and highlight the article's key points. Summarize the article in fewer than 100 words, paraphrasing the key points.

11.13 Analyzing Data: Calculating the Mean Your boss has asked you to analyze and report on your division's sales for the first nine months of this year. Using the following data from company invoices, calculate the mean for each quarter and all averages for the year to date. Then identify and discuss the quarterly sales trends.

January	$24,600	April	$21,200	July	$29,900
February	25,900	May	24,600	August	30,500
March	23,000	June	26,800	September	26,600

11.14 Teamwork: Unsolicited Proposal Break into small groups and identify an operational problem occurring at your campus that involves either registration, university housing, food services, parking, or library services. Then develop a workable solution to that problem. Finally, develop a list of pertinent facts that your team will need to gather to convince the reader that the problem exists and that your solution will work.

11.15 Analyzing the Situation: Statement of Purpose Sales at The Style Shop, a clothing store for men, have declined for the third month in a row. Your boss is not sure if this decline is due to a weak economy or if it's due to another unknown reason. She has asked you to investigate the situation and to submit a report to her highlighting some possible reasons for the decline. Develop a statement of purpose for your report.

11.16 Organizing Reports: Structuring Analytical Reports Three years ago, your company (a carpet manufacturer) modernized its Georgia plant in anticipation of increasing demand for carpets. Because of the depressed housing market, the increase in demand for new carpets has been slow to materialize. As a result, the company has excess capacity at its Georgia and California plants. On the basis of your research, you have recommended that the company close the California plant. The company president, J. P. Lawrence, has asked you to prepare a justification report to support your recommendation. Here are the facts you gathered by interviewing the respective plant managers:

OPERATIONAL STATISTICS

- *Georgia plant:* This plant has newer equipment, productivity is higher, it employs 100 nonunion production workers, and it ships $12 million in carpets a year. The hourly base wage is $16.
- *California plant:* California plant employs 80 union production workers and ships $8 million in carpets a year. The hourly base wage is $20.

FINANCIAL IMPLICATIONS

- *Savings by closing California plant:* (1) Increase productivity by 17%; (2) reduce labor costs by 20% (total labor savings would be $1 million per year; see assumptions); (3) annual local tax savings of $120,000 (Georgia has a more favorable tax climate).
- *Sale of Pomona, California, land:* Purchased in 1952 for $200,000. Current market value $2.5 million. Net profit (after capital gains tax) over $1 million.
- *Sale of plant and equipment:* Fully depreciated. Any proceeds a windfall.
- *Costs of closing California plant:* One-time deductible charge of $250,000 (relocation costs of $100,000 and severance payments totaling $150,000).

ASSUMPTIONS

- Transfer 5 workers from California to Georgia.
- Hire 45 new workers in Georgia.
- Lay off 75 workers in California.
- Georgia plant would require a total of 150 workers to produce the combined volume of both plants.
    a. Which approach (focus on conclusions, recommendations, or logical arguments) will you use to structure your report to the president? Why?
    b. Suppose this report were to be circulated to plant managers and supervisors instead. What changes, if any, might you make in your approach?
    c. List some conclusions that you might draw from the above information to use in your report.
    d. Using the structure you selected for your report to the president, draft a final report outline with first- and second-level informative headings.

Expand Your Knowledge

LEARNING MORE ON THE WEB
CHECK OUT THIS 24-HOUR LIBRARY

www.ipl.org

Start your business research by visiting the Internet Public Library (IPL). Visit the reference center and explore the many online references available. These cover topics such as business, economics, law, government, science, technology, computers, education, and more. You can even submit questions for the IPL staff. Visit the reference center and explore the many business and economics resources. Click on "Business" and then "Business Directories" and perform these tasks:

1. Select five companies and use the links provided to find contact information (address, phone, website, officers' names, and so on) for each company. What kinds of contact information did you find at the company websites?
2. Click on the "E-Commerce" link and find information that helps consumers shop online safely. Is this informa-

tion presented in a way that is easy for the average consumer to understand?

3. Go back to the library's main reference center and click on "Ready Reference." Follow some of the reference links. How might these links help you when performing business research?

SURFING YOUR WAY TO CAREER SUCCESS

Bovée and Thill's Business Communication Headline News offers links to hundreds of online resources that can help you with this course, your other college courses, and your career. Visit **www.businesscommunicationblog.com** and click on "Web Directory." The "Research" section connects you to a variety of websites and articles on such important topics as using research tools, analyzing and evaluating research materials, checking facts, interviewing, and using online research tools. Identify three websites from this section that could be useful in your business career. For each site, write a two-sentence summary of what the site offers and how it could help you launch and build your career.

Learn Interactively

INTERACTIVE STUDY GUIDE

Visit **www.prenhall.com/thill**, locate your book and click on its "Companion Website" link. Select Chapter 11 to take advantage of the interactive "Chapter Quiz" to test your knowledge of chapter concepts. Receive instant feedback on whether you need to do additional studying. Also, visit the "Study Hall," where you'll find an abundance of valuable resources that will help you succeed in this course.

PEAK PERFORMANCE GRAMMAR AND MECHANICS

If your instructor has required the use of "Peak Performance Grammar and Mechanics," either in your online course or on CD, you can improve your skill with question marks and exclamation points by using the "Peak Performance Grammar and Mechanics" module. Click on "Punctuation II." Take the Pretest to determine whether you have any weak areas. Then review those areas in the Refresher Course. Take the Follow-Up Test to check your grasp of question marks and exclamation points. For an extra challenge or advanced practice, take the Advanced Test. Finally, for additional reinforcement, go to the "Improve Your Grammar, Mechanics, and Usage" section that follows and complete those exercises.

Improve Your Grammar, Mechanics, and Usage

The following exercises help you improve your knowledge of and power over English grammar, mechanics, and usage. Turn to the Handbook of Grammar, Mechanics, and Usage at the end of this book and review all of Sections 2.1 (Periods), 2.2 (Question Marks), and 2.3 (Exclamation Points). Then look at the following 10 items. Circle the letter of the preferred choice in the following groups of sentences. (Answers to these exercises appear on page AK-4.)

1. a. Dr. Eleanor H Hutton has requested information on TaskMasters, Inc.?
   b. Dr. Eleanor H. Hutton has requested information on TaskMasters, Inc.

2. a. That qualifies us as a rapidly growing new company, don't you think?
   b. That qualifies us as a rapidly growing new company, don't you think.

3. a. Our president is a C.P.A. On your behalf, I asked him why he started the firm.
   b. Our president is a CPA. On your behalf, I asked him why he started the firm.

4. a. Contact me at 1358 N. Parsons Ave., Tulsa, OK 74204.
   b. Contact me at 1358 N. Parsons Ave, Tulsa, OK. 74204.

5. a. Jeb asked, "Why does he want to know! Maybe he plans to become a competitor."

   b. Jeb asked, "Why does he want to know? Maybe he plans to become a competitor!"

6. a. The debt load fluctuates with the movement of the U.S. prime rate.
   b. The debt load fluctuates with the movement of the US prime rate.

7. a. Is consumer loyalty extinct? Yes and no!
   b. Is consumer loyalty extinct? Yes and no.

8. a. Will you please send us a check today so that we can settle your account.
   b. Will you please send us a check today so that we can settle your account?

9. a. Will you be able to speak at the conference, or should we find someone else.
   b. Will you be able to speak at the conference, or should we find someone else?

10. a. So I ask you, "When will we admit defeat?" Never!
    b. So I ask you, "When will we admit defeat"? Never!

For additional exercises focusing on periods, question marks, and exclamation points, go to **www.prenhall.com/thill**, then locate your text and click on its "Companion Website" link. Click on Chapter 11, click on "Additional Exercises to Improve Your Grammar, Mechanics and Usage," and click on "17. Punctuation B."

Chapter 12

Writing Business Reports and Proposals

Learning Objectives

AFTER STUDYING THIS CHAPTER, YOU WILL BE ABLE TO

1 Explain how to adapt to your audiences when writing reports and proposals

2 List the topics commonly covered in the introduction, body, and close of informational and analytical reports

3 Name five characteristics of effective report content

4 Name six strategies to strengthen your proposal argument

5 List the topics commonly covered in a proposal's introduction, body, and close

6 Identify five characteristics of effective writing in online reports

7 Describe the communication power that visuals add to your writing

8 Explain how to choose which points in your message to illustrate

9 Discuss six principles of graphic design that can improve the quality of your visuals

10 Name three qualities to look for before including a visual in a report or presentation

On the Job

COMMUNICATING AT TELLABS

REDEFINING THE ANNUAL REPORT WITH AUDIENCE-FOCUSED WRITING

Few reports get as much scrutiny as corporate annual reports, and the feedback from many readers is not particularly positive.

These compliance reports are required of every company listed on U.S. stock exchanges, and investors pore over them, looking for clues about a company's financial health and prospects. However, investor surveys suggest that many readers don't believe they are getting the information they need in order to make intelligent decisions about investing in a company's stock. Some companies have even been sued in recent years over their annual reports, with investors accusing them of withholding or obscuring vital information.

In this environment of uncertainty and outright mistrust, writers who communicate clearly and openly tend to stand out from the crowd. One such writer is George Stenitzer, vice president of corporate communication for Tellabs, a major producer of equipment for Internet service providers based in Naperville, Illinois. According to one widely respected consultant who assesses the quality of annual reports, Stenitzer's work practically demands to be read, thanks to its brevity, forthright style, full disclosure of important financial information, numerous features that enhance readability, and attractive design.

While annual report writers must comply with a complex array of legal compliance requirements, Stenitzer's view is that accuracy and compliance—while vital—are not enough. He recognizes that many companies still lean in the direction of minimal disclosure, saying just enough to satisfy government regulations,

The annual reports written by Tellabs's George Stenitzer go beyond regulatory compliance to helping investors understand the business and its financial performance.

but Stenitzer's goal is to help investors truly understand the nature of Tellabs's business and its financial performance. As he puts it, "The test for investor communications is shifting from technical accuracy and legal compliance to clear communication and investor understanding."

The proof of his approach seems to bear out in investor surveys. In an environment in which many investors are extremely skeptical of, or even confused by, what they read in annual reports, one of Tellabs's recent annual reports was rated "good" or "very good" by an overwhelming 83 percent of readers.[1]

www.tellabs.com

411

CRAFTING REPORTS AND PROPOSALS

George Stenitzer (profiled in the chapter opener) can tell you how important the writing stage is in the development of successful reports and proposals. This chapter builds on the writing techniques and ideas you learned in Chapter 5, focusing on issues that are particularly important when preparing longer message formats (see Figure 12.1). In addition, you'll get an introduction to creating effective visuals, which are a vital aspect of many reports and proposals.

As with shorter messages, take a few moments before you start writing to make sure you're ready to adapt your approach to your audience.

ADAPTING TO YOUR AUDIENCE

Successful report writers adapt to their intended audiences as much as possible. This means being sensitive to audience needs, building strong relationships with the audience, and controlling style and tone.

Chapter 5 introduces four aspects of audience sensitivity, and all four apply to reports and proposals: adopting the "you" attitude, maintaining a strong sense of etiquette, emphasizing the positive, and using bias-free language. Reports and proposals that are highly technical, complex, or lengthy can put heavy demands on your readers, so the "you" attitude is especially important with these long messages.

Be sure to plan how you will adapt your style and your language to reflect the image of your organization. Many companies have specific guidelines for communicating with public audiences, so make sure you're aware of these preferences before you start writing.

If you know your readers reasonably well and your report is likely to meet with their approval, you can adopt a fairly informal tone (as long as this is appropriate in your organization, of course). To make your tone less formal, speak to readers in the

Long or complex reports demand a lot from readers, making the "you" attitude especially important.

Many companies have specific guidelines for reports, particularly those intended for external audiences.

FIGURE 12.1
Step Two in the Three-Step Writing Process for Reports and Proposals
As you get ready to write a report or proposal, consider how you should adapt to your audience's needs and expectations.

Planning → Writing → Completing

Adapt to Your Audience
Be sensitive to audience needs with a "you" attitude, politeness, positive emphasis, and bias-free language. Build a strong relationship with your audience by establishing your credibility and projecting your company's image. Control your style with a tone and voice appropriate to the situation.

Compose the Message
Choose strong words that will help you create effective sentences and coherent paragraphs throughout the introduction, body, and close of your report or proposal.

1   2   3

first person, refer to them as *you*, and refer to yourself as *I* (or *we* if there are multiple report authors).

To make your tone more formal, use the impersonal journalism style: Emphasize objectivity, ensure that content is free from personal opinion, and build your argument on provable facts. When creating a formal tone, eliminate all references to *you* and *I* (including *we*, *us*, and *our*). Your tone should also be businesslike and unemotional. Be careful to avoid jokes, similes, and metaphors, and try to minimize the use of colorful adjectives or adverbs.

A more formal tone is appropriate for longer reports, especially those that deal with controversial or complex information. You also need a more formal tone when your report will be sent to other parts of the organization or to outsiders, such as customers, suppliers, or members of the community (see Figure 12.2).

Communicating with people in other cultures often calls for more formality—for two reasons. First, the business environment outside the United States tends to be more formal in general, and that formality must be reflected in your communication. Second, the things you do to make a document informal (such as using humor and idiomatic language) tend to translate poorly or not at all from one culture to another. Using a less formal tone in cross-cultural reports and proposals increases the risk of offending people and the chance of miscommunicating information.

> Reports destined for audiences outside the United States often require a more formal tone to match the expectations of audiences in many other countries.

COMPOSING REPORTS AND PROPOSALS

When you compose reports and proposals, follow the writing advice offered in Chapter 5: Select the best words, create the most effective sentences, and develop coherent paragraphs. As with other written business communications, the text of

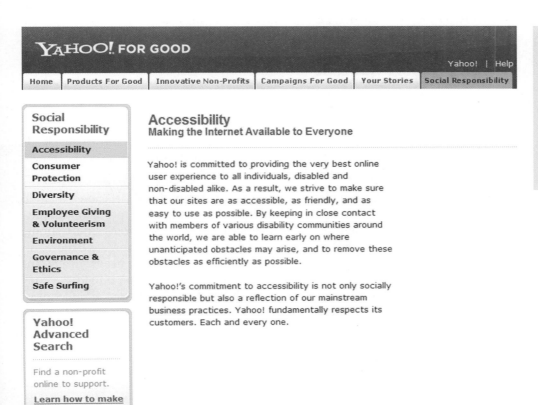

FIGURE 12.2
Choosing the Right Tone for Business Reports
Yahoo! is known for using a playful, informal tone in its advertising and in most communication with customers, but the company's tone is more formal when communicating with the public on more serious matters.

reports and proposals has three main sections: an introduction, a body, and a close.

The *introduction* (or *opening*) is the first section in the text of any report or proposal. An effective introduction accomplishes at least four things:

- Puts the report or proposal in a broader context by tying it to a problem or an assignment

- Introduces the subject or purpose of the report or proposal and indicates why the subject is important

- Previews the main ideas and the order in which they'll be covered

- Establishes the tone of the document and the writer's relationship with the audience

The *body*, or main section, usually consists of major sections with various levels of headings. These divisions present, analyze, and interpret the information gathered during your investigation, and they support the recommendations or conclusions discussed in your document. The body contains the proof, the detailed information necessary to support your conclusions and recommendations (see Figure 12.3).

The *close* has three important functions:

- Emphasizes the main points of the message

- Summarizes the benefits to the reader if the document suggests a change or some other course of action

- Brings all the action items together in one place and gives the details about who should do what, when, where, and how

Research shows that the final section of a report or proposal leaves a lasting impression. The close gives you one last chance to make sure your report says what you intended.[2] In fact, readers who are in a hurry might skip the body of the report and read only the summary, so make sure it carries a strong, clear message.

Drafting Report Content

Your credibility and career advancement are on the line with every business report you write, so make sure your content is

- **Accurate.** Be sure to double-check your facts and references and to check for typos. If an audience ever gets an inkling that your information is shaky, they'll start to view all your work with skepticism.

- **Complete.** To help colleagues or supervisors make informed decisions, include everything necessary for readers to understand the situation, problem, or proposal. Support all key assertions using an appropriate combination of illustrations, explanations, and facts.[3] Tell your readers what they need to know—no more, no less—and present the information in a way that is geared to their needs. In a recent Tellabs annual report, for example, George Stenitzer and his team provided a concise and easily understandable overview of the company's complex and technical product line. The subject matter is presented in a way that any investor interested in the company's stock can comprehend.[4]

- **Balanced.** Present all sides of the issue fairly and equitably and include all the essential information, even if some of the information doesn't support your line of reasoning. Omitting relevant information or facts can bias your report.

- **Clear and logical.** Clear sentence structure and good transitions are essential.[5] Save your readers time by making sure your sentences are uncluttered, contain well-chosen words, and proceed logically. To help your readers move from one

Your introduction needs to put the report in context for the reader, introduce the subject, preview main ideas, and establish the tone of the document.

The body of your report presents, analyzes, and interprets the information you gathered during your investigation.

The close might be the only part of your report some readers have time for, so make sure it conveys the full weight of your message.

MEMO

DATE: July 7, 2008
TO: Board of Directors, Executive Committee members
FROM: Alycia Jenn, Business Development Manager
SUBJECT: Website expansion

In response to your request, my staff and I investigated the potential for expanding our website from its current "brochureware" status (in which we promote our company and its products but don't provide any way to place orders online) to full e-commerce capability (including placing orders and checking on order delivery status). After analyzing the behavior of our customers and major competitors and studying the overall development of electronic retailing, we have three recommendations:

1. We should expand our online presence from "brochureware" to e-commerce capability within the next 6 months.

2. We should engage a firm that specializes in online retailing to design and develop the new e-commerce capabilities.

3. We must take care to integrate online retailing with our store-based and mail-order operations.

1. WE SHOULD EXPAND THE WEBSITE TO FULL E-COMMERCE CAPABILITY

First, does e-commerce capability make sense today for a small company that sells luxury housewares? Even though books and many other products are now commonly sold online, in most cases, this enterprise involves simple, low-cost products that don't require a lot of hands-on inspection before purchasing. As we've observed in our stores, shoppers like to interact with our products before purchasing them. However, a small but growing number of websites do sell specialty products, using such tactics as "virtual product tours" (in which shoppers can interactively view a product in three dimensions, rather than simply looking at a static photograph) and generous return policies (to reduce the perceived risk of buying products online).

Second, do we need to establish a presence now in order to remain competitive in the future? The answer is an overwhelming "yes." The initial steps taken by our competitors are already placing us at a disadvantage among those shoppers who are already comfortable buying online, and every trend indicates our minor competitive weakness today will turn into a major weakness in the next few years:

• Several of our top competitors are beginning to implement full e-commerce, including virtual product tours. Our research suggests that these companies aren't yet generating significant financial returns from these online investments, but their online sales are growing.

• Younger consumers who grew up with the World Wide Web will soon be reaching their peak earning years (ages 35–54). This demographic segment expects e-commerce in nearly every product category, and we'll lose them to the competition if we don't offer it.

• The web is erasing geographical shopping limits, presenting both a threat and an opportunity. Even though our customers can now shop websites anywhere in the world (so that we have thousands of competitors instead of a dozen), we can now target customers anywhere in the world.

(continued)

Reminds readers of the origin and purpose of the report

Clarifies the recommendation by listing the necessary actions in clear, direct language

Presents logical reasons for recommending that the firm expand its website to include e-commerce

Supports the reasoning with evidence

FIGURE 12.3
Effective Problem-Solving Report Focusing on Recommendations
In this report recommending that her firm expand its website to full e-commerce capability, Alycia Jenn uses the body of her report to provide enough information to support her argument, without burdening her high-level readership with a lot of tactical details.

---

point to the next, make your transitions just as clear and logical. For a successful report, identify the ideas that belong together and organize them in a way that's easy to understand.[6]

• **Documented properly.** If you use primary and secondary sources for your report or proposal, be sure to properly document and give credit to your sources, as Chapter 11 explains.

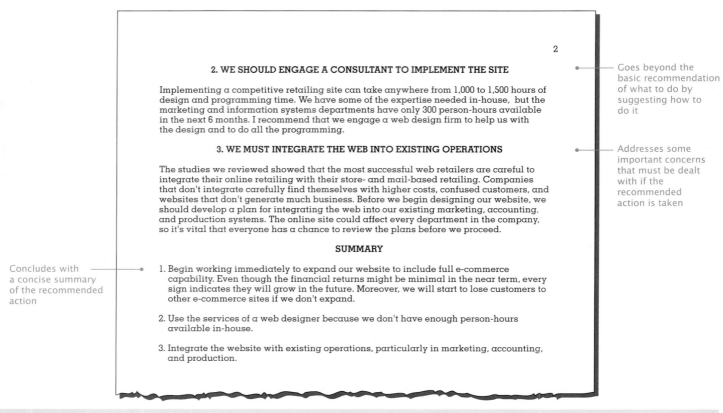

2

2. WE SHOULD ENGAGE A CONSULTANT TO IMPLEMENT THE SITE

Implementing a competitive retailing site can take anywhere from 1,000 to 1,500 hours of design and programming time. We have some of the expertise needed in-house, but the marketing and information systems departments have only 300 person-hours available in the next 6 months. I recommend that we engage a web design firm to help us with the design and to do all the programming.

Goes beyond the basic recommendation of what to do by suggesting how to do it

3. WE MUST INTEGRATE THE WEB INTO EXISTING OPERATIONS

The studies we reviewed showed that the most successful web retailers are careful to integrate their online retailing with their store- and mail-based retailing. Companies that don't integrate carefully find themselves with higher costs, confused customers, and websites that don't generate much business. Before we begin designing our website, we should develop a plan for integrating the web into our existing marketing, accounting, and production systems. The online site could affect every department in the company, so it's vital that everyone has a chance to review the plans before we proceed.

Addresses some important concerns that must be dealt with if the recommended action is taken

SUMMARY

Concludes with a concise summary of the recommended action

1. Begin working immediately to expand our website to include full e-commerce capability. Even though the financial returns might be minimal in the near term, every sign indicates they will grow in the future. Moreover, we will start to lose customers to other e-commerce sites if we don't expand.

2. Use the services of a web designer because we don't have enough person-hours available in-house.

3. Integrate the website with existing operations, particularly in marketing, accounting, and production.

FIGURE 12.3
(continued)

Keeping these points in mind will help you draft the most effective introduction, body, and close for your report (see Figure 12.4).

Carefully select the elements to include in your introduction; strive for a balance between necessary, expected information and brevity.

Report Introduction The specific elements you should include in an introduction depend on the nature and length of the report, the circumstances under which you're writing the report, and your relationship with the audience. An introduction could contain any or all of the following:

- **Authorization.** When, how, and by whom the report was authorized; who wrote it; and when it was submitted. This material is especially important when you don't accompany the report with a *letter of transmittal* (see Chapter 13).

- **Problem/opportunity/purpose.** The reason the report was written and what is to be accomplished as a result of your having written it.

- **Scope.** What is and what isn't covered in the report. The scope also helps with the critical job of setting the audience's expectations.

- **Background.** Any relevant historical conditions or factors that can help readers grasp the report's message.

- **Sources and methods.** The primary and secondary sources of information used. As appropriate, this section can also explain how the information was collected.

- **Definitions.** Definitions of important terms used in the report. Define any terms that might be unfamiliar to the audience or any terms you use in an unfamiliar way.

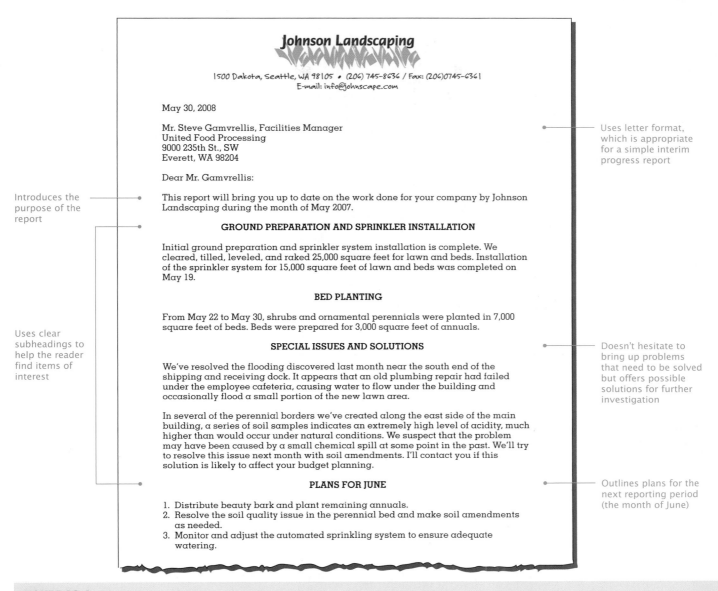

Uses letter format, which is appropriate for a simple interim progress report

Introduces the purpose of the report

Uses clear subheadings to help the reader find items of interest

Doesn't hesitate to bring up problems that need to be solved but offers possible solutions for further investigation

Outlines plans for the next reporting period (the month of June)

The content of the letter shown in the figure:

Johnson Landscaping

1500 Dakota, Seattle, WA 98105 • (206) 745-8636 / Fax: (206)0745-6361
E-mail: info@johnscape.com

May 30, 2008

Mr. Steve Gamvrellis, Facilities Manager
United Food Processing
9000 235th St., SW
Everett, WA 98204

Dear Mr. Gamvrellis:

This report will bring you up to date on the work done for your company by Johnson Landscaping during the month of May 2007.

GROUND PREPARATION AND SPRINKLER INSTALLATION

Initial ground preparation and sprinkler system installation is complete. We cleared, tilled, leveled, and raked 25,000 square feet for lawn and beds. Installation of the sprinkler system for 15,000 square feet of lawn and beds was completed on May 19.

BED PLANTING

From May 22 to May 30, shrubs and ornamental perennials were planted in 7,000 square feet of beds. Beds were prepared for 3,000 square feet of annuals.

SPECIAL ISSUES AND SOLUTIONS

We've resolved the flooding discovered last month near the south end of the shipping and receiving dock. It appears that an old plumbing repair had failed under the employee cafeteria, causing water to flow under the building and occasionally flood a small portion of the new lawn area.

In several of the perennial borders we've created along the east side of the main building, a series of soil samples indicates an extremely high level of acidity, much higher than would occur under natural conditions. We suspect that the problem may have been caused by a small chemical spill at some point in the past. We'll try to resolve this issue next month with soil amendments. I'll contact you if this solution is likely to affect your budget planning.

PLANS FOR JUNE

1. Distribute beauty bark and plant remaining annuals.
2. Resolve the soil quality issue in the perennial bed and make soil amendments as needed.
3. Monitor and adjust the automated sprinkling system to ensure adequate watering.

FIGURE 12.4
Effective Progress Report Offering Complete Content (Excerpt)
Note how Carlyce Johnson offers her client a complete but efficient update of her company's landscaping services. In addition to providing routine information, she also informs the client of progress in two problem areas—one that her firm has been able to resolve and one that it's just discovered. Johnson does the right thing by telling the client about the problems as early as possible, giving the client time to react and plan.

- **Limitations.** Factors beyond your control that affect the quality of the report, such as budgets, schedule constraints, or limited access to information or people. However, don't apologize or try to explain away personal shortcomings, such as your own poor planning.

- **Report organization.** The organization of the report. This "road map" helps readers understand what's coming in the report and why.

In a brief report, these topics may be discussed in only a paragraph or two. Here's an example of a brief indirect opening, taken from the introduction of a memo on why a new line of luggage has failed to sell well. The writer's ultimate goal is to recommend a shift in marketing strategy:

> The performance of the Venturer line can be improved. In the two years since its introduction, this product line has achieved a sales volume lower than we expected, resulting in a drain on the company's overall earnings. The purpose of this report is to review the luggage-buying habits of consumers in all markets where the Venturer line is sold so that we can determine where to put our marketing emphasis.

This paragraph quickly introduces the subject (disappointing sales), tells why the problem is important (drain on earnings), and indicates the main points to be addressed in the body of the report (review of markets where the Venturer line is sold), without revealing what the conclusions and recommendations will be.

In a longer formal report, the discussion of these topics may span several pages and constitute a significant section within the report.

Report Body   As with the introduction, the body of your report can require some tough decisions about which elements to include and how much detail to offer. Here again, your decisions depend on many variables, including the needs of your audience. Provide only enough detail in the body to support your conclusions and recommendations.

As with the introduction, the report body should contain only enough information to convey your message in a convincing fashion; don't overload the body with interesting but unnecessary material.

The topics commonly covered in a report body include

- Explanations of a problem or opportunity
- Facts, statistical evidence, and trends
- Results of studies or investigations
- Discussion and analyses of potential courses of action
- Advantages, disadvantages, costs, and benefits of a particular course of action
- Procedures or steps in a process
- Methods and approaches
- Criteria for evaluating alternatives and options
- Conclusions and recommendations
- Supporting reasons for conclusions or recommendations

For analytical reports that use the direct approach, you generally state your conclusions or recommendations in the introduction and use the body to provide your evidence and support (as illustrated in Figures 12.3 and 12.4). If you're using the indirect approach, you're likely to use the body to discuss your logic and reserve your conclusions or recommendations until the very end.

The nature of your close depends on the type of report (informational or analytical) and the approach (direct or indirect).

Report Close   The content and length of your report close depend on your choice of direct or indirect order, among other variables. If you're using the direct approach, you can end with a summary of key points, listed in the order in which they appear in the report body. If you're using the indirect approach, you can use the close to present your conclusions or recommendations if you didn't end the body with them. Just remember that a conclusion or recommendation isn't the place to introduce new facts; your readers should have all the information they need by the time they reach this point in your report.

If your report is intended to prompt others to action, use the ending to spell out exactly what should happen next and who is responsible for each task. If you'll be

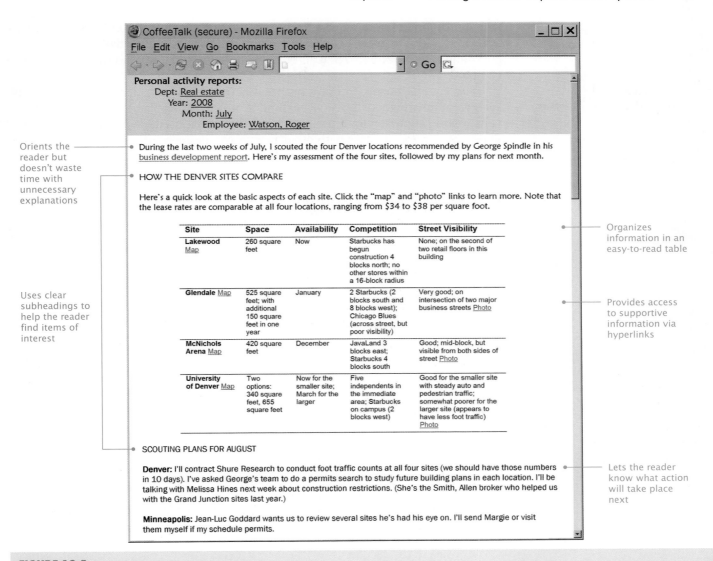

Orients the reader but doesn't waste time with unnecessary explanations

Uses clear subheadings to help the reader find items of interest

Organizes information in an easy-to-read table

Provides access to supportive information via hyperlinks

Lets the reader know what action will take place next

FIGURE 12.5
Effective Report Expressing Action Plan in the Close
Roger Watson's personal activity report for July is a good example of efficiently conveying key information points, including a clear plan of action in the close. Note the use of hyperlinks to maps, photos, and a related report, all of which are stored on the same secure intranet site.

taking all the actions yourself, make sure your readers understand this fact so that they know what to expect from you (see Figure 12.5).

In a short report, the close may be only a paragraph or two. However, the close of a long report may have separate sections for conclusions, recommendations, and actions. Using separate sections helps your reader locate this material and focus on each element. Such an arrangement also gives you a final opportunity to emphasize this important content. If you have multiple conclusions, recommendations, or actions, you may want to number and list them as well for easier reference.

For long reports, you may need to divide your close into separate sections for conclusions, recommendations, and actions.

Drafting Proposal Content

With proposals, the content for each section is governed by many variables—the most important of which is the source of your proposal. If your proposal is unsolicited, you have some latitude in the scope and organization of content. However, if you are responding to a request for proposals (RFP), you need to follow the instructions in the RFP in every detail. Most RFPs spell out precisely what a proposal must cover and in what order so that all bids will be similar in form and therefore easier to compare.

The general purpose of any proposal is to persuade readers to do something, such as purchase goods or services, fund a project, or implement a program. Thus, your writing approach for a proposal is similar to that used for persuasive sales messages (see Chapter 10). As with other persuasive messages, the AIDA model of gaining attention, building interest, creating desire, and motivating action is an effective structure. Here are some additional strategies to strengthen your argument:[7]

- Demonstrate your knowledge in terms that are meaningful to the audience.

- Provide concrete information and examples.

- Research the competition so you know what other proposals your audience is likely to read.

- Prove that your proposal is appropriate and feasible for your audience.

- Relate your product, service, or personnel to the reader's exact needs.

- Package your proposal attractively.

In addition, make sure your proposal is letter perfect, inviting, and readable. Readers will prejudge the quality of your products, services, and capabilities by the quality of the proposal you submit. Errors, omissions, or inconsistencies will work against you—and might even cost you important career and business opportunities.

Proposal Introduction   The introduction of a proposal presents and summarizes the problem or opportunity you want to address, along with your proposed solution. If your proposal is solicited, follow the RFP's instructions about indicating which RFP you're responding to. If your proposal is unsolicited, your introduction should mention any factors that led you to submit your proposal, such as previous conversations you've had with readers. The following topics are commonly covered in a proposal introduction:

- **Background or statement of the problem or opportunity.** Briefly reviews the reader's situation and establishes a need for action. Readers may not perceive a problem or an opportunity the same way you do. In unsolicited proposals, you need to convince them that a problem or an opportunity exists before you can convince them to accept your solution. In a way that is meaningful to your reader, discuss the current situation and explain how things could be better.

- **Solution.** Briefly describes the change you propose and highlights your key selling points and their benefits, showing how your proposal will help readers meet their business objectives. In a sales proposal, the solution would be the products or services you offer, along with any accessories, warranties, professional services such as installation, and other enhancements. In other types of proposals, the solution would be defined by the nature of the proposal.

- **Scope.** States the boundaries of the proposal—what you will and will not do. Sometimes called "Delimitations."

- **Organization.** Orients the reader to the remainder of the proposal and calls attention to the major divisions of information.

In short proposals, your discussion of these topics will be brief—perhaps only a sentence or two for each. For long, formal proposals, each topic may warrant separate subheadings and several paragraphs of discussion.

Approach proposals the same way you approach persuasive messages.

In an unsolicited proposal, your introduction needs to convince readers that a problem or an opportunity exists.

Proposal Body   The proposal's body gives complete details on the proposed solution and specifies what the anticipated results will be. Because a proposal is by definition a persuasive message, your audience expects you to promote your offering in a confident but professional manner.

In addition to providing facts and evidence to support your conclusions, an effective body covers this information:

- **Proposed solution.** Describes what you have to offer: your concept, product, or service. Stress the benefits of your product, service, or investment opportunity that are relevant to your readers' needs and point out any advantages that you have over your competitors.

- **Work plan.** Describes how you'll accomplish what must be done. Explain the steps you'll take, their timing, the methods or resources you'll use, and the person(s) responsible. Specifically include when the work will begin, how it will be divided into stages, when you will finish, and whether any follow-up is involved. For solicited proposals, make sure your dates match those specified in the RFP. Keep in mind that if your proposal is accepted, the work plan is contractually binding, so don't promise more than you can deliver.

- **Statement of qualifications.** Describes your organization's experience, personnel, and facilities—all in relation to reader needs. The qualifications section can be an important selling point, and it deserves to be handled carefully. You can supplement your qualifications by including a list of client references, but get permission ahead of time to use those references.

- **Costs.** Covers pricing, reimbursable expenses, discounts, and so on. Coverage can vary widely, from a single price amount to detailed breakdowns by part number, service category, and so on. If you're responding to an RFP, follow the instructions it contains. In other cases, your firm probably has a set policy for discussing costs.

In an informal proposal, discussion of some or all of these elements may be grouped together and presented in a letter format, as the proposal in Figure 12.6 does. In a formal proposal, the discussion of these elements can be quite long and thorough. The format may resemble long reports with multiple parts, as Chapter 13 discusses.

Proposal Close   The final section of a proposal generally summarizes the key points, emphasizes the benefits that readers will realize from your solution, summarizes the merits of your approach, restates why you and your firm are a good choice, and asks for a decision from the reader. The close is your last opportunity to persuade readers to accept your proposal. In both formal and informal proposals, make this section relatively brief, assertive (but not brash or abrupt), and confident.

Drafting Online Content

When you're writing for an audience online, follow the basic guidelines for writing a report presented earlier in this chapter along with these five additional steps to make your web content as effective as possible. First, take special care to build trust with your intended audiences because careful readers can be skeptical of online content. Make sure your content is accurate, current, complete, and authoritative. Indicate the date material was originally posted and when it is updated so that readers can judge your content's currency.

Second, even though it can be complicated and expensive, adapt your content for a global audience. Translating content is expensive, and going a step beyond—to *localizing* it so that it reflects not only the native language of your readers but their cultural norms, weights, measures, time, money, and so on—costs even more. Some

Readers understand that a proposal is a persuasive message, so they're willing to accommodate a degree of promotional emphasis in your writing—as long as it is professional and focused on their needs.

The work plan indicates exactly how you will accomplish the solution presented in the proposal.

The close is your last chance to convince the reader of the merits of your proposal, so make especially sure it's clear, compelling, and audience oriented.

Localizing web content involves both translating the content and adapting it to local cultural norms and practices.

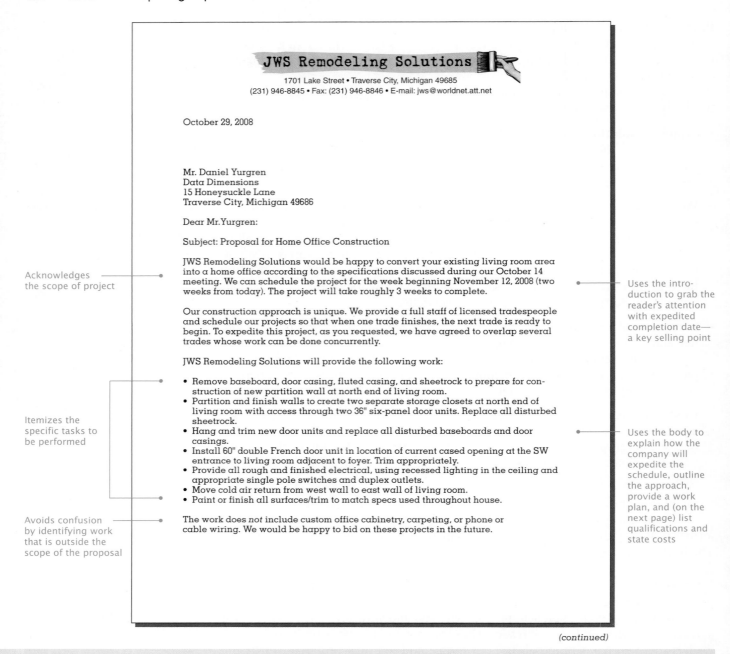

Acknowledges the scope of project

Itemizes the specific tasks to be performed

Avoids confusion by identifying work that is outside the scope of the proposal

Uses the introduction to grab the reader's attention with expedited completion date—a key selling point

Uses the body to explain how the company will expedite the schedule, outline the approach, provide a work plan, and (on the next page) list qualifications and state costs

(continued)

FIGURE 12.6

Effective Solicited Proposal in Letter Format

This informal solicited proposal provides the information the customer needs to make a purchase. Note that by signing the proposal and returning it, the customer enters into a legal contract to pay for the services described.

companies compromise by localizing the homepage and key secondary pages while keeping the deeper, more detailed content in its original language.

Third, compose web-friendly content. In an environment that presents many reading challenges, careful attention to composition is critical. Compelling, reader-oriented content is the key to success for any website.[8] Most readers don't return to websites that don't offer interesting, helpful content—it's too easy to find websites that serve them better. Wherever possible, use the *inverted pyramid* style, in which you cover the most important information briefly at first, then gradually reveal successive layers of detail—letting readers choose to see those additional layers if they

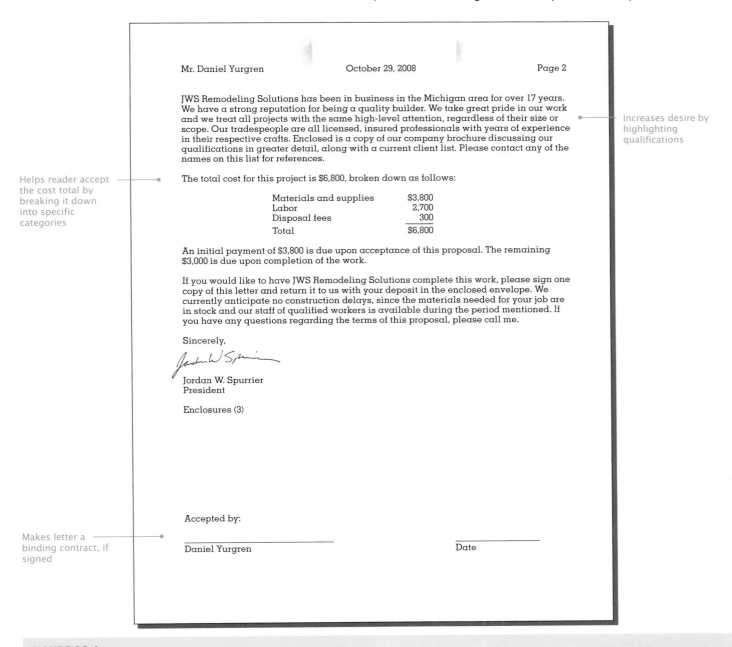

Mr. Daniel Yurgren   October 29, 2008   Page 2

JWS Remodeling Solutions has been in business in the Michigan area for over 17 years. We have a strong reputation for being a quality builder. We take great pride in our work and we treat all projects with the same high-level attention, regardless of their size or scope. Our tradespeople are all licensed, insured professionals with years of experience in their respective crafts. Enclosed is a copy of our company brochure discussing our qualifications in greater detail, along with a current client list. Please contact any of the names on this list for references.

Increases desire by highlighting qualifications

The total cost for this project is $6,800, broken down as follows:

Materials and supplies	$3,800
Labor	2,700
Disposal fees	300
Total	$6,800

Helps reader accept the cost total by breaking it down into specific categories

An initial payment of $3,800 is due upon acceptance of this proposal. The remaining $3,000 is due upon completion of the work.

If you would like to have JWS Remodeling Solutions complete this work, please sign one copy of this letter and return it to us with your deposit in the enclosed envelope. We currently anticipate no construction delays, since the materials needed for your job are in stock and our staff of qualified workers is available during the period mentioned. If you have any questions regarding the terms of this proposal, please call me.

Sincerely,

Jordan W. Spurrier
President

Enclosures (3)

Accepted by:

_____   _____
Daniel Yurgren   Date

Makes letter a binding contract, if signed

FIGURE 12.6
(continued)

want to. (Links to subpages are ideal for this.) Also, make sure your writing is compact and efficient; material on the web needs to be short because online readers tend to skip over long chunks of text.

Fourth, present your information in a concise, skimmable format. Effective websites use a variety of means to help readers skim pages quickly, including lists, careful use of color and boldface, informative headings (clever headings with lots of wordplay are usually more annoying than effective), and helpful summaries that give readers a choice of learning more if they want to.

Fifth, write effective links that serve for both site navigation and content skimming. Above all else, clearly identify where a link will take readers; don't force them to click through and try to figure out where they're going. If necessary, include a brief summary that explains what readers will experience if they click on the link—

Effective links in online reports let readers know exactly what to expect before they click on them.

particularly if the link downloads or opens a file or does anything else that might be unexpected. Also, try to avoid using directional words such as *back*, *forward*, *next*, *above*, *below*, *bottom*, or *top*. Such words are meaningful in a linear document but not necessarily in a hypertext document, where visitors can enter your site at many places and from many directions. Instead, use absolute directions such as *Return to Tables*, *Next Learning Step*, or *Beginning of Tutorial*.[9]

Helping Report Readers Find Their Way

Help your audiences navigate through your reports by providing clear directions to key pieces of content.

Today's time-pressed readers want to browse reports and quickly find information of interest. To help them find what they're looking for and stay on track as they navigate through your documents, learn to make good use of headings and links, smooth transitions, and previews and reviews:

- **Headings and links.** Readers should be able to follow the structure of your document and pick up the key points of your message from the headings and subheadings. (See Chapter 6 for a review of what makes an effective heading.) Follow a simple, consistent arrangement that clearly distinguishes levels.

- **Transitions.** Chapter 5 defines transitions as words or phrases that tie ideas together and show how one thought is related to another. In a long report, an entire paragraph might be used to highlight transitions from one section to the next, such as in this example:

As you can see alerts readers to the fact that they are reading a summary of the information just presented

this decline in profits lets readers know that the text will be saying something else about that previous topic

First, *second*, and *third* help readers stay on track as the three alternatives are introduced

However alerts readers to the fact that evaluating the three alternatives requires some additional discussion

> . . . <u>As you can see</u>, our profits have decreased by 12 percent over the past eight months.
>
> To counteract <u>this decline in profits</u>, we have three alternatives. <u>First</u>, we can raise our selling prices of existing products. <u>Second</u>, we can expand our offering by adding new products. <u>Third</u>, we can reduce our manufacturing costs. <u>However</u>, each of these alternatives has both advantages and disadvantages.

✓ CHECKLIST: Composing Business Reports and Proposals

A. Review and fine-tune your outline.

- ✓ Match your parallel headings to the tone of your report or proposal.
- ✓ Understand how the introduction, body, and close work together to convey your message.

B. Draft report content.

- ✓ Use the introduction to establish the purpose, scope, and organization of your report or proposal.
- ✓ Use the body to present and interpret the information you gathered.
- ✓ Use the close to summarize major points, discuss conclusions, or make recommendations.

C. Draft proposal content.

- ✓ Use the introduction to discuss the background or problem, your solution, the scope, and organization.

- ✓ Use the body to persuasively explain the benefits of your proposed approach.
- ✓ Use the close to emphasize reader benefits and summarize the merits of your approach.

D. Help readers find their way.

- ✓ Provide headings to improve readability and clarify the framework of your ideas.
- ✓ Use hyperlinks online to allow readers to jump from section to section.
- ✓ Create transitions that tie together ideas and show how one thought relates to another.
- ✓ Preview important topics to help readers get ready for new information.
- ✓ Review key information to help readers absorb details and keep the big picture in mind.

- **Previews and reviews.** *Preview sections* introduce important or complex topics by helping readers get ready for new information. *Review sections* come after a body of material and summarize key points to help readers absorb the information just read.

Previews help readers prepare for upcoming information, and reviews help them verify and clarify what they've just read.

To review the tasks discussed in this section, see "Checklist: Composing Business Reports and Proposals."

USING TECHNOLOGY TO CRAFT REPORTS AND PROPOSALS

Creating lengthy reports and proposals can be a huge task, so take advantage of technological tools that can help you throughout the process. You've read about some of these tools in earlier chapters; here are some of the most important ones for developing reports and proposals:

Look for ways to use technology to reduce the mechanical work involved in writing long reports.

- **Templates.** Beyond simply formatting documents, report templates can identify the specific sections required for each type of report and even automatically insert headings for each section.

- **Linked and embedded documents.** In many reports and proposals, you need to include graphics, spreadsheets, databases, and other elements produced in other software programs. Make sure you know how the software handles the files, or you may receive some unpleasant surprises. For instance, in Microsoft Office, you can choose to either *link* or *embed* an incoming element, such as a table from a spreadsheet. If you link, the element will be updated whenever you or someone else updates the spreadsheet. In contrast, if you embed it, the files are no longer connected; changes in the spreadsheet will not show up in the report document.

- **Electronic forms.** For recurring forms such as sales reports and compliance reports, consider creating a word processing file that combines boilerplate text for material that doesn't change from report to report. To accommodate information that does change (such as last week's sales results), use *form tools* such as text boxes (in which users can type new text) and check boxes (which can be used to select from a set of predetermined choices).

- **Electronic documents.** Portable Document Format (PDF) files have become a universal replacement for printed reports and proposals. With a copy of Adobe Acrobat (a separate product from the free Acrobat Reader), you can quickly convert reports and proposals to PDF files that are easy and safe to share electronically.

- **Multimedia documents.** When the written word isn't enough, combine your report with video clips, animation, presentation software slides, and other elements.

- **Proposal-writing software.** Basic features of proposal-writing software include the ability to automatically personalize proposals, ensure proper structure (making sure you don't forget any sections, for instance), and organize storage of all your boilerplate text. At a more advanced level, products such as Pragmatech's RFP Machine and Sant's RFPMaster can scan RFPs to identify questions and requirements and fill in potential answers from a centralized knowledge base that contains input from all the relevant experts in your company.[10]

Today's computer technology also makes it easy to add a wide variety of compelling visuals to reports, which you'll learn more about in the next section.

ILLUSTRATING YOUR REPORTS WITH EFFECTIVE VISUALS

Well-designed visual elements can enhance the communication power of textual messages and, in some instances, even replace textual messages. Visuals can often convey some message points (such as spatial relationships, correlations, procedures, and emotions) more effectively and more efficiently than words. Generally speaking, in a given amount of time, well-designed images can convey much more information than text.[11] In the numbers-oriented world of work, people rely heavily on trend lines, distribution curves, and visual presentations of numeric quantities. Visuals attract and hold people's attention, helping your audience understand and remember your message. Busy readers often jump to visuals to try to get the gist of a message, and attractive visuals can draw readers more deeply into your reports and presentations. Using pictures is also an effective way to communicate with the diverse audiences that are common in today's business environment.

Like words, visuals often carry connotative or symbolic meanings.

In addition to their direct information value, visuals often have connotative meaning as well. As you read in Chapter 5, many words and phrases carry connotative meanings, which are all the mental images, emotions, and other impressions that the word or phrase evokes in audience members. A significant part of the power—and risk—of visual elements derives from their connotative meanings as well. Even something as simple as a watermark symbol embedded in letterhead stationery can boost reader confidence in whatever message is printed on the paper.[12] Many colors, shapes, and other design elements have **visual symbolism**; and their symbolic, connotative meaning can evolve over time and mean different things in different cultures (see Figure 12.7). Being aware of these symbolic meanings and using them to your advantage are important aspects of being an effective business communicator.

Understanding Visual Design Principles

Visual literacy is the ability to create and interpret visual messages.

Given the importance of visuals in today's business environment, **visual literacy**—the ability (as a sender) to create effective images and (as a receiver) to correctly interpret visual messages—has become a key business skill.[13] Just as creating effective sentences, paragraphs, and documents requires working knowledge of the principles of good writing, creating effective visuals requires some knowledge of the principles of

FIGURE 12.7
Visual Symbolism
A red cross (with equal-length arms) on a white background is the well-known symbol of the Red Cross relief organization. It is also used to indicate the medical branches of many nations' military services. The red cross symbol is based on the flag of Switzerland (where the first Red Cross organization was formed), which over the course of hundreds of years developed from battle flags that originally used the Christian cross symbol. Although the Red Cross emblem is not based directly on the Christian symbol, the organization uses a red crescent in countries where Islam is the dominant religion and is known as the Red Crescent. To avoid association with religious symbols, the International Federation of Red Cross and Red Crescent Societies (the global umbrella organization for all national Red Cross and Red Crescent organizations) recently adopted the Red Crystal as its new symbol.

Communication Challenge	Effective Visual Choice

Presenting Data

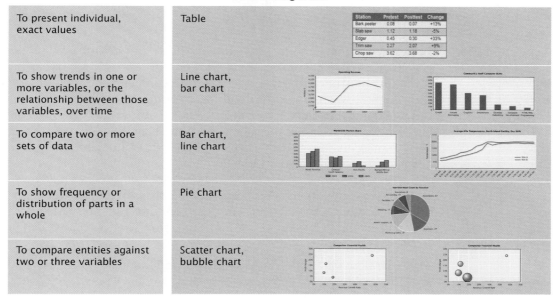

To present individual, exact values	Table
To show trends in one or more variables, or the relationship between those variables, over time	Line chart, bar chart
To compare two or more sets of data	Bar chart, line chart
To show frequency or distribution of parts in a whole	Pie chart
To compare entities against two or three variables	Scatter chart, bubble chart

Presenting Information, Concepts, and Ideas

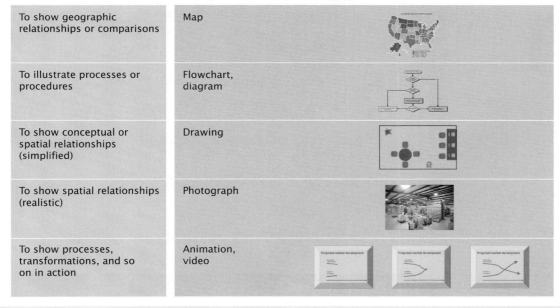

To show geographic relationships or comparisons	Map
To illustrate processes or procedures	Flowchart, diagram
To show conceptual or spatial relationships (simplified)	Drawing
To show spatial relationships (realistic)	Photograph
To show processes, transformations, and so on in action	Animation, video

FIGURE 12.9
Selecting the Best Visual
For each point you want to illustrate, make sure to choose the most effective type of visual.

ple, your audience is likely to expect line charts and bar charts to show trends. Line charts usually show data variations relative to a time axis (such as sales month by month), whereas bar charts more often compare discrete groups (such as sales by demographic segment). Although a bar chart can show the percentages that make up a whole, this job is usually reserved for pie charts.

The following sections explore the most common types of visuals in more detail, starting with visuals designed to present data.

Visuals for Presenting Data Business professionals have a tremendous number of choices for presenting data, from general-purpose line, bar, and pie charts to specialized charts for product portfolios, financial analysis, and other professional functions. The visuals most commonly used to present data include tables, line and surface charts, bar charts, and pie charts.

Tables When you need to present detailed, specific information, choose a **table**, a systematic arrangement of data in columns and rows. Most tables contain the standard parts illustrated in Table 12.2. For printed documents, you can adjust font size and column/row spacing to fit a considerable amount of information on the page and still maintain readability. For online documents, you often need to reduce the number of columns and rows to make sure your tables are easily readable online. Tables for oral presentations usually need to be the simplest of all because you can't expect audiences to read detailed information from the screen.

Although complex information may require formal tables that are set apart from the text, you can present some data more simply within the text. Such text tables are usually introduced with a sentence that leads directly into the tabular information. Here's an example:[21]

> Printed tables can display extensive amounts of data, but tables for online display and electronic presentations need to be simpler.

Here is how the five leading full-service restaurant chains compare in terms of number of locations and annual revenue:

	OSI Restaurant Partners	Applebee's	Carlson	Brinker	Darden
Major chain(s)	Outback Steakhouse, Carrabba's	Applebee's	TGI Friday's, Pick Up Stix	Chili's, Romano's	Red Lobster, Olive Garden
Locations	1,400	1,900	900	1,600	1,400
Revenue ($ million)	$3,940	$1,338	$2,400	$4,151	$5,721

Source: Hoover's Online [accessed 7 April 2007] www.hoovers.com.

When you prepare tables, follow these guidelines to make your tables easy to read:

- Use common, understandable units and clearly identify the units you're using.
- Express all items in a column in the same unit and round off for simplicity.

Table 12.2   PARTS OF A TABLE

			Multicolumn Head*	
Subhead	**Subhead**	**Subhead**	**Single-Column Head**	**Single-Column Head**
Row head	XXX	XXX	XX	XX
Row head				
Subhead	XX	XXX	XX	X
Subhead	XX	XXX	XX	XX
Total	XXX	XXX	XX	XX

Source (In the same format as a text footnote; see Appendix B.)

*Footnote (For an explanation of elements in the table, a superscript number or small letter may be used instead of an asterisk or other symbol.)

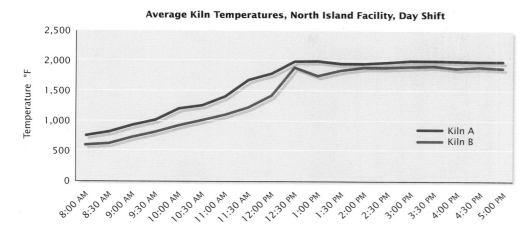

FIGURE 12.10
Line Chart
This two-line line chart compares the temperatures measured inside two cement kilns from 8:00 A.M. to 5:00 P.M.

- Label column headings clearly and use a subhead, if necessary.

- Separate columns or rows with lines or extra space to make the table easy to follow; in complex tables, consider highlighting every other row or column in a pale contrasting color.

- Provide totals or averages of columns or rows when relevant.

- Document the source of the data, using the same format as for a text footnote (see Appendix B).

Line Charts and Surface Charts A **line chart**, or *line graph*, illustrates trends over time or plots the relationship of two variables. In line charts that show trends, the vertical, or *y*, axis shows the amount, and the horizontal, or *x*, axis shows the time or other quantity against which the amount is being measured. Moreover, you can plot just a single line or overlay multiple lines to compare different entities (see Figure 12.10).

A **surface chart**, also called an **area chart**, is a form of line chart that shows a cumulative effect; all the lines add up to the top line, which represents the total (see Figure 12.11). This form of chart helps you illustrate changes in the composition of something over time. When preparing a surface chart, put the most important segment against the baseline and restrict the number of strata to four or five.

Bar Charts and Pie Charts A **bar chart**, or *bar graph*, portrays numbers with the height or length of its rectangular bars, making one or more series of numbers easy to read or understand. Bar charts are particularly valuable when you want to show or

Line charts are commonly used to show trends over time or the relationship between two variables.

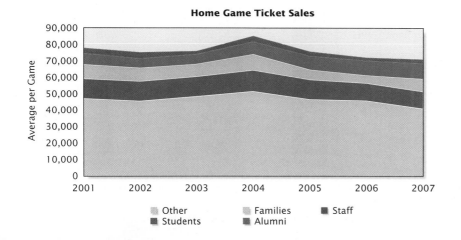

FIGURE 12.11
Surface Chart
Surface, or area, charts can show a combination of trends over time and the individual contributions of the components of a whole.

FIGURE 12.12
The Versatile Bar Chart
Here are six of the dozens of
variations possible with bar
charts: singular (12.12a), grouped
(12.12b), deviation (12.12c),
segmented (12.12d), combination
(12.12e), and paired (12.12f).

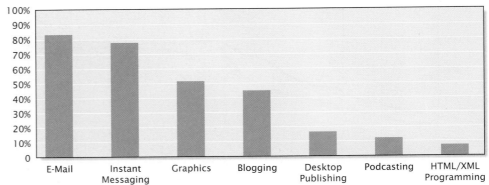

(a) CommuniCo Staff Computer Skills

(b) Worldwide Market Share

(c) CommuniCo Stock Price

(d) CommuniCo Preferred Communication Media

(continued)

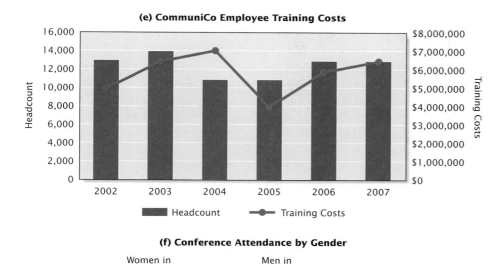

(e) CommuniCo Employee Training Costs

(f) Conference Attendance by Gender

Women in Attendance / Men in Attendance

750	600	San Diego Conference
590	800	Las Vegas Conference
950	450	Miami Conference

FIGURE 12.12
(continued)

compare quantities over time. As the charts in Figure 12.12 suggests, bar charts can appear in various forms. *Grouped* bar charts compare more than one set of data, using a different color or pattern for each set. *Deviation* bar charts identify positive and negative values, or winners and losers. *Segmented* bar charts, also known as stacked bar charts, show how individual components contribute to a total number, using a different color or pattern for each component. *Combination* bar and line charts compare quantities that require different intervals. *Paired* bar charts show the correlations between two items.

Like segmented bar charts and area charts, a **pie chart** shows how the parts of a whole are distributed (see Figure 12.13). However, pie charts have the advantage of familiarity; most people expect parts of a whole to be displayed via a pie chart. Each segment represents a slice of a complete circle, or *pie*.

When creating pie charts, try to restrict the number of slices in the pie. Otherwise, the chart looks cluttered and is difficult to label. If necessary, lump the smallest pieces together in a "miscellaneous" or "other" category. Ideally, the largest or most important slice of the pie, the segment you want to emphasize, is placed at the

Most readers expect pie charts to show the distribution of parts within a whole.

Year-End Head Count by Function

Executives, 8; Accounting, 14; Facilities, 14; Shipping, 17; Admin Support, 25; Marketing/Sales, 27; Engineers, 28; Assemblers, 67

FIGURE 12.13
Pie Chart
When creating pie charts, use different colors or patterns to distinguish the various pieces. Label all the segments and indicate their value in either percentages or units of measure so that your readers can judge the values of the wedges.

twelve o'clock position; the rest are arranged clockwise either in order of size or in some other logical progression.

Use different colors or patterns to distinguish the various pieces. If you want to draw attention to the segment that is of the greatest interest to your readers, use a brighter color for that segment, draw an arrow to the segment, or explode it; that is, pull the segment away from the rest of the pie. In any case, label all the segments and indicate their values in either percentages or units of measure so that your readers can judge the values of the wedges. Remember that the segments must add up to 100 percent if percentages are used or to the total number if numbers are used.

Line, surface, bar, and pie charts will meet most of your data presentation needs, but for specialized needs, explore the other chart options available in software such as Microsoft Excel.

Visuals for Presenting Information, Concepts, and Ideas In addition to facts and figures, you need to present other types of information, from spatial relationships (such as the floor plan for a new office building) to abstract ideas (such as progress or competition). The most common types of visuals for these applications include flowcharts, organization charts, maps, drawings, diagrams, photographs, animation, and video.

Flowcharts and Organization Charts A **flowchart** (see Figure 12.14) illustrates a sequence of events from start to finish; it is an indispensable tool for illustrating processes, procedures, and sequential relationships. For general business purposes, you don't need to be too concerned about the specific shapes in a flowchart, but use

FIGURE 12.14
Flowchart
Flowcharts show sequences of events and are most valuable when the process or procedure has a number of decision points and variable paths.

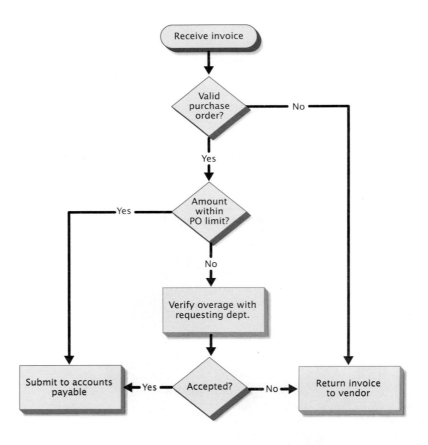

them consistently. However, you should be aware of the formal flowchart "language," in which each shape has a specific meaning (diamonds are decision points, rectangles are process steps, and so on). If you're communicating with computer programmers and others who are accustomed to formal flowcharting, make sure you use the correct symbols to avoid confusion.

As the name implies, an **organization chart** illustrates the positions, units, or functions of an organization and the way they interrelate. An organization's normal communication channels are almost impossible to describe without the benefit of a chart like the one in Figure 12.15. These charts aren't limited to organization structures, of course; as you saw in Chapter 4, they can also be used to outline messages.

Maps, Drawings, Diagrams, and Photographs Maps are useful for showing market territories, distribution routes, facilities locations, and other geographically significant data (see Figure 12.16). Simple maps are available via clip art libraries for word processing and presentation software, but more powerful uses (such as automatically generating color-coded maps based on data inputs) usually require the specialized capabilities of *geographic information systems*. You may also want to explore online resources such as Google Earth (http://earth.google.com) and Windows Live (http://maps.live.com), which offer a variety of mapping and aerial photography features.

> Use maps to represent statistics by geographic area and to show spatial relationships.

Although drawings, diagrams, and photographs are often created by people working in communication specialties such as web design or technical writing, all managers encounter situations in which such images can help get their messages

FIGURE 12.15
Organization Chart
Using an organization chart is the expected way to illustrate the hierarchy of positions in an organization.

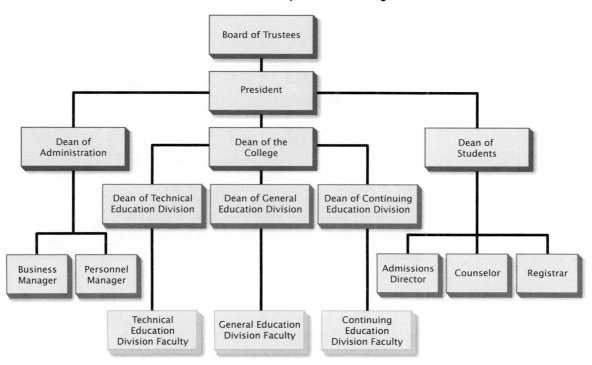

FIGURE 12.16

Map

Maps offer many opportunities for displaying data and information. The map in Figure 12.16a shows population projections for each state in the United States. Figure 12.16b is a simple version of a geographic information system, in this case showing hotels and motels in a neighborhood near New York's La Guardia Airport. A company looking for sites to build a hotel in this area could use such a map to identify potential competitors, traffic patterns, and other important variables.

(a) Map Showing Statistical Data

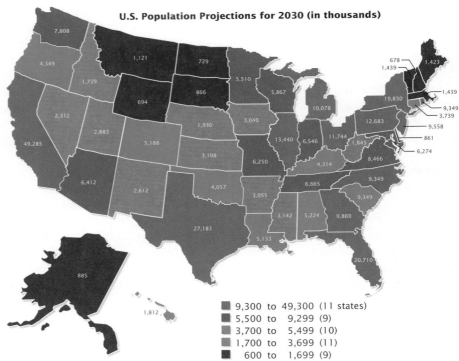

U.S. Population Projections for 2030 (in thousands)

9,300 to 49,300 (11 states)
5,500 to 9,299 (9)
3,700 to 5,499 (10)
1,700 to 3,699 (11)
600 to 1,699 (9)

(b) Map Generated by a Geographic Information System

across (see Figure 12.17). For example, when Brian Lamkin, an executive at Adobe Systems, wants to inform his staff about new competitive products being demonstrated at trade shows or the way Adobe products are being displayed in a particular retail store, he uses his digital camera to share images.[22] Simple drawings can show the network of suppliers in an industry, the flow of funds through a company, or the

FIGURE 12.17
Diagram
Clearly drawn diagrams can help audiences grasp technical information quickly.

process for completing the payroll each week. More complex diagrams can convey technical topics such as the operation of a machine or repair procedures.

Word processing programs and presentation software provide basic drawing capabilities, but for more precise drawings or complex illustrations, you need a specialized package such as Microsoft Visio or Adobe Illustrator. Moving to a level beyond those programs, computer-aided design (CAD) systems such as Autodesk's AutoCAD can produce extremely detailed architectural and engineering drawings.

Photographs offer both functional and decorative value. In the past, their use was limited to specialized documents such as annual reports and product brochures; however, with low-cost digital photography now widely available, virtually all writers have the ability to add photographs to printed documents, presentations, and webpages. In addition, photo libraries such as Getty Images (www.gettyimages.com) and photo search engines such as the one provided by AltaVista (www.altavista.com/image) make it easy to find digital photographs. Some of these photos are available for free, but the professional collections, such as Getty Images, require either a one-time payment for unlimited use (often called *royalty free*) or an annual payment or other limited-use purchase (often called *rights managed*).

Nothing else can demonstrate the exact appearance of a new facility, a piece of property, a new product, or even a retiring co-worker the way a photograph can. However, in some situations, a photograph may show too much detail, which is one reason repair manuals frequently use drawings instead of photos, for instance. With a drawing, you can select how much detail to show, and you can focus the reader's attention on particular parts or places. The disadvantage of such technical illustrations is the time, skill, and special tools often required to create them.

Technology makes it easy to use photographs in reports and presentations, but it also presents an important ethical concern. Software tools such as Photoshop and

Use photographs for visual appeal and to show exact appearances.

To show investors what a new building would look like in its environment, an artist combined a photograph of a scale model of the building with a photograph of the actual street scene. Because the target audience clearly understands that the building doesn't exist, this sort of image manipulation is not unethical.

Paint Shop Pro allow you to easily make dramatic changes to photos—without leaving a clue that they've been altered. Altering photos in small ways has been possible for a long time (more than a few students have had blemishes airbrushed out of their yearbook photos), but computers make drastic changes easy and undetectable. You can remove people from photographs, put Person A's head on Person B's body, and make products look more attractive than they really are. Most people would agree that it's acceptable to make cosmetic improvements, such as brightening an underexposed photo to make it easier to view. But to avoid ethical lapses, don't make any alterations that mislead the viewer or substantially change the message conveyed by the photo—at least not without informing your audience of the changes.[23]

Animation and Video Computer animation and video are among the most specialized forms of business visuals. When they are appropriate and done well, they offer unparalleled visual impact. At a simple level, you can animate shapes and text within Microsoft PowerPoint, although the possibilities are somewhat limited. At a more sophisticated level, software programs such as Adobe Flash enable the creation of multimedia files that include computer animation, digital video, and other elements. A wide variety of tools are also available for digital video production. Chances are, you won't have to use these tools yourself, but if you employ a specialist to create animation or video for websites or presentations, make sure the results follow all the guidelines for effective business messages.

PRODUCING AND INTEGRATING VISUALS

Now that you understand the communication power of visuals and have chosen the best visuals to illustrate key points in your report, website, or presentation, it's time to get creative. This section offers advice on creating visuals, integrating them with your text, and verifying the quality of your visual elements.

Creating Visuals

Computer software offers a variety of tools but doesn't automatically give you the design sensibility that is needed for effective visuals.

Computers make it easy to create visuals, but they also make it easy to create ineffective, distracting, and even downright ugly visuals. However, by following the basic design principles discussed on pages 426 to 428, you can create all the basic visuals you need—visuals that are attractive and effective. If possible, have a professional designer set up a *template* for the various types of visuals you and your colleagues need to create. In addition to helping ensure an effective design, using templates saves you the time of making numerous design decisions every time you create a chart or graphic.

Remember that the style and quality of your visuals communicates a subtle message about your relationship with the audience. A simple sketch might be fine for a working meeting but inappropriate for a formal presentation or report. On the other hand, elaborate, full-color visuals may be viewed as extravagant for an informal report but may be entirely appropriate for a message to top management or influential outsiders.

Integrating Visuals with Text

For maximum effectiveness and minimum disruption for the reader, visual elements need to be carefully integrated with the text of your message so that readers can move back and forth between text and visuals with as little disruption as possible. Successful integration involves four decisions: maintaining a balance between visuals and text, referring to visuals in the text, placing the visuals in the document, and writing titles and other descriptions.

Balancing Illustrations and Words   Strong visuals enhance the descriptive and persuasive power of your writing, but putting too many visuals into a report can distract your readers. Constantly referring to visuals makes it difficult for readers to maintain focus on the thread of your message. The space occupied by visuals can also disrupt the flow of text on the page or screen. The pacing of visuals throughout the text is also an important consideration. Although it isn't always possible to have perfect distribution throughout the report, try to have a fairly even flow of text and visuals from page to page or screen to screen.

As always, take your readers' specific needs into account. If you're addressing an audience with multiple language backgrounds or widely varying reading skills, you can shift the balance toward more visual elements to help get around any language barriers. The professional experience, education, and training of your audience should influence your approach as well. For instance, detailed statistical plots and mathematical formulas are everyday reading material for quality-control engineers but not for most salespeople or top executives.

Referencing Visuals   Unless a visual element clearly stands on its own, as in the *sidebars* you often see in magazines, visuals should be clearly referred to by number in the text of your report. Some report writers refer to all visuals as "exhibits" and number them consecutively throughout the report; many others number tables and figures separately (everything that isn't a table is regarded as a figure). In a long report with numbered sections, illustrations may have a double number (separated by a period or a hyphen) representing the section number and the individual illustration number within that section. Whichever scheme you use, make sure it's clear and consistent.

Help your readers understand the significance of visuals by referring to them before readers encounter them in the document or onscreen. The following examples show how you can make this connection in the text:

> Figure 1 summarizes the financial history of the motorcycle division over the past five years, with sales broken into four categories.
>
> Total sales were steady over this period, but the mix of sales by category changed dramatically (see Figure 2).
>
> The underlying reason for the remarkable growth in our sales of youth golf apparel is suggested by Table 4, which shows the growing interest in junior golf around the world.

When describing the data shown in your visuals, be sure to emphasize the main point you are trying to make. Don't make the mistake of simply repeating the data to be shown.

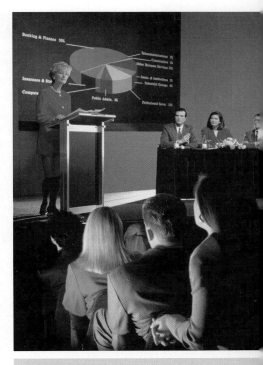

The use of color in visuals accelerates learning, retention, and recall by 55 percent to 78 percent, and it increases motivation and audience participation by up to 80 percent.

Maintain a balance between text and visuals and pace your visuals in a way that emphasizes your key points.

To tie visuals to the text, introduce them in the text and place them near the points they illustrate.

Placing Visuals Try to position your visuals so that your audience doesn't have to flip back and forth (in printed documents) or scroll (onscreen) between the visuals and the text. Ideally, it's best to place each visual within, beside, or immediately after the paragraph it illustrates so that readers can consult the explanation and the visual at the same time. If possible, try to avoid bunching several visuals in one section of the document.

Writing Titles, Captions, and Legends
Titles, captions, and legends provide more opportunities to connect your visual and textual messages. A **title** is similar to a subheading, providing a short description that identifies the content and purpose of the visual, along with whatever label and number you're using to refer to the visual. A **caption** usually offers additional discussion of the visual's content and can be several sentences long, if appropriate. Captions can also alert readers that additional discussion is available in the accompanying text. Titles usually appear above visuals and captions appear below, but effective designs can place these two elements in other positions. Sometimes titles and captions are combined in a single block of text as well. As with all other design decisions, be consistent throughout your report or website. A **legend** helps readers "decode" the visual by explaining what various colors, symbols, or other design choices mean.

The title of a visual functions in the same way as a subheading; the caption provides any additional detail needed.

Readers should be able to grasp the point of a visual without digging into the surrounding text. For instance, a title that says simply "Refineries" doesn't say much at all. A **descriptive title** that identifies the topic of the illustration, such as "Relationship Between Petroleum Demand and Refinery Capacity in the United States" provides a better idea of what the chart is all about. An **informative title** tells even more by calling attention to the conclusion that ought to be drawn from the data, such as "Refinery Capacity Declines as Petroleum Demand Continues to Grow."

Verifying the Quality of Your Visuals

Visuals have a particularly strong impact on your readers and on their perceptions of you and your work, so verifying their quality is vital. Take a few extra minutes to make sure your visuals are absolutely accurate, properly documented, and honest:

Review each visual to make sure it doesn't intentionally or unintentionally distort the meaning of the underlying information.

- **Is the visual accurate?** Be sure to check visuals for mistakes such as typographical errors, inconsistent color treatment, confusing or undocumented symbols, and misaligned elements. Does each visual deliver your message accurately? Have you inserted the right visuals in the right places? Also verify that information in visuals and accompanying text matches. For data presentations, particularly if you're producing charts with a spreadsheet, verify any formulas used to generate the numbers and make sure you've selected the right numbers for each chart.

- **Is the visual properly documented?** As with the textual elements in your reports and presentations, visuals based on other people's research, information, and ideas require full citation. (Note that in many books, including this one, source notes for visuals are collected in one place at the end of the book.) Also, try to anticipate any

PRACTICING ETHICAL COMMUNICATION

Distorting the Data

Take a quick look these three line charts, all of which display the level of impurities found in a particular source of drinking water. Chart A suggests that the source has a consistently high level of impurities throughout the year, Chart B indicates that the level of impurities jumps up and down throughout the year, and Chart C shows an impurity level that is fairly consistent throughout the year—and fairly low.

Here's the catch: All three charts are displaying *exactly the same data*.

Look again at Chart A. The vertical scale is set from 0 to 120, sufficient to cover the range of variations in the data. However, what if you wanted to persuade an audience that the variations from month to month were quite severe? In Chart B, the scale is "zoomed in" on 60 to 110, making the variations look much more dramatic. The result could be a stronger emotional impact on the reader, creating the impression that these impurities are out of control.

On the other hand, what if you wanted to create the impression that things were humming along just fine, with low levels of impurities and no wild swings from month to month? You would follow the example in Chart C, where the scale is expanded from 0 to 200, which appears to minimize the variations in the data. This graph is visually "calmer," potentially creating the impression that there's really nothing to worry about.

If all three graphs show the same data, is any one of them more honest than the others? The answer to this question depends on your intent and your audience's information needs. For instance, if dramatic swings in the measurement from month to month suggest a problem with the quality of your product or the safety of a process that affects the public, then visually minimizing the swings might well be considered dishonest.

CAREER APPLICATIONS

1. What sort of quick visual impression would such a chart give if the vertical scale is set to 0 to 500? Why?

2. If the acceptable range of impurities in this case is from 60 to 120 parts per million, which of these three charts is the fairest way to present the data? Why?

questions or concerns your audience may have and address them with additional information as needed. For instance, if you're presenting the results of survey research, many readers will want to know who participated in the survey, how many people responded, and when the questions were asked. You could answer these questions with a note in the caption.

- **Is the visual honest?** As a final precaution, step back and make sure your visuals communicate truthful messages (see "Practicing Ethical Communication: Distorting the Data"). Make sure they don't hide information the audience needs, imply conclusions that your information doesn't support, or play on audience emotions in manipulative or coercive ways.

For a review of the important points to remember when creating visuals, see "Checklist: Creating Effective Visuals."

✓ CHECKLIST: Creating Effective Visuals

- ✓ Emphasize visual consistency to connect parts of a whole and minimize audience confusion.
- ✓ Avoid arbitrary changes of color, texture, typeface, position, or scale.
- ✓ Highlight contrasting points through color, position, and other design choices.
- ✓ Decide whether you want to achieve formal or informal balance.
- ✓ Emphasize dominant elements and de-emphasize less important pieces in a design.
- ✓ Understand and follow (at least most of the time) the visual conventions your audience expects.
- ✓ Strive for simplicity and clarity; don't clutter your visuals with meaningless decoration.
- ✓ Follow the guidelines for avoiding ethical lapses.
- ✓ Carefully consider your message, the nature of your information, and your audience to choose which points to illustrate.

- ✓ Select the proper types of graphics for the information at hand and for the objective of the message.
- ✓ Be sure the visual contributes to overall understanding of the subject.
- ✓ Understand how to use your software tools to maximize effectiveness and efficiency.
- ✓ Integrate visuals and text by maintaining a balance between illustrations and words, clearly referring to visuals within the text, and placing visuals carefully.
- ✓ Use titles, captions, and legends to help readers understand the meaning and importance of your visuals.
- ✓ Verify the quality of your visuals by checking for accuracy, proper documentation, and honesty.

On the Job

SOLVING COMMUNICATION DILEMMAS AT TELLABS

You wanted to start your career in corporate communications with an opportunity to learn from one of the best, so you're excited to be on George Stenitzer's team at Tellabs. Using the skills you've been practicing in this course, respond to these challenges.

1. The *CEO's letter* in a corporate annual report serves as an introduction to the rest of the report. In Tellabs's 2006 report, CEO Krish Prabhu opened his letter with the following:

> More. I can't think of a better word to describe what's happening in communications today. All across the world, people want to see more. Do more. Interact more. Learn more. And everywhere we look, the world's communications providers are rushing to respond.
>
> This transition to tomorrow's networks represents a unique growth opportunity for Tellabs. That's because making more possible is what this company is all about. We do it by supplying the solutions that providers need to make their networks smarter, faster and better-suited to the kinds of high-bandwidth applications that will define the future of communications.
>
> In fact, that future is already with us. As I write this, YouTube, the immensely popular videosharing Web site, is already one of the top

15 Web sites in the world, even though it has yet to celebrate its second birthday. YouTube originates an average of 100 million video streams each day. And thanks to a partnership with Verizon, those videos are now accessible even when we're away from our computers.

> The YouTube success story is merely one illustration of the remarkable changes that are taking place in the way we communicate and entertain ourselves.

After reviewing a draft, Stenitzer suggested that a heading would help intrigue and prepare readers for the information in this section. Which of the following headings does the best job of introducing this section of Prabhu's letter? (The purpose of discussing these changes in online communication and networking is to convince investors that the market opportunities for Tellabs's products will continue to grow.)

a. There's No Stopping Us Now!
b. Exciting Opportunities in the Exciting New World of High-Bandwidth Communication
c. Growth Opportunities in a Growing Market
d. Growth Opportunities: Market Drivers

2. Like many other companies associated with the Internet, Tellabs's business declined when the dot-com boom of the late 1990s began to fizzle out by

early 2001. The following excerpt from the company's 2005 annual report describes the effect this had on the company's operations. (The *carriers* and *service providers* referred to are the companies that buy Tellabs's products; *material charges* are expenses that are significant enough to affect the company's stock price.) As you review these two paragraphs (don't worry about all the technical and financial details), you can see that the first discusses the period from 2001 to 2003, when the company's financial results suffered. The second discusses the upturn that began in 2003 and continued through 2005.

The markets for our products have undergone dynamic change over the last few years. Beginning in 2001, carrier overcapacity, a softening economy and other factors caused our customers to reduce their capital spending significantly. The impact on Tellabs was a dramatic decline in revenue for each of the years 2001 through 2003. In addition, we had manufacturing overcapacity, excess inventories and a cost structure that could not be supported by our smaller revenue base. We responded by closing manufacturing facilities, reducing global head count, consolidating office space, exiting certain product lines and instituting cost controls across the organization. We also reviewed our product portfolio and cut back or stopped development efforts on some products. In addition, at the end of 2003, we moved to outsource the majority of our remaining manufacturing operations to third-party electronics manufacturing services providers to take advantage of their greater purchasing power and other efficiencies. These actions caused us to record material charges in 2001 through 2005 for excess and obsolete inventory and excess purchase commitments, severance costs, facilities shutdown costs, including accelerated depreciation on certain manufacturing and office buildings and equipment due to shortened useful lives, and various contractual obligations. We also recorded charges for other impaired and surplus assets.

Market stability began in 2003 and continued in 2004 and 2005 as service providers invested in their networks at levels at or above 2003. This stability enabled us to post year-over-year revenue growth in 2004 for the first time since fiscal 2000. Growing demand for wireless services, including third-generation (3G) services, drove capital investments by both wireless and wireline service providers and helped drive sales of our transport and managed access products.

Which of the following transition sentences would be the best choice to add at the beginning of the second paragraph, signaling to readers that the story is about to change from the negative news of 2001–2003 to the more positive results that began in 2003?

a. Were we glad to see the dark days of 2001–2003 behind us!
b. Fortunately, those bad times didn't last forever.
c. These aggressive measures helped the company survive the extended downturn and prepared us to grow again when the market recovered.
d. Transitioning forward, the situation began to improve beginning in 2003.

3. You've just helped a team from the marketing and engineering departments draft a report on the prospects for the electronic communication market over the next five years. Thanks to the team's diligent research, you're confident that the information is about as current as it could possibly be. However, so many things associated with the Internet can change so quickly that you can't guarantee the information will be accurate several months from now, much less several years from now. Which of the following statements would be the best way to express this limitation of the report?

a. It must be pointed out that the information in this report may become obsolete as market conditions change. This is a function of the dynamic nature of the market and is not an issue with the quality of our research.
b. The information contained herein was current as of the time of publication. We cannot guarantee its accuracy in the future.
c. The dynamic nature of the electronic communication industry means that information is likely to change over time. Please accept our apologies for this limitation.
d. The dynamic nature of the electronic communication industry means that information is likely to change over time. Please check with us for the latest news and insights before making any major strategic or financial decisions based on the content of this report.

4. To help readers quickly assess the relative contributions of Tellabs's various product lines to the company's overall revenues, year by year over a 10-year period, which type of visual would be most effective?

a. Ten pie charts, one per year, showing the breakdown of sales by product line
b. A table, with the years in columns and the product lines in rows
c. An area chart
d. A bar chart

Assess your understanding of the principles in this chapter by reading each learning objective and studying the accompanying exercises. For fill-in-the-blank items, write the missing text in the blank provided; for multiple-choice items, circle the letter of the correct answer. You can check your responses against the answer key on page AK-2.

Objective 12.1: Explain how to adapt to your audiences when writing reports and proposals.

1. Why is the "you" attitude particularly important with long or complex reports and proposals?
   a. The "you" attitude takes less time to write, so you'll save considerable time with long documents.
   b. Professionals are accustomed to reading long reports, so they don't require a lot of "hand holding."
   c. People simply don't read reports that don't demonstrate good business etiquette.
   d. The length and complexity of these reports put a heavy demand on readers, making it particularly important to be sensitive to their needs.

2. Which of these sentences has the most formal tone?
   a. We discuss herein the possibility of synergistic development strategies between our firm and U.S. Medical.
   b. This report explores the potential for a strategic partnership with U.S. Medical.
   c. My report is the result of a formal investigation into the possibility of a strategic partnership with U.S. Medical.
   d. In this report, I address the potential for a strategic partnership with U.S. Medical.

Objective 12.2: List the topics commonly covered in the introduction, body, and close of informational and analytical reports.

3. Which of these does not belong in the body of an informational or analytical report?
   a. An explanation of weaknesses in the report
   b. Facts, statistical evidence, and trends
   c. Conclusions and recommendations
   d. Criteria for evaluating alternatives and options

4. Where would you list action items in a report?
   a. In the opening
   b. In the body
   c. In the close
   d. Action items are never listed in reports.

Objective 12.3: Name five characteristics of effective report content.

5. Which of the following is *not* a characteristic of effective report content?
   a. Balanced
   b. Logical
   c. Entertaining
   d. Accurate

6. How are audiences likely to react if they spot several errors in your reports?
   a. They'll become skeptical about the quality of all your work.

b. They'll forgive you and move on without thinking any more about it; everybody makes mistakes.
   c. They'll stop reading your reports.
   d. They'll respect the fact that you don't waste time proofreading.

Objective 12.4: Name six strategies to strengthen your proposal argument.

7. Which of the following is not a recommended strategy for strengthening your proposal argument?
   a. Provide concrete examples of the value of your proposal.
   b. Demonstrate your knowledge.
   c. Identify the amount of time you've invested in the proposal.
   d. Adopt a "you" attitude.

8. If packaging and presentation are only superficial, why are they so important in proposal writing?
   a. Readers tend to prejudge the quality of your products and services based on the quality of your proposal.
   b. They show that you're more than just a "numbers" person—that you can think creatively.
   c. They show the audience that you're willing to invest time and money in getting your proposal accepted.
   d. Attractive documents always have high-quality information in them.

Objective 12.5: List the topics commonly covered in a proposal's introduction, body, and close.

9. Which of the following elements is usually *not* part of a proposal's introduction?
   a. Background or statement of the problem
   b. Detailed cost analysis
   c. Organization of the proposal
   d. Scope of the proposal

10. The primary purpose of the body of a proposal is to
   a. List your firm's qualifications for the project in question
   b. Explain why the recipient needs to address a particular problem or opportunity
   c. Communicate your passion for solving the problem or addressing the opportunity
   d. Give complete details on the proposed solution and its anticipated benefits

11. If a proposal is being sent in response to an RFP, how should the body of the proposal address the issue of costs?
   a. It should avoid any mention of costs.
   b. It should provide a total cost figure without wasting the reader's time with a lot of details.
   c. It should follow whatever your company's policy is regarding cost estimates.
   d. It should follow the instructions in the RFP exactly.

Objective 12.6: Identify five characteristics of effective writing in online reports.

12. _____ goes a step beyond translating, making sure web content reflects not only the native language of

your readers but their cultural norms, weights, measures, time, money, and other specific elements.

13. Which of the following is the most effectively worded link to a webpage that describes a company's products and services?
    a. <u>Click here</u> to learn more about what we do.
    b. Learn more about <u>our products and services</u>.
    c. <u>Next page</u>
    d. You have problems? We have <u>solutions</u>.

Objective 12.7: Describe the communication power that visuals add to your writing.

14. Visuals can enhance the communication impact of your writing by
    a. Conveying some types of information better than text can
    b. Reaching audiences of diverse professional and cultural backgrounds
    c. Communicating your most important points to audiences that are too busy to read your entire report
    d. Delivering all of the above benefits

Objective 12.8: Explain how to choose which points in your message to illustrate.

15. Which of the following is a good candidate for illustrating in a report?
    a. Comparison of customer satisfaction ratings of 12 stores across a 12-month period
    b. Percentage of employees who have attended 10 different training courses
    c. Ranking of webpages on a website, from most visited to least visited
    d. All of the above

16. Which of the following is *not* a good reason to use a visual in a report?
    a. To communicate more effectively with multilingual audiences
    b. To help unify the separate parts of a process, an organization, or another entity, such as by using a flowchart to depict the various steps in a process
    c. To simplify access to specific data points, such as by listing them in a quick-reference table
    d. To demonstrate your creative side

Objective 12.9: Discuss six principles of graphic design that can improve the quality of your visuals.

17. Why is consistency important in visual design?
    a. It shows the audience that you're not wasting precious time doing artistic designs.
    b. It reduces confusion by eliminating arbitrary changes that force people to relearn your design scheme every time they encounter another visual.
    c. It saves on ink and toner when reports are printed.
    d. It shows the audience that you're serious and businesslike.

18. Which of the following steps could you take to call attention to the most important elements in a visual?
    a. Use a dominant color for the important elements.
    b. Call attention to the important elements in the caption or in the text of your report.
    c. Make the important elements larger.
    d. Do all of the above.

Objective 12.10: Name three qualities to look for before including a visual in a report or presentation.

19. Which of the following steps should you take to verify the accuracy of the visuals in your reports?
    a. Make sure that data presentations such as line charts and bar charts accurately portray the data that you intended to show.
    b. Make sure flowcharts and other computer-generated artwork are correct and clear.
    c. Make sure that you've inserted the correct visuals at each place in your report.
    d. Do all of the above.

20. Assume that you have a line chart with a vertical axis scaled from 0 to 100 and data points that vary within a range of roughly 10 to 90. How would you influence audience perceptions if you increased the vertical scale so that it stretched from 0 to 200 instead of 0 to 100?
    a. The scaling change would have no effect on audience perceptions.
    b. The scaling change would maximize the perceived variations in the data.
    c. The scaling change would minimize the perceived variations in the data.
    d. You have no way of predicting in advance how the scaling change would affect perceptions.

Apply Your Knowledge

1. Should a report always explain the writer's method of gathering evidence or solving a problem? Why or why not?
2. Besides telling readers why an illustration is important, why refer to it in the text of your document?
3. When you read a graph, how can you be sure that the visual impression you are receiving is an accurate reflection of reality? Please explain.
4. If you want your audience to agree to a specific course of action, should you exclude any references to alternatives that you don't want the audience to consider? Why or why not?
5. **Ethical Choices** If a company receives a solicited formal proposal outlining the solution to a particular problem, is it ethical for the company to adopt the proposal's recommendations without hiring the firm that submitted the proposal? Why or why not?

Practice Your Knowledge

MESSAGE FOR ANALYSIS: EVALUATING A PROPOSAL

Read Figure 12.18, a solicited memo proposal, and then (1) analyze the strengths and weaknesses of this document and (2) revise the document so that it follows this chapter's guidelines.

EXERCISES

For active links to all websites discussed in this chapter, visit this book's website, at www.prenhall.com/thill. Locate your book and click on its "Companion Website" link. Then select Chapter 12 and click on "Featured Websites." Locate the name of the page or the URL related to the material in the text. Please note that links to sites that become inactive after publication of the book will be removed from the "Featured Websites" section.

12.1 Adapting Reports to the Audience Review the reports shown in Figures 12.3 and 12.4. Give specific examples of how each of these reports establishes a good relationship with the audience. Consider such things as using the "you" attitude, emphasizing the positive, establishing credibility, being polite, using bias-free language, and projecting a good company image.

12.2 Composing Reports: Report Content You are writing an analytical report on the U.S. sales of your newest product. Of the following topics, identify those that

FIGURE 12.18
Solicited Proposal

PROPOSAL

DATE: April 18, 2008
TO: Ken Estes, Northern Illinois Concrete
FROM: Kris Beiersdorf, Memco Construction
PROJECT: IDOT Letting Item #83, Contract No. 79371, DuPage County

Memco Construction proposes to furnish all labor, material, equipment, and supervision to provide Engineered Fill—Class II and IV—for the following unit prices.

Engineered Fill—Class II and IV

Description	Unit	Quantity	Unit Price	Total
Mobilization*	Lump Sum	1	$4,500.00	$4,500.00
Engineered Fill Class II	Cubic Yards	1,267	$33.50	$42,444.50
Engineered Fill Class IV	Cubic Yards	1,394	$38.00	$52,972.00

* Mobilization includes one move-in. Additional move-ins to be billed at $1,100.00 each.

The following items clarify and qualify the scope of our subcontracting work:
1. All forms, earthwork, clearing, etc., to be provided and maintained by others at no cost to Memco Construction.
2. General Contractor shall provide location for staging, stockpiling material, equipment, and storage at the job site.
3. Memco Construction shall be paid strictly based upon the amount of material actually used on the job.
4. All prep work, including geotechnical fabrics, geomembrane liners, etc., to be done by others at no cost to Memco Construction.
5. Water is to be available at project site at no charge to Memco Construction.
6. Dewatering to be done by others at no cost to Memco Construction.
7. Traffic control setup, devices, maintenance, and flagmen are to be provided by others at no cost to Memco Construction.
8. Memco Construction LLC may withdraw this bid if we do not receive a written confirmation that we are the apparent low sub-bidder within 10 days of your receipt of this proposal.
9. Our F.E.I.N. is 36-4478095.
10. Bond is not included in above prices. Bond is available for an additional 1 percent.

If you have any questions, please contact me at the phone number listed below.

Kris Beiersdorf
Memco Construction
187 W. Euclid Avenue, Glenview, IL 60025
Office: (847) 352-9742, ext. 30
Fax: (847) 352-6595
E-mail: Kbeiersdorf@memco.com
www.memco.com

should be covered in the report's introduction, body, and close. Briefly explain your decisions.

a. Regional breakdowns of sales across the country
b. Date the product was released in the marketplace
c. Sales figures from competitors selling similar products worldwide
d. Predictions of how the struggling U.S. economy will affect sales over the next six months
e. Method used for obtaining the above predictions
f. The impact of similar products being sold in the United States by Japanese competitors
g. Your recommendation as to whether the company should sell this product internationally
h. Actions that must be completed by year end if the company decides to sell this product internationally

12.3 Composing Business Reports Your boss, Len Chow (vice president of corporate planning), has asked you to research opportunities in the cosmetics industry and to prepare a report that presents your findings and your recommendation for where you think the company should focus its marketing efforts. Here's a copy of your note cards (data were created for this exercise):

Sub: Demand   ref: 1.1
Industrywide sales have grown consistently for several decades, fueled by both a growing population and increased per capita consumption

Sub: Competition   ref: 1.2
700 companies currently in cosmetics industry

Sub: Niches   ref: 1.3
Focusing on special niches avoids head-on competition with industry leaders

Sub: Competition   ref: 1.4
Industry dominated by market leaders: Revlon, Procter & Gamble, Avon, Gillette

Sub: Demand   ref: 1.5
Industry no longer recession-proof: Past year, sales sluggish; consumer spending is down; most affected were mid- to high-priced brands; consumers traded down to less expensive lines

Sub: Competition   ref: 1.6
Smaller companies (Neutrogena, Mary Kay, Softsoap, and Noxell) survive by: specializing in niches, differentiating product line, focusing on market segment

Sub: Demand   ref: 1.7
Consumption of cosmetics relatively flat for past five years

Sub: Competition   ref: 1.8
Prices are constant while promotion budgets are increasing

Sub: Niches   ref: 1.9
Men: 50 percent of adult population; account for one-fifth of cosmetic sales; market leaders have attempted this market but failed

Sub: Demand   ref: 1.10
Cosmetic industry is near maturity but some segments may vary. Total market currently produces annual retail sales of $14.5 billion: Cosmetics/lotions/fragrances—$5.635 billion; Personal hygiene products—$4.375 billion; Hair-care products—$3.435 billion; Shaving products—$1.055 billion

Sub: Niches   ref: 1.11
Ethnic groups: Some firms specialize in products for African Americans; few firms oriented toward Hispanic, Asian, or Native Americans, which tend to be concentrated geographically

Sub: Demand   ref: 1.12
Average annual expenditure per person for cosmetics is $58

Sub: Competition   ref: 1.13
Competition is intensifying and dominant companies are putting pressure on smaller ones

Sub: Demand   ref: 1.14
First quarter of current year, demand is beginning to revive; trend expected to continue well into next year

Sub: Niches   ref: 1.15
Senior citizens: large growing segment of population; account for 6% of cosmetic sales; specialized needs for hair and skin not being met; interested in appearance

Sub: Demand   ref: 1.16
Demographic trends: (1) Gradual maturing of baby-boomer generation will fuel growth by consuming greater quantities of shaving cream, hair-coloring agents, and skin creams; (2) population is increasing in the South and Southwest, where some brands have strong distribution

List the main idea of your message (your recommendation), the major points (your conclusions), and supporting evidence. Then construct a final report outline with first- and second-level informative headings focusing on your conclusions. Because Chow requested this report, you can feel free to use the direct approach. Finish by writing a draft of your memo report to Chow.

12.4 Composing Reports Find an article in a business newspaper or journal (in print or online) that recommends a solution to a problem. Identify the problem, the recommended solution(s), and the supporting evidence provided by the author to justify his or her recommendation(s). Did the author cite any formal or informal studies as evidence? What facts or statistics did the author include? Did the author cite any criteria for evaluating possible options? If so, what were they?

12.5 Composing Reports: Navigational Clues Review a long business article in a journal or newspaper. Highlight examples of how the article uses headings, transitions, and previews and reviews to help the readers find their way.

12.6 Ethical Choices Your boss has asked you to prepare a feasibility report to determine whether the company should advertise its custom-crafted cabinetry in the weekly neighborhood newspaper. Based on your primary research, you think they should. As you draft the introduction to your report, however, you discover that the survey administered to the neighborhood newspaper subscribers was flawed. Several of the questions were poorly written and misleading. You used the survey results, among other findings, to justify your recommendation. The report is due in three days. What actions might you want to take, if any, before you complete your report?

12.7 Improving Visual Design Find a communication example that you believe could be improved by applying the visual design principles you learned in this chapter. It can be from any medium—a webpage, a magazine ad, a promotional e-mail message, an illustration from a report—anything that you can either copy or scan into a word processing file. With the image in your word processing program, annotate it with notes that identify visual weaknesses and describe ways to fix those weaknesses. (In Microsoft Word, for example, you can use the "AutoShapes Callouts" feature to place notes wherever you'd like on the page.) In a paragraph of accompanying text, explain why you believe the message isn't as effective as it could be and how your suggestions would make it more effective.

12.8 Preparing Line Charts The pet food manufacturer you work for is interested in the results of a recent poll of U.S. pet-owning households. Look at the statistics that follow and decide on the most appropriate scale for a chart; then create a line chart of the trends in cat ownership. What conclusions do you draw from the trend you've charted? Draft a paragraph or two discussing the results of this poll and the potential conse-

quences for the pet food business. Support your conclusions by referring readers to your chart.

> In 1990, 22 million U.S. households owned a cat. In 1995, 24 million households owned a cat. In 2000, 28 million households owned a cat. In 2005, 32 million households owned a cat.

12.9 Selecting the Right Visual You're preparing the annual report for FretCo Guitar Corporation. For each of the following types of information, select an appropriate chart or visual to illustrate the text. Explain your choices.

a. Data on annual sales for the past 20 years
b. Comparison of FretCo sales, product by product (electric guitars, bass guitars, amplifiers, acoustic guitars), for this year and last year
c. Explanation of how a FretCo acoustic guitar is manufactured
d. Explanation of how the FretCo Guitar Corporation markets its guitars
e. Data on sales of FretCo products in each of 12 countries
f. Comparison of FretCo sales figures with sales figures for three competing guitar makers over the past 10 years

12.10 Selecting the Right Chart Here are last year's sales figures for the appliance and electronics megastore where you work. Construct charts based on these figures to help explain to the store's general manager seasonal variations in each department.

Store Sales in 2007 (in $ thousands)

Month	Home Electronics	Computers	Appliances
January	$68	$39	$36
February	72	34	34
March	75	41	30
April	54	41	28
May	56	42	44
June	49	33	48
July	54	31	43
August	66	58	39
September	62	58	36
October	66	44	33
November	83	48	29
December	91	62	24

12.11 Creating Maps You work for C & S Holdings, a company that operates coin-activated, self-service car washes. Research shows that the farther customers live from a car wash, the less likely they are to visit. You know that 50 percent of customers at each of your car washes live within a 4-mile radius of the location, 65 percent live within 6 miles, 80 percent live within 8 miles, and 90 percent live within 10 miles. C & S's owner wants to open two new car washes in your city and has asked you to prepare a report recommending locations. Using a map of your city (print or online), choose two possible locations for car washes and create a visual depicting the customer base surrounding each location. (Make up whatever population data you need.)

12.12 Internet One of the best places to see how data can be presented visually is in government statistical publications, which are often available on the Internet. For example, the International Trade Administration (ITA), a branch of the U.S. Department of Commerce, publishes monthly reports about U.S. trade with other

countries. Visit the report page of its website, at http://trade.gov, and follow the link to the latest monthly International Trade Update (you should find the link on the right side of the homepage). Download the complete issue as a PDF file. Using what you learned in this chapter, evaluate the charts in the report. Do they present the data clearly? Are they missing any elements? What would you do to improve the charts? Print a copy of the report to turn in with your answers and indicate which charts you are evaluating.

Expand Your Knowledge

LEARNING MORE ON THE WEB
BRUSH UP ON YOUR COMPUTER-GRAPHICS SKILLS

http://graphicssoft.about.com

Need some help using graphics software? Get started at the About.com Graphics Software website. Take the tutorials and learn how to manage fonts, images, and perform a variety of graphics-related tasks. View the illustrated demonstrations. Read the instructional articles. Learn how to use the most common file formats for graphics. Expand your knowledge of the basic principles of graphic design. And master some advanced color tips and theory. Don't leave without following the links to recommended books and magazines. Explore About.com's Graphics Software section and answer these questions:

1. What are the most common file formats for online visuals?

2. What does color depth mean in computer visuals?
3. What is dithering and how can it affect your visuals?

SURFING YOUR WAY TO CAREER SUCCESS

Bovée and Thill's Business Communication Headline News offers links to hundreds of online resources that can help you with this course, your other college courses, and your career. Visit www.businesscommunicationblog.com and click on "Web Directory." The "Online Videos" section provides links to a wide variety of free online videos on numerous business communication topics, from blogging and business plans to podcasting and résumé writing. Identify three websites from this section that could be useful in your business career. For each site, write a two-sentence summary of what the site offers and how it could help you launch and build your career.

Learn Interactively

INTERACTIVE STUDY GUIDE

Visit www.prenhall.com/thill, locate your book and click on its "Companion Website" link. Select Chapter 12 to take advantage of the interactive "Chapter Quiz" to test your knowledge of chapter concepts. Receive instant feedback on whether you need to do additional studying. Also, visit the "Study Hall," where you'll find an abundance of valuable resources that will help you succeed in this course.

PEAK PERFORMANCE GRAMMAR AND MECHANICS

If your instructor has required the use of "Peak Performance Grammar and Mechanics," either in your online course or on

CD, you can improve your skill with dashes and hyphens by using the "Peak Performance Grammar and Mechanics" module. Click on "Punctuation II." Take the Pretest to determine whether you have any weak areas. Then review those areas in the Refresher Course. Take the Follow-Up Test to check your grasp of dashes and hyphens. For an extra challenge or advanced practice, take the Advanced Test. Finally, for additional reinforcement, go to the "Improve Your Grammar, Mechanics, and Usage" section that follows and complete those exercises.

Improve Your Grammar, Mechanics, and Usage

The following exercises help you improve your knowledge of and power over English grammar, mechanics, and usage. Turn to the Handbook of Grammar, Mechanics, and Usage at the end of this book and review all of Sections 2.7 (Dashes)

and 2.8 (Hyphens). Then look at the following 10 items. Circle the letter of the preferred choice in the following groups of sentences. (Answers to these exercises appear on page AK-4.)

1. a. Three qualities—speed, accuracy, and reliability are desirable in any applicant.
   b. Three qualities—speed, accuracy, and reliability—are desirable in any applicant.

2. a. A highly placed source explained the top-secret negotiations.
   b. A highly-placed source explained the top-secret negotiations.
   c. A highly placed source explained the top secret negotiations.

3. a. The file on Mary Gaily—yes—we finally found it reveals a history of tardiness.
   b. The file on Mary Gaily, yes—we finally found it— reveals a history of tardiness.
   c. The file on Mary Gaily—yes, we finally found it— reveals a history of tardiness.

4. a. They're selling a well designed machine.
   b. They're selling a well-designed machine.

5. a. Argentina, Brazil, Mexico—these are the countries we hope to concentrate on.
   b. Argentina, Brazil, Mexico—these are the countries— we hope to concentrate on.

6. a. Only two sites maybe three—offer the things we need.
   b. Only two sites—maybe three—offer the things we need.

7. a. How many owner operators are in the industry?
   b. How many owner—operators are in the industry?
   c. How many owner-operators are in the industry?

8. a. Your ever-faithful assistant deserves—without a doubt— a substantial raise.
   b. Your ever faithful assistant deserves—without a doubt— a substantial raise.

9. a. The charts are well placed—on each page—unlike the running heads and footers.
   b. The charts are well-placed on each page—unlike the running heads and footers.
   c. The charts are well placed on each page—unlike the running heads and footers.

10. a. Your devil-may-care attitude affects everyone in the decision-making process.
    b. Your devil may care attitude affects everyone in the decision-making process.
    c. Your devil-may-care attitude affects everyone in the decision making process.

For additional exercises focusing on dashes and hyphens, go to www.prenhall.com/thill, then locate your text and click on its "Companion Website" link. Click on Chapter 12, click on "Additional Exercises to Improve Your Grammar, Mechanics and Usage," and click on "18. Punctuation C."

Cases

Applying the Three-Step Writing Process to Cases
Apply each step to the following cases, as assigned by your instructor.

Planning

1

Analyze the Situation
Clarify the problem or opportunity at hand, develop an audience profile, and develop a work plan.

Gather Information
Determine audience needs and obtain the information necessary to satisfy those needs; conduct a research project if necessary.

Select the Right Medium
Choose the best medium for delivering your message; consider delivery through multiple media.

Organize the Information
Define your main idea, limit your scope, select a direct or an indirect approach, and outline your content using an appropriate structure for an informational report, analytical report, or proposal.

Writing

2

Adapt to Your Audience
Be sensitive to audience needs with a "you" attitude, politeness, positive emphasis, and bias-free language. Build a strong relationship with your audience by establishing your credibility and projecting your company's image. Control your style with a tone and voice appropriate to the situation.

Compose the Message
Choose strong words that will help you create effective sentences and coherent paragraphs throughout the introduction, body, and close of your report or proposal.

Completing

3

Revise the Message
Evaluate content and review readability, edit and rewrite for conciseness and clarity.

Produce the Message
Use effective design elements and suitable layout for a clean, professional appearance; seamlessly combine text and graphical elements.

Proofread the Message
Review for errors in layout, spelling, and mechanics.

Distribute the Message
Deliver your report using the chosen medium; make sure all documents and all relevant files are distributed successfully.

INFORMATIONAL REPORTS

1. My progress to date: Interim progress report on your academic career As you know, the bureaucratic process involved in getting a degree or certificate is nearly as challenging as any course you could take.

Your task: Prepare an interim progress report detailing the steps you've taken toward completing your graduation or certification requirements. After examining the requirements listed in your college catalog, indicate a realistic schedule for completing those that remain. In addition to course requirements, include steps such as completing the residency requirement, filing necessary papers, and paying necessary fees. Use memo format for your report, and address it to anyone who is helping or encouraging you through school.

2. Gavel to gavel: Personal activity report of a meeting Meetings, conferences, and conventions abound in the academic world, and you have probably attended your share.

Your task: Prepare a personal activity report on a meeting, convention, or conference that you recently attended. Use memo format and direct the report to other students in your field who were not able to attend.

3. Check that price tag: Informational report on trends in college costs Your college's administration has asked you to compare your college's tuition costs with those of a nearby college and determine which has risen more quickly. Research the trend by checking your college's annual tuition costs for each of the most recent four years. Then research the four-year tuition trends for a neighboring college. For both colleges, calculate the percentage change in tuition costs from year to year and between the first and fourth years.

Your task: Prepare an informal report (using letter format) that presents your findings and conclusions to the president of your college. Include graphics that explain and support your conclusions.

4. Get a move on it: Lasting guidelines for moving into college dormitories Moving into a college dormitory is one experience you weren't quite prepared for. In addition to lugging all your earthly belongings up four flights of stairs in 90-degree heat, channeling electrical cords to the one room outlet tucked in the corner of the room, lofting your beds, and negotiating with your roommate over who gets the bigger closet, you had to hug your parents goodbye in the parking lot in front of the entire freshman class—or so it seemed. Now that you're a pro, you've offered to write some lasting guidelines for future freshmen so they know what is expected of them on moving day.

Your task: Prepare an informational report for future freshmen classes, outlining the rules and procedures to follow when moving into a college dorm. Lay out the rules, such as starting time, handling trash and empty boxes, items permitted and not permitted in dorm rooms, common courtesies, parking,

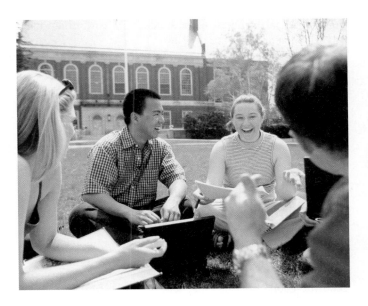

and so on. Be sure to mention what the policy is for removing furniture from the room, lofting beds, and overloading electrical circuits. Of course, any recommendations on how to handle disputes with roommates would be helpful. So would some brief advice on how to cope with anxious parents. Direct your memo report to the college dean.

ANALYTICAL REPORTS

5. My next career move: Feasibility report organized around recommendations If you've ever given yourself a really good talking-to, you'll be quite comfortable with this project.

Your task: Write a memo report directed to yourself and signed with a fictitious name. Indicate a possible job that your college education will qualify you for, mention the advantages of the position in terms of your long-range goals, and outline the actions you must take to get the job.

6. Staying the course: Unsolicited proposal using the 2 + 2 = 4 approach Think of a course you would love to see added to the core curriculum at your school. Conversely, if you would like to see a course offered as an elective rather than being required, write your e-mail report accordingly.

Your task: Write a short e-mail proposal using the 2 + 2 = 4 approach (refresh your memory in Chapter 11, if necessary). Prepare your proposal to be submitted to the academic dean by e-mail. Be sure to include all the reasons that support your idea.

7. Planning my program: Problem-solving report using the yardstick approach Assume that you will have time for only one course next term.

Your task: List the pros and cons of each of four or five courses that interest you and use the yardstick approach to settle on the course that is best for you to take at this time. Write your report in memo format and address it to your academic adviser.

8. Restaurant review: Troubleshooting report on a restaurant's food and operations Visit any restaurant, possibly your school cafeteria. The workers and fellow customers will assume that you are an ordinary customer, but you are really a spy for the owner.

Your task: After your visit, write a short letter to the owner, explaining (a) what you did and what you observed, (b) any violations of policy that you observed, and (c) your recommendations for improvement. The first part of your report (what you did and what you observed) will be the longest. Include a description of the premises, inside and out. Tell how long it took for each step of ordering and receiving your meal. Describe the service and food thoroughly. You are interested in both the good and bad aspects of the establishment's décor, service, and food. For the second section (violations of policy), use some common sense. If all the servers but one have their hair covered, you may assume that policy requires hair to be covered; a dirty window or restroom obviously violates policy. The last section (recommendations for improvement) involves professional judgment. What management actions will improve the restaurant?

9. On the books: Troubleshooting report on improving the campus bookstore Imagine that you are a consultant hired to improve the profits of your campus bookstore.

Your task: Visit the bookstore and look critically at its operations. Then draft a letter to the bookstore manager, offering recommendations that would make the store more profitable, perhaps suggesting products it should carry, hours it should remain open, or added services that it should make available to students. Be sure to support your recommendations.

10. Day and night: Problem-solving report on stocking a 24-hour convenience store When a store is open all day, every day, when's the best time to restock the shelves? That's the challenge at Store 24, a retail chain that never closes. Imagine you're the assistant manager of a Store 24 branch that just opened near your campus. You want to set up a restocking schedule that won't conflict with prime shopping hours. Think about the number of customers you're likely to serve in the morning, afternoon, evening, and overnight hours. Consider, too, how many employees you might have during these four periods.

Your task: Write a problem-solving report in letter form to the store manager (Isabel Chu) and the regional manager (Eric Angstrom), who must agree on a solution to this problem. Discuss the pros and cons of each of the four periods, and include your recommendation for restocking the shelves.

PROPOSALS

11. "Would you carry it?" Unsolicited sales proposal recommending a product to a retail outlet Select a product you are familiar with and imagine that you are the manufacturer trying to get a local retail outlet to carry it. Use the Internet and other resources to gather information about the product.

Your task: Write an unsolicited sales proposal in letter format to the owner (or manager) of the store, proposing that the item be stocked. Use the information you gathered to describe some of the product's features and benefits to the store. Then make up some reasonable figures, highlighting what the item costs, what it can be sold for, and what services your company provides (return of unsold items, free replacement of unsatisfactory items, necessary repairs, and so on).

12. Where is everybody? Proposal to sell GPS fleet tracking system As a sales manager for Air-Trak, one of your responsibilities is writing sales proposals for potential buyers of your company's Air-Trak tracking system. The system uses a global positioning system (GPS) to track the location of vehicles and other assets. For example, the dispatcher for a trucking company can simply click on a map display on a computer screen to find out where all the company's trucks are at that instant. Air-Trak lists the following as benefits of the system:

- Making sure vehicles follow prescribed routes with minimal loitering time

- "Geofencing," in which dispatchers are alerted if vehicles leave

- Route optimization, in which fleet managers can analyze routes and destinations to find the most time- and fuel-efficient path for each vehicle

- Comparisons between scheduled and actual travel

- Enhanced security to protect both drivers and cargos

Your task: Write a brief proposal to Doneta Zachs, fleet manager for Midwest Express, 338 S.W. 6th, Des Moines, Iowa, 50321. Introduce your company, explain the benefits of the Air-Trak system, and propose a trial deployment in which you would equip five Midwest Express trucks. For the purposes of this assignment, you don't need to worry about the technical details of the system; focus on promoting the benefits and asking for a decision regarding the test project. (You can learn more about Air-Trak at www.air-trak.com.)[24]

Completing Business Reports and Proposals

Learning Objectives

AFTER STUDYING THIS CHAPTER, YOU WILL BE ABLE TO

1 Characterize the four tasks involved in completing business reports and proposals

2 Explain how computers have both simplified and complicated the report-production process

3 Identify the circumstances in which you should include letters of authorization and letters of acceptance in your reports

4 Explain the difference between a synopsis and an executive summary

5 Describe the three supplementary parts of a formal report

6 Explain how prefatory parts of a proposal differ, depending on whether the proposal is solicited or unsolicited

On the Job

COMMUNICATING AT THE BILL & MELINDA GATES FOUNDATION

CREATING EFFECTIVE PARTNERSHIPS TO TACKLE SOME OF THE WORLD'S MOST CHALLENGING PROBLEMS

Microsoft co-founder Bill Gates is accustomed to creating change on a global scale, and he now applies the same energy and strategic thinking to charitable causes. Backed by billions of dollars in endowments, the Bill & Melinda Gates Foundation acts as a catalyst, bringing resources together in a way that "increases the momentum, scale, and sustainability of change." The strategy is applied to such important social challenges as containing the AIDS epidemic, eradicating malaria, improving high schools, and making sure people everywhere have access to the digital revolution made possible by the Internet.

Meeting challenges of such staggering complexity and coordinating the resources of organizations all over the world is obviously no small task, and communication plays a vital role in this effort. In particular, reports and proposals link the various groups involved in the foundation's activities and inform the public about ongoing challenges and progress.

The foundation is staffed with people who have demonstrated effective leadership and communication skills, including Patty Stonesifer, a former Microsoft executive, who serves as chief executive officer. Stonesifer is deeply involved in reports and proposals, both as a writer and a reader. In addition to co-authoring the foundation's annual report, she reads numerous proposals from organizations asking for part of the $1.5 billion the foundation provides every year. The foundation receives some 3,000 formal grant requests every month, and the review process is thorough.

For Patty Stonesifer, co-chair and president of the Bill & Melinda Gates Foundation, much of her communication effort involves one-on-one conversations with both the people the foundation helps and the researchers who create solutions to health and education challenges. However, written reports and proposals play an equally important role in her work.

Stonesifer examines proposals from various angles, listening to her colleagues' perspectives and asking all sorts of questions: Is this really the best approach? What's going to make the biggest difference? Could this proposal be a catalyst that attracts other organizations to participate?

Stonesifer and her colleagues recognize that they are tackling problems of almost unimaginable complexity, but with systematic thinking, unstoppable optimism, unmatched financial resources, and effective communication skills, they remain committed to improving life for people the world over.[1]

www.gatesfoundation.org

PUTTING THE FINAL TOUCHES ON REPORTS AND PROPOSALS

Experienced business communicators such as Patty Stonesifer (profiled in the chapter opener) recognize that the process of writing a report or proposal doesn't end with a first draft. This chapter addresses all four tasks involved in completing longer messages: revising, producing, proofreading, and distributing (see Figure 13.1). Although the tasks covered in this chapter are similar in concept to those you studied for short messages in Chapter 6, the completion stage for reports and proposals can require considerably more work. And as you've probably experienced with school reports already, computers, copiers, and other resources have an uncanny knack for going haywire when you're frantic to finish and have no time to spare. When completing an important report on the job, try to leave yourself double or even triple the amount of time you think you'll need so that last-minute glitches don't compromise the quality of all your hard work.

Formal reports have a higher degree of polish and production quality, and they often contain elements not found in informal reports.

Most of the discussion in this chapter applies to *formal* reports and proposals—documents that require an extra measure of polish and professionalism. Few reports and proposals require every component described in this chapter, but be sure to carefully select the elements you want to include in each of your documents.

REVISING YOUR REPORTS AND PROPOSALS

The revision process is essentially the same for reports as for any other business message, although it may take considerably more time, depending on the length of your document. Evaluate your organization, style, and tone to make sure you've said what you want to say in a logical, audience-focused way. Then work to improve the report's readability by varying sentence length, keeping paragraphs short, using lists and bul-

FIGURE 13.1
Step Three in the Three-Step Writing Process for Reports
As you prepare to complete your report or proposal, allow plenty of time for the four tasks needed to complete your project.

Planning

Writing

Completing

Revise the Message
Evaluate content and review readability, then edit and rewrite for conciseness and clarity.

Produce the Message
Use effective design elements and suitable layout for a clean, professional appearance; seamlessly combine text and graphical elements.

Proofread the Message
Review for errors in layout, spelling, and mechanics.

Distribute the Message
Deliver your report using the chosen medium; make sure all documents and all relevant files are distributed successfully.

1   2   3

lets, and adding headings and subheadings. Keep revising the content until it is clear, concise, and compelling.

Tight, efficient writing that is easy to skim is always a plus, but it's especially important for impatient online audiences.[2] Review online report content carefully; strip out all information that doesn't meet audience needs and condense everything else as much as possible. Audiences will gladly return to sites that deliver quality information quickly—and they'll avoid sites that don't.

The virtually unlimited graphical and technical possibilities of web design have had the unfortunate side effect of producing too many websites that are difficult to read. You've no doubt visited some of these hard-to-read sites yourself—webpages with backgrounds so busy that you can't make out the words, tiny type that has you reaching for a magnifying glass, quirky fonts that are difficult to read at any size, lines of text that are stretched and wrapped around images, unlabeled graphical hyperlinks that force you to click on them to see what each page is about, and so on. Even when these sites are visually attractive, which isn't often, they fail to meet the primary objective of providing information to the reader. Web-design expert Dean Allen put it perfectly when he wrote that "the primary goal of communication design is to make vital, engaging work intended above all to be read."[3]

Revising for clarity and conciseness is especially important for online reports because reading online can be difficult.

PRODUCING YOUR REPORTS AND PROPOSALS

When you are satisfied with your text, you're ready to produce your report by incorporating the design elements discussed in Chapter 6. At this point, you should also start to add charts, graphs, and other visuals, as well as any missing textual elements, such as previews and reviews.

In some organizations, you'll be able to rely on the help of specialists in design and production, particularly when you are working on important, high-visibility reports or proposals. You may also have clerical help available to assist with mechanical assembly and distribution. However, for most reports in many of today's lean-staffed companies, you should count on doing most or all of the production work yourself.

The good news is that computer tools are now generally easy enough for the average businessperson to use productively. A software suite such as Microsoft Office or WordPerfect Office lets you produce reports that incorporate graphics, spreadsheet data, and database records. Even features such as photography are relatively simple to include these days, thanks to low-cost digital cameras, color desktop scanners, and photo-quality printers.

The bad news is that these continually improving computer tools increase your audience's expectations. People are influenced by packaging, so a handsomely bound report with full-color graphics will impress your audience more than a plain report, even though the two documents may contain the same information. In other words, you may find yourself spending more time on production just to keep up with the competition.

Components of a Formal Report

The parts you include in a report depend on the type of report you are writing, how long it is, what your audience expects and requires, and what your organization dictates. The components listed in Figure 13.2 fall into three categories, depending on where they are found in a report: prefatory parts, text of the report, and supplementary parts. For an illustration of how the various parts fit together, see Linda Moreno's Electrovision report in "Report Writer's Notebook: Analyzing a Formal Report."

Many of the components in a formal report start on a new page, but not always. Inserting page breaks consumes extra paper and adds to the bulk of your report. On the other hand, starting a section on a new page helps your readers navigate the report and recognize transitions between major sections or features.

Length, audience expectations, and organizational traditions all dictate what you should include in a formal report.

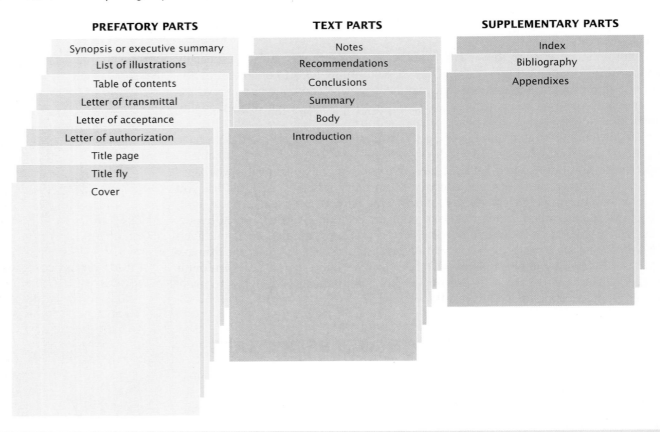

FIGURE 13.2
Parts of a Formal Report
Depending on the level of formality you need to achieve, you can select from these elements to complete your formal report.

If you want a section to stand out, start it on a new page.

When you want a particular section to stand apart, start it on a new page (in the same way that each chapter in this book starts on a new page). Most prefatory parts, such as the table of contents, should also be placed on their own pages. However, the various parts in the report text are often run together. If your introduction is only a paragraph long, don't bother with a page break before moving into the body of your report. If the introduction runs longer than a page, however, a page break can signal the reader that a major shift is occurring in the flow of the report.

Formal reports can contain a variety of prefatory parts, from a cover page to a synopsis or an executive summary.

Prefatory Parts Prefatory parts are front-end materials that provide key preliminary information so that readers can decide whether and how to read the report.[4] Note that many of these parts—such as the table of contents, list of illustrations, and executive summary—are easiest to prepare after the text has been completed because they directly reflect the contents. When your text is complete, you can use your word processor to automatically compile the table of contents and the list of illustrations. You can prepare other parts at almost any time.

Cover Many companies have standard covers for reports, made of heavy paper and imprinted with the company's name and logo. If your company doesn't have such covers, you can usually find something suitable in a good stationery store. Look for a cover that is attractive, convenient, and appropriate to the subject matter. Also, make sure it can be labeled with the report title, the writer's name (optional), and the submission date (also optional).

(*Text continues on page 476.*)

REPORT WRITER'S NOTEBOOK
Analyzing a Formal Report

The report presented in the following pages was prepared by Linda Moreno, manager of the cost accounting department as Electrovision, a high-tech company based in Los Gatos, Cailfornia. Electrovision's main product is optical character recognition equipment, which is used by the U.S. Postal Service for sorting mail. Moreno's job is to help analyze the company's costs. She has this to say about the background of the report:

> For the past three or four years, Electrovision has been on a roll. Our A-12 optical character reader was a real breakthrough, and the post office grabbed up as many as we could make. Our sales and profits kept climbing, and morale was fantastic. Everybody seemed to think that the good times would last forever. Unfortunately, everybody was wrong. When the Postal Service announced that it was postponing all new equipment purchases because of cuts in its budget, we woke up to the fact that we are essentially a one-product company with one customer. At that point, management started scrambling around looking for ways to cut costs until we could diversify our business a bit.

> The vice president of operations, Dennis McWilliams, asked me to help identify cost-cutting opportunities in travel and enter-tainment. On the basis of his personal observations, he felt that Electrovision was overly generous in its travel policies and that we might be able to save a significant amount by controlling these costs more carefully. My investigation confirmed his suspicion.

> I was reasonably confident that my report would be well received. I've worked with Dennis for several years and know what he likes: plenty of facts, clearly stated conclusions, and specific recommendations for what should be done next. I also knew that my report would be passed on to

other Electrovision executives, so I wanted to create a good impression. I wanted the report to be accurate and thorough, visu-ally appealing, readable, and appropriate in tone.

When writing the analytical report that follows, Moreno based the organization on conclu-sions and recommendations presented in direct order. The first two sections of the report corre-spond to Moreno's two main conclusions: that Electrovision's travel and entertainment costs are too high and that cuts are essential. The third section presents recommendations for achieving better control over travel and entertainment expenses. As you review the report, analyze both the mechanical aspects and the way Moreno pre-sents her ideas. Be prepared to discuss the way the various components convey and reinforce the main message.

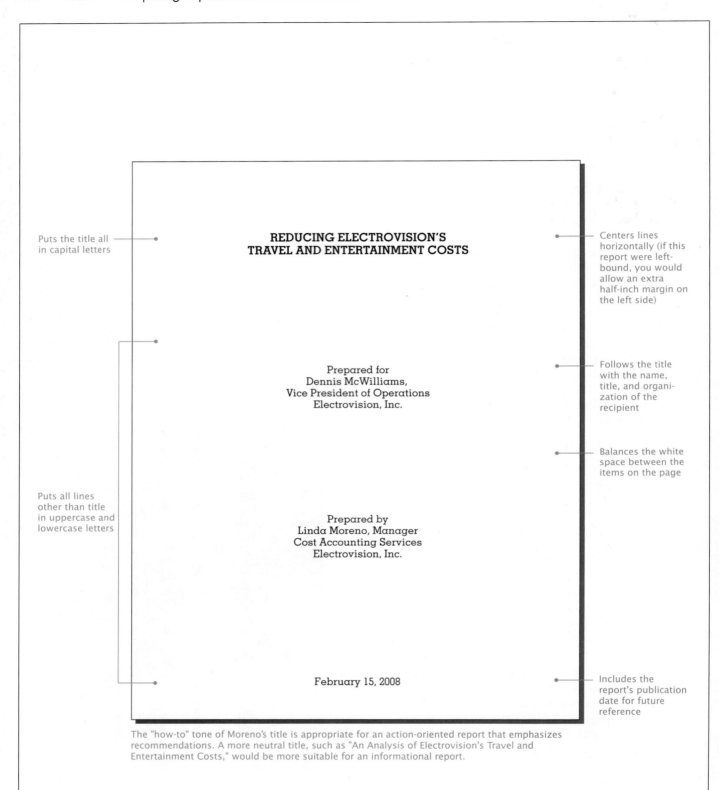

Puts the title all in capital letters

Puts all lines other than title in uppercase and lowercase letters

Centers lines horizontally (if this report were left-bound, you would allow an extra half-inch margin on the left side)

Follows the title with the name, title, and organization of the recipient

Balances the white space between the items on the page

Includes the report's publication date for future reference

REDUCING ELECTROVISION'S
TRAVEL AND ENTERTAINMENT COSTS

Prepared for
Dennis McWilliams,
Vice President of Operations
Electrovision, Inc.

Prepared by
Linda Moreno, Manager
Cost Accounting Services
Electrovision, Inc.

February 15, 2008

The "how-to" tone of Moreno's title is appropriate for an action-oriented report that emphasizes recommendations. A more neutral title, such as "An Analysis of Electrovision's Travel and Entertainment Costs," would be more suitable for an informational report.

Uses memo format for transmitting this internal report; otherwise, letter format would be used for transmitting external reports

Uses a conversational style

Acknowledges help that has been received

Presents the main conclusion right away (because Moreno expects a positive response)

Closes with thanks and an offer to discuss results (when appropriate, you could also include an offer to help with future projects)

MEMORANDUM

DATE: February 15, 2008
TO: Dennis McWilliams, Vice President of Operations
FROM: Linda Moreno, Manager of Cost Accounting Services *LM*
SUBJECT: Reducing Electrovision's Travel and Entertainment Costs

Here is the report you requested January 28 on Electrovision's travel and entertainment costs.

Your suspicions were right. We are spending far too much on business travel. Our unwritten policy has been "anything goes," leaving us with no real control over T&E expenses. Although this hands-off approach may have been understandable when Electrovision's profits were high, we can no longer afford the luxury of going first class.

The solutions to the problem seem rather clear. We need to have someone with centralized responsibility for travel and entertainment costs, a clear statement of policy, an effective control system, and a business-oriented travel service that can optimize our travel arrangements. We should also investigate alternatives to travel, such as videoconferencing. Perhaps more important, we need to change our attitude. Instead of viewing travel funds as a bottomless supply of money, all traveling employees need to act as if they were paying the bills themselves.

Getting people to economize is not going to be easy. In the course of researching this issue, I've found that our employees are deeply attached to their generous travel privileges. I think some would almost prefer a cut in pay to a loss in travel status. We'll need a lot of top management involvement to sell people on the need for moderation. One thing is clear: People will be very bitter if we create a two-class system in which top executives get special privileges while the rest of the employees make the sacrifices.

I'm grateful to Mary Lehman and Connie McIllvain for their help in rounding up and sorting through five years' worth of expense reports. Their efforts were truly Herculean.

Thanks for giving me the opportunity to work on this assignment. It's been a real education. If you have any questions about the report, please give me a call.

In this report, Moreno decided to write a brief memo of transmittal and include a separate executive summary. Short reports (fewer than 10 pages) often combine the synopsis or executive summary with the memo or letter of transmittal.

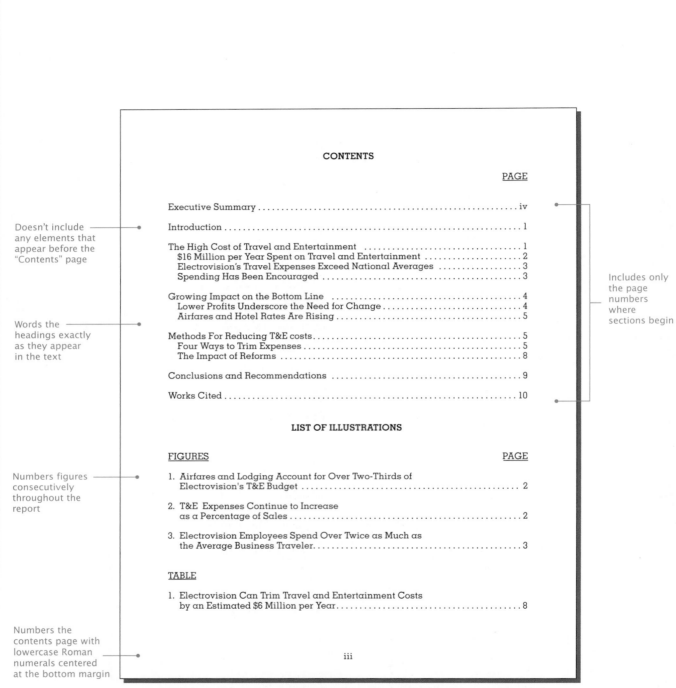

Doesn't include any elements that appear before the "Contents" page

Words the headings exactly as they appear in the text

Numbers figures consecutively throughout the report

Numbers the contents page with lowercase Roman numerals centered at the bottom margin

Includes only the page numbers where sections begin

CONTENTS

LIST OF ILLUSTRATIONS

iii

Moreno included only first- and second-level headings in her table of contents, even though the report contains third-level headings. She prefers a shorter table of contents that focuses attention on the main divisions of thought. She used informative titles, which are appropriate for a report to a receptive audience.

Begins by stating the purpose of the report

Presents the points in the executive summary in the same order as they appear in the report, using subheadings that summarize the content of the main sections of the report

EXECUTIVE SUMMARY

This report analyzes Electrovision's travel and entertainment (T&E) costs and presents recommendations for reducing those costs.

Travel and Entertainment Costs Are Too High

Travel and entertainment is a large and growing expense category for Electrovision. The company spends over $16 million per year on business travel, and these costs have been increasing by 12 percent annually. Company employees make roughly 3,390 trips each year at an average cost per trip of $4,720. Airfares are the biggest expense, followed by hotels, meals, and rental cars.

The nature of Electrovision's business does require extensive travel, but the company's costs are excessive: Our employees spend more than twice the national average on travel and entertainment. Although the location of the company's facilities may partly explain this discrepancy, the main reason for our high costs is a management style that gives employees little incentive to economize.

Cuts Are Essential

Electrovision management now recognizes the need to gain more control over this element of costs. The company is currently entering a period of declining profits, prompting management to look for every opportunity to reduce spending. At the same time, rising airfares and hotel rates are making T&E expenses more significant.

Electrovision Can Save $6 Million per Year

Fortunately, Electrovision has a number of excellent opportunities for reducing T&E costs. Savings of up to $6 million per year should be achievable, judging by the experience of other companies. A sensible travel-management program can save companies as much as 35 percent a year (Gilligan 39–40), and we should be able to save even more, since we purchase many more business-class tickets than the average. Four steps will help us cut costs:

1. Hire a director of travel and entertainment to assume overall responsibility for T&E spending, policies, and technologies, including the hiring and management of a national travel agency.
2. Educate employees on the need for cost containment, both in avoiding unnecessary travel and reducing costs when travel is necessary.
3. Negotiate preferential rates with travel providers.
4. Implement technological alternatives to travel, such as virtual meetings.

As necessary as these changes are, they will likely hurt morale, at least in the short term. Management will need to make a determined effort to explain the rationale for reduced spending. By exercising moderation in their own travel arrangements, Electrovision executives can set a good example and help other employees accept the changes. On the plus side, using travel alternatives such as web conferencing will reduce the travel burden on many employees and help them balance their business and personal lives.

Targets a receptive audience with a hard-hitting tone in the executive summary (a more neutral approach would be better for hostile or skeptical readers)

Executive summary uses the same font and paragraph treatment as the text of the report

Continues numbering the executive summary pages with lowercase Roman numerals

iv

Moreno decided to include an executive summary because her report is aimed at a mixed audience, some of whom are interested in the details of her report and others who just want the "big picture." The executive summary is aimed at the second group, giving them enough information to make a decision without burdening them with the task of reading the entire report.

Her writing style matches the serious nature of the content without sounding distant or stiff. Moreno chose the formal approach because several members of her audience are considerably higher up in the organization, and she did not want to sound too familiar. In addition, her company prefers the impersonal style for formal reports.

**REDUCING ELECTROVISION'S
TRAVEL AND ENTERTAINMENT COSTS**

INTRODUCTION

Electrovision has always encouraged a significant amount of business travel. To compensate employees for the stress and inconvenience of frequent trips, management has authorized generous travel and entertainment (T&E) allowances. This philosophy has been good for morale, but last year Electrovision spent $16 million on travel and entertainment—$7 million more than it spent on research and development.

This year's T&E costs will affect profits even more, due to increases in airline fares and hotel rates. Also, the company anticipates that profits will be relatively weak for a variety of other reasons. Therefore, Dennis McWilliams, Vice President of Operations, has asked the accounting department to explore ways to reduce the T&E budget.

The purpose of this report is to analyze T&E expenses, evaluate the effect of recent hotel and airfare increases, and suggest ways to tighten control over T&E costs. The report outlines several steps that could reduce Electrovision's expenses, but the precise financial impact of these measures is difficult to project. The estimates presented here provide a "best guess" view of what Electrovision can expect to save.

In preparing this report, the accounting department analyzed internal expense reports for the past five years to determine how much Electrovision spends on travel and entertainment. These figures were then compared with average statistics compiled by Dow Jones (publisher of the *Wall Street Journal*) and presented as the Dow Jones Travel Index. We also analyzed trends and suggestions published in a variety of business journal articles to see how other companies are coping with the high cost of business travel.

THE HIGH COST OF TRAVEL AND ENTERTAINMENT

Although many companies view travel and entertainment as an incidental cost of doing business, the dollars add up. At Electrovision the bill for airfares, hotels, rental cars, meals, and entertainment totaled $16 million last year. Our T&E budget has increased by 12 percent per year for the past five years. Compared to the average U.S. business traveler, Electrovision's expenditures are high, largely because of management's generous policy on travel benefits.

1

In her brief introduction, Moreno counts on topic sentences and transitions to indicate that she is discussing the purpose, scope, and limitations of the study.

2

Uses arabic
numerals to
number the
second and
succeeding pages
of the text in the
upper right-hand
corner where the
top and right-hand
margins meet

$16 Million per Year Spent on Travel and Entertainment

Electrovision's annual budget for travel and entertainment is only 8 percent of sales. Because this is a relatively small expense category compared with such things as salaries and commissions, it is tempting to dismiss T&E costs as insignificant. However, T&E is Electrovision's third-largest controllable expense, directly behind salaries and information systems.

Last year Electrovision personnel made about 3,390 trips at an average cost per trip of $4,720. The typical trip involved a round-trip flight of 3,000 miles, meals, and hotel accommodations for two or three days, and a rental car. Roughly 80 percent of trips were made by 20 percent of the staff—top management and sales personnel traveled most, averaging 18 trips per year.

Figure 1 illustrates how the T&E budget is spent. The largest categories are airfares and lodging, which together account for $7 out of $10 that employees spend on travel and entertainment. This spending breakdown has been relatively steady for the past five years and is consistent with the distribution of expenses experienced by other companies.

Figure 1
Airfares and Lodging Account for Over
Two-Thirds of Electrovision's T&E Budget

Although the composition of the T&E budget has been consistent, its size has not. As mentioned earlier, these expenditures have increased by about 12 percent per year for the past five years, roughly twice the rate of the company's sales growth (see Figure 2). This rate of growth makes T&E Electrovision's fastest-growing expense item.

Figure 2
T&E Expenses Continue to Increase as a
Percentage of Sales

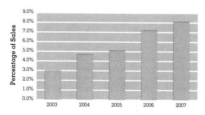

Moreno opens the first main section of the body with a topic sentence that introduces an
important fact about the subject of the section. Then she orients the reader to the three major
points developed in the section.

Places the visual
as close as possible
to the point it
illustrates

Gives each visual
a title that clearly
indicates what it's
about; titles are
consistently placed to
the left of each visual

3

Electrovision's Travel Expenses Exceed National Averages

Much of our travel budget is justified. Two major factors contribute to Electrovision's high T&E budget:

- With our headquarters on the West Coast and our major customer on the East Coast, we naturally spend a lot of money on cross-country flights.

- A great deal of travel takes place between our headquarters here on the West Coast and the manufacturing operations in Detroit, Boston, and Dallas. Corporate managers and division personnel make frequent trips to coordinate these disparate operations.

However, even though a good portion of Electrovision's travel budget is justifiable, the company spends considerably more on T&E than the average business traveler (see Figure 3).

Figure 3
Electrovision Employees Spend Over Twice as Much as the Average Business Traveler

Source: *Wall Street Journal* and company records

Dollars Spent per Day

The Dow Jones Travel Index calculates the average cost per day of business travel in the United States, based on average airfare, hotel rates, and rental car rates. The average fluctuates weekly as travel companies change their rates, but it has been running at about $1,000 per day for the last year or so. In contrast, Electrovision's average daily expense over the past year has been $2,250—a hefty 125 percent higher than average. This figure is based on the average trip cost of $4,720 listed earlier and an average trip length of 2.1 days.

Spending Has Been Encouraged

Although a variety of factors may contribute to this differential, Electrovision's relatively high T&E costs are at least partially attributable to the company's philosophy and management style. Since many employees do not enjoy business travel, management has tried to make the trips more pleasant by authorizing business-class airfare, luxury hotel accommodations, and full-size rental cars. The sales staff is encouraged to entertain clients at top restaurants and to invite them to cultural and sporting events.

Numbers the visuals consecutively and refers to them in the text by their numbers

Introduces visuals before they appear and indicates what readers should notice about the data

The chart in Figure 3 is simple but effective; Moreno includes just enough data to make her point. Notice how she is as careful about the appearance of her report as she is about the quality of its content.

4

The cost of these privileges is easy to overlook, given the weakness of
Electrovision's system for keeping track of T&E expenses:

- The monthly financial records do not contain a separate category for travel
  and entertainment; the information is buried under Cost of Goods Sold and
  under Selling, General, and Administrative Expenses.

- Each department head is given authority to approve any expense report,
  regardless of how large it may be.

- Receipts are not required for expenditures of less than $100.

- Individuals are allowed to make their own travel arrangements.

- No one is charged with the responsibility for controlling the company's total
  spending on travel and entertainment.

GROWING IMPACT ON THE BOTTOM LINE

During the past three years, the company's healthy profits have resulted in
relatively little pressure to push for tighter controls over all aspects of the
business. However, as we all know, the situation is changing. We're projecting flat
to declining profits for the next two years, a situation that has prompted all of us
to search for ways to cut costs. At the same time, rising airfares and hotel rates
have increased the impact of T&E expenses on the company's financial results.

Lower Profits Underscore the Need for Change

The next two years promise to be difficult for Electrovision. After several years of
steady increases in spending, the Postal Service is tightening procurement
policies for automated mail-handling equipment. Funding for the A-12 optical
character reader has been canceled. As a consequence, the marketing
department expects sales to drop by 15 percent. Although Electrovision is
negotiating several other promising R&D contracts, the marketing department
does not foresee any major procurements for the next two to three years.

At the same time, Electrovision is facing cost increases on several fronts. As we
have known for several months, the new production facility now under
construction in Salt Lake City, Utah, is behind schedule and over budget. Labor
contracts in Boston and Dallas will expire within the next six months, and plant
managers there anticipate that significant salary and benefits concessions may
be necessary to avoid strikes.

Moreover, marketing and advertising costs are expected to increase as we
attempt to strengthen these activities to better cope with competitive pressures.
Given the expected decline in revenues and increase in costs, the Executive
Committee's prediction that profits will fall by 12 percent in the coming fiscal
year does not seem overly pessimistic.

Moreno designed her report to include plenty of white space so even those pages that lack visuals
are still attractive and easy to read.

5

Airfares and Hotel Rates Are Rising

Business travelers have grown accustomed to frequent fare wars and discounting in the travel industry in recent years. Excess capacity and aggressive price competition, particularly in the airline business, made travel a relative bargain.

Documents the facts to add weight to Moreno's argument

However, that situation has changed as weaker competitors have been forced out and the remaining players have grown stronger and smarter. Airlines and hotels are better at managing inventory and keeping occupancy rates high, which translates into higher costs for Electrovision. Last year saw some of the steepest rate hikes in years. Business airfares (tickets most likely to be purchased by business travelers) jumped more than 40 percent in many markets. The trend is expected to continue, with rates increasing another 5 to 10 percent overall (Phillips 331; "Travel Costs Under Pressure" 30; Dahl B6).

Given the fact that air and hotel costs account for 70 percent of our T&E budget, the trend toward higher prices in these two categories will have serious consequences, unless management takes action to control these costs.

METHODS FOR REDUCING T&E COSTS

Gives recommendations an objective flavor by pointing out both the benefits and the risks of taking action

By implementing a number of reforms, management can expect to reduce Electrovision's T&E budget by as much as 40 percent. This estimate is based on the general assessment made by American Express (Gilligan 39) and on the fact that we have an opportunity to significantly reduce air travel costs by eliminating business-class travel. However, these measures are likely to be unpopular with employees. To gain acceptance for such changes, management will need to sell employees on the need for moderation in T&E allowances.

Four Ways to Trim Expenses

By researching what other companies are doing to curb T&E expenses, the accounting department has identified four prominent opportunities that should enable Electrovision to save about $6 million annually in travel-related costs.

Institute Tighter Spending Controls

A single individual should be appointed director of travel and entertainment to spearhead the effort to gain control of the T&E budget. More than a third of all U.S. companies now employ travel managers ("Businesses Use Savvy Managers" 4). The director should be familiar with the travel industry and should be well versed in both accounting and information technology. The director should also report to the vice president of operations. The director's first priorities should be to establish a written T&E policy and a cost-control system.

Electrovision currently has no written policy on travel and entertainment, a step that is widely recommended by air travel experts (Smith D4). Creating a policy

Moreno creates a forceful tone by using action verbs in the third-level subheadings of this section. This approach is appropriate to the nature of the study and the attitude of the audience. However, in a status-conscious organization, the imperative verbs might sound a bit too presumptuous coming from a junior member of the staff.

6

would clarify management's position and serve as a vehicle for communicating the need for moderation. At a minimum, the policy should include the following:

- All travel and entertainment should be strictly related to business and should be approved in advance.

Breaks up text with bulleted lists, which not only call attention to important points but also add visual interest

- Except under special circumstances to be approved on a case-by-case basis, employees should travel by coach and stay in mid-range business hotels.

- The T&E policy should apply equally to employees at all levels.

To implement the new policy, Electrovision will need to create a system for controlling T&E expenses. Each department should prepare an annual T&E budget as part of its operating plan. These budgets should be presented in detail so that management can evaluate how T&E dollars will be spent and can recommend appropriate cuts. To help management monitor performance relative to these budgets, the director of travel should prepare monthly financial statements showing actual T&E expenditures by department.

The director of travel should also be responsible for retaining a business-oriented travel service that will schedule all employee business trips and look for the best travel deals, particularly in airfares. In addition to centralizing Electrovision's reservation and ticketing activities, the agency will negotiate reduced group rates with hotels and rental car firms. The agency selected should have offices nationwide so that all Electrovision facilities can channel their reservations through the same company. This is particularly important in light of the dizzying array of often wildly different airfares available between some cities. It's not uncommon to find dozens of fares along commonly traveled routes (Rowe 30). In addition, the director can help coordinate travel across the company to secure group discounts whenever possible (Barker 31; Miller B6).

Specifies the steps required to implement recommendations

Reduce Unnecessary Travel and Entertainment

One of the easiest ways to reduce expenses is to reduce the amount of traveling and entertaining that occurs. An analysis of last year's expenditures suggests that as much as 30 percent of Electrovision's travel and entertainment is discretionary. The professional staff spent $2.8 million attending seminars and conferences last year. Although these gatherings are undoubtedly beneficial, the company could save money by sending fewer representatives to each function and perhaps by eliminating some of the less valuable seminars.

Similarly, Electrovision could economize on trips between headquarters and divisions by reducing the frequency of such visits and by sending fewer people on each trip. Although there is often no substitute for face-to-face meetings, management could try to resolve more internal issues through telephone, electronic, and written communication.

Electrovision can also reduce spending by urging employees to economize. Instead of flying business class, employees can fly coach class or take advantage

Moreno takes care not to overstep the boundaries of her analysis. For instance, she doesn't analyze the value of the seminars that employees attend every year, so she avoids any absolute statements about reducing travel to seminars.

7

of discount fares. Rather than ordering a $50 bottle of wine, employees can select a less expensive bottle or dispense with alcohol entirely. People can book rooms at moderately priced hotels and drive smaller rental cars.

Obtain Lowest Rates from Travel Providers

Apart from urging employees to economize, Electrovision can also save money by searching for the lowest available airfares, hotel rates, and rental car fees. Currently, few employees have the time or knowledge to seek out travel bargains. When they need to travel, they make the most convenient and comfortable arrangements. A professional travel service will be able to obtain lower rates from travel providers.

Judging by the experience of other companies, Electrovision may be able to trim as much as 30 to 40 percent from the travel budget simply by looking for bargains in airfares and negotiating group rates with hotels and rental car companies. Electrovision should be able to achieve these economies by analyzing its travel patterns, identifying frequently visited locations, and selecting a few hotels that are willing to reduce rates in exchange for guaranteed business. At the same time, the company should be able to save up to 40 percent on rental car charges by negotiating a corporate rate.

The possibilities for economizing are promising; however, making the best travel arrangements often requires trade-offs such as the following:

- The best fares might not always be the lowest. Indirect flights are usually cheaper, but they take longer and may end up costing more in lost work time.

- The cheapest tickets often require booking 14 or even 30 days in advance, which is often impossible for us.

- Discount tickets are usually nonrefundable, which is a serious drawback when a trip needs to be canceled at the last minute.

Replace Travel with Technological Alternatives

Less-expensive travel options promise significant savings, but the biggest cost reductions over the long term might come from replacing travel with virtual meeting technology. Both analysts and corporate users say that the early kinks that hampered online meetings have largely been worked out, and the latest systems are fast, easy to learn, and easy to use (Solheim 26). For example, Webex (a leading provider of webconferencing services) offers everything from simple, impromptu team meetings to major online events with up to 3,000 participants ("Online Meeting Solutions").

One of the first responsibilities of the new travel director should be an evaluation of these technologies and a recommendation for integrating them throughout Electrovision's operations.

Points out possible difficulties to show that all angles have been considered and to build confidence in her judgment

---

Note how Moreno makes the transition from section to section. The first sentence under the second heading on this page refers to the subject of the previous paragraph and signals a shift in thought.

8

The Impact of Reforms

By implementing tighter controls, reducing unnecessary expenses, negotiating more favorable rates, and exploring alternatives to travel, Electrovision should be able to reduce its T&E budget significantly. As Table 1 illustrates, the combined savings should be in the neighborhood of $6 million, although the precise figures are somewhat difficult to project.

Table 1
Electrovision Can Trim Travel and Entertainment Costs
by an Estimated $6 Million per Year

SOURCE OF SAVINGS	ESTIMATED SAVINGS
Switching from business-class to coach airfare	$2,300,000
Negotiating preferred hotel rates	940,000
Negotiating preferred rental car rates	460,000
Systematically searching for lower airfares	375,000
Reducing interdivisional travel	675,000
Reducing seminar and conference attendance	1,250,000
TOTAL POTENTIAL SAVINGS	**$6,000,000**

To achieve the economies outlined in the table, Electrovision will incur expenses for hiring a director of travel and for implementing a T&E cost-control system. These costs are projected at $115,000: $105,000 per year in salary and benefits for the new employee and a one-time expense of $10,000 for the cost-control system. The cost of retaining a full-service travel agency is negligible, even with the service fees that many are now passing along from airlines and other service providers.

The measures required to achieve these savings are likely to be unpopular with employees. Electrovision personnel are accustomed to generous T&E allowances, and they are likely to resent having these privileges curtailed. To alleviate their disappointment

- Management should make a determined effort to explain why the changes are necessary.
- The director of corporate communication should be asked to develop a multifaceted campaign that will communicate the importance of curtailing T&E costs.
- Management should set a positive example by adhering strictly to the new policies.
- The limitations should apply equally to employees at all levels in the organization.

Note how Moreno calls attention in the first paragraph to items in the following table, without repeating the information in the table.

9

CONCLUSIONS AND RECOMMENDATIONS

Electrovision is currently spending $16 million per year on travel and entertainment. Although much of this spending is justified, the company's costs are high relative to competitors' costs, mainly because Electrovision has been generous with its travel benefits.

Electrovision's liberal approach to travel and entertainment was understandable during years of high profitability; however, the company is facing the prospect of declining profits for the next several years. Management is therefore motivated to cut costs in all areas of the business. Reducing T&E spending is particularly important because the bottom-line impact of these costs will increase as airline fares increase.

Electrovision should be able to reduce T&E costs by as much as 40 percent by taking four important steps:

1. *Institute tighter spending controls.* Management should hire a director of travel and entertainment who will assume overall responsibility for T&E activities. Within the next six months, this director should develop a written travel policy, institute a T&E budget and a cost-control system, and retain a professional, business-oriented travel agency that will optimize arrangements with travel providers.

2. *Reduce unnecessary travel and entertainment.* Electrovision should encourage employees to economize on T&E spending. Management can accomplish this by authorizing fewer trips and by urging employees to be more conservative in their spending.

3. *Obtain lowest rates from travel providers.* Electrovision should also focus on obtaining the best rates on airline tickets, hotel rooms, and rental cars. By channeling all arrangements through a professional travel agency, the company can optimize its choices and gain clout in negotiating preferred rates.

4. *Replace travel with technological alternatives.* With the number of computers already installed in our facilities, it seems likely that we could take advantage of desktop videoconferencing and other distance-meeting tools. Technological alternatives won't be quite as feasible with customer sites, since these systems require compatible equipment at both ends of a connection, but such systems are certainly a possibility for communication with Electrovision's own sites.

Because these measures may be unpopular with employees, management should make a concerted effort to explain the importance of reducing travel costs. The director of corporate communication should be given responsibility for developing a plan to communicate the need for employee cooperation.

10

WORKS CITED

Barker, Julie. "How to Rein in Group Travel Costs." *Successful Meetings* Feb. 2004: 31.

"Businesses Use Savvy Managers to Keep Travel Costs Down." *Christian Science Monitor* 17 July 2004: 4.

Dahl, Jonathan. "2000: The Year Travel Costs Took Off." *Wall Street Journal* 29 Dec. 2004: B6.

Gilligan, Edward P. "Trimming Your T&E Is Easier Than You Think." *Managing Office Technology* Nov. 2004: 39–40.

"Meet With Anyone, Anywhere, Anytime, "*Webex.com*. 2006. WebEx, 15 November 2006, <http://www.webex.com/solutions/online-meeting-suc.html>.

Miller, Lisa. "Attention, Airline Ticket Shoppers." *Wall Street Journal* 7 July 2004: B6.

Phillips, Edward H. "Airlines Post Record Traffic." *Aviation Week & Space Technology* 8 Jan. 2005: 331.

Rowe, Irene Vlitos. "Global Solution for Cutting Travel Costs." *European* 12 Oct. 2004: 30.

Smith, Carol. "Rising, Erratic Airfares Make Company Policy Vital." *Los Angeles Times* 2 Nov. 2004: D4.

Solheim, Shelley. "Web Conferencing Made Easy." *eWeek* 22 Aug. 2005: 26.

"Travel Costs Under Pressure." *Purchasing* 15 Feb. 2004: 30.

Lists references alphabetically by the author's last name, and when the author is unknown, by the title of the reference (see Appendix B for additional details on preparing reference lists)

Moreno's list of references follows the style recommended in The MLA Style Manual. The box below shows how these sources would be cited following APA style.

10

REFERENCES

Barker, J. (2004, February). How to rein in group travel costs. *Successful Meetings*, 31.

Businesses use savvy managers to keep travel costs down. (2004, July 17). *Christian Science Monitor*, 4.

Dahl, J. (2004, December 29). 2000: The year travel costs took off. *Wall Street Journal*, B6.

Gilligan, E. (2004, November). Trimming your T&E is easier than you think. *Managing Office Technology*, 39–40.

Miller, L. (2004, July 7). Attention, airline ticket shoppers. *Wall Street Journal*, B6.

Phillips, E. (2005, January 8). Airlines post record traffic. *Aviation Week & Space Technology*, 331.

Rowe, I. (2004, October 12). Global solution for cutting travel costs. *European*, 30.

Smith, C. (2004, November 2). Rising, erratic airfares make company policy vital. *Los Angeles Times*, D4.

Solheim, S. (2005, August 22). Web conferencing made easy. *eWeek*, 26.

Travel costs under pressure. (2004, February 15). *Purchasing*, 30.

Webex.com. (2006). *Meet With Anyone, Anywhere, Anytime*. Retrieved 15 November 2006, from http://www.webex.com/solutions/online-meeting-suc.html.

Think carefully about the title you put on the cover. A business report is not a mystery novel, so give your readers all the information they need: the who, what, when, where, why, and how of the subject. At the same time, try to be concise. You can reduce the length of your title by eliminating phrases such as *A Report of*, *A Study of*, or *A Survey of*.

Title Fly and Title Page The **title fly** is a single sheet of paper with only the title of the report on it. You don't really need one, but it adds a touch of formality. The **title page** includes four blocks of information: (1) the title of the report; (2) the name, title, and address of the person(s), group, or organization that authorized the report (if anyone); (3) the name, title, and address of the person(s), group, or organization that prepared the report; and (4) the date on which the report was submitted. On some title pages, the second block of information is preceded by the words *Prepared for* or *Submitted to*, and the third block of information is preceded by *Prepared by* or *Submitted by*. In some cases, the title page serves as the cover of the report, especially if the report is relatively short and is intended solely for internal use.

Letter of Authorization and Letter of Acceptance If you received written authorization to prepare a report, you may want to include that letter or memo in your report. This **letter of authorization** (or *memo of authorization*) is a document you received, asking or directing you to prepare the report. If you wrote a **letter of acceptance** (or *memo of acceptance*) in response to that communication, accepting the assignment and clarifying any conditions or limitations, you might also include that letter in the report's prefatory parts. If there is any chance that your report might not meet your audience's expectations, the letter of acceptance can remind your readers what you agreed to do and why.

In general, letters of authorization and acceptance are included in only the most formal reports. However, in any case in which a significant amount of time has passed since you received the letter of authorization or you do not have a close working relationship with the audience, consider including both letters to make sure everyone is clear about the report's intent and the approach you took to create it. You don't want your weeks or months of work to be diminished by any misunderstandings.

> A letter of authorization is the document that instructed you to produce a report; a letter of acceptance is your written agreement to produce the report.

> A letter or memo of transmittal introduces your report to your audience.

Letter of Transmittal The **letter of transmittal** (or *memo of transmittal*), a specialized form of a cover letter, introduces your report to your audience. The letter of transmittal says what you'd say if you were handing the report directly to the person who authorized it, so its style is often less formal than that of the rest of the report.

The transmittal letter usually appears right before the table of contents. If your report will be widely distributed, however, you may decide to include the letter of transmittal only in selected copies so that you can make certain comments to a specific audience. If your report discusses layoffs or other issues that affect people in the organization, you might want to discuss your recommendations privately in a letter of transmittal to top management. If your audience is likely to be skeptical of or even hostile to something in your report, the transmittal letter is a good opportunity to acknowledge their concerns and explain how the report addresses the issues they care about.

Depending on the nature of your report, your letter of transmittal can follow either the direct approach for routine and positive messages described in Chapter 8 or the indirect approach for negative messages described in Chapter 9. Open by officially conveying the report to your readers and summarizing its purpose. Such a letter typically begins with a statement such as "Here is the report you asked me to prepare on . . ." The rest of the introduction includes information about the scope of the report, the methods used to complete the study, limitations, and any special messages you need to convey. For instance, in Patty Stonesifer's introduction to a recent Gates Foundation annual report, she began by explaining that while annual reports usually cover an organization's own accomplishments for the prior year, she wanted to focus on the good work that the foundation's partners had done instead.[5]

In the body of the transmittal letter, you may also highlight important points or sections of the report, give suggestions for follow-up studies, and offer any details that will help readers understand and use the report. You may also want to acknowledge help given by others. The conclusion of the transmittal letter often includes a note of thanks for having been given the report assignment, an expression of willingness to discuss the report, and an offer to assist with future projects.

If the report does not have a synopsis, the letter of transmittal may summarize the major findings, conclusions, and recommendations. This material would be placed after the opening of the letter.

> If you don't include a synopsis, you can summarize the report's content in your letter of transmittal.

Table of Contents The table of contents (usually titled simply *Contents*) indicates in outline form the coverage, sequence, and relative importance of the information in the report. The headings used in the text of the report are the basis for the table of contents. Depending on the length and complexity of the report, you may need to decide how many levels of headings to show in the contents; you want to strike a balance between simplicity and completeness. Contents that show only first-level heads are easy to scan but could frustrate people looking for specific subsections in the report. Conversely, contents that show every level of heading—down to fourth or fifth level in detailed reports—identify all the sections but can intimidate readers and blur the focus by detracting from your most important message points. If a detailed table of contents could have dozens or even hundreds of entries, consider including two tables: a high-level table that shows only major headings, followed by a detailed table that includes everything (as this and many other textbooks do). No matter how many levels you include, make sure readers can easily distinguish between them.

Also, take extra care to verify that your table of contents is accurate, consistent, and complete. To ensure accuracy, construct the table of contents after your report is complete, thoroughly edited, and proofed. This way, the headings and subheadings aren't likely to change or move from page to page. And if at all possible, use the automatic features in your word processor to generate the table of contents. Doing so helps improve accuracy by eliminating typing mistakes, and it keeps your table current in the event that you do have to repaginate or revise headings late in the process.

> To save time and reduce errors, use the table of contents generator in your word processor.

List of Illustrations If you have more than a handful of illustrations in your report, or if you want to call attention to your illustrations, include a list of illustrations after the table of contents. For simplicity's sake, some reports refer to all visuals as *illustrations* or *exhibits*. In other reports, as in Moreno's Electrovision report, tables are labeled separately from other types of visuals, which are called *figures*. Regardless of the system you use, be sure to include titles and page numbers.

If you have enough space on a single page, include the list of illustrations directly beneath the table of contents. Otherwise, put the list on the page after the contents page. When tables and figures are numbered separately, they should also be listed separately.

Synopsis or Executive Summary A **synopsis** is a brief overview (one page or less) of a report's most important points, designed to give readers a quick preview of the contents (see Figure 13.3). A synopsis is often included in long informational reports dealing with technical, professional, or academic subjects and can also be called an **abstract**. Because it's a concise representation of the whole report, it may be distributed separately to a wide audience; based on the information it contains, interested readers can request a copy of the entire report. The synopsis or abstract can also be indexed as a separate entry in electronic databases, so think carefully about the best way to preview the report's contents.

> A synopsis is a brief preview of the most important points in your report.

The phrasing of a synopsis can be either informative or descriptive. An informative synopsis presents the main points of the report in the order in which they appear in the text. A descriptive synopsis, on the other hand, simply tells what the report is about, using only moderately greater detail than the table of contents; the actual findings of the report are omitted. Here are examples of statements from each type:

Informative Synopsis	**Descriptive Synopsis**
Sales of super-premium ice cream make up 11 percent of the total ice cream market.	This report contains information about super-premium ice cream and its share of the market.

The way you handle a synopsis reflects the approach you use in the text. If you're using an indirect approach in your report, you're better off with a descriptive synopsis because an informative synopsis "gives away the ending" of your report. No matter which type of synopsis you use, be sure to present an accurate picture of the report's contents.[6]

Many business report writers prefer to include an **executive summary** instead of a synopsis or an abstract. Whereas a synopsis is a prose table of contents that outlines the main points of the report, an executive summary is a fully developed "mini" version of the report itself. An executive summary is more comprehensive than a synopsis; many contain headings, well-developed transitions, and even visual elements. They are usually organized in the same way as the report, using a direct or an indirect approach, depending on the audience's receptivity.

An executive summary is a "mini" version of your report.

Executive summaries are intended for readers who lack the time or motivation to study the complete text. As a general rule, keep the length of an executive summary proportionate to the length of the report. A brief business report may have only a one-page or shorter executive summary. A longer business report may have a two- or three-page summary. Anything longer, however, might cease to be a summary.[7]

Many reports require neither a synopsis nor an executive summary. Length is usually the determining factor. Most reports of fewer than 10 pages either omit such a preview or combine it with the letter of transmittal. However, if your report is over 20 or 30 pages long, you'll probably want to include either a synopsis or an executive summary as a convenience for readers. Which one you'll provide depends in part on the traditions of your organization.

Text of the Report   Although reports may contain a variety of components, the heart of a report is always composed of three main parts: an introduction, a body, and a close (which may consist of a summary, conclusions, or recommendations or some combination of the three). As Chapter 11 points out, the length and content of each of these parts vary with the length and type of report, the organizational structure, and the reader's familiarity with the topic. Following is a brief review of the three major parts of the report text.

> No matter how many separate elements are in a formal report, the heart of the report is still the introduction, body, and close.

Introduction A good introduction invites audience members to continue reading by telling them what the report is about, why the audience should be concerned, and how the report is organized. If your report has a synopsis or an executive summary, minimize redundancy by balancing the introduction with the material in your summary—as Linda Moreno does in her Electrovision report. For example, Moreno's executive summary is fairly detailed, so she keeps her introduction brief. If you believe that your introduction needs to repeat information that has already been covered in one of the prefatory parts, try to vary the wording to minimize the feeling of repetition.

Body The body of a report contains the information that supports your conclusions and recommendations as well as your analysis, logic, and interpretation of the information. See the body of Linda Moreno's Electrovision report for an example of the types of supporting detail commonly included in this section. Pay close attention to her effective use of visuals. Most inexperienced writers have a tendency to include too much data in their reports or place too much data in paragraph format instead of using tables and charts. Such treatment increases the chance of boring or losing an audience. If you find yourself with too much information, include only the essential supporting data in the body, use visuals, and place any additional information in an appendix.

Close The close of your report should summarize your main ideas, highlight your conclusions or recommendations (if any), and list any courses of action that you expect readers to take or that you will be taking yourself. In a long report, this section may be labeled "Summary" or "Conclusions and Recommendations." If you have organized your report in a direct pattern, your close should be relatively brief, like Linda Moreno's. With an indirect organization, you may use this section to present your conclusions and recommendations for the first time, in which case this section might be fairly extensive.

Supplementary Parts   Supplementary parts follow the text of the report and provide information for readers who seek more detailed discussion. For online reports, you can put supplements on separate webpages and allow readers to link to them from the main report pages. Supplements are more common in long reports than in short ones, and they typically include appendixes, a bibliography, and an index.

Appendixes An **appendix** contains materials related to the report but not included in the text because they are lengthy, bulky, or perhaps not relevant to everyone in the audience. If your company has an intranet, shared workspaces, or other means of

> Use an appendix for materials that are too lengthy for the body or not directly relevant to all audience members.

storing and accessing information online, consider putting your detailed supporting evidence there and referring readers to those sources for more detail.

The content of report appendixes varies widely; an appendix can include sample questionnaires and cover letters, sample forms, computer printouts, statistical formulas, financial statements and spreadsheets, copies of important documents, and multipage illustrations that would break up the flow of text. You might also include a glossary as an appendix or as a separate supplementary part.

If you have multiple categories of supporting material, give each type a separate appendix. Appendixes are usually identified with a letter and a short, descriptive title—for example, "Appendix A: Questionnaire," "Appendix B: Computer Printout of Raw Data," and so on. All appendixes should be mentioned in the text and listed in the table of contents.

A bibliography fulfills your ethical obligation to credit your sources, and it allows readers to consult those sources for more information.

Bibliography To fulfill your ethical and legal obligation to credit other people for their work and to assist readers who may want to research your topic further, include a **bibliography**, a list of the secondary sources you consulted when preparing your report. In her Electrovision report, Linda Moreno labeled her bibliography "Works Cited" because she listed only the works that were mentioned in the report. You might call this section "Sources" or "References" if it includes works consulted but not mentioned in your report. Moreno uses the author-date system to format her bibliographic sources. An alternative is to use numbered footnotes (bottom of the page) or endnotes (end of the report). For more information on citing sources, see Appendix B, "Documentation of Report Sources."

In addition to providing a bibliography, some authors prefer to cite references in the report text. Acknowledging your sources in the body of your report demonstrates that you have thoroughly researched your topic. Furthermore, mentioning the names of well-known or important authorities on the subject helps build credibility for your message. On the other hand, you don't want to make your report read like an academic treatise, dragging along from citation to citation. The source references should be handled as conveniently and inconspicuously as possible. One approach, especially for internal reports, is simply to mention a source in the text:

> According to Dr. Lewis Morgan of Northwestern Hospital, hip replacement operations account for 7 percent of all surgery performed on women age 65 and over.

However, if your report will be distributed to outsiders, include additional information on where you obtained the data. Most college students are familiar with citation methods suggested by the Modern Language Association (MLA) or the American Psychological Association (APA). *The Chicago Manual of Style* is a reference often used by typesetters and publishers. All these sources encourage the use of in-text citations (inserting the author's last name and a year of publication or a page number directly in the text).

If your report is lengthy, an index can help readers locate specific topics quickly.

Index An **index** is an alphabetical list of names, places, and subjects mentioned in a report, along with the pages on which they occur. (See the indexes in this book for examples.) If you think your readers will need to access specific points of information in a lengthy report, consider including an index that lists all key topics, product names, markets, important persons—whatever is relevant to your subject matter. As with your table of contents, accuracy is critical. The good news is that you can also use your word processor to compile the index. Just be sure to update the index (and any automatically generated elements, for that matter) right before you produce and distribute the format.

Components of a Formal Proposal

The goal of a proposal is to impress readers with your professionalism and to make your offering and your company stand out from the competition. Consequently, proposals addressed to external audiences, including potential customers and investors, are nearly always formal. For smaller projects and situations in which you already have a working relationship with the audience, the proposal can be less formal and skip some of the components described in this section.

Formal proposals contain many of the same components as other formal reports (see Figure 13.4). The difference lies mostly in the text, although a few of the prefatory parts are also different. With the exception of an occasional appendix, most proposals have few supplementary parts. As always, if you're responding to a request for proposal (RFP), follow its specifications to the letter, being sure to include everything it asks for and nothing it doesn't ask for.

Formal proposals must be produced with a high degree of polish and professionalism.

Prefatory Parts   The cover, title fly, title page, table of contents, and list of illustrations are handled in formal proposals the same as in other formal reports. However, you'll want to handle other prefatory parts a bit differently, such as the copy of the RFP, the synopsis or executive summary, and the letter of transmittal.

Copy of the RFP RFPs usually have specific instructions for referring to the RFP itself in the proposal because the organizations that issue RFPs need a methodical way to track all their active RFPs and the incoming responses. Some organizations require that you include a copy of the entire RFP in your proposal; others simply want you to refer to the

An RFP may require you to include a copy of the RFP in your prefatory section; just be sure to follow instructions carefully.

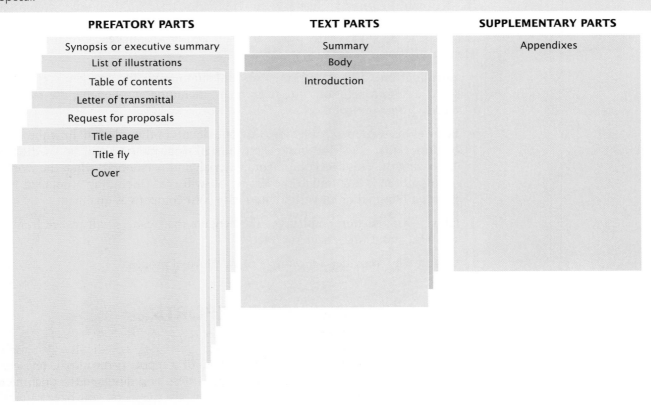

FIGURE 13.4
Parts of a Formal Proposal
As with formal reports, you can select from a variety of components to complete a formal proposal.

PREFATORY PARTS	TEXT PARTS	SUPPLEMENTARY PARTS
Synopsis or executive summary	Summary	Appendixes
List of illustrations	Body	
Table of contents	Introduction	
Letter of transmittal		
Request for proposals		
Title page		
Title fly		
Cover		

RFP by name or number or perhaps include just the introductory section of the RFP. Make sure you follow the instructions in every detail. If there are no specific instructions, use your best judgment, based on the length of the RFP and whether you received a printed copy or accessed it online. In any event, make sure your proposal refers to the RFP in some way so that the audience can associate your proposal with the correct RFP.

Document Makeover

IMPROVE THIS EXECUTIVE SUMMARY

To practice correcting drafts of actual documents, visit your online course or the access-code-protected portion of the Companion Website. Click on "Document Makeovers" and then click on Chapter 13. You will find an excerpt from an executive summary that contains problems and errors related to what you've learned in this chapter about completing formal reports and proposals. Use the "Final Draft" decision tool to create an improved version of this document. Check the executive summary for an appropriate degree of formality, parallel structures, the skillful inclusion or exclusion of detail, and a consistent time perspective.

Synopsis or Executive Summary Although you may include a synopsis or an executive summary for your reader's convenience when your proposal is quite long, these components are often less useful in a formal proposal than they are in a formal report. If your proposal is unsolicited, your transmittal letter will already have caught the reader's interest, making a synopsis or an executive summary redundant. It may also be less important if your proposal is solicited because the reader is already committed to studying your proposal to find out how you intend to satisfy the terms of a contract. The introduction of a solicited proposal would provide an adequate preview of the contents.

Letter of Transmittal The way you handle the letter of transmittal depends on whether the proposal is solicited or unsolicited. If the proposal is solicited, approach the transmittal letter as a positive message, highlighting the aspects of your proposal that may give you a competitive advantage. If the proposal is unsolicited, approach the transmittal letter as a persuasive message. The letter must persuade the reader that you have something worthwhile to offer, something that justifies the time required to read the entire proposal.

Text of the Proposal   Just as with reports, the text of a proposal is composed of three main parts: an introduction, a body, and a close. The content and depth of each part depend on whether the proposal is solicited or unsolicited, formal or informal. Here's a brief overview:[8]

- **Introduction.** This section presents and summarizes the problem you intend to solve and your solution to that problem, including any benefits the reader will receive from your solution.

- **Body.** This section explains the complete details of the solution: how the job will be done, how it will be broken into tasks, what method will be used to do it (including the required equipment, material, and personnel), when the work will begin and end, how much the entire job will cost (including a detailed breakdown, if required or requested), and why your company is qualified.

- **Close.** This section emphasizes the benefits that readers will realize from your solution, and it urges readers to act.

    Figure 13.5 provides an example of an informal proposal.

PROOFREADING YOUR REPORTS AND PROPOSALS

After you have assembled all the components of a report or proposal, revised the entire document's content for clarity and conciseness, and designed the document to ensure readability and a positive impression on your readers, you have essentially produced your document in its final form. Now you need to review it thoroughly one last time, looking for inconsistencies, errors, and missing components. For instance, if you changed a heading in the report's text part, make sure that you also changed the corresponding heading in the table of contents and in all references to that heading in your report. Proofing can catch minor flaws that might diminish your credibility—and major flaws that might damage your career.

Proofreading the textual part of your report is essentially the same as proofreading any other business message—you check for typos, spelling errors, and mistakes

FIGURE 13.5
Dixon O'Donnell's Informal Solicited Proposal
This proposal was submitted by Dixon O'Donnell, vice president of O'Donnell & Associates, a geotechnical engineering firm that conducts a variety of environmental testing services. As you review this document, pay close attention to the specific items addressed in the proposal's introduction, body, and close.

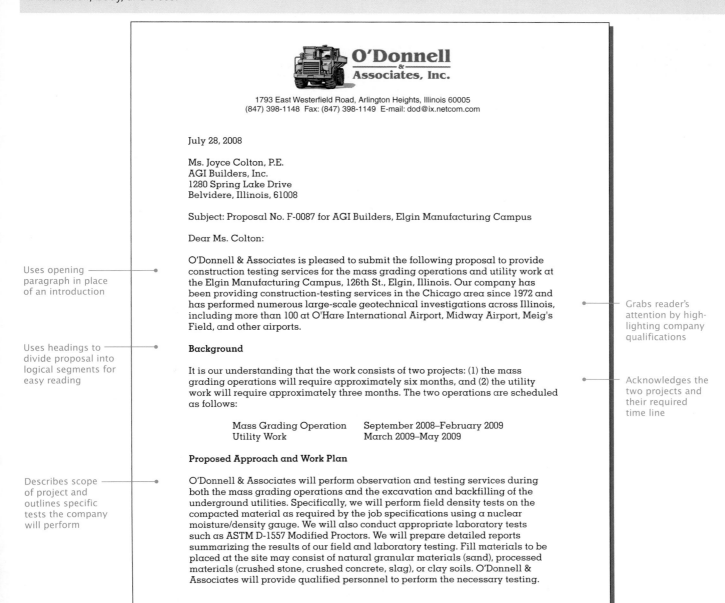

O'Donnell & Associates, Inc.

1793 East Westerfield Road, Arlington Heights, Illinois 60005
(847) 398-1148 Fax: (847) 398-1149 E-mail: dod@ix.netcom.com

July 28, 2008

Ms. Joyce Colton, P.E.
AGI Builders, Inc.
1280 Spring Lake Drive
Belvidere, Illinois, 61008

Subject: Proposal No. F-0087 for AGI Builders, Elgin Manufacturing Campus

Dear Ms. Colton:

Uses opening paragraph in place of an introduction

O'Donnell & Associates is pleased to submit the following proposal to provide construction testing services for the mass grading operations and utility work at the Elgin Manufacturing Campus, 126th St., Elgin, Illinois. Our company has been providing construction-testing services in the Chicago area since 1972 and has performed numerous large-scale geotechnical investigations across Illinois, including more than 100 at O'Hare International Airport, Midway Airport, Meig's Field, and other airports.

Grabs reader's attention by highlighting company qualifications

Uses headings to divide proposal into logical segments for easy reading

Background

It is our understanding that the work consists of two projects: (1) the mass grading operations will require approximately six months, and (2) the utility work will require approximately three months. The two operations are scheduled as follows:

Acknowledges the two projects and their required time line

| Mass Grading Operation | September 2008–February 2009 |
| Utility Work | March 2009–May 2009 |

Proposed Approach and Work Plan

Describes scope of project and outlines specific tests the company will perform

O'Donnell & Associates will perform observation and testing services during both the mass grading operations and the excavation and backfilling of the underground utilities. Specifically, we will perform field density tests on the compacted material as required by the job specifications using a nuclear moisture/density gauge. We will also conduct appropriate laboratory tests such as ASTM D-1557 Modified Proctors. We will prepare detailed reports summarizing the results of our field and laboratory testing. Fill materials to be placed at the site may consist of natural granular materials (sand), processed materials (crushed stone, crushed concrete, slag), or clay soils. O'Donnell & Associates will provide qualified personnel to perform the necessary testing.

(continued)

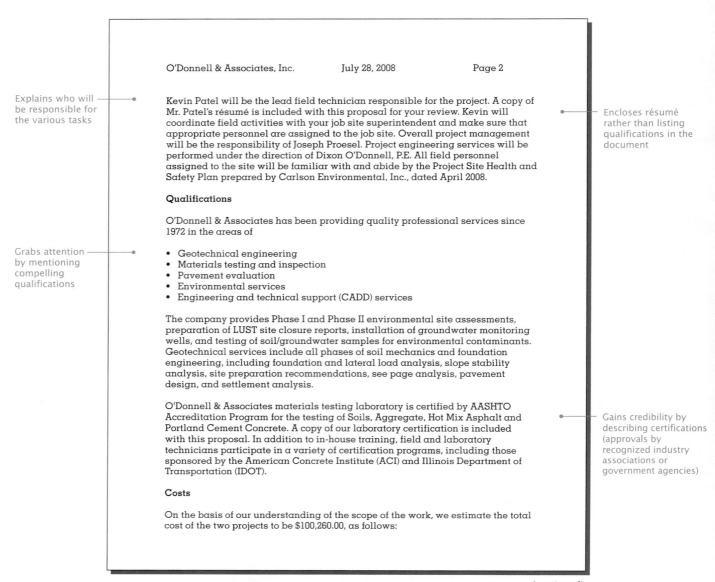

Explains who will be responsible for the various tasks

Grabs attention by mentioning compelling qualifications

Encloses résumé rather than listing qualifications in the document

Gains credibility by describing certifications (approvals by recognized industry associations or government agencies)

O'Donnell & Associates, Inc.   July 28, 2008   Page 2

Kevin Patel will be the lead field technician responsible for the project. A copy of Mr. Patel's résumé is included with this proposal for your review. Kevin will coordinate field activities with your job site superintendent and make sure that appropriate personnel are assigned to the job site. Overall project management will be the responsibility of Joseph Proesel. Project engineering services will be performed under the direction of Dixon O'Donnell, P.E. All field personnel assigned to the site will be familiar with and abide by the Project Site Health and Safety Plan prepared by Carlson Environmental, Inc., dated April 2008.

Qualifications

O'Donnell & Associates has been providing quality professional services since 1972 in the areas of

- Geotechnical engineering
- Materials testing and inspection
- Pavement evaluation
- Environmental services
- Engineering and technical support (CADD) services

The company provides Phase I and Phase II environmental site assessments, preparation of LUST site closure reports, installation of groundwater monitoring wells, and testing of soil/groundwater samples for environmental contaminants. Geotechnical services include all phases of soil mechanics and foundation engineering, including foundation and lateral load analysis, slope stability analysis, site preparation recommendations, see page analysis, pavement design, and settlement analysis.

O'Donnell & Associates materials testing laboratory is certified by AASHTO Accreditation Program for the testing of Soils, Aggregate, Hot Mix Asphalt and Portland Cement Concrete. A copy of our laboratory certification is included with this proposal. In addition to in-house training, field and laboratory technicians participate in a variety of certification programs, including those sponsored by the American Concrete Institute (ACI) and Illinois Department of Transportation (IDOT).

Costs

On the basis of our understanding of the scope of the work, we estimate the total cost of the two projects to be $100,260.00, as follows:

(continued)

FIGURE 13.5
(continued)

in punctuation. However, reports often have elements that may not be included in other messages, so don't forget to proof your visuals thoroughly and make sure they are positioned correctly. If you need specific tips on proofreading documents, refer to Chapter 6 for some reminders on what to look for when proofreading text and how to proofread like a pro.

Ask for proofreading assistance from someone who hasn't been involved in the development of your proposal; he or she might see errors that you've been overlooking.

Whenever possible, arrange for someone with "fresh eyes" to proofread the report, somebody who hasn't been involved with the text so far. At this point in the process, you are so familiar with the content that your mind is likely to fill in missing words, fix misspelled words, and subconsciously compensate for other flaws without your even being aware of it. Someone with fresh eyes might see mistakes that you've passed over a dozen times without noticing. An ideal approach is to have two people review it—one who is an expert in the subject matter and one who isn't. The first person can ensure its technical accuracy, and the second can ensure that a wide range of readers will understand it.[9]

O'Donnell & Associates, Inc.   July 28, 2008   Page 3

Cost Estimates

Cost Estimate: Mass Grading	Units	Rate ($)	Total Cost ($)
Field Inspection			
Labor	1,320 hours	$38.50	$ 50,820.00
Nuclear Moisture Density Meter	132 days	35.00	4,620.00
Vehicle Expense	132 days	45.00	5,940.00
Laboratory Testing			
Proctor Density Tests (ASTM D-1557)	4 tests	130.00	520.00
Engineering/Project Management			
Principal Engineer	16 hours	110.00	1,760.00
Project Manager	20 hours	80.00	1,600.00
Administrative Assistant	12 hours	50.00	600.00
Subtotal			**$ 65,860.00**

Cost Estimate: Utility Work	Units	Rate ($)	Total Cost ($)
Field Inspection			
Labor	660 hours	$ 38.50	$ 25,410.00
Nuclear Moisture Density Meter	66 days	5.00	2,310.00
Vehicle Expense	66 days	45.00	2,970.00
Laboratory Testing			
Proctor Density Tests (ASTM D-1557)	2 tests	130.00	260.00
Engineering/Project Management			
Principal Engineer	10 hours	110.00	1,100.00
Project Manager	20 hours	80.00	1,600.00
Administrative Assistant	15 hours	50.00	750.00
Subtotal			**$ 34,400.00**
Total Project Costs			**$100,260.00**

This estimate assumes full-time inspection services. However, our services may also be performed on an as-requested basis, and actual charges will reflect time associated with the project. We have attached our standard fee schedule for your review. Overtime rates are for hours in excess of 8.0 hours per day, before 7:00 a.m., after 5:00 p.m., and on holidays and weekends.

Itemizes costs by project and gives supporting details

Provides alternative option in case full-time service costs exceed client's budget

(continued)

FIGURE 13.5
(continued)

DISTRIBUTING YOUR REPORTS AND PROPOSALS

All the distribution issues you explored in Chapter 6 apply to reports and proposals, as long as you take into account the length and complexity of your documents. For physical distribution, consider spending the few extra dollars for a professional courier or package delivery service, if doing so will help your document stand apart from the crowd. The online tracking offered by FedEx, UPS, and other services can verify that your document arrived safely. On the other hand, if you've prepared the document for a single person or small group, delivering it in person can be a nice touch. Not only can you answer any immediate questions about it, you can promote the results in person—reminding the recipient of the benefits contained in your report or proposal.

O'Donnell & Associates, Inc.   July 28, 2008   Page 4

Authorization

With a staff of over 30 personnel, including registered professional engineers, resident engineers, geologists, construction inspectors, laboratory technicians, and drillers, we are convinced that O'Donnell & Associates is capable of providing the services required for a project of this magnitude.

If you would like our firm to provide the services as outlined in this proposal, please sign this letter and return it to us along with a certified check in the amount of $10,000 (our retainer) by August 15, 2008. Please call me if you have any questions regarding the terms of this proposal or our approach.

Sincerely,

Dixon O'Donnell

Dixon O'Donnell
Vice President

Enclosures

Accepted for AGI BUILDERS, INC.

By_____   Date _____

Uses brief close to emphasize qualifications and ask for client decision

Provides deadline and makes response easy

Makes letter a binding contract, if signed

FIGURE 13.5
(continued)

Adobe's PDF is a safe and common way to distribute reports electronically.

For electronic distribution, unless your audience specifically requests a word-processor file, provide documents as Portable Document Format (PDF) files. Many people are reluctant to open word-processor files these days, particularly from outsiders, given the vulnerability of such files to macro viruses and other contaminations. Moreover, using PDF files lets you control how your document is displayed on your audience's computer, ensuring that your readers see your document as you intended. In addition, making documents available as downloadable PDF files is almost universally expected these days, if only for the sake of convenience.

If your company or client expects you to distribute your reports via a web-based content management system, intranet, or extranet, be sure to upload the correct file(s) to the correct online location. Verify the onscreen display of your report after you've posted it, too; make sure graphics, charts, links, and other elements are in place and operational.

✓ CHECKLIST: Producing Formal Reports and Proposals

A. Prefatory parts

✓ Use your company's standard report covers, if available.

✓ Include a concise, descriptive title on the cover.

✓ Include a title fly only if you want an extra-formal touch.

✓ On the title page, list the (1) report title; (2) name, title, and address of the group or person(s) who authorized the report; (3) name, title, and address of the group or person(s) who prepared the report; and (4) date of submission.

✓ Include a copy of the letter of authorization, if appropriate.

✓ Include a copy of the RFP (or its introduction only, if the document is long), if appropriate.

✓ Include a letter of transmittal that introduces the report.

✓ Provide a table of contents in outline form, with headings worded exactly as they appear in the body of the report.

✓ Include a list of illustrations if the report contains a large number of them.

✓ Include a synopsis (a brief summary of the report) or an executive summary (a condensed, "mini" version of the report) for longer reports.

B. Text of the report

✓ Draft an introduction that prepares the reader for the content that follows.

✓ Provide information that supports your conclusions, recommendations, or proposals in the body of the report.

✓ Don't overload the body with unnecessary detail.

✓ Close with a summary of your main idea.

C. Supplementary parts

✓ Use appendixes to provide supplementary information or supporting evidence.

✓ List any secondary sources you used in a bibliography.

✓ Provide an index if your report contains a large number of terms or ideas and is likely to be consulted over time.

When you've completed your formal report or proposal and sent it off to your audience, your next task is to wait for a response. If you don't hear from your readers within a week or two, you might want to ask politely whether the report arrived. (Some RFPs specify a response time frame. In such a case, *don't* pester the recipient ahead of schedule, or you'll hurt your chances.) In hope of stimulating a response, you might ask a question about the report, such as "How do you think accounting will react to the proposed budget increase?" You might also offer to answer any questions or provide additional information. To review the ideas presented in this chapter, see "Checklist: Producing Formal Reports and Proposals."

On the Job

SOLVING COMMUNICATION DILEMMAS AT THE BILL & MELINDA GATES FOUNDATION

A decade into your business career, you've decided to put your communication skills to use in an effort to improve global health. You recently joined the Gates Foundation as a program officer in global health strategies.

Malaria is one of the foundation's primary health concerns. This mosquito-borne disease has been largely eradicated in many parts of the world, but it remains an active and growing menace in other areas (particularly sub-Saharan Africa). Worldwide, malaria kills more than a million people every year, most of whom are children.

You are writing an informational report that will be made available on the foundation's website, summarizing the current crisis and progress being made toward the eventual control and eradication of malaria. How will you handle the following challenges?[10]

1. A wide variety of people visit the foundation's website, from researchers who are interested in applying for grants to reporters writing about health and education issues to members of the general public. Consequently, you can't pin down a specific audience for your report. In addition, because people will

simply download a PDF file of the report from the website, you don't have the opportunity to write a traditional letter or memo of transmittal. How should you introduce your report to website visitors?

a. Write a brief description of the report, explaining its purpose and content; post this information on the website, above the link to the PDF file so that people can read it before they decide whether to download the file.

b. Provide an e-mail link that people can use to send you an e-mail message if they'd like to know more about the report before reading it.

c. Write a news release describing the report and post this document on the website's "Newsroom" section.

d. Count on the title of the report to introduce its purpose and content; don't bother writing an introduction.

2. Which of the following report titles would do the best job of catching readers' attention with an emotional "hook" that balances the urgency of the crisis with the reasons for hope?

a. Children Who Don't Need to Die: The Urgent Global Malaria Crisis

b. Preventing a Million Malaria Deaths Every Year: The Urgent Global Challenge—And Reasons for Hope

c. Malaria: It Killed Two Thousand More Children Today

d. Malaria: Progress Toward Eradicating This Global Disease

3. The Gates Foundation is known around the world for the quality of its work, and that includes the quality of its communication efforts. Which of the following proofreading strategies should you use to make sure your report is free of errors?

a. Take advantage of technology. Double-check the settings in your word processor to make sure every checking tool is activated as you type, including the spell checker, grammar checker, and style checker. When you're finished with the first draft, run each of these tools again, just to make sure the computer didn't miss anything.

b. Recognize that no report, particularly a complex 48-page document with multiple visuals and more than 60 sources, is going to be free of errors. Include a statement on the title page apologizing for any errors that may still exist in the report. Provide your e-mail address and invite people to send you a message when they find errors.

c. As soon as you finish typing the first draft, immediately review it for accuracy while the content is still fresh in your mind. After you done this, you can be reasonably sure that the document is free from errors. If you wait a day or two, you'll start to forget what you've written, thereby lowering your chances of catching errors.

d. Put the report aside for at least a day and then proofread it carefully. Also, recruit two colleagues to review it for you—one who can review the technical accuracy of the material and one you has a good eye for language and clarity.

4. One of the sources used in your report is an article titled "Making Antimalarial Agents Available in Africa," by Kenneth J. Arrow, Hellen Gelband, and Dean T. Jamison. The article appeared in the July 28, 2005, edition (volume 353, issue 4) of the *New England Journal of Medicine*, on pages 333 to 335. Which of the following is the correct way to cite this source using APA guidelines?

a. Arrow, K. J., Gelband H., & Jamison, D. T. (2005). Making antimalarial agents available in Africa. *New England Journal of Medicine, 353* (4), 333–335.

b. Kenneth J. Arrow, Hellen Gelband, and Dean T. Jamison, "Making Antimalarial Agents Available in Africa," *New England Journal of Medicine*, 28 July 2005, 333 (3 pgs).

c. "Making Antimalarial Agents Available in Africa," *New England Journal of Medicine*: Vol. 353, Iss. 4, Pgs. 333–335.

d. Arrow, Kenneth J., Gelband, Hellen, and Jamison, Dean T. "Making Antimalarial Agents Available in Africa." *New England Journal of Medicine* 353.4 (2005): 333–335.

Learning Objectives Checkup

Assess your understanding of the principles in this chapter by reading each learning objective and studying the accompanying exercises. For fill-in-the-blank items, write the missing text in the blank provided; for multiple-choice items, circle the letter of the correct answer. You can check your responses against the answer key on page AK-2.

Objective 13.1: Characterize the four tasks involved in completing business reports and proposals.

1. Which of the following is *not* one of the four major tasks involved in completing business reports and proposals?

a. Revising the report's organization, style, tone, and readability

b. Formatting the report
c. Deciding which visuals to create for the report
d. Proofreading the report

2. The following sentence appears in your first draft of a report that analyzes perceived shortcomings in your company's employee health benefits: "Among the many criticisms and concerns expressed by the workforce, at least among the 376 who responded to our online survey (out of 655 active employees), the issues of elder care, health insurance during retirement, and the increased amount that employees are being forced to pay every month as the company's contribution to health insurance coverage has declined over the past two years were identified as the most important." You realize that this 69-word sentence could be shorter, more direct, and more powerful. Which of these revisions is the most effective?
   a. The employees who responded to our online survey (376 out of 655 active employees) identified these three issues as the most important: elder care, insurance coverage after they retire, and rising monthly payments.
   b. Elder care, insurance coverage after they retire, and rising monthly payments were the three most important issues identified in our survey of employees regarding their complaints and criticisms of health care benefits. Out of a current active workforce of 655 people, 376 employees completed the online survey. They complained about quite a range of issues, but these three were the most important to them overall.
   c. The top three employee concerns: elder care, insurance coverage after they retire, and increases in the amounts that employees pay every month for health insurance.
   d. The top three concerns our employees have regarding their health benefits are elder care, insurance coverage after they retire, and increases in the monthly cost of insurance. These results are based on responses from the 376 employees (out of 655) who participated in our online survey.

Objective 13.2: Explain how computers have both simplified and complicated the report-production process.

3. How have computers and related technology (such as low-cost color printers) made it easier in recent years for all businesspeople to product top-quality reports and proposals?
   a. Tasks that once required expensive equipment and specialized skills can now be accomplished on most desktop computers by regular businesspeople with minimal training.
   b. Most companies now have dedicated desktop publishing departments, so business professionals are no longer expected to create their own charts, graphs, and other report elements.
   c. The support personnel who will do all your typing for you can now produce all your visuals and other report

elements, so you no longer need to work with a variety of different people.
   d. The Internet has improved everyone's design sensibilities.

4. How has the widespread availability of computer publishing tools made life more difficult for report writers?
   a. The Internet is slower than ever before.
   b. Since prices have fallen so low, most companies expect employees to purchase their own computers.
   c. More and more readers are growing tired of the slick, overproduced reports available these days; they want to see more simple, black-and-white, "typewriter-style" reports.
   d. In terms of production quality, audience expectations are higher, and the competition is tougher than ever before.

Objective 13.3: Identify the circumstances in which you should include letters of authorization and letters of acceptance in your reports.

5. In what situation should you consider including a letter or memo of authorization in a formal report?
   a. If you're getting paid to write the report
   b. If you received written authorization to write the report
   c. If the audience outranks you
   d. If you outrank the audience

6. What is the purpose of including a letter of acceptance in a formal report?
   a. It reminds your audience what you previously agreed to address in the report and why you were assigned to write it.
   b. It makes your report feel more formal and official.
   c. It prevents others from taking credit for your work.
   d. It summarizes the key points of your report for people who are too busy to read the report itself.

Objective 13.4: Explain the difference between a synopsis and an executive summary.

7. A/an _____ is a brief overview (usually one page or less) of a report's most important points.

8. A/an _____ is a fully developed "mini" version of the report itself.

9. Which of the following may contain headings, visual aids, and enough information to help busy executives make quick decisions?
   a. An executive summary
   b. A synopsis
   c. Both
   d. Neither

Objective 13.5: Describe the three supplementary parts of a formal report.

10. Which of the following is *not* a typical supplementary part of a formal report?
    a. Appendixes
    b. Bibliography
    c. Letter of authorization
    d. Index

Objective 13.6: Explain how prefatory parts of a proposal differ, depending on whether the proposal is solicited or unsolicited.

11. If you've submitted a proposal that is in response to an RFP, what steps can you take to make sure the recipient understands which RFP you're responding to?
    a. Include the formal title of the RFP (and its reference number, if it has one) as a footnote in the first appendix of your report.
    b. If the RFP is short, include it with the other prefatory parts of your proposal; if the RFP is lengthy, include just the introductory page(s) from it.
    c. Include the entire RFP in the body of your proposal, no matter how long it is.
    d. The RFP was written by someone else, so you can ignore it in your report.
12. How should you handle the letter of transmittal for an unsolicited proposal?
    a. Treat the letter as a routine message; businesspeople get proposals all the time, so they don't expect anything more than a simple announcement that identifies you and your proposal.
    b. Treat the letter as a positive message, highlighting the good news that you have to offer in the proposal.
    c. Treat the letter as a persuasive message, persuading the reader that your proposal offers something of value.
    d. Don't waste the reader's time with a letter of transmittal; get right to the point with the body of your proposal.

Apply Your Knowledge

1. Is an executive summary a persuasive message? Explain your answer.
2. Under what circumstances would you include more than one index in a lengthy report?
3. If you were submitting a solicited proposal to build a small shopping center, would you include as references the names and addresses of other clients for whom you recently built similar facilities? Where in the proposal would you include these references? Why?
4. If you included a bibliography in your report, would you also need to include in-text citations? Please explain.
5. **Ethical Choices** How would you report on a confidential survey in which employees rated their managers' capabilities? Both employees and managers expect to see the results. Would you give the same report to employees and managers? What components would you include or exclude for each audience? Explain your choices.

Practice Your Knowledge

MESSAGE FOR ANALYSIS

Visit the website of the U.S. Citizenship and Immigration Services (a division of the U.S. Department of Homeland Security), at http://uscis.gov. Click on "About USCIS," followed by "Reports and Studies" then find the report titled "The Triennial Comprehensive Report on Immigration." Download this PDF file and read the executive summary. Using the information in this chapter, analyze the executive summary and offer specific suggestions for revising it.

EXERCISES

For active links to all websites discussed in this chapter, visit this book's website at www.prenhall.com/thill. Locate your book and click on its "Companion Website" link. Then select Chapter 13 and click on "Featured Websites." Locate the name of the page or the URL related to the material in the text. Please note that links to sites that become inactive after publication of the book will be removed from the "Featured Websites" section.

13.1 Revising for Clarity and Conciseness The following sentence appears in your first draft of a report: "Most analysts agree that Google needs to stake out a sizable presence in the mobile phone services market in order to maintain anything close to the phenomenal growth rates the company has enjoyed in recent years because the wireless industry represents tremendous opportunity for the growth of all kinds of both for-fee and advertising-supported services, from voice and video to search, navigation, and game playing." Revise this sentence to make it shorter, more direct, and more powerful.

13.2 Teamwork You and a classmate are helping Linda Moreno prepare her report on Electrovision's travel and entertainment costs (see "Report Writer's Notebook"). This time, however, the report is to be informational rather than analytical, so it will not include recommendations. Review the existing report and determine what changes would be needed to make it an informational report. Be as specific as possible. For example, if your team decides the report needs a new title, what title would you use? Draft a transmittal memo for Moreno to use in conveying this informational report to Dennis McWilliams, Electrovision's vice president of operations.

13.3 Producing Reports: Letter of Transmittal You are president of the Friends of the Library, a nonprofit group that raises funds and provides volunteers to support your local library. Every February, you send a report of the previous year's activities and accomplishments to the County Arts Council, which provides an annual grant of $1,000 toward your group's summer reading festival. Now it's February 6, and you've completed your formal report. Here are the highlights:

- Back-to-school book sale raised $2,000.
- Holiday craft fair raised $1,100.
- Promotion and prizes for summer reading festival cost $1,450.
- Materials for children's program featuring local author cost $125.
- New reference databases for library's career center cost $850.
- Bookmarks promoting library's website cost $200.

Write a letter of transmittal to Erica Maki, the council's director. Because she is expecting this report, you can use the direct approach. Be sure to express gratitude for the council's ongoing financial support.

13.4 Internet Government reports vary in purpose and structure. Read through the U.S. Department of Education's report "Helping Your Child Become a Reader," available at www.ed.gov. What is the purpose of this document? Does the title communicate this purpose? What type of report is this, and what is the report's structure? Which prefatory and supplementary parts are included? Analyze the visuals. What types are included in this report? Are they all necessary? Are the titles and legends sufficiently informative? How does this report take advantage of the online medium to enhance readability?

13.5 Ethical Choices: Team Challenge You submitted what you thought was a masterful report to your boss over three weeks ago. The report analyzes current department productivity and recommends several steps that you think will improve employee output without increasing individual workloads. Brilliant, you thought. But you haven't heard a word from your boss. Did you overstep your boundaries by making recommendations that might imply that she has not been doing a good job? Did you overwhelm her with your ideas? You'd like some feedback. In your last e-mail to her, you asked if she had read your report. So far, you've received no reply. Yesterday, you overheard the company vice president talk about some productivity changes in your department. The changes were ones that you recommended in your report. Now you're worried that your boss submitted your report to senior management and will take full credit for your terrific ideas. What, if anything, should you do? Should you confront your boss about this? Should you ask to meet with the company vice president? Discuss this situation with your teammates and develop a solution to this sticky situation. Present your solution to the class, explaining the rationale behind your decision.

Expand Your Knowledge

LEARNING MORE ON THE WEB
PREVIEW BEFORE YOU PRODUCE

www.dogpile.com
A good way to get ideas for the best style, organization, and format of a report is by looking at copies of professional business reports. To find samples of various types of reports, you can use a metasearch engine such as Dogpile. Choose a metasearch engine (refer to Table 11.4 on page 380). Try several search terms—such as *status report, progress report, sales report, business plan,* or *marketing plan*—until you uncover an interesting-looking report. Review the report and then answer the following questions:

1. What is the purpose of the report you read? Who is its target audience? Explain why the structure and style of the report make it easy or difficult to follow the main idea.
2. What type of report did you read? Briefly describe the main message. Is the information well organized? If you answer yes, explain how you can use the report as a guide for a report you might write. If you answer no, explain why the report is not helpful.
3. Drawing on what you know about the qualities of a good business report, review a report and describe the features that contribute to its readability.

SURFING YOUR WAY TO CAREER SUCCESS

Bovée and Thill's Business Communication Headline News offers links to hundreds of online resources that can help you with this course, your other college courses, and your career. Visit www.businesscommunicationblog.com and click on "Web Directory." The "Search Engines and Directories" section connects you to a variety of search and metasearch engines, online directories and libraries, specialized search engines for multimedia content, newsfeed aggregators, and other helpful tools. Identify three websites from this section that could be useful in your business career. For each site, write a two-sentence summary of what the site offers and how it could help you launch and build your career.

Learn Interactively

INTERACTIVE STUDY GUIDE

Visit www.prenhall.com/thill, locate your book and click on its "Companion Website" link. Select Chapter 13 to take advantage of the interactive "Chapter Quiz" to test your knowledge of chapter concepts. Receive instant feedback on whether you need to do additional studying. Also, visit the "Study Hall," where you'll find an abundance of valuable resources that will help you succeed in this course.

PEAK PERFORMANCE GRAMMAR AND MECHANICS

If your instructor has required the use of "Peak Performance Grammar and Mechanics," either in your online course or on

CD, you can improve your skill with apostrophes, quotation marks, parentheses, and ellipses by using the "Peak Performance Grammar and Mechanics" module. Click on "Punctuation" and then "Vocabulary II." Take the Pretest to determine whether you have any weak areas. Then review those areas in the Refresher Course. Take the Follow-Up Test to check your grasp of quotation marks, parentheses, and ellipses. For an extra challenge or advanced practice, take the Advanced Test. Finally, for additional reinforcement, go to the "Improve Your Grammar, Mechanics, and Usage" section that follows and complete those exercises.

Improve your Grammar, Mechanics, and Usage

The following exercises help you improve your knowledge of and power over English grammar, mechanics, and usage. Turn to the Handbook of Grammar, Mechanics, and Usage at the end of this book and review all of Sections 2.10 (Quotation Marks), 2.11 (Parentheses), and 2.12 (Ellipses). Then look at the following 10 items. Circle the letter of the preferred choice in the following groups of sentences. (Answers to these exercises appear on page AK-4.)

1. a. Be sure to read (How to Sell by Listening) in this month's issue of *Fortune*.
   b. Be sure to read "How to Sell by Listening" in this month's issue of *Fortune*.
   c. Be sure to read "How to Sell by Listening . . ." in this month's issue of *Fortune*.
2. a. Her response . . . see the attached memo . . . is disturbing.
   b. Her response (see the attached memo) is disturbing.
   c. Her response "see the attached memo" is disturbing.
3. a. We operate with a skeleton staff during the holidays (December 21 through January 2).
   b. We operate with a skeleton staff during the holidays "December 21 through January 2".
   c. We operate with a skeleton staff during the holidays (December 21 through January 2.)
4. a. "The SBP's next conference . . ." the bulletin noted, " . . . will be held in Minneapolis."
   b. "The SBP's next conference," the bulletin noted, "will be held in Minneapolis."
   c. "The SBP's next conference," the bulletin noted, "will be held in Minneapolis".
5. a. The term "up in the air" means "undecided."
   b. The term "up in the air" means *undecided*.
   c. The term *up in the air* means "undecided."

6. a. Her assistant (the one who just had the baby) won't be back for four weeks.
   b. Her assistant (the one who just had the baby), won't be back for four weeks.
   c. Her assistant . . . the one who just had the baby . . . won't be back for four weeks.
7. a. "Ask not what your country can do for you," begins a famous John Kennedy quotation.
   b. " . . . Ask not what your country can do for you" begins a famous John Kennedy quotation.
   c. "Ask not what your country can do for you . . ." begins a famous John Kennedy quotation.
8. a. Do you remember who said, "And away we go?"
   b. Do you remember who said, "And away we go"?
9. a. Refinements may prove profitable. (More detail about this technology appears in Appendix A).
   b. Refinements may prove profitable. (More detail about this technology appears in Appendix A.)
10. a. The resignation letter begins, "Since I'll never regain your respect . . . ," and goes on to explain why that's true.
    b. The resignation letter begins, "Since I'll never regain your respect, . . ." and goes on to explain why that's true.
    c. The resignation letter begins, "Since I'll never regain your respect . . ." and goes on to explain why that's true.

For additional exercises focusing on quotation marks, parentheses, and ellipses, go to www.prenhall.com/thill, then locate your text and click on its "Companion Website" link. Click on Chapter 13, click on "Additional Exercises to Improve Your Grammar, Mechanics and Usage," and then click on "19. Punctuation D."

Cases

Applying the Three-Step Writing Process to Cases

Apply each step to the following cases, as assigned by your instructor.

Planning ➤ Writing ➤ Completing

Analyze the Situation
Clarify the problem or opportunity at hand, develop an audience profile, and develop a work plan.

Gather Information
Determine audience needs and obtain the information necessary to satisfy those needs; conduct a research project if necessary.

Select the Right Medium
Choose the best medium for delivering your message; consider delivery through multiple media.

Organize the Information
Define your main idea, limit your scope, select a direct or an indirect approach, and outline your content using an appropriate structure for an informational report, analytical report, or proposal.

Adapt to Your Audience
Be sensitive to audience needs with a "you" attitude, politeness, positive emphasis, and bias-free language. Build a strong relationship with your audience by establishing your credibility and projecting your company's image. Control your style with a tone and voice appropriate to the situation.

Compose the Message
Choose strong words that will help you create effective sentences and coherent paragraphs throughout the introduction, body, and close of your report or proposal.

Revise the Message
Evaluate content and review readability, edit and rewrite for conciseness and clarity.

Produce the Message
Use effective design elements and suitable layout for a clean, professional appearance; seamlessly combine text and graphical elements.

Proofread the Message
Review for errors in layout, spelling, and mechanics.

Distribute the Message
Deliver your report using the chosen medium; make sure all documents and all relevant files are distributed successfully.

1   **2**   **3**

SHORT FORMAL REPORTS THAT REQUIRE NO ADDITIONAL RESEARCH

Portfolio BUILDER

1. Giving it the online try: Report that analyzes the advantages and disadvantages of corporate online learning As the newest member of the corporate training division of Paper Products, Inc., you have been asked to investigate and analyze the merits of creating online courses for the company's employees. The president of your company thinks e-learning might be a good employee benefit as well as a terrific way for employees to learn new skills that they can use on the job. You've already done your research and compiled a list of notes (shown on page 494).

Your task: Write a short (3- to 5-page) memo report to the director of human resources, Kerry Simmons, presenting the advantages and disadvantages of e-learning and making a recommendation as to whether Paper Products, Inc., should invest time and money in training its employees this way. Be sure to organize your information so that it is clear, concise,

and logically presented. Simmons likes to read the "bottom line" first, so be direct: Present your recommendation up front and support your recommendation with your findings.[11]

Portfolio BUILDER

2. Grumbling in the ranks: When departments can't agree on the value of work You've been in your new job as human resources director for only a week, and already you have a major personnel crisis on your hands. Some employees in the marketing department got their hands on a confidential salary report and learned that, on average, marketing employees earn less than engineering employees. In addition, several top performers in the engineering group make significantly more than anybody in marketing. The report was passed around the company instantly by e-mail, and now everyone is discussing the situation. You'll deal with the data security issue later; for now, you need to address the dissatisfaction in the marketing group.

Table 13.1 lists the salary and employment data you were able to pull from the employee database. You also had the opportunity to interview the engineering and marketing

---

Research notes for Exercise 13.1

Online courses open up new horizons for working adults, who often find it difficult to juggle conventional classes with jobs and families.

Adults over 25 now represent nearly half of higher-ed students; most are employed and want more education to advance their careers.

Some experts believe that online learning will never be as good as face-to-face instruction.

Online learning requires no commute and is appealing for employees who travel regularly.

Enrollment in courses offered online by postsecondary institutions is expected to increase from 2 million students in 2001 to 5 million students in 2006.

E-learning is a cost-effective way to get better-educated employees.

More than one-third of the $50 billion spent on employee training every year is spent on e-learning.

At IBM, some 200,000 employees received education or training online last year, and 75 percent of the company's Basic Blue course for new managers is online. E-learning cut IBM's training bill by $350 million last year—mostly because online courses don't require travel.

There are no national statistics, but a recent report from the *Chronicle of Higher Education* found that institutions are seeing dropout rates that range from 20 to 50 percent for online learners. The research does not adequately explain why the dropout rates for e-learners are higher.

A recent study of corporate online learners reported that employees want the following things from their online courses: college credit or a certificate; active correspondence with an online facilitator who has frequent virtual office hours; access to 24-hour, seven-day-a-week technical support; and the ability to start a course anytime.

Corporate e-learners said that their top reason for dropping a course was lack of time. Many had trouble completing courses from their desktops because of frequent distractions caused by co-workers. Some said they could only access courses through the company's intranet, so they couldn't finish their assignments from home.

Besides lack of time, corporate e-learners cited the following as e-learning disadvantages: lack of management oversight; lack of motivation; problems with technology; lack of student support; individual learning preferences; poorly designed courses; substandard/inexperienced instructors.

A recent study by GE Capital found that finishing a corporate online course was dependent on whether managers gave reinforcement on attendance, how important employees were made to feel, and whether employee progress in the course was tracked.

Sun Microsystems found that interactivity can be a critical success factor for online courses. Company studies showed that only 25 percent of employees finish classes that are strictly self-paced. But 75 percent finish when give similar assignments and access to tutors through e-mail, phone, or online discussion groups.

Company managers must supervise e-learning just as they would any other important initiative.

For online learning to work, companies must develop a culture that takes online learning just as seriously as classroom training.

For many e-learners, studying at home is optimal. Whenever possible, companies should offer courses through the Internet or provide intranet access at home. Having employees studying on their own time will more than cover any added costs.

Corporate e-learning has flared into a $2.3 billion market, making it one of the fastest-growing segments of the education industry.

Rather than fly trainers to 7,000 dealerships, General Motors University now uses interactive satellite broadcasts to teach salespeople the best way to highlight features on the new Buick.

Fast and cheap, e-training can shave companies' training costs while it saves employees travel time.

Pharmaceutical companies such as Merck are conducting live, interactive classes over the web, allowing sales reps to learn about the latest product information at home rather than fly them to a conference center.

McDonald's trainers can log into Hamburger University to learn such skills as how to assemble a made-to-order burger or properly place the drink on a tray.

One obstacle to the spread of online corporate training is the mismatch between what employees really need—customized courses that are tailored to a firm's products and its unique corporate culture—and what employers can afford.

80 percent of companies prefer developing their own online training courses in-house. But creating even one customized e-course can take months, involve armies of experts, and cost anywhere from $25,000 to $50,000. Thus, most companies either stick with classroom training or buy generic courses on such topics as how to give performance appraisals, understanding basic business ethics, and so on. Employers can choose from a wide selection of noncustomized electronic courses.

For online learning to be effective, content must be broken into short "chunks" with lots of pop quizzes, online discussion groups, and other interactive features that let students demonstrate what they've learned. For instance, Circuit City's tutorial on digital camcorders consists of three 20-minute segments. Each contains audio demonstrations of how to handle customer product queries, tests on terminology, and "try-its" that propel trainees back onto the floor to practice what they've learned.

Dell Computer expects 90 percent of its learning solutions to be totally or partially technology enabled.

The Home Depot has used e-training to cut a full day from the time required to train new cashiers.

Online training has freed up an average of 17 days every year for Black & Decker's sales representatives.

---

directors to get their opinions on the pay situation; their answers are listed in Table 13.2.

Your task: The CEO has asked for a short report, summarizing whatever data and information you have on engineering and marketing salaries. Feel free to offer your own interpretation of the situation as well (make up any information you need), but keep in mind that as a new manager with almost no experience in the company, your opinion might not have a lot of influence.

SELECTED EMPLOYMENT DATA FOR ENGINEERS AND MARKETING STAFF

Table 13.1

Employment Statistic	Engineering Department	Marketing Department
Average number of years of work experience	18.2	16.3
Average number of years of experience in current profession	17.8	8.6
Average number of years with company	12.4	7.9
Average number of years of college education	6.9	4.8
Average number of years between promotions	6.7	4.3
Salary range	$58k–$165k	$45k–$85k
Median salary	$77k	$62k

Table 13.2   SUMMARY STATEMENTS FROM DEPARTMENT DIRECTOR INTERVIEWS

Question	Engineering Director	Marketing Director
1. Should engineering and marketing professionals receive roughly similar pay?	In general, yes, but we need to make allowances for the special nature of the engineering profession. In some cases, it's entirely appropriate for an engineer to earn more than a marketing person.	Yes.
2. Why or why not?	Several reasons: (1) top engineers are extremely hard to find and we need to offer competitive salaries; (2) the structure of the engineering department doesn't provide as many promotional opportunities, so we can't use promotions as a motivator the way marketing can; (3) many of our engineers have advanced degrees and nearly all pursue continuous education to stay on top of the technology.	Without marketing, the products the engineers create wouldn't reach customers and the company wouldn't have any revenue. The two teams make equal contributions to the company's success.
3. If we decide to balance pay between the two departments, how should we do it?	If we do anything to cap or reduce engineering salaries, we'll lose key people to the competition.	If we can't increase payroll immediately to raise marketing salaries, the only fair thing to do is freeze raises in engineering and gradually raise marketing salaries over the next few years.

Portfolio BUILDER

3. Building a new magazine: Finding opportunity in the remodeling craze Spurred in part by the success of such hit shows as *Changing Rooms*, *Trading Spaces*, and *Designers' Challenge*, homeowners across the country are redecorating, remodeling, and rebuilding. Many people are content with superficial changes, such as new paint or new accessories, but some are more ambitious. These homeowners want to move walls, add rooms, redesign kitchens, convert garages to home theaters—the big stuff.

Publishers try to create magazines that appeal to carefully identified groups of potential readers and the advertisers who'd like to reach them. The do-it-yourself (DIY) market is already served by numerous magazines, but you see an opportunity in the homeowners who tackle the heavy-duty projects. Tables 13.3 through 13.5 summarize the results of some preliminary research you asked your company's research staff to conduct.

Table 13.3	ROOMS MOST FREQUENTLY REMODELED BY DIYERS	
	Room	**Percentage of Homeowners Surveyed Who Have Tackled or Plan to Tackle at Least a Partial Remodel**
	Kitchen	60
	Bathroom	48
	Home office/study	44
	Bedroom	38
	Media room/home theater	31
	Den/recreation room	28
	Living room	27
	Dining room	12
	Sun room/solarium	8

Table 13.4	AVERAGE AMOUNT SPENT ON REMODELING PROJECTS	
	Estimated Amount	**Percentage of Surveyed Homeowners**
	Under $5k	5
	$5k–$10k	21
	$10k–$20k	39
	$20k–$50k	22
	More than $50k	13

Table 13.5	TASKS PERFORMED BY HOMEOWNER ON A TYPICAL REMODELING PROJECT	
	Task	**Percentage of Surveyed Homeowners Who Perform or Plan to Perform Most or All of This Task Themselves**
	Conceptual design	90
	Technical design/architecture	34
	Demolition	98
	Foundation work	62
	Framing	88
	Plumbing	91
	Electrical	55
	Heating/cooling	22
	Finish carpentry	85
	Tile work	90
	Painting	100
	Interior design	52

Your task: You think the data show a real opportunity for a "big projects" DIY magazine, although you'll need more extensive research to confirm the size of the market and refine the editorial direction of the magazine. Prepare a brief analytical report that presents the data you have, identifies the opportunity or opportunities you've found (suggest your own ideas, based on Tables 13.3 through 13.5), and requests funding from the editorial board to pursue further research.

SHORT FORMAL REPORTS THAT REQUIRE ADDITIONAL RESEARCH

4. Picking the better path: Research report assisting a client in a career choice You are employed by Open Options, a career-counseling firm, where your main function is to help clients make career choices. Today, a client with the same name as yours (a truly curious coincidence!) came to your office and asked for help deciding between two careers— careers that you yourself had been interested in (an even greater coincidence!).

Your task: Do some research on the two careers and then prepare a short report that your client can study. Your report should compare at least five major areas, such as salary, working conditions, and education required. Interview the client to understand her or his personal preferences regarding each of the five areas. For example, what is the minimum salary the client will accept? By comparing the client's preferences with the research material you collect, such as salary data, you will have a basis for concluding which of the two careers is best. The report should end with a career recommendation. (Note: One good place for career-related information is the *Occupational Outlook Handbook*, published by the U.S. Bureau of Labor Statistics, which is available at www.bls.gov/oco.)

Portfolio BUILDER

5. Selling overseas: Research report on the prospects for marketing a product in another country Select a fairly inexpensive product that you currently own and a country that you're not very familiar with. The product could be a moderately priced watch, radio, or other device. Now imagine that you are with the international sales department of the company that manufactures and sells the item and that you are proposing to make it available in the country you have selected.

The first step is to learn as much as possible about the country where you plan to market the product. Check almanacs, encyclopedias, the Internet, and library databases for the most recent information, paying particular attention to descriptions of the social life of the inhabitants, their economic conditions, and cultural traditions that would encourage or discourage use of the product.

Your task: Write a short report that describes the product you plan to market abroad, briefly describes the country you have selected, indicates the types of people in this country who would find the product attractive, explains how the product

would be transported into the country (or possibly manufactured there, if materials and labor are available), recommends a location for a regional sales center, and suggests how the product should be sold. Your report is to be submitted to the chief operating officer of the company, whose name you can either make up or find in a corporate directory. The report should include your conclusions (how the product will do in this new environment) and your recommendations for marketing (steps the company should take immediately and those it should develop later).

Portfolio BUILDER

6. A ready-made business: Finding the right franchise opportunity After 15 years in the corporate world, you're ready to strike out on your own. Rather than build a business from the ground up, however, you think that buying a franchise is a better idea. Unfortunately, some of the most lucrative franchise opportunities, such as the major fast-food chains, require significant start-up costs—some more than a half million dollars. Fortunately, you've met several potential investors who seem willing to help you get started in exchange for a share of ownership. Between your own savings and these investors, you estimate that you can raise from $350,000 to $600,000, depending on how much ownership share you want to concede to the investors.

You've worked in several functional areas already, including sales and manufacturing, so you have a fairly well-rounded business résumé. You're open to just about any type of business, too, as long as it provides the opportunity to grow; you don't want to be so tied down to the first operation that you can't turn it over to a hired manager and expand into another market.

Your task: To convene a formal meeting with the investor group, you need to first draft a report that outlines the types of franchise opportunities you'd like to pursue. Write a brief report, identifying five franchises that you would like to explore further. (Choose five based on your own personal interests and the criteria identified above.) For each possibility, identify the nature of the business, the financial requirements, the level of support the company provides, and a brief statement of why you could run such a business successfully. (Make up any details you need.) Be sure to carefully review the information you find about each franchise company to make sure you can qualify for it. For instance, McDonald's doesn't allow investment partnerships to buy franchises, so you won't be able to start up a McDonald's outlet until you have enough money to do it on your own.

For a quick introduction to franchising, see How Stuff Works (www.howstuffworks.com/franchising). You can learn more about the business of franchising at Franchising.com (www.franchising.com) and search for specific franchise opportunities at FranCorp Connect (www.francorpconnect.com). In addition, many companies that sell franchises, such as Subway, offer additional information on their websites.

LONG FORMAL REPORTS THAT REQUIRE NO ADDITIONAL RESEARCH

▌Portfolio
▌BUILDER

7. You can get anything online these days: Shopping for automobiles on the Internet As a researcher in your state's consumer protection agency, you're frequently called on to investigate consumer topics and write reports for the agency's website. Thousands of consumers have arranged the purchase of cars online, and millions more do at least some of their research online before heading to a dealership. Some want to save time and money, some want to be armed with as much information as possible before talking to a dealer, and others want to completely avoid the often-uncomfortable experience of negotiating prices with car salespeople. In response, a variety of online services have emerged to meet these consumer needs. Some let you compare information on various car models, some connect you to local dealers to complete the transaction, and some complete nearly all the transaction details for you, including negotiating the price. Some search the inventory of thousands of dealers, whereas others search only a single dealership or a network of affiliated dealers. In other words, a slew of new tools are available for car buyers, but it's not always easy to figure out where to go and what to expect. That's where your report will help.

By visiting a variety of car-related websites and reading magazine and newspaper articles on the car-buying process, you've compiled a variety of notes related to the subject:

- **Process overview.** The process is relatively straightforward and fairly similar to other online shopping experiences, with two key differences. In general, a consumer identifies the make and model of car he or she wants and then the online car buying service searches the inventories of car deal-

ers nationwide and presents the available choices. The consumer chooses a particular car from that list and then the service handles the communication and purchase details with the dealer. When the paperwork is finished, the consumer visits the dealership and picks up the car. The two biggest differences with online auto buying are that (1) you can't actually complete the purchase over the Internet (in most cases, you must visit a local dealer to pick up the car and sign the papers, although in some cities, a dealer or a local car buying service will deliver it to your home) and (2) in most states, it's illegal to purchase a new car from anyone other than a franchise dealer (that is, you can't buy directly from the manufacturer, the way you can buy a Dell computer directly from Dell, for instance).

- **Information you can find online (not all information is available at all sites).** You can find information on makes, models, colors, options, option packages (often, specific options are available only as part of a package; you need to know these constraints before you select your options), photos, specifications (everything from engine size to interior space), mileage estimates, performance data, safety information, predicted resale value, reviews, comparable models, insurance costs, consumer ratings, repair and reliability histories, available buyer incentives and rebates, true ownership costs (which include fuel, maintenance, repair, and so on), warranty, loan and lease payments, and maintenance requirements.

- **Advantages of shopping online.** Advantages of shopping online include shopping from the comfort and convenience of home, none of the dreaded negotiating at the dealership (in many cases), the ability to search far and wide for a specific car (even nationwide on many sites), rapid access to considerable amounts of data and information, and reviews from both professional automotive journalists and other consumers. In general, online auto shopping reduces a key advantage that auto dealers used to have, which was control of most of the information in the purchase transaction. Now consumers can find out how reliable each model is, how quickly it will depreciate, how often it is likely to need repairs, what other drivers think of it, how much the dealer paid the manufacturer for it, and so on.

- **Changing nature of the business.** The relationship between dealers and third-party websites (such as CarsDirect.com and Vehix.com) continues to evolve. At first, the relationship was more antagonistic, as some third-party sites and dealers frequently competed for the same customers, and both sides made bold proclamations about driving the other out of business. However, the relationship is more collaborative in many cases now, with dealers realizing that some third-party sites already have wide brand awareness and nationwide audiences. As the percentage of new car sales that originate via the Internet continues to increase, dealers are more receptive to working with third-party sites.

- **Comparing information from multiple sources.** Consumers shouldn't rely solely on information from a single website. Each site has its own way of organizing information, and many have their own ways of evaluating car models and connecting buyers with sellers.

- **Understanding what each site is doing.** Some sites search thousands of dealers, regardless of ownership connections. Others, such as AutoNation, search only affiliated dealers. A search for a specific model might yield only a half dozen cars on one site but dozens of cars on another site. Find out who owns the site and what their business objectives are, if you can; this will help you assess the information you receive.

- **Leading websites** Consumers can check out a wide variety of websites, some of which are full-service operations, offering everything from research to negotiation; others provide more specific and limited services. For instance, CarsDirect (www.carsdirect.com) provides a full range of services, whereas CARFAX (www.carfax.com) specializes in uncovering the repair histories of individual used cars. Table 13.6 lists some of the leading car-related websites.

Your task: Write an informational report based on your research notes. The purpose of the report is to introduce consumers to the basic concepts of integrating the Internet into their car-buying activities and to educate them about important issues.[12]

Portfolio BUILDER

8. **Moving the workforce: Understanding commute patterns** Your company is the largest private employer in your metropolitan area, and the 43,500 employees in your workforce have a tremendous impact on local traffic. A group of city and county transportation officials recently approached your CEO with a request to explore ways to reduce this impact. The CEO has assigned you the task of analyzing the workforce's transportation habits and attitudes as a first step toward identifying potential solutions. He's willing to consider anything from subsidized bus passes to company-owned shuttle buses to telecommuting, but the decision requires a thorough understanding of employee transportation needs. Tables 13.7 through 13.11 summarize data you collected in an employee survey.

Your task: Using the data provided in Tables 13.7 through 13.11, present the results of your survey in an informational report.

Table 13.6

LEADING AUTOMOTIVE WEBSITES

Site	URL
AutoAdvice	www.autoadvice.com
Autobytel	www.autobytel.com
AutoDirectory.com	www.autodirectory.com
Autos.com	www.autos.com
AutoVantage	www.autovantage.com
Autoweb	www.autoweb.com
CarBargains	www.carbargains.com
CARFAX	www.carfax.com
CarPrices.com	www.carprices.com
Cars.com	www.cars.com
CarsDirect	www.carsdirect.com
CarSmart	www.carsmart.com
Consumer Reports	www.consumerreports.com
eBay Motors	www.ebaymotors.com
Edmunds	www.edmunds.com
iMotors	www.imotors.com
IntelliChoice	www.intellichoice.com
InvoiceDealers	www.invoicedealers.com
J.D. Power	www.jdpower.com
Kelley Blue Book	www.kbb.com
MSN Autos	http://autos.msn.com
PickupTruck.com	www.pickuptruck.com
The Car Connection	www.thecarconnection.com
Vehix.com	www.vehix.com
Yahoo! Autos	www.autos.yahoo.com

Table 13.7

EMPLOYEE CARPOOL HABITS

Frequency of Use: Carpooling	Portion of Workforce
Every day, every week	10,138 (23%)
Certain days, every week	4,361 (10%)
Randomly	983 (2%)
Never	28,018 (64%)

Table 13.8

USE OF PUBLIC TRANSPORTATION

Frequency of Use: Public Transportation	Portion of Workforce
Every day, every week	23,556 (54%)
Certain days, every week	2,029 (5%)
Randomly	5,862 (13%)
Never	12,053 (28%)

Table 13.9

EFFECT OF POTENTIAL IMPROVEMENTS TO PUBLIC TRANSPORTATION

Which of the Following Would Encourage You to Use Public Transportation More Frequently? (Check All That Apply)	Portion of Respondents
Increased perceptions of safety	4,932 (28%)
Improved cleanliness	852 (5%)
Reduced commute times	7,285 (41%)
Greater convenience: fewer transfers	3,278 (18%)
Greater convenience: more stops	1,155 (6%)
Lower (or subsidized) fares	5,634 (31%)
Nothing could encourage me to take public transportation	8,294 (46%)

Note: This question was asked of those respondents who use public transportation randomly or never, a subgroup that represents 17,915 employees or 41 percent of the workforce.

Table 13.10

DISTANCE TRAVELED TO/FROM WORK

Distance You Travel to Work (One Way)	Portion of Workforce
Less than 1 mile	531 (1%)
1–3 miles	6,874 (16%)
4–10 miles	22,951 (53%)
11–20 miles	10,605 (24%)
More than 20 miles	2,539 (6%)

Table 13.11

IS TELECOMMUTING AN OPTION?

Does the Nature of Your Work Make Telecommuting a Realistic Option?	Portion of Workforce
Yes, everyday	3,460 (8%)
Yes, several days a week	8,521 (20%)
Yes, random days	12,918 (30%)
No	18,601 (43%)

LONG FORMAL REPORTS THAT REQUIRE ADDITIONAL RESEARCH

▌Portfolio
▌BUILDER

9. **Face-off: Informational report that compares and contrasts two companies in the same industry** Your boss, Dana Hansell, has been searching for some solid companies to personally invest in for the long term. After reviewing security analysts' reports and financial statements for several candidates, Hansell has narrowed the list to these leading industry competitors:

- Boeing; Airbus (aerospace and airline industry)
- HP; Dell (computers and software industry)
- Merrill Lynch; Schwab (finance, banking, and insurance industry)
- Barnes & Noble; Amazon.com (online retailing)
- UPS; FedEx (trucking and freight industry)

According to Hansell, all these candidates have about the same financial outlook for the future, so she is not interested in obtaining more financial performance detail. Instead, your boss is looking for more qualitative information, such as

- Fundamental philosophical differences in management styles, launching and handling products and services, marketing products and services, and approach to e-commerce that sets one rival company apart from the other
- Future challenges that each competitor faces
- Important decisions made by the two competitors and how those decisions have affected their company
- Fundamental differences in each company's vision of its industry's future (for instance, do they both agree on what consumers want, what products to deliver, and so on?)
- Specific competitive advantages held by each rival
- Past challenges each competitor has faced and how each met those challenges

- Strategic moves made by one rival that might affect the other

- Company success stories

- Brief company background information (Hansell already has some from the brokers' reports)

- Brief comparative statistics such as annual sales, market share, number of employees, number of stores, types of equipment, number of customers, sources of revenue, and so on

Hansell has heard that you are the department's most proficient researcher and an effective writer. You have been assigned the task of preparing a formal, long informational report for her. You need not make a recommendation or come to any conclusions; Hansell will do that based on the informational content of your report.

Your task: Select two industry competitors from the above list (or another list provided by your instructor) and write a long formal informational report comparing and contrasting how the two companies are addressing the topics outlined by Hansell. Of course, not every topic will apply to each company, and some will be more important than others—depending on the companies you select. Hansell will invest in only one of the two companies in your report. (Note: Because these topics require considerable research, your instructor may choose to make this a team project.)

10. Is there any justice? Report critiquing legislation Plenty of people complain about their state legislators, but few are specific about their complaints. Here's your chance.

Your task: Write a long formal report about a law that you believe should not have been enacted or should be enacted. Be objective. Write the report using specific facts to support your beliefs. Reach conclusions and offer your recommendation at the end of the report. As a final step, send a copy of the report to an appropriate state official or legislator.

11. Travel opportunities: Report comparing two destinations You are planning to take a two-week trip abroad sometime within the next year. A couple destinations appeal to you, and you are going to have to do some research before you can make a decision.

Your task: Prepare a lengthy comparative study of two countries that you would like to visit. Begin by making a list of important questions you will need to answer. Do you want a relaxing vacation or an educational experience? What types of services will you require? What will your transportation needs be? Where will you have the least difficulty with the language? Using resources in your library, the Internet, and perhaps travel agencies, analyze the suitability of these two destinations with respect to your own travel criteria. At the end of the report, recommend the better country to visit this year.

Portfolio BUILDER

12. Secondary sources: Report based on library and online research As a college student and an active consumer, you may have considered one or more of the following questions at some point in the past few years:

a. What criteria distinguish the top-rated MBA programs in the country? How well do these criteria correspond to the needs and expectations of business? Are the criteria fair for students, employers, and business schools?

b. Which of three companies you might like to work for has the strongest corporate ethics policies?

c. What will the music industry look like in the future? What's next after online stores such as Apple iTunes and digital players such as the iPod?

d. Which industries and job categories are forecast to experience the greatest growth—and therefore the greatest demands for workers—in the next 10 years?

e. What has been the impact of Starbucks's aggressive growth on small, independent coffee shops? On midsized chains or franchises? In the United States or in another country?

f. How large is the "industry" of major college sports? How much do the major football or basketball programs contribute—directly or indirectly—to other parts of a typical university?

g. How much have minor league sports—baseball, hockey, arena football—grown in small- and medium-market cities? What is the local economic impact when these municipalities build stadiums and arenas?

Your task: Answer one of those questions using secondary research sources for information. Be sure to document your sources in the correct form. Give conclusions and offer recommendations where appropriate.

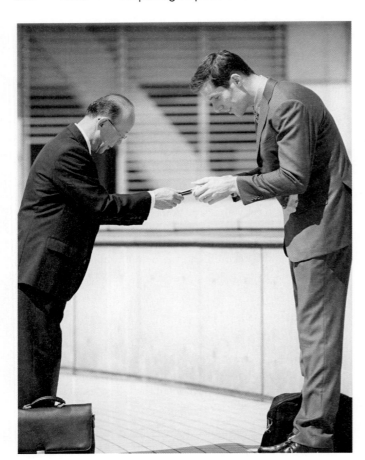

ate, and deliver more effective presentations, you offer a three-day workshop that covers the essentials of good presentations:

- Understanding your audience's needs and expectations
- Formulating your presentation objectives
- Choosing an organizational approach
- Writing openings that catch your audience's attention
- Creating effective graphics and slides
- Practicing and delivering your presentation
- Leaving a positive impression on your audience
- Avoiding common mistakes with Microsoft PowerPoint
- Making presentations online using webcasting tools
- Handling questions and arguments from the audience
- Overcoming the top 10 worries of public speaking (including *How can I overcome stage fright?* and *I'm not the performing type; can I still give an effective presentation?*)

Workshop benefits: Students will learn how to prepare better presentations in less time and deliver them more effectively.

Who should attend: Top executives, project managers, employment recruiters, sales professionals, and anyone else who gives important presentations to internal or external audiences.

Your qualifications: 18 years of business experience, including 14 years in sales and 12 years in public speaking. Experience speaking to audiences as large as 5,000 people. More than a dozen speech-related articles published in professional journals. Have conducted successful workshops for nearly 100 companies.

Workshop details: Three-day workshop (9 A.M. to 3:30 P.M.) that combines lectures, practice presentations, and both individual and group feedback. Minimum number of students: 6. Maximum number of students per workshop: 12.

Pricing: The cost is $3,500, plus $100 per student. 10 percent discount for additional workshops.

Other information: Each attendee will have the opportunity to give three practice presentations that will last from three to five minutes. Everyone is encouraged to bring PowerPoint files containing slides from actual business presentations. Each attendee will also receive a workbook and a digital video recording of his or her final class presentation on DVD. You'll also be available for phone or e-mail coaching for six months after the workshop.

Your task: Identify a company in your local area that might be a good candidate for your services. Learn more about the company by visiting its website so you can personalize your pro-

Portfolio BUILDER

13. Doing business abroad: Report summarizing the social and business customs of a foreign country Your company would like to sell its products overseas. Before it begins negotiating on the international horizon, however, the management team must have a clear understanding of the social and business customs of the countries where it intends to do business.

Your task: Choose a non-English-speaking country and write a long formal report summarizing the country's social and business customs. Review Chapter 3 and use Table 3.1 as a guide for the types of information you should include in your report.

FORMAL PROPOSALS
Portfolio BUILDER

14. Polishing the presenters: Offering your services as a presentation trainer Presentations can make—or break—careers and businesses. A good presentation can bring in millions of dollars in new sales or fresh investment capital. A bad presentation might cause any number of troubles, from turning away potential customers to upsetting fellow employees to derailing key projects. To help business professionals plan, cre-

posal. Using the information listed above, prepare a sales proposal that explains the benefits of your training and what students can expect during the workshop.

Portfolio BUILDER

**15. Healthy alternatives: Proposal to sell snacks and bever-
ages at local schools** For years, a controversy has been brewing over the amount of junk food and soft drinks being sold
through vending machines in local schools. Schools benefit
from revenue-sharing arrangements, but many parents and
health experts are concerned about the negative effects of these
snacks and beverages. You and your brother have almost a
decade of experience running espresso and juice stands in
malls and on street corners, and you'd love to find some way
to expand your business into schools. After a quick brainstorming session, the two of you craft a plan that makes good
business sense while meeting the financial concerns of school
administrators and the nutritional concerns of parents and
dietitians. Here are the notes from your brainstorming session:

- Set up portable juice bars on school campuses, offering
  healthy fruit and vegetable drinks along with simple,
  healthy snacks

- Offer schools 30 percent of profits in exchange for free
  space and long-term contracts

- Provide job training opportunities for students (such as
  during athletic events)

- Provide detailed dietary analysis of all products sold

- Establish a nutritional advisory board composed of parents,
  students, and at least one certified health professional

- Assure schools and parents that all products are safe (for
  example, no stimulant drinks, no dietary supplements)

- Support local farmers and specialty food preparers by buying locally and giving these vendors the opportunity to test-
  market new products at your stands

Your task: Based on the ideas listed, draft a formal proposal to
the local school board, outlining your plan to offer healthier
alternatives to soft drinks and prepackaged snack foods.
Invent any details you need to complete your proposal.

Portfolio BUILDER

**16. Career connections: Helping employees get the advice
they need to move ahead** Seems like everybody in your firm
is frustrated. On the one hand, top executives complain about
the number of lower-level employees who want promotions
but just don't seem to "get it" when it comes to dealing with
customers and the public, recognizing when to speak out and
when to be quiet, knowing how to push new ideas through the
appropriate channels, and performing other essential but diffi-
cult-to-teach tasks. On the other hand, ambitious employees

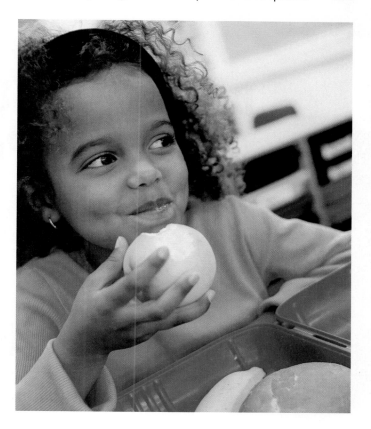

who'd like to learn more feel that they have nowhere to turn
for career advice from people who've been there. In between, a
variety of managers and midlevel executives are overwhelmed
by the growing number of mentoring requests they're getting,
sometimes from employees they don't even know.

You've been assigned the challenge of proposing a formal
mentoring program—and a considerable challenge it is:

- The number of employees who want mentoring relationships far exceeds the number of managers and executives
  willing and able to be mentors; how will you select people
  for the program?

- The people most in demand for mentoring also tend to be
  some of the busiest people in the organization.

- After several years of belt tightening and staff reductions,
  the entire company feels overworked; few people can imagine adding another recurring task to their seemingly endless to-do lists.

- What's in it for the mentors? Why would they be motivated
  to help lower-level employees?

- How will you measure the success or failure of the mentoring effort?

Your task: Identify potential solutions to the issues (make up
any information you need) and draft a proposal to the executive committee for a formal, company-wide mentoring program that would match selected employees with successful
managers and executives.

Chapter 14

Designing and Delivering Oral and Online Presentations

Learning Objectives

AFTER STUDYING THIS CHAPTER, YOU WILL BE ABLE TO

1 Explain the importance of presentations in your career success

2 Explain how to adapt the three-step writing process to oral presentations

3 Discuss the three functions of an effective introduction

4 Identify six ways to keep your audience's attention during your presentation

5 Explain how visuals enhance oral presentations and list several popular types of visuals

6 Explain the importance of design consistency in electronic slides and other visuals

7 Highlight seven major issues to consider when you're preparing to give a presentation online

8 Identify six ways that effective speakers handle questions responsively

On the Job

COMMUNICATING AT HEWLETT-PACKARD

MAKING A COMPELLING PRESENTATION WITH $3 BILLION ON THE LINE

Making presentations with millions or billions of dollars on the line? That's business as usual for Dan Talbott of HP Managed Services, a unit of Hewlett-Packard that manages computer operations for other companies.

A great example was the pursuit of a huge contract with Procter & Gamble (P&G), the consumer-products giant that markets more than 300 brands, including Charmin, Crest, and Tide. P&G was looking to lower its costs by hiring an outside organization to take over its global information system—a network of more than 80,000 computers. HP faced two tough competitors for the contract, Electronic Data Systems (EDS) and IBM, and was considered a distant third-place contender because it had never landed a contract the size of the P&G deal. And as if that weren't enough, P&G had published a 10,000-page request for proposals (RFP) and limited the response time to just 56 days—when 9 to 12 months is typical on projects of this magnitude.

Dan Talbott (far right) led a team whose presentation skills helped land a multibillion-dollar contract for Hewlett-Packard.

As a seasoned industry veteran but a rookie at HP, Talbott was eager to show that he could bring his new employer this mammoth piece of business. He moved his team into an HP office near P&G's Cincinnati headquarters, tapped the brainpower of 80 colleagues from around the world, and began developing the series of presentations that were specified in the RFP. Talbott told the group, "Our job is to ensure that every conversation is a win." However, HP's initial presentation was shaky, so he asked the presenters to print their PowerPoint slides—over 200 in all—and post them on the walls of a conference room. He conducted a slide-by-slide critique, questioning every slide that lacked a clear message. The team revised and kept revising until the presentation was audience centered and crystal clear from beginning to end.

That rigorous review produced a string of successful presentations that ultimately helped Talbott and his team win a 10-year contract worth $3 billion—a stunning success that announced HP's arrival as a serious contender in computer services.[1]

www.hp.com

505

BUILDING YOUR CAREER WITH PRESENTATIONS

Presentations involve all your communication skills, from research through nonverbal communication.

Dan Talbott's experience (profiled in the chapter opener) is solid proof that presentation skills are vital in today's business environment. Oral presentations offer important opportunities to put all your communication skills on display—not just in research, planning, writing, and visual design but also in interpersonal and nonverbal communication. Presentations can also let you demonstrate your ability to think on your feet, grasp complex issues, and handle challenging situations—all attributes that executives look for when searching for talented employees to promote.

Feeling nervous is perfectly normal when you're faced with an oral presentation; the good news is there are positive steps you can take to reduce your anxiety.

If the thought of giving a speech or presentation makes you nervous, try to keep three points in mind. First, everybody gets nervous when speaking in front of a group. Even with years of experience, professional speakers and entertainers get nervous. Second, being nervous is actually a good thing; it means you care about the topic, your audience, and your career success. With practice, you can convert those nervous feelings into positive energy. Third, you don't have to be a victim of your own emotions when it comes to oral presentations. You can take control of the situation by using the three-step writing process to prepare for successful presentations.

ADAPTING THE THREE-STEP PROCESS FOR PRESENTATIONS

While you don't usually write oral presentations word for word, the three-step writing process is easily adaptable to oral presentations.

Although you don't often write out presentations word for word, nearly every task in the three-step writing process applies to oral presentations, with some modifications (see Figure 14.1). In addition, a few extra steps help you prepare both your material

FIGURE 14.1
The Three-Step Process for Developing Oral and Online Presentations
Although you rarely "write" a presentation or speech in the sense of composing every word ahead of time, the tasks in the three-step writing process adapt quite well to the challenge of planning, creating, and delivering oral and online presentations.

Planning

Analyze the Situation
Define your purpose and develop a profile of your audience, including their emotional states and language preferences.

Gather Information
Determine audience needs and obtain the information necessary to satisfy those needs.

Select the Right Medium
Choose the best medium or combination of media for delivering your presentation, including hand-outs and other support materials.

Organize the Information
Define your main idea, limit your scope and verify timing, select a direct or an indirect approach, and outline your content.

Writing

Adapt to Your Audience
Be sensitive to audience needs and expectations with a "you" attitude, politeness, positive emphasis, and bias-free language. Build a strong relationship with your audience by establishing your credibility and projecting your company's image. Adjust your delivery style to fit the situation, from casual to formal.

Compose Your Presentation
Outline an effective introduction, body, and close. Prepare supporting visuals and speaking notes.

Completing

Revise the Message
Evaluate your content and speaking notes.

Master Your Delivery
Choose your delivery mode and practice your presentation.

Prepare to Speak
Verify facilities and equipment, including online connections and software setups. Hire an interpreter if necessary.

Overcome Anxiety
Take steps to feel more confident and appear more confident on stage.

1   **2**   **3**

and yourself for the actual presentation. As with written reports, people often judge the quality of the content by the quality of the presentation, so your delivery style and the packaging of any visual support materials can be as important as your message.

STEP 1: PLANNING YOUR PRESENTATION

Planning oral presentations is much like planning any other business message: You (1) analyze the situation, (2) gather information, (3) select the right medium, and (4) organize the information. Gathering information for oral presentations is essentially the same as it is for written communication projects (see Chapter 10). The other three planning tasks have some special applications when it comes to oral presentations; they are covered in the following sections.

Analyzing the Situation

As with written communications, in oral communications, analyzing the situation involves defining your purpose and developing an audience profile. The purpose of most of your presentations will be to inform or to persuade, although you may occasionally need to make a collaborative presentation, such as when you're leading a problem-solving or brainstorming session. The guidelines in Chapter 4 will help you identify and refine your purpose.

When you develop your audience profile, start with the advice in Chapter 4 and then consider two other issues that are particularly important for oral presentations. First, try to anticipate what sort of emotional state your audience members are likely to be in. Consider what you know about the audience, the topic of your presentation, and your relationship with the audience. Will your listeners be supportive, hostile, or somewhere in between? Here are some tips on preparing for audiences in various mindsets:

Knowing your audience's state of mind will help you adjust your message and your delivery.

- **Supportive.** Speaking to people who welcome both you and your message is a pleasant opportunity. Reward their goodwill with a presentation that is clear, concise, and upbeat. Provide enough information to confirm their belief in you and your message but don't belabor points they already accept or drone on about endless details. Speak in a relaxed, confident manner.

- **Interested but neutral.** If people are interested in your message but unsure whether they'll accept it, plan to build your credibility as you present your main idea and key support points. Address possible objections as you move along to show that you've considered all sides of the issue. Be confident in what you have to say while remaining open to questions and challenges from the audience.

- **Uninterested.** In some respects, an uninterested audience can be even more challenging than an apprehensive or hostile audience. If people don't care, it doesn't matter how good your presentation is. Think creatively to find a way to connect your message with some aspect of their personal or professional lives. Use the techniques in Table 14.2 (page 516) to get their attention. Prepare interesting questions, eye-opening facts, or thought-provoking quotations to engage the audience intellectually or emotionally. Make sure your presentation is concise and well organized to avoid the appearance of rambling.

- **Apprehensive.** Audiences that are worried about your message are obviously going to be in an emotionally negative state before you even begin. Treat their emotions with respect. Don't dismiss their fears or tell them they are mistaken for feeling that way. Avoid trying to diffuse the tension with humor, or people might conclude that you don't take their concerns seriously. If your message will calm their fears, use the direct approach to share the good news immediately. If your message will confirm their fears, consider using the indirect approach to build up rational support for the negative message.

- **Hostile.**   No one looks forward to addressing an angry audience, but when you face this challenge, you have one major factor working in your favor: The audience definitely cares about your message, so they are sure to pay attention. As with an apprehensive audience, treat their emotions with respect and avoid humor. Prepare thoroughly so you can provide complete information in a calm, rational manner. In most situations, use the indirect approach to build support for your message while addressing points of concern along the way. As you're speaking, do your best to remain calm; avoid engaging in emotional exchanges with the audience.

After considering your audience's emotional state, determine whether they are comfortable listening to the language you speak. Listening to an unfamiliar language is much more difficult than reading that language, so an audience that might be able to read a written report might not be able to understand an oral presentation covering the same material (see "Communicating Across Cultures: Five Tips for Making Presentations Around the World").

Be sure to research the setting and circumstances of your presentation, from the size of the audience to potential interruptions.

As you analyze the situation, also consider the specific circumstances in which you'll be making your presentation. Will you speak in a conference room, where you can control everything from light to sound to temperature? Or will you be demonstrating a product on the floor of a trade show and have little control over the environment? Will everyone be in the same room, or will your audience participate from

COMMUNICATING ACROSS CULTURES

Five Tips for Making Presentations Around the World

When making presentations to international audiences, language fluency might vary widely, so take special care to ensure clear communication:

- *Speak slowly and distinctly.* The most common complaint of international audiences is that English speakers talk too fast. Articulate every word carefully, emphasize consonants for clarity, and pause frequently.

- *Repeat key words and phrases.* When audiences are not terribly familiar with your language, they need to hear important information more than once. Also, they may not be familiar with various synonyms, so word key points in the same way throughout your presentation.

- *Aim for clarity.* Keep your message simple. Eliminate complex sentence structure, abbreviations, and acronyms. Replace two-word verbs with one-word alternatives (such as *review* instead of *look over*). Two-word verbs are confusing because the definition of each separate word differs from the meaning of the two words combined. Avoid cultural idioms, such as *once in a blue moon*, which may be unfamiliar to an international audience.

- *Communicate with body language.* Emphasize and clarify verbal information with gestures and facial expressions. For

instance, smile to emphasize positive points and use gestures to illustrate the meaning of words such as *up*, *down*, or *under*.

- *Support your oral message with visuals.* For most audiences, visual messages support and clarify spoken words. To eliminate problems with rapid speech, unclear pronunciations, or strange accents, prepare captions both in English and in your audience's native language.

CAREER APPLICATIONS

1. One of the most important changes speakers need to make when addressing audiences in other cultures is to avoid colloquial figures of speech. Replace each of these phrases with wording that is more likely to be understood by non-native English speakers or audiences in other countries: "hit one out of the park," "go for broke," and "get your ducks in a row."

2. Make a list of 10 two-word verbs. How does the meaning of each separate word differ from the definition of the combined words? Replace each two-word verb with a single, specific word that will be clearer to an international audience.

ANALYZING AN AUDIENCE FOR AN ORAL PRESENTATION		Table 14.1
Task	**Actions**	
To determine audience size and composition	• Estimate how many people will attend and whether they will all attend in person, online, or a mix of both. • Consider whether they share professional interests or other affiliations that can help you establish common ground with them. • Analyze the mix of men and women, age ranges, socio-economic and ethnic groups, occupations, and geographic regions represented.	
To predict the audience's probable reaction	• Analyze why audience members are attending the presentation. • Determine the audience's general attitude toward the topic—interested, moderately interested, unconcerned, open-minded, or hostile. • Analyze the mood that people will be in when you speak to them. • Find out what kind of backup information will most impress the audience: technical data, historical information, financial data, demonstrations, samples, and so on. • Consider whether the audience has any biases that might work against you. • Anticipate possible objections or questions.	
To gauge the audience's level of understanding	• Analyze whether everybody has the same background and experience. • Determine what the audience already knows about the subject. • Decide what background information the audience will need to better understand the subject. • Consider whether the audience is familiar with your vocabulary. • Analyze what the audience expects from you. • Think about the mix of general concepts and specific details you will need to present.	

remote locations via the Internet? What equipment will you use? All these variables can influence not only the style of your presentation but even the content.

Table 14.1 offers a summary of the key steps in analyzing an audience for oral presentations. For even more insight into audience evaluation (including emotional and cultural issues), consult a good public-speaking textbook.

Selecting the Right Medium

The task of selecting the right medium might seem obvious—after all, you are speaking, so it's an oral medium. However, technology offers an array of choices these days, ranging from live, in-person presentations to webcasts that people view on your website whenever doing so fits their individual schedules. Explore these options early on so that you can take full advantage of the ones at your disposal. For example, to reach an international audience, you might want to conduct a live presentation with a question-and-answer session for the audience in your home office and then post a video archive of this meeting on your website for audience members in other time zones. Planning is key to media selection.

Expect to give many online presentations during your career.

Organizing Your Presentation

Organizing a presentation involves the same tasks as organizing a written message: Define your main idea, limit your scope, select a direct or an indirect approach, and outline your content. As you work through these tasks, keep in mind that audiences for oral presentations are more or less trapped in your time frame and sequence. When reading written reports, audiences can skip back and forth, backing up if they miss a point or become confused and jumping ahead if they aren't interested in a particular part or are already familiar with the content. However, unless they interrupt you, presentation audiences have no choice but to listen to your content in exactly the order in which you present it.

For instance, say that your presentation is a proposal and you expect your audience to be hostile to the idea. You plan to structure your proposal using the indirect approach. Simple enough, until … surprise—the members of your audience have already heard of your idea through other channels, and they like it. Now they have to sit through an extended presentation of your reasons so that you can convince them to accept an idea they have already accepted. With a printed report, your audience would simply skip ahead, but they can't do that with an oral presentation. Fortunately, you can use hyperlinks (see page 180) to build flexibility into your presentation, but only if you plan ahead.

Define Your Main Idea   If you've ever heard a speaker struggle to get his or her main point across ("What I really mean to say is …"), you know how frustrating such an experience can be for an audience. To avoid that struggle, figure out the one message you want audience members to walk away with. Then compose a one-sentence summary that links your subject and purpose to your audience's frame of reference, much as an advertising slogan points out how a product can benefit consumers. Here are some examples:

- Convince management that reorganizing the technical support department will improve customer service and reduce employee turnover.

- Convince the board of directors that we should build a new plant in Texas to eliminate manufacturing bottlenecks and improve production quality.

- Reduce employee concerns regarding a new health-care plan by showing how the plan will lower costs and improve the quality of their care.

Each of these statements puts a particular slant on the subject, one that directly relates to the audience's interests. By focusing on your audience's needs and using the "you" attitude, you help keep their attention and convince them that your points are relevant. For example, a group of new employees will be much more responsive to your discussion of plant safety procedures if you focus on how the procedures can save lives and prevent injuries rather than on adhering to company rules, saving the company money, or conforming to Occupational Safety and Health Administration (OSHA) guidelines.

Limit Your Scope   Effective presentations not only focus on the audience's needs but also tailor the material to the time allowed, which is often strictly regulated. Moreover, in many situations, multiple presenters are scheduled to speak one right after the other, so time allotments are rigid, permitting little or no flexibility. If you overestimate the amount of material you can cover within your allotted time, you're left with only unpleasant alternatives: rushing through your presentation, skipping some of the information you've so carefully prepared, or trying to steal a few minutes from the next presenter. On the other hand, if you don't have enough material prepared to fill your time slot, you might be left standing in front of the audience trying to ad lib information you haven't prepared.

Margin notes:

If you can't express your main idea in a single sentence, you probably haven't defined it clearly enough.

Limiting your scope is important for two reasons: to fit your allotted time and to make sure your content meets audience needs and expectations.

Limiting your scope also involves matching your message with your audience's needs and expectations. Studies show that audience attention levels and retention rates drop sharply after 20 minutes, and venture capitalists (investors who fund many new companies) expect entrepreneurs to get to the point within 15 minutes.[2] In addition, if you try to cover too many details in a presentation, you can leave the audience feeling confused and frustrated. Often a better approach is to explain important concepts in your oral presentation and refer your audience to printed documents or websites for supporting details.

When you've decided on the right amount of information to cover, do your best to estimate the time required to present that material or to estimate the amount of material you can cover within a fixed amount of time. The only sure way to do this is to practice. As an alternative to doing a complete practice run, you can try several techniques for estimating time requirements. First, if you're in one of those rare situations in which you're reciting your material verbatim or reading from a prepared script (more on this later in the chapter), you can divide your word count by 125 (if you speak slower than average) or 150 (if you're faster than average) to get a rough idea of how many minutes you'll need. Most speakers can comfortably deliver between 125 and 150 words per minute. Second, you can measure how long it takes to talk through a small portion of your presentation and then extrapolate how long the entire presentation will take. This method isn't terribly accurate, but it can help identify major timing problems. Third, after you get some experience giving presentations with either overhead transparencies or electronic slides, you'll get a feel for the time you typically need to cover a single slide. As a general guideline, figure on 3 or even 4 minutes per slide.[3] For instance, if you have 20 minutes, plan on being able to cover roughly six or seven slides. If you're whipping through slides faster than that, chances are your slides are too simple or you're not engaging the audience with enough discussion about each one.

> As a rough guideline, allow 3 or 4 minutes per slide.

Of course, be sure to factor in time for introductions, coffee breaks, demonstrations, question-and-answer sessions, and anything else that takes away from your speaking time.

Choose Your Approach   With a well-defined main idea to guide you and a clear idea about the scope of your presentation, you can begin to arrange your message. If you have 10 minutes or less to deliver your message, organize your presentation much as you would a letter or a brief memo: Use the direct approach if the subject involves routine information or good news, and use the indirect approach if the subject involves bad news or persuasion. Plan your introduction to arouse interest and to give a preview of what's to come. For the body of the presentation, be prepared to explain the who, what, when, where, why, and how of your subject. In the final section, review the points you've made, and close with a statement that will help your audience remember the subject of your speech. Figure 14.2 presents an outline of a short presentation that updates management on the status of a key project; the presenter has some bad news to deliver, so she opted for an indirect approach to lay out the reasons for the delay before sharing the news of the schedule slip.

> Organize short presentations the same way you would a letter or brief memo.

Longer presentations are organized like reports. If the purpose is to motivate or inform, use a direct approach and a structure imposed naturally by the subject: importance, sequence, chronology, spatial orientation, geography, or category (as discussed in Chapter 11). If your purpose is to analyze, persuade, or collaborate, organize your material around conclusions and recommendations or around a logical argument. Use a direct approach if the audience is receptive and an indirect approach if you expect resistance.

Regardless of the length of your presentation, remember that simplicity of organization is especially valuable in oral communication. If listeners lose the thread of your presentation, they'll have a hard time catching up and following your message in the rest of your speech. Look for the most obvious and natural way to organize

> Simplicity is critical in the organization of oral presentations.

Progress Report: August 2008

Purpose: To update the Executive Committee on our product development schedule.

I.   Review goals and progress.
   A. Mechanical design:
     1. Goal: 100%
     2. Actual: 80%
     3. Reason for delay: Unanticipated problems with case durability
   B. Software development:
     1. Goal: 50%
     2. Actual: 60%
   C. Material sourcing:
     1. Goal: 100%
     2. Actual: 45% (and materials identified are at 140% of anticipated costs)
     3. Reason for delay: Purchasing is understaffed and hasn't been able to research sources adequately.
II. Discuss schedule options.
   A. Option 1: Reschedule product launch date.
   B. Option 2: Launch on schedule with more expensive materials.
III. Suggest goals for next month.
IV. Q&A

your ideas, using a direct approach whenever possible. Explain at the beginning how you've organized your material and try to limit the number of main points to three or four—even when the speech or presentation is lengthy.

Finally, remind yourself that just like every other good business message, an effective presentation has a clear introduction, body, and close. In fact, one noted presentation expert even advises a three-act storytelling structure (the approach used in many novels, movies, and TV shows). Act I introduces the "story" you're about to tell and grabs the audience's attention. Act II explores the complications, evidence, support points, and other information needed to understand the story and its conclusion. Act III resolves all the complications and presents a solution that addresses the problem introduced in Act I and that is strongly supported by all the evidence introduced in Act II.[4]

A presentation outline helps you plan your speaking notes as well as your presentation.

Prepare Your Outline   A presentation outline performs the same function as an outline for a written report: It helps you organize your message in a way that maximizes its impact on your audience. To ensure effective organization, prepare your outline in several stages:[5]

- State your purpose and main idea and then use these to guide the rest of your planning.
- Organize your major points and subpoints in logical order, expressing each major point as a single, complete sentence.
- Identify major points in the body first and then outline the introduction and close.
- Identify transitions between major points or sections and then write these transitions in full-sentence form.

- Prepare your bibliography or source notes; highlight the sources you want to identify by name during your talk.

- Choose a compelling title; even if the title won't be published, it will help you focus your thoughts around your main idea.

The outline in Figure 14.3 is for a 30-minute analytical presentation. It is organized around conclusions and presented in direct order. This outline is based on Chapter 13's Electrovision report, written by Linda Moreno.

FIGURE 14.3

Effective Outline for a 30-Minute Presentation

This outline clearly identifies the purpose and the distinct points to be made in the introduction, body, and close. Notice also how the speaker wrote her major transitions in full-sentence form to be sure she can clearly phrase these critical passages when it's time to speak.

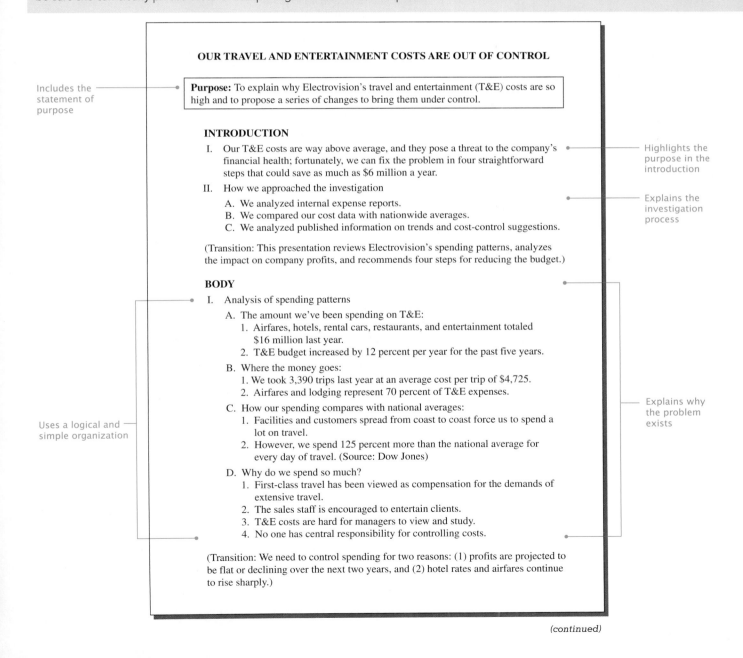

OUR TRAVEL AND ENTERTAINMENT COSTS ARE OUT OF CONTROL

Includes the statement of purpose →

Purpose: To explain why Electrovision's travel and entertainment (T&E) costs are so high and to propose a series of changes to bring them under control.

INTRODUCTION

I. Our T&E costs are way above average, and they pose a threat to the company's financial health; fortunately, we can fix the problem in four straightforward steps that could save as much as $6 million a year. *(← Highlights the purpose in the introduction)*

II. How we approached the investigation *(← Explains the investigation process)*

   A. We analyzed internal expense reports.
   B. We compared our cost data with nationwide averages.
   C. We analyzed published information on trends and cost-control suggestions.

(Transition: This presentation reviews Electrovision's spending patterns, analyzes the impact on company profits, and recommends four steps for reducing the budget.)

BODY

I. Analysis of spending patterns

   A. The amount we've been spending on T&E:
      1. Airfares, hotels, rental cars, restaurants, and entertainment totaled $16 million last year.
      2. T&E budget increased by 12 percent per year for the past five years.

   B. Where the money goes:
      1. We took 3,390 trips last year at an average cost per trip of $4,725.
      2. Airfares and lodging represent 70 percent of T&E expenses.

   C. How our spending compares with national averages: *(← Explains why the problem exists)*
      1. Facilities and customers spread from coast to coast force us to spend a lot on travel.
      2. However, we spend 125 percent more than the national average for every day of travel. (Source: Dow Jones)

   D. Why do we spend so much?
      1. First-class travel has been viewed as compensation for the demands of extensive travel.
      2. The sales staff is encouraged to entertain clients.
      3. T&E costs are hard for managers to view and study.
      4. No one has central responsibility for controlling costs.

(Uses a logical and simple organization)

(Transition: We need to control spending for two reasons: (1) profits are projected to be flat or declining over the next two years, and (2) hotel rates and airfares continue to rise sharply.)

(continued)

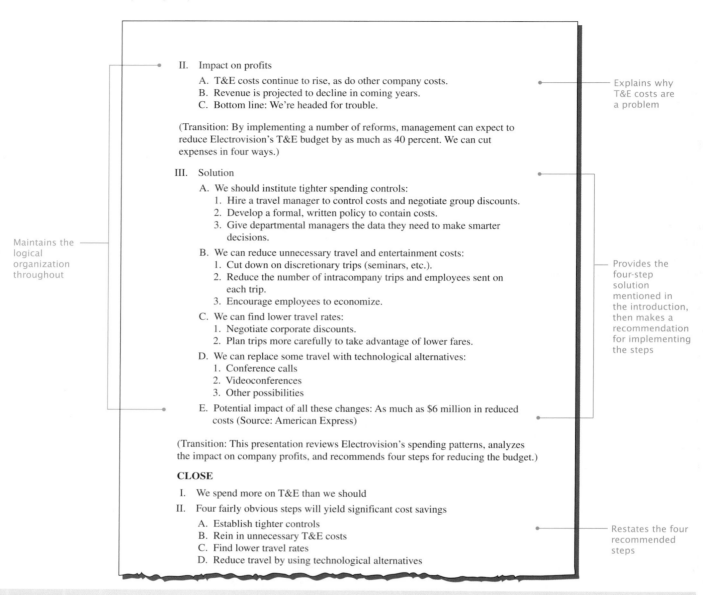

The following annotations appear alongside the outline:

- Explains why T&E costs are a problem
- Maintains the logical organization throughout
- Provides the four-step solution mentioned in the introduction, then makes a recommendation for implementing the steps
- Restates the four recommended steps

The outline content reads:

II.   Impact on profits

    A. T&E costs continue to rise, as do other company costs.

    B. Revenue is projected to decline in coming years.

    C. Bottom line: We're headed for trouble.

(Transition: By implementing a number of reforms, management can expect to reduce Electrovision's T&E budget by as much as 40 percent. We can cut expenses in four ways.)

III.   Solution

    A. We should institute tighter spending controls:

        1. Hire a travel manager to control costs and negotiate group discounts.

        2. Develop a formal, written policy to contain costs.

        3. Give departmental managers the data they need to make smarter decisions.

    B. We can reduce unnecessary travel and entertainment costs:

        1. Cut down on discretionary trips (seminars, etc.).

        2. Reduce the number of intracompany trips and employees sent on each trip.

        3. Encourage employees to economize.

    C. We can find lower travel rates:

        1. Negotiate corporate discounts.

        2. Plan trips more carefully to take advantage of lower fares.

    D. We can replace some travel with technological alternatives:

        1. Conference calls

        2. Videoconferences

        3. Other possibilities

    E. Potential impact of all these changes: As much as $6 million in reduced costs (Source: American Express)

(Transition: This presentation reviews Electrovision's spending patterns, analyzes the impact on company profits, and recommends four steps for reducing the budget.)

CLOSE

I.   We spend more on T&E than we should

II.   Four fairly obvious steps will yield significant cost savings

    A. Establish tighter controls

    B. Rein in unnecessary T&E costs

    C. Find lower travel rates

    D. Reduce travel by using technological alternatives

FIGURE 14.3
(continued)

You might find it helpful to create a simpler speaking outline from your planning outline.

Many speakers like to prepare both a detailed *planning outline* and a simpler *speaking outline* that provides all the cues and reminders they need to present their material.[6] To prepare an effective speaking outline, follow these steps:[7]

- Start with the planning outline and then strip away anything you don't plan to say to your audience (statement of general purpose, main idea, bibliography, and so on).

- Condense points and transitions to key words or phrases, choosing words that will prompt you to remember what each point is about.

- Add delivery cues, such as places in your outline where you plan to pause for emphasis or use a visual.

- Arrange your notes on cards (or sheets of paper, if you prefer); number your cards (or sheets of paper) so that you can keep them in order. (If you plan to use PowerPoint or other presentation software, you can also use the "notes" field on each slide for speaking notes.)

STEP 2: WRITING YOUR PRESENTATION

Although you may never actually write out a presentation word for word, you still engage in the writing process—developing your ideas, structuring support points, phrasing your transitions, and so on. Depending on the situation and your personal style, your presentation might follow these initial words closely or might express your thoughts in fresh, spontaneous language. Before you get to the actual writing phase, consider how you should adapt your style to your audience.

Adapting to Your Audience

Your audience's size, your subject, your purpose, your budget, and the time available for preparation all influence the style of your presentation. If you're speaking to a small group, particularly people you already know, you can use a casual style that encourages audience participation. A small conference room, with your audience seated around a table, may be appropriate. Use simple visuals and invite your audience to interject comments. Deliver your remarks in a conversational tone, using notes to jog your memory, if necessary.

Adapting to your audience involves a number of issues, from speaking style to technology choices.

If you're addressing a large audience or if the event is important, establish a more formal atmosphere. During formal presentations, speakers are often located on a stage or platform, standing behind a podium and using a microphone so that their remarks can be heard throughout the room or captured for broadcasting or webcasting.

Whether your presentation is formal or informal, strive for simple, familiar vocabulary and define any special terms you need to use. And keep things simple. If you repeatedly stumble over a word as you rehearse, use a different one.[8]

Finally, when you're pondering how you'll adapt to your audience, take public speaking etiquette into account. Plan to show consideration for your audience by making good use of their time, addressing them respectfully, and maintaining a professional presence during your speech.

Composing Your Presentation

Just like written documents, oral presentations are composed of three distinct elements: the introduction, the body, and the close.

Introduction   A good introduction arouses the audience's interest in your topic, establishes your credibility, and prepares the audience for what will follow. That's a lot to pack into the first few minutes of your presentation, so give yourself plenty of time to develop the words and visuals you'll use to get your presentation off to a great start.

An effective introduction arouses interest in your topic, establishes your credibility, and prepares the audience for the body of your presentation.

Arousing Audience Interest   Some subjects are naturally interesting; others call for more imagination. For example, how do you get people to listen if you're explaining your pension program to a group of new clerical employees, none of whom will be fully eligible for the program for another five years and many of whom might leave the company within two? The best approach to dealing with an uninterested audience is to appeal to human nature and encourage people to take the subject personally. Show them how they'll be affected as individuals. For example, you might begin by addressing the new clerical employees like this:

If somebody offered to give you $200,000 in exchange for $40 per week, would you be interested? That's the amount you might reasonably expect to collect during your retirement years if you choose to participate in the voluntary retirement savings plan. During the next two weeks, you will have to

> decide whether you want to participate. Although retirement is many years away for most of you, it is an important financial decision. During the next 20 minutes, I hope to give you the information you need to make a decision that's best for you and your families.

Table 14.2 suggests six techniques you can use to arouse audience interest during your introduction, and "Holding Your Audience's Attention" on page 517 lists six ways to keep audience members' attention throughout your presentation. Regardless of which technique you choose, make sure you can give audience members a reason to care and to believe that the time they're about to spend listening to you will be worth their while.[9]

Building Your Credibility In addition to grabbing the audience's attention, your introduction has to establish your credibility. If you're a well-known expert in the subject matter or have earned your audience's trust in other situations, you're ahead of the game. However, if you have no working relationship with your audience or if you're speaking in an area outside your presumed expertise, you need to establish your credibility and do so quickly; people tend to decide within a few minutes whether you're worth listening to.[10]

Techniques for building credibility vary, depending on whether you will be introducing yourself or having someone else introduce you. If a master of ceremonies, conference chair, or other person will introduce you, he or she can present your credentials so that you won't appear boastful. If you will be introducing yourself, keep

> If someone else will be introducing you to the audience, you can ask this person to present your credentials as well.

Table 14.2	SIX WAYS TO GET ATTENTION DURING YOUR INTRODUCTION	
	Task	**Actions**
	Unite the audience around a common goal	Invite them to help solve a problem, capitalize on an opportunity, or otherwise engage in the topic of your presentation.
	Tell a story	Slice-of-life stories are naturally interesting and can be compelling. Be sure your story illustrates an important point.
	Pass around a sample	Psychologists say that you can get people to remember your points by appealing to their senses. The best way to do so is to pass around a sample. If your company is in the textile business, let the audience handle some of your fabrics. If you sell chocolates, give everybody a taste.
	Ask a question	Asking questions will get the audience actively involved in your presentation and, at the same time, will give you information about them and their needs.
	State a startling statistic	People love details. If you can interject an interesting statistic, you can often wake up your audience.
	Use humor	Even though the subject of most business presentations is serious, including a light comment now and then can perk up the audience. Just be sure the humor is relevant to the presentation and not offensive to the audience. In general, avoid humor when you and the audience don't share the same native language.

your comments simple but don't be afraid to mention your accomplishments. Your listeners will be curious about your qualifications, so tell them briefly who you are and why you're there. Generally, you need to mention only a few aspects of your background: your position in an organization, your profession, the name of your company. You might say something like this:

> I'm Karen Whitney, a market research analyst with Information Resources Corporation. For the past five years, I've specialized in studying high-technology markets. Your director of engineering, John LaBarre, has asked me to talk to you about recent trends in computer-aided design so that you'll have a better idea of how to direct your research efforts.

This speaker establishes credibility by tying her credentials to the purpose of her presentation. By mentioning her company's name, her specialization and position, and the name of the audience's boss, she lets her listeners know immediately that she is qualified to tell them something they need to know. She connects her background to their concerns.

Previewing Your Message In addition to arousing audience interest and building your credibility, a good introduction gives your audience a preview of what's ahead. Your preview should summarize the main idea of your presentation, identify major supporting points, and indicate the order in which you'll develop those points. Tell your listeners in so many words, "This is the subject, and these are the points I will cover." Once you've established the framework, you can be confident that the audience will understand how the individual facts and figures are related to your main idea as you move into the body of your presentation.

> Use the preview to help your audience understand the importance, the structure, and the content of your message.

Body The bulk of your speech or presentation is devoted to a discussion of the main points in your outline. Use the same organizational patterns you'd use in a letter, memo, or report but keep things simple. Your goals are to make sure that (1) the organization of your presentation is clear and (2) your presentation holds the audience's attention.

Connecting Your Ideas In written documents, you can show how ideas are related on the page or screen by using a variety of design clues: headings, paragraph indentions, white space, and lists. However, with oral communication—particularly when you aren't using visuals for support—you have to rely primarily on words to link various parts and ideas.

For the small links between sentences and paragraphs, use one or two transitional words: *therefore, because, in addition, in contrast, moreover, for example, consequently, nevertheless,* or *finally*. To link major sections of a presentation, use complete sentences or paragraphs, such as "Now that we've reviewed the problem, let's take a look at some solutions." Every time you shift topics, be sure to stress the connection between ideas. Summarize what's been said and then preview what's to come.

The longer your presentation, the more important your transitions. If you will be presenting many ideas, audience members may have trouble absorbing them and seeing the relationships among them. Your listeners need clear transitions to guide them to the most important points. Furthermore, they'll appreciate brief, interim summaries to pick up any ideas they may have missed. By repeating key ideas in your transitions, you can compensate for lapses in your audience's attention. When you actually give your presentation, you might also want to call attention to the transitions by using gestures, changing your tone of voice, or introducing a new visual.

> Use transitions to repeat key ideas, particularly in longer presentations.

Holding Your Audience's Attention When you've successfully captured your audience's attention in your introduction, you need to work to keep it throughout the

The most important way to hold an audience's attention is to show how your message relates to their individual needs and concerns.

body of your presentation. Here are a few helpful tips for keeping the audience tuned into your message:

- **Relate your subject to your audience's needs.** People are interested in things that affect them personally. As much as possible, present every point in light of your audience's needs and values.

- **Anticipate your audience's questions.** Try to anticipate as many questions as you can and address these questions in the body of your presentation or during the question-and-answer period.

- **Use clear, vivid language.** People become bored quickly when they don't understand the speaker. If your presentation will involve abstract ideas, show how those abstractions connect with everyday life. Use familiar words, short sentences, and concrete examples. Avoid repeating the same words and phrases, too.

- **Explain the relationship between your subject and familiar ideas.** Show how your subject is related to ideas that audience members already understand and give people a way to categorize and remember your points.[11]

- **Ask for opinions or pause occasionally for questions or comments.** Audience feedback helps you determine whether your listeners understand a key point before you launch into another section. Feedback also gives your audience members a chance to switch for a time from listening to participating, which helps them engage with your message and develop a sense of shared ownership.

- **Illustrate your ideas with visuals.** Visuals enliven your message, help you connect with audience members, and help them remember your message more effectively (see "Enhancing Your Presentations with Effective Visuals," page 519).

When attempting to hold an audience's attention, public speakers sometimes encounter distractions in the background. It takes a focused speaker to overcome such physical interruptions and get his or her message across.

Plan your close carefully so that your audience leaves with your main idea fresh in their minds.

Close   The close of a speech or presentation is critical for two reasons: Audiences tend to focus more carefully as they wait for you to wrap up, and they leave with your final words ringing in their ears. Before closing your presentation, tell listeners that you're about to finish so they'll make one final effort to listen intently. Don't be afraid to sound obvious. Consider saying something such as "In conclusion" or "To sum it all up." You want people to know this is the final segment of your presentation.

Restating Your Main Points After you announce your close, repeat your main idea and reinforce it with your key support points. Emphasize what you want your audience to do or to think and stress the key motivating factor that will encourage them to respond that way. For instance, to conclude a presentation on your company's executive compensation program, you can repeat your specific recommendations and finish with a memorable statement to motivate your audience to take action:

We can all be proud of the way our company has grown. However, if we want to continue that growth, we need to adjust our executive compensation program to reflect competitive practices. If we don't, our best people will look for opportunities elsewhere.

In summary, our survey has shown that we need to take four steps to improve executive compensation:

- Increase the overall level of compensation
- Install a cash bonus program
- Offer a variety of stock-based incentives
- Improve our health insurance and pension benefits

By making these improvements, we can help our company remain competitive with the industry's largest competitors.

Such repetition of key ideas greatly improves the chance that your audience will hear your message in the way you intended.

Describing Next Steps Some presentations require the audience to reach a decision or agree to take specific action, in which case the close provides a clear wrap-up. If the audience agrees on an issue covered in the presentation, briefly review the consensus. If they don't agree, make the lack of consensus clear by saying something like, "We seem to have some fundamental disagreement on this question." Then be ready to suggest a method of resolving the differences.

If you expect any action to occur as a result of your speech, be sure to explain who is responsible for doing what. One effective technique is to list the action items, with an estimated completion date and the name of the person or team responsible. You can present this list in a visual and ask each person on the list to agree to accomplish his or her assigned task by the target date. This public commitment to action is good insurance that something will happen.

> If you need to have the audience make a decision or agree to take action, make sure the responsibilities for doing so are clear.

Ending on a Strong Note Make sure your final remarks are upbeat and memorable. After summarizing your key points, conclude with a quote, a call to action, or some encouraging words. For instance, you might stress the benefits of action or express confidence in the listeners' ability to accomplish the work ahead. An alternative is to end with a question or a statement that will leave your audience thinking.

At the completion of your presentation, your audience should feel satisfied. The close is not the place to introduce new ideas or to alter the mood of the presentation. Even if parts of your presentation are downbeat, try to close on a positive note. Compose your closing remarks carefully. You don't want to wind up on stage with nothing to say but "Well, I guess that's it."

> Plan your final statement carefully so you can end on a strong, positive note.

Enhancing Your Presentations with Effective Visuals

Visuals can improve the quality and impact of your oral presentation by creating interest, illustrating points that are difficult to explain in words alone, adding variety, and increasing the audience's ability to absorb and remember information. Behavioral research has shown that visuals can improve learning by up to 400 percent because humans can process visuals 60,000 times faster than text.[12]

You can select from a variety of visuals to enhance oral presentations, each of which has unique advantages and disadvantages:

- **Overhead transparencies.** Overhead transparencies have been the workhorses of business presentations for decades, and some professionals still prefer them to

> Thoughtfully designed visuals create interest, illustrate complex points in your message, add variety, and help the audience absorb and remember information.

Document Makeover

IMPROVE THIS PRESENTATION

To practice correcting drafts of actual documents, visit your online course or the access-code-protected portion of the Companion Website. Click on "Document Make-overs" and then click on Chapter 14. You will find a presentation draft that contains problems and errors related to what you've learned in this chapter about preparing effective oral presentations. Use the "Final Draft" decision tool to create an improved version of this presentation. Check the message for effective choices in scope, style, opening, use of transitions, and close.

electronic presentations. Transparencies don't require the latest computer or projection equipment, you can write on them during a presentation, and they never crash on you—as computers have been known to do. However, they're limited to static displays, and they're impossible to edit once you've printed them.

- **Electronic presentations.** Electronic presentations are the visual aid of choice in most business situations today. An **electronic presentation**, or *slide show*, consists of a series of **electronic slides** composed using popular computer software such as Microsoft PowerPoint or Apple Keynote. To display an electronic presentation, you simply connect your computer to a portable projector (some are now small enough to carry around in your pocket) or a built-in unit that's part of a multimedia system in a conference room. Electronic presentations are easy to edit and update; you can add sound, photos, video, and animation; they can be incorporated into online meetings, webcasts, and *webinars* (a common term for web-based seminars); and you can record self-running presentations for trade shows, websites, and other uses. The primary disadvantage is the complexity involved in relying on a computer and a display projector.

- **Chalkboards and whiteboards.** Chalkboards and whiteboards are effective tools for the flexible, spontaneous nature of workshops and brainstorming sessions. Electronic whiteboards let you capture the information written on them.

- **Flip charts.** Flip charts are great for recording comments and questions during your presentation and for keeping track of ideas during a brainstorming session.

- **Other visuals.** Be creative when choosing visuals to support your presentation. A video recording of a group of customers talking about your company can have a lot more impact than a series of slides that summarize what they said. Samples of products and materials let your audience experience your subject directly. Designers and architects use mock-ups and models to help people envision what a final creation will look like. For software products, *screencasting* lets presenters capture software operation in action and replay it for audiences.

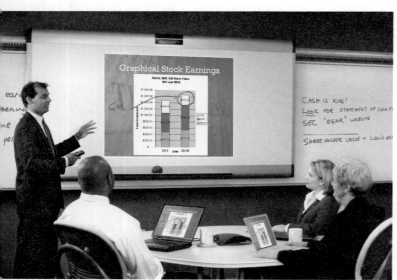

Electronic whiteboards let you capture notes and feedback during presentations and then print them out or e-mail them to audience members.

This chapter focuses on electronic presentations, the mainstay of business presentations today, although most of the following design tips apply to overhead transparencies as well.

Creating Effective Slides When it comes time to make design choices, from selecting fonts to deciding whether to include a photo, let accuracy and simplicity guide you. Doing so has several advantages. First, simple materials take less time to create than complex materials. Second, simple visuals reduce the chances of distraction and misinterpretation. Third, the more "bells and whistles" you have in your presentation, the more likely something will go wrong.

Writing Readable Content Effective text slides supplement your words and help the audience follow the flow of ideas. They are simplified outlines of your presentation that you can use to highlight key points, summarize and preview your message, signal major shifts in thought, illustrate concepts, or help create interest in your oral message. Slides are not intended to display your entire script or highlight every single point you plan to make.[13] Keep your message short and simple:

- Limit each slide to one thought, concept, or idea.

- Limit the content of each slide to about 40 words—with no more than 6 lines of text containing about 6 or 7 words per line.

- Write short bulleted phrases rather than long sentences or blocks of text.
- Phrase list items in parallel grammatical form to facilitate quick reading.
- Make your slides easy to read by using the active voice.
- Include short, informative titles.

Figure 14.4 is a good example of text slides that have been revised according to these principles to make their content more readable.

FIGURE 14.4
Writing Readable Content

Figure 14.4a—Inefficient paragraph style

Figure 14.4b—Efficient bulleted phrases

The paragraph style in Figure 14.4a is much more difficult to read, particularly from a distance, than the bulleted style in Figure 14.4b. The speaker will explain these bullet points while showing the slide.

Figure 14.4c—Wordy bullets

Figure 14.4d—Concise bullets

Unnecessary words in Figure 14.4c make these bullets harder to read. With the concise bullets in Figure 14.4d, the audience can quickly grasp key message points as the speaker provides additional information. Note also how the phrases in Figure 14.4d are parallel and the font is larger, both of which make this slide easier to read.

Visuals created for printed documents may need to be simplified for use in presentations.

Modifying Graphics for Slides The visual design principles you learned in Chapter 12 apply to presentation visuals as well, with one important caution: Visuals for presentations need to be simpler than visuals for printed documents. Detailed images that look fine on the printed page can be too dense and complicated for presentations.

If you're adapting visuals originally created for a written report, start by reducing the level of detail, eliminating anything that is not absolutely essential to the message. If necessary, break information into more than one illustration. Whenever you can do so without confusing the audience, look for shorter variations of numeric values. For instance, round off a number such as $12,500.72 to $12 or $12.5, and then label the axis to indicate thousands.

With the basic design in place, use graphical elements to highlight key points. Leave plenty of white space, use colors that stand out from the slide's background, and choose a font that's clear and easy to read. Use arrows, boldface type, and color to direct your audience's eyes to the main point of a visual.

To design effective slides, consider the six principles of effective design: consistency, contrast, balance, emphasis, convention, and simplicity.

Color is more than just decoration; colors have meanings themselves, based on both cultural experience and the relationships you establish between the colors in your designs.

Selecting Design Elements Chapter 12 highlights six principles of effective design: consistency, contrast, balance, emphasis, convention, and simplicity (see page 426). Pay close attention to these principles as you select the color, background and foreground designs, artwork, fonts, and type styles for your slides:

- **Color.** Color is a critical design element that can grab attention, emphasize important ideas, and create contrast. Research shows that color visuals can account for 60 percent of an audience's acceptance or rejection of an idea. Color can increase willingness to read by up to 80 percent, and it can enhance learning and improve retention by more than 75 percent.[14] Your color choices can also stimulate various emotions, as Table 14.3 suggests. Limit your choices to a few complementary ones, and keep in mind that some colors work better together than others. Contrasting colors, for example, increase readability. So when selecting color for backgrounds, titles, and text, avoid choosing colors that are close in hue, such as brown on green or blue on purple.[15]

- **Background designs and artwork.** Electronic slides have two layers or levels of graphic design: the background and foreground. The *background* is the equivalent

Table 14.3 **COLOR AND EMOTION**

Color	Emotional Associations	Best Uses
Blue	Peaceful, soothing, tranquil, cool, trusting	Background for electronic business presentations (usually dark blue); safe and conservative
White	Neutral, innocent, pure, wise	Font color of choice for most electronic business presentations with a dark background
Yellow	Warm, bright, cheerful, enthusiastic	Text bullets and subheadings with a dark background
Red	Passionate, dangerous, active, painful	Promote action or stimulate audience; seldom used as a background ("in the red" specifically refers to financial losses)
Green	Assertive, prosperous, envious, relaxed	Highlight and accent color (green symbolizes money in the United States but not in other countries)

of paper in a printed report. Keep the background simple; cluttered or flashy backgrounds distract from your message. As part of the background, you may want to add a company logo, the date, the presentation title, and a slide number. Just be sure to keep all these elements small and unobtrusive.

- **Foreground designs and artwork.** The *foreground* contains the unique text and graphic elements that make up each individual slide. In the foreground, artwork can be either functional or decorative. *Functional artwork* includes photos, technical drawings, charts, and other visual elements containing information that's part of your message. In contrast, *decorative artwork* simply enhances the look of your slides. Decorative artwork is the least important element of any slide, but it tends to cause the most trouble for anyone inexperienced in designing slides (see Figure 14.5).

> Artwork in the foreground of your slides can be either decorative or functional; use decorative artwork sparingly.

- **Fonts and type styles.** Type is harder to read onscreen than on the printed page because projectors have lower *resolution* (the ability to display fine details) than most printed pages. Sans serif fonts are usually easier to read than serif fonts (see Figure 14.6). In general, avoid script or decorative fonts and italicized type. Use both uppercase and lowercase letters, with extra white space between lines of text, and limit the number of fonts to two or three. Choose font sizes that are easy to read from anywhere in the room, usually between 24 and 36 points. After you select fonts and type styles, test them for readability by viewing sample slides from a distance.

> Many of the fonts available on your computer are difficult to read onscreen, so they aren't good choices for presentation slides.

With so many choices at your fingertips, maintaining consistency in your design is critical. Audiences start to assign meaning to visual elements beginning with the first slide. For instance, if yellow is used to call attention to the first major point in your presentation, audience members will expect the next occurrence of yellow to also signal an important point. Fortunately, the *slide master* feature makes consistency easy to achieve (see Figure 14.7).

> Design inconsistencies confuse and annoy audiences; don't change colors and other design elements randomly throughout your presentation.

Adding Animation and Special Effects Today's presentation software offers many options for livening up your slides, including sound, animation, video clips, transition effects, and hyperlinks. Think about the impact that all these effects will have on your audience and use only those special effects that support your message.[16]

> You can animate just about everything in an electronic presentation; resist the temptation to do so—make sure an animation has a purpose.

FIGURE 14.5
Distractions from Decorative Artwork
Clip art and other pieces of purely decorative artwork must be used with great care to avoid distracting your audience members by giving them extra visual elements to decode—particularly if the artwork is inconsistent from piece to piece or slide to slide. The clip art in this slide doesn't add any information value, and it creates a cartoonish, unprofessional look.

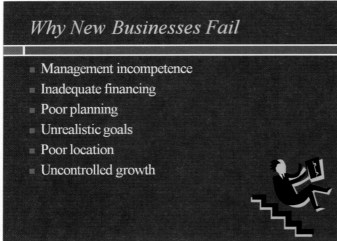

Figure 14.6a Times New Roman font   Figure 14.6b Arial font

Times New Roman is a standard font for many print documents; however, as Figure 14.6a demonstrates, the serifs at the end of each letter make this font difficult to read on screen, and so does the italicized type. As Figure 14.6b shows, sans serif fonts such as Arial are a better choice for slides; they are clearer and easier to read from a distance.

FIGURE 14.6
Selecting Readable Fonts and Type Styles

Functional animation involves motion that is directly related to your message, such as a highlight arrow that moves around the screen to emphasize specific points in a technical diagram. Such animation is also a great way to demonstrate sequences and procedures. In contrast, *decorative animation*, such as having a block of text cartwheel in from offscreen, needs to be used with great care. These effects don't add any functional value, and they easily distract audiences.

FIGURE 14.7
PowerPoint Slide Master
A *slide master* helps maintain consistency by ensuring that colors are used consistently and that bulleted lists, charts, graphics, and other elements show up in predictable places on each slide. The less readers have to work to interpret your slide designs, the more attention they can pay to your message.

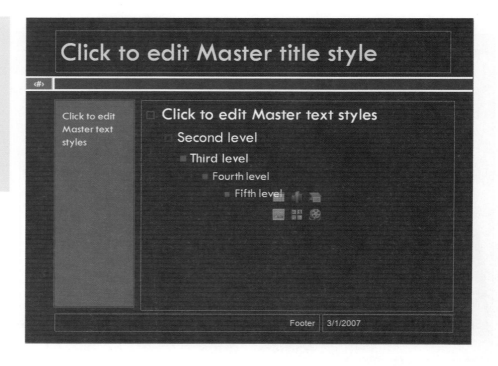

Transitions control how one slide replaces another, such as having the current slide gently fade out before the next slide fades in. Subtle transitions like this can ease your viewers' gaze from one slide to the next, but many of the transition effects now available are little more than distractions, so choose carefully. **Builds** control the release of text, graphics, and other elements on individual slides. With builds, you can make your bullet points appear one at a time rather than having all of them appear on a slide at once, thereby making it easier for you and the audience to focus on each new message point.

Some of the slide transitions available in presentation software are distracting and can quickly begin to annoy audiences.

A **hyperlink** instructs your computer to jump to another slide in your presentation, to a website, or to another program entirely. Hyperlinks can also be assigned to **action buttons**, which are a variety of preprogrammed icons available in PowerPoint. Action buttons let you perform such common tasks as jumping forward or backward to a specific slide and opening a document or spreadsheet. Using hyperlinks and action buttons is also a great way to build flexibility into your presentations so that you can instantly change the flow of your presentation in response to audience feedback.

You can increase the flexibility of your presentation slides with hyperlinks that let you jump to different slides, websites, or other displays.

Multimedia elements offer the ultimate in active presentations. Integrating short video clips can be a great way to add interest to your presentation. However, keep these clips short; audiences dislike being forced to sit through long speeches online.[17] For more advanced digital video, you can use such specialized products as Adobe Premiere Pro or Macromedia Director (you can learn more about both products at www.adobe.com).

Video clips can add memorable, engaging content to your presentations; just make sure they are relevant, interesting, and brief.

Giving Presentations Online   With the global reach of today's business organizations, you can expect to deliver a presentation online at some point in your career. In some companies, online presentations have already become a routine matter, conducted via internal groupware, virtual meeting systems, or webcast systems designed specifically for online presentations. In most cases, you'll communicate through some combination of audio, video, and data presentations (with PowerPoint slides, for instance). Your audience will view your presentation either on their individual computer screens or via a projector in a conference room.

The benefits of online presentations are considerable, including the opportunity to communicate with a geographically dispersed audience at a fraction of the cost of travel and the ability for a project team or an entire organization to meet at a moment's notice. Online presentations can also be less disruptive for the members of your audience, giving them the options of viewing your presentation from their desks and listening to only those parts that apply to them. However, the challenges for a presenter can be significant, thanks to that layer of technology between you and your audience. Many of those "human moments" that guide and encourage you through an in-person presentation don't travel across the digital divide. For instance, it's often difficult to tell whether your audience is bored or confused because your view of them is usually confined to

Online presentations let you reach a wide audience, but the lack of direct contact forces you to take a more active role in engaging your audience.

small video images. Moreover, the technology itself can be a source of trouble from time to time, with dropped Internet connections, untrained users, and other problems. However, as online systems continue to improve, presenters who master this new mode of communication will definitely have an advantage in tomorrow's business environment.

Online presentations give you a way to reach many people in a short time, but they require special preparation and skills.

To ensure successful online presentations, regardless of the system you're using, keep the following advice in mind:

- **Consider sending preview study materials ahead of time.** Doing so lets your audience familiarize themselves with any important background information.

- **Keep your content—and your presentation of it—as simple as possible.** Break complicated slides down into multiple slides, if necessary, and keep the direction of your discussion clear so that no one gets lost. Moreover, make sure any prerecorded video presentations are short; audiences dislike being forced to sit through long speeches online.[18]

- **Ask for feedback frequently.** You won't have as much of the visual feedback that alerts you when audience members are confused, and many online viewers will be reluctant to call attention to themselves by interrupting you to ask for clarification.

- **Consider the viewing experience from the audience's side.** Will they be able to see what you think they can see? For instance, webcast video is typically displayed in a small window onscreen, so viewers may miss important details.

- **Make sure your audience can receive the sort of content you intend to use.** For example, some corporate *firewalls* don't allow *streaming media* (audio and video files that continue to download while audiences listen to or watch them), so your webcast video might not survive the trip.[19]

- **Allow plenty of time for everyone to get connected and familiar with the screen they're viewing.** Build extra time into your schedule to ensure that everyone is connected and ready to start.

Last but not least, don't get lost in the technology. Use these tools whenever they'll help, but remember that the most important aspect of any presentation is getting the audience to receive, understand, and embrace your message.

STEP 3: COMPLETING YOUR PRESENTATION

With a draft of your presentation in hand, you're ready to complete the development of your presentation. As with written communication, this third step starts with the all-important task of revising your message to ensure appropriate content. Edit your presentation for clarity and conciseness as you would any other business message. If you're using electronic slides, make sure they are readable, concise, consistent from slide to slide, and fully operational (including transitions, builds, and animations). The first step in completing your presentation is finalizing your slides and support materials.

Finalizing Slides and Support Materials

Electronic presentation software can help you throughout the editing and revision process. As Figure 14.8 shows, the *slide sorter view* lets you see some or all of the slides in your presentation on a single screen. Use this view to add and delete slides, reposition slides, check slides for design consistency, and verify the operation of animation and transition effects.

In addition to the content slides that you've already created, you can help your audience follow the flow of your presentation by creating slides for your title, agenda and program details, and navigation flow:

- **Title slide(s).** Make a good first impression on your audience with one or two title slides, the equivalent of a report's cover and title page (see Figures 14.9a and

When you master the technology, you can spend less time thinking about it and more time thinking about the most important elements of the presentation: your message and your audience.

Use the slide sorter view to verify and modify the organization of your slides.

Navigational slides help your audience keep track of what you've covered already and what you plan to cover next.

FIGURE 14.8
Slide Sorter View
Examining thumbnails of slides on one screen is the best way to check the overall design of your final product. The slide sorter also makes it easy to ponder the order and organization of your presentation; you can change the position of any slide simply by clicking and dragging it to a new position.

14.9b). A title slide should contain the title of your presentation (and subtitle, if appropriate), your name, your department affiliation (for internal audiences), and your company affiliation (for external audiences).

- **Agenda and program details.** These slides communicate both the agenda for your presentation and any additional information your audience might need, such as lunch plans (see Figures 14.9c and 14.9d).

- **Navigation slides.** To tell your audience where you're going and where you've been, you can use a series of **navigation slides** based on your outline or agenda. This technique is most useful in longer presentations with several major sections. As you complete each section, repeat the slide but indicate which material has been covered and which section you are about to begin (see Figure 14.10). This

Figure 14.9a

Figure 14.9b

Figure 14.9c

Figure 14.9d

FIGURE 14.9
Navigation and Support Slides
You can use a variety of navigation and support slides to introduce yourself and your presentation, to let the audience know what your presentation will cover, and to provide essential details.

sort of slide is sometimes referred to as a *moving blueprint*. You can use the original slide again in the close of your presentation to review the points you've covered. As an alternative to the repeating agenda slide, you can insert a simple *bumper slide* at each major section break, announcing the title of the section you're about to begin.[20]

Use handout materials to support the points made in your presentation and to offer the audience additional information on your topic.

With your slides working properly and in clear, logical order, consider whether some additional material will help your audience either during or after your presentations. *Handouts* are a great way to offer your audience additional material without overloading your slides with information. Possibilities for good handout materials include complex charts and diagrams that are too unwieldy for the screen, articles and technical papers, case studies, lists of websites, and printed copies of your slides.[21]

Figure 14.10a

Figure 14.10b

FIGURE 14.10
Moving Blueprint Slides
Here are two of the ways you can use a *blueprint slide* as a navigational aid to help your audience stay on track with the presentation. Figure 14.10a visually "mutes" and checks off the sections of the presentation that have already been covered. In contrast, Figure 14.10b uses a sliding highlight box to indicate the next section to be covered.

Finally, think about a backup plan. What will you do if your laptop won't boot up or the projector dies? Can you get by without your slides? For important presentations, consider having backup equipment on standby, loaded with your presentation and ready to go. Having a backup copy of your presentation slides on a CD-ROM or flash drive is often a good idea, too. At the very least, have enough printed handouts ready to give the audience so that, as a last resort, you can give your presentation "on paper."

Preparing to Speak

With all your materials ready, your next step is to decide which method of speaking you want to use. You have three options: memorizing your material word for word, reading a printout of your material, or speaking from notes. Memorizing is usually not a good choice. In the best of circumstances, you'll probably sound stilted; in the worst, you might forget your lines. Besides, you'll often need to address audience questions during your speech, so you must be flexible enough to adjust your speech as you go. However, memorizing a quotation, an opening paragraph, or a few concluding remarks can bolster your confidence and strengthen your delivery.

Reading your speech is sometimes necessary, such as when delivering legal information, policy statements, or other messages that must be conveyed in an exact manner. However, for most business presentations, reading is a poor choice because it limits your interaction with the audience and lacks the fresh, dynamic feel of natural talking. (In any event, *never* stand in front of an audience and simply read the text on your slides.) If you do plan to read a prepared speech, practice enough so that you can still maintain eye contact with your audience. Print your speech with triple-spaced lines, wide margins, and large type. You might even want to include stage cues, such as *pause*, *raise hands*, or *lower voice*.

Speaking from notes, with the help of an outline, note cards, or visuals, is usually the most effective and easiest delivery mode. This approach gives you something to

Speaking from carefully prepared notes is the easiest and most effective delivery mode for most speakers.

refer to and still allows for plenty of eye contact, interaction with the audience, and improvisation in response to audience feedback.

From time to time, you may have to give an *impromptu*, or unrehearsed, speech when you have virtually no time at all to prepare. If you have the option, avoid speaking unprepared unless you're well versed in the topic or have lots of experience at improvising in front of a live audience. When you're asked to speak "off the cuff," take a moment to think through what you'll say and then focus on your key points. If you absolutely cannot say something intelligent and effective on the subject at hand, it's usually better to explain that you can't and ask for an opportunity to prepare some remarks for a later time or date.

Practicing Your Delivery

The more you practice, the more confidence you'll have in yourself and your material.

You're now just one step away from giving your presentation, and it's a step that many novice presenters overlook: practicing the delivery of your presentation. Many things can go wrong in a major presentation, including equipment glitches, timing problems, and that sinking feeling that you don't know what to say next. That's why experienced speakers always practice important presentations. If you can arrange an audience of several helpful colleagues, by all means do so. They can tell you if your slides are understandable and whether your delivery is effective. A day or two before you're ready to step on stage for an important talk, make sure you can give a positive response to the following questions:

You'll know you've practiced enough when you can present the material at a comfortable pace and in a conversational tone, without the need to read your slides or constantly refer to your notes.

- Can you present your material naturally, without reading your slides word-for-word?
- Is the equipment working—and do you know how to work it?
- Is your timing on track?
- Can you easily pronounce all the words you plan to use?
- Have you decided how you're going to introduce your slides?
- Have you anticipated likely questions and objections?

With experience, you'll get a feel for how much practice is enough in any given situation. For an important presentation, four or five practice runs is not excessive. Your credibility is dramatically enhanced when you move seamlessly through your presentation, matching effective words with each slide. Practicing helps keep you on track, helps you maintain a conversational tone with your audience, and boosts your confidence and composure.

If you're addressing an audience that doesn't speak your language, consider using an interpreter. Working with an interpreter does constrain your presentation somewhat. For one thing, you must speak slowly enough for the interpreter to keep up with you; however, don't speak so slowly that the rest of your audience loses interest. Send your interpreter a copy of your speech and visuals as far in advance of your presentation as possible. If your audience is likely to include persons with hearing impairments, be sure to team up with a sign-language interpreter as well.

Any time you deliver an oral presentation to people from other cultures, you may need to adapt the content of your presentation. It is also important to take into account any cultural differences in appearance, mannerisms, and other customs. Your interpreter or host will be able to suggest appropriate changes for a specific audience or particular occasion.

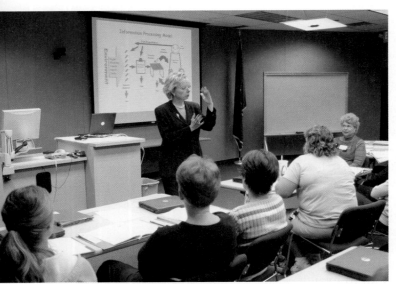

Learning to focus on and interact with the audience while using electronic slides or other visuals takes practice.

Overcoming Anxiety

If you're nervous about facing an audience, you're not alone: Even speakers with years of experience feel some anxiety about getting up in front of an audience. Polished speakers know how to use that nervous energy to their advantage. For starters, think of nervousness as an indication that you care about your audience, your topic, and the occasion. If your palms get wet or your mouth goes dry, don't think of it as nerves—think of it as excitement. Such stimulation can give you the extra energy you need to make your presentation sparkle. Here are some ways to harness your nervous energy to become a more confident speaker:[22]

- **Prepare more material than necessary.** Combined with having a genuine interest in your topic, having extra knowledge will reduce your anxiety.

- **Practice.** The more familiar you are with your material, the less panic you'll feel.

- **Think positively.** See yourself as polished and professional, and your audience will, too.

- **Visualize your success.** Use the few minutes before you actually begin speaking to tell yourself you're on and you're ready. Visualize mental images of yourself in front of the audience, feeling confident, prepared, and able to handle any situation that might arise.[23]

- **Take a few deep breaths.** Before you begin to speak, remember that your audience wants you to succeed, too.

- **Be ready.** Have your first sentence memorized and on the tip of your tongue.

- **Be comfortable.** Dress appropriately for the situation but as comfortably as possible. Drink plenty of water before your scheduled presentation time to ensure that your voice is well hydrated (bring a bottle of water with you, too). If possible, adjust the temperature in the room to your personal preference. The fewer physical distractions you have, the better you'll perform.

- **Don't panic.** If you sense that you're starting to race—a natural response when you're nervous—stop for a second and arrange your notes or perform some other small task while taking several deep breaths. Then start again at your normal pace. If you feel that you're losing your audience, try to pull them back by involving them in the action; ask for their opinions or pause for questions.

- **Concentrate on your message and your audience, not on yourself.** When you're busy thinking about your subject and observing your audience's response, you tend to forget your fears.

- **Maintain eye contact with friendly audience members.** When your presentation is under way, be particularly careful to maintain eye contact with your audience, shifting your gaze periodically around the room. Looking directly at your listeners will make you appear sincere, confident, and trustworthy. It also helps you get an idea of the impression you're creating.

- **Keep going.** Things usually get better as you move along, with each successful minute giving you more and more confidence.

Preparation is the best antidote for anxiety.

Handling Questions Responsively

The question-and-answer period is one of the most important parts of an oral presentation. Questions give you a chance to obtain important information, to emphasize your main idea and supporting points, and to build enthusiasm for your point

Don't leave the question-and-answer period to chance: Anticipate likely questions and think through your answers.

of view. When you're speaking to high-ranking executives in your company, the question-and-answer period will often consume most of the time allotted for your presentation.[24]

Preparation is essential. Even if you can't anticipate every question, learn enough about your audience to get an idea of their concerns. Think through answers to questions you're likely to get, even those that you don't have a complete answer to. Don't assume that you can handle whatever comes up.[25]

Pay attention to the questioner's body language and facial expression to help determine what the person really means (assuming that you can see your audience). Repeat the question to confirm your understanding and to ensure that the entire audience has heard it. If the question is vague or confusing, ask for clarification; then give a simple, direct answer. If you're asked to choose between two alternatives, don't feel you must do so. Offer your own choice instead, if it makes more sense.[26]

Be sure to answer the question you're asked. Don't sidestep it, ignore it, laugh it off, or get so caught up in the situation that you forget to respond. If giving an adequate answer would take too long, simply say, "I'm sorry, we don't have time to get into that issue right now, but if you'll see me after the presentation, I'll be happy to discuss it with you." If you don't know the answer, don't pretend that you do. Instead, say something like "I don't have those figures. I'll get them for you as quickly as possible."

You have less control over the proceedings during the question-and-answer session than during the rest of your presentation, but establish some ground rules up front. If appropriate—and it wouldn't be appropriate to do so if your audience consists of potential investors or your company's top managers—announce a time limit or a question limit per person. Plus, give as many audience members as possible a chance to participate by calling on people from different parts of the room.

If audience members try to turn a question into an opportunity to make their own minipresentations, remember that it's up to you to stay in control. You might admit that you and the questioner have differing opinions and, before calling on someone else, offer to get back to the questioner once you've done more research. Or you might simply respond with a brief answer, avoiding a lengthy debate or additional questions.[27]

If a question ever puts you on the hot seat, respond honestly but keep your cool. Look the person in the eye, answer the question as well as you can, and keep your emotions under control. Avoid getting into a heated argument. Defuse hostility by paraphrasing the question and asking the questioner to confirm that you've understood it correctly. Maintain a businesslike tone of voice and a pleasant expression.[28]

When the time allotted for your presentation is up, call a halt to the question-and-answer session. Prepare the audience for the end by saying something like, "Our time is almost up. Let's have one more question." After you've made your reply, summarize the main idea of the presentation and thank people for their attention. Conclude the way you opened: by looking around the room and making eye contact. Then gather your notes and leave the podium, maintaining the same confident demeanor you've had from the beginning. For a reminder of the steps to take in developing an oral presentation, refer to "Checklist: Developing Oral Presentations."

Maintaining control during the question-and-answer session can be a challenge, particularly if any audience members outrank you in the corporate hierarchy.

If you ever face hostile questions, don't duck; respond honestly and directly while keeping your cool.

The question-and-answer session is often the most valuable part of a presentation, so prepare for it by researching answers to likely questions.

✓ CHECKLIST: Developing Oral Presentations

A. Plan your oral presentation.

✓ Analyze the situation by defining your purpose and developing an audience profile.
✓ Select the right medium.
✓ Organize your presentation by defining the main idea, limiting the scope, choosing your approach, and preparing your outline.

B. Write your oral presentation.

✓ Adapt to your audience by tailoring your style and language.
✓ Compose your presentation by preparing an introduction, a body, and a close.
✓ Use your introduction to arouse audience interest, build your credibility, and preview your message.

✓ Use the body to connect your ideas and hold your audience's attention.
✓ Use the close to restate your main points and describe the next steps.

C. Complete your oral presentation.

✓ Master the art of delivery by choosing a delivery method, knowing your material, and practicing your delivery.
✓ Check the location and equipment in advance.
✓ Determine whether you should use an interpreter.
✓ Overcome anxiety by preparing thoroughly.
✓ Handle questions responsively.

On the Job

SOLVING COMMUNICATION DILEMMAS AT HEWLETT-PACKARD

After leading the successful effort to land the huge Procter & Gamble computer services contract, Dan Talbott is now HP's senior client relationship director for the P&G program. You work for him as an assistant manager on the program, and one of your key responsibilities is coordinating communication efforts across the far-flung team of people who now operate P&G's computer network. When HP landed the contract to take over P&G's information systems, it not only acquired several P&G facilities but also hired a large number of P&G employees who had previously worked on those systems. Although both companies have highly respected—and widely emulated—corporate cultures, you appreciate that the transition is difficult for some of the P&G staff. Many of these people joined P&G right out of college, and some have worked there for 20 years or more. They might be doing the same jobs as before and even working in the same facilities, but they have a new employer with different policies, different leadership, and so on. They also need to adjust to working for a high-technology firm instead of a consumer-goods firm. How will you address these challenges?[29]

1. You've been preparing a series of presentations on what it's like to work at HP, and the presentation you're developing now is on the concept of the "agile organization." Here's how HP's website describes the concept:

By working together, we become a smart organization that thinks imaginatively, acts decisively and delivers quickly. Time-to-market, time-to-customer, time-to-revenue and time-to-profit are our critical drivers, as we take calculated risks to outpace competitors and anticipate market changes.

Which of the following main idea statements does the best job of encapsulating this rather complicated thought?

a. Talk about how speed is critical to HP's success—creating new products quickly, acquiring new customers quickly, generating new revenue quickly, and realizing profits quickly.
b. Explain how teamwork plays a vital role in HP's ability to outpace competitors and anticipate market changes.
c. Make sure the ex-P&G people understand that business moves quickly at HP and that everyone is responsible for making HP an agile organization.
d. By working together, we become a smart organization that thinks imaginatively, acts decisively, and delivers quickly.

2. Eventually, some of the people who've recently joined from P&G may be transferred to other positions within HP, including working on HP's own internal information systems or working on programs for

other HP clients. However, the vast majority are still focused on the P&G program, so HP's overall mission and competitive concerns are probably not of immediate interest to many of them. What approach should you take in your presentation to encourage them to care about the concept of the "agile organization" and their individual roles in it?

a. Begin your presentation by immediately asking them what they've heard about the "agile organization" so far. Encourage them to ask any questions before you begin your presentation. This way you can squash any rumors before explaining what the "agile organization" means.

b. Start your introduction with a few recent news items about layoffs in other high-technology companies and then emphasize that in order to avoid that fate, everyone who works for HP needs to embrace the idea of agility. This will scare them into paying attention.

c. Share with them an insider's view of the sales process that Dan Talbott's team used to land the P&G contract, focusing on how the team responded so quickly to the opportunity. It's a great example of agility in action, and this situation affected all of them personally (and many of them probably wonder why HP was able to win the contract when EDS and IBM seemed to most people in the industry as more obvious choices for such a huge project). As HP employees now, they will care about how HP will continue to win big contracts and thereby avoid layoffs, keep providing good benefits, and create opportunities for career advancement.

d. Start your presentation with several short video clips that communicate the idea of speed, such as race cars, rockets, foot races at the Olympics, and a microwave oven cooking a meal in a matter of minutes. From these scenes, they'll get the idea that speed is vital in today's fast-paced world.

3. In the body of your presentation, you plan to show a PowerPoint slide that explains the various aspects of the company's description of what it means to be an agile organization. You'll present a text slide, talk the audience through the description, and then open the floor to questions. Which of the following is the best way to arrange the text for this slide?

a.

> ### The Agile Organization
> By working together, we become a smart organization that thinks imaginatively, acts decisively and delivers quickly. Time-to-market, time-to-customer, time-to-revenue and time-to-profit are our critical drivers, as we take calculated risks to outpace competitors and anticipate market changes.

b.

> ### What Does It Mean to Be Agile?
> By working together, we become a smart organization that thinks imaginatively, acts decisively and delivers quickly. Time-to-market, time-to-customer, time-to-revenue and time-to-profit are our critical drivers, as we take calculated risks to outpace competitors and anticipate market changes.

c.

> ### What Does It Mean to Be Agile?
> - Teamwork creates a smart organization:
>   - Imaginative thinking
>   - Decisive action
>   - Quick delivery
> - Time is our primary motivating force:
>   - Time-to-market
>   - Time-to-customer
>   - Time-to-revenue
>   - Time-to-profit
> - A strategy of taking calculated risks yields major benefits:
>   - Outpace competitors
>   - Anticipate market changes

d.

> ### What Does It Mean to Be Agile?
> - Teamwork creates a smart organization
> - Time is our primary motivating force
> - A strategy of taking calculated risks yields major benefits

4. You've completed your slide show on the agile organization, and you've been looking forward to giving the presentation for the first time. The presentation is going along nicely until you notice one employee in the back of the room snickering from time to time and whispering to people next to him. You've never met this person, and you're not even sure what his position is, but he's starting to distract you. After a few more minutes of this annoying behavior, the employee begins openly laughing at some of your remarks about corporate agility. Unfortunately, your emotions get the best of you, and you lose your cool, stop the presentation, and demand to know what the employee finds so funny. You realize immediately that you've made a mistake, particularly when the employee responds, "If HP is so freakin' agile, why have you been forced to lay off thousands of employ-

ees in the past couple of years? How soon until we lose our jobs, too?" You're not prepared to respond to such a complex question (the layoffs were the result of both the merger with Compaq and the general downturn in the technology market a few years ago), nor are you authorized to speak for the company on such a sensitive subject. On the other hand, you don't want to appear weak or ill prepared. After you take a deep breath and calm down a bit, how should you respond?

a. Use humor to defuse the situation. Tell the questioner, "HP laid off other employees to make room for charming new additions like you."

b. Recognize that this is not a question you should try to handle under these circumstances, particularly since you don't know how many other people might share the questioner's anxiety; you might lose control of the situation entirely. Respond by saying, "This is not an appropriate time or place to discuss such matters, and I'd like to return to the focus of our discussion today so that those employees who would like to learn more can get the information they came for."

c. Express empathy with the questioner's anxiety and explain that the best way to avoid layoffs in the future is for everyone to contribute to the company's efforts of becoming more agile: "As a fellow employee, I certainly share your concern about job security. However, I also know that the only part I can control is my contribution to the company's efforts to become more agile. Rather than digressing into past difficulties, why don't we focus on what each of us can do to ensure profitable growth into the future?"

d. Ignore the question entirely. Count to 10 silently, look back around the room at the friendly faces you were making eye contact with earlier, and resume your presentation.

Learning Objectives Checkup

Assess your understanding of the principles in this chapter by reading each learning objective and studying the accompanying exercises. For fill-in-the-blank items, write the missing text in the blank provided; for multiple-choice items, circle the letter of the correct answer. You can check your responses against the answer key on page AK-2.

Objective 14.1: Explain the importance of presentations in your career success.

1. Which of the following is a good reason to look for opportunities to give presentations during your career?
   a. Presentations let you demonstrate your ability to think on your feet, grasp complex issues, and handle challenging situations.
   b. Presentations give you a nice break from the routine of your regular job.
   c. Presentations let you demonstrate what a social person you are.
   d. Presentations are usually just a distraction from your main job; avoid them as much as possible.

2. Which of the following is an effective way to respond if you feel nervous right before giving a presentation?
   a. Think up a short joke to begin your presentation; the audience's laughter will help you relax.
   b. Begin your presentation by telling people that you're nervous and asking them to be sympathetic if you make any mistakes.
   c. Begin your presentation by telling the audience how much you dislike speaking in public; most of them dislike public speaking, too, so they'll be more sympathetic toward you.
   d. Remind yourself that everybody gets nervous and that being nervous simply means you care about doing well;

use the nervousness to be more energetic when you begin speaking.

Objective 14.2: Explain how to adapt the three-step writing process to oral presentations.

3. Which of the following is true about "writing" a presentation?
   a. You should always write every word of every presentation, leaving nothing to chance.
   b. You should never write presentations in the sense of writing a memo or a report.
   c. In most cases, you don't write out every word of a presentation; instead, you think through key phrases and perhaps draft your opening and closing statements.
   d. The three-step writing process does not apply to presentations.

4. A/an _____ outline is similar to an outline for a written memo or report, whereas a/an _____ outline is a simplified version designed to help you during the delivery of the your presentation.

5. How does the completion stage of the three-step writing process differ between reports and presentations?
   a. Completion is exactly the same for reports and presentations.
   b. Presentations are never proofread or tested ahead of time; doing so would destroy the spontaneity of your delivery.
   c. You never revise presentation slides because they're locked in place once you create them.
   d. The completion state for presentations involves a wider range of tasks, including testing your presentation slides, verifying equipment operation, practicing your speech, and creating handout materials.

Objective 14.3: Discuss the three functions of an effective introduction.

6. Which of the following is the best way to arouse interest in a presentation to a group of fellow employees on the importance of taking ownership of the problem whenever a customer calls in with a complaint?
   a. "If customers leave, so do our jobs."
   b. "Everything we want as employees of this company—from stable jobs to pay raises to promotional opportunities—depends on one thing: satisfied customers."
   c. "How are customers supposed to get their problems solved if we keep passing the buck from one person to the next without ever doing anything?"
   d. "The company's profit margins depend on satisfied customers, and it's up to us to make sure those customers are satisfied."

7. If you suspect that your audience doesn't really care about the topic you plan to discuss, how can you generate interest in your presentation?
   a. Look for ways to help them relate to the information on a personal level, such as helping the company ensure better job security.
   b. Speak louder and, if possible, use lots of sound effects and visual special effects in your presentation.
   c. Show your passion for the material by speaking faster than normal and pacing the room in an excited fashion.
   d. Show that you care about their feelings by saying up front that you don't really care about the topic either, but you've been assigned to talk about it.

8. If you're giving a presentation in a subject area that you've researched thoroughly but in which you don't have any hands-on experience (suppose your topic is coordinating a major facility relocation or hiring a tax attorney, for instance), which of these steps should you take to build credibility?
   a. During your introduction, explain that your presentation is the result of research that you've done and briefly explain the extent of the research.
   b. Explain that you don't have any experience in the subject area, but you've done some research.
   c. Emphasize that you know a great deal about the subject matter.
   d. Sidestep the issue of credibility entirely in the introduction and let your knowledge shine through during the body of your presentation.

Objective 14.4: Identify six ways to keep your audience's attention during your presentation.

9. Which of the following would do the best job of holding an audience's attention during a presentation on the growing importance of blogs (web logs) in corporate communication? In this particular case, the audience members are all managers of the same company, but they represent a half dozen countries and speak four different native languages (although they all have basic English skills).
   a. "Blogs are now an important feature in the corporate communication landscape."
   b. "Successful managers around the world now view blogging as an essential tool in their communication efforts."
   c. "Millions of customers and employees are now hip to the latest wave to blow through corporate communication, the clumsily named but nevertheless vital blog."
   d. "I personally read more than a dozen blogs every day, which is solid evidence of how important blogs have become."

10. Your company recently relocated from another state, and the owners are eager to begin building a positive relationship with the local community. You've been asked to speak to employees about volunteering in various community organizations. Which of the following statements does the best job of communicating the owners' wishes while appealing to employees' personal interests?
   a. "Becoming involved in community organizations is a great way for you and your families to meet new people and feel more at home in your new city."
   b. "Becoming involved in community organizations shows our new neighbors that we're an organization of positive, caring people—and it's a great way for you and your families to meet new people and feel more at home in your new city."
   c. "We really owe it to our new community to give back by volunteering."
   d. "The owners feel it is vital for us to become more involved in the community."

11. Which of these techniques is mentioned in the chapter as a way to hold an audience's attention during a presentation?
   a. Speak louder than average
   b. Tell people that management expects them to pay attention
   c. Use clear and vivid language
   d. None of the above

Objective 14.5: Explain how visuals enhance oral presentations, and list several popular types of visuals.

12. Which of the following is true about visuals?
   a. They can add interest to your presentations.
   b. They can help you illustrate and clarify important points.
   c. They can help your audience absorb and understand information.
   d. They can do all of the above.

13. Which of these is an advantage of electronic presentations over transparencies?
   a. You can edit and update your slides right up to the beginning of your presentation.
   b. Electronic presentations are less expensive.
   c. Electronic presentations require you to talk less.
   d. None of the above.

Objective 14.6: Explain the importance of design consistency in electronic slides and other visuals.

14. Why is consistent use of colors, fonts, size, and other design elements important in presentations?
   a. Consistency is not important; in fact, it's a sign of a dull presentation.

b. Consistency shows that you're a smart businessperson who doesn't waste time on trivial details.

c. Consistency simplifies the viewing and listening process for your audience and enables them to pay closer attention to your message rather than spending time trying to figure out your visuals.

d. Consistency shows that you're a team player who can follow instructions.

Objective 14.7: Highlight seven major issues to consider when you're preparing to give a presentation online.

15. Which of the following is a disadvantage of conducting presentations online?
    a. The lack of audio communication
    b. The inability of most people to participate, since most businesses don't have Internet access
    c. The inability to use PowerPoint slides online
    d. The shortage (or sometimes complete lack) of nonverbal signals such as posture, which can provide vital feedback during a presentation

16. Which of the following is an advantage of online presentations?
    a. Lower travel costs
    b. Less disruption for audiences
    c. The ability to meet on a moment's notice
    d. All of the above

Objective 14.8: Identify six ways that effective speakers handle questions responsively.

17. Which of these actions should you take when an audience member asks you a question?
    a. Observe the questioner's body language and facial expression to help determine what the person really means.
    b. Nod your head or show some other sign that you acknowledge the question.
    c. Repeat the question to confirm your understanding and to ensure that the entire audience has heard it.
    d. Do all of the above.

18. If you receive a question that is important and relevant to the topic you're presenting but you lack the information needed to answer it, which of the following would be the best response?
    a. "I'm sorry; I don't know the answer."
    b. "You've asked an important question, but I don't have the information needed to answer it properly. I'll research the issue after we're finished here today and then send everyone an e-mail message with the answer."
    c. "Let me get back to you on that."
    d. "I'd really like to stay focused on the material that I prepared for this presentation."

Apply Your Knowledge

1. Would you rather (a) deliver an oral presentation to an outside audience, (b) be interviewed for a news story, or (c) make a presentation to a departmental meeting? Why? How do the communication skills differ among those situations? Explain.

2. How might the audience's attitude affect the amount of audience interaction during or after a presentation? Explain your answer.

3. If you were giving an oral presentation on the performance of a company product, what three attention-getters might you use to enliven your speech?

4. How can you use a slide master to enhance the effectiveness of your slides?

5. **Ethical Choices** Is it ethical to use design elements and special effects to persuade an audience? Why or why not?

Practice Your Knowledge

MESSAGES FOR ANALYSIS

MESSAGE 14.A: IMPROVING A SLIDE

Examine the slide in Figure 14.11 and point out any problems you notice. How would you correct these problems?

MESSAGE 14.B: SIMPLIFYING A GRAPH

Examine the graph in Figure 14.12 and explain how to modify it for an electronic presentation using the guidelines discussed in this chapter.

MESSAGE 14.C: ANALYZING ANIMATION

To access this PowerPoint presentation, visit www.businesscommunicationblog.com and click on Textbook Resources. Locate *Excellence in Business Communication*, 8th

ed., click on Chapter 14, and then select Page 537, Message 14.C. Download and watch the presentation in slide show mode. (After you select Slide Show from the View menu, click your mouse to advance through the slides.) After you've watched the presentation, identify at least three ways in which various animations, builds, and transitions either enhanced or impeded your understanding of the subject matter.

EXERCISES

For active links to all websites discussed in this chapter, visit this book's website, at www.prenhall.com/thill. Locate your book and click on its "Companion Website" link. Then select Chapter 14 and click on "Featured Websites." Locate the name of the page or the URL related to the material in the text.

FIGURE 14.11
Piece of Cake Bakery
Electronic Slide #8

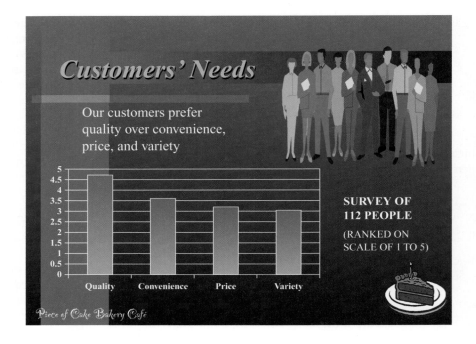

Please note that links to sites that become inactive after publication of the book will be removed from the "Featured Websites" section.

14.1 Mastering Delivery: Analysis Attend a presentation at your school or in your town or watch a speech on television. Categorize the presentation or speech as one that motivates or entertains, one that informs or analyzes, or one that persuades or urges collaboration. Then compare the speaker's delivery with this chapter's "Checklist: Developing Oral Presentations." Write a two-page report analyzing the speaker's performance and suggesting improvements.

14.2 Mastering Delivery: Nonverbal Signals Observe and analyze the delivery of a speaker in a school, at work, or in another setting. What type of delivery did the speaker use? Was this delivery appropriate for the occasion? What nonverbal signals did the speaker use to emphasize key points? Were these signals effective? Which nonverbal signals would you suggest to further enhance the delivery of this oral presentation—and why?

14.3 Ethical Choices Think again about the oral presentation you observed and analyzed in Exercise 14.2. How could the speaker have used nonverbal signals to unethically manipulate the audience's attitudes or actions?

14.4 Teamwork You've been asked to give an informative 10-minute presentation on vacation opportunities in your home state. Draft your introduction, which should last no more than 2 minutes. Then pair off with a classmate and analyze each other's introductions. How well do these two introductions arouse the audience's interest, build credibility, and preview the presentation? Suggest how these introductions might be improved.

14.5 Completing Oral Presentations: Self-Assessment How good are you at planning, writing, and delivering oral presentations? Rate yourself on each of the following elements of the oral presentation process. Then examine your ratings to identify where you are strongest and where you can improve, using the tips in this chapter.

FIGURE 14.12
CommuniCo Employee
Training Costs

Element of Presentation Process	Always	Frequently	Occasionally	Never
1. I start by defining my purpose.				
2. I analyze my audience before writing an oral presentation.				
3. I match my presentation length to the allotted time.				
4. I begin my oral presentations with an attention-getting introduction.				
5. I look for ways to build credibility as a speaker.				
6. I cover only a few main points in the body of my presentation.				
7. I use transitions to help listeners follow my ideas.				
8. I review main points and describe next steps in the close.				
9. I practice my presentation beforehand.				
10. I prepare in advance for questions and objections.				
11. I conclude oral presentations by summarizing my main idea.				

14.6 Creating Effective Slides: Content Look through recent issues (print or online) of *BusinessWeek*, *Fortune*, or other business publications for articles that discuss challenges that a specific company or industry is facing. Using the articles and the guidelines discussed in this chapter, create three to five slides that summarize these issues.

14.7 Creating Effective Slides: Content and Design You've been asked to give an informative 10-minute talk to a group of conventioneers on great things to see and do while visiting your hometown. Write the content for three or four slides (including a cover slide). Then think about the design elements for your slides. Describe design choices you would make, particularly in terms of colors, fonts, drawings, and photography.

14.8 Completing Electronic Presentations: Slide Sorter View Download any PowerPoint presentation from the "Business Communication Multimedia Resources" page at www.businesscommunicationblog.com. Then use the *slide sorter view* to critique the content, layout, and design elements of this presentation. Edit and revise the slides to improve their overall effectiveness.

14.9 Internet Creating hyperlinks to live websites can perk up an electronic presentation, but it also means being prepared for the unexpected. What are some of the obstacles you might encounter when creating live Internet links? How can you prepare in advance to overcome such obstacles?

Expand Your Knowledge

LEARNING MORE ON THE WEB
LEARN FROM THE PRESENTATION PROS

www.presentations.com

The online home of *Presentations* magazine offers a wealth of articles that offer practical advice on creating and delivering business presentations. Under the "Presentations" tab, browse the "Creation," "Delivery," "Venue," "Technology," and "Products" sections to find resources that will help you complete the following tasks.

1. Find several articles that discuss the unique challenges of making presentations at trade shows. Identify three to five tips that will help you succeed in these environments.
2. Find a recent article that discusses tips, techniques, or traps of using PowerPoint for business presentations. Summarize the article's advice in a brief message that could be posted on your company's internal blog.
3. Find one or more articles that discuss techniques for improving vocal delivery. Identify three points that speakers can use to make more effective use of their voice during presentations.

SURFING YOUR WAY TO CAREER SUCCESS

Bovée and Thill's Business Communication Headline News offers links to hundreds of online resources that can help you with this course, your other college courses, and your career. Visit www.businesscommunicationblog.com and click on "Web Directory." The "Oral Communication" section connects you to a variety of websites and articles on speeches, stage fright, presentations, PowerPoint tips, podcasts, webcasts, and videoconferencing. Identify three websites from this section that could be useful in your business career. For each site, write a two-sentence summary of what the site offers and how it could help you launch and build your career.

Learn Interactively

INTERACTIVE STUDY GUIDE

Go to the Companion Website at www.prenhall.com/thill and locate your book, then click on "Companion Website." Select Chapter 14 to take advantage of the interactive "Chapter Quiz" to test your knowledge of chapter concepts. Receive instant feedback on whether you need to do additional studying. Also, visit the "Study Hall," where you'll find an abundance of valuable resources that will help you succeed in this course.

PEAK PERFORMANCE GRAMMAR AND MECHANICS

If your instructor has required the use of "Peak Performance Grammar and Mechanics," either in your online course or on

CD, you can continue to improve your skill with mechanics by using the "Peak Performance Grammar and Mechanics" module. Click on "Mechanics of Style." Take the Pretest to determine whether you have any weak areas. Then review those areas in the Refresher Course. Take the Follow-Up Test to check your grasp of mechanics. For an extra challenge or advanced practice, take the Advanced Test. Finally, for additional reinforcement, go to the "Improve Your Grammar, Mechanics, and Usage" section that follows, and complete those exercises.

Improve Your Grammar, Mechanics, and Usage

The following exercises help you improve your knowledge of and power over English grammar, mechanics, and usage. Turn to the Handbook of Grammar, Mechanics, and Usage at the end of this book and review all of Sections 3.1 (Capitalization), 3.2 (Underscores and Italics), and 3.3 (Abbreviations). Then look at the following 10 items. Circle the letter of the preferred choice in the following groups of sentences. (Answers to these exercises appear on page AK-4.)

1. a. Send this report to Mister H. K. Danforth, RR 1, Albany, NY 12885.
   b. Send this report to Mister H. K. Danforth, Rural Route 1, Albany, New York 12885.
   c. Send this report to Mr. H. K. Danforth, RR 1, Albany, NY 12885.
2. a. She received her MBA degree from the University of Michigan.
   b. She received her Master of Business Administration degree from the university of Michigan.
3. a. Sara O'Rourke (a reporter from The <u>Wall Street Journal</u>) will be here Thursday.
   b. Sara O'Rourke (a reporter from <u>The Wall Street Journal</u>) will be here Thursday.
   c. Sara O'Rourke (a reporter from The *Wall Street Journal*) will be here Thursday.
4. a. The building is located on the corner of Madison and Center streets.
   b. The building is located on the corner of Madison and Center Streets.
5. a. Call me at 8 a.m. tomorrow morning, PST, and I'll have the information you need.
   b. Call me at 8 tomorrow morning, PST, and I'll have the information you need.
   c. Call me tomorrow at 8 a.m. PST, and I'll have the information you need.

6. a. Whom do you think *Time* magazine will select as its Person of the Year?
   b. Whom do you think *Time magazine* will select as its *Person of the Year*?
   c. Whom do you think *Time magazine* will select as its Person of the Year?
7. a. The art department will begin work on Feb. 2, just one wk. from today.
   b. The art department will begin work on February 2, just one week from today.
   c. The art department will begin work on Feb. 2, just one week from today.
8. a. You are to meet him on friday at the UN building in NYC.
   b. You are to meet him on Friday at the UN building in NYC.
   c. You are to meet him on Friday at the un building in New York city.
9. a. You must help her distinguish between *i.e.* (which means "that is") and *e.g.* (which means "for example").
   b. You must help her distinguish between <u>i.e.</u> (which means "that is") and *e.g.* (which means "for example").
   c. You must help her distinguish between *i.e.* (which means <u>that is</u>) and *e.g.* (which means <u>for example</u>).
10. a. We plan to establish a sales office on the West coast.
    b. We plan to establish a sales office on the west coast.
    c. We plan to establish a sales office on the West Coast.

For additional exercises focusing on mechanics, go to www.prenhall.com/thill, then locate your text and click on its "Companion Website" link. Click on Chapter 14, click on "Additional Exercises to Improve Your Grammar, Mechanics and Usage," and then click on "20. Capitals" or "21. Word division."

Cases

Applying the Three-Step Writing Process to Cases

Apply each step to the following cases, as assigned by your instructor (refer to Figure 14.1).

Portfolio BUILDER

1. Is anybody out there? Explaining Loopt's social mapping service How many times have you been out shopping or clubbing and wondered if any of your friends were in the neighborhood? A new *social mapping* service from Loopt can provide the answer. It lets you put yourself on a map that your friends can see on their mobile phones, and you can see their locations as well. You can even get automatic alerts whenever friends are near.

Your task: Create a brief presentation explaining the Loopt concept to someone who is comfortable using text messaging and other mobile phone features. Be sure to explain what type of phone is required and include one slide that discusses safety issues. You can learn more about it at www.loopt.com.[30]

Portfolio BUILDER

2. I'll find my space somewhere else, thanks: Promoting alternatives to MySpace With a user base well on its way toward 200 million people, MySpace is the king of social networking sites. However, it doesn't appeal to everyone. Some people want to be able to customize their online presence more than MySpace allows, while others want more control over who sees what aspects of their online profiles.

Your task: Choose one of the lesser-known alternatives to MySpace, such as Ning (www.ning.com), Vox (www.vox.com), Esnips (www.esnips.com), or any other site that offers some degree of social networking. Compare its features and functions to those of MySpace and prepare a brief presentation that highlights the similarities and differences of the two sites. In your presentation, identify the sort of people most likely to prefer the site you've chosen over MySpace.[31]

3. Face to face: Updating management on your monthly progress Imagine that you've just completed the impressive-looking online progress report shown in Figure 12.5 (page 419), when your boss decides he'd like to hear a presentation from you instead.

Your task: Adapt the information in Figure 12.5 to a brief electronic slide show. Your boss might want to see maps of the four locations listed, so have slides with maps ready. (Because you don't have the specific addresses, just capture an online map for each general area; Lakewood and Glendale are suburbs of Denver, and Pepsi Center is a sports arena in Denver.)

Portfolio BUILDER

4. Hot topics: Identifying key elements in an important business issue In your job as a business development researcher for a major corporation, you're asked to gather and process information on a wide variety of subjects. Management has gained confidence in your research and analysis skills and would now like you to begin making regular presentations at management retreats and other functions. Topics are likely to include the following:

- Offshoring of U.S. jobs
- Foreign ownership of U.S. firms
- Employment issues involving immigrants
- Tax breaks offered by local and state governments to attract new businesses
- Economic impact of environmental regulations

Your task: Choose one of the topics from this list and conduct enough research to familiarize yourself with the topic. Identify at least three important issues that anyone involved with this topic should know about. Prepare a 10-minute presentation that introduces the topic, comments on its importance to the U.S. economy, and discusses the issues you've identified. Assume that your audience is a cross-section of business managers who don't have any particular experience in the topic you've chosen.

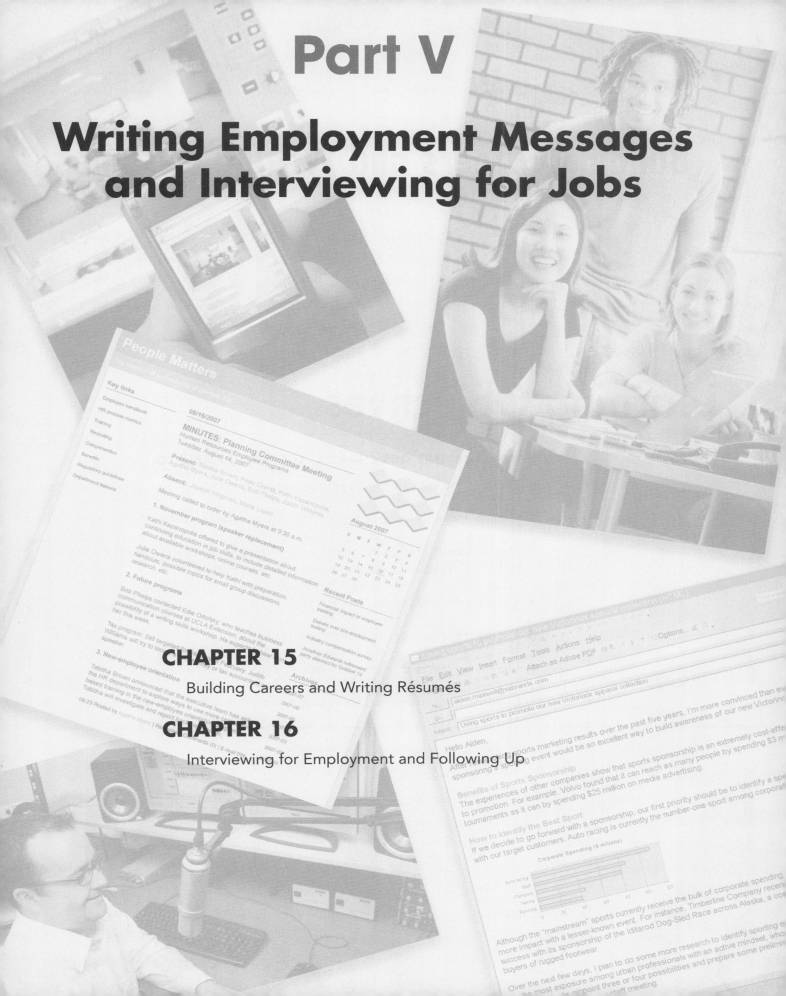

Part V

Writing Employment Messages and Interviewing for Jobs

CHAPTER 15
Building Careers and Writing Résumés

CHAPTER 16
Interviewing for Employment and Following Up

Chapter 15

Building Careers and Writing Résumés

Learning Objectives

AFTER STUDYING THIS CHAPTER, YOU WILL BE ABLE TO

1   Describe the approach most employers take to finding potential new employees

2   Explain the importance of networking in your career search

3   Discuss how to choose the appropriate résumé organization and list the advantages and disadvantages of the three common options

4   Describe the problem of résumé fraud

5   List the major sections of a traditional résumé

6   Identify six different formats in which you can produce a résumé

7   Describe what you should do to adapt your résumé to a scannable format

On the Job

COMMUNICATING AT HERSHA HOSPITALITY MANAGEMENT

SERVING UP THE RIGHT CANDIDATES FOR A SERVICE-DRIVEN ORGANIZATION

For applicants, the job search process might be long and grueling, but at least it has a definite beginning, middle, and end. But for managers in charge of recruiting, such as Hersha Hospitality Management's vice president of human resources, Jeffrey Wade, the process never ends. Hersha provides operational management services to a growing number of hotels in the eastern United States, and as the company grows, its need to add top-quality employees continues.

Growth is not the only force that puts demands on Wade and his team. "Recruiting in the hospitality industry is always a challenge because many of the positions are lower-wage jobs, and front-office positions are often filled by college students who want to move on with their careers," he explains. In other words, even as the company expands and needs to bring in more new employees, many existing employees are looking to move up and out. The result is relentless pressure to select new people to join the Hersha family. Moreover, Wade isn't interested in hiring just anybody; the company has extremely high customer-service

An applicant tracking system has helped Jeffrey Wade and his team at Hersha Hospitality Management efficiently recruit the service-driven employees that Hersha relies on.

standards for everyone from entry-level hotel workers to top management.

Many managers in Wade's position, particularly in small to midsize companies, *outsource* the recruiting function, paying an outside company to find and filter candidates. However, Wade believes that recruiting is too essential to Hersha's success to be left in the hands of an outsider.

His answer to the challenge of endless hiring is to use an *applicant tracking system* (ATS), a computer-based solution that integrates the entire recruiting and employee records management effort—from job seekers' submission of online résumés and applications through interviewing, hiring, orientation, promotions, and eventual leaving of the company. Although it is highly computerized, the process is far from impersonal. In fact, by managing all the details, the system frees up Wade and his staff to spend time with applicants, assessing their personalities and potential fit with Hersha's service-oriented culture.[1]

www.hershahotels.com

SECURING EMPLOYMENT IN TODAY'S JOB MARKET

Hersha's approach to managing the employee application process (profiled in the chapter opener) highlights the ever-evolving nature of the job market. To keep up with the demand for good employees—and the flood of résumés coming in from all over the Internet—many companies now use some form of automation to find the best candidates and shepherd them through the selection process.

Understanding how employers approach the hiring process is just one of many insights and skills you need to conduct a successful job search. After you've armed yourself with knowledge of today's workplace and your potential role in it, it's time to launch an efficient, productive process to find that ideal position. (Before you read this chapter, make sure you've read the Prologue, "Building a Career with Your Communication Skills," which starts on page xxxiii.) Figure 15.1 shows the six most important tasks in the job search process. This chapter and the Prologue discuss the first two, and Chapter 16 explores the final four.

Understanding Employers' Approach to the Employment Process

You can save considerable time and effort by understanding how employers approach the recruiting process (see Figure 15.2). Generally, employers prefer to look for candidates within their own organization or through referrals from people they know and trust. Overall, personal contacts appear to be the prime source of jobs, regardless of whether a candidate has just graduated from college or has been out of school for several years.[2] Increasingly, these personal referrals can come through social networking websites, a fact that highlights the importance of networking (see page 550).

Many employers send representatives to college campuses to conduct student interviews, which are usually coordinated by the campus placement office. In addition, many employers accept unsolicited résumés, and most keep unsolicited résumés on file or in a database. **Applicant tracking systems**, such as the one used by Hersha, help employers sift through the hundreds or thousands of résumés they receive each year. Employers also recruit candidates through employment agencies, state employment services, temporary staffing services, and the employment bureaus operated by some trade associations. They also post jobs through advertisements in newspapers, trade magazines, campus publications, their own websites, and job sites such as Monster.com. In fact,

FIGURE 15.1
The Employment Search Process
Finding the ideal job opportunity is a six-step process that you might repeat a number of times during your career.

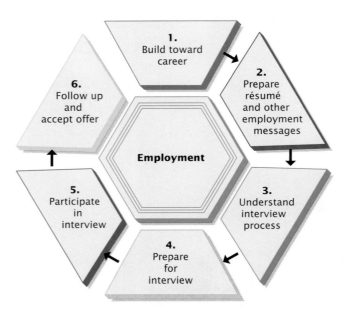

1. Build toward career
2. Prepare résumé and other employment messages
3. Understand interview process
4. Prepare for interview
5. Participate in interview
6. Follow up and accept offer

Employment

FIGURE 15.2
How Organizations Prefer to Find Employees
Employers usually prefer to look at their existing workforce to find candidates for newly created jobs and promotional opportunities. If no suitable candidates can be found, they begin to look outside the firm, starting with people whom company insiders already know.

major job boards such as Monster.com and CareerBuilder.com have grown so popular that some employers feel deluged with résumés, and some job seekers fear it's becoming impossible to stand out from the crowd when hundreds or thousands of people are applying for the same jobs. As a result, many specialized websites are now springing up to focus on narrow parts of the job market or offer technology that promises to do a better job of matching employers and job searchers. For example, Jobfox, www.jobfox.com, uses in-depth questionnaires to match employers and employees.[3]

Look again at Figure 15.2, and you'll notice that the easiest way for you to find out about new opportunities—that is, through the employer's outside advertising—is the employer's least-preferred way of finding new employees. As many as 80 percent of all job openings are never advertised, a phenomenon known as the *hidden job market*.[4] In other words, employers have looked in quite a few other places before they come looking for you. It's up to you to take action to get yourself noticed. But fear not; throughout this course, you've developed the communication skills to present yourself to the world effectively.

> It's important to understand that the easiest way for you to find jobs (that is, through companies' help-wanted advertising) is the least-preferred channel for many companies to find new employees.

Organizing Your Approach to the Employment Process

The employment process can be time-consuming, so organize your efforts carefully to save time and maximize your chances. Begin by finding out where the job opportunities are, which industries are strong, which parts of the country are booming, and which specific job categories offer the best prospects for the future. From there you can investigate individual organizations, doing your best to learn as much about them as possible. If you plan to search in another country, heed the advice in "Communicating Across Cultures: Looking for Work Around the World."

Staying Abreast of Business and Financial News   Thanks to the Internet, staying on top of business news is easy today. In fact, your biggest challenge will be selecting new material from the many available sources. To help you get started, here is a selection of websites of periodicals that offer business news (in some cases, you need to be a subscriber to access all the material, including archives):

> With so many print and electronic resources available today, it's easy to stay in touch with what's happening in the business world.

- *Wall Street Journal:* www.wsj.com
- *New York Times:* www.nyt.com
- *BusinessWeek:* www.businessweek.com
- *Business 2.0:* www.business2.com
- *Fast Company:* www.fastcompany.com
- *Fortune:* www.fortune.com
- *Forbes:* www.forbes.com

COMMUNICATING ACROSS CULTURES

Looking for Work Around the World

With his eyes fixed on a career in international law, University of Michigan (UM) graduate Andrew Jaynes knew that overseas work experience would help his law school admission chances and expand his intercultural background.

Jaynes started with the Overseas Opportunities Office at UM's International Center, which offers UM students extensive information on its website and access to advisers and students who have international work experience. With that information, he signed on with one of several companies that offer students assistance with foreign work permits and provide housing and job leads. He eventually found a job on his own, working at the American Library in Paris. "It took longer than I expected, but every day I learned more about the real lives of working Parisians—an awareness you can't get as a tourist."

To help ensure success in your own search for employment abroad, keep these points in mind:

- *Give yourself plenty of time.* Finding a job in another country is a complicated process that requires extensive and time-consuming research.

- *Research thoroughly, both online and off.* In addition to your school's resources, you can find numerous websites that offer advice, job listings, and other information. For a good look at the range of international opportunities, visit www.InternAbroad.com, www.VolunteerAbroad.com, www.TeachAbroad.com, and www.JobsAbroad.com. However, Jaynes and others with international experience will tell you that you can't limit your research to the web. With any

job search, networking is crucial, so join cultural societies with international interests, volunteer with exchange student programs, or find other ways to connect with people who have international experience.

- *Consider all the possibilities.* Keep an open mind when you're exploring your options; you'll probably run across situations you hadn't considered at the beginning of your search. For instance, you might find that an unpaid internship in your future profession would help your career prospects more than a paying position in some other industry.

- *Be flexible.* If you have to settle for something less than your dream job, focus on the big picture, which for most students is the cultural opportunity.

Finding a job in another country can be a lot of work, but the rewards can be considerable. "I had studied abroad for a year and traveled through many countries around the world," Jaynes says, "but nothing gives you the same feel for a culture as working in it."

CAREER APPLICATIONS

1. How might international work experience help you in a career in the United States, even if you never work abroad again?

2. If your work history involves religious or political activities, either paid or volunteer, explain how you might present this information on a *curriculum vitae* (the version of a résumé used in many countries) intended for international readers?

In addition, thousands of bloggers and podcasters offer news and commentary on the business world. To identify those you might find helpful, start with directories such as Technorati (www.technorati.com/blogs/business) for blogs or Podcast Alley (www.podcastalley.com; select the "Business" genre) for podcasts. For all these online resources, use a newsfeed aggregator to select the type of stories you're interested in and have them delivered to your screen automatically.

Of course, with all the business information available today, it's easy to get lost in the details. Try not to get too caught up in the daily particulars of business. Start by examining "big picture" topics—trends, issues, industrywide challenges, and careers—before delving into specific companies that look attractive.

Researching Specific Companies   Chapter 11 discusses how to find information on individual industries and companies, and it provides a list of helpful research resources. Review those sources, as well as professional journals and websites in the fields that interest you. When you've identified a promising industry and career field, consult directories of employers at your college library, at your career center, or on the web and compile a list of specific organizations that appeal to you.

Go beyond every company's own communication materials; find out what others in their industries and communities think about them.

In addition to using the web to find detailed information about prospective employers, you can use it to look for and respond to job openings. Most companies, even small firms, offer at least basic information about themselves on their websites.

Look for the "About Us" or "Company" part of the site to find a company profile, executive biographies, press releases, financial information, and information on employment opportunities. You'll often find information about an organization's mission, products, annual reports, and employee benefits. Plus, you can often download annual reports, brochures, and other materials. Any company's website is going to present the firm in the most positive light possible, of course, so look for outside sources as well, including the business sections of local newspapers and trade publications that cover the company's industries and markets.

Table 15.1 lists some of the many websites where you can learn more about companies and find job openings. Start with The Riley Guide, www.rileyguide.com, which offers links to hundreds of specialized websites that post openings in specific industries and professions. Your college's career center placement office probably maintains an up-to-date list as well.

Table 15.1	NETTING A JOB ON THE WEB	
Website*	**URL**	**Highlights**
The Riley Guide	www.rileyguide.com	Vast collection of links to both general and specialized job sites for every career imaginable; don't miss this one—it'll save you hours and hours of searching
CollegeRecruiter.com	www.collegerecruiter.com	Focused on opportunities for graduates with less than three years of work experience
Monster.com	www.monster.com	One of the most popular job sites, with hundreds of thousands of openings, many from hard-to-find smaller companies; extensive collection of advice on the job search process
MonsterTrak	www.monstertrak.com	Focused on job searches for new college grads; your school's career center site probably links here
Yahoo! HotJobs	http://hotjobs.yahoo.com	Another leading job board, formed by recent merger of HotJobs and Yahoo! Careers
CareerBuilder.com	www.careerbuilder.com	Fast-growing site affiliated with more than 100 local newspapers around the country
USA Jobs	www.usajobs.opm.gov	The official job search site for the U.S. government, featuring everything from economists to astronauts to border patrol agents
IMDiversity	www.imdiversity.com	Good resource on diversity in the workplace, with job postings from companies that have made a special commitment to promoting diversity in their workforces
Dice.com	www.dice.com	One of the best sites for high-technology jobs
Net-Temps	www.net-temps.com	Popular site for contractors and freelancers looking for short-term assignments
Internship Programs.com	www.internships.wetfeet.com	Posts listings from companies looking for interns in a wide variety of professions
SimplyHired.com Indeed.com	www.simplyhired.com www.indeed.com	Specialized search engines that look for job postings on hundreds of websites worldwide; find many postings that aren't listed on "job board" sites such as Monster.com

*Note: This list represents only a small fraction of the hundreds of job-posting sites and other resources available online; be sure to check with your college's career center for the latest information.

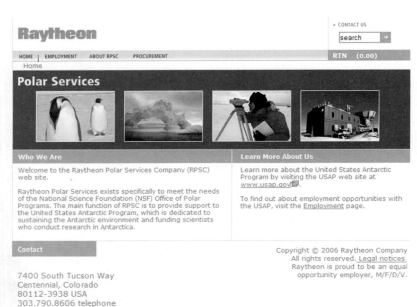

Are you willing to go to the ends of the earth to pursue your career? Raytheon Polar Services, which staffs U.S. research bases in Antarctica, might be the company for you. No matter what your interests, be creative in your job search and look for fascinating challenges such as this.

Networking   **Networking** is the process of making informal connections with a broad sphere of mutually beneficial business contacts. According to one recent survey, networking is the most common way that employees find jobs.[5] Networking takes place wherever and whenever people communicate: at industry functions, at social gatherings, at sports events and recreational activities, in online newsgroups, at alumni reunions, and so on. Increasingly, business-oriented social networking sites such as LinkedIn (www.linkedin.com) and Ryze (www.ryze.com) have become important ways to get connected with job openings. Some of these sites are even linked to job posting websites, and when you apply for a job at a particular company, you can see a list of people in your network who work at that company.

To find helpful networks, both the in-person and online variety, read news sites, blogs, and other online sources. Participate in student business organizations and visit *trade shows* that cater to an industry you're interested in. You will learn plenty about that sector of the work-

Start thinking like a networker now; your classmates could turn out to be some of your most important business contacts.

place and rub shoulders with people who actually work in the industry.[6] Don't overlook volunteering in social, civic, and religious organizations. As a volunteer, you meet people and also demonstrate your ability to solve problems, plan projects, and so on.

Novice job seekers sometimes misunderstand networking and unknowingly commit breaches of etiquette. Networking isn't a matter of walking up to strangers at social events, handing over your résumé, and asking them to find you a job. Rather, it involves the sharing of information between people who might be able to offer mutual help at some point in the future. Think of it as an organic process in which you cultivate the possibility of finding that perfect opportunity. Networking can take time, so start early and make it part of your lifelong program of career management.

Remember that you need to contribute to the networking process, too.

To become a valued network member, you need to be able to help others in some way. You may not have any influential contacts yet, but because you're actively researching a number of industries and trends in your own job search, you probably have valuable information to share. Or you might simply be able to connect one person with another who can help. The more you network, the more valuable you become in your network—and the more valuable your network becomes to you.

Don't overlook the many resources available through your college's placement office.

Seeking Career Counseling   College placement offices offer individual counseling, credential services, job fairs, on-campus interviews, and job listings. They can give you advice on résumé-writing software and provide workshops in job search techniques, résumé preparation, interview techniques, and more.[7] You can also find job counseling online. You might begin your self-assessment, for example, with the Keirsey Temperament Sorter, an online personality test, at www.advisorteam.com. For excellent job-seeking pointers and counseling, visit college- and university-run online career centers. Major online job boards such as Monster.com also offer a variety of career planning resources.

PREPARING RÉSUMÉS

The job search process involves many forms of communication, but the centerpiece of this effort is a well-written résumé. In fact, your success in finding a job may well depend on how carefully you plan, write, and complete your résumé. Some job seekers are intimidated by the prospect of writing a résumé, but it is really just another specialized business message. Follow the three-step writing process, and it'll be easier than you think (see Figure 15.3).

Planning Your Résumé

Your résumé must be more than a simple list of the jobs you've held. It needs to tell the "story of you"—who you are, what you've accomplished, and, most importantly, what you can contribute to any organization that hires you. As with other business messages, planning a résumé means analyzing your purpose and your audience, gathering information, choosing the best medium, and organizing your content. Be prepared to craft several or perhaps many versions of your résumé. By making some simple changes in wording or organization, you'll probably be able to match your value more closely to the specific opportunities offered by particular employers.

Career fairs give companies the chance to meet potential employees—and for you to learn more about career opportunities.

FIGURE 15.3

Three-Step Writing Process for Résumés

Following the three-step writing process will help you create a successful résumé in a short time. Remember to pay particular attention to the "you" attitude and presentation quality; your résumé will probably get tossed aside if it doesn't speak to audience needs or if it contains mistakes.

Planning

Analyze the Situation
Recognize that the purpose of your résumé is to get an interview, not to get a job.

Gather Information
Research target industries and companies so that you know what they're looking for in new hires; learn about various jobs and what to expect; learn about the hiring manager, if possible.

Select the Right Medium
Start with a traditional paper résumé and develop scannable, electronic plain text, HTML, or PDF versions as needed.

Organize the Information
Choose an organizational model that highlights your strengths and downplays your shortcomings; use the chronological approach unless you have a strong reason not to.

Writing

Adapt to Your Audience
Plan your wording carefully so that you can catch a recruiter's eye within seconds; translate your education and experience into attributes that target employers find valuable.

Compose the Message
Write clearly and succinctly, using active, powerful language that is appropriate to the industries and companies you're targeting; use a professional tone in all communications, even when using e-mail.

Completing

Revise the Message
Evaluate content and review readability, then edit and rewrite for conciseness and clarity.

Produce the Message
Use effective design elements and suitable layout for a clean, professional appearance; seamlessly combine text and graphical elements.

Proofread the Message
Review for errors in layout, spelling, and mechanics; mistakes can cost you interview opportunities.

Distribute the Message
Deliver your résumé following the specific instructions of each employer or job board website.

1   2   3

When you view your résumé as a persuasive business message, it's easier to decide what should and shouldn't be in it.

Analyzing Your Purpose and Audience   A **résumé** is a structured, written summary of a person's education, employment background, and job qualifications. Recognize that your résumé is a persuasive business message intended to stimulate an employer's interest in meeting you and learning more about you. (Table 15.2 lists some of the common misconceptions about résumés.) In other words, your purpose in writing your résumé is to create interest—*not* to tell readers every little detail.[8]

Because you've already completed a good deal of research on specific companies, you should know quite a bit about the organizations you'll be applying to. But take some time now to learn what you can about the individuals who may be reading your résumé. For example, if you learned of an opportunity through your networking efforts, chances are you'll have both a contact name and some personalized advice to help fine-tune your writing. Search online using the person's name; you might find him or her mentioned in a news release, magazine article, or blog. Any bit of information can help you craft a more effective message. Even if you can't identify a specific hiring manager, try to put yourself in his or her shoes so that you can tailor your résumé to satisfy your audience's needs. Why would that person be interested in learning more about you?

By the way, if employers ask to see your "CV," they're referring to your *curriculum vitae*, the term used instead of *résumé* in some professions and in many countries outside the United States. Résumés and CVs are essentially the same, although CVs can be more detailed. If you need to adapt a U.S.-style résumé to CV format, or vice versa, see Monster.com, which offers helpful guidelines on the subject.

Gathering Pertinent Information   If you haven't been building an employment portfolio thus far, you may need to do some research on yourself at this point. Gather all the pertinent personal history you can think of, including all the specific dates, duties, and accomplishments from any previous jobs you've held. Collect every piece of relevant educational experience that adds to your qualifications—formal degrees,

Table 15.2	FALLACIES AND FACTS ABOUT RÉSUMÉS	
	Fallacies	*Facts*
	• The purpose of a résumé is to list all your skills and abilities.	• The purpose of a résumé is generate interest and an interview.
	• A good résumé will get you the job you want.	• All a résumé can do is get you in the door.
	• Your résumé will be read carefully and thoroughly.	• In most cases, your résumé needs to make a positive impression within 30 or 45 seconds; moreover, it may be screened by a computer looking for keywords first—and if it doesn't contain the right keywords, a human being may never see it.
	• The more good information you present about yourself in your résumé, the better.	• Recruiters don't need that much information about you at the initial screening stage, and they probably won't read it.
	• If you want a really good résumé, have it prepared by a résumé service.	• You have the skills needed to prepare an effective résumé, so prepare it yourself—unless the position is especially high level or specialized. Even then, you should check carefully before using a service.

skills certificates, academic awards, or scholarships. Also, gather any relevant information about personal endeavors: dates of your membership in an association, offices you may have held in a club or professional organization, any presentations you might have given to a community group. You probably won't use every piece of information you come up with, but you'll want to have it at your fingertips before you begin composing your résumé.

Selecting the Best Medium   Selecting the medium for your résumé used to be a simple matter: You typed it on paper. These days, though, your job search might involve various forms, including an uploaded Word document, a plain-text document that you paste into an online form, or a multimedia résumé that is part of your online e-portfolio. Explore all your options and choose those that (a) meet the requirements of target employers and (b) allow you to present yourself in a compelling fashion. For instance, if you're applying for a sales position, in which your personal communication skills would be a strong point, a vidcast showing you making a sales presentation (even a mock presentation) could be a strong persuader.

No matter how many different media you eventually use, it's always a good idea to prepare a basic paper résumé and keep copies on hand. You'll never know when someone might ask for it, and not all employers want to bother with electronic media when all they want to know is your basic profile. In addition, starting with a traditional paper résumé is a great way to organize your background information and identify your unique strengths.

Organizing Your Résumé Around Your Strengths   Organize your résumé to highlight several qualities employers seek: that you (1) think in terms of results, (2) know how to get things done, (3) are well rounded, (4) show signs of career progress and professional development, (5) have personal standards of excellence, (6) are flexible and willing to try new things, and (7) communicate effectively.

Although you may want to include some information in all categories, you'll naturally want to emphasize the information that does the best job of aligning your career objectives with the needs of your target employers—and that does so without distorting or misrepresenting the facts.[9] While you're pondering your strengths, you also need to consider any perceived weaknesses you may have. Do you have something in your history that might trigger an employer's red flag? Here are some common problems and quick suggestions for overcoming them:[10]

> The key to organizing a résumé is aligning your personal strengths with both the general and specific qualities that your target employers are looking for.

- **Frequent job changes.**   If you've had a number of short-term jobs of a similar nature, such as independent contracting and temporary assignments, see if you can group them under a single heading. Also, if past job positions were eliminated as a result of layoffs or mergers, find a subtle way to convey that information (if not in your résumé, then in your cover letter). Reasonable employers understand that many otherwise stable employees have been forced to job hop in recent years.

> Frequent job changes and gaps in your work history are two of the most common issues that employers may perceive as weaknesses, so plan to address these if they pertain to you.

- **Gaps in work history.**   Mention relevant experience and education you gained during employment gaps, such as volunteer or community work. If gaps are due to personal problems such as drug or alcohol abuse or mental illness, you can use a cover letter to offer honest but general explanations about your absences ("I had serious health concerns and had to take time off to fully recover").

- **Inexperience.**   Mention related volunteer work. List relevant course work and internships. If appropriate, offer hiring incentives such as "willing to work nights and weekends."

- **Overqualification.**   Tone down your résumé, focusing exclusively on the experience and skills that relate to the position.

- **Long-term employment with one company.** Itemize each position held at the firm to show career progress with increasing responsibilities.

- **Job termination for cause.** Be honest with interviewers. Show that you're a hard-working employee and counter their concerns with proof, such as recommendations and examples of completed projects.

- **Criminal record.** You don't necessarily need to disclose a criminal record or time spent incarcerated on your résumé, but you may be asked about it on a job application form. Laws regarding what employers may ask (and whether they can conduct a criminal background check) vary by state and profession, but if you are asked and the question applies to you, you must answer truthfully, or you risk being terminated later if the employer finds out. Use the interview process to explain any mitigating circumstances and to emphasize your rehabilitation and commitment to being a law-abiding, trustworthy employee.[11]

To focus attention on your strongest points, adopt the appropriate organizational approach for your résumé, based on your background and your goals.

The Chronological Résumé In a **chronological résumé**, the work experience section dominates and is placed in the most prominent slot, immediately after your name and address and optional objective. Develop this section by listing your jobs sequentially in reverse order, beginning with the most recent position. Under each listing, describe your responsibilities and accomplishments, giving the most space to the most recent and most relevant positions. If you're just graduating from college and have limited professional experience, you can vary this chronological approach by putting your educational qualifications before your experience, thereby focusing attention on your academic credentials.

The chronological résumé is the most common approach, but it might not be right for you at a particular stage in your career.

The chronological approach is the most common way to organize a résumé, and many employers prefer it. This approach has three key advantages: (1) Employers are familiar with it and can easily find information, (2) it highlights growth and career progression, and (3) it highlights employment continuity and stability.[12] As vice president with Korn/Ferry International, Robert Nesbit speaks for many hiring managers and recruiters when he says, "Unless you have a really compelling reason, don't use any but the standard chronological format. Your résumé should not read like a treasure map, full of minute clues to the whereabouts of your jobs and experience. I want to be able to grasp quickly where a candidate has worked, how long, and in what capacities."[13]

The chronological approach is especially appropriate if you have a strong employment history and are aiming for a job that builds on your current career path (see Figures 15.4 and 15.5).

The functional résumé is often used by people with little employment history or gaps in their work history, but some employers suspect that people who use this approach are trying to hide weaknesses in their backgrounds.

The Functional Résumé A **functional résumé**, sometimes called a *skills résumé*, emphasizes your skills and capabilities while identifying employers and academic experience in subordinate sections. This pattern stresses individual areas of competence, so it's useful for people who are just entering the job market, who want to redirect their careers, or who have little continuous career-related experience. The functional approach also has three advantages: (1) Without having to read through job descriptions, employers can see what you can do for them; (2) you can emphasize earlier job experience; and (3) you can de-emphasize any lengthy unemployment or lack of career progress. However, you should be aware that because the functional résumé can obscure your work history, many employment professionals are suspicious of it—and some assume that candidates who use it are trying to hide something. In fact, Monster.com lists the functional résumé as one of employers' "Top 10 Pet Peeves."[14] If you don't have a strong, uninterrupted history of relevant work, the combination résumé might be a better choice.

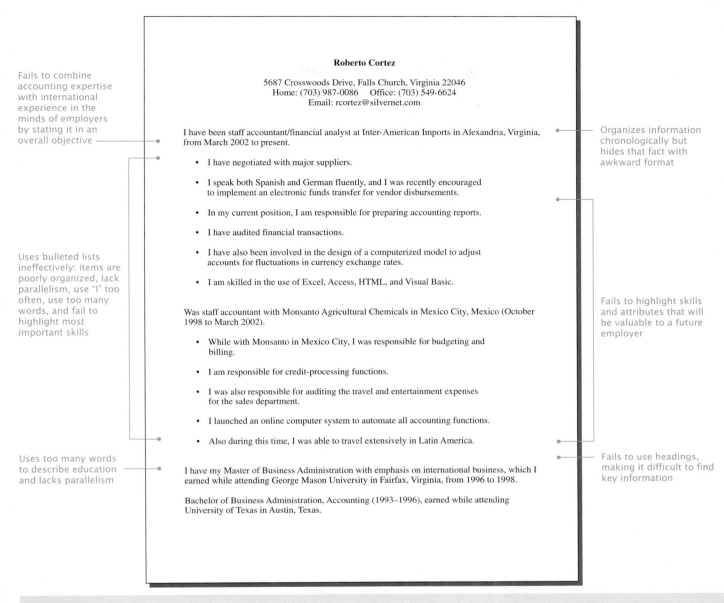

Roberto Cortez

5687 Crosswoods Drive, Falls Church, Virginia 22046
Home: (703) 987-0086   Office: (703) 549-6624
Email: rcortez@silvernet.com

I have been staff accountant/financial analyst at Inter-American Imports in Alexandria, Virginia, from March 2002 to present.

- I have negotiated with major suppliers.

- I speak both Spanish and German fluently, and I was recently encouraged to implement an electronic funds transfer for vendor disbursements.

- In my current position, I am responsible for preparing accounting reports.

- I have audited financial transactions.

- I have also been involved in the design of a computerized model to adjust accounts for fluctuations in currency exchange rates.

- I am skilled in the use of Excel, Access, HTML, and Visual Basic.

Was staff accountant with Monsanto Agricultural Chemicals in Mexico City, Mexico (October 1998 to March 2002).

- While with Monsanto in Mexico City, I was responsible for budgeting and billing.

- I am responsible for credit-processing functions.

- I was also responsible for auditing the travel and entertainment expenses for the sales department.

- I launched an online computer system to automate all accounting functions.

- Also during this time, I was able to travel extensively in Latin America.

I have my Master of Business Administration with emphasis on international business, which I earned while attending George Mason University in Fairfax, Virginia, from 1996 to 1998.

Bachelor of Business Administration, Accounting (1993–1996), earned while attending University of Texas in Austin, Texas.

Annotations (left side):

Fails to combine accounting expertise with international experience in the minds of employers by stating it in an overall objective

Uses bulleted lists ineffectively: items are poorly organized, lack parallelism, use "I" too often, use too many words, and fail to highlight most important skills

Uses too many words to describe education and lacks parallelism

Annotations (right side):

Organizes information chronologically but hides that fact with awkward format

Fails to highlight skills and attributes that will be valuable to a future employer

Fails to use headings, making it difficult to find key information

FIGURE 15.4
Ineffective Chronological Résumé
This chronological résumé exhibits a wide range of problems. The language is self-centered and unprofessional, and the organization forces the reader to dig out essential details—and today's recruiters don't have the time or the patience for that. Compare this with the improved version in Figure 15.5.

The Combination Résumé A **combination résumé** includes the best features of the chronological and functional approaches (see Figure 15.6 on page 557). Nevertheless, it is not commonly used, and it has two major disadvantages: (1) It tends to be longer than a chronological résumé, and (2) it can be repetitious if you have to list your accomplishments and skills in both the functional section and the chronological job descriptions.[15]

As you look at a number of sample résumés, you'll probably notice variations on the three basic formats presented here. Study these other options; if you find one that seems like the best fit for your unique situation, by all means use it—but always apply the principles of effective business communication you've learned in this course.

If you don't have a lot of work history, consider a combination résumé to highlight your skills while still providing a chronological history of your employment.

FIGURE 15.5 Effective Chronological Résumé
Compared to the version in Figure 15.4, this version does a much better job of presenting the candidate's ability to contribute to a new employer. Notice in particular how easy it is to scan through this résumé to find sections of interest.

Combines accounting expertise with international experience in a clearly stated objective

Makes each description concise, easy to read, and informative; avoids "I" throughout

Makes special skills easy to find (note that multiple bullets in the last line could cause problems with a scannable résumé format; see page 566)

ROBERTO CORTEZ
5687 Crosswoods Drive
Falls Church, Virginia 22046
Home: (703) 987-0086   Office: (703) 549-6624
E-mail: RCortez@silvernet.com

OBJECTIVE

Accounting management position requiring hands-on knowledge of international finance

EXPERIENCE

March 2002 to present — **Staff Accountant/Financial Analyst,** Inter-American Imports (Alexandria, Virginia)
- Prepare accounting reports for wholesale giftware importer ($15 million annual sales)
- Audit financial transactions with suppliers in 12 Latin American countries
- Created a computerized model to adjust accounts for fluctuations in currency exchange rates
- Negotiated joint-venture agreements with major suppliers in Mexico and Colombia
- Implemented electronic funds transfer for vendor disbursements, improving cash flow and eliminating payables clerk position

October 1998 to March 2002 — **Staff Accountant,** Monsanto Agricultural Chemicals (Mexico City, Mexico)
- Handled budgeting, billing, and credit-processing functions for the Mexico City branch
- Audited travel & entertainment expenses for Monsanto's 30-member Latin American sales force
- Assisted in launching an online system to automate all accounting functions, improving reporting accuracy by 65%

EDUCATION

1996 to 1998 — Master of Business Administration with emphasis in international business, George Mason University, Fairfax, Virginia

1993 to 1996 — Bachelor of Business Administration, Accounting, University of Texas, Austin

INTERCULTURAL AND TECHNICAL SKILLS

- Fluent in Spanish and German
- Traveled extensively in Latin America
- Excel • Access • HTML • Visual Basic

Translates experience into general accomplishments that will appeal to any company that employs international accountants

Uses active language to describe past and present responsibilities and accomplishments

Makes good use of headings so that major content sections are easy to identify

Planning

Analyze the Situation
Decide on the best way to combine finance and international experience.

Gather Information
Research target positions to identify key employer needs.

Select the Right Medium
Start with a traditional paper résumé and develop scannable or plain-text versions as needed.

Organize the Information
Choose the chronological format since it fits this strong employment history perfectly.

Writing

Adapt to Your Audience
Translate specific experience into general qualifications that all international companies will find valuable.

Compose the Message
Write clearly and succinctly, using active, powerful language that is appropriate to the financial management profession.

Completing

Revise the Message
Evaluate your content and review readability, clarity, and accuracy.

Produce the Message
Use effective design elements and suitable layout for a clean, professional appearance.

Proofread the Message
Review for errors in layout, spelling, and mechanics.

Distribute the Message
Deliver your résumé and other employment messages following the specific instructions of each employer or job board website.

1   2   3

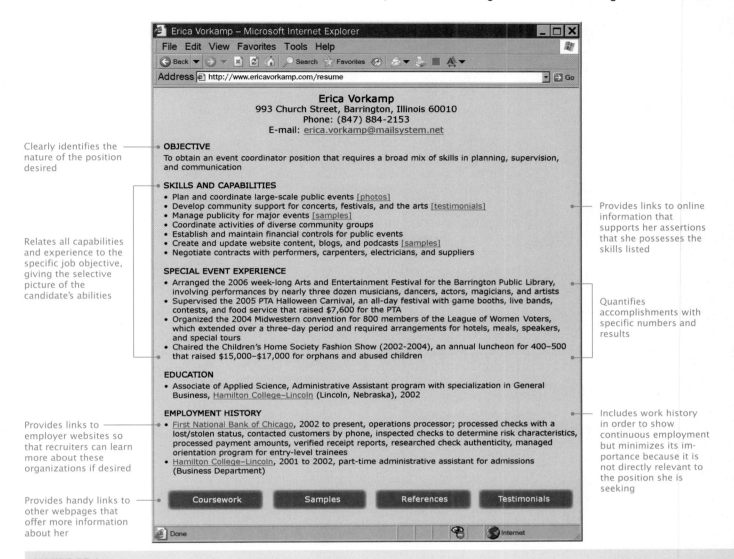

Clearly identifies the nature of the position desired

Relates all capabilities and experience to the specific job objective, giving the selective picture of the candidate's abilities

Provides links to employer websites so that recruiters can learn more about these organizations if desired

Provides handy links to other webpages that offer more information about her

Provides links to online information that supports her assertions that she possesses the skills listed

Quantifies accomplishments with specific numbers and results

Includes work history in order to show continuous employment but minimizes its importance because it is not directly relevant to the position she is seeking

FIGURE 15.6
Combination Résumé
With her limited work experience in her field of interest, Erica Vorkamp opted for a combination résumé to highlight her skills. Her employment history is complete and easy to find, but it isn't featured to the same degree as the other elements. Also, because she created an HTML version and posted it on her personal website, she is able to provide instant links to other information, such as samples of her work and testimonials from people who have worked with her in the past.

Writing Your Résumé

Your résumé is one of the most important documents you will ever write. Even so, you needn't work yourself into a panic; all the advice you need to write effective résumés is presented in this chapter. Follow the three-step process and help ensure success by remembering four key points: First, treat your résumé with the respect it deserves. Until you're able to meet with employers in person, you *are* your résumé, and a single mistake or oversight can cost you interview opportunities. Second, give yourself plenty of time. Don't put off preparing your résumé until the last second and then try to write it in one sitting. Third, learn from good models. You can find thousands of sample résumés online at college websites and job sites such as Monster.com. Fourth, don't get frustrated by the conflicting advice you read about

Until employers meet you in person, your résumé (and perhaps your cover letter) is usually the only information they have about you, so make sure that information is clear and compelling.

résumés; they are more art than science. Consider the alternatives and choose the approach that makes the most sense to you, given everything you know about successful business communication.

You can take some comfort in the fact that many people, even accomplished writers, find it difficult to write their own résumés. Part of this problem stems from the challenge of writing a compelling message in limited space, and part from the awkward feeling of talking about oneself to strangers. You might find it helpful to distance yourself emotionally from the task; you can even pretend you're writing about someone else. You might also find a classmate or friend who's writing a résumé and swap projects for a while. By working on each other's résumés, you might be able to speed up the process for both of you.

Keeping Your Résumé Honest   At some point in the writing process, you're sure to run into the question of honesty. A claim may be clearly wrong ("So what if I did not get those last two credits—I got the same education as people who did graduate, so it's okay to say that I graduated, too"). Or a rationalization may be more subtle ("Organizing snacks for the company picnic—that qualifies as 'project management'"). Either way, the information is dishonest.

Somehow, the idea that "everybody lies on their résumés" has crept into popular consciousness, and résumé fraud has reached epidemic proportions. As many as half of the résumés now sent to employers contain false information. And we're not just talking about the simple fudging of facts here and there. Dishonest applicants are getting bolder all the time—buying fake diplomas online, paying computer hackers to insert their names into prestigious universities' graduation records, and signing up for services that offer phony employment verification.[16]

> Applicants with integrity know they don't need to lie on their résumés to catch the attention of potential employers.

Applicants with integrity know they don't need to stoop to lying to compete in the job market. If you are tempted to stretch the truth, bear in mind that professional recruiters have seen every trick in the book, and employers who are fed up with the dishonesty are getting more aggressive at uncovering the truth. Roughly 80 percent now contact references and conduct criminal background checks when allowed, and many do credit checks when the job involves financial responsibility.[17] In a recent survey in Great Britain, 25 percent of employers reported withdrawing job offers after discovering that applicants had lied on their résumés.[18] And even if you were to get past these filters, you'd probably be exposed on the job when you couldn't live up to your own résumé. From college coaches to CEOs, résumé fabrications have been known to catch up to people many years into their careers, with embarrassing consequences.[19]

If you're not sure whether to include something in your résumé, ask yourself this: Would you be willing to say the same thing to an interviewer in person? If you wouldn't be comfortable saying it in person, don't say it in your résumé. Keep your résumé honest so that it represents who you really are and leads you toward jobs that are truly right for you.

> One of the biggest challenges in writing a résumé is to make your unique qualities apparent to readers *quickly*; they won't search through details if you don't look like an appealing candidate.

Adapting Your Résumé to Your Audience   Your résumé needs to make a positive impression in a matter of seconds, so be sure to adopt a "you" attitude and think about your résumé from the employer's perspective. Ask yourself: What key qualifications will this employer be looking for? Which of these qualifications are your greatest strengths? What quality would set you apart from other candidates in the eyes of a potential employer? What are three or four of your greatest accomplishments, and what has resulted from these accomplishments? No matter which format you use or what information you include, the single most important concept to keep in mind as you write is to translate your past accomplishments into perceived future potential. In other words, employers are certainly interested in what you've done in the past, but they're more interested in what you can do for them in the future. If necessary, customize your résumé for individual companies, too.

You may also need to translate your skills and experiences into the terminology of the hiring organization. For instance, military experience can develop a number of skills that are valuable in business, but military terminology can sound like a foreign language to people who aren't familiar with it. Isolate the important general concepts and present them in common business language. Similarly, educational achievements in other countries might not align with U.S. definitions of high schools, community colleges, technical and trade schools, and universities. If necessary, include a brief statement explaining how your degree or certificate relates to U.S. expectations—or how your U.S. degree relates to expectations in other countries, if you're applying for work abroad.

Regardless of your background, it's up to you to combine your experiences into a straightforward message that communicates what you can do for your potential employer.[20] Think in terms of an image or a theme you'd like to project. Are you academically gifted? A strong leader? A well-rounded person? A creative genius? A technical wizard? By knowing yourself and your audience, you'll focus successfully on the strengths needed by potential employers.

Although your résumé is a highly factual document, it should still tell the "story of you," giving readers a clear picture of the sort of employee you are.

Composing Your Résumé   To save readers time and to state your information as forcefully as possible, write your résumé using a simple and direct style. (You may need to modify your approach for other countries.) Use short, crisp phrases instead of whole sentences and focus on what your reader needs to know. Avoid using the word *I*, which can sound self-involved and repetitive by the time you identify all your skills and accomplishments. Instead, start your phrases with strong action verbs such as these:[21]

Draft your résumé using short, crisp phrases built around strong verbs and nouns.

accomplished	coordinated	initiated	participated	set up
achieved	created	installed	performed	simplified
administered	demonstrated	introduced	planned	sparked
approved	developed	investigated	presented	streamlined
arranged	directed	joined	proposed	strengthened
assisted	established	launched	raised	succeeded
assumed	explored	maintained	recommended	supervised
budgeted	forecast	managed	reduced	systematized
chaired	generated	motivated	reorganized	targeted
changed	identified	operated	resolved	trained
compiled	implemented	organized	saved	transformed
completed	improved	oversaw	served	upgraded

For instance, you might say, "Created a campus organization for students interested in entrepreneurship" or "Managed a fast-food restaurant and four employees." Whenever you can, quantify the results so that your claims don't come across as empty puffery. Don't just say you're a team player or detail oriented—show who you are by offering concrete proof.[22] Here are some examples of phrasing accomplishments using active statements that show results:

Avoid Weak Statements	**Use Active Statements That Show Results**
Responsible for developing a new filing system	Developed a new filing system that reduced paperwork by 50 percent
I was in charge of customer complaints and all ordering problems	Handled all customer complaints and resolved all product order discrepancies
I won a trip to Europe for opening the most new customer accounts in my department	Generated the highest number of new customer accounts in my department
Member of special campus task force to resolve student problems with existing cafeteria assignments	Assisted in implementing new campus dining program that balances student wishes with cafeteria capacity

In addition to presenting your accomplishments effectively, think carefully about the way you will craft the major sections of a traditional résumé: your name and contact information, career objective or summary of qualifications, educational credentials, employment history, activities and achievements, and relevant personal data.

Be sure to provide complete and accurate contact information; mistakes in this section of the résumé are surprisingly common.

Name and Contact Information The first thing an employer needs to know is who you are and where you can be reached. Your name and contact information constitute the heading of your résumé, so include the following:

- Name

- Physical address (both permanent and temporary, if you're likely to move during the job search process; however, if you're posting a résumé in an unsecured location online, leave off your physical address for security purposes)

- E-mail address

- Phone number(s)

- The URL of your personal webpage or e-portfolio (if you have one)

Be sure that everything in your résumé heading is well organized and clearly laid out on the page.

If you don't already have one, get a professional-sounding e-mail address for business correspondence (such as firstname.lastname@something.com).

If the only e-mail address you have is through your current employer, get a free personal e-mail address from one of the many services that offer them. It's not fair to your current employer to use company resources for a job search; moreover, it sends a bad signal to potential employers. Also, if your personal e-mail address is anything like precious.princess@something.com or PsychoDawg@something.com, get a new e-mail address for your business correspondence.

Career Objective or Summary of Qualifications Experts disagree about the need to state a career objective on your résumé. Some argue that your objective is obvious from your qualifications, so stating your objective seems redundant. Some also maintain that such a statement labels you as being interested in only one thing and thus limits your possibilities as a candidate (especially if you want to be considered for a variety of openings). Other experts argue that employers will try to categorize you anyway, so you might as well make sure they attach the right label. They maintain that stating your objective up front gives employers an immediate idea of what you're all about.

Whether you choose to open with a career objective or a summary of qualifications, remember that the important point is to generate interest immediately.

Remember, your goal is to generate interest immediately. Consider the situation and the qualities the employer is looking for. If a stated objective will help you look like the perfect fit, then you should definitely consider adding it. Consider the following objectives:

> A software sales position in a growing company requiring international experience
>
> Advertising assistant with multimedia emphasis requiring strong customer-contact skills

With some careful writing, you can phrase your career objective in terms that highlight the reader's needs.

Both these objectives have an important aspect: Even though they are stating "your" objective, they are really about the employer's needs. Avoid such self-absorbed (but all too common) statements such as "A fulfilling position that provides ample opportunity for career growth and personal satisfaction." Writers who include such statements have completely forgotten about audience focus and the "you" attitude.

A good alternative to a simple statement of career objectives is to highlight your strongest points in a brief *summary of qualifications*. A good summary of qualifications not only identifies the type of job you're interested in but also gives employers a compelling reason to consider you. Use short, direct phrases that highlight what you can bring to a new employer, as in this example:

> **Summary of qualifications:** Ten years of experience in commission selling, consistently meeting or exceeding sales goals through creative lead generation, effective closing techniques, and solid customer service.

If you include either a career objective or a summary of qualifications, make it strong, concise, and convincing.

Education If you're still in school, education is probably your strongest selling point. Present your educational background in depth, choosing facts that support your "theme." Give this section a heading such as "Education," "Technical Training," or "Academic Preparation," as appropriate. Then, starting with the most recent, list the name and location of each school you have attended, along with the term of your enrollment (in months and years), your major and minor fields of study, significant skills and abilities you've developed in your course work, and the degrees or certificates you've earned. If you're still working toward a degree, include in parentheses the expected date of completion. Showcase your qualifications by listing courses that have directly equipped you for the job you are seeking and indicate any scholarships, awards, or academic honors you've received.

The education section also includes off-campus training sponsored by business or government. Include any relevant seminars or workshops you've attended, as well as the certificates or other documents you've received. Mention high school or military training only if the associated achievements are pertinent to your career goals.

Whether you list your grade-point average depends on the job you want and the quality of your grades. If you choose to show a grade-point average, be sure to mention the scale, especially if a five-point scale is used instead of a four-point scale. If you don't show your GPA on your résumé—and there's no rule saying you have to—be prepared to answer questions about it during the interview process because many employers will assume that your GPA is not spectacular if you didn't show it on your résumé. If your grades are better within your major than in other courses, you can also list your GPA as "Major GPA" and include only those courses within your major. (This way, that D you received in scuba diving or Sanskrit doesn't need to hurt your accounting career.)

Education is usually given less emphasis in a résumé after you've worked in your chosen field for a year or more. If work experience is your strongest qualification, save the section on education for later in the résumé and provide less detail.

Work Experience, Skills, and Accomplishments Like the education section, the work experience section should focus on your overall theme. Align your past with the employer's future. Call attention to the skills you've developed on the job and to your ability to handle increasing responsibility.

List your jobs (including military service) in reverse chronological order and include part-time, summer, or intern positions, even if they're unrelated to your current career objective. Employers will see that you have the ability to get and hold a job. If you have worked your way through school and contributed significantly to your education expenses, say so. Many employers interpret this accomplishment as a sign of character and the ability to manage your time.

In each listing, include the name and location of the employer. If readers are unlikely to recognize the organization, briefly describe what it does. When you want to keep the name of your current employer confidential, you can identify the firm by industry only ("a large video-game developer"). Alternatively, you might use the

---

Margin notes:

Your education is likely to be one of your strongest selling points, so think carefully about how you will present it.

When you describe past job responsibilities, be sure to relate them to the needs of potential employers; identify the skills and knowledge from these previous jobs that you can apply to a future job.

firm's name and request confidentiality in your application letter or include an under-lined note at the top or bottom of your résumé: "Résumé submitted in confidence."

Before or after each job listing, state your functional title, such as "records clerk" or "salesperson." Don't try to make your role seem more important by glamorizing your job title, functions, or achievements. List the years you worked in the job and use the phrase "to present" to denote current employment. If a job was part-time, indicate so.

Whenever you can, quantify your accomplishments in numeric terms: sales increases, customer satisfaction scores, measured productivity, and so on.

Devote the most space to the jobs that are related to your target position. If you were personally responsible for significant achievements, be sure to mention it ("Devised a new collection system that accelerated payment of overdue receivables"). Facts about your skills and accomplishments are the most important information you can give a prospective employer, so quantify them whenever possible:

Designed a new ad that increased sales by 9 percent

Raised $2,500 in 15 days for cancer research

One helpful exercise is to write a 30-second "commercial" for each major skill you want to highlight. The commercial should offer proof that you really do possess the skill. For your résumé, distill the commercials down to brief phrases; you can use the more detailed proof statements in cover letters and as answers to interview questions.[23]

You may also include information describing other aspects of your background that pertain to your career objective, such as fluency in another language. If you have an array of special skills, group them together and include them near your education or work experience section. You might categorize such additional information as "Special Skills," "Work-Related Skills," "Other Experience," "Language Skills," or "Computer Skills." If samples of your work might increase your chances of getting the job, insert a line at the end of your résumé offering to supply them on request or indicate that they're available in your e-portfolio.

Don't overlook personal accomplishments that indicate special skills or qualities but make sure they are relevant to the jobs you're seeking.

Activities and Achievements Many employers look beyond your formal employment to assess your total character and personality. Your activities and achievements out-side work speak volumes about who you are and what you value. Use this section to list volunteer activities that demonstrate important abilities such as leadership, orga-nization, teamwork, and cooperation. Emphasize career-related activities such as "member of the Student Marketing Association." List skills you learned in these activ-ities and explain how these skills are related to your target job. Include speaking, writing, or tutoring experience; participation in athletics or creative projects; fundraising or community-service activities; and offices held in academic or profes-sional organizations. (However, mention of political or religious organizations may be a red flag to someone with differing views, so use your judgment.)

Note any relevant awards you've received. Again, quantify your achievements whenever possible. Instead of saying that you addressed various student groups, state how many and the approximate audience sizes. If your activities have been extensive, you may want to group them into divisions such as "College Activities," "Community Service," "Professional Associations," "Seminars and Workshops," and "Speaking Activities."

Personal Data The question of what personal data to provide is a common source of confusion with résumés. Most experts advise you to skip personal interests unless including them enhances the employer's understanding of why you would be the best candidate for the job.[24] Just make sure that any personal interests and accomplish-ments relate to the employer's business, culture, or customers. For example, your achievements as an amateur artist could appeal to an advertising agency, even if you're applying for a technical or business position, because they show an appreciation for the creative process.

Some information is best excluded from your résumé. Civil rights laws prohibit employers from discriminating on the basis of gender, marital or family status, age (although only persons aged 40 to 70 are protected), race, religion, national origin, and physical or mental disability. Exclude any items that could encourage discrimination, even subconsciously. Experts also recommend excluding salary information, reasons for leaving jobs, names of previous supervisors, your Social Security number, and other identification codes. Save these items for the interview, and then offer them only if the employer specifically requests them.

The availability of references is usually assumed, so you don't necessarily need to put "References available upon request" at the end of your résumé. Whether you include this line or not, be sure to have a list of several references available when you begin applying for jobs. You will probably be asked for it at some point in the selection process. Prepare your reference sheet with your name and contact information at the top. For a finished look, use the same design and layout you use at the top of your résumé. Then list three or four people who have agreed to serve as references. (Don't list anyone who hasn't agreed to be listed.) Include each person's name, job title, organization, address, telephone number, and e-mail address (if the reference prefers to be contacted by e-mail).

Completing Your Résumé

When you're creating your résumé, the last step in the three-step writing process is no less important than the other two. As with any other business message, you need to revise your résumé, produce it in an appropriate form, and proofread it for any errors before distributing it to your target employers.

As a general guideline, if you have less than 10 years of professional experience, try to keep your résumé to one page. If you have more experience and are applying for a higher-level position, you may need to prepare a somewhat longer résumé. For highly technical positions, longer résumés are often the norm as well because the qualifications for these jobs can require more space to describe.

Revising Your Résumé   Ask professional recruiters to list the most common mistakes they see on résumés, and you'll hear the same things over and over again. Keep your résumé out of the recycling bin by avoiding these flaws:

Avoid the common errors that will get your résumé excluded from consideration.

- **Too long.** The résumé is not concise, relevant, and to the point.
- **Too short or sketchy.** The résumé does not give enough information for a proper evaluation of the applicant.
- **Hard to read.** The résumé lacks enough white space and devices such as indentions and boldfacing to make the reader's job easier.
- **Wordy.** Descriptions are verbose, using numerous words to describe simple concepts.
- **Too slick.** The résumé appears to have been written by someone other than the applicant, which raises the question of whether the qualifications have been exaggerated.
- **Amateurish.** The résumé includes the wrong information or presents it awkwardly, which indicates that the applicant has little understanding of the business world or of a particular industry.
- **Poorly produced.** The print is faint and difficult to read or the paper is cheap and inappropriate.

- **Misspelled and ungrammatical throughout.** The document contains spelling and grammar mistakes which indicate that the candidate lacks communication skills and attention to quality.

- **Boastful.** The overconfident tone makes the reader wonder whether the applicant's self-evaluation is realistic.

- **Generic.** Customize your résumé to fit specific industries, companies, and positions.

- **Gimmicky.** The words, structure, decoration, or material used in the résumé depart so far from the usual as to make the résumé ineffective.

Effective résumé designs are simple, clean, and professional—not gaudy, clever, or cute.

Producing Your Résumé   Good design is a must, and it's not hard to achieve. As you can see in Figures 15.5 and 15.6, good designs feature simplicity, order, plenty of white space, and straightforward typefaces, such as Times Roman or Arial. (Keep in mind that many of the fonts on your computer are not appropriate for a résumé.) Make your subheadings easy to find and easy to read, placing them either above each section or in the left margin. Use lists and leave plenty of white space. Color is not necessary by any means, but if you add color, make it subtle and sophisticated, such as in a thin horizontal line under your name and address. If any part of the design "jumps out at you," tone it down. To see how jarring and unprofessional a truly poor design looks to an employer, compare Figures 15.5 and 15.6 with the "creative" design in Figure 15.7. An amateurish design could end your chances of getting an interview. As one experienced recruiter put it recently, "At our office, these résumés are rejected without even being read."[25]

Start with a traditional printed résumé but realize that you may need to create several other versions during your job search.

Depending on the companies you apply to, you might want to produce your résumé in as many as six forms (all are explained in the following sections):

- Printed traditional résumé

- Printed scannable résumé

- Electronic plain-text file

- Microsoft Word file

- HTML format

- PDF file

Most of these versions are easy to create, as you'll see in the following sections.

In addition to these six common options, you might consider creating a résumé slide show in Microsoft PowerPoint. Two key advantages of a PowerPoint résumé are the flexibility and multimedia capabilities. For instance, you can present a menu of choices on the opening screen and allow viewers to click through to such items as a brief biography, photos that document important accomplishments (such as an event you planned or a project you created for a class), or screen shots of websites that you were involved in creating. Be creative—and make sure you don't simply re-create your résumé in PowerPoint; doing so would result in a rather dull presentation that is actually harder to read than a regular printed version.

Strive for a clean, classy look in your printed résumé, using professional-grade paper and a clean, high-quality printer.

Printing a Traditional Résumé The traditional paper résumé still has a place in this world of electronic job searches, if only to have a few copies ready whenever one of your networking contacts asks for one. Avoid basic, low-cost white bond paper intended for general office use and gimmicky papers with borders and backgrounds. Choose a heavier, higher-quality paper designed specifically for résumés and other important documents. White or slightly off-white is the best color choice. This paper is more expensive than general office paper, but you don't need much, and it's a worthwhile investment.

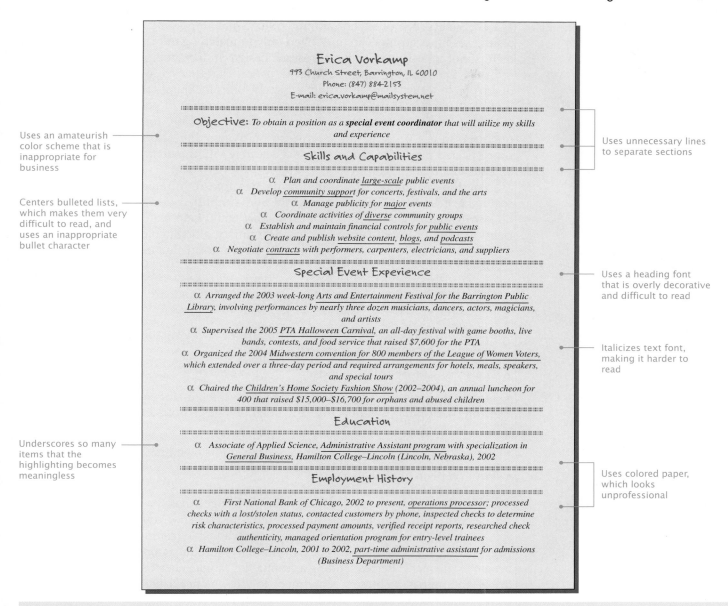

FIGURE 15.7
Ineffective Résumé Design
This truly jarring résumé exhibits numerous flaws, including distracting lines, bad font choices, and unprofessional colors. The well-written information is completely lost in all the visual "noise."

When you're ready to print your résumé, use a well-maintained, quality printer. Don't tolerate any streaks, stray lines, or poor print quality. You wouldn't walk into an interview looking messy, so make sure your résumé doesn't look that way, either.

Printing a Scannable Résumé To cope with the flood of unsolicited paper résumés in recent years, many companies now optically scan incoming résumés into a database that hiring managers can search for attractive candidates. Whether they use simpler keyword matching or sophisticated linguistic analysis, these systems display lists of possible candidates, each with a percentage score indicating how closely the résumé reflects a given position's requirements.[26] Nearly all large companies now use these systems, as do many midsized companies and even some small firms.[27]

Converting your résumé to scannable format is easy—and extremely important.

The emergence of such scanning systems has important implications for your résumé. First, computers are interested only in matching information to search parameters, not in artistic attempts at résumé design. In fact, complex designs can cause errors in the scanning process. Second, *optical character recognition (OCR)* software doesn't technically "read" anything; it merely looks for shapes that match stored profiles of characters. If the OCR software can't make sense of your fancy fonts or creative page layout, it will enter gibberish into the database (for instance, your name might go in as "W<$..3r ?00!#" instead of "Walter Jones"). Third, even the most sophisticated databases cannot conduct a search with the nuance and intuition of an experienced human recruiter.

For job searchers, this situation creates two requirements for a successful scannable résumé: (1) Use a plain font and simplified design and (2) compile a **keyword summary** that lists all the terms that could help match your résumé to the right openings. Other than the keyword summary, a scannable résumé contains the same information as your traditional résumé but is formatted to be OCR friendly (see Figure 15.8):[28]

- Use a clean sans serif font such as Optima or Arial and size it between 10 and 14 points.

- Make sure that characters do not touch one another (whether numbers, letters, or symbols—including the slash [/]).

- Don't use side-by-side columns.

- Don't use ampersands (&), percent signs (%), foreign-language characters (such as é and ö), or bullet symbols (use a hyphen or a dash, not a lowercase *o*, in place of a bullet symbol).

- Put each phone number and e-mail address on its own line.

- Print on plain white paper.

Your scannable résumé will probably be longer than your traditional résumé because you can't compress text into columns and because you need plenty of white space between headings and sections. If your scannable résumé runs more than one page, make sure your name appears on every subsequent page (in case the pages become separated). Before sending a scannable résumé, check the company's website or call the human resources department to see whether it has any specific requirements other than those discussed here.

Think carefully about the keywords you include in your scannable résumé; they need to appeal to recruiters and reflect your qualities accurately.

When adding a keyword summary (see Figure 15.8) to your résumé, keep your audience in mind. Employers generally search for nouns (because verbs tend to be generic rather than specific to a particular position or skill), so make your keywords nouns as well. Use abbreviations sparingly and only when they are well known and unambiguous, such as *MBA*. List 20 to 30 words and phrases that define your skills, experience, education, and professional affiliations as they relate to your target position. (Review job descriptions to find words most relevant to a given position.) Place this list right after your name and address.

If you're tempted to toss in impressive keywords that don't really apply to you, don't. Increasingly sophisticated résumé analysis systems can now detect whether your keywords truly relate to the job descriptions and other information on your résumé. If a system suspects that you've padded your keyword list, it could move you to the bottom of the ranking or delete your résumé.[29]

A plain-text version of your résumé is simply a computer file without any of the formatting that you typically apply using a word processor.

Creating a Plain-Text File of Your Résumé An increasingly common way to get your information into an employer's database is by entering a **plain-text version** (sometimes referred to as an *ASCII text version*) of your résumé into an online form. This approach has the same goal as a scannable résumé, but it's faster, easier, and less

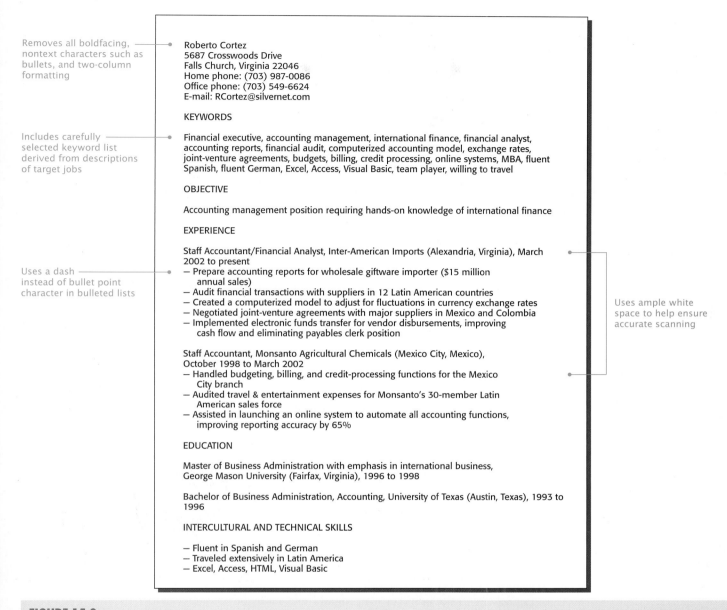

Removes all boldfacing, nontext characters such as bullets, and two-column formatting

Includes carefully selected keyword list derived from descriptions of target jobs

Uses a dash instead of bullet point character in bulleted lists

Uses ample white space to help ensure accurate scanning

Roberto Cortez
5687 Crosswoods Drive
Falls Church, Virginia 22046
Home phone: (703) 987-0086
Office phone: (703) 549-6624
E-mail: RCortez@silvernet.com

KEYWORDS

Financial executive, accounting management, international finance, financial analyst, accounting reports, financial audit, computerized accounting model, exchange rates, joint-venture agreements, budgets, billing, credit processing, online systems, MBA, fluent Spanish, fluent German, Excel, Access, Visual Basic, team player, willing to travel

OBJECTIVE

Accounting management position requiring hands-on knowledge of international finance

EXPERIENCE

Staff Accountant/Financial Analyst, Inter-American Imports (Alexandria, Virginia), March 2002 to present
— Prepare accounting reports for wholesale giftware importer ($15 million annual sales)
— Audit financial transactions with suppliers in 12 Latin American countries
— Created a computerized model to adjust for fluctuations in currency exchange rates
— Negotiated joint-venture agreements with major suppliers in Mexico and Colombia
— Implemented electronic funds transfer for vendor disbursements, improving cash flow and eliminating payables clerk position

Staff Accountant, Monsanto Agricultural Chemicals (Mexico City, Mexico), October 1998 to March 2002
— Handled budgeting, billing, and credit-processing functions for the Mexico City branch
— Audited travel & entertainment expenses for Monsanto's 30-member Latin American sales force
— Assisted in launching an online system to automate all accounting functions, improving reporting accuracy by 65%

EDUCATION

Master of Business Administration with emphasis in international business, George Mason University (Fairfax, Virginia), 1996 to 1998

Bachelor of Business Administration, Accounting, University of Texas (Austin, Texas), 1993 to 1996

INTERCULTURAL AND TECHNICAL SKILLS

— Fluent in Spanish and German
— Traveled extensively in Latin America
— Excel, Access, HTML, Visual Basic

FIGURE 15.8
Scannable Résumé
This version of the chronological résumé from Figure 15.5 shows the changes necessary for it to be successfully scanned. Notice that it doesn't have any special characters or design elements that are likely to confuse the scanning software.

prone to errors than the scanning process. If you have the option of mailing a scannable résumé or submitting plain text online, go with plain text.

In addition, when employers or networking contacts ask you to e-mail your résumé, they'll often want to receive it in plain-text format in the body of your e-mail message. Thanks to the prevalence of computer viruses these days, many employers will refuse to open an e-mail attachment. Plain text is also helpful when you're completing online application forms; simply copy and paste from your plain-text file into the appropriate fields.

Plain text is just what it sounds like: no font selections, no bullet symbols, no colors, no lines or boxes, and so on. A plain-text version is easy to create with a word processor. Start with the file you used to create your traditional printed résumé, use the "Save As" choice to save it as "plain text" or whichever similarly labeled option your software has, and then verify the result.

The verification step is crucial because you need to be sure what happens to your layout. Open the text file to view the layout but don't use your word processor; instead, open the file with a basic text editor (such as Microsoft's Notepad) so that the text doesn't get reformatted in any way. If necessary, adjust the page manually, moving text and inserting spaces as needed. For simplicity's sake, left justify all your headings rather than try to center them manually. You can put headings in all caps or underline them with a row of hyphens to separate them from blocks of text.

Creating a Word File of Your Résumé In some cases, an employer or job-posting website will let you upload a Microsoft Word file directly. (Although there are certainly other word processors on the market, Microsoft Word is the de facto standard in business these days.) Read the instructions on each site carefully. For instance, you can upload a Word résumé to Monster.com, but the site asks you to follow some specific formatting instructions to make sure your file isn't garbled.[30]

Before you submit a Word file to anyone, make sure your system is free from computer viruses. Infecting a potential employer's PC is not a way to make a good first impression.

Creating an HTML Version of Your Résumé You can probably find several uses for an HTML (webpage) version of your résumé, including sending it as a fully formatted e-mail message and including it in your e-portfolio. A key advantage of an HTML version is that you can provide links to supporting details and other materials from within your résumé. Even if you don't have HTML experience, you can save your résumé as a webpage from within Word. This method won't necessarily create the most spectacularly beautiful webpage, but it should at least be functional.

As you design your HTML résumé, think of important keywords to use as hyperlinks—words that will grab an employer's attention and make the recruiter want to click on that hyperlink to learn more about you. You can link to papers you've written, recommendations you've received, and sound or video clips that directly support your résumé. However, be sure to have permission to publish or link to material created for a previous employer.

Creating a PDF Version of Your Résumé Creating a PDF version of your résumé is a simple procedure, but you need the right software. Adobe Acrobat (not the free Acrobat Reader) is the best-known program, but many others are available, including some free versions. You can also use Adobe's online service at http://createpdf.adobe.com to create PDFs without buying software.

Proofreading Your Résumé   Employers view your résumé as a concrete example of how you will prepare material on the job. It doesn't need to be good or pretty good; it needs to be *perfect*. Job seekers have committed every error from forgetting to put their own names on their résumés to misspelling "Education."[31] Even seemingly tiny errors signal that you don't pay attention to details.[32] Not only is your résumé one of the most important documents you'll ever write, it's also one of the shortest, so there's no reason not to make it perfect. Check all headings and lists for clarity and parallelism and be sure that your grammar, spelling, and punctuation are correct. Ask at least three or four other people to read it, too. As the creator of the material, you could stare at a mistake for weeks and not see it.

You also need to make sure your résumé works in every format you create, so double- and triple-check your scannable and plain-text résumés closely. Many personal computer users now have low-cost scanners with OCR software, so you can even test the scannability of your résumé. These OCR tools aren't as accurate as commercial systems, but you'll get a rough idea of what your résumé will look like on the other end of the scanning process. Test your plain-text version by copying it into an e-mail message and sending it to yourself and several friends on different e-mail systems.

Distributing Your Résumé   What you do to distribute your résumé depends on the number of employers you target and their preferences for receiving résumés. Employers usually list their preferences on their websites, so verify this information to make sure your résumé ends up in the right format and in the right channel. Beyond that, here are some general delivery tips:

- **Mailing your traditional and scannable résumés.** Take some care with the packaging. Spend a few extra cents to mail these documents in a flat 9 by 12 envelope, or better yet, use Priority Mail, which gives you a sturdy cardboard mailer and faster delivery for just a few more dollars. Consider sending both versions to each employer. In your cover letter, explain that for the employer's convenience, you're sending both standard and scannable versions.

When distributing your résumé, pay close attention to the specific wishes of each employer.

- **Faxing your traditional and scannable résumés.** If you know that an employer prefers résumés via fax, be sure to include a standard fax cover sheet, along with your cover letter, followed by your résumé. Set the fax machine to "fine" mode to help ensure a high-quality printout on the receiving end.

- **E-mailing your résumé.** Unless someone specifically asks for a Word document as an attachment, don't send it—it probably won't be opened. Instead, insert plain text into the body of the e-mail message, attach a PDF file, or include a hyperlink in the e-mail that links to your HTML résumé. If you know a reference number or a job ad number, include it in your e-mail subject line.

- **Submitting your résumé online.** The details of submitting résumés online vary from site to site, so be sure to read the instructions thoroughly. Some sites let you upload files directly from your computer; others instruct you to copy and paste blocks of plain text into specific fields in an online form. Whenever you do this, be sure to copy and paste rather than retype information; you've already proofed this material, and you don't want to create any new mistakes while rekeying it.

- **Posting a résumé on your website.** If you want to post your résumé on your website, you need to find some way of providing potential employers with your URL; recruiters won't take the time to use search engines to find your site.[33]

- **Posting your résumé with an index service or job site.** Make sure you explore all your online options. Websites such as Monster.com, CareerBuilder.com, and Yahoo! HotJobs have rapidly become a major force in recruiting. Don't forget to check specialty sites as well, such as those maintained by professional societies in your fields of interest. However, before you upload your résumé to any site, learn about its confidentiality protection. Some sites allow you to specify levels of confidentiality, such as letting employers search your qualifications without seeing your personal contact information or preventing your current employer from seeing your résumé. In any case, carefully limit the amount of personal information you provide online. Never put your home address, Social Security number, student ID number, or driver's license number online.

For a quick summary of the steps to take when planning, writing, and completing your résumé, refer to "Checklist: Writing an Effective Résumé."

✓ CHECKLIST: Writing an Effective Résumé

A. Plan your résumé.

✓ Analyze your purpose and audience carefully to make sure your message meets employers' needs.

✓ Gather pertinent information about your target companies.

✓ Select the best medium by researching the preferences of each employer.

✓ Organize your résumé around your strengths, choosing the chronological, functional, or combination structure. (Be careful about using the functional structure.)

B. Write your résumé.

✓ Keep your résumé honest.

✓ Adapt your résumé to your audience to highlight the qualifications each employer is looking for.

✓ Use powerful language to convey your name and contact information, career objective or summary of qualifications, education, work experience, skills, work or school accomplishments, and personal activities and achievements.

C. Complete your résumé.

✓ Revise your résumé until it is clear, concise, and compelling.

✓ Produce your résumé in all the formats you might need: traditional printed résumé, scannable, plain-text file, Microsoft Word file, HTML format, or PDF.

✓ Proofread your résumé to make sure it is letter perfect.

✓ Distribute your résumé using the means that each employer prefers.

On the Job

SOLVING COMMUNICATION DILEMMAS AT HERSHA HOSPITALITY MANAGEMENT

You recently joined Jeffrey Wade's recruiting team at Hersha, and your responsibilities include analyzing résumés and applications to help the company identify the most promising candidates to be interviewed. Your current task is finding candidates to fill a staff accountant position in the corporate finance group.

1. You've learned to pay close attention to the career objectives on résumés to make sure you match applicants' interests with appropriate job openings. You've selected four résumés for the accountant position; from them, which of the following is the most compelling statement of objectives for this position?

   a. An entry-level financial position in a large company

   b. To invest my accounting and financial talent and business savvy in shepherding Hersha toward explosive growth

   c. A position in which my degree in business administration and my experience in cash management will make a valuable contribution

   d. To learn all I can about accounting in an exciting environment with a company whose reputation is as outstanding as Hersha's

2. Of the education sections included in the résumés, which of the following is the most effective?

   a. Morehouse College, Atlanta, GA, 2001–2004. Received BA degree with a major in Business Administration and a minor in Finance. Graduated with a 3.65 grade-point average. Played varsity football and basketball. Worked 15 hours per week in the library. Coordinated the local student chapter of the American Management Association. Member of Alpha Phi Alpha social fraternity.

   b. I attended Wayne State University in Detroit, Michigan, for two years and then transferred to the University of Michigan at Ann Arbor, where I completed my studies. My major was economics, but I also took many business management courses, including employee motivation, small business administration, history of business start-ups, and organizational behavior. I selected courses based on the professors' reputation for excellence, and I received mostly A's and B's. Unlike many college students, I viewed the acquisition of knowledge—rather than career preparation—as my primary goal. I believe I have received a well-rounded education that has prepared me to approach management situations as problem-solving exercises.

c. University of Connecticut, Storrs, Connecticut. Graduated with a BA degree in 2004. Majored in Physical Education. Minored in Business Administration. Graduated with a 2.85 average.

d. North Texas State University and University of Texas at Tyler. Received BA and MBA degrees. I majored in business as an undergraduate and concentrated in financial management during my MBA program. Received a special $2,500 scholarship offered by Rotary International recognizing academic achievement in business courses. I also won the MEGA award in 2003. Dean's List.

3. Which of the résumés does the best job of portraying each candidate's work experience?

a. **McDonald's, Peoria, IL, 2000–2001. Part-time cook.** Worked 15 hours per week while attending high school. Prepared all menu items. Received employee-of-the-month award for outstanding work habits.
University Grill, Ames, IA, 2001–2004. Part-time cook. Worked 20 hours per week while attending college. Prepared hot and cold sandwiches. Helped manager purchase ingredients. Trained new kitchen workers. Prepared work schedules for kitchen staff.

b. Although I have never held a full-time job, I have worked part-time and during summer vacations throughout my high school and college years. During my freshman and sophomore years in high school, I bagged groceries at the A&P store three afternoons a week, where I was generally acknowledged as one of the hardest-working employees. During my junior and senior years, I worked at the YMCA as an after-school counselor for elementary school children. I know I made a positive difference in their lives because I still get letters from some of them. During summer vacations while I was in college, I did construction work for a local homebuilder. The job paid well, and I also learned a lot about carpentry. I also worked part-time in college in the student cafeteria.

c. **Macy's Department Store, Sherman Oaks, CA, Summers, 2002–2005. Sales Consultant, Furniture Department.** Interacted with a diverse group of customers while endeavoring to satisfy their individual needs and make their shopping experience efficient and enjoyable. Under the direction of the sales manager, prepared employee schedules and completed departmental reports. Demon-

strated computer skills and attention to detail while assisting with inventory management, working the cash register, and handling a variety of special orders and customer requests. Received the CEO Award (for best monthly sales performance) three times.

d. **Athens, GA, Civilian Member of Public Safety Committee, January–December 2004.**
• Organized and promoted a lecture series on vacation safety and home security for the residents of Athens, GA; recruited and trained seven committee members to help plan and produce the lectures; persuaded local businesses to finance the program; designed, printed, and distributed flyers; wrote and distributed press releases; attracted an average of 120 people to each of three lectures
• Developed a questionnaire to determine local residents' home security needs; directed the efforts of 10 volunteers working on the survey; prepared written report for city council and delivered oral summary of findings at town meeting; helped persuade city to fund new home security program
• Initiated the Business Security Forum as an annual meeting at which local business leaders could meet to discuss safety and security issues; created promotional flyers for the first forum; convinced 19 business owners to fund a business security survey; arranged press coverage of the first forum

4. While you are analyzing four résumés suggested by your applicant tracking system, a fellow employee hands you the following résumé and says this person would be great for the opening in accounting. What action will you take?

a. Definitely recommend that Hersha take a look at this outstanding candidate.
b. Reject the application. He doesn't give enough information about when he attended college, what he majored in, or where he has worked.
c. Review the candidate's web-based e-portfolio, in which he has posted many of his school projects. If the assessment contains the missing information and the candidate sounds promising, recommend him for a closer look. If vital information is still missing, send the candidate an e-mail requesting additional information. Make the decision once you receive all necessary information.
d. Consider the candidate's qualifications relative to those of other applicants. Recommend him if you cannot find three or four other applicants with more directly relevant qualifications.

Darius Jaidee

809 N. Perkins Rd, Stillwater, OK 74075
Phone: (405) 369-0098
E-mail: dariusj@okstate.edu

Career Objective: To build a successful career in accounting and/or financial management

Summary of Qualifications: As a student at the University of Oklahoma, Stillwater, completed a wide variety of assignments that demonstrate skills related to accounting and management. For example:

Planning skills: As president of the university's foreign affairs forum, organized six lectures and workshops featuring 36 speakers from 16 foreign countries within a nine-month period. Identified and recruited the speakers, handled their travel arrangements, and scheduled the facilities.

Communication skills: Wrote more than 25 essays and term papers on various academic topics, including at least 10 dealing with business and finance. As a senior, wrote a 20-page analysis of financial trends in the petroleum industry, interviewing five high-ranking executives in accounting and finance positions at ConocoPhillip's refinery in Ponca City, Oklahoma, and company headquarters in Houston, Texas.

Accounting and computer skills: Competent in all areas of Microsoft Office, including Excel spreadsheets and Access databases. Assisted with bookkeeping activities in parents' small business, including the conversion from paper-based to computer-based accounting (Peachtree software). Have taken courses in accounting, financial planning, database design, web design, and computer networking.

For more information, please access my e-portfolio at http://dariusjaidee.tripod.com

Learning Objectives Checkup

Assess your understanding of the principles in this chapter by reading each learning objective and studying the accompanying exercises. For fill-in-the-blank items, write the missing text in the blank provided; for multiple-choice items, circle the letter of the correct answer. You can check your responses against the answer key on page AK-3.

Objective 15.1: Describe the approach most employers take to finding potential new employees.

1. What is the first step that employers usually take when they need to find candidates to interview for a job opening?
   a. They search online for personal websites and e-portfolios that might contain information about potential candidates.
   b. They look inside the company for likely candidates.

   c. They post job openings on job boards such as Monster.com and CareerBuilder.com.
   d. They run ads in the local newspaper.
2. Which of these most accurately characterizes the respective approaches that employers use to find new employees and employees use to find new opportunities?
   a. Employers and employees look in the same places, in the same general sequence.
   b. The respective approaches of employers and employees are essentially opposite, with employers starting inside the firm and gradually moving toward help wanted ads as a last resort and employees starting with help wanted ads and moving in the other direction.
   c. Because websites are the only places that employers now communicate news of job openings, the web is the only place employees should look.

d. The approaches of employees and employers have nothing in common.

3. According to the chapter, what percentage of job openings are never advertised (a phenomenon known as the *hidden job market*)?
   a. 15 percent
   b. 5 percent
   c. 28 percent
   d. 80 percent

Objective 15.2: Explain the importance of networking in your career search.

4. Which of the following best describes the process of networking as it applies to your career?
   a. Making sure you are plugged into the online scene so that you don't miss out on any new Internet developments
   b. Making informal connections with a broad sphere of mutually beneficial business contacts
   c. Asking as many people as possible to alert you to interesting job opportunities
   d. Making sure you get to know everyone in your company shortly after accepting a new position

5. If you don't yet have significant work experience but still want to become a valued network member, which of the following tactics should you consider?
   a. Limit your networking to people whose work experience is similar to yours so that you can share similar information.
   b. Create a convenient, foldable, business-card-size version of your résumé that you can give to everyone you meet so they don't have to carry a full-size copy of your résumé.
   c. Avoid networking until you have enough work experience to be able to offer insider tips on the job market in your industry.
   d. Research recent trends in the business world in order to have interesting and useful information at your fingertips whenever you encounter people in your network.

Objective 15.3: Discuss how to choose the appropriate résumé organization, and list the advantages or disadvantages of the three common options.

6. A/an _____ résumé highlights employment experience, listing jobs in reverse order from most recent to earliest.

7. A/an _____ résumé focuses on a person's particular skills and competencies, without itemizing his or her job history.

8. A/an _____ résumé uses elements of both the chronological and functional formats.

9. Which of the following is an advantage of the chronological résumé?
   a. It helps employers easily locate necessary information.
   b. It highlights your professional growth and career progress.
   c. It emphasizes continuity and stability in your employment background.
   d. It performs all of these communication functions.

10. Why are many employers suspicious of the functional résumé?
    a. It allows applicants to hide or downplay lengthy periods of unemployment or a lack of career progress.
    b. It doesn't scan into computer databases as effectively as other résumé formats.
    c. It doesn't provide any information about education.
    d. It encourages applicants to include accomplishments that were the result of teamwork rather than individual efforts.

11. Which of the following is a disadvantage of the combination résumé?
    a. It is impossible to convert to scannable format.
    b. It tends to be longer than other formats and can be repetitive.
    c. It doesn't work for people who have extensive job experience.
    d. The combination résumé has no disadvantages.

Objective 15.4: Describe the problem of résumé fraud.

12. Roughly what percentage of employers now contact references and conduct criminal background checks when allowed as part of the effort to combat résumé fraud?
    a. 30 percent
    b. 80 percent
    c. 99.8 percent
    d. 4 percent

Objective 15.5: List the major sections of a traditional résumé.

13. Which of the following sections should be included in any résumé, regardless of the format you've chosen?
    a. Contact information, education, and work experience
    b. Contact information, education, and personal references
    c. Personal data, contact information, and education
    d. Education, personal references, and career objectives

14. Why do some experts recommend not including a career objective on your résumé?
    a. It can limit your possibilities as a candidate, particularly if you want to be considered for a variety of positions.
    b. It shows that you're selfish and only thinking about your own success.
    c. It shows that you're unrealistic, since no one can plan a career that might last for 40 or 50 years.
    d. It helps focus you as a candidate in the minds of potential employers.

15. Should a summary of qualifications focus on the past or the future?
    a. It should focus on the past, covering things that you've already accomplished.
    b. It should focus on the future, identifying valuable traits that you can offer a new employer.
    c. It should combine elements of both the past and the future, offering solid evidence of what you've accomplished while being phrased in a way that relates to a future employer's needs.
    d. It should focus on the future, explaining what you'd like to accomplish in your career in the coming years.

Objective 15.6: Identify six different formats in which you can produce a résumé.

16. A/an _____ version of your résumé has the same content as a traditional résumé but has had all the formatting removed so that it can be easily e-mailed or copied into online forms.

17. Which of these is a significant advantage of an HTML format résumé?
    a. You can save money on printing paper résumés.
    b. You can provide links to additional information, such as samples of your work.
    c. You can use lots of color.
    d. You can use the flexibility of the web to provide extensive details on your life history.

Objective 15.7: Describe what you should do to adapt your résumé to a scannable format.

18. Which of the following formatting steps is necessary to convert a traditional résumé to a scannable format?
    a. Remove all font formatting, such as boldface and italics.
    b. Replace bullet point characters with hyphens.
    c. Convert all multiple columns to a single column.
    d. Do all of the above.

19. What is the primary purpose of the list of keywords in a scannable résumé?
    a. It shows employers that you've done your research.
    b. It increases the probability that a computer database will select your résumé for the types of opportunities in which you're interested.
    c. It fills up space when you don't have enough work experience.
    d. Keywords should never be included in a scannable résumé.

Apply Your Knowledge

1. If you're still a year or two away from graduation, should you worry about your job search? Explain your answer.

2. One of the disadvantages of computerized résumé scanning is that some qualified applicants will be missed because the technology isn't perfect. However, more and more companies are using this approach to deal with the flood of résumés they receive. Do you think that scanning is a good idea? Explain.

3. Stating your career objective on a résumé or an application might limit your opportunities by labeling you too narrowly. Not stating your objective, however, might lead an employer to categorize you incorrectly. Which outcome is riskier? Do summaries of qualifications overcome such drawbacks? If so, how? Explain briefly.

4. Some people don't have a clear career path when they enter the job market. If you're in this situation, how would your uncertainty affect the way your write your résumé?

5. **Ethical Choices** Between your sophomore and junior years, you quit school for a year to earn the money to finish college. You worked as a loan-processing assistant in a finance company, checking references on loan applications, typing, and filing. Your manager made a lot of the fact that he had never attended college. He seemed to resent you for pursuing your education, but he never criticized your work, so you thought you were doing okay. After you'd been working there for six months, he fired you, saying that you failed to be thorough enough in your credit checks. You were actually glad to leave, and you found another job right away at a bank, doing similar duties. Now that you've graduated from college, you're writing your résumé. Will you include the finance company job in your work history? Explain.

Practice Your Knowledge

MESSAGE FOR ANALYSIS

Read the following résumé information and then (1) analyze the strengths or weaknesses of the information and (2) create a résumé that follows the guidelines presented in this chapter.

Sylvia Manchester
765 Belle Fleur Blvd.
New Orleans, LA 70113
(504) 312-9504
smanchester@rcnmail.com

PERSONAL:	Single, excellent health, 5′8″, 116 lbs.; hobbies include cooking, dancing, and reading.
JOB OBJECTIVE:	To obtain a responsible position in marketing or sales with a good company.
EDUCATION:	BA degree in biology, University of Louisiana, 1998. Graduated with a 3.0 average. Member of the varsity cheerleading squad. President of Panhellenic League. Homecoming queen.
WORK EXPERIENCE	*Fisher Scientific Instruments, 2004 to now, field sales representative.* Responsible for calling on customers and explaining the features of Fisher's line of laboratory instruments. Also responsible for writing sales letters, attending trade shows, and preparing weekly sales reports.

Fisher Scientific Instruments, 2001–2003, customer service representative. Was responsible for handling incoming phone calls from customers who had questions about delivery, quality, or operation of Fisher's line of laboratory instruments. Also handled miscellaneous correspondence with customers.

Medical Electronics, Inc., 1998–2001, administrative assistant to the vice president of marketing. In addition to handling typical secretarial chores for the vice president of marketing, I was in charge of compiling the monthly sales reports, using figures provided by members of the field sales force. I also was given responsibility for doing various market research activities.

New Orleans Convention and Visitors Bureau, 1995–1998, summers, tour guide. During the summers of my college years, I led tours of New Orleans for tourists visiting the city. My duties included greeting conventioneers and their spouses at hotels, explaining the history and features of the city during an all-day sightseeing tour, and answering questions about New Orleans and its attractions. During my fourth summer with the bureau, I was asked to help train the new tour guides. I prepared a handbook that provided interesting facts about the various tourist attractions, as well as answers to the most commonly asked tourist questions. The Bureau was so impressed with the handbook they had it printed up so that it could be given as a gift to visitors.

University of Louisiana, 1995–1998, part-time clerk in admissions office. While I was a student in college, I worked 15 hours a week in the admissions office. My duties included filing, processing applications, and handling correspondence with high school students and administrators.

EXERCISES

For active links to all websites discussed in this chapter, visit this book's website at www.prenhall.com/thill. Locate your book and click on its "Companion Website" link. Then select Chapter 15 and click on "Featured Websites." Locate the name of the page or the URL related to the material in the text. Please note that links to sites that become inactive after publication of the book will be removed from the "Featured Websites" section.

15.1 Internet Based on the preferences you identified in your career self-assessment (see page xxxvi) and the academic, professional, and personal qualities you have to offer, perform an online search for a career that matches your interests (starting with the websites listed in Table 15.1). Draft a brief report for your instructor, indicating how the career you select and the job openings you find match your strengths and preferences.

15.2 Teamwork Working with another student, change the following statements to make them more effective for a résumé by using action verbs.
  a. Have some experience with database design.
  b. Assigned to a project to analyze the cost accounting methods for a large manufacturer.
  c. I was part of a team that developed a new inventory control system.
  d. Am responsible for preparing the quarterly department budget.
  e. Was a manager of a department with seven employees working for me.
  f. Was responsible for developing a spreadsheet to analyze monthly sales by department.
  g. Put in place a new program for ordering supplies.

15.3 Résumé Preparation: Work Accomplishments Using your team's answers to Exercise 15.2, make the statements stronger by quantifying them. (Make up any numbers you need.)

15.4 Ethical Choices Assume that you achieved all the tasks shown in Exercise 15.2 not as an individual employee but as part of a work team. In your résumé, must you mention other team members? Explain your answer.

15.5 Résumé Preparation: Electronic Plain-Text Version Using your revised version of Message for Analysis 15.A, prepare a fully formatted print résumé. What formatting changes would Sylvia Manchester need to make if she were uploading her résumé to a website as a plain-text file? Develop a keyword summary and make all the changes needed to complete this plain-text résumé.

15.6 Résumé Preparation: HTML Version Using your revised version of the résumé in Message for Analysis 15.A, prepare a webpage version. Your instructor may direct you to a particular HTML editing tool, or you can use the "Save as Web Page" function in Microsoft Word. Word also lets you insert hyperlinks, so somewhere in the Work Experience section, create a hyperlink that takes the reader to a secondary page in order to show a work sample. For this new page, you can either use one of your own assignments from this course or simply create a blank page titled "Work Sample for Sylvia Manchester." On this page, create a hyperlink that takes the reader back to the main résumé page. Be sure to test your finished files using a web browser. Adjust your formatting as necessary to ensure a clean, professional design. When your files are complete, submit as your instructor indicates.

15.7 It's Show Time: Creating a Vidcast to Supplement Your Application Imagine that you are applying for work in a field that involves speaking in front of an audience, such as sales, consulting, management, or training. Using material you created for any of the exercises or cases in Chapter 14, plan a 2- to 3-minute video demonstration of your speaking and presentation skills. Using a digital camcorder, a digital camera with video capability, or a webcam, record yourself speaking to an imaginary audience. If possible, use PowerPoint slides or other visuals. As your instructor directs, either submit this movie clip or use it to create a video podcast. For a good tutorial on creating vidcasts on Apple computers running Mac OS X, visit www.apple.com/quicktime/tutorials/videopodcasts.html; for Windows computers, visit www.apple.com/quicktime/tutorials/videopodcasts_win.html.

Expand Your Knowledge

LEARNING MORE ON THE WEB
POST AN ONLINE RÉSUMÉ

www.careerbuilder.com

At CareerBuilder, you'll find sample résumés, tips on preparing different types of résumés (including scannable ones), links to additional articles, and expert advice on creating résumés that bring positive results. After you've polished your résumé-writing skills, you can search for jobs online using the site's numerous links to national and international industry-specific websites. You can access the information at CareerBuilder to develop your résumé and then post it with prospective employers—all free of charge. Use the site's advice to complete these tasks:

1. Before writing a new résumé, make a list of action verbs that describe your skills and experience.
2. Describe the advantages and disadvantages of chronological and functional résumé formats. Do you think a com-

bination résumé would be an appropriate format for your new résumé? Explain why or why not.

3. List some of the tips you learned for preparing an electronic résumé.

SURFING YOUR WAY TO CAREER SUCCESS

Bovée and Thill's Business Communication Headline News offers links to hundreds of online resources that can help you with this course, your other college courses, and your career.

Visit www.businesscommunicationblog.com and click on "Web Directory." The "Employment" section connects you to a variety of articles and websites covering such key topics as career planning, résumé writing, employment portfolios, background checks, and salary information. Identify three websites from this section that could be useful in your business career. For each site, write a two-sentence summary of what the site offers and how it could help you launch and build your career.

Learn Interactively

INTERACTIVE STUDY GUIDE

Visit www.prenhall.com/thill and locate your book, then click on its "Companion Website" link. Select Chapter 15 to take advantage of the interactive "Chapter Quiz" to test your knowledge of chapter concepts. Receive instant feedback on whether you need to do additional studying. Also, visit the "Study Hall," where you'll find an abundance of valuable resources that will help you succeed in this course.

PEAK PERFORMANCE GRAMMAR AND MECHANICS

If your instructor has required the use of "Peak Performance Grammar and Mechanics," either in your online course or on CD, you can improve your skill with frequently confused, mis-

used, and misspelled words by using the "Peak Performance Grammar and Mechanics" module. Click on "Spelling." Take the Pretest to determine whether you have any weak areas. Then review those areas in the Refresher Course. Take the Follow-Up Test to check your grasp of handling these tricky words. For an extra challenge or advanced practice, take the Advanced Test. Finally, for additional reinforcement, go to the "Improve Your Grammar, Mechanics, and Usage" section that follows and complete those exercises.

Improve Your Grammar, Mechanics, and Usage

The following exercises help you improve your knowledge of and power over English grammar, mechanics, and usage. Turn to the Handbook of Grammar, Mechanics, and Usage at the end of this book and review all of Sections 4.1 (Frequently Confused Words), 4.2 (Frequently Misused Words), and 4.3 (Frequently Misspelled Words). Then look at the following 10 items. Underline the preferred choice within each set of parentheses. (Answers to these exercises appear on page AK-4.)

1. Everyone (*accept/except*) Barbara King has registered for the company competition.
2. We need to find a new security (*device/devise*).
3. The Jennings are (*loath/loathe*) to admit that they are wrong.
4. That decision lies with the director, (*who's/whose*) in charge of this department.
5. In this department, we see (*a lot, alot*) of mistakes like that.
6. In my (*judgement, judgment*), you'll need to redo the cover.

7. He decided to reveal the information, (*irregardless, regardless*) of the consequences.
8. Why not go along when it is so easy to (*accomodate, accommodate*) his demands?
9. When you say that, do you mean to (*infer, imply*) that I'm being unfair?
10. All we have to do is try (*and, to*) get along with him for a few more days.

For additional exercises focusing on frequently confused, misused, or misspelled words, go to www.prenhall.com/thill, then locate your text and click on its "Companion Website" link. Click on Chapter 15, click on "Additional Exercises to Improve Your Grammar, Mechanics and Usage," and then click on "21. Frequently confused words," "22. Frequently misused words," or "23. Frequently misspelled words."

Cases

Applying the Three-Step Writing Process to Cases

Apply each step to the following cases, as assigned by your instructor.

1. Taking stock and taking aim: Résumé tailored for the right job Think about yourself. What are some things that come easily to you? What do you enjoy doing? In what part of the country would you like to live? Do you like to work indoors? Outdoors? A combination of the two? How much do you like to travel? Would you like to spend considerable time on the road? Do you like to work closely with others or more independently? What conditions make a job unpleasant? Do you delegate responsibility easily, or do you like to do things yourself? Are you better with words or numbers? Better at speaking or writing? Do you like to work under fixed deadlines? How important is job security to you? Do you want your supervisor to state clearly what is expected of you, or do you like the freedom to make many of your own decisions?

Your task: After answering these questions, gather information about possible jobs that suit your profile by consulting reference materials (from your college library or placement center) and by searching the Internet (using some of the search strategies discussed in Chapter 11). Next, choose a location, a company, and a job that interests you. With guidance from your instructor, decide whether to apply for a job you're qualified for now or one you'll be qualified for with additional education. Then, as directed by your instructor, write a résumé.

2. Scanning the possibilities: Résumé for the Internet In your search for a position, you discover Career Magazine, a website that lists hundreds of companies advertising on the Internet. Your chances of getting an interview with a leading company will be enhanced if you submit your résumé and cover letter electronically. On the web, explore www.careermag.com.

Your task: Prepare a scannable résumé that could be submitted to one of the companies advertising at the Career Magazine website. Print out the résumé for your instructor.

3. "Help wanted": Application for a job listed in the classified section Among the jobs listed in today's *Chicago Tribune* (435 N. Michigan Avenue, Chicago, IL 60641) are the following:

Accounting Assistant

Established leader in the vacation ownership industry has immediate opening in its Northbrook corp. accounting dept. for an Accounting Assistant. Responsibilities include: bank reconciliation, preparation of deposits, AP, and cash receipt posting. Join our fast-growing company and enjoy our great benefits package. Flex work hours, medical, dental insurance. Fax résumé to Lisa: 847-564-3876.

Administrative Assistant

Fast-paced Wood Dale office seeks professional with strong computer skills. Proficient in MS Word & Excel, PowerPoint a plus. Must be detail oriented, able to handle multiple tasks, and possess strong communication skills. Excellent benefits, salary, and work environment. Fax résumé to 630-350-8649.

Customer Service

A nationally known computer software developer has an exciting opportunity in customer service and inside sales support in its fast-paced downtown Chicago office. You'll help resolve customer problems over the phone, provide information, assist in account management, and administer orders. If you're friendly, self-motivated, energetic, and have 2 years of experience, excellent problem-solving skills, organizational, communication, and PC skills, and communicate well over the phone, send résumé to J. Haber, 233 North Lake Shore Drive, Chicago, IL 60641.

Sales-Account Manager

MidCity Baking Company is seeking an Account Manager to sell and coordinate our programs to major accounts in the Chicago market. The candidate should possess strong analytical and selling skills and demonstrate computer proficiency. Previous sales experience with major account level assignment desired. A degree in business or equivalent experience preferred. For confidential consideration please mail résumé to Steven Crane, Director of Sales, MidCity Baking Company, 133 N. Railroad Avenue, Northlake, IL 60614.

Your task: Write a résumé for one of these potential employers. (Make up any information you need or adapt your résumé.)

Chapter 16

Interviewing for Employment and Following Up

Learning Objectives

AFTER STUDYING THIS CHAPTER, YOU WILL BE ABLE TO

1 Define the purpose of application letters and explain how to apply the AIDA organizational model to them

2 Describe the typical sequence of job interviews

3 Describe briefly what employers look for during an employment interview and pre-employment testing

4 List six tasks you need to complete to prepare for a successful job interview

5 Explain the three stages of a successful employment interview

6 Identify the most common employment messages that follow an interview and explain when you would use each one

On the Job

COMMUNICATING AT GOOGLE

THE SEARCH ENGINE LEADER'S SEARCH FOR THE BEST TALENT ON THE WEB

As you prepare for your job interviews, knowing just the basic facts and figures about a company isn't always enough to impress top recruiters. For instance, most web surfers know Google as the leading online search engine, but the company is also helping to revolutionize advertising, publishing, geographic information systems, shopping—if it involves digital information, chances are Google has looked into opportunities to build a business out of it.

As Google continues its rapid growth, recruiting manager Arnnon Geshuri and his staff dedicate considerable time, energy, and resources to

Arnnon Geshuri heads Google's recruiting effort as the company looks to hire thousands of the most innovative online business and technical specialists in the world.

employee recruiting. However, finding the right people is so important to the company that contributing to the recruiting effort is considered the responsibility of virtually every manager and employee. In fact, John Sullivan of San Francisco State University, who has studied the company's recruiting efforts closely, says that recruiting permeates the company so thoroughly that Google has created what he terms the world's first "recruiting culture."

Moreover, as befits a company focused on innovation, Google pursues people who don't fit the traditional corporate mold. Most are either risk takers with adventurous outside interests or experienced superstars from top research labs or respected technology firms. Googlers, as employees are informally known, hail from every corner of the business world—and beyond. As the company puts it, "Googlers have been Olympic athletes and Jeopardy champions; professional chefs and independent filmmakers."

You may never apply to Google, but gaining similar insights about the companies you are interested in will give you a competitive edge. Google provides quite a bit of information on its website about work life at the company, but you can't always hop on a company website to find these insights. Doing some extra digging through magazines, reading employment-related blogs, networking with others in your chosen field, and taking every other opportunity to learn will help you prepare for every stage of the employment search process.[1]

www.google.com

WRITING APPLICATION LETTERS AND OTHER EMPLOYMENT MESSAGES

Whether you plan to apply to Google (profiled in the chapter opener) or any other company, your résumé will usually be the centerpiece of your job search package. However, it needs support from several other employment messages, including application letters, job-inquiry letters, application forms, and follow-up notes.

Application Letters

Use the three-step process to create attention-getting application letters.

Whenever you submit your résumé, accompany it with an application letter (also known as a *cover letter*) to let readers know what you're sending, why you're sending it, and how they can benefit from reading it. The three-step process of planning, writing, and completing an application letter involves the same steps you've used throughout this course. Start by researching the organization and then focus on your audience so that you can show you've done your homework. During your research, try to find out the name, title, and department of the person you're writing to. If you can't find a specific name, use something like "Dear Hiring Manager."[2] If you're applying for work in another country, be sure to research the hiring practices that are prevalent in that culture and adjust your letter format as needed.

Impress your reader with knowledge and professionalism—not gimmicks.

Remember that your reader's in-box is probably overflowing with résumés and cover letters, so respect his or her time. Avoid gimmicks and don't repeat information that already appears in your résumé. Keep your letter straightforward, fact based, short, upbeat, and professional. Here are some quick tips to help you write effective cover letters:[3]

- Be as clear as possible about the kind of opportunity you seek.
- Show that you understand the company and the position.
- Never volunteer salary information unless an employer asks for it.
- Keep it short—and keep e-mail cover letters even shorter; in just two or three paragraphs, convey how your strengths and character would fit the position.
- Show some personality; this will help balance the choppy, shorthand style of your résumé.
- Meticulously check your spelling, mechanics, and grammar; errors will send your message directly to the recycling bin. And be aware that potential employers will treat your e-mail messages every bit as seriously as formal, printed letters.[4]

If you're sending a **solicited application letter** in response to an announced job opening, you'll usually know what qualifications the organization is seeking (see Figure 16.1). In contrast, if you're sending an **unsolicited application letter** to an organization that has not announced an opening, you'll need to do some research to identify the requirements the position is likely to have (see Figure 16.2). (Note that even though these documents are referred to as letters, they can be e-mail messages as well.)

Solicited and unsolicited application letters present your qualifications similarly. The main difference is in the opening paragraph. In a solicited letter, you need no special attention-getter because you have been invited to apply. In an unsolicited letter, you need to start by capturing the reader's attention and interest.

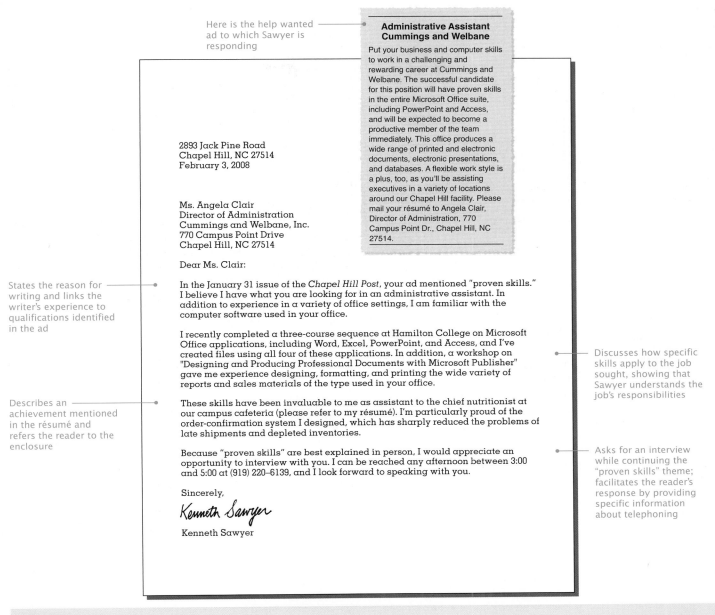

Here is the help wanted ad to which Sawyer is responding

**Administrative Assistant
Cummings and Welbane**

Put your business and computer skills to work in a challenging and rewarding career at Cummings and Welbane. The successful candidate for this position will have proven skills in the entire Microsoft Office suite, including PowerPoint and Access, and will be expected to become a productive member of the team immediately. This office produces a wide range of printed and electronic documents, electronic presentations, and databases. A flexible work style is a plus, too, as you'll be assisting executives in a variety of locations around our Chapel Hill facility. Please mail your résumé to Angela Clair, Director of Administration, 770 Campus Point Dr., Chapel Hill, NC 27514.

2893 Jack Pine Road
Chapel Hill, NC 27514
February 3, 2008

Ms. Angela Clair
Director of Administration
Cummings and Welbane, Inc.
770 Campus Point Drive
Chapel Hill, NC 27514

Dear Ms. Clair:

States the reason for writing and links the writer's experience to qualifications identified in the ad

In the January 31 issue of the *Chapel Hill Post*, your ad mentioned "proven skills." I believe I have what you are looking for in an administrative assistant. In addition to experience in a variety of office settings, I am familiar with the computer software used in your office.

I recently completed a three-course sequence at Hamilton College on Microsoft Office applications, including Word, Excel, PowerPoint, and Access, and I've created files using all four of these applications. In addition, a workshop on "Designing and Producing Professional Documents with Microsoft Publisher" gave me experience designing, formatting, and printing the wide variety of reports and sales materials of the type used in your office.

Discusses how specific skills apply to the job sought, showing that Sawyer understands the job's responsibilities

Describes an achievement mentioned in the résumé and refers the reader to the enclosure

These skills have been invaluable to me as assistant to the chief nutritionist at our campus cafeteria (please refer to my résumé). I'm particularly proud of the order-confirmation system I designed, which has sharply reduced the problems of late shipments and depleted inventories.

Because "proven skills" are best explained in person, I would appreciate an opportunity to interview with you. I can be reached any afternoon between 3:00 and 5:00 at (919) 220-6139, and I look forward to speaking with you.

Asks for an interview while continuing the "proven skills" theme; facilitates the reader's response by providing specific information about telephoning

Sincerely,

Kenneth Sawyer

Kenneth Sawyer

FIGURE 16.1
Effective Solicited Application Letter
In this letter written in response to a help-wanted ad, notice how Kenneth Sawyer highlights his qualifications and mirrors the requirements specified in the ad. He grabs attention by focusing on the phrase "proven skills," which was used in the ad: He not only elaborates on his own proven skills throughout the letter but even mentions the term in his closing paragraph.

Getting Attention   Like your résumé, your application letter is a form of advertising, so organize it as you would a sales letter: Use the AIDA model, focus on your audience, and emphasize reader benefits (as discussed in Chapter 10). Make sure your style projects confidence without being arrogant.

The opening paragraph of your application letter has two important tasks to accomplish: (1) clearly stating your reason for writing and (2) giving the recipient a reason to keep reading. Why would a recruiter want to keep reading your letter instead of the hundred others piling up on his or her desk? Because you show some

The opening paragraph of your application letter needs to clearly convey the reason you're writing and give the recipient a compelling reason to keep reading.

457 Mountain View Rd.
Clear Lake, IA 50428
June 16, 2008

Ms. Patricia Downings, Store Manager
Wal-Mart
840 South Oak
Iowa Falls, IA 50126

Dear Ms. Downing:

You want retail clerks and managers who are accurate, enthusiastic, and experienced. You want someone who cares about customer service, who understands merchandising, and who can work with others to get the job done. When you're ready to hire a manager trainee or a clerk who is willing to work toward promotion, please consider me for the job.

Working as a clerk and then as an assistant manager in a large department store has taught me how to anticipate customer problems and deliver the type of service that keeps customers coming back. Moreover, my recent BA degree in retailing, which encompassed such courses as retailing, marketing, management, and business information systems, will provide your store with a well-rounded associate. (Please refer to my enclosed résumé for more information.) You'll find that I'm interested in every facet of retailing, eager to take on responsibility, and willing to continue learning throughout my career.

I understand that Wal-Mart prefers to promote its managers from within the company, and I would be pleased to start out with an entry-level position until I gain the necessary experience. Could we meet in the near future to discuss my qualifications for the next available associate position? I will phone you early next Wednesday to arrange a meeting at your convenience.

Sincerely,

Glenda Johns

Glenda Johns

Enclosure

Annotations:
- Gains attention in the first paragraph by speaking directly to the reader's needs
- Builds the reader's interest by demonstrating knowledge of the company's policy toward promotion
- Points out personal qualities that aren't specifically stated in her résumé
- Focuses on the reader and displays the "you" attitude, even though the last paragraph uses the word "I"

FIGURE 16.2
Effective Unsolicited Application Letter
Glenda Johns's experience as a clerk and an assistant manager gives her a good idea of the qualities that Wal-Mart is likely to be looking for in future managers. She uses these insights to craft the opening of her letter.

immediate potential for meeting the company's needs. You've researched the company and the position, and you know something about the industry and its current challenges. Consider this opening:

> With the recent slowdown in corporate purchasing, I can certainly appreciate the challenge of new fleet sales in this business environment. With my high energy level and 16 months of new-car sales experience, I believe I can produce the results you listed as vital in your September 23 ad in the Baltimore Sun.

This applicant does a smooth job of mirroring the company's stated needs while highlighting his personal qualifications along with evidence that he understands the broader market.

TIPS FOR GETTING ATTENTION IN APPLICATION LETTERS

Table 16.1

Tip	*Example*
Unsolicited Application Letters	
• Show how your strongest skills will benefit the organization	If you need a regional sales specialist who consistently meets sales targets while fostering strong customer relationships, please consider my qualifications.
• Describe your understanding of the job's requirements and then show how well your qualifications fit them	Your annual report stated that improving manufacturing efficiency is one of the company's top priorities for next year. Through my postgraduate research in systems engineering and consulting work for several companies in the industry, I've developed reliable methods for quickly identifying ways to cut production time while reducing resource usage.
• Mention the name of a person known to and highly regarded by the reader	When Janice McHugh of your franchise sales division spoke to our business communication class last week, she said you often need promising new marketing graduates at this time of year.
• Refer to publicized company activities, achievements, changes, or new procedures	Today's issue of the *Detroit News* reports that you may need the expertise of computer programmers versed in robotics when your Lansing tire plant automates this spring.
• Use a question to demonstrate your understanding of the organization's needs	Can your fast-growing market research division use an interviewer with two years of field survey experience, a B.A. in public relations, and a real desire to succeed? If so, please consider me for the position.
• Use a catchphrase opening if the job requires ingenuity and imagination	*Haut monde*—whether said in French, Italian, or Arabic, it still means "high society." As an interior designer for your Beverly Hills showroom, not only could I serve and sell to your distinguished clientele, but I could do it in all these languages. I speak, read, and write them fluently.
Solicited Application Letters	
• Identify where you discovered the job opening; describe what you have to offer	Your ad in the April issue of *Travel & Leisure* for a cruise-line social director caught my eye. My eight years of experience as a social director in the travel industry would allow me to serve your new Caribbean cruise division well.

Table 16.1 highlights some ways you can spark interest and grab attention in your opening paragraph. All these openings demonstrate the "you" attitude, and many indicate how the applicant can serve the employer.

Building Interest and Increasing Desire   The middle section of your application letter presents your strongest selling points in terms of their potential benefit to the organization, thereby building interest in you and creating a desire to interview you. As with the opening, the more specific you can be, the better. And back up your assertions with some convincing evidence of your ability to perform:

Use the middle section of your letter to expand on your opening, presenting a more complete picture of your strengths.

Poor: I completed three college courses in business communication, earning an A in each course, and have worked for the past year at Imperial Construction.

> **Improved:** Using the skills gained from three semesters of college training in business communication, I developed a collection system for Imperial Construction that reduced annual bad-debt losses by 25 percent. Emphasizing a win-win scenario for the company and its clients with incentives for on-time payment, the system was also credited with improving customer satisfaction.

When writing a solicited letter, be sure to discuss each requirement specified in the ad. If you are deficient in any of these requirements, stress other solid selling points to help strengthen your overall presentation.

Don't restrict your message to just core job duties, either. Also highlight personal characteristics that apply to the targeted position, such as your diligence or your ability to work hard, learn quickly, handle responsibility, or get along with people:

> While attending college full-time, I trained 3 hours a day with the varsity track team. In addition, I worked part-time during the school year and up to 60 hours a week each summer in order to be totally self-supporting while in college. I can offer your organization the same level of effort and perseverance.

Don't bring up salary in your application letter unless the recipient has previously asked you to include your salary requirements.

Another matter you might bring up in this section is your salary requirements—but *only* if the organization has asked you to state them. If you don't know the salary that's appropriate for the position and someone with your qualifications, you can find salary ranges for hundreds of jobs at the Bureau of Labor Statistics website, **www.bls.gov** or a number of commercial sites, including Monster.com. If you do state a target salary, tie it to the benefits you would bring to the organization:

> For the past two years, I have been helping a company similar to yours organize its database marketing efforts. I would therefore like to receive a salary in the same range (the mid-60s) for helping your company set up a more efficient customer database.

Toward the end of this section, refer the reader to your résumé by citing a specific fact or general point covered there:

> As you can see in the enclosed résumé, I've been working part-time with a local publisher since my sophomore year. During that time, I've used client interactions as an opportunity to build strong customer service skills.

In the final paragraph of your application letter, respectfully ask for specific action and make it easy for the reader to respond.

Motivating Action   The final paragraph of your application letter has two important functions: to ask the reader for a specific action and to facilitate a reply. Don't demand an interview, however; try to sound natural and appreciative. Offer to come to the employer's office at a convenient time or, if the firm is some distance away, to meet with its nearest representative or arrange a telephone interview. Make the request easy to fulfill by stating your phone number and the best time to reach you—or, if you want to be in control, by mentioning that you will follow up with a phone call in a few days. Refer again to your strongest selling point and, if desired, your date of availability:

> After you have reviewed my qualifications, could we discuss the possibility of putting my marketing skills to work for your company? Because I will be on spring break the week of March 8, I would like to arrange a time to talk then. I will call in late February to schedule a convenient time when we could discuss employment opportunities at your company.

✓ CHECKLIST: Writing Application Letters

✓ Open the letter by capturing the reader's attention in a businesslike way.
✓ Use specific language to clearly state your interests and objectives.
✓ Build interest and desire in your potential contribution by presenting your key qualifications for the job.
✓ Link your education, experience, and personal qualities to the job requirements.

✓ Outline salary requirements only if the organization has requested that you provide them.
✓ Request an interview at a time and place that is convenient for the reader.
✓ Make it easy to comply with your request by providing your complete contact information and good times to reach you.
✓ Adapt your style for cultural variations, if required.

After you have edited and proofread your application letter, give it a final quality check by referring to "Checklist: Writing Application Letters." Then print it and send it (or e-mail it) along with your résumé promptly, especially if you are responding to an ad or online job posting.

Application Follow-Ups

If your application letter and résumé fail to bring a response within a month or so, follow up with a second letter to keep your file active. This follow-up letter also gives you a chance to update your original application with any recent job-related information:

> Since applying to you on May 3 for a position in your management training program, I have completed three courses in business and management at South River Community College and received straight A's.
>
> Please keep my application in your active file; I would welcome another opportunity to apply for the program.

Even if you've received a letter acknowledging your application and saying that it will be kept on file, don't hesitate to send a follow-up letter three months later to show that you are still interested:

> Three months have elapsed since I applied to you for an underwriting position, but I want to let you know that I am still very interested in joining your company.
>
> I recently completed a four-week temporary work assignment at a large local insurance agency. I learned several new verification techniques and gained experience in using the online computer system. This experience could increase my value to your underwriting department.
>
> Please keep my application in your active file and let me know when a position opens for a capable underwriter.

You can write this sort of follow-up message even if you have no new accomplishments to share. Do some quick research on the company and its industry to find something that you can feature in your message ("I've been reading about the new technical challenges facing your industry . . ."). Your initiative and knowledge will impress recruiters. Without a follow-up communication from you, the human resources office is likely to assume that you've already found a job and are no

Think creatively about a follow-up message; show that you've continued to add to your skills or that you've learned more about the company or the industry.

longer interested in the organization. Moreover, a company's requirements change. A follow-up letter can demonstrate that you're sincerely interested in working for the organization, persistent in pursuing your goals, and committed to upgrading your skills. And it might just get you an interview.

UNDERSTANDING THE INTERVIEWING PROCESS

Like Google's Arnnon Geshuri, all recruiters have lists of qualities and accomplishments they are looking for in job candidates. An **employment interview** is a formal meeting during which you and a prospective employer ask questions and exchange information. These meetings have a dual purpose: (1) The organization's main objective is to find the best person available for the job by determining whether you and the organization are a good match, and (2) your main objective is to find the job best suited to your goals and capabilities. While recruiters such as those at Google are trying to decide whether you are right for them, you must decide whether Google or any other company is right for you.

Large organizations that hire hundreds of new employees every year typically take a more systematic approach to the recruiting and interviewing process than small local businesses that hire only a few new people each year. You'll need to adjust your job search according to the company's size and hiring practices. In general, the easiest way to connect with a big company is through your campus placement office; the most efficient way to approach a smaller business is often contacting the company directly.

Regardless of which path you choose, interviewing takes time, so start seeking jobs well in advance of the date you want to start work. Some students begin their job search as much as nine months before graduation. During downturns in the economy, early planning is especially crucial. During downturns, many employers become more selective, and many corporations reduce their campus visits and campus hiring programs, so more of the job-search burden falls on you. Whatever shape the economy is in, try to secure as many interviews as you can, both to improve the chances of receiving a job offer and to give yourself more options when you do get offers.

The Typical Sequence of Interviews

Not all organizations interview potential candidates the same way. At Southwest Airlines, for example, each candidate undergoes a rigorous interview process that can take as long as six weeks.[5] However, most employers interview an applicant two or three times before deciding to make a job offer. Applicants often face a sequence of interviews, each with a different purpose.

First is the preliminary *screening stage*, which may be conducted in person (at a company site or on campus for new college hires), over the telephone, or online. Those candidates who best meet the organization's requirements are invited to visit company offices for further evaluation. Interviews at the screening stage are fairly structured, so applicants are often asked roughly the same questions. Many companies use standardized evaluation sheets to "grade" the applicants so that all the candidates will be measured against the same criteria. In some cases, technology has transformed the initial, get-to-know-you interview, allowing employers to screen candidates by phone, video interview, or computer.[6]

Your best approach to an interview at the screening stage is to follow the interviewer's lead. Keep your responses short and to the point. Time is limited, so talking too much can be a big mistake. However, to give the interviewer a way to differentiate you from other candidates and to demonstrate your strengths and qualifications, try to emphasize the "theme" you used in developing your résumé.

Asking questions of your own is as important as answering the interviewer's questions. Not only do you get vital information, but you show initiative and curiosity.

Most organizations interview an applicant several times before extending a job offer.

During the screening stage, try to differentiate yourself from other candidates.

The next stage of interviews helps the organization narrow the field a little further. Typically, if you're invited to visit a company, you will talk with several people in succession, such as a member of the human resources department, one or two potential colleagues, and one or more managers, including your potential supervisor. You might face a **panel interview**, during which several interviewers ask questions during a single session. Your best approach during this *selection stage* of interviews is to show interest in the job, relate your skills and experience to the organization's needs, listen attentively, ask insightful questions, and display enthusiasm.

During the selection stage, you may interview with several people, perhaps at the same time.

If the interviewers agree that you're a good candidate, you may receive a job offer, either on the spot or a few days later by phone or mail. In other cases, you may be invited back for a final evaluation by a higher-ranking executive who has the authority to make the hiring decision and to decide on your compensation. An underlying objective of the *final stage* is often to sell you on the advantages of joining the organization.

During the final stage, the interviewer may try to sell you on working for the firm.

Common Types of Interviews

Organizations use various types of interviews to discover as much as possible about you and other applicants. A **structured interview** is generally used in the screening stage. The employer controls the interview by asking a series of prepared questions in a set order. Working from a checklist, the interviewer asks you each question, staying within an allotted time period. All answers are noted. Although useful for gathering facts, the structured interview is generally regarded as a poor measure of an applicant's personal qualities. Nevertheless, some companies use structured interviews to create uniformity in their hiring process.[7]

The goal of a structured interview is to gather facts.

By contrast, the **open-ended interview** is less formal and is unstructured. The interviewer poses broad, open-ended questions and encourages you to talk freely. This type of interview is good for bringing out your personality and for testing professional judgment. However, some candidates reveal too much, rambling on about personal or family problems that have nothing to do with their qualifications for employment, their ability to get along with co-workers, or any personal interests that could benefit their performance on the job. So be careful. You need to strike a balance between being friendly and remembering that you're in a business situation.

In an open-ended interview, the recruiter encourages you to speak freely.

Some organizations perform **group interviews**, meeting with several candidates simultaneously to see how they interact. This type of interview isn't as common as the other types, but some companies use it to assess interpersonal skills and the ability to work as part of a team.[8] In contrast, the **panel interview**, in which a single candidate faces a panel of interviewers, is becoming more common. One key advantage of this approach for employers is the chance for everyone on the interview team to see the candidate's response to every question rather than replying on reports from each interviewer. To succeed in a panel interview, keep in mind that the panel is made up of individuals who represent different parts of the organization and therefore have different concerns about job candidates. Address each interviewer individually in your answers, tailoring each response to that person's concerns.[9]

Group interviews help recruiters see how several candidates interact with one another.

The most unnerving type of interview is the **stress interview**, during which you might be asked pointed questions designed to irk or unsettle you, or you might be subjected to long periods of silence, criticisms of your appearance, deliberate interruptions, and abrupt or even hostile reactions by the interviewer. The theory behind this approach is that you'll reveal how well you handle stressful situations, although some experts find the technique of dubious value—particularly if the stress induced during the interview has no relationship to the job in question.[10] If you find yourself

Stress interviews help recruiters see how you handle yourself under pressure.

in a stress interview, pause for a few seconds to collect your thoughts and then continue, knowing what the interviewer is up to.

Many companies have learned that no strong correlation exists between how well people answer interview questions in a traditional interview and how well they perform on the job. In response, these firms have adopted a variety of new interviewing strategies. In the **situational interview**, various on-the-job scenarios are described, and candidates are asked how they would respond. Similarly, a **behavioral interview** asks candidates to describe real situations in the past and explain how they responded.[11] The most realistic approach is the **working interview**, in which the candidate is asked to perform the actual work that he or she would be doing on the job. For instance, a copywriting candidate in an advertising agency could be asked to write text for a webpage.[12]

> In situational interviews, you're asked to explain how you would handle a specific set of circumstances.

Interview Media

In addition to encountering a variety of interview formats, expect to be interviewed through a variety of media. Employers trying to cut travel costs and the demands on staff time now interview candidates via telephone, e-mail, instant messaging, virtual online systems, and videoconferencing. These alternative media options are used most frequently in the screening stage but can be used into the selection stage as well.

To succeed at a telephone interview, make sure you treat it as seriously as an in-person interview. Be prepared with a copy of all the materials you have sent the employer, including your résumé and any correspondence. In addition, prepare some note cards with key message points you'd like to make and your supporting evidence (such as an impressive success story from your current job). If possible, arrange to speak on a landline so you don't have to worry about mobile phone reception problems. And remember that you won't be able to use a pleasant smile, a firm handshake, and other nonverbal signals to create a good impression. A positive, alert tone of voice is therefore vital.[13]

> Treat a telephone interview as seriously as you would an in-person interview.

E-mail and IM are also sometimes used in the screening stage. While you have even less opportunity to send and receive nonverbal signals with these formats, you do have the major advantage of being able to review and edit each response before you send it. Maintain a professional style in your responses and be sure to ask questions that demonstrate your knowledge of the company and the position.[14]

> When interviewing via e-mail or IM, be sure to take a moment to review your responses before sending them.

Virtual online interviews can range from simple structured interviews to sophisticated job simulations that are similar to working interviews. People applying for teller positions at SunTrust, a regional bank based in Atlanta, interact with video-game-like characters while performing job-related tasks. These job simulations not only identify good candidates but also reduce the risk of employment discrimination lawsuits because they closely mimic actual job skills.[15] The latest innovation in simulators uses prerecorded video of real people asking questions and records the candidate's answers on video as well.[16] And as one might expect from an innovator in search technology, Google is testing an extensive online interview system that measures attitudes, behaviors, personality, and personal history in an attempt to find candidates who match the profiles of successful Google employees.[17]

> Computer-based virtual interviews range from simple structured interviews to realistic job simulations.

Many large companies use videoconferencing systems to screen middle-management candidates or to interview new recruits at universities. Experts recommend that candidates prepare a bit differently for a video interview than for an in-person meeting:[18]

> In a video interview, speak to the camera as though you are addressing the interviewer in person.

- Ask for a preliminary phone conversation to establish rapport with the interviewer.

- Dress conservatively, in solid colors with minimal jewelry.

- Arrive early enough to get used to the equipment and setting.

- During the interview, speak clearly but not more slowly than normal.

- Sit straight.

- Talk to the camera.

- Keep your mannerisms lively without looking forced or fake.

What Employers Look for in an Interview

Chapter 15 points out the attributes employers look for when reviewing résumés. The interview process gives them a chance to go beyond this basic information to answer two essential questions: Will the candidate be a good fit with the organization? and Can the candidate handle the responsibilities of the position? For instance, TechTarget, an interactive media company, gives employees an unusual amount of freedom, including the freedom to set their own hours and take as many days off for illness, personal matters, and vacation as they want or need—provided that they meet their work objectives. It may sound like a wonderful arrangement, but CEO Greg Strakosch recognizes that some people can't handle the responsibility that comes with such independence. As a result, TechTarget's hiring process is focused on filtering out candidates who need a more structured environment.[19]

Some interviewers believe that personal background indicates how well a candidate will fit in, so they might ask about your interests, hobbies, awareness of world events, and so forth. You can expand your potential along these lines by reading widely, making an effort to meet new people, and participating in discussion groups, seminars, and workshops. For instance, Google (see page 581) values diverse interests and experiences, and rampant curiosity about virtually any subject is always welcome.

Beyond your organizational fit, interviewers are likely to consider your personal style as well. You're likely to impress an employer by being open, enthusiastic, and interested. Some interviewers also look for courtesy, sincerity, willingness to learn, and a style that is positive and self-confident. All these qualities help a new employee adapt to a new workplace and new responsibilities.

Preemployment Testing

In an effort to improve the predictability of the selection process and reduce the reliance on the brief interaction that an interview allows, many employers now conduct a variety of preemployment tests.[20] These tests attempt to assess such factors as integrity, personality, job skills, and substance use. Google uses testing in creative ways not only to measure skills of potential hires but also to build interest in the company as a fun place to work. Thousands of computer programmers compete in the annual Google Code Jam, vying for valuable prizes and the chance to visit Google to explore job opportunities.[21]

Testing is a complex topic that varies widely by industry and position, and it also involves a wide range of legal and ethical issues, including discrimination and privacy. For instance, any testing that can be construed as a preemployment medical examination is prohibited by the Americans with Disabilities Act.[22] Here is an overview of the most common types of tests:

- **Integrity tests.** You might not think that a test could identify job candidates who are more likely than others to steal from their employers or commit other ethical or legal infractions, but employers have had some success in using integrity tests, such as reducing employee theft.[23]

- **Personality tests.** Personality tests are used to assess either general character or suitability for the demands of a specific profession. General tests attempt to profile

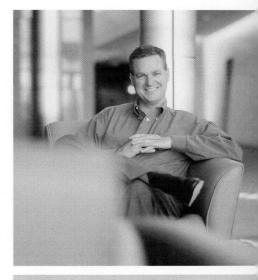

TechTarget CEO Greg Strakosch offers his employees extraordinary amounts of freedom, so he works hard to find employees who can handle the responsibility of setting their own schedules.

Compatibility with an organization is judged on the basis of personal background, attitudes, and style.

Suitability for a specific job is judged on the basis of
- Academic preparation
- Work experience
- Job-related personality traits

Preemployment tests attempt to provide objective, quantitative information about a candidate's skills, attitudes, and habits.

overall intellectual ability, attitudes toward work, interests, and managerial potential, as well as such characteristics as dependability, commitment, honesty, and motivation.[24]

- **Job skills tests.** The most common type of preemployment tests are those designed to assess the competency or specific abilities needed to perform a job.[25]

- **Substance tests.** Drug and alcohol testing is one of the most controversial issues in business today. Some employers believe such testing is absolutely necessary to maintain workplace safety, whereas others view it as an invasion of employee privacy and a sign of disrespect. Some companies test only applicants but not employees.[26] Companies test for three reasons: (1) to cut the costs (approximately $100 billion a year) and the reduced productivity associated with drug abuse, (2) to reduce the number of accidents (substance abusers have two to four times as many accidents as other employees, and drug use is linked to 40 percent of industrial fatalities), and (3) to reduce legal liability for negligent hiring practices if an employee harms an innocent party on the job.[27] In recent years, as many as 80 percent of U.S. employers have conducted drug testing, but that percentage appears to be declining.[28]

- **Background checks.** The use of background checks has been growing rapidly; 80 percent of U.S. employers now conduct criminal background checks, for instance. Other types of background checks try to verify the credentials on your résumé, see how well you manage credit, or determine whether you might be on a terrorist watch list.[29] Despite concerns about privacy, many employers believe they have no choice but to conduct background checks. Employers can be held liable for the actions of employees who obtained jobs under false pretenses—and lying by job candidates is depressingly common these days. In one recent survey of more than 2 million job applicants, 44 percent lied about their employment history, 41 percent lied about their education, and 23 percent claimed to have professional credentials or licenses they didn't have.[30]

If you're concerned about any preemployment test, ask the employer for more information or ask your college placement office for advice. You can also get more information from the Equal Employment Opportunity Commission, at www.eeoc.gov. Also, make sure your college transcript and credit record are correct and up to date so that any errors don't cause problems when a potential employer looks into your background.[31]

Your college's career center has numerous resources to help you prepare for interviews.

PREPARING FOR A JOB INTERVIEW

The more prepared you are, the less nervous you'll be about the interviewing process. Be sure to consider any cultural differences when preparing for interviews, and base your approach on what your audience expects. To prepare for a successful interview, learn about the organization, think ahead about questions, bolster your confidence, polish your interview style, plan to look good, and be ready when you arrive.

Learning About the Organization

Today's companies expect serious candidates to demonstrate an understanding of a company's operations, its markets, and its strategic and tactical challenges.[32] When you were planning your employment search, you probably already researched the companies you sent your résumé to. But now that you've been invited for an interview, you'll want to fine-tune your research and brush up on the facts you've collected. Table 16.2 offers tips on researching both companies and jobs.

FINDING OUT ABOUT AN ORGANIZATION AND A JOB OPPORTUNITY

Table 16.2

Where to Look and What You Can Learn

- Company website: Overall information about the company, including key executives, products and services, locations and divisions, employee benefits, job descriptions

- Competitors' websites: Similar information from competitors, including the strengths these companies claim to have

- Industry-related websites: Objective analysis and criticism of the company, its products, its reputation, and its management

- Marketing materials (brochures, catalogs, etc.): The company's marketing strategy and customer communication style

- Company publications (both print and electronic): Key events, stories about employees, new products

- Blogs: Analysis and criticism (not always fair or unbiased) of the company, its products and services, its reputation, and its management

- Periodicals (newspapers and trade journals, both print and online): In-depth stories about the company and its strategies, products, successes, and failures; you may find profiles of top executives

- Career center at your college: Often provides wide array of information about companies that hire graduates

- Current and former employees: Insights into the work environment

Points to Learn About the Organization

- Full name
- Location (headquarters and divisions, branches, subsidiaries, or other units)
- Age and brief history
- Products and services
- Industry position (is the company a leader or a minor player; is it an innovator or more of a follower)
- Key financial points (such as stock price and trend, if a public company)
- Growth prospects (is the company investing in its future through research and development; is it in a thriving industry)

Points to Learn About the Position

- Title
- Functions and responsibilities
- Qualifications and expectations
- Career path
- Salary range
- Travel expectations and opportunities
- Relocation expectations and opportunities

Thinking Ahead About Questions

As you plan your responses to potential interview questions, be prepared to relate your qualifications to the organization's needs.

Planning ahead for the interviewer's questions will help you handle them more confidently and successfully. As you consider answers to questions you might encounter, think about how you can relate your qualifications to the organization's needs. In addition, you will want to prepare insightful questions of your own.

Planning for the Employer's Questions   Employers usually gear their interview questions to specific organizational needs. You can expect to be asked about your skills, achievements, and goals, as well as about your attitudes toward work and school, your relationships with others, and occasionally your hobbies and interests. You'll also need to anticipate and give a little extra thought to a few particularly tough questions, such as these:

- **What is the hardest decision you've ever had to make?** Be prepared with a good example, explaining why the decision was difficult and how you finally made it.

- **What are your greatest weaknesses?** This question seems to be a stock favorite of some interviewers, although it probably rarely yields useful information. The standard ways to reply are to describe a weakness so that it sounds like a virtue—such as driving yourself too hard—or to describe a relatively minor shortcoming and explain how you're working to improve.

- **What didn't you like about previous jobs you've held?** State what you didn't like and discuss what the experience taught you. Avoid making negative references to former employers or colleagues. Be aware that when employers ask this question, they're trying to predict if you'll be an unhappy or difficult employee, so plan your answer with care.[33]

- **Where do you want to be five years from now?** This questions tests (1) whether you're merely using this job as a stopover until something better comes along and (2) whether you've given thought to your long-term goals. Whatever you plan to say, your answer should reflect your desire to contribute to the employer's long-term goals.

- **Tell me something about yourself.** Answer that you'll be happy to talk about yourself and ask what the interviewer wants to know. If this point is clarified, respond. If it isn't, explain how your skills can contribute to the job and the organization. This is a great chance to sell yourself.

Practice answering typical interview questions so that you can respond with confidence and complete answers.

For a look at the types of interview questions often asked, see Table 16.3. Jot down a brief answer to each one. Then read over the answers until you feel comfortable with each of them. You might also have a friend ask you these questions so you can practice giving answers.

Planning Questions of Your Own   Interviewers expect you to have questions, so be prepared with a dozen of them or so. By asking insightful questions, you can demonstrate your understanding of the organization, you can steer the discussion into areas that allow you to present your qualifications to best advantage, and you can verify for yourself whether this is the right opportunity for you.

Plan questions that will help you decide whether the work and the organization are compatible with your goals and values.

Don't limit your questions to those you think will impress the interviewer, or you won't get the information you need to make a wise decision if you're offered the job. Craft questions to help you explore such issues as these:

- Are these my kind of people?

- Can I do this work?

- Will I enjoy the work?

- Is the job what I want?

- Does the job pay what I'm worth?

- What kind of person would I be working for?

- What sort of future can I expect with this organization?

Rather than bombarding the interviewer with questions the minute you walk in the room, work them into the conversation naturally, without trying to take control

You don't necessarily have to wait until the interviewer asks if you have any questions of your own; look for smooth ways to work prepared questions into the conversation.

TWENTY-FIVE COMMON INTERVIEW QUESTIONS   Table 16.3

Questions About College

1. What courses in college did you like most? Least? Why?
2. Do you think your extracurricular activities in college were worth the time you spent on them? Why or why not?
3. When did you choose your college major? Did you ever change your major? If so, why?
4. Do you feel you did the best scholastic work you are capable of?
5. Which of your college years was the toughest? Why?

Questions About Employers and Jobs

1. What jobs have you held? Why did you leave?
2. What percentage of your college expenses did you earn? How?
3. Why did you choose your particular field of work?
4. What are the disadvantages of your chosen field?
5. Have you served in the military? What rank did you achieve? What jobs did you perform?
6. What do you think about how this industry operates today?
7. Why do you think you would like this particular type of job?

Questions About Personal Attitudes and Preferences

1. Do you prefer to work in any specific geographic location? If so, why?
2. How much money do you hope to be earning in 5 years? In 10 years?
3. What do you think determines a person's progress in a good organization?
4. What personal characteristics do you feel are necessary for success in your chosen field?
5. Tell me a story.
6. Do you like to travel?
7. Do you think grades should be considered by employers? Why or why not?

Questions About Work Habits

1. Do you prefer working with others or by yourself?
2. What type of boss do you prefer?
3. Have you ever had any difficult getting along with colleagues or supervisors? With instructors? With other students?
4. Would you prefer to work in a large or small organization? Why?
5. How do you feel about overtime work?
6. What have you done that shows initiative and willingness to work?

Table 16.4	**TEN QUESTIONS TO ASK AN INTERVIEWER**

1. What are the job's major responsibilities?
2. What qualities do you want in the person who fills this position?
3. How do you measure success for someone in this position?
4. What is the first problem that needs the attention of the person you hire?
5. Would relocation be required now or in the future?
6. Why is this job now vacant?
7. What makes your organization different from others in the industry?
8. How would you define your organization's managerial philosophy?
9. What additional training does your organization provide?
10. Do employees have an opportunity to continue their education with help from the organization?

of the interview. For a list of good questions you might use as a starting point, see Table 16.4.

Impress the interviewer with your ability to organize and be thorough by bringing a list of questions to the job interview.

Write your list of questions on a notepad and take it to the interview. If you need to, jot down brief notes during the meeting and be sure to record answers in more detail afterward. Having a list of questions should impress the interviewer with your organization and thoroughness. It will also show that you're there to evaluate the organization and the job as well as to promote yourself.

Bolstering Your Confidence

By building your confidence, you'll make a better impression and make the whole process less stressful. The best way to counteract any apprehension is to remove its source. You may feel shy or self-conscious because you think you have some flaw that will prompt others to reject you. Bear in mind, however, that you're often much more conscious of your limitations than other people are.

If some aspect of your appearance or background makes you uneasy, correct it or offset it by emphasizing positive traits such as warmth, wit, intelligence, or charm. Instead of dwelling on your weaknesses, focus on your strengths. Instead of worrying about how you will perform in the interview, focus on how you can help the organization succeed. Remember that all the other candidates for the job are just as nervous as you are. The interviewers may be nervous, too; after all, they're judged on how well they assess candidates, so help them see your positive qualities clearly.

Polishing Your Interview Style

Competence and confidence are the foundation of your interviewing style, and you can enhance them by giving the interviewer an impression of poise, good manners, and good judgment. Some job seekers hire professional coaches and image consultants to create just the right impression. These experts teach clients how to adopt appropriate communication styles, using role-playing, videotaping, and audiotaping.[34] You can use these techniques, too.

Staging mock interviews with a friend is a good way to hone your style.

For example, you can develop an adept style by staging mock interviews with a friend. You can record these practice sessions and then evaluate them yourself. The taping process can be intimidating, but it helps you work out any problems before you begin actual job interviews. Also, see if your career center has one of the com-

FIGURE 16.3
Interview Simulators
Experts advise you to practice your interview skills as much as possible. You can use a friend or classmate as a practice partner, or you might be able to use one of the interview simulators now available, such as this system from Perfect Interview. Ask at your career center for more information.

puter-based interview simulators that are now available (see Figure 16.3). You can search online for "practice interviews" or "interview simulators."

After each practice session, try to identify opportunities for improvement. Have your mock interview partner critique your performance, or critique yourself if you're able to record your practice interviews, using the list of warning signs shown in Table 16.5.

As you stage your mock interviews, pay particular attention to your nonverbal behavior. In the United States, you are more likely to have a successful interview if

Nonverbal behavior has a significant effect on the interviewer's opinion of you.

WARNING SIGNS: 25 ATTRIBUTES THAT INTERVIEWERS DON'T LIKE TO SEE — Table 16.5

- Poor personal appearance
- Overbearing, overaggressive, conceited demeanor; a "superiority complex" or know-it-all attitude
- Inability to express ideas clearly; poor voice, diction, grammar
- Lack of knowledge or experience
- Poor preparation for the interview
- Lack of interest in the job
- Lack of planning for career; lack of purpose, goals
- Lack of enthusiasm; passive and indifferent demeanor
- Lack of confidence and poise; appearance of being nervous and ill at ease
- Insufficient evidence of achievement
- Failure to participate in extracurricular activities
- Overemphasis on money; interest only in the best dollar offer
- Poor scholastic record; just got by
- Unwillingness to start at the bottom; expecting too much too soon
- Tendency to make excuses
- Evasive answers, hedges on unfavorable factors in record
- Lack of fact
- Lack of maturity
- Lack of courtesy; ill-mannered
- Condemnation of past employers
- Lack of social skills
- Marked dislike for schoolwork
- Lack of vitality
- Failure to look interviewer in the eye
- Limp, weak handshake

you maintain eye contact, smile frequently, sit in an attentive position, and use frequent hand gestures. These nonverbal signals convince the interviewer that you're alert, assertive, dependable, confident, responsible, and energetic.[35] Some companies based in the United States are owned and managed by people from other cultures, so during your research, find out about the company's cultural background and preferences regarding nonverbal behavior.

The way you speak is almost as important as what you say.

The sound of your voice can also have a major impact on your success in a job interview.[36] You can work with a tape recorder to overcome voice problems. If you tend to speak too rapidly, practice speaking more slowly. If your voice sounds too loud or too soft, practice adjusting it. Work on eliminating speech mannerisms such as *you know*, *like*, and *um*, which might make you sound inarticulate.

Planning to Look Good

Dress conservatively and be well groomed for every interview; you will be judged on how well you can sense what is appropriate in the work environment.

Physical appearance is important because clothing and grooming reveal something about a candidate's personality, professionalism, and ability to sense the unspoken "rules" of a situation. When it comes to clothing, the best policy is to dress conservatively. Wear the best-quality businesslike clothing you can, preferably in a dark, solid color. Wearing clothes that are appropriate and clean is far more important than wearing clothes that are expensive. Avoid flamboyant styles, colors, and prints. Even in companies in which interviewers may dress casually, it's important to show good judgment by dressing—and acting—in a professional manner. Even minor points of etiquette can make a lasting impression on recruiters. Refer to Table 2.3 on page 60 for tips on selecting appropriate business attire.

Some candidates ask interviewers ahead of time what they should wear. One human resources executive tells job seekers to dress business casual because dressing in a suit, for example, looks awkward at his company.[37] However, in other companies, business casual would be completely out of place in a job interview. Your research into various industries and professions should give you insight into expectations for business attire, too. If you're not sure, being a little too formal is a better guess than being too casual.

Make a positive first impression with careful grooming and attire. You don't need to spend a fortune on new clothes, but you do need to look clean, prepared, and professional.

Good grooming makes any style of clothing look better. Make sure your clothes are clean and unwrinkled, your shoes unscuffed and well shined, your hair neatly styled and combed, your fingernails clean, and your breath fresh. If possible, check your appearance in a mirror before entering the room for the interview. Finally, remember that one of the best ways to look good is to smile at appropriate moments.

Make professional appearance and habits a routine part of your day after you land that first job, too. Some students fail to recognize the need to adjust their dress and personal habits when they make the transition to professional life. Behaviors you may not think about, such as showing up five minutes late to every meeting or wearing a T-shirt to a client's office, could limit your career potential. Again, these may seem like minor issues, but many people are sensitive to these points of business etiquette and consider them signs of mutual respect.

Being Ready When You Arrive

Be ready to go the minute you arrive at the interviewing site; don't fumble around for your résumé or your list of questions.

When you go to your interview, take a small notebook, a pen, a list of the questions you want to ask, two copies of your résumé (protected in a folder), an outline of what you have learned about the organization, and any past correspondence about the position. You may also want to take a small calendar, a transcript of your college grades, a list of references, and a portfolio containing samples of your work, performance reviews, and certificates of achievement.[38]

Be sure you know when and where the interview will be held. The worst way to start any interview is to be late. Check the route you will take, even if it means phon-

✓ CHECKLIST: Planning for a Successful Job Interview

- ✓ Learn about the organization, including its operations, markets, and challenges.
- ✓ Plan for the employer's questions, including questions about tough decisions you've made, your weaknesses, what you didn't like about previous jobs, and your career plans.
- ✓ Plan questions of your own to find out whether this is really the job and the organization for you and to show that you've done your research.
- ✓ Bolster your confidence by removing as many sources of apprehension as you can.

- ✓ Polish your interview style by staging mock interviews.
- ✓ Plan to look good with appropriate dress and grooming.
- ✓ Be ready when you arrive and bring along a pen, paper, list of questions, two résumés, an outline of your research on the company, and any correspondence you've had regarding the position.
- ✓ Double-check the location and time of the interview and map out the route beforehand.
- ✓ Relax and be flexible; the schedule and interview arrangements may change when you arrive.

ing ahead to ask. Find out how much time it takes to get there; then plan to arrive early. Allow a little extra time in case you run into a problem on the way.

When you arrive, remind yourself that you are fully prepared and confident and then try to relax. You may have to wait, so bring along something business oriented to read. If company literature is available in the lobby, read it while you wait. At every step, show respect for everyone you encounter. If the opportunity presents itself, ask a few questions about the organization or express enthusiasm for the job. Refrain from smoking before the interview (nonsmokers can smell smoke on the clothing of interviewees) and avoid chewing gum or otherwise eating or drinking in the waiting room. Anything you do or say while you wait may well get back to the interviewer, so make sure your best qualities show from the moment you enter the premises. That way, you'll be ready for the interview itself when it actually begins. To review the steps for planning a successful interview, see "Checklist: Planning for a Successful Job Interview."

INTERVIEWING FOR SUCCESS

Your approach to interviews evolves as you move through each stage of the process. The techniques for success are similar throughout, even though the focus and purpose of the interviews change—for both you and the employer. To increase your chances of success, follow tips from successful interviewers about how to make a positive impression by avoiding mistakes (see "Sharpening Your Career Skills: Make Sure You Don't Talk Yourself Right Out of a Job").

If you're being interviewed for the first time, your main objective is to differentiate yourself from the many other candidates who are also being screened. Without resorting to gimmicks, call attention to one key aspect of your personal or professional background so that the recruiter can say, "Oh yes, I remember Brenda Jones—the one who built a computerized home weather station to wake her up a few minutes early whenever it snowed overnight." Just be sure the trait you accentuate is relevant to the job in question. In addition, you'll want to be prepared in case an employer expects you to demonstrate a particular skill (perhaps problem solving) during the screening interview.

Present a memorable "headline" during an interview at the screening stage.

If you progress to the initial selection interview, broaden your promotional message. Instead of telegraphing the "headline," give the interviewer the whole story. Touch briefly on all your strengths but explain three or four of your best qualifications in depth. At the same time, probe for information that will help you evaluate the position objectively.

Cover all your strengths during an interview at the selection stage.

SHARPENING YOUR CAREER SKILLS

Make Sure You Don't Talk Yourself Right Out of a Job

Even well-qualified applicants sometimes talk themselves right out of an opportunity by making avoidable blunders during a job interview. Take care to avoid these all-too-common mistakes:

- *Being defensive.* An interview isn't an interrogation, and the interviewer isn't out to get you. Treat interviews as business conversations, an exchange of information in which both sides have something of value to share. You'll give (and get) better information that way.

- *Failing to ask questions.* Interviewers expect you to ask questions, both during the interview and at its conclusion, when they ask if you have any questions. If you have nothing to ask, you come across as someone who isn't really interested in the job or the company. Prepare a list of questions before every interview.

- *Failing to answer questions—or trying to bluff your way through difficult questions.* If you simply can't answer a question, don't try to talk your way around it or fake your way through it. Remember that sometimes interviewers ask strange questions just to see how you'll respond. What kind of fish would you like to be? How would you go about nailing jelly to the ceiling? Why are manhole covers round? Some of these questions are designed to test your grace under pressure, whereas others are used to get you to think through a logical answer. (Manhole covers are round because that's the only shape that can't fall through an open hole of slightly smaller size, by the way.) Don't act like the question is stupid or refuse to answer it. Sit quietly for a few seconds, try to imagine why the interviewer has asked the question, and then frame an answer that links your strengths to the company's needs.

- *Freezing up.* The human brain seems to have the capacity to just freeze up in stressful situations. An interviewer might have asked you a simple question, or perhaps you are halfway through an intelligent answer, and poof—all your thoughts disappear and you can't organize words in any logical order. Try to quickly replay the last few seconds of the conversation in your mind to see if you can recapture the conversational thread. If that fails, you're probably better off explaining to the interviewer that your mind has gone blank and asking him or her to repeat the question. Doing so is embarrassing but not as embarrassing as chattering on and on with no idea of what you're saying, hoping you'll stumble back onto the topic.

- *Failing to understand your potential to contribute to the organization.* Interviewers care less about your history than about how you can help their organization in the future. Unless you've inventoried your own skills, researched their needs, and found a match between the two, you won't be able to answer these questions quickly and intelligently.

CAREER APPLICATIONS

1. What should you do if you suddenly realize that something you said earlier in the interview is incorrect or incomplete? Explain your answer.

2. How would you answer the following question: "How do you respond to colleagues who make you angry?" Explain your answer.

Emphasize your personality, motivations, and values during a final interview.

If you're asked back for a final visit, your chances of being offered a position have improved considerably. At this point, you'll probably talk to a person who has the authority to make an offer and negotiate terms. This individual may have already concluded that your background is right for the job and may be most concerned with sizing up your personality. Both you and the employer need to find out whether there is a good psychological fit. Be honest about your motivations and values. If the interview goes well, your objective should be to clinch the deal on the best possible terms.

Regardless of where you are in the interview process, every interview will proceed through three stages: the warm-up, the question-and-answer session, and the close.

The Warm-Up

The first minute of an interview is crucial, so be ready and stay on your toes.

Of the three stages, the warm-up is the most important, even though it may account for only a small fraction of the time you spend in the interview. Studies suggest that many interviewers, particularly those who are poorly trained in interviewing techniques, make up their minds within the first 20 seconds of contact with a candidate.[39] Don't let your guard down if the interviewer wants to engage in what feels like small talk; these exchanges are every bit as important as structured questions.

Body language is important at this point. Because you won't have time to say much in the first minute or two, you must sell yourself nonverbally. Begin by using the interviewer's name if you're sure you can pronounce it correctly. If the interviewer extends a hand, respond with a firm but not overpowering handshake; don't sit down until you're asked to be seated or the interviewer has taken his or her own seat. Let the interviewer start the discussion, and listen for cues that tell you what he or she is interested in knowing about you as a potential employee.

The Question-and-Answer Stage

Questions and answers will consume the greatest part of the interview. The interviewer will ask you about your qualifications and discuss many of the points mentioned in your résumé. You'll also be asking questions of your own.

Dealing with Questions   Let the interviewer lead the conversation and never answer a question before he or she has finished asking it—the last few words of the question might alter how you respond. As questions are asked, tailor your answers to make a favorable impression. Don't limit yourself to yes or no answers. If the interviewer asks you a difficult question, be sure you pause to think before responding. The recruiter may know that you can't answer a question and may only want to know how you'll respond.

Tailor your answers to emphasize your strengths.

If you periodically ask a question or two from the list you've prepared, you'll not only learn something but also demonstrate your interest. Probe for what the company is looking for in its new employees so that you can show how you meet the firm's needs. Also try to zero in on any reservations the interviewer might have about you so that you can dispel them.

Listening to the Interviewer   Paying attention when an interviewer speaks can be as important as giving good answers or asking good questions. Review the tips on listening offered in Chapter 2.

The interviewer's facial expressions, eye movements, gestures, and posture may tell you the real meaning of what is being said. Be especially aware of how your comments are received. Does the interviewer nod in agreement or smile to show approval? If so, you're making progress. If not, you might want to introduce another topic or modify your approach.

Paying attention to both verbal and nonverbal messages can help you turn the question-and-answer stage to your advantage.

Fielding Discriminatory Questions   Employers cannot legally discriminate against a job candidate on the basis of race, color, gender, age (at least if you're between 40 and 70), marital status, religion, national origin, or disability. Accordingly, federal regulations are in place to prevent interviewers from asking questions in ways that would allow them to discriminate according to any of these factors. Individual states and cities have enacted a variety of laws concerning interview questions, so you may have additional protections beyond the federal standards.[40] Table 16.6 compares specific questions that may and may not be asked during an employment interview.

Well-trained interviewers are aware of questions they shouldn't ask.

If your interviewer asks these personal questions, how you respond depends on how badly you want the job, how you feel about revealing the information asked for, what you think the interviewer will do with the information, and whether you want to work for a company that asks such questions. Remember that you always have the option of simply refusing to answer or of telling the interviewer that you think a particular question is unethical—although either of these responses is likely to leave an unfavorable impression.[41] If you do want the job, you might (1) ask how the question

Think about how you might respond if you are asked a potentially unlawful question.

Table 16.6	INTERVIEW QUESTIONS THAT MAY AND MAY NOT BE ASKED	
	Interviewers May Ask This . . .	*But Not This . . .*
	What is your name?	What was your maiden name?
	Are you over 18?	When were you born?
	Did you graduate from high school?	When did you graduate from high school?
	[No questions about race are allowed.]	What is your race?
	Can you perform [specific tasks]?	Do you have physical or mental disabilities?
		Do you have a drug or alcohol problem?
		Are you taking any prescription drugs?
	Would you be able to meet the job's requirements to frequently work weekends?	Would working on weekends conflict with your religion?
	Do you have the legal right to work in the United States?	What country are you a citizen of?
	Have you ever been convicted of a felony?	Have you ever been arrested?
	This job requires that you speak Spanish. Do you?	What language did you speak in your home when you were growing up?

is related to your qualifications, (2) explain that the information is personal, (3) respond to what you think is the interviewer's real concern, or (4) answer both the question and the concern.

If you do answer an unethical or unlawful question, you run the risk that your answer may hurt your chances, so think carefully before answering.[42] In any event, don't forget the two-way nature of the interview process: The organization is learning about you, and you're learning about the organization. Would you want to work for an organization that condones illegal or discriminatory questions or that doesn't train its employees enough to avoid them?

If you believe an interviewer's questions are unreasonable, unrelated to the job, or an attempt to discriminate, you may complain to the nearest field office of the EEOC (find offices online at www.eeoc.gov) or to the agency in your state that regulates fair employment practices. To report discrimination on the basis of age or physical disability, contact the employer's equal opportunity officer or the U.S. Department of Labor. If you file a complaint, be prepared to spend a lot of time and effort on it—and keep in mind that you may not win.[43]

The Close

Like the warm-up, the end of the interview is more important than its brief duration would indicate. In the last few minutes, you need to evaluate how well you've done. You also need to correct any misconceptions the interviewer might have.

Conclude an interview with courtesy and enthusiasm.

Concluding Gracefully   You can generally tell when the interviewer is trying to conclude the session. He or she may ask whether you have any more questions, sum up the discussion, change position, or indicate with a gesture that the interview is over. When you get the signal, respond promptly but don't rush. Be sure to thank the interviewer for the opportunity and express interest in the organization. If you can do so comfortably, try to pin down what will happen next but don't press for an immediate decision.

If this is your second or third visit to the organization, the interview may culminate with an offer of employment. You have two options: Accept it or request time to think it over. The best course is usually to wait. If no job offer is made, the interviewer may not have reached a decision yet, but you may tactfully ask when you can expect to know the decision.

Discussing Salary If you receive an offer during the interview, you'll naturally want to discuss salary. However, let the interviewer raise the subject. If you are asked your salary requirements during the interview or on a job application, you can say that your salary requirements are open or negotiable or that you would expect a competitive compensation package.[44] If you have added qualifications, point them out: "With my 18 months of experience in the field, I would expect to start in the middle of the normal salary range." You can find industry salary ranges at the Bureau of Labor Statistics website, www.bls.gov, and at several of the popular job websites.

> Research salary ranges in your job, industry, and geographic region before you try to negotiate salary.

If you don't like the offer, you might try to negotiate, provided that you're in a good bargaining position and the organization has the flexibility to accommodate you. You'll be in a fairly strong position if your skills are in short supply and you have several other offers. It also helps if you're the favorite candidate and the organization is booming. However, many organizations are relatively rigid in their salary practices, particularly at the entry level. In the United States and some European countries, it is perfectly acceptable to ask, "Is there any room for negotiation?"

Salary will probably be the most important component of your compensation and benefits package, but it's not the only factor by any means. And even if salary isn't negotiable, you may find flexibility in a signing bonus, profit sharing, pension and other retirement benefits, health coverage, vacation time, stock options, and other valuable elements in the overall compensation and benefits package.[45]

> Negotiating benefits may be one way to get more value from an employment package.

To review the important tips for successful interviews, see "Checklist: Making a Positive Impression in Job Interviews."

✓ CHECKLIST: Making a Positive Impression in Job Interviews

A. Understand the warm-up.

- ✓ Stay on your toes; even initial small talk is part of the interviewing process.
- ✓ Greet the interviewer by name, with a smile and direct eye contact.
- ✓ Offer a firm (not crushing) handshake if the interviewer extends a hand.
- ✓ Take a seat only after the interviewer invites you to sit or has taken his or her own seat.
- ✓ Listen for cues about what the questions are trying to reveal about you and your qualifications.

B. Understand the question-and-answer stage.

- ✓ Let the interviewer lead the conversation.
- ✓ Never answer a question before the interviewer finishes asking it.
- ✓ Listen carefully to the interviewer and watch for non-verbal signals.
- ✓ Don't limit yourself to simple yes or no answers; expand on the answer to show your knowledge of the company (but don't ramble on).
- ✓ If you encounter a potentially discriminatory question, decide how you want to respond before you say anything.
- ✓ When you have the opportunity, ask questions from the list you've prepared; remember that interviewers expect you to ask questions.

C. Close the interview.

- ✓ Watch and listen for signs that the interview is about to end.
- ✓ Quickly evaluate how well you've done and correct any misperceptions the interviewer might have.
- ✓ If you receive an offer and aren't ready to decide, it's entirely appropriate to ask for time to think about it.
- ✓ Don't bring up salary but be prepared to discuss it if the interviewer raises the subject.
- ✓ End with a warm smile and a handshake and thank the interviewer for meeting with you.

Interview Notes

Keep a written record of your job interviews, and keep your notes organized so that you can compare companies and opportunities.

If yours is a typical job search, you'll have many interviews before you accept an offer. For that reason, keeping a notebook or simple database of interview notes can help you refresh your memory of each conversation. As soon as you leave the interview facility, jot down the names and titles of the people you met. Briefly summarize the interviewer's answers to your questions. Then quickly evaluate your performance during the interview, listing what you handled well and what you didn't. Going over these notes can help you improve your performance in the future.[46] In addition to improving your performance during interviews, interview notes help you keep track of any follow-up messages you'll need to send.

FOLLOWING UP AFTER THE INTERVIEW

Six types of follow-up messages:
- Thank-you message
- Message of inquiry
- Request for a time extension
- Letter of acceptance
- Letter declining a job offer
- Letter of resignation

Touching base with the prospective employer after the interview, either by phone or in writing, shows that you really want the job and are determined to get it. Doing so also gives you another chance to demonstrate your communication skills and sense of business etiquette. Following up brings your name to the interviewer's attention once again and reminds him or her that you're actively looking and waiting for the decision.

The two most common forms of follow-up are the thank-you message and the message of inquiry. These messages are often handled by letter, but an e-mail or a phone call can be just as effective, particularly if the employer seems to favor a casual, personal style. Other types of follow-up messages—letters requesting a time extension, letters of acceptance, letters declining a job offer, and letters of resignation—are best handled in writing to document any official actions related to your employment.

Thank-You Message

A note or phone call thanking the interviewer should be organized like a routine message and close with a request for a decision or future consideration.

Express your thanks within two days after the interview, even if you feel you have little chance for the job. Not only is this good etiquette, but it leaves a positive impression. Acknowledge the interviewer's time and courtesy and convey your continued interest; then ask politely for a decision (see Figure 16.4).

Keep your thank-you message brief (less than five minutes for a phone call or just two or three paragraphs for a letter or an e-mail message) and organize it like a routine message. Demonstrate the "you" attitude and sound positive without sounding overconfident. Even if the interviewer has said that you are unqualified for the job, a thank-you message may keep the door open to future opportunities.

Message of Inquiry

To inquire about a hiring decision, follow the model for a direct request.

If you're not advised of the interviewer's decision by the promised date or within two weeks, you might make an inquiry. A message of inquiry is particularly appropriate if you've received a job offer from a second firm and don't want to accept it before you have an answer from the first. The following message illustrates the general plan for a direct request; the writer assumes that a simple oversight or routine delay, and not outright rejection, is the reason for the delay:

Identifies the position and introduces the main idea →

> When we talked on April 7 about the fashion coordinator position in your Park Avenue showroom, you indicated that a decision would be made by May 1. I am still enthusiastic about the position and eager to know what conclusion you've reached.

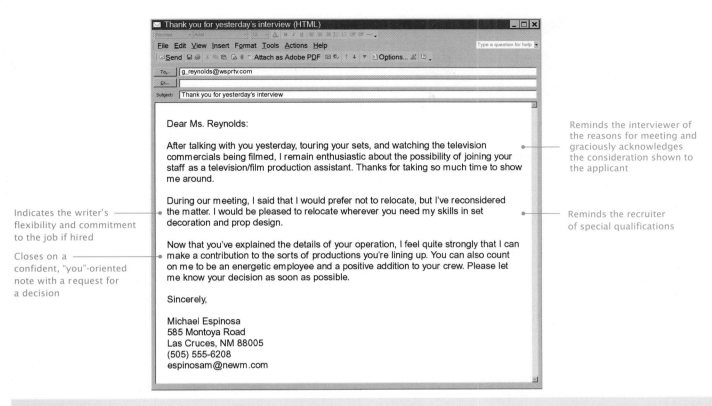

Reminds the interviewer of the reasons for meeting and graciously acknowledges the consideration shown to the applicant

Reminds the recruiter of special qualifications

Indicates the writer's flexibility and commitment to the job if hired

Closes on a confident, "you"-oriented note with a request for a decision

(email message shown in figure:)

To...: g_reynolds@wsprtv.com

Subject: Thank you for yesterday's interview

Dear Ms. Reynolds:

After talking with you yesterday, touring your sets, and watching the television commercials being filmed, I remain enthusiastic about the possibility of joining your staff as a television/film production assistant. Thanks for taking so much time to show me around.

During our meeting, I said that I would prefer not to relocate, but I've reconsidered the matter. I would be pleased to relocate wherever you need my skills in set decoration and prop design.

Now that you've explained the details of your operation, I feel quite strongly that I can make a contribution to the sorts of productions you're lining up. You can also count on me to be an energetic employee and a positive addition to your crew. Please let me know your decision as soon as possible.

Sincerely,

Michael Espinosa
585 Montoya Road
Las Cruces, NM 88005
(505) 555-6208
espinosam@newm.com

FIGURE 16.4

Thank-You Message
In three brief paragraphs, Michael Espinosa acknowledges the interviewer's time and consideration, expresses his continued interest in the position, explains a crucial discussion point that he has reconsidered, and asks for a decision.

To complicate matters, another firm has now offered me a position and has asked that I reply within the next two weeks.

Places the reason for the request second

Because your company seems to offer a greater challenge, I would appreciate knowing about your decision by Thursday, May 12. If you need more information before then, please let me know.

Makes a courteous request for specific action last, while clearly stating a preference for this organization

Request for a Time Extension

If you receive a job offer while other interviews are still pending, you'll probably want more time to decide, so write to the offering organization and ask for a time extension. Employers understand that candidates often interview with several companies. They want you to be sure you're making the right decision, so most are happy to accommodate you with a reasonable extension.

Preface your request with a friendly opening. Ask for more time, stressing your enthusiasm for the organization. Conclude by allowing for a quick decision if your request for additional time is denied. Ask for a prompt reply

Document Makeover

IMPROVE THIS LETTER

To practice correcting drafts of actual documents, visit your online course or the access-code-protected portion of the Companion Website. Click on "Document Makeovers" and then click on Chapter 16. You will find a letter that contains problems and errors related to what you've learned in this chapter about applying and interviewing for employment. Use the "Final Draft" decision tool to create an improved version of this request for a time extension. Check the letter for all the elements necessary to reassure the potential employer, ask for the extension, explain the reasons for the request, offer to compromise, and facilitate a quick reply.

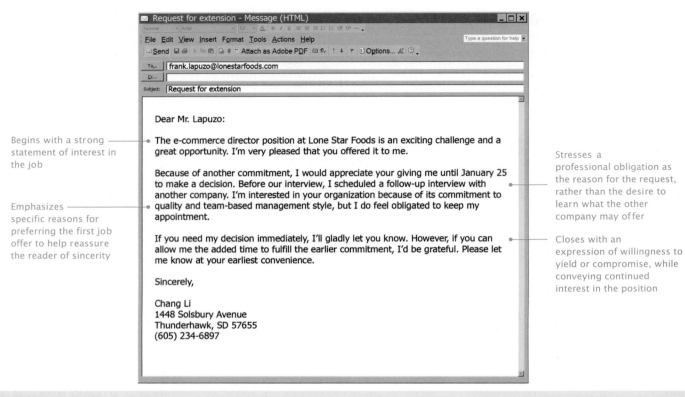

Begins with a strong statement of interest in the job

Emphasizes specific reasons for preferring the first job offer to help reassure the reader of sincerity

Stresses a professional obligation as the reason for the request, rather than the desire to learn what the other company may offer

Closes with an expression of willingness to yield or compromise, while conveying continued interest in the position

FIGURE 16.5
Request for a Time Extension
If you need to request more time to make a decision about a job offer, be sure to explain why you need the extension and reaffirm that you are still interested in the job.

confirming the time extension if the organization grants it. This type of message is, in essence, a direct request. However, because the recipient may be disappointed, be sure to temper your request for an extension with statements indicating your continued interest (see Figure 16.5).

Letter of Acceptance

Use the model for positive messages when you write a letter of acceptance.

When you receive a job offer that you want to accept, reply within five days. Begin by accepting the position and expressing thanks. Identify the job that you're accepting. In the next paragraph, cover any necessary details. Conclude by saying that you look forward to reporting for work. As always, a positive message such as this should convey your enthusiasm and eagerness to cooperate:

Confirms the specific terms of the offer with a good-news statement at the beginning

I'm delighted to accept the graphic design position in your advertising department at the salary of $2,975 a month.

Covers miscellaneous details in the middle

Enclosed are the health insurance forms you asked me to complete and sign. I've already given notice to my current employer and will be able to start work on Monday, January 18.

Closes with another reference to the good news and a look toward the future

The prospect of joining your firm is exciting. Thank you for giving me this opportunity for what I'm sure will be a challenging future.

Be aware that a job offer and a written acceptance of that offer can constitute a legally binding contract—for you and the employer. Before you write an acceptance letter, be sure you want the job.

Letter Declining a Job Offer

After all your interviews, you may find that you need to write a letter declining a job offer. Use the techniques for negative messages (see Chapter 9): Open warmly, state the reasons for refusing the offer, decline the offer explicitly, and close on a pleasant note, expressing gratitude. By taking the time to write a sincere, tactful letter, you leave the door open for future contact:

> A letter declining a job offer follows the model for negative messages.

> Thank you for your hospitality during my interview at your Durham facility last month. I'm flattered that you would offer me the computer analyst position that we talked about.
>
> During my job search, I applied to five highly rated firms like your own, each one a leader in its field. Both your company and another offered me a position. Because my desire to work abroad can more readily be satisfied by the other company, I have accepted that job offer.
>
> I deeply appreciate the time you spent talking with me. Thank you again for your consideration and kindness.

Uses a buffer in the opening paragraph

Precedes the bad news with tactfully phrased reasons for the applicant's unfavorable decision and leaves the door open

Lets the reader down gently with a sincere and cordial ending

Letter of Resignation

If you get a job offer and are currently employed, you can maintain good relations with your current employer by writing a letter of resignation to your immediate supervisor. Follow the approach for negative messages and make the letter sound as positive as possible, regardless of how you feel. Don't take this letter as an opportunity to vent any frustrations you may have. Say something favorable about the organization, the people you work with, or what you've learned on the job. Then state your intention to leave and give the date of your last day on the job. Be sure you give your current employer at least two weeks' notice:

> Letters of resignation should always be written in a gracious and professional style that avoids criticism of your employer or your colleagues.

> My sincere thanks to you and to all the other Emblem Corporation employees for helping me learn so much about serving the public these past two years. You have given me untold help and encouragement.
>
> You may recall that when you first interviewed me, my goal was to become a customer relations supervisor. Because that opportunity has been offered to me by another organization, I am submitting my resignation. I will miss my friends and colleagues at Emblem, but I want to take advantage of this opportunity.
>
> I would like to terminate my work here two weeks from today but can arrange to work an additional week if you want me to train a replacement.
>
> Best wishes to all of you.

Uses an appreciative opening to serve as a buffer

States reasons before the bad news itself, using tactful phrasing to help keep the relationship friendly, should the writer later want letters of recommendation

Discusses necessary details in an extra paragraph

Tempers any disappointment with a cordial close

To verify the content and style of your follow-up messages, consult the tips in "Checklist: Writing Follow-up Messages."

✓ CHECKLIST: Writing Follow-Up Messages

A. Thank-You Messages

✓ Write a brief thank-you letter within two days of the interview.
✓ Acknowledge the interviewer's time and courtesy.
✓ Restate the specific job you're applying for.
✓ Express your enthusiasm about the organization and the job.
✓ Add any new facts that may help your chances.
✓ Politely ask for a decision.

B. Messages of Inquiry

✓ If you haven't heard from the interviewer by the promised date, write a brief message of inquiry.
✓ Use a direct approach: main idea, necessary details, specific request.

C. Requests for a Time Extension

✓ Request an extension if you have pending interviews and need time to decide about an offer.
✓ Open on a friendly note.
✓ Explain why you need more time and express continued interest in the company.
✓ In the close, promise a quick decision if your request is denied and ask for a confirmation if your request is granted.

D. Letters of Acceptance

✓ Send this message within five days of receiving the offer.
✓ State clearly that you accept the offer, identify the job you're accepting, and confirm vital details such as salary and start date.
✓ Make sure you want the job; an acceptance letter can be treated as a legally binding contract.

E. Letters Declining a Job Offer

✓ Use the model for negative messages.
✓ Open on a warm and appreciative note and then explain why you are refusing the offer.
✓ End on a sincere, positive note.

F. Letters of Resignation

✓ Send a letter of resignation to your current employer as soon as possible.
✓ Begin with an appreciative buffer.
✓ In the middle section, state your reasons for leaving and actually state that you are resigning.
✓ Close cordially.

On the Job

SOLVING COMMUNICATION DILEMMAS AT GOOGLE

Much of Google's recruiting effort focuses on the software engineers and other technical specialists who create and refine the company's search technologies. However, as those technologies get put to use in a wider array of commercial applications, business specialists will play an increasingly important role in the company's future. You're on the interview team assigned to fill one such position, that of corporate development analyst/associate in Google's Mountain View, California, offices. Here is how Google's website describes the position ("M&A" is an abbreviation for mergers and acquisitions):

This is a great opportunity to join the team at Google focusing on enhancing our corporate mission through M&A transactions. We are looking for an associate to join our corporate development team where you will be mentored by some of the best deal people in the business. In this role, you will screen external inquiries for potential acquisition deals, research domestic and international market segments, and participate in deal activities working closely with corporate development managers, principals and the director.

Our ideal candidate is a top performer who brings high levels of energy and enthusiasm, works well with large and diverse teams, and has a demonstrated ability to think creatively.

Requirements:

- Bachelor's degree required.
- 1–3 years of experience in strategic consulting, investment banking or relevant corporate experience preferred.
- Strong quantitative and qualitative analytical ability required.
- Excellent oral and written communication skills.

- Demonstrated ability to manage multiple projects simultaneously.
- Must be a team player with a sense of humor.

With these job requirements in mind, how would you respond to these recruiting situations?[47]

1. Because written communication skills are such an important part of the job, you pay close attention to application letters. Based on the following opening paragraphs, which of these four candidates has done the best job of capturing your attention and interest?

   a. I LOVE GOOGLE! I relied on your awesome search engine to get me through a zillion research papers in college, and I continue to use it in my new job as a legislative analyst in the mayor's office (that would be the Honorable Jack R. Spiker, mayor of Cheyenne, Wyoming, in whose employ I currently serve).
   b. Guess what I found when I Googled myself? A five-page listing of all the awards I've received, speeches I've given, articles I've written, and projects I've managed. Try it yourself and see what you can see about my work.
   c. Given Google's reputation for hiring only the best and brightest, the big question is why the heck don't I work there yet? I'm driven, way smarter than the average bear, and not afraid to tell my mom I work at some place called "Google"!
   d. It's amazing how many times Google's name keeps popping up around the espresso machine here at Ignito Strategic Consulting, whenever my colleagues and I discuss smart acquisitions. Your firm continues to execute strategic moves that are creatively imagined, carefully researched, and cleverly implemented—exactly the kind of business deals I've been training for my entire career. And although that career is only one year old at the moment, my first annual performance review just said that I already have the deal-making acumen of a five-year veteran.

2. You like to put applicants at ease right away, so you usually start by asking a humorous question to break the tension while also revealing something about the candidate's personality and knowledge. For this round of interviews, which of these questions would you choose to start each interview?

   a. What's the dumbest business deal you've ever heard of?
   b. If we wanted to lose $10 million on a business deal, what would you suggest we do?
   c. Ever have one of those days when life seems like one endless job interview?
   d. So…buying that weekly lottery ticket still hasn't worked out, eh?

3. Google places a great deal of emphasis on creative thinking, so you and your colleagues spend much of your time probing candidates' abilities to think through challenges and propose clever solutions. Which of these questions would you use to judge a candidate's ability to grasp a problem and begin developing a solution?

   a. You're a scientist with the Environmental Protection Agency, specializing in toxic waste from electronic products. You're testifying before a congressional committee, and a senator wants to know how many mobile phone batteries will be thrown away in the next 10 years. Without access to any additional information, how would you start to construct an estimate of this number?
   b. Guess how old I am.
   c. Why do telephone numbers in movies and TV shows always start with 555?
   d. How would you explain the concept of a human family to a creature from another planet?

4. At the end of each interview, you make a point to ask candidates if they have any questions for you. Which of the following responses impresses you the most?

   a. No, thanks. I think I'm all set.
   b. Hey, if I have any questions, I'll just Google away when I get back to my computer, right?
   c. Yes, one of my top priorities in searching for a new job is finding a greater sense of intellectual and professional freedom. Is Google the kind of place where top performers can really pursue their own dreams?
   d. Yes, a couple of questions, actually. First, Google's stated mission of organizing the world's information and making it universally accessible leaves the door open to a lot of different possibilities. For instance, do you see the company ever moving into traditional publishing, with books or magazines?

Learning Objectives Checkup

Assess your understanding of the principles in this chapter by reading each learning objective and studying the accompanying exercises. For fill-in-the-blank items, write the missing text in the blank provided; for multiple-choice items, circle the letter of the correct answer. You can check your responses against the answer key on page AK-3.

Objective 16.1: Define the purpose of application letters, and explain how to apply the AIDA organizational model to them.

1. What is the primary reason for sending an application letter?
   a. To encourage the reader to look at your résumé

b. To ask for a job

c. To itemize your qualifications

d. To ask for an application form

2. Which of the following is a good technique to gain attention in the opening paragraph of an application letter?

a. Explain how your work skills could benefit the organization.

b. Explain how your qualifications fit the job.

c. Show that you understand the organization's needs.

d. Do all of the above.

Objective 16.2: Describe the typical sequence of job interviews.

3. Which of these interview stages happens first?

a. The selection stage

b. The screening stage

c. The filtering stage

d. The sorting stage

4. A/an _____ interview, often used in the screening stage, features a series of prepared questions in a set order.

5. A/an _____ interview is a relatively informal and unstructured format, in which the interviewer poses broad, open-ended questions.

6. A/an _____ interview tries to uncover how the candidate would behave when faced with various challenges on the job.

Objective 16.3: Describe briefly what employers look for during an employment interview and pre-employment testing.

7. What are the two most important factors that employers look for during interviews?

a. Fit with the organization and motivation

b. Motivation and ability to perform the job

c. Motivation and years of experience

d. Fit with the organization and ability to perform the job

8. Which of the following pre-employment tests might you encounter while applying for jobs?

a. Integrity tests

b. Substance tests

c. Personality tests

d. All of the above

9. Approximately what percentage of U.S. companies require applicants to undergo pre-employment drug testing?

a. 3 percent

b. 12 percent

c. 50 percent

d. 80 percent

Objective 16.4: List six tasks you need to complete to prepare for a successful job interview.

10. If an interviewer asks you to describe your biggest weakness, which of the following is the best strategy for your response?

a. Explain the weakness in depth; doing so will convince the interviewer of your honesty.

b. Describe a weakness so that it sounds like a strength, such as saying that you drive yourself too hard.

c. Respectfully explain to the interviewer that the question is illegal.

d. Explain that you don't have any major weaknesses.

11. What is the best strategy for asking questions of your own during an interview?

a. Try to ask all of them at the beginning of the interview so that you don't run out of time.

b. Wait until after the interview and then e-mail your questions to the interviewer.

c. Try to work your questions in naturally throughout the course of the interview.

d. Wait until the interviewer asks if you have any questions.

12. If you believe that you have a particular disadvantage related to some aspect of your appearance, interviewing skills, job skills, or work experience, how should you handle the situation when preparing for an interview?

a. Plan to make a joke about your weakness early in the interview; this will break the tension and allow you to focus on the interviewer's questions.

b. Compensate by focusing on your strengths, both while you're preparing and during the interview.

c. Correct the perceived shortcoming if possible; if not, focus on your positive attributes.

d. Ignore the situation; there's nothing you can do about a weakness at this point.

13. If you're not sure what style of clothing to wear to a particular interview and you're not able to ask someone at the company for advice, what should you do?

a. Dress in a fairly conservative style; it's better to be a little too dressy than too casual.

b. Dress as you would like to dress on the job.

c. Dress in an eye-catching style that will make a lasting impression on the interviewer.

d. Arrive early with several different changes of clothes; try to see what people there are wearing, then find a place to change into whichever outfit you have that most closely matches.

Objective 16.5: Explain the three stages of a successful employment interview.

14. Studies show that many interviewers, particularly those with poor training, make up their minds about candidates

a. In the first 20 seconds of the interview

b. In the final 20 seconds of the interview

c. On the basis of the résumé

d. On the basis of the cover letter

15. What do you do if a job interviewer asks you about your marital status, how many children you have, and what their ages are?

a. Answer them; it is perfectly within the interviewer's right to ask you such personal questions, even if they are not directly related to the job you are applying for.

b. Tell the interviewer that such questions are illegal and threaten to sue for invasion of privacy.

c. Sidestep the questions—which are illegal in many states—by asking if the interviewer has some specific concerns about your commitment to the job, your willingness to travel, or some other factor.

d. If you want the job, refuse to answer the questions but promise that you won't report the illegal questioning to the EEOC.

16. What should you do if the interviewer tells you the salary for the job being offered?
a. Always take whatever the company offers.
b. Respond with a figure higher than what is offered.
c. Respond with a figure lower than what is offered.
d. Ask if there is any room to negotiate on salary.

Objective 16.6: Identify the most common employment messages that follow an interview, and explain when you would use each one.

17. Following a job interview, you should send a thank-you message
a. Within two days after the interview
b. Only if you think you got the job
c. That follows the AIDA organizational model
d. That does all of the above

18. A letter declining a job offer should follow
a. The direct approach
b. The AIDA model
c. A negative news approach
d. The polite plan

Apply Your Knowledge

1. How can you distinguish yourself from other candidates in a screening interview and still keep your responses short and to the point? Explain.

2. What can you do to make a favorable impression when you discover that an open-ended interview has turned into a stress interview? Briefly explain your answer.

3. If you want to switch jobs because you can't work with your supervisor, how can you explain this situation to a prospective employer? Give an example.

4. If you lack one important qualification for a job but have made it past the initial screening stage, how should you prepare to handle this issue during the next round of interviews? Explain your answer.

5. **Ethical Choices** Why is it important to distinguish unethical or illegal interview questions from acceptable questions? Explain.

Practice Your Knowledge

MESSAGES FOR ANALYSIS

Read the following documents and then (1) analyze the strengths or weaknesses of each document and (2) revise each document so that it follows this chapter's guidelines.

MESSAGE 16.A: WRITING AN APPLICATION LETTER

I'm writing to let you know about my availability for the brand manager job you advertised. As you can see from my enclosed résumé, my background is perfect for the position. Even though I don't have any real job experience, my grades have been outstanding, considering that I went to a top-ranked business school.

I did many things during my undergraduate years to prepare me for this job:

• Earned a 3.4 out of a 4.0, with a 3.8 in my business courses
• Elected representative to the student governing association
• Selected to receive the Lamar Franklin Award
• Worked to earn a portion of my tuition

I am sending my résumé to all the top firms, but I like yours better than any of the rest. Your reputation is tops in the industry, and I want to be associated with a business that can pridefully say it's the best.

If you wish for me to come in for an interview, I can come on a Friday afternoon or anytime on weekends when I don't have classes. Again, thanks for considering me for your brand manager position.

MESSAGE 16.B: WRITING APPLICATION FOLLOW-UP MESSAGES

Did you receive my résumé? I sent it to you at least two months ago and haven't heard anything. I know you keep résumés on file, but I just want to be sure that you keep me in mind. I heard you are hiring health-care managers and certainly would like to be considered for one of those positions.

Since I last wrote you, I've worked in a variety of positions that have helped prepare me for management. To wit, I've become lunch manager at the restaurant where I work, which involved a raise in pay. I now manage a waitstaff of 12 girls and take the lunch receipts to the bank every day.

Of course, I'd much rather be working at a real job, and that's why I'm writing again. Is there anything else you would *like to know about me or my background? I would really like to know more about your company. Is there any literature you could send me? If so, I would really appreciate it.*

I think one reason I haven't been hired yet is that I don't want to leave Atlanta. So I hope when you think of me, it's for a position that wouldn't require moving. Thanks again for considering my application.

MESSAGE 16.C: THANK-YOU MESSAGE

Thank you for the really marvelous opportunity to meet you and your colleagues at Starret Engine Company. I really enjoyed touring your facilities and talking with all the people there. You have quite a crew! Some of the other companies I have visited have been so rigid and uptight that I can't imagine how I would fit in. It's a relief to run into a group of people who seem to enjoy their work as much as all of you do.

I know that you must be looking at many other candidates for this job, and I know that some of them will probably be more experienced than I am. But I do want to emphasize that my two-year hitch in the Navy involved a good deal of engineering work. I don't think I mentioned all my shipboard responsibilities during the interview.

Please give me a call within the next week to let me know your decision. You can usually find me at my dormitory in the evening after dinner (phone: 877-9080).

MESSAGE 16.D: LETTER OF INQUIRY

I have recently received a very attractive job offer from the Warrington Company. But before I let them know one way or another, I would like to consider any offer that your firm may extend. I was quite impressed with your company during my recent interview, and I am still very interested in a career there.

I don't mean to pressure you, but Warrington has asked for my decision within 10 days. Could you let me know by Tuesday whether you plan to offer me a position? That would give me enough time to compare the two offers.

MESSAGE 16.E: LETTER DECLINING A JOB OFFER

I'm writing to say that I must decline your job offer. Another company has made me a more generous offer, and I have decided to accept. However, if things don't work out for me there, I will let you know. I sincerely appreciate your interest in me.

EXERCISES

For active links to all websites discussed in this chapter, visit this book's website at www.prenhall.com/thill. Locate your book and click on its "Companion Website" link. Then select Chapter 16 and click on "Featured Websites." Locate the name of the page or the URL related to the material in the text. Please note that links to sites that become inactive after publication of the book will be removed from the "Featured Websites" section.

16.1 Internet Select a large company (one that you can easily find information on) where you might like to work. Use Internet sources to gather some preliminary research on the company; don't limit your search to the company's own website.
1. What did you learn about this organization that would help you during an interview there?
2. What Internet sources did you use to obtain this information?
3. Armed with this information, what aspects of your background do you think might appeal to this company's recruiters?
4. Based on what you've learned about this company's culture, what aspects of your personality should you try to highlight during an interview?

16.2 Teamwork Divide the class into two groups. Half the class will be recruiters for a large chain of national department stores looking to fill manager trainee positions (there are 16 openings). The other half of the class will be candidates for the job. The company is specifically looking for candidates who demonstrate these three qualities: initiative, dependability, and willingness to assume responsibility.
1. Have each recruiter select and interview an applicant for 10 minutes.
2. Have all the recruiters discuss how they assessed the applicant in each of the three desired qualities. What questions did they ask or what did they use as an indicator to determine whether the candidate possessed the quality?
3. Have all the applicants discuss what they said to convince the recruiters that they possessed each of these qualities.

16.3 Interviews: Understanding Qualifications Write a short e-mail to your instructor, discussing what you believe are your greatest strengths and weaknesses from an employment perspective. Next, explain how these strengths and weaknesses would be viewed by interviewers evaluating your qualifications.

16.4 Interviews: Being Prepared Prepare written answers to 10 of the questions listed in Table 16.3, "Twenty-Five Common Interview Questions."

16.5 Ethical Choices You have decided to accept a new position with a competitor of your company. Write a letter of resignation to your supervisor, announcing your decision.
1. Will you notify your employer that you are joining a competing firm? Please explain.
2. Will you use the direct or the indirect approach? Please explain.
3. Will you send your letter by e-mail, send it by regular mail, or place it on your supervisor's desk?

Expand Your Knowledge

LEARNING MORE ON THE WEB
PREPARE AND PRACTICE BEFORE THAT FIRST INTERVIEW

www.job-interview.net

How can you practice for a job interview? What are some questions you might be asked? How should you respond? What questions are you not obligated to answer? Job-interview.net, www.job-interview.net, provides mock interviews based on actual job openings. It provides job descriptions, questions and answers for specific careers and jobs, and links to company guides and annual reports. You'll find a step-by-step plan that outlines key job requirements, lists practice interview questions, and helps you put together practice interviews. The site offers tips on the keywords to look for in a job description, which will help you narrow your search and anticipate the questions you might be asked on your first or next job interview. Explore the site and then answer these questions.

1. What are some problem questions you might be asked during a job interview? How would you handle these questions?

2. Choose a job title from the list and read more about it. What did you learn that could help during an actual interview for the job you selected?
3. Developing an "interview game plan" ahead of time helps you make a strong, positive impression during an interview. What are some of the things you can practice to help make everything you do during an interview seem to come naturally?

SURFING YOUR WAY TO CAREER SUCCESS

Bovée and Thill's Business Communication Headline News offers links to hundreds of online resources that can help you with this course, your other college courses, and your career. Visit www.businesscommunicationblog.com and click on "Web Directory." The "Reference" section connects you to a variety of websites that can help in all aspects of business communication, from writing centers and online libraries to dictionaries. encyclopedias, and more. Identify three websites from this section that could be useful in your business career. For each site, write a two-sentence summary of what the site offers and how it could help you launch and build your career.

Learn Interactively

INTERACTIVE STUDY GUIDE

Go to the Companion Website at www.prenhall.com/thill and locate your book, then click on "Companion Website." Select Chapter 16 to take advantage of the interactive "Chapter Quiz" to test your knowledge of chapter concepts. Receive instant feedback on whether you need to do additional studying. Also, visit the "Study Hall," where you'll find an abundance of valuable resources that will help you succeed in this course.

PEAK PERFORMANCE GRAMMAR AND MECHANICS

If your instructor has required the use of "Peak Performance Grammar and Mechanics," either in your online course or on CD, you can review the grammar and mechanics skills you've learned throughout this course. Retake the Pretests, Follow-Up Tests, and the Advanced Tests to measure your progress; review weak areas in the Refresher Courses. Finally, for additional reinforcement, go to the "Improve Your Grammar, Mechanics, and Usage" section that follows and complete those exercises.

Improve Your Grammar, Mechanics, and Usage

The following exercises help you improve your knowledge of and power over English grammar, mechanics, and usage. Turn to the Handbook of Grammar, Mechanics, and Usage at the end of this book and review all of Section 3.4 (Numbers). Then look at the following 10 items. Circle the letter of the preferred choice in the following groups of sentences. (Answers to these exercises appear on page AK-4.)

1. a. We need to hire one office manager, four bookkeepers, and 12 clerk-typists.
   b. We need to hire one office manager, four bookkeepers, and twelve clerk-typists.
   c. We need to hire 1 office manager, 4 bookkeepers, and 12 clerk-typists.

2. a. The market for this product is nearly 6 million people in our region alone.
   b. The market for this product is nearly six million people in our region alone.
   c. The market for this product is nearly 6,000,000 million people in our region alone.

3. a. Make sure that all 1,835 pages are on my desk no later than 9:00 a.m.
   b. Make sure that all 1835 pages are on my desk no later than nine o'clock in the morning.
   c. Make sure that all 1,835 pages are on my desk no later than nine o'clock a.m.

4. a. Our deadline is 4/7, but we won't be ready before 4/11.

b. Our deadline is April 7, but we won't be ready before April 11.

c. Our deadline is 4/7, but we won't be ready before April 11.

5. a. 95 percent of our customers are men.

b. Ninety-five percent of our customers are men.

c. Of our customers, ninety-five percent are men.

6. a. More than half the U.S. population is female.

b. More than 1/2 the U.S. population is female.

c. More than one-half the U.S. population is female.

7. a. Last year, I wrote 20 15-page reports, and Michelle wrote 24 three-page reports.

b. Last year, I wrote 20 fifteen-page reports, and Michelle wrote 24 three-page reports.

c. Last year, I wrote twenty 15-page reports, and Michelle wrote 24 three-page reports.

8. a. Our blinds should measure 38 inches wide by 64 and one-half inches long by 7/16 inches deep.

b. Our blinds should measure 38 inches wide by 64-1/2 inches long by 7/16 inches deep.

c. Our blinds should measure 38 inches wide by 64-8/16 inches long by 7/16 inches deep.

9. a. Deliver the couch to 783 Fountain Rd., Suite 3, Procter Valley, CA 92074.

b. Deliver the couch to 783 Fountain Rd., Suite three, Procter Valley, CA 92074.

c. Deliver the couch to seven eighty-three Fountain Rd., Suite three, Procter Valley, CA 92074.

10. a. Here are the corrected figures: 42.7% agree, 23.25% disagree, 34% are undecided, and the error is 0.05%.

b. Here are the corrected figures: 42.7% agree, 23.25% disagree, 34.0% are undecided, and the error is .05%.

c. Here are the corrected figures: 42.70% agree, 23.25% disagree, 34.00% are undecided, and the error is 0.05%.

For an overall review of your grammar, mechanics, and usage skills, go to www.prenhall.com/thill, then locate your text, and click on its "Companion Website" link. Click on Chapter 16, click on "Additional Exercises to Improve Your Grammar, Mechanics and Usage," and then click on "25. Grammar and usage."

Cases

Applying the Three-Step Writing Process to Cases

Apply each step to the following cases, as assigned by your instructor.

PREPARING OTHER TYPES OF EMPLOYMENT MESSAGES

1. Online application: Electronic cover letter introducing a résumé While researching a digital camera purchase, you stumble on the webzine *Megapixel* (www.megapixel.net), which offers product reviews on a wide array of camera models. The quality of the reviews and the stunning examples of photography on the site inspire you to a new part-time business idea—you'd like to write a regular column for *Megapixel*. The webzine does a great job addressing the information needs of experienced camera users, but you see an opportunity to write for "newbies," people who are new to digital photography and need a more basic level of information.

Your task: Write an e-mail message that will serve as your cover letter and address your message to Denys Bouton, who edits the English edition of *Megapixel*. (It is also published in French.) Try to limit your message to one screen (generally 20–25 lines). You'll need a creative "hook" and a reassuring approach that identifies you as the right person to launch this new feature in the webzine. (Make up any details about your background that you may need to complete the letter.)

2. All over the map: Application letter to Google Earth You've applied yourself with vigor and resolve for four years, and you're just about to graduate with your business degree. While cruising the web to relax one night, you stumble on something called Google Earth. You're hooked instantly by the ability to zoom all around the globe and look at detailed satellite photos of places you've been to or dreamed of visiting. You can even type in the address of your apartment and get an aerial view of your neighborhood. You're amazed at the three-dimensional renderings of major U.S. cities. Plus, the photographs and maps are linked to Google's other search technologies, allowing you to locate everything from ATMs to coffee shops in your neighborhood.

You've loved maps since you were a kid, and discovering Google Earth is making you wish you'd majored in geography. Knowing how important it is to follow your heart, you decide to apply to Google anyway, even though you don't have a strong background in geographic information systems. You do have a ton of passion for maps and a good head for business.

Your task: Visit http://earth.google.com and explore the system's capabilities. (You can download a free copy of the software.) In particular, look at the business and government applications of the technology, such as customized aerial photos and maps for real estate sales, land use and environmental impact analysis, and emergency planning for homeland security agencies. Be sure to visit the Community pages as well, where you can learn more about the many interesting applications of this technology. Draft an application e-mail to Google (address it to jobs@google.com), asking to be considered for the Google Earth team. Think about how you could help the company develop the commercial potential of this product line and make sure your enthusiasm shines through in the message.

INTERVIEWING WITH POTENTIAL EMPLOYERS

3. Interviewers and interviewees: Classroom exercise in interviewing Interviewing is clearly an interactive process that involves at least two people. The best way to practice for interviews is to work with others.

Your task: You and all other members of your class are to write letters of application for an entry-level or management-trainee position that requires a pleasant personality and intelligence but a minimum of specialized education or experience. Sign your letter with a fictitious name that conceals your identity. Next, polish (or create) a résumé that accurately identifies you and your educational and professional accomplishments.

Now, three members of the class who volunteer as interviewers divide up all the anonymously written application letters. Then each interviewer selects a candidate who seems the most pleasant and convincing in his or her letter. At this time, the selected candidates identify themselves and give the interviewers their résumés.

Each interviewer then interviews his or her chosen candidate in front of the class, seeking to understand how the items on the résumé qualify the candidate for the job. At the end of the interviews, the class may decide who gets the job and discuss why this candidate was successful. Afterward, retrieve your letter, sign it with the right name, and submit it to the instructor for credit.

4. Internet interview: Exercise in interviewing Locate the website of a company in an industry in which you might like to work and then identify an interesting position within the company. Study the company, using any of the online business resources discussed in Chapter 11, and prepare for an interview with that company.

Your task: Working with a classmate, take turns interviewing each other for your chosen positions. Interviewers should take notes during the interview. When the interview is complete, critique each other's performance. (Interviewers should critique how well candidates prepared for the interview and answered the questions; interviewees should critique the quality of the questions asked.) Write a follow-up letter, thanking your interviewer, and submit the letter to your instructor.

FOLLOWING UP AFTER THE INTERVIEW

5. A slight error in timing: Letter asking for delay of an employment decision Thanks to a mix-up in your job application scheduling, you accidentally applied for your third-choice job before going after what you really wanted. What you want to do is work in retail marketing with the upscale department store Neiman Marcus in Dallas; what you have been offered is a similar job with Longhorn Leather and Lumber, 55 dry and dusty miles away in Commerce, just south of the Oklahoma panhandle.

You review your notes. Your Longhorn interview was three weeks ago with the human resources manager, R. P. Bronson, a congenial person who has just written to offer you the position. The store's address is 27 Sam Rayburn Drive, Commerce, TX 75428. Mr. Bronson notes that he can hold the position open for 10 days. You have an interview scheduled with Neiman Marcus next week, but it is unlikely that you will know the store's decision within this 10-day period.

Your task: Write to R. P. Bronson, requesting a reasonable delay in your consideration of his job offer.

6. Job hunt: Set of employment-related letters to a single company Where would you like to work? Choose one of your favorite products, find out which company either manufactures it or sells it in the United States (if it's manufactured in another country). Assume that a month ago you sent your résumé and application letter. Not long afterward, you were invited to come for an interview, which seemed to go very well.

Your task: Use your imagination to write the following: (a) a thank-you letter for the interview, (b) a note of inquiry, (c) a request for more time to decide, (d) a letter of acceptance, and (e) a letter declining the job offer.

FORMAT AND LAYOUT OF BUSINESS DOCUMENTS

The format and layout of business documents vary from country to country; they even vary within regions of the United States. In addition, many organizations develop their own variations of standard styles, adapting documents to the types of messages they send and the kinds of audiences they communicate with. The formats described here are more common than others.

FIRST IMPRESSIONS

Your documents tell readers a lot about you and about your company's professionalism. So all your documents must look neat, present a professional image, and be easy to read. Your audience's first impression of a document comes from the quality of its paper, the way it is customized, and its general appearance.

Paper

To give a quality impression, businesspeople consider carefully the paper they use. Several aspects of paper contribute to the overall impression:

- **Weight.** Paper quality is judged by the weight of four reams (each a 500-sheet package) of letter-size paper. The weight most commonly used by U.S. business organizations is 20-pound paper, but 16- and 24-pound versions are also used.

- **Cotton content.** Paper quality is also judged by the percentage of cotton in the paper. Cotton doesn't yellow over time the way wood pulp does, plus it's both strong and soft. For letters and outside reports, use paper with a 25 percent cotton content. For memos and other internal documents, you can use a lighter-weight paper with lower cotton content. Airmail-weight paper may save money for international correspondence, but make sure it isn't too flimsy.[1]

- **Size.** In the United States, the standard paper size for business documents is 8½ by 11 inches. Standard legal documents are 8½ by 14 inches. Executives sometimes have heavier 7-by-10-inch paper on hand (with matching envelopes) for personal messages such as congratulations and recommendations.[2] They may also have a box of note cards imprinted with their initials and a box of plain folded notes for condolences or for acknowledging formal invitations.

- **Color.** White is the standard color for business purposes, although neutral colors such as gray and ivory are sometimes used. Memos can be produced on pastel-colored paper to distinguish them from external correspondence. In addition, memos are sometimes produced on various colors of paper for routing to separate departments. Light-colored papers are appropriate, but bright or dark colors make reading difficult and may appear too frivolous.

Customization

For letters to outsiders, U.S. businesses commonly use letterhead stationery, which may be either professionally printed or designed in-house using word processing templates and graphics. The letterhead includes the company's name and address, usually at the top of the page but sometimes along the left side or even at the bottom. Other information may be included in the letterhead as well: the company's telephone number, fax number, cable address, website address, product lines, date of establishment, officers and directors, slogan, and symbol (logo). Well-designed letterhead gives readers[3]

- Pertinent reference data

- A favorable image of the company

- A good idea of what the company does

For as much as it's meant to accomplish, the letterhead should be as simple as possible. Too much information makes the page look cluttered, occupies space needed for the message, and might become outdated before all the stationery can be used. If you correspond frequently with people abroad, your letterhead must be intelligible to foreigners. It must include the name of your country in addition to your cable, telex, e-mail, or fax information.

In the United States, businesses always use letterhead for the first page of a letter. Successive pages are usually plain sheets of paper that match the letterhead in color and quality. Some companies use a specially printed second-page letterhead that bears only the company's name. Other countries have other conventions.

Many companies also design and print standardized forms for memos and frequently written reports that always require the same sort of information (such as sales reports and expense reports). These forms may be printed in sets for use with carbon paper or in carbonless-copy sets that produce multiple copies automatically. More and more organizations use computers to generate their standardized forms, which can save them both money and time.[4]

Appearance

Nearly all business documents are produced using an inkjet or laser printer; make sure to use a clean, high-quality printer. Certain documents, however, should be handwritten (such as a short informal memo or a note of condolence). Be sure to handwrite, print, or type the envelope to match the document. However, even a letter on the best-quality paper with the best-designed letterhead may look unprofessional if it's poorly produced. So pay close attention to all the factors affecting appearance, including the following:

- **Margins.** Companies in the United States make sure that documents (especially external ones) are centered on the page, with margins of at least 1 inch all around. Using word processing software, you can achieve this balance simply by defining the format parameters.

- **Line length.** Lines are rarely justified, because the resulting text looks too much like a form letter and can be hard to read (even with proportional spacing). Varying line length makes the document look more personal and interesting.

- **Line spacing.** You can adjust the number of blank lines between elements (such as between the date and the inside address) to ensure that a short document fills the page vertically or that a longer document extends at least two lines of the body onto the last page.

- **Character spacing.** Use proper spacing between characters and after punctuation. For example, U.S. conventions include leaving one space after commas, semicolons, colons, and sentence-ending periods. Each letter in a person's initials is followed by a period and a single space. However, abbreviations such as U.S.A. or MBA may or may not have periods, but they never have internal spaces.

- **Special symbols.** Take advantage of the many special symbols available with your computer's selection of fonts. (In Microsoft Word, click on the Insert menu, then select Symbol.) Table A.1 shows some of the more common symbols used in business documents. In addition, see if your company has a style guide for documents, which may include other symbols you are expected to use.

- **Corrections.** Messy corrections are unacceptable in business documents. If you notice an error after printing a document with your word processor, correct the mistake and reprint. (With informal memos to members of your own team or department, the occasional small correction in pen or pencil is acceptable, but never in formal documents.)

LETTERS

All business letters have certain elements in common. Several of these elements appear in every letter; others appear only when desirable or appropriate. In addition, these letter parts are usually arranged in one of three basic formats.

Standard Letter Parts

The letter in Figure A.1 shows the placement of standard letter parts. The writer of this business letter had no letterhead available but correctly included a heading. All business letters typically include these seven elements.

Heading

Letterhead (the usual heading) shows the organization's name, full address, telephone number (almost always), and e-mail address (often). Executive letterhead also bears the name of an individual within the organization. Computers allow you to design your own letterhead (either one to use for all correspondence or a new one for

each piece of correspondence). If letterhead stationery is not available, the heading includes a return address (but no name) and starts 13 lines from the top of the page, which leaves a 2-inch top margin.

Date

If you're using letterhead, place the date at least one blank line beneath the lowest part of the letterhead. Without letterhead, place the date immediately below the return address. The standard method of writing the date in the United States uses the full name of the month (no abbreviations), followed by the day (in numerals, without *st, nd, rd,* or *th*), a comma, and then the year: July 14, 2008 (7/14/08). Some organizations follow other conventions (see Table A.2). To maintain the utmost clarity in international correspondence, always spell out the name of the month in dates.[5]

When communicating internationally, you may also experience some confusion over time. Some companies in the United States refer to morning (A.M.) and afternoon (P.M.), dividing a 24-hour day into 12-hour blocks so that they refer to four o'clock in the morning (4:00 A.M.) or four o'clock in the afternoon (4:00 P.M.). The U.S. military and European companies refer to one 24-hour period so that 0400 hours (4:00 A.M.) is always in the morning and 1600 hours (4:00 P.M.) is always in the afternoon.[6] Make sure your references to time are as clear as possible, and be sure you clearly understand your audience's time references.

Inside Address

The inside address identifies the recipient of the letter. For U.S. correspondence, begin the inside address at least one line below the date. Precede the addressee's name with a courtesy title, such as *Dr., Mr.,* or *Ms.* The accepted courtesy title for women in business is *Ms.,* although a woman known to prefer the title *Miss* or *Mrs.* is always accommodated. If you don't know whether a person is a man or a woman (and you have no way of finding out), omit the courtesy title. For example, *Terry Smith* could be either a man or a woman. The first line of the inside address would be just *Terry Smith,* and the salutation would be *Dear Terry Smith.* The same is true if you know only a person's initials, as in *S. J. Adams.*

Spell out and capitalize titles that precede a person's name, such as *Professor* or *General* (see Table A.3 for the proper forms of address). The person's organizational title, such as *Director,* may be included on this first line (if it is short) or on the line below; the name of a department may follow. In addresses and signature lines, don't forget to capitalize any professional title that follows a person's name:

> Mr. Ray Johnson, Dean
>
> Ms. Patricia T. Higgins
>
> Assistant Vice President

However, professional titles not appearing in an address or signature line are capitalized only when they directly precede the name.

> President Kenneth Johanson will deliver the speech.
>
> Maria Morales, president of ABC Enterprises, will deliver the speech.
>
> The Honorable Helen Masters, senator from Arizona, will deliver the speech.

If the name of a specific person is unavailable, you may address the letter to the department or to a specific position within the department. Also, be sure to spell out company names in full, unless the company itself uses abbreviations in its official name.

Table A.1

SPECIAL SYMBOLS ON A COMPUTER

	Computer symbol
Case fractions	$\frac{1}{2}$
Copyright	©
Registered trademark	®
Cents	¢
British pound	£
Paragraph	¶
Bullets	●,◆,■,□,✓,☑,⊗
Em dash	—
En dash	–

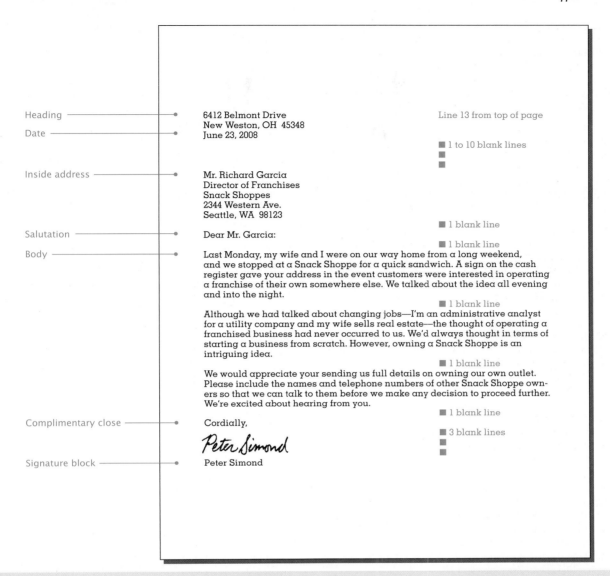

FIGURE A.1
Standard Letter Parts

Table A.2	COMMON DATE FORMS		
Convention	**Description**	**Date—Mixed**	**Date—All Numerals**
U.S. standard	Month (spelled out) day, year	July 14, 2008	7/14/08
U.S. government and some U.S. industries	Day (in numerals) month (spelled out) year	14 July 2008	14/7/08
European	Replace U.S. solidus (diagonal line) with periods	14 July 2008	14.7.2008
International standard	Year month day	2008 July 14	2008,7,14

Table A.3   FORMS OF ADDRESS

Person	In Address	In Salutation
PERSONAL TITLES		
Man	Mr. [first & last name]	Dear Mr. [last name]:
Woman[1]	Ms. [first & last name]	Dear Ms. [last name]:
Two men (or more)	Mr. [first & last name] and Mr. [first & last name]	Dear Mr. [last name] and Mr. [last name] *or* Messrs. [last name] and [last name]:
Two women (or more)	Ms. [first & last name] and Ms. [first & last name]	Dear Ms. [last name] and Ms. [last name] *or* Mses. [last name] and [last name]:
One woman and one man	Ms. [first & last name] and Mr. [first & last name]	Dear Ms. [last name] and Mr. [last name]:
Couple (married)	Mr. [husband's first name] and Ms. [wife's first name] [couple's last name]	Dear Mr. and Mrs. [last name]:
Couple (married with different last names)	Mr. [first & last name of husband] Ms. [first & last name of wife]	Dear Mr. [husband's last name] and Ms. [wife's last name]:
Couple (married professionals with same title and same last name)	[title in plural form] [husband's first name] and [wife's first name] [couple's last name]	Dear [title in plural form] [last name]:
Couple (married professionals with different titles and same last name)	[title] [first & last name of husband] and [title] [first & last name of wife]	Dear [title] and [title] [last name]:
PROFESSIONAL TITLES		
President of a college or university	[title] [first & last name], President	Dear [title] [last name]:
Dean of a school of college	Dean [first & last name] *or* Dr., Mr., or Ms. [first & last name], Dean of (title)	Dear Dean [last name]: *or* Dear Dr., Mr., or Ms., [last name]:
Professor	Professor *or* Dr. [first & last name]	Dear Professor *or* Dr. [last name]:
Physician	[first & last name], M.D.	Dear Dr. [last name]:
Lawyer	Mr., *or* Ms. [first & last name] Attorney at Law	Dear Mr., *or* Ms. [last name]:
Military personnel	[full rank, first & last name, abbreviation of service designation] (add *Retired* if applicable)	Dear [rank][last name]:
Company or corporation	[name of organization]	Ladies and Gentlemen: *or* Gentlemen and Ladies:
GOVERNMENTAL TITLES		
President of the United States	The President	Dear Mr. *or* Madam President:
Senator of the United States	Honorable [first & last name]	Dear Senator [last name]:
Cabinet member	Honorable [first & last name]	Dear Mr. *or* Madam Secretary:
Postmaster General		Dear Mr. *or* Madam Postmaster General:
Attorney General		Dear Mr. *or* Madam Attorney General:
Mayor	Honorable [first & last name], Mayor of [name of city]	Dear Mayor [last name]:
Judge	The Honorable [first & last name]	Dear Judge [last name]:

[1]Use *Mrs.* or *Miss* only if the recipient has specifically requested that you use one of these titles; otherwise *always* use *Ms.* in business correspondence. A never refer to a woman by her husband's name (e.g., Mrs. Robert Washington) unless she specifically requests that you do so.

Table A.4	INSIDE ADDRESS INFORMATION	
Description		**Example**
Capitalize building names.		Empire State Building
Capitalize locations within buildings (apartments, suites, rooms).		Suite 1073
Use numerals for all house or building numbers, except the number *one*.		One Trinity Lane; 637 Adams Ave., Apt. 7
Spell out compass directions that fall within a street address		1074 West Connover St.
Abbreviate compass directions that follow the street address		783 Main St., N.E., Apt. 27

Other address information includes the treatment of buildings, house numbers, and compass directions (see Table A.4). The following example shows all the information that may be included in the inside address and its proper order for U.S. correspondence:

Ms. Linda Coolidge, Vice President
Corporate Planning Department
Midwest Airlines
Kowalski Building, Suite 21-A
7279 Bristol Ave.
Toledo, OH 43617

Canadian addresses are similar, except that the name of the province is usually spelled out:

Dr. H. C. Armstrong
Research and Development
Commonwealth Mining Consortium
The Chelton Building, Suite 301
585 Second St. SW
Calgary, Alberta T2P 2P5

The order and layout of address information vary from country to country. So when addressing correspondence for other countries, carefully follow the format and information that appear in the company's letterhead. However, when you're sending mail from the United States, be sure that the name of the destination country appears on the last line of the address in capital letters. Use the English version of the country name so that your mail is routed from the United States to the right country. Then, to be sure your mail is routed correctly within the destination country, use the foreign spelling of the city name (using the characters and diacritical marks that would be commonly used in the region). For example, the following address uses *Köln* instead of *Cologne*:

H. R. Veith, Director	Addressee
Eisfieren Glaswerk	Company name
Blaubachstrasse 13	Street address
Postfach 10 80 07	Post office box
D-5000 Köln I	District, city
GERMANY	Country

For additional examples of international addresses, see Table A.5.

Be sure to use organizational titles correctly when addressing international correspondence. Job designations vary around the world. In England, for example, a managing director is often what a U.S. company would call its chief executive officer or president, and a British deputy is the equivalent of a vice president. In France, responsibilities are assigned to individuals without regard to title or organizational structure, and in China the title *project manager* has meaning, but the title *sales manager* may not.

To make matters worse, businesspeople in some countries sign correspondence without their names typed below. In Germany, for example, the belief is that employees represent the company, so it's inappropriate to emphasize personal names.[7] Use the examples in Table A.5 as guidelines when addressing correspondence to countries outside the United States.

Salutation

In the salutation of your letter, follow the style of the first line of the inside address. If the first line is a person's name, the salutation is *Dear Mr.* or *Ms. Name*. The formality of the salutation depends on your relationship with the addressee. If in conversation you would say "Mary," your letter's salutation should be *Dear Mary*, followed by a colon. Otherwise, include the courtesy title and last name, followed by a colon. Presuming to write *Dear Lewis* instead of *Dear Professor Chang* demonstrates a disrespectful familiarity that the recipient will probably resent.

If the first line of the inside address is a position title such as *Director of Personnel*, then use *Dear Director*. If the addressee is unknown, use a polite description, such as *Dear Alumnus, Dear SPCA Supporter*, or *Dear Voter*. If the first line is plural (a department or company), then use *Ladies and Gentlemen* (look again at Table A.3). When you do not know whether you're writing to an individual or a group (for example, when writing a reference or a letter of recommendation), use *To whom it may concern*.

In the United States some letter writers use a "salutopening" on the salutation line. A salutopening omits *Dear* but includes the first few words of the opening paragraph along with the recipient's name. After this line, the sentence continues a double space below as part of the body of the letter, as in these examples:

Thank you, Mr. Brown,	Salutopening Body
for your prompt payment of your bill.	
Congratulations, Ms. Lake!	Salutopening Body
Your promotion is well deserved.	

Whether your salutation is informal or formal, be especially careful that names are spelled right. A misspelled name is glaring evidence of carelessness, and it belies the personal interest you're trying to express.

Body

The body of the letter is your message. Almost all letters are single-spaced, with one blank line before and after the salutation or salutopening, between paragraphs, and before the complimentary close. The body may include indented lists, entire paragraphs indented for emphasis, and even subheadings. If it does, all similar elements

Table A.5   INTERNATIONAL ADDRESSES AND SALUTATIONS

Country	Postal Address	Address Elements	Salutations
Argentina	Sr. Juan Pérez Editorial Internacional S.A. Av. Sarmiento 1337, 8° P. C. C1035AAB BUENOS AIRES – CF ARGENTINA	S.A. = Sociedad Anónima (corporation) Av. Sarmiento (name of street) 1337 (building number) 8° = 8th. P = Piso (floor) C (room or suite) C1035AAB (postcode + city) CF = Capital Federal (federal capital)	Sr. = Señor (Mr.) Sra. = Señora (Mrs.) Srta. = Señorita (Miss) Don't use given names except with people you know well.
Australia	Mr. Roger Lewis International Publishing Pty. Ltd. 166 Kent Street, Level 9 GPO Box 3542 SYDNEY NSW 2001 AUSTRALIA	Pty. Ltd. = Proprietory Limited (corp.) 166 (building number) Kent Street (name of street) Level (floor) GPO Box (post office box) city + state (abbrev.) + postcode	Mr. and Mrs. used on first contact. Ms. not common (avoid use). Business is informal—use given name freely.
Austria	Herrn Dipl.-Ing.J.Gerdenitsch International Verlag Ges.m.b.H. Glockengasse 159 1010 WIEN AUSTRIA	Herrn = To Mr. (separate line) Dipl.-Ing. (engineering degree) Ges.m.b.H. (a corporation) Glockengasse (street name) 159 (building number) 1010 (postcode + city) WIEN (Vienna)	Herr (Mr.) Frau (Mrs.) Fräulein (Miss) obsolete in business, so do not use. Given names are almost never used in business.
Brazil	Ilmo. Sr. Gilberto Rabello Ribeiro Editores Internacionais S.A. Rua da Ajuda, 228–6° Andar Caixa Postal 2574 20040–000 RIO DE JANEIRO – RJ BRAZIL	Ilmo. = Ilustrissimo (honorific) Ilma. = Ilustrissima (hon. female) S.A. = Sociedade Anônima (corporation) Rua = street, da Ajuda (street name) 228 (building number) 6° = 6th. Andar (floor) Caixa Postal (P.O. box) 20040–000 (postcode + city) – RJ (state abbrev.)	Sr. = Senhor (Mr.) Sra. = Senhora (Mrs.) Srta. = Senhorita (Miss) Family name at end, e.g., Senhor Ribeiro (Rabello is mother's family—as in Portugal) Given names readily used in business.
China	Xia Zhiyi International Publishing Ltd. 14 Jianguolu Chaoyangqu BEIJING 100025 CHINA	Ltd. (limited liability corporation) 14 (building number) Jianguolu (street name), lu (street) Chaoyangqu (district name) (city + postcode)	Family name (single syllable) first. Given name (2 syllables) second, sometimes reversed. Use Mr. or Ms. at all times (Mr. Xia).
France	Monsieur LEFÈVRE Alain Éditions Internationales S.A. Siège Social Immeuble Le Bonaparte 64–68, av. Galliéni B.P. 154 75942 PARIS CEDEX 19 FRANCE	S.A. = Société Anonyme (corporation) Siège Social (head office) Immeuble (building + name) 64–68 (building occupies 64, 66, 68) av. = avenue (no initial capital) B.P. = Boîte Postale (P.O. box) 75942 (postcode) CEDEX (postcode for P.O. box)	Monsieur (Mr.) Madame (Mrs.) Mademoiselle (Miss) Best not to abbreviate. Family name is sometimes in all caps with given name following.
Germany	Herrn Gerhardt Schneider International Verlag GmbH Schillerstraße 159 44147 DORTMUND GERMANY	Herrn = To Mr. (on a separate line) GmbH (inc.—incorporated) –straße (street—'ß' often written 'ss') 159 (building number) 44147 (postcode + city)	Herr (Mr.) Frau (Mrs.) Fräulein (Miss) obsolete in business. Business is formal: (1) do not use given names unless invited, and (2) use academic titles precisely.

Table A.5   Continued

Country	Postal Address	Address Elements	Salutations
India	Sr. Shyam Lal Gupta International Publishing (Pvt.) Ltd. 1820 Rehaja Centre 214, Darussalam Road Andheri East BOMBAY – 400049 INDIA	(Pvt.) (privately owned) Ltd. (limited liability corporation) 1820 (possibly office #20 on 18th floor) Rehaja Centre (building name) 214 (building number) Andheri East (suburb name) (city + hyphen + postcode)	Shri (Mr.), Shrimati (Mrs.) but English is common business language, so use Mr., Mrs., Miss. Given names are used only by family and close friends.
Italy	Egr. Sig. Giacomo Mariotti Edizioni Internazionali S.p.A. Via Terenzio, 21 20138 MILANO ITALY	Egr. = Egregio (honorific) Sig. = Signor (not nec. a separate line) S.p.A. = Società per Azioni (corp.) Via (street) 21 (building number) 20138 (postcode + city)	Sig. = Signore (Mr.) Sig.ra = Signora (Mrs.) Sig.a (Ms.) Women in business are addressed as Signora. Use given name only when invited.
Japan	Mr. Taro Tanaka Kokusai Shuppan K.K. 10–23, 5-chome, Minamiazabu Minato-ku TOKYO 106 JAPAN	K.K. = Kabushiki Kaisha (corporation) 10 (lot number) 23 (building number) 5-chome (area #5) Minamiazabu (neighborhood name) Minato-ku (city district) (city + postcode)	Given names not used in business. Use family name + job title. Or use family name + "-san" (Tanaka-san) or more respectfully, add "-sama" or "-dono."
Korea	Mr. Kim Chang-ik International Publishers Ltd. Room 206, Korea Building 33–4 Nonhyon-dong Kangnam-ku SEOUL 135–010 KOREA	English company names common Ltd. (a corporation) 206 (office number inside the building) 33–4 (area 4 of subdivision 33) -dong (city neighborhood name) -ku (subdivision of city) (city + postcode)	Family name is normally first but sometimes placed after given name. A two-part name is the given name. Use Mr. or Mrs. in letters, but use job title in speech.
Mexico	Sr. Francisco Pérez Martínez Editores Internacionales S.A. Independencia No.322 Col. Juárez 06050 MEXICO D.F.	S.A. = Sociedad Anónima (corporation) Independencia (street name) No. = Número (number) 322 (building number) Col. = Colonia (city district) Juárez (locality name) 06050 (postcode + city) D.F. = Distrito Federal (federal capital)	Sr. = Señor (Mr.) Sra. = Señora (Mrs.) Srta. = Señorita (Miss) Family name in middle: e.g., Sr. Pérez (Martínez is mother's family). Given names are used in business.
South Africa	Mr. Mandla Ntuli International Publishing (Pty.) Ltd. Private Bag X2581 JOHANNESBURG 2000 SOUTH AFRICA	Pty. = Proprietory (privately owned) Ltd. (a corporation) Private Bag (P.O. Box) (city + postcode) or (postcode + city)	Mnr = Meneer (Mr.) Mev. = Mevrou (Mrs.) Mejuffrou (Miss) is not used in business. Business is becoming less formal, so the use of given names is possible.
United Kingdom	Mr. N. J. Lancaster International Publishing Ltd. Kingsbury House 12 Kingsbury Road EDGEWARE Middlesex HA8 9XG ENGLAND	N. J. (initials of given names) Ltd. (limited liability corporation) Kingsbury House (building name) 12 (building number) Kingsbury Road (name of street/road) EDGEWARE (city—all caps) Middlesex (county—not all caps) HA8 9XG	Mr. and Ms. used mostly. Mrs. and Miss sometimes used in North and by older women. Given names—called Christian names—are used in business after some time. Wait to be invited.

should be treated in the same way. Your department or company may select a format to use for all letters.

Complimentary Close

The complimentary close begins on the second line below the body of the letter. Alternatives for wording are available, but currently the trend seems to be toward using one-word closes, such as *Sincerely* and *Cordially*. In any case, the complimentary close reflects the relationship between you and the person you're writing to. Avoid cute closes, such as *Yours for bigger profits*. If your audience doesn't know you well, your sense of humor may be misunderstood.

Signature Block

Leave three blank lines for a written signature below the complimentary close, and then include the sender's name (unless it appears in the letterhead). The person's title may appear on the same line as the name or on the line below:

> Cordially,
>
>
> Raymond Dunnigan
> Director of Personnel

Your letterhead indicates that you're representing your company. However, if your letter is on plain paper or runs to a second page, you may want to emphasize that you're speaking legally for the company. The accepted way of doing that is to place the company's name in capital letters a double space below the complimentary close and then include the sender's name and title four lines below that:

> Sincerely,
>
> WENTWORTH INDUSTRIES
>
>
> (Mrs.) Helen B. Taylor
> President

If your name could be taken for either a man's or a woman's, a courtesy title indicating gender should be included, with or without parentheses. Also, women who prefer a particular courtesy title should include it:

> Mrs. Nancy Winters
>
> (Miss) Juana Flores
>
> Ms. Pat Li
>
> (Mr.) Jamie Saunders

Additional Letter Parts

Letters vary greatly in subject matter and thus in the identifying information they need and the format they adopt. The letter in Figure A.2 shows how these additional parts should be arranged. The following elements may be used in any combination, depending on the requirements of the particular letter:

- **Addressee notation.** Letters that have a restricted readership or that must be handled in a special way should include such addressee notations as *Personal, Confidential,* or *Please Forward*.

This sort of notation appears a double space above the inside address, in all-capital letters.

- **Attention line.** Although not commonly used today, an attention line can be used if you know only the last name of the person you're writing to. It can also direct a letter to a position title or department. Place the attention line on the first line of the inside address and put the company name on the second.[8] Match the address on the envelope with the style of the inside address. An attention line may take any of the following forms or variants of them:

> Attention Dr. McHenry
>
> Attention Director of Marketing
>
> Attention Marketing Department

- **Subject line.** The subject line tells recipients at a glance what the letter is about (and indicates where to file the letter for future reference). It usually appears below the salutation, either against the left margin, indented (as a paragraph in the body), or centered. It can be placed above the salutation or at the very top of the page, and it can be underscored. Some businesses omit the word *Subject*, and some organizations replace it with *Re:* or *In re:* (meaning "concerning" or "in the matter of"). The subject line may take a variety of forms, including the following:

> Subject: RainMaster Sprinklers
>
> About your February 2, 2008, order
>
> FALL 2008 SALES MEETING
>
> Reference Order No. 27920

- **Second-page heading.** Use a second-page heading whenever an additional page is required. Some companies have second-page letterhead (with the company name and address on one line and in a smaller typeface). The heading bears the name (person or organization) from the first line of the inside address, the page number, the date, and perhaps a reference number. Leave two blank lines before the body. Make sure that at least two lines of a continued paragraph appear on the first and second pages. Never allow the closing lines to appear alone on a continued page. Precede the complimentary close or signature lines with at least two lines of the body. Also, don't hyphenate the last word on a page. All the following are acceptable forms for second-page headings:

> Ms. Melissa Baker
>
> May 10, 2008
>
> Page 2
>
> Ms. Melissa Baker, May 10, 2008, Page 2
>
> Ms. Melissa Baker   -2-   May 10, 2008

- **Company name.** If you include the company's name in the signature block, put it all in capital letters a double space below the complimentary close. You usually include the company's name in the signature block only when the writer is serving as the company's official spokesperson or when letterhead has not been used.

- **Reference initials.** When businesspeople keyboard their own letters, reference initials are unnecessary, so they are becoming

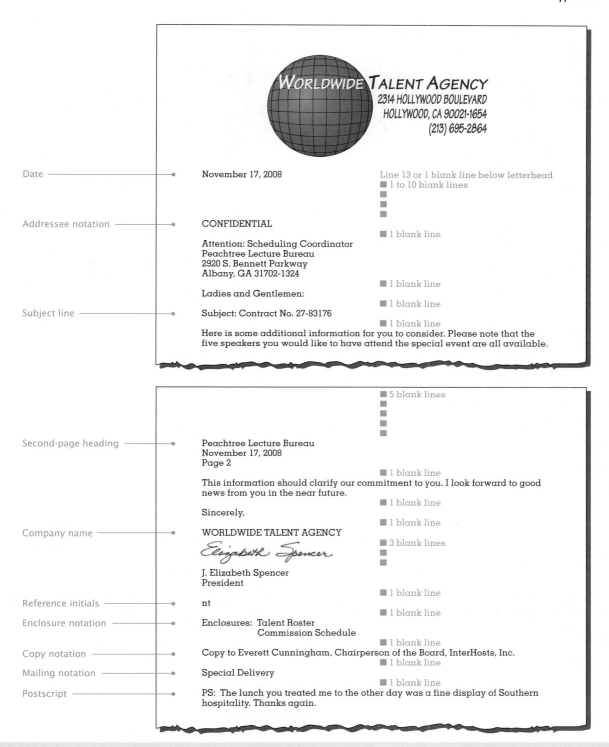

FIGURE A.2
Additional Letter Parts

rare. When one person dictates a letter and another person produces it, reference initials show who helped prepare it. Place initials at the left margin, a double space below the signature block. When the signature block includes the writer's name, use only the preparer's initials. If the signature block includes only the

department, use both sets of initials, usually in one of the following forms: *RSR/sm, RSR:sm,* or *RSR:SM* (writer/preparer). When the writer and the signer are different people, at least the file copy should bear both their initials as well as the typist's: *JFS/RSR/sm* (signer/writer/preparer).

- **Enclosure notation.** Enclosure notations appear at the bottom of a letter, one or two lines below the reference initials. Some common forms include the following:

Enclosure

Enclosures (2)

Enclosures: Résumé

      Photograph

      Attachment

- **Copy notation.** Copy notations may follow reference initials or enclosure notations. They indicate who's receiving a *courtesy copy* (*cc*). Some companies indicate copies made on a photocopier (*pc*), or they simply use *copy* (*c*). Recipients are listed in order of rank or (rank being equal) in alphabetical order. Among the forms used are the following:

cc: David Wentworth, Vice President

pc: Dr. Martha Littlefield

Copy to Hans Vogel

748 Chesterton Road

Snowhomish, WA 98290

c: Joseph Martinez with brochure and technical sheet

When sending copies to readers without other recipients knowing, place *bc, bcc,* or *bpc* ("blind copy," "blind courtesy copy," or "blind photocopy") along with the name and any other information only on the copy, not on the original.

- **Mailing notation.** You may place a mailing notation (such as *Special Delivery* or *Registered Mail*) at the bottom of the letter, after reference initials or enclosure notations (whichever is last) and before copy notations. Or you may place it at the top of the letter, either above the inside address on the left side or just below the date on the right side. For greater visibility, mailing notations may appear in capital letters.

- **Postscript.** A postscript is an afterthought to the letter, a message that requires emphasis, or a personal note. It is usually the

FIGURE A.3
Block Letter Format

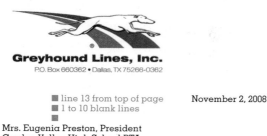

Greyhound Lines, Inc.
P.O. Box 660362 • Dallas, TX 75266-0362

■ line 13 from top of page   November 2, 2008
■ 1 to 10 blank lines
■

Mrs. Eugenia Preston, President
Garden Valley High School PTA
P.O. Box 335
Garden Valley, ID 83622
        ■ 1 blank line
Dear Mrs. Preston:
        ■ 1 blank line
Thank you for inviting us to participate in your "Day of Government" program.
So that your honors students can experience state government firsthand, we
will be delighted to provide one of our motor coaches next May at a 15% dis-
count to transport up to 40 students and 7 advisers from Garden Valley to Boise
and back.
        ■ 1 blank line
Our buses seat 47 passengers, are fully equipped with restrooms and reclining
seats, and are climate controlled for year-round comfort. You can rely on us for
your charter transportation needs:
        ■ 1 blank line
• Our intensive, ongoing driver-training program ensures your safety and
  satisfaction.
• Our competitive pricing allows us to compete both locally and nationwide.
• Our state-of-the-art maintenance facilities are located in all major U.S. cities
  to ensure quality, reliability, and excellent service.
        ■ 1 blank line
Please give me a call at (208) 997-4646 to discuss the specific date of your event,
departure times, and the discounted price for your trip. Together, we'll make
sure your students have a day that's not only fun and educational but safe and
secure. I look forward to hearing from you.
        ■ 1 blank line
                                        Sincerely,
        ■ 3 blank lines
        ■
        ■   *Ronald Struthers*

                                        Ronald Struthers
                                        Vice President, Public Relations
        ■ 1 blank line
pf
        ■ 1 blank line
Enclosure

last thing on any letter and may be preceded by *P.S., PS., PS:*, or nothing at all. A second afterthought would be designated *P.P.S.* (post postscript). Since postscripts usually indicate poor planning, generally avoid them. However, they're common in sales letters as a punch line to remind readers of a benefit for taking advantage of the offer.

Letter Formats

A letter format is the way of arranging all the basic letter parts. Sometimes a company adopts a certain format as its policy; sometimes the individual letter writer or preparer is allowed to choose the most appropriate format. In the United States, three major letter formats are commonly used:

• **Block format.** Each letter part begins at the left margin. The main advantage is quick and efficient preparation (see Figure A.3).

• **Modified block format.** Same as block format, except that the date, complimentary close, and signature block start near the center of the page (see Figure A.4). The modified block format does permit indentions as an option. This format mixes preparation speed with traditional placement of some letter parts. It also looks more balanced on the page than the block format does.

• **Simplified format.** Instead of using a salutation, this format often weaves the reader's name into the first line or two of the body and often includes a subject line in capital letters (see Figure A.5). With no complimentary close, your signature appears after the body, followed by your printed (or typewritten) name (usually in all capital letters). This format is convenient when you don't know the reader's name; however, some people object to it as mechanical and impersonal (a drawback you can overcome with a warm writing style). Because certain letter parts are eliminated, some line spacing is changed.

These three formats differ in the way paragraphs are indented, in the way letter parts are placed, and in some punctuation. However, the elements are always separated by at least one blank line, and the printed (or typewritten) name is always separated from the line above by at least three blank lines to allow space for a signature. If paragraphs are indented, the indention is normally five spaces. The most

FIGURE A.5
Simplified Letter Format

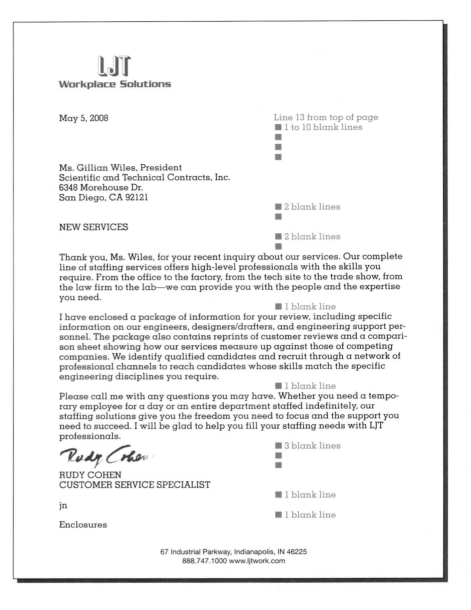

common formats for intercultural business letters are the block style and the modified block style.

In addition to these three letter formats, letters may also be classified according to their style of punctuation. *Standard,* or *mixed, punctuation* uses a colon after the salutation (a comma if the letter is social or personal) and a comma after the complimentary close. *Open punctuation* uses no colon or comma after the salutation or the complimentary close. Although the most popular style in business communication is mixed punctuation, either style of punctuation may be used with block or modified block letter formats. Because the simplified letter format has no salutation or complimentary close, the style of punctuation is irrelevant.

ENVELOPES

For a first impression, the quality of the envelope is just as important as the quality of the stationery. Letterhead and envelopes should be of the same paper stock, have the same color ink, and be imprinted with the same address and logo. Most envelopes used by U.S. businesses are No. 10 envelopes (9½ inches long), which are sized for an 8½-by-11-inch piece of paper folded in thirds. Some occasions call for a smaller, No. 6¾, envelope or for envelopes pro-

portioned to fit special stationery. Figure A.6 shows the two most common sizes.

Addressing the Envelope

No matter what size the envelope, the address is always single-spaced with all lines aligned on the left. The address on the envelope is in the same style as the inside address and presents the same information. The order to follow is from the smallest division to the largest:

1. Name and title of recipient
2. Name of department or subgroup
3. Name of organization
4. Name of building
5. Street address and suite number, or post office box number
6. City, state, or province, and zip code or postal code
7. Name of country (if the letter is being sent abroad)

Because the U.S. Postal Service uses optical scanners to sort mail, envelopes for quantity mailings, in particular, should be addressed in the prescribed format. Everything is in capital letters, no punctuation

Gary J. Marshall
PACIFIC ELECTRONICS
1325 Ocean Boulevard
Santa Monica, California 90415-1216

3 lines

<u>Please Forward</u>

4¹/₂ inches

Line 9

REGISTERED

Line 13

MS. ELEANOR R. FLEMING
246 SHASTA AVENUE
REDDING, CA 96001-2436

Line 3

¹/₂ inch

Helen Richmond
6295 Glenwood Drive
Albuquerque, NM 87001

Line 12

2¹/₂ inches

Dr. Alexander Morris
Avondale Medical Center
453 Camilla Drive
Atlanta, GA 30300

Large envelope, No. 10, is 9¹/₂ by 4¹/₈ inches.

Small envelope, No. 6³/₄, is 6¹/₂ by 3⁵/₈ inches.

FIGURE A.6
Prescribed Envelope Format

is included, and all mailing instructions of interest to the post office are placed above the address area (see Figure A.6). Canada Post requires a similar format, except that only the city is all in capitals, and the postal code is placed on the line below the name of the city. The post office scanners read addresses from the bottom up, so if a letter is to be sent to a post office box rather than to a street address, the street address should appear on the line above the box number. Figure A.6 also shows the proper spacing for addresses and return addresses.

The U.S. Postal Service and the Canada Post Corporation have published lists of two-letter mailing abbreviations for states, provinces, and territories (see Table A.6). Postal authorities prefer no punctuation with these abbreviations, but some executives prefer to have state and province names spelled out in full and set off from city names by a comma. The issue is unresolved, although the comma is most often included. Quantity mailings follow post office requirements. For other letters, a reasonable compromise is to use traditional punctuation, uppercase and lowercase letters for names and street addresses, but two-letter state or province abbreviations, as shown here:

Mr. Kevin Kennedy
2107 E. Packer Dr.
Amarillo, TX 79108

For all out-of-office correspondence, use zip and postal codes that have been assigned to speed mail delivery. The U.S. Postal Service has divided the United States and its territories into 10 zones (0 to 9); this digit comes first in the zip code. The second and third digits represent smaller geographical areas within a state, and the last two digits identify a "local delivery area." Canadian postal codes are alphanumeric, with a three-character "area code" and a

three-character "local code" separated by a single space (K2P 5A5). Zip and postal codes should be separated from state and province names by one space. Canadian postal codes may be treated the same or may be put in the bottom line of the address all by itself.

The U.S. Postal Service has added zip + 4 codes, which add a hyphen and four more numbers to the standard zip codes. The first two of the new numbers may identify an area as small as a single large building, and the last two digits may identify one floor in a large building or even a specific department of an organization. The zip + 4 codes are especially useful for business correspondence. The Canada Post Corporation achieves the same result with special postal codes assigned to buildings and organizations that receive a large volume of mail.

Folding to Fit

The way a letter is folded also contributes to the recipient's overall impression of your organization's professionalism. When sending a standard-size piece of paper in a No. 10 envelope, fold it in thirds, with the bottom folded up first and the top folded down over it (see Figure A.7); the open end should be at the top of the envelope and facing out. Fit smaller stationery neatly into the appropriate envelope simply by folding it in half or in thirds. When sending a standard-size letterhead in a No. 6¾ envelope, fold it in half from top to bottom and then in thirds from side to side.

International Mail

Postal service differs from country to country, so it's always a good idea to investigate the quality and availability of various services before sending messages and packages internationally. Also, compare the services offered by delivery companies such as UPS, FedEx,

Table A.6	TWO-LETTER MAILING ABBREVIATIONS FOR THE UNITED STATES AND CANADA

State/Territory/Province	Abbreviation	State/Territory/Province	Abbreviation	State/Territory/Province	Abbreviation
United States		Massachusetts	MA	Texas	TX
Alabama	AL	Michigan	MI	Utah	UT
Alaska	AK	Minnesota	MN	Vermont	VT
American Samoa	AS	Mississippi	MS	Virginia	VA
Arizona	AZ	Missouri	MO	Virgin Islands	VI
Arkansas	AR	Montana	MT	Washington	WA
California	CA	Nebraska	NE	West Virginia	WV
Canal Zone	CZ	Nevada	NV	Wisconsin	WI
Colorado	CO	New Hampshire	NH	Wyoming	WY
Connecticut	CT	New Jersey	NJ	Canada	
Delaware	DE	New Mexico	NM	Alberta	AB
District of Columbia	DC	New York	NY	British Columbia	BC
Florida	FL	North Carolina	NC	Labrador	NL
Georgia	GA	North Dakota	ND	Manitoba	MB
Guam	GU	Northern Mariana	MP	New Brunswick	NB
Hawaii	HI	Ohio	OH	Newfoundland	NL
Idaho	ID	Oklahoma	OK	Northwest Territories	NT
Illinois	IL	Oregon	OR	Nova Scotia	NS
Indiana	IN	Pennsylvania	PA	Nunavur	NU
Iowa	IA	Puerto Rico	PR	Ontario	ON
Kansas	KS	Rhode Island	RI	Prince Edward Island	PE
Kentucky	KY	South Carolina	SC	Quebec	PQ
Louisiana	LA	South Dakota	SD	Saskatchewan	SK
Maine	ME	Tennessee	TN	Yukon Territory	YT
Maryland	MD	Trust Territories	TT		

and DHL to find the best rates and options for each destination and type of shipment. No matter which service you choose, be aware that international mail requires more planning than domestic mail. For example, for anything beyond simple letters, you generally need to prepare *customs forms* and possibly other documents, depending on the country of destination and the type of shipment. You are responsible for following the laws of the United States and any countries to which you send mail and packages.

The U.S. Postal Service currently offers four classes of international delivery, listed here from the fastest (and most expensive) to the slowest (and least expensive):

- **Global Express Guaranteed** is the fastest option. This service, offered in conjunction with FedEx, provides delivery in one to three business days to more than 190 countries and territories.

- **Express Mail International** guarantees delivery in three to five business days to a limited number of countries, including Australia, China, Hong Kong, Japan, South Korea.

- **Priority Mail International** offers delivery guarantees of six to ten business days to more than 190 countries and territories.

No. 10 Envelope

No. 6³/₄ Envelope

FIGURE A.7
Folding Standard-Size
Letterhead

- **First Class Mail International** is an economical way to send correspondence and packages weighing up to four pounds to virtually any destination worldwide.

To prepare your mail for international delivery, follow the instructions provided at **www.usps.com/business/international/welcome.htm**. There you'll find complete information on the international services available through the U.S. Postal Service, along with advice on addressing and packaging mail, completing customs forms, and calculating postage rates and fees. The *International Mail Manual*, also available on this website, offers the latest information and regulations for both outbound and inbound international mail. For instance, you can click on individual country names to see current information about restricted or prohibited items and materials, required customs forms, and rates for various classes of service.[9] Various countries have specific and often extensive lists of items that may not be sent by mail at all or that must be sent using particular postal service options.

MEMOS

Many organizations have memo forms preprinted, with labeled spaces for the recipient's name (or sometimes a checklist of all departments in an organization or all persons in a department), the sender's name, the date, and the subject (see Figure A.8). If such forms don't exist, you can use a memo template (which comes with word processing software and provides margin settings, headings, and special formats), or you can use plain paper.

On your document, include a title such as MEMO or INTEROFFICE CORRESPONDENCE (all in capitals) centered at the top of the page or aligned with the left margin. Also at the top, include the words *To, From, Date,* and *Subject*—followed by the appropriate information—with a blank line between as shown here:

MEMO

TO:

FROM:

DATE:

SUBJECT:

Sometimes the heading is organized like this:

MEMO

TO: DATE:

FROM: SUBJECT:

You can arrange these four pieces of information in almost any order. The date sometimes appears without the heading *Date*. The subject may be presented with the letters *Re:* (in place of *SUBJECT:*) or may even be presented without any heading (but in capital letters so that it

MEMO

TO: _____

DEPT: _____   FROM: _____

DATE: _____   TELEPHONE: _____

SUBJECT: _____   *For your*
☐ APPROVAL ☐ INFORMATION ☐ COMMENT

FIGURE A.8
Preprinted Memo Form

stands out clearly). You may want to include a file or reference number, introduced by the word *File*.

The following guidelines will help you effectively format specific memo elements:

- **Addressees.** When sending a memo to a long list of people, include the notation *See distribution list* or *See below* in the *To* position at the top; then list the names at the end of the memo. Arrange this list alphabetically, except when high-ranking officials deserve more prominent placement. You can also address memos to groups of people—*All Sales Representatives, Production Group, New Product Team*.

- **Courtesy titles.** You need not use courtesy titles anywhere in a memo; first initials and last names, first names, or even initials alone are often sufficient. However, use a courtesy title if you would use one in a face-to-face encounter with the person.

- **Subject line.** The subject line of a memo helps busy colleagues quickly find out what your memo is about. Although the subject "line" may overflow onto a second line, it's most helpful when it's short (but still informative).

- **Body.** Start the body of the memo on the second or third line below the heading. Like the body of a letter, it's usually single-spaced with blank lines between paragraphs. Indenting paragraphs is optional. Handle lists, important passages, and subheadings as you do in letters. If the memo is very short, you may double-space it.

- **Second page.** If the memo carries over to a second page, head the second page just as you head the second page of a letter.

- **Writer's initials.** Unlike a letter, a memo doesn't require a complimentary close or a signature, because your name is already prominent at the top. However, you may initial the memo—either beside the name appearing at the top of the memo or at the bottom of the memo—or you may even sign your name at the bottom, particularly if the memo deals with money or confidential matters.

- **Other elements.** Treat elements such as reference initials, enclosure notations, and copy notations just as you would in a letter.

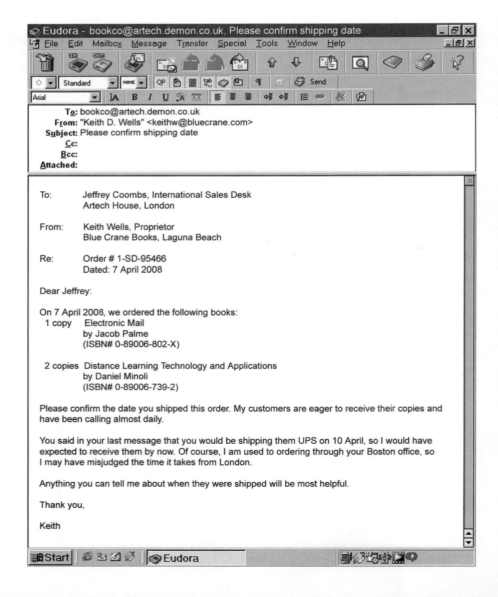

FIGURE A.9
A Typical E-Mail Message

Memos may be delivered by hand, by the post office (when the recipient works at a different location), or through interoffice mail. Interoffice mail may require the use of special reusable envelopes that have spaces for the recipient's name and department or room number; the name of the previous recipient is simply crossed out. If a regular envelope is used, the words *Interoffice Mail* appear where the stamp normally goes, so that it won't accidentally be stamped and mailed with the rest of the office correspondence.

Informal, routine, or brief reports for distribution within a company are often presented in memo form. Don't include report parts such as a table of contents and appendixes, but write the body of the memo report just as carefully as you'd write a formal report.

E-MAIL

Because e-mail messages can act both as memos (carrying information within your company) and as letters (carrying information outside your company and around the world), their format depends on your audience and purpose. You may choose to have your e-mail resemble a formal letter or a detailed report, or you may decide to keep things as simple as an interoffice memo. A modified memo format is appropriate for most e-mail messages.[10] All e-mail programs include two major elements: the header and the body (see Figure A.9).

Header

The e-mail header depends on the particular program you use. Some programs even allow you to choose between a shorter and a longer version. However, most headers contain similar information.

- **To:** Contains the audience's e-mail address (see Figure A.10). Most e-mail programs also allow you to send mail to an entire group of people all at once. First, you create a distribution list. Then you type the name of the list in the *To:* line instead of typ-

ing the addresses of every person in the group.[11] The most common e-mail addresses are addresses such as

nmaa.betsy@c.si.edu (Smithsonian Institute's National Museum of American Art)

webwsj@dowjones.com (*Wall Street Journal home page*)

relpubli@mairie-toulouse.mipnet.fr (Municipal Services, Toulouse, France)

- **From:** Contains your e-mail address.
- **Date:** Contains the day of the week, date (day, month, year), time, and time zone.
- **Subject:** Describes the content of the message and presents an opportunity for you to build interest in your message.
- **Cc:** Allows you to send copies of a message to more than one person at a time. It also allows everyone on the list to see who else received the same message.
- **Bcc:** Lets you send copies to people without the other recipients knowing—a practice considered unethical by some.[12]
- **Attachments:** Contains the name(s) of the file(s) you attach to your e-mail message. The file can be a word processing document, a digital image, an audio or video message, a spreadsheet, or a software program.[13]

Most e-mail programs now allow you the choice of hiding or revealing other lines that contain more detailed information, including

- **Message-Id:** The exact location of this e-mail message on the sender's system
- **X-mailer:** The version of the e-mail program being used

FIGURE A.10
Anatomy of an E-Mail Address

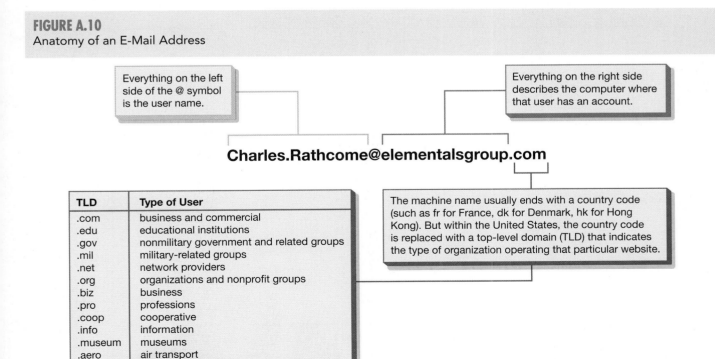

- **Content type:** A description of the text and character set that is contained in the message

- **Received:** Information about each of the systems your e-mail passed through en route to your mailbox.[14]

Body

The rest of the space below the header is for the body of your message. In the *To:* and *From:* lines, some headers actually print out the names of the sender and receiver (in addition to their e-mail addresses). Other headers do not. If your mail program includes only the e-mail addresses, you might consider including your own memo-type header in the body of your message, as in Figure A.9. The writer even included a second, more specific subject line in his memo-type header. Some recipients may applaud the clarity of such second headers; however, others will criticize the space it takes. Your decision depends on how formal you want to be.

Do include a greeting in your e-mail. As pointed out in Chapter 7, greetings personalize your message. Leave one line space above and below your greeting to set it off from the rest of your message. You may end your greeting with a colon (formal), a comma (conversational), or even two hyphens (informal)—depending on the level of formality you want.

Your message begins one blank line space below your greeting. Just as in memos and letters, skip one line space between paragraphs and include headings, numbered lists, bulleted lists, and embedded lists when appropriate.

One blank line space below your message, include a simple closing, often just one word. A blank line space below that, include your signature. Whether you type your name or use a signature file, including your signature personalizes your message.

REPORTS

Enhance your report's effectiveness by paying careful attention to its appearance and layout. Follow whatever guidelines your organization prefers, always being neat and consistent throughout. If it's up to you to decide formatting questions, the following conventions may help you decide how to handle margins, headings, spacing and indention, and page numbers.

Margins

All margins on a report page are at least 1 inch wide. For double-spaced pages, use 1-inch margins; for single-spaced pages, set margins between 1¼ and 1½ inches. The top, left, and right margins are usually the same, but the bottom margins can be 1½ times deeper. Some special pages also have deeper top margins. Set top margins as deep as 2 inches for pages that contain major titles: prefatory parts (such as the table of contents or the executive summary), supplementary parts (such as the reference notes or bibliography), and textual parts (such as the first page of the text or the first page of each chapter).

If you're going to bind your report at the left or at the top, add half an inch to the margin on the bound edge (see Figure A.11): The space taken by the binding on left-bound reports makes the center point of the text a quarter inch to the right of the center of the paper. Be sure to center headings between the margins, not between the edges of the paper. Computers can do this for you automatically. Other guidelines for report formats are in the Chapter 13 samples.

FIGURE A.11
Margins for Formal Reports

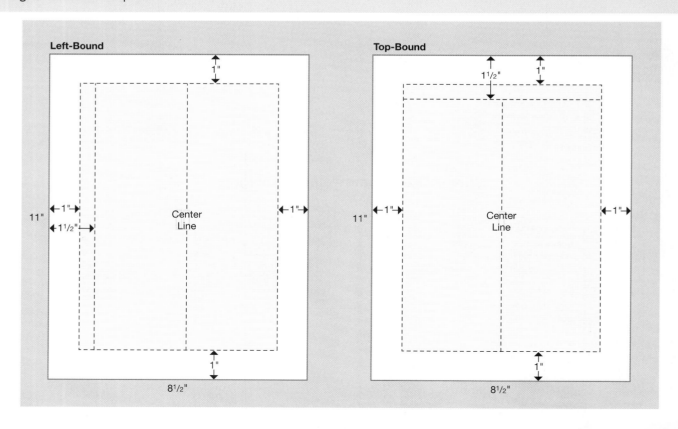

Headings

Headings of various levels provide visual clues to a report's organization. Figure 12.3, on page 415, illustrates one good system for showing these levels, but many variations exist. No matter which system you use, be sure to be consistent.

Spacing and Indentions

If your report is double-spaced (perhaps to ease comprehension of technical material), indent all paragraphs five character spaces (or about half an inch). In single-spaced reports, block the paragraphs (no indentions) and leave one blank line between them.

Make sure the material on the title page is centered and well balanced, as on the title page of the sample report in Chapter 13. When using a typewriter, proper spacing takes some calculation. To center text in left-bound reports, start a quarter inch to the right of the paper's center. From that point, backspace once for each two letters in the line. The line will appear centered when the report is bound.

To place lines of type vertically on the title page, follow these steps:

1. Count the number of lines in each block of copy, including blank lines.
2. Subtract that total from 66 (the number of lines on an 11-inch page); the result is the number of unused lines.
3. Divide the number of unused lines by the number of blank areas (always one more than the number of blocks of copy). The result is the number of blank lines to allocate above, between, and below the blocks of copy.

A computer with a good word processing program will do these calculations for you at the click of a mouse.

Page Numbers

Remember that every page in the report is counted; however, not all pages show numbers. The first page of the report, normally the title page, is unnumbered. All other pages in the prefatory section are numbered with a lowercase roman numeral, beginning with *ii* and continuing with *iii, iv, v,* and so on. The unadorned (no dashes, no period) page number is centered at the bottom margin.

Number the first page of the text of the report with the unadorned arabic numeral 1, centered at the bottom margin (double- or triple-spaced below the text). In left-bound reports, number the following pages (including the supplementary parts) consecutively with unadorned arabic numerals (2, 3, and so on), placed at the top right-hand margin (double- or triple-spaced above the text). For top-bound reports and for special pages having 2-inch top margins, center the page numbers at the bottom margin.

BIBLIOGRAPHY

Journal article with volume and issue numbers

Assira, James. "Are They Speaking English in Japan?" *Journal of Business Communication* 36, no. 4 (Fall 2002): 72.

Brochure

BestTemp Staffing Services. *An Employer's Guide to Staffing Services.* 2d ed. Denver: BestTemp Information Center, 2000.

Newspaper article, no author

"Buying Asian Supplies on the Net." *Los Angeles Times,* 12 February 2000, sec. D, p. 3.

Annual report

Eurotec. *2001 Annual Report.* New York: Eurotec, Inc., 2001.

Magazine article

Graves, Holly. "Prospecting Online." *BusinessWeek,* 17 November 2002, 43–5.

Television broadcast

Han, Daniel. "Trade Wars Heating Up Around the Globe." *CNN Headline News.* Atlanta: CNN, 5 March 2002.

Internet, World Wide Web

"Intel—Company Capsule." *Hoover's Online* [cited 8 March 2003]. 3 screens; Available from www.hoovers.com/capsules/13787.html.

Book, component parts

Kuntz, Sonja. "Moving Beyond Benefits." In *Our Changing Workforce*, edited by Randolf Jacobson. New York: Citadel Press, 2001.

Unpublished dissertation or thesis

Morales, George H. "The Economic Pressures on Industrialized Nations in a Global Economy." Ph.D. diss., University of San Diego, 2001.

Paper presented at a meeting

Myers, Charles. "HMOs in Today's Environment." Paper presented at the Conference on Medical Insurance Solutions, Chicago, Ill., August 2001.

Online magazine article

Norwalk, Preston. "Training Managers to Help Employees Accept Change." In *Business Line* [online]. San Francisco, 2002 [updated 17 September 2002; cited 3 October 2002]. Available from www.busline.com/news.

CD-ROM encyclopedia article, one author

Parkings, Robert. "George Eastman." *The Concise Columbia Encyclopedia.* New York: Columbia University Press, 1998. [CD-ROM].

Interview

Stainer, Georgia, general manager, Day Cable and Communications. Interview by author. Topeka, Kan., 2 March 2000.

Newspaper article, one author

Standish, Evelyn. "Global Market Crushes OPEC's Delicate Balance of Interests." *Wall Street Journal,* 19 January 2002, sec. A, p. 1.

Book, two authors

Toller, Miriam, and Jay Fielding. *Global Business for Smaller Companies.* Rocklin, Calif.: Prima Publishing, 2001.

Government publication

U.S. Department of Defense. *Stretching Research Dollars: Survival Advice for Universities and Government Labs.* Washington, D.C.: GPO, 2002.

FIGURE B.2
Sample Bibliography—Chicago Humanities Style

- Explain how electronic references can be reached: Available from www.spaceless.com/WWWVL.

- Give the citation date for online references: Cited 23 August 2007.

APA STYLE

The American Psychological Association (APA) recommends the author-date system of documentation, which is popular in the physical, natural, and social sciences. When using this system, you simply insert the author's last name and the year of publication within parentheses following the text discussion of the material cited. Include a page number if you use a direct quote. This approach briefly identifies the source so that readers can locate complete information in the alphabetical reference list at the end of the report. The author-date system is both brief and clear, saving readers time and effort.

In-Text Citation—APA Style

To document report sources in text using APA style, insert the author's surname and the date of publication at the end of a statement. Enclose this information in parentheses. If the author's name is referred to in the text itself, then the name can be omitted from parenthetical material.

Some experts recommend both translation and back-translation when dealing with any non-English-speaking culture (Assira, 2001).

Toller and Fielding (2000) make a strong case for small companies succeeding in global business.

Personal communications and interviews conducted by the author would not be listed in the reference list at all. Such citations would appear in the text only.

> Increasing the role of cable companies is high on the list of Georgia Stainer, general manager at Day Cable and Communications (personal communication, March 2, 2007).

List of References—APA Style

For APA style, list only those works actually cited in the text (so you would not include works for background or for further reading). Report writers must choose their references judiciously. Following are the major conventions for developing a reference list according to APA style (see Figure B.3):

- Format entries as hanging indents.

- List all author names in reversed order (last name first), and use only initials for the first and middle names.

- Arrange entries in the following general order: (1) author name, (2) date, (3) title information, (4) publication information, (5) periodical page range.

- Follow the author name with the date of publication in parentheses.

- List titles of articles from magazines, newspapers, and journals without underlines or quotation marks. Capitalize only the first word of the title, any proper nouns, and the first word to follow an internal colon.

FIGURE B.3
Sample References—APA Style

REFERENCES

Journal article with volume and issue numbers
Assira, J. (2002). Are they speaking English in Japan? *Journal of Business Communication, 36*(4), 72.

Brochure
BestTemp Staffing Services. (2000). *An employer's guide to staffing services* (2d ed.) [Brochure]. Denver: BestTemp Information Center.

Newspaper article, no author
Buying Asian supplies on the net. (2000, February 12). *Los Angeles Times*, p. D3.

Annual report
Eurotec. (2001). *2001 annual report*. New York: Eurotec.

Magazine article
Graves, H. (2002, November 17). Prospecting online. *BusinessWeek*, 43–45.

Television broadcast
Han, D. (2002, March 5). Trade wars heating up around the globe. *CNN Headline News*. [Television broadcast]. Atlanta, GA: CNN.

Internet, World Wide Web
Hoover's Online. (2003). *Intel—Company Capsule*. Retrieved March 8, 2002, from http://www.hoovers.com/capsules/13787.html

Book, component parts
Kuntz, S. (2001). Moving beyond benefits. In Randolph Jacobson (Ed.), *Our changing workforce* (pp. 213–227). New York: Citadel Press.

Unpublished dissertation or thesis
Morales, G. H. (2001). *The economic pressures on industrialized nations in a global economy*. Unpublished doctoral dissertation, University of San Diego.

Paper presented at a meeting
Myers, C. (2001, August). *HMOs in today's environment*. Paper presented at the Conference on Medical Insurance Solutions, Chicago, IL.

Online magazine article
Norwalk, P. (2002, July 17). Training managers to help employees accept change. *Business Line*. Retrieved March 8, 2002, from http://www.busline.com/news

CD-ROM encyclopedia article, one author
Parkings, R. (1998). George Eastman. On *The concise Columbia encyclopedia*. [CD-ROM]. New York: Columbia University Press.

Interview
Cited in text only, not in the list of references.

Newspaper article, one author
Standish, E. (2002, January 19). Global market crushes OPEC's delicate balance of interests. *Wall Street Journal*, p. A1.

Book, two authors
Toller, M., & Fielding, J. (2001). *Global business for smaller companies*. Rocklin, CA: Prima Publishing.

Government publication
U.S. Department of Defense. (2002). *Stretching research dollars: Survival advice for universities and government labs*. Washington, DC: U.S. Government Printing Office.

- Italicize titles of books, capitalizing only the first word, any proper nouns, and the first word to follow a colon.

- Italicize names of magazines, newspapers, journals, and other complete publications—capitalizing all the important words.

- For journal articles, include the volume number (in italics) and, if necessary, the issue number (in parentheses). Finally, include the page range of the article: *Journal of Business Communication, 36*(4), 72. (In this example, the volume is 36, the number is 4, and the page number is 72.)

- Include personal communications (such as letters, memos, e-mail, and conversations) only in text, not in reference lists.

- Electronic references include author, date of publication, title of article, name of publication (if one), volume, date of retrieval (month, day, year), and the source.

- For electronic references, indicate the actual year of publication and the exact date of retrieval.

- For electronic references, specify the URL; leave periods off the ends of URLs.

MLA STYLE

The style recommended by the Modern Language Association of America is used widely in the humanities, especially in the study of language and literature. Like APA style, MLA style uses brief parenthetical citations in the text. However, instead of including author name and year, MLA citations include author name and page reference.

In-Text Citation—MLA Style

To document report sources in text using MLA style, insert the author's last name and a page reference inside parentheses following

FIGURE B.4
Sample Works Cited—MLA Style

WORKS CITED

Journal article with volume and issue numbers	Assira, James. "Are They Speaking English in Japan?" *Journal of Business Communication* 36, 4 (2002): 72.
Brochure	BestTemp Staffing Services. *An Employer's Guide to Staffing Services*. 2d ed. Denver: BestTemp Information Center, 2000.
Newspaper article, no author	"Buying Asian Supplies on the Net." *Los Angeles Times* 12 Feb. 2000: D3.
Annual report	Eurotec. *2000 Annual Report*. New York: Eurotec, Inc., 2001.
Magazine article	Graves, Holly. "Prospecting Online." *BusinessWeek* 17 Nov. 2002: 43–45.
Television broadcast	Han, Daniel. "Trade Wars Heating Up Around the Globe." *CNN Headline News*. CNN, Atlanta. 5 Mar. 2002.
Internet, World Wide Web	"Intel—Company Capsule." *Hoover's Online*. 2003. Hoover's Company Information. 8 Mar. 2002 <http://www.hoovers.com/capsules/13787.html>.
Book, component parts	Kuntz, Sonja. "Moving Beyond Benefits." *Our Changing Workforce*. Ed. Randolf Jacobson. New York: Citadel Press, 2001. 213–27.
Unpublished dissertation or thesis	Morales, George H. "The Economic Pressures on Industrialized Nations in a Global Economy." Diss. U of San Diego, 2001.
Paper presented at a meeting	Myers, Charles. "HMOs in Today's Environment." Conference on Medical Insurance Solutions. Chicago. 13 Aug. 2001.
Online magazine article	Norwalk, Preston. "Training Managers to Help Employees Accept Change." *Business Line* 17 July 2002. 8 Mar. 2002 <http://www.busline.com/news>.
CD-ROM encyclopedia article, one author	Parkings, Robert. "George Eastman." *The Concise Columbia Encyclopedia*. CD-ROM. New York: Columbia UP, 1998.
Interview	Stainer, Georgia, general manager, Day Cable and Communications. Telephone interview. 2 Mar. 2000.
Newspaper article, one author	Standish, Evelyn. "Global Market Crushes OPEC's Delicate Balance of Interests." *Wall Street Journal* 19 Jan. 2002: A1.
Book, two authors	Toller, Miriam, and Jay Fielding. *Global Business for Smaller Companies*. Rocklin, CA: Prima Publishing, 2001.
Government publication	United States. Department of Defense. *Stretching Research Dollars: Survival Advice for Universities and Government Labs*. Washington: GPO, 2002.

the cited material: (Matthews 63). If the author's name is mentioned in the text reference, the name can be omitted from the parenthetical citation: (63). The citation indicates that the reference came from page 63 of a work by Matthews. With the author's name, readers can find complete publication information in the alphabetically arranged list of works cited that comes at the end of the report.

> Some experts recommend both translation and back-translation when dealing with any non-English-speaking culture (Assira 72).

> Toller and Fielding make a strong case for small companies succeeding in global business (102–03).

List of Works Cited—MLA Style

The *MLA Style Manual* recommends preparing the list of works cited first so that you will know what information to give in the parenthetical citation (for example, whether to add a short title if you're citing more than one work by the same author, or whether to give an initial or first name if you're citing two authors who have the same last name). The list of works cited appears at the end of your report, contains all the works that you cite in your text, and lists them in alphabetical order. Following are the major conventions for developing a reference list according to MLA style (see Figure B.4):

- Format entries as hanging indents.

- Arrange entries in the following general order: (1) author name, (2) title information, (3) publication information, (4) date, (5) periodical page range.

- List the lead author's name in reverse order (last name first), using either full first names or initials. List second and succeeding author names in normal order.

- Use quotation marks around the titles of articles from magazines, newspapers, and journals—capitalize all important words.

- Italicize the names of books, newspapers, journals and other complete publications, capitalizing all main words in the title.

- For journal articles, include the volume number and the issue number (if necessary). Include the year of publication inside parentheses and follow with a colon and the page range of the article: *Journal of Business Communication* 36, 4 (2001): 72. (In this source, the volume is 36, the number is 4, and the page is 72.)

- Electronic sources are less fixed than print sources, and they may not be readily accessible to readers. So citations for electronic sources must provide more information. Always try to be as comprehensive as possible, citing whatever information is available.

- The date for electronic sources should contain both the date assigned in the source and the date accessed by the researcher.

- The URL for electronic sources must be as accurate and complete as possible, from access-mode identifier (http, ftp, gopher, telnet) to all relevant directory and file names. Be sure to enclose this path inside angle brackets: <http://www.hoovers.com/capsules/13787.html>.

Appendix C

CORRECTION SYMBOLS

Instructors often use these short, easy-to-remember correction symbols and abbreviations when evaluating students' writing. You can use them too, to understand your instructor's suggestions and to revise and proofread your own letters, memos, and reports. Refer to the Handbook of Grammar, Mechanics, and Usage (pp. H-1–H-23) for further information.

CONTENT AND STYLE

Acc	Accuracy. Check to be sure information is correct.
ACE	Avoid copying examples.
ACP	Avoid copying problems.
Adp	Adapt. Tailor message to reader.
App	Follow proper organization approach.
Assign	Assignment. Review instructions for assignment.
AV	Active verb. Substitute active for passive.
Awk	Awkward phrasing. Rewrite.
BC	Be consistent.
BMS	Be more sincere.
Chop	Choppy sentences. Use longer sentences and more transitional phrases.
Con	Condense. Use fewer words.
CT	Conversational tone. Avoid using overly formal language.
Depers	Depersonalize. Avoid attributing credit or blame to any individual or group.
Dev	Develop. Provide greater detail.
Dir	Direct. Use direct approach; get to the point.
Emph	Emphasize. Develop this point more fully.
EW	Explanation weak. Check logic; provide more proof.
Fl	Flattery. Avoid compliments that are insincere.
FS	Figure of speech. Find a more accurate expression.
GNF	Good news first. Use direct order.
GRF	Give reasons first. Use indirect order.
GW	Goodwill. Put more emphasis on expressions of goodwill.
H/E	Honesty/ethics. Revise statement to reflect good business practices.
Imp	Imply. Avoid being direct.
Inc	Incomplete. Develop further.
Jar	Jargon. Use less specialized language.
Log	Logic. Check development of argument.
Neg	Negative. Use more positive approach or expression.
Obv	Obvious. Do not state point in such detail.
OC	Overconfident. Adopt humbler language.
OM	Omission.
Org	Organization. Strengthen outline.
OS	Off the subject. Close with point on main subject.
Par	Parallel. Use same structure.
Pom	Pompous. Rephrase in down-to-earth terms.
PV	Point of view. Make statement from reader's perspective rather than your own.
RB	Reader benefit. Explain what reader stands to gain.
Red	Redundant. Reduce number of times this point is made.
Ref	Reference. Cite source of information.
Rep	Repetitive. Provide different expression.
RS	Resale. Reassure reader that he or she has made a good choice.
SA	Service attitude. Put more emphasis on helping reader.
Sin	Sincerity. Avoid sounding glib or uncaring.
SL	Stereotyped language. Focus on individual's characteristics instead of on false generalizations.
Spec	Specific. Provide more specific statement.
SPM	Sales promotion material. Tell reader about related goods or services.
Stet	Let stand in original form.
Sub	Subordinate. Make this point less important.
SX	Sexist. Avoid language that contributes to gender stereotypes.
Tone	Tone needs improvement.
Trans	Transition. Show connection between points.
UAE	Use action ending. Close by stating what reader should do next.
UAS	Use appropriate salutation.
UAV	Use active voice.
Unc	Unclear. Rewrite to clarify meaning.
UPV	Use passive voice.
USS	Use shorter sentences.
V	Variety. Use different expression or sentence pattern.
W	Wordy. Eliminate unnecessary words.
WC	Word choice. Find a more appropriate word.
YA	"You" attitude. Rewrite to emphasize reader's needs.

GRAMMAR, MECHANICS, AND USAGE

Ab	Abbreviation. Avoid abbreviations in most cases; use correct abbreviation.
Adj	Adjective. Use adjective instead.
Adv	Adverb. Use adverb instead.
Agr	Agreement. Make subject and verb or noun and pronoun agree.
Ap	Appearance. Improve appearance.
Apos	Apostrophe. Check use of apostrophe.
Art	Article. Use correct article.
BC	Be consistent.
Cap	Capitalize.
Case	Use cases correctly.
CoAdj	Coordinate adjective. Insert comma between coordinate adjectives; delete comma between adjective and compound noun.
CS	Comma splice. Use period or semicolon to separate clauses.
DM	Dangling modifier. Rewrite so that modifier clearly relates to subject of sentence.
Exp	Expletive. Avoid expletive beginnings, such as it is, there are, there is, this is, and these are.
F	Format. Improve layout of document.
Frag	Fragment. Rewrite as complete sentence.
Gram	Grammar. Correct grammatical error.
HCA	Hyphenate compound adjective.
lc	Lowercase. Do not use capital letter.

M	Margins. Improve frame around document.
MM	Misplaced modifier. Place modifier close to word it modifies.
NRC	Nonrestrictive clause (or phrase). Separate from rest of sentence with commas.
P	Punctuation. Use correct punctuation.
Par	Parallel. Use same structure.
PH	Place higher. Move document up on page.
PL	Place lower. Move document down on page.
Prep	Preposition. Use correct preposition.
RC	Restrictive clause (or phrase). Remove commas that separate clause from rest of sentence.

RO	Run-on sentence. Separate two sentences with comma and coordinating conjunction or with semicolon.
SC	Series comma. Add comma before *and*.
SI	Split infinitive. Do not separate *to* from rest of verb.
Sp	Spelling error. Consult dictionary.
S-V	Subject-verb pair. Do not separate with comma.
Syl	Syllabification. Divide word between syllables.
WD	Word division. Check dictionary for proper end-of-line hyphenation.
WW	Wrong word. Replace with another word.

PROOFREADING MARKS

Symbol	Meaning	Symbol Used in Context	Corrected Copy
≡	Align horizontally	meaningful result	meaningful result
‖	Align vertically	1. Power cable 2. Keyboard	1. Power cable 2. Keyboard
≡	Capitalize	Pepsico, Inc.	PepsiCo, Inc.
⊐⊏	Center	Awards Banquet	Awards Banquet
◡	Close up space	self- confidence	self-confidence
ℓ	Delete	harrassment and abuse	harassment
(ds)	Double-space	text in first line text in second line (ds)	text in first line text in second line
∧	Insert	tirquoise shirts (u) (and white)	turquoise and white shirts
∨	Insert apostrophe	our teams goals	our team's goals
∧	Insert comma	a, b and c	a, b, and c
= ∧	Insert hyphen	third quarter sales	third-quarter sales
⊙	Insert period	Harrigan et al	Harrigan et al.
∀ ∀	Insert quotation marks	This team isn't cooperating.	This "team" isn't cooperating.
#	Insert space	real estate testcase	real estate test case
/	Lowercase	TULSA, South of here	Tulsa, south of here
⌐⌐	Move down	Sincerely,	Sincerely,
⊏	Move left	Attention: Security	Attention: Security
⊐	Move right	February 2, 2003	February 2, 2003
⌐⌐	Move up	THIRD-QUARTER SALES	THIRD-QUARTER SALES
(STET)	Restore	staff talked openly and frankly (STET)	staff talked openly
⌒	Run lines together	Manager, Distribution	Manager, Distribution
(ss)	Single space	text in first line text in second line	text in first line text in second line
⬯	Spell out	COD	cash on delivery
(sp)	Spell out	Assn. of Biochem. Engrs.	Association of Biochemical Engineers
⌐	Start new line	Marla Fenton, Manager, Distri-bution	Marla Fenton, Manager, Distribution
¶	Start new paragraph	¶The solution is easy to determine but difficult to implement in a competitive environment like the one we now face.	The solution is easy to determine but difficult to implement in a competitive environment like the one we now face.
∼	Transpose	airy, light, casual tone	light, airy, casual tone
(bf)	Use boldface	Recommendations (bf)	**Recommendations**
(ital)	Use italics	Quarterly Report (ital)	*Quarterly Report*

Your instructor may elect to show you one or more of the videos described on the following pages. These programs supplement course concepts with real-life examples of businesspeople meeting important communication challenges. This video guide includes several review and analysis questions as well as exercises for each video. Be sure to review the appropriate page ahead of time so that you'll know what to look for when you watch the video.

EFFECTIVE COMMUNICATION
Learning Objectives

After viewing this video, you will be able to

1. Recognize the importance of communication in the business environment
2. Recognize the elements that distinguish effective from ineffective communication
3. Understand why brevity is an important part of effective communication

Background Information

Effective communication delivers a number of business benefits, including stronger decision making and faster problem solving, earlier warning of potential problems, increased productivity and steadier workflow, stronger business relationships, clearer and more persuasive marketing messages, enhanced professional images for both employers and companies, lower employee turnover and higher employee satisfaction, better financial results, and higher return for investors. To be considered effective, communication efforts need to provide practical information, give facts rather than vague impressions, present information concisely, clarify expectations and responsibilities, and offer persuasive arguments and recommendations.

The Video

This video portrays a new employee at an advertising agency as he learns the importance of effective communication—and learns how to improve his communication efforts. As he goes through a typical day accompanied by a "message mentor," he observes the results of both effective and ineffective communication.

Discussion Questions

1. Why might new hires fresh out of college face challenges in learning how to communicate in the workplace?
2. How should you handle situations in which you are asked to provide solid information but the only information available to you is imprecise and potentially unreliable?
3. How can effective communication improve employee morale?
4. How can you judge how much information to provide your audience in any given situation?
5. Can communication efforts be both effective and unethical? For example, what about a marketing campaign that uses compelling information to persuade people to buy an inferior product when a better product is available from the competition?

Follow-up Assignment

Most companies make an effort to define external communication strategies, but many don't have a formal strategy for internal communication—which is every bit as essential to their success. Read the article, "Internal Communication Strategies—The Neglected Strategic Element," at http://workhelp.org/content/view/171/46/ and then answer the following questions:

1. What are the advantages of effective internal communication?
2. How does communication help align the efforts of everyone in the organization toward common goals?
3. Why is it important to have a companywide strategy for internal communication?

For Further Research

The *HR Magazine* article, "Great Communicators, Great Communication," at www.shrm.org/hrmagazine/articles/0706/0706gptw_pomeroy.asp (or go to www.shrm.org and search on the article title) emphasizes the role communication plays in creating great workplaces. After reading the article, summarize the steps companies have taken to be included among the magazine's list of the 50 best small and medium companies to work for in the United States.

ETHICAL COMMUNICATION
Learning Objectives

After viewing this video, you will be able to

1. Describe a process for deciding what is ethical or unethical
2. Explain the importance of meeting your personal and professional responsibilities in an ethical manner
3. Discuss the possible consequences of ethical and unethical choices and talk about the impact of these choices on direct and related audiences

Background Information

Communication is ethical when it includes all relevant information, when it's true in every sense, and when it isn't deceptive in any way. In contrast, communication is unethical when it includes false information, fails to include important information, or otherwise misleads an audience. To avoid unethical choices in your communication efforts, you must consider not only legal issues but also the needs of your audience and the expectations of society and your employer. In turn, companies that demonstrate high standards of ethics maintain credibility with employees, customers, and other stakeholders.

The Video

This video identifies two important tools in a communicator's toolbox: honesty and objectivity. These tools help businesspeople resolve ethical dilemmas and avoid ethical lapses, both within the company and during interactions with outside audiences. Poor ethical choices can damage a company's credibility and put employees, customers, and the surrounding community at risk. Unfortunately, some ethical choices are neither clear nor simple, and you may face situations in which the needs of one group or individual must be weighed against the needs of another.

Discussion Questions

1. Would you ever consider compromising your ethics for self-gain? If so, under what circumstance? If not, why?

2. The video mentions the role of misrepresentations in the collapse of Enron. If you were the head of communications at Enron and had some knowledge of the true nature of the company's financial condition, what would you have done?

3. Identify risks involved when you choose to act in an unethical manner.

4. How can you be an effective business communicator without credibility?

5. Is it ethical to call in sick to work, even though you are not ill? What happens to your credibility if someone finds out you were not sick?

Follow-up Assignment

Many businesses, from small companies to large corporations, formulate codes of ethics that outline ethical standards for employees. Review IBM's guidelines, which are posted on its website, at www.ibm.com/investor/corpgovernance/cgbeg.phtml. Now answer the following questions:

1. What does IBM want employees to do if they are aware of unethical situations within the organization?

2. How does IBM view misleading statements or innuendos about competitors?

3. What advice does IBM give employees on the subject of receiving gifts from people outside the company?

For Further Research

Advertising communications, particularly advertising aimed at children, can present a variety of ethical concerns. The article provided at www.mediascope.org/pubs/ibriefs/cha.htm reports statistics on the advertising of alcohol and tobacco products and discusses the negative effect these advertisements can have on children. To what extent was it ethical for Anheuser Busch to use the Budweiser frog or for Philip Morris to use Joe Camel in their advertisements, given that many children were able to identify with both characters?

BUSINESS ETIQUETTE
Learning Objectives

After viewing this video, you will be able to

1. Recognize the negative impact that poor etiquette can have in the workplace

2. Identify the five goals that every bad-news message should seek to achieve

3. Identify situations in which the indirect approach is likely to be more effective than the direct approach

Background Information

Etiquette strikes some people as a fine idea for tea parties but something that has little relevance in the contemporary workplace. However, the stresses and strains of today's business environment make etiquette more important than ever. Poor etiquette harms relationships, hinders communication, lowers morale and productivity, and limits career potential. Successful professionals know that taking the time and effort to treat others with respect—through their words and their actions—pays off for everyone in the long run.

The Video

This video shows a young employee learning firsthand the value of business etiquette. A business associate whom he has offended through clumsy communication turns the tables and helps him understand the negative effect that poor etiquette has on people in the workplace. She then helps him grasp the steps needed to present himself respectably and to communicate in ways that get his point across without unnecessarily stirring up negative emotions.

Discussion Questions

1. Is paying attention to standards of etiquette likely to save time or cost time in the workplace? Why?

2. If you need to deliver bad news to a person with whom you will probably never interact again, how can you justify taking extra time and effort to communicate carefully and respectfully? Are you wasting your company's money by spending time on such efforts?

3. How does a well-written buffer in an indirect negative message help the receiver accept the bad news?

4. Can a buffer also make the task of delivering negative messages less stressful? Why or why not?

5. Is the indirect approach to negative messages deceptive? Shouldn't communication always be straightforward and direct? Be prepared to explain your answer.

Follow-up Assignment

Visit www.executiveplanet.com and click on any country that interests you. Explore the "Public Behaviour" section(s) for that country and identify three tips that would help anyone from the United States who is preparing to do business there.

For Further Research

Take the brief business etiquette quiz at www.gradview.com/careers/etiquette.html. Were you able to figure out answers to these situations? Do you agree with the responses that the website identifies as being correct?

LEARNING TO LISTEN: SECOND CITY COMMUNICATIONS
Learning Objectives

After viewing this video, you will be able to

1. Understand the functions of interpersonal communication in the workplace

2. Identify the ways to overcome barriers to effective communication

3. Discuss the importance of active listening both socially and professionally

Background Information

Chicago's Second City Improv is more than the world's best-known comedy theater. Second City now brings its famous brand of humor to corporate giants such as Coca-Cola, Motorola, and Microsoft. With over 40 years of experience in corporate services, Second City's teachers help business professionals develop communication skills through lessons in improvisational theater. Business Communications Training is Second City's fastest-growing practice, fueled by the demands of more than two hundred Fortune 500 companies. Workshops are tailored to client's needs in such areas as listening and giving presentations, collaborative leadership and team skills, interviewing, breaking down barriers to successful communication, and using humor to convey important messages. The next time you watch improvisational sketch comedy, ask yourself how a lesson in the art of "Improv" might give your career a boost.

The Video

In these two video segments, you'll see Second City's training techniques in action. The first segment addresses the need to listen actively, and the second explores techniques for encouraging innovation. The second clip is less focused on communication, but you can see how the techniques for stimulating innovation work equally well for fostering meaningful, two-way conversation that encourages people to open up rather than shut down.

Discussion Questions

1. How do the exercises featured in this video address the contrasting needs of the trial lawyer, the divorce lawyer, and the media buyer?
2. Would ABC's talkative guest Kay Jarman, the 47-year-old award-winning salesperson, be a good candidate for Second City's training workshop?
3. What other workshops might Tom Yorton want to offer companies in response to the current economic and political climate?
4. How might the "Yes and" rule of improvisation be used to train customer service representatives at an L.L. Bean or a Dell computer call center? Without physical cues, such as facial expression and body language, is the "Yes and" rule still effective?
5. As president and managing director of Second City Communications, Tom Yorton says the following: "You have to be willing to fail to be able to get the results you want... to connect with an audience." Do you agree that this statement is as true in business as it is in comedy? Support your chosen position.

Follow-up Assignment

Enjoy Second City Communications's website at www.secondcity.com. If you are a loyal fan, you might want to check out the book titles offered and read more about the group's history. Now explore Second City's Corporate Services: Scan the client roster, read the testimonials, and then select a case study that you find compelling. If you are currently employed, which workshop would be most beneficial to you and to your work team? Explain your choice. If you are not currently employed, how might you and your fellow business students benefit from a Second City workshop? Which workshop would you most like to participate in? Explain how you think it might help you in terms of your social life, your career planning, and your interviewing skills.

For Further Research

The importance of active listening is at the core of *consultative selling*, an approach that emphasizes posing questions to the potential buyer in order to identify needs and expectations—rather than rattling off a prepared sales speech. PublicSpeakingSkills.com (www.publicspeakingskills.com) is one of many companies that offer training in consultative selling. Review the description of the company's Consultative Selling and Negotiating Skills course. Do the principles espoused match the concept of the "you" attitude and the elements of ethical communication that you've learned so far?

COMMUNICATING IN THE GLOBAL WORKPLACE
Learning Objectives

After viewing this video, you will be able to

1. Discuss the challenges of communicating in the global workplace
2. Identify barriers to effective communication across borders
3. Explain the critical role of time in global communication efforts

Background Information

Many businesses are crossing national boundaries to engage in international business. However, operating in a global environment presents a variety of challenges related to culture and communication. Understanding and respecting these challenges can mean the differ-

ence between success and failure, so executives must make sure that employees are educated on cultural issues before attempting to do business in other countries.

The Video

This video identifies the challenges to effective communication in the global marketplace, including the barriers posed by language, culture, time, and technology. You will see that a significant amount of research needs to be conducted before a company can engage in successful global business ventures. For instance, if communicators are unaware of differences in gestures, expressions, and dialect, they can inadvertently offend or confuse their audiences. In addition, time zone differences require organizations to plan carefully in advance so that they can develop, translate, and deliver information in a timely manner.

Discussion Questions

1. Language can be a barrier to effective communication. What steps can a company take to minimize language barriers across borders?
2. What characteristics of a country's culture need to be researched to ensure business success across borders?
3. How does a company ensure that a message is properly translated into the local language and dialect of the people it conducts business with?
4. What challenges does a company face when trying to hold a conference call or video meeting with affiliates and employees around the world?
5. The video mentions that some companies have trusted contacts in a country they wish to do business with, while other companies rely on a significant amount of research to learn more about culture and other local characteristics. What method do you feel is most effective for gathering useful, accurate, and up-to-date information regarding cultural issues?

Follow-up Assignment

The Coca-Cola Company has local operations in more than 200 countries throughout the world. Visit www.coca-cola.com to learn more about the company's business activities in a variety of countries. What steps does Coke take to communicate through its website with customers around the world? Does the company strive to develop products that meet local tastes and needs? If so, how and why?

For Further Research

Choose a country other than the United States, and research your selection using both online and library resources to identify important cultural characteristics specific to that country. For example, you may want to gather information about gestures and other nonverbal communication that would be considered offensive, about work habits, or about laws related to conducting business in that country. The characteristics you identify should be useful and accurate.

Based on what you've learned about this country and your personal beliefs, values, and life experiences, is there any risk that you might have a prejudiced or ethnocentric viewpoint regarding people from this country? Why or why not?

IMPACT OF CULTURE ON BUSINESS: SPOTLIGHT ON LATIN AMERICA
Learning Objectives

After viewing this video, you will be able to

1. List key aspects of Latin American cultures and indicate the influences on their development

2. Identify factors that might lead to cultural change in Latin America

3. Explain some of the major cultural contrasts within Latin America and their impact on international business operations

Background Information

To a large degree, culture defines the way all human beings interpret and respond to life's changing circumstances. When you interact with people from your own culture, your shared experiences and expectations usually enhance the communication process by providing a common language and frame of reference. However, when you communicate across cultural boundaries, a lack of awareness of your audience's culture—and the subconscious ways that your own culture shapes your perceptions—can result in partial or even total failure of the communication process. Moreover, culture is rarely static, so impressions you may have gathered at one point in your life may need to be revisited and revised over time.

The Video

This video takes a broad look at Latin America's various countries and cultures and explores the business implications of cultural similarities and differences. You'll learn how cultural groups that may appear identical on the surface can in fact have subtle but profound differences. Although communication is just one of many topics discussed in the video, you will get a sense of just how important—and challenging—communication can be when conducting business across cultural boundaries.

Discussion Questions

1. Explain what the video means when it says that your own culture can "sneak up on you."
2. How is business influencing the economic gulf between urban and rural populations in Latin America?
3. How have imperial conquests and slavery affected the populations and cultures of Latin America?
4. How do many outsiders view the issue of business and government corruption in Latin America?
5. Is business etiquette in most of Latin America considered relatively formal or relatively informal?

Follow-up Assignment

The World Bank plays an important role in today's fast-changing, closely meshed global economy. Visit the bank's website, at www. worldbank.org, and explore the programs and initiatives under way in the Latin American region. How is the bank using this website to foster better communication between Latin America and the rest of the world?

For Further Research

In today's global marketplace, knowing as much as possible about your international customers' business practices and customs could give you a strategic advantage. To help you successfully conduct business around the globe, navigate the resources at the U.S. Government Export portal. Start at www.export.gov, then click on "Market Research" and then on "Country Information—Quick Reference (TIC)." Click anywhere on the world map to learn more about each country.

How can resources such as this website help U.S. businesses communicate more successfully with customers, employees, and other groups in Latin America?

TECHNOLOGY AND THE TOOLS OF COMMUNICATION
Learning Objectives

After viewing this video, you will be able to

1. Identify technology-related issues to consider when developing communication strategies
2. Identify advantages of using technology as a tool for effective communication
3. Differentiate between "push" and "pull" communication

Background Information

From instant messaging to online meetings, technology has become an integral element of business communication. When used with care, technological tools can help you reach more people in less time with more effective messages. However, when technology is misused or misunderstood, it can cause more problems than it solves. Knowing which technologies to use in every situation—and knowing how to use each one—are vital to your success.

The Video

This video discusses how the Internet, e-mail, voicemail, and other devices have revolutionized the way people communicate. These technological tools increase the speed, frequency, and range of business communication. The video also discusses factors to consider when choosing the most appropriate vehicle for your communication, including the all-important challenge of getting and keeping your audience's attention. The advantages of using technological communication tools are presented throughout the video.

Discussion Questions

1. Identify six questions you need to consider when choosing a technology vehicle for your messages.
2. List the advantages of communicating via e-mail within an organization.
3. What role does technology play in ensuring effective communication within an organization?
4. What are some of the more common challenges that business communicators can encounter when they use technology for communication purposes?
5. Identify the difference between "push" and "pull" communications, and provide an example of each method.

Follow-up Assignment

VolResource (at www.volresource.org.uk/samples/olcomms.htm) provides practical and informative resources for volunteer organizations that are trying to develop online communication strategies. The VolResource website further details questions that need to be addressed in the process of developing an effective communication strategy for any organization. What issues do you think are the most important to consider? Why?

For Further Exploration

Visit the Yellow Transportation website, at www.myyellow.com, and explore the various e-commerce tools this company utilizes to communicate effectively with its customers. Examine these tools and consider their effectiveness. What are some of the advantages of these online communication tools? How do they benefit the client? How do they benefit Yellow Transportation?

EFFECTIVE ORAL PRESENTATIONS
Learning Objectives

After viewing this video, you will be able to

1. Reiterate the importance of knowing your audience before creating and delivering oral presentations
2. Discuss the role of teamwork in preparing and delivering complex presentations
3. Explain the importance of anticipating objections likely to be raised during a presentation

Background Information

Oral presentations are a vital communication medium in most companies. In particular, important decisions often involve one or more presentations, either in person or online, in which people advocating a specific choice present their case to the people responsible for making the decision. Such presentations usually combine informational and analytical reporting, along with the persuasive aspects of a proposal. Beyond the mere delivery of information, however, presentations also involve an element of performance. Audiences search for both verbal and nonverbal clues to help them assess presenters' knowledge, confidence, and credibility.

The Video

This video follows three colleagues as they create and deliver a presentation that seeks to convince the audience to approve the purchase of a particular software system that will be used to manage the company's sales force. The presenters explain the importance of understanding the expectations of their audience, from the types of visuals they prefer to the objections they are likely to raise. The team also explains how they took advantage of each member's individual strengths to create a more effective presentation.

Discussion Questions

1. How did the presenters demonstrate their knowledge of the audience?
2. Why did one presenter use a $100 bill as a prop?
3. What are the risks of using props such as the $100 bill?
4. How did the presenters prepare for objections raised by the audience?
5. How would the team need to modify its presentation for an online webcast instead of an in-person oral presentation?

Follow-up Assignment

Podcasts (audio only) and vidcasts (podcasts with video) are quickly catching on as a medium for business presentations. Visit **www.technorati.com** and click on the Business category. Select any three podcasts. Listen to them while taking careful notes so that you can compare the three selections in terms of grabbing your attention, keeping your attention, and effectively communicating the podcast's information. Which of the three podcasts is the most effective? Why?

For Further Research

Musicians, actors, jugglers—virtually everyone who performs in public experiences *performance anxiety* or *stage fright*, as it is commonly known. This anxiety is simply the natural outcome of caring about how well you do. After all, if you didn't care, you wouldn't feel anxious. Seasoned performers not only recognize that anxiety is natural but they also have learned how to use this emotion to their advantage by giving them extra energy. Visit **www.petethomas.co.uk/performance-nerves.html** and **www.jugglingdb.com** (search for "stage fright," then click on the "Collective wisdom on stage fright") and read how these accomplished performers handle the anxiety of performing in public. How can you adapt their techniques to business presentations?

INTERVIEWING SKILLS
Learning Objectives

After viewing this video, you will be able to

1. Explain how the AIDA approach helps create effective application letters
2. Identify mistakes that can cause an otherwise qualified candidate to lose out on a job opportunity
3. Explain why planning for tough questions is such an important part of your interviewing strategy

Background Information

Most companies would admit that the employment interview is an imperfect test of a candidate's skills and personality fit with the organization. In response, some are beginning to add testing, job simulations, and other evaluation tools to the selection process. However, the classic face-to-face interview remains the dominant decision-making tool in the hiring process, so developing your interviewing skills will be vital to your success at every stage in your career.

The Video

This video follows the progress of two candidates applying and interviewing for a technical writing position. One candidate has more experience in this area, but his approach to the interview process ends up costing him the job opportunity. In contrast, a candidate with less experience takes a confident and creative approach that nets her the job.

Discussion Questions

1. Why are multiple StayCom managers involved in this interviewing process? Couldn't one manager handle it?
2. Why does one of the managers compare an application letter to a news story?
3. What steps did Cheryl Yung take to overcome a potential shortcoming in her qualifications?
4. What mistakes did candidate Buddy McCoy make in his interview?
5. Why would the interviewers care about the interpersonal skills of someone who will be writing for a living?

Follow-up Assignment

Nonverbal cues are important in every communication scenario, but perhaps never more important than in job interviews. Not only are interviewers looking for any clues they can find that will guide their decisions but they tend to make up their minds quickly—perhaps even before the candidate has said anything at all. Read the advice on nonverbal communication in interviews at **www.careerjournal.com/jobhunting/interviewing/20021205-raudsepp.html**. Distill this information down to a half dozen or so key points that you can write on a note card to study before you step into your next job interview.

For Further Research

You look great in your new interview outfit, your hair is perfect but not too perfect, your smile radiates positive energy, and you're ready to dazzle the interviewer. Then, oops—you discover that your first interview will be held over the telephone, so none of your visual cues will help you at this stage. Don't fret; read the telephone interviewing advice at **http://www.collegegrad.com/jobsearch/phone-Interviewing-Success/**, and you'll be ready to dazzle the interviewer long distance.

Handbook of Grammar, Mechanics, and Usage

Grammar and mechanics are nothing more than the way words are combined into sentences. Usage is the way words are used by a network of people—in this case, the community of businesspeople who use English. You'll find it easier to get along in this community if you know the accepted standards of grammar, mechanics, and usage. This handbook offers you valuable opportunities in three sections:

- **Diagnostic Test of English Skills.** Testing your current knowledge of grammar, mechanics, and usage helps you find out where your strengths and weaknesses lie. This test offers 50 items taken from the topics included in this Handbook.

- **Assessment of English Skills.** After completing the diagnostic test, use the assessment form to highlight those areas you most need to review. (To check your answers, you will need to get an answer sheet from your instructor.)

- **Essentials of Grammar, Mechanics, and Usage.** This section helps you brush up on the basics. You can study issues that you've probably already learned but may have forgotten related to the parts of speech, sentence construction, punctuation, capitalization, abbreviations, number style, spelling, proper word usage, and so on. Use this essential review not only to study and improve your English skills but also as a reference for any questions you may have during this course.

Without a firm grasp of the basics of grammar, mechanics, and vocabulary, you risk being misunderstood, damaging your company's image, losing money for your company, and possibly even losing your job. However, once you develop strong English skills, you should be able to create clear and concise messages, to enhance your company's image as well as your own, and to expand your chances of success.

DIAGNOSTIC TEST OF ENGLISH SKILLS

Use this test to help you determine whether you need more practice with grammar, punctuation, mechanics, or vocabulary. When you've answered all the questions, ask your instructor for an answer sheet so that you can score the test. On the Assessment of English Skills form (page H-2), record the number of questions you answered correctly in each section.

The following choices apply to items 1–10. In each blank, write the letter of the choice that best describes the problem with each sentence.

A. sentence incomplete
B. too many phrases/clauses strung together
C. modifying elements misplaced (dangling)
D. structure not parallel
E. nothing wrong

_____ 1. Stop here.
_____ 2. Your duties are interviewing, hiring, and also to fire employees.
_____ 3. After their presentation, I was still undecided.
_____ 4. Speaking freely, the stock was considered a bargain.
_____ 5. Margaret, pressed for time, turned in unusually sloppy work.
_____ 6. Typing and filing, routine office chores.
_____ 7. What do you think he is up to?
_____ 8. When Paul came to work here, he brought some outmoded ideas that were not useful, now he has accepted our modern methods.
_____ 9. To plan is better than improvising.
_____ 10. Hoping to improve performance, practice is advisable.

The following choices apply to items 11–20. In each blank, write the letter of the choice that identifies the underlined word(s) in each sentence.

A. subject
B. predicate (verb)
C. object
D. modifier
E. conjunction/preposition

_____ 11. Take his <u>memo</u> upstairs.
_____ 12. Before leaving, he <u>repaired</u> the photocopier.
_____ 13. <u>Velnor, Inc.</u>, will soon introduce a new product line.
_____ 14. We must hire only <u>qualified</u>, ambitious graduates.
_____ 15. They <u>are having</u> trouble with their quality-control systems.
_____ 16. <u>After</u> she wrote the report, Jill waited eagerly for a response.
_____ 17. The route to the plant isn't paved <u>yet</u>.
_____ 18. See <u>me</u> after the meeting.
_____ 19. Your new <u>home</u> is ready and waiting.
_____ 20. BFL is large <u>but</u> caring.

In the blanks for items 21–30, write the letter of the word that best completes each sentence.

_____ 21. Starbucks (A. is, B. are) opening five new stores in San Diego in the next year.
_____ 22. There (A. is, B. are) 50 applicants for the job opening.
_____ 23. Anyone who wants to be (A. their, B. his or her) own boss should think about owning a franchise.
_____ 24. Neither of us (A. was, B. were) prepared for the meeting.
_____ 25. Another characteristic of a small business is that (A. they tend, B. it tends) to be more innovative than larger firms.
_____ 26. After he had (A. saw, B. seen) the revised budget, Raymond knew he wouldn't be getting a new desk.
_____ 27. The number of women-owned small businesses (A. has, B. have) increased sharply in the past two decades.
_____ 28. If I (A. was, B. were) you, I'd stop sending personal e-mails at work.
_____ 29. Eugene (A. lay, B. laid) the files on the desk.
_____ 30. Either FedEx or UPS (A. has, B. have) been chosen as our preferred shipping service.

The following choices apply to items 31–40. In each blank, write the letter of the choice that best describes each sentence.

A. error in punctuation
B. error in use of abbreviations or symbols
C. error in use of numbers
D. error in capitalization
E. no errors

_____ 31. Most of last year's sales came from the midwest.
_____ 32. We can provide the items you are looking for @ $2 each.
_____ 33. Alex noted: "few of our competitors have tried this approach."
_____ 34. Address the letter to professor Elliott Barker, Psychology Department, North Dakota State University.
_____ 35. They've recorded 22 complaints since yesterday, all of them from long-time employees.
_____ 36. Leslies' presentation—'New Markets for 2010'—was well-organized.
_____ 37. We're having a sale in the childrens' department, beginning Wednesday, August 15.
_____ 38. About 50 of the newly inducted members will be present.
_____ 39. Mister Spencer has asked me to find eleven volunteers.
_____ 40. Let's meet in Beth and Larry's office at one o'clock.

In the blanks for items 41–50, write the letter of the word that best completes each sentence.

_____ 41. Will having a degree (A. affect, B. effect) my chances for promotion?
_____ 42. Place the latest drawings (A. beside, B. besides) the others.
_____ 43. Try not to (A. loose, B. lose) this key; we will charge you a fee to replace it.
_____ 44. Let us help you choose the right tie to (A. complement, B. compliment) your look.
_____ 45. The five interviewers should discuss the candidates' qualifications (A. among, B. between) themselves.
_____ 46. New employees spend their time looking for (A. perspective, B. prospective) clients.
_____ 47. Are the goods you received different (A. from, B. than) the goods you ordered?
_____ 48. He took those courses to (A. farther, B. further) his career.
_____ 49. We are (A. anxious, B. eager) to see you next Thursday.
_____ 50. All commissions will be (A. disbursed, B. dispensed, C. dispersed) on the second Friday of every month.

ASSESSMENT OF ENGLISH SKILLS

In the space provided, record the number of questions you answered correctly.

Questions	Number you Got Correct	Skill Area
1–10	_____	Sentence structure
11–20	_____	Grammar; Parts of speech
21–30	_____	Grammar; Verbs and agreement
31–40	_____	Punctuation and mechanics
41–50	_____	Vocabulary

If you scored 8 or lower in any of the skills areas, focus on those areas in the appropriate sections of this handbook.

ESSENTIALS OF GRAMMAR, MECHANICS, AND USAGE

The following sentence looks innocent, but is it really?

> We sell tuxedos as well as rent.

You sell tuxedos, but it's highly unlikely that you sell rent—which is what this sentence says. Whatever you're selling, some people will ignore your message because of a blunder like this. The following sentence has a similar problem:

> Vice President Eldon Neale told his chief engineer that he would no longer be with Avix, Inc., as of June 30.

Is Eldon or the engineer leaving? No matter which side the facts are on, the sentence can be read the other way. Now look at this sentence:

> The year before we budgeted more for advertising sales were up.

Confused? Perhaps this is what the writer meant:

> The year before, we budgeted more for advertising. Sales were up.

Or Maybe you meant this:

> The year before we budgeted more for advertising, sales were up.

These examples show that even short, simple sentences can be misunderstood because of errors on the part of the writer. As you've learned in numerous courses over your schooling, an English sentence consists of the parts of speech being combined with punctuation, mechanics, and vocabulary to convey meaning. Making a point of brushing up on your grammar, punctuation, mechanics, and vocabulary skills will help ensure that you create clear, effective business messages.

1.0 GRAMMAR

Grammar is the study of how words come together to form sentences. Categorized by meaning, form, and function, English words fall into various parts of speech: nouns, pronouns, verbs, adjectives, adverbs, prepositions, conjunctions, articles, and interjections. You will communicate more clearly if you understand how each of these parts of speech operates in a sentence.

1.1 Nouns

A **noun** names a person, a place, a thing, or an idea. Anything you can see or detect with one of your senses has a noun to name it. Some things you can't see or sense are also nouns—ions, for example, or space. So are things that exist as ideas, such as accuracy and height. (You can see that something is accurate or that a building is tall, but you can't see the idea of accuracy or the idea of height.) These names for ideas are known as **abstract nouns**. The simplest nouns are the names of things you can see or touch: *car, building, cloud, brick;* these are termed **concrete nouns**. A few nouns, such as *algorithm, software,* and *code,* are difficult to categorize as either abstract or concrete but can reasonably be considered concrete even though they don't have a physical presence.

1.1.1 Proper Nouns and Common Nouns

So far, all the examples of nouns have been common nouns, referring to general classes of things. The word *building* refers to a whole class of structures. Common nouns such as *building* are not capitalized.

If you want to talk about one particular building, however, you might refer to the Glazier Building. The name is capitalized, indicating that *Glazier Building* is a **proper noun**.

Here are three sets of common and proper nouns for comparison:

Common	Proper
city	Kansas City
company	Blaisden Company
store	Books Galore

1.1.2 Nouns as Subject and Object

Nouns may be used in sentences as subjects or objects. That is, the person, place, thing or idea that is being or doing (subject) is represented by a noun. So is the person, place, idea, or thing that is being acted on (object). In the following sentence, the nouns are underlined:

The <u>web designer</u> created the <u>homepage</u>

The web designer (subject) is acting in a way that affects the home page (object). The following sentence is more complicated:

The <u>installer</u> delivered the <u>carpet</u> to the <u>customer</u>.

Installer is the subject. *Carpet* is the object of the main part of the sentence (acted on by the installer), whereas *customer* is the object of the phrase *to the customer*. Nevertheless, both *carpet* and *customer* are objects.

1.1.3 Plural Nouns

Nouns can be either singular or plural. The usual way to make a plural noun is to add *s* or *es* to the singular form of the word:

Singular	Plural
file	files
tax	taxes
cargo	cargoes

Many nouns have other ways of forming the plural. Some plurals involve a change in a vowel (*mouse/mice, goose/geese, woman/women*), the addition of *en* or *ren* (*ox/oxen, child/children*), the change from a *y* to an *ie* (*city/cities, specialty/specialties*), or the change of an *f* to *v* (*knife/knives, half/halves*; some exceptions: *fifes, roofs*). Some words of Latin origin offer a choice of plurals (*phenomena/phenomenons, indexes/indices, appendixes/appendices*). It's always a good idea to consult a dictionary if you are unsure of the correct or preferred plural spelling of a word.

The plurals of compound nouns are usually formed by adding *s* or *es* to the main word of the compound (*fathers-in-law, editors-in-chief, attorneys-at-law*).

Some nouns are the same whether singular or plural (*sleep, deer, moose*). Some nouns are plural in form but singular in use (*ethics, measles*). Some nouns are used in the plural only (*scissors, trousers*).

Letters, numbers, and words used as words are sometimes made plural by adding an apostrophe and an *s* (*A's, Ph.D.'s, I's*). However, if no confusion would be created by leaving off the apostrophe, it is common practice to just add the *s* (*1990s, RFPs, DVDs*).

1.1.4 Possessive Nouns

A noun becomes possessive when it's used to show the ownership of something. Then you add *'s* to the word:

the man's car   the woman's apartment

However, ownership does not need to be legal:

the secretary's desk   the company's assets

Also, ownership may be nothing more than an automatic association:

a day's work   the job's prestige

An exception to the rule about adding *'s* to make a noun possessive occurs when the word is singular and already has two "s" sounds at the end. In cases like the following, an apostrophe is all that's needed:

crisis' dimensions   Mr. Moses' application

When the noun has only one "s" sound at the end, however, retain the *'s*:

Chris's book   Carolyn Nuss's office

With compound (hyphenated) nouns, add *'s* to the last word:

Compound Noun	Possessive Noun
mother-in-law	mother-in-law's
mayor-elect	mayor-elect's

To form the possessive of plural nouns, just begin by following the same rule as with singular nouns: add *'s*. However, if the plural noun already ends in an *s* (as most do), drop the one you've added, leaving only the apostrophe:

the clients' complaints   employees' benefits

To denote joint possession by two or more proper nouns, add the *'s* to the last name only (*Moody, Nation, and Smith's* ad agency). To denote individual possession by two or more persons, add an *'s* to each proper noun (*Moody's, Nation's, and Smith's* ad agencies).

1.1.5 Collective Nouns

Collective nouns encompass a group of people or objects: *crowd, jury, committee, team, audience, family, couple, herd, class.* They are often treated as singular nouns. (For more on collective nouns, see Section 1.3.4, Subject-Verb Agreement.)

1.2 Pronouns

A **pronoun** is a word that stands for a noun; it saves repeating the noun:

Employees have some choice of weeks for vacation, but *they* must notify the HR office of *their* preference by March 1.

The pronouns *they* and *their* stand in for the noun *employees*. The noun that a pronoun stands for is called the **antecedent** of the pronoun; *employees* is the antecedent of *they* and *their*.

When the antecedent is plural, the pronoun that stands in for it has to be plural; *they* and *their* are plural pronouns because *employees* is plural. Likewise, when the antecedent is singular, the pronoun has to be singular:

We thought the contract had expired, but we soon learned that *it* had not.

1.2.1 Multiple Antecedents

Sometimes a pronoun has a double (or even a triple) antecedent:

> Kathryn Boettcher and Luis Gutierrez went beyond *their* sales quotas for January.

If taken alone, *Kathryn Boettcher* is a singular antecedent. So is *Luis Gutierrez*. However, when together they are the plural antecedent of a pronoun, so the pronoun has to be plural. Thus the pronoun is *their* instead of *her* or *his*.

1.2.2 Unclear Antecedents

In some sentences the pronoun's antecedent is unclear:

> Sandy Wright sent Jane Brougham *her* production figures for the previous year. *She* thought they were too low.

To which person does the pronoun *her* refer? Someone who knew Sandy and Jane and knew their business relationship might be able to figure out the antecedent for *her*. Even with such an advantage, however, a reader might receive the wrong meaning. Also, it would be nearly impossible for any reader to know which name is the antecedent of *she*.

The best way to clarify an ambiguous pronoun is usually to rewrite the sentence, repeating nouns when needed for clarity:

> Sandy Wright sent her production figures for the previous year to Jane Brougham. Jane thought they were too low.

The noun needs to be repeated only when the antecedent is unclear.

1.2.3 Pronoun Classes

Personal pronouns consist of *I, you, we/us, he/him, she/her, it,* and *they/them.*

Compound personal pronouns are created by adding *self* or *selves* to simple personal pronouns: *myself, ourselves, yourself, yourselves, himself, herself, itself, themselves.* Compound personal pronouns are used either *intensively*, to emphasize the identity of the noun or pronoun (I *myself* have seen the demonstration), or *reflexively*, to indicate that the subject is the receiver of his or her own action (I promised *myself* I'd finish by noon). Compound personal pronouns are used incorrectly if they appear in a sentence without their antecedent:

> Walter, Virginia, and *me* (not *myself*) are the top salespeople.

> You need to tell *her* (not *herself*) about the mixup.

Relative pronouns refer to nouns (or groups of words used as nouns) in the main clause and are used to introduce clauses:

> Purina is the brand *that* most dog owners purchase.

The relative pronouns are *which, who, whom, whose,* and *what.* Other words used as relative pronouns include *that, whoever, whomever, whatever,* and *whichever.*

Interrogative pronouns are those used for asking questions: *who, whom, whose, which, what.*

Demonstrative pronouns point out particular persons, places or things:

> *That* is my desk.   *This* can't be correct.

The demonstrative pronouns are *this, these, that,* and *those.*

Indefinite pronouns refer to persons or things not specifically identified. They include *anyone, someone, everyone, everybody, somebody, either, neither, one, none, all, both, each, another, any, many,* and similar words.

1.2.4 Case of Pronouns

The case of a pronoun tells whether it's acting or acted upon:

> *She* sells an average of five packages each week.

In this sentence, *she* is doing the selling. Because *she* is acting, *she* is said to be in the **nominative case**. Now consider what happens when the pronoun is acted upon:

> After six months, Ms. Browning promoted *her*.

In this sentence, the pronoun *her* is acted upon and is thus said to be in the objective case.

Contrast the nominative and objective pronouns in this list:

Nominative	Objective
I	me
we	us
he	him
she	her
they	them
who	whom
whoever	whomever

Objective pronouns may be used as either the object of a verb (such as *promoted*) or the object of a preposition (such as *with*):

> Rob worked with *them* until the order was filled.

In this example, *them* is the object of the preposition *with* because Rob acted upon—worked with—them. Here's a sentence with three pronouns, the first one nominative, the second the object of a verb, and the third the object of a preposition:

> He paid *us* as soon as the check came from *them*.

He is nominative; *us* is objective because it's the object of the verb *paid*; *them* is objective because it's the object of the preposition *from*.

Every writer sometimes wonders whether to use *who* or *whom*:

> (Who, Whom) will you hire?

Because this sentence is a question, it's difficult to see that *whom* is the object of the verb *hire*. You can figure out which pronoun to use if you rearrange the question and temporarily try *she* and *her* in place of *who* and *whom*: "Will you hire *she*?" or "Will you hire *her*?" *Her* and *whom* are both objective, so the correct choice is "Whom will you hire?" Here's a different example:

> (Who, Whom) logged so much travel time?

Turning the question into a statement, you get:

> He logged so much travel time.

Therefore, the correct statement is:

Who logged so much travel time?

1.2.5 Possessive Pronouns

Possessive pronouns work like possessive nouns: They show ownership or automatic association.

her job	their preferences
his account	its equipment

However, possessive pronouns are different from possessive nouns in the way they are written. That is, possessive pronouns never have an apostrophe.

Possessive Noun	Possessive Pronoun
the woman's estate	her estate
Roger Franklin's plans	his plans
the shareholders' feelings	their feelings
the vacuum cleaner's attachments	its attachments

The word *its* is the possessive of *it*. Like all other possessive pronouns, *its* has no apostrophe. Some people confuse *its* with *it's*, the contraction of *it is*. (Contractions are discussed in Section 2.9, Apostrophes.)

1.2.6 Pronoun-Antecedent Agreement

Like nouns, pronouns can be singular or plural. Pronouns must agree in number with their antecedents: a singular antecedent requires a singular pronoun:

The president of the board tendered *his* resignation.

Multiple antecedents require a plural pronoun:

The members of the board tendered *their* resignations.

A pronoun referring to singular antecedents connected by *or* or *nor* should be singular:

Neither Sean nor Terry made *his* quota.

But a pronoun referring to a plural and a singular antecedent connected by *or* or *nor* should be plural:

Neither Sean nor the twins made *their* quotas.

Formal English prefers the nominative case after the linking verb *to be*:

It is *I*.	That is *he*.

However, for general usage it's perfectly acceptable to use the more natural "It's me" and "That's him."

1.3 Verbs

A **verb** describes an action or acts as a link between a subject and words that define or describe that subject:

They all *quit* in disgust.

Working conditions *were* substandard.

The English language is full of **action verbs**. Here are a few you'll often run across in the business world:

verify	perform	fulfill
hire	succeed	send
leave	improve	receive
accept	develop	pay

You could undoubtedly list many more.

The most common linking verbs are all the forms of *to be*: I *am, was,* or *will be*; you *are, were,* or *will be*. Other words that can serve as linking verbs include *seem, become, appear, prove, look, remain, feel, taste, smell, sound, resemble, turn,* and *grow*:

It *seemed* a good plan at the time.

She *sounds* impressive at a meeting.

The time *grows* near for us to make a decision.

These verbs link what comes before them in the sentence with what comes after; no action is involved. (See Section 1.7.5 for a fuller discussion of linking verbs.)

An **auxiliary verb** is one that helps another verb and is used for showing tense, voice, and so on. A verb with its helpers is called a **verb phrase**. Verbs used as auxiliaries include *do, did, have, may, can, must, shall, might, could, would,* and *should*.

1.3.1 Verb Tenses

English has three simple verb tenses: present, past, and future.

Present:	Our branches in Hawaii *stock* other items.
Past:	We *stocked* Purquil pens for a short time.
Future:	Rotex Tire Stores *will stock* your line of tires when you begin a program of effective national advertising.

With most verbs (the regular ones), the past tense ends in *ed*, and the future tense always has *will* or *shall* in front of it. But the present tense is more complex, depending on the subject:

	First Person	Second Person	Third Person
Singular	I stock	you stock	he/she/it stocks
Plural	we stock	you stock	they stock

The basic form, *stock*, takes an additional *s* when *he, she,* or *it* precedes it. (See Section 1.3.4 for more on subject-verb agreement.)

In addition to the three simple tenses, the three **perfect tenses** are created by adding forms of the auxiliary verb *have*. The present perfect tense uses the past participle (regularly the past tense) of the main verb, *stocked*, and adds the present-tense *have* or *has* to the front of it:

(I, we, you, they) *have stocked*.

(He, she, it) *has stocked*.

The past perfect tense uses the past participle of the main verb, *stocked*, and adds the past-tense *had* to the front of it:

(I, you, he, she, it, we, they) *had stocked*.

The future perfect tense also uses the past participle of the main verb, *stocked*, but adds the future-tense *will have:*

(I, you, he, she, it, we, they) *will have stocked.*

Verbs should be kept in the same tense when the actions occur at the same time:

When the payroll checks *came in,* everyone *showed up* for work.

We *have found* that everyone *has pitched* in to help.

When the actions occur at different times, you may change tense accordingly:

The shipment *came* last Wednesday, so if another one *comes* in today, please return it.

The new employee *had been* ill at ease, but now she *has become* a full-fledged member of the team.

1.3.2 Irregular Verbs

Many verbs don't follow some of the standard patterns for verb tenses. The most irregular of these verbs is *to be:*

Tense	Singular	Plural
Present:	I *am*	we *are*
	you *are*	you *are*
	he, she, it *is*	they *are*
Past:	I *was*	we *were*
	you *were*	you *were*
	he, she, it *was*	they *were*

The future tense of *to be* is formed in the same way that the future tense of a regular verb is formed.

The perfect tenses of *to be* are also formed as they would be for a regular verb, except that the past participle is a special form, *been,* instead of just the past tense:

Present perfect:	you have been
Past perfect:	you had been
Future perfect:	you will have been

Here's a sampling of other irregular verbs:

Present	Past	Past Participle
begin	began	begun
shrink	shrank	shrunk
know	knew	known
rise	rose	risen
become	became	become
go	went	gone
do	did	done

Dictionaries list the various forms of other irregular verbs.

1.3.3 Transitive and Intransitive Verbs

Many people are confused by three particular sets of verbs:

lie/lay   sit/set   rise/raise

Using these verbs correctly is much easier when you learn the difference between transitive and intransitive verbs.

Transitive verbs require a receiver; they "transfer" their action to an object. Intransitive verbs do not have a receiver for their action. Some intransitive verbs are complete in themselves and need no help from other words (prices *dropped;* we *won*). Other intransitive words must be "completed" by a noun or adjective called a **complement.** Complement's occur with linking verbs.

Here are some sample uses of transitive and intransitive verbs:

Intransitive	Transitive
We should include in our new offices a place to *lie* down for a nap.	The workers will be here on Monday to *lay* new carpeting.
Even the way an interviewee *sits* is important.	That crate is full of stemware, so *set* it down carefully.
Salaries at Compu-Link, Inc., *rise* swiftly.	They *raise* their level of production every year.

The workers *lay* carpeting, you *set down* the crate, they *raise* production; each action is transferred to something. In the intransitive sentences, a person *lies down,* an interviewee *sits,* and salaries *rise* without affecting anything else. Intransitive sentences are complete with only a subject and a verb; transitive sentences are not complete unless they also include an object; or something to transfer the action to.

Tenses are a confusing element of the lie/lay problem:

Present	Past	Past Participle
I *lie*	I *lay*	I *have lain*
I *lay* (something down)	I *laid* (something down)	I *have laid* (something down)

The past tense of *lie* and the present tense of *lay* look and sound alike, even though they're different verbs.

1.3.4 Subject-Verb Agreement

Whether regular or irregular, every verb must agree with its subject, both in person (first, second, or third) and in number (single or plural).

	First Person	Second Person	Third Person
Singular	I *am;* I *write*	you *are;* you *write*	he/she/it *is;* he/she/it *writes*
Plural	we *are;* we *write*	you *are;* you *write*	they *are;* they *write*

In a simple sentence, making a verb agree with its subject is a straightforward task:

Hector Ruiz *is* a strong competitor. (third-person singular)

We *write* to you every month. (first-person plural)

Confusion sometimes arises when sentences are a bit more complicated. For example, be sure to avoid agreement problems when words come between the subject and verb. In the following examples, the verb appears in italics, and its subject is underlined:

The <u>analysis</u> of existing documents *takes* a full week.

Even though *documents* is a plural, the verb is in the singular form. That's because the subject of the sentence is *analysis,* a singular noun.

The phrase *of existing documents* can be disregarded. Here is another example:

> The <u>answers</u> for this exercise *are* in the study guide.

Take away the phrase *for this exercise* and you are left with the plural subject *answers*. Therefore, the verb takes the plural form.

Verb agreement is also complicated when the subject is a collective noun or pronoun or when the subject may be considered either singular or plural. In such cases, you often have to analyze the surrounding sentence to determine which verb form to use.

> The <u>staff</u> *is* quartered in the warehouse.
>
> The <u>staff</u> *are* at their desks in the warehouse.
>
> The <u>computers</u> and the <u>staff</u> *are* in the warehouse.
>
> Neither the staff nor the <u>computers</u> *are* in the warehouse.
>
> <u>Every</u> computer *is* in the warehouse.
>
> Many a <u>computer</u> *is* in the warehouse.

Did you notice that words such as *every* use the singular verb form? In addition, when an *either/or* or a *neither/nor* phrase combines singular and plural nouns, the verb takes the form that matches the noun closest to it.

In the business world, some subjects require extra attention. Company names, for example, are considered singular and therefore take a singular verb in most cases—even if they contain plural words:

> Stater Brothers *offers* convenient grocery shopping.

In addition, quantities are sometimes considered singular and sometimes plural. If a quantity refers to a total amount, it takes a singular verb; if a quantity refers to individual, countable units, it takes a plural verb:

> Three hours *is* a long time.
>
> The eight dollars we collected for the fund *are* tacked on the bulletin board.

Fractions may also be singular or plural, depending on the noun that accompanies them:

> One-third of the warehouse *is* devoted to this product line.
>
> One-third of the products *are* defective.

To decide whether to use a singular or plural verb with subjects such as *number* and *variety*, follow this simple rule: If the subject is preceded by *a*, use a plural verb:

> A number of products *are* being displayed at the trade show.

If the subject is preceded by *the*, use a singular verb:

> *The* variety of products on display *is* mind-boggling.

For a related discussion, see Section 1.7.1, Longer Sentences.

1.3.5 Voice of Verbs

Verbs have two voices, active and passive. When the subject comes first, the verb is in **active voice**; when the object comes first, the verb is in **passive voice**:

Active:	The buyer *paid* a large amount.
Passive:	A large amount *was paid* by the buyer.

The passive voice uses a form of the verb *to be*, which adds words to a sentence. In the example, the passive-voice sentence uses eight words, whereas the active-voice sentence uses only six to say the same thing. The words *was* and *by* are unnecessary to convey the meaning of the sentence. In fact, extra words usually clog meaning. So be sure to opt for the active voice when you have a choice.

At times, however, you have no choice:

> Several items *have been taken*, but so far we don't know who took them.

The passive voice becomes necessary when you don't know (or don't want to say) who performed the action; the active voice is bolder and more direct.

1.3.6 Mood of Verbs

Verbs can express one of three moods: indicative, imperative, or subjunctive. The **indicative mood** is used to make a statement or to ask a question:

> The secretary mailed a letter to each supplier.
>
> Did the secretary mail a letter to each supplier?

Use the **imperative mood** when you wish to command or request:

> Please mail a letter to each supplier.

With the imperative mood, subject is the understood *you*.

The **subjunctive mood** is used to express doubt or a wish or a condition contrary to fact:

> If I *were* you, I wouldn't send that e-mail.

The subjunctive is also used to express a suggestion or a request:

> I asked that Rosario *be* [not *is*] present at the meeting.

1.3.7 Verbals

Verbals are verbs that are modified to function as other parts of speech. They include infinitives, gerunds, and participles.

Infinitives are formed by placing a *to* in front of the verb (*to go, to purchase, to work*). They function as nouns. Although many of us were taught that it is "incorrect" to split an infinitive—that is, to place an adverb between the *to* and the verb—that rule is not a hard and fast one. In some cases, the adverb is best placed in the middle of the infinitive to avoid awkward constructions or ambiguous meaning:

> Production of steel is expected to *moderately exceed* domestic use.

Gerunds are verbals formed by adding *ing* to a verb (*going, having, working*). Like infinitives, they function as nouns. Gerunds and gerund phrases take a singular verb:

> *Borrowing* from banks *is* preferable to getting venture capital.

Participles are verb forms used as adjectives. The present participle ends in *ing* and generally describes action going on at the same time as other action:

> *Checking* the schedule, the contractor was pleased with progress on the project.

The past participle is usually the same form as the past tense and generally indicates completed action:

> When *completed*, the project will occupy six city blocks.

The **perfect participle** is formed by adding *having* to the past participle:

> *Having completed* the project, the contractor submitted his last invoice.

1.4 Adjectives

An **adjective** modifies (tells something about) a noun or pronoun. Each of the following phrases says more about the noun or pronoun than the noun or pronoun would say alone.

an *efficient* staff	a *heavy* price
brisk trade	*light* web traffic

Adjectives modify nouns more often than they modify pronouns. When adjectives do modify pronouns, however, the sentence usually has a linking verb:

They were *attentive*.	It looked *appropriate*.
He seems *interested*.	You are *skillful*.

1.4.1 Types of Adjectives

Adjectives serve a variety of purposes. **Descriptive adjectives** express some quality belonging to the modified item (*tall, successful, green*). **Limiting or definitive adjectives**, on the other hand, point out the modified item or limit its meaning without expressing a quality. Types include:

- Numeral adjectives (*one, fifty, second*)

- Articles (*a, an, the*)

- Pronominal adjectives: pronouns used as adjectives (*his* desk, *each* employee)

- Demonstrative adjectives: *this, these, that, those* (*these* tires, *that* invoice)

Proper adjectives are derived from proper nouns:

Chinese customs	*Orwellian* overtones

Predicate adjectives complete the meaning of the predicate and are introduced by linking verbs:

The location is *perfect*.	Prices are *high*.

1.4.2 Comparative Degree

Most adjectives can take three forms: simple, comparative, and superlative. The simple form modifies a single noun or pronoun. Use the comparative form when comparing two items. When comparing three or more items, use the superlative form.

Simple	Comparative	Superlative
hard	harder	hardest
safe	safer	safest
dry	drier	driest

The comparative form adds *er* to the simple form, and the superlative form adds *est*. (The *y* at the end of a word changes to *i* before the *er* or *est* is added.)

A small number of adjectives are irregular, including these:

Simple	Comparative	Superlative
good	better	best
bad	worse	worst
little	less	least

When the simple form of an adjective is two or more syllables, you usually add *more* to form the comparative and *most* to form the superlative:

Simple	Comparative	Superlative
useful	more useful	most useful
exhausting	more exhausting	most exhausting
expensive	more expensive	most expensive

The most common exceptions are two-syllable adjectives that end in *y*:

Simple	Comparative	Superlative
happy	happier	happiest
costly	costlier	costliest

If you choose this option, change the *y* to *i* and tack *er* or *est* onto the end.

Some adjectives cannot be used to make comparisons because they themselves indicate the extreme. For example, if something is perfect, nothing can be more perfect. If something is unique or ultimate, nothing can be more unique or more ultimate.

1.4.3 Hyphenated Adjectives

Many adjectives used in the business world are actually combinations of words: *up-to-date* report, *last-minute* effort, *fifth-floor* suite, *well-built* engine. As you can see, they are hyphenated when they come before the noun they modify. However, when such word combinations come after the noun they modify, they are not hyphenated. In the following example, the adjectives appear in italics and the nouns they modify are underlined:

> The <u>report</u> is *up to date* because of our team's *last-minute* <u>efforts</u>.

Hyphens are not used when part of the combination is a word ending in *ly* (because that word is usually not an adjective). Hyphens are also omitted from word combinations that are used so frequently that readers are used to seeing the words together:

We live in a *rapidly shrinking* world.

Our *highly motivated* employees will be well paid.

Please consider renewing your *credit card* account.

Send those figures to our *data processing* department.

Our new intern is a *high school* student.

1.5 Adverbs

An **adverb** modifies a verb, an adjective, or another adverb:

Modifying a verb:	Our marketing department works *efficiently*.
Modifying an adjective:	She was not dependable, although she was *highly* intelligent.
Modifying another adverb:	When signing new clients, he moved *extremely* cautiously.

An adverb can be a single word (*clearly*), a phrase (*very clearly*), or a clause (*because it was clear*).

1.5.1 Types of Adverbs

Simple adverbs are simple modifiers:

The door opened *automatically*.

The order arrived *yesterday*.

Top companies were *there*.

Interrogative adverbs ask a question:

Where have you been?

Conjunctive adverbs connect clauses:

We can't start *until* Maria gets here.

Jorge tried to explain *how* the new software works.

Words frequently used as conjunctive adverbs include *where, wherever, when, whenever, while, as, how, why, before, after, until,* and *since.*

Negative adverbs include *not, never, seldom, rarely, scarcely, hardly,* and similar words. Negative adverbs are powerful words and therefore do not need any help in conveying a negative thought. Avoid using double negatives like these:

I don't want no mistakes.
(Correct: "I don't want any mistakes," or "I want no mistakes.")

They couldn't hardly read the report.
(Correct: "They could hardly read the report," or "They couldn't read the report.")

They scarcely noticed neither one.
(Correct: "They scarcely noticed either one," or "They noticed neither one.")

1.5.2 Adverb–Adjective Confusion

Many adverbs are adjectives turned into adverbs by adding *ly: highly, extremely, officially, closely, really.* In addition, many words can be adjectives or adverbs, depending on their usage in a particular sentence:

The *early* bird gets the worm. [adjective]	We arrived *early*. [adverb]
It was a *hard* decision. [adjective]	He hit the wall *hard*. [adverb]

Because of this situation, some adverbs are difficult to distinguish from adjectives. For example, in the following sentences, is the underlined word an adverb or an adjective?

They worked <u>well</u>.

The baby is <u>well</u>.

In the first sentence, *well* is an adverb modifying the verb *worked*. In the second sentence, *well* is an adjective modifying the noun *baby*. To choose correctly between adverbs and adjectives, remember that linking verbs are used to connect an adjective to describe a noun. In contrast, you would use an adverb to describe an action verb:

Adjective	Adverb
He is *good* worker. (What kind of worker is he?)	He works *well*. (How does he work?)
It is a *real* computer. (What kind of computer is it?)	It *really* is a computer. (To what extent is it a computer?)
The traffic is *slow*. (What quality does the traffic have?)	The traffic moves *slowly*. (How does the traffic move?)
This food tastes *bad* without salt. (What quality does the food have?)	This food *badly* needs salt. (How much is it needed?)

1.5.3 Comparative Degree

Like adjectives, adverbs can be used to compare items. Generally, the basic adverb is combined with *more* or *most*, just as long adjectives are. However, some adverbs have one-word comparative forms:

One Item	Two Items	Three Items
quickly	more quickly	most quickly
sincerely	less sincerely	least sincerely
fast	faster	fastest
well	better	best

1.6 Other Parts of Speech

Nouns, pronouns, verbs, adjectives, and adverbs carry most of the meaning in a sentence. Four other parts of speech link them together in sentences: prepositions, conjunctions, articles, and interjections.

1.6.1 Prepositions

A **preposition** is a word or group of words that describes a relationship between other words in a sentence. A simple preposition is made up of one word: *of, in by, above, below.* A *compound preposition* is made up of two prepositions: *out of, from among, except for, because of.*

A **prepositional phrase** is a group of words introduced by a preposition that functions as an adjective (an adjectival phrase) or as an adverb (adverbial phrase) by telling more about a pronoun, noun, or verb:

> The shipment will be here *by next Friday.*

> Put the mail *in the out-bin.*

Prepositional phrases should be placed as close as possible to the element they are modifying:

> Shopping *on the Internet* can be confusing for the uninitiated. (*not* Shopping can be confusing for the uninitiated *on the Internet.*)

Some prepositions are closely linked with a verb. When using phrases such as *look up* and *wipe out,* keep them intact and do not insert anything between the verb and the preposition.

You may have been told that it is unacceptable to put a preposition at the end of a sentence. However, that is not a hard-and-fast rule, and trying to follow it can sometimes be a challenge. You can end a sentence with a preposition as along as the sentence sounds natural and as long as rewording the sentence would create awkward wording:

> I couldn't tell what they were interested in.

> What did she attribute it to?

> What are you looking for?

Avoid using unnecessary prepositions. In the following examples, the prepositions in parentheses should be omitted:

> All (of) the staff members were present.

> I almost fell off (of) my chair with surprise.

> Where was Mr. Steuben going (to)?

> They couldn't help (from) wondering.

The opposite problem is failing to include a preposition when you should. Consider these two sentences:

> Sales were over $100,000 for Linda and Bill.

> Sales were over $100,000 for Linda and for Bill.

The first sentence indicates that Linda and Bill had combined sales over $100,000; the second, that Linda and Bill each had sales over $100,000, for a combined total in excess of $200,000. The preposition *for* is critical here.

When the same preposition can be used for two or more words in a sentence without affecting the meaning, only the last preposition is required:

> We are familiar (with) and satisfied with your company's products.

But when different prepositions are normally used with the words, all the prepositions must be included:

> We are familiar with and interested in your company's products.

Some prepositions have come to be used in a particular way with certain other parts of speech. Here is a partial list of some prepositions that have come to be used with certain words:

according to	independent of
agree to (a proposal)	inferior to
agree with (a person)	plan to
buy from	prefer to
capable of	prior to
comply with	reason with
conform to	responsible for
differ from (things)	similar to
differ with (person)	talk to (without interaction)
different from	talk with (with interaction)
get from (receive)	wait for (person or thing)
get off (dismount)	wait on (like a waiter)

If you are unsure of the correct idiomatic expression, check a dictionary.

Some verb-preposition idioms vary depending on the situation: You agree *to* a proposal but *with* a person, *on* a price, or *in* principle. You argue *about* something, *with* a person, and *for* or *against* a proposition. You compare one item *to* another to show their similarities; you compare one item *with* another to show differences.

Here are some other examples of preposition usage that have given writers trouble:

> **among/between:** *Among* is used to refer to three or more (Circulate the memo *among* the staff); *between* is used to refer to two (Put the copy machine *between* Judy and Dan).

> **as if/like:** As *if* is used before a clause (It seems *as if* we should be doing something); *like* is used before a noun or pronoun (He seems *like* a nice guy).

> **have/of:** *Have* is a verb used in verb phrases (They should *have* checked first); *of* is a preposition and is never used in such cases.

> **in/into:** *In* is used to refer to a static position (The file is *in* the cabinet); *into* is used to refer to movement toward a position (Put the file *into* the cabinet).

1.6.2 Conjunctions

Conjunctions connect the parts of a sentence: words, phrases, and clauses. A **coordinating conjunction** connects two words, phrases, or clauses of equal rank. The simple coordinating conjunctions include *and, but, or, nor, for, yet,* and *so.* **Correlative conjunctions** are coordinating conjunctions used in pairs: *both/and, either/or, neither/nor, nor only/but also.* Constructions with correlative conjunctions should be parallel, with the same part of speech following each element of the conjunction:

> The purchase was *not only* expensive *but* unnecessary.

> The purchase *not only was* expensive *but was* unnecessary.

Conjunctive adverbs are adverbs used to connect or show relationships between clauses. They include *however, nevertheless, consequently, moreover,* and *as a result.*

A **subordinate conjunction** connects two clauses of unequal rank; it joins a dependent (subordinate) clause to the independent clause on which it depends (for more on dependent and independent clauses, see Section 1.7.1). Subordinate conjunctions include *as, if, because, although, while, before, since, that, until, unless, when, where,* and *whether.*

1.6.3 Articles and interjections

Only three **articles** exist in English: *the, a,* and *an.* These words are used, like adjectives, to specify which item you are talking about. *The* is called the *definite article* because it indicates a specific noun; *a* and *an* are called the *indefinite articles* because they are less specific about what they are referring to.

If a word begins with a vowel (soft) sound, use *an;* otherwise use *a.* It's *a history,* not *an history, a hypothesis,* not *an hypothesis.* Use *an* with an "h" word only if it is a soft "h," as in *honor* and *hour.* Use *an* with words that are pronounced with a soft vowel sound even if they are spelled beginning with a consonant (usually in the case of abbreviations): *an SEC application, an MP3 file.* Use *a* with words that begin with vowels if they are pronounced with a hard sound: *a university, a Usenet account*

Repeat an article if adjectives modify different nouns: *The red house and the white house are mine.* Do not repeat an article if all adjectives modify the same noun: *The red and white house is mine.*

Interjections are words that express no solid information, only emotion:

Wow!	Well, well!
Oh, no!	Good!

Such purely emotional language has its place in private life and advertising copy, but it only weakens the effect of most business writing.

1.7 Sentences

Sentences are constructed with the major building blocks, the parts of speech. Take, for example, this simple two-word sentence:

Money talks.

It consists of a noun (*money*) and a verb (*talks*). When used in this way, the noun works as the first requirement for a sentence, the **subject**, and the verb works as the second requirement, the **predicate**. Without a subject (who or what does something) and a predicate (the doing of it), you have merely a collection of words, not a sentence.

1.7.1 Longer Sentences

More complicated sentences have more complicated subjects and predicates, but they still have a simple subject and a predicate verb. In the following examples, the subject is underlined once, the predicate verb twice:

<u>Marex</u> and <u>Contron</u> <u>enjoy</u> higher earnings each quarter.

Marex [and] *Contron* do something; *enjoy* is what they do.

My <u>interview</u>, coming minutes after my freeway accident, <u>did</u> not <u>impress</u> or <u>move</u> anyone.

Interview is what did something. What did it do? It *did* [not] *impress* [or] *move.*

In terms of usable space, a steel <u>warehouse</u>, with its extremely long span of roof unsupported by pillars, <u>makes</u> more sense.

Warehouse is what *makes.*

These three sentences demonstrate several things. First, in all three sentences, the simple subject and predicate verb are the "bare bones" of the sentence, the parts that carry the core idea of the sentence. When trying to find the subject and predicate verb, disregard all prepositional phrases, modifiers, conjunctions, and articles.

Second, in the third sentence, the verb is singular (*makes*) because the subject is singular (*warehouse*). Even though the plural noun *pillars* is closer to the verb, *warehouse* is the subject. So *warehouse* determines whether the verb is singular or plural. Subject and predicate must agree.

Third, the subject in the first sentence is compound (*Marex* [and] *Contron*). A compound subject, when connected by *and,* requires a plural verb (*enjoy*). Also, the second sentence shows how compound predicates can occur (*did* [not] *impress* [or] *move*).

Fourth, the second sentence incorporates a group of *words— coming minutes after my freeway accident*—containing a form or a verb (*coming*) and a noun (*accident*). Yet, this group of words is not a complete sentence for two reasons:

- Not all nouns are subjects: *Accident* is not the subject of *coming.*

- Not all verbs are predicates: A verb that ends in *ing* can never be the predicate of a sentence (unless preceded by a form of *to be,* as in *was coming*).

Because they don't contain a subject and a predicate, the words *coming minutes after my freeway accident* (called a **phrase**) can't be written as a sentence. That is, the phrase cannot stand alone; it cannot begin with a capital letter and end with a period. So a phrase must always be just one part of a sentence.

Sometimes a sentence incorporates two or more groups of words that do contain a subject and a predicate; these word groups are called **clauses**:

My <u>interview</u>, because it <u>came</u> minutes after my freeway accident, <u>did</u> not <u>impress</u> or <u>move</u> anyone.

The **independent clause** is the portion of the sentence that could stand alone without revision:

My <u>interview</u> <u>did</u> not <u>impress</u> or <u>move</u> anyone.

The other part of the sentence could stand alone only by removing *because.*

(because) <u>It</u> <u>came</u> minutes after my freeway accident.

This part of the sentence is known as a **dependent clause**; although it has a subject and a predicate (just as an independent clause does), it's linked to the main part of the sentence by a word (*because*) showing its dependence.

In summary, the two types of clauses—dependent and independent—both have a subject and a predicate. Dependent clauses, however, do not bear the main meaning of the sentence and are therefore linked to an independent clause. Nor can phrases stand alone, because they lack both a subject and a predicate. Only independent clauses can be written as sentences without revision.

1.7.2 Types of Sentences

Sentences come in four main types, depending on the extent to which they contain clauses. A **simple sentence** has one subject and one predicate; in short, it has one main independent clause:

> Boeing is the world's largest aerospace company.

A **compound sentence** consists of two independent clauses connected by a coordinating conjunction (*and*, *or*, *but*, etc.) or a semicolon:

> Airbus outsold Boeing for several years, but Boeing has recently regained the lead.

A **complex sentence** consists of an independent clause and one or more dependent clauses:

> Boeing is betting, [independent clause] that airlines will begin using moderately smaller planes to fly passengers between smaller cities [dependent clause introduced by *that*].

A **compound-complex sentence** has two main clauses, at least one of which contains a subordinate (dependent clause):

> Boeing is betting [independent clause] that airlines will begin using moderately smaller planes to fly passengers between smaller cities [dependent clause], and it anticipates that new airports will be developed to meet passenger needs [independent clause].

1.7.3 Sentence Fragments

An incomplete sentence (a phrase or a dependent clause) that is written as though it were a complete sentence is called a **fragment**. Consider the following sentence fragments:

> Marilyn Sanders, having had pilferage problems in her store for the past year. Refuses to accept the results of our investigation.

This serious error can easily be corrected by putting the two fragments together:

> Marilyn Sanders, having had pilferage problems in her store for the past year, refuses to accept the results of our investigation.

The actual details of a situation will determine the best way for you to remedy a fragment problem.

The ban on fragments has one exception. Some advertising copy contains sentence fragments, written knowingly to convey a certain rhythm. However, advertising is the only area of business in which fragments are acceptable.

1.7.4 Fused Sentences and Comma Splices

Just as there can be too little in a group of words to make it a sentence, there can also be too much:

> All our mail is run through a postage meter every afternoon someone picks it up.

This example contains two sentences, not one, but the two have been blended so that it's hard to tell where one ends and the next begins. Is

the mail run through a meter every afternoon? If so, the sentences should read:

> All our mail is run through a postage meter every afternoon. Someone picks it up.

Perhaps the mail is run through a meter at some other time (morning, for example) and is picked up every afternoon;

> All our mail is run through a postage meter. Every afternoon someone picks it up.

The order of words is the same in all three cases; sentence division makes all the difference. Either of the last two cases is grammatically correct. The choice depends on the facts of the situation.

Sometimes these so-called **fused sentences** have a more obvious point of separation:

> Several large orders arrived within a few days of one another, too many came in for us to process by the end of the month.

Here, the comma has been put between two independent clauses in an attempt to link them. When a lowly comma separates two complete sentences, the result is called a **comma splice**. A comma splice can be remedied in one of three ways:

- Replace the comma with a period and capitalize the next word: ". . . one another. Too many . . ."

- Replace the comma with a semicolon and do not capitalize the next word: ". . . one another; too many . . ." This remedy works only when the two sentences have closely related meanings.

- Change one of the sentences so that it becomes a phrase or a dependent clause. This remedy often produces the best writing, but it takes more work.

The third alternative can be carried out in several ways. One is to begin the sentence with a subordinating conjunction:

> Whenever several large orders arrived within a few days of one another, too many came in for us to process by the end of the month.

Another way is to remove part of the subject or the predicate verb from one of the independent clauses, thereby creating a phrase:

> Several large orders arrived within a few days of one another, too many for us to process by the end of the month.

Finally, you can change one of the predicate verbs to its *ing* form:

> Several large orders arrived within a few days of one another, too many coming in for us to process by the end of the month.

In many cases, simply adding a coordinating conjunction can separate fused sentences or remedy a comma splice:

> You can fire them, or you can make better use of their abilities.

Margaret drew up the designs, and Matt carried them out.

We will have three strong months, but after that sales will taper off.

Be careful with coordinating conjunctions: Use them only to join simple sentences that express similar ideas.

Also, because they say relatively little about the relationship between the two clauses they join, avoid using coordinating conjunctions too often: *and* is merely an addition sign; *but* is just a turn signal; *or* only points to an alternative. Subordinating conjunctions such as *because* and *whenever* tell the reader a lot more.

1.7.5 Sentences with Linking Verbs

Linking verbs were discussed briefly in the section on verbs (Section 1.3). Here, you can see more fully the way they function in a sentence. The following is a model of any sentence with a linking verb:

A *(verb)* B.

Although words such as *seems* and *feels* can also be linking verbs, let's assume that the verb is a form of *to be:*

A *is* B.

In such a sentence, A and B are always nouns, pronouns, or adjectives. When one is a noun and the other is a pronoun, or when both are nouns, the sentence says that one is the same as the other:

She is president.

Rachel is president.

She is forceful.

Recall from Section 1.3.3 that the noun or adjective that follows the linking verb is called a *complement*. When it is a noun or noun phrase, the complement is called a *predicate nominative*, when the complement is an adjective, it is referred to as a *predicate adjective*.

1.7.6 Misplaced Modifiers

The position of a modifier in a sentence is important. The movement of *only* changes the meaning in the following sentences:

Only we are obliged to supply those items specified in your contract.

We are obliged only to supply those items specified in your contract.

We are obliged to supply only those items specified in your contract.

We are obliged to supply those items specified only in your contract.

In any particular set of circumstances, only one of those sentences would be accurate. The others would very likely cause problems. To prevent misunderstanding, place such modifiers as close as possible to the noun or verb they modify.

For similar reasons, whole phrases that are modifiers must be placed near the right noun or verb. Mistakes in placement create ludicrous meanings:

Antia Information Systems has bought new computer chairs for the programmers with more comfortable seats.

The anatomy of programmers is not normally a concern of business writers. Obviously, the comfort of the chairs was the issue:

Antia Information Systems has bought new computer chairs with more comfortable seats for the programmers.

Here is another example:

I asked him to file all the letters in the cabinet that had been answered.

In this ridiculous sentence, the cabinet has been answered, even though no cabinet in history is known to have asked a question. *That had been answered* is too far from *letters* and too close to *cabinet*. Here's an improvement:

I asked him to file in the cabinet all the letters that had been answered.

The term **dangling modifier** is often used to refer to a clause or phrase that because of its position in the sentence seems to modify a word that it is not meant to modify. For instance:

Lying motionless, co-workers rushed to Barry's aid.

Readers expect an introductory phrase to modify the subject of the main clause. But in this case it wasn't the *co-workers* who were lying motionless but rather *Barry* who was in this situation. Like this example, most instances of dangling modifiers occur at the beginning of sentences. The source of some danglers is a passive construction:

To find the needed information, the whole book had to be read.

In such cases, switching to the active voice can usually remedy the problem:

To find the needed information, you will need to read the whole book.

1.7.7 Parallelism

Two or more sentence elements that have the same relation to another element should be in the same form. Otherwise, the reader is forced to work harder to understand the meaning of the sentence. When a series consists of phrases or clauses, the same part of speech (preposition, gerund, etc.) should introduce them. Do not mix infinitives with participles or adjectives with nouns. Here are some examples of non-parallel elements:

Andersen is hiring managers, programmers, and people who work in accounting. [nouns not parallel]

Andersen earns income by auditing, consulting, and by bookkeeping. [prepositional phrases not parallel]

Andersen's goals are to win new clients, keeping old clients happy, and finding new enterprises. [infinitive mixed with gerunds]

2.0 PUNCTUATION

On the highway, signs tell you when to slow down or stop, where to turn, and when to merge. In similar fashion, punctuation helps readers negotiate your prose. The proper use of punctuation keeps readers from losing track of your meaning.

2.1 Periods

Use a period (1) to end any sentence that is not a question, (2) with certain abbreviations, and (3) between dollars and cents in an amount of money.

2.2 Question Marks

Use a question mark after any direct question that requests an answer:

> Are you planning to enclose a check, or shall we bill you?

Don't use a question mark with commands phrased as questions for the sake of politeness:

> Will you send us a check today.

A question mark should precede quotation marks, parentheses, and brackets if it is part of the quoted or parenthetical material; otherwise, it should follow:

> This issue of *Inc.* has an article titled "What's Your Entrepreneurial IQ?"

> Have you read the article "Five Principles of Guerrilla Marketing"?

Do not use the question mark with indirect questions or with requests:

> Mr. Antonelli asked whether anyone had seen Nathalia lately.

Do not use a comma or a period with a question mark; the question mark takes the place of these punctuation marks.

2.3 Exclamation Points

Use exclamation points after highly emotional language. Because business writing almost never calls for emotional language, you will seldom use exclamation points.

2.4 Semicolons

Semicolons have three main uses. One is to separate two closely related independent clauses:

> The outline for the report is due within a week; the report itself is due at the end of the month.

A semicolon should also be used instead of a comma when the items in a series have commas within them:

> Our previous meetings were on November 11, 2004; February 20, 2005; and April 28, 2006.

Finally, a semicolon should be used to separate independent clauses when the second one begins with a conjunctive adverb such as

however, *therefore*, or *nevertheless* or a phrase such as *for example* or *in that case*:

> Our supplier has been out of part D712 for 10 weeks; however, we have found another source that can ship the part right away.

> His test scores were quite low; on the other hand, he has a lot of relevant experience.

Section 4.4 has more information on using transitional words and phrases.

Semicolons should always be placed outside of question marks or parenthesis.

2.5 Colons

Use a colon after the salutation in a business letter. You should also use a colon at the end of a sentence or phrase introducing a list or (sometimes) a quotation:

> Our study included the three most critical problems: insufficient capital, incompetent management, and inappropriate location.

A colon should not be used when the list, quotation, or idea is a direct object of the verb or preposition. This rule applies whether the list is set off or run in:

> We are able to supply
> staples
> wood screws
> nails
> toggle bolts

> This shipment includes 9 DVDs, 12 CDs, and 4 USB flash drives.

Another way you can use a colon is to separate the main clause and another sentence element when the second explains, illustrates, or amplifies the first:

> Management was unprepared for the union representatives' demands: this fact alone accounts for their arguing well into the night.

However, in contemporary usage, such clauses are frequently separated by a semicolon.

Colons should always be placed outside of question marks or parenthesis.

2.6 Commas

Commas have many uses; the most common is to separate items in a series:

> He took me job, learned it well, worked hard, and succeeded.

> Put paper, pencils, and paper clips on the requisition list.

Company style may dictate omitting the final comma in a series. However, if you have a choice, use the final comma; it's often necessary to prevent misunderstanding.

A second place to use a comma is between independent clauses that are joined by a coordinating conjunction (*and*, *but*, or *or*) unless one or both are very short:

> She spoke to the sales staff, and he spoke to the production staff.

> I was advised to proceed and I did.

A third use for the comma is to separate a dependent clause at the beginning of a sentence from an independent clause:

> Because of our lead in the market, we may be able to risk introducing a new product.

However, a dependent clause at the end of a sentence is separated from the independent clause by a comma only when the dependent clause is unnecessary to the main meaning of the sentence:

> We may be able to introduce a new product, although it may involve some risk.

A fourth use for the comma is after an introductory phrase or word:

> Starting with this amount of capital, we can survive in the red for one year.

> Through more careful planning, we may be able to serve more people.

> Yes, you may proceed as originally planned.

However, with short introductory prepositional phrases and some one-syllable words (such as *hence* and *thus*), the comma is often omitted:

> Before January 1 we must complete the inventory.

> Thus we may not need to hire anyone.

> In July we will complete the move to Tulsa.

Fifth, paired commas are used to set off nonrestrictive clauses and phrases. A **restrictive clause** is one that cannot be omitted without altering the meaning of the main clause, whereas a **nonrestrictive clause** can be:

> The *Time Magazine* website, which is produced by Steve Conley, has won several design awards. [nonrestrictive: the material set off by commas could be omitted]

> The website that is produced by Steve Conley has won several design awards. [restrictive: no commas are used before and after *that is produced by Steve Conley* because this information is necessary to the meaning of the sentence—it specifies which website]

A sixth use for commas is to set off appositive words and phrases. (An **appositive** has the same meaning as the word it is in apposition to.) Like nonrestrictive clauses, appositives can be dropped without changing or obscuring the meaning of the sentence:

> Conley, a freelance designer, also produces the websites for several nonprofit corporations.

Seventh, commas are used between adjectives modifying the same noun (coordinate adjectives):

> She left Monday for a long, difficult recruiting trip.

To test the appropriateness of such a comma, try reversing the order of the adjectives: *a difficult, long recruiting trip*. If the order cannot be reversed, leave out the comma (a *good old friend* isn't the same as an *old good friend*). A comma should not be used when one of the adjectives is part of the noun. Compare these two phrases:

> a distinguished, well-known figure

> a distinguished public figure

The adjective-noun combination of *public* and *figure* has been used together so often that it has come to be considered a single thing: *public figure*. So no comma is required.

Eighth, commas are used both before and after the year in sentences that include month, day, and year:

> It will be sent by December 15, 2007, from our Cincinnati plant.

Some companies write dates in another form: 15 December 2007. No commas should be used in that case. Nor is a comma needed when only the month and year are present (December 2007).

Ninth, commas are used to set off a variety of parenthetical words and phrases within sentences, including state names, dates, abbreviations, transitional expressions, and contrasted elements:

> They were, in fact, prepared to submit a bid.

> Habermacher, Inc., went public in 1999.

> Our goal was increased profits, not increased market share.

> Service, then, is our main concern.

> The factory was completed in Chattanooga, Tennessee, just three weeks ago.

> Joanne Dubiik, M.D., has applied for a loan from First Savings.

> I started work here on March 1, 2003, and soon received my first promotion.

Tenth, a comma is used to separate a quotation from the rest of the sentence:

> Your warranty reads, "These conditions remain in effect for one year from date of purchase."

However, the comma is left out when the quotation as a whole is built into the structure of the sentence:

> He hurried off with an angry "Look where you're going."

Finally, a comma should be used whenever it's needed to avoid confusion or an unintended meaning. Compare the following:

> Ever since they have planned new ventures more carefully.

> Ever since, they have planned new ventures more carefully.

2.7 Dashes

Use a dash to surround a comment that is a sudden turn in thought:

> Membership in the IBSA—it's expensive but worth it—may be obtained by applying to our New York office.

A dash can also be used to emphasize a parenthetical word or phrase:

> Third-quarter profits—in excess of $2 million—are up sharply.

Finally, use dashes to set off a phrase that contains commas:

> All our offices—Milwaukee, New Orleans, and Phoenix—have sent representatives.

Don't confuse a dash with a hyphen. A dash separates and emphasizes words, phrases, and clauses more strongly than commas or parentheses can; a hyphen ties two words so tightly that they almost become one word.

When using a computer, use the em dash symbol. When typing a dash in e-mail or on a typewriter, type two hyphens with no space before, between, or after.

A second type of dash, the en dash, can be produced with computer word processing and page-layout programs. This kind of dash is shorter than the regular dash and longer than a hyphen. It is reserved almost exclusively for indicating "to" or "through" with numbers such as dates and pages: *2001–2002, pages 30–44.*

2.8 Hyphens

Hyphens are mainly used in three ways. The first is to separate the parts of compound words beginning with such prefixes as *self-, ex-, quasi-,* and *all-*:

self-assured	quasi-official
ex-wife	all-important

However, do not use hyphens in words that have prefixes such as *pro, anti, non, re, pre, un, inter,* and *extra*:

prolabor	nonunion
antifascist	interdepartmental

Exceptions occur when (1) the prefix occurs before a proper noun or (2) the vowel at the end of the prefix is the same as the first letter of the root word:

pro-Republican	anti-American
anti-inflammatory	extra-atmospheric

When in doubt, consult your dictionary.

Hyphens are used in some types of spelled-out numbers. For instance, they are used to separate the parts of a spelled-out number from *twenty-one* to *ninety-nine* and for spelled-out fractions: *two-thirds, one-sixth* (although some style guides say not to hyphenate fractions used as nouns).

Certain compound nouns are formed by using hyphens: *secretary-treasurer, city-state.* Check your dictionary for compounds you're unsure about.

Hyphens are also used in some compound adjectives, which are adjectives made up of two or more words. Specifically, you should use hyphens in compound adjectives that come before the noun:

> an interest-bearing account   well-informed executives

However, you need not hyphenate when the adjective follows a linking verb:

> This account is interest bearing.

> Their executives are well informed.

You can shorten sentences that list similar hyphenated words by dropping the common part from all but the last word:

> Check the costs of first-, second-, and third-class postage.

Finally, hyphens may be used to divide words at the end of a typed line. Such hyphenation is best avoided, but when you have to divide words at the end of a line, do so correctly (see Section 3.5). A dictionary will show how words are divided into syllables.

2.9 Apostrophes

Use an apostrophe in the possessive form of noun (but not in a pronoun):

> On his desk was a reply to Bette *Ainsley's* application for the *manager's* position.

Apostrophes are also used in place of the missing letter(s) of a contraction:

Whole Words	Contraction
we will	we'll
do not	don't
they are	they're

2.10 Quotation Marks

Use quotation marks to surround words that are repeated exactly as they were said or written:

> The collection letter ended by saying, "This is your third and final notice."

Remember: (1) When the quoted material is a complete sentence, the first word is capitalized. (2) The final comma or period goes inside the closing quotation marks.

Quotation marks are also used to set off the title of a newspaper story, magazine article, or book chapter:

> You should read "Legal Aspects of the Collection Letter" in *Today's Credit.*

Quotation marks may also be used to indicate special treatment for words or phrases, such as terms that you're using in an unusual or ironic way:

> Our management "team" spends more time squabbling than working to solve company problems.

When you are defining a word, put the definition in quotation marks:

> The abbreviation *etc.* means "and so forth."

When using quotation marks, take care to insert the closing marks as well as the opening ones.

Although periods and commas go inside any quotation marks, colons and semicolons go outside them. A question mark goes inside the quotation marks only if the quotation is a question:

> All that day we wondered, "Is he with us?"

If the quotation is not a question but the entire sentence is, the question mark goes outside:

> What did she mean by "You will hear from me"?

For quotes within quotes, use single quotation marks within double:

> As David Pottruck, former co-CEO of Charles Schwab, told it, "I assembled about 100 managers at the base of the Golden Gate Bridge and gave them jackets emblazoned with the phrase 'Crossing the Chasm' and then led them across the bridge."

Otherwise, do not use single quotation marks for anything, including titles of works—that's British style.

2.11 Parentheses and Brackets

Use parentheses to surround comments that are entirely incidental or to supply additional information:

> Our figures do not match yours, although (if my calculations are correct) they are closer than we thought.

> These kinds of supplements do not require FDA (Food and Drug Administration) approval.

Parentheses are used in legal documents to surround figures in arabic numerals that follow the same amount in words:

> Remittance will be One Thousand Two Hundred Dollars ($1,200).

Be careful to put punctuation marks (period, comma, and so on) outside the parentheses unless they are part of the statement in parentheses. And keep in mind that parentheses have both an opening and a closing mark; both should always be used, even when setting off listed items within text: *(1)*, not *1)*.

Brackets are used for notation, comment, explanation, or correction within quoted material:

> In the interview, multimillionaire Bob Buford, said, "One of my major influences was Peter [Drucker], who encourages people and helps them believe in themselves."

Brackets are also used for parenthetical material that falls within parentheses:

> Drucker's magnum opus (*Management: Tasks, Responsibilities, Practices* [Harper & Row, 1979]) has influenced generations of entrepreneurs.

2.12 Ellipses

Use ellipsis points, or three evenly spaced periods, to indicate that material has been left out of a direct quotation. Use them only in direct quotations and only at the point where material was left out. In the following example, the first sentence is quoted in the second:

> The Dow Jones Industrial Average fell 276.39 points, or 2.6%, during the week to 10292.31.

> According to the *Wall Street Journal*, "The Dow Jones Industrial Average fell 276.39 points . . . to 10,292.31."

The number of dots in ellipses is not optional; always use three. Occasionally, the points of ellipsis come at the end of a sentence, where they seem to grow a fourth dot. Don't be fooled: One of the dots is a period. Ellipsis points should always be preceded and followed by a space.

Avoid using ellipses to represent a pause in your writing; use a dash for that purpose:

> At first we had planned to leave for the conference on Wednesday—but then we changed our minds. [not *on Wednesday . . . but than*]

3.0 MECHANICS

The most obvious and least tolerable mistakes that a business writer makes are probably those related to grammar and punctuation. However, a number of small details, known as writing mechanics, demonstrate the writer's polish and reflect on the company's professionalism.

When it comes to mechanics, also called *style*, many of the "rules" are not hard and fast. Publications and organizations vary in their preferred styles for capitalization, abbreviations, numbers, italics, and so on. Here, we'll try to differentiate between practices that are generally accepted and those that can vary. When you are writing materials for a specific company or organization, find out the preferred style (such as *The Chicago Manual of Style* or Webster's *Style Manual*). Otherwise, choose a respected style guide. The key to style is consistency: If you spell out the word *percent* in one part of a document, don't use the percent sign in a similar context elsewhere in the same document.

3.1 Capitalization

With capitalization, you can follow either an "up" style (when in doubt, capitalize: *Federal Government, Board of Directors*) or a "down" style (when in doubt, use lowercase: *federal government, board of directors*). The trend over the last few decades has been toward the down style. Your best bet is to get a good style manual and consult it when you have a capitalization question. Following are some rules that most style guides agree on.

Capital letters are used at the beginning of certain word groups:

- **Complete sentence:** Before hanging up, he said, "We'll meet here on Wednesday at noon."

- **Formal statement following a colon:** She has a favorite motto: Where there's a will, there's a way.

- **Phrase used as sentence:** Absolutely not!

- **Quoted sentence embedded in another sentence:** Scott said, "Nobody was here during lunch hour except me."

- **List of items set off from text:** Three preliminary steps are involved:
  Design review
  Budgeting
  Scheduling

Capitalize proper adjectives and proper nouns (the names of particular persons, places, and things):

> Darrell Greene lived in a Victorian mansion.

> We sent Ms. Larson an application form, informing her that not all applicants are interviewed.

> Let's consider opening a branch in the West, perhaps at the west end of Tucson, Arizona.

> As office buildings go, the Kinney Building is a pleasant setting for TDG Office Equipment.

> We are going to have to cancel our plans for hiring French and German sales reps.

Larson's name is capitalized because she is a particular applicant, whereas the general term *applicant* is left uncapitalized. Likewise, *West* is capitalized when it refers to a particular place but not when it means a direction. In the same way, *office* and *building* are not capitalized when they are general terms (common nouns), but they are capitalized when they are part of the title of a particular office or building (proper nouns). Some proper adjectives are lowercased when they are part of terms that have come into common use, such as *french fries* and *roman numerals*.

Titles within families or companies as well as professional titles may also be capitalized:

> I turned down Uncle David when he offered me a job. I wouldn't be comfortable working for one of my relatives.

> We've never had a president quite like President Sweeney.

People's titles are capitalized when they are used in addressing a person, especially in a formal context. They are not usually capitalized, however, when they are used merely to identify the person:

> Address the letter to Chairperson Anna Parmer.

> I wish to thank Chairperson Anna Palmer for her assistance.

> Anna Palmer, chairperson of the board, took the podium.

Also capitalize titles if they are used by themselves in addressing a person:

> Thank you, Doctor, for your donation.

Always capitalize the first word of the salutation and complimentary close of a letter:

> *Dear* Mr. Andrews: *Yours* very truly,

The names of organizations are capitalized, of course; so are the official names of their departments and divisions. However, do not use capitals when referring in general terms to a department or division, especially one in another organization:

> Route this memo to Personnel.

> Larry Tien was transferred to the Microchip Division.

> Will you be enrolled in the Psychology Department?

> Someone from the personnel department at EnerTech stopped by the booth.

Capitalization is unnecessary when using a word like *company, corporation*, or *university* alone:

> The corporation plans to issue 50,000 shares of common stock.

Likewise, the names of specific products are capitalized, although the names of general product types are not:

> Apple computer   Tide laundry detergent   Xerox machine

When it comes to government terminology, here are some guides to capitalization: (1) Lowercase *federal* unless it is part of an agency name; (2) capitalize names of courts, departments, bureaus, offices, and agencies, but lowercase such references as *the bureau* and *the department* when the full name is not used; (3) lowercase the titles of government officers unless they precede a specific person's name: *the secretary of state, the senator, the ambassador, the governor, the mayor*, but *Mayor Gonzalez* (note: style guides vary on whether to capitalize *president* when referring to the president of the United States without including the person's name); capitalize the names of laws and acts: *the Sherman Antitrust Act, the Civil Rights Act*; (5) capitalize the names of political parties, but lowercase the word *party: Democratic party, Libertarian party*.

One problem that often arises in writing about places is the treatment of two or more proper nouns of the same type. When the common word comes before the specific names, it is capitalized; when it comes after the specific names, it is not:

> Lakes Ontario and Huron

> Allegheny and Monongahela rivers

The names of languages, races, and ethnic groups are capitalized: Japanese, Caucasian, Hispanic. But racial terms that denote only skin color are not capitalized: black, white.

When referring to the titles of books, articles, magazines, newspapers, reports, movies, and so on, you should capitalize the first and last words and all nouns, pronouns, adjectives, verbs, and adverbs, and capitalize prepositions and conjunctions with five letters or more. Except for the first and last words, do not capitalize articles:

> *Economics During the Great War*

> "An Investigation into the Market for Long-Distance Services"

> "What Successes Are Made Of"

When *the* is part of the official name of a newspaper or magazine, it should be treated this way too:

> *The Wall Street Journal*

Style guides vary in their recommendations regarding capitalization of hyphenated words in titles. A general guide is to capitalize the second word in a temporary compound (a compound that is hyphenated for grammatical reasons and not spelling reasons), such as *Law-Abiding Citizen*, but to lowercase the word if the term is always hyphenated, such as *Son-in-law*).

References to specific pages, paragraphs, lines, and the like are not capitalized: *page 73, line 3*. However, in most other numbered or lettered references, the identifying term is capitalized:

> Chapter 4, Serial No. 382-2203, Item B-11

Finally, the names of academic degrees are capitalized when they follow a person's name but are not capitalized when used in a general sense:

> I received a bachelor of science degree.
>
> Thomas Whitelaw, Doctor of Philosophy, will attend.

Similarly, general courses of study are not capitalized, but the names of specific classes are:

> She studied accounting as an undergraduate.
>
> She is enrolled in Accounting 201.

3.2 Underscores and Italics

Usually a line typed underneath a word or phrase either provides emphasis or indicates the title of a book, magazine, or newspaper. If possible, use italics instead of an underscore. Italics (or underlining) should also be used for defining terms and for discussing words as words:

> In this report *net sales* refers to after-tax sales dollars.
>
> The word *building* is a common noun and should not be capitalized.

Also use italics to set off foreign words, unless the words have become a common part of English:

> Top Shelf is considered the *sine qua non* of comic book publishers.
>
> Chris uses a laissez-faire [no italic] management style.

3.3 Abbreviations

Abbreviations are used heavily in tables, charts, lists, and forms. They're used sparingly in prose. Here are some abbreviation situations to watch for:

- In most cases do not use periods with acronyms (words formed from the initial letter or letters of parts of a term): *CEO, CD-ROM, DOS, YWCA, FDA*; but: *Ph.D., M.A., M. D.*

- Use periods with abbreviations such as *Mr., Ms., Sr., Jr., a.m., p.m., B.C.,* and *A.D.*

- The trend is away from using periods with such units of measure as *mph, mm,* and *lb.*

- Use periods with such Latin abbreviations as *e.g., i.e., et al.,* and *etc.* However, style guides recommend that you avoid using

these Latin forms and instead use their English equivalents (*for example, that is, and others, and,* respectively). If you must use these abbreviations, such as in parenthetical expressions or footnotes, do not put them in italics.

- Some companies have abbreviations as part of their names (*&, Co., Inc., Ltd.*). When you refer to such firms by name, be sure to double-check the preferred spelling, including spacing: *AT&T; Barnes & Noble; Carson Pirie Scott & Company; PepsiCo; Kate Spade, Inc.; National Data Corporation; Siemens Corp.; Glaxo Wellcome PLC; US Airways; U.S. Business Reporter.*

- Most style guides recommend that you spell out *United States* as a noun and reserve *U.S.* as an adjective.

One way to handle an abbreviation that you want to use throughout a document is to spell it out the first time you use it, follow it with the abbreviation in parentheses, and then use the abbreviation in the remainder of the document.

3.4 Numbers

Numbers may be correctly handled many ways in business writing, so follow company style. In the absence of a set style, however, generally spell out all numbers from one to nine and use arabic numerals for the rest.

There are some exceptions to this general rule. For example, never begin a sentence with a numeral:

> Twenty of us produced 641 units per week in the first 12 weeks of the year.

Use numerals for the numbers one through nine if they're in the same list as larger numbers:

> Our weekly quota rose from 9 to 15 to 27.

Use numerals for percentages, time of day (except with o'clock), dates, and (in general) dollar amounts:

> Our division is responsible for 7 percent of total sales.
>
> The meeting is scheduled for 8:30 a.m. on August 2.
>
> Add $3 for postage and handling.

When using numerals for time, be consistent: It should be *between 10:00 a.m. and 4:30 p.m.*, not *between 10 a.m. and 4:30 p.m.* Expressions such as *4:00 o'clock* and *7 a.m. in the morning* are redundant.

Use a comma in numbers expressing thousands (1,257), unless your company specifies another style. When dealing with numbers in the millions and billions, combine words and figures: 7.3 million, 2 billion.

When writing dollar amounts, use a decimal point only if cents are included. In lists of two or more dollar amounts, use the decimal point either for all or for none:

> He sent two checks, one for $67.92 and one for $90.00.

When two numbers fall next to each other in a sentence, use figures for the number that is largest, most difficult to spell, or part of a physical measurement; use words for the other:

> I have learned to manage a classroom of 30 twelve-year-olds.

She's won a bonus for selling 24 thirty-volume sets.

You'll need twenty 3-inch bolts.

In addresses, all street numbers except One are in figures. So are suite and room numbers and zip codes. For street names that are numbered, practice varies so widely that you should use the form specified on an organization's letterhead or in a reliable directory. All the following examples are correct:

One Fifth Avenue	297 Ninth Street
1839 44th Street	11026 West 78 Place

Telephone numbers are always expressed in figures. Parentheses may separate the area code from the rest of the number, but a slash or a hyphen may be used instead, especially if the entire phone number is enclosed in parentheses.

382-8329   (602/382-8329)   602-382-8329

Percentages are always expressed in figures. The word *percent* is used in most cases, but % may be used in tables, forms, and statistical writing.

Physical measurements such as distance, weight, and volume are also often expressed in figures: *9 kilometers, 5 feet 3 inches, 7 pounds 10 ounces.*

Decimal numbers are always written in figures. In most cases, add a zero to the left of the decimal point if the number is less than one and does not already start with a zero:

1.38   .07   0.2

In a series of related decimal numbers with at least one number greater than one, make sure that all numbers smaller than one have a zero to the left of the decimal point: 1.20, 0.21, 0.09.

Simple fractions are written in words, but more complicated fractions are expressed in figures or, if easier to read, in figures and words:

two-thirds   9/32   2 hundredths

Most style guides recommend that you use a comma with numbers consisting of four digits: *2,345,* not *2345.*

When typing ordinal numbers, such as *3rd edition* or *21st century* your word processing program may automatically make the letters *rd* (or *st, th,* or *nd*) into a superscript. Do yourself a favor and turn that formatting function off in your "Preferences," as superscripts should not be used in regular prose or even in bibliographies.

3.5 Word Division

In general, avoid dividing words at the end of lines. When you must do so, follow these rules:

- Don't divide one-syllable words (such as *since, walked,* and *thought*), abbreviations (*mgr.*), contractions (*isn't*), or numbers expressed in numerals (*117,500*).

- Divide words between syllables, as specified in a dictionary or word-division manual.

- Make sure that at least three letters of the divided words are moved to the second line: *sin-cerely* instead of *sincere-ly.*

- Do not end a page or more than three consecutive lines with hyphens.

- Leave syllables consisting of a single vowel at the end of the first line (*impedi-ment* instead of *imped-iment*), except when the single vowel is part of a suffix such as *-able, -ible, -ical,* or *-ity* (*re-spons-ible* instead of *re-sponsi-ble*).

- Divide between double letters (*tomor-row*), except when the root word ends in double letters (*call-ing* instead of *cal-ling*).

- Wherever possible, divide hyphenated words at the hyphen only: instead of *anti-inde-pendence,* use *anti-independence.*

4.0 VOCABULARY

Using the right word in the right place is a crucial skill in business communication. However, many pitfalls await the unwary.

4.1 Frequently Confused Words

Because the following sets of words sound similar, be careful not to use one when you mean to use the other:

Word	Meaning
accede	to comply with
exceed	to go beyond
accept	to take
except	to exclude
access	admittance
excess	too much
advice	suggestion
advise	to suggest
affect	to influence
effect	the result
allot	to distribute
a lot	much or many
all ready	completely prepared
already	completed earlier
born	given birth to
borne	carried
capital	money; chief city
capitol	a government building
cite	to quote
sight	a view
site	a location
complement	complete amount; to go well with
compliment	expression of esteem; to flatter
corespondent	party in a divorce suit
correspondent	letter writer
council	a panel of people
counsel	advice; a lawyer
defer	to put off until later
differ	to be different
device	a mechanism
devise	to plan
die	to stop living; a tool
dye	to color
discreet	careful
discrete	separate
envelop	to surround
envelope	a covering for a letter

Word	Meaning
forth	forward
fourth	number four
holey	full of holes
holy	sacred
wholly	completely
human	of people
humane	kindly
incidence	frequency
incidents	events
instance	example
instants	moments
interstate	between states
intrastate	within a state
later	afterward
latter	the second of two
lead	a metal; to guide
led	guided
lean	to rest at an angle
lien	a claim
levee	embankment
levy	tax
loath	reluctant
loathe	to hate
loose	free; not tight
lose	to mislay
material	substance
materiel	equipment
miner	mineworker
minor	underage person
moral	virtuous; a lesson
morale	sense of well-being
ordinance	law
ordnance	weapons
overdo	to do in excess
overdue	past due
peace	lack of conflict
piece	a fragment
pedal	a foot lever
peddle	to sell
persecute	to torment
prosecute	to sue
personal	private
personnel	employees
precedence	priority
precedents	previous events
principal	sum of money; chief; main
principle	general rule
rap	to knock
wrap	to cover

Word	Meaning
residence	home
residents	inhabitants
right	correct
rite	ceremony
write	to form words on a surface
role	a part to play
roll	to tumble; a list
root	part of a plant
rout	to defeat
route	a traveler's way
shear	to cut
sheer	thin, steep
stationary	immovable
stationery	paper
than	as compared with
then	at that time
their	belonging to them
there	in that place
they're	they are
to	a preposition
too	excessively; also
two	the number
waive	to set aside
wave	a swell of water; a gesture
weather	atmospheric conditions
whether	if
who's	contraction of "who is" or "who has"
whose	possessive form of who

In the preceding list, only enough of each word's meaning is given to help you distinguish between the words in each group. Several meanings are left out entirely. For more complete definitions, consult a dictionary.

4.2 Frequently Misused Words

The following words tend to be misused for reasons other than their sound. Reference books (including the *Random House College Dictionary*, revised edition; Follett's *Modern American Usage*; and Fowler's *Modern English Usage*) can help you with similar questions of usage:

a lot: When the writer means "many," *a lot* is always two separate words, never one.

aggravate/irritate: *Aggravate* means "to make things worse." Sitting in the smoke-filled room *aggravated* his sinus condition. *Irritate* means "to annoy." Her constant questions *irritated* [not *aggravated*] me.

anticipate/expect: *Anticipate* means "to prepare for": Macy's *anticipated* increased demand for athletic shoes in spring by ordering in November. In formal usage, it is incorrect to use *anticipate* for *expect*: I *expected* (not *anticipated*) a better response to our presentation than we actually got.

compose/comprise: The whole comprises the parts:

The company's distribution division *comprises* four departments.

It would be incorrect usage to say

> The company's distribution division *is comprised of* four departments.

In that construction, *is composed of* or *consists of* would be preferable. It might be helpful to think of *comprise* as meaning "encompasses" or "contains."

continual/continuous: *Continual* refers to ongoing actions that have breaks:

> Her *continual* complaining will accomplish little in the long run.

Continuous refers to ongoing actions without interruptions or breaks:

> A *continuous* stream of paper came out of the fax machine.

convince/persuade: One is *convinced* of a fact or that something is true; one is *persuaded* by someone else to do something. The use of *to* with *convince* is unidiomatic—you don't convince someone to do something, you persuade them to do it.

correspond with: Use this phrase when you are talking about exchanging letters. Use *correspond to* when you mean "similar to." Use either *correspond with* or *correspond to* when you mean "relate to."

dilemma/problem: Technically, a *dilemma* is a situation in which one must choose between two undesirable alternatives. It shouldn't be used when no choice is actually involved.

disinterested: This word means "fair, unbiased, having no favorites, impartial." If you mean "bored" or "not interested," used *uninterested*.

etc.: This abbreviated form of the Latin phrase *et cetera* means "and so on" or "and so forth," so it is never correct to write *and etc.* The current tendency among business writers is to use English rather than Latin.

flaunt/flout: To *flaunt* is to be ostentatious or boastful; to *flout* is to mock or scoff at.

impact: Avoid using *impact* as a verb when *influence* or *affect* is meant.

imply/infer: Both refer to hints. Their great difference lies in who is acting. The writer *implies*, the reader *infers*, sees between the lines.

lay: This word is a transitive verb. Never use it for the intransitive *lie*. (See Section 1.3.3.)

lend/loan: *Lend* is a verb; *loan* is a noun. Usage such as "Can you loan me $5?" is therefore incorrect.

less/fewer: Use *less* for uncountable quantities (such as amounts of water, air, sugar, and oil). Use *fewer* for countable quantities (such as numbers of jars, saws, words, page, and humans). The same distinction applies to *much* and *little* (uncountable) versus *many* and *few* (countable).

liable/likely: *Liable* means "responsible for": I will hold you *liable* if this deal doesn't go through. It is incorrect to use *liable* for "possible": Anything is *likely* (not *liable*) to happen.

literally: *Literally* means "actually" or "precisely"; it is often misused to mean "almost" or "virtually." It is usually best left out entirely or replaced with *figuratively*.

many/much: See *less/fewer*.

regardless: The *less* suffix is the negative part. No word needs two negative parts, so don't add *ir* (a negative prefix) to the beginning. There is no such word as *irregardless*.

try: Always follow with *to*, never *and*.

4.3 Frequently Misspelled Words

All of us, even the world's best spellers, sometimes have to check a dictionary for the spelling of some words. People who have never memorized the spelling of commonly used words must look up so many that they grow exasperated and give up on spelling words correctly.

Don't expect perfection, and don't surrender. If you can memorize the spelling of just the words listed here, you'll need the dictionary far less often and you'll write with more confidence:

absence	disappoint
absorption	disbursement
accessible	discrepancy
accommodate	dissatisfied
accumulate	dissipate
achieve	
advantageous	eligible
affiliated	embarrassing
aggressive	endorsement
alignment	exaggerate
aluminum	exceed
ambience	exhaust
analyze	existence
apparent	extraordinary
appropriate	
argument	fallacy
asphalt	familiar
assistant	flexible
asterisk	fluctuation
auditor	forty
bankruptcy	gesture
believable	grievous
brilliant	
bulletin	haphazard
	harassment
calendar	holiday
campaign	
category	illegible
ceiling	immigrant
changeable	incidentally
clientele	indelible
collateral	independent
committee	indispensable
comparative	insistent
competitor	intermediary
concede	irresistible
congratulations	
connoisseur	jewelry
consensus	judgment
convenient	judicial
convertible	
corroborate	labeling
criticism	legitimate
	leisure
definitely	license
description	litigation
desirable	
dilemma	maintenance
disappear	mathematics
	mediocre
	minimum

necessary
negligence
negotiable
newsstand
noticeable

occurrence
omission

parallel
pastime
peaceable
permanent
perseverance
persistent
personnel
persuade
possesses
precede
predictable
preferred
privilege
procedure
proceed
pronunciation
psychology
pursue

questionnaire

receive
recommend

repetition
rescind
rhythmical
ridiculous

salable
secretary
seize
separate
sincerely
succeed
suddenness
superintendent
supersede
surprise

tangible
tariff
technique
tenant
truly

unanimous
until

vacillate
vacuum
vicious

4.4 Transitional Words and Phrases

The following sentences don't communicate as well as they could because they lack a transitional word or phrase:

Production delays are inevitable. Our current lag time in filling orders is one month.

A semicolon between the two sentences would signal a close relationship between their meanings, but it wouldn't even hint at what that relationship is. Here are the sentences again, now linked by means of a semicolon, with a space for a transitional word or phrase:

Production delays are inevitable; _____, our current lag time in filling orders is one month.

Now read the sentence with *nevertheless* in the blank space. Then try *therefore, incidentally, in fact,* and *at any rate* in the blank. Each substitution changes the meaning of the sentence.

Here are some transitional words (conjunctive adverbs) that will help you write more clearly:

accordingly
anyway
besides
consequently
finally

furthermore
however
incidentally
likewise
meanwhile

moreover
otherwise
still
therefore

The following transitional phrases are used in the same way:

as a result
at any rate
for example
in fact

in other words
in the second place
on the other hand
to the contrary

When one of these words or phrases joins two independent clauses, it should be preceded by a semicolon and followed by a comma:

The consultant recommended a complete reorganization; moreover, she suggested that we drop several products.

Answer Keys

ANSWER KEY FOR "LEARNING OBJECTIVES CHECKUP"

CHAPTER 1
1. e
2. b
3. b
4. c
5. a, d, f, and h
6. c
7. c
8. d
9. b
10. c
11. b
12. improvement
13. a
14. sense, select, perceive
15. d
16. enhances or supports
17. a
18. c
19. d
20. dilemma, lapse

CHAPTER 2
1. d
2. d
3. d
4. a
5. e
6. dysfunctional
7. b
8. constructive, destructive
9. virtual
10. decode
11. c
12. d
13. a
14. d
15. d
16. c
17. a
18. a

CHAPTER 3
1. d
2. d
3. b
4. b
5. c
6. d
7. ethnocentrism
8. stereotyping
9. d
10. a
11. c
12. b
13. a
14. nonverbal
15. d
16. a
17. b
18. b

CHAPTER 4
1. b
2. c
3. d
4. a
5. general purpose
6. e
7. b
8. a
9. c
10. c
11. d
12. d
13. richness
14. d
15. b
16. direct
17. indirect
18. a

CHAPTER 5
1. a
2. d
3. d
4. b
5. c
6. c
7. passive
8. active
9. b
10. b
11. c
12. a
13. a
14. c
15. c
16. examples
17. similarities, differences
18. a

CHAPTER 6
1. d
2. a
3. c
4. a
5. b
6. d
7. d
8. b
9. b
10. a
11. c
12. b
13. white space
14. c
15. a
16. d
17. a
18. b

CHAPTER 7

1. b
2. a
3. c
4. c
5. b
6. b
7. a
8. CC, BCC
9. c
10. d
11. b
12. a
13. b
14. viral marketing
15. c
16. c
17. d
18. podcast channel
19. syndication
20. a

CHAPTER 8

1. b
2. a
3. d
4. c
5. b
6. d
7. b
8. the good news
9. d
10. d
11. b
12. a
13. b
14. d
15. c

CHAPTER 9

1. g
2. d
3. c
4. a
5. a
6. c
7. c
8. buffer
9. d
10. a

11. a
12. d
13. b
14. c
15. b
16. a
17. a

CHAPTER 10

1. c
2. d
3. d
4. b
5. b
6. c
7. d
8. c
9. emotional
10. logical
11. b
12. d
13. b
14. d
15. c
16. b
17. d
18. d

CHAPTER 11

1. d
2. a
3. informational
4. analytical
5. proposals
6. d
7. d
8. primary
9. secondary
10. a
11. c
12. a
13. c
14. c
15. a
16. b
17. summary
18. conclusion
19. recommendation
20. a
21. logic

CHAPTER 12

1. d
2. b
3. a
4. c
5. c
6. a
7. c
8. a
9. b
10. d
11. d
12. localizing
13. b
14. d
15. d
16. d
17. b
18. d
19. d
20. c

CHAPTER 13

1. c
2. d
3. a
4. d
5. b
6. a
7. synopsis
8. executive summary
9. a
10. c
11. b
12. c

CHAPTER 14

1. a
2. d
3. c
4. planning, speaking
5. d
6. b
7. a
8. a
9. b
10. b
11. c
12. d
13. a
14. c

15. d
16. d
17. d
18. b

CHAPTER 15

1. b
2. b
3. d
4. b
5. d
6. chronological
7. functional
8. combination
9. d

10. a
11. b
12. b
13. a
14. a
15. c
16. plain-text
17. b
18. d
19. b

CHAPTER 16

1. a
2. d
3. b

4. structured
5. open-ended
6. situational
7. d
8. d
9. d
10. b
11. c
12. c
13. a
14. a
15. c
16. d
17. a
18. c

ANSWER KEY FOR "IMPROVE YOUR GRAMMAR, MECHANICS, AND USAGE" EXERCISES

CHAPTER 1

1. boss's (1.1.4)
2. sheep (1.1.3)
3. 1990s (1.1.3)
4. Joneses, stopwatches (1.1.3)
5. attorneys (1.1.3)
6. copies (1.1.3)
7. employees' (1.1.4)
8. sons-in-law, businesses (1.1.3, 1.1.4)
9. parentheses (1.1.3)
10. Ness's, week's (1.1.4)

CHAPTER 2

1. its (1.2.5)
2. their (1.2.5)
3. its (1.2.5)
4. their (1.2.1)
5. his or her (1.2.3)
6. his or her (1.2.3)
7. a, them (1.2.3, 1.2.4)
8. who (1.2.4)
9. whom (1.2.4)
10. its (1.2.5)

CHAPTER 3

1. b (1.3.1)
2. b (1.3.1)
3. a (1.3.1)
4. b (1.3.5)
5. a (1.3.5)
6. a (1.3.4)
7. b (1.3.4)
8. b (1.3.4)
9. a (1.3.4)
10. b (1.3.4)

CHAPTER 4

1. greater (1.4.2)
2. perfect (1.4.2)
3. most interesting (1.4.2)
4. hardest (1.4.2)
5. highly placed, last-ditch (1.4.3)
6. top-secret (1.4.3)
7. 30-year-old (1.4.3)
8. all-out, no-holds-barred struggle (1.4.3)
9. tiny metal (2.6)
10. usual cheerful, prompt service (2.6)

CHAPTER 5

1. good (1.5)
2. surely (1.5)
3. sick (1.5)
4. well (1.5)
5. good (1.5)
6. faster (1.5.3)
7. better (1.5.3)
8. any (1.5.1)
9. ever (1.5.1)
10. can, any (1.5.1)

CHAPTER 6

1. leading (1.6.1)
2. off (1.6.1)
3. aware of (1.6.1)
4. to (1.6.1)
5. among (1.6.1)
6. for (1.6.1)
7. to (1.6.1)
8. from (1.6.1)
9. not only in (1.6.2)
10. into (1.6.1)

CHAPTER 7

1. b (1.6.2)
2. b (1.6.1)
3. a (1.6.1)
4. b (1.6.1)
5. b (1.6.1)
6. a (1.6.1)
7. a (1.6.3)
8. b (1.6.2)
9. b (1.6.3)
10. b (1.6.3)

CHAPTER 8

1. b (1.7.3)
2. a (1.7.1)
3. b (1.7.6)
4. a (1.7.4)
5. b (1.7.4)
6. b (1.7.6)
7. a (1.7.6)
8. b (1.7.4)
9. a (1.7.3)
10. b (1.7.1)

CHAPTER 9

1. c (2.6)
2. a (2.6)
3. b (2.6)
4. a (2.6)
5. b (2.6)
6. c (2.6)
7. b (2.6)
8. a (2.6)
9. c (2.6)
10. b (2.6)

CHAPTER 10

1. a (2.4)
2. a (2.5)
3. c (2.4)
4. a (2.5)
5. b (2.5)
6. b (2.4)
7. a (2.4)
8. c (2.4)
9. b (2.4)
10. c (2.5)

CHAPTER 11

1. b (2.1)
2. a (2.2)
3. b (2.1)
4. a (2.1)
5. b (2.2, 2.3)
6. a (2.1)
7. b (2.2, 2.1)
8. a (2.2)
9. b (2.2)
10. a (2.2, 2.3)

CHAPTER 12

1. b (2.7)
2. a (2.8)
3. c (2.7)
4. b (2.8)
5. a (2.7)
6. b (2.7)
7. c (2.8)
8. a (2.8, 2.7)
9. c (2.8, 2.7)
10. a (2.8)

CHAPTER 13

1. b (2.10)
2. b (2.11)
3. a (2.11)
4. b (2.10)
5. c (2.10)
6. a (2.11)
7. c (2.10, 2.12)
8. b (2.10)
9. b (2.11)
10. c (2.10, 2.12)

CHAPTER 14

1. c (3.1, 3.3)
2. a (3.1, 3.3)
3. b (3.2)
4. a (3.1)
5. c (3.3)
6. a (3.1, 3.2)
7. b (3.1, 3.3)
8. b (3.1, 3.3)
9. a (3.2)
10. c (3.1)

CHAPTER 15

1. except (4.1)
2. device (4.1)
3. loath (4.1)
4. who's (4.1)
5. a lot (4.2)
6. judgment (4.3)
7. regardless (4.2)
8. accommodate (4.3)
9. imply (4.2)
10. to (4.2)

CHAPTER 16

1. c (3.4)
2. a (3.4)
3. a (3.4)
4. b (3.4)
5. b (3.4)
6. a (3.4)
7. b (3.4)
8. c (3.4)
9. a (3.4)
10. c (3.4)

References

PROLOGUE

1. Maureen Jenkins, "Yours for the Taking," *Boeing Frontiers Online*, June 2004 [accessed 25 September 2005] www.boeing.com; "Firm Predicts Top 10 Workforce/Workplace Trends for 2004, *Enterprise*, 8–14 December 2003, 1–2; Scott Hudson, "Keeping Employees Happy," *Community Banker*, September 2003, 34+; Marvin J. Cetron and Owen Davies, "Trends Now Changing the World: Technology, the Workplace, Management, and Institutions," *Futurist* 35, no. 2 (March/April 2001): 27–42.

2. Jim Puzzanghera, "Coalition of High-Tech Firms to Urge Officials to Help Keep U.S. Competitive," *San Jose Mercury News*, 8 January 2004 [accessed 14 February 2004] www.ebscohost.com.

3. Amanda Bennett, "GE Redesigns Rungs of Career Ladder," *Wall Street Journal*, 15 March 1993, B1, B3.

4. Robin White Goode, "International and Foreign Language Skills Have an Edge," *Black Enterprise*, May 1995, 53.

5. Nancy M. Somerick, "Managing a Communication Internship Program," *Bulletin of the Association for Business Communication* 56, no. 3 (1993): 10–20.

6. Fellowforce website [accessed 8 July 2007] www.fellowforce.com.

7. Joan Lloyd, "Changing Workplace Requires You to Alter Your Career Outlook," *Milwaukee Journal Sentinel*, 4 July 1999, 1; Camille DeBell, "Ninety Years in the World of Work in America," *Career Development Quarterly* 50, no.1 (September 2001): 77–88.

8. Jeffrey R. Young, "'E-Portfolios' Could Give Students a New Sense of Their Accomplishments," *The Chronicle of Higher Education*, 8 March 2002, A31.

9. Brian Carcione, e-portfolio [accessed 20 December 2006] http:// eportfolio.psu.edu.

CHAPTER 1

1. Six Apart website [accessed 4 August 2006] www.sixapart.com; David Kirkpatrick and Daniel Roth, "Why There's No Escaping the Blog," *Fortune*, 10 January 2005, 44–50; "People of the Year," *PC Magazine*, 12 December 2004 [accessed 21 June 2005] www.pcmag.com; Thomas Mucha, "A Motor City Marketing Lesson," *Business 2.0*, 10 March 2005 [accessed 13 March 2005] www.business2.com; Lee Gomes, "How the Next Big Thing in Technology Morphed into a Really Big Thing," *Wall Street Journal*, 4 October 2004, B1; David Kirkpatrick, "It's Hard to Manage if You Don't Blog," *Fortune*, 4 October 2004, 46.

2. Julie Connelly, "Youthful Attitudes, Sobering Realities," *New York Times*, 28 October 2003, E1, E6; Nigel Andrews and Laura D'Andrea Tyson, "The Upwardly Global MBA," *Strategy + Business*, no. 36, 6069; Jim McKay, "Communication Skills Found Lacking," *Pittsburgh Post-Gazette*, 28 February 2005 [accessed 28 February 2005] www.delawareonline.com.

3. Richard L. Daft, *Management*, 6th ed. (Cincinnati: Thomson South-Western, 2003), 580.

4. Based in part on Nicholas Carr, "Lessons in Corporate Blogging," *BusinessWeek*, 18 July 2006, 9; Susan Meisinger, "To Keep Employees, Talk—and Listen—to Them!" *HR Magazine*, August 2006, 10.

5. Daft, *Management*, 147.

6. Gareth R. Jones and Jennifer M. George, *Contemporary Management*, 3rd ed. (New York: McGraw-Hill Irwin, 2003), 512, 517.

7. Donald O. Wilson, "Diagonal Communication Links with Organizations," *Journal of Business Communication* 29, no. 2 (Spring 1992): 129–143.

8. J. David Johnson, William A. Donohoe, Charles K. Atkin, and Sally Johnson, "Differences Between Formal and Informal Communication Channels," *Journal of Business Communication* 31, no. 2 (1994): 111–122.

9. David Pescovitz, "Technology of the Year: Social Network Applications," *Business 2.0*, November 2003, 113–114.

10. Tim Laseter and Rob Cross, "The Craft of Connection," *Strategy + Business*, Autumn 2006, 26–32.

11. Philip C. Kolin, *Successful Writing at Work*, 6th ed. (Boston: Houghton Mifflin, 2001), 17–23.

12. "Do-It-Yourself Skills Enhancement: CFOs Value Communication Skills, but Few Firms Provide Training, Survey Shows," press release, Accountemps, 28 July 2006 [accessed 8 August 2006] www.accountemps.com.

13. Don Hellriegel, Susan E. Jackson, and John W. Slocum, Jr., *Management: A Competency-Based Approach* (Cincinnati: Thomson South-Western, 2002), 447.

14. Ann Pomeroy, "Great Communicators, Great Communication," SHRMOnline [accessed 15 April 2007] www.shrm.org.

15. Jonathan Baldwin and Lucienne Roberts, *Visual Communication: From Theory to Practice* (Lausanne, Switzerland: AVA, 2006), 5.

16. Jeff Davidson, "Fighting Information Overload," *Canadian Manager*, Spring 2005, 16+.

17. Scott Ginsberg, "How to Give Your Staff Permission to Talk to You," Hello My Name Is Scott [accessed 11 August 2006] www. hellomynameisscott.com.

18. Paul Martin Lester, *Visual Communication: Images with Messages* (Belmont, Calif.: Thomson South-Western, 2006), 6–8.

19. Michael R. Solomon, *Consumer Behavior: Buying, Having, and Being*, 6th ed. (Upper Saddle River, N.J.: Pearson Prentice Hall, 2004), 65.

20. Anne Field, "What You Say, What They Hear," *Harvard Management Communication Letter*, Winter 2005, 3–5.

21. Chuck Williams, *Management*, 2nd ed. (Cincinnati: Thomson South-Western, 2002), 690.

22. Charles G. Morris and Albert A. Maisto, *Psychology: An Introduction*, 12th ed. (Upper Saddle River, N.J.: Pearson Prentice Hall, 2005), 226–239; Saundra K. Ciccarelli and Glenn E. Meyer, *Psychology* (Upper Saddle River, N.J.: Prentice Hall, 2006), 210–229; Mark H. Ashcraft, *Cognition*, 4th ed. (Upper Saddle River, N.J.: Prentice Hall, 2006), 44–54.

23. Stephanie Armour, "Music Hath Charms for Some Workers—Others It Really Annoys," *USA Today*, 24 March 2006, B1–B2.

24. Debbie Weil, *The Corporate Blogging Book* (New York: Portfolio, 2006), 60.

25. Hellriegel., *Management: A Competency-Based Approach*, 451.

26. Laura L. Myers and Mary L. Tucker, "Increasing Awareness of Emotional Intelligence in a Business Curriculum," *Business Communication Quarterly*, March 2005, 44–51.

27. John Owens, "Good Communication in Workplace Is Basic to Getting Any Job Done," *Knight Ridder/Tribune Business News*, 9 July 2003, 1.

28. Tamar Lewin, "Study Finds Widespread Neglect of Writing Skills," *Desert Sun*, 26 April 2003, A12.

29. Williams, *Management*, 706–707.

30. Del Jones, "Watch Your Language, Ladies," *USA Today*, 24 November 2004, 3B.

31. "Employers, Beware: 'Techno Addicts' May Be More Liability Than Boon," Lockergnome.com, 18 August 2006 [accessed 23 August 2006] www.lockergnome.com.

32. Eric J. Sinrod, "Perspective: It's My Internet—I Can Do What I Want," News.com, 29 March 2006 [accessed 12 August 2006] www.news.com.

33. "The Hidden Dangers of Instant Messaging," Newsfactor.com, 5 July 2006 [accessed 12 August 2006] www.newsfactor.com.

34. Eric J. Sinrod, "Time to Crack Down on Tech at Work?" News.com, 14 June 2006 [accessed 12 August 2006] www.news.com.

35. A. Thomas Young, "Ethics in Business: Business of Ethics," *Vital Speeches*, 15 September 1992, 725–730.

36. "Undercover Marketing Uncovered," CBSnews.com, 25 July 2004 [accessed 11 April 2005] www.cbsnews.com; Stephanie Dunnewind, "Teen Recruits Create Word-of-Mouth 'Buzz' to Hook Peers on Products," *Seattle Times*, 20 November 2004 [accessed 11 April 2005] www.seattletimes.com.

37. Kolin, *Successful Writing at Work*, 24–30.

38. Nancy K. Kubasek, Bartley A. Brennan, and M. Neil Browne, *The Legal Environment of Business*, 3rd ed. (Upper Saddle River, N.J.: Prentice Hall, 2003), 172.

39. Kelli Esters, "Insurance Company to Repay $1.1 Million to Georgia Soldiers," *Ledger-Enquirer* (Columbus, Ga.), 26 May 2005 [accessed 28 June 2005] www.ebsco.com; Diana B. Henriques, "Insurer to Refund Money to Soldiers Who Bought High-Cost Life Policies," *New York Times*, 23 September 2004, C1, C4; Diana B. Henriques, "Going Off to War, and Vulnerable to the Pitches of Salesmen," *New York Times*, 20 July 2004, C1, C6.

40. Daft, *Management*, 155.

41. "Less Than Half of Companies Encourage Discussion of Ethical Issues at the Workplace," press release, International Association of Business Communicators Research Foundation, 23 May 2006 [accessed 12 August 2006] www.iabc.com.

42. Joanne Sammer, "United Technologies Offers a Model for Reporting Ethical Issues," *Workforce Management*, August 2004, 64–66.

43. Based in part on Robert Kreitner, *Management*, 9th ed. (Boston: Houghton Mifflin, 2004), 163.

44. Henry R. Cheeseman, *Contemporary Business and E-Commerce Law*, 4th ed. (Upper Saddle River, N.J.: Prentice Hall, 2003), 841–843.

45. Cheeseman, *Contemporary Business and E-Commerce Law*, 201.

46. John Jude Moran, *Employment Law: New Challenges in the Business Environment*, 2nd ed. (Upper Saddle River, N.J.: Prentice Hall, 2002), 186–187; Kubasek et al., *The Legal Environment of Business*, 562.

47. Cheeseman, *Contemporary Business and E-Commerce Law*, 325.

48. Kubasek et al., *The Legal Environment of Business*, 306.

CHAPTER 2

1. The Container Store website [accessed 5 February 2007] www.containerstore.com; "2005: Best Companies to Work For," *Fortune*, 24 January 2005 [accessed 11 March 2005] www.fortune.com; Bob Nelson, "Can't Contain Excitement at The Container Store," BizJournals.com [accessed 11 March 2005] www.bizjournals.com; Mike Duff, "Top-Shelf Employees Keep Container Store on Track," *DSN Retailing Today*, 8 March 2004, 7, 49; Bob Nelson, "The Buzz at The Container Store," *Corporate Meetings & Incentives*, June 2003, 32; Jennifer Saba, "Balancing Act," *Potentials*, 1 October 2003 [accessed 15 April 2004] www.highbeam.com; Peter S. Cohan, "Corporate Heroes," *Financial Executive*, 1 March 2003 [accessed 15 April 2004] www.highbeam.com; Margaret Steen, "Container Store's Focus on Training a Strong Appeal to Employees," *Mercury News* (San Jose, Calif.), 6 November 2003 [accessed 15 April 2004] www.highbeam.com; Holly Hayes, "Container Store Brings Clutter Control to San Jose, Calif.," 17 October 2003, *Mercury News* (San Jose, Calif.), 1F; "Performance Through People Award," press release, Business Wire, 10 September 2003; David Lipke, "Container Store's CEO: People Are Most Valued Asset," 13 January 2003, *HFN* [accessed 9 March 2003] www.highbeam.com; Lorrie Grant, "Container Store's Workers Huddle Up to Help You Out," 30 April 2002, *USA Today*, B1.

2. Courtland L. Bovée and John V. Thill, *Business in Action*, 3rd ed. (Upper Saddle River, N.J.: Prentice Hall, 2005), 175.

3. "Five Case Studies on Successful Teams," *HR Focus*, April 2002, 18+.

4. Stephen R. Robbins, *Essentials of Organizational Behavior*, 6th ed. (Upper Saddle River, N.J.: Prentice Hall, 2000), 98.

5. Max Landsberg and Madeline Pfau, "Developing Diversity: Lessons from Top Teams," *Strategy + Business*, Winter 2005, 10–12.

6. "Groups Best at Complex Problems," *Industrial Engineer*, June 2006, 14.

7. Lynda McDermott, Bill Waite, and Nolan Brawley, "Executive Teamwork," *Executive Excellence*, May 1999, 15.

8. Nicola A. Nelson, "Leading Teams," *Defense AT&L*, July–August 2006, 26–29; Larry Cole and Michael Cole, "Why Is the Teamwork Buzz Word Not Working?" *Communication World*, February–March 1999, 29; Patricia Buhler, "Managing in the 90s: Creating Flexibility in Today's Workplace," *Supervision*, January 1997, 24+; Allison W. Amason, Allen C. Hochwarter, Wayne A. Thompson, and Kenneth R. Harrison, "Conflict: An Important Dimension in Successful Management Teams," *Organizational Dynamics*, Autumn 1995, 20+.

9. Richard L. Daft, *Management*, 6th ed. (Cincinnati: Thomson South-Western, 2003), 614.

10. Geoffrey Colvin, "Why Dream Teams Fail," *Fortune*, 12 June 2006, 87–92.

11. Vijay Govindarajan and Anil K. Gupta, "Building an Effective Global Business Team," *MIT Sloan Management Review*, Summer 2001, 63+.

12. Louise Rehling, "Improving Teamwork Through Awareness of Conversational Styles," *Business Communication Quarterly*, December 2004, 475–482.

13. Jon Hanke, "Presenting as a Team," *Presentations*, January 1998, 74–82.

14. William P. Galle, Jr., Beverly H. Nelson, Donna W. Luse, and Maurice F. Villere, *Business Communication: A Technology-Based Approach* (Chicago: Irwin, 1996), 260.

15. Mary Beth Debs, "Recent Research on Collaborative Writing in Industry," *Technical Communication*, November 1991, 476–484.

16. "TWiki Success Stories," TWiki website [accessed 18 August 2006] www.twiki.org.

17. Mark Choate, "What Makes an Enterprise Wiki?" CMS Watch website, 28 April 2006 [accessed 18 August 2006] www.cmswatch.com.

18. Choate, "What Makes an Enterprise Wiki?"

19. "Codex: Guidelines," WordPress website [accessed 18 August 2006] www.wordpress.org; Michael Shanks, "Wiki Guidelines," Traumwerk website [accessed 18 August 2006] http://metamedia.stanford.edu/projects/traumwerk/home; Joe Moxley, M.C. Morgan, Matt Barton, and Donna Hanak, "For Teachers New to Wikis," Writing Wiki [accessed 18 August 2006] http://writingwiki.org; "Wiki Guidelines," PsiWiki [accessed 18 August 2006] http://psi-im.org.

20. Tony Kontzer, "Learning to Share," *InformationWeek*, 5 May 2003, 28; Jon Udell, "Uniting Under Groove," *InfoWorld*, 17 February 2003 [accessed 9 September 2003] www.elibrary.com; Alison Overholt, "Virtually There?" *Fast Company*, 14 February 2002, 108.

21. Colvin, "Why Dream Teams Fail," 87–92.

22. Tiziana Casciaro and Miguel Sousa Lobo, "Competent Jerks, Lovable Fools, and the Formation of Social Networks," *Harvard Business Review*, June 2005, 92–99.

23. Stephen P. Robbins and David A. DeCenzo, *Fundamentals of Management*, 4th ed. (Upper Saddle River, N.J.: Prentice Hall, 2004), 266–267; Jerald Greenberg and Robert A. Baron, *Behavior in Organizations*, 8th ed. (Upper Saddle River, N.J.: Prentice Hall, 2003), 279–280.

24. "Team Building: Managing the Norms of Informal Groups in the Workplace," Accel-Team.com [accessed 16 August 2006] www.accelteam.com.

25. B. Aubrey Fisher, *Small Group Decision Making: Communication and the Group Process*, 2nd ed. (New York: McGraw-Hill, 1980), 145–149; Robbins and De Cenzo, *Fundamentals of Management*, 334–335; Daft, *Management*, 602–603.

26. Michael Laff, "Effective Team Building: More Than Just Fun at Work," *Training+Development*, August 2006, 24–35.

27. Claire Sookman, "Building Your Virtual Team," *Network World*, 21 June 2004, 91.

28. Jared Sandberg, "Brainstorming Works Best if People Scramble for Ideas on Their Own," *Wall Street Journal*, 13 June 2006, B1.

29. Mark K. Smith, "Bruce W. Tuckman—Forming, Storming, Norming, and Performing in Groups," Infed.org [accessed 5 July 2005] www.infed.org.

30. Robbins and DeCenzo, *Fundamentals of Management*, 258–259.

31. Daft, *Management*, 609–612.

32. Andy Boynton and Bill Fischer, *Virtuoso Teams: Lessons from Teams That Changed Their Worlds* (Harrow, England: FT Prentice Hall, 2005), 10.

33. Thomas K. Capozzoli, "Conflict Resolution—A Key Ingredient in Successful Teams," *Supervision*, November 1999, 14–16.

34. Janis Graham, "Sharpen Your Negotiating Skills," *Sylvia Porter's Personal Finance*, December 1985, 54–58.

35. Amason, et al., "Conflict."

36. Jesse S. Nirenberg, *Getting Through to People* (Paramus, N.J.: Prentice Hall, 1973), 134–142.

37. Nirenberg, *Getting Through to People*.

38. Nirenberg, *Getting Through to People*.

39. "Better Meetings Benefit Everyone: How to Make Yours More Productive," *Working Communicator Bonus Report*, July 1998, 1.

40. Ken Blanchard, "Meetings Can Be Effective," *Supervisory Management*, October 1992, 5.

41. "Better Meetings Benefit Everyone."

42. Nicole Ridgway, "A Safer Place to Meet," *Forbes*, 28 April 2003, 97.

43. IBM InnovationJam website [accessed 15 August 2006] www.globalinnovationjam.com; "Big Blue Brainstorm," *BusinessWeek*, 7 August 2006 [accessed 15 August 2006] www.businessweek.com.

44. Linda Zimmer, "Second Life: What Is It Good For?" Business Communicators of Second Life blog, 24 January 2007 [accessed 7 February 2007] http://freshtakes.typepad.com/sl_communicators; Robert D. Hof, "My Virtual Life," *BusinessWeek*, 1 May 2006 [accessed 7 February 2007] www.businessweek.com; David Needle, "Sun Finds a Home in Second Life," Internetnews.com, 11 October 2006 [accessed 7 February 2007] www.internetnews.com.

45. Judi Brownell, *Listening*, 2nd ed. (Boston: Allyn & Bacon, 2002), 9, 10.

46. Augusta M. Simon, "Effective Listening: Barriers to Listening in a Diverse Business Environment," *Bulletin of the Association for Business Communication* 54, no. 3 (September 1991): 73–74.

47. Robyn D. Clarke, "Do You Hear What I Hear?" *Black Enterprise*, May 1998, 129.

48. Larry Barker and Kittie Watson, *Listen Up* (New York: St. Martin's, 2000), 24–27.

49. Terri Somers, "Gen-Probe's Nordhoff Listens Well, Then Acts," *San Diego Union-Tribune*, 2 November 2004, C1, C6.

50. Dennis M. Kratz and Abby Robinson Kratz, *Effective Listening Skills* (New York: McGraw-Hill, 1995), 45–53; J. Michael Sproule, *Communication Today* (Glenview, Ill.: Scott Foresman, 1981), 69.

51. Brownell, *Listening*, 230–231.

52. Kratz and Kratz, *Effective Listening Skills*, 78–79; Sproule, *Communication Today*.

53. Tyner Blain, "Ten Supercharged Active Listening Skills to Make You More Successful," Tyner Blain blog, 15 March 2007 [accessed 16 April 2007] http://tynerblain.com/blog/; Bill Brooks, "The Power of Active Listening," *American Salesman*, June 2003, 12; "Active Listening," Study Guides and Strategies [accessed 5 February 2005] www.studygs.net.

54. Bob Lamons, "Good Listeners Are Better Communicators," *Marketing News*, 11 September 1995, 13+; Phillip Morgan and H. Kent Baker, "Building a Professional Image: Improving Listening Behavior," *Supervisory Management*, November 1985, 35–36.

55. Clarke, "Do You Hear What I Hear?"; Dot Yandle, "Listening to Understand," *Pryor Report Management Newsletter Supplement* 15, no. 8 (August 1998): 13.

56. Brownell, *Listening*, 14; Kratz and Kratz, *Effective Listening Skills*, 8–9; Sherwyn P. Morreale and Courtland L. Bovée, *Excellence in Public Speaking* (Orlando, Fla.: Harcourt Brace, 1998), 72–76; Lyman K. Steil, Larry

L. Barker, and Kittie W. Watson, *Effective Listening: Key to Your Success* (Reading, Mass.: Addison-Wesley, 1983), 21–22.

57. Patrick J. Collins, *Say It with Power and Confidence* (Upper Saddle River, N.J.: Prentice Hall, 1997), 40–45.

58. Morreale and Bovée, *Excellence in Public Speaking*, 296.

59. Judee K. Burgoon, David B. Butler, and W. Gill Woodall, *Nonverbal Communication: The Unspoken Dialog* (New York: McGraw-Hill, 1996), 137.

60. "Study: Human Lie Detectors Rarely Wrong," CNN.com, 14 October 2004 [accessed 14 October 2004] www.cnn.com.

61. Dale G. Leathers, *Successful Nonverbal Communication: Principles and Applications* (New York: Macmillan, 1986), 19.

62. Gerald H. Graham, Jeanne Unrue, and Paul Jennings, "The Impact of Nonverbal Communication in Organizations: A Survey of Perceptions," *Journal of Business Communication* 28, no. 1 (Winter 1991): 45–62.

63. Virginia P. Richmond and James C. McCroskey, *Nonverbal Behavior in Interpersonal Relations* (Boston: Allyn & Bacon, 2000), 153–157.

64. Carmine Gallo, "Body Language: Key to Success in the Workplace," *BusinessWeek*, 14 February 2007 [accessed 16 April 2007] www.businessweek.com.

65. Richmond and McCroskey, *Nonverbal Behavior in Interpersonal Relations*, 2–3.

66. John Hollon, "No Tolerance for Jerks," *Workforce Management*, 12 February 2007, 34.

67. Dana May Casperson, *Power Etiquette: What You Don't Know Can Kill Your Career* (New York: AMACOM, 1999), 9.

68. Marilyn Pincus, *Everyday Business Etiquette* (Hauppauge, N.Y.: Barron's Educational Series, 1996), 7, 133.

69. Pincus, *Everyday Business Etiquette*, 136.

70. Casperson, *Power Etiquette*, 23.

71. Graham, et al., "The Impact of Nonverbal Communication," *Journal of Business Communication* 28, no. 1 (Winter 1991): 45–62.

72. Pincus, *Everyday Business Etiquette*, 100–101.

73. Maggie Jackson, "Turn Off That Cellphone. It's Meeting Time," *New York Times*, 2 March 2003, sec. 3, 12.

74. Casperson, *Power Etiquette*, 10–14; Ellyn Spragins, "Introducing Politeness," *Fortune Small Business*, November 2001, 30.

75. Tanya Mohn, "The Social Graces as a Business Tool," *New York Times*, 10 November 2002, sec. 3, 12.

76. Casperson, *Power Etiquette*, 19; Pincus, *Everyday Business Etiquette*, 7–8.

77. Casperson, *Power Etiquette*, 44–46.

78. Casperson, *Power Etiquette*, 109–110.

CHAPTER 3

1. Regina Tosca and Rima Matsumoto, "Diversity and Inclusion: A Driving Force for Growth and Innovation at IBM," 2 February 2007, Hispanic Association on Corporate Responsibility website [accessed 12 February 2007] www.hacr.org; IBM website [accessed 12 February 2007] www.ibm.com; "Executive Corner: Letter from IBM's Vice President, Global Workforce Diversity," IBM website [accessed 12 February 2007] www.ibm.com; "IBM—Diversity as a Strategic Imperative," *Global Diversity @ Work* [accessed 6 July 2005] www.diversityatwork.com; Cliff Edwards, "The Rewards of Tolerance," *BusinessWeek*, 15 December 2003 [accessed 6 July 2005] www.businessweek.com; David A. Thomas, "IBM Finds Profit in Diversity," *HBS Working Knowledge*, 27 September 2004 [accessed 5 July 2005] http://hbswk.hbs.edu; "IBM Diversity Executive to Speak at the University of Virginia," *University of Virginia News*, 7 November 2003 [accessed 5 July 2005] www.virginia.edu.

2. Michael R. Carrell, Everett E. Mann, and Tracey Honeycutt Sigler, "Defining Workforce Diversity Programs and Practices in Organizations: A Longitudinal Study," *Labor Law Journal*, Spring 2006, 5–12.

3. "Top Trading Partners—Total Trade, Exports, Imports June 2006," U.S. Census Bureau [accessed 23 August 2006] www.census.gov.

4. Ford Motor Co. website [accessed 12 July 2005] www.ford.com.

5. Nancy R. Lockwood, "Workplace Diversity: Leveraging the Power of Difference for Competitive Advantage," *HR Magazine*, June 2005, special section 1–10.

6. Carol Hymowitz, "Managers Err if They Limit Their Hiring to People Like Them," *Wall Street Journal*, 12 October 2004, B1.

7. Rona Gindin, "Dealing with a Multicultural Workforce," *Nation's Restaurant News*, September–October 1998, 31, 83; Howard Gleckman, "A Rich Stew in the Melting Pot," *BusinessWeek*, 31 August 1998, 76+; Toby B. Gooley, "A World of Difference," *Logistics Management and Distribution Report*, June 2000, 51–55; William H. Miller, "Beneath the Surface," *Industry Week*, 20 September 1999, 13–16.

8. Robert Kreitner, *Management*, 9th ed. (Boston: Houghton Mifflin, 2004), 84.

9. Linda Beamer and Iris Varner, *Intercultural Communication in the Workplace*, 2nd ed. (New York: McGraw-Hill Irwin, 2001), xiii.

10. Tracy Novinger, *Intercultural Communication, A Practical Guide* (Austin, Tex.: University of Texas Press, 2001), 15.

11. Beamer and Varner, *Intercultural Communication in the Workplace*, 3.

12. Randolph E. Schmid, "Asians, Americans See World Differently," *SF Gate*, 22 August 2005 [accessed 23 August 2006] http://chineseculture. about.com.

13. "Languages of the USA," Ethnologue.com [accessed 22 August 2006] www.ethnologue.com.

14. Philip R. Harris and Robert T. Moran, *Managing Cultural Differences*, 3rd ed. (Houston: Gulf, 1991), 394–397, 429–430.

15. Lillian H. Chaney and Jeanette S. Martin, *Intercultural Business Communication*, 2nd ed. (Upper Saddle River, N.J.: Prentice Hall, 2000), 6.

16. Beamer and Varner, *Intercultural Communication in the Workplace*, 4.

17. Chaney and Martin, *Intercultural Business Communication*, 2nd ed., 9.

18. Richard L. Daft, *Management*, 6th ed. (Cincinnati: Thomson South-Western, 2003), 455.

19. Lillian H. Chaney and Jeanette S. Martin, *Intercultural Business Communication*, 4th ed. (Upper Saddle River, N.J.: Pearson Prentice Hall, 2007), 53.

20. Project Implicit website [accessed 12 July 2005] https://implicit. harvard.edu/implicit.

21. Larry A. Samovar and Richard E. Porter, "Basic Principles of Intercultural Communication," in *Intercultural Communication: A Reader*, 6th ed., edited by Larry A. Samovar and Richard E. Porter (Belmont, Calif.: Wadsworth, 1991), 12.

22. Linda Beamer, "Teaching English Business Writing to Chinese-Speaking Business Students," *Bulletin of the Association for Business Communication* 57, no. 1 (1994): 12–18.

23. Edward T. Hall, "Context and Meaning," in *Intercultural Communication*, edited by Samovar and Porter, 46–55.

24. Daft, *Management*, 459.

25. Beamer, "Teaching English Business Writing to Chinese-Speaking Business Students."

26. Charley H. Dodd, *Dynamics of Intercultural Communication*, 3rd ed. (Dubuque, Iowa: Brown, 1991), 69–70.

27. Daft, *Management*, 459.

28. Beamer and Varner, *Intercultural Communication in the Workplace*, 230–233.

29. James Wilfong and Toni Seger, *Taking Your Business Global* (Franklin Lakes, N.J.: Career Press, 1997), 277–278.

30. Harris and Moran, *Managing Cultural Differences*, 260.

31. Ishbel Matheson, "Kenyans Dance Against Graft," *BBC News*, 18 September 2001 [accessed 23 August 2006] http://news.bbc.co.uk.

32. Skip Kaltenheuser, "Bribery Is Being Outlawed Virtually Worldwide," *Business Ethics*, May–June 1998, 11; Thomas Omestad, "Bye-Bye to Bribes," *U.S. News & World Report*, 22 December 1997, 39, 42–44.

33. "Big Oil's Dirty Secrets," *The Economist*, 10 May 2003, 62; Skip Kaltenheuser, "A Little Dab Will Do You?" *World Trade*, January 1999, 58–63; James Walsh, "A World War on Bribery," *Time*, 22 June 1998, 16.

34. Guo-Ming Chen and William J. Starosta, *Foundations of Intercultural Communication* (Boston: Allyn & Bacon, 1998), 288–289.

35. Mark Landler and Michael Barbaro, "Wal-Mart Finds That Its Formula Doesn't Fit Every Culture," *New York Times*, 2 August 2006 [accessed 23 August 2006] www.nytimes.com.

36. Mary A. DeVries, *Internationally Yours* (New York: Houghton Mifflin, 1994), 194.

37. Chaney and Martin, *Intercultural Business Communication*, 2nd ed., 122–123.

38. Erin Richards, "Are You the Ugly American?" CNN.com, 1 November 2006 [accessed 16 April 2007] www.cnn.com.

39. Novinger, *Intercultural Communication: A Practical Guide*, 54.

40. Peter Coy, "Old. Smart. Productive." *BusinessWeek*, 27 June 2005 [accessed 24 August 2006] www.businessweek.com; Beamer and Varner, *Intercultural Communication in the Workplace*, 107–108.

41. Beamer and Varner, *Intercultural Communication in the Workplace*, 107–108.

42. Michael Kinsman, "Respect Helps Mix of Generations Work Well Together," *San Diego Union-Tribune*, 19 September 2004, H2.

43. Archer Daniels Midland website [accessed 23 August 2006] www.admworld.com; Ann Harrington and Petra Bartosiewicz, "50 Most Powerful Women," *Fortune*, 16 October 2006 [accessed 13 February 2007] www.fortune.com.

44. Tonya Vinas, "A Place at the Table," *Industry Week*, 1 July 2003, 22.

45. Daft, *Management*, 445.

46. John Gray, *Mars and Venus in the Workplace* (New York: HarperCollins, 2002), 10, 25–27, 61–63.

47. Chaney and Martin, *Intercultural Business Communication*, 4th ed., 62.

48. Todd Henneman, "A New Approach to Faith at Work," *Workforce Management*, October 2004, 76–77.

49. IBM Accessibility Center [accessed 24 August 2006] www-3.ibm.com/ able; AssistiveTech.net [accessed 24 August 2006] www.assistivetech.net; Business Leadership Network website [accessed 24 August 2006] www.usbln.org; National Institute on Disability and Rehabilitation Research website [accessed 24 August 2006] www.ed.gov/about/offices/ list/osers/nidrr; Rehabilitation Engineering & Assistive Technology Society of North America website [accessed 24 August 2006] www.resna.org.

50. Sana Reynolds and Deborah Valentine, *Guide for Internationals: Culture, Communication, and ESL* (Upper Saddle River, N.J.: Prentice Hall, 2006), 3–11, 14–19, 25.

51. P. Christopher Earley and Elaine Mosakowsi, "Cultural Intelligence," *Harvard Business Review*, October 2004, 139–146.

52. Wendy A. Conklin, "An Inside Look at Two Diversity Intranet Sites: IBM and Merck," *The Diversity Factor*, Summer 2005.

53. Craig S. Smith, "Beware of Green Hats in China and Other Cross-Cultural Faux Pas," *New York Times*, 30 April 2002, C11.

54. Francesca Bargiela-Chiappini, Anne Marie Bülow-Møller, Catherine Nickerson, Gina Poncini, and Yunxia Zhu, "Five Perspectives on Intercultural Business Communication," *Business Communication Quarterly*, September 2003, 73–96.

55. Paul Johnson, "Must the Whole World Speak English?" *Forbes*, 29 November 2004, 39; Randolph E. Schmid, "Study Says English Language Is Losing Cultural Dominance," *Desert Sun*, 29 February 2004, A25.

56. Mary Beth Sheridan, "Learning the New Language of Labor," *Washington Post*, 20 August 2002, A1.

57. Bob Nelson, "Motivating Workers Worldwide," *Global Workforce*, November 1998, 25–27.

58. Mona Casady and Lynn Wasson, "Written Communication Skills of International Business Persons," *Bulletin of the Association for Business Communication* 57, no. 4 (1994): 36–40.

59. "From Plain English to Global English," Quickit Limited website [accessed 24 August 2006] www.webpagecontent.com.

60. Myron W. Lustig and Jolene Koester, *Intercultural Competence*, 4th ed., (Boston: Allyn & Bacon, 2003), 196.

61. Mark Lasswell, "Lost in Translation," *Business 2.0*, August 2004, 68–70.

62. Sheridan Prasso, ed., "It's All Greek to These Sites," *BusinessWeek*, 22 July 2002, 18.

CHAPTER 4

1. Complete Idiot's Guide website [accessed 28 August 2006] www.idiotsguides.com; Chris Taylor, "One-Minute Photo Smile!" *Time*, 23 December 2002, 80; "Writers Seek Simple Ways to Describe New Products," *Washington Times*, 7 November 2002 [accessed 28 October 2003] www.elibrary.com; Caroline E. Mayer, "Why Won't We Read the Manual?" *Washington Post*, 26 May 2002, H01.

2. Sanford Kaye, "Writing Under Pressure," *Soundview Executive Book Summaries* 10, no. 12, part 2 (December 1988): 1–8.

3. Peter Bracher, "Process, Pedagogy, and Business Writing," *Journal of Business Communication* 24, no. 1 (Winter 1987): 43–50.

4. Laurey Berk and Phillip G. Clampitt, "Finding the Right Path in the Communication Maze," *IABC Communication World*, October 1991, 28–32.

5. Linda Duyle, "Get Out of Your Office," *HR Magazine*, July 2006, 99–101.

6. Skype website [accessed 30 August 2006] www.skype.com.

7. Kris Maher, "The Jungle," *Wall Street Journal*, 5 October 2004, B10.

8. Kevin Maney, "Surge in Text Messaging Makes Cell Operators :-)," *USA Today*, 28 July 2005, B1–B2.

9. David Kirkpatrick, "It's Hard to Manage if You Don't Blog," *Fortune*, 4 October 2004, 46; Lee Gomes, "How the Next Big Thing in Technology Morphed into a Really Big Thing," *Wall Street Journal*, 4 October 2004, B1; Jeff Meisner, "Cutting Through the Blah, Blah, Blah," *Puget Sound Business Journal*, 19–25 November 2004, 27–28; Lauren Gard, "The Business of Blogging," *BusinessWeek*, 13 December 2004, 117–119; Heather Green, "Online Video: The Sequel," *BusinessWeek*, 10 January 2005, 40; Michelle Conlin and Andrew Park, "Blogging with the Boss's Blessing," *BusinessWeek*, 28 June 2004, 100–102.

10. Berk and Clampitt, "Finding the Right Path in the Communication Maze."

11. Berk and Clampitt, "Finding the Right Path in the Communication Maze."

12. Berk and Clampitt, "Finding the Right Path in the Communication Maze."

13. Raymond M. Olderman, *10 Minute Guide to Business Communication* (New York: Alpha Books, 1997), 19–20.

14. Mohan R. Limaye and David A. Victor, "Cross-Cultural Business Communication Research: State of the Art and Hypotheses for the 1990s," *Journal of Business Communication* 28, no. 3 (Summer 1991): 277–299.

15. Holly Weeks, "The Best Memo You'll Ever Write," *Harvard Management Communication Letter*, Spring 2005, 3–5.

CHAPTER 5

1. Creative Commons website [accessed 17 February 2007] www.creativecommons.org; Ariana Eunjung Cha, "Creative Commons Is Rewriting Rules of Copyright," *Washington Post*, 15 March 2005 [accessed 3 August 2005] www.washingtonpost.com; Steven Levy, "Lawrence Lessig's Supreme Showdown," *Wired*, October 2002 [accessed 3 August 2005] www.wired.com; "Happy Birthday: We'll Sue," Snopes.com [accessed 3 August 2005] www.snopes.com.

2. Elizabeth Blackburn and Kelly Belanger, "You-Attitude and Positive Emphasis: Testing Received Wisdom in Business Communication," *Bulletin of the Association for Business Communication* 56, no. 2 (June 1993): 1–9.

3. Placard at Alaska Airlines ticket counters, Seattle-Tacoma International Airport, 3 October 2003.

4. Annette N. Shelby and N. Lamar Reinsch, Jr., "Positive Emphasis and You Attitude: An Empirical Study," *Journal of Business Communication* 32, no. 4 (1995): 303–322.

5. Sherryl Kleinman, "Why Sexist Language Matters," *Qualitative Sociology* 25, no. 2 (Summer 2002): 299–304.

6. Judy E. Pickens, "Terms of Equality: A Guide to Bias-Free Language," *Personnel Journal*, August 1985, 24.

7. Lisa Taylor, "Communicating About People with Disabilities: Does the Language We Use Make a Difference?" *Bulletin of the Association for Business Communication* 53, no. 3 (September 1990): 65–67.

8. Susan Benjamin, *Words at Work* (Reading, Mass.: Addison-Wesley, 1997), 136–137.

9. Stuart Crainer and Des Dearlove, "Making Yourself Understood," *Across the Board*, May/June 2004, 23–27.

10. Plain English Campaign website [accessed 3 October 2003] www.plainenglish.co.uk.

11. Creative Commons website [accessed 20 September 2006] www.creativecommons.org.

12. Joseph Kimble, "Answering the Critics of Plain Language," The Plain Language Network website, 12 April 2003 [accessed 22 September 2006] www.plainlanguagenetwork.org.

13. Peter Crow, "Plain English: What Counts Besides Readability?" *Journal of Business Communication* 25, no. 1 (Winter 1988): 87–95.

14. Susan Jaderstrom and Joanne Miller, "Active Writing," *Office Pro*, November/December 2003, 29.

15. Gap website [accessed 20 September 2006] www.gap.com.

16. Mary Munter, *Guide to Managerial Communication*, 7th ed. (Upper Saddle River, N.J.: Prentice Hall, 2006), 41.

17. Portions of this section are adapted from Courtland L. Bovée, *Techniques of Writing Business Letters, Memos, and Reports* (Sherman Oaks, Calif.: Banner Books International, 1978), 13–90.

18. Janice Obuchowski, "Communicate to Inform, Not Impress," *Harvard Management Communication Letter*, Winter 2006, 3–4; Robert Hartwell Fiske, *The Dimwit's Dictionary* (Oak Park, Ill.: Marion Street Press, 2002), 1620.

19. Beverly Ballaro and Christina Bielaszka-DuVernay, "Building a Bridge over the River Boredom," *Harvard Management Communication Letter*, Winter 2005, 3–5.

20. David A. Fryxell, "Lost in Transition?" *Writer's Digest*, January 2005, 24–26.

21. Adapted from Creative Commons website [accessed 18 February 2007] www.creativecommons.org.

22. Food Allergy Initiative website [accessed 23 September 2006] www.foodallergyinitiative.org; Diana Keough, "Snacks That Can Kill; Schools Take Steps to Protect Kids Who Have Severe Allergies to Nuts," *Plain Dealer*, 15 July 2003, E1; "Dawdling Over Food Labels," *New York Times*, 2 June 2003, A16; Sheila McNulty, "A Matter of Life and Death," *Financial Times*, 10 September 2003, 14.

23. Apple iTunes website [accessed 23 September 2006] www.apple.com/itunes.

CHAPTER 6

1. Mercedes-AMG website [accessed 23 February 2007] www.mercedes-amg.com; Avenue A | Razorfish website [accessed 25 September 2006] www.avenuea-razorfish.com; "Mercedes-AMG Website Wins Webby Award," 12 June 2006, eMercedesBenz website [accessed 25 September 2006] www.emercedesbenz.com.

2. William Zinsser, *On Writing Well*, 5th ed. (New York: HarperCollins, 1994), 9.

3. Zinsser, *On Writing Well*, 7, 17.

4. Mary A. DeVries, *Internationally Yours* (Boston: Houghton Mifflin, 1994), 160.

5. Zinsser, *On Writing Well*, 126.

6. Deborah Gunn, "Looking Good on Paper," *Office Pro*, March 2004, 10–11.

7. Jennifer Saranow, "Memo to Web Sites: Grow Up!" *Wall Street Journal*, 15 November 2004, R14–R15.

8. Jacci Howard Bear, "Desktop Publishing Rules of Page Layout," About.com [accessed 22 August 2005] www.about.com.

9. Jacci Howard Bear, "Desktop Publishing Rules for How Many Fonts to Use," About.com [accessed 22 August 2005] www.about.com.

10. Adapted from Mercedes-AMG website [accessed 23 February 2007] www.mercedes-amg.com.

11. The writing sample in this exercise was adapted from material on the Marsh Risk Consulting website [accessed 2 October 2006] www.marshriskconsulting.com.

12. Podium website [accessed 24 February 2007] www.podiumpodcasting.com.

CHAPTER 7

1. Bill Owens, "Why Can't I Make Reservations Further in Advance?" Nuts About Southwest blog, 24 January 2007 [accessed 15 May 2007] www.blogsouthwest.com; Bill Owens, "I Blogged. You Flamed. We Changed." Nuts About Southwest blog, 18 April 2007 [accessed 10 May 2007] www.blogsouthwest.com; "Welcome to the Nuts About Southwest Blog—A User's Guide," Nuts About Southwest blog, [accessed 15 May 2007] www.blogsouthwest.com; "Southwest Airlines Is Nuts About Blogging," Southwest Airlines press release, 27 April 2007 [accessed 15 May 2007] www.prnewswire.com.

2. Dave Carpenter, "Companies Discover Marketing Power of Text Messaging," *Seattle Times*, 25 September 2006 [accessed 25 September 2006] www.seattletimes.com.

3. "A Definition of Social Media," Technology in Translation blog, 6 April 2007 [accessed 11 June 2007] http://technologyintranslation.blockwork.org; Robert Scoble, "What Is Social Media?" Scobleizer blog, 16 February 2007 [accessed 11 June 2007] www.scobleizer.com; Paul Gillin, *The New Influencers* (Sanger, Calif.: Quill Driver Books, 2007), xi–xii.

4. Hilary Potkewitz and Rachel Brown, "Spread of E-mail Has Altered Communication Habits at Work," *Los Angeles Business Journal*, 18 April 2005 [accessed 30 April 2006] www.findarticles.com; Nancy Flynn, *Instant Messaging Rules* (New York: AMACOM, 2004), 47–54.

5. "Employee Communication Is Cause for Concern," Duane Morris LLP website, 23 August 2006 [accessed 4 October 2006] www.duanemorris.com.

6. Greg Burns, "For Some, Benefits of E-mail Not Worth Risk," *San Diego Union-Tribune*, 16 August 2005, A1, A8; Pui-Wing Tam, Erin White, Nick Wingfield, and Kris Maher, "Snooping E-mail by Software Is Now a Workplace Norm," *Wall Street Journal*, 9 March 2005, B1+.

7. Matt Cain, "Managing E-mail Hygiene," ZD Net Tech Update, 5 February 2004 [accessed 19 March 2004] www.techupdate.zdnet.com.

8. Lizette Alvarez, "Got 2 Extra Hours for Your E-mail?" *New York Times*, 10 November 2005 [accessed 10 November 2005] www.nytimes.com.

9. Jack Trout, "Beware of 'Infomania,'" *Forbes*, 11 August 2006 [accessed 5 October 2006] www.forbes.com.

10. Reid Goldsborough, "'Creeping Informality' Can Be Big Mistake in Business E-mails," *New Orleans City Business*, 14 March 2005, 18; Jack E. Appleman, "Bad Writing Can Cost Insurers Time & Money," *National Underwriter*, 27 September 2004, 34; Adina Genn, "RE: This Is an Important Message, Really," *Long Island Business News*, 5–11 December 2003, 21A; Lynn Lofton, "Regardless of What You Thought, Grammar Rules *Do* Apply to E-mail," *Mississippi Business Journal*, 23–29 May 2005, 1.

11. Mary Munter, Priscilla S. Rogers, and Jone Rymer, "Business E-mail: Guidelines for Users," *Business Communication Quarterly*, March 2003, 26+; Renee B. Horowitz and Marian G. Barchilon, "Stylistic Guidelines for E-mail," *IEEE Transactions on Professional Communication* 37, no. 4 (December 1994): 207–212.

12. "E-mail Is So Five Minutes Ago," *BusinessWeek Online*, 28 November 2005 [accessed 3 May 2006] www.businessweek.com.

13. Robert J. Holland, "Connected—More or Less," Richmond.com, 8 August 2006 [accessed 5 October 2006] www.richmond.com.

14. Vayusphere website [accessed 22 January 2006] www.vayusphere.com; Christa C. Ayer, "Presence Awareness: Instant Messaging's Killer App," *Mobile Business Advisor*, 1 July 2004 [accessed 22 January 2006] www.highbeam.com; Jefferson Graham, "Instant Messaging Programs Are No Longer Just for Messages," *USA Today*, 20 October 2003, 5D; Todd R. Weiss, "Microsoft Targets Corporate Instant Messaging Customers," *Computerworld*, 18 November 2002, 12; "Banks Adopt Instant Messaging to Create a Global Business Network," *Computer Weekly*, 25 April 2002, 40; Michael D. Osterman, "Instant Messaging in the Enterprise," *Business Communications Review*, January 2003, 59–62; John Pallato, "Instant Messaging Unites Work Groups and Inspires Collaboration," *Internet World*, December 2002, 14+.

15. Paul Kedrosky, "Why We Don't Get the (Text) Message," *Business 2.0*, 2 October 2006 [accessed 4 October 2006] www.business2.com; Carpenter, "Companies Discover Marketing Power of Text Messaging."

16. Mark Gibbs, "Racing to Instant Messaging," *NetworkWorld*, 17 February 2003, 74.

17. "E-mail Is So Five Minutes Ago."

18. Elizabeth Millard, "Instant Messaging Threats Still Rising," Newsfactor.com, 6 July 2005 [accessed 5 October 2006] www.newsfactor.com.

19. Walaika K. Haskins, "New Virus Spreads by Chatting with You," Newsfactor.com, 9 December 2005 [accessed 5 October 2006] www.newsfactor.com.

20. Clint Boulton, "IDC: IM Use Is Booming in Business," InstantMessagingPlanet.com, 5 October 2005 [accessed 22 January 2006] www.instantmessagingplanet.com; Jenny Goodbody, "Critical Success Factors for Global Virtual Teams," *Strategic Communication Management*, February/March 2005, 18–21; Ann Majchrzak, Arvind Malhotra, Jeffrey Stamps, and Jessica Lipnack, "Can Absence Make a Team Grow Stronger?" *Harvard Business Review*, May 2004, 131–137; Christine Y. Chen, "The IM Invasion," *Fortune*, 26 May 2003, 135–138; Yudhijit Bhattacharjee, "A Swarm of Little Notes," *Time*, September 2002, A3–A8; Mark Bruno, "Taming the Wild Frontiers of Instant Messaging," *Bank Technology News*, December 2002, 30–31; Richard Grigonis, "Enterprise-Strength Instant Messaging," Convergence.com, 10–15 [accessed March 2003] www.convergence.com.

21. Pallato, "Instant Messaging Unites Work Groups and Inspires Collaboration," 14+.

22. Anita Hamilton, "You've Got Spim!" *Time*, 2 February 2004 [accessed 1 March 2004] www.time.com.

23. Robert Scoble and Shel Israel, *Naked Conversations* (Hoboken, N.J.: Wiley, 2006), 15–18.

24. GM FastLane blog [accessed 4 May 2006] http://fastlane.gmblogs.com.

25. Fredrik Wackå, "Six Types of Blogs—A Classification," CorporateBlogging.Info website, 10 August 10 2004 [accessed 5 October 2006] www.corporateblogging.info; Stephen Baker, "The Inside Story on Company Blogs," *BusinessWeek*, 14 February 2006 [accessed 15 February 2006] www.businessweek.com; Jeremy Wright, *Blog Marketing* (New York: McGraw-Hill, 2006), 45–56; Paul Chaney, "Blogs: Beyond the Hype!" 26 May 2005 [accessed 4 May 2006] http://radiantmarketinggroup.com.

26. Evolve24 website [accessed 5 October 2006] www.evolve24.com.

27. Stephen Baker and Heather Green, "Blogs Will Change Your Business," *BusinessWeek*, 2 May 2005, 57–67.

28. Julie Moran Alterio, "Podcasts a Hit Inside and Outside IBM," *The Journal News* (White Plains, N.Y.), 9 January 2006 [accessed 5 May 2006] www.thejournalnews.com.

29. "Turn Your Feed into a Podcast," Lifehacker blog, 12 January 2006 [accessed 6 May 2006] www.lifehacker.com.

30. "Set Up Your Podcast for Success," FeedForAll website [accessed 4 October 2006] www.feedforall.com.

31. Shel Holtz, "Ten Guidelines for B2B Podcasts," Webpronews.com, 12 October 2005 [accessed 9 March 2006] www.webpronews.com.

32. Todd Cochrane, *Podcasting: The Do-It-Yourself Guide* (Indianapolis, Ind.: Wiley, 2005), 107–109.

9. Shel Holtz, "Writing for the Wired World," *International Association of Business Communicators*, 1999, 6–9.

10. Sant Corporation website [accessed 16 August 2007] www.santcorp.com; Pragmatech Software website [accessed 16 August 2007] www.pragmatech.com.

11. Alexis Gerard and Bob Goldstein, *Going Visual* (Hoboken, N.J.: Wiley, 2005), 18.

12. Charles Kostelnick and Michael Hassett, *Shaping Information: The Rhetoric of Visual Conventions* (Carbondale, Ill.: Southern Illinois University Press, 2003), 177.

13. Gerard and Goldstein, *Going Visual*, 103–106.

14. Edward R. Tufte, *Visual Explanations: Images and Quantities, Evidence and Narrative* (Cheshire, Conn.: Graphics Press, 1997), 82.

15. Joshua David McClurg-Genevese, "The Principles of Design," *Digital Web Magazine*, 13 June 2005 [accessed 23 November 2006] www.digital-web.com.

16. Kostelnick and Hassett, *Shaping Information: The Rhetoric of Visual Conventions*, 17.

17. Kostelnick and Hassett, *Shaping Information: The Rhetoric of Visual Conventions*, 216.

18. Edward R. Tufte, *The Visual Display of Quantitative Information* (Cheshire, Conn.: Graphic Press, 1983), 113.

19. Tufte, *Visual Explanations: Images and Quantities, Evidence and Narrative*, 73.

20. Based in part on Tufte, *Visual Explanations: Images and Quantities, Evidence and Narrative*, 29–37, 53; Paul Martin Lester, *Visual Communication: Images with Messages*, 4th ed. (Belmont, Calif.: Thomson Wadsworth, 2006), 95–105, 194–196.

21. Hoover's Online [accessed 30 December 2003] www.hoovers.com.

22. Gerard and Goldstein, *Going Visual*, 49.

23. Sheri Rosen, "What Is Truth?" *IABC Communication World*, March 1995, 40.

24. Adapted from Air-Trak website [accessed 12 September 2005] www.air-trak.com.

CHAPTER 13

1. Gates Foundation website [accessed 13 November 2006] www.gatesfoundation.org; Richard Klausner and Pedro Alonso, "An Attack on All Fronts," *Nature*, 19 August 2004, 930–931; "Richard Klausner Spends to Save Lives," *Fast Company*, November 2002, 128; Kent Allen, "The Gatekeeper," *U.S. News & World Report*, 8 December 2003, 64–66.

2. John Morkes and Jakob Nielsen, "Concise, Scannable, and Objective: How to Write for the Web," UseIt.com [accessed 13 November 2006] www.useit.com.

3. Dean Allen, "Reading Design," *A List Apart*, 23 November 2001 [accessed 9 November 2004] www.alistapart.com.

4. Michael Netzley and Craig Snow, *Guide to Report Writing* (Upper Saddle River, N.J.: Prentice Hall, 2001), 57.

5. Patty Stonesifer, "Partners and Progress: A Message from Patty Stonesifer," Gates Foundation website [accessed 15 September 2005] www.gatesfoundation.org.

6. Oswald M. T. Ratteray, "Hit the Mark with Better Summaries," *Supervisory Management*, September 1989, 43–45.

7. Netzley and Snow, *Guide to Report Writing*, 43.

8. Alice Reid, "A Practical Guide for Writing Proposals" [accessed 31 May 2001] http://members.dca.net/areid/proposal.htm.

9. Toby B. Gooley, "Ocean Shipping: RFPs That Get Results," *Logistics Management*, July 2003, 47–52.

10. See Note 1.

11. Adapted from "Home Depot Says E-Learning Is Paying for Itself," *Workforce Management*, 25 February 2004 [accessed 28 February 2004] www.workforce.com; Robert Celaschi, "The Insider: Training," *Workforce Management*, August 2004, 67–69; Joe Mullich, "A Second Act for E-learning," *Workforce Management*, February 2004, 51–55; Gail Johnson, "Brewing the Perfect Blend," *Training*, December 2003, 30+; Tammy

Galvin, "2003 Industry Report," *Training*, October 2003, 21+; William C. Symonds, "Giving It the Old Online Try," *BusinessWeek*, 3 December 2001, 76–80; Karen Frankola, "Why Online Learners Drop Out," *Workforce*, October 2001, 52–60; Mary Lord, "They're Online and on the Job; Managers and Hamburger Flippers Are Being E-trained at Work," *U.S. News & World Report*, 15 October 2001, 72–77.

12. Adapted from Ieva M. Augstumes, "Buyers Take the Driver's Seat," *Dallas Morning News*, 20 February 2004 [accessed 30 June 2004] www.highbeam.com; Jill Amadio, "A Click Away: Automotive Web Sites Are Revved Up and Ready to Help You Buy," *Entrepreneur*, 1 August 2003 [accessed 30 June 2004] www.highbeam.com; Dawn C. Chmielewski, "Car Sites Lend Feel-Good Info for Haggling," *San Jose Mercury News*, 1 August 2003 [accessed 30 June 2004] www.highbeam.com; Cromwell Schubarth, "Autoheroes Handle Hassle of Haggling," *Boston Herald*, 24 July 2003 [accessed 30 June 2004] www.highbeam.com; Rick Popely, "Internet Doesn't Change Basic Shopping Rules," *Chicago Tribune*, 28 February 2004 [accessed 30 June 2004] www.highbeam.com; Matt Nauman, "Walnut Creek, Calif., Firm Prospers as Online Car Buying Becomes More Popular," *San Jose Mercury News*, 21 June 2004 [accessed 30 June 2004] www.highbeam.com; Cliff Banks, "e-Dealer 100," *Ward's Dealer Business*, 1 April 2004 [accessed 30 June 2004] www.highbeam.com; Cars.com website [accessed 30 June 2004] www.cars.com; CarsDirect.com website [accessed 30 June 2004] www.carsdirect.com.

CHAPTER 14

1. "Culture and Philosophy" and "Procter & Gamble Case Study," HP website [accessed 20 September 2005] www.hp.com; Paul McDougall, "Procter & Gamble's Deal with HP Grows," *InformationWeek*, 16 August 2004 [accessed 20 September 2005] www.outsourcingpipeline.com; Bill Breen, "The Big Score," *Fast Company*, September 2003, 64; "HP Finalizes $3 Billion Outsourcing Agreement to Manage Procter & Gamble's IT Infrastructure," press release, HP website, 6 May 2003 [accessed 10 October 2003] www.hp.com; "HP Selected by P&G for $3 Billion, 10-Year Services Contract," press release, HP website, 11 April 2003 [accessed 10 October 2003] www.hp.com.

2. Carmine Gallo, "Loaded for Bore," *BusinessWeek Online*, 5 August 2005 [accessed 19 September 2005] www.businessweek.com.

3. Sarah Lary and Karen Pruente, "Powerless Point: Common PowerPoint Mistakes to Avoid," *Public Relations Tactics*, February 2004, 28.

4. Cliff Atkinson, *Beyond Bullet Points: Using Microsoft PowerPoint to Create Presentations That Inform, Motivate, and Inspire* (Redmond, Wash.: Microsoft Press, 2005), 29, 55, 65.

5. Sherwyn P. Morreale and Courtland L. Bovée, *Excellence in Public Speaking* (Fort Worth, Tex.: Harcourt Brace, 1998), 234–237.

6. Morreale and Bovée, *Excellence in Public Speaking*, 230.

7. Morreale and Bovée, *Excellence in Public Speaking*, 241–243.

8. "Choose and Use Your Words Deliberately," *Soundview Executive Book Summaries*, 20, no. 6, pt. 2 (June 1998): 3.

9. Carmine Gallo, "Grab Your Audience Fast," *BusinessWeek*, 13 September 2006, 19.

10. Walter Kiechel III, "How to Give a Speech," *Fortune*, 8 June 1987, 180.

11. *Communication and Leadership Program* (Santa Ana, Calif.: Toastmasters International, 1980), 44, 45.

12. "Polishing Your Presentation," 3M Meeting Network [accessed 25 May 2007] www.3m.com/meetingnetwork/readingroom/meetingguide_pres.html.

13. Claudyne Wilder and David Fine, *Point, Click & Wow* (San Francisco: Jossey-Bass Pfeiffer, 1996), 50.

14. "The Power of Color in Presentations," 3M Meeting Network [accessed 25 May 2007] www.3m.com/meetingnetwork/readingroom/meetingguide_power_color.html.

15. Jon Hanke, "Five Tips for Better Visuals," 3M Meeting Network [accessed 25 May 2007] www.3m.com/meetingnetwork/presentations/pmag_better_visuals.html.

16. Lary and Pruente, "Powerless Point: Common PowerPoint Mistakes to Avoid."

17. Jeff Yocom, "TechRepublic Survey Yields Advice on Streaming Video," TechRepublic website [accessed 16 February 2004] www.techrepublic.com.

18. Yocom, "TechRepublic Survey Yields Advice on Streaming Video."

19. "Webcasting Tips & Advice," Spider Eye Studios [accessed 13 February 2004] www.spidereye.com.

20. Jerry Weissman, *Presenting to Win: The Art of Telling Your Story* (Upper Saddle River, N.J.: Pearson Prentice-Hall, 2006), 162.

21. Ted Simons, "Handouts That Won't Get Trashed," *Presentations*, February 1999, 47–50.

22. Morreale and Bovée, *Excellence in Public Speaking*, 24–25.

23. Jennifer Rotondo and Mike Rotondo, Jr., *Presentation Skills for Managers* (New York: McGraw-Hill, 2002), 9.

24. Rick Gilbert, "Presentation Advice for Boardroom Success," *Financial Executive*, September 2005, 12.

25. Rotondo and Rotondo, Jr., *Presentation Skills for Managers*, 151.

26. "Control the Question-and-Answer Session," *Soundview Executive Book Summaries* 20, no. 6, pt. 2 (June 1998): 4.

27. Teresa Brady, "Fielding Abrasive Questions During Presentations," *Supervisory Management*, February 1993, 6.

28. Robert L. Montgomery, "Listening on Your Feet," *The Toastmaster*, July 1987, 14–15.

29. See Note 1.

30. Adapted from Loopt website [accessed 9 December 2006] www.loopt.com; Boost Mobile website [accessed 9 December 2006] www.boostmobile.com.

31. Adapted from Robert D. Hof, "There's Not Enough 'Me' in MySpace," *BusinessWeek*, 4 December 2006, 40.

CHAPTER 15

1. Charles Handler, "What You Need to Know About What's Happening in the Pre-Employment Assessment Market," Ere.net, 20 July 2006 [accessed 12 December 2006] www.ere.net; Fay Hansen, "Growing into Applicant Tracking Systems, *Workforce Management*, 10 October 2006 [accessed 12 December 2006] www.workforce.com; Connie Winkler, "Job Tryouts Go Virtual," *HR Magazine*, September 2006, 131–134; "Hersha Hospitality Management Selects ERC's Selectech Workforce Management Recruiting Solution," 7 December 2006, ERC Dataplus website [accessed 12 December 2006] www.ercdataplus.com.

2. Robert J. Gerberg, *Robert Gerberg's Job Changing System*, summarized by Macmillan Book Clubs, Inc., in the "Macmillan Executive Summary Program," April 1987, 4.

3. Jobfox website [accessed 24 August 2007] www.jobfox.com; Olga Kharif, "The Job of Challenging Monster," *BusinessWeek*, 6 September 2005 [accessed 25 September 2005] www.businessweek.com; "Job Sites: The 'Second Generation,'" *BusinessWeek*, 7 September 2005 [accessed 25 September 2005] www.businessweek.com.

4. Caroline A. Drakeley, "Viral Networking: Tactics in Today's Job Market," *Intercom*, September–October 2003, 4–7.

5. Drakeley, "Viral Networking: Tactics in Today's Job Market," 5.

6. Anne Fisher, "Greener Pastures in a New Field," *Fortune*, 26 January 2004, 48.

7. Cheryl L. Noll, "Collaborating with the Career Planning and Placement Center in the Job-Search Project," *Business Communication Quarterly* 58, no. 3 (1995): 53–55.

8. Rockport Institute, "How to Write a Masterpiece of a Résumé" [accessed 25 September 2005] www.rockportinstitute.com.

9. Pam Stanley-Weigand, "Organizing the Writing of Your Resume," *Bulletin of the Association for Business Communication* 54, no. 3 (September 1991): 11–12.

10. Susan Vaughn, "Answer the Hard Questions Before Asked," *Los Angeles Times*, 29 July 2001, W1–W2.

11. John Steven Niznik, "Landing a Job with a Criminal Record," About.com [accessed 12 December 2006] http://jobsearchtech.about.com.

12. Richard H. Beatty and Nicholas C. Burkholder, *The Executive Career Guide for MBAs* (New York: Wiley, 1996), 133.

13. Adapted from Burdette E. Bostwick, *How to Find the Job You've Always Wanted* (New York: Wiley, 1982), 69–70.

14. Norma Mushkat Gaffin, "Recruiters' Top 10 Resume Pet Peeves," Monster.com [accessed 19 February 2004] www.monster.com; Beatty and Burkholder, *The Executive Career Guide for MBAs*, 151.

15. Rockport Institute, "How to Write a Masterpiece of a Résumé."

16. "Resume Fraud Gets Slicker and Easier," CNN.com [accessed 11 March 2004] www.cnn.com.

17. "Resume Fraud Gets Slicker and Easier"; Employment Research Services website [accessed 18 March 2004] www.erscheck.com.

18. "Employers Turn Their Fire on Untruthful CVs," *Supply Management*, 23 June 2005, 13.

19. Lore Croghan, Candidates Unafraid to Fudge Résumés, Study Finds," *Seattle Times*, 12 March 2006 [accessed 12 March 2006] www.seattletimes.com.

20. Sal Divita, "If You're Thinking Résumé, Think Creatively," *Marketing News*, 14 September 1992, 29.

21. Rockport Institute, "How to Write a Masterpiece of a Résumé."

22. Lora Morsch, "25 Words That Hurt Your Resume," CNN.com, 20 January 2006 [accessed 20 January 2006] www.cnn.com.

23. Karl L. Smart, "Articulating Skills in the Job Search," *Business Communication Quarterly* 67, no. 2 (June 2004): 198–205.

24. Annie Fisher, "What Makes a Résumé Scream: Don't Hire Me," *Fortune*, 6 June 2006 [accessed 6 June 2006] http://money.cnn.com; Rockport Institute, "How to Write a Masterpiece of a Résumé."

25. Ed Tazzia, "Wanted: A Résumé That Really Works," *Brandweek*, 15 May 2006, 26.

26. Ellen Joe Pollock, "Sir: Your Application for a Job Is Rejected; Sincerely, Hal 9000," *Wall Street Journal*, 30 July 1998, A1, A12.

27. "Scannable Resume Design," ResumeEdge.com [accessed 19 February 2004] www.resumeedge.com.

28. Kim Isaacs, "Tips for Creating a Scannable Resume," Monster.com [accessed 19 February 2004] www.monster.com.

29. Sarah E. Needleman, "Why Sneaky Tactics May Not Help Resume; Recruiters Use New Search Technologies to Ferret Out Bogus Keywords," *Wall Street Journal*, 6 March 2007, B8.

30. Kim Isaacs, "Enhance Your Resume for Monster Upload," Monster.com [accessed 19 February 2004] www.monster.com.

31. "The Rogue's Gallery of 25 Awful Résumé Mistakes," Career Explorer [accessed 19 February 2004] www.careerexplorer.net.

32. Lore Croghan, "Recruiters Cite Litany of Mistakes They've Seen on Résumés," *Seattle Times*, 20 November 2005 [accessed 20 November 2005] www.seattletimes.com.

33. Regina Pontow, "Electronic Résumé Writing Tips," ProvenResumes.com [accessed 18 October 1998] www.provenresumes.com/reswkshps/electronic/scnres.html.

CHAPTER 16

1. John Sullivan, "A Case Study of Google Recruiting," 5 December 2005, *Electronic Recruiting Exchange* [accessed 16 December 2006] www.ere.net; "What's It Like to Work at Google?" Google website [accessed 26 September 2005] www.google.com; Fred Vogelstein, "Can Google Grow Up?" *Fortune*, 8 December 2003, 102; Quentin Hardy, "All Eyes on Google," *Forbes*, 26 May 2003, 100; Keith H. Hammonds, "Growth Search," *Fast Company*, April 2003, 74–81; Stanley Bing, "How Not to Success (*sic*) in Business," *Fortune*, 30 December 2002, 210; Pierre Mornell, "Zero Defect Hiring," *Inc.*, March 1998, 74.

2. "The Writer Approach," *Los Angeles Times*, 17 November 2002, W1.

3. Toni Logan, "The Perfect Cover Story," *Kinko's Impress* 2 (2000): 32, 34.

4. James Gonyea, "Money Talks: Salary History Versus Salary Requirements," Monster.com [accessed 19 October 2004] www.monster.com; Marguerite Higgins, "Tech-Savvy Job Hunters Not So Suave in Writing;

E-Mail Résumés Appall Employers," *Washington Times*, 17 December 2002 [accessed 22 February 2004] www.highbeam.com; "Keep Goal in Mind When Crafting a Résumé," *Register-Guard* (Eugene, Ore.), 3 August 2003 [accessed 22 February 2004] www.highbeam.com; Anis F. McClin, "Effects of Spelling Errors on the Perception of Writers," *Journal of General Psychology*, January 2002 [accessed 22 February 2004] www.highbeam.com.

5. George Donnelly, "Recruiting, Retention & Returns," CFO.com, March 2000 [accessed 10 April 2000] www.cfonet.com.

6. Stephanie Armour, "The New Interview Etiquette," *USA Today*, 23 November 1999, B1, B2.

7. Samuel Greengard, "Are You Well Armed to Screen Applicants?" *Personnel Journal*, December 1995, 84–95.

8. Caroline Levchuck, "Survival Tips for Group Interviews," Yahoo! HotJobs [accessed 16 December 2006] http://hotjobs.yahoo.com.

9. "Panel Interview," Job-Employment-Guide.com [accessed 2 June 2007] www.job-employment-guide.com; Carole Martin, "The Panel Interview," JobBank USA [accessed 2 June 2007] www.jobbankusa.com.

10. William Poundstone, "Beware the Interview Inquisition," *Harvard Business Review*, May 2003, 18+.

11. "Interview Preparation," Madison MacArthur website [accessed 13 December 2006] www.mmsearch.com.

12. Lynda M. Bassett, "Work the Working Interview," Monster.com [accessed 13 December 2006] www.monster.com.

13. Peter Vogt, "Mastering the Phone Interview," Monster.com [accessed 13 December 2006] www.monster.com; Nina Segal, "The Global Interview: Tips for Successful, Unconventional Interview Techniques," Monster.com [accessed 13 December 2006] www.monster.com.

14. Segal, "The Global Interview: Tips for Successful, Unconventional Interview Techniques."

15. Connie Winkler, "Job Tryouts Go Virtual," *HR Magazine*, September 2006, 131–134.

16. Steven Isbitts, "Virtual Interview," *Tampa Tribune*, 20 March 2006 [accessed 13 December 2006] www.ebscohost.com.

17. Saul Hansell, "Google Answer to Filling Jobs Is an Algorithm," *New York Times*, 3 January 2007 [accessed 3 January 2007] www.nytimes.com.

18. Carole Martin, "Smile, You're on Camera: Videoconference Interviews," Monster.com [accessed 13 December 2006] www.monster.com; Marcia Vickers, "Don't Touch That Dial: Why Should I Hire You?" *New York Times*, 13 April 1997, F11.

19. Patrick J. Sauer, "Open-Door Management," *Inc.*, June 2003, 44.

20. Dino di Mattia, "Testing Methods and Effectiveness of Tests," *Supervision*, August 2005, 4–5.

21. Sullivan, "A Case Study of Google Recruiting."

22. Steven Mitchell Sack, "The Working Woman's Legal Survival Guide: Testing," FindLaw [accessed 22 February 2004] www.findlaw.com; David W. Arnold and John W. Jones, "Who the Devil's Applying Now?" *Security Management*, March 2002, 85–88.

23. Arnold and Jones, "Who the Devil's Applying Now?" 86.

24. Arnold and Jones, "Who the Devil's Applying Now?" 86.

25. Adam Agard, "Preemployment Skills Testing: An Important Step in the Hiring Process," *Supervision*, June 2003, 7+.

26. Andy Meisler, "Negative Results," *Workforce Management*, October 2003, 35+.

27. Tyler D. Hartwell, Paul D. Steele, and Nathaniel F. Rodman, "Workplace Alcohol-Testing Programs: Prevalence and Trends," *Monthly Labor Review*, June 1998, 27–34; "Substance Abuse in the Workplace," *HR Focus*, February 1997, 1, 4+.

28. "Drug Test Company Official Disputes Report Pre-Employment Tests Falling," *Drug Detection Report*, 23 March 2006, 43.

29. Hope A. Comisky and Christopher P. Zubowicz, "The Law of Criminal Background Checks," *Employee Relations Law Journal* 32, no. 3 (Winter 2006): 66–85.

30. Thomas A. Buckhoff, "Preventing Fraud by Conducting Background Checks," *CPA Journal*, November 2003, 52.

31. "Check Yourself Before Employer Does," *CA Magazine*, June/July 2005, 12.

32. Nancy K. Austin, "Goodbye Gimmicks," *Incentive*, May 1996, 241.

33. Katherine Spencer Lee, "Tackling Tough Interview Questions," *Certification Magazine*, May 2005, 35.

34. Leigh Dyer, "Job Hunters Should Think Carefully Before Using Job Counselor," *Charlotte Observer*, 30 July 2001 [accessed 29 September 2005] www.ebsco.com; Anne Field, "Coach, Help Me Out with This Interview," *BusinessWeek*, 22 October 2001, 134E2, 134E4.

35. Robert Gifford, Cheuk Fan Ng, and Margaret Wilkinson, "Nonverbal Cues in the Employment Interview: Links Between Applicant Qualities and Interviewer Judgments," *Journal of Applied Psychology* 70, no. 4 (1985): 729.

36. Dale G. Leathers, *Successful Nonverbal Communication* (New York: Macmillan, 1986), 225.

37. Armour, "The New Interview Etiquette."

38. William S. Frank, "Job Interview: Pre-Flight Checklist," *The Career Advisor* [accessed 28 September 2005] http://careerplanning.about.com.

39. T. Shawn Taylor, "Most Managers Have No Idea How to Hire the Right Person for the Job," *Chicago Tribune*, 23 July 2002 [accessed 29 September 2005] www.ebsco.com.

40. Sack, "The Working Woman's Legal Survival Guide."

41. Gerald L. Wilson, "Preparing Students for Responding to Illegal Selection Interview Questions," *Bulletin of the Association for Business Communication* 54, no. 2 (1991): 44–49.

42. Jeff Springston and Joann Keyton, "Interview Response Training," *Bulletin of the Association for Business Communication* 54, no. 3 (1991): 28–30; Gerald L. Wilson, "An Analysis of Instructional Strategies for Responding to Illegal Selection Interview Questions," *Bulletin of the Association for Business Communication* 54, no. 3 (1991): 31–35.

43. Stephen J. Pullum, "Illegal Questions in the Selection Process: Going Beyond Contemporary Business and Professional Communication Textbooks," *Bulletin of the Association for Business Communication* 54, no. 3 (1991): 36–43; Alicia Kitsuse, "Have You Ever Been Arrested?" *Across the Board*, November 1992, 46–49; Christina L. Greathouse, "Ten Common Hiring Mistakes," *Industry Week*, 20 January 1992, 22–23, 26.

44. "Negotiating Salary: An Introduction," *InformationWeek* online [accessed 22 February 2004] www.infoweek.com.

45. "Negotiating Salary: An Introduction."

46. Harold H. Hellwig, "Job Interviewing: Process and Practice," *Bulletin of the Association for Business Communication* 55, no. 2 (1992): 8–14.

47. See Note 1.

APPENDIX A

1. Mary A. De Vries, *Internationally Yours* (Boston: Houghton Mifflin, 1994), 9.

2. Patricia A. Dreyfus, "Paper That's Letter Perfect," *Money*, May 1985, 184.

3. "When Image Counts, Letterhead Says It All," *Stamford (Conn.) Advocate and Greenwich Times*, 10 January 1993, F4.

4. Mel Mandell, "Electronic Forms Are Cheap and Speedy," *D&B Reports*, July–August 1993, 44–45.

5. Linda Driskill, *Business and Managerial Communication: New Perspectives* (Orlando, Fla.: Harcourt Brace Jovanovich, 1992), 470.

6. Driskill, *Business and Managerial Communication*, 470.

7. Lennie Copeland and Lewis Griggs, *Going International: How to Make Friends and Deal Effectively in the Global Marketplace*, 2d ed. (New York: Random House, 1985), 24–27.

8. De Vries, *Internationally Yours*, 8.

9. U.S. Postal Service, *International Mail Manual*, Issue 34, 14 May 2007 [accessed 23 October 2007] www.usps.gov.

10. U.S. Postal Service, *Postal Addressing Standards* (Washington, D.C.: GPO, 1992).

11. Copeland and Griggs, *Going International*, 24–27.

12. Renee B. Horowitz and Marian G. Barchilon, "Stylistic Guidelines for E-Mail," *IEEE Transactions on Professional Communications*, 37, no. 4 (1994): 207–212.

13. Jill H. Ellsworth and Matthew V. Ellsworth, *The Internet Business Book* (New York:Wiley, 1994), 93.

14. William Eager, *Using the Internet* (Indianapolis: Que Corporation, 1994), 11.

15. Eager, *Using the Internet*, 10.

16. William Eager, Larry Donahue, David Forsyth, Kenneth Mitton, and Martin Waterhouse, *Net.Search* (Indianapolis: Que Corporation, 1995), 221.

17. Rosalind Resnick and Dave Taylor, *Internet Business Guide* (Indianapolis: Sams.net Publishing, 1995), 117.

18. James L. Clark and Lyn R. Clark, *How 7: A Handbook for Office Workers*, 7th ed. (Cincinnati: South-Western, 1995), 431–432.

Acknowledgments

TEXT

10 (Using the Power of Technology: Is Web 2.0 the Future or the Past Revisited?) Adapted from Russell Shaw, "Web 2.0? It Doesn't Exist," ZDNet blogs, 17 December 2005 [accessed 13 August 2006] http://blogs.zdnet.com; Tim O'Reilly, "What Is Web 2.0? Design Patterns and Business Models for the Next Generation of Software," *O'Reilly*, 30 September 2005 [accessed 13 August 2006] www.oreillynet.com; John Dvorak, "Web 2.0 Baloney," *PC Magazine* online, 1 March 2006 [accessed 13 August 2006] www.pcmag.com; Nicholas Carr, "The Amorality of Web 2.0" (blog entry), 3 October 2005 [accessed 13 August 2006] http://roughtype.com; Shayne Bowman and Chris Willis, "We Media: How Audiences Are Shaping the Future of News and Information," 21 September 2003, Hypergene.net [accessed 4 February 2007] www.hypergene.net. 56 (Checklist: Overcoming Barriers to Effective Listening) Source: Robert A. Luke, Jr., "Improving Your Listening Ability," *Supervisory Management*, June 1992, 7; Madelyn Burley-Allen, "Listening for Excellence in Communication," *The Dynamics of Behavior Newsletter* 2, no. 2 (Summer 1992): 1; Bob Lamons, "Good Listeners Are Better Communicators," *Marketing News*, 11 September 1995, 13+. 59 (Checklist: Improving Nonverbal Communication Skills) Source: Gerald H. Graham, Jeanne Unrue, and Paul Jennings, "The Impact of Nonverbal Communication in Organizations: A Survey of Perceptions," *Journal of Business Communication* 28, no. 1 (Winter 1991): 45–62; Dianna Booher, *Communicate with Confidence* (New York: McGraw-Hill, 1994), 363–370. 76 (Communicating Across Cultures: Test Your Intercultural Knowledge) Adapted from David A. Ricks, "International Business Blunders: An Update," *Business & Economic Review*, January–March 1988, 25; Valerie Frazee, "Keeping Up on Chinese Culture," *Global Workforce*, October 1996, 16–17; Valerie Frazee, "Establishing Relations in Germany," *Global Workforce*, April 1997, 16–17; James Wilfong and Toni Seger, *Taking Your Business Global* (Franklin Lakes, N.J.: Career Press, 1997), 282. 120 (Using the Power of Technology: Create and Collaborate with Powerful Outlining Tools) Adapted from Microsoft Word Help text; Microsoft website [accessed 2 December 2003] www.microsoft.com/office; "What Electronic Outlining Tools Can Do for You," Web Writing That Works website [accessed 7 March 2004] www.webwritingthatworks.com. 143 (Communicating Across Cultures: Communicating with a Global Audience on the Web) Adapted from Laura Morelli, "Writing for a Global Audience on the Web," *Marketing News*, 17 August 1998, 16; Yuri and Anna Radzievsky, "Successful Global Web Sites Look Through Eyes of the Audience," *Advertising Age's Business Marketing*, January 1998, 17; Sari Kalin, "The Importance of Being Multiculturally Correct," *Computerworld*, 6 October 1997, G16–G17; B. G. Yovovich, "Making Sense of All the Web's Numbers," *Editor & Publisher*, November 1998, 30–31; David Wilford, "Are We All Speaking the Same Language?" *The Times* (London), 20 April 2000, 4. 202 (Using the Power of Technology) *Makezine* website [accessed 22 January 2006] www.makezine.com; Jane Spencer, "The Annoying New Face of Customer Service—Virtual Phone Reps Replace the Old Touch-Tone Menus; Making Claire Less Irritating," *Wall Street Journal*, 21 January 2003, D1; Allison Fass, "Speak Easy," *Forbes*, 6 January 2003, 135. 254 (What's Right to Write in a Recommendation Letter?) Adapted from Diane Cadrain, "HR Professionals Stymied by Vanishing Job References," *HR Magazine*, November 2004, 31–40; "Five (or More) Ways You Can Be Sued for Writing (or Not Writing) Recommendation Letters," *Fair Employment Practice Guidelines*, July 2006, 1, 3–4; Rochelle Kaplan, "Writing a Recommendation Letter," National Association of Colleges and Employers website [accessed 12 October 2006] www.naceweb.org; Maura Dolan and Stuart Silverstein, "Court Broadens Liability for Job References," *Los Angeles Times*, 28 January 1997, A1, A11; David A. Price, "Good References Pave Road to Court," *USA Today*, 13 February 1997, 11A; Frances A. McMorris, "Ex-Bosses Face Less Peril Giving Honest Job References," *Wall Street Journal*, 8 July 1996, B1, B8; Dawn Gunsch, "Gray Matters: Centralize Control of Giving References," *Personnel Journal*, September 1992, 114, 116–117; Betty Southard Murphy, Wayne E. Barlow, and D. Diane Hatch, "Manager's Newsfront: Job Reference Liability of Employees," *Personnel Journal*, September 1991, 22, 26;

Ross H. Fishman, "When Silence Is Golden," *Nation's Business*, July 1991, 48–49. 301 (Controlling Online Rumors) Adapted from Melissa Allison, "Corporations Seek to Clean Up Online Rumors," *Seattle Times*, 4 March 2007 [accessed 4 March 2007] www.seattletimes.com; Charles Wolrich, "Top Corporate Hate Web Sites," Forbes.com, 8 March 2005 [accessed 16 August 2005] www.forbes.com; PlanetFeedback.com [accessed 3 December 2003] www.planetfeedback.com; "Health Related Hoaxes and Rumors," Centers for Disease Control and Prevention website [accessed 16 August 2005] www.cdc.gov; Snopes.com [accessed 16 August 2005] www.snopes.com; "Pranksters, Activists and Rogues: Know Your Adversaries and Where They Surf," *PR News*, 26 June 2000 [accessed 3 December 2003] www.elibrary.com. 327 (Building an Audience Through Search Engine Optimization) Adapted from "Law Firm Marketing Now Dependent on Search Engine Optimization," *Law Office Management & Administration Report*, June 2006, 1, 10–12; *Pandia Search Engine Marketing 101*, Pandia website [accessed 25 March 2007] www.pandia.com; Mike Grehan, "Does Textbook SEO Really Work Anymore?" 17 April 2006, Clickz.com [accessed 25 March 2007], www.clickz.com; Shari Thurow, "Web Positioning Metrics and SEO," 24 October 2005, Clickz.com [accessed 25 March 2007], www.clickz.com. 389 (Sharpening Your Career Skills: Creating an Effective Business Plan) Adapted from Michael Gerber, "The Business Plan That Always Works," *Her Business*, May/June 2004, 23–25; J. Tol Broome, Jr., "How to Write a Business Plan," *Nation's Business*, February 1993, 29–30; Albert Richards, "The Ernst & Young Business Plan Guide," *R & D Management*, April 1995, 253; David Lanchner, "How Chitchat Became a Valuable Business Plan," *Global Finance*, February 1995, 54–56; Marguerita Ashby-Berger, "My Business Plan—And What Really Happened," *Small Business Forum*, Winter 1994–1995, 24–35; Stanley R. Rich and David E. Gumpert, *Business Plans That Win $$$* (New York: Harper Row, 1985). 508 (Five Tips for Making Presentations Around the World) Adapted from Patricia L. Kurtz, *The Global Speaker* (New York: AMACOM, 1995), 35–47, 56–68, 75–82, 87–100; David A. Victor, *International Business Communication* (New York: HarperCollins, 1992), 39–45; Lalita Khosla, "You Say Tomato," *Forbes*, 21 May 2001, 36; Stephen Dolainski, "Are Expats Getting Lost in the Translation?" *Workforce*, February 1997, 32–39. 548 (Looking for Work Around the World) Adapted from University of Michigan International Center Website [accessed 18 February 2004] www.umich.edu; Allan Hoffman, "Five Strategies for Finding Work Abroad," Monster.com [accessed 18 February 2004] www.monster.com; personal communication, Andrew Jaynes, 18 February 2004. 600 (Make Sure You Don't Talk Yourself Right out of a Job) Adapted from Thomas Pack, "Good Answers to Job Interview Questions," *Information Today*, January 2004, 35+; John Lees, "Make Them Believe You Are the Best," *The Times* (London), 21 January 2004, 3; "Six Interview Mistakes," Monster.com [accessed 23 February 2004] www.monster.com.

FIGURES AND TABLES

18 (Figure 1.7): From Six Apart website [accessed 17 December 2005] www.sixapart.com 55 (Table 2.2): Source: Madelyn Burley-Allen, *Listening: The Forgotten Skill*, (New York: Wiley, 1995), 70–71, 119–120; Judi Brownell, *Listening: Attitudes, Principles, and Skills*, (Boston: Allyn and Bacon, 2002), 3, 9, 83, 89, 125; Larry Barker and Kittie Watson, *Listen Up*, (New York: St. Martin's, 2000), 8, 9, 64. 61 (Table 2.4): Source: Alf Nucifora, "Voice Mail Demands Good Etiquette from Both Sides," *Puget Sound Business Journal*, 5–11 September 2003, 24; Ruth Davidhizar and Ruth Shearer, "The Effective Voice Mail Message," *Hospital Material Management Quarterly*, 45–49; "How to Get the Most out of Voice Mail," *The CPA Journal*, February 2000, 11; Jo Ind, "Hanging on the Telephone," *Birmingham Post*, 28 July 1999, PS10; Larry Barker and Kittie Watson, *Listen Up* (New York: St. Martin's Press, 2000), 64–65; Lin Walker, *Telephone Techniques*, (New York: Amacom, 1998), 46–47; Dorothy Neal, *Telephone Techniques*, 2nd ed. (New York McGraw-Hill, 1998), 31; Jeannie Davis, Beyond "Hello" (Aurora, Colo.: Now Hear This, Inc., 2000), 2–3; "Ten Steps to Caller-Friendly Voice Mail," *Managing Office Technology*, January 1995, 25; Rhonda Finniss, "Voice Mail:

Tips for a Positive Impression," *Administrative Assistant's Update*, August 2001, 5; "How to Get the Most out of Voice Mail," *The CPA Journal*, February 2000, 11; Ruth Davidhizar and Ruth Shearer, "The Effective Voice Mail Message," *Hospital Material Management Quarterly*, 45–49; "How to Get the Most out of Voice Mail," *The CPA Journal*, February 2000, 11. **77** (Figure 3.2): Source: Mary O'Hara-Devereaux and Robert Johansen, *Global Work: Bridging Distance, Culture, and Time* (San Francisco: Jossey Bass, 1994), 55, 59. **79** (Figure 3.3): Source: "New ILO Study Highlights Labour Trends Worldwide," International Labour Organization [accessed 15 September 2003] www.ilo.org **80** (Figure 3.4): Source: Roger Axtell, *Gestures: The Do's and Taboos of Body Language Around the World* (New York: Wiley, 1991), 117–119. **100** (Figure 4.1): Source: Adapted from Kevin J. Harty and John Keenan, *Writing for Business and Industry: Process and Product* (New York: Macmillan Publishing Company, 1987), 3–4; Richard Hatch, *Business Writing* (Chicago: Ill., Science Research Associates, 1983), 88–89; Richard Hatch, *Business Communication Theory and Techniques* (Chicago, Ill., Science Research Associates, 1983), 74–75; Center for Humanities, *Writing as a Process: A Step-by-Step Guide, Four Filmstrips and Cassettes*, Mount Kisco, New York, 1987; Michael L. Keene, *Effective Professional Writing* (New York: D.C. Heath, 1987), 28–34. **213** (Table 7.2): Robert Scoble and Shel Israel, *Naked Conversations* (Hoboken, N.J.: John Wiley & Sons, 2006), 78–81, 190–194; Paul McFedries, *The Complete Idiot's Guide to Creating a Web Page & Blog*, 6th ed. (New York: Alpha, 2004), 206–208, 272–276; Shel Holtz and Ted Demopoulos, *Blogging for Business* (Chicago: Kaplan, 2006), 54–59, 113–114: Denise Wakeman, "Top 10 Blog Writing Tips," Blogarooni.com [accessed 1 February 2006] www.blogarooni.com; Dennis A. Mahoney, "How to Write a Better Weblog," 22 February 2002, A List Apart [accessed 1 February 2006] www.alistapart.com. **250** Source: Courtesy Herman Miller. **256** Source: Courtesy Discovery Communications. **325** (Table 10.1): Source: Adapted from Saundra K. Ciccarelli and Glenn E. Meyer, *Psychology* (Upper Saddle River, N.J.: Prentice Hall, 2006), 336–346; Courtland L. Bovée, John V. Thill, and Michael H. Mescon, *Excellence in Business*, 3rd ed. (Upper Saddle River, N.J.: Prentice Hall, 2006), 327–333; Abraham H. Maslow, "A Theory of Human Motivation," *Psychological Review* 50 (1943): 370–396. **376** (Table 11.3): Source: Adapted from "Industry Information," Thomas J. Long Business and Economics Library website, University of California, Berkley [accessed 6 November 2006] www.lib.berkeley.edu; Hoover's website [accessed 6 November 2006] www.hoovers.com; MarketResearch.com [accessed 6 November 2006] www.marketresearch.com; Risk Management Association website [accessed 6 November 2006] www.rmahq.org; "Subscribed Sites," Sno-Isle Regional Library System [accessed 18 December 2003] www.sno.isle.org; "Business Directories: A Research Guide," University of Delaware Library website [accessed 6 November 2006] www.lib.udel.edu; Thomas P. Bergman, Stephen M. Garrison, and Gregory M. Scott, *The Business Student Writer's Manual and Guide to the Internet* (Paramus, N.J.: Prentice Hall, 1998), 67–80; Ernest L. Maier, Anthony J. Faria, Peter Kaatrude, and Elizabeth Wood, *The Business Library and How to Use It* (Detroit: Omnigraphics, 1996), 53–76. **516** (Table 14.2): Source: Adapted from Carmen Matthews, "Speaker's Notes," *Presentations*, April 2005, 42; Eric J. Adams, "Management Focus: User-Friendly Presentation Software," *World Trade*, March 1995, 92. **522** (Table 14.3): Source: Adapted from Claudyne Wilder and David Fine, *Point, Click & Wow* (San Francisco: Jossey-Bass Pfeiffer, 1996), 63, 527. **549** (Table 15.1): Source: The Riley Guide [accessed 22 September 2005] www.rileyguide.com; Bethany McLean, "A Scary Monster," *Fortune*, 22 December 2003, 19+; Alan

Cohen, "Best Job Hunting Sites," *Yahoo! Internet Life*, May 2002, 90–92; Richard N. Bolles, "Career Strategizing, or What Color Is Your Web Parachute?" *Yahoo! Internet Life*, May 1998, 116, 121; Tara Weingarten, "The All-Day, All-Night, Global, No-Trouble Job Search," *Newsweek*, 6 April 1998, 14; Michele Himmelberg, "Internet an Important Tool in Employment Search," *San Diego Union-Tribune*, 7 September 1998, D2; Gina Imperato, "35 Ways to Land a Job Online," *Fast Company*, August 1998, 192–197; Roberta Maynard, "Casting the Net for Job Seekers," *Nation's Business*, March 1997, 28–29. **552** (Table 15.2): Source: Adapted from Richard Nelson Bolles, *What Color Is Your Parachute?* (Berkeley, Calif.: Ten Speed Press, 1997), 67. **595** (Table 16.3): Source: Adapted from *The Northwestern Endicott Report* (Evanston Ill.: Northwestern University Placement Center). **596** (Table 16.4): Source: Adapted from Marilyn Sherman, "Questions R Us: What to Ask at a Job Interview," *Career World*, January 2004, 20; H. Lee Rust, *Job Search: The Complete Manual for Jobseekers* (New York: American Management Association, 1979), 56. **597** (Table 16.5): Source: Adapted from The Northwestern Endicott Report (Evanston: Ill.: Northwestern University Placement Center). **602** (Table 16.6): Source: Deanna G. Kucler, "Interview Questions: Legal or Illegal?" *Workforce Management* [accessed 28 September 2005] www.workforce.com; "Illegal Interview Questions," *USA Today*, 29 January 2001 [accessed 28 September 2005] www.usatoday.com; "Dangerous Questions," *Nation's Business*, May 1999, 22.

PHOTO CREDITS

39 Joe McDonald **40** Masterfile Corporation **47** Getty Images, Stone Allstock **54** Getty Images, Photodisk **57** Getty Images, Photodisk **71** IBM Corporation **73** Mark Richards **75** Mark Gibson/Mark and Audra Gibson Photography **81** Getty Images, Photodisk **87** CORBIS-NY **99** Alpha Books/Penguin Group, USA **101** Michael Newman/PhotoEdit **108** Walter Hodges/Getty Images **131** Stanford Law School **140** Corbis RF **165** Mercedes-AMG **180** Frederic Neema/Corbis/Sygma **200** Chung Sung-Jun/Getty Images **201** Chris Strangemore/Craig Strangemore; **212** Ric Feld/AP Wide World Photos **217** Promethius Consulting, LLC **230** Bill Stevenson/The Stock Connection **235** SuperStock, Inc. **237** Cone, Inc. **252** David Deal **268** Andrew Brooks/CORBIS-NY **270** Amy C. Etra/PhotoEdit **272** Mark Jenkinson/CORBIS-NY **274** PhotoEdit **276** Ed Kashi/Corbis/Bettmann **278** Paul Sakuma/AP Wide World Photos **281** Landov LLC **283** Jeffrey Sauger/Bloomberg News **286** Lawrence Jackson/AP Wide World Photos **314** CORBIS-NY **315** Tom Raymond/Getty Images, Stone Allstock **317** Thomas Babb/AP Wide World Photos **319** Reggie Casagrande/Getty Images **326** Paul Sakuma/AP Wide World Photos **354** Todd Bigelow/Aurora & Quanta Productions Inc. **356** AP Wide World Photos, Alex Wong/Getty Images, Inc. –Liaison **360** Masterfile Corporation **362** AP Wide World Photos **365** Getty Images **411** Robert Seale/Tellabs **440** Alan Gough/Alan Gough Photography **441** Getty Images **453** Corbis/Bettmann **454** John Decker/Landov LLC **457** Corbis/Sygma **461** Masterfile Royalty Free Division **497** Myrleen Ferguson Cate/PhotoEdit **509** B. Roland/The Image Works **502** SuperStock, Inc. **503** SuperStock, Inc. **505** Hewlett Packard **518** AP Wide World Photos **520** Lance Davies Photography/Polyvision, A Steelcase Company **525** CORBIS-NY **530** Dennis MacDonald/PhotoEdit Inc. **532** Noel Hendrickson/Getty Images **545** Hersha Hospitality Management **550** Raytheon Polar Services **551** Mark Richards/PhotoEdit, Inc. **581** Google Inc. **588** Photolibrary.com **591** David Carmack Photography **592** SuperStock, Inc. **598** Jon Feingersh/zefa-CORBIS-NY

Company/Name/Product Index

Subject Index